PREFACE

On behalf of the Conference Organisers, Editorial Board and Organising Committee, it is my great pleasure to present to you the Conference Proceedings of the *Muslim World in Transition: Contributions of the Gülen Movement.*

The underlying aim of this conference is to examine the impact of the Gülen movement on the contemporary Muslim world in transition and the relations between the West and Islam in general.

As a leading religious movement in contemporary Turkey with a universal educational and interfaith agenda, the Gülen movement aims to promote creative and positive relations between the West and the Muslim world and articulate a constructive position on issues such as democracy, multiculturalism, globalisation, and interfaith dialogue in the context of secular modernity. Gülen's re-reading of religious texts in the context of a renewal and re-interpretation in Islam that can take part in the building of a fully human society in Europe also features in the deliberations of the conference. The conference also examines the theological and intellectual contributions of Fethullah Gülen, situates him in the context of the modern intellectual history of Islam and discusses his own interpretations of the above central issues. As a religious intellectual and peace activist from Turkey, Gülen has influenced a whole generation of Muslims worldwide and inspired them to play an important role in dialogue and educational projects towards lasting peace.

The conference Call for Paper attracted 150 abstract submissions. The Conference Editorial Board, responsible for all decisions pertaining to paper review and selection, read and scored each submitted abstract. Successful authors were then invited to submit full papers three months in advance of the conference for further review by the Editorial Board. Each submitted paper was then read by at least three members of the Board. Papers were classed as either 'accepted', 'conditionally accepted pending revision' or 'declined'. Conditionally accepted papers were reviewed a second time on re-submission. In short, our authors and Editorial Board worked extremely hard to produce 48 quality papers of high academic standard and objective critique of the title in hand. I would therefore like to acknowledge all authors for their efforts and all members of the Editorial Board for their painstaking scrutiny and review of papers.

In particular, I would like to extend my special gratitude and appreciation to Muharrem Atlig, Dr Cem Erbil, Selvinaz Erbil, Ozcan Keles, Fatih Tedik, Erkan Kaymak, Arzu Ayaz, Tugrul Olcer, Mehtap Meric and Ahmet Alver, members of the Conference Organising Committee, who were the main driving force behind this conference. I am extremely grateful to our organisers and sponsors for helping to put together, what I believe, has already become a most worthwhile and stimulating academic enterprise. Finally, I would like to acknowledge the support of all whose names I cannot list here for their contribution to the conference.

Please note that papers have not been copy-edited but are provided in advance circulation of the conference as draft copies to facilitate meaningful discussion on the day.

Dr Ihsan Yilmaz

Conference Coordinator

MUSLIM WORLD IN TRANSITION: CONTRIBUTIONS OF THE GÜLEN MOVEMENT

CONFERENCE PROCEEDINGS

Leeds Metropolitan University Press
London
October 2007

First published in Great Britain 2007

ISBN 978-0-9555017-5-3

EDITORS

Dr Ihsan Yilmaz

PhD in law in 1999 from SOAS, University of London. 1999-2001: Research Fellow at the University of Oxford where he undertook two separate research projects: the Turkish diaspora in London, and the faith-based movement of Fethullah Gülen, its neo-ijtihad and renewal of Islam. Since 2001, he has been teaching comparative law, legal sociology, Islamic law and Turkish politics at the University of London. Research interests: Turkish diaspora, Turkish politics, Islamic movements, Muslim legal pluralism, neo-ijtihad and Fethullah Gülen's faith-based movement.

Prof. Eileen Barker OBE, FBA

Professor Emeritus of Sociology with Special Reference to the Study of Religion. (PhD, London School of Economics; and an Honorary Doctorate from the University of Copenhagen.) Main research: cults, sects and new religious movements, and the social reactions to which they give rise. Since 1989 she has also spent much time studying the state of religion in post-communist societies. In 1988, with the support of the Home Office and the mainstream churches, she set up INFORM, an NGO, which supplies information about alternative religions.

She has over 250 publications, translated into 27 languages. These include the award-winning The *Making of a Moonie: Brainwashing or Choice*? and *New Religious Movements: A Practical Introduction*, published in eight languages.

She has given guest lectures in over 200 universities around the world, and is a familiar commentator on religious matters on both radio and television.

Prof. Henri J. Barkey

Chair of the Department of International Relations and The Bernard and Bertha Cohen Chair at Lehigh University. Dr Barkey is the foremost scholar on Turkish Politics in the US. 1998-2000: a Member of the Policy Planning Staff at the State Department. He has taught at Princeton, Columbia, the State University of New York, and at the University of Pennsylvania. He is co-author of *Turkey's Kurdish Question* (1998); editor of *Reluctant Neighbour: Turkey's Role in the Middle East* (1996); and author of *The State and the Industrialization Crisis in Turkey* (1990). His articles have appeared in *Brookings Policy Briefs, Journal of International Affairs, Middle East Policy, Middle East Journal, World Policy Journal, Journal of Democracy, Comparative Political Studies, Survival, Studies in Comparative International Development,* and *Armed Forces and Society*. His op-ed pieces have been published in the *New York Times*, the *Washington Post*, and the *Los Angeles Times*.

Prof. Muhammad Abdul Haleem

Director of the Centre of Islamic Studies at SOAS, Chief Editor of the *Journal of Qur'anic Studies* (EUP), BA (Cairo), PhD (Cambridge), Fellow of the Chartered Institute of Linguists, participant in the Building Bridges programme, chaired by the Archbishop of Canterbury, and the Cambridge Interfaith Programme; Member of the Scientific Committee of the Foundation for Inter-religious/Inter-cultural Research/ Dialogue (FIIRD), University of Geneva.

Recent publications: *The Qur'an: a New Translation*, (OUP 2004); *Understanding the Qur'an: Themes and Style*, (IB Tauris, 2001); 'The Politics of Peace in Islam', in *Religions and the Politics of Peace and War*, ed. Linda Hogan, Wipf and Stock, (USA, 2007); 'Islam, Religion of the Environment' in *Yearbook of Islamic and Middle Eastern Law*, Vol. 10 (2003-4), editors Eugene Cotran and Martin Lau, (Brill 2006).

Prof. George S. Harris

Currently a Research Fellow at Bilkent University, Ankara, and a Consultant on Eurasian and Middle East Affairs carrying out research on Turkey and the Middle East. He received his PhD in History of the Middle East from Harvard University in 1957 and then served in the Department of State, ending as Director of Analysis for Near East and South Asia at the time of his retirement in January 1996. He has published numerous articles and books on Turkey, including *Troubled Alliance, Turkish-American Problems in Historical Perspective 1945-1971* and most recently *The Communists and the Kadro Movement: Shaping Ideology in Ataturk's Turkey*. He is presently researching Turkish foreign policy and its practitioners in the Ataturk era.

Prof. Thomas Michel

Currently Secretary for Interreligious Dialogue for the Society of Jesus and as Ecumenical Secretary for the Federation of Asian Bishops' Conferences, Professor Michel was director of the Islamic Office of the Vatican's Council for Interreligious Dialogue for 13 years. He belongs to the Indonesian Province of the Jesuits. He regularly conducts seminars on Christian–Muslim relations in Indonesia, the Philippines and Malaysia.

Prof. Rev. Simon Robinson

Professor of Applied and Professional Ethics, Leeds Metropolitan University, Associate Director, Ethics Centre of Excellence, and Visiting Fellow in Theology, University of Leeds. Educated at Oxford and Edinburgh universities, Professor Robinson entered psychiatric social work before ordination in the Church of England in 1978. He served in university chaplaincy at Heriot-Watt and Leeds universities, developing research in areas of applied ethics and practical theology. Ongoing research interests: religious ethics and care; interfaith pastoral care; professional ethics; ethics in higher education; spirituality and professional practice; corporate social responsibility; and ethics in global perspective. Among his publications: *Moral Meaning and Pastoral Counselling*; (ed. with Chris Megone) *Case Histories in Business Ethics*; *Living Wills*; (with Kevin Kendrick and Alan Brown) *Spirituality and Healthcare*; *Ministry Amongst Students*; (ed. with Clement Katulushi) *Values in Higher Education*; (with Ross Dixon, Chris Preece and Kris Moodley) *Engineering, Business and Professional Ethics*.

Prof. Zeki Saritoprak

The Bediuzzaman Said Nursi Chair in Islamic Studies at John Carroll University in Cleveland, Ohio. PhD in Islamic theology, University of Marmara, Turkey; and several years studying the Arabic language in Cairo while researching his dissertation on 'The Antichrist (*al-Dajjal*)'. He has researched and taught a range of subjects – at Harran University (Turkey), Georgetown University, the Catholic University of America in Washington D.C. and Berry College in Rome, Georgia – Islamic theology, Introduction to Islam, World Religions, Biblical Elements in the Qur'an, Islamic Spirituality, classical and contemporary Islamic movements, and interfaith dialogue, notably courses on Islamic personalities such as al-Ghazzali and Bediuzzaman Said Nursi.

Prof. David Thomas

Professor of Christianity and Islam at the University of Birmingham. His main interests: Islamic theology and philosophy, the history and theology of Christian-Muslim relations, Islam and culture, and textual studies in Arabic. Among recent publications: 'Dialogue with other Faiths as an Aspect of Islamic Theology' in T.L. Hettema and A. van der Kooij (eds.), *Religious Polemics in Context* (Assen, The Netherlands 2004); *Muslim-Christian Polemic during the Crusades. The letter from the People of Cyprus and Ibn Abi Talib's Response*; (ed. with R. Ebied) *The History of Christian-Muslim Relations 2* (Leiden, 2005); 'Receiving and Acquiring Wisdom in Islam', *Journal of Chinese Philosophy* 33 (2006). He is currently working on 'Christian Doctrine in Islamic Theology'. He is the editor for entries on Islam in *The Encyclopaedia of the Bible and its Reception*; general editor of *Christian-Muslim Relations: a Bibliographical History 1*; and editor of the journal *Islam and Christian-Muslim Relations*.

Prof. Paul Weller

Professor of Inter-Religious Relations at the University of Derby and Head of Research and Commercial Development in its Faculty of Education, Health and Sciences; Visiting Fellow in the Oxford Centre for Christianity and Culture at Regent's Park College, University of Oxford; and Vice Chair of the Multi-Faith Centre at the University of Derby. Current interests: issues in the relationships between religion, state and society. Recent publications: *Time for Change: Reconfiguring Religion, State and Society* (London: T. & T. Clark, 2005) and 'Fethullah Gülen, Religions, Globalisation and Dialogue', in R. Hunt and Y. Aslandoğan (eds.), *Muslim Citizens of the Globalized World: Contributions of the Gülen Movement* (Somerset, NJ: The Light Inc. and IID Press, 2006). He is editor of *Religions in the UK: Directory*, 2007-2010 (Derby: University of Derby and Multi-Faith Centre at the University of Derby, 2007).

Prof. Ian G. Williams

Senior Lecturer & Subject Leader in Religious Education, University of Central England, Faculty of Education, Birmingham. (PhD in Islamic Studies, University of Derby; after ordination, served in Church of England parish ministry and religious education.) He has lectured in Religious Studies at the Universities of Chester and Derby, and taught and researched in the Middle East, the USA, and India. Current interests: the Fethullah Gülen movement in Turkish Islam; sacred violence and martyrdom in contemporary Islam; Sufi movements in the UK. Among recent publications: 'Modern Movements in Islam and Zoroastrianism' in *Dictionary of Contemporary Religion in the Western World* (IVP: Leicester, 2003); 'In the Aftermath of 9/11. Jihad and Martyrdom in Contemporary Islam', *Sea of Faith Journal* (Sept. 2002); 'Sufism in British Islam' in *Contemporary Mysticism* (Exeter: Paternoster, 2001); 'Fundamentalist Movements amongst British Muslims' in *Fundamentalisms: Studies in Contemporary Religious Radicalism* (Exeter: Paternoster, 2000).

Dr Alan Godlas

Associate Professor in the Department of Religion at the University of Georgia. In addition, he is the Co-Director of the UGA-Morocco Maymester program. At UGA he teaches Islamic Studies and Arabic courses as well as a survey course on the world's religions. Dr Godlas received his MA (1983) and PhD (1991) in Near Eastern Studies from the University of California at Berkeley. Dr Godlas has conducted extensive research in manuscript libraries in Egypt, Morocco, and Turkey. His professional experience includes being on the editorial board of the journal, *Sufi Illuminations*, and being a member of the steering committee of the Study of Mysticism and Study of Islam sections of the American Academy of Religion. In January 2003, Dr Godlas was chosen by the US Department of State and the Emir of Kano to give two presentations on Islam for a bilateral conference in Northern Nigeria.

Dr Asaf Hussain

An academic from the University of Leicester. He teaches modules on Islamic civilisation. He has been writing and publishing books on Islamic fundamentalism since the early 1980s, and in the course of his research visited many fundamentalist groups in the Middle East and South Asia. Currently he is engaged in writing three studies on 'Islamic civilisation', 'Islamic fundamentalism in Britain' and 'Islamic fundamentalism in Pakistan'.

Rev. Dr Johnston McMaster

Lecturer and Programme Co-ordinator of Education in the Irish School of Ecumenics, Trinity College Dublin, and Chair of the Northern Ireland Youth Service Curriculum and Policy Development at the Joined in Equity, Diversity and Interdependence (JEDI). (Doctorate of Ministry at Garrett-Evangelical Seminary in North Western University, Illinois.) Among his areas of expertise and research: Broadcasting, Public Theology, Socio-Political Biblical Hermeneutics, Celtic Spirituality and Contemporary Social Ethics, Communities of Reconciliation, Overcoming Violence: A Faith Perspective, The Shape of Faith in a Post-Christendom Era.

Dr Colin Turner

Lecturer in Islamic Studies and Persian at the University of Durham, where he also completed his PhD on the rise of religious nomocentrism in 17th century Persia. Dr Turner is the author of the best-selling *Islam: The Basics* (Routledge) and *Islam without Allah? The Rise of Religious Externalism in Safavid Iran* (Curzon Press). His main research interests include Islamic theology and philosophy; the anthropology of Islam; Quranic exegesis; Shi'ism and Sufism. He is currently engaged in research on the issue of immortality motifs in the Quran and an annotated translation of Mulla Sadra's *Three Principles*.

Dr Tim Winter

University Lecturer in Islamic Studies at the University of Cambridge, and Director of Studies in Theology at Wolfson College. He is the author of several translations of texts by al-Ghazali (d.1111), and of two books in Turkish on Islam and modernity. His edited volume 'The Cambridge Companion to Classical Islamic Theology' is scheduled for publication in 2008. His main research interests are Sufism, the development of the Ottoman learned institution, computerised hadith databases and Muslim-Christian relations.

TABLE OF CONTENTS

WHAT MADE THE GÜLEN MOVEMENT POSSIBLE?

Mustafa Akyol

Abstract

Turkey's most powerful and popular Islamic community, the Fethullah Gülen movement, is also a very moderate one, which embraces liberal democracy and promotes inter-faith tolerance and dialogue. This paper asks what socio-political conditions enabled this movement to emerge, get established and grow as successfully as it has.

The legacy of late Ottoman modernisation, which sought a synthesis of Islamic and modern Western values, assisted the Muslims of Republican Turkey to embrace democracy and establish good relations with the West. Post-war Turkey's peaceful interaction with the West — via free markets and international institutions — must have been a factor. So too it must be relevant that Turkey was never colonised by Western powers or even occupied for a long time (military interventions by the West in other Muslim countries have provoked quite radical, not moderate, Islamic responses).

The paper discusses the historical roots and social dynamics in Turkey that enabled the kind of 'moderate Islam' represented by the Gülen movement. That effort could provide lessons for other Muslim countries. It is all but taken for granted that the Islamic world needs some kind of 'reform'. Élitist and autocratic calls for 'top–down' efforts to reshape Islam notwithstanding, what is really needed is to build the social environment (security, freedom, democracy, economic opportunity) that will enable a new kind of Muslim, who will, eventually, search for new meanings in traditional texts.

Ottoman Modernization Revisited

To see that, one should first examine the Turks' experience with Islam. Compared with the Arabs, the Turks were latecomers to the Muslim faith. The former were politically and intellectually more advanced until the 13th century, when the Arabs' brilliant civilization was nearly destroyed by one of the most devastating conquests ever, the Mongol catastrophe. The chance of world trade roots, from the Middle East and the Levant to the oceans, was an additional misfortune that would steadily impoverish the Arab world, which owed much of its wealth to trade. The long-term result was the stagnation of the Arab peoples.

Meanwhile, the leadership of Islam was passing to the Turks, who created powerful states under the Seljuk, and especially the subsequent Ottoman dynasty. The Ottoman state extended its borders both towards the West and the East, and in the 16th and much of the 17th centuries, acted as the world's foremost superpower.

The political power of the Turks, and their continual interaction with the West, gave them an important insight: They faced the rise of modernity. The Ottoman elite had to rule an empire, make practical decisions, adopt new technologies, and reform existing structures — all of which allowed them to understand and cope with secular realities. Sociologist Şerif Mardin defines the consequential praxis as "Ottoman secularity," and gives examples of Ottoman bureaucrats who started to discover "Western ways," more than two centuries before the Turkish Republic:

> ... It is quite clear that the eighteenth century brought about a number of cumulative changes that promoted the "secularist" aspect of the discourse of Ottoman bureaucracy. One of these changes was the creation of a new bureau (Amedî Odası) through which flowed all communication with Western states. The employees of this bureau were now increasingly exposed to information about the major European states. Antedating this change already in the 1730s there had been an increase in the number of bureaucrats who were sent to various European capitals to observe Western "ways." An innovation of the same years was the practice of these envoys to write reports about their missions upon their return. What is striking about these reports is the "materiality" of their content. The reports did not contrast the religious or political institutions they found in the West with their Ottoman equivalents, but focused on the material elements of life. They detailed technological advances such as the construction of stone buildings, both military and civilian, and they described the splendour of Versailles, its organization of leisure activities and in particular the theatre. The precision of the tables of astronomical observatories also impressed them.[1]

According to Mardin, such practices helped formulating "Turkish-Islamic exceptionalism," which is overlooked by most contemporary Western scholars on Islam because of their "concentration on Arab or Salafi Islam." Mardin adds that the exceptionalism is not solely produced by the Turkish Republic, as it is often thought, but was built in a long historical evolution thanks to milestones such as "the earlier rise of a Turkish bureaucratic class (circa 1780)... the type of institution building policy that goes back to the reign of Sultan Abdulhamid II (r. 1876–1909) and the type of synthesis between Islam and modernity that was promoted by an intellectual elite between 1908 and 1923."[2]

---

1 Şerif Mardin, "Turkish Islamic Exceptionalism Yesterday and Today: Continuity, Rupture and Reconstruction in Operational Codes," Turkish Studies 6, (2), Summer 2005, pp. 149-150
2 Ibid., p. 145

Tanzimat and Equal Citizenship

The 18th century discovery of Europe by Ottoman bureaucrats resulted in the famous "Imperial Gulhane Decree of 1839," also known as the Tanzimat Edict, which introduced the idea of supremacy of law and modern citizenship to the empire. In a second substantive reform edict, in 1856, the dhimmi ("protected") status was abolished, and Jews and Christians gained equal citizenship rights.

That dhimmi status that Islamic states have traditionally given to Jews and Christians —and actually any other traditional faith except Arab idolaters— has been the subject of much criticism recently. There are writers who present it as a slavish life that Islam imposes on non-Muslims.[3] Although it is true that the dhimma was an unequal status that grew out from and should remain in pre-modern times, it was actually quite generous according to norms of that period. One interesting fact which would support that conclusion is that many non-Muslims of the Ottoman State were actually content with the dhimma so that they resisted its abolition. According to historian Roderick H. Davison:

> The program of equality between Christian and Muslim in the empire remained largely unrealized not because of bad faith on the part of leading Ottoman statesmen but because many of the Christians wanted it to fail... The ecclesiastical hierarchies that ruled the Christian millet's also opposed equality. Osmanlilik [Ottomanhood] would both decrease their authority and lighten their purses. This was especially true of the Greek Orthodox hierarchy, which had the most extensive prerogatives and by far the largest flock. When the Hatt-i Sherif [Tanzimat Edict] was solemnly read in 1839 and then put back into its red satin pouch it is reported that the Greek Orthodox patriarch, who was present among the notables, said, "Inshallah-God grant that it not be taken out of this bag again." In short, the doctrine of equality faced formidable opposition from Christians of the empire who were leaders in the churches and the nationalist movements...[4]

Davidson also notes,

> Both in 1839 and 1856 the sultan proclaimed that his Christian subjects should be equally privileged to serve in the armed forces along with the Muslims, instead of paying an exemption tax as they had previously done. It soon became obvious that the Christians would rather continue to pay than serve, despite the step toward equality which military service might mean.[5]

In the 19th century, the Ottoman state also started to accept the principle of religious freedom. As early as May 1844, an official Ottoman edict read, "No subject of the Sublime [Ottoman] State shall be forced by anyone to convert to Islam against their wishes."[6] In the Reform Edict of 1856 the Sultan proclaimed, "All forms of religion are and shall be freely professed in my dominions. No subject of my empire shall be hindered in the exercise of the religion that he professes."[7] The Ottoman Constitution of 1876 established a limited monarchy all of whose subjects were considered "Osmanli (Ottoman), whatever religion or creed they hold." The constitution further affirmed that "all Osmanli are equal before the law . . .

---

3 Bat Ye'or, Islam and Dhimmitude: Where Civilizations Collide, (Trans. By Miriam Kochan and David Littman) Cranbury, NJ: Associated University Presses. 2002

4 Roderick H. Davison, Turkish Attitudes Concerning Christian-Muslim Equality in the Nineteenth Century, American Historical Review, Vol. 59, No. 4 (Jul., 1954), pp. 844-864

5 Ibid.

6 Selim Deringil, "There Is No Compulsion in Religion": On Conversion and Apostasy in the Late Ottoman Empire: 1839–18561," Comparative Studies in Society and History (2000), 42: 547-575 Cambridge University Press

7 Ibid.

without distinction as to religion."[8]

What is striking about these events is the fact that the Ottoman Empire — an Islamic state which many Muslims around the world still respect — gave full citizenship rights to Jews and Christians. These would create a precedent for the ecumenical approach towards Jews and Christians that would be articulated in Turkey's Republican era by scholars like Said Nursi and Fethullah Gülen.

One crucial point was that the Ottoman Empire wasn't abandoning Islam by reforming the sharia laws. It was rather modernizing itself from within the tradition. The Qur'anic verse "There is no compulsion in religion" was stressed by the Ottoman religious elite to justify the reforms.[9] Under the auspices of Sultan Abdulhamid II, Ahmet Cevdet Pasha, an Ottoman bureaucrat and an Islamic scholar, prepared the Mecelle, a new legal code which was based on traditional Islamic law but which also included many important modifications with the idea of updating the shariah according to "the requirements of the time."[10]

The Ottoman Islamic modernization ended with the demise of the empire in the First World War. From its ruins, what we now call the Middle East arose-with a doomed legacy: All post-Ottoman states, except Turkey and Saudi Arabia, were colonized by European powers, a phenomenon that would soon breed anti-colonialism and anti-Westernism throughout the entire region. That was also one of the reasons of the end of what the great historian of the Middle East, Albert Hourani, called the "liberal age" of the Arab world[11] — which was, basically, the Arabic counterpart of Ottoman modernization.

The Two Trends

The Ottoman reforms were articulated and carried out by the intellectual elite of the empire. Most of these men — and some women —spoke English and French, and were very well versed in European thought, not to mention the Islamic tradition. Among them were different trends, but to generalize, we can speak of two main camps. One of these was what one can call the "modernization within the tradition" camp. Its proponents realized the need for reforms, but were hoping to realize these without abandoning traditional values, and especially the religious ones.

The second trend was what one can call the "modernization despite the tradition" line, which found its most radical expressions among some radical Young Turks such as Abdullah Cevdet. "The Young Turk Weltanschauung, as it developed between 1889 and 1902," according to historian Şükrü Hanioğlu, "was vehemently antireligious, viewing religion as the greatest obstacle to human progress."[12] In later years, the Young Turks played down their secularist views for political purposes, but the Weltanschauung remained intact.

During Turkey's War of Liberation (1919-22), both of these intellectual trends — and all other segments of the society, which included Islamic clerics, Kurdish leaders, and local notables — were united against the occupying powers and under the roof of the Turkish Parliament. But even during those years, the two different political lines became evident

8   Ibid.

9   Ibid.

10   Kemal Karpat, The Politicization of Islam, p. 189

11   Albert Hourani, *Arabic Thought in the Liberal Age, 1798-1939*, Cambridge University Press, 1983

12   Şükrü Hanioğlu, *Preparation for a Revolution: The Young Turks, 1902-1908*, Oxford University Press, 2001, p. 305

within Parliament. "The First Group" consisted of the enthusiastic supporters of Mustafa Kemal, the leader of the War of Liberation who was also a follower of the secularist and revolutionary line of thinking. "The Second Group," on the other hand, included those who had reservations about Mustafa Kemal's increasing political power.

The Fate of Terakkiperver Fırka

When the war was won and the Republic was announced in 1923, the First Group turned into the People's Party ("Halk Fırkası"), which was directed by Mustafa Kemal (Atatürk) and his closest ally, İsmet İnönü. About a year later, The Second Group established the Progressive Party (Terakkiperver Fırka), whose leaders were also war heroes such as Kazım Karabekir, Refet Bele or Rauf Orbay.

There were three main differences between the conservative Progressive Party and the revolutionary People's Party:

i.   The Progressive Party believed in free markets and individual entrepreneurship, an idea that had been advanced by Prince Sabahattin, the nephew of the late Sultan Abdulhamid II. The People's Party, on the other hand, held a more "statist" approach towards the economy, which would carry corporatist tones in the 30's.

ii.   The Progressive Party was friendly to religion. Its founding document included the famous Article six, which read, "We are respectful to religious ideas and sentiments."

iii.   On political issues such as the fate of the Kurds, the Progressive Party was tolerant and liberal. Kazım Karabekir, its leader, prepared a detailed report arguing that Kurds needed to be integrated into Turkish society gradually by encouraging agriculture and trade, and by keeping the spirit of common Muslim values. The People's Party, on the other hand, believed in what its leader İsmet İnönü called the "Turkification" of the Kurds, by using authoritarian methods such as banning their language and destroying their culture.

Yet the disagreement between the parties would not last long. On June 5, 1925 the Progressive Party was closed down by the regime. The party was actually able to survive for only six months and two weeks. Then, not only was it destroyed, but also its leaders were excluded from politics. Its top figure, Kazım Karabekir, lived under house arrest for many years. All of his works were collected and burned on the orders of the government.

The announced reason was Article six in its program: the "We are respectful to religious ideas and sentiments" clause. For the new regime, this was a statement that encouraged "backward minded thought and action," and which could not be tolerated.

The Post-1925 Trauma

From 1925 to 1950, Turkey lived under a "single party regime," which was characterized by its self-style secularism. Unlike the separation between church and state, which defines the American version of secularism, the Kemalist model was "based on the radical Jacobin laicism that aimed to transform society through the power of the state and eliminate religion from the public sphere."[13]

---

13   M. Hakan Yavuz, John L. Esposito, "Islam in Turkey: Retreat from the Secular Path?" in Turkish Islam and the Secular State, (ed. by M. Hakan Yavuz, John L. Esposito) Syracuse University Press, 2003, p. xvi

This effort had the negative effect of establishing the perception that religion and modernity are incompatible. Turkey's practicing Muslims felt themselves forced to abandon the former for the sake of the latter. The authoritarian secularist effort also drove Turkey into an acute version of the problem that Richard John Neuhaus points out to: The vacuum created by absent religion was filled by ersatz religion.[14] In just a decade, Islam was replaced by a new public faith based on Turkishness and the cult of personality created around Mustafa Kemal Atatürk. "Let the Ka'aba be for the Arabs," wrote poet Kemalettin Kamu, "for us, Çankaya is enough." That new shrine was Atatürk's residence.

The people who bought into this new faith became known as the "secular elite." They were a small minority in a very traditional society. That's why they have decided that they have no time to lose with democracy. The people needed not to be represented and served, but to be ruled and indoctrinated. That's why, unlike the American Republic which is traditionally defined as "a government by the people, for the people, of the people," the Turkish Republic was defined in its early decades as a government "for the people, in spite of the people."

The two main segments of the society that the Republic acted "in spite of" were practicing Muslims and Kurds. Both groups were suppressed. The former got their religious institutions destroyed, the latter got their language and identity banned. Not surprisingly, both of these alienated groups had a hard time in digesting this undemocratic republic, and instead hoped for a democracy through which they could realize their longing for freedom. In the first free and fair elections in 1950, they brought the Democrat Party in power, whose motto was, "Enough! The nation has the word." The first thing the DP did was to set the Muslim call for prayer (the daily "ezan") free, and to ease the burden in Kurdish areas. It also brought some suppressed Kurdish leaders to the parliament. Moreover it put Turkey into NATO, accepted the Marshall Plan, and brought in Western capital, which many "Republicans," who had socialist views, saw as "imperialism."

The democratic honeymoon did not last long, tough. In 1960 the military staged a coup, closed down the DP, and, after a controversial show trial, executed Prime Minister Adnan Menderes and two of his ministers.

Said Nursi and His Heritage

The iron hand of "the Republic" led some Kurds to initiate a terrorist war against it (carried out by the bloody PKK and its forerunners), but the reaction of the practicing Muslims has been peaceful. After all, Turkey does not have a tradition of Islamist violence and there is a synthesis of Islam and democracy that goes way back to the Ottoman Empire.

Thus, instead of fighting against "the Republic", practicing Muslims have preferred to vote for conservative parties that would soften its autocratic nature. Some of them hoped to bring an "Islamic rule" via elections, while others only demanded a democratic rule which would respect their religious freedom. A very prominent name in the latter camp would be Said Nursi (1878-1960), whose treaties on Islamic faith and morality has created Turkey's most important Islamic movement.

Turkish scholar Yasin Aktay defines Nursi as a "very apolitical, other-worldly and loyal character," the latter feature referring to his allegiance to Republican Turkey. Unlike Sheik Said, another Kurdish Islamic leader who led a popular but unsuccessful revolt against the

---

14   Richard John Neuhaus, The Naked Public Square: Religion and Democracy in America, William B. Eerdmans Publishing, 1984, pp. 80-84

secular Turkish Republic in 1925, Nursi rejected political radicalism and focused his energy to articulating a godly worldview and moral code compatible with the modern world. According to Aktay, he, in his books, developed "a very elective and appropriate combination of the elements of the popular culture, mystical discourses, orthodox Islam and science and rationality."[15]

In his thought, Nursi was closer to someone like C.S. Lewis — the Oxford professor who is widely regarded as one of the most important Christian apologists of the 20th century — than to Muslim contemporaries such as Hassan al-Banna, the founder of Egypt's Muslim Brotherhood. His enemies were not Zionism or Western imperialism but materialist philosophy and communist ideology, and he saw the Christian West as an ally against both. In 1951, Nursi sent one of his books to the Vatican, along with a letter in which he called for an Islamo-Christian alliance against atheism. During the Korean War, which Turkey joined as an American ally, Nursi encouraged his followers to enlist in the army to fight against the communists.

Nursi's millions of followers who constituted the Nur ("Light") movement, have always steered away from Islamist political parties and voted for centre-right parties which promised not shariah but religious freedom. According to Hakan Yavuz, Nursi, unlike the Young Turks and Kemalists who praised the state, "treated the state as the servant of the people and argued for a neutral state without any ideology."[16] Moreover he was very much in favour of modernizing Turkey, and the Islamic world in general, by importing Western science and technology.

But even that modernist Islam was too much for the secularist establishment. "In spite of all [their] compatibility with the modernization process, Said Nursi and his movements have been prosecuted by the state," notes Yasin Aktay. "Because... in order to constitute themselves as Western, Kemalists had to deny and repress any traces of the Orient."[17]

The Rise of the Gülen Movement

After the death of Nursi in 1960, his followers ("nurcus") divided into several camps with differing views on how to interpret his legacy and, also, how to engage with politics. In the 70's a cleric in Izmir who had been influenced by some of Nursi's ideas but also who had new approaches of his own, started to attract attention and following. He was Fethullah Gülen, whose popularity and influence would soon exceed those of all other Islamic movements in Turkey. According to Aktay,

> Fethullah Hoca, as a preacher famed in İzmir, following the same path of the Nurcu movement in that sense, seems to have been discovered by the state at least since the mid-eighties. He left the mainstream Nurcu movement at the early seventies and began to publish a monthly named, Sızıntı. The underlying idea of the name implies that it represents the leakage of the essence of the absolute truth, of the revelation. The major themes in the journal turn around catching the dispatches from the God which is embodied through a striking and mysterious order of the world. Undoubtedly a relevant discourse analysis of the journal may clarify various aspects of the community in terms of also the constitution of the self-identity in relation with the nature, religion and

15   Yasin Aktay, Body, Text, Identity: The Islamist Discourse Of Authenticity In Modern Turkey, PhD Thesis, 1997, The Graduate School Of Social Sciences of the Middle East Technical University, Ankara

16   M. Hakan Yavuz, "Islam in the Public Square: The Case of the Nur Movement," in Turkish Islam and the Secular State, (ed. by M. Hakan Yavuz, John L. Esposito) Syracuse University Press, 2003, p. 11

17   Aktay, Ibid.

the political body. After leaving the mainstream movement he found an alternative community which depended on his personal charisma achieved by his strong ability in preaching and organising, and of course, on his deep intelligence.[18]

Gülen had a vision that would take him and his followers to a point where no other Muslim community in Turkey even dreamed of. Instead of simply trying to create a limited living space for itself in public life, like many other Islamic groups do, Gülen movement decided to engage with society and create publications and institutions that would appeal to people from all walks of life. Their newspapers and TV channels, such as Zaman or STV, are not in-house community outlets but they speak to the whole society. Their schools, which are famed for their high education quality and moral integrity, have students with diverse backgrounds. Their initiatives such as the Abant Platform or Intercultural Dialogue Platform — which are both supported by the Journalists and Writers Foundation, whose honorary president is Fethullah Gülen — address not sectarian issues, but deal with virtually all social problems of Turkey.

Moreover, since the mid-90's, Gülen movement started to become a global phenomenon. They first started by opening schools in ex-Soviet Republics, which proved to be a very successful enterprise. Soon the schools spread out to four corners of the world, ranging from South Africa to Mongolia, or from Australia to Denmark. Gülen's move to United States in late 90's also contributed to the globalism of the movement. And while the movement was hoping to help changing the world for the better with all these activities, they were also being changed by the world for the better: Their engagement with different cultures, and especially that of the West, helped Gülen's followers to develop a more liberal and cosmopolitan mindset and discourse.

Incorporating Capitalism

Today the Gülen movement represents the most powerful element of the rising "Muslimhood" of Turkey, as sociologist Jenny B. White defines as an alternative to Islamism.[19] This Muslimhood is in favour of democracy, secularity, pluralism and even capitalism — something which even many modern Muslims perceive as alien to Islam.

Some striking examples of the latter phenomenon have emerged in Turkey in the past two decades. Turkey is not the richest country the Islamic world, but it is arguably the most developed. The richest are the oil-rich Arab nations, most of which, despite their petro-dollars, remain socially pre-modern and tribal. Regrettably, oil brings wealth, but it does not modernize. Modernization comes through rationality, which can be achieved only through organization, order, exchange, and risk-taking in pursuit of goals. The late Turgut Özal, one of Turkey's wiser Presidents, once said, "We are lucky that we don't have oil; we have to work hard to make money."

Özal was a pro-Western politician and a Muslim believer. His revolutionary, Reaganesque reforms during the 1980s transformed the Turkish economy from import subsidization to free markets. In this new setting the conservative Muslim masses of Anatolia have found fertile ground for a socio-economic boom. Thanks to their astounding successes in business, they have been called "Anatolian Tigers." They constitute a new class that rivals

---

18 Ibid.

19 Jenny B. White, "The End of Islamism? Turkey's Muslimhood Model", *Modern Muslim Politics*, Robert Hefner, ed., Princeton University Press, 2005

lished, privileged, highly secularized and utterly condescending "Istanbul

n Stability Initiative (ESI), a Berlin-based think tank, conducted an extensive
"Anatolian tigers" in 2005. ESI researchers interviewed hundreds of conservative businessmen in the central Anatolian city of Kayseri. They discovered that "individualistic, pro-business currents have become prominent within Turkish Islam," and a "quiet Islamic
Reformation" was taking place in the hands of Muslim entrepreneurs. The term they used to
define these godly capitalists was also the title of their report: "Islamic Calvinists."[20]

Some of these "Islamic Calvinists", apparently, are also the followers of Fethullah Gülen.[21]
Gülen movement is well known for its success in business, which create financial support for
the movement's cultural and educational institutions.

This amalgamation of Islamic values with the practical rationality of the free market indeed
reminds of the spirit of the real Calvinists, who, according to sociologist Max Weber, spearheaded the rise of capitalism in the West. Interestingly Weber was not very hopeful for Islam
in this regard. For him Islam was an obstacle to capitalist development, for it could foster
only aggressive militancy (jihad) or contemplative austerity. However, one of the greatest
Turkish sociologists, Sabri F. Ülgener — both a student and a critic of Weber — argued that
Weber, despite his genius in analyzing the origins of capitalism in the West, misjudged Islam
and overlooked its inherent compatibility with a "liberal market system."[22]

The rise of an Islamic entrepreneurial class is a remarkable phenomenon, because it marks
the beginning a whole new stage for Islamic civilization. People understand religion according not only to its textual teachings, but also their social environment. As for Islam, this
environment has been feudal, imperial, or bureaucratic. But now, in Turkey and in a few other
Muslim counties such as Malaysia, Islam is being transformed into a religion of the middle
class and its rational, independent individuals. And the Gülen movement plays a leading
role in this silent yet crucial transformation. "Gülen is the engine behind the construction of
a 'new' national Islam of Turkey," argues Hakan Yavuz, "marked by the logic of a market
economy and the Ottoman legacy."[23]

The Rediscovery of the West

A related aspect of the new "Muslimhood" in Turkey, and that of the Gülen movement, is its
growing advocacy of Western-style democracy. One reason of this phenomenon is a significant discovery that Turkey's observant Muslims — especially the ones who had a chance to
know the West, such as the Gülen movement — had in the past quarter century: that the West
is better than the Westernisers.

What this means is that they recognized that Western democracies give their citizens all the

---

20 European Stability Initiative, Islamic Calvinists: Change and Conservatism in Central Anatolia, September 19,
2005; http://www.esiweb.org/pdf/esi_document_id_69.pdf
21 Following a heated public discussion on the term "Islamic Calvinists" in Turkey, Gülen announced that he does
not endorse the term, and, unlike the original Calvinists, he is not seeking a reform in religion. But this seems to be
negation of the extravagant meanings that the Turkish media attributed to "Islamic Calvinism," not the meaning that
the ESI report suggested, which is the rise of a business-friendly and dynamic Muslim identity.
22 Sabri Ülgener, Zihniyet ve Din (Mindset and Religion), Derin Yayınları, 2006, pp. 57-64
23 M. Hakan Yavuz, "The Gülen Movement: The Turkish Puritans," in Turkish Islam and the Secular State, (ed. by
M. Hakan Yavuz, John L. Esposito) Syracuse University Press, 2003, p. 21

religious freedoms that Turkey has withheld from its own. In fact, no country in the free world has secularism as illiberal as Turkey's self-styled laicité. Any society or club which has an Islamic name or purpose is illegal, and religious education is very limited. A woman wearing a Muslim headscarf has no chance of any kind of learning in Turkey, whether in public or private schools. There is also the bitter language used the by secular elite towards observant Muslims.

For many decades, devout Muslims in Turkey have perceived this entire secular fundamentalism as a product of the West, and hoped that de-Westernization would end their feelings of being "a pariah in their own land," as the late Islamic poet Necip Fazil once put it. Yet, the more they learned about the West, the more they realized that the problem is in Ankara — not in Washington, London, or Brussels. In Europe and North America, one can establish Islamic centres, Sufi clubs, and independent mosques, none of which are allowed in their homeland. It is possible to attend American or European universities with the headscarf, while it is banned by law in Turkey.

All those facts transformed the way Turkish Muslim perceive the West. Having realized that the real West is preferable to the caricature of it they have at home, they have re-routed their search for freedom. Instead of trying to Islamize the state, they have decided to liberalize it.

In this regard, Gülen's comments about his own discovery of the West, which he made during an interview in 2000, is quite illuminating:

> We all change, don't we? There is no escape from change. By visiting the United States and many other European countries, I realized the virtues and the role of religion in these societies. Islam flourishes in America and Europe much better than in many Muslim countries. This means freedom and the rule of law are necessary for personal Islam. Moreover, Islam does not need the state survive, but rather needs educated and financially rich communities to flourish. In a way, not the state but rather community is needed under a full democratic system."

The line of reasoning that Gülen articulates — the argument for an Islam which demands a liberal democratic, not Islamic, state — also explains the remarkable alliance in today's Turkey between Muslim conservatives, and especially the Gülen movement, and the secular liberals. Their coalition is in favour of the EU bid and democratization, whereas the nationalist front—which includes die-hard secular Kemalists, ultra-right wing Turkish nationalists, and hardliner Islamists—abhors both of those objectives. It is no accident the daily Zaman and its English-language sister publication, Today's Zaman — which both belong to the Gülen movement — hosts many liberal columnists.

Conclusion

In today's Turkey Gülen movement represents an Islam which is liberal and tolerant, which is in favour of the country's EU bid and democratizing reforms. And this means that it is a "modern" movement. Yet this modernity has not been achieved by the authoritarian secularist policies of the state. It has been achieved thanks to Turkey's heritage of Ottoman modernization, engagement with the Western world, and its social progress.

The experience of Turkish Islam also hints us how the much-sought renaissance of the Islamic world will come about: through the flourishing of democracy, freedom and economic opportunity. Only these social dynamics create individuals and communities who are willing to adapt to modernity. On the other hand, if Muslim societies are forced to accept modernity— through, say, secularist tyrannies or Western military interventions—they simply react to it, and the backlash fuels radicalism.

Just remember the fact that Christianity surpassed its dark ages thanks to its godly—not secular—renovators. Islamic civilization needs to follow a similar route to accomplish its renewal. And the Turkish experience, and in particular the Gülen movement, hints that there are reasons to be hopeful.

THE INFLUENCE OF THE GÜLEN MOVEMENT IN THE EMERGENCE OF A TURKISH CULTURAL THIRD WAY

Marie-Elisabeth Maigre

Abstract

This paper aims to understand the role of Fethullah Gülen's movement in the emergence of the new Islamic culture in Turkey. Among the Islamic dynamics that emerged in the 80s, the movement based on Gülen's ideas is unique not in that it spread through an intellectual, healthcare and media network – this is true of other Sufi communities – but in its development of an effective educational programme now comprising more than 300 schools around the world.

In the 1990s, this movement favoured a 'Turkish Islam' encompassing the principles of democracy and moderation, and so rejected the radical ideals of Necmettin Erbakan's Refah party. After the 1997 'soft coup' removed the Erbakan government, pro-Islamic businesspeople became more disinclined to support a party that could threaten their business interests. A reformist branch led by Istanbul mayor, Recep Tayyip Erdoğan, began to adopt the principles of democracy and religious freedom as part of a new political argument, and eventually won the general elections of November 2002.

It seems that three actors – the Islamist reformists, the businessmen, and Gülen's followers – converged around the common concepts of Turkish Islam, Conservative Democracy, and Business to re-elaborate the cultural content of the Islamic movement with a more Western-democratic and capitalist orientation. The phrase 'Islam de marché', coined by Patrick Haenni, refers to the culture, born of globalisation, in which business success is efficiently used to translate thinking or religious beliefs into something practical and derive some cultural influence from association with the state.

Fethullah Gülen, whose movement is a paradigm of these new approaches, could be considered a far-sighted visionary since he anticipated the need for Turkish people, whether secular or Islamist, to adapt to the present times, and the strong potential of globalisation to diffuse his vision of Islam.

For the last 5 years, the debate on democratization in the Islamic world has been very lively. As the result of a shift in the studies of the Islamic countries in the 1990s when the opposition between authoritarian regimes and "political Islam" stopped being considered as the only socio-political framework to study the Islamic countries, many specialists started promoting the idea that the "fourth wave of democratization" was about to rise in the Middle East and North Africa (after Southern Europe, South America, and South-East Asia). The focus of the current US administration on promoting the democracy in a "Greater Middle East" has had a strong impact on the academia and research centres. The topic of "democratization in the Middle East" has become the latest thing. But in spite of some symbolic policies to "pull the wool" over western eyes, the grounding of democracy in most of the Muslim countries remains only intentional; very few Muslim-majority countries are considered indeed as fully democratic.

In this still pessimistic surrounding, Turkey represents a unique case, due to exceptional historical opportunities. From 1923, Mustapha Kemal "Atatürk" annihilated the old institutions of the Ottoman Empire and introduced a secular, bureaucratic, and centralized system; the latter earned a democratic facade in 1946 when the electoral system authorized bi-partism. In fact, until very recently, the military controlled the system through the National Security Council, a half-military half-civilian organism in charge of defending the spirit of the secular republic as conceived by Atatürk; this council had the power to force ministers to implement certain policies and the legitimacy to instigate a coup whenever it was believed necessary – which occurred four times in the history of the Turkish republic, in 1960, 1971, 1980, and again in 1997 against the Islamist Prime Minister Erbakan. However, the conditions set up by Brussels to start the process of EU membership stimulated a reform of the system. In 2002, the Turkish Parliament adopted a series of legislative and constitutional amendments that took effects in 2003. Moreover, since the 1980s, during the governments of Turgut Özal, social activities have increased and diversified. Among the actors of the blooming civil society, the pro-Islamic organizations have had an important influence by their support to the cultural reislamilisation of the society within the constraints of its secular political system.

At the heart of those pro-Islamic partakers of the democratization process, the movement based on Gülen's ideas spread in the last two decades through an intellectual, educative, healthcare, and media network. Articulated around the concepts of education, tolerance and inter-religious dialogue and unity, the movement pretends to encourage a return to the dialogue between the religious and scientific worlds since "science and religion as two manifestations of the same truth" – God's existence and purpose (Gülen, 2004: 82) The notions of compassion, love, and tolerance dominates the vision of the Islamic master in every aspects of life including politics, international relations and any kind of relationships. This paper intends to answer the following question: what has been the specific role of Gülen's movement in the emergence of a new Turkish culture? I will argue that Gülen's cultural and religious influence on both the business and political classes within the Islamic movement has driven the moderation of political Islam and open the way toward the integration into the new reality of globalization where the frontier between religion and business are blurred and those notions are brought together within a new conception of Culture.

The first part of this paper will focus on how Fethullah Gülen introduced his own style in Turkey, universalizing the Ottoman heritage of religious tolerance, emphasizing the points of convergence of all the monotheist religions in the world, and encouraging the achievability of his vision through a solid network of schools, charity, and media. The second part contrasts the evolution of political Islam in Turkey from radical ideas (for instance, the creation of an

Islamic State) to a moderate and pro-democratic with Gülen's political ideas. In the 1990s, his movement favoured a "Turkish Islam" encompassing the principles of democracy and moderation, therefore rejecting the radical ideals of Necmettin Erbakan's Refah party. After the soft coup of 1997 to bring the Erbakan's government to an end, the pro-Islamic business-men became more disinclined to support a party that could threat their business interests and position. Consequently, a reformist branch led by Istanbul Mayor Recep Tayyip Erdoğan also started adopting those principles of democracy and religious freedom as part of its new political line and finally won the general elections of November 2002.

Finally, observing the convergence of three groups, the religious-conservative businesspeo-ple, the followers of Gülen, and the Muslim democrats of Recep Tayyip Erdoğan, the third section will try to situate this socio-cultural alliance in the context of globalization. "*Islam de marché*", a concept of Patrick Haenni, refers to this new culture born from Globalization where business activities and success are efficiently used to translate thinking or religious beliefs into something practical and take cultural influence from the State.

Gülen and His Followers within the Turkish Islamic Movement

First of all, the Gülen community occupies a unique place in what Jenny B. White has ana-lyzed as the "Islamic movement" (White, 2001). Far from being homogeneous, the latter encompasses different ideologies, motivations, goals, or organizations, all united around a strong commitment to Islam; Jenny B. White also associates the movement with the local roots and values of its members such as the constant use of interpersonal relations – but, despite local, middle class roots and volunteer networks, this aspect will be leveraged in the case of the Gülen movement given that this group has usually been perceived as based on elitist institutions pretending to go beyond the local tradition (Anatolian bonds and pious-ness) or the national ideology (Kemalism[1]) joining forces with other religions to revitalize universal principles of faith and moral.

During the prime ministership of Turgut Özal in the 1980s, the policies of socio-economic liberalization that were carried out triggered the rise of Islamic-oriented activities and life-styles that the Kemalist ideology had tried to eradicate since the beginning of the Republic in the 1920s. The Islamic movement relied on people based either in the rural parts of Anatolia or the underprivileged suburbs (*varoş*) of Istanbul and Ankara where they had recently mi-grated in search of a better life. These people organized themselves in networks of solidarity that reproduced the imece (mutual support), "the rural tradition which villagers help one another at harvest, without then be obliged to help that particular family back" (White, 2001: 68). Refah, the Islamist party that was the latest continuation of previous political organiza-tions led by Necmettin Erbakan, took advantage of this "community-based form of coopera-tion" to develop a door-to-door activism and secure the vote of a large segment of the Turkish society. Concurrently, new media, holdings related to old Sufi tarikatlar (brotherhoods), even

---

1 We regard Kemalism as the ideology promoted by Mustafa Kemal (Atatürk) after the creation of the Republic of Turkey in 1922: "Kemalism as a political doctrine cohered loosely around certain principles that came to be known as the Six Arrows: republicanism, laicism, nationalism, populism, statism, and reformism." (White, 2002: 36) In this contexture, "laicism" is different from "secularism" (the separation of the State and religion) since the State fully controls religious affairs (through an organ called Diyanet) and independent Islamic institutions are virtually illicit.

Islamic banks[2] and business associations like MÜSİAD[3] or İŞHAD (linked to F Gülen), have represented a bridge between modernity and the traditional Anatolian society.

Among those many manifestations of an Islamic blooming, the followers of Fethullah Gülen occupy a pre-eminent place as the agents of an alternative elitist culture. Initially, the Gülen movement was entirely based on the personality and teachings of Fethullah Gülen because, as we mentioned, the Hocaefendi (beloved master) had been able to bring back "Turkish Islam"[4], highlighting the universality of its principles that could be found in other religions and the need for an inter-religious dialogue. Books and articles have been already dedicated to his life but it is still important to recall it briefly and to show how his trajectory itself symbolizes what we call a form of Turkish "cultural third way" that is neither Kemalism nor Islamism but a mix of "Turkishness", Islamic Sufi thought, and the appropriation of the Americanized globalization.

Born in 1941 in Erzurum, Eastern Anatolia, Fethullah Gülen was raised in a very pious family. His father, an Imam, taught him very early Arabic and Persian. When he became an adolescent, he attended lectures in religious sciences from the professor Muhammed Lütfi, a member of the Qadiri Sufi order, but also received a "modern" education in literature, philosophy, and history; he also sympathized with students of Bediüzzaman Said Nursi (1877-1961) and was introduced to his writings, the "Letters of Light" (Risale-i Nur), that supported the idea that Islam was compatible with science, reason, and modernity. The discovery of the contemporary Sufi thought was a major step in F Gülen's intellectual and spiritual training. Around the age of 20, he left his homeland to teach in the mosque of Edirne and later joined the Kestanepazari Qur'anic School in Izmir. At that time, the success of his lessons was so high that a first "community of Izmir" emerged spontaneously. After the coup of March 12, 1971, Gülen was arrested for clandestine religious activities and spent seven months in prison. He spent the rest of the decade visiting several cities of western Anatolia and preaching his vision of Islam with great popularity. Through his sermons, private conversations, and conferences on topics as religious as social, economic, and philosophical, he became a magnet for students, doctors, academics, civil servants, and businessmen. In the 80s, although he was under the protection of the Prime Minister Turgut Özal, Gülen remained highly suspicious for

---

2 From the very start of his first mandate, Turgut Özal deleted the article 163 of the new constitution repressing all those who, "exploiting religion... endangers the State's safety", and carried out on December 16, 1983 a Decree-Law 83/ 7506 relative to the "special financing institutions" (ÖFK/ Özel Finans Kurumları), in other words, the "Islamic banks". This decree legitimates the right to have recourse to an interest-free financial system taking into account the prohibition of riba (interest on money).

3 The "Independent Association of Industrialists and Businessmen" (MÜSİAD – *Müstakil Sanayiciler ve İşadamları Derneği*) was created by five pro-Islamic businessmen – among whom Erol Yarar, Ali Bayramoğlu, Natık Akyol and Abdurrahman Esmerer - on May 5, 1990 in Istanbul. The principal objective of MÜSİAD is to help the small and medium-sized entrepreneurs of Anatolia to increase their business potential and to export. The association especially will make it possible to create networks between the provincial towns and the national level.

4 Aras and Çaha (2000) affirm that the concept of "Turkish Islam" was formulated by the Nurcu movement and some nationalist thinker. They give a definition: "The main premise of "Turkish Islam" is moderation. Since people of Turkish origin first accepted Islam, they perceived and practiced it under the influence of Sufi ideas. Sufi-oriented Islamic movements kept a certain distance from the politics of their times in contrast to other Islamic movements. For example, the Shiites or Haricis defined themselves according to an imagined other (those who do not support the truth) and became associated with specific political stances over the proper nature of the state and who should hold power. Sufi tradition, however, has described itself as being based on the philosophy that all creatures should be loved as God's physical reflection and objects of the Creator's own love. There is no place for enemies or "others" in this system."

the laic and military elites. His efforts to promote the inter-faith dialogue whose climax was a visit to the Pope John Paul II in 1998 did not have the softening effect that could have been expected from the State authorities in those circumstances, since not only Gülen was promoting a peaceful and tolerant vision of Islam in the Western world but he was also, in some way, publicizing Turkey as a religiously modern and open-minded Muslim country. Nevertheless, victim of the anti-Islamic repression wave of the late 1990s, Gülen was forced to migrate to the United States. He is currently the honorary president of the Rumi Forum, a platform of inter-cultural and inter-faith dialogue founded in 1999 and located in Virginia.

One can perhaps wonder whether Fethullah Gülen would benefit from such recognition in Turkey and abroad if his ideas had not been practically applied and had not influenced the life of thousands of young people around the world. One should not neglect the key role of his group of followers. Privileging education for the integration in the modern world, the Gülen community holds and manages today around one hundred Turkish schools whose instructors graduated from the best Turkish universities. The message of the "Hoca" also dragged young people from the cities, in particular doctors, professors and some businessmen, who regard as an honour to take part in the activities of two of his foundations, the Turkish Teachers' Foundation (TOV) and the Turkish Journalists' and Writers' Foundation. At the beginning of the 1990s, the movement of Fethullah Gülen grew rapidly, expanding its presence in Central Asia through the support of the successive governments which, after the fall of the Soviet empire, tried to impose Turkey as a new leader in the newly independent Turkic republics - Azerbaijan, Turkmenistan, Uzbekistan, Kazakhstan and Kyrgyzstan. The Community founded about 200 schools throughout the world, from Tanzania to China, and mainly in these Turkic republics. The objective was, and still is, to form local elites regarding Turkey as a model. Beyond the strong educational network, the followers of Gülen have built a reputation in the media and even the business at large. Outside the bank Asya Finans that was created to finance projects in the Turkic republics, the community manages the daily newspaper Zaman, the television channel STV (Samanyolu or "Milky Way"), the radio station Burç, and an advertising agency, IŞIK. Rather intellectual and available in English, Zaman proposes insightful articles on national and international issues, economy, sciences and new technologies. Finally, İŞHAD, the Business Life Solidarity Association, was created in 1993 and based in Istanbul. It pretends not to have any Islamic ideology, even if the majority of its 500 members back Gülen's educative activities; besides, many have responsibilities in the school boards. They also recognize bonds with the Journalists' and Writers' Foundation of Fethullah Gülen. Their objective is triple: to improve the business outside Turkey, to reinforce the structure of the companies-members, and to support the dialogue with the various actors of political and economic life. Like the Gülen movement, they do not acknowledge any political view nor support any party in particular (we will outline Gülen's views on politics, democracy, secularism, and the West later on this paper).

One can argue that the Gülen movement was not the only one to use this network-implantation strategy. Using the donations of their members, other brotherhoods or communities became true companies, when the informal bonds between the members were progressively rationalized. Some even succeeded in creating their own holdings. A former popular brotherhood founded by Bahaeddin Nakşibend (1318-1389), the Nakşibendiyya knew how to adapt to modernity and addresses today to its two million followers a modernizing speech where Muslim moral values and worship mix with instruction, technocracy and middle-class values (see Manço, 1999). At the media level, the Nakşibendi owns three reviews: Islam, printing 100000 copies, Mektup ("The Letter") and Kadin ve Aile ("Woman and Family"), designed for women. Within the Nakşibendiler, the community of the İskender Paşa mosque in Istanbul is regarded as the most famous branch. The leaders of the community strongly encourage their members to become rich as a means to compete with the Kemalist establishment in the economic, political, and intellectual life and so prove the superiority of the Islamic ethics This community set up its own businesses thanks to its relationship with powerful families, chiefly the Özal and the Topbaş.

Not only the Nakşibendiler but also another community considered as a dissenting and conservative branch of the Nakşibendiyya, founded by the sheik Sayyid Abdhülhakim Arvasi (1865-1943) and known for its nationalist and very conservative ideology, organized itself in such a way. İhlas Holding, founded and chaired by Enver Oren, is considered the most powerful "cemaat holding". Able to compete with the Turkish largest conglomerates, namely Sabancı and Koç, İhlas is an immense company, especially present in publishing activities (books, newspapers, and magazines), construction, healthcare, and education. Among its publications, the daily newspaper Türkiye is very popular. The TV channel TGTR and the advertising agency ÖNCÜ are as renown as STV or IŞIK (see Buğra, 1999).

So, if other Sufi-inspired communities have followed the same path as Gülen's, what make his movement so unique inside and outside the Turkish Islamic movement? The similarities between the three Sufi communities are actually very strong in the media; nevertheless, only the Gülen movement has developed an extended network of schools, and that is by far their main achievement. Furthermore, the other communities are Turkish-centred and do not especially look for a better dialogue with the West. By preparing a future generation as confident with the principles of Turkish Islam as with modernity and scientific knowledge, the community is not only looking for present but future influence – like the private schools called Imam Hatip have influenced a generation of Islamist activists in the 80s-90s. And doing so, it is expected to become stronger and stronger, gaining gradually "share" on the socio-cultural realm in Turkey and abroad.

As a consequence of the personality and message of Hoca Gülen on top of the leadership in activities of its most educated followers(students, teachers, businessmen, journalists, and educated professionals), this community may have been perceived, inside the Islamic movement, as quite sophisticated and potentially out of reach for the poorest and least learned people that felt more attracted by populist leaders such as the Islamist Necmettin Erbakan (see White, 2001: 112-113).

Addressing the Question of the Influence of Gülen on the Moderation of Political Islam in Turkey

Now that we established what distinguishes the socio-economic organization of the Gülen community from the other Sufi communities, we would like to consider its political stance and its potential role in the evolution of political Islam since this possibility has not been really addressed. Could it be possible that the Gülen movement, especially the idea of its Hoca, have influenced the whole political dimension of the Islamic movement? Initially this assumption may look odd as the link between Gülen and the political Islam is far from being obvious, contrary to what many Kemalists have claimed. Instead, in the 80s and 90s, the relationship between the Gülen movement and the Islamist Refah party were rather cold, each accusing the other of "secretive fanaticism" (White, 2001: 112). Aras and Çaha (2000) reported: "Relations with Refah supporters are tense given that Refah supporters widely believe that the secular establishment uses Gülen's community to obstruct their path. Necmettin

Erbakan, Refah's long-time chairman, even accused Gülen of accepting government support to threaten Refah." Considered as an elitist movement, the Gülen movement had "little recognition in rural and working-class areas" (White, 2001: 112) while Refah had developed since the 60s as a result of the support of the voters from the eastern and central Anatolian towns since the 1960s. Therefore, the two groups attracted different publics and send out different messages, one asking for the compromise with the secular system and the other proposing a rupture with the Kemalist principles.

Furthermore, contrary to the Islamist Erbakan, Fethullah Gülen has always been against the application of the Shariah Islamic law by the State and considers the democracy as the best kind of government, accepting "Western civilization as a suitable foundation for material life while considering Islamic civilization suitable for spiritual life" (Aras and Çaha, 2000). In an interview in 1995 quoted by Kuru (2005: 265), he criticized anti-Western feelings: "Anti-Westernism should force us out of civilization". The only political positions he has consistently advocated have been: 1) the return to the relations of independence between the State and the religion as they were fairly maintained at the time of the Ottoman Empire – and that also exists today in most of the Western Democracy - and 2) the integration of Turkey to the European Union – which should secure religious freedom and a neat separation between the State and religion. In July 2005, The Muslim World published a special issue on Fethullah Gülen and his works, including a series of academic articles and a long interview of the religious leader. In this interview, Gülen stated that the Muslim religion included a moral duty of political control by the believers' community, as well as the respect for the rights and freedoms of the other religious minorities. The Hoca did not perceive the necessity of establishing an Islamic State based on the principles of the Shariah since he distinguished the rules of Islam, such as they appear in the Koran and the Sunnah, from the successive historic experiences which corresponded to the appropriate needs of their times. But today, as the consensus or "mutual contract" between Muslims was essential in government, a "caliphate" could not be imposed on the populations by force, as it would probably occur in the case of hypothetical application: "the revival of the Caliphate would be very difficult [today] and making Muslims accept such a revived Khilafah would be impossible". On the other hand, Islam is particularly related to democracy because if "in a democratic society the source of law is colour-blind and free from ethnic prejudice" favouring then the "development of human rights, political participation protection of minority rights…", "no one can ignore the universal values that the Qur'an and the Sunnah have represented with regard to the rights mentioned above". For the Muslims who live in democracy, "there is [thus] no need to seek an alternative state".

Between 1982 and 1998, i.e. the rise and decline of Refah, Gülen's ideas had little influence on the Islamists that privileged a more aggressive stance, including the introduction of the Shariah, the establishment of a Islamic common market, and an Islamic pact of defence. The party became stronger when it started attracting not only the Anatolian poor and middle class and the urban immigrants but also a new Islamic bourgeoisie with Anatolian origins and represented through the MÜSİAD association (see note 3). In the elections of March 27, 1994, Refah collected 19.1% of the votes becoming the ruling party in the city halls of Ankara and Istanbul. But its major breakthrough was the victory at the general elections of December 1995 which caused a great surprise. Without majority, Refah achieved a coalition with Doğru Yol (the "Party of the Right Way" or DYP) that was very quickly called the government Refahyol. Under Refahyol, the high aspirations of social justice and Islamisation of the Turkish society were quickly passed over due to the need to cooperate with Doğu Yol to remain in the government. In spite of the lack of real Islamist policies, the officers of the Turkish army supervised closely Refahyol; certain initiatives, like the trips to Iran and Libya or the will to remove the headscarf ban in universities and public administrations, worried the authorities and the most laic segment of the population. Finally, on June 18, 1997, after one year in the government as Prime Minister, Erbakan was constrained to resign, under the pressure of the military. In the months following this "soft" coup d'état, all the Islamic-oriented organizations, especially the Refah politicians and the pro-Islamic businessmen suffered severe pursuits. Even Fethullah Gülen who had tried to remain outside the tensions between Refah and the military was accused of fanaticism for an interview he had had on TV, slightly criticizing the Turkish system.

All of a sudden, after this anti-Islamist repressive wave, the discourse of the Islamist changed dramatically, endorsing the democratic ideal, and became very similar to the views that Gülen had invariably prescribed. This shift surprised many observers, for example Marvine Howe: "During a six-week visit to Istanbul the summer of 1998, I talked to a wide range about Islamic activists and found little echo of the old anti-American, anti-NATO, anti-Israel, anti-Europe rhetoric. Instead, even militant Islamists were now asking for basic American rights: freedom of religion, assembly, enterprise, speech, and dress. " (Howe, 2000: 179-180). Thus, the new party which succeeded Refah, Fazilet or the "Virtue party", adopted a different ideology. In a discussion with Marvine Howe, Abdullah Gül, then appointed of Fazilet, recommended "democratic moderation"; he who formerly qualified Refah of "Islamic-oriented party", now described Fazilet in these words: "this is not a religious party; we are open to all citizens, not only religious people." (Howe, 2000: 183). Proof of a major change in their speech, the Islamists now supported the accession of Turkey to the European Union in order to accelerate the adoption of the basic rights associated with the Western democracies, starting with religious freedom. At the end of July 1999, the "renovating" branch of Fazilet, led by Recep Tayyip and Abdullah Gül, split with the "old guard" of Erbakan's followers. The "Party of Justice and Development" (or AKP) was founded in 2001 and ran against Erbakan's Saadet (the "Happiness Party") for the prime ministership in the general elections November 2002. As we know, the AKP was largely victorious gaining 34% of the votes, while Saadet did not reach 3%. Erdoğan, once Prime Minister, continued to promote the new discourse, advocating for the "Muslim democracy" or "conservative democracy" which he compared to the German Christian democracy, stressing the complementarities, not antagonism, of Islam and democracy.

This little detour off Gülen and his movement was necessary to show how the Islamic movement shifted politically from a radical anti-western stance to the endorsement of democracy and religious tolerance through a moderate communication and behaviour. They understand that if they wanted to promote their vision of a tolerant society where women would be able to wear headscarves in public places including administrations and universities and where private Islamic schools (Imam Hatip) would be fully recognized as an option in the Turkish educative system, moderation and the recourse to a Western democratic rhetoric were the answer. Indeed, that was what Fethullah Gülen strongly believed and had advocated for years.

However, how to verify the influence of the Hoca on the moderation of political Islam, especially knowing that the relationships between the followers of Gülen and the Islamists has been consistently very distant? At the moment, there is no clear explanation for the moderation of the Islamists. Seda Demiralp and Todd A. Eisenstadt (2006) believe that the 120-day prison stay of Erdoğan in 1999 for a discourse he had pronounced may have been a key factor: "As Erdoğan sat in the darkness of a prison cell, he must have wondered whether it had been worth it. While in jail, he met with RP party members Abdulkadir Aksu and Azmi Ates. The three talked about the future of the party and criticized its leadership for the party's vote share decline in the 1999 national parliamentary elections… Radical confrontation between the RP and the military-secularist establishment was not beneficial to Erdoğan and its party anymore." For these authors, moderation would have only relied upon one man and his ambition. Another explanation has been outlined by Ziya Öniş (2006) regarding the role of the Islamic bourgeoisie in this moderation process: "The fact that winners of globalization are part of the broad electoral coalition [of Erdoğan's AKP] also explains, in part, why Islamist politics in Turkey has been evolving in a moderate direction in recent years since these groups, far more than the poor and underprivileged strata of society, have a lot to lose from open confrontation with the secular establishment and the state elites". The "winners of globalization" he refers to are that class of businessmen that emerged in the 80s[5] and gained a significant economic power in the next decade. Usually members of the MÜSİAD, an association created to represent them (see note 3), these entrepreneurs were proud to belong to the employers' class and therefore aspired to a place among the elites, which was denied[6] (see Buğra, 1999). As a reaction, those businessmen assumed openly Islamist positions[7] and benefited from the political ascension of the Islamist party.

As a result, the "process of February 28" following the destitution of Erbakan in 1997 had also an impact on these businessmen as they were clearly considered as related with political Islam. The director of the MÜSİAD and some companies-members were prosecuted. At that point, the specific positioning of the "Islamist bourgeoisie" revealed its limits: how to reconcile the aspiration for social recognition, which requires the integration in the pre-existing system, and political identity, which conversely shocks with this established order? For the "other", more intellectual Islamic bourgeoisie who followed Gülen's principles rather than Erbakan's, there was no dilemma since their belief in a strict separation of the public and private spheres made compatible religious commitments at home and through social, apolitical activities, with the respect of the current institutions of the Turkish Republic. Furthermore, for the middle class observant Muslims including the businessmen and politicians, Gülen's Ulama background gave his discourse a legitimate Islamic authority that Erbakan did not have as he was an engineer.

At the end of the 90s, most of the Islamic businessmen had understood that keeping a low profile concerning their political views was the only way to secure their social position and, in the same time, to keep growing as key economic actors of the civil society. We may still wonder who had the major influence on the new moderate thinking: Erdoğan himself after his hard experience in prison. The Islamist businessmen worried to loose their privileged lifestyle and economic welfare? Or Hoca Gülen that was the first ideologue to insist on ideas that became those of almost the whole Islamic movement at the beginning of the new century?

---

5 Coming from the interior of the Turkey, they are often referred as the "Anatolian Tigers" (*Anadolu Aslanı*) due their strong attachment to the provincial identity and the preservation of their traditional and religious values.

6 The traditional Turkish elites (senior executives, staff officers, and industrialists protected by the State and generally brought together within the TÜSİAD, the "Turkish Association of the industrialists and the business men") are characterised by their determination to preserve the laic, Kemalist principles. These established elites had have little will to share their hegemony with businessmen, mainly owners of small and medium-size companies, that had not been raised in the city and were self-confessed very religious.

7 This ideological affiliation seemed to obey a strange mechanism of re-conquest of an undergone mechanism. The emergence of SMEs relying on the Anatolian and Islamic values was the consequence of total economic opportunities. Nevertheless, the contractors of the MÜSİAD tried to adapt this reality, by conceiving it like the effect of a practical application conscious of the Islamic economic principles. The entrepreneurship became thus an act of faith.

While it is quite difficult to tell which group has had the foremost influence, researchers and academics have outlined the inter-connexion between the Islamic bourgeoisie, the moderate Islamists, and the Gülen movement. It is noteworthy that many of these business people as well as some Virtue and later AK Party politicians sent their children to Gülen's schools. Furthermore, Zaman is the second largest daily newspaper, the largest in Anatolian towns, and the majority of Virtue & AK party's supporters, including the businessmen, are regular readers. The triangulation appears clearly in a report of the European Stability Initiative (ESI) on the recent economic development of central Anatolia (Orta Anadolu), especially in the city of Kayseri. With the growth of the main cities of central Anatolia in the last fifteen years, the traditional Anatolian society has profoundly changed. Living henceforth mostly in urban areas, the population of central Anatolia is more educated, more industrious and infinitely more modern in its tastes and modes of consumption.

All of this success is due to the multiplications of private enterprises that used their money to modernize and improve the living conditions of the local population. Surprisingly, the businessmen of Kayseri refer openly to entrepreneurial values that have been associated with the Protestants since the publication of The Protestant Ethic and the Spirit of Capitalism by Max Weber in 1905: hard work, productive investment, honesty in business relations, risk-taking, charity, and community service. Unexpectedly, the interviews carried out to 94 businessmen of Kayseri reveal an iterative reference to Protestantism and its values. To support its observations in theory, ESI refers to the Turkish sociologist M. Hakan Yavuz, a specialist of the Gülen movement[8]; an aspect is particularly underlined by the article: the impact of the Nur movement on the "Muslim renewal" (tajdid) – similar in some ways to the protestant reform. In the Nurcu speech[9], the search for profit and for the welfare of the Muslim community became as important as prayer and fast. There would be thus a convergence between the modern Nurcu thought and the new Anatolian entrepreneurship. The Islamic capitalist speech grew within the new industrial districts of Anatolian and an effervescent associative life whose activities are mainly financed by the private contributions of the local businessmen. Interestingly, Abdullah Gül, the second leader of the new Muslim-democrat AK party, comes from Kayseri. It seems that Islamic factions came together at some point: the Islamic bourgeoisie, emblematized by the MÜSİAD association or the companies linked to powerful brotherhoods and communities, and the Islamic intellectual elite writing columns in Zaman) or participates in the Writers' and Journalists' Foundation.

Finally, the Abant platform was a strong source of inspiration and creativity for the pro-Islamic intellectual elite. Consisting of participants with really diverse opinions (atheists, agnostics, Marxists, leftists, Islamists etc.), this regular conference held all over the world[10] aimed to discuss sensitive issues such as laicism, democracy and Islam, globalization, diversification, education, liberalism, the Middle East and the EU and confirmed that it was possible to reach an agreement through dialogue - as Gülen had repeatedly advocated. Many of AK party founders, MPs, ministers attended its meetings well before they founded AK Party. Through this kind of initiatives and intellectual approximation, the concepts of Business, Turkish Islam, and Conservative Democracy have gradually converged to re-elaborate the

---

8 See Hakan Yavuz, M., and Esposito, John L. (2003) Turkish Islam and the Secular State: The Gülen Movement (Syracuse, New York, Syracuse University Press)

9 Even if Gülen denies being a Nurcu, he was highly influenced by Nursi and both communities are considered close in terms of discourse and beliefs.

10 Abant meetings have been held in important cities such as Washington, D.C., Paris, Brussels, Moscow and Cairo.

cultural content of the Islamic movement in a more western-democratic and capitalist way.

To conclude with the topic of Islamists' political moderation, the apparent division inside the Islamic movement between an elitist and intellectual minority linked to and a more down-to-earth majority related with the Refah party of Necmettin Erbakan has tended to be blurred as the Islamic bourgeoisie move apart of political Islam and took over the leadership of a new pro-democratic and pro-European party at the beginning of the 21st century. While we cannot establish the role of Gülen in this process, the cultural change in the direction of his long-claimed socio-political ideals was highly beneficial giving more significance to his movement in Turkey and abroad

Gülen's Contribution: Enlightening the Cultural Content of Globalization

Finally, we find very important to place the new Muslim culture in a broader context, that of globalization. The intensification of trans-national relations, especially in the socio-cultural and economic fields can also explain the shift to a more moderate Islamic culture in Turkey since the means offered by globalization are huge, including better media coverage of the thinking of the socio-cultural actors and precious business tools to finance and implement their activities and economic power. Ahmet T. Kuru (2005: 258) sees the extraordinary potential for the organizations that, in the past, were limited by a strong State control:

> "The relationship between globalization and the nation-state is not a zero-sum game. Globalization empowers the free market system at the expense of the statist regimes… It weakens state monopolies in different areas (that is, the economy, the media, and education) through a free market system and the spread of communication technologies".

Referring to the Gülen movement, Kuru considers it as a perfect illustration of the success that Islamic institutions that are both able to benefit from "international opportunity structure shaped by globalization" and develop a "tolerant normative framework open to cross-cultural interactions" can have. He especially insists on the international opportunity structures:

> "First the movement has been very successful in English instruction, which has been in high demand in many countries… The second resource of the movement is that it has created a synergy based on cooperation between educators and businesspeople. The sympathizers of the Gülen movement have been powerful enough to establish an interest-free bank and insurance company. Without the financial donations of businesses, the movement's schools could not have afforded to operate." (Kuru, 2005: 62)

The link between business and religious communitarism appears clearly here: developing business activities seems to be only way to translate a thinking or religious believes into something practical. In the case of Gülen, the international opportunity structure has been the need for English-speaking elitist schools in Turkey and abroad. But only what Kuru called a "tolerant normative framework", which is a positive thinking, could make the vision of the community come true. This "recipe" of success through moderation and opening can also explain the change operated by the Anatolian Tigers and the political faction of Recep Tayyip Erdoğan. To succeed in their businesses, the Anatolian Tigers needed excellent relationship with the businessmen of diverse export countries – Europe, Russia, and some Muslim countries as well; on the other side, a friendly relationship with the European Union leading to a future membership would secure the political settlement of Erdoğan and his followers, and avoid any ban from the military. The benefits of adaptation to the new international system, highly superior to any form of resistance, explains\ perfectly why these three movements have joined their force at the beginning of the 21st century to promote a new culture, neither Islamist nor Kemalist but in-between, and at one with globalisation.

The business dimension of the new pro-democratic Muslim culture is very important because it allowed its actors to bring back the benefit of globalization to the local ground and influence their peers' thinking through their new instruments (namely marketing and advertisement). From their broad media representation, the Muslim communities that we mentioned in the first part of this paper made Islam more visible in a public field that had been monopolized by the Kemalists. Their advertising agencies (IŞIK, Öncü and Panel Ajans) and television channels (STV, TGTR and Kanal 7) benefited from the growing demand of the urban, young, and Islamized generation in search of consumer goods compatible with their religious identity and their need to distinguish themselves from the prevalent laic culture. Using inventiveness and persuasion, the Islamic companies created an alternative culture going beyond the Western copy-paste offered by the classic media. By using a language more adapted to the lower layers of the population, these communities created a bridge between them and modernity, opening people's mind to the capitalist culture but, at the same time, keeping control of media instruments allowing them to influence morally and culturally modernity.

So gaining "market share" as a media holding and gaining "cultural share" as a thinking movement over concurrent philosophies in a given society are converging today and redefining to some extent the concept of culture. To describe this phenomenon in the Islamic context, the sociologist Patrick Haenni uses the concept of Islam de marché (market Islam) which, I believe, is extremely relevant for explaining the cultural move in Turkey: "Au croisement d'une Islamisation qui s'embourgeoise et de son découplage avec la matrice Islamiste, une nouvelle configuration religieuse est en train de naître que nous qualifierons d'Islam de marché en raison de ses affinités avec des institutions du champ économique qui lui servent de support, et avec la nouvelle culture d'entreprise à laquelle elle emprunte les categories de son discours. " (At the crossroad of an Islamisation becoming more bourgeois and its separation with the Islamist matrix, a new religious configuration is being born which we will describe as Islam de marché because of its affinities with institutions of the economic field it uses as a support, and with the new business culture from which it borrows the categories of its speech) Basically, the market religious culture (religion entrepreneuriale) trusts in private enterprise (not State interventionism) and piety. For Haenni, the globalization is allowing the market religious culture to expand in many different context, in the Muslim communities as in other groups – as the Christian churches in the United States that have been using for years capitalist methods to build up their circle of believers.

When Fethullah Gülen decided to stay in the USA and to keep promoting his ideas from there through an American NGO of inter-religious dialogue, he ultimately changed the fate of his movement. By mixing with the American society and people from other religions, many of them Christians, he is making his message even more universal. In this country where hundred of different religious movements operate, his ideas are very well received, not only by the Muslim and Turkish minorities but also the Christian communities. The book written by Jill Carroll and published last April, A Dialogue of Civilization: Gülen's Islamic Ideals and Humanistic Discourse, received excellent response. Living in the United States, the centre of this new religious market thinking, undeniably places the Hoca as a key interlocutor of the Muslim version of a culture well established there.

Conclusive Remarks on Fethullah Gülen and His Movement: What Impact on the Muslim World?

The movement became the strong network that it is today because it has been able to combine successfully the peaceful discourse of the Hoca supported by intellectual institutions and a solid media group and a network of schools where these ideas can develop and guide new generations all around the world. This movement benefited from a set of opportunities that help its influence to increase within the society and indirectly politics. For example, the quality of the education provided by its schools while the Imam-Hatip schools were becoming obsolete convinced many pro-Islamic businessmen and politicians to put their children in its schools and therefore they become familiar to the movement's principles and purpose. On the other end, the climate of hostility against the Islamic businessmen and politicians favoured, among them, new behaviours of opening to the West and the secular elites so Gülen and its inter-religious dialogue became gradually a point of reference. At the end of the 1990s, more of the Islamist politicians abandoned their extremist discourse and adopted pro-Democratic views very similar to those of Gülen who advocated for "Tajdid", the Islamic renewal through social reform.

By anticipating the need to adapt Islam to the present times, confident that the Turkish republic would have to adapt too and open itself to more diversity, Gülen has been a visionary. He has unlocked the way to a new global culture that places Muslim Democrats ahead of any radical thinking and he has sent a strong message to the Muslim world showing a successful way towards democratic transition and gradual adaptation to Globalization without loosing landmarks and religious background. To the Muslim world, the "Hoca" says that there is nothing to fear about democracy and globalization because the Qur'an teaches compassion, love and tolerance and, through these principles, nothing should impede a Muslim to be, at the same time, a servant of God and a first-class citizen within a democratic country. Nothing should hinder him either to seize the benefits of a business-oriented society that will improve his lifestyle and help him promote the splendour of his religious beliefs.

Gülen's new social movement has been able to benefit from the capitalist globalization by efficiently using newly-available marketing instruments and become a bridge between modernity and a large segment of the Turkish society. At that point, cultural influence relies on the gain of market share in the media realms, which a new way of putting things because it means that only the people able to be in command of the capitalist game will triumph culturally in the long run. So not only the followers of Gülen participate in the emergence of a new Turkish culture but also to a new understanding of what culture consists of.

THE FETHULLAH GÜLEN MOVEMENT AS A TRANSNATIONAL PHENOMENON

Bill Park

Abstract

This paper investigates the apparent paradox thrown up by the distinctively Turkish roots and contents of Fethullah Gülen's philosophy on the one hand, and the movement's educational activities beyond Turkey and its promotion of interfaith dialogue on the other. It considers how far the movement has been able to transcend its 'Turkishness'. In the Turkic world, primarily in Central Asia and Azerbaijan, the paper offers an assessment of the extent to which the movement generates an emulative or transformational response, perhaps contributing to the emergence of a non-territorial 'Turkic' nation or identity. In that context, the paper considers the degree to which the movement can be seen as 'pan-Turkic' in terms of its aspirations and effects. Turning to its activities in the non-Turkic world, the paper tries to establish whether the movement should be regarded as a primarily Turkish or primarily Muslim agency, and what kind of impact this creates in host countries. In chiefly Islamic host countries, to what degree is the movement engaged, intentionally or otherwise, in a competition with more radical interpretations of Islam? Or is the movement's approach to Islam rooted too exclusively in a Turkish context? This leads into a consideration of whether the movement is an agency for a 'Turkish model' approach to blending Islam with modernity and democratisation, and whether this suggests either competition or tacit alliance with the Turkish state in this regard. Finally, with respect to interfaith dialogue, is the movement's contribution seen as narrowly Turkish in its applicability, or as resonating in and of utility to the wider Muslim world?

Introduction

This study will not confine its purpose to determining the extent to which the 'movement' inspired by the thoughts and writings of Fethullah Gülen can be regarded as an agency of transnationalism. It also intends to address the difficult question of what impact the movement, as an agency of transnationalist phenomena, might have. Robert O. Keohane and Joseph S. Nye famously defined transnational relations as 'contacts, coalitions and interactions across state boundaries that are not controlled by the central foreign policy organs of government' (Keohane and Nye, 1972, p.xi). One possible outcome of the activities of transnational agencies might be the creation of transnational networks of individuals and groups that interact, where possible, without direct reference to state authorities or territorial boundaries. These new social formations might impact on the power structures, values and ultimately state policies of both 'sending' and 'receiving' societies. Another outcome might be the generation of blurred, multiple, shared or shifting identities and value systems amongst individuals and groups that by their very existence offset the territorialisation of global politics and might even consciously resist it. This might take the form of a loosely-constructed transnationally shared ideational consciousness, or a much tighter, emulative cultural reproduction or hybridity. This article will consider the Fethullah Gülen movement in the light if these observations. However, although we can trace the interactions, ties, and influences linking individuals, groups and institutions across the borders of Westphalian states, the impact of transnational phenomena cannot readily be measured or even defined with precision. We must bear this in mind too when seeking to assess the Gülen movement's significance.

When considering the Gülen movement's transnational activities, or indeed those of any comparable phenomena, we must also guard against the risk of slipping into an unexamined assumption that transnational activities are necessarily welcome, especially in 'receiving' countries, or that they invariably produce positive outcomes - at least not in an unambiguous and unmitigated way. Transnational phenomena might be simultaneously transcending in their impact, and perceived as competitive and threatening by receiving states and societies. A state can and might choose to mediate between its citizens and external influences, and existing social values and structures might generate defensive reactions to unwelcome externally-derived intrusions and challenges. 'Receiving' societies should not be assumed to resemble 'blank pages' on which anything can be written, or pliable material out of which we can construct anything we wish. The more transnational phenomena are seen as intrusive, as imports from one state, society or value-system into another, the more they might generate nationalist or otherwise culturally-protective forms of resistance. Transnational interactions can as easily highlight differences, and attachments to such differences, as they can create new, transformative and shared social formations. They might generate negative reactions, in other words. They might also be broadly neutral in impact. In our exploration of the Gülen movement's impact, we must open our minds to the possibility of reactions, outcomes and consequences such as these.

'Islam was 'transnational'...long before there were nations' (Vertovec, 2003 p324), and the notion of a global Muslim ummah has continued to provide a source of resistance to the territorialization and nationalization of global politics. The current discourse on Islam, at least in much of the western media, sometimes implicitly assumes that it is solely as a radicalized and violent variant that modern Islam adopts a transnational garb. The kind of radical Islam associated with the al-Qaeda network is additionally seen as resistant to globalization understood as Americanization or westernization, although it is simultaneously enabled by globalization via its exploitation of the modern media, the internet, international travel and emigration.

This type of Islam seeks to protect an idealized and essentialist Islam from the impurities, temptations and corruption of a Godless and materialist west. The often unstated assumption in the west is that traditional, moderate, and locally-flavoured Islamic tradition and practices are passive, defensive or vulnerable in the face of this globalised onslaught from an angry, violent Salafi inspired interpretation that appears to vindicate Samuel Huntington's 'Clash of Civilizations' thesis.

Yet the traffic in the trans-border exchange of ideas and influence that is taking place within the Islamic world is not all one way, so much so that it might even be argued that non-essentialist and more distinctly culture-bound variants of Islam are also undergoing something of a revival. This certainly appears to apply in Turkey's case (Mardin, 2005 p157). The Fethullah Gülen movement,[1] named after its Turkish founder and inspiration, is actively engaged in disseminating to a world beyond Turkey's state boundaries, as well as within them, an approach to Islam and to its relationship to politics and other faiths quite at odds with that propagated by Islamic fundamentalism. Although the Gülen movement is far from being the only source of moderate Islamic ideas actively engaged in the competition for influence in today's globalised Islamic space, it is one of the largest and most active. It is a major participant in a global contestation over what Islam is and what role it should play, and its message could hardly be more at odds with that brand of Islam typically dubbed 'fundamentalist'.[2] Specifically, it qualifies to be considered as a transnational phenomenon, and as contributing to and manifesting the spirit of globalization, via both its geographically dispersed educational activities and its commitment to dialogue with other faiths. Each of these areas of activity will be discussed below.

The Gülen Movement's 'Turkishness'

Yet its roots are quintessentially Turkish, located in Turkey's historical baggage, its domestic political circumstances, and in a version of Islam that arguably has more currency in Turkey than elsewhere. This rich 'Turkishness' endows this globally-engaged movement with a paradoxical and sometimes quixotic character. The Gülen movement offers an example of a transnational phenomenon that nevertheless retains and indeed lauds its national flavour. Although the purpose here is to explore the transnationalism of the movement rather than the ideas of its founder, so powerful is Fethullah Gülen's inspiration that mention must be made of him. He began his career in Turkish fashion as a state-appointed religious preacher in 1953, and began to acquire a serious following, sometimes referred to as the Fethullahci, in the wake of his appointment to Izmir in 1966, where a loose network of students, teachers, professionals, businessmen and the like took on his name. The movement's first venture into the wider propagation of its philosophy came in the form of summer schools in and around Izmir. It soon established teaching centres (dershane), largely to prepare religious students for university admission. As its activities blossomed, so it attracted the attention of Turkey's secularist state establishment. Gülen himself served a 7-month spell in prison in the early 1970s for propagating religion, and again attracted uncomfortable attention both during the1980s and in the late 1990s, in the wake of the 'soft coup' of 1997. Gülen and his followers are regarded with suspicion by Turkey's secular establishment to this day, and this partly

---

1 Articles, speeches, interviews etc by Fethullah Gülen can be found at the movement's website at www.fGülen. org. See also Yavuz and Esposito (eds), 2003; Hunt and Aslandogan (eds), 2006; The Muslim World, 95(3), July 2005: Special Issue; West, 2006; Aras and Caha, 2000.

2 For a comparison of these two approaches to a globalised Islam, see Hendrick, 2006 pp11-29.

explains his preference for domicile in the US.[3]

The network did not openly emerge as a major educational, social and religious movement until 1983, when in the wake of the military coup of 1980 the Turkish General Staff expanded the space for religious activity. Such policies were inspired by the so-called 'Turkish-Islamic synthesis', which emphasised a fusion between Turkish national identity and the Islamic faith. The hope was that religiosity would offer a more conservative and spiritual, and politically less threatening, antidote to the leftism that had contributed to the social chaos of the preceding decade. Thus the rise of the Gülen movement formed one element in the more general 'Islamisation' of Turkish public life that has been in evidence since the 1980s (Narli, 1999). Under the protective cover of the premiership of Turgut Özal, himself a sympathiser, the movement opened schools (there are now around 150 such schools in Turkey alone), universities, a television channel (Samanyolu TV), a radio station (Burc FM), a daily newspaper (Zaman), several other periodicals, and a bank (Asya Finans) set up in 1996 to raise investment funds for the Turkic republics. The network also spawned a Journalists and Writers Foundation[4] and a Teachers Foundation, each of which publishes journals and organizes symposiums and conferences, frequently abroad.

Notwithstanding its subsequent phenomenal growth, in many respects the nature of the movement remains true to its origins. It consists of a mix of largely professional male members, sympathisers, and affiliates, whose relationship to the movement varies considerably. It ranges from extremely pious individuals, often teachers and preachers, whose lives are dedicated to the propagation of the values and ideas of Fethullah Gülen, to more occasional and functional fellow-travellers, such as businessmen and even politicians. Partly for this reason, and the blurred distinction between members, followers, and sympathisers, estimates of the movement's 'membership' vary considerably. One source suggests a figure anywhere between two hundred thousand and four million Turks (Aras and Caha, 2000 p33). The movement should not be envisaged as a centrally-organized body. It is loosely structured and decentralized, and each of its ventures are individually financed and run on a voluntary basis by members of and sympathisers with the network. This explains why estimates of the number of schools and other educational establishments run by the movement can also vary.

Although the thinking of Fethullah Gülen has continued to evolve, with an intensified emphasis on the philosophy's more universalistic, pluralistic, liberal, and democratic qualities in recent years (Yavuz, 2005 p45), it remains rooted in Turkish-Ottoman experience. His belief is that, as Turkish society is overwhelmingly Muslim in faith, the state and its citizens should not have become as alienated from each other as he insists has been the case in Republican Turkey. The 'top-down' imposition of the sometimes anti-religious secular dogma associated with Turkey's Kemalist state has served to distance its citizens from the governing elite. As the Turkish novelist Rasim Ozdenoren expressed it, modern Turkey is 'like a transgendered body with the soul of one gender in the body of another'.[5] Gülen draws inspiration from the Ottoman rather than the Republican model of state-society relationships. Although the empire's rulers were guided by their faith, and indeed held custody of the Caliphate, the leadership of the Muslim world, the Ottoman system of governance was not theocratic. Public laws were formulated on the basis of the state's needs rather than in accordance with Islamic law (Shari'a). Indeed, Gülen's thinking is quite distinctly state-centric, and this too gives a quite Turkish flavour to Gülen's ideas. This statism might be thought to overlap with Atatürk's,

---

3 For details of allegations made against Gülen in 1999, see Özdalga, 2005 pp439-440.

4 Its website can be found at www.gyv.org.tr.

5 Quoted in Aktay, 2003 p.134.

but again Gülen prefers to look back beyond the Republic to the Ottoman era. The state has a functionally secular role to provide internal and external security and stability for its citizens. It would be preferable if a state's rulers are people of faith, but they should not use their secular authority to implement religious dogma. Gülen is not in favour of the political implementation of Shari' a, which in any case is mostly concerned with private and personal faith-inspired behavioural expectations.

Thus, for Gülen, the key to Islam's influence and utility in the modern world does not lie through direct political activity and organization, and he is opposed to 'political Islam' as such. Indeed, he sympathised with the 1997 'post-modern coup' that removed Erbakan's Welfare Party from power, although Gülen was himself caught up in the crackdown on religious activity that came in its wake. He believed that Erbakan and his followers were embarked on the first steps towards an 'Iranianization' of Turkish political and social life. Gülen sympathised with the 1980 coup too, regarding it as appropriate and necessary that the state protect itself and its citizens against the chaos and violence that was threatening to engulf Turkish society. According to Gülen, Turkish Islam's more flexible, adaptable, spiritual and less doctrinal traditions have enabled Republican Turkey and Turkish society more broadly, with its democratization, free market economy, and secular political system, to incorporate aspects of modernity to an extent barely found elsewhere in the Muslim world. All this very much accords with Gülen's vision of an Islamic, but modern and progressive, Turkey of the future. The movement has itself profited from Turkey's post-1980 economic, social and political liberalization, of course, which has created a space for its media, educational and financial activities free from the control of the statist secular establishment. In this sense, we might argue that the movement is in large measure a by-product of the impact of globalization on the wider evolution of Turkish politics and economic management.

Thus, Gülen sees no contradiction between Islam and modernity. Indeed, he insists on the desirability of Islam's embrace of science, reason, democratization, and tolerance. Although Gülen shares Atatürk's assessment that the relative economic and moral poverty of the Islamic world is explained by its spiritual and intellectual decline, for Gülen the problem is not Islam per se. His assessment of the Turkish and Ottoman experience of Islam is that religion should not become a dogma, but can be adaptive, open, flexible, rational, and tolerant, and not closed and shielded from other faiths, other ideas, and from scientific and technological progress. Indeed, another root of Gülen's thinking is the 'folk Islam' and pronounced Sufism, or spirituality, of Anatolian Turkish Islam.[6] Specifically, and as with a number of other Turkish sects and brotherhoods, Gülen derives inspiration from the writings of the prominent Kurdish religious authority Said Nursi (1877-1961). The Nur (Light) or Nurcu movement that Said inspired was distinguished by its advocacy of reason, progress, tolerance, and a distance from direct political involvement. It too did not regard western science, openness and modernity as necessarily contrary to the spirit of Islam.

Modern Turkish society is also intensely nationalistic, and some of this flavour too has been absorbed by the Gülen movement. Perhaps Gülen's Erzurum birthplace – a kind of Turkish frontier town abutting the Caucasus, Kurdish regions, and former Armenian-populated lands, where both Turkish nationalism and Islamic faith is particularly strongly felt – has influenced his thinking. In any case, the movement's philosophy fuses its brand of Islam with a Turkish nationalism. After all, its theological and cultural roots, as well as its key personnel and resource base, lie in Turkish practice and experience. This conscious 'Turkishness'

---

6 For more on this, see Gokcek, 2006; Saritoprak, 2003; Michel, 2005; Yavuz, 2004. Not all are convinced of the uniquely Sufi-influenced or distinctiveness of Turkish Islam, however. See Özdalga, 2006.

has encouraged the movement to engage far more actively with the Turkic world than any-where else. Turkish society and much of its political elite was quick to make overtures to Central Asia, Azerbaijan, and other traces of an ethnically and culturally pan-Turkic world in the immediate aftermath of the Soviet break-up. Turks enthused over the rediscovery of a world from which their forefathers originated and with whom they shared ancient cultural and linguistic roots. At its headiest, the hope in Turkey was that a political, economically and culturally tightly-knit entity would emerge that would take modern Turkey as its in-spiration.[7] Gülen followers too were swept up in this mood, and this largely explains why the full-scale emergence of the Gülen movement as a transnational educational community essentially coincided with the 1991 Soviet collapse, which opened the way for an exten-sion of its activities into Turkic Central Asia and Azerbaijan, purportedly Turkic republics and regions of the Russian Federation such as Dagestan, Karachai-Cherkessiya, Tataristan, and Bashkotorstan, other former Soviet states containing Turkic minorities such as Ukraine, Georgia, and Moldova, and into the Balkans. Even in Iraq, the Gülen School's pupils are mainly ethnic Turkmen (Balci, 2003a. p156). Thus, the Gülen movement can be said to have thrived largely as a response to international, as well as domestic, 'opportunity structures' that presented themselves (Kuru, 2005).

The Gülen Movement's Transnational Educational Activities

Gülen propagates a kind of 'educational Islamism' as opposed to a 'political Islamism' (Agai, 2003 p50). Furthermore, education curricula should emphasise science and technology as much, or more than, they incorporate faith teaching. Gülen also advocates the transmission of spiritual, moral and behavioural values, of tolerance, respect, openness, and the like.[8] Through the internalized spiritual transformation of individuals will come a wider social transformation and, at least in Islamic societies (including Turkey) in which Gülen institu-tions operate, a (re-) 'Islamisation' of modernity. Thus, politics in Turkey and perhaps in other Islamic societies in which the movement operates should be 'Islamized' only via a bottom-up process and indirectly, in which people and state are reunited in a kind of organic way, through a shared attachment to and internalization of faith. In this sense, the Gülen movement's mission in the Islamic societies in which it operates can be said to be a political project, but one that aspires to achieve its goals indirectly. People of faith as well as learn-ing, a 'Golden Generation', should be cultivated and encouraged to dedicate their lives to the service (hizmet) of the people. It is an approach that resembles a kind of 'long march through the institutions', and Turkey's secular establishment, and some secularists elsewhere, are oc-casionally unsettled by it.

Yet overt religious teaching, and even explicit mention of Fethullah Gülen, is generally ab-sent from Gülen educational establishments, both in the Islamic world and elsewhere. This is partly but not entirely explained by the need to tread carefully in the presence of political au-thorities suspicious of religious or foreign activities within their borders. This delicacy about the movement's nature and involvement raises a question of whether the Gülen movement's educational establishments, especially beyond Turkey or the wider Turkic world, constitute much more than a commercially-based transnational educational foundation. For example, one searches in vain for any sign either of Gülen's inspiration or of any notable religious focus on the website of the Gülen-sourced Virginia International University in the US (www.

---

7 For an in-depth study of this phenomenon, see Bal, 2000.

8 For a discussion of the movement's approach to education, see Agai, 2003; Michel, 2003; Aslandogan and Cetin, 2006.

viu.edu). There has even been speculation as to whether the movement's universalist ethos and its emphasis on 'activism through good deeds' is leading to a kind of secularism akin to that which befell those earlier Protestant missionaries that the Gülen movement can be said to resemble (Özdalga, 2003).

The Gülen movement's external activities are characterized by a marked concentration in Turkic Central Asia and Azerbaijan. There are half a dozen Gülen-sponsored universities in Central Asia, and numerous other educational, welfare and economic institutions and activities. One can readily see why the movement might have assumed that in Turkic Central Asia and Azerbaijan the likely receptivity to its overtures would be high. After all, the Turkish state made a similar assessment in the immediate aftermath of the Soviet collapse. The region shares a linguistic and ethnic root with Turkey, and a 'folk Islam' that, as in Turkey, incorporates numerous Sufi sects and has absorbed pre-Islamic traditions, beliefs and rituals. In fact, the very existence of a Turkic world is a reminder that many of the processes that we associate with globalization are not at all new. The history of the Turkic peoples is part of 'world history' - of the rise and fall of empires, cultures, and civilisations; of their interpenetration with and resistance to other cultures; of their capacity to absorb and reconstitute. Modern Turkish interest in this 'Diaspora' can be seen as a resuscitation of this earlier global interconnectedness. Furthermore, the Soviet era left behind a legacy of secular education and a commitment to science, progress and modernity that might broadly be thought to correspond with Turkey's circumstances and the Gülen movement's aspirations (Yavuz, 2003 pp39-40). This suggests some scope for cultural reproduction in the region, whereby the Gülen network's Central Asian elites could in time take on the forms of their Turkish counterparts, blending to generate a new, distinct and perhaps de-territorialized transnational social formation. In the longer term, this could have important ramifications, and lend support to the emergence of a pan-Turkic world linked by overlapping and fused identities. This could in turn ease the development of economic interactions, and even encourage closer state-to-state relationships. Such an evolution would not quite accord with the adoption of the 'Turkish model' that Ankara's secularists and some of its western advocates had hoped for, but it might dovetail with the aspirations of pan-Turkic nationalist elements in Turkey.

In the Turkic territories of Central Asia and elsewhere, much of the push behind the network's penetration of the region came from devout and conservative Turkish businessmen who were willing to finance educational activities 'because of their commitment to Gülen's Turko-Islamic worldview' (Yavuz, 2003 p39). This sector of society has been instrumental in 'Islamizing' Turkey's face too, via its support for the AKP (Adalet ve Kalkinma Partisi), its backing for MUSIAD (the Independent Industrialists and Businessmen's Association), and by generally offering a model of a religious, conservative Anatolian elite quite distinct from and at odds with the secular Kemalists. In other words, they are inclined to see themselves, and indeed are, an ascendant class. Furthermore, these business groups have frequently fused their commercial ventures with their support for the Gülen network's activities in Central Asia (Balci, 2003a. pp154-155; Peuch 2004a). As an illustration of the form the Turkish presence in the region can take, in Kazakhstan, the most important location for the Gülen network's activities abroad, the Kazakh-Turkish Education Foundation (KATEV) in Almaty functions as a cornerstone of the resident Turkish community, and is supported and frequented by Turkish business and charitable groups and by the Gülen network (Turam, 2003 pp188-189). This kind of presence has in turn generated a close working relationship with Turkish embassies in the region, whose staff readily facilitate the activities of Turkish religious networks that are otherwise frowned upon by the state in Ankara (Balci, 2003b). The Gülen network's transnationalist activities might in this way be furthering Turkey's economic interests abroad as well as contributing to a shifting of Turkey's domestic political arrangements.

However, some caution is necessary here. To begin with, and as with so many transnational phenomena, the receiving country can affect the impact of the transnational agency, positively or negatively. Intentions do not always readily translate into outcomes, and cross-border 'intrusions' can sometimes stimulate or further entrench an essentialist nationalism. The pan-Turkic strain that runs through the Gülen movement's approach stresses the shared ethnic and cultural origins if the Turkic people. As one observer has expressed it, '…the followers of the Gülen community aspire to reconnect Central Asians with their Turkic origins by spreading Turkish Muslim culture and morality to that region' (Turam, 2003, p187). It appears that the movement's followers in the region typically regard Central Asians as their Turkic blood brothers, and aspire to create individuals oriented towards Turkey and 'Turkishness' as well towards Islamic progress and enlightenment. Indeed, there may have been a greater receptivity to 'Turkism' than to Islam in the region (Balci, 2003a. p153; Turam, 2004).

However, there are indications that a shared Turkic ethnic and linguistic root might not be sufficient to remove all barriers to a fuller interpenetration and blending. The movement's educational establishments in the region are frequently referred to simply as 'Turkish schools', and at least initially some inhabitants of Central Asia seem to have resented the speed with which Turkish institutions replaced Soviet/Russian ones after 1991 (Peuch, 2004b). Furthermore, there have been indications of a Turkish chauvinism towards the Turkic peoples of Central Asia, whether intentional or not. Students in the movement's schools abroad might be expected to sing the Turkish national anthem as well as their own, and raise the Turkish as well as their own national flag (Peuch, 2004b). Instruction is chiefly in English, but Turkish is also extensively used, in addition to local languages where necessary. Furthermore, the overwhelming majority of the teachers and administrators in the movement's institutions abroad are Turks from Turkey rather than locals (Balci, 2003b). This sense of a 'foreign' and intrusive penetration has occasionally combined with a dislike of the perceived religious, missionary self-righteousness of the movement's teachers, whose piety and dedication can grate with more secular, perhaps non believing, Central Asians. They can even seem to be imbued with a distasteful 'big brother' attitude (Miller, 2003).

Additionally, the determined and autocratic secularity of the region's political leaderships, and their post-Soviet prickly sensitivity to anything they perceive as external meddling in their affairs, puts the Gülen movement's reception in the Turkic world very much at the mercy of the region's governments. In 1994 and again four years later, Uzbek President Islam Karimov cracked down on the movement's activities in his country, including a ban on the distribution of Zaman, such that the movement has minimal presence there today. It is unclear whether this was a reaction to the presence in his country of a religious group that he did not control, or whether it indicated retaliation against the Turkish state's harbouring of Uzbek opposition leaders. Either way, Turkish prime minister Bülent Ecevit felt obliged to deny any Turkish wrongdoing towards Uzbekistan, which served to strengthen the perception that the Gülen movement was in some way representative of the Turkish state (Peuch, 2004b; Aras and Caha, 2000 p28; Balci 2003a. pp155-157). In 2005, Turkish teaching staff at the Islamic theology school at a university in Turkmenistan was sacked by the country's autocratic leader President Saparmurat Niyazov. The move was linked with a suspicion that the regime was becoming increasingly aware of and uneasy about both the pan-Turkic and Islamic ideology of the Gülen network in the country (Institute for War and Peace Reporting, 2005). Beyond former Soviet Central Asia, the Taliban regime closed own the Gülen movement's activities in Afghanistan in the late 1990s owing to its disapproval both of its brand of Islam and of external interference in the country (Kuru, 2005, p262), and Fethullah Gülen has also claimed that his movement was denied permission to open a school in an Azeri (Turkic) region of Iran through Tehran's suspicion of its pan-Turkic aspirations (Kosebalaban, 2003 pp179-180). Such incidents constitute examples of how the non-state activities of transnational enterprises can nevertheless become entangled with state-to-state interactions, and can as easily reinforce negative tendencies in such relationships as help overcome them by transcending them.

An additional source of resentment at the activities of the movement in Central Asia is its elitist nature, a notable feature of its activities in Turkey too. In this sense, the movement's activities can be seen as 'translocal' rather than transnational, as a vehicle for relatively exclusive and restricted interpenetration by narrow sectors of societies rather than more mass-based trans-border interactions. It is relatively rare for children of the disadvantaged, even if devout, to gain entry into Gülen schools. The fees and entrance requirements are high, and the good reputations the schools have acquired for the quality of their technical education, their use of English as a language of instruction, and the high behavioural standards they set, have combined to ensure that places are at a premium. Typically, successful applicants in Central Asia and elsewhere in the post-communist world are the children either of the wealthy or of government officials (Miller, 2003; Balci, 2003a. pp164-165). This has to be appreciated against the background of a collapsed educational, social, and economic infrastructure throughout much of the region. State spending on education has plummeted throughout Central Asia in particular, leading to school closures, a shortage of teachers, a degradation of the physical infrastructure, and widespread corruption surrounding school and college admissions and test results (Silova, Johnson and Heyneman, 2007). It should not be a surprise to anyone that foreign-owned schools providing quality education to the offspring of those best placed to profit from or to protect themselves against the wider social collapse might be resented by those whose future is likely to consist of poverty, unemployment, and emigration. In so far as this is true, then the laudable long-term aspirations of the Gülen movement's activists could be obstructed or derailed by the more immediate injustices with which they become associated.

However, we should be wary of excessive generalization concerning the nature and impact of the Gülen movement's activities abroad. Largely as a consequence of its devolved and voluntaristic nature, the precise characteristics of each establishment might differ just as the motives behind their establishment can vary (Peuch, 2004b). It might also be that from the mid-1990s onwards the movement, or at any rate Gülen's own thinking, shifted from a chauvinistic Turkish Islamic identity towards 'global educational activities that encourage the national identities of the countries in which it is operating' (Agai, 2003 p63). In this context, it is worth noting that the movement has a presence in the form of a variety of educational institutions in around fifty countries, and now supervises as many or more schools abroad as it does in Turkey – in excess of 150, although the unstructured nature of the movement means no precise figure can be given. Gülen schools and other educational establishments are globally far-flung, and can be found in such places as the Balkans, Russia, Armenia, the US, Australia, China, Cambodia, sub-Saharan Africa, India, and in western countries where Turkish minorities are located, such as Germany and France. Indeed, in western Europe the movement's schools have served to reinforce or preserve Turkish and Muslim identities otherwise vulnerable to dilution and distortion as a result of interaction with host societies, although the simultaneous commitment to accommodation to and tolerance of host country customs is strong (Bilir, 2004: Irvine, 2006). A quite different assessment might be made of a Gülen educational initiative in a non-Turkic location such as the Philippines. Here, in an area where the denominational split between Muslims and Christians is roughly half and half, a Gülen school employs many Philipino teachers (some of whom are Christian) and admits many Christian students. Furthermore, and in keeping with the movement's commitment to interfaith dialogue, strong and healthy links are maintained with nearby Christian institutions. Even in Central Asia, non-Muslim students might be granted admission to Gülen establishments (Michel, 2003).

Interestingly, even in decidedly non-Turkic countries such as India and Mongolia, portraits of Atatürk are on show, Turkish is taught, and the Turkish national anthem sung. The Turkishness of Gülen schools is certainly more evident than their Islamism. This emphasis on Turkish language and culture has even won over some of the usually suspicious representatives of Turkey's secularist political class.[9] It should also be noted that, wherever they are found, Gülen educational establishments abide by local curricula requirements. They do not directly propagate Islam, but rather emphasise virtues such as respect for elders, politeness, modesty, and hard work. In other words, they teach by example. As elsewhere, this approach accounts for the popularity of Gülen schools in Africa, where there are over fifty Turkish schools in thirty countries, many of them in largely Christian sub-Saharan Africa.[10] It is difficult to assess, however, what the ultimate impact might be of a globally-scattered body of well-behaved, hard-working, well-educated individuals with a knowledge of and sympathy with Turkish culture. It is hardly likely to do harm to Turkey's image and interests abroad, or to the more general cause of global understanding and tolerance. On the other hand, the relative scale of the Gülen movement's presence is so small, and Turkey's footprint in such regions otherwise so light, that it is hard to see what measurable good it might do either.

Is it possible to assess the contribution the Gülen movement's educational activities are making to Islam, to Turkey's interests and image, and to global dialogue and tolerance? As we have noted, we would surely be well advised to differentiate in our assessments, and to avoid conclusiveness. It is too early to tell, and too difficult to estimate. This is especially so with respect to the movement's ventures in non-Turkic, and non-Muslim, worlds. In any case, their role in the Turkic world looms larger and is conceivably more portentous. Fethullahci schools represent only around ten percent of Central Asia's education system (Peuch, 2004b), albeit a share disproportionately patronized by the economic, intellectual and social elite. It could be that, in a tacit partnership with the Turkish state, the movement's activities will over the longer term intensify the emotive and material bonds between Turkic peoples – or their elites - and states (Balci, 2003a. pp166-167). As one observer has expressed it, the Gülen movement has 'an ethnic agenda, which calls for the realisation of Turkic homogeneity in Central Asia. It is this ethnic politics that makes Gülen an effective international actor' (Turam, 2003 p192). Alternatively, if its activities serve to 'encourage the national identities of the countries in which it is operating'(Agai, 2003 p63) and perhaps also assist the survival of local variants of the Islamic faith, it might help generate local bulwarks against a de-nationalized Islamic fundamentalism and increase belief in the viability of a Turkish-style fusion of modernity and Islam. There is scope for differences of view as to which of these two propositions is closest to reality, but both might contain elements of truth. Even in the face of opposition, unease or ambivalence from Turkey's Kemalist elite the movement could in time have a transformative impact on the region – although we should be wary of looking for an

9 'CHP deputies: Turkish schools abroad are a source of pride', Zaman, 21 March 2007.

10 'What are Gülen's missionaries after?' Sabah, 19 February 2007.

'arrival' at rather than a potential journey towards a more 'Turkish Islamic' future.

The movement might also help generate emulative reactions more widely throughout the Islamic world. Kemalist Turkey has often been presented as a model of modernity and democratisation, but 'the primary condition for being a model is its chance of being accepted. The Turkish model, with its radical interpretation of secularism and confrontation with religion, does not have a strong chance of being accepted other than as a western Trojan horse in the Islamic world' (Kosebalaban, 2003 p183). The Gülen movement, on the other hand, with its heady and promising combination of faith, identity, material progress, democratization and dialogue, might offer a model more attractive to and more worthy of emulation by Muslim states and societies struggling to orientate themselves towards a more dynamic and open future. For this reason, a more determined engagement by the Gülen movement in those parts of the Islamic world seemingly prone to take a quite different course, such as parts of the Arab world and Iran, would be especially interesting. Yet the movement has largely shunned involvement in the Arab world or Iran. This is partly explained by its occasionally dismissive attitude towards the role and practice of Islam in these countries (West, 2006 p292). Even so, overtures to the Arab and Iranian worlds occur, and may be intensifying. Thus, the 12th meeting of the network's Journalists and Writers Foundation, the Abant Platform, and its first anywhere in the Muslim world outside Turkey, was held in Cairo in February 2007.[11] In such guises, the movement has already emerged as an element in Turkey's 'soft' power, whether the state appreciates it or not. Indeed, it forms part of a more general challenge to Kemalist power and tenets, both in domestic Turkish politics and society and in the face Turkey turns towards the outside world.

Interfaith Dialogue

In its sponsorship and support for interfaith and intercivilisational dialogue, the Gülen movement seeks both to counter the impact of the more violent fundamentalist strains in modern Islam and to undermine wherever it can Huntington's 'Clash of Civilizations' thesis. These are transnational activities, but are global in their reach and potential impact. Fethullah Gülen's championing of interfaith dialogue has varied and complex roots. In part it springs from a profound recognition and embrace of the shared theological origins of Islam, Christianity and Judaism – although in his appeal for interfaith dialogue and tolerance Gülen incorporates Buddhism and Hinduism too – and the Prophet's injunction to respect the 'people of the book'. The transcendental quality of faith itself is for Gülen a unifying force that outweighs theological differences. His commitment to dialogue with the western or Judeo-Christian world is also related to his admiration for western modernity, liberalism and technological and economic prowess, and his belief that the Islamic world can and should adopt elements of the west's dynamism. Gülen's explicit references to the 'Global Village' express an assumption that the phenomena of globalization have so bound together the fates of peoples that conflict between them serves no-one's interests. Characteristically, he again draws upon the multi-faith and multi-cultural example of the Ottoman Empire, which he adduces as evidence of and inspiration for the capacity of diverse peoples to live together harmoniously and fruitfully. The empire was officially tolerant towards its non-Muslim subjects, and sought to incorporate many western practices, such as female education, the rule of law, and constitutionalism, in addition to its technology. It is fitting, therefore, that the Gülen movement's dialogue activities focus on interfaith relations within Turkey as well as at the regional and

---

11 'Abant meeting in Muslim state for the first time', Turkish Daily News, 26 February 2007. For the official website of the Journalists and Writers Foundation, see www.gyv.org.tr

global levels.

If judged by the words and thoughts of Fethullah Gülen, his movement not only embraces glo-balization, but also seeks to contribute to and shape its direction. However, little is achieved by words and thoughts alone. More substantively, Gülen met with Pope John Paul II in Rome in 1998, and has also met with Patriarch Barthelomeous, head of the Greek Orthodox Fener Patriarchate in Istanbul, the former Chief Rabbi of Turkey's Jewish community David Aseo, and with numerous other high-profile Jewish and Christian figures.[12] Tracing the range of interfaith activities of the Gülen movement is difficult, given its devolved nature and its sometimes coy approach to self-publicity, but the movement has sponsored or contributed to, and sometimes dominates, a confusing diversity of often overlapping interfaith organiza-tions. Many of the movement's interfaith platforms are US based, perhaps partly owing to the considerable market for interfaith dialogue among segments of the large actively Christian US population. Examples are the Institute of Interfaith Dialog (www.interfaithdialog.org) and the Interfaith Cultural Organization (www.uga.edu/ifco). The Gülen movement takes the credit for organizing the Inter-Civilization Dialogue Conference in 1997 to counter the 'Clash of Civilizations' thesis. In 1998 it initiated the annual Eurasian Meetings, and in Turkey it has brought together leaders of the three Abrahamic religious communities (Kuru, 2005 p.263). The movement also claims to have provided much of the inspiration for the European Union-Organization of Islamic Conference summit in Istanbul in 2002, in the wake of the 9/11 at-tacks (Kosebalaban, 2003 pp181-182).

Its chief instrument of interfaith and intercultural dialogue is the Abant Platform of the Gülen-inspired Journalists and Writers Foundations, which itself sponsors the Intercultural Dialogue Platform and the Dialogue Eurasia Platform. In its various meetings, conferences, panels, and publications, the Abant Platform seeks to propagate tolerance and modernity and the contribution Gülen's ideas might make to them, and brings together intellectuals, writers, activists and others to discuss a wide range of current issues. For example, early in 2007 it organized a panel in Turkey aimed at encouraging dialogue between the Sunni majority and the Alevi minority. The Platform's initial meetings were held at Abant in Turkey, but the first of its annual meetings to take place abroad was held in Washington DC in 2004, followed by Brussels and Paris. As we have noted, it was not until February 2007 that it held its first inter-national meeting in the Islamic world, in Egypt. This can be interpreted in a number of ways, but it can appear to reinforce the impression that the movement has at least until recently been inclined to turn its back somewhat on the non-Turkic Islamic world in its interfaith as well as its educational ventures.

In its very nature, interfaith dialogue is more about the dissemination of ideas and the bat-tle for hearts and minds than it is an institutional power struggle. This is a process, not an event that produces winners and losers. As such, it is not and may never be possible to definitively assess the impact of the Gülen movement's transnational interfaith engagement. Nevertheless, and particularly in light of the international atmosphere in the wake of the 9/11 events, any initiative that seeks to reduce the suspicion, hostility and misunderstanding be-tween the Islamic and other worlds will be welcomed in most quarters. This is true not only at the macro or global level, but also on a more local scale, where intercommunal and interfaith relations have sometimes been threatened by the ripple effects of 9/11 and its aftermath. This is an area where a local sense of alienation and exclusion can generate acts of global signifi-cance, as the UK discovered with the July 2005 London bombings and other terrorist acts

---

12 Fethullah Gülen's website contains transcripts of speeches and interviews in which he outlines his reasoning on interfaith dialogue. Also, see Sarıtoprak and Griffith, 2005; Weller, 2006.

planned or carried out by British-based Muslims, and where globally-significant events such as those of 9/11 can undermine neighbourhood harmony across the globe.

Interfaith dialogue is a growth area. There are over 250 interfaith groups, councils and forums in the UK alone. At both local and national levels in the west (although less so in most of the Muslim world and anywhere else where civil society is less developed), and at a transnational level globally, religious representatives and thinkers find themselves engaged in a constant round of initiatives, conferences, panels, and the like. Websites, publications and fora proliferate. This is a truly transnational phenomenon, and has created a transnational consciousness among its participants. Members of the Gülen movement are at the heart of much of this activity, and have come to be seen by many not of the Muslim faith as inhabiting a place very much towards the more accessible end of the spectrum of Muslim opinion. However, an empirically-inclined and sceptical political scientist is obliged to ask some hard questions about the impact of much of this activity. First of all, those engaged in interfaith dialogue are, after all, preaching largely to the converted – to each other. It is not at all clear that the fruits of this intense activity spill over into areas of society or consciousness that are not engaged. Secondly, for many secularists, rationalists and disbelievers, faith is the problem more than it is the solution. The history of interfaith violence, oppression and intolerance is long and rich. It is useful and constructive to be reminded that not all Muslims think and act as do adherents of al Qaeda. However, such reminders will not dislodge the observation that al Qaeda's activists are also devout and sincere in their faith, and they too claim to act in the name of Islam. And there is a third observation that the hardened political scientist is obliged to make, which is that even those committed to interfaith dialogue can commit acts or make statements that put back the cause of inter-religious harmony. Pope Benedict XVI's comments in September 2006, appearing to question the scope for reform of Islam and whether it had ever contributed anything that was good, offer a case in point.

None of this is intended to decry the virtue of interfaith dialogue. Nor is it even to deny its value. In the present atmosphere, it is a welcome antidote to the 'Clash of Civilizations' thesis, and counter to those who seem determined to prove Huntington right. Rather, the point is that intense interfaith activity at the transnational level should not too readily be assumed to convert into expanded transnational understanding. In a battle for hearts and minds, it is those not yet won that need to be reached.

Conclusions

The Gülen movement's Islamic inspiration combine with its Turkic identity to serve as a reminder that transnationalism is not at all a recent phenomenon. Historically, neither religions nor ethnic groups and cultures have been great respecters of artificially-constructed politico-geographic boundaries. Furthermore, both the spread of faith and the movement of peoples have long been central features in the unfolding of the human story, and in their diversity and their unity both the Islamic and the Turkic worlds demonstrate how unifying and centripetal forces are in perennial competition with pressures towards fragmentation and separation. The Gülen movement's embrace of dialogue with other faiths, particularly the Abrahamic, and its approach to a Turkic world from which Turks themselves have been for centuries largely estranged, indicate how even deep ruptures between societies and cultures can conceal the scope for rediscovery, commonality, and perhaps transformation. Yet, if transnationalism isn't new, more recent historical developments have intensified and expanded its scope. Both the capacity of the Gülen movement to grow in its country of origin, Turkey, and the opportunity it has exploited to expand its activities and influence on such a global scale, including into region's of the world long kept secluded, are testimony to the increased interconnectedness and transparency of the modern world.

It is evident that the Gülen movement is a transnational actor on a major scale, through both its educational and its interfaith programmes. Its non-state nature is clear and its global reach substantial. Its activities will impact on 'the Clash of Civilizations' and the evolution and image of Islam in the modern world. It stands to play a substantial role in the evolution of the Turkic world, in terms of its cultural unity, its modernity, and the role Islam assumes in the region. It has become part of Turkey's face abroad and an expression of Turkey's 'soft power' in particular. In this respect, it could offer to much of the Islamic world a more digestible and accessible 'model' for development and democratization than that usually associated with Turkey's ardently secular Republic. Yet the movement's transnationalism is in some respects bounded, limited in its scope, reach and impact by the prioritization inherent in the movement's various activities. Its disproportionately heavy presence in the Turkic world is more than matched by its seeming indifference to the non-Turkic Islamic world, especially its Arab neighbourhood – much of which, it must be said, is unlikely to welcome its presence in any case. Its educational elitism leaves many – perhaps those most in need of its services – untouched, both inside and beyond Turkey. Its interfaith dialogue too focuses largely on the cultivation of those (mostly in the west) who share its commitment to such activities. It leaves those who do not share this commitment, or who otherwise have limited access to it, vulnerable to the proselytizing of less savoury groups. Its activities in non-Turkic and largely non-Islamic parts of the world might be likened to the work of the cultural agencies of the major globally-active western powers such as the US, the UK and France. They are unlikely to harm Turkey's economic prospects and diplomatic image, and are indeed likely to benefit them.

However, in the relative absence of so many of the other attributes of power possessed and disseminated by the major powers – military, political, technological and economic – it is hard to calculate just how much direct advantage will accrue to Turkey and its people as a spill-over from the movement's activities abroad. There is perhaps insufficient Turkish political, technological and economic presence and 'follow up' to the Gülen movement's activities for Turkish influence to fully take root and make a truly lasting impact. Consider by contrast the substantial cultural, economic, political, linguistic, and even religious interpenetration between the UK and France and the Anglophone and Francophone worlds respectively. On the other hand, through Turkey's large Diaspora, its writers, artists, and film-makers, its economic output, and its more transparent social and political system, non-Turks – especially in the west - are acquiring a more nuanced and sophisticated appreciation of the complexities of Turkish society than that traditionally afforded by the Kemalist regime. The Gülen movement's contribution to that enriched understanding is substantial indeed, and almost entirely positive. This thought in turn raises the prospect that the most interesting ramification of the movement's transnational activities will be the indirect contribution they might make to domestic developments in Turkey itself. In understanding Turkey differently, external expectations of and policies towards Turkish domestic developments might gradually alter, and in directions that could help create space for a Turkey that is more 'comfortable in its own skin' to emerge.

THE CULTIVATION OF MEMORY IN THE GÜLEN COMMUNITY

Marcia Hermansen

Abstract

This paper explores the cultivation of 'memory' as reflected in the teachings of Fethullah Gülen and the practices of the community inspired by him. For example, it discusses how particular places, themes, and images are remembered within the movement, evoked and re-enacted so as to create community and inspire a sense of participation and allegiance.

Although the history of the Gülen movement is relatively brief-some forty years or less, practices of sharing memories inspires a collective sense of community and even sacrality.

In this paper memory within the Gülen movement will be presented in terms of its resonance with broader themes in Turkish collective memory such as Anatolian/Turkish Islam, the Ottoman cultural ideal, etc. In addition, the relationship of particular remembered symbols and experiences in the history of the Gülen movement to its current practices will be elaborated, for example 'the Light Houses' and 'camps'.

All of this will be set against the background of the topography of a movement that has expanded its imagination and its practice from local to national and ultimately global contexts.

*"In great and magnificent nations, dervish lodges
and even gravestones are ornamented. One can read
a nation's concept of beauty and art on its places of
worship and its tombstones" (Gülen)*[1]

In this paper I will explore the cultivation of "memory" as reflected in the teachings of Fethullah Gülen and the practices of the community inspired by him. For example, I will indicate how particular images, places, and themes are remembered within the movement, evoked and reenacted so as to create community and inspire a sense of participation and allegiance.

The Gülen movement has emerged as a significant phenomenon in Turkey and now globally so that this community inspired by Islamic preacher and teacher Fethullah Gülen (b. ca 1938) now comprises over six million followers. Beginning with a small circle of members of his mosque congregation in Izmir that crystallized around Gülen the late 1970s, the movement now focuses on globalized service projects, especially in the fields of education and interfaith and intercultural dialogue. The movement prefers not to conceive of itself as a formal organization. While outsiders may refer to it as a "Gülen movement" or in the Turkish style to its members as Fethullahcilar (followers of Fethullah--this may have a somewhat deprecatory ring), it is informally called **Hizmet** (service) by insiders.[2]

Hizmet has established a global network of over 500 schools world wide that offer a curriculum compatible with the highest local standards and avoid Islamic or other sorts of indoctrination. In the United States and Europe the movement involves itself in various forms of community outreach, cooperating with universities, cultural institutions, and local interreligious dialogue platforms. Within Turkey, students, teachers, and businessmen support *Hizmet*, many believing that it imparts Islamic values, while bettering humanity and fostering peace and cooperation. The Gülen movement is influential in the Turkish media (Zaman newspaper, Samanyolu television and Burc FM radio), the educational system, in financial companies (Asya Finans-now Bank Asya), as well as in publishing and book distribution. Within Turkey a bookstore chain, NT Stores with over 300 outlets, disseminates the publications of the movement, as well as many other titles, stationery and software items deemed suitable and useful both for supporters of the movement and the general public.

History and Cultural and Political Background: Turkey and the Role of Religion in Society

If we think of the Gülen community as an Islamic religious movement, it puts their status in Turkey under some scrutiny. Turkey is among the most modern and Westernized of the

---

1 M. Fethullah Gülen, *Pearls of Wisdom* (Somerset NJ: Light, 2005), 109.

2 Etienne Copeaux has discussed the use of the term hizmet as used to represent the valuable contribution of Turks to the Muslim world and the world as a whole. He finds this to be an expressional of national pride that is an element of the representations of Turkish history in public discourse and in government sanctioned textbooks. The use of hizmet in the Gülen community may draw on this resonance, however, Copeaux seems to think that the term in narrowed from the world to the Muslim world whereas in the Gülen community the object of hizmet is increasingly widened. It also would probably represent a sense of "humble" selfless service, without the recipients being "indebted". (p. 107) Etienne Copeaux, "Hizmet: A Keyword in Turkish Historical Narrative" in New Perspectives on Turkey 13 (1996):97-114.

countries of the Muslim world. Even today, almost a century after the time of the fall of the Ottoman Empire and the rise of Kemal Ataturk (d. 1938), this path to being a secular state is both celebrated and contested. Turks are fiercely nationalistic and portraits of the founder of the modern Turkish nation, Kemal Ataturk, adorn all public institutions while his statues dominate every town and village square. Kemalism, the philosophy inspired by Ataturk, is widely espoused in Turkey. It is categorized by strong nationalistic sentiments as embodied in Ataturk's declaration, memorized by school children and inscribed in many public paces, "How happy is the person who can say 'I am a Turk'". Another pillar of Kemalism is the idea of the secular state. Ataturk was a lover of things modern and for him that meant Western European. His biographers note the powerful influence that his early posting as a military attaché to Sofia Bulgaria in 1913 made on Ataturk. In fact, he came to blame religion, that is, a sort of popular and superstitious version of Islam, for the economic and cultural backwardness of his countrymen.

Emerging from the debacle of Turkey's having taking the side of the Axis powers during World War 1, and in the aftermath of great civil upheavals, Ataturk, who had become a national war hero during the battle of Gallipoli, was seen as a strong man and a rallying point for salvaging the disintegrating nation. Once in power as a virtual dictator, Ataturk instituted unprecedented secularizing and modernizing reforms. For example, after he took power in the 1920s the Ottoman law codes based on the Islamic law (*shari'a*) were abolished and a new legal system based on French and Swiss models was implemented. Visible signs of religio-cultural identity such as the face veil (*yashmak*) and the headscarf for women and the fez for men were banned. A massive reeducation of the population in European tastes and mores was undertaken by the state.

The linguistic reform of the Turkish language that took place in 1927 was another remarkable sea change. Linguists from around the world assisted in adapting the Latin alphabet used by the western world to Turkish, itself a language with a complex system of vowel harmony that was more easily configured to the Latin phonetic letters. Vocabulary items associated with the Arabic and Persian tastes espoused by courtly circles--usages that defined a sort of cultural class and religious elitism and could be perceived as obscurantist, were pushed aside in favor of Turkish words and idioms. If these were not easily located, old Turkish ballads and folklore were combed for ozturk--"ur" or authentically, Turkish equivalents. A more dramatic illustration of an erasure of archived collective memory could hardly be found.

The new generation of Turks was thus cut off from the literate heritage of their forebears. At the same time, of course, great changes in literacy were taking place in many Muslim societies due to the advent of compulsory primary and secondary education.[3] Large numbers of the rural Turkish population, especially those living away from Istanbul in central regions of Anatolia and eastern Turkey were thus encountering literacy for the first time through the new medium of the Turkish language written in the Latin script. A new generation of Turks would be educated using new texts that promoted a nationalistic, secular and modern identity. No doubt pockets of resistance to these reforms existed and persisted, but overall the change in Turkish national consciousness was pervasive and dominant.

In the light of this historical background, the nature of contemporary Turkish collective memory is necessarily complex and contested. Among the elements that may be drawn on to constitute this memory are the Ottoman heritage and Turkish regional traditions. However, the

---

3 Dale, Eickelman, "Mass Higher Education and the Religious Imagination in Contemporary Arab Societies," *American Ethnologist* 19, no. 4 (November): 643-55.

Ottoman period may be variously understood as glorious or decadent, and regional traditions potentially subvert the unity of the imagined community of the nation.

Within recent Turkish intellectual life the search for a specifically Turkish articulation of the religion has been undertaken by nationalism intellectuals as well as, on the religious side, some of the followers of the Nur movement inspired by the teachings of Said Nursi (d. 1960).[4] Some scholars have discussed the relationship of the Gülen movements with the teachings of Said Nursi and the spectrum of groups inspired by him. Nursi is highly respected by followers of *hizmet* where he is referred to as "*ustad*" (venerable teacher). His writings, especially the Risale-i Nur, as often invoked and read within Gülen study circles. Recently the Gülen community is offering its own translations of the classic writing of Nursi, in a sense offering an alternative reading of Nursi for the English speaking world. Among the themes associated with Islam in the eyes of the Gülen movement are the Ottoman heritage, Anatolian Islam, and Islamic mysticism (Sufism).

Fethullah Gülen is a retired Islamic preacher and teacher "Hoca". It is clear that Islamic teachings and values pervade the regular practices of the members of the movement. Negotiating this Islamic element in the highly secularized Turkish public sphere, and with international expansion, in a predominantly non-Muslim world stage, presents numerous challenges to the symbolic articulation of the movement.

Islam and Turkish Public Memory

Another aspect of the "Turkish" Islam concept has political implications in terms of relation to the official state ideology and apparatus. The formulation of a "Turkish" Islam allowed accommodation as it presented classical Islamic political thought as a sort of precursor to modern secularism. For example, in such a reading of Islamic political theory, the ruler himself was presented as being the guarantee of a proper religious order.

> The dominant belief was that a truly religious Sultan would govern the state according to the principles of justice, equality, and piety. This approach of keeping religion apart from worldly affairs led to a collective memory that regarded Islam as a flexible and tolerant belief system. Thus, it was assumed that religious institutions should adapt flexible attitudes toward the changing situations of their times. In the Ottoman era there was never a full-fledged theocratic system.[5]

The Ottoman Empire's social and political order known as the millet system (community-based organization) in which diverse religious communities were governed by their own laws and officials may also be involved positively in this regard. By analogy to this Ottoman system, the heritage of Turkish Islam is portrayed as being able to offer a pluralistic model for society.

For example, Aras and Caha observe that, "Turkish" Islam is characterized by "moderation", i. e. "That all creatures should be loved as God's physical reflection and objects of the Creator's own love. There is no place for enemies or "others" in this system".[6] According to the construction of a "Turkish" Islam, Islamic law (*shari'a*) primarily regulated areas of private life for Muslims such as marriage and divorce. Mush of the public law, however was based on "custom". This aspect of Islamic law is invoked today by many moderate Muslim

---

4 Bulent Aras and Omer Chaha, "Fethullah Gülen and his Liberal "Turkish Islam" Movement. *MERIA* 4 (Dec. 2000): 30 ff.

5 Ibid., 31

6 Ibid.

reformers in order to demonstrate the flexibility of Islam and its possibility to adapt to diverse cultural and political situations. This view also supports the proposition that Islamic regulations could work in a secular context and even provide an accommodating and pluralistic environment, should Islamic government become the dominant system in a modern state. Of course, this is in contrast to the more rigid and totalizing formulations of an Islamic state espoused by contemporary political Islamist movements such as the Muslim Brotherhood and the Jama'at-e Islami. In these, the shari'a is conceived of as a total system that should ideally regulate every detail of public and private life and the Qur'an should be acceded to as the constitution over which only God has sovereignty.

A prominent intellectual of the Gülen community, Enes Ergene, articulates Turkish Islam in terms of the movement's philosophy as follows.

> The values of individualism and tolerance which are said to characterize the twenty first century are identified with "the essence of the synthesis created by the coming together of Turkish culture with Islam. Muslim Turks have practiced tolerance and concurrence, which are the essence of the contemporary democracy, over a vast geography for centuries. Islam has been interpreted in this geography with the same tolerance for a thousand years... Gülen, following this very basis, regenerates this tolerant interpretation and understanding of Muslim-Turkish Sufism within contemporary circumstances, albeit high lighting a broader, more active, and more socially oriented vision.[7]

Anatolian Islam

Some academic observers of Gülen and his movement trace some of its distinctive attitudes to an "Anatolian" historical and cultural context.

Anatolia is the large plateau that defines this central Turkish region. Until recently, Anatolia could represent the heart of Turkey, but also the area less impacted by European and modern behaviors and tastes.

The concept of an Anatolian practice of Islam draws on elements such as the image of Jelaluddin Rumi (d. 1273). Rumi, whose shrine is located in Konya, a central Anatolia city, was the founder of the Mevlevi or Whirling Dervish order. His poetry is pervaded by love and is often read as promoting religious pluralism.

One observer of the Gülen movement suggests that Rumi has become emblematic of its position of dialogue and tolerance.

> The philosophy that comes closest to this kind of humanism within the Muslim tradition is, of course, Sufism, and above all the teachings of Mevlana or Celaluddin Rumi (d. 1273). From this point of view it is no coincidence that there has been a general reorientation in recent years within the Gülen community away from Said Nursi (d. 1960), the original source of inspiration for the movement. Instead, there is greater interest in the works of Mevlana, the initiator of the whirling dervishes and a master of poetry and tevhid (mystic unity).[8]

In fact, during 2007, UNESCO declared "year of Rumi", Gülen communities world wide promoted cultural events celebrating Rumi's life and poetry.

---

7 Enes Ergene "Introduction" *Toward a Global Civilization of Love and Tolerance* (Somerset NJ: Light, 2004), viii.

8 Elisabeth Özdalga, "Secularizing Trend sin Fethullah Gülen's Movement: Impasse or Opportunity for Further Renewal" Critique (12, 2003), 70.

Another association that makes embracing a Sufi heritage attractive is "moderation". This strand of Islamic contemporary thought is not unique to the Turkish context. Similar attempts to recover a Sufi background so as to inspire pluralistic, tolerant, and moderate attitudes have been made by intellectuals and government officials, in Pakistan, for example.[9]

History of the Movement

Broadly speaking, the development of the Gülen movement can be described as occurring through three phases. The first and initial period would be from the 1970s until 1983 and that could be characterized as a time for community building by Gülen and his immediate circle. From 1983-1997 the movement focused on educational projects, such as providing dormitories for college students and establishing primary and secondary institutes with a focus on achievements in math and science while forging strong relationship among dedicated teachers and their pupils.

Internationalization of the movement began with an expansion of business and educational projects into the Turkish speaking ex-Soviet republics in Central Asia with the collapse of the Soviet Union in 1994. With Gülen's move to the United State since 1997 the focus has further expanded to inter religious dialogue and a global expansion of projects and institutions.[10]

The expansion of the Gülen movement from a local to a national to a global one, correlated with developments both in Turkey and worldwide. With the collapse of the Soviet Union, its state monopoly on economic and cultural life ended in Central Asia and in other areas of the world. Into the vacuum in the Turkish speaking ex-Soviet republics in Central Asia came Gülen students--initially to explore the possibilities of replicated the success of the movement's Turkish schools in those regions. Soon delegations of businessmen supporters (*esnaf*) followed. The pioneers in these new regions learned on the ground, often facing daunting physical and political challenges.

In difficult political and economic times, a significant Turkish Diaspora of migrant workers and small businessmen had occurred since the 1970s, not only to Western Europe, in particular Germany and the Benelux countries, but also to the United States. With economic prosperity and a more open society of the 1990s, Turkish economic and political relations with non-Muslim societies also increased.

In constructing a narrative of the movement's origins in modern Turkish history, recollections of senior members of *Hizmet* portray the period of the 1970s as a dark one in Turkish history.[11] This era of the 20th century was the full-blown cold war. At the global level the capitalist West faced off against the communist Soviet Union. In individual buffer nations similar conflicts boiled over, often accentuated by class and ethnic divides.

In Turkey the forces of the right and left battled in the streets and many educational institutions became polarized or were dominated by one group or the other.

Those who eventually felt drawn to *Hizmet* seem to be those who eschewed violent conflict. They were, however, often students from more traditional backgrounds and perspectives who felt their faith and values assaulted by their militantly secular teachers. They often felt

---

9 Hasssan N. Gardezi "Sufi Mysticism of the Indus Valley" http://www.apnaorg.com/articles/sufi.html Viewed Sept. 21, 2007.

10 Hakan Yavuz, for example, discusses this development of the movement in *Turkish Islam and the Secular State. The Gülen Movement*. Syracuse:Syracuse University Press, 2003.

11 Interviews.

personally and physically intimidated. The emergence of Gülen's teachings was like a refuge and a ray of hope for such individuals who were rejected in their immediate environment.

The 1980 military coup was a watershed event in Turkish economic and political development. The social violence and ongoing clashes between rightists and leftists had provoked a state of continuous violence. To bring this to a halt the army arrested 30,000 people in the month after the coup. Ideological activity, especially that on the left, was curtailed. In fact, the new military regime, however, supported the idea of a Turkish Islamic synthesis as a way of containing leftist radicalism.

Under the premiership and presidency of Turgut Ozal (1983-1993) Turkey opened up to capitalist economics rather than state control, and to the rest of the world.

> The expansion of the Gülen Movement in the early 1980s was the result of two structural opportunities opened under the Ozal regime. First Turkey's economic liberalization schemes gave rise to a conservative central Anatolian bourgeoisie. Second, the 1982 constitution opened up new spaces for social and religious organizing. Such social reforms opened doors for previously restricted religious expression, and led to religious revival throughout the country.[12]

In a complex set of ramifications, space for an expansion of moderate Islamic expression was cleared in the early 1980s. This was, by coincidence, the very period when Gülen and his early circle were poised to take their activities to a new level.

According to the Turkish scholar, Atasoy, Ozal's Motherland Party contained with it a strong pro-Islamic faction. This was able to link Muslim cultural values and economic development.

> The political decision to develop a religious educational system played a significant role in the creation of a new genre of Muslim professionals employed mainly as engineers in the state bureaucracy and private sector. These professionals were the children of religiously minded rural small producers and urban lower classes.[13]

On the whole, this was the period of negotiating a new national culture that reincorporated religion. Religion as a subject could now be taught in the state schools that seemed to be in competition with private and Qur'an schools.

An explosion of private religious education was also taking place. at this time Statistics cite that there were only seventy (70) Imam hatip (religious) schools in 1951-2 , while by 1980 there were 588. From 1980 to 1986 this increased to 717--about 22%.[14]

My point in citing these numbers is to make a connection between the expansion of *Hizmet* and its reception in a new Turkish public sphere, to a general shift in Turkish public culture during these decades that facilitated a synthesis of nationalist and Islamic religious values, symbols, and memories.

However, the strategy of the Gülen movement schools was not to promote religious education. Rather the focus was on excellence in science and mathematics in particular, the skills needed for a prosperous and successful modernity. At the same time a concern with the moral formation of students was to be addressed by dedicated teachers who would befriend and

---

12 Joshua D. Hendrick, "The Regulated Potential of Kinetic Islam: Antithesis in Global Islamic Activism" in *Muslim Citizes of a Gloalized World: Contributins of the Gülen Movement* ed. Robert A. Hunt and Yuksel Asladogan (Somerset NJ: Light, 2007), 23.

13 Atasoy *Turkey, Islamists, and Democracy* (London: I. B. Taurus, 2005), 154.

14 Atasoy, 155.

advise their students as true "older siblings" (*abis* and *ablas*).

> The emphasis on religious topics and practices, which was characteristic of the Evangelical missions, has never been a distinguishing quality of the Gülen schools. From the start, their syllabi have been under the strict control of the Turkish Ministry of Education, which means that they have applied the same program as other Turkish public or private schools, with no special emphasis on religious topics. Religion has permeated the activities through the religious zeal on the part of the teachers and other personnel, but it has never been part of the curriculum. [15]

Topographies of the Movement

The development in Gülen's outlook from earlier Ottoman/Turkish nationalism to a pan-Turkic and ultimately more global and even universal perspective may be represented by "the map story". In my interviews I heard the story as follows from a businessman and early supporter, Ali Riza Tanrısever:

On the wall in his dormitory room, Hoca Effendi used to have a map of the Ottoman empire with the inscription 'you are still in my dreams'. Later this was exchanged for a world map and finally for a satellite view from space'[16]

As Gülen's own vision expanded from the local Turkish context in the 1990s with educational projects in the ex-Soviet republics and the initiation of dialogue with non-Muslims, his followers also broadened their horizons. For example, when outreach to non-religious Turks commenced, one follower explained how Hocaeffendi told followers to distinguish the dinsiz (non-religious) persons from the *din-düşmanı* (enemies of religion).[17] At the same time, some negative impressions by outsiders of Gülen's use of the Ottoman and world map as suggesting an imperialistic drive were noted by Ünal Bilir.[18]

Symbols used to represent the movement are thus subject to negotiation and reinterpretation depending on the audience and on the expanding horizons of its outreach activities.

The Asian Side

The dilemma of Turkey, situated on both sides of the Europe/ Asia divide may also be seen as representing the polarities modernity/tradition, secular/Islamic.

Associating with members of the Gülen community and studying the itineraries of many of the trips on which their foreign guests are taken discloses some of the principles of selection as to which sites are considered meaningful and memorable.

Turkish culture is represented on such tours by monuments familiar to all tourist itineraries-
-the Topkapi museum. Dolmabache Palace and the Covered Bazaar. However, less familiar sites generally visited by *Hizmet's* guests are situated on Istanbul's Asian side, in particular Camlica Hill and Uskudar. It is unlikely that many of these visitors will pause to inquire about the significance of Uskudar and Camlica in the history and historical memory of the Gülen movement.

In addition to the Turkish perception that the Asian Side represents religiosity and tradition,

---

15 Ozdalga, "Secularizing Trends", 71.

16 Interview, Ali Riza Tanrısever, Istanbul, Aug. 13, 2005.

17 Interview, Davut Ay, Ankara, July 22, 2005.

18 Ünal Bilir.(2004: 270).

specific associations pervade Camlica hill. It played a role in Ottoman times as a place of repose and even today the restaurant at the top of Büyük Camlica takes the form of a recon-structed chalet in the Ottoman style complete with poetry inscribed in the Osmanli script adorning the walls. Camlica is also near *Hizmet* institutions including Coskun school and the "Academy", which is the intellectual center of the movement. Here Gülen's corpus of lectures and writings as well as other material related to the movement are translated and edited for distribution in multiple languages around the world. The function of the Academy in preserving, shaping, and archiving the "memory" and the intellectual life of the Gülen community is central. It is in close touch with a number of the more "intellectual" *abis* drawn from the early students of Gülen. The model of a movement intellectual would be the graduate of an Islamic studies program with a knowledge of Arabic who then is able to internalize and interpret the teachings of Gülen. The major *Abis* are known to many members of the movement who tend to be drawn from the ranks of teachers and students, i. e. have an interest and affinity for intellectual life and discourse. Examples of such intellectuals are Ali Unal, translator of the Qur'an, biographer of Gülen, and now translator of the new editions of Nursi's works. Another intellectual is Enes Ergene, an early student who presents the move-ment in sociological terms in his book, *Geleneğin Modern Çağa Tanıklığı*.[19]

Even at more grass roots levels there is scope for the training and development of intellectual within the movement. For example, small "at home" gathering may be convened weekly. An example would be women's study groups at which one or two members take the lead, of-fering moral discourses on Islamic teachings or the Qur'an, providing fellowship and moral support to a confirmed circle and also new potentially interested housewives and friends of the group's members.

Within the Light Houses or dormitories, similar groups often convene. There is usually a space reserved for such meetings, perhaps an auditorium where outreach can occur. During the summer holidays, for example, I observed busloads of teachers in Gülen schools from other areas of Turkey coming to a large dorm located in Libadiye on the Asian side. In sev-eral days of meetings they may compare notes on pedagogy and other educational issues. At the same time, there will be a motivational component at which *Abis* will address them on inspirational topics, and they may watch DVDs on Gülen's sermons or on his life.

Beside the Academy is a large mosque in Ottoman style (as almost all Turkish mosques are) used by members.

Down the hill is the town of Uskudar, a ferry ride across the Bosphorus from Europe and the Sultan Ahmet area. The Uskudar Valide Sultan mosque is also a site of memory for the *Hizmet* community for it is here that Gülen delivered a series of lectures on the Prophet Muhammad during the year 1989-1990. These are still available on DVD and the substance of them forms the background of the book, Infinite Light (*Sonsuz Nur*).[20]

The Early Days of the Movement Memorialized and Reenacted

Several themes of the 70s period, the earliest in the development of Gülen's work continue to be used to evoke memories and in some cases continuities with those times. In the following section of this article I will discuss several of these: the "light houses", the golden generation, the "fifth floor" and camps.

---

19 Ergene, M. Enes, *Geleneğin Modern Çağa Tanıklığı* (Istanbul, Yeni Akademi, 2005).
20 *Sonsuz Nur*

Light Houses

One symbol related to the educational and inspirational function of the group is the *Işık evi* (light house):

> Gülen calls the *Işık evleri* a tree, the seed of which was planted in the times of the Prophet Muhammad himself (1997: 12). He sees their roots within the Qur'an (24:36f) itself (Gülen 2004: 2), thus giving the cemaat's own form of organization the highest Islamic virtue. For Gülen the ışık evleri are the essence of Islamic education par excellence and are viewed to be the basis for the educational activities.[21] (This gives the teachers a high religious prestige.[22]

Balcı describes the houses of light as "flats rented by the cemaat or purchased by cemaat businessmen where students—usually from poor families—are allowed to stay during their studies. Each "house of light" is under the direction of an abi (older brother) who helps to educate the students".[23] Over time the dormitory system has evolved so that most of the students now pay their own way except for those who may receive scholarship support. Based on my observations of life in a girl's dorm (Istanbul 2006), students from a wide range of backgrounds and lifestyles opt to avail themselves of the facilities that are clean, modern, and well-equipped. The "light house" concept, today, may more likely apply to smaller units of students who form study circles within a dorm or in housing they privately rent.

Beyond this more concrete and specific role of the light houses, they are compared to the ideal functions of madrasas, tekyes, and zawiyas (Islamic schools, dervish lodges, and Sufi retreat houses) that they are said to revive and combine. Their function of ihya (revival) is envisioned to have expanded from Anatolia to the world as the movement's horizons broadened.[24] This is an example of collective memory because the "light house" is a term particular to this movement. It may overlap in usage with the term "dershane" (place of study), which is typically used within the Nur movement.[25]

The fact that the light houses are functionally associated by Gülen with madrasas and Sufi lodges, demonstrates how they symbolically bridge the spheres of modern and traditional, Islamic and secular education. In another association, the imagery of "light' evokes the linguistic coinage for being "enlightened" or in a sense modern, whether in terms of the Turkish "*aydın*", or the Arabic "*manar*" group.

This idea of "function:" also evokes a story about Gülen that is repeatedly told. In the 70s in Izmir he was addressing his early circle of businessmen followers. He told them that since Turkey already had a great number of mosques; their zeal to contribute to good works should therefore be channeled to functions that were more practical and necessary for Turkish society. More practical and useful would be the building of dormitories for the many students who were relocating to new cities or moving to larger cities from the country in the pursuit of education. This Gülen's vision was put into effect in various Turkish cities and the businessmen drew of their networks in cities around the country to clone the success of the dormitory

---

21 Gülen 1998e: 193

22 Agai, forthcoming

23 Bayram Balcı, "Fethullah Gülen's Missionary Schools in Central Asia and their Role in the Spreading of Turkism and Islam" in *Religion, State and Society* 31, no. 2 (June 2003): 151-77. P. 158

24 M. Fethullah Gülen, *Prizma* 2 (Prism 2) Izmir: Nil, 1997, 13. . "Dünden Bugüne Işık Evler" (Light Houses from Yesterday to Today) http://tr.fGülen.com/a.page/eserleri/prizma/perspektif/a696.html

25 Hakan Yavuz, "Towards an Islamic liberalism? The Nurcu movement and Fethullah Gülen" *Middle East Journal* (53, # 4 Autumn): 584-605.

projects.

The strategy of imitating successful projects is highly representative of Gülen movement activities. If an event or program, for example sponsoring a performance of the dervishes or distributing "Noah's pudding" on Ashura day works in one city. The word is quickly spread and the program is replicated elsewhere. Information on what worked and what could be improved is also shared and a healthy spirit of cooperative competition is engendered among the various Hizmet centers.

The Golden Generation

A senior activist in the movement (Sait Aksoy, Chicago, October 23, 2005) described its activism in terms of a relay race in which the current generations are running and passing the torch or flag on to the next generation. Sighing, he explained how they have to run very quickly because previous generations had lagged behind. Various participants in the movement would probably construe the nature of the torch that is being carried differently--but all would agree on the need to make all efforts and sacrifices (fedakarlık) to bear it onward and on high.

Gülen uses the term Golden Generation (*altın nesil*) to refer to future Hizmet members or perhaps more broadly to those positively impacted by the movement, for example, graduates of the schools. This concept has historical resonance with the Islamic idea of the "best generations" of early Muslims. Within the evolving discourse of *nesil* (generation) the Golden Generation has been transformed from indicating a specifically Turkish Islam to a universal ideal.[26] A conference was convened on this topic in 1977, whose proceedings are available on two cassette tapes or CDs [Istanbul, Nil, 2004]. Key concepts articulated in those sessions included the idea of inner self-evaluation (*muhasaba*), love, friendliness (*dostane*), self-control, and reflection (*muraqaba*). Since these terms refer to particular practices and spiritual stages of the Sufi path the influence of Sufism on these formulations is quite clear. The Golden Generation is also seen as being antithetical to the chaos and hopelessness that some Hizmet members believe marks the current age.[27] Gülen has written that he has

> always dreamed of a generation with minds enlightened by positive science, with hearts purified by faith, who would be an example of virtue and who would burn with the desire to serve their nation and humanity, and who would live, not for themselves, but for others. Inspired by the verse and hadith I just mentioned, I called them the "Altın Nesil" (Golden Generation). I described the characteristics of this generation twenty-two years ago in conferences I gave in some cities. This is an expression that I coined and used. But without making any distinctions it's being used in the accusations for all the activities done by our Muslim people. This strange situation shows how well things are or are not understood.[28]

Balcı describes the significance of the Golden Generation in terms of the educational activities of the movement.

> The concept of altın nesil (the Golden Generation) is an important one for Gülen and his followers. The aim is to provide 'a perfect education for a perfect generation in order to obtain a perfect

26   Bekim Agai, *Zwischen Netzwerk und Diskurs: Das Bildungsnetzwerk um Fethullah Gülen* (Schenefeld: EB Verlag, 2004), 255.
27   Ibid.
28   Gülen, "Claims and Answers" Aksiyon, 06.06.1998 , Claim #19. http://en.fGülen.com/a.page/press/interview/a1216p2.html Viewed Nov. 2, 2005. Aksiyon, (1998:2).

society'. 'Altın nesil' also requires the young people of the community to show a great respect for religious and national values. This generation has to be modern and disciplined. The community therefore offers it members the best schools and the best teachers.[29]

Members of the Turkish left have suggested that the altin nesil concept could inculcate neo-conservative, elitist attitudes (Bilir 2005: 265).[30] There is also some question as to whether the phrase's meaning is context specific depending on whether the audience is within or outside Turkey, and what its political implications might be. Agai argues that the Golden Generation constructs an alternate version of modernity in which religion will remain an essential component.[31]

As in other elements of Gülen's thought, the Golden Generation concept has evolved from a nationalistic project of saving Turkey to a project of offering hope to the entire world through imbuing the pursuit of science and progress with spiritual and moral values.[32] While the term Golden Generation evokes the *hadith* that the early generations of Muslims were the best and a model for those who come later, in Gülen's thought this admiration of tradition persists along with an evocation of "hope" that a "new generation" may restore and recover what has been lost, and perhaps even continue to evolve, at least in the sphere of scientific knowledge and accomplishment.

The Fifth Floor (*Beşinci Kat*)

Another designation for aspects of the Gülen movement that carries a special spatial referent is the *Beşinci Kat* (fifth floor) (Gülen 2003c: 196). This originally referred to the top floor of a dormitory in which Gülen stayed in the mid 1980s. This period is remembered fondly by the senior students who had to humbly serve any guests that came so that the students would not develop a "*hoca*" mentality.[33] It also has the sense of representing "another world" so that its interpretation could be further related to the concept of levels of heaven, as in the Mi'raj, or Night Journey of the Prophet Muhammad. Indeed, the atmosphere of the fifth floor represents a "sacred space" in which, for example, followers would cultivate attitudes of utmost kindness, service, and tranquility becoming almost "angelic". The number "five" in itself is not supposed to be significant – Gülen states that it could have been the fifteenth floor, for example—it is rather the concept of "height" or sublimity that is important.[34] The fifth floor also represents an experience of a spiritual retreat, and a vantage point at which Gülen received inspiration for future projects, "seeing" them on the horizons from the terrace of the fifth floor.

The "fifth floor" motif would be an element of community identity generally known only to insiders. It is, therefore, noteworthy for demonstrating that among the metaphors used for describing the Hizmet community there appear to be both exoteric social definitions and esoteric/spiritual symbolism.

---

29 Balcı 2003a: 159

30 Ünal Bilir, "'Turkey-Islam': Recipe for Success or Hindrance to the Integration of the Turkish Diaspora Community in Germany" *Journal of Muslim Minority Affairs* (24, #2, Oct.2004): 259-283

31 Agai, Zwischen *Netzwerk und Diskurs*. 256.

32 Bekim Agai, "Fethullah Gülen and his Movement's Islamic Ethic of Education". *Critique:critical Middle Eastern Studies* 11 (1): 27-48. pp. 36-7

33 Reşit Haylamaz, Istanbul, August 9, 2005.

34 Gülen, *Işığın Görüngüğü Ufuk* (The Horizon of Light) (Çag ve Nesil-7) Istanbul: Nil, 197).

Camps

I was first invited to a *Hizmet* "camp" during the winter season, in fact, the Christmas Holidays of 2005 in the Chicago area. My pre-existing impression of camps was of tents pitched in a forest. This camp however, was held in a summer resort hotel for which a very appealing rate could be negotiated during the winter season, especially at a time when most American families are at home with relatives.

The activities of this camp consisted of reading and discussing *Risale Nur* and Gülen's book on the Prophet Muhammad.[35] No dramatic religious practices took place, just a simple round of communal ritual prayers and devotions.[36] Evening lectures were presented by visiting senior *Abis* and a few outside guests. Almost all sessions were conducted in Turkish. It was a family atmosphere with special classes and activities for children and young people.

It did not occur to me to ask--why call it a "camp", and it was only later that I learned about the first *Hizmet* camps and their place in the memory of the Gülen movement. This I was to hear from one of the first members of Gülen's circle in Turkey, a man who was an early follower of *Hoca Effendi* from the Days of the Kastanepazari mosque in Izmir, Ismail Büyükcelebi.[37]

After an evening (*sohbet*) with members of the movement in Chicago, I was granted an interview, conducted in Turkish. The following account of the first camp is based on my notes.

> At the first camp in 1968 (check date) there were about 50 students. They lived in tents in an open field at Kaynaklar village near Izmir. It was in the open air and there was a row of pine tress on one side of the field. There was a one room house that had been used as a barn and had to be cleaned up. For cooking they made a hearth out of stones.
>
> All the students (male) were used to dorm life and had never cooked. They learned by experience, taking turns and having Hoca Effendi comment on the meals as they were progressing.
>
> The water came from a well and there was no electricity, only the light of oil lamps.
>
> The only place to do laundry was in a stream about 30 minutes away.
>
> The second year of the camp there were 120 students and in the third 275.
>
> In the 70s Hoca Effendi moved to the city of Enderem and so did the camps for four years. During this period, in fact, after the 1971 coup there was more pressure on the movement from the state authorities. Gülen himself was jailed for holding the camps as they were viewed as being potentially subversive.
>
> Soldiers would routinely come and check for clandestine activities.[38]

When the students were alerted that such a raid was immanent they would hide their religious books such as copies of the *Risale-i Nur*. In order to give the impression that fewer attendees were at the camp, they used to put one bed roll on top of another.

They recited litanies of protection such as the prayer (*du'a*) of those who were at the early Islamic battle of Badr. Once Gülen saw a dream of the Prophet's uncle, Hamza, just as a raid

---

35   *Infinite Light/ Sonsuz Nur*

36   Primarily from *al-Jawshan al-Kabir* (Somerset NJ: Light, 2006).

37   Interview Chicago April 16, 2007.

38   At that point visibly practicing Islam was considered subversive.

was immanent. They later learned that at that very time the jeep of a party of soldiers who were coming to investigate had an accident on the road delaying the raid.

At one time in the late 1960s the future leader of the Refah party, Najmettin Erbakan, came to the camps to attempt to rally support for his party. This type of political solicitation, however, was not an interest for Gülen's students.

In addition to its intrinsic historical interest, my purpose in recounting this camp narrative is that it typifies the type of account that members of the movement would listen to in a group session (*sohbet*). Often senior Abis will visit local groups and tell then stories of early struggles to establish schools in new and remote areas of the world. In fact, just prior to the interview at which Ismail Büyükcelebi told me about the camp, he had been presenting a *sohbet* at which he recounted his adventures in starting schools in South East Asian countries such as Thailand and Malaysia.

This would be an example of the sharing and implantation of shared memories--shared very explicitly of events some thirty or forty years old--clearly before the birth of many of the young followers of the movement, yet still relatively recent.

The fact is that such camps may be held by Gülen communities in far-flung situations and locations. They may be viewed as new seeds that are being planted in the hopes that they will flourish and inspire as those first camps did. There is also, perhaps a note of relief that the persecution of the 1970s had abated.

But has it entirely? I was staying at a *Hizmet* girls dorm in central Istanbul (summer 2006). In the middle of the night there was a loud banging at my locked dorm room door. I awoke, bewildered, and was told that the "*mufattishler*" (inspectors) might show up any time and my door must be kept unlocked.

According to the wardens, these official dorm inspectors were not so much concerned about who was in the dorm, but apparently would be offended by conspicuous signs of religious practice such as Qur'ans or prayer carpets unrolled for easy use. How much of this was substantial I never ascertained, because I did not encounter any actual "inspectors". The story does, however, resonate with the account of students needing to clean up or secularize the early *Hizmet* camps.

This in turn leads back to reflection on the dynamic of shared, overlapping, and potently conflicting stores of memories. Nationalist memories are part of Turkish experience and followers of *Hizmet* in my experience, are very comfortable with combining the paradigms and creating a space of identity/memory in which they can comfortably co-exist.

For example, in *Hizmet* public institutions such as schools and dorms, one finds prominent displays of the obligatory pictures of Kemal Ataturk and his proverbial sayings. In fact, the selection of which of the founder's sayings will be prominently displayed on the walls of the entrances seems to consciously strive to conjoin moral and nationalist elements.

Images and Symbolism in the Creation of Memory

It is also worth noting how certain symbols and themes seem to be evoked in literature, imagery, and means of identification among the *Hizmet* community.

This provokes a reflection as to whether such "symbolic" names are an obfuscation of the identity and purpose of the group. There is a preference for natural symbols, some of which may have some vaguely Islamic relevance.

The earliest journal "*Sizinti*" began in the 1970s--the later English version is called the "*The Fountain*". "The underlying idea of the name implies that it represents the leakage of the essence of the absolute truth, of the revelation." The major themes in the journal turn around catching the dispatches from the God which are embodied through a striking and mysterious order of the world.[39] Many later books of Gülen are compiled from his articles that were regularly prepared for this journal.

The preference for water associated names was explained by one movement scholar as follows,

> Water refers to purity. It also refers to humility, simplicity etc. It also refers to universality as everyone needs it and nobody would object to it... Generally, river names are used[40] -but never lake names-emphasizing dynamism and constant action... Sometimes ocean or sea names may be used to refer to the horizon, vision and so on... Similarly, star or planet names or celestial references[41] are also used to convey the same meanings, i.e. the horizon, high and lofty ideals etc.[42]

A relatively early publication of the movement is the book, Truth through Colours.[43] It contains images, composite photographs geared to evoke emotional responses. Each is accompanied by a brief textual observation or query designed to inspire the reader to reflection.

This undertone of emotion, perhaps a sadness, longing, and so on, is carried through in the choice of music played at Gülen meetings or in the dervish flute scores played on Burc FM. Certain pieces of instrumental music are repeated used as background on DVDs and at Hizmet community dinners etc. so as to become almost emblematic anthems.

Media and Memory

Having the ability to create narratives and have them performed is a very important means of influencing public consciousness in the contemporary period. This would be the characteristics of some of the popular programs produced by Samanyolu TV which merit separate study on their own. For example, the popular series, "Fifth Dimension", could be considered a Turkish Islamic version of "Touched by an Angel" where the hero Salih is an observer and occasionally a participant in human affairs. Another major drama is "*Büyük Buluşma*", the "Final Meeting"--or "Great Encounter" the premise of which is a newly deceased person's arriving at the gate of judgment where they encounter an ambiguous, figure--an angel or as the program notes describe him, a personification of their conscience. Their life at this point, "passes before their eyes" and the audience views the sequence of moral decisions and circumstances leading up to the moment of the individual's death.

The ambiguity of whether such imaginary productions are geared at moralizing or Islamicizing the society remains. "Good characters" may be portrayed as rural or urban, they may be identifiable as practicing Muslims, for example, women wearing Islamic dress, or secular.

---

39 Yasin Aktay, "*Body, Text, Identity: The Islamist Discourse Of Authenticity In Modern Turkey*", PhD Thesis, 1997, The Graduate School Of Social Sciences of the Middle East Technical University, Ankara).

40 For example "nil" (Nile) publishing.

41 "Light" TV was used for a time. Mehtap (Moonlight) is the name of a satellite network, Samanyolu (Milky Way) the Gülen movement TV station.

42 Personal e--mail communication Sept. 30, 2007 drawing on the expertise of Ahmet Kurucan.

43 Fethullah Gülen, *Truth through Colours* (Izmir: Nil, 1992). Turkish original *Renkler Kusaginda Hakikat Tomurcuklari* (1985).

The dialogue certainly makes reference to specifically Islamic concepts and teachings, and on some occasions the symbols of moral reform or repentance are portrayed in terms of Islamic observance and tranquil domesticity.

Additional "dramas" or "soap opera" type programs may deal allegorically with challenges faced by the movement in Turkey, and certain characters have been identified with the role of Gülen himself.

An interesting example of the evolving role of media and the arts in the movement is that of a sort of cultural center, *Firat Kultur Merkezi* (FKM), sponsored by the community near Sultan Ahmet. Here discussions may be held. There is a coffee bar, art on the walls, the sort of space that would appeal to university students or graduates. I was also told that plays are performed at this center and films shown. One of the plays, *Tuna Boyu*, was written based on the story of a Gülen teacher who so loved his students in a remote area of Central Asia that when one of them fell into a river he attempted to save him, and in the course of this action lost his own life.[44] Naturally, this touching story is inspirational and emblematic of the role of the ideal teacher.

Conclusion

The Gülen community, despite its relative youth, has developed a rich array of symbolic self-understandings and representations. This development of shared symbols and memories creates a sense of unity and collective identification beyond the interests and experiences of individual members. These memories combine elements of Turkish identity such as Ottoman cultural achievements with a range of references to Islamic spirituality including Sufism. In addition they serve to bridge various realms of symbolic identification, the nationalist/Kemalist ethos of modern Turkey with its Islamic Ottoman heritage; and now with the group's expansion, a sort of global universalist consciousness with the sharing of specific features of Turkish cultural symbols, whirling dervishes, *ebru* arts, and so on. This symbolic exchange is concretized in the Turkish Olympiad, in which school children from Gülen sponsored schools around the world gather in Istanbul and perform songs and recite poems in the Turkish language.

The movement as it develops is also in the process of creating certain "heroes", Gülen himself, the second layer of *Abis*, and the teacher as a hero. Among these heroes are Haci Ata, the late Haci Kemal Erimez (d. 1997), Gülen's friend since 1968 who passed away while trying to open schools in Tajikistan. A play has been written about him, a web site is dedicated to his memory and DVDs about *Hizmet* containing video images from his funeral are presented as part of the narrative of heroic sacrifice.[45] A further example is the 2006 publication of a book written by Harun Tokak, head of the Writers and Journalists Union in Istanbul, eulogized various Turkish teachers who had gone to far-flung reaches of the world to work in Gülen schools.[46] For example, Adem Tatlı, a 39 year old teacher and school officer in Mongolia, was tragically killed in an auto accident on his way to see his family in Turkey. It is said that his last request was to be buried in Mongolia, near his school.[47]

---

44 Ali Fuat, *Marallar İnince Suya*, (Ankara: FM Yayınları, 2005) features the plot of a teacher who goes to Central Asia, and loses his life there while trying to save one of his students in a lake.

45 This may be viewed on Youtube http://www.youtube.com/watch?v=KIwtBAzmrgE. See also the book by M. Kücük, *Adanmış, Bir Gönül İnsanı Hacı Ata*. (Istanbul: Kaynak, 2006).

46 Harun Tokak, *Önden Giden Atlılar* (Istanbul, 2006).

47 http://tr.fGülen.com/content/view/10242/94/

Some of these memories are replicable and performable while others are spontaneously generated around particular times and spaces. In the study of this contemporary movement, we are able to see the making of "sacred history" from the perspective of insiders, almost as it happens.

Interviews

Davut Ay	July 22, 2005
Enes Ergene	July 23, 2005
Cemal Türk	July 24, 2005
Reşit Haylamaz	August 9, 2005
Ali Ünal	August 9, 2005
Ali Rıza Tanrısever	August 13, 2005
Ismail Büyükcelebi	Chicago, April 2007

FETHULLAH GÜLEN: KEMALIST AND ISLAMIC REPUBLICANISM AND THE TURKISH DEMOCRATIC FUTURE

Louis J. Cantori

Abstract

To put it bluntly, the claim that liberal democracy is a universal concept is false. Its prerequisites of individualism, equality, secularism, pluralism etc. have a minority status in the world. On the other hand, what can be termed Islamic conservatism does apply to Islamic societies: 1) the past incorporates within it the revelations of God as expressed in the Qur'an as the spiritual centre of gravity; 2) community and family take precedence over the individual and 3) the goal of society is the enjoining of that which is good and the prohibition of that which is evil. Islamic conservatism can also be analytically attached to republicanism as an alternative to democracy. Referred to here is the republicanism of ancient Rome which argues for (a) the limitation of the powers of a strong and benevolent and moral state, (b) an elite pledged to serve the public good (*maslahah*), (c) a citizenry also pledged to serve society, and (d) an embedded law respected and upheld by all.

Kemalism in contemporary Turkey represents the principles of republicanism as formulated in the famous 'Six Arrows', which centred more on the need for a strong centralised state than on the obligations of the state to its citizens. If measured against the four criteria of the ancient Roman republican ideal, the Turkish state clearly falls far short. By contrast, this paper argues, the Gülen movement does, rather remarkably, meet those high standards. As a consequence, there are present in Turkey today, two interacting modes of republicanism that are increasingly beginning to overlap with and resemble one another.

Introduction

The Problem

From the point of view of the study of Middle Eastern politics, Turkey appears so exceptional that it is seldom ever grouped comparatively with the other states of the region. After all, it represented a historically impressive ability under the Ottoman Empire to resolutely pursue the reformist goals of virtually uninterrupted self-directed reform under the Tanzimat from 1839 onwards and then it was also able to resist European colonialism until the end of World War I . Then, under the nationalist leadership of Kemal Atatürk, it denied the occupation of the Anatolian peninsular to the voraciousness of an array of European armies. Turkey subsequently then undertook a successful program of modernization in which the philosophical positivism of Comte and Durkheim established parallel deep roots with a modernizing Islamic theology. The Arab countries of the Middle East , by contrast, have had a far more fractured experience in resisting European colonialism and imperialism. Culturally, they were conflicted by the competing rivalries of Arabism and nationalism and have faltered and slowed in the efforts at a self-modernizing Islam . Riding the wave of these national accomplishments, the Turks also found within themselves, the cultural quiet place of a political Sufism where they could communicate among themselves in even casual and graceful conversation about how to link their hearts to their minds. The preceding remarks suggest the profoundness and depth of their self-directed historical change . The story is even more monumental than what has been said thus far. Present day Turkey, somewhat paradoxically, under the resolute leadership of its mainstream Muslim political organizations is also said to be on the cusp of entry into the European Union. In addition, perhaps the most important summary indication of their political and cultural accomplishments has been their ability to creatively hold to religious belief while at the same time interpolating it and causing it to wax and prosper. Finally, to return to the beginning of these remarks, there is also the continued ability of the Turkish people to face the tyranny of the military which in another country might have led to political polarization and violent conflict, instead has witnessed a sustained level of extraordinary level of civility. As one observes the military itself at this moment in time, it is also possible that the ameliorating views of Fethullah Gülen and those influenced by him has contributed to this level of collective political maturity.

Turkey has achieved what outside powers are continually berating the Arab countries of the region for failing to have achieved , namely democratization. The reason for this success can be attributed to the fact that Turkey has managed to avoid that Anglo-Saxon "disease", namely subscribing to a liberal democracy whose political cultural assumptions are inappropriate and incongruent to those of a civilization standing outside of the influence of the European Enlightenment. This disease thus consists of attempting to embrace an alien political culture of individualism, secularism, pluralism etc . Instead, as is argued in the present paper, Turkey has subscribed to a version of republican democracy. In addition, for reasons of historical opportunity and gifted political leadership, Turkey also has been able to successfully contest European tyrannical rule when it put in its appearance. Much of the remainder of the Middle East on the other hand permitted itself to be beguiled by the Anglo Saxons to seek an unachievable liberal democracy and for their leaders to be seduced into mimicking the soft corruption of tyrannical , colonial and imperial rulers. This "double tackle " has left the other Middle East players disabled and suffering from numbing brain concussions. While admittedly, Turkey has much about it that is exceptional in it opportunities and its successes, there are, however, important analytical lessons to be learned and applied to the politics of the countries in the remainder of the Middle East. The present paper is organized around the important distinction of republicanism versus tyranny . This distinction is important for the following reasons:

i.   Political science at the beginning of the Twenty first Century remains without a typology adequate to the understanding of what is still called in some circles the politics of "Third World states" i.e. terminology of a now non-existent Cold War. In the terminology of the present paper, a so-called "Third World state" most often is a tyrannical republican state e.g. Tunisia, Egypt etc.

ii.   The absence of a meaningful and informing typology in fact has been noted in some well known and important scholarly exchanges which in fact are said to also have had a mischievous impact upon politics and policy in the post-World War I era as well. The point is that if one does not possess a rigorous political science typology of regimes, one can not know what the sign posts are to successfully navigate a complex political world.

iii.   What lies at the base of the difficulty of developing such a typology is the intellectual vise grip of a presumed "value free" behavioural social science. This social science is "presumed value free" because in reality it mimics the liberal culturally dominant thought of individualism, equality, pluralism etc. This has interfered with the ability to ask the questions of underlying teleological political values so as to delineate the value direction that is being pursued in political behaviour.[1]

iv.   The preceding cosmological question can be brought closer to ground if one is to direct these questions to one particular political region in the world, that of the Middle East. What persuasive political typology has been developed in order to understand this, perhaps the most strategically important and dangerous of the regions of the world? The answer, based on counts of word frequency , might be misleadingly "democracy" and "authoritarianism" instead of the prevalent republicanism and tyranny.

v.   The present paper in the interest of brevity passes over these latter terms in order to join the intellectual debate in the following way. If "democracy" is so illuminating, how is that one does not see more of it? The answer is because "democracy" is in fact distant from the ground in the Middle East and what is close to the ground are the deaths and tortured cries of something old fashioned, called tyranny. If "tyranny" is so prevalent there is a need to address it in a meaningful way. A way to the end of the political domination that cultivates tyranny needs to be developed and a well established historical way in the long history of Western political theory is to accomplish this is via "republicanism". It is useful to recall , that the historical solutions to achieve this objective are well known e.g. the bloody confrontations and revolutions on the model of those of 1649(England), 1776(America), 1789(France) etc .[2]

---

1 When the political science discipline is looked at critically, one discovers that far from being "scientific 'and "objective" it is in fact joined at the hip ideologically to liberal democracy. The consequence is that political analysis utilizing such a "discipline" becomes an advocate for a liberal democracy that will find little resonating supporting political culture of individualism, equality, secularism etc in so much of the world that has not shared the experience of the Enlightenment. . See James Creaser, Liberal Democracy and Political Science (Baltimore, MD: Johns Hopkins University Press, 1990) for a particularly acute presentation of this point of view.

2 The valuable general sources utilized in the present paper to make the transition from its theoretical concepts to the Turkish case study are, M. Hakan Yavuz, Islamic Political Identity In Turkey (New York: Oxford University Press, (2005) (See especially p. 32 for a summary historical table of Islamic organizations) and M. Hakan Yavuz

Defining Republicanism

First, however, there is the necessity to define what is meant by "republicanism":

While liberty is central to republicanism, the key objective of republicanism is not political participation but the more practical imperative of first gaining freedom from domination. One can have liberty without necessarily having democratic representation. The achievement of this freedom depends upon four prerequisites :

i.   First, the state takes precedence over the individual so that it becomes the "free state" (civitas libera) from which the citizen gains his freedom from domination by means of a mixed constitution(politeia) accompanied by a system of political checks and balances.

ii.   The second is that there should be a system of law (legis) which is embedded in history and tradition so that its principles are instinctive to its citizens.

iii.   The third is that the political culture of the state should be one of civic virtue (virtu) which results in the welfare of one's fellow citizens being of first importance.

iv.   The fourth is related to the foregoing and that is there should be virtuous ruling elite whose privileges in society are earned by its attention to the welfare of the society as a whole.[3]

This definition is a composite one due to the fact that there is hardly not a single agreed upon definition of republicanism in scholarly literature. Instead, most scholars appear to have adopted a definition that fits their specific scholarly concern . The definition presented here begins and remains true to Rome and especially Cicero, as indicated in the use of technical Latin terms. This careful attention to definition is what is called for in the case of a paper whose theme is the somewhat unfamiliar one of Roman republicanism.

"Republicanism" is used in the present paper as a concept of two analytical varieties. The first variety is the one of self-description which means that an actor or movement begins with a self conscious definition or concept which they denote as "republicanism". The second variety is the case when a pattern of behaviour begins to implicitly take on the characteristics of "republicanism". Thus the two varieties are either respectively self-descriptive or implicit republicanisms. The first variety in the case of Turkey is illustrated by what has come to be called in effect self-described "Kemalism" . The second variety in the case of Turkey is the implicit one of Islamic republicanism. The self-described version in the case of Turkey actually self-consciously adopts the label of "republicanism". The implicit variety becomes one whose characteristics approximate those of the Roman republic. Republicanism is also an ideal type as an ideal type that stands for the limitation upon the exercise of political power . It is this latter type of republicanism that in this paper constitutes what is termed "Islamic republicanism". This paper identifies Fethullah Gülen as the single Turkish leader whose thinking and writing can be said to constitute Islamic republicanism. The republican curtailing of the excesses of the exercise of political power might appear to resemble liberalism as some scholars writing about republicanism claim. In fact, however,

---

and John Esposito, Eds., Turkish Islam And The Secular State: The Gülen Movement (Syracuse, N.Y.: Syracuse University Press, 2003.

3 Sources on republicanism: Philip Pettit, Republicanism: A Theory of Freedom and Government (New York, NY: Oxford University Press, 1997); Quentin Skinner, Liberty Before Liberalism Cambridge, UK: Cambridge University Press, 1998); Maurizio Viroli, Republicanism, Translated from the Italian by Antony Shugar (New York, New York: Hill and Wang, 2002): Cicero, The Republic and The Laws. Translated from the Latin by Niall Rudd (Oxford, UK: Oxford University Press, 1980).

its objective of limiting political domination predates liberalism by some 2000 years. Note, for example, the typical haste with which proponents of liberal democracy proclaim the universal importance of the later concept of democracy with little attention to the intermediate steps necessary to its achievement. From this perspective, there is something akin to a "miraculous birth" of democracy resembling the concept "miraculous birth" in Christianity ! In practical, down to earth terms, it is not democracy that urgently imposes itself upon peoples, but rather something as simple as the security and safety of home and hearth . The key assurance of republicanism is that it stands for freedom from domination but it does not necessarily stand for political representation. The latter expectation, for example, might very well be undertaken by a responsive "free" state or by a socially virtuous ruling elite. Thus the definition of republicanism can be elegantly defined as a political system that assures that the individual be free from domination and this is to be achieved by a mixed constitution of checks and balances, a system of law that originates in the tradition of the people and a ruling elite and citizens possessing a culture of civic virtue and collective responsibility .

Republicanism has a polar opposite and this is the typology of "tyranny". Tyranny is nearly as elusive to define as republicanism .[4] One reason for this is perhaps due to the fact that political science is as much out of practice in utilizing this concept as it is in the instance of republicanism. This is a concept which has shared a similar political science fate of neglect as that of republicanism itself. Perhaps the best definition remains that of Aristotle who points out that tyrannies resemble the single person rule of the monarchy but it is without the accompanying political constraints of law or tradition.[5] He points out that there are two varieties of tyrannies: The "bad" variety in which the ruler rules self indulgently and the "good " variety in which the ruler rules with the welfare of the people in mind. An example of a good tyranny might be the case of tyrannical republican military rule in Turkey that also rules without the constraint of law or tradition, but does so with the self-justification of doing so in order to benefit the Turkish people. In the West, tyranny like republicanism also was delivered a conceptual coup de grace by the European Enlightenment . In the passions and exhilaration of la Terreur and the apparent end of monarchies, the time of tyrannies seemed to have come to an end, to be replaced by democracies. In addition, in the theories of Hegel and Comte, the state was not to be a tyranny but rather was to be neutrally bureaucratic as part of the optimism of the anticipated process of modernization. Instead of the tyranny of the state, one now used the term in a rather trivializing fashion e.g. "the tyranny of the minority" or "the tyranny of public opinion". One consequence of this was that when the repressiveness of Russia and Germany put in an appearance in the 20th Century, instead of instantly recognizing these political forms as tyrannies to be resolutely opposed, the West instead dawdled about debating the merits of the so called new ideologies . Meanwhile, this was occurring while European peoples were brutally conquered and abused while settling upon the self descriptions of the regimes themselves as "communism" and "fascism". The "new" labels of "communism" and "fascism" were to lead to further conceptual confusions with the advent of the Cold War. Additional terminology such as "totalitarianism " was to

---

4 "Authoritarianism" would seem to claim some equal status to tyranny as a concept, but whereas tyranny is a previously prominent concept in political science, "authoritarianism" appears to be an afterthought. Note, for example, that in an edited book containing contributions from a number of well known scholars, and with "authoritarianism" in its title, Marsha Pristine Posusney and Michele Penner Angrist, Eds. Authoritarianism in the Middle East: Regimes and Resistance(Boulder, CO: Lynne Reiner, 2005), the concept is not even defined, let alone utilized in an illuminating and suggestive fashion. It turns out; the book is really about the failure of democracy in the Middle East.

5 Aristotle, Politics and the Constitution of Athens (Cambridge, UK: Cambridge University Press, 1984).

lead to the paradoxical confusing and sometimes even irrelevant intellectual nuances similar to those directed to fascism and communism. Clearly, the so called "Third World states" were in fact tyrannical regimes resembling those accompanying the advent of communism and fascism. Time and millions of lives were lost as a consequence. History was to repeat itself more recently in Bosnia and the Balkans and the repetition of the debates of the interwar period.[6]

More so than many Middle Eastern countries, the political appearance of Turkey belies its political reality. The appearance is one of a fierce patriotism which is evident in the ocean-like flood of the blood red Turkish flag that flies everywhere from the highest natural and man-made elevations. In addition, religiously, the flag is accented by the symbolism of a white crescent and the star of Islam. Perhaps the greatest indication of the strength of commitment to Islam is that, in contrast to many other Muslim countries, there is the sheer enormous numbers of persons committed to a variety of local Sufi organizations. The most popular of these was the Naksibendi order, including the enormous number of followers of Said Nursi(1881-1960) and now those of Fethullah Gülen (1938-)who is the subject of the present paper. The scale of Sufi activity can be underestimated given its "invisibility" as a consequence of the humbleness and humility of its practice, perhaps most often in the home of friends and not in a physical lodge(tekke) . This is reinforced symbolically by the extraordinary gentleness of voices in group meetings of the movement's adherents. Conversation in these groups possesses the quality of hushed respect to God and to one's brothers. The result is therefore neither argument nor elevated voices, but rather the intentness of focused appreciative listening. It is also the case, however, that Kemal Atatürk as the great militant secular founder of the Turkish republic, pursued his secular and republican goals relentlessly and aggressively. Therefore, there is an accurate preconception about Turkish politics which recognizes that there exists a gulf between the secular policies of the state on the one hand, and the pious sentiment of the majority of the population on the other. This preconception, however, can also be exaggerated.

In fact, it is the thesis of the present paper that Kemal Atatürk's (1881-1938) "republicanism" and the secularism associated with the term that creates the religious divide in the society. Nonetheless, in fact this division also contributes to a surprising degree to the linkage between the two segments of the society. Thus, when analyzed dialectically, patriotic Kemalism and pious Islam may be said to operate in discernable and interactive parallels with one another. In fact one can even detect evidence of a degree of a convergent trend towards the possible synthesis of the two. It remains the case, however, that a great deal of subtle theoretical and empirical analysis has yet to be undertaken in order to support this assertion .

It is the case that Turkish politics are commonly understood to be beset by an authoritarian republican state led by a military elite upholding the secularism of Kemal Atatürk against an increasingly strong Islamic resurgence, one of whose most important leaders is Fethullah Gülen . The argument advanced here, however, is somewhat to the contrary. Rather than Kemalism and Gülen being separated by republicanism , it is arguably the case that they are possibly joined rather than separated by the concept.

While the foregoing sets the Turkish stage for what follows, this paper also locates its argument within a second, broader analytical social frame work which itself is novel and

---

6 For a critical discussion of the concept of "tyranny", see Mark Lilla, "The New Age of Tyranny', The New York Review of Books, October 24, 2002, XLLI, No 16, 28-9.

challenging. This story begins by noting that the political science utilized in the study of Middle Eastern politics is severely handicapped by the absence in the discipline of even a single significant post-Enlightenment intellectual figure who even approaches the eminence of those scholars found within other social sciences in the formative two hundred years period since the Enlightenment. Note, for example, the cascade of the eminent names of those from adjoining disciplines: Smith plus Marx in economics; Comte plus Durkheim plus Toennies plus Weber in sociology; Fustel de Coulange plus Radclyffe-Brown in anthropology, plus von Gierke and Vinogratov in history.[7] There is not even a single political scientist who appears among them and therefore, there is also not a single American scholar. What this qualitative penuriousness illustrates is the tardiness of this discipline to make the intellectual transition from political philosophy to becoming a social science. As a result, there is an absence of a universal typology of regime types in political science that might otherwise illuminate global or regional politics such as those of the Middle East. In the Middle East, a political scientist visiting from Mars would be led to believe that the widespread references to "democracy "is because it is a classification that is authoritatively revealing of the political process of that region. Similarly, he might think the same about the prevalence of the Cold war concept of "totalitarianism". In fact, it is tyranny that more accurately describes the widespread bloody repression and political injustice of the region. But, as already noted, even the concept of tyranny is absent from political science. Thus in spite of the fact that the Middle East is awash in political injustice of the cruellest variety, tyranny seldom appears as a concept employed by the Middle East analyst. If tyranny is therefore the Middle East norm, than a more accurate label to apply to Turkey is in fact not democracy, but rather "republicanism". As will be noted, however, Turkey also has its own familiarity with tyranny. This is due to the fact that it appears to be a quite appropriate label to describe the fact of not only four major military coups of the government by the Turkish army in the Twentieth Century, but also the manner in which the army has statutorily written into regulations its own ability to continuously interfere in Turkish politics whenever it sees fit to exert political influence. Thus, the casual outside observer of Turkish politics little appreciates the nearly constant interference of the Turkish military in Turkish politics.

Turkish democracy, however, also eludes an accurate and appropriate political science label. When political science asserts that "democracy" has a universal application, once again, a conceptual error is being made. The "democracy" applied by the discipline is in fact "liberal" democracy. It is an ethnocentric concept expressing the liberal philosophy of the West that was itself only developed in the two hundred year period since the Enlightenment . The alternative and more accurate label developed in the present paper is that of republicanism and republican democracy. It is the latter concept that is in consort with Middle Eastern political and Islamic culture. Individualism, secularism, equality etc and the principle of liberty of non-interference with the individual are virtually absent in the Middle East. What is present in the Middle East instead is the moral authority of religion anchored in the past, the community and the family preceding the individual and the societal goal of prohibiting that which is evil and promoting that which is good. In addition, the criteria of republicanism also presents the opportunity for Turkish religious leadership to join in the pursuit of a religiously based republicanism whose criteria rather remarkably resemble those of the ummah. The principle of liberty of republicanism is founded in the "free state" (civatis libera) to which the individual surrenders him/herself. The ruler of the republican state safeguards the welfare of the citizen, the republican political class does the same, and most of all, the state is also the guardian of

---

7 See Lilla, Ibid. for this discussion of the intellectual weakness of political science.

a system of secular law and potentially of religious law which is also committed to the same objective. The principle is that of the freedom bestowing republican "free state" preventing a basic political domination and not necessarily that of the assurance of the more ambitious and perhaps theoretically unachievable liberal "free man".

Liberal democracy has its origins in the West and specifically in the European Enlightenment. It therefore is attached organically to liberal political philosophy.

Republicanism , on the other hand, dates from Roman times and the pre-Enlightenment and has the label of philosophical conservatism underpinning it. Philosophical conservatism is a subject far more complex than liberalism for the reason that unlike the latter, conservatism tends to be more of a minority point of view and it also tends to contain a greater variety of ideas within it. Liberalism and Marxism are two bodies of thought which are firmly anchored in the Enlightenment. Conservatism, on the other hand , is significantly defined as being pre- or counter-Enlightenment. Conservativism can be defined as: 1) respect for the past as the source of the tradition and the religious revelation that guides society, 2) the ascendancy of the family and community over the individual, and 3) the goal of society is the seeking of social virtue or, enjoining of the good and prohibition of evil.[8]

Thus far, republicanism and conservatism have been suggested as alternative typologies to those of liberal political science (liberal democracy and liberalism). In addition, the concept of tyranny has also been suggested as a contrasting and contesting concept to republicanism. Tyranny has been defined as the exercise of abusive political power outside of legal and constitutional restraints. It has also been said that Turkey is a rare instance of democracy in the Middle East. Therefore, how and in what way might one speak of tyranny in the Turkish case? One can do this by carefully noting the attachment of the label of "republicanism" to Kemalism on the one hand and what can be termed "tyranny" to the interventionist militarism of the Turkish army on the other hand. As the "founder" of the modern Turkish republic, Kemal Atatürk succeeded in articulating an ideology of "republicanism "from the time of the "war of independence" to his death in 1938. In the years since his death, however, the gradual development of a political party system began to reduce the ability of the army to rule directly and therefore when the army seized direct political power at intervals of several or more years; it also had less of an opportunity to develop ideological republicanism. This was accompanied also by the moribund ideology of the Republican political parties prepared to support the army's point of view. Therefore, when the army took power in a military coup it did so accompanied by the ideological dead hand of its military bureaucratic instincts and its ruling by military decree. Therefore, on the one hand, "Kemalism" has remained as a patriotic sentiment of republicanism to which all patriotic Turks can commit themselves with national pride. On the other hand, however, the army and its militaristic principles, has been left exposed as an uninspiring tyrannical institution. In other words, arguably, what might be called Kemalist and Islamic democratic republicanism have much in common whereas the army's tyrannical republicanism tends to alienate it from society.

In what follows, the theory of republicanism and tyranny is more fully elaborated. This is

---

8 The ordinary definitions of "conservatism" are said to also to date from the Enlightenment in what is conventionally termed the "counter-Enlightenment" and in the respect for tradition. For an accessible presentation of this approach to conservatism by a leading conservative American scholar, see, Robert Nisbet, *Conservatism* (Minneapolis,
MI: University of Minneapolis Press, 1986). The definition utilized here is adapted from the conservative scholar,
Georg Wilhelm Friedrich Hegel the Philosophy of History. Translator. S. Sibree (New York: Dover, 1956) and his
philosophical method of dialectical analysis, pp. 8 ff.

followed by an analysis of the republicanism of the Kemalism of Kemal Atatürk and by what is argued to be the republicanism of Islam in general and to the teachings of the two great Turkish Islamic intellectuals, Said Nursi and Fethullah Gülen . This paper presents this as a dialectical process in which the republicanism of Islam and of Fethullah Gülen interact with that of Kemalism to achieve succeeding stages of synthesis. In the process, both varieties of republicanism can be observed as drawing closer to one another. One can therefore draw a speculative conclusion that developmentally, Turkish republicanism in general may be proceeding in a politically and socially mutually reinforcing manner.

In light of the foregoing, while the chief political problem of the Middle East is widely said to be the absence of democracy i.e. the so-called "democratic deficit ", is this the question, is it really the priority problem , or is the most important problem that of the tyranny of repression, torture, imprisonment and death elsewhere in the Middle East and political repression in Turkey? When the legions of policy makers and scholars spot- light the alleged priority problem of democracy, it never occurs to them, that their version of what they term a universal theory of democracy is that it is in fact an Euro-centric liberal democracy. The latter is a theory of democracy whose preconditions are individualism, equality , secularism and pluralism. These preconditions are the ethnocentric ones of the European Enlightenment and those areas of the world intensely exposed to these values; North America, Western Europe, India, Australia etc. Once said, the obvious difficulties of these preconditions are instantly apparent. In addition, it is paradoxically notable that when critics speak of the "democratic deficit" , they pass over, often without comment, the exceptional cases by their criteria, of the label of democracy in Turkey, Lebanon, Israel , Palestine and Iran. This absence of systematic comment is perhaps also further evidence of the inadequacy of their liberal democratic label. Is it possible that these efforts at indigenous democracy are further illustrations of possible republican and not liberal democracy?

There is however an additional less apparent factor that is more directly relevant to the problem of tyranny and that is the underlying theory of change of liberalism. Liberalism's theory of change is one of incremental pluralism and gradualism, commonly expressed as reformism. Whether expressed academically as in the so-called theory of "transition to democracy" or in policy by the members of the so-called "community of democracy promotion" by the U.S. Government , liberal theory is silent on the subject of revolution and internal coups as means to end tyranny. Even the present activism of the Bush administration in advocating violence to end tyranny has its own limitations. How many countries will the United States invade in order to democratize them? Can "coercive democracy" work?

If liberal democracy has these shortcomings and limitations, what might be an alternative ? Isaiah Berlin has pithily and influentially summarized the alternatives. He defines liberalism as a doctrine of being left alone , as non-interference. As an alternative to what he terms this type of negative of liberalism, he suggests there is a philosophy of freedom which stands for something i.e. positive liberty. He , and other scholars in interpreting his ideas, suggests that positive freedom contains within it what he terms the "harmonization" of ideas. By this he means that all human thought that was part of the European Enlightenment possesses a residual commitment to an intellectual monism and not the pluralism that is customarily assumed to be attached to the Enlightenment. This challenging proposition is made even more challenging by a further consideration. He has hinted in his writings and other scholars have gone further in their commentary on his ideas that this monism is in fact a "harmony" of agreement on the pre-Enlightenment importance of religion. As a result, Enlightenment influenced thinkers therefore assume that all are involved in a dispute that can be expected to respond to reason and end in a compromise of differences, even in the matter of religion and secularism. Berlin, and other scholars have speculated that Western thinkers can begin a political encounter that can be pursued because of the fact that because they all share Enlightenment values, a comfortable compromise can be arrived at. This is the basis of the claim that democracies do not make war on one another. What is overlooked however, is that when the adversary is a non-Enlightenment state , the West will fight to the last man e.g. as presently in Iraq. [9]Berlin also speculated , however, that in addition, his principle of latent monism might also be applied to the very question of religion that provoked the long wars of religion prior to the Enlightenment. He, and others, have also noted that while the Enlightenment has held firmly to religious secularism, it was also the case that many Enlightenment thinkers who were overtly secularist, also reserved their judgment to the effect that the existence of God in fact was attested to by the scientific principles of positivism. In other words, in nature, God is everywhere. A further observation is that Kemal Atatürk held to the tenets of scientific positivism , but it also has been said that that he also identified with the scientific proof of the existence of God in what is known as Deism.[10] It is important to also note that Gülen has referred to nature as a scientific "book" which can be "read" to validate the comprehensiveness of the authority of God. This suggests a possible further way in which two of Turkey's greatest figures have something possibly in agreement with one another.

In the case of the Middle East and much of the Asian world, popular political culture is communal and not individualistic. This emphasis upon community also exists in Western political theory from at least the Roman republic forward. There is, of course, also the persistency of republicanism as in the Italian city state system of the Renaissance. Even the Holy Roman Empire as the earthly rule of the Papacy kept important ancient Roman values and institutions intact until its dissolution in 1804. This is a philosophy that is intent to control the state on the one hand and to use it for the social good on the other. This quality is by and large consistent with Middle Eastern political culture. And, as argued in this article , it is also consistent with the values of Islam.

Republican democracy begins with the fact, as is the case of the tradition of the Ottoman state in Turkey, that it is the state that controls society and not the other way around. It is the case, however, that the state that controls society is created in the first instance by the voluntary surrender of the individual to the state. The control of the state by republicans can originate in revolution as in the cases of the regicide of King Charles I in England in 1649, in America in 1776 or those of Turkey (1923), and Iran (1970), or by coup d'etat in other Middle Eastern states or as the outcome of civil war as in the case of Lebanon. The point is that struggle, violence and warfare as suggested by Dankwart Rustow is even the customary mid-wife of democratic rule.[11] These demonstrated historical examples are what politically dominant Western liberal democracy chooses to forget about from within its own political traditions. It is not only "revolution that comes out of the barrel of a gun" but so can politically meaningful democracy. The current political impasse in Iraq illustrates this as well.

---

9 Berlin first laid these ideas out in a famous lecture series at Cambridge University, Isaiah Berlin, Two Concepts of Liberty (Oxford, UK: Oxford University Press, 1958). They were subsequently and critically elaborated upon in John Gray, "The Case for Decency", The New York Review of Books, July 13, 2006, LIII, No. 12, 20-22. For further analysis, see Mark Lilla, Ed.The Legacy of Isaiah Berlin (New York City: New York Review, 2001).

10 It has been said that the prominent American revolutionary founders, Thomas Jefferson, Thomas Paine, and Alexander Hamilton and others were Deists. For a comprehensive collection of authoritative writings on Deism, see Peter Gay, Ed. Deism: An Anthology (New York. NYC: Van Nostrand, 1968).

11 Dankwart Rustow, "Transitions to Democracy: Towards a Dynamic Model" Comparative Politics, 2(3), April 1970, 337-363.

Even the republicanism of the French Revolution remains present in the establishment of a law on the model of the law of the Roman republic that now has nearly universally adopted (called the Code Napoleon or Code Civil) world wide. This includes the Swiss Civil Code adopted by Kemal Atatürk as the present Turkish law. The counterpart of this near ubiquitous law elsewhere in the world is that of Islamic law (shari'a). What is striking about republicanism in Turkey is the apparent consensus about the fact that where one might anticipate that the shari'a or Islamic law might be insisted upon as a prerequisite for adopting republicanism, in fact this is not only not the case, but one can also speak of a plurality of such laws.[12] It is the defence of this law that marks the republican and intensifies his commitment both to the restraint and the safe guarding of the state. It is said that in a republic, the citizen looks the ruler straight in the eye.

The present framework begins by noting that in order to correct the problem of the absence of a typological framework for a viable political science, at this, the beginning of the 21st Century, it is necessary to return to the 19th Century and earlier. When this is done, one can return to more politically relevant historical political philosophical foundations.

The necessity for this, as already noted, is what is sought is a typology that possesses the universality absent in those of the parochial 20th Century such as authoritarianism and totalitarianism. Such more genuine universal political typologies begin with the fact of the existence of universal and teleological goals (illustrating this are Aristotle's typologies in his Politics). The quality of universality in political typologies is found in their political philosophical foundations. Therefore the first distinction to be made is between liberal and republican democratic regimes i.e. between individualism, equality, secularism, pluralism on the one hand and a free state, a socially responsible ruler and elite, and the rule of law on the other hand. In the case of the Middle East and the present study of Turkey, the typology to be employed is that of republicanism of either a democratic or tyrannical variety. This suggests the combination of some degree of political accountability in the former on the one hand and the common phenomenon of abusive political rule on the other. This permits one to consider the possibilities in the case of Turkey of a democratic republicanism to apply to the Gülen movement and by extension to the Turkish state. This could apply also to what appear to be the increasingly democratic Kemalist political parties as well versus the tyrannical republican army on the other hand.

He who subscribes to republicanism also subscribes to democratic elitism. This is clearly stated in terms of the criterion of the need for socially responsible elite. This also dovetails with de Tocqueville's suggestion that all political systems can be said to be "dual societies". [13] The dualism consists of an internal division consisting of a political state and a social state. The political state is where the ruling elite is located. It contains the important national political institutions and it is where wealth is concentrated. The dual state begins with the assumption that in many if not most states, power and authority is concentrated in the top of the political system and authority is directed downward. The political state in Turkey has meant that this is the location where the intra-elite competition between the beneficiaries of Kemalist republicanism has met the newly mobilized Anatolian Islamic republicanism. The consequence is that in viewing present day Turkish politics, it is the Kemalists who have had

---

12   See Ihsan Yilmaz, "*Ijtihad* and *Tajdid* by Conduct" in Yavuz and Esposito, pp. 208-237.
13   This distinction arose in Alexis de Tocqueville's *Democracy in America*, 2 Vols. Translated by Harvey C. Mansfield and Delba Winthrop. (Chicago, IL. University of Chicago Press, 2000) as he grappled with the challenge of generalizing about American politics. He began with Chapter Three as the "Social State of the Anglo-Americans"pp.45 ff. See also Louis J. Cantori, "The Dual Arab State and Islamic Radicalism", August 29, 2002.

to vigorously work to gain the electoral support of the social state. This suggests that the social state and its masses is now increasingly integrated into the political process. There is in effect a varying distance between the political and the social state. The more democratic the state, the closer the proximity of the two segments. One assumes that a democratic state is more closely knit, whereas in the conservative republican state the political distance can be great. The dual state is also, however, an organic society. This suggests that such a state is a clientelistic or corporatistic state which is functionally organized according to the division of economic labour in the society.[14] Thus the concept of the dual state is increasingly important in permitting an estimation of the democratization of Turkish politics.

Republican democracy had its origins in the opposition that developed in the Roman Empire against arbitrary rule. As Shakespeare's Julius Caesar tells us in dramatic form, the idealists of the virtu of Roman rule, struggled valiantly against the oppression of imperial rule in this case, the person of Caesar. They were struggling to uphold the virtue of the Roman citizen as expressed in Roman law. The persons engaged in the struggle were, moreover, patrician members of the Roman elite struggling for justice on behalf of Roman plebeians. In other words, not only does republicanism stand for the justice of the state, but it is also the responsibility of the few to do this on behalf of the many. In the case of Julius Caesar, this meant that under Roman law, the republican elite had the obligation to resort to tyranicide in order to relieve the Roman citizens of the burden of Caesar's tyranny. Therefore the features of republicanism so far elaborated upon suggests the centrality and not the marginality of the state, the need for both the constraint and the support of the state , the compelling of the state to abide by the law and the fact that the democracy implied in this is top down with the expectation of an elite prepared to provide democratic responsibility and leadership.

These were the features of republicanism that were to echo down through the centuries until Machiavelli adopted them in his political philosophy of the Italian city states of the sixteenth century. It was to be the French philosopher Montesquieu who was to take them up again in the seventeenth century and influence the thinking of the regicides of 1649 and the Glorious Revolution of 1688 in England . Equally important, he was to influence the Founding Fathers of the United States , especially Alexander Hamilton and James Madison in their Federalist Papers as well as George Washington. It was in these events, however, that republicanism in America began to mix with and was eventually eclipsed by liberalism. It is the experience of Turkey and the resiliency of these ideas ,however, and their potential resonance in Middle Eastern political culture and especially possibly in Islam, that is central to the present article. It also is the case that the political cultural underpinnings of Turkey and the Middle East are such that republicanism will remain the appropriate concept to be used in the analysis of the region's politics.

Republicanism and Kemalism

The Pragmatic Beginning of Turkish Republicanism

The origins of republicanism as an expression of the reforms of Kemal Atatürk lies more in the venue of revolutionary praxis than in ideology. The reason for this rests with the nature of the practical challenges that Atatürk faced in the two phases of his determination to first set his country free from foreign military occupation and then second , to modernize it in

---

14 This subject remains unaddressed in the present paper due to space limitations, but reference here is to the attraction of Durkheim's functionalism and corporatism to Kemalism. This leads analytically to the internally organic nature of the republican state.

order to achieve the national military strength necessary to protect the success of his military achievement. It is the combination of inspiring leadership and political pragmatism that is the hallmark of his success. It has been pointed out that it has been tyranny rather than democracy which has been the priority challenge to the other states of the Middle East . For these states, tyranny was never identified as a first objective and instead the distracting issue of liberal democracy was permitted to confuse the priorities of the indigenous political leadership. Tyranny as the challenge for the Turks, on the other hand, was very clear and consisted of a widespread European invasion that presented itself as a clear cut nationalist issue within a limited time framework due to the effectiveness of Atatürk's military and political leadership. After securing the military success of his two phased military objectives(to defeat the European invaders and then to compel these defeated nations to agree to the 1923 Treaty of Lausanne that assured Turkish sovereignty over the regained territories), he turned to a program of the modernization of the country. Just as his military successes showed his ability to work pragmatically towards his goals, so too was the case with his modernization program.

His program consisted of what he termed the "Six Arrows" , the first of which in presumed priority order was in fact " republicanism". The reason for presuming this is that there is other evidence indicating this priority . In addition, however, it is noteworthy that not only did he wish political power to be concentrated in the centre in the "top down" republican model, but he also had "nationalism" and étatism" as two additional political "arrows" suggesting that he understood that his modernization program was predicated upon political authority being concentrated in the political centre. The question was, of course, towards what specific objective was this concentration of political power to be directed ? Essentially what occurred is that Atatürk was able to capitalize upon the institutions and cultural achievements that the Ottoman Empire had created in its own drive towards a significantly successful defensive modernization program in the preceding century. This had unfurled in three phases. In the first phase, there was the success of the creation of the institution of an authoritative autonomous Ottoman state. This was a state that was not dependent upon single ruling family nor was it dependent upon a socially cohesive ruling class. In fact, it has been pointed out that the nature of the Turkish state was such that it was the state that validated and constructed the Turkish nation. This is the opposite of what is said to occur in the case of other instances of nation building. This had the effect of continuing a state institution to which Turks were able to direct their loyalty, free from parochial ethnic and local loyalties. It is precisely this objective that significantly motivates Gülen to make the Ottoman state and its accompanying culture as the cornerstone of the new Turkey. Instead, the state possessed an administrative structure staffed by modern educated bureaucrats. In fact, it was to be the establishment of modern professional schools that were to not only serve the empire well but also were to provide the education of the members of the Modern Turk Movement /Committee of Union and Progress that was to initiate a modernization program of its own prior to WW I and to provide the modern military education of the Turkish army that Atatürk was to so brilliantly lead in the war itself. The result was that at the war's end, Atatürk was able to smoothly adopt the state as an institution around which the nation could be rallied . There was an additional attribute of the state that was advantageous as well. The Islam of the Ottoman Empire was the Islam of what has been termed "frontier" Islam. This was itself also a pragmatic attribute that began with the establishment of the Ottoman Empire in 1299. The formation of the empire was predicated upon its cosmopolitan ability to negotiate the incorporation within it a diversity of ethnic and religious groups as it expanded its political boundaries. Therefore, when the secularist Atatürk faced the successive challenges to gather to himself Muslim Turks , he was able tactically to do so on the basis of nationalist secular loyalty to the state. In doing so, he was already recruiting the Turkish people to rally to the nationalist cause that was in fact his primary objective. Likewise, when after 1923 he now wanted to appeal to Turkish patriotism, he was able to do this as well. From this beginning, there was to develop the ideological basis for him to rally the Turkish people to him in the name of Turkish patriotism. This latter appeal was to be synonymous with a far more comprehensive modernization appeal that was to preoccupy him and his immediate successors in the period 1923-1950.

Kemalist Republicanism

Atatürk's "republicanism" does not appear to have had any kind of indigenous ideological depth to it, or, alternatively, the adoption of a particularly well worked out set of borrowed ideas.[15] What is known about it is that the concept appeared coincidently with the passage from the scene of particularly monarchical systems of government in the politically tumultuous post -World War I period, including the Ottoman Empire itself. . Thus, for example, the first nation in at least the 20th Century to appear with the name "republic" was the Republic of Azerbaijan in 1918, also a Muslim state. . This was a period of political instability and even radicalism, for example in the case of the Russian revolution and of the failure of the Republic of Hungary revolution in 1920 . The characteristics of republicanism can be summarized as consisting of four elements. The first is the existence of a strong state as an institution. This is of course very much the case of the pre-existence of the Ottoman Empire. The state should be a "free state" taking precedence over the so-called "free man" of liberalism. This signalled that in exchange for the surrender of the individual to the state, the state would set the individual free , very much as Fethullah Gülen has also described the relation of the state to the Turkish people. In addition, there was also the desirability for a mixed constitution and political checks and balances. The second is that there should be a system of law embedded in history and tradition so that its principles are instinctive to its citizens. The code of law of the new Turkey was the adopted one of the Swiss Civil Code. This law was an especially clear instance of the Code Civil as a direct descendant of the legal system of the Roman Republic. This legal code is one which places the welfare of the republican state above that of the individual. It was widely adopted in Europe in the aftermath of the Enlightenment. It has already been noted , that the path away from the potential controversy of an insistence upon implementing religious/shariah law was already avoided.[16] The third is that there should be a political culture of civic virtue(virtu/maslaha) . The fourth is that there should be a ruling elite whose privileges are justified by its attention to the welfare of the people. This is the importance of the Islam in Turkey which of course was opposed to by Atatürk's secularism while at the same time, however, he also called for civic self-sacrifice . As will be noted, while initially Atatürk stood firmly in support of secularization during the turbulence of the period of the imparting of republicanism, by the1940's, Kemalism began to relent on this principle. The effort to introduce republicanism in Turkey met some violent resistance such as for example in revolts that occurred in 1925 and 1930. By the late 1930's there began a policy of relenting some of the cascade of requirements that had been levied on Turkey. This relenting was preceded however, by a strenuous attack upon traditional Islamic institutions and figures at the local level . This was accompanied by the eventually unsuccessful effort to create substitute state sponsored organizations at the local level e.g. the failed effort of secular "Peoples Houses" to substitute for dissolved local religious bodies. What was in fact occurring at the local level in this first period of republicanisation,

---

15 For a succinct account of Kemalism as a program of political and social reform, see, Yavuz, pp. 46-58.
16 Yilmaz in Yavuz and Esposito, pp. 208-237.

was that Kemalism was in effect repressing traditional Islam at the local level, and in the process inadvertently preparing the way for the creation of more spontaneous and vigorous opportunities for the emergence of modern Islamic organizations such as those of the neo -Nur movement .[17] This in effect was the opportunity for the establishment of intermediary religious discussion groups of Said Nursi and of the Naksibendi Sufi organizations. These groups plus the later ones of Fethullah Gülen 's movement became equivalent Islamic republican organizations.

What is clear is that Atatürk had pragmatically adopted the loose but effective framework of republicanism as a guide to focus and concentrate the political energy of the nationalism of the Turkish people in the pursuit of modernization.

Republicanism and Islam

Republicanism, Islam and Political Sovereignty

All political analysis begins with the question of political sovereignty i.e. where does political power and legitimacy lie ? In liberalism, for example, it is said to reside in the individual in what is termed popular sovereignty. In both republicanism and in Islam it also lies in the individual but only in combination with a communal solidarity that is expressed ultimately in the state or the ummah. In republicanism this is the result of the philosophical conviction that it is the citizen that is its repository with it being locked, in effect, within the republican state. The citizen brings this sovereignty to the political table and by surrendering to the state, he/ she is then able to share in the guarantee of the liberty of that state. Islam reinforces this process in the fact that sovereignty is theologically mandated. This results from the fact that God deputizes the individual to be His vicegerent (khilafa) and to express the will of God in all that he does. When the individual engages the state, the state then becomes legitimate and gains its power from the citizenry. The state therefore undertakes activities to serve the needs of the citizen and at the same time, the state serves God. It is also the case both in republicanism and in Islam that while the individual citizen possesses sovereignty , there are those who gain greater moral merit as members of the elite who have a particular responsibility as the social few to act on behalf of the many.

There are a number of key concepts of striking similarity in republicanism and Islam. Perhaps the most fundamental of these is that of conservatism. It is this conservatism that further distinguishes republicanism from liberalism. While republicanism may differ from liberalism in this respect, its resemblance to Islam is striking. This can be seen in a review of the three principles of conservatism:

Tradition in republicanism represents the past where its guiding values are located in history and myth. Its path inspires its future. The tradition of Islam can be said to begin with the concept of asala , meaning the roots of religious and social identity . In Islam this begins with the revelation of God's word in the Quran and the sunnah of the sayings and practices of the Prophet Muhammad. This tradition is also divine so that what occurred historically in the past continues to the present and transcends into the future. Its resemblance to republicanism lies in the role of history and myth in setting the goals of the republic.

i.   In republicanism, the individual is in a subordinate relationship to family and com-
      munity. In modern day Europe this relationship is preserved in the system of law
      derived directly from the Roman Republic called variously, Code Civil or Code

---

17 Yavuz, p. 54.

Napoleon whose principles put the needs of the community before those of the individual. In Islam, the individual is defined in terms of his obligations to family and to the community of believers (ummah). In behavioural terms, this is expressed as patrimonialism in an organic society. It is the family and the community of believers that defines the individual , not the other way around . There is a further expectation related to the preceding one and that is maslaha or the duty of promoting the welfare of the community by the elite(virtu is the Latin equivalent in Roman republicanism). The symbolic expression of this is the orderliness of prayer (salah) in which the individual is submerged in the prostrations of the community of believers.

ii. As already noted, the ethical and moral principles of virtue or social responsibility in republicanism represent its moral compass. The moral purpose of Islam is evident everywhere in the Quran . This is summarized in the concept of khilafa or the "vicegerency" of God. This means that every Muslim understands that he has a personal responsibility to carry out the teachings of God in his daily life just as this is also the guiding moral principle for the state, hence the advisory role of the clergy discussed above. In the case of the state, it is written that it is expected "To enjoin that which is evil and promote that which is good."

There are additional shared features of republicanism and Islam . Even the word republic (res publica) has a close Arabic and Islamic equivalent, jumhur (republic). Res publica or public things has virtually the same meaning as jumhur , also public things. But the deeper meaning is also nearly the same, in both cases, the management of public things by the privileged on behalf of the many. Jumhur is not only a prominent technical term, but it is also an active and contemporary political one as well. In the analysis of representative contemporary Islamic writings below, it will be noted that the term appears frequently sometimes as a contested term. Increasingly, it appears in the formal names of states along with the name Islamic e.g. The Islamic Republic of Iran. The name of the latter country was adopted after a popular referendum. Even more telling, is the case that in the latter country, there was also a popular slogan, Nah Gharbinah Nah Sharqi, Jumhuriy-ti Islam ("Neither Eastern nor Western, But An Islamic Republic") that was adopted by referendum of the Iranian people. .

Whenever democracy is broached as a subject in contemporary Islamic discourse, there are two fundamental concepts that are invariably addressed, sometimes in a somewhat misleading way. These are shura and bay'a. Shura has the meaning of consultation. The Quran in fact has a surah or chapter bearing this name. As a consequence it is widely held in the Muslim world that all political authority should be exercised on the basis of the receiving of advice from what is now increasingly common in the Islamic world, a consultative council (majlis al-shura) . Such councils are elected or appointed and consist of persons of some particular functional expertise e.g. law, medicine, engineering etc and persons of political importance. The representatives on these councils are from the social elite(tribal leaders, family leaders etc or members of the educated elite or ayyan) and they arrive at decisions according to the principle of consensus or ijma'a . These representatives engage in an oath of allegiance to the ruler called a baya'a . This allegiance extends ridwan or "felicity" to the ruler, contingent , however, on the ruler exercising authority in an expected manner. Otherwise, the baya'a can be withdrawn. This tradition dating from the time of the Prophet himself is a powerful one, and all proposals for democracy in the Middle East begin with these specifics or the principles upon which they are based. What is often misleading about this linkage to democracy, however, is that these concepts are frequently interpreted as the shura meaning a representative body of individuals and the bay'a is interpreted as an expression of individual want or desire. The more accurate interpretation is that these two concepts resemble more the practice of communal republicanism rather than individualistic liberalism. What is important here is that either shura or republican representation is not the representation of liberalism. Liberal representation sets as an ideal the priority of individual wishes over those of the community. Shura and republicanism on the other hand is predicated on the role of an elite on behalf of the masses. As a consequence this theory of representation is more directly collectively political than individually representational. The elite in Islam and especially in republicanism expect to share in ruling. It is this political avidness of the few that contributes to the executive authority of the state and the containment of the power of the state. This is a theory of democracy and politics from the top down . It is one in which the citizen insists on having an important voice in order to direct the state in a proper moral direction. . It is this insistence that results in the containment of the state.

Islam like republicanism and unlike liberalism views the state positively. For Islam, the state supports the social structure and organizations vital to Islam. It also provides the administrative structure for the Islamic law whose celebration represents freedom in republican democracy. This does not mean, however, that the Islamic state is monolithic and fails to make a distinction between religion (din) and the state (dawla). This is the Western stereotype and not the reality. According to this stereotype , the Islamic state is said to be intrinsically non-democratic. Scholarly research is increasingly proving this to be incorrect. From the time of the Prophet Muhammad in his constitution of the city of Medina (622-634AD) until the present, what is remarkable is that the state under Islam has not had a structure that gave religion a predominant role. Instead, Islamic political theory, underdeveloped as it is, has stated that the state exists to collect taxes to assure the stability and maintenance of order under which worship can occur. In other words, political order and stability in Islam goes beyond a universal human desire for these conditions, to the desire for them as a precondition for worship. This illustrates the collective importance of the republican principle of non-domination to Muslims. This concept of disorder (fitna) which is considered so objectionable in Islamic society is a reinforcing factor in the strength of the unacceptability of disorder in present day Turkey in the words of Gülen and presently also in Iraq. Order is religiously mandated. What is important to understand, however, is that as far as the formal role of religious clerics are concerned, these are to remain indirect in the exercise of power . Their expected political role is advisory. The Islamic state must be one in which Islamic law and practices must be upheld. In order to achieve this, the ulama or clerics are expected to form an advisory council to the ruler. The struggle for democracy in the modern period often centres on the rules governing the role of this council. Thus, for example, in the informal discussions that have occurred already in the new Iraq, this council is expected to be formed but its role is also expected to be circumscribed. This issue is most dramatically at work in present day Iran. From the time of the Iranian revolution in 1979, the Ayatollah Khomeini promoted the doctrine of velayet-e faqih or "The Counsel of the Jurisprudents". This idea drawn from Shiite Islam provided for near total authority of the clergy. A substantial political struggle has been waged since 1979 between those who support this vision and those who in large numbers opposed it at one time under the leadership of democratically elected President Khatemi. This issue is intensified because of the particular principles of Shiism, but the point is that this is also an unresolved issue within Islam more generally. This contest regarding the proper political role of the clergy in Islam, while far less important in Sunni Islam can also be viewed as an expression of the constraining role of republicanism.

Turkish Republican Islam

Foundations of Contemporary Turkish Islam

There are a number of special characteristics of Turkish Islam that are important to understand in terms of the strength of its appeal and its ability to endure the tyrannical repression of a heavy ideological secular military regime. One point is the fact that from the year 1229 AD and the founding of the Ottoman Turkish Empire, what has become modern Turkey developed what is termed "frontier" Islam. The meaning of this results from the fact that the empire was to expand outwards from what was initially a smaller geographical bounded area. This meant that as it expanded to all four compass points to what was to become a gigantic regional empire, it had to in effect negotiate this expansion with the diverse practices of Islam that it encountered. Therefore Turkish Islam tended to be a pragmatic, cosmopolitan and perhaps a bit of a "political" faith. Turkish Islam has carried this cultural imprint down to the present age. It is also the case that Turkish Islam is also a pious and religiously resilient faith. The explanation for this is due to two of its defining characteristics. The first is a more or less conventionally organized Islam at the local level consisting of religious schools and the religious authority of its ulama. What reinforced this localism , however, has been the density and vibrant nature of Sufism in the form of the Naksibendi Sufi order. Sufism gave Turkish Islam a liveliness and durability that served it well during practically the entire life of the Ottoman Empire.

Turkish Islam also benefited from the fact that while Kemal Atatürk shared the secularism of one segment of the Young Turk's Movement, it was he who also rallied the Turkish people to rise up against the invasion of Turkey by the British, the French and several other foreign armies in the aftermath of World War I and he did this successfully due in no small measure to his appeals to an Islamic inspired Turkish patriotism. The Treaty of Lausanne in 1923 brought this fighting to a successful conclusion which then permitted Atatürk to direct his full attention to what was to become an aggressive policy of secularism. His objective was to rigorously strip religion entirely from representation in the new Republic of Turkey . In fact, the name "Republic" was chosen in order to signal that secularism in Turkey was to be the draconian one of the French revolution and would not be the negotiated Anglo-Saxon one of Britain and America.

The policy of secularism also, however, unintentionally benefited the resistance to secularism as well. This was due to the fact that Atatürk's policy was so aggressive that he tore up the organizational roots of Islam at the village level to such a degree so as to make the work easier for their being supplanted by what was to become the educated leaders of the Islamic resistance. These leaders were in effect to come from the Sufi orders who could far more easily than what might have been otherwise the case to introduce modern, deshanes, readings of Islam which were to become the basis for resistance to Kemalism. Unlike the modernization of Islam in other Muslim countries , the educated elite was to possess a high degree of agreement with one another while at the time they were able to communicate their ideas for reform to an emerging, increasingly better educated middle class. In effect, the modernization of Islam was able to skip an entire generation in the drive for an Islamic modernity. In addition, while Atatürk was in effect creating his own opportunities for his Western formula of modernization, in fact Islam was in effect "neck and neck" in the race for its version of modernity. It is perhaps nearly unique in the case of Middle East that in Turkey there was this near equality of historical opportunity for intellectual secularism and religious modernization . In other words, consistent with the theme of this paper, while Kemalist republicanism supported secularism and Islamic republicanism did not, the latter , however, was intent on the pursuit on the modernization of Islam. In other words, both republicanisms were intent on the pursuit of what was significantly a similar agenda of national modernization.

As already noted, organized Islam and especially the Naksibendi Sufi orders in Turkey historically has shown evidence of its steadfastness to the defense of Turkey whether it was in the war against Russia in 1878 or the "War of Independence" led by Kemal Atatürk from 1918-1923 . Therefore, Turkish Islam has never had to stand nationalistically apologetic on the sidelines while it pursued a political agenda possibly different from that of Turkey's ruler, Kemal Atatürk. Instead, Turkish Islam, unlike Arab Islam, has also been in the forefront of defining that which is modern for Turkish Muslims. As a result, Turkish Islam has faced the challenge of countering the more limited, single issue Kemalist program of secularism rather than the totality of what have been a far more complex and larger modernization agenda. In other words, Turkish Muslims have had the intellectual self-confidence to sit at the same table as secular intellectuals and debate the content of the meaning of modernism for Turkish society.

The Islamic response to modernization has had two important intertwined dimensions. The first was the fact that the efforts of Atatürk to modernize the society had the effect of causing rural to urban population movements that became the beginning of the creation of a modern educated urban bourgeois class. This class, moreover, tended to re-establish their rural bonds in the city and thus as intact local/mahalle and extended family units sought to continue their religious commitments. In short, the rural to urban population movement preserved the solidarity of the bonds of rural society. The retention of this degree of sociological solidarity appears to have assisted in the modernization transition from the oral celebration of Islam to a written one. The written one was able to smoothly establish itself in the new urban environment. At the same time, this historical deshanes tradition also became the vehicle within which the teachings of a remarkable theologian and intellect, Said Nursi (1876-1960), came to be read. The combination of this deshanes tradition and the appearance of Nursi and other thinkers like him also benefited from a further cultural persistency and that is the "interior" or highly personalized nature of the Sufi spiritual experience. In addition, whereas the village practice of deshanes took place in a tekke or special meeting place, now this was being done socially in private homes. Thus, just as Kemalism was aggressively Westernizing the country, a counter religious message of cultural modernization was also being pursued.

The Advent of Party Politics

With the death of Atatürk, "Kemalism" lost its charismatic leader and the person who also possibly had the intellectual capacity to change and adapt to new political challenges. Perhaps due to this or more simply due to a generational ideological change in the search for a more intellectually coherent statement of Kemalism, there next occurred an experiment with the creation of a multiparty system . This served as an opportunity for the Islamic opposition to attempt to pursue its own political objectives. Meanwhile, what came to be called the Nursi movement after Said Nursi in turn spawned a new generation of similarly inspiring religious leaders, among whom was Fethullah Gülen (1941-). This in turn came to be called the neo-Nur movement. What became apparent from the 1960's onwards were the ideological weaknesses of Kemalism. Kemalism always has had the army to rely upon politically in extreme circumstances, but as a movement its ideological appeal was largely restricted to its Turkish patriotism. As a movement, it consisted at first of a single official party which then underwent organizational and ideological change with decreasing electoral appeal., backed always, however, by the army. Its ideological appeal continues to be the nostalgic one of the veneration of Kemal Atatürk. Beyond that, however, is little in the way of the appeal of sophisticated ideas. When the army has imposed its authority, it has done so by edict and force and not by persuasion.

With the military always lurking in the background and nearly always prepared to exert influence or to physically intervene, Islam has had to search for spaces and opportunities in order to gain political representation. One can see camera instances of this in each of the military inventions that occurred in 1960 and 1980. In 1960 the military felt that the Democratic Party (DP) was making too much of an opening to Islam, so it intervened and cashiered 2000 officers and finally introduced the revised constitution of 1961 which gave the bureaucracy authority for policy decisions and also favoured interest groups rather than political parties. In the 1980 coup it sought to control religion not by repressing it but by co-opting it in schools it controlled etc. Its fears, however, were more from the political left, so the army actually created opportunities for religion to be used against what it considered the Marxist left. It sought therefore to co-opt and manipulate religion.

The preceding suggests that the republicanism of Kemalism is defective. To begin with, the fact of the free license that army exercises in its interventions is sabotaging of the possibilities of political freedom. The situation is made worse by the regularity with which the army not only does this, but does so also with a similar regularity of tearing up and rewriting constitutions. Under these conditions, there can be no possibility of the containment of political power developing from checks and balances. The army in effect has a veto power claim on this possibility. The Turkish system of law is that of the adopted one of the Swiss Code of Law . This "foreign" code of law has in fact had a perhaps surprising high degree of acceptance. The reason for this acceptance may be because it is itself indirectly adopted from the system of the law of the Roman Republic i.e. it originated as a republican system of law in which the state takes precedence over the individual. Finally, while a self-consciously Muslim society is governed by the social responsibility of maslaha , once again, the army's intervention tends to restrict this quality to itself. In short, Kemalism fails to achieve the liberating goals of republicanism. Instead, certainly, militarism, if not Kemalism, is an example of tyrannical republicanism. The pattern of the preceding is clear, politics in Turkey were becoming more complex and far more difficult for the military to control.

AKP, the February 1997 Coup and the Parliamentary Elections of July 2002

The Justice and Development Party (AKP)

The February 28, 1997 military coup was the fourth and most recent of the military corrective actions taken against the Turkish state as an expression of its version of republicanism. The reason given by the coup leaders was that the Kemalist principle of secularism was being violated and the case that the military put forward to support its claims was clear and to the point. The Welfare Party (RP) and its leader Erbakan as prime minister were accused of offending the Turkish "way of life" and jailed i.e. the military had the temerity to advocate a moral direction for the Muslim society. The specific consequence of this was to force a generational change in the leadership of the Islamic political opposition. Erbakan as the perennial leader of this opposition was now replaced by the younger Erdoğan who had established his reputation as the energetic mayor of Istanbul. Therefore , the coup was the opening offensive of a cultural war. The events leading up to the coup, however, were hardly spiritually edifying in their details. With Erdoğan and the revived RP on the political ascendancy, the military worked behind the scenes to encourage two secular political parties, The True Path Party (DYP) and The Motherland Party (ANAP) to enter into a political alliance in order to marginalize the RP. There were already, however, major accusations of corruption charges against the leader of the DYP but the military agreed to ignore these in their eagerness to achieve their tactical political objective. At first this appeared to succeed, but Erdoğan, saw a political opportunity in the situation and he entered into an alliance of his own with Tansu Çiller ,the head of the DYP, thus splitting the army's planned alliance. Erdoğan had pulled off a shrewd manoeuvre of his own, so that the military were now faced with the first avowed Muslim Prime Minister in Turkish history. This was an achievement much appreciated by the Muslim masses of the population, but it was an outcome that the military could not permit to stand. The consequence was the inauguration of a "Roll Back" campaign against Islam launched against not only the RP and Erdoğan, but also the closing of thousands of Muslim educational , business, banking institutions, cultural organizations etc. These decrees were promulgated in the "Eighteen Directives" dated the day of the coup, February 28, 1997. The latter "Directives" were further stark evidence of the arbitrariness of the army in unilaterally rewriting the law of the country at its own tactical convenience. This is a vivid transgression of the law so important to the operation of republicanism. The army went so far as to alter its strategic planning document so that some objectively serious security issues were given less priority and that "reactionary Islam" became the national target. The April 1999 elections were won by right wing parties in an electoral campaign conducted in a climate of national fear and hysteria. One of the unusual outcomes of this was that the Islamic groupings in the country turned wholeheartedly to advocating Turkish entry into the EU in order to possibly gain the protection of European Union civil rights protection. The military had gone so far in this campaign that by the parliamentary elections of 2002, the Islamic party of the AKP under the leadership of the outspoken Erdoğan won 363 seats out of 550.This movement towards the stabilization of republican politics in Turkey was reinforced in the July 2007 parliamentary elections where the Islamic republican AKP was able to increase the size of its popular vote to 47% and the Kemalist republican vote of the CHP and the MHP also increased its percentage slightly. [18] This election then set the stage for successive votes by the parliament which on August28, 2007 finally elected Foreign Minister Abdullah Gül to the politically powerful position of president. The fact that the army has accepted this constitutionally arrived at outcome and that President Gül has sworn to uphold the constitutional principle of secularism speaks soundly to the continued constitutional development of republican Turkey. The AKP had run the June 2007 parliamentary campaign ironically on the slogan, "The Good Life" with its undertones of religious morality and over tones of moral hypocrisy directed at the military! It is possible to say these parliamentary and presidential elections support the point made at the outset of this paper, namely that Turkey may be witnessing the evidence of an emerging distinction between the democratic republicanism of the Islamic and Kemalist political parties versus the tyranny of the republicanism of the army.[19]

---

18 For an analysis of the July 2007 elections, see Reuters (http.//www.reuters.com article/world news).
19 For a summary of these complex developments, see Yavuz, pp. 244-259. For an analysis of the presidential elections, see, Guardian Unlimited, August 29, 2007.

Fethullah Gülen and Islamic Republicanism

Fethullah Gülen and Islamic Republicanism

In the aftermath of the fourth and most recent intervention by the military in Turkish politics on February 28, 1997 in what was called somewhat misleadingly a "soft coup", it is remarkable that Fethullah Gülen has perhaps emerged as the single most important religious personality in contemporary Turkey. This is especially remarkable in light of his personal history of having been sentenced to prison and in fact going into political exile abroad. This "soft coup" after all was called a "roll back" of "totalitarian" Islam in which Islam had been elevated to the status of a strategic target by the army. The story of how a soft spoken Islamic scholar without any explicitly political organization to support him has in fact weathered this storm and rebounded to emerge politically strengthened is a story of how deeply he has affected Muslims in Turkey and perhaps how representative of religious sentiment he has become.[20]

Fethullah Gülen is a fitting conclusion to this comparative analysis of Kemalist and Islamic conceptions of republicanism in Turkey. The thesis has been that contrary to the claims of Kemalists and also those of most scholars , both groups are in significant agreement about the meaning and importance of republicanism. A careful application of the concept reveals that Kemalist and Islamist alike find general agreement upon its criteria . The only significant disagreement is Kemalism's claim to secularism. It is also possible, however, that even this convention of the Kemalist polemic may conceal the possibility of a similarity on this criterion as well. We will return to this admittedly controversial point by way of conclusion.

It is well to begin this discussion of the enormous importance of Gülen to Turkish Islam by noting that his education in Islam occurred in the Erzurum region of Turkey . There he was the beneficiary of the scholarship of Naksibendi Sufi Islam at a time when its already formidable tradition was itself undergoing change as the result of the challenge of Kemalist secularist and modernist policy. This change was initiated by the remarkable intellectual leadership of Said Nursi whose prescience was the quickness with which he supported the newly emerging nationalism of the Young Turk movement prior to World War One. At the same time, however, he began to have reservations about the religious direction of this reformation. Thus, when Kemal Atatürk began his patriotic attack upon the European occupation of Turkey, he was also prepared to support this, while also harbouring reservations about the spiritual direction that reform was moving in. Therefore, when Gülen began his studies in the 1950's, he like other young scholars, was able to benefit from thinking which possessed a remarkable understanding of the Enlightenment thinking that laid behind the European thinking that Atatürk and the Kemalists was so uncritically borrowing from. Gülen also benefited from the manner in which Nursi's shift to textual rather than oral discussion undermined the authority of the traditional ulama and placed it in the hands of this new class of Islamic intellectuals . Nursi's ideas, as a result of political repression, had however, remained "internal" in the tradition of Sufism. Due to the fact that Gülen was appearing later in the historical process, his extraordinarily influential ideas became more "external" and public with the consequence that he was able to target with some precision his audience of young journalists , engineers and members of other professions.

---

20 For a careful and balanced analysis of Gülen, see Yavuz, "The Gülen Movement: The Turkish Puritans" in Yavuz and Esposito, pp. 19-47. Yavuz's account is an especially nuanced one in which he notes, as has been argued in this paper, that in Yavuz's terms, Gülen is not a liberal and strongly implies that he is a conservative.

Consistent with the foregoing, Gülen 's ideas became increasingly practical and applied in nature. His thinking was that of praxis or, in his own terms, that of aksiyon (action). He is thus a bridging figure between being a dominant interpreter of Islam and being an animator of Islamic practice. He always had adhered to the foundational principles of orthodox Islamic theology . So much so, that his theological arguments proceed in the formal logic and building block strategy of classical kallam. What is astonishing about his ideas, however, is that while effectively convincing the reader in this fashion by traditional means, he is then able to turn adroitly to an emphasis upon a supplementary argument of reason and an insistence upon independent and critical thinking. A consequence of this intellectual style is that he has become an authoritative intermediary between the sunnah and the Quran on the one hand and modern Western thought on the other. This intermediary approach (wasta in Arabic) also applied to his practical recommendations as well. For example, rather then urge the building of mosques as a spiritual act he suggested instead, the construction of what has become some astonishing very large scale, internationally state of the art research hospitals or huge publishing and broadcasting enterprises.[21] A particularly striking further example of this, was his calling to people's attention what he referred to as "the humiliation of materialism" . This statement is an admonition that in the midst of the wealth now being earned by the new urban, modern educated professional middle class, which is his special audience, conspicuous consumption was said to be spiritually humiliating and not something to take pride in. In fact, this modesty of appearance and personal life style is characteristic of his supporters.

In turning now to the subject of "republicanism", it is well to recall what was said at the outset that reference here is to two varieties of republicanism. The first one is the self-descriptive one of Kemalism while the second is the implicit one developed from within the context of the Muslim political opposition. It is also well to recall what was said at the beginning of this paper about how one conceptualizes this concept. The distinction was made between the concreteness of the concept as self-description on the one hand and the implicit abstractness of the concept on the other . The concreteness of the concept is well illustrated in the case of the Kemalists . They begin by using it as a descriptive label. They tend to use it as means to characterize a political system that is non-monarchical and possesses the quality of being an especially modern political form in the era in which it was adopted, . This modernity further implied that it was populist in nature and perhaps even committed to democratic practices. In addition, it is clear that Atatürk intended that the new state would be "étatiste", that is, it would have a strong executive leadership and that it would not be liberally democratic.

The implicit concept of Islamic republicanism, on the other hand, is one that emerges gradually and pragmatically. What is required in this instance is that the definition of republicanism is constructed from the pragmatic approach to politics of the Islamists. It was the discrete and considered choices of Fethullah Gülen that has led to a de facto Islamic republicanism.

One can begin with evidence that Gülen very self consciously embraces republicanism by noting his pragmatic references to its four principles . To begin with, he very explicitly embraces republicanism. As one scholar has noted, Gülen and Mehmet Kirkinci (another

---

21 What is remarkable about this is that these enterprises appear to be accomplished on the basis of the auftrag-stactik or mission order tactics of the German army of World War I and the U.S. Marine Corps. This is devolution of authority in which the subordinate knows what is to be accomplished because he knows the mind of his superior. Therefore, in the Gülen movement, one can have the experience of a conversation with a wealthy business man who has donated possibly hundreds of thousands of dollars or possibly more for a school project, but who has never met Hojaefendi Fethullah Gülen personally. He also did not think that there was anything unusual about this.

neo- Nur scholar) represent a degree of accommodation that has been attained by neo-Nur leaders with republican principles of the state.[22] What follows from this commitment to republicanism is very strong additional evidence of support of the further criteria of republicanism. Gülen is quoted as saying that: " I am always on the side of the state and the military. Without the state, there is anarchy and chaos."[23] This conservative sentiment seems to apply to the contemporary political era, but it is also explicitly consonant with the theory of the historical Islamic state where Muslims are counselled against the advent of fitna and disorder.

Gülen also strongly upholds the principle of civic virtue as a second republican principle. For example, he makes frequent references to the requirements of hizmet or service; himmet or donations; and ihlas or the seeking the appreciation of God. The latter requirement is especially revealing of this because what is expected is that the individual must engage in spiritual self-scrutiny in order for him/her to be accountable to God. As for the republican principle of law as a third criteria , Gülen on the one hand upholds the principles of the shariah governing human behaviour, but he is also accepting of the Swiss Civil Code as having been accepted by the Turkish people . [24]

Finally, the fourth criteria of republicanism of the noblesse oblige of the ruling elite is roundly and repetitively upheld by Gülen. What is very clear is that the privileged few must justify their prominence by assuming responsibility for the welfare of society as a whole. In Islamic terms this is termed maslaha and the Quranic phrase supporting this role of the elite is, ahl al hal wa al'aqd ("Those who loosen and those who bind"). A particularly dramatic illustration of this expectation is what he refers to as the education of the "golden generation".(altin nesil).

Conclusion

Politically, it is the case that unlike other political leaders in Turkey, Gülen has not sought to construct an independent organization.. An interesting point related to the foregoing is the answer to the question of where might he be located in the Turkish political spectrum? There are to begin with his personal political assumptions. There is little doubt that for him, politics is a "top down" process with authority concentrated at the top. He is reconciled to democracy and secularism, but, however, without full democracy and full secularism.. For example, it has been said of him that he is not a liberal. He is intent on building the state, not civil society.[25]

What is important to understand is that while he does not possess a political organization, in fact years of religious instruction in his informal but authoritative role as Hocaefendi has, however, cast a vast network of hundreds of outstanding world class high schools in Turkey and abroad where his example and the standards of teachers modelled on him, are maintained; a very influential television network has been established and he has a whole series of high quality magazine and newspaper publications.

It is the case that Gülen and his movement have been interwoven with the Turkish political process. Thus in the mid-1980's Özal was able to use Gülen to strengthen his government

---

22 Rusen Sakir, "Devlet Babanin Nurcu Oglu: Kiirkinci Hoca, Artheber (Dec. 20.1997: 19 in Yavuz, p. 195, fn.45.

23 Interview with Gülen in Sabah, 27Jan. 1995 quoted in Yavuz, p. 27.

24 His commitment to law is cited at length in "Third Abant Platform Final Declaration, on "Islam and democracy", (July 2000) as an appendix in Yavuz and Esposito, pp.253-55.

25 Quoted in Zaman, June 21, 1993.

politically while at the same time, enhancing the reputation of Gülen himself. Looking ahead to the mid-1990's on the other hand, Gülen true to his instincts to support the state, stood with the military against Erbakan in the 1997 coup. Suddenly, however, the military in the coup of February 28, 1997 declared the Turkish enemy to be "reactionary Islam". Gülen came to be one of the enemy and he left Turkey to go into political exile. The situation had reached such an extreme, however, that Islamic groups rallied around Erdoğan, a very popular and successful mayor of Istanbul and a new victorious alliance that in 2002 and again in 2007 swept to victory. Gülen, on the other hand, seems to have emerged more prominent than previously, but now in a different role as the spokesman for contemporary reformist Turkish Islam.

It is notable that while other Muslim leaders are playing more overt political roles, he has become the bridge between the modernization of Islam and the robust market driven capitalism of contemporary Turkey. In addition, to anticipate the overall conclusion, this bridge has been constructed from his ability to draw Kemalist and Islamic republicanism ever so closer to one another. In other words, Gülen can be viewed as a unifier of Turkish society.

Conclusion

i.   Why is it that Turkey appears to be so exceptional in the study of Middle Eastern politics? The conceptual explanation is that the study of the Arab countries of the region is dominated conceptually by the ethnocentrism of liberal democracy and the failure to address the question of tyranny and the victimization of the peoples of the Middle East.

ii.   What is clear in the present paper is that "republicanism" better explains the politics of the Middle East because it better accounts for the favour with which the state is viewed.

iii.   In addition, republicanism has perhaps the greater promise of ending the domination of the tyrants in the Middle East. This is, after all, what has historically occurred in the tenacity with which the Turks retained their political independence and the Iranians gained theirs.[26] Likewise, the utilization of the concept of "tyranny" better describes the brutal repression and injustice of the region.

iv.   This paper also raises a deeper and more profound question regarding how one studies the politics of the Middle East. What is clear is that the academic political science employed in the study of the Middle East has become intellectually trapped into the liberal biases of individualism, equality, secularism etc from the Enlightenment onwards. In contrast, the sister social sciences of economics, sociology etc originating at the same time are far less susceptible to this. Therefore, this paper critically advances both the study of Turkish politics, Middle Eastern politics and politics in general.

v.   This paper also addresses what has become a perennial and possibly distracting question in the study of Turkish politics, and that is what appears to be a highly polarized conflict between the secularization of Kemalist republicanism on the one hand, and the Islamic piety of the republican masses of the population on the other hand. This paper suggests that this is perhaps not the most useful way of addressing the relationship of the masses of the population and the "Kemalists". This distinction is perhaps too provocative and too confrontational. The more

---

26 Similarly, Hamas has forced the Israeli settler evacuation of Gaza in 2005 and subsequently gained electoral success in some movement towards Palestinian independence. Louis J. Cantori, "Islamic Republicanism, Hamas and the Emergence of the Palestinian State", American Political Science Association, Chicago, August 29, 2007.

profound question is what amounts to the principle of legitimacy of "republicanism". Viewed from this perspective, it would appear that "republicanism" is possibly what is called the political and social state in the present paper have in common. "Kemalism" has selected the label of "republicanism" to rally the nation about. In the concepts of the present paper, this has become self-descriptive. It utilizes "republicanism" to denote the state, but at the same time, it has assumed the implicit features of republicanism as well. The consequence is that the features of Kemalism have come to resemble those of Islamic republicanism as well. In the process, Kemalism and Islamic republicanism have come to resemble one another i.e. Turkey is becoming more united politically. To summarize the point, the "republicanism" of the Kemalists and Islamic republicanism have possibly dialectically drawn closer to one another. The consequence is a gradual rapprochement while the military as an institution has become increasingly isolated and defensive in its secularist and less democratic position. Even the latter point could face the possibility of attenuation in the process of possible further dialectical process in the aftermath of the election of President Gül.

vi. Perhaps the key facilitator in bringing about this rapprochement of Kemalist republicanism and republican Islam has been Fethullah Gülen . As has been shown, he very dramatically fits the republican profile in terms of his advocacy of the state, his respect for the law, his instructional role in promoting civic virtue, and his consistent emphasis upon the recruitment and formation of the character of the Turkish elite. In addition, his historical importance as one of the greatest of the neo-Nur intellectuals was sufficient to mark him as perhaps the most pre-eminent of contemporary Islamic Turkish scholars. What has occurred is that this prominence has permitted him to bring to bear his remarkable understanding of Western contemporary thought in order to facilitate the advance of the spiritual and intellectual modernization of Turkey. In the process of achieving this, he is also facilitating the greater growth of the cultural unity of Turkey while at the same time, contributing to the diminution of internal conflict on issues of defining what it means to be a modern Turk.

vii. Finally, Fethullah Gülen in an alternative venue has generated a most interesting discussion of the "New Islamic Discourse". In that discussion, Voll has raised the possibility that at the beginning of the new century it is now time to draw the final curtain on the old and intellectually tired subject of modernity and secularization. His point is that Fethullah Gülen is symptomatic of the fact that what is occurring in a remarkably rapidly modernizing Turkey is "desecularisation " i.e. the increase of commitment to religion as a process that sees the expansion of public space for religion and not the anticipated shrinkage of private space. From this perspective, secularism is not innately tied to modernity, but instead, itself has become a separate ideology and belief system. If modernization is indeed a process of equalization and competition, than secularism is thus reduced in significance. He quotes Abdullah An-Na'im as observing that the an implication of this emerging conclusion is that those debating the question of secularism will now be able to perhaps choose their own version of secularism and not necessarily that of Europe. He says that this process will retain an Islamic imperative and will also be in "strict observance of the principle of pluralism and the protection of human rights." This is an interesting suggestion, but alternatively, the Muslim future of "desecularisation" might well contain within it not the "pluralism" of liberalism, but rather the republicanism of "conservatism".[27]

---

27   Voll in Yavuz and Esposito, pp. 242-44. The German scholar Stauth has noted similarly that with the "…Islamic revolution in Iran in 1978-79 that Islam has reentered the Weltgeschichte. In good Hegelian fashion he is reminding us that this ideological discussion of secularization also is accompanied by real world events. In other words, by thought and by deed, Islam in the new century will be more insistently requiring serious intellectual attention to the Islamic cultural dynamic. Georg Stauth, Ed. Islam-Motor or Challenge of Modernity? (Hamburg, Germany: Lit Verlag, 1998)

PERFORMING MORAL OPPOSITION: MUSINGS ON THE STRATEGY AND IDENTITY IN THE GÜLEN MOVEMENT

Mustafa Gurbuz

Abstract

This paper investigates the Gülen movement's repertoires of action in order to determine how it differs from traditional Islamic revivalist movements and from the so-called 'New Social Movements' in the Western world.

Two propositions lead the discussion: First, unlike many Islamic revivalist movements, the Gülen movement shaped its identity against the perceived threat of a trio of enemies, as Nursi named them a century ago – ignorance, disunity, and poverty. This perception of the opposition is crucial to understanding the apolitical mind-set of the Gülen movement's followers. Second, unlike the confrontational New Social Movements, the Gülen movement has engaged in 'moral opposition', in which the movement's actors seek to empathise with the adversary by creating (what Bakhtin calls) 'dialogic' relationships. 'Moral opposition' has enabled the movement to be more alert strategically as well as more productive tactically in solving the everyday practical problems of Muslims in Turkey. A striking example of this 'moral opposition' was witnessed in the Merve Kavakci incident in 1999, when the movement tried to build bridges between the secular and Islamist camps, while criticising and educating both parties during the post-February 28 period in Turkey. In this way the Gülen movement's performance of opposition can contribute new theoretical and practical tools for our understanding of social movements.

Recent works on social movements have criticized the longstanding tradition of classifying social movement types as "strategy-oriented" versus "identity-oriented" (Touraine 1981; Cohen 1985; Rucht 1988) and "identity logic of action" versus "instrumentalist logic of action" (Duyvendak and Giugni 1995) by regarding identities as a key element of a movement's strategic and tactical repertoire (see Bernstein 1997, 2002; Gamson 1997; Polletta 1998a; Polletta and Jasper 2001; Taylor and Van Dyke 2004). Bifurcation of identity versus strategy suggests the idea that some movements target the state and the economy, thus, they are "instrumental" and "strategy-oriented"; whereas some other movements so-called "identity movements" challenge the dominant cultural patterns and codes and are considered "expressive" in content and "identity-oriented." New social movement theorists argue that identity movements try to gain recognition and respect by employing expressive strategies wherein the movement itself becomes the message (Touraine 1981; Cohen 1985; Melucci 1989, 1996).

Criticizing these dualisms, some scholars have shown the possibility of different social movement behaviour under different contextual factors (e.g. Bernstein 1997; Katzenstein 1998). In contrast to new social movement theory, this work on the Gülen movement indicates that identity movements are not always expressive in content and do not always follow an identity-oriented approach; instead, identity movements can synchronically be strategic as well as expressive.

In her article on strategies and identities in Black Protest movements during the 1960s, Polletta (1994) criticizes the dominant theories of social movements, which a priori assume challengers' unified common interests. Similarly, Jenkins (1983: 549) refers to the same problem in the literature by stating that "collective interests are assumed to be relatively unproblematic and to exist prior to mobilization." By the same token, Taylor and Whittier (1992: 104) criticize the longstanding lack of explanation "how structural inequality gets translated into subjective discontent." The dominant social movement theory approaches such as resource mobilization and political process regard these problems as trivial because of their assumption that identities and framing processes can be the basis for interests and further collective action but cannot change the final social movement outcome. Therefore, for the proponents of the mainstream theories, identities of actors are formed in evolutionary processes wherein social movements consciously frame their goals and produce relevant discourses; yet, these questions are not essential to explain why collective behaviour occurs (see McAdam, McCarthy, and Zald 1996). This reductionist view of movement culture has been criticized by a various number of scholars (e.g. Goodwin and Jasper 1999; Polletta 1997, 1999a, 1999b; Eyerman 2002).

In fact, the debate over the emphases (interests vis-à-vis identities) is a reflection of the dissent between American and European sociological traditions. As Eyerman and Jamison (1991: 27) note, the American sociologists focused on "the instrumentality of movement strategy formation, that is, on how movement organizations went about trying to achieve their goals," whereas the European scholars concerned with the identity formation processes that try to explain "how movements produced new historical identities for society." Although the social movement theorists had recognized the deficiencies within each approach, the attempts to synthesize these two traditions in the literature failed to address the empirical problems and methodological difficulties.

While criticizing the mainstream American collective behaviour approaches that treat the collective identities as given, many leading European scholars fell into a similar trap by a priori assuming that the collective identities are socio-historical products rather than cognitive processes (see, for instance, Touraine 1981). New Social Movement (NSM) theory, which is an offshoot of European tradition, has lately been involved in the debate over "cognitive praxis" (Eyerman and Jamison 1991), "signs" (Melucci 1996), "identity as strategy" (Bernstein 1997), protest as "art" (Jasper 1997), "moral performance" (Eyerman 2006), and "storytelling" (Polletta 2006). In general, these new formulations attempt to bring mental structures of social actors and symbolic nature of social action back in the study of collective behaviour. The mental structures of the actors should be considered seriously because they have a potential to change the social movement behaviours, tactics, strategies, timing, alliances and outcomes. The most important failure, I think, in the dominant SM approaches lies behind the fact that they hinder the possibility of the construction of divergent collective identities under the same structures (cf. Polletta 1994: 91).

This study investigates on how the Gülen movement differed from other Islamic social movements under the same structural factors that were realized by the organized opposition against Islamic activism after the soft coup in 1997. Two propositions shall lead my discussion here: First, unlike many Islamic revivalist movements, the Gülen movement shaped its identity against perceived threat of the triple enemies, what Nursi defined a century ago: ignorance, disunity, and poverty. This perception of the opposition is crucial to grasp non-political mental structures of the Gülen movement followers. Second, unlike the confrontational nature of the new social movements, the Gülen movement engaged in a "moral opposition," in which the movement actors try to empathize with the enemy by creating "dialogic" relationships.

Turkey after the Post-Modern Coup: Organized Opposition against Islamic Social Movements

As many scholars pointed out, the neo-liberal policies of the Turgut Özal cabinet paved the way to a rapid growth of Islamic revivalist movements in 1980s (e.g., Onis 1997, Cavdar 2006). The secularist elite favoured the incorporation of Islamists into the larger system because of the threat posed by the radical left movements at the time being. Özal's free market policies enabled small-scale provincial businesses and the large city petit bourgeoisie to develop rapidly in late 1980s and formed MUSIAD, an association of Islamic capitalists, in 1990. This new Anatolian bourgeoisie had envisioned both a socially Islamic public and an economically liberal society (Yavuz 2003). The new bourgeoisie, however, is consistently excluded by the big corporations and isolated from the centre in economical terms. The economic isolation, together with political marginalization, has produced a political Islamic movement, which is mostly supported by the "Black Turks" (Yavuz 2000).[1]

The rise of the new bourgeoisie was powerful enough to alarm the secularist elite. A recent report of the European Stability Initiative, a research organization in Berlin, argues that,

---

1 The term, Black Turks, itself suggests center-periphery approach to Turkish politics. According to Serif Mardin (1973), one of the prominent Turkish sociologists, the Turkish politics can only be conceptualised by identifying two forces date back to late Ottoman modernization period: (1) the centre, which is composed of the civil-bureaucratic elite, and (2) the periphery, who represents the ordinary modern citizen. For Mardin, the Turkish modernization process provided the conditions for the estrangement of the periphery from the centre and therefore, the peripheral forces at an increasing rate began to define themselves with religious rituals and identities. Technological developments and neo-liberal policies led to better penetration of the centre into the periphery; however, the peripheral forces have been excluded from the control mechanisms of the centre. In his late writings, Mardin argues that the centre-periphery duality remained the basic duality into the Republican period and still very influential in shaping current Turkish politics. See, for example, Mardin 2006.

from the 1990s onwards, Anatolia has experienced a silent revolution due to the economic success of the emerging "Islamist Calvinists," who frequently attribute their achievements to their "Protestant ethic."[2] As a number of analysts pointed out, however, the new bourgeoisie was not largely based in small towns of the Anatolia, rather, a significant component of the political Islam supporters were well-educated professionals or businessmen living in largest urban areas (Onis 1997, Yavuz 2003). In this regard, it is very important to see the appeal of Islamist discourse, which was an ideological unifying force among the all different sorts of "excluded" Black Turks from poor peasants to urban professionals. Since the secularist "centre" of the society was radically "elitist" and exclusionary, social forces of the periphery, those who are alienated, became so diverse.[3] As Onis (1997: 748) convincingly puts,

> The religious symbolism associated with political Islam provides the unifying bond that helps to engineer a cross-class alliance, bringing together individuals with markedly different status in society. What is common to both groups is that they are part of the 'excluded,' but excluded in a very different sense of the term. The poor and the disadvantaged who form the principal electoral base of political Islam are excluded in the sense that they do not share in the benefits of growth in the age of globalisation. The professionals, the businessmen and the intellectuals whom we would classify as the rising 'Islamic bourgeoisie,' are clearly benefiting from globalisation and modernity, yet also feel part of the excluded by not being part of the real elite in society. In this sense, political Islam as a protest movement and the ideology of the excluded constitutes a challenge to both left and right-wing parties of the established secular political order.

> The civil and military establishment of Turkish Republic, which consists of the military leaders and the secularists among the civilian population, has expressed its deep concern about the growing success of the pro-Islamic Welfare Party (WP) during 1990s. The municipal elections of March 1994 were the turning point in the transformation of the WP into a nationwide political force. As many scholars note (Onis 1997; White 2002), WP have capitalised on the weakness of the social-democratic left municipalities of the large metropolitan centres. The WP ranked first in the 1995 general election after receiving 21.4 percent of the popular vote. The party's charismatic leader Professor Necmettin Erbakan managed to be elected prime minister, on July 8, 1996, in a coalition with the centre-right True Path Party. This was unprecedented in the sense that, for the first time in the 73 year history of the modern Turkish Republic, a person who had so openly challenged the secular pro-Western orientation of the country had come to power (Gruen 1999).

The WP's economic and political program was based on a project entitled Just Order (Adil Düzen), understood as a third way between capitalism and socialism. The party's program, which has a particular interest in establishing a common market with Muslim countries, was essentially a collectivist program having a semi-socialist outlook (Caha 2003). The Just Order discourse, which openly aims to transform the whole society upon the basis of traditional values and symbols, increased the scepticism of the secular elites about the "true" intentions of the party and its leadership. Although the leaders of the party did not clearly express their favour for Sharia, an Islamic order, they seemed to criticize the secular order

---

2 "Islamic Calvinists: Change and Conservatism in Central Anatolia," *European Stability Initiative Report*, September 19, 2005. Accessed from www.esiweb.org, January 30, 2006. Although the report's title offers that there are "Islamist Calvinists" in Anatolia, the theory/practice gap evidenced in the work was plain to see in the following pages: "It is hard to say whether the rise of 'Islamic Calvinism'…is a cause of their commercial success…, or whether increasing prosperity has led them to embrace interpretations of Islam that emphasize its compatibility with the modern world" (p. 25). For criticism, see Author (forthcoming).

3 The diverse nature of the periphery against the secularist center is usually omitted in the scholarship on Turkish Islamic movements. The Gülen movement's impact has proved that a very significant amount of individuals from the new Muslim bourgeoisie have rejected to support political Islam and joined non-political Islamic groups.

and many values connected to it.

Due to the growing scepticism among the secularist circles, the WP's exercise of power as the government did not even survive for a year. On February 28, 1997, the National Security Council (NSC) issued a long list of measures to be urgently implemented by the Erbakan government. This kind of military intervention was unprecedented in Turkey in the sense that the action was not a direct intervention of politics by brute force. Therefore, some commentators called the intervention as a "soft" coup or a "postmodern" coup (Yavuz 2003, Bulac 2007). In fact, the February 28 coup was not the effect or outcome of a single memo, but was rather a transformation into a "process" (Cizre and Cinar 2003; Author 2007). The Erbakan government was forced to resign in June 1997 as a result of behind-the-scenes pressure from the military; however, it was not the end of the story, instead, it was the first step of the February 28th process, a process "of monitoring, controlling, and criminalizing all Islamic activism as a security threat and institutionalizing a permanent legal framework for ostracizing devout and active Turkish Muslims from the market, educational, and political spheres" (Yavuz 2003: 277).

After the fall of the Erbakan cabinet, following governments began to implement the list of measures. Mandated by the Turkish military and the NSC, the governments' consequent legislative and administrative steps towards elimination of irtica , religious reactionism, include the proposals that all activities of Islamic movements should be under strict scrutiny and surveillance of the state; eight-year uninterrupted and compulsory elementary education should be enforced in order to unite the all educational activities across the country under the supervision of the state; Imam-Hatip (preacher) schools should be limited in number; and, Kemalist modern dress code should be strictly implemented in public sphere (Gruen 1999).

The February 28th process was a typical example of what political scientists call "securitization", the process of defining an issue "as an existential threat, requiring emergency measures and justifying actions outside the normal bounds of political procedure" (Buzan et. al., 1998: 23-24). During the February 28th process, the securitization agenda was primarily held as well. Censorship, the police and an extreme network of spies and informers were activated by the "deep state"[4]; so that free exchange of political ideas was suppressed. In the process,

---

4   The concept "deep state" refers to illegal enterprises within the state, which is an important aspect of Turkish politics. The Susurluk accident in 1996 revealed illegal organizations operating in the name of the state, taking considerable help and support from the civil and military bureaucrats. These organizations have justified their presence by claiming that they are protecting "state interest" or "national interest" (Turkone 2007). The emerging threat of Kurdistan Worker's Party (PKK), a Kurdish terrorist organization, in 1980s, further legitimized the presence of some forces that carries out illegal operations for the sake of the state. In November 2005, a renegade member of the PKK currently employed as an 'informant' by the security forces, two officers of the local gendarmerie and possibly higher level officers were allegedly involved in bombing a local bookstore and forming illegal networks that targeted suspected 'sympathizing' citizens of the PKK (TESEV 2006). This event, known as Semdinli affair, was followed by some other events and, in a couple of months, five different illegal organizations were found and some army officers were arrested. See "Nice çetelere," Radikal, June 2, 2006. The events hinted the existence of shadowy formations within the security forces and raised questions about the 'legality' of the measures in fighting terrorism in respect to citizens' rights. For Hanioglu (2007), the deep state is not a new phenomenon; rather, it is a legacy of late Ottoman period. As William Hale (1994: 8) points out, Machiavelli's observations about the Ottoman Empire still relevant in terms of the strong state culture in Turkish politics: "It would be very difficult to acquire the state of the Turk; but, having conquered it, it would be very easy to hold it." Lately, Christopher de Bellaigue of The New York Review of Books noted that "some members of the armed forces, afraid of losing the prestige, political autonomy, and big budgets that they have enjoyed since the PKK rebellion gained momentum in the late 1980s, do not want peace at all... The relative freedom with which Ocalan's (the captured leader of the PKK) lawyers have been able to pass on

two parties (Welfare Party and its successor Virtue Party) have been abolished because of their allegedly Islamic roots[5], about 900 military officers were removed from their posts; certain corporations were defined as "green capital" and discriminated against in governmental contracts and bids; hundreds of Qur'an courses and Imam-Hatip (religious preacher) schools were closed; thousands of university students were expelled from the public and private universities due to their adoption of headscarf (Kuru 2006). The military unilaterally organized briefings and speeches delivered to businessmen, owners of the mass media companies, and most importantly to members of the judiciary, demanding a total elimination of the religious threat.[6] The briefings were organized by Batı Çalışma Grubu (BÇG), an illegal organization within the military.[7] The BCG was working as secret information service that had recorded thousands of individuals as a threat to the regime of the Republic.[8] The secularist elite were so confident in durability of their policies. In 1999, the Chief of the Turkish General Staff General Hüseyin Kıvrıkoğlu declared that "the February 28th process will persist for a thousand year."[9] Yet, the February 28th process has ended by the 2001 economic crisis, when the financial supporters of the process experienced a vicious bankruptcy.

The Gülen Movement against the Organized Opposition

Especially after 1994, the Gülen movement has tried to form a vast network including some secularist members of the academia, business elite, popular artists, journalists and the Alevi opinion leaders under the umbrella of some fashionable causes such as "dialogue," "tolerance," "democracy," "liberty," and an inclusive "Anatolian platform." This Anatolian Platform was named as "Abant Platform," in which prominent writers, journalists, and professors gather on a yearly basis to discuss Turkey's problems and prospects for the future. This intellectual endeavour has been organized by Journalist and Writers Foundation, of which honorary president is Fethullah Gülen himself, since 1998 and it has provided both a great sympathy

---

his messages has led some to suspect that he is cooperating with his captors—that he has defected, in effect, to the 'deep state'". See C. Bellaigue "The Uncontainable Kurds," The New York Review of Books 54: 3, 2007.

5 Welfare Party of Necmettin Erbakan was closed in January 1998 and Erbakan was banned from politics for ten years. The successor party of Erbakan followers was Virtue Party, which was closed in 2001. Another important event during the process was the imprisonment of Tayyip Erdoğan, renowned Istanbul Mayor from Welfare Party. Erdoğan was a popular opinion leader within the party, who was likely to succeed Erbakan. He was arrested because of reciting the following verses in a public speech: "The mosques are our barracks, the minarets are our bayonets, their domes are our helmets and the believers are our soldiers." Ironically, the poem was written by a famous Turkish nationalist, Ziya Gokalp, whom the secularists elite admire. Erdoğan was spent four months in prison. Yet, this experience made him more popular in the public image. Erdoğan took the advantage of the imprisonment and broadcasted his new album, "This Song is Not Yet Over," in which his recites some famous poems. It was a clear message to the audience that he would return back to politics. Later, he established a new party, Justice and Development Party, and succeeded to become Prime Minister.

6 M. Yetkin, "10. Yilinda 28 Subat," Radikal, February 26, 2007. Sevket Kazan, the Minister of Justice at the time being, pointed out that the briefings to the members of the judiciary were organized without any official request for permit from the Ministry of Justice. See "28 Subat- Derin Darbe Belgeseli" www.stv.com.tr (Accessed May 10, 2007).

7 The generals of the time later confessed the presence of the BCG but still defended its rationale. According to them, they needed such kind of organization to save the Kemalist regime from the Islamist threat. See, for example, interview with General Ozkasnak: "BCG Cevik Bir'in Fikriydi," Sabah, February 26, 2006.

8 According to Bayramoglu, six million people, in one way or another, had been recorded on the lists. Some of the lists were revealed to the public after the February 28th process. See Nese Duzel, "Bayramoglu: Izleniyoruz," Radikal, April 12, 2004.

9 "İlk Kez Konuştu," Sabah, September 4, 1999.

and prestige to the movement from various circles. Since 2004, the Abant Conventions has started to be held internationally as well as domestically. In its seventh annual meeting in 2004, the Platform was held in Washington D.C. on "Islam, Secularism, and Democracy: The Turkish Experience"; in December 2004, it was in Brussels, titled "Culture, Identity, and Religion in Turkey's EU Accession Process." The Platform brought together the French and Turkish academia in the name of Turkey-France conversations in March 2006 and in April 2007 to discuss religion, secularism, and pluralism in democracies. In February 2007, the Platform organized its annual conference with Arab intellectuals in Egypt on "Islam, the West, and Modernization." The most recent subject in domestic gathering was on Alevi identity in Turkey, held in March 2007. The movement had never mentioned the sensitive and symbolic issues such as the headscarf issue as an urgent problem at any instance; instead, the compromising attitude was the dominant characteristic of the events they organized.

Ironically, however, as the Gülen Movement took compromising behaviour; it led to a further schism between the Kemalist elite and the movement. For the Kemalists, the Gülen movement has tried to break the monopoly over the civilisational project, which has been employed as a symbolic capital in their hands. The greatest challenge to the secular establishment was the movement's outstanding success of absorbing "the global language of human rights and democracy in its efforts to counter Kemalist exclusiveness" (Yavuz 1999). As Özdalga (2005: 438) asserts, "it is true that this religious community particularly promotes modern developments, but this has not prevented it from being degraded by the leading elites in Turkish society into the position of an Outsider."

As the Gülen movement became apparently different from political Islam, the secularists denounced it as a "secret Islamist" organization. The routine Kemalist opposition became an organized opposition in June 1999 when the military decided to eliminate the threat of "Gülen-led Islamism." Özdalga (2005: 439-40) sums up the main accusations against Fethullah Gülen in the mainstream media as the following:

i.   Fethullah Gülen is trying to infiltrate important state institutions like the judiciary, the police and the military.
ii.   The purpose behind that is to prepare the ground for a seizure of state power.
iii.   The struggle for the final takeover of the state has been going on for a long time and takes place in great secrecy.
iv.   Fethullah Gülen's strategy is to pretend that he and his adherents fully favour Mustafa Kemal Atatürk and the existing regime, while in reality he is preparing himself and his followers for an Islamist revolution.
v.   What is so disturbing about Gülen is that he has been so skilful in hiding his real purposes from the public.
vi.   Fethullah Gülen controls "gigantic" (korkunç) sums of money. How and where these resources are appropriated is unknown. Since he lives in the US, it is hinted that he is supported by this superpower (allegedly to undermine the interests of his native Turkey).
vii.   In the schools, dormitories and home-like student houses (ışık evleri) set up in the name of Gülen, students are pressured to accept his teachings (brainwashed).
viii. Gülen and his adherents constitute a greater threat to the regime than either the Kurdish "terror organization" PKK and Abdullah Öcalan or the Welfare Party and its most militant demagogue Sevket Yilmaz. The fact that the Welfare Party functions openly must count in its favour compared to Gülen's secretiveness.

Following the media accounts, the State Security Court Prosecutor opened a court case against Fethullah Gülen by demanding a death penalty. This massive attack on the Gülen movement was astonishing for many individuals given the fact that the movement's constant representation of Islam's moderate face, opening educational centres and worldwide schools, its emphasis upon diversity, dialogue, and tolerance as well as its strong loyalty to the state policies have constituted a bulwark against radical Islamic revivalism and all sorts of political Islamic parties. The uneasiness of the secularists, however, has emerged exactly at this point: the Gülen movement has projected a re-construction of the society in every aspect without any confrontational means. Therefore, the Gülen's movement identity for education, which gives strong legitimacy to the movement to challenge the monopoly of the state elite, became the source of the problem itself. As Özdalga (2005: 440) adequately puts,

> Regarding class, the urge for social mobility is strong among Gülen adherents, who are largely average urban middle class in character. This means that the socioeconomic composition of the Gülen movement is not markedly different from that of the official elite. The same is true of ethnic belonging, since Gülen adherents are of mainly Turkish, not Kurdish, origin, and of religious belonging, since they, like the establishment, are mainly Sunni Muslims, not Alevis. It is a characteristic of an Established-Outsider relationship that hostility tends to be stronger the more similar the groups are with respect to their socioeconomic, ethnic or racial backgrounds.

Although the movement had first faced with such a fierce organized opposition, its reaction was not radical. Parallel to earlier strategy of deploying educational identities, the movement aimed to defend itself by public speeches, media accounts, and lobbying. Since the movement was not a political movement, it has been "inclusive" in its organizational infrastructure; in other words, the movement's access to the polity has been very broad due to its practical aims such as being the centre of an "Anatolian Platform" (see fig.1. path 1b). In the following section, I will specifically discuss on the Gülen movement's moral opposition against the organized opposition of the secularist elite.

Performing Moral Opposition

The most distinguishing feature of the Gülen movement is its ability to define the Kemalist opposition as non-unified entity. Therefore, the Gülen movement has been eager to ally with the passive secularists (Kemalist doves); whereas opposing assertive secularists (Kemalist hawks).[10] Ron Eyerman (2006) provides the basic principle for moral performance in social movement activism as the following:

> If the first step in dehumanization is to reduce an other to a simple phrase, an enemy, a parasite, or a terrorist, the first step in moral performance or empathy is attentiveness to the complexity of another's status and situation, something which can be viewed as an attribution of subjectivity. This may involve seeing the other as an agent or victim of historical or natural forces and "forced" to act in certain ways.

Eyerman gives the example of diversification of the opposition movements in France against the French government policies during the war with Algeria between 1954 and 1962. There were two groups that opposed to French invasion: reformists and Marxists. According to the reformists, associated with L'Express, Algerian rebels were potential partners in a dialogue to renegotiate the relationship between France and a somewhat independent Algeria. On the other hand, Marxists associated with Les temps modernes viewed the rebels as historical agents of "world historical dimension ushering a new stage of development," in which

---

10 For the distinction between assertive secularism and passive secularism, see Kuru (2006).

violence is accepted as a necessary means. Therefore, Marxists had a morally more tolerant view of the other, the Algerians (Eyerman 2006: 201).

The Gülen movement, from its very beginning, has expressed a moral tolerance toward the secularist power centre. Inspired from the Jasper's (1997) concept of "moral protest" and Eyerman's concept of "moral performance," I shall call this non-confrontational engagement as "moral opposition." As a challenging movement, on the one hand, the Gülen movement has launched an opposition to the centre; however, on the other hand, the movement's use of non-confrontational means and its deployment of educational identity distinguished it from other social movements.

The moral opposition of the Gülen movement stems from twofold reasons: mental structures of the movement and its organizational features (see figure 1). Unlike political Islamic movements in Turkey, the Gülen followers believe that their actual enemy is the triple monster that was defined by Said Nursi: (1) ignorance of the Muslims in religious as well as scientific terms (2) poverty of the ummah, Muslim nation, in general (3) disunity among the believers. Therefore, their perception of the oppositional cultural domination led them to employ cultural and educational means to overcome the problems in Turkey (see figure 2).

Mental Structures of the Movement

Pointing out the vicious circle that Islamic community has found itself for centuries, Gülen (2005: 22) believes that the problems can only be solved by "the inheritors of the earth," a cadre of "physicians of the soul and reality whose hearts are open to all fields of all knowledge: perspicacity, culture, spiritual knowledge, inspirations and divine blessings, abundance and prosperity, enlightenment; from physics to metaphysics, from mathematics to ethics, from chemistry to spirituality, from astronomy to subjectivism, from fine arts to Sufism, from law to jurisprudence, from politics to special training of religious Sufi orders." Gülen calls this ideal type of man as the "new human model"[11] and employs "the inheritors of the earth" concept interchangeably with some other concepts such as "golden generation," "hero of thought and action," and "devout" to refer this new model throughout his writings.[12] In this regard, the Gülen schools have played an important mission and envisioned a "new society" that is full of "new humans."

A typical reader of Gülen can understand that there is a Divine mission in the course of history and this mission will be accomplished by "the inheritors".[13] Becoming an inheritor, however, is not that being "chosen by God." Gülen specifically mentions the difference between "becoming" and "being", where he explains meaning of one verse in the Qur'an.[14] Since becoming depends on the conditions that should be fulfilled rather than being chosenness beforehand, the state of "becoming" can be lost in future if the necessary duties ignored. This belief implies that there are no God-favoured people; instead, there are God-favoured attributes. Therefore, "inheritors of the earth" as personalities are intentionally remained ambiguous in Gülen's thought; but, the characteristics and attributes of the inheritors are clearly

---

11 See Gülen 1991; Ergene 2005: 270.

12 For the concepts of "hero of thought and action" and "devout," see Gülen 2005: 67-83, 91-97. On the concept of "golden generation," Gülen's tape-recorded conferences have been in circle from as far as 1980es, which are available from the official web-site of Gülen: www.fGülen.org.

13 For Gülen's philosophy of history, see Gülen 2005: 129-34.

14 The verse was translated by Gülen as the following: "You *became* the best of people, evolved for mankind, enjoining what is right, forbidding what is wrong, and believing in Allah." (3: 110) See, Gülen 1998: 36.

described.[15] True inheritors are those who live "at the expense of their own selves in order to make others live"; who never claim that they are inheritors; who "do not ever desire that the masses follow them" (Gülen 2005: 95). Nobody knows the genuine "inheritors of the earth" because it resembles an ideal form of a true believer who is very open to worldly affairs and science, while seeking the hereafter and spiritual nobility:

> To reach such a degree of spirituality and saintliness is dependent on being open to perception, logic, and reasoning, and thence to thoughts and inspiration from the Divine. In other words, it is very difficult for a person to reach this peak, to acquire such a state, unless experience has been sieved by the filter of the reason, reason has surrendered to the greatest intellect and foresight of the prophets, logic has turned completely into love, and love has evolved into love of God (Gülen 2005: 62).

Thus, the Gülen movement has defined the enemy as "attributes" rather than the "objects." In other words, bad attributes such as selfishness, ego-centrism, and fraudulence that sustain the triple enemies of ignorance, poverty, and disunity in Muslim world specifically, and the world in general, can only be solved by the "new human" attributes such as love, saintliness, and perceptive reasoning. In this sense, the Gülen thought is not a utopian vision[16]; instead, it refers to a dualistic situation of an ideal human, "whose world of thought stretches from the material to the immaterial, from physics to metaphysics, from philosophy to Sufism" (Gülen 2005: 64). Gülen perfectly describes this paradox as the following:

> Using Rumi's expression, such a person is like a compass with one foot *well-established in the centre of belief and Islam* and the other foot with people of many nations. If this apparently du-alistic state can be caught by a person who believes in God, it's most desirable. *So deep in his or her own inner world, so full of love…so much in touch with God; but at the same time an active member of society.*[17]

The Gülen movement's inclusive nature in its mental structures and its well-expressed identity for education (cf. Bernstein 1997) has provided a strong base for moral opposition toward the Kemalist organized attacks during the February 28th process. Unlike the Milli Gorus (National View) Movement, the Gülen movement did not openly criticize the regime; rather, it interpreted the Kemalist opposition as fuzzy, which includes those who have been ignorant about Islam and Muslims due to the bad representations in the media. For Gülen followers, they were "victims of the historical forces" (cf. Eyerman 2006), who should see the real lovely face of Muslims. Therefore, the Gülen movement took a mission to find a middle way to gather non-ideological Kemalists (passive secularists) and non-ideological Islamists in order to represent the all-encompassing nature of the Anatolian Islam. One of the most striking examples of the Gülen movement's inclusive strategy was witnessed in the Kavakci affair in 1999.

The April 18 general country-wide elections in 1999 introduced the election of two Muslim women with headscarves for the first time in Turkish modern history: Nesrin Unal, a rep-resentative of the Nationalist Action Party (MHP), and Merve Kavakci, an Istanbul deputy from the pro-Islamic Virtue Party (FP). What produced a tense public debate was not the

---

15 For an extensive description of the attributes of the inheritors, see Gülen 2005: 31-42. Gülen exhaustively stresses on altruism as the main characteristic: "What we are always stressing is that it is those who live their lives in sincerity, loyalty, and altruism at the expense of their own selves in order to make others live who are the true inheritors of the historical dynamics to whom we can entrust our souls" (p. 95).

16 For a comparison of Gülen, Confucius, and Plato on ideal human, see Carroll 2007: 35-58.

17 Cited in Ünal and Williams 2000: 207. Emphases added.

election of "covered" deputies but, instead, the possibility of having covered women in the parliament. The mainstream mass media, which has predominantly secularist writers and commentators, started a campaign against the presence of headscarf in the parliament. The media also interviewed the each deputy, asking if they would remove the headscarf in the parliament, as they were demanded to do. The MHP member, Unal, replied that if she absolutely had to she would uncover her head, though she did not want to.[18] Yet, the FP member Merve Kavakci declared that she would not take off her headscarf nor would she resign (Shively 2005). All Islamic groups and their media outlets defended Kavakci's right to appear in parliament with the headscarf given the fact that there is no explicit statement in the Parliamentary legal rules of conduct.[19] The secularist opposition, in turn, replied that no woman had ever worn the headscarf in the parliament and it would be an explicit offense to the secular Kemalist ideology of the Republic.[20]

Thus, the Merve Kavakci incident in the Turkish Parliament inflamed a furious historical debate between the secular elites and the Islamic groups, and thus, threatened the implicit social contract in the Turkish society. Yet, the Gülen movement's emphasis on the non-confrontational means (cf. Turam 2007) and educational identity prevented a further contention in a society of turbulent crisis (see figure 2).

The Organizational Base of the Moral Opposition

The structural factors have also played a decisive role in the Gülen movement's moral opposition. The Gülen movement has been a civic, cultural social movement (see Figure 3). Unlike political movements, cultural movements have inclusive organizational structures, in which active participation of the movement is open to everyone and the access to the polity is straightforward. This characteristic, besides with the inclusive peaceful message in content, led to a unique stance of the Gülen movement compared to other Islamic movements in Turkey (see Figure 1 and 3).

Implications for Social Movements Literature

The Gülen movement's distinctive feature might extend the new social movement theory in two important respects. First, New Social Movement theory regards all cultural movements as "expressive" and "confrontational" social movements. Instead, as proved in the Gülen movement case, cultural movements are more prone to combine strategic and expressive elements simultaneously when they are compared to political movements (see Figure 4). Political movements, on the other hand, seem liking to play extremes in both (strategic vs. expressive) directions. One possible suggestion of this fact would be that cultural movements have always keep an "expressive" content in their nature; however, when they are targeted by political power holders (cf. Eyerman 2006), the movements are strategically trying to find a way to escape from deadlock, which may put an end to the movement itself. Unlike cultural

---

18 It should be noted that the MHP leaders put an explicit pressure on Nesrin Unal to take off her scarf. See, "Bahceli: Meclis Krizle Baslamamali," *Hurriyet*, May 1, 1999.

19 See, for example, Fehmi Koru, "Vahim Hata," *Yeni Safak*, April 25, 1999; Nedim Odabas, "Neler Olacak?," *Milli Gazete*, April 28, 1999; Ahmet Ridvan, "Merve-Nesrin ve MHP," *Yeni Safak*, April 29, 1999; Kazim Gulecyuz, "Meclis Acilirken," *Yeni Asya*, May 2, 1999.

20 "Turban Yasagi Ata'nin Emri," *Milliyet*, May 1, 1999; "64 Yildir Turban Sorunu Olmadi," *Hurriyet*, May 2, 1999; Emin Colasan, "Merve'nin Ortusu," *Hurriyet*, May 1, 1999; Derya Sazak, "Merve Krizi," *Milliyet*, May 1, 1999.

movements, political movements are extremely eager to convince more people around their movements. The conventional wisdom suggests the political movements to become more opportunistic and strategic in order to reach many more people. Yet, it is equally easy to understand that when a political movement becomes more expressive and resisting, there is a high possibility of appealing certain type of people. Therefore, playing the extremes in both directions are feasible options for political mobilization.

Second, regarding the social protest aspect of the new social movements, Katzenstein (1998: 7) persuasively illustrated that feminist activism inside the church and the military has taken unusual forms of protest that are very different from the traditional demonstrations in the street:

> Feminist organizing in institutional contexts may not press for the instant cessation of daily business sought by the earlier sit-ins or the demonstrations that led to the destruction of property or clashes with the police. But feminist organizing (in its most adversarial and even sometimes in its more accommodative forms) does seek to transform the world. Even some of the most narrow versions of feminist politics that decline to embrace antiracist, antiheterosexist, and antipoverty agendas intend through their focus on equal jobs, promotions, harassment, rape, and other forms of sexual violence to fundamentally change the way American institutions function.

Parallel to feminist activism, Islamic activism in Turkey in its all forms aims to challenge the unwritten assertive secularist codes of the society. In this regard, we can turn the Kavakci case: all Islamic movements in Turkey, for example, ardently support the headscarf liberation. Yet, the Gülen movement strategies such as discursive activism and dialogue activism are not usually considered as protest behaviour. The Gülen movement supporters who do not attending the sit-ins in the universities to favour the headscarf ban protestors were conscious and collective actors. Instead of taking that type of confrontational protest, they call for a discursive action through educating the society. Headscarf ban protest literature, however, omits this dimension of moral protest and therefore disregards the Gülen community's collective action. Thus, by indicating the possibility of new types of protest, we may unfold "the art of moral protest" (cf. Jasper 1997). Viewing the social movements as dynamic agents that using full of artistic imaginaries (Eyerman and Jamison 1998) and the social life as artful (Jasper 1997), in which people play on cultural meanings and strategic expectations in multiple ways, we can understand the Islamic moral protestors better. Moral protestors in moral opposition, as Jasper (1997: 13) asserts, are "at the cutting edge of society's understanding of itself as it changes."

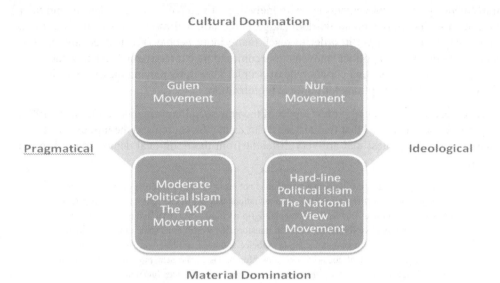

Table 1: Islamic Movements' Perception of the dominant opposition ("other") and operation of power politics in Turkey.

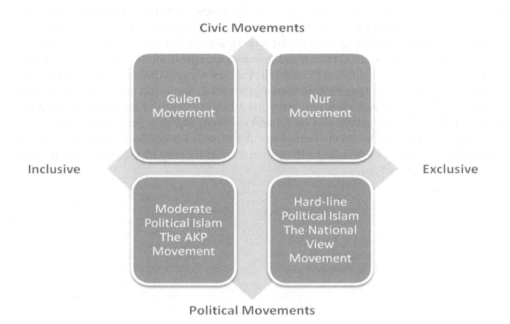

Table 2: Diversification of Islamic Movements in Turkey.

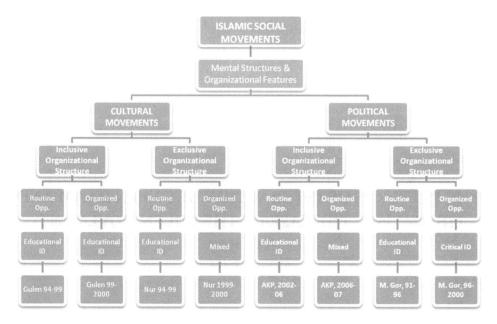

Figure 3: General model of identity as perceived strategies in the context of Islamic activism

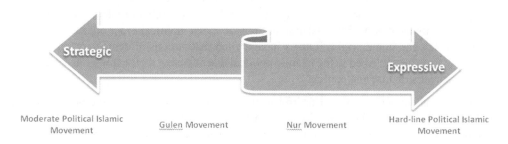

Figure 4: Islamic Movement Behavior in Turkey.

THE PATTERNS OF INTERACTION BETWEEN ISLAM AND LIBERALISM: THE CASE OF THE GÜLEN MOVEMENT[1]

Ramazan Kilinc

Abstract

The unprecedented resurgence of religious organisations in the public sphere in recent years has given particular urgency to the old question of the compatibility of Islam and liberalism. Some scholars have argued that Islamic notions of social–political order are not hospitable to democracy and human rights. Others have argued that notions of democracy and human rights are firmly established in the Islamic political discourse but their expression depends on history, social structure and context.

Although this debate has proved fruitful in framing the role of Islam in the public sphere, both sides have generally focused on essential sources of Islam. The debate needs to be extended to the empirical realm through study of particular Islamic movements and their responses to liberalisation trends. Such study should take into account local context, the organisational capabilities of the movement, and the Islamic repertoire that it deploys in mobilising its followers.

This paper looks at the Gülen movement's response to liberalisation processes in Turkey in the 1990s and 2000s. Since liberalism has radically transformed the economic and political system of the country over the last two decades, Turkey is a good example for our purposes. Furthermore, the increased influence of the Gülen movement in Turkey provides rich empirical data of an Islamic movement engaging with liberalisation in civil society and politics. The paper concludes that, while the movement's discourse and practice are compatible with liberalism, its Islamic ethos means that at some points it must engage liberalism critically.

---

1 The author wishes to thank Carolyn Warner, Etga Uğur, Ahmet T Kuru, Miriam Elman, Eren Tatari, Mustafa Özgür Tuna, Miki Kittilson, Ibrahim Abu-Rabi, Mustafa Tağma, Ihsan Yilmaz, and Halide Görgün Kılınç for their critical comments and suggestions.

Introduction

To what extent are Islam and liberalism compatible? How have Islamic movements responded to liberalization trends in the last two decades?[2] Some scholars argue that liberalism can flourish in the Muslim world[3] while others contend that developing a liberal economic and political system within the Islamic tradition is almost impossible.[4] I argue that there is no general answer to this question and scholars should instead analyze the Islamic movements empirically. Each group's compatibility with a liberal system depends on some contextual conditions. One should consider environmental factors within which an Islamic movement is located, the organizational capabilities that the movement possesses, and the Islamic repertoire that the movement uses in mobilizing its followers. My objective in this study is to specify certain conditions under which Islamic movements and liberal economic and political systems co-exist peacefully.

In this paper, I aim to reach an answer to this question by looking at the Gülen movement's response to liberalization processes in Turkey in the 1990s and 2000s.[5] Analyzing the Gülen movement in 1990s and 2000s offers many analytical opportunities. First of all, liberalism has transformed the Turkish economic and political system radically in the last two decades. Turkey is a good case at hand to analyze the responses of Islamic movements to the liberalization of social and political life. Second, the Gülen movement is not a political movement; it is a social movement which is active in many spheres of social life. Earlier studies on Islam and liberalism have generally focused on political movements. This study aims to enlarge those analyses toward social movements to get a larger picture of the interactions between Islam and liberalism. Finally, the Gülen movement has become an influential transnational Islamic movement in the last two decades. Analyzing the movement's engagement with liberalism is also instructive in understanding the patterns of interactions between Islamic movements and liberalism at large. The conclusions that we get from this inquiry may contribute to larger debates on democratization in the Muslim world.

I analyze the Gülen movement's engagement with liberalization in two spheres: economic liberalization and political liberalization. In analyzing the movement's engagement with economic liberalization, I look at what normative position the followers have taken against free market economy, which diffused in 1990s and 2000s in Turkey; and in what ways they have implemented the rules of free market economy. Although the movement has run many

---

2 Adopting James Beckford's definition of "religious movement," I define an Islamic movement as "formal or informal mobilization of people, material resources, ideas, and feelings in pursuit of objectives dictated by concerns deemed ultimately significant but largely outside the framework of conventional religious activities." See James Beckford, "Religious Movements and Globalization," In *Global Social Movements*, edited by Robin Cohen and Shirin M. Rai (New Brunswick, NJ: Athlone Press, 2000), p. 169.

3 See Khaled Abou El-Fadl, *Islam and the Challenge of Democracy: A Boston Review Book* (Princeton: Princeton University Press, 2004), Charles Kurzman, *Liberal Islam: A Source Book* (New York: Oxford University Press, 1998); and Michaelle Browers and Charles Kurzman (eds), *An Islamic Reformation?* (Oxford: Lexington Books, 2004).

4 See Bernard Lewis, *What Went Wrong?: The Clash between Islam and Modernity in the Middle East* (New York, Perennial, 2003); and Bernard Lewis, *The Crisis of Islam: Holy War and Unholy Terror* (New York: Modern Library, 2003). Many years ago, Max Weber argued that Islam was an obstacle against the development of a capitalist spirit in the Muslim-majority countries. Max Weber, *The Protestant Ethic and the Spirit of Capitalism* (New York: Scribner, 1958).

5 For an earlier study which depicts the Gülen movement as a liberal Islamic movement see: Bülent Aras and Ömer Çaha, "Fethullah Gülen and His Liberal 'Turkish Islam' Movement," *Middle East Review of International Affairs*, Volume 4 No 4 (December 2000).

economic activities without any serious contradiction with the liberal economic system, the followers have strived to transform it by adding some components from Islamic teachings. Under the heading of political liberalization, I analyze the movement's response to the expansion of the civil and political liberties which strengthened the democratization process in Turkey in the last two decades. In line with a liberal participatory philosophy, the movement has developed amicable relations with different segments of the society and defended a pluralist understanding in its relations with the others. However, the followers, without interfering the others' preferences, have also developed some communitarian responses to the individualist emphasis of liberal philosophy.

Thus, this paper argues that the Gülen movement has reinterpreted Islamic activism in a way to make it compatible with the liberalization process.[6] This movement has used the opportunities offered by the liberalization process in Turkey and abroad. Moreover, it has strived to transform liberalization processes by re-evaluating them within an Islamic perspective.[7] The conditions which made this possible will become clear after the detailed examination of the Gülen movement's social and political practices within a liberalizing society in the last two decades. Before analyzing the Gülen movement, I will briefly summarize the discussions on Islam and liberalism.

Islam and Liberalism: The Question of Compatibility

We can identify three different approaches on the relationship between Islam and liberalism. The first group of scholars argues that Islam and liberalism are incompatible. These scholars consist of two essentialist camps: those who present Islam as a backward ideology which

6   Ihsan Yilmaz argues that the inherent pluralistic nature of Islamic jurisprudence allows the emergence of many authorities who eclectically and pragmatically construct their own interpretations of the Islamic law against the challenges of modern times. This results in the postmodern fragmentation of the Islamic legal sphere. The Islamic social movements, which have the capacity to transform the public sphere, may prevent the fragmentation of the Islamic legal sphere by gathering their followers around certain discourses and practices. Yilmaz argues that by its increasing influence, the Gülen movement has the capacity to renew the Islamic discourse and practices so as to empower it to meet the challenges of modernity. See Ihsan Yilmaz, "Ijtihad and Tajdid by Conduct: The Gülen Movement" in *Turkish Islam and the Secular State: The Gülen Movement*, edited by M. Hakan Yavuz and John L. Esposito, (Syracuse, NY: Syracuse University Press, 2003), pp. 208-237. See also: Ihsan Yilmaz, "State, Law, Civil Society and Islam in Contemporary Turkey," *Muslim World*, Volume 95 No 3 (July 2005), pp. 385-412; Ugur Komecoglu, "Kutsal ile Kamusal: F. Gülen Cemaat Hareketi", *İslamın Yeni Kamusal Yüzleri*, ed. Nilufer Göle. Istanbul: Metis Yayınları, 2000, 148-94; Elizabeth Özdalga, "Secularizing Trends in Fethullah Gülen's Movement: Impasse or Opportunity for Further Renewal," *Critique: Critical Middle Eastern Studies*, Volume 12 No 1 (Spring 2003), pp. 61-73.

7   Not all of Islamic groups embrace liberalism in Turkey. The recent spread of neo-liberal policies in Turkey produced two diverging outcomes on the identities of Islamic groups. While some Islamic groups embraced liberalism and developed a pro-liberal stance, others took a more nationalist/illiberal position. For example, the Justice and Development Party moved toward a more liberal stance, while the Haydar Baş movement and the Felicity Party leaned toward a more nationalist one. For the transformation of Islamic movements toward a more liberal stance see Ihsan Dağı, "Transformation of Islamic Political Identity in Turkey: Rethinking the West and Westernization," *Turkish Studies*, Vol. 6, No 1 (2005) and Ihsan Dağı, Rethinking Human Rights, Democracy and the West: Post-Islamist Intellectuals in Turkey?," *Critique: Critical Middle Eastern Studies*, Vol. 13, No 2 (2004). For a comparative study of Turkish Islamic movements' responses to globalization see Ahmet T. Kuru, "Globalization and Diversification of Islamic Movements," *Political Science Quarterly*, Vol. 120, No 2 (2005), pp. 253-74. For a study that compares Turkish Islamic movements' reaction to liberalism, see Ramazan Kılınç, "Transformative Role of Liberalism in Turkey after 1990s: The Case of Turkish Islamic Groups," Paper Presented at the 7th Annual Kokkalis Program Graduate Student Workshop, Harvard University, Cambridge, MA, 3-4 February 2005.

cannot develop a liberal discourse within its existing set of ideas and institutions; and those Islamist thinkers who see liberalism as an inimical threat to Islam. The second group argues that Islam and liberalism are not inherently incompatible. Two different kinds of studies prevail in this thinking: theological studies that look at the discursive resources of Islam and sociological studies that look at Muslim politics empirically. The final group of scholars argues that Islam gives no hint to understand the fate of liberalism in Muslim countries; social and political context and strategic interactions of actors matter.

The first group of scholars such as Daniel Pipes, Elie Kedourie, Samuel Huntington, Bassam Tibi, and Bernard Lewis argue that Islamic political values are incompatible with the basic principles of liberal democracy.[8] Pipes, for example, argues that the lack of the distinction between spiritual and secular in Islam is an obstacle for liberal democracy. He states that political participation is an alien concept in Muslim societies.[9] Elie Kedourie, in answering the question of why democracy failed in the Middle East, argues that Islamic models of society and government are in conflict with central elements of European constitutionalism. Popular sovereignty and separation of powers are two most important principles that are in conflict with Islamic political theory. Her conclusion, then, is "the idea of democracy is quite alien to the mindset of Islam."[10] Huntington shares the same conclusion and writes that Islam "has not been hospitable to democracy."[11] He reiterates his position in his later work: "the underlying problem for the West is not Islamic fundamentalism. It is Islam."[12] Tibi writes that Islamic modernization is impossible unless Muslims embrace cultural modernization along with the instrumental modernization in the technological realm.[13] He identifies the past modernization efforts in the Muslim world as an "Islamic dream of semi-modernity," since Muslims only took the technology of the West and failed to internalize its cultural values.[14] In analyzing the reasons of the democratic backwardness of Middle Eastern states, Bernard Lewis argues that the problem stems from Islam's inability to adapt to the modern age.[15] According to him, Islam and liberal democracy are fundamentally incompatible and the only solution for the Muslim world for democratization is to modernize their systems by denouncing the authentic Islam.[16] Scholars in this vein describe the relationship between Islam and the West as "the contemporary outgrowth of tensions between the secular worldview of secular modernity and the cosmological worldview of Islamic monotheism."[17]

On the other side, there is a group of Muslim thinkers, who also agrees that Islam and democracy are incompatible. Sayyid Qutb (1906-1966), who is accepted as the ideologue of

---

8 Daniel Pipes, *In the Path of God: Islam and Political Power* (New York: Basic Books, 1983); Elie Kedourie, *Democracy and Arab Political Culture*, (Washington, DC: Washington Institute for Near East Policy, 1992); Samuel Huntington, "Will More Countries Become Democratic," *Political Science Quarterly,* Volume 99 No 2 (1984), pp. 193-218; Bassam Tibi, *The Challenge of Fundamentalism: Political Islam and the New World Disorder* (Berkeley, CA: California University Press, 1998); Bernard Lewis, *What Went Wrong?: The Clash between Islam and Modernity in the Middle East,* (New York: Prennial, 2003).

9 Pipes, *In the Path of God: Islam and Political Power,* pp. 48-69, 144-47.

10 Kedourie, *Democracy and Arab Political Culture*, p. 1.

11 Huntington, "Will More Countries Become Democratic," p. 208

12 Samuel P. Huntington, *The Clash of Civilizations and the Remaking of World Order* (New York: Simon & Schuster, 1996), p. 217.

13 Tibi, *The Challenge of Fundamentalism*, p. 66.

14 *Ibid.*, p. 66.

15 Lewis, *What Went Wrong?: The Clash between Islam and Modernity in the Middle East*

16 For a similar argument see: Daniel Lerner, *The Passing of Traditional Society*, (Glenco, IL: Free Press, 1958).

17 Tibi, *The Challenge of Fundamentalism*, p. 68.

the Muslim Brotherhood in Egypt, sees democracy as a threat to Islam's authenticity. As if concurring the above-mentioned authors, he argues that democracy is antithetical to Islam since it is against the Islamic notion of God's sovereignty.[18] He wrote that "as long as there is a group of people legislating for others, equality and absolute dignity cannot be realized."[19] The followers of Qutb saw democracy as a Western plot against Muslims and considered it a religion and worldview that poses a threat to the Islamic faith instead of a political system.[20]

Abul Ala Mawdudi (1903-1979), founder of the Jamaat-i Islami in Indian subcontinent, is another Muslim thinker who argues that the notion of popular sovereignty that democracy entails is not compatible with the Islamic teachings. Based on this argument, he concludes that Islam is "the very antithesis of secular Western democracy."[21] However, unlike Qutb, he does not deny democracy fully and suggests an Islamic version of democracy, what he calls "theo-democracy." Accordingly, he talks about a system of governance which allows a "limited form of popular sovereignty, restricted and directed by God's law."[22] The Islamic concept of "shura," which means consultation, is much more pronounced in Mawdudi's concept of theo-democracy.[23]

Along similar lines, Ayatollah Khomeini, the leader of Iranian revolution, argues that democracy is anathema to Islam. He states that humans are responsible to God and they do not have individual rights. Khomeini's idea of the primacy of the common good is also against the democratic philosophy. He claims that every individual must first think the Islamic community's good. The primacy of the community in Khomeini's worldview allows the violation of human rights if they constitute a challenge to the common good.[24]

The thesis that Islam and democracy are incompatible has been contested by a group of theological or sociological studies. The scholars who contest the incompatibility of Islam and democracy from a theological point of view compare Islamic political discourse with the notions of democracy. They point to the concepts such as *shura* (consultation), *ijtihad* (independent reasoning) and *ijma* (consensus) in the Islamic tradition to provide some basis for their argument. The main argument that repeats itself in the writings of these scholars is that Islam does not impose a specific form of government; and the form of government is left to the human agency, who makes its decision according to the changing historical, social and political conditions. Thus, democracy is one of the alternatives that Muslims can agree on. For example, Anoushiravan Ehteshami writes that "there are simply no single set of canons which can be said to provide a 'blueprint' for Islamic government."[25] Along the same lines, Tassaquq Hussain Jillani argues that the "Quran did not prescribe any particular political system of governance."[26] Rachid al-Ghannuchi claims that the primary focus of the religion

---

18 Nasr Abu Zayd, *Reformation of Islamic Thought: A Critical Historical Analysis*, (Amsterdam: Amsterdam University Press, 2006), p. 47.

19 Quoted in John L. Esposito and James P. Piscatori, "Democratization and Islam," *Middle East Journal*, Volume 45 No 3, (Summer 1991), p. 436.

20 Azzam Tamimi, "Islam and Democracy from Tahtawi to Ghannouchi," *Theory, Culture & Society*, Volume 24 No 2, (March 2007), p. 51.

21 Quoted in Esposito and Piscatori, "Democratization and Islam," p. 436.

22 Esposito and Piscatori, "Democratization and Islam," p. 436.

23 Hugh Goddard, "Islam and Democracy," *The Political Quarterly*, Volume 73 No 3, (2002), p. 6.

24 Zayd, *Reformation of Islamic Thought: A Critical Historical Analysis*, p. 70.

25 Anoushiravan Ehteshami, "Islam, Muslim Polities and Democracy," *Democratization*, Volume 11 No 4, (August 2004), p. 93.

26 Tassaduq Hussain Jillani, "Democracy and Islam: An Odyssey in Braving the Twenty-First Century," *BYU Law Review* (2006), p. 732.

is not politics but morality. He states that the Islamic contribution to society is primarily in the form of "a code of ethics, a transcendent morality that seems to have no place in today's democratic practice."[27] These points have been elaborated by a number of scholars.

Khaled Abou El Fadl, for example, shares the idea that Qur'an does not specify any particular form of government; but Qur'an identifies a set of social and political values that are central to Islamic political entity.[28] According to him, three values that Qur'an sets for Islamic polities constitute the basis for governance in Islam: "pursuing justice through social cooperation and mutual assistance; establishing a non-autocratic, consultative method of governance; and institutionalizing mercy and compassion in social interactions."[29] He argues that constitutional democracy is the system which suits best to these Islamic social and political values.

Ahmad Moussalli argues that the seeds of the notions of democracy, pluralism and human rights are embedded in many notions of government and politics found in Islamic religious thought.[30] Examining classical, medieval and modern Islamic discourse, Moussalli explores how Islamic concepts of shura (consultation), ikhtilaf (difference) and al-huquq al-shar'iyya (legal rights) are in tune with the notions of democracy, pluralism and human rights respectively. As opposed to fundamentalist thinkers' insistence on God's sovereignty as an obstacle for democracy, Moussalli makes a sharp distinction between "Islam as a divine belief system and the Islamic state as a humanly developed political system" and argues that humanly developed system requires the intervention of human agency.[31] According to Moussalli, the practical implementation of the liberal Islamic theology depends on the existence of pluralistic societies and democratic institutions. He argues that nationalist and socialist tendencies in the Muslim world, which had emerged as responses to oppression by imperial powers, have strengthened the authoritarian secular governments, and prevented the emergence of liberal democratic alternatives.[32]

Abdulaziz Sachedina also argues that democratic pluralism is inscribed into the fabric of Qur'an.[33] For Sachedina, the purpose of revelation is not to govern but to guide humankind.[34] Qur'an has a distinction between the obligations that humans perform as part of their relationship to God and duties they perform as part of their interpersonal responsibility. According to Islamic jurisprudence, human beings are not entitled to interfere God-human relationship; this brings up the opportunities for religious toleration. On the interpersonal responsibility of humans, Qur'an also has a distinction between inter-communal and intra-communal relations. For Sachedina, the vision of inter-communal relations in Islam is "firmly founded upon the diverse communities' sharing in cross-religious moral concern with egalitarianism, peace and justice."[35] For intra-communal relations, Qur'an sets some normative principles which

27 Tamimi, "Islam and Democracy from Tahtawi to Ghannouchi," p. 54.

28 Khaled Abou El Fadl, *Islam and the Challenge of Democracy*, (Princeton: Princeton University Press, 2004). See also Khaled Abou El Fadl, "Islam and the Challenge of Democratic Commitment," *Fordham International Law Journal*, Volume 27 No 4 (2003-2004), pp. 4-71.

29 El Fadl, *Islam and the Challenge of Democracy*, p. 5.

30 Ahmad S. Mousalli, *The Islamic Quest for Democracy, Pluralism, and Human Rights*, (Tampa: University Press of Florida, 2001).

31 Mousalli, *The Islamic Quest for Democracy, Pluralism, and Human Rights*, p. 6.

32 Mousalli, *The Islamic Quest for Democracy, Pluralism, and Human Rights*, p. 12.

33 Abdul-Aziz Sachedina, *The Role of Islam in the Public Square: Guidance or Governance* (Amsterdam, Amsterdam University Press, 2006). See also: Abdul-Aziz Sachedina, *The Islamic Roots of Democratic Pluralism*, (Oxford: Oxford University Press, 1998).

34 Sachedina, *The Role of Islam in the Public Square: Guidance or Governance*, p. 9.

35 Sachedina, *The Role of Islam in the Public Square: Guidance or Governance*, p. 8.

bound only Muslims. In sum, the universal message of Qur'an, for him, provides a mini-malist and thin description of moral principles for humanity that is very inclusive while the particular Qur'anic message provides a maximalist and thick description of moral language that speaks to only Muslims.[36] This distinction, for Sachedina, opens up the possibilities for democratic pluralism in Islam.

To test the validity of these philosophical/theological views on compatibility of Islam and democracy, some sociological/empirical studies have analyzed the social and political prac-tices of Muslim societies. The main conclusion of these studies is that Islam may facilitate both democratic and totalitarian tendencies depending on which the actors are and in what the social and political conditions they reside.

John Esposito and John Voll, in their seminal study, argue that Islam and democracy are not inherently incompatible, and they can be compatible under certain political conditions.[37] They claim that there are potential democratic resources in the Islamic tradition to develop a democratic discourse. They state that in analyzing Islamic movements, scholars should be attentive to individual political systems and specific historical contexts rather than making broad generalizations. They conclude that moderate Islamic movements, which are more open to compromise with the state, facilitate democratization; and if Islamic groups are al-lowed to compete for votes, they become integral part of the democratic system and facilitate democratization.

Examining radical and cosmopolitan transnational Islamic movements, Peter Mandaville challenges the widely held idea that "transnational Islam is not conducive to discourses of political civility, pluralism and democracy."[38] In his study, he shows both examples of fun-damentalist militant groups (Hizb ut-Tahrir, Al-Muhajiroun, the Jihadis) and cosmopolitan social/educational movements (Gülen Movement, Tariq Ramadan's European Islam). While militant groups centre their attention to the ideal of the Islamic state, moderate groups focus on individual morality and responsibility toward others. For them, the institutional form of the state does not matter if it delivers good governance. He concludes that we observe two kinds of groups side by side: "moderate discourses that produce the kind of social capital that Putnam and others have identified as a cornerstone of civil societies, and groups for whom democratic pluralism represents the greatest of dangers."[39] Although Mandaville successfully presents the diversity of Islamic movements, he does not offer a strong explanation for this variation.

Robert W. Hefner, in his analysis of democratization in Indonesia in 1990s, argues that cul-tural Islamic discourse in Indonesia, both in intellectual and practical level, contributed to democratization in various ways.[40] He analyzes how the discourses of Islamic intellectu-als have influenced the political community in a way to facilitate democratization and to destroy Suharto's authoritarian government. Drawing on Putnam's civic culture approach, Hefner explains the Islamic groups' support for democracy with three factors, which are

---

36 Sachedina, *The Role of Islam in the Public Square: Guidance or Governance*, p. 15.

37 John L. Esposito and John O. Voll, *Islam and Democracy*, (Oxford: Oxford University Press, 1996).

38 Peter Mandeville, "Sufis and Salafis: The Political Discourse of Transnational Islam,'"" In Robert W. Hefner (ed), *Remaking Muslim Politics: Pluralism, Contestation, Democratization,* (Princeton: Princeton University Press, 2005), p. 3. See also Peter Mandaville, *Transnational Muslim Politics: Reimagining the Umma,* (London: Routledge, 2001).

39 Mandaville, "Sufis and Salafis: The Political Discourse of Transnational Islam," p. 322.

40 Robert Hefner, *Civil Islam: Muslims and Democratization in Indonesia,* (Princeton: Princeton University Press, 2000).

the foundations for a working democracy: abundance of civic organizations through which people can develop habits of voluntarism and tolerance, a pluralistic and democratic public culture, and a state willing to protect the rights of the people. He concludes that in Indonesia, the cultural Islamic tradition made the first two possible while authoritarian state of Suharto made the possibility of the third condition very low.

Vali Nasr argues that there is not a generalized answer to the question of whether Islam is compatible with democracy; the answer lies in the participation of Islamic groups into the democratic political institutions.[41] As along as Islamic movements are allowed to compete in elections, they become integrated into the mainstream political institutions of the country. For Islamic movements to become fully democratized, Nasr suggests two more conditions: (1) the military should withdraw from politics formally even if they are still influential over politicians; and (2) an Islamic middle class which gain from economic liberalization should emerge.

Sharing the theoretical premise of the final group of scholars who argue that Islam and liberalism are not necessarily incompatible, I suggest the analysis of the interaction of both textual sources and social and political structures. A full answer requires an empirical inquiry of how Muslim actors interpret the textual sources in responding to the liberalization process. In this direction, drawing on Doug McAdam, Sidney Tarrow, and Charles Tilly's effort to develop a synthetic theory of social movements,[42] I argue that the Islamic movements' engagements with liberalism are shaped by economic and political structures, these movements' own efforts to take advantage of these structures, and the normative repertoires that motivate these movements.[43] In the Gülen movement case, economic and political liberalization provided the movement with the opportunities to increase its influence both in Turkey and abroad. However, this would not have been possible if the leaders of the movement had failed to mobilize the followers in contributing to the movement with their money, time, and energy. This mobilization would have been very difficult, if not impossible, if the movement had not revived the normative repertoires that were inherent in the Islamic resources; and the integration with the liberal structures was not beneficial to the interests of the movement. In line with Jose Casanova[44], I argue that the end result of developing a liberalism-friendly Islamic

---

41   Vali Nasr, "The Rise of Muslim Democracy," *Journal of Democracy*, Volume 16 No 2, (April 2005), pp. 13-27.

42   Doug McAdam, Sidney Tarrow, and Charles Tilly, *Dynamics of Contention* (New York: Cambridge University Press, 2001). McAdam, Tarrow, and Tilly attempt to combine three mainstream social movement theories: opportunity structures, resource mobilization, and framing processes. For a work on opportunity structures, see Herbert Kitschelt, "Political Opportunity Structures and Political Protest: Anti-Nuclear Movements in Four Democracies," *British Journal of Political Science,* Vol. 16 (1986), pp. 57-85. For a work on resource mobilization, see John D. McCarthy and Mayer N. Zald, *The Trend of Social Movements in America: Professionalization and Resource Mobilization* (Morristown, NJ: General Learning Press, 1973); and John D. McCarthy and Mayer N. Zald, "Resource Mobilization and Social Movements: A Partial Theory," *American Journal of Sociology*, Vol.82 (1977), pp. 1212-41. For a work on framing processes, see Bert Klandermans, "The Social Construction of Protest and Multiorganizational Fields," In *Frontiers in Social Movement Theory,* edited by Aldon Morris and Carol McClurg Mueller (New Haven and London: Yale University Press, 1992).

43   Developing a synthetic approach in explaining the variation among Turkish Islamic groups with respect to their responses to globalization, Ahmet Kuru argues that Islamic movements' attitudes toward globalization is determined by two variables: domestic and international opportunity structures, and movements' normative frameworks. Kuru aptly synthesizes structural and cultural approaches, however his analysis lack the mobilizing structures that the movements use in increasing their efficacy. See: Kuru, "Globalization and Diversification of Islamic Movements."

44   Jose Casanova, *Public Religions in the Modern World,* (Chicago: University of Chicago Press, 1994).

interpretation was two-fold: (1) enriching the public sphere and civil society; (2) and integrating the religious people to the political structures of liberal democratic regime.

In the following paragraphs, I will examine the Gülen movement's engagement with economic and political liberalization in Turkey respectively. In each section, I will first describe the structural liberal transformations that the movement was encircled. Then I will show how the movement used these structures in increasing its sphere of influence in Turkey and abroad. Finally, I will explain how the movement used the Islamic repertoire both in organizing its followers and reinterpreting liberalization in the light of an Islamic discourse.

Economic Liberalization

Structural Transformations

Systematic integration of the Turkish economy into the global market started after the 1983 elections when Turgut Özal became the prime minister. Being in close contact with the key international institutions such as the World Bank, the International Monetary Fund (IMF), and the Organization for Economic Cooperation and Development, Turkey experienced a radical structural transformation in the economic realm.[45] Throughout the 1980s, trade became liberalized, the Turkish lira gained convertibility against the foreign currency after the removal of ban on foreign currency. Liberalization was extended to financial markets in the late 1980s and throughout the 1990s.[46] Turkey transferred new technologies in the 1980s and 1990s, modernized its infrastructure especially in the area of telecommunications. The government gradually privatized state-owned enterprises. In the 1990s, the number of privately-owned industrial enterprises, educational institutions, radios, and televisions increased tremendously.

Economic liberalization efforts, especially in the financial realm, continued after Özal's death. Thanks to Turkey's loan agreements with the IMF throughout the late 1990s and 2000s, Turkey adopted an institutional structure, which was integrated into the global liberal economic system. The retreat of the state from the economic life, and incentives for economic investments allowed the emergence of new economic actors from the periphery. These actors, who felt themselves confident to penetrate domestic and international markets, challenged the monopoly of mainstream businessmen who have revolved around Turkish Industrialists and Businessmen Association (TUSIAD). The emergence of new social forces that constituted an alternative to state-supported bourgeoisie opened new opportunities for the building of a new social and economic make-up which constituted more diverse and competitive social and political realm within which civil society can flourish in Turkey.

---

45   This transformation was not restricted to the economic realm. Özal also had a great impact on Turkey's political and social transformation. See Ihsan Dağı, "Human Rights, Democratization, and the European Community in Turkish Politics: The Özal Years, 1983-1987," *Middle Eastern Studies*, Vol. 37, No 1 (2001); and Berdal Aral, "Dispensing with Tradition?: The Özal Decade, 1983-1993," *Middle Eastern Studies*, Vol. 37, No 1, (January 2001), pp. 72-88.

46   Özal was a staunch believer in economic liberalization. He went so further as to violate the rule of law in implementing liberal policies; because these policies were difficult to implement in the existence of strong étatism in Turkey. For a balanced evaluation of Özal's economic reforms see Ziya Öniş, "Turgut Özal and His Economic Legacy: Turkish Neo-Liberalism in Critical Perspective," *Middle Eastern Studies*, Volume 40 Number 4, (July 2004), pp. 113-34.

Mobilizing Resources

The followers of the Gülen movement, along with many other Islamic groups, took part in this new economic transformation. Under the favourable conditions of a gradually liberalizing economic environment, they established new enterprises in different economic sectors, from finance to tourism, from media to education.[47] In the financial sector, the followers of the movement established Asya Finans in 1996, which changed its name to Bank Asya in 2006, as a private finance house in Turkey.[48] As of July 2007, it has 117 domestic branches. It was established in accordance with the principles of interest-free banking. In its constitution, Bank Asya states its two fundamental objectives as "to develop new interest free banking products" and "to take products that are already being offered at conventional banks and adapt them in such a way as to fit into the system of interest-free banking."[49] By offering similar services that conventional banks offer, such as internet banking, telephone banking, credit cards, and ATM and POS terminals, Bank Asya competes with conventional banks. However, at the same time, it strives to offer a banking service, which is congruent with the Islamic teachings. Most of its work principles (as declared in its mission statement) are derived from Islamic ethics: honesty, respect, and trust. Even describing "innovation" as one of its work principles, Asya Finans quotes from Prophet Muhammad: "We feel that 'two days spent in the same way' are in loss."[50]

The movement also has enterprises in the tourism sector. Asya Kızılcahamam Resort and SPA is a five-star thermal springs facility owned by Bank Asya. It was opened in 2004 in a small town in the Ankara region. Located in a 100 acres of land, the facility has a five-star thermal hotel, almost 400 luxury condominiums, a cultural and convention centre, a shopping and entertainment centre, a health and beauty centre, and thermal spring pools. It is considered to be the second best in thermal tourism in the world.[51] Asya Hotel attracts many Turkish tourists whose socio-economic level is high enough to have an expensive vacation. Many of the customers of Asya Hotel are religious people; thus Asya Hotel offers an alternative to many other hotels in Turkey. For example, the hotel offers separate swimming pools for women and men.[52] Unusual to other hotels in Turkey, the facility has a mosque. In my interviews, many customers of the hotel told me that they were happy to find a place where they could have a vacation without sacrificing their religious values.[53] This is also what the managers of the facility stated as their objective in running this facility.[54]

In addition to its financial institution and hotel, the Gülen movement also has media outlets.

---

47 Although these corporations do not belong to Fethullah Gülen himself or any organization associated with him, the owners of these corporations fund the activities that Fethullah Gülen encourages.

48 "Private finance house" is the name given to the banks that offer interest-free banking to their customers. Asya Finans was not the first of its kind in Turkey. It was established as the 6th private finance house.

49 The objectives of Asya Finans are available http://www.bankasya.com.tr/en/hakkimizda/. Last accessed on September 22, 2007.

50 See http://www.bankasya.com.tr/en/hakkimizda/calisma_prensipleri.jsp Last accessed on September 22, 2007.

51 "Başbakan: Dünyayı gezdim böyle bir tesis görmedim" ["Prime Minister: I have visited all over the world but never seen such a facility"], *Zaman*, 3 June 2004.

52 There are also some other hotels in Turkey which offers the same opportunities. For a study on Caprice Hotel which is the first of its kind see: Mücahit Bilici, "İslam'ın Bronzlaşan Yüzü: Caprice Hotel Örnek Olayı [Tanning Face of Islam: The Case of the Caprice Hotel," In *İslam'ın Yeni Kamusal Yüzleri* [New Public Faces of Islam], edited by Nilüfer Göle, (İstanbul: Metis, 2000).

53 The author's interviews with Asya Finans customers in Kızılcahamam, Ankara, 30 June-1 July 2005.

54 The author's interviews with Asya Finans managerial team, 30 June-1 July 2005.

Zaman newspaper and Samanyolu television (STV) are the two most important enterprises of the movement in the media sector. Zaman was established in 1986. It is now among top three national newspapers in Turkey with an average of a 500.000 daily circulation. It also has international editions published in more than 15 foreign countries including the United States. STV was established in 1993. Zaman and STV have spread the movement's perspectives on various social and political issues. Through many commentaries and programs, they have validated the movement's conciliatory rhetoric with the state and different social segments.[55] They also aim to promote moral values. Zaman has a number of weekly publications such as Ailem (My Family), Akademi (Academy), and Arkadaşım (My Friend) which aim to increase religious awareness. Along the same lines, STV produces movies that are coloured with religious and spiritual messages. However, these movies are not produced in the format of traditional religious sermons, which generally have transmitted the religious messages in a didactic way.[56] This strengthens STV's competitiveness against other TV stations, which in turn increases its income from commercials.

Probably the most important sector for the Gülen movement is education. The movement started building educational institutions in Turkey in the 1980s. The first educational institutions were tutor centres (dershane) to prepare students for the university entrance examinations. Later on, the movement opened private high schools with English as the language of instruction. Today, the movement has at least one high school in almost each major city in Turkey. Since the 1990s, the movement has opened schools abroad.[57] These schools have offered a quality education to their students; they became among the best schools in many countries. For instance, students of the movement's schools have won several prizes in international science contests.[58] Although many of these schools require their students to pay their own tuition, they are basically supported by Turkish businessmen. The tuitions in many developing countries are very low. Furthermore, many students who are from the less

---

55 For a study on the roots of Gülen's conciliatory rhetoric see Yasin Aktay, "Diaspora and Stability: Constitutive Elements in a Body of Knowledge," in Turkish Islam and the Secular State: The Gülen Movement (Syracuse, NY: Syracuse University Press, 2003), edited by M. Hakan Yavuz and John L. Esposito, pp. 131-54.

56 Three series produced by STV are worth mentioning. 1. *Büyük Buluşma* [Grand Meeting]: In this TV series, people are questioned about their life immediately after their death. The conscience questions people's desires, feelings, and the actions in the world and shows the misdeeds. This questioning somehow represents the judgment day. 2. *Beşinci Boyut* [Fifth Dimension]: In Islam it is believed that martyr are not aware of their death. In this series, a martyr helps people to make appropriate decisions when they find themselves in trouble. This series emphasizes the allegiance to God and recommends forbearance against the troubles that peoples confront. 3. *Sırlar Dünyası* [The World of Secrets]: It dramatizes real mysterious stories that have religious and spiritual dimensions.

57 For a comprehensive work on Gülen schools around the world see Toktamış Ateş, Eser Karakaş and İlber Ortaylı, Barış Köprüleri: Dünyaya Açılan Türk Okulları, [Bridges of Peace: Turkish Schools Opening to the World], İstanbul: Ufuk Kitap, 2005. For a study that focuses on Gülen schools in Central Asia see: Bayram Balcı, Orta Asya'da İslam Misyonerleri: Fethullah Gülen Okulları [Muslim Missionaries in the Central Asia: Fethullah Gülen Schools], İstanbul: İletişim Yayınları, 2005; Thomas Michel, "Fethullah Gülen as Educator," in Turkish Islam and the Secular State: The Gülen Movement, edited by M. Hakan Yavuz and John L. Esposito, pp. 69-84. (Syracuse, NY: Syracuse University Press, 2003).

58 See Ahmet T. Kuru, "Fethullah Gülen's Search for a Middle Way between Modernity and Muslim Tradition," in *Turkish Islam and the Secular State: The Gülen Movement*, edited by M. Hakan Yavuz and John L. Esposito,(Syracuse, NY: Syracuse University Press, 2003), p. 120. Some scholars criticize these schools as offering a heavy science curriculum while ignoring social sciences and humanities. For an example, see Süleyman Seyfi Öğün, "Türk Okullarına Dair Gözlem ve Tespitler [Some Observations and Points on Turkish Schools]," In *Barış Köprüleri: Dünyaya Açılan Türk Okulları*, [Bridges of Peace: Turkish Schools Opening to the World], edited by Toktamış Ateş, Eser Karakaş and İlber Ortaylı, (İstanbul: Ufuk Kitap, 2005), pp. 99-104.

developed regions in their countries are financially supported by these schools. This provides the integration of lower social groups into the political system in those countries. In purely economic terms, many of these schools do not make a profit. The motive that mobilizes the sponsors of these schools is a mixture of patriotism and religious pietism. These schools generally offer Turkish as a secondary foreign language along with English and the native language. Islam is not taught in these schools, but the teachers educate the students with universal moral and ethical values.[59]

Normative Repertoires

Although the Gülen movement has benefited from the opportunities that economic liberalization offered, it has also tried to transform it in at least two ways so as to make it congruent with the Islamic worldview. First, the movement has used market forces not only for capital accumulation and profit maximization, but also to create a new social and economic environment for Muslims who wanted to practice their faith in an era of rapid globalization. The movement created new social milieus where religious piety meets with modern capitalist economic system. For example, Bank Asya's modern banking services are both compatible with religious teachings and contemporary economic principles. Private hospitals that the movement owns pay a special attention to religious sensitivities in providing their service.[60] The movement's schools have focused on science and thus contributed to bridging the gap between religion and science in Turkish society.[61] The businessmen running these economic enterprises have found innovative ways to reconcile Islamic teachings and liberal market rules within the domestic legal framework as in the example of Bank Asya. The movement has also invented new entertainment and socialization patterns that meet Islamic ethical standards. As previously noted, Asya Hotel's five-star facilities, for example, watch for the religious demands of their customers while offering a first class vacation service. Moreover, the movement's firms have produced[62] new forms of TV and radio programs,[63] drama performances,[64] literary works,[65] and music CDs.[66] The movement also produced an alternative social environment among university students for the purpose of reconciling mod-

---

59 See Bekim Agai, "The Gülen Movement's Islamic Ethic of Education," in Turkish Islam and the Secular State: The Gülen Movement, edited by M. Hakan Yavuz and John L. Esposito, pp. 48-68. (Syracuse, NY: Syracuse University Press, 2003); and Michel, "Fethullah Gülen as Educator.".

60 Author's observations at Konya Vakif Hospital in June 2001.

61 Ali Bulaç sees these schools as Turkey's sole contribution to the globalization process especially for two reasons: upbringing of a new elite who is in peace with religion and the expansion of Turkish language worldwide. See: Ali Bulaç, "Küresel Bir Açılım Olarak Türk Okulları [Turkish Schools as a Global Opening]," In Barış Köprüleri: Dünyaya Açılan Türk Okulları, [Bridges of Peace: Turkish Schools Opening to the World], edited by Toktamış Ateş, Eser Karakaş and İlber Ortaylı, (İstanbul: Ufuk Kitap, 2005), pp. 181-98.

62 In my interviews, many followers emphasized Said Nursi's point that there was enough legitimate room in Islam for joy. See Said Nursi, Sözler [Words], (İstanbul: Sözler Publications, 1977), p. 30.

63 STV and the movement's radio stations (such as Burç FM and the Dünya Radyo) feature music and entertainment programs that watch for the religious sensitivities of the audience.

64 Ankara Sanat Evi (Ankara Art House), for example, is a drama group which performs its plays in different cities both in Turkey and abroad. The group was in the US during 10-15 January 2006. They performed dramas in different cities of the US including Phoenix, Seattle, San Francisco, and Denver. The play was both amusing and colored with spiritual messages (Author's observation in Phoenix, Arizona on 14 January 2006 during the group's performance).

65 For example, Yağmur is a literary journal published by Journalists and Writers Foundation.

66 For example, a number of musicians produced music CDs from Fethullah Gülen's poems. They include Reşit Muhtar, Bilal Ercan, Ahmet Özhan, Ertuğrul Erkişi, and Metin Haboğlu.

ern science, religious pietism, and social activism.[67] The movement has also striven to create its own intellectual elite.[68]

Some scholars see the creation of new entertainment and socialization patterns as a secularization trend in the movement. For example, Hakan Yavuz argues that in the existence of alternative public spaces, the Islamic movements in Turkey experience a process of "internal secularization of Islam."[69] However, it should be noted that these new entertainment and socialization patterns are efforts to meet the modern challenges with an Islamic orientation. The motive that propels the followers to open alternative sites is "religious" rather than "profane." Furthermore, Gülen, when talking about the activities of the movement, generally emphasizes the religious sources of its world-wide activism.[70]

Second, the Gülen movement has embraced the capitalist system without necessarily being capitalist. Two concepts are particularly important in the movement's effort to transform the "homo economicus" of capitalism: aspiration (*himmet*)[71] and emigration (*hicret*). From the beginning, Gülen has encouraged his followers not to be passive subjects; instead, he has encouraged them to do their best for the spread of the Islamic message. He has consistently reminded followers that they have to use all of their potential to spread the Islamic message. In mobilizing his followers in this regard, the concept of aspiration (*himmet*) has played an important role. Gülen defines aspiration (*himmet*) as follows:

"Aspiration (*himmet*) is the attitude of a passenger of the Right (*Hak yolcusu*), who dedicates all the moments of his life to acquire for the sake of God. He is ready to renounce his material, even his spiritual expectations, and career goals for this aim. He thinks only of Him [God], watches for His forgiveness, and prefers His sake over all other attainments. [...] Aspiration (*himmet*) also means to strive, to endeavour, to work hard, and to struggle for the fulfilment of a duty."[72]

The discourse of aspiration motivated the followers to give their property, time, and energy to the activities of the movement. In his speeches, Gülen weaves this concept with examples from Islamic tradition up to modern times. Stories about the Prophet Muhammad and his companions have an important mobilizing force among the followers of the movement. Businessmen among the movement's followers finance the establishment of the schools abroad, pay the salaries of the teachers, and finance the establishment of new institutions. Not only do the businessmen but also other followers and even students contribute to the

---

67 The author's observations and interviews in Ankara in 2001 and in Istanbul in 2002.

68 *Zaman* daily, *Aksiyon* weekly, forums like Journalists and Writers Foundation, and the movement's print houses (such as Nil Publications), all have contributed to the creation and performance of this new elite. For a study on the Gülen movement and the emergence of a new elite see Yilmaz, "Ijtihad and Tajdid."

69 Yavuz, *Islamic Political Identity in Turkey*.

70 Fethullah Gülen's recent speeches can be reached at http://www.herkul.org. For one of his recent talks that elaborates this point see: Fethullah Gülen, "*Himmet*: Teveccüh, İnfak ve Gayret [Assiduity: Favour, Charity, and Perseverance]," Herkül, 12 December 2005, available at: http://www.herkul.org/kiriktesti/index.php?article_id=2720. Last accessed on September 22, 2007.

71 A note on the translation of the word "*himmet*": It is difficult to find an exact word in English that reflects the meaning of "*himmet*." The meaning of "*himmet*" includes concentrating on a cause with an extreme energy and zeal; giving one's property for the realization of that cause, etc. I thank to Alan Godlas who suggested me "aspiration" for the translation of the word "*himmet*."

72 Fethullah Gülen, "*Himmet*: Teveccüh, İnfak ve Gayret [Assiduity: Favour, Charity, and Perseverance]," Herkül, 12 December 2005, available at: http://www.herkul.org/kiriktesti/index.php?article_id=2720. Last accessed on September 22, 2007.

movement financially. For the followers, the motive to earn more is not to accumulate personal wealth but to give more charity in the service of God.[73]

The concept of "emigration" (hicret) is another resource for the mobilization of the followers in transforming the image of "homo economicus." Gülen has strongly recommended his followers to emigrate from one city to another or to other countries. For him, he/she who emigrates for the supreme cause will feel more responsibility for the cause; and will arrange his/her life according to his/her spiritual principles.[74] He argues that emigration has historically been a precondition for the establishment of great civilizations. He reminds his followers that Islam's early expansion became possible after early Muslims migrated from Mecca to Medina.[75] Many followers of the movement have moved to different places around the world without knowing what would meet them there. Teachers for the schools abroad are recruited from the graduates of Turkey's most prestigious universities.[76] Although many of these graduates can find well-paid jobs in Turkey, they often choose to immigrate to other countries, including poor and undeveloped ones, working under very difficult conditions.[77]

The activities of the followers demonstrate that they have transformed the image of the self-interested capitalist individual within the movement. Is it irrational to sacrifice one's own interests for the cause and community? Gülen's answer to this question is "absolutely no." He argues that the activities of his followers "stem from the differences between the world of our values and of theirs."[78] Altruism for Gülen makes believers happy both in this world and hereafter. It not only helps to get a better place in the hereafter, it also ties them to the world.[79] In short, the movement constructs a different form of rationality than the one developed within the liberal tradition.

Throughout this section, I have attempted to show how the Gülen movement succeeded in forming new kinds of social and economic practices and ethics, which are compatible with economic liberalization, while at the same time being faithful to Islamic principles.

Political Liberalization

Structural Transformations

In the 1980s and 1990s, Turkey's liberalization reforms also penetrated the political realm. Significantly, a number of political restrictions which were enacted after the 1980 coup were

---

73 The author's interviews with the followers in Ankara in 2001 and in İstanbul in 2002.

74 Fethullah Gülen, "Mukaddes Göç [Sacred Emigration]," Sızıntı, Volume 7 No. 81 (October 1985).

75 Gülen brings examples from the Islamic history. The most sacred emigration for him was Prophet Muhammad's emigration from Mecca to Medina. He also adds that other prophets had to emigrate to spread their message. See Gülen, "Mukaddes Göç."

76 The most prominent ones are Boğaziçi and ODTÜ universities. The author's interviews with the followers in Ankara in 2001 and in İstanbul in 2002.

77 Fethullah Gülen, "Bu hareket devlete alternatif mi? [Is this movement an alternative to the state?]," Herkül, 14 November 2005, available at: http://www.herkul.org/kiriktesti/index.php?article_id=2418 Last accessed on September 22, 2007.

78 Fethullah Gülen, "Fedakarlıkta Mantığın Ölçüsü [The Limits of Rationality in Altrusim]," Zaman, 10 February 2006.

79 Gülen asserts that the real rationality is the one that considers both this world and the hereafter. Paying attention to the difference of this kind of rationality, he quotes from a previous Islamic scholar, Hasan Basrî: "If you had seen the companions of the Prophet, you would think that they were mad. If they had seen you they would doubt that you were Muslims." See Gülen, "Fedakarlıkta Mantığın Ölçüsü."

abolished. In the Özal years, the parliament abolished the 141st, 142nd, and 163rd articles of the Turkish penal code, which forbade ideological advocacy of communism and religious movements. The global surge of liberalism after the Cold War had a remarkable impact on Turkey. Although Turkey had statist politicians in the 1990s, liberalization still continued. Along with other global influences, Turkey's bid for European Union membership has also promoted liberalism in the country.

Under these circumstances, Turkey implemented several liberalizing reforms throughout the 1990s: Some restrictions on the use of Kurdish language were removed; private broadcasting companies have ended the state's monopoly over broadcasting; limitations on the political participation by trade unions, academicians, and students were eased; and a Parliamentary Human Rights Commission were established.[80] Liberalizing reforms reached its culmination point between 2002 and 2005 when Turkey worked towards getting candidacy status from the European Union.[81]

These structural changes led the emergence of a vibrant civil society in Turkey in the last two decades. Although civil society organizations were mostly under the control of the state until then, they got an autonomous position in 1990s and 2000s and they represented various social groups which had not been represented in the civil society earlier. As Augustus Richard Norton argues, the civil society constituted a public space "where a mélange of associations, clubs, guilds, syndicates, federations, unions, parties, and groups come together to provide a buffer between state and citizen."[82] Norton assumes that "a vital and autonomous civil society is a necessary condition for democracy;"[83] because it counterweights the power of the state, dilutes state control over society, and advances societal interests against the dominant elites.

Mobilizing Resources

The political liberalization of Turkey has offered new opportunities to the Gülen movement. The movement picked up these opportunities in at least three ways. First, the movement found a medium through which it could spread its message to the masses. Both Zaman and STV have been instrumental in this regard. The movement has also founded the Journalists and Writers Foundation (JWF) to get involved in the public debates.[84] Founded in 1994, the JWF has three platforms through which it involves in the public debates: the Abant Platform[85], the

---

80 Ergun Özbudun and Serap Yazıcı, *Democratizing Reforms in Turkey*, (İstanbul: TESEV Publications, 2004).

81 For a comprehensive analysis of the democratization reforms in this period see: Özbudun and Yazıcı, *Democratizing Reforms*. The reforms implemented in this period not only increased the opportunities for political participation of Islamic groups, but also they granted new rights to non-Muslim religious groups. The third reform laws package which went into force on 9 August 2002 recognized the right of community foundations (meaning non-Muslim foundations) to own immovable properties and to dispose of them freely. The sixth reform package which went into force on 19 July 2003 recognized the right of non-Muslim communities to build places of worship subject to the approval of the competent administrative authorities (Özbudun and Yazıcı, *Democratizing Reforms in Turkey*).

82 Augustus Richard Norton, "Introduction," In Augustus Richard Norton (ed), *Civil Society in the Middle East, Volume 1*, (Leiden: EJ Brill, 1995), p. 7.

83 Norton, "Introduction," p. 9.

84 See Etga Uğur, "Political Culture, Civil Society, and Public Religion: Musings on the Gülen Movement" Paper Presented In *Second Middle East and Central Asia Politics, Economy, and Society Conference (MECA)*, University of Utah, (September 2004); and Etga Uğur, "Civic Islam in the Public Sphere: The Gülen Movement, Civil Society, and Social Capital in Turkey," Paper Presented In *Second International Conference on Islam*, University of Wisconsin-Madison, (March 2006).

85 "Abant" is a city in Northwestern Turkey. The Foundation organized workshops first in this city.

Dialogue Eurasia Platform, and the Intercultural Dialogue Platform. The Abant Platform organizes annual workshops[86] in which leading intellectuals are invited to debate certain political and social issues. Since 1998, the JWF has organized nine workshops on several topics including Islam and secularism; religion, state, and society; pluralism and social compromise; and war and democracy.[87] The Dialogue Eurasia Platform aims to increase the interactions between the peoples of Eurasia, particularly Turkey and the former Soviet Republics. This platform publishes a bilingual quarterly journal, DA, in Russian and Turkish. The platform also organizes annual workshops known as "Dialogue Eurasia Meetings" through which writers and journalists of Eurasian countries get together.[88] The Intercultural Dialogue platform aims to increase interaction and dialogue between different faiths in Turkey as well as in the world. It also organizes events, which bring representatives of different religions together. In sum, through involvement in the public debates, the Gülen movement has increased its influence in both domestic and international realms.

Second, within the democratic environment in Turkey, the Gülen movement has gained the support of certain politicians to obviate the bureaucratic elite's efforts to inactivate the movement. Although it has not openly supported any specific political party, the competitive nature of democratic politics provided the Gülen movement (which has a few millions followers) with an opportunity to gain the support of several political parties since 1994. Gülen himself met with several politicians including former Presidents Turgut Özal and Süleyman Demirel, former Prime Ministers Tansu Çiller, Mesut Yılmaz and Bülent Ecevit, former Ministers Hikmet Çetin and Deniz Baykal. In his meetings with the politicians, Gülen found the opportunity to express his views and also gave the message that his movement had nothing to do with any activity that was against the state. Gülen met with all sorts of politicians who represent different views. Many of these parties have shied away from taking a hostile attitude towards Gülen and his movement.

For example, when the secular mass media in Turkey launched a major attack on Gülen in June 1999, accusing him of possessing a hidden agenda to take over the state, many politicians during these days refrained from speaking out against the movement. Furthermore, several politicians including the president, the prime minister, several ministers, and the leaders of opposition parties gave support to Gülen at a time when it would be easier to criticize him.[89]

---

86 The foundation organized two workshops in 2004.

87 For more information about the activities of the foundation see its website at: http://www.gyv.org.tr/. The themes of the nine Abant workshops were as follows: Islam and secularism in 1998; religion, state, and society in 1999; democratic rule of law in 2000; pluralism and social compromise in 2001; globalization in 2002; war and democracy in 2003; Islam, secularism, and democracy; The Turkish experience in 2004; Culture, Identity, and Religion in Turkey's EU Integration Process in 2004; New Perspectives on Education in 2005. The Abant workshops gained an international character since 2004. In 2004 JWF organized the workshops in Washington, DC, and Brussels; and the 10th workshop will be organized in Paris in March 2006.

88 For further information see the platform's website at: http://www.daplatform.org/default.asp?caid=78 Last accessed on September 22, 2007.

89 For example, when asked his views about the issue, President Süleyman Demirel said that "I do not want to make any comment without any verdict of the court." "Cumhurbaşkanı Süleyman Demirel: Yargısız İnfaz Yapmayın [President Süleyman Demirel: No comment without verdict]," Zaman, 21 June 1999. Prime Minister Bülent Ecevit said that "The government officials who has the these kinds of documents should have given them to the Premiership Prosecution and Coordination Committee or their ministries instead of infiltrating them to the media. This situation is not compatible with the solemnity of the state ("Başbakan Ecevit: Nerede Ciddiyet? [Prime Minister Ecevit: Where is solemnity]", Zaman, 23 June 1999). The leader of the Grand Union Party Muhsin Yazıcıoğlu stated that some

Furthermore, several politicians supported the Gülen movement's international activities, especially its schools abroad. Presidents Turgut Özal and Süleyman Demirel wrote credentials to the leaders of the countries abroad to facilitate the opening of new schools.[90] Turgut Özal visited Turkish schools in Central Asian countries during his official visit.[91] Süleyman Demirel also visited the schools in Central Asia; he opened the Süleyman Demirel University, which was founded by the initiatives of the movement's followers, in Kazakhstan with his Kazak counterpart Nursultan Nazarbayev.[92] Former Prime Minister Bülent Ecevit, after his visit to movement's schools in Albania, even went so far as to say that "I know they [implying anti-Gülen groups within the state] will get angry at me but I would like to congratulate these schools."[93] In sum, liberal political reforms that have strengthened Turkey's democratic structure favoured the Gülen movement. The movement had the opportunity to gain the support of the politicians. In the absence of a democratic liberal environment, it would have been more difficult for the movement to have amicable relations with the governments.

Finally, the liberalizing environment in the 1980s and 1990s provided the Gülen movement with the opportunities to expand its influence globally. The spread of English learning in the 1990s through newly-formed high schools,[94] communication technologies, private radio and television stations eased reaching to the international opportunities.[95] The collapse of communism and its global effects in the 1990s also facilitated this process. The Gülen movement now is a transnational movement, which has about 500 high schools in more than 90 countries. The movement leads several worldwide interfaith dialogue activities, as well.[96]

Normative Repertoires

Although the Gülen movement has embraced political liberalization, its understanding of such notions as democracy and liberty is somewhat different from that the liberal philosophy suggests. This difference comes from the movement's interpretation of Islam, the movement's

---

people within the state wanted to press over the Prime Minister Ecevit to get concessions from him; these concessions for Yazıcıoğlu would be used to press over religious groups in Turkey ("Ecevit'i sıkıştırıp taviz koparacaklar [They will press Ecevit to get concessions]", *Zaman*, 23 June 1999). The Minister of Public Works and Settlement Koray Aydın said that "Gülen's ideas should live. If Gülen is to be punished, who would not?" ("Bayındırlık ve İskan Bakanı Koray Aydın: Gülen Çizgisi Yaşamalı [The Minister of Public Works and Settlement Koray Aydın: Gülen's ideas should live]", *Zaman* 25 June 1999).

90 To see two examples written by former Presidents Turgut Özal and Süleyman Demirel see: Ateş et. al., *Barış Köprüleri*, appendix.

91 Hulusi Turgut, "Özal son gezisine okullar için çıktı [Özal's last visit was for the schools]," *Yeni Yüzyıl*, 16 January 1998.

92 Hulusi Turgut, "Fethullah Gülen ve Okullar [Fethullah Gülen and Schools]," *Yeni Yüzyıl*, 22 January 1998.

93 Bülent Ecevit, "Türk Okullarının Türk Dili ve Türkiye'ye Katkısı [The Contributions of Turkish Schools to Turkey and Turkish Language]," In *Barış Köprüleri: Dünyaya Açılan Türk Okulları*, [Bridges of Peace: Turkish Schools Opening to the World], edited by Toktamış Ateş, Eser Karakaş and İlber Ortaylı, (İstanbul: Ufuk Kitap, 2005), p. 25.

94 In the Özal years English instruction became widespread in Turkey. Özal led the establishment of new high schools which specialize on English language instruction. Before the establishment of these schools, English language was thought at a number of high schools established by the foreigners. These new schools were called as Anatolian High Schools, implying the spread of English language instruction throughout Anatolia.

95 Ahmet T Kuru contends that English instruction and synergy between educators and businessmen are the two resources that have helped the Gülen movement to benefit from the international opportunity structures. See Kuru, "Globalization and Diversification of Islamic Movements," p. 262.

96 For example Rumi Forum is a Washington-based organization which works for interfaith and intercivilizational dialogue. See its website at: http://www.rumiforum.org/.

motive to expand the Islamic message of tolerance and morality, and the socio-historical conditions of Turkey where the movement has matured. Three of these differences deserve to be mentioned: (1) extensive emphasis on dialogue and reconciliation, (2) enriching democracy by adding a spiritual dimension, and (3) the idea of restrained individualism.

First, the Gülen movement's emphasis on dialogue and reconciliation have some differences from the notion of pluralistic society that liberal democracy suggests. Gülen's conception of politics sees the society as an organism, and this approach aims to achieve harmony among different segments of the society. Dialogue and reconciliation are used to eliminate conflict in society. While identifying the virtues of the individuals that would constitute the ideal society, Gülen writes that in the ideal society individuals would "treat the others so gently so that they search for the paths to the universal peace. They do not fight with others; rather they fight with their own flaws, their own dilemmas so that they clean themselves."[97] Gülen believes that treating others in a good manner will contribute for the elimination of conflicts: "Approach unbelievers so gently that their envy and hatred melt away. Like a Messiah, revive people with your breath."[98] Liberal democracy does not aim to eliminate the conflicting issues; rather it focuses on the ways to manage these conflicts.[99] However, the movement's dialogue activities since the mid-1990s show that the notion of reconciliation has not been perceived in ignoring differences; dialogue activities since 1990s have aimed at living together with the existing commonalities and differences. The movement gradually changed its discourse from reconciliation to tolerance, which is much more compatible with the liberal understanding of pluralism.[100]

Second, Gülen thinks that democracy should be enriched in a way to meet the needs of believers. On the one hand, he makes a distinction between religion and political regimes: "One should remember that the former [Islam] is a divine and heavenly religion, while the latter [democracy] is a form of government developed by humans."[101] For him, the principles that are related to the state administration constitute only 5% of the religion while the remaining 95% are related to the articles of faith, the pillars of Islam, and the moral principles of religion.[102] His view on democracy is shaped by this distinction. Gülen says that "In Islam, which is based on the Qur'an and the sayings of the Prophet, there is neither absolute monarchy nor classical democracy as known in the West."[103] Thus, the type of government in Islam is determined by the historical, social, and political conditions. Democracy, for Gülen, is the best possible system in the contemporary era.[104]

On the other hand, however, he contends that there are many different types of democracies, such as social democracy and liberal democracy; and that Muslims should develop a kind of

---

97 Fethullah Gülen, "Buhran Ufku ve Beklentilerimiz [The Scope of Crisis and Our Expectations]," *Işığın Göründüğü Ufuk* [The Horizon that Light Appears], (İzmir: Nil, 2000).

98 Quoted in Ali Ünal and Alphonse Williams, *Advocate of Dialogue: Fethullah Gülen*, Fairfax, VI: Fountain, 2000), p. 193.

99 For example see: Robert Dahl, *Polyarchy: Participation and Opposition* (New Haven: Yale University Press, 1971)

100 I owe this point to Mustafa Özgür Tuna.

101 Fethullah Gülen, (translated by Zeki Sarıtoprak and Ali Ünal) "An Interview with Fethullah Gülen," *Muslim World*, Volume 95 Number 3, (July 2005), p. 451.

102 Ibid., p. 451. Having such a view on Islam and political life makes the Gülen movement less political. Gülen states that the exaggeration of the political dimension of Islam is very harmful to the religion. Ibid., p. 452.

103 Ibid., p. 450.

104 Fethullah Gülen, "A Comparative Approach to Islam and Democracy," *SAIS Review*, Volume 21 No 2, pp. 133-38.

democracy which would support them in reaching spiritual satisfaction. Such a democracy, which he calls "democracy with spiritual dimensions" (mana boyutlu demokrasi), respects human rights and freedoms, watches for religious liberty, prepares necessary conditions for its citizens to experience their beliefs, and helps the citizens to fulfil their spiritual needs.[105]

Finally, although Gülen movement's understanding of individual liberty approves of the basic rights that classical liberal theory emphasizes (namely, liberty, life, property), Gülen criticizes liberal individualism in two respects. First, according to Gülen, having an unrestricted individualism in Islam is impossible. Individualism gains a negative connotation along the lines of selfishness and lack of care for social matters.[106] In his writings, Gülen depicts a typology of an individual who is restricted by moral values.[107] Gülen argues that "humans are either both free with no acceptance of any moral values and rebellious with no moral criteria, or they are servants who are dependent on God and seriously obedient to His commands."[108] Individuals that are servants of God should not be enslaved by worldly belongings, considerations of selfish interests, greed for more material earnings, and different kinds of material desires that destroys morality.[109] Gülen's followers are self-disciplined individuals who follow very strict rules in their daily life. Their difference from others can easily be noticed in their consumption behaviours, entertainment habits, commitment to religious practices, and involvement in community services.[110] Although the Gülen movement criticizes absolute individualism and idealizes a moral-based individual, this attitude does not translate into limiting other individuals' lifestyles in the society.[111]

Second, the movement does not agree with liberalism's preference of the individual over the collectivity. Gülen has an organic view of society; according to which humans should dedicate themselves to the well-being of the community. However, as Mücahit Bilici states, Gülen's view on the state is anti-anarchist rather than statist.[112] This leads Gülen to attach

---

105 Fethullah Gülen, "Demokrasi Yokuşu [Acclivity of Democracy]," Herkül, 2 January 2006, (Online portal to which Fethullah Gülen's speeches are posted), available at: http://www.herkul.org/kiriktesti/index.php?article_id=2846 Last accessed on September 22, 2007. Gülen's suggestions to enrich democracy with sprorutal elements do not conradict liberal ideals. However, if these elements are thought within the context of only one religion, and if the spiritual elements go deeper, then there is a danger for democracy to become sacralized. Making democracy sacralized is as dangerous as relegating religion to a narrow ideology.

106 Many Christian groups think along the same lines. This reminds us the fact that the question of the compatibility of religion and liberalism is not restricted to the Muslim world. The question of the compatibility of religion and liberalism can be asked in other contexts. I owe this point to Carolyn Warner.

107 See for example: Fethullah Gülen, *Ruhumuzun Heykelini Dikerken*, (Izmir, Nil Publications, 1998).

108 Gülen, "An Interview with Fethullah Gülen," p. 447.

109 Ibid., p. 447. See also Fethullah Gülen, "Hür Yaşadım, Hür Yaşarım… [I have lived free and I will live free]," Herkül, 15 August 2005, (Online portal to which Fethullah Gülen's speeches are posted), available at: http://www.herkul.org/kiriktesti/index.php?article_id=2061 Last accessed on September 22, 2007.

110 The author's observations and interviews with the followers in Ankara in 2001 and in Istanbul in 2002.

111 Berna Turam, "National Loyalties and International Undertakings: The Case of the Gülen Community in Kazakhstan;" in *Turkish Islam and the Secular State: The Gülen Movement,* edited by M. Hakan Yavuz and John L. Esposito, pp. 184-207. (Syracuse, NY: Syracuse University Press, 2003). See also Berna Turam, "The Politics of Engagement between Islam and the Secular State: The Ambivalences of 'Civil Society'," *The British Journal of Sociology,* Volume 55 Issue 2 (2004), pp. 259-281. See also Elizabeth Özdalga, "Following in the Footsteps of Fethullah Gülen: Three Women Teacher's Tell Their Stories," in *Turkish Islam and the Secular State: The Gülen Movement,* edited by M. Hakan Yavuz and John L. Esposito, pp. 85-114. (Syracuse, NY: Syracuse University Press, 2003).

112 Mücahit Bilici, "The Fethullah Gülen Movement and Its Politics of Representation in Turkey, The Muslim World, Volume 96, (January 2006), pp. 1-20.

a special importance to the concepts of "order" and "stability." Gülen says that "The worst state is better than statelessness; because statelessness brings anarchy."[113] While explaining the motives behind establishing schools abroad, Gülen emphasizes the importance of serving humanity and the local communities where schools are established.[114]

Conclusion

Turkey has experienced a liberal transformation in the last two decades. The Gülen movement's response to this liberalization process created new forms of social and political practices that are compatible with both Islam and liberalism. The Gülen movement used the opportunities offered by economic and political liberalization to raise its domestic and international sphere of influence. The followers established businesses, media corporations and schools in this environment. They also gained the support of the politicians and involved in worldwide educational and interfaith dialogue activities. At the same time, the movement transformed liberal principles and practices so as to align them with the Islamic teachings. This transformation, by increasing the legitimate room for Muslims, increased the followers' involvement in social and economic life and made their smooth integration to liberal economic and political structures possible. The movement in this process applied the normative repertoire in mobilizing its followers. Aspiration (*himmet*), emigration (*hicret*), dialogue and reconciliation, and spirituality have been the most-emphasized concepts in this process.

This analysis shows that it is impossible to reach generalisable conclusions on the compatibility of Islam and democracy. Scholars on Islam should examine this relationship by conducting in-depth studies on each Islamic movement. They should examine each movement within its own context that includes the environmental conditions, the organizational capabilities of the movement, and the movement's ability to communicate with the Islamic repertoire. The Gülen movement's experience is instructive in thinking about the institutionalization of liberalism in contemporary Turkey and Muslim world at large. For democracy to emerge in the Muslim world, economic and political liberalization should be adapted to the local contexts. For this to happen, liberalization should offer a number of opportunities to domestic groups, and the domestic groups should find innovative ways to make it compatible with the local conditions. The Islamic groups can mobilize their followers by using their Islamic normative repertoire.

Fethullah Gülen's theological answer to the question of the compatibility of Islam and liberalism is positive. Along with other scholars (such as Abou El Fadl, Mousalli, Sachedina), Gülen also argues that the interpretation of Islam which can best fit the needs of the modern times is possible since Islam leaves the type of government to the human reason. He doe not see any contradiction between Islamic teachings on governance and liberal democracy. However, what make the Gülen movement unique are the social and political practices that the followers have produced in a challenging liberal environment. These practices, which fitted both with Islamic teachings and the liberal philosophy, provided the movement with the opportunity to integrate in the global system. This integration is important with respect to the interactions between Islamic movements and liberalism in two ways. First, it transformed the

---

113 Fethullah Gülen, "Bu hareket devlete alternatif mi? [Is this movement an alternative to the state?], Herkül, 14 November 2005, available at http://www.herkul.org/kiriktesti/index.php?article_id=2418 Last accessed on September 22, 2007.

114 Gülen, "Bu Hareket...," For a study that analyzes Gülen's position toward the state see Aktay, "Diaspora and Stability: Constitutive Elements in a Body of Knowledge."

social and political practices of Islamic groups to make them compatible with the dominant discourses. Islamic renewal (tajdid) and interpretation (ijtihad) became the main instrument of these groups in this process. Second, these movements also influenced the transformation of social and political structures through becoming public. These two dynamics increased the level of compatibility between Islam and liberalism by making them much closer to one another. A few points can be made to characterize the conditions under which Islamic groups develop a peaceful rhetoric with liberalism.

First, the institutional environment is a very important factor in explaining Islamic movements' responses to liberalization. As the institutions liberalize, the Islamic movements adopt their discourses and strategies so as to integrate into liberalizing social, economic and political system. Gülen movement's liberal friendly social and political practices cannot be explained without any reference to economic and political liberalizing reforms that Turkey has experienced in the last decades. A survey of Muslim societies can be instructive to see the validity of this claim. Liberal Islamic groups are generally found in those countries where we see a liberalizing and/or liberalized economy and politics. The Indonesian and Turkish examples are very illustrative in this regard. The democratic practices of those Muslims living in Western liberal societies can also shed light on this argument. When judging the compatibility of Islam and democracy, it is analytically problematic to see the Islamic movements in the countries where authoritarian institutions prevail. A nuanced analysis should compare the political behaviours of Muslims living under authoritarian and liberal regimes.

Second, institutional environment cannot explain the patterns of Islam and liberalism alone; one should also analyze whether or not liberalization is beneficial to the Islamic groups. The Gülen movement's integration with the market economy created huge opportunities for the followers. Economic liberalization led the emergence of a new bourgeoisie, which had been less influential in the past when the market was not competitive and the state supported only certain business groups. Political liberalization also enhanced the manoeuvre room for Islamic groups so that the number of Islamic civil society organizations increased tremendously. A viable policy which aims the incorporation of Islamic groups to the liberal economic and political system should be attentive to the interests of Islamic groups as well. The Islamic movements under authoritarian systems should be autonomous from the state to develop a liberal-friendly discourse. The Islamic groups which have close links with the authoritarian state apparatus are less likely to have a liberal-friendly discourse since their interests depend on the maintenance of authoritarianism.

Finally, if an Islamic group has a cooperative normative repertoire, it is more likely to develop liberal-friendly discourse. Even when the interests of Islamic groups coincide with liberalization, it may be difficult to develop a liberal-friendly discourse if a group embraces a conflict-ridden political and social discourse. The Gülen movement, through its moderate and reconciliatory rhetoric, contributed to Turkey's civic life. If a movement has a reconciliatory rhetoric, its involvement in the public debates strengthens democracy.[115] The Gülen movement, by entering into the public sphere, is forced to confront and possibly come to terms with liberal normative structures, while it also influenced the formation of social and political practices at large. This, as Casanova argues, activates the potential role of religious norms and institutions in the formation of civil society and the process of democratization.[116] The

---

115 Jose Casanova, "Civil Society and Religion: Retrospective Reflections on Catholicism and Prospective Reflections on Islam," *Social Research*, Volume 68 No 4, (2001), pp. 1041-1080.
116 Casanova, "Civil Society and Religion: Retrospective Reflections on Catholicism and Prospective Reflections on Islam," p. 1074.

rise of moderate Islamic groups in the Muslim world is, then, a good start for a democratic future.

CHANGING PERSPECTIVES ON ISLAMISM AND SECULARISM IN TURKEY: THE GÜLEN MOVEMENT AND THE AK PARTY

Ahmet T. Kuru

Abstract

The debate between secularists and Islamic groups, a conspicuous feature of Turkish politics for decades, changed in the late 1990s when the political discourse of mainstream Islamic groups embraced secularism. The establishment elite advocate the existing French model of an 'assertive secularism', meaning that, in the public domain, the state supports only the expression of a secular worldview, and formally excludes religion and religious symbols from that domain. The pro-Islamic conservatives, on the other hand, favour the American model of 'passive secularism', in which the state permits the expression of religion in the public domain. In short, what Turkey has witnessed over the last decade is no longer a tussle between secularism and Islamism, but between two brands of secularism.

Two actors have played crucial roles in this transformation: the Gülen movement and the Justice and Development (AK) Party. Recently the Gülen movement became an international actor and a defendant of passive secularism. Similarly, although the AK Party was originated from an Islamist Milli Görüş (National Outlook) movement, it is now a keen supporter of Turkey's membership to the European Union and defends (passive) secularist, democratic regime. This paper analyses the transformation of these important social and political actors with regard to certain structural conditions, as well as the interactions between them.

In April 2007, the international media covered Turkey for the protest meetings of more than a million people in three major cities, the military intervention to politics, and the abortive presidential election. According to several journalists and columnists, Turkey was experiencing another phase of the ongoing tension between the secularists and Islamists. Some major Turkish newspapers, such as Hürriyet, were asserting that the secularists finally achieved to bring together millions of opponents of the ruling Adalet ve Kalkınma (Justice and Development) (AK) Party. In addition to their dominance in military and judicial bureaucracy, the secularists appeared to be maintaining the support of the majority of the people.

The parliamentary elections that took place few months later, in July, revealed that the mainstream Turkish media's presentation was misleading and the so-called secularists' aspirations were unrealistic. The AK Party received 47 percent of the national votes, an unusual ratio for a multiparty system where there were 14 contesting parties. The main opposition, Cumhuriyet Halk (Republican People's) Party (CHP), only received 21 percent of the votes, despite its alliance with the other leftist party. Both the national and international media's misleading presentation of Turkish politics was not confined by the preferences of the voters. Moreover, the media was primarily misleading with its use of the terms "Islamists" and "secularists."

What Turkey has witnessed for the last decade has not been a struggle between secularism and Islamism; but it has been a conflict between two types of secularism. As I elaborated elsewhere, the AK Party is not an Islamist party.[1] It defends a particular understanding of secularism that differs from that of the CHP. Although several leaders of the AK Party historically belonged to an Islamist -Milli Görüş (National Outlook)- movement, they later experienced an ideational transformation and embraced a certain type of secularism that tolerates public visibility of religion. This transformation was not an isolated event, but part of a larger experience that several other Islamic groups took part in. I argue that the AKP leaders' interaction with the Gülen movement, in this regard, played an important role in the formation of the party's new perspective toward secularism. In another article, I analyzed the transformation of the AK Party and Gülen movement with certain external (globalization process) and internal (the February 28 coup) conditions.[2] In this essay, I will focus on the interaction between these two entities to explore their changing perspectives.

I will first discuss the two different types of secularism that the Kemalists and conservatives defend in Turkey. Then, I will briefly summarize diverse discourses of the Milli Görüş and Gülen movements. Finally, I will examine the exchanges between the Gülen movement and the AK Party with regard to their rethinking of Islamism and secularism.

Assertive Secularism and its Critics in Turkey

The Turkish Republic is the first secular state with a Muslim majority society. I define secular states by two main characteristics: 1) their legal and judicial processes are out of institutional religious control, and 2) they constitutionally lack official religions.[3] Besides this general

---

1 Kuru 2006.

2 Kuru 2005.

3 Many scholars emphasize two other dimensions while defining a secular state: a) Separation of church/mosque and state, and b) religious freedom. See Smith 1999, esp. 178-183. A complete separation is, in fact, neither constitutionally declared in many secular states nor a practical issue. Religious freedom, on the other hand, is both constitutionally declared and practical; yet, it is neither necessary nor sufficient to be secular for a state to provide religious freedom.

definition, secularism is not a monolithic concept. There are two different types of secularism, with distinct normative backgrounds and policy implications. I call these two types "passive" and "assertive" secularism.[4] Passive secularism allows for the public visibility of religion. It requires that the state play a "passive" role in avoiding the establishment of any religions. Assertive secularism, on the other hand, excludes religion from the public sphere.[5] It demands that the state plays an "assertive" role as the agent of a social engineering project that confines religion to the private domain.[6]

Assertive secularism has been the dominant ideology in Turkey since the foundation of the Republic. The Kemalists, who have embraced Mustafa Kemal Atatürk's principles as non-negotiable dogmas, have been the main supporters of this ideology.[7] They have included the CHP, military generals, majority of the high court members, and major media outlets. Despite its some disagreements with the Kemalists, the Association of Turkish Industrialists and Businessmen (TÜSİAD), has also supported assertive secularism. The assertive secularists currently refer to the Turkish Constitutional Court's definition of secularism as the official and unchangeable depiction of secularism in Turkey.[8] According to the court, secularism does not denote the separation of religion and state, but it implies "separation of religion and worldly affairs." Secularism means separation of "social life, education, family, economy, law, manners, dress codes, etc. from religion."[9] Like the court, the former President Ahmet Sezer was also attaching importance to separating religion from "this-worldly affairs." For him, "Religion only belongs to its sacred and special place in individuals' conscience."[10]

One may argue that assertive secularism is not the dominant ideology in Turkey because the Turkish state favours Islam through the existence of obligatory religious instruction in all schools, state funding of religious education (in Imam-Hatip schools), and public funding of the imams in mosques, who are all civil servants of the state's Directorate of Religious Affairs (Diyanet).[11] Yet these policies do not mean that the Turkish state has a positive attitude toward Islam for four main reasons. First, the main rationale behind these institutions is not to support Islam, but rather it is to take Islam under state control.[12] Public schools provide religious instruction and the state runs the Imam-Hatip schools because any type of private religious education is banned in Turkey, despite the popular demand for such an education. Similarly, the Diyanet controls the mosques, including all vaazs (sermons before Friday prayer) and hutbes (sermons during the Friday prayer).[13] Second, through these institutions, the state also aims to create an "individualized" version of Islam, which exists behind

---

4 Kuru 2008.

5 I follow Charles Taylor's definition of the public sphere: "The public sphere is a common space in which the members of society are deemed to meet through a variety of media: print, electronic, and also face-to-face encounters; to discuss matters of common interest; and thus to be able to form a common mind about these." Taylor 2004, 83. See also Habermas 1999; Habermas 1989.

6 See Taylor 1999; McClay 2002.

7 See Turam 2006, 144-145.

8 As an example, see the speech of General Staff Deputy Chief General İlker Başbuğ, May 27, 2004, accessed at http://www.tsk.mil.tr/genelkumay/bashalk/2004basinbringleri/mayis2004/sempozyum1.htm, June 1, 2004.

9 The Turkish Constitutional Court's ruling on the *Welfare Party* case on January 16, 1997; no. 1998/1. For a critique of the Court's decision, see Erdoğan 1999.

10 Quoted in "Laiklik Özgürlük Demek," *Radikal*, February 6, 2004.

11 See Selçuk 1999, esp. 48.

12 Kara 2003, 92-106; Canatan 1997, 33-34; Keyder 2004, 69.

13 Çakır and Bozan 2005, 34.

the walls of private homes or within one's own conscience.[14] Third, the state expropriated the financial sources of the Islamic foundations in the founding period and still controls these foundations. Since the state historically confiscated Islamic funds and currently does not allow independent financing of the imams, it has to pay their salaries. Last but not least, the Turkish state pursues restrictive policies toward Islam, such as the ban on headscarves in all educational institutions, the prohibition on teaching the Qur'an to children under 15 year (with the exception of summer courses for those who are above 12), and the disallowance of the Imam-Hatip schools' graduates to attend universities (except the Schools of Theology).

There have been two main opponents of assertive secularism in Turkey. One has been the central rightist/conservative parties, such as the Demokrat (Democratic) Party (1950-1960), Adalet (Justice) Party (1961-1980), Anavatan (Motherland) Party (1983-), and True Path (Doğru Yol) Party (DYP) (1983-2007). These parties have generally opposed the policies of the assertive secularists. They have tolerated public visibility of religion, in general, Islam, in particular. The other set of opponents has been pro-Islamic conservative movements, particularly the two most influential ones--the Milli Görüş and Gülen movements. Despite their common critique of assertive secularism, these two movements had several disagreements as explained below.[15]

The Gülen Movement vs. the Milli Görüş Movement: Faith Service vs. Political Islamism

Up until the late 1990s, the Gülen and Milli Görüş movements were representing almost opposite perspectives. The Gülen movement was focusing on faith service (iman hizmeti), by publishing magazines and books about Islamic faith, opening student housings and dormitories, and bringing business people together to fund this activities. This movement was avoiding party politics arguing that the most important project would be training the youth to create a "golden generation", instead of seeking the state power. The Milli Görüş movement, however, was representing political Islamism in Turkey, by founding Islamist political parties.

Fethullah Gülen initiated his movement in the early 1970s, in the Izmir region, where he was a preacher of Diyanet. Throughout the 1970s, the movement was focusing on mosque activities and providing student housings. In the 1980s, it started to open dormitories, university preparation courses, and schools in all around Turkey. The movement also founded a media network, including publication companies (e.g., Nil Publication), magazines (e.g., Sızıntı and Yeni Ümit), and a newspaper (Zaman). Before the mid-1990s, the Gülen movement was focusing on education and avoiding political debates, following Said Nursi's statement "I seek refuge in God from Satan and [party] politics."[16] The leader of the movement, Fethullah Gülen, was contacting with the public only through his preaching in mosques and his articles published in the movement's magazines.

Necmettin Erbakan initiated the Milli Görüş movement in the early 1970s too. The parties he led—Milli Nizam (National Order) Party (1970-1971) and Milli Selamet (National Salvation) Party (1972-1980)—were accused as anti-secular Islamist and disbanded following the 1971 and 1980 military coups. In 1983, Erbakan and his followers founded the Refah (Welfare) Party (RP). The RP became successful in local elections in 1994 and won mayor

---

14 See Bozarslan 2004; Ulusoy 1999.

15 See Turam 2006

16 Nursi 1996, 368.

posts of Istanbul and Ankara. In terms of national parliamentary elections, The RP increased its share of the votes from 7.2 percent in 1987 to 21.4 percent in 1995 and became the leading party. Erbakan became the prime minister in 1996 in the RP-DYP coalition.[17]

In the mid-1990s the disparity and tension between the Gülen and Milli Görüş movements got deeper. At that time the Gülen movement experienced two transformations. First, it became an international movement with its schools and business network in different parts of the world.[18] The movement first opened schools in former Soviet Republics following their in-dependence. Then, it expanded its educational institutions to other Asian, European, African, and North American countries, which would eventually result six universities and more than 500 schools in about 100 different countries.[19] Moreover, the movement developed an in-ternational media network, which included a newspaper that printed in about ten countries (Zaman), an internationally broadcasting TV channel (STV), and an international magazine in English (The Fountain). The more the Gülen movement became international benefiting the opportunities of globalization, the more it developed a pro-globalization discourse.[20] The movement began to support Turkey's membership to the European Union (EU).[21] Gülen him-self initiated certain interfaith dialogue activities in Turkey and abroad. He met with religious leaders, including Pope John Paul II, the Panahriot Greek Patriarch Bartholomeos, and Israeli Sephardic Head Rabbi Eliyahu B. Doron. For him, there were two main motives behind these activities. One is theological: Islam had many things in common with other two Abrahamic religions and that required interfaith dialogue.[22] The other is contextual: in the post-Cold War world Samuel Huntington's "clash of civilization" thesis was taken seriously. Gülen was aiming to prevent such an inter-religious clash with interfaith dialogue.[23]

Erbakan and his cadre, however, had opposite views about globalization, Turkey's member-ship to the EU, and interfaith dialogue. The RP clearly opposed Turkey's membership to the EU seeing it as a "Christian club."[24] As a part of his Islamist foreign policy agenda, Erbakan gave his first visits to countries such as Iran and Libya. He also led the foundation of an in-ternational organization among eight Muslim countries, known as Developing Eight (D-8).[25] The tension between the two movements on these issues was clear on Gülen's speeches and writings. For example, he defined D-8 as a vain project and a "cheap message" to Erbakan's constituency.[26]

The second transformation the Gülen movement experienced was its public outreach in the mid-1990s.[27] To coordinate its public activities the movement founded the Gazeteciler ve Yazarlar Vakfı (Journalists and Writers' Foundation) (GYV). The GYV organized dinners at five star hotels in Istanbul and Ankara to maintain the movement's outreach to Turkish

---

17 Yavuz 1997.

18 Yavuz and Esposito 2003.

19 Agai 2003. For the list of the schools run by the Gülen movement worldwide, see *Yeni Aktüel*, No.13, October 11-17, 2005.

20 Kuru 2005.

21 Kösebalaban 2003.

22 Gülen 2006; M. Fethullah Gülen, "The Necessity of Interfaith Dialogue," *The Fountain*, No. 31 (July-September 2000).

23 Gülen 2004; M. Fethullah Gülen, "At the Threshold of the New Millennium," *The Fountain*, No. 29 (January-March 2000).

24 Dağı 1998.

25 The members of D-8 are Turkey, Iran, Egypt, Pakistan, Bangladesh, Indonesia, Malaysia, and Nigeria.

26 Gülen's interview with Nevval Sevindi. Sevindi 2002, 33.

27 Yilmaz 2003.

elite. Numerous politicians, journalists, and academics attended to these dinners and other meetings of the GYV, where Gülen delivered key note speeches. In those speeches, as well as his interviews at top circulating newspapers (e.g., Sabah and Hürriyet), Gülen stressed the importance of democracy, tolerance, and dialogue. His messages were largely welcomed by country's secular elite.

Erbakan's discourse, on the other hand, was almost the opposite. He was accusing those who did not vote for RP as belonging to "religion of potato," instead of Islam. Erbakan was claiming that the political regime in Turkey would be certainly changed but the question was whether it would be done "with or without blood." Erbakan's discourse provided an excuse to the military, particularly a junta within it, Batı Çalışma Grubu (Western Working Group), to stage a soft coup d'état on February 28, 1997.[28] The generals and their civilian supporters justified the military intervention arguing that Erbakan's premiership encouraged irtica (Islamic reactionism). Following the intervention, several people and institutions asked Erbakan to resign. Gülen joined them on April 16, 1997, by giving an interview to the TV channel Kanal D, where he encouraged Erbakan to leave the office. The following day two major newspapers (Hürriyet and Milliyet) made Gülen's critique of Erbakan their headlines. That meant the deepest tension between the two movements. Yet a new period in Turkish politics, in general, and the relationship between the Gülen and the Milli Görüş movements, in particular, began following this crisis.

The Gülen Movement and the AK Party: Passive Secularism and Globalization

Erbakan resigned in June 1997. Seven months later, the Constitutional Court dissolved the RP. Following that, the RP's parliamentarians founded the Fazilet (Virtue) Party (FP). Within the FP, there emerged a disagreement between the Milli Görüş's old generation led by Erbakan and the new generation led by three figures: Tayyip Erdoğan, Abdullah Gül, and Bülent Arınç. These leaders had better personal relations with the Gülen movement than Erbakan did. Erdoğan had attended the GYV's dialog meetings and made a key note speech. Arınç became the first politician who defended Gülen when assertive secularist media launched a lynching campaign against him in June 1999. Beyond personal relations, the young generation was ideationally resembled to the Gülen movement. In terms of foreign policy, they supported Turkey's membership to the EU. In terms of domestic politics, they developed a new discourse that emphasized democracy and dialogue.

The Milli Görüş's young generation and the Gülen movement had two main venues to interact their ideas. One is the Gülen movement's media network, especially newspaper Zaman. For example, in February 2000, Erdoğan and Arınç first publicized their new discourse in Zaman. In two separate interviews, these two leaders emphasized democracy as their priority and embraced (passive) secularism while criticizing the idea of an Islamic state.[29] These two interviews received the attention of other newspapers. Assertive secularist Hürriyet positively announced them in its headline "Political Islam at the Crossroads," while Islamist Vakit criticized them arguing that Zaman corrupted Erdoğan and Arınç's mind.[30]

The second venue was the Abant meetings organized by the Gülen movement's GYV. The GYV has organized the Abant meetings to head off socio-political polarization and to search

---

28 Yavuz 2000.
29 Erdoğan and Arınç's interviews, *Zaman*, February 6, 2000.
30 See "Siyasal İslam Yol Ayrımında," *Hürriyet*, February 8, 2000.

for a new social contract in Turkey.[31] Each annual Abant workshop has included about fifty Turkish intellectuals (academics, politicians, and journalists) from sharply different ideological backgrounds (Islamists, liberals, socialists, nationalists, and Kemalists). The first meeting was organized in 1998 and devoted to Islam and secularism. Its press declaration emphasized that God's ontological sovereignty was compatible with the political sovereignty of the people.[32] The second meeting also examined the relationships among state, society, and religion.[33] The third meeting focused on democracy and the rule of law, while the fourth one discussed pluralism and social consensus.[34] Among the attendants were several leaders of the Milli Görüş's new generation, such as Gül, Arınç, Cemil Çiçek, Ali Coşkun, and Nevzat Yalçıntaş. Moreover the chairperson of the meetings, Mehmet Aydın, and some frequent participants, such as Hüseyin Çelik and Burhan Kuzu, joined them, when the new generation founded the AK Party.[35] These meetings contributed to a new discourse based on democracy and a liberal (read passive) version of secularism that the Milli Görüş's new generation and the Gülen movement shared. This new discourse was critical of both Erbakan's political Islamism and the Kemalists' assertive secularism.

In 2001, the Constitutional Court dissolved the FP arguing that it defended the freedom to wear headscarves and was therefore anti-secular. Following the closure of FP, the followers of Erbakan founded the Saadet (Felicity) Party (SP), while those of Erdoğan, Gül, and Arınç founded the AK Party. The SP had an Islamist and anti-EU discourse. The AK Party, on the other hand, declined to be defined as Islamist and defended Turkey's membership to the EU. In the elections of November 3, 2002, the SP was marginalized with 2.5 percent of the national votes while the AK Party became the leading party with 34.3 percent of the votes and about two third of the seats in the parliament. Erdoğan became prime minister, while Gül became the vice prime minister and minister of foreign affairs, and Arınç became the speaker of the parliament.

The AK Party completely cut its ties with the Milli Görüş movement.[36] It embraced (passive) secularism as a principle that "maintains peace among diverse beliefs, schools of thoughts, and perspectives."[37] Its party program depicts secularism as "an assurance of the freedom of religion and conscience" and rejects "the interpretation and distortion of secularism as enmity against religion."[38] The AK Party identified its ideology as "conservative democracy."[39] Erdoğan emphasized that the AK Party's understanding of conservatism did not mean the conservation of established institutions and relations but implied the protection of important values and principles while pursuing progress. He stressed that using religion as a political instrument was harmful to social peace, political diversity, and religion itself. For him, the AK Party aims to synthesize local and universal values, tradition and modernity, and morality

---

31   The author's personal interviews with the GYV representatives, Istanbul, June 14, 1998.

32   Gazetciler ve Yazarlar Vakfı 1998.

33   Gazetciler ve Yazarlar Vakfı 1999.

34   Gazetciler ve Yazarlar Vakfı 2000; Gazetciler ve Yazarlar Vakfı 2001.

35   In the first AK Party government, in late 2002, Çiçek became the minister of justice, Coşkun became the minister of industry, Mehmet Aydın became the minister in charge of religious affairs (the Diyanet), and Çelik became the minister of education. At that time, Kuzu became the chairman of the Constitutional Affairs Committee in the Turkish Parliament.

36   "Erdoğan: Millî Görüş'ün Değil Demokrat Parti'nin Devamıyız," *Zaman*, May 17, 2003.

37   AK Parti N.d., 13-14.

38   AK Parti 2002.

39   The author's personal interviews with AK Party politicians, September 2004, Ankara, Turkey. See also Akdoğan 2003.

and rationality.[40]

Besides their similar emphasis on democracy and (passive) secularism, the Gülen movement and the AK Party have had a tacit agreement on two important points. One is that both are pro-globalization, in the sense that they try to take advantage of globalization's opportunities, rather than pursuing an isolationist policy to avoid its challenges.[41] A clear indicator of being pro-globalization in Turkey is to defend the country's membership to the EU. For the last five years, the AK Party government has been active on this issue. The AK Party group in the parliament led the passing of seven legal reform packets, which resulted in Turkey's adaptation to EU legal structure, by the liberalization of the political system. The Gülen movement has also tried to contribute Turkey's membership. The movement's media network has played an important role in promoting pro-EU sentiments, particularly among the conservative people. Moreover, the eight Abant meeting in 2004 took place in the European Parliament in Brussels to discuss Turkey's membership with the participation of several European academics and politicians.[42] Similarly, in 2006 and 2007, the GYV organized Abant meetings in Paris to engage with French intellectuals.

Another aspect of being pro-globalization is to adapt global economy. The AK Party has been a keen supporter of privatization and foreign direct investments to Turkey, despite the opposition of statist judges. The Gülen movement supported the AK Party government's such policies in its newspapers and TV channels. In addition to its international educational and media institutions, the movement is also active in international business. In 2005, the businesspeople affiliated with the movement initiated the Confederation of Businessmen and Industrialists of Turkey (TUSKON), which included 124 business unions and 9500 businesspeople. In 2006, Bank Asya, the interest-free bank affiliated with the movement, publicly traded its stocks to Turkish and international buyers.

Due to their pro-globalization stands, the AK Party and the Gülen movement have been criticized by both the SP and the anti-globalization nationalists (ulusalcıs), who are a strange combination of some Kemalists, nationalists, and leftists.[43] The ulusalcıs, such as certain columnists in Yeniçağ, accused the AK Party and the Gülen movement of selling the country to global capitalists, as well as being a spy of the EU, an agent of the "moderate Islam project" of the US, or even a servant of Israel.

The second major point that the Gülen movement and the AK Party have been in tacit agreement is the importance of interfaith dialogue. As I already mentioned, the Gülen movement has been very active in interfaith dialogue in Turkey and abroad. Each year the movement organizes dozens of dialogue dinners in the US, European countries, and other parts of the world. Domestically, the movement has supported rights of non-Muslim minorities. For example, Gülen has repeatedly stressed that Turkey should allow the reopening of Halki Seminary of Greek Orthodox Patriarch in Istanbul.

The AK Party also tried to pursue benevolent policies toward non-Muslim communities in Turkey. Non-Muslim communities in Turkey have faced several official restrictions since the founding of the Republic, such as the "absence of legal personality, education and training of

---

40 Erdoğan 2004. Erdoğan's view on synthesizing seemingly opposite things resembles to Gülen's understanding of the "middle way." See Kuru 2003.

41 Kuru 2005.

42 The author's personal observation and interviews in the Abant Meeting, Brussels, December 3-4, 2004.

43 Kösebalaban 2005.

ecclesiastic personnel as well as full enjoyment of property rights."[44] The AK Party initiated certain reforms to alleviate such conditions.[45] In 2003, the AK Party group in the parliament led the legal reform concerning religious places, replacing the word "mosque" in the law with "place of worship." This allowed all religions to open temples in Turkey.[46] In 2004, the AK Party government cancelled the state surveillance over non-Muslims citizens by abolishing the Subcommittee for Minorities, which had been monitoring non-Muslim citizens for 42 years.[47] Moreover, Erdoğan has made several visits to Jewish synagogues and Christian churches in Turkey, a gesture which has been appreciated by these communities. That is why the Armenian Orthodox Patriarch Mesrob II announced that they would vote for the AK Party in the July 2007 elections.[48]

AK Party's benevolent policies toward non-Muslim communities are also a reflection of its adoption of passive secularism. The assertive secularists, such as CHP, have not been active on this issue. Since the assertive secularists have focused on the exclusion of religion from the public sphere, they have not taken non-Muslim communities' problems seriously. Moreover, they have been worried about non-Muslims' rights of association because if the Christians and Jews were free to have legal entities, found associations, and open private temples, then independent Muslim communities in Turkey would want these freedoms too.[49] For example, in 2006, assertive secularist President Sezer vetoed a parliamentary bill that recognized the legal status and full property rights of non-Muslim foundations. He argued that the bill would wrongly allow the expansion of the economic activities and social status of these foundations.[50]

The AK Party has also embraced interfaith, or inter-civilisational, dialogue as a foreign policy principle. It has presented Turkey's membership to the EU as the marriage of two civilizations. Erdoğan has also taken personal initiatives on this issue. He became the co-sponsor, with the Spanish Prime Minister Jose Zapatero, of the UN General Secretary Kofi Annan's "Alliance of Civilization" project. The ulusalcıs and some marginal Islamic groups, such as the Haydar Baş community with its newspaper (Yeni Mesaj) and TV channels (Meltem TV and Mesaj TV), have targeted the Gülen movement and the AK Party for their interfaith dialogue activities. They particularly blamed Gülen as a fifth-column of Christian missionaries. The attacks of their common enemies deepened the friendship between the Gülen movement and the AK Party as explained below.

The Gülen Movement and the AK Party: Protecting Democracy

The Gülen movement had close relations with Turgut Özal in the early 1990s and Bülent Ecevit in the late 1990s. Yet it has avoided explicitly supporting one single party at the expense of others. Recently, the movement largely dropped its neutrality principle and supported the AK Party in the national elections of July 22, 2007. The chief editor of Zaman accepted the movement's indirect support and explained it with the aim of protecting demococ-

---

44 WRR 2004, 30.
45 "Members of Turkey's non-Muslim communities are unanimous in declaring that, since the ruling ...AK Party came to power in November 2002, relations with the government have improved considerably." Jenkins 2004, 54.
46 The law passed in the Parliament on July 15, 2003. See Öktem 2004.
47 Şükrü Küçükşahin, "Sessiz Azınlık Devrimi, *Hürriyet*, February 23, 2004.
48 "Ermeni Cemaati Seçimlerde Ak Parti'yi Destekleyecek," *Yeni Şafak*, June 4, 2007.
49 See İsmet Berkan, "AB ve Din Özgürlüğü Eksikliği," *Radikal*, May 26, 2004.
50 "Sezer Vakıflar Yasası'nı Lozan'a Aykırı Buldu," *Zaman*, November 30, 2006.

racy against authoritarian assaults.[51]

The assaults against Turkish democracy took place from mid-2006 to mid-2007, because of the presidential election scheduled in April 2007. The presidential post was very vital for the dominance of assertive secularism in Turkey. The conservative and central rightist parties, including the AK Party, MHP, DYP, and ANAP, won about 70 percent of votes in national elections for decades. Yet they had limited impacts on state policies toward religion due to the assertive secularist dominance in the military and the judicial bureaucracy. Presidency played the key role for the preservation of the assertive secularist domination in these state institutions, since the president would sign the appointment of high ranking generals and top civil bureaucrats, as well as appointing high court judges and presidents of universities. The president was elected for seven years by the parliament. The military kept intervening to the presidential elections to force the parliamentarians to elect an assertive secularist candidate. Yet the assertive secularists were very concerned about the April 2007 election since it would not be easy to force the AK Party majority in the parliament to elect an assertive secularist president. That resulted in a political crisis that took more than a year.

In February 2006, the Council of State decided that it was inappropriate for a teacher to wear headscarf even on the street. The conservatives condemned the decision as a violation of religious freedom. Two months later, an assassin shot the judges who made this decision and killed one of them. The assertive secularists accused the AK Party government for targeting the judges following their decision. Yet the police and conservative media uncovered that the assassin was linked to some ulusalcı retired military officers. The Gülen movement's Zaman and STV led other conservative newspapers (e.g., Yeni Şafak, Star, and Bugün) and TV channels (e.g., Kanal 7) in revealing this link. That created serious doubts that the murderer was a puppet used by some paramilitary organizations that wanted to topple the AK Party government.

In April 2007, the assertive secularists brought together the total of more than one million protesters in meetings in major cities to prevent the AK Party to elect the new president. The AK Party, however, nominated Gül for presidency. Gül needed to receive two third of the votes (367/550) in the first two rounds. In the third round, however, more than half (276/550) would be enough. Gül received 357 votes out of 361 participant deputies in the first round, when the CHP, DYP, and ANAP boycotted the voting. He was planning to be easily elected in the third round. Conservative media, including Zaman and STV, was fully supporting Gül. At that midnight, the military issued a statement in its web site threatening with intervention. It was particularly shocking that the statement included explicitly negative words about certain Islamic values, such as the birthday celebrations of the Prophet. The CHP supported the military's statement, while the AK Party government declared that the military was under its authority. Zaman and STV, alongside with other newspapers (e.g., Sabah) directly rejected a possible military intervention. Gül did not quit his candidacy. Nevertheless, the CHP had already applied to the Constitutional Court arguing that at least 367 parliamentarians should have been present at the first round. The court supported the CHP's claim, cancelled the first round, and put the 367 quorum as a requirement.

During this process, Zaman, which reached the largest national circulation (700,000) at the time, published several op-eds written by respectful scholars to criticize the CHP, military, and Constitutional Court, in terms of their attitudes during the presidential election. An example is Ergun Özbudun, who is Turkey's top professor of constitutional law. In his op-ed in

---

51 Ekrem Dumanlı, "Medya, Kendi Seçim Karnesine de Bakmalı," *Zaman*, July 23, 2007.

Zaman, Özbudun criticized the court's decision as a political manoeuvre that clearly contradicted the text and original intent of the Constitution, as well as the precedents of presidential elections.[52]

In short, the presidential election polarized Turkish politics. The CHP and other assertive secularists tried to prevent AK Party to elect the new presidents by encouraging the military to stage a coup. In response, the Gülen and some other democratic forces, which were not explicitly supporting the AK Party before, provided an unprecedented support to this party. As a result, the AK Party received 47 percent of national votes in July 2007 parliamentary elections. The CHP lost about half of its seats, while the DYP (which got the name DP) and ANAP remained completely out of the new parliament, mainly as a result of the voters' disapproval of their boycotting the presidential election. The new parliament re-initiated the presidential election. This time all parties, except CHP, participated in the election and Gül became 11th President of Turkey on August 28, 2007.

Conclusion

The debate between the assertive secularists and Islamic groups had been a major aspect of Turkish politics for decades. In the late 1990s, however, mainstream pro-Islamic groups changed their political discourse by embracing passive secularism. Currently, the Kemalists defend the dominant assertive secularist ideology, which excludes religion from the public sphere. The pro-Islamic conservatives, such as the Gülen movement and the AK Party, on the other hand, try to promote a new passive secularist ideology, which allows public visibility of religion. What Turkey has witnessed for the last decade has no longer been a struggle between secularism and Islamism, but it has been a conflict between the two types of secularism.

In addition to secularism, this paper also pointed to the second fault line of Turkish politics: globalization. Besides the assertive secularists, the ulusalcıs are the main critic of the Gülen movement and the AK Party. The Gülen movement and the AK Party are pro-globalization, in a sense of supporting Turkey's membership to the EU and its integration to global economy, as well as promoting interfaith dialogue. The ulusalcıs and some marginal Islamic groups have allied in their opposition to globalization and their critique of the Gülen movement and the AK Party on these three particular issues.

Although the AK Party had originated from the Islamist Milli Görüş movement, it embraced passive secularism and became pro-globalization. Throughout this transformation, the AK Party leaders have been in direct interaction with the Gülen movement. The movement's media outlets and Abant meetings played important roles in this interaction. The movement and the party have also many other overlapping: they address to a similar set of conservative businesspeople (generally called Anatolian Tigers), several party members send their children to movement's schools, and several movement sympathizers politically support the party. In short, scholars who simply focused on the "political" actor (i.e., the AK Party) of ideational transformation in Turkey make a mistake by undermining the important role of a "social" agent (i.e., the Gülen movement).

It has been long debated whether Turkey can become a model for other Muslim countries with its democratic and secular regime. It is very difficult to give a positive answer to such a question because of Turkey's own political problems and several peculiar characteristics that make its political system hard to transfer elsewhere. Yet the Turkish experience is still

---

52 "Cumhurbaşkanlığı Krizinin Götürdükleri," *Zaman*, May 14, 2007.

very important to understand dynamics of democratization and political secularization in a Muslim country. This essay particularly reveals three lessons from the Turkish case. First, Islamic groups do not have monolithic and frozen relationships with secularism and democracy. Instead, these groups may and do reinterpret their political views and revise their attitudes towards secularism and democracy in a dynamic manner. Second, the democratic process helps moderation of Islamic actors' perspectives and discourses. Free, fair, and frequent elections are especially important to marginalize radical discourses and to empower realistic, pragmatic, and moderate voices. Finally, a political project can only be successfully materialized if it has a social basis. Political actors always need some social counterparts to appeal majority of the people and to redesign political debates.

RELIGION AS A SOURCE OF SOCIAL CAPITAL? THE GÜLEN MOVEMENT IN THE PUBLIC SPHERE

Etga Ugur

Abstract

This paper asks: when and under what conditions does religion become a source of cooperation rather than conflict? The Gülen movement is an Islamic social movement that bases its philosophy on increasing religious consciousness at the individual level and making Islam an important social force in the public sphere. It is this intellectual and social activism that has made the movement a global phenomenon and the focus of socio-political analysis.

The Gülen community brings different sectors of society together to facilitate 'collective intellectual effort' and offer 'civil responses' to social issues, seeing this as a more subtle and legitimate way of influencing public debate and policy. To this end, the movement initiated a series of symposiums, known as Abant Workshops in Turkey. The scope of these meetings was later expanded to include a wider audience in Europe, the U.S., and the Middle East.

This paper looks specifically at the Abant Workshops and the movement's strategy of bridge building and problem-solving. It uses the press releases, transcripts and audio-visual records of the past 14 meetings to discuss their objectives and outcomes. This material is supplemented by interviews with key organisers from the Journalists and Writer Foundation and other participants. The discussion aims to understand how far religiously inspired social groups can contribute to the empowerment of civil society vis-à-vis the state and its officially secular ideology. Beyond that, it aims to explain the role of civil society organisations in democratic governance, and the possibility of creating social capital in societies lacking a clear 'overlapping consensus' on issues of citizenship, morality and national identity.

The hesitancy at the beginning turns into friendship,

the distance into understanding, stiff looks and tensions into humorous jokes, and differences into richness.[1]

Abant is boldly moving towards an institutionalization. The objective is evident: Talking about some of the problems the country is facing, debating them and offering solutions; on a civil ground, within the framework of knowledge and deliberation. Some labelled the ideas in the concluding declarations as "revolutionary," "renaissance," and "first indications of a religious reform." Some others (in minority) saw them "dangerous" and "non-sense." In fact, the result is neither a "revolution" nor "non-sense" It is an indication of a quest for opening new horizons or creating a novel vision.[2]

When and under what conditions does religion become a source of cooperation rather than conflict in the civil society? The Gülen movement is an Islamic social movement that bases its philosophy on increasing religious consciousness at the individual level and making Islam an important social force in the public sphere. It is this intellectual and social activism that raises the Gülen movement of Turkey as a global phenomenon to the focus of socio-political analysis.

The Gülen community brings different sectors of the society together to create and facilitate a 'common intellect' to brainstorm and offer 'civil responses' to social issues. The movement sees this as a more subtle, but more effective, and legitimate way of influencing public debate and policy. Hence, the movement initiated a series of symposiums, known as Abant Workshops in Turkey. The scope of the meetings was later expanded to include a wider audience in Europe, the U.S., and the Middle East.

In early 1990s the Gülen Movement launched a silent but persistent public relations campaign. Fethullah Gülen openly met with the prominent figures of government and politics, and gave interviews to some popular newspapers and magazines. With a thriving media network, private schools, and business associations the movement seemed to have entered a new stage in its relations with the outside world. This new stage was not a simple outreach effort; it was rather a confident step to carve a niche in the increasingly diversified Turkish public sphere. The instigation of a series of workshops known as Abant Platforms was one of the biggest steps in this process. The workshops brought academics, politicians, and intellectuals together to discuss some of the thorniest issues of, first, Turkey, such as secularism and pluralism, and then the Muslim World, such as war, globalization and modernization. This paper seeks to explain the motives behind this kind of an ambitious project and its possible implications for the movement itself, for Turkey and for the Muslim World in transition.

---

1 The 13th Abant Meeting Opening Video Presentation.
2 Mehmet S. Aydin, Opening Remarks for the 2nd Abant Meetings, *Abant Platformu: Din, Devlet ve Toplum* (Gazeteciler ve Yazarlar Vakfi Yayinlari, 2000), pp.9-12.

Religion as a Source of Social Capital in Civil Society

In order to understand the involvement of religious groups in public life one needs to look at the three domains of the public sphere: the state, the political society and the civil society (Casanova, 1994). The state refers to the continuous administrative, legal, bureaucratic and coercive system with institutions, regulations, and enforcement. The state level primarily includes symbolic and legal functions. The constitution, civil service and judiciary are some examples of venues in which religion can work within the state apparatus. The political society is an arena in which societal groups contest to gain control over the state apparatus and influence public policy. This contestation usually takes place through political parties, interest groups and lobbies. Many religious groups directly or indirectly become part of governing coalitions, political parties and interest groups.

The civil society is made up of a body of associations, groups and organizations beyond the immediate reach and control of the state. The civil society requires a certain reference to the public good, as opposed to pure economic market rationality and self-interest. Voluntary organizations and members of the associational life in civil society offer social services in education, health care, gender equality, minority rights, and issue-based platforms. Religious groups choose to utilize a combination of these three domains. The specific domains used by a group depend on its worldview and the cultural and political context. The Gülen movement primarily operates within the civil society, and sometimes interacts with politicians in order to promote some of their objectives in the civil society, such as dialogue, freedom of religion and democratization.[3]

The quality of public life and the performance of political institutions are significantly influenced by the norms and networks of civic engagement. Robert Putnam defines social capital as "features of social organization such as networks, norms and social trust that facilitate coordination and cooperation for mutual benefit."[4] Civic engagement facilitates communication and creates social bonds, and social trust, which in turn makes collective action easier, and opportunism and cheating less likely. Participation in voluntary civic associations advances the socialization of individuals and cultivates values and mores regarding communal life, such as reciprocity, trustworthiness and friendship. Engagement in civic life exposes the citizens to politically relevant information and enhances their social skills (Putnam, 2000).

Social capital, or networks of civic engagement, is crucial to create a vibrant society with a meaningful dialogue among its constituents. Social capital can be understood at two separate but interrelated levels. One is the individual level pertaining to the degree to which individuals are "community minded" with a sense of the common good. The other level is more intersubjective and structural, and relates to the absence or existence of trust between individuals in a society. In a way, voluntary organizations in the civil society play an important role in transforming anonymous masses into communities, and trust "lubricates" cooperation for mutual benefit (Smidt, 2003).

Religion is an important source of social capital in many modern societies. Religion as a body of beliefs, values and norms motivates believers to volunteer in community affairs to provide social services such as health care, soup kitchens, education, and helping the poor. Religion also provides a source of common identity to its followers and creates bonds

---

3 The movement has had dialogue with most of the center right and center left political parties in Turkey, with a notable exception of the Islamist Welfare Party. However, because of the overlaps between the constituencies, the movement has been closer to conservative (center right) parties, such as ANAP, and most recently the AK Party.

4 Putnam (1995), p. 67.

between them. Obviously, religion is only one source of social capital or civic engagement, albeit an important one.

Is there anything unique about religion when it comes to generating social capital? In comparison to 'secular' sources, religion can be an asset to promote a strong sense of reciprocity given its teachings of an after life and all-seeing omnipotent higher authority. In that sense, non-material basis of volunteering and self-sacrifice are key aspects of religious social capital. Additionally, most religions claim universal appeal, which in turn fosters a sense of common identity and purpose across ethnic, racial and economic classes. Some religious groups get involved in politics more directly while some others prefer to invoke 'prophetic politics', working as an outside critique especially in 'moral issues'. Also, the fact that most religions are motivated with salvation rather than strict definitions of worldly success makes it possible for them to take bold initiatives and politically risky ventures. Other than these concrete aspects, religion also provides a symbolic language enmeshed in the grammar of the society by speaking the language of the masses and utilizing the 'cultural capital' (Smidt, 2003).

Then, is religion a source of conflict or cooperation in the civil society? The answer to this question depends on the way religion is used in the civic realm. Religious groups whose organizations are congregational tend to promote a more active and engaged laity than hierarchically structured groups (Harris, 2003). Teachings of religion also play a role in enhancing or hindering social capital formation. Religions that emphasize distinctiveness of their beliefs, especially the ones with exclusive evangelism, are more likely to be inward looking whereas religions that emphasize social justice and interfaith dialogue are more likely to work across faiths and socio-economic classes.

The Gülen movement demonstrates elements of a congregational organizational structure. Although there is a core cadre of devotees around Fethullah Gülen who provide the inspiration and know-how to others for building schools, opening cultural centres and language courses, the bulk of the movement is in the periphery. The idea of volunteering and committing one's time and money plays a key role in the activities of the group. The movement employs an inclusive language vis-à-vis other religious, ethnic and ideological groups and claims to promote the religio-national[5] interest of the host country. This has proven to be an important tool to appeal to the society at large and legitimate the movement's social projects in face of questions on the basis of secular and national commitment of the movement.[6]

Abant Platform is a good example of a religiously inspired social capital formation in a society with ideological, ethnic and religious fault lines. The Gülen movement has been quite successful in utilizing its cultural and human capital in order to empower the civil society and expand the democratic space available for the formally excluded periphery vis-à-vis the centre.

A Brief History of the Abant Platform

In June 1994, Gülen movement introduced the Journalists and Writers Foundation (JWF) to the media in a much publicized cocktail. Fethullah Gülen, as the honorary president, made

---

5 A key term used by the movement in Turkey is "milli" which has religious connotations as well as national, as opposed to "ulusal" which is more secular.

6 The movement has been criticized on two contradictory grounds: Aiming to 'infiltrate' into the system to create an Islamic state; cooperating with Christian missionaries and Jews through interfaith dialogue activities to undermine the Muslim identity and territorial integrity of Turkey.

his first media appearance and gave warm messages to the public, emphasizing dialogue, tolerance, pluralism and democracy. In the subsequent years, the foundation organized iftar (fast-breaking) dinners every year with participants from different walks of life and gave "tolerance awards" to people who were seen as key contributors to social peace in Turkey. Later, the JWF formed three platforms with particular missions and focus: The Abant Platform, which has organized annual and semi-annual workshops on social issues in Turkey, Europe, U.S., and the Middle East. The Intercultural Dialogue Platform, which focused on increasing understanding between different religious, ethnic and cultural groups[7]. The Dialogue Eurasia Platform, which has worked with mostly former Soviet Republics to forge close cultural ties, and has since been publishing the DA Magazine in Turkish and Russian (with contributions from Russia, Turkic Republics of Central Asia and Turkey).[8]

The Abant Platform is a self-governing entity supported by the JWF. Its executive committee includes some key members of the foundation's board of trustees as well as some independent academics.[9] The themes of annual meetings, participants to be invited and organizational issues are addressed by the executive committee.

The mission statement of the platform mentions 'dialogue and reconciliation in light of knowledge and expertise' as the key principle. The platform aims to create a 'common intellect' that can define social problems, break them down into pieces, and brainstorm in a collective manner to deliberate the public and propose solutions. The idea is finding a common ground without necessarily giving up personal beliefs and values.[10] The philosophical guru of the platform, Mehmet S. Aydin explains the notable success of the platform by stressing five traits of Abant:

i.   Disengaging the so called controversial issues in deadlock from ideological and fanatical realm and bringing them into the world of knowledge and rationality.

ii.   Formation of an "Abant spirit" that is intellectually brave and tolerant of opposing ideas.

iii.   A democratic attitude by which a free debate and deliberation is possible.

iv.   Based on dialogic logic with three steps: accumulation of knowledge, critical and analytical mind, and the existential step in touch with reality.

v.   The possibility of meeting on the common denominator in spite of seemingly irreconcilable philosophical and ideological positions.[11]

---

7 This platform organized interfaith trips and meetings in Harran, Urfa (Turkey), where Prophet Abraham was believed to have spent the earlier years of his life. The concept of "Abrahamic Religions" and commonalities between them were emphasized with Muslim, Jewish and Christian participants. The platform also raised awareness about the tragedy of Bosnian Muslims, organized interfaith prayer services for peace, and a celebration of the 700th anniversary of the asylum granted to the Jews, who escaped from persecution in Spain, by the Ottoman Empire.

8 For the mission statement and the board of trustee of the JWF, see the foundation's official website: www.gyv.org.tr

9 The theology professor Mehmet S. Aydin, who served as the minister of state in charge of religious affairs in Justice and Development Party (AKP) cabinet (2002-2007) chaired the committee until recently. Another academic, professor of history, Mete Tuncay of Istanbul University, took over the position since 2006. Mete Tuncay defines himself as agnostic and his support for the platform gives the Abant Platform credit as an inclusive and non-confessional organization.

10 Harun Tokak, "Abant and the Feeling of Responsibility," Opening Speech for the 1st Abant Meeting (1998).

11 Mehmet S. Aydin, Opening Remarks for the 2nd Abant Meetings, *Abant Platformu: Din, Devlet ve Toplum*, op. cit., pp. 10-11.

Format of the Meetings and the Participants

The platform chose Abant, a remote recreational area in Northern Turkey, as the venue for the first six meetings. Hence, the notions of "Abant Platform" and "Abant spirit" have been used to refer to the initiative. The participants can be divided into two categories. First group is the 'core' participants that include the platform's executive committee, most members of the JWF's board of trustee, and some other well-known academics.[12] These people have participated in almost all of the fourteen meetings. The second group consists of academics and intellectuals who are invited based on their expertise and the theme of the workshop, politicians depending on the political climate, and media representatives.[13] The academics are primarily from the fields of theology, political science, history, law, philosophy and economics. The politicians who participated have been primarily from conservative parties and movements.

The workshop starts with an opening session where the executive committee introduces the topic, the participants and operational aspects of the meeting. Usually, politicians and a select number of community leaders deliver speeches on the importance of the Abant Platforms and their reflections on that year's theme. Later, the workshops proceed either with some specialized committee meetings or thematic panels.

Meeting No	Academic	Media	Politician	Bureaucracy - State	Civil Society
1st Meeting-1998	71	6	2	1	10
2nd Meeting-1999	67	24	5	0	4
3rd Meeting-2000	61	16	8	3	12
4th Meeting-2001	55	13	16	0	16
5th Meeting-2002	69	17	5	0	9
6th Meeting-2003	63	21	0	8	8
7th Meeting-2004	64	8	8	0	20
8th Meeting-2004	68	4	10	8	10
9th Meeting-2005	85	10	0	0	5
10th Meeting-2006	36	20	0	9	35
11th Meeting-2006	51	19	7	13	10
12th Meeting-2007	55	27	0	6	12
13th Meeting-2007	47	18	7	4	24
Average	61	16	5	4	14

Earlier the meetings were more in the form of workshops where different aspects of issues were debated to come up with some consensus conclusions-for the press release and concluding declaration. Later, however, this format was criticized to work as a forcing mechanism to forge consensus. Since the sixth workshop, the meetings were reorganized to be more like academic conferences with presentations and panels. This format change is also evident in the concluding documents. The first five meetings produced declarations with specific points and

---

12   Harun Tokak, Cemal Ussak, Huseyin Gulerce, and Serif Ali Tekalan from the JWF administration; and academics including Mehmet S. Aydin, Mete Tuncay, Niyazi Oktem, Durmus Hocaoglu, Hayreddin Karaman.

13   Politicians who have participated include Abdullah Gul, Bulent Arinc, Kemal Dervis, Mehmet Agar, Riza Akcali, Huseyin Celik, Ali Babacan, Ali Coskun, Cemil Cicek, Celal Adan, Ali Mufit Gurtuna. Journalists from a wide range of media outlets also attended: Toktamis Ates (Cumhuriyet), Fehmi Koru (Yeni Safak), Cuneyt Ulsever (Hurriyet), Cengiz Candar (Referans), Ali Bulac (Zaman), Nevval Sevindi (Zaman), Sahin Alpay (Zaman), Alev Alatli (Zaman), Mustafa Armagan (Zaman), Besir Ayvazoglu (Zaman), Mustafa Erdoğan (Star), Ali Bayramoglu (Yeni Safak), Rusen Cakir (Vatan), Yasin Aktay (Yeni Safak), Emre Akoz (Sabah), Osman Ozsoy (Tercuman), Tarhan Erdem (Radikal), Ani Ozgurel (Radikal), among others.

the later meetings were summarized with concluding remarks and conference proceedings.

Themes

i.   Islam and Secularism- Abant, Turkey (1998)
ii.   Religion, State and Society- Abant, Turkey (1999)
iii.   Democratic State and the Rule of Law- Abant, Turkey (2000)
iv.   Pluralism and Social Reconciliation- Abant, Turkey (2001)
v.   Globalization- Abant, Turkey (2002)
vi.   War and Democracy- Abant, Turkey (2003)
vii.   Islam, Secularism and Democracy: The Turkish Experience- Washington DC, US (2004)
viii.   Culture, Identity and Religion in the Process of Turkey's EU Membership- Brussels, Belgium (2004)
ix.   New Pursuits in Education- Erzurum, Turkey (2005)
x.   Republic, Multiculturalism, and Europe- Paris, France (2006)
xi.   Global Politics and the Future of the Middle East- Abant, Turkey (2006)
xii.   Turkey-Egypt Colloquium: Islam, West and Modernization - Cairo, Egypt (2007)
xiii.   Historic, Cultural, Folkloric and Contemporary Dimensions of Alevism- Abant, Turkey (2007)
xiv.   Turkey-French Conversations II- Istanbul, Turkey (2007)

The topics discussed in the meetings underscore two important points. Firstly, the specific topics are chosen based on the context (time and space). After the indirect military intervention in politics against the Islamist Welfare Party government, Turkey struggled its way towards normalization of civil-military relations between 1997 and 2002. The first four meetings search in this context for consensus building on some of the intractable issues polarizing the country along the lines of Islamist vs. Secularist and the state vs. the society. After 2002, the themes were based more on global context than local. The 2003 meeting tackled the question of bringing democracy by force in face of escalating US threat to intervene in Iraq. The platform discussed the question of Islam and democracy in 2004 during the euphoria right after the 'success' of Operation Iraqi Freedom. It seems, by having this meeting at the very birth place of the Greater Middle East Initiative, the platform aimed to speak to the Western audience. The two Turkey-France conversations (2004 and 2007) were more focused on Turkey's EU membership with a broad multiculturalism outlook. France was symbolic in being one of the most vocal opponents of Turkey's full membership and its historical influence over Turkish intelligentsia in issues of secularism, republicanism and citizenship. In 2006, the Gülen movement, which has been criticized not paying enough attention to the Muslim World as much as they emphasize dialogue with non-Muslims, invited intellectuals from the Middle East including Arab, Jewish and Turkish to discuss the future of the Middle East. And most recently in February 2007, the platform co-organized a meeting in Egypt with the prominent Al-Ahram Institute to discuss Turkish and Egyptian experience with democracy, modernization and secularism.

Along with the platform's close consideration of socio-political setting, the second striking point is the increased frequency of the meetings by time. As a result, the participants and the target audience also expanded, becoming more diverse every year. The first meetings probe Turkey's chronic problems that are at the source of significant tension in the country. Secularism, state-society relations, Alevi-Sunni relations are just a few of those issues that are still at the centre of public debate. Later, the platform looks into issues that are more global in nature but with clear implications for Turkey, such as democratization, war, and globalization. The meetings in the U.S. and Europe are more tuned toward bringing Turkey and Turkey's experiences with democracy, secularism and Islam to the forefront of discussion. This also aims to put up bridges between Turkish and the Western intellectual, and possibly policy, circles.

Results of the Meetings

The Abant workshops close with a concluding declaration or a conference report. These documents are then shared with the public with a press release and either sent or presented to statesmen and members of the political society. The JWF have also published transcripts and proceedings of some of the earlier workshops. Most recently, the Mehtap TV, a channel that specializes in cultural and educational programs and known for its ties with the Gülen movement, started to air the Abant meetings live. This is an important move to make these meetings more accessible to the general population.

The public declarations consist of three broad items:

i.   A belief in social harmony
ii. A commitment to liberal-democratic values
iii. A referral to Turkish and/or Islamic perspective.

The starting point for Abant meetings is the possibility and necessity of dialogue across different beliefs, values and identities. The organizers, sponsors, participants and supporters of Abant frequently stress the need for dialogue, open debate, consensus building and conflict resolution. One can see references to this conviction in almost every meeting declaration. The fourth meeting is in essence an embodiment of this position with philosophical and analytical underpinnings. The main purpose of pluralism is described as the recognition of difference and achieving a societal consensus. The consensus is not defined as transformation of differences, rather as finding a social compromise (similar to the concept of social contract) to be able to live together in spite of differences. Obviously, the virtue is to live in peace with a meaningful dialogue among the constituents of the society. The document celebrates diversity and openly calls for a new constitution based on a manifestation of the new social contract. The Kemalist ideology is criticized for attempting to homogenize the society in the prolonged period of nation-state building and blamed for "social engineering" in the name of modernization to attain the desired ideological and political outcomes. [14]

Another characteristic of the declarations is their liberal democratic tone. Freedom of religion and conscious along with the right of individuals to practice their beliefs is the central thesis of 1st and 2nd meetings, which examine secularism, and the social role of religion. There is also a clear liberal position in regards to state-society relations. By questioning the sacralisation of the state, participants portray the state in service to its citizens, contrary to the traditional state dominant Turkish political culture. In that sense, the state is urged to liberate itself from totalitarian, authoritarian and top-down ideological-doctrinal tendencies. The concept of raison d'Etat[15] is rejected in favour of a full fledged rule of law and a neutral referee state.[16] This speaks to the fallacy of creating a police state with human rights violations in

---

14   The concluding declaration of the 4th Abant meeting, www.gyv.gov.tr.
15   The French term used to describe the justification of overriding state power.
16   3rd meeting concluding declaration, www.gyv.gov.tr.

the name of national security and war on terror. The strongest critique of laïcité also comes from this avenue: Turkish secularism is not simply a separation of religious and political authorities, but a subjugation of religion to state control, which raises serious questions about the freedom of religious practice (e.g. the headscarf ban in public schools). [17] Finally, the platform maintains that Turkey needs more democracy not less to solve its ethnic, religious and social problems. [18]

The Abant platform departs from a belief that religion, and particularly Islam, can be a positive factor in social, political and economic life. The 1st Abant meeting undertook the challenging question of the relationship between Islam and secularism. Being the first of its kind in Turkey and organized by a religiously-based civil society group, this meeting not only attracted quite an attention at the beginning, but also provoked some interesting public debate afterwards. The meeting ended with casting some doubts on some clichés and taboos in Turkey about the position of Islam on secularism and democracy. The participants agreed on positions such as:

i.   There is no contradiction between revelation and reason according to the prevalent position in the Islamic scholarship.

ii. No person or group has a monopoly or divine authority over the understanding and interpretation of Islam.

iii. Muslims in the earlier periods of Islam engaged in more independent judgment (ijtihad) to solve problems in accordance with the general principles of the religion and necessities of the time. (This was a direct challenge to the orthodox position in Sunni Islam about the closing of the gates of ijtihad since the 12th century AD).

iv. There is not a necessary contradiction between the sovereignty of God in religious cosmos and sovereignty of people in politics.

v.   State is a human construct, rather than a metaphysically and politically sacred entity (in response to the question of the existence and nature of an "Islamic state")

vi. Other than the universal and basic democratic rights and the rule of law principles, Islam leaves the specifics of the regime type to societies. (Islam and democracy are compatible)

vii. Turkey should develop a more freedom based form of secularism (Anglo-Saxon version of secularism investigated in depth during the workshop) [19]

The reactions to these bold statements were mixed. Some Islamic intellectuals, such as Ahmet Tasgetiren, declined the invitation to participate and criticized its concluding document for being limited by the conditions of 1997 indirect military intervention in politics[20]. Most liberals and conservative intellectuals, on the hand, praised the meeting for its brevity and sincerity.

The question of Islam and modernity assumes another pivotal position in the 7th Abant meeting in Johns Hopkins University, US. The American and Turkish intellectuals scrutinized the Turkish experience with Islam, modernization, secularism and democracy. Unlike the 1st meeting, the 7th meeting did not produce a consensus public declaration, the general tone was about the unique historical and contemporary dynamics in Turkey's experience with Islam. I believe the intentions of the Gülen movement to sponsor such a meeting are twofold.

---

17 2nd meeting concluding declaration www.gyv.gov.tr.

18 3rd meeting concluding declaration, www.gyv.gov.tr.

19 1st meeting, (the comments in the parentheses are mine)

20 Tasgetiren is in the board of trustees of the JWF. He later participated in the 4th workshop.

Firstly, to offer an alternative face to Islam and Muslims after the negative effects of the 9/11: There are moderate Muslims who denounce violence, appear in public discussion and engage in open exchange with non-Muslims. Second is to make a statement in the US, and the world, public sphere that there are organic-native Muslim groups who take the responsibility to discuss the problems of the Muslim world in a genuinely open and sincere manner. Thus, the US policy-makers and the media are expected to pay closer attention to the people 'on the ground' before engaging into ambitious projects, such as the Greater Middle East Initiative.

The Gülen movement is very much in tune with globalization in terms of an increased connection between societies and a freer flow of information, ideas and economic goods across the boundaries of the nation-states. In spite of the global reach of the movement, the local characteristics are still salient. In the case of Turkey, the movement sees its Turkish and Islamic roots complementary and inseparable. According to Gülen, Turks played a significant role in Islamic history not only by defending the Muslim World militarily, but also by producing a remarkable civilization based on Islamic principles. He argues that by the 10th century Turkish Muslim scholars in Central Asia were able to understand the 'universality' and 'spirit' of the Islamic teachings and use new methodological tools for interpretation and inference. The Seljuk and Ottoman Empires benefited from this comprehensive jurisprudence to freely borrow from other civilizations and legal systems to make their Shari'a based rule more flexible and in touch with the realities.[21] From this historical account, the Turkish interpretation and practice of Islam is tacitly presented to other Muslim societies as an alternative to the more literal salafi Islam, popular in some parts of the Arab World. Although one can see this Turkish bias in most of the Abant workshops, the 6th meeting in Washington DC was the one that directly addressed the theoretical and practical meaning of Turkish Islam.

Broader Meaning and Implications of Abant

In many respects Abant is a unique enterprise. First, it is a genuine civil society initiative. It is 'civil' as it does not have any links with any branches of the state apparatus. It also does not directly promote economic or political interest of a group. This difference from an interest group is important to underline because it suggests a more civic and collective purpose to contribute to the public good as opposed to particular understanding of public good from an economic, political or ideological perspective. Think-tanks, business associations, labour unions, environmental groups and even human rights advocates are examples of interest groups that are formed by like-minded individuals with very particular goals. The Abant platform is primarily supported by the Gülen movement, yet its mission statement points to the interest of the society as a whole. This is in fact not more than a logistical and moral support. However, this does not mean that the movement gains nothing out of this leadership in the end. If you ask the activists in the executive committee, they will stress that a society in peace and harmony is in the interest of everyone including the members of the Gülen movement.[22] In addition to this, I believe that the Abant platform along with JWF presents a much needed visibility to overcome the suspicions regarding the informal structure, and a possible secrecy, of the movement.[23] This in turn contributes to the legitimacy of the movement in the public

---

21 For an analysis of Gülen's ideas and the concept of Turkish Islam, see Ugur (2004).

22 Author's interview with members of the JWF, June 2007.

23 After a media campaign against him, Fethullah Gülen was tried by the State Security Court on grounds of forming a secret organization to change the secular nature of the Turkish state (2000-2003). He was acquitted, yet there is still an uneasy relationship between the movement and the Kemalist state bureaucracy. The popular support behind the movement, its economic power and the education and media network worry the state that the movement might

eye, which is quite crucial for the uninterrupted prospering of the educational and business network of the movement.

Another unique feature of the Abant initiative is its religious based inspiration and motivation. The Gülen movement is not exceptional in forming civil society organizations and using religion as a source of social capital. However, other religious groups mainly offer social services, such as health care, private education, and food and clothing for the needy. When it comes to public policy, most religious groups act as an interest group. In other words, they take open positions in moral issues, such as social justice, war, abortion, drugs among others. Many Christian churches participate in the democratic process, even hire registered lobbyists. Even if they form coalitions, they still retain their positions as a distinct group.[24] The Gülen movement, in contrast, does not openly take position in many issues, including the much debated headscarf question in Turkey. Rather, the movement takes a more indirect way to influencing the public opinion. Promoting platforms where different groups in the society, including non-religious and atheists, is an outcome of this indirect approach. In a way, the Abant Platform does not only consume the existing social capital by bonding (within the Gülen movement fellowship) but also creates more social capital by bridging (across different groups).[25] One needs to take into account the influence of the political culture in shaping such an approach. Unlike the liberal pluralist political culture in the US, for historical reasons[26] Turkey is closer to the republican tradition that emphasizes the 'general will' and public order over public sphere that legitimizes inclusion of particular moral, philosophical and ideological values. As we mentioned in the previous section, the Gülen movement uses a national (interest) based rhetoric, and this becomes the basis for their legitimacy in the Turkish public sphere.

A critical contribution of Abant in Turkey is the empowerment of the civil society vis-à-vis the state. Many civil society organizations in Turkey function as agents of the state, jeopardizing the autonomy of the civil society as a whole. One can see this especially in some Kemalist organizations, which are orchestrated by some retired army generals. During the most recent series of public demonstrations against the Justice and Development Party (AKP) in Turkey, the links between the military and the "civil" society organizations were hotly debated.[27]

The success of Abant depends on two factors: its continued commitment to the democratic process (without getting entangled in every day politics) and its faith in the power of civil society. As a result of the public deliberations about various aspects of the social problems, a more informed, educated and cohesive public have already started to emerge, which in turn developed a self-esteem for challenging the state in matters of democracy, freedoms and the rule of law. The open dialogue and reconciliation that takes place in Abant demystifies social problems that were seen as intractable. This in turn depoliticizes social problems. And paradoxically, depoliticisation opens more space for the political society against the resentment of the state bureaucracy to reform. A civil society mindful of its interest in balancing the coercive power of the state and a political society that can transmit the societal preferences into policy and legislation are two indispensable elements of a functioning democracy.

---

want to capitalize this influence into political power in the future.

24 The New Christian Right and the Interfaith Alliance are good examples from the US.

25 For an extensive discussion of bonding vs. bridging social capital, see Robert D. Putnam, *Bowling Alone: The Collapse and Revival of American Community* (New York: Simon and Schuster, 2000).

26 The strong Ottoman state tradition and the French influence on Turkish modernization.

27 See for example, "Vatanseverlik' yarışındaki örgütler emekli asker dolu. Al sana 'sivil' toplum!" [Organizations competing for 'patriotism' are full of retired army generals, a 'civil' society!], *Radikal*, 17 February 2007.

CIVILITY IN ISLAMIC ACTIVISM: TOWARDS A BETTER UNDERSTANDING OF SHARED VALUES FOR CIVIL SOCIETY DEVELOPMENT

Wanda Krause

Abstract

Fethullah Gülen's works and movement have aimed to mend the tensions and fissures, specifically along racial and ideological lines on both practical and theoretical levels that are emerging in this rapidly globalising world. Within a civil society theoretical framework, this paper addresses the knowledge developed on Islamically inspired forms of activism, before proceeding to an examination of key civil society actors with focus on the Gülen movement.

Islam-based forms of organisation are conventionally presented as deficient in 'civility' or even antithetical to civil principles. The danger is that they are then simply excluded from normative definitions of civil society and their positive role in it diminished. In this respect, this paper argues for expanding the concepts through which we view and come to judge civility and citizenship. The role of shared values in building civil society is facilitated by expanding the concepts through which we measure and exclude crucial components. Recognising the value systems behind Islamic forms of organisation helps develop better tools for deciphering the shared values among various parts of civil society.

Focusing on the Gülen movement, through an investigation of its beliefs, values and practices, the paper illustrates not only its contribution in terms of expanding civil societies internationally, but also how – according to the criteria used for measuring its effect – it is positioned as a leading example of dealing with contemporary challenges. It is hoped that this work will contribute to laying the epistemological groundwork for those struggling against Islamophobia and striving to expose the values shared among all actors in a healthy and vibrant civil society.

Introduction

Within a civil society theoretical framework, the paper addresses the knowledge developed on Islamically inspired forms of activism and proceeds with an examination of the Gülen movement as a key component of civil society. A critical rethinking is required of the dominant theoretical understandings of civil society and views within the existing body of literature on the forms of organisation that contribute to its vibrancy and expansion. The dominant discourse or assemblage of ideas is 'a clash of civilizations,' spearheaded by Samuel Huntington. Huntington theorised that a clash of civilisations will occur as different civilisations are more likely to fight each other.[1] Issues have emerged because of factors, such as, the increased interaction among peoples of different civilisations and a global resurgence of religious identity, and demographic and economic changes that threaten to shift the balance of power among western and non-western civilisations. Consequently, as Özdalga points out, there has been an upsurge in the visibility of Islam.[2] For Huntington, religion is the central defining characteristic that defines identities.[3] Such theorisation needs to be contested and revealed of its fallacies for a clearer understanding of global politics and the role of faith-based movements.

Islamic-based forms of organisation are classically presented as deficient in 'civility' or, in fact, antithetical to civil principles. As Özdalga further points out, "in spite of the increasing awareness that Islam and Islamic movements play a decisive role in modern society, they are most often brought to the notice of the public when large and sensational events take place. The result of this sporadic and sensationalistic attention is a general lack of focus on not only non-violent forms of Islam, but also on long-term analytical perspectives."[4] They become, therefore, excluded from normative definitions on civil society and their positive role in it diminished. Ever more pressing, a dilemma faces, more generally, theorists and leaders in terms of how best to tackle the growing security threats of terrorism and Islamophobia. In a globalised world in which terrorism has become one the of the major challenges facing individuals and state leaders, narrowly constructed frames - of actors and institutions that have the ability not only to create greater civility but to counter anti-civil movements and actors - are actually exacerbating the problems of terrorism and racism.

Thus, the Gülen movement will be analysed in this paper and argued to be a leading model of Islamically-based associations and movements that contribute to the development of civil societies.[5] It is an example that challenges these mainstream readings. It is crucial that policy makers and theorists, alike: a) question not only the basis but the effect of such framing and b) expand their theoretical framework of civil society in practical terms by seeking the inclusion of model civil society movements, such as the Gülen movement, that are in a position to best address and tackle these major problems.

The Gülen movement is discussed in an attempt to contribute to a questioning of the knowledge

1 Huntington, Samuel P. (1993) The Clash of Civilizations? Foreign Affairs, vol. 72, no. 3:22-49 and S. P. Huntington. 1996. The Clash of Civilizations and the Remaking of World Order (New York: Simon and Schuster).

2 Özdalga, Elisabeth. (2005) Redeemer or Outsider? The Gülen Community in the Civilizing Process. The Muslim World, vol. 95 (July), 429.

3 Huntington 1996, 47.

4 Özdaga . (2005), 430.

5 Berna Turam similarly argues Gülen's significant role in civil society. See Turam, Berna (2001) National Loyalties and International Undertakings. Islamic Modernism: Fethullah Gülen and Contemporary Islam. Georgetown University (26-27 April).

developed on civility and citizenship globally. Through an investigation of beliefs, values and practices, the paper will argue that the Gülen movement functions as a mechanism to counter threats to civility and security. The paper illustrates not only its crucial contribution in terms of expanding civil societies internationally, but how – through an examination of its empowering effects and the civility components of trust, cooperation, reciprocity, and tolerance, it is positioned as a leading example for dealing effectively with contemporary challenges by countering forces that threaten civil societies. Its founder, Fethullah Gülen, and his movement have aimed to mend the tensions fissuring in this fast emerging globalised world, specifically cleavages along racial and ideological lines on both practical and theoretical levels.

In the first section, 'Fethullah Gülen and the Gülen Movement, Gülen's philosophy will be outlined as a backdrop to an analysis of the movement and his works. In the second section, 'Islam and the Idea of Civil Society,' the theoretical underpinnings of civil society which reject religiously, specifically Islamically, motivated action will be contested. The paper proceeds in the next section, 'Indicators for the Development of Civil Society in a Globalised World,' with a brief description of the indicators that will be used to assess the impact of the Gülen movement, specifically in the current political context. The analysis through the two main indicators used for the purpose of this project will follow in the subsequent sections: 'Empowerment: The Gülen Movement's Role in Individual and Societal Development,' and 'Civility: Terrorism and Racism,' respectively. Lastly, the 'Conclusions' summarise the findings and discusses future prospects and dilemmas.

Fethullah Gülen and the Gülen Movement

The Gülen movement is based on an Islamic philosophy that embraces a 'common good,' and emphasises the universality of values, spirituality and principles of justice – in short, the welfare of society and all individuals within that society. Gülen's work and movement has become an active force within civil societies, as can be seen in the numerous activities pursued, and its growing presence in an increasing number of countries outside its origins, Turkey.

Gülen is a peace activist, intellectual, religious scholar, mentor, author and poet, great thinker and spiritual guide who has devoted his life to seeking the solutions for society's ills and spiritual needs. The movement depends on members' recognition of a set of shared and meaningful references to Gülen's ideal cognitive schemetas and the Nur (Light) doctrines that together lead to a collectivity.[6] Many of Gülen's ideas are influenced by Said Nursi's magnum opus, written discourse of Bediüzzaman Said Nursi (1876 – 1960), who authored several volumes of Qur'anic exegesis known as Risale-i Nur Kulliyati (The Epistles of Light).[7] Other Turkish Muslim figures that have influenced Gülen include Alvarli Muhammed Lutfi, Mehmet Akif, Necip Fazil, Elmalili Hamdi, Nurettin Topcu, and Sezai Karakoc.[8]

Gülen envisions a world in which we will witness a revival of long-dormant moral values, an age of tolerance, dialogue, and cooperation that will ultimately lead to a single, inclusive civilization. In this vein, Gülen and his supporters have struggled for worldwide peace

---

6 Komecoglu, Ugur, quoted in Ihsan Yilmaz (2000) Changing Turkish-Muslim Discourses on Modernity, West and Dialogue. Paper presented at the Congress of the International Association of Middle East Studies, Berlin (October 5-7), 2.

7 Yilmaz, 2000, 2.

8 Thanks to Dr Ihsan Yilmaz for providing this information.

through conferences and symposiums. Gülen contributes to a number of journals and magazines and writes the editorial page for several magazines. He has written more than forty books, hundreds of articles, and recorded thousands of audio and videocassettes. He has delivered innumerable speeches on many social and religious issues. Some of his books have been best-sellers in Turkey and translated into German, Russian, Albanian, Japanese, Indonesian, and Spanish.[9]

He has lead the establishment of many charitable organisations. He has influenced the use of mass media, in particular television, to inform the public of matters of pressing concern. Gülen has opened high quality schools and institutions for learning in over 100 countries, illustrating its wide reach and exponential growth. He believes the road to justice for all is dependent on the provision of an adequate and appropriate universal education. Volunteerism is a cornerstone to the success of his educational institutions, as well as the support of small businessmen, the social elite and community leaders, and powerful industrialists. With donations from these sources, educational trusts have been able to establish these schools and scholarships to help students.

The discourse of any movement is of crucial importance in assessing any impact on civil society. Some of the main ideas Gülen espouses are *ijtihad*, democracy, and harmony between science and religion.[10] *Ijtihad* refers generally to some form of 're-interpretation,' in which the Islamic scripts are understood in line with modern and civil values. Gülen embraces interpretation, which includes the rethinking of issues based on new contexts, environments, and differing cultures.[11] He encourages Muslims to resort to 'civil *ijtihad*.' As such, he encourages work on issues such as genetic engineering, organ transplantation, music, art, secularism, modern law, etc.[12]

He argues that in spite of its many shortcomings, democracy is now the only viable political system. He argues that science and religion are actually two different aspects that emanate from the same truth. He strives against terrorism by lecturing on Islam's principles and against those who seek to use Islam's name in their acts of terror. He strongly advocates pluralism in theory and practice. For example, he argues for a pluralism of ideas and that open contestation and persuasion is the route to toleration and co-operation, as will be elaborated on later. For Gülen, pluralism must also exist in Islamic legal opinions.[13]

Gülen's movement becomes a powerful civil society force for a number of aspects. In more quantitative terms, it forms a loose entity that transcends cultures, ethnicities, and even religion due to its breadth over several countries at a growing rate. The movement draws on Islamic teachings that are mostly no different from most other religious teachings, thus enabling the movement to build bridges between faiths and the pursuance of common interests for the good of mankind and society. In this way the movement is positioned to root itself in a variety of contexts making it an 'outward-looking' form of organisation, as opposed to an 'inward-looking' form of organisation which comprises the dominant mode of religious-based and interest-based organisation. The movement, thus, has the capacity to be more effectual in

---

9 Gülen, Fethullah (2005) Pearls of Wisdom (Light: New Jersey), xii.

10 His ideas on inter-faith dialogue and education will be elaborated on below.

11 Yilmaz, Ihsan (2003), *Ijtihad* and Tadjdid by *Conduct: The Gülen Movement*, in: M. Hakan Yavus and John Esposito. Turkish Islam and the Secular State: The Impact of Fethullah Gülen's Nur Movement (Syracuse: Syracuse University Press), 221.

12 Ibid., 223.

13 Ibid., 224.

its ambitions for greater world peace and individual and societal development.

But just as important to note is its firm philosophy and goals. In considering the impact of any organisation or movement, qualitative terms are just as, if not more, important. It is true that many forms of organisation preach principles of civility and world peace, all which are necessary for attaining such ambitions globally. But for the 21st century, I argue that the form of organisation that is best suited to the major challenges of terrorism and racism must not only embrace principles of democracy and universal principles of justice and rights, but also be rooted in Islamic philosophy. The core texts of Islam share and preach the same values of tolerance, understanding and peace as do the core texts of the other main faiths. However, cleavages are along racial lines that predominantly follow religious adherence. Moreover, Islam has been successfully framed by the doings of both Muslim and non-Muslim supporters of division, misunderstanding, and hierarchy. Thus, it must necessarily be a movement that understands and advocates the purposes of Islamic teachings as being for the welfare of individuals and society for this framing to be countered effectively and a 'clash of civilizations' to be avoided. The recent RAND report,[14] developed by numerous high-level thinkers, has concluded that the way forward to the eradication of terrorism is through embracing liberal Islamic thinkers that are still rooted in the mainstream Muslim populace. The Gülen movement straddles this delicate balance and achieves much more.

Islam and the Idea of Civil Society

The inclusion or exclusion of Islamic groups or associations as civil society institutions has been a matter of considerable disagreement. Many argue that Islamic groups or associations fall outside the realm of civil society. Most research on Islamic movements has been directed to Islamist groups,[15] particularly violent groups or movements, as opposed to Islamic organisations or organisations inspired by Islamic principles. Thus, mainstream and majority Islamic faith-based forms of association have been glossed over in much of the literature and theorisation. Apart from grievous misunderstandings, much research has been influenced by the orientalist bias. Additionally, civil society's progressive teleology often embraces anti-religious positions and particularly those with some Islamic component. Thus, the behaviours, norms and practices that are ideologically motivated are seen as incongruous with the project of civil society.

Scholars, such as Clark, Verhagen, Göle, and Kandil assert that religious organisations have an important function in civil society. Clark shows that a danger in analyses has been the blurring between the minority of violent Islamist groups and the majority of non-violent Islamist groups, in which Islamic associations are characterised as instruments of the undemocratic and extremist Islamic groups.[16] As Verhagen notes, the contribution of religious organisations is in terms of the value systems they furnish and also of the catalyst for social transformation they often become. Göle, in fact, in her study on Turkey, speaks of the

---

14 Please see Rand's 2007 report at http://www.rand.org/pubs/monographs/MG483/

15 I use Laura Guazzone's definition of the term, *Islamism*, referring to "an ideology and the set of movements associated with it." *Islamists* consciously choose an Islamic doctrine as a guide for political action. *Islamist movements* can vary significantly in their doctrines and should not be confused with *Islam*, which is a much broader concept referring to the Islamic religion. See Guazzone, Laura (1995) Islamism and Islamists in the Contemporary Arab World, in: Laura Guazzone (Ed) The Islamist Dilemma: The Political Role of Islamist Movements in the Contemporary Arab World (Reading: Ithaca Press), 4.

16 Clark, Janine A. (1994) "Islamic Social-Welfare Organizations and the Legitimacy of the State in Egypt: Democratization or Islamization From Below?" unpublished PhD dissertation, University of Toronto, Canada, 35.

creation of an autonomous sphere in society due to Islamic values and the Islamicisation of politics.[17] Kandil recognises that religion plays a key role as a motivating factor for women's voluntary initiatives since it encourages them to volunteer time and give charity and thus enables them to assume a profound role in civil society.[18] Ghannouchi argues that Islam is naturally strengthening to 'civility'.[19]

This paper will emphasise, through a notable example, that Islamically inspired groups are equally relevant to the sphere in which dominant discourses are challenged and competing views are put forward. Excluding forms of collaboration and movements inspired by Islam means ignoring the fact that, as well as contributing to civility, they can be the most effective means for responding to the needs of citizens[20] and challenges facing many governments today. It is also important to recognise that a 'common good' is a contested domain. As Carothers explains, "struggles over public interest are not between civil society on the one hand and bad guys on the other but within civil society itself."[21]

The 'common good', although a contested domain, is however best accomplished when different groupings can experience peaceful co-existence through shared value systems. Since tensions between various ethnic, racial and religious or ideological groupings are increasing, as can be evinced in many European capitals today, to the point that individual safety is a growing concern, there has never been greater need to establish common principles and values among these groupings and leanings. Therefore, those civil society actors that espouse ideas and practices that strengthen intra-group unity and cooperation, as opposed to those whose interests and aspirations result in greater tensions or hatred, must be facilitated and supported by citizens and policy-makers alike.

Indicators for the Development of Civil Society in a Globalised World

Civility will take greater focus in analysing the Gülen movement, in way of demonstrating the key role this movement inspired by Islamic teachings plays in moving – including western societies – to greater civility and, thus, demonstrating the dysfunction of the mainstream conception of civil society from which Islamic forms of organising are often not included. Empowerment will be a further indicator used for analysing its role and importance in civil society.

Civility is understood here as the conduct of a person whose individual self-consciousness is partly superseded by his or her collective self-consciousness, with the society as a whole and the institution of civil society being the referents of her collective self-consciousness.[22] As Seligman stresses, "The continuity of ethnic loyalties and solidarities (and so also the

---

17 Nilüfer Göle (1994) Towards an Autonomization of Politics and Civil Society in Turkey, in: Metin Heper (Ed), Politics in the Third Turkish Republic (Boulder: Westview Press), 221.

18 Kandil, Amani (1999) Women and Civil Society", in: Civil Society at the Millennium (Civicus, Connecticut: Kumarian Press), 63. Kandil (1999, p. 63) accredits the large number of women in Egyptian private voluntary organisations (PVOs) essentially to their traditional mothering roles.

19 Ghannouchi, Rached (1999) Muqarabat fi al-`ilmaniyya w'al-mujtam' al-madani [Papers on Secularism and Civil Society] (London: Maghreb Center for Research and Translation), 83.

20 Schwedler, Jillian (1995) Introduction, in: Jillian Schwedler (Ed) Toward Civil Society in the Middle East? A Primer (Boulder CO: Lynne Rienner), 16.

21 Carothers, Thomas (1999) Civil Society: Think Again. Foreign Policy, no. 117, 21.

22 Shils, Edward (1992) The Virtue of Civil Society. Government and Opposition., vol. 26, no. 1 (winter), 335.

potential for ethnic exclusion) within groups undercuts the very definition of universal citizenship within the nation-state...."[23] While "tolerance towards the other", most often defined as synonymous with 'civility', is an indictor,[24] a wider range of "civil acts", or what are referred to as "values" for the normative part of civil society, are considered here. While agreeing with Schwedler that "tolerance toward those with different views is paramount,"[25] following Antoun's contribution to the definition of civility, "the practices and ideas that generate cooperation and trust for the purpose of accomplishing social goals"[26] must necessarily be part and parcel of the concept. Singerman also emphasises the important factors of "cooperation, trust, and mutual dependence";[27] which is especially crucial for deciphering which activities and philosophies promote these values in an increasingly globalised world. Underpinning the concept of civility in dealings and behaviour, thus, are the values of trust, reciprocity, cooperation and tolerance.

The empowerment process has traditionally been left out of the analysis of social movements and associational activism. It is mostly feminists who have defined empowerment, and have emphasised the effects a woman has on her institutional environment as "circumventing, changing, or eliminating the society's values, practices, norms and laws in order to lessen the extent to which they constrain her activities and choices."[28] The mainstream conceptualisation of empowerment is, indeed, important to civil society development in a broader sense. Empowerment also involves the attainment of freedoms from injustice among threatened or oppressed individuals, groups, or nations. The language of freedoms must include broader categories where the systematic violation of rights and freedoms results in the same dynamics of oppression as has been widely described for women as a category. Any form of agency from which greater fulfilment, satisfaction, consciousness-raising, skills development, or piety may result is important not to overlook. As Adam Ferguson comments, "The happiness of individuals is the great end of civil society: For, in what sense can a public enjoy any good, if its members, considered apart, be unhappy?"[29]

Empowerment: The Gülen Movement's Role in Individual and Societal Development

Analysing empowering effects that result from the Gülen movement's efforts, captures a deeper understanding of how their mode of action enables greater well-being, health and the ability of individuals to be in better positions to take greater control over their choices. Empowerment is achieved through its educational and charitable efforts. The movement is dedicated to education in a broad sense. It is an education of the heart and soul as well as of the mind, aimed at invigorating the whole being to achieve personal competence and the

---

23 Seligman, Adam B. (1992) The Idea of Civil Society (New York: The Free Press), 165.

24 Norton, Richard (1995) Introduction, in: Augustus Richard Norton (Ed) Civil Society in the Middle East, Vol. 1 (Leiden: E. J. Brill), 213.

25 Schwedler 1995, 6.

26 Antoun, Richard T. (2000) Civil Society, Tribal Process, and Change in Jordan: An Anthropological View. International Journal of Middle East Studies, vol. 32, no. 4 (November), 456.

27 Singerman Diane (1995) Avenues of Participation: Family, Politics, and Networks in Urban Quarters of Cairo (Princeton: Princeton University Press), 50.

28 Ackerly Brooke (1997) What's in a Design? The Effects of NGO Programme Delivery Choices on Women's Empowerment in Bangladesh, in: Anne Marie Goetz (Ed) Getting Institutions Right for Women in Development (London: Zed Books), 141.

29 Quoted in Schwedler 1995, p. 5.

ability to be a useful citizen for the benefit of others.[30]

Education has taken centrality in Gülen's philosophy for attaining existential rewards. Teachers in Gülen schools do not overtly proclaim their adherence to Islam nor teach the sciences from a religious perspective. Gülen explains that it is enough to be a faithful Muslim while imparting secular knowledge because "knowledge itself becomes an Islamic value when it is imparted by teachers with Islamic values and who can show students how to employ knowledge in the right and beneficial Islamic way."[31] What Gülen has been inspired to achieve from the inception of the schools is a quality of education that surpasses rivalries and stagnation. This began when he confronted the problem, first in Turkey, of secular schools having been unable to free themselves of the prejudices and conventions of modernist ideology and the madrasas of having shown little desire and ability to break with the past or enact change and to integrate technology and scientific thought.[32] An empowerment from stagnation in educational systems and philosophies and rivalry is achieved in his endeavours now on a global scale.

In Gülen's educational philosophy, scientific learning is not dissected from development of spirituality. As Gülen has continually emphasised, faith and science are not separate entities for individual and societal development and advancement. Piety and spirituality are part and parcel of developing the conscientious citizen. He asks people to "judge your worth in the Creator's sight by how much space. He occupies in your heart, and your worth in people's eyes by how you treat them. Do not neglect the Truth even for a moment. And yet, 'be a human being among other human beings'."[33] For Gülen, improving a community is possible by elevating the coming generations to the rank of humanity through spiritual consciousness and the consciousness of others' rights. Gülen stresses:

> Civilization lies in people's spiritual evolution and continuous self-renewal toward true humanity and personal integrity-to realizing their full potential as the "best pattern of creation." People must realize that civilization is not ... something to be bought from a store and worn. Rather, it is a final destination that can be reached only by following a rational way passing through time and circumstances.[34]

As such, for a strengthened global civil society to be achieved, one must understand that to be civilised entails first the building of the self. This responsibilisation sought through 'secular' learning and spiritual consciousness consequently effects a stronger and healthier community, which in effect contributes to the wider civilization. Gülen repeats, "Magnificent nations produce magnificent governments. It is the generations with high spirituality, scientific advancement, financial opportunities, broad consciousness, and the individuals struggling to be 'themselves,' that form magnificent nations."[35]

More deeply, one must look at the value systems which furnish and drive this whole process. Gülen expresses that a core component of this process involves jihad. He explains jihad occurs on two fronts: the internal and the external, both of which are based on struggling in

30 Gülen (2005) Pearls of Wisdom.
31 Agai, Bekim (2002) Fethullah Gülen and His Movement's Islamic Ethic of Education. *Critique*: Critical Middle Eastern Studies, vol. 11, 41.
32 Michel, Thomas (2001) Fethullah Gülen and the Gülen Schools. Islamic Modernism: Fethullah Gülen and Contemporary Islam. Georgetown University (26-27 April), 4.
33 Gülen (2005) Pearls of Wisdom, 76.
34 Gülen, Fethullah. Civilization and the Confusion of Conceptions, http://en.fGülen.com/
35 Gülen (2005) Pearls of Wisdom, 88.

the path of God. His focus is on the internal struggle, which he calls 'the greater jihad' and defines as the effort to attain one's essence. The external struggle (the lesser jihad) is the process of enabling someone else to attain his or her essence. The first, he comments, "is based on overcoming obstacles between oneself and one's essence, and the soul's reaching knowledge, and eventually divine knowledge, divine love, and spiritual bliss."[36] The second is based on removing obstacles between people and faith so they have free choice in belief and unbelief. For him, jihad is the purpose of our creation and our most important duty.

When one conquers one's selfish desires through internal jihad, one becomes more giving, sacrificial, and conscious of others' rights to well-being and happiness. Establishing a true civilization, for Gülen, is assisted when one learns to seek existential reward over worldly riches and status. He explains, "those who want to reform the world must first reform themselves. If they want to lead others to a better world, they must purify their inner worlds of hatred, rancour, and jealousy, and adorn their outer worlds with virtue."[37]

His movement has worked towards inculcating individuals with this desire and practice, and the effects can be seen through the numerous charitable works its members have developed. As such, the movement can be said to have an important effect in building civil societies as the bases of civilization, through individual empowerment and societal empowerment. Empowerment is achieved one, when the individual develops and advances his/her own skills, education and consciousness and two, when other individuals benefit from that person's charity, education, or guidance. True civilization is premised on the empowerment of humanity.

Civility: Terrorism and Racism

The Gülen movement exemplifies an institution and mode of action that is indispensable to decision makers and policy makers struggling with the strains of ideological cleavages and growing fear and threats of terrorist and racist action. A look at four major components of civility – tolerance, cooperation, reciprocity, trust - illustrate how the teachings and philosophy of the Gülen movement is a vehicle for the development and securing of civil societies.

Tolerance is the "willingness to recognise and respect the beliefs or practices of others."[38] It is something one needs to build from the inside. Gülen asks people to "be so tolerant that your heart becomes wide like the ocean. Become inspired with faith and love for others. Offer a hand to those in trouble, and be concerned about everyone. He emphasises the meaning of tolerance in his article, "Islam – A Religion of Tolerance:"[39]

Islam is a word derived from the root words silm and salamah. It means surrendering, guiding to peace and contentment, and establishing security and accord.... How unfortunate it is that Islam, which is based on this understanding and spirit, is shown by some circles to be synonymous with terrorism. This is a great historical mistake; wrapping a system based on safety and trust in a veil of terrorism just shows that the spirit of Islam remains unknown.[40]

In this article and many of his other works, Gülen refers to the core text of Islam, the Qur'an,

---

36 Gülen, Fethullah, Lesser and Greater Jihad, http://en.fGülen.com/
37 Gülen (2005) Pearls of Wisdom, 105.
38 Word Reference Com: World Dictionary. http://www.wordreference.com/definition/tolerance Last accessed 5 May, 2006.
39 Gülen (2005) Pearls of Wisdom, 75.
40 Gülen, Fethullah, Islam – A Religion of Tolerance, http://en.fGülen.com/

and the sunnah, the traditions of Prophet Mohammed, and practices of the companions of the Prophet and Islamic scholars throughout history, to show how the message of peace and tolerance is repeated throughout.

Again and again, he underscores how misguided those people are who hijack Islam in legitimising terrorisation of innocents. Gülen warns of present-day manifestations of groups in Islamic history that threaten civility. He refers to the Karmatis, Kharijites, and Anarchists,[41] to explain the groups today that often follow a literal meaning of the Qur'an, create chaos, hatred and warfare not only between Muslims and Non-Muslims but between Muslims.

Toleration of another person's beliefs and practices does not mean that one must like them, accept them for oneself, or even believe that they are correct. But one must accept the condition of a co-existence with people of diverse beliefs, traditions and practices, with the appreciation that others have the same right as oneself to personal beliefs and ways of behaving, given that legal parameters must be in place that will curtail behaviour that harms society. As Gülen most aptly puts it:

No matter how charming and enchanting the atmosphere that catches the eye or fills the heart is there is no permission for us to forget the truth to which we are committed. We cannot stay alien toward each other while we are in the same camp. We do not have a monopoly of the good and the beautiful; therefore we cannot be allowed to wage a war with the passengers who are heading to the same destination but on a different path.[42]

Gülen believes that through education there will be sufficient understanding and tolerance to secure respect for the rights of others. In securing tolerance he however emphasises the need to view science or reason as part of religious understanding. He states:

Humankind from time to time has denied religion in the name of science and denied science in the name of religion, arguing that the two present conflicting views. All knowledge belongs to God and religion is from God. How then can the two be in conflict? To this end, our joint efforts directed at inter-religious dialogue can do much to improve understanding and tolerance among people.[43]

For the Gülen movement, tolerance is achieved through a form of education that does not deny the place of religion, nor denies the place of what is known as 'secular' learning. This is merely a constructed dichotomy that bears little relevance in the true attainment of building a holistic self and society.

Cooperation is, indeed, another value the Gülen movement strives for, as can been observed

---

41 As Gülen explains, Karmatism is a heretical esoteric sect founded by Hamdan ibn Karmat in the ninth century AD. Hamdan ursupted the poor and claimed shares from the rich in Iraq and its surroundings as "collective property." and claiming shares from the rich. His group was religious only in appearance. Among many things, members rebeled against the Abbasid caliphate, tortured Sunni Muslims, ambushed pilgrims on their way to the Hajj, attacked the sacred city of Makka (at one time stole the Hajar al-Aswad from the Ka'ba), treated women as collective property, institutionalised prostitution widely, and legitimized alcohol. The Kharijites was another faction which blamed Caliph Ali, one for conceding to arbitration and accepting the treaty at the Battle of Siffin and two for not handing over the caliphate to Muawiya. They declared all others who did not think likewise—including the Companions of the Prophet—infidels. Gülen explains, further, they were dragged into bigotry, hostility, and intolerance, getting mired in harshness, violence, and crudity. Anarchists legitimized the actions of some tyrants against Muslims and have positioned themselves rebels against the state. See, Fethullah Gülen, "Three Groups Opposing Dialogue – Kharajites, Karmatis, and Anarchists," http://en.fGülen.com/
42 Gülen, Fethullah, Respect for Humankind, http://en.fGülen.com/
43 Gülen (2005) Pearls of Wisdom.

in its philosophy and practice. Cooperation is important not only between groups but within groups for civility to take root and grow in any context. The movement enables the crucial civility component of cooperation in its endeavours to establish interfaith dialogue and within its institution establish an ethic of inclusivity.

Gülen argues,

> Interfaith dialogue seeks to realize religion's basic oneness and unity, and the universality of belief. Religion embraces all beliefs and races in brotherhood, and exalts love, respect, tolerance, forgiveness, mercy, human rights, peace, brotherhood, and freedom via its Prophets.... For interfaith dialogue to succeed, we must forget the past, ignore polemics, and focus on common points. [44]

He, furthermore, believes that, "The Islamic social system seeks to form a virtuous society and thereby gain God's approval. It recognizes right, not force, as the foundation of social life. Hostility is unacceptable. Relationships must be based on belief, love, mutual respect, assistance, and understanding instead of conflict and realization of personal interest."[45] Similarly, Gülen refers to the modern-day Karmatis, Kharajites, and Anarchists as those who threaten cooperation between those of different faiths.[46]

Since non-discriminatory forms of cooperation are a key to establishing norms that support plurality, the inclusivity of individuals is noted. The Gülen movement supports educational and work opportunities for women. Many women work particularly as educators in schools and universities, and as administrators in certain areas.[47] With regard to religious minorities, Gülen schools have been established in various countries with communities of various faiths. Students of all backgrounds attend these schools because of the high quality of education they offer. Observers will attest to, even sometimes how surprised they are at, the high level of educational abilities of the students the professionalism of teaching staff.[48] As Özdalga notes in her observation of the staff of the schools, they give primary loyalty to their work and students as opposed to their families.[49] This is of particular importance to the formation of a civil society as in many, especially developing, countries, and particularly in the wider Middle East, internal loyalties supersede external loyalties, causing one major source of problems to the development of healthy civil societies. When travelling to visit some of the Gülen schools, Turan attests he witnessed a "pluralist nature of the student bodies - Christian and Muslim in Zamboanga, and Buddhist and Hindu as well in Kyrgyzstan - that what they sought to communicate were universal Islamic values such as honesty, hard work, harmony, and conscientious service rather than any confessional instruction."[50] He further comments, "in the Sebat International School in Bishkek, students from U.S.A., Korea, and Turkey appeared to be studying comfortably with those coming from Afghanistan and Iran."[51]

Gülen also pioneered the establishment of the Journalists and Writers Foundation in 1994, whose activities promote dialogue and tolerance widely within society. Gülen is the honorary

---

44 Gülen, Fethullah, The Necessity of Interfaith Dialogue, http://en.fGülen.com/
45 Gülen, quoted in Yilmaz 2003, 230.
46 Gülen, Fethullah, Three Groups Opposing Dialogue – Kharajites, Karmatis, and Anarchists, http://en.fGülen.com/
47 Afsarrudin, Asma. The Philosophy of Religious Education: Classical Views and Fethullah Gülen's Perspectives, 21.
48 Michel (2001) 3.
49 Özdalga (2005), 435.
50 Michel (2001), 3.
51 Ibid.

president of the foundation. The aim of the Foundation, according to its president, Harun Tokak, is the development and consolidation of love, tolerance, and dialogue, among journalists and writers, throughout Turkish society, and humankind.[52] The Foundation has held several conferences and publishes books that promote its aim. In its aim for wider participation among various groups, the Foundation attracts scholars and intellectuals of different ethnic, ideological, religious, and cultural backgrounds.

Importantly, the Journalists and Writers Foundation also functions as a think-tank. The Abant Conference - its success, the first of its kind in Turkey - is a result of the Foundation's attempt to work together with people of various backgrounds to find solutions to some of the issues facing intellectuals in regards to Turkey, such as laicism, secularism, religion, and the state. The convention takes place yearly and ends with a declaration. In 1998, the theme was "Islam and secularism"; in 1999, "religion and state relations"; and in 2000, "the democratic state within the framework of rule of law."[53]

Reciprocity is also a major component of civility. Inclusivity, as found within the Gülen school system, establishes a basis upon which individuals can share knowledge and can further an ethic of tolerance and understanding. Thereby, an ethic of giving, receiving and sacrifice are spread among those who participate in such projects, as well those who are educated through them. Norms of reciprocity help communities to better achieve their interests in a peaceful and civil manner. Reciprocity strengthens relations between the members, organisations they work with, and consequently communities. In short, it solidifies networks in which people can rely on one another to cooperate and struggle towards the goal of global peace.

Trust is the last component of civility that we will discuss, though no less important the building of a civil society than tolerance, cooperation, and reciprocity. Gülen emphasises the need for trust between individuals to facilitate cooperation and success in any endeavour. Gülen argues for the individual to be trustworthy so as to facilitate the bonds between people. This requires individual integrity and sense of responsibility to others' rights and needs. This is a "virtue related self-discipline and sensitivity."[54] He furthers the centrality of the principle of trust in admonishing its importance to the wider community: "If a state cannot protect its secrets from its enemies, it cannot develop. If an army reveals its strategy to its antagonists, it cannot attain victory. If key workers are won over by the competitors, their employers cannot succeed."[55] However, trust is broader than the terms of keeping secrets. Trust is, for example, also about entrusting another with one's possessions. This can be seen to be put into practice among members who sacrifice their time and material resources, in faith that their works and charity will be put into worthy causes by others who believe in and support Gülen's dreams and philosophy.

Conclusions

The Gülen movement takes a sizeable and important role in the development of a number of civil societies around the world. This can be seen in their educational and charitable projects. Of importance, however, are the ambitions, philosophy, and dreams with which the movement aspires and the principles upon which members are motivated and they base their activism. The movement aptly demonstrates how its Islamic principles are put into practice to

---

52 Yilmaz 2003, 231.
53 Ibid., 231, 232.
54 Gülen (2005) Pearls of Wisdom, 81.
55 Ibid., 83.

create a better world. Its impact can be more readily seen through a systematic analysis of its contribution in terms of empowerment strategies and modes of civil action.

The Gülen movement contributes to empowerment on a massive scale as its projects and schools have spread to over 100 countries. The features of its empowerment strategies include, first and foremost, the merging of the secular and spiritual to educate an all-rounded, capable and responsible individual who has acquired the desire to be a source of inspiration and help in the modern market economy and global world. As many observers have attested through visits to the Gülen educational establishments, individuals thrive in often multiracial/religious and supportive environments; hence, they gain the ability to provide a solid foundation to a healthy community, which Gülen views as crucial component to a healthy civilization and civilized world.

Not unconnected, thus, is the impact the movement has on developing civil societies globally through the developing of civility – a crucial component to their stability and productivity. This is observed through the Gülen movement's strong commitment to civil components of tolerance, reciprocity, trust, and co-operation. Practice in this direction is found in the participation of hundreds of thousands of individuals in the numerous establishments, the Foundation, schools, and charitable projects that establish these values and spread them to the wider societies in which they operate. An important example includes Gülen's fervent commitment to inter-faith dialogue which takes place through all these venues on various scales.

This example as a humanistic movement inspired by Islamic principles should convince scholars and policy makers of its importance to the development of civil society on a theoretical level. Equally crucial, it should be viewed as a leading example of the forms of organisation that should be promoted for the benefit of civil societies, whether in predominantly Islamic countries or what one might commonly refer to as secular countries. Forms of organisation that promote empowerment and civility through Islamic teachings are crucial in a world in which civility seems to be increasingly threatened.

The challenge of the future of civil societies lies not only in the ability of such forms of faith-based movements to empower, provide example, and create better conditions for civility. We are entering a time in our history where proponents of a 'clash of civilizations' are influencing public opinion towards increased hatred and polarisation with growing terrorist action and the distortion of global politics and meaning of civil society. Terrorism and Islamophobia will continue to be on the increase if movements that have popular opinion in the Muslim world and solidly espouse values of democracy, human rights, and civility - and decisively establish through its discourse the compatibility of belief and these values - are not supported.

"ISLAMIC PURITANISM" AS A SOURCE OF ECONOMIC DEVELOPMENT: THE CASE OF THE GÜLEN MOVEMENT

Selcuk Uygur

Abstract

Turkey has been going through significant transformations over the last two decades, which might be studied under diverse rubrics. The focus in this paper is on the emergence of a new bourgeoisie that is overwhelmingly religious; its aim is to describe the motives behind the attitudes of religious business people and to discuss the contribution of the Gülen movement.

The paper begins by clarifying relevant concepts that appear vague – such as 'Islamic Puritanism' and 'Islamic work ethic' – following the particular interpretation by Wilhelm Hennis of Max Weber's familiar 'Protestant ethic' thesis. Rather than looking for mechanical causal relationships, this paper focuses on life goals and ways of living and discusses the Gülen movement's contribution to the way of living related to economic activities. (The movement is considered as a new interpretation of Islam – Turkish and strongly influenced by Sufism.) Next, the institutional and moral sources enabling an enterprise culture are discussed. This paper considers the transformation in Turkey to be securely founded on the moral sources and suggests that Turkish Islam might be considered as a source enabling a particular type of entrepreneurs, and that this type is helpful to Turkey's modernisation project as it anticipates membership of the European Union.

Introduction

Lately, it has been discussed that religious people in Turkey are in transition. This paper will be stressing on the economic aspect of this transition, particularly focussing on the emergence of religious businessmen, and the contribution of the Gülen movement to this transition. We argue that Turkey's effort of economic development can benefit from this transition. In order to support this argument, we intend to explain the religious businessmen phenomenon with a Weberian approach. In this respect, first, the study evaluates the emergence of religious businessmen in Turkey. Then, Max Weber's Protestant ethic thesis and its different interpretations will be assessed. We intend to explain the above-mentioned phenomenon with a distinctive Weber reading which is made by Wilhelm Hennis. Hennis's Weber interpretation, in terms of the relation between religion and economic activity, focuses on how a religion shapes individuals' way of living rather than suggesting any causal relation between religion and economic development. This particular interpretation seems a useful instrument to explain the economic impacts of the Gülen movement. At the same time, this study intends to clarify probable misunderstandings and concept confusion regarding the using of such terms as "Muslim Calvinists" or "Islamic Puritanism" in the relevant literature.

The Emergence of Religious Businessmen in Turkey

Turkey has been facing a significant transformation in its social structure for two decades. This transformation process might be classified under several subheadings; however, we intend to focus in this piece on the emergence of religious businessmen and their economic activities and dynamics. Newly emerging religious business people and SME (small and medium sized enterprise) owners, and their new entrepreneurship culture seem quite unique, especially in the Muslim world. This new entrepreneurship culture has been considered as a new attitude concerning worldly activities, particularly in business circles. It is considered as new because religious people were not for a long time interested in doing economic activities in a rational and modern way. Consequently, the development has been the subject of a heated debate in Turkish intellectual and economic circles. The controversy has been intensified, especially after a recent report entitled "Islamic Calvinists" by European Stability Initiative (ESI)[1].

The report has focused on the central Anatolia, Kayseri a city known for its conservative and religious leanings. Basically, the report has attributed the business boom in Kayseri to the "protestant work ethic" values of its people (esiweb.org). In turn, such terms as "Muslim Calvinists" or "Islamic puritans" have been frequently used by some journalists and academics alike, to describe the business elite of the region. This transformation process has been considered as a struggle for creating an indigenous Muslim ethic (Ozdemir, 2006). This opinion also claims that it is a unique and yet highly compatible step for Turkey's ongoing modernisation project. In this sense, this new development has been argued to be creating a new Turkish bourgeoisie and an enterprise culture in Turkey.

Obviously, in the context of this controversy, the concept of enterprise culture gains special importance. According to Keat (1991) and Carr (2000) creating enterprise culture has two dimensions. First, it requires institutional and structural changes, such as changes on regulations, privatization, encouraging private business sector, reducing taxes, etc. But, these changes are not sufficient as such. Creating enterprise culture also requires moral foundations.

---

1   For more information and the full text of the report, see http://www.esiweb.org/index.php?lang=en&id=117

As it is seen in the example of the United Kingdom (UK), Thatcher's endeavours were covering both, namely institutional changes on one hand and moral foundations of the country's enterprise culture, on the other. Thatcher frequently stressed the importance of UK's historical moral values, principally the Protestant ethic, to facilitate creating enterprise culture. In fact, what is at issue here may be claimed to be a long term struggle to modify people's way of thinking and transform their 'souls' (Roberts, 1992:15). In short, religion may be argued to be a source of creating particular type of individuals in terms of economic activities and enterprise culture.

In this piece, we will focus on the Gülen movement in Turkey that emerged with its flexible ideas to stimulate a patriotic, global and free market orientation with an emphasis on the spiritual and intellectual consciousness of the individuals (Yavuz, 2003: 19, 29). Fethullah Gülen is a well known Islamic scholar in Turkey. His ideas have inspired many people in Turkey to establish educational institutions that integrate modern science, ethics and spirituality. Berberoglu (2000), a Turkish journalist, describes him as an opinion leader, and Aras (1998) sees him as "a most likely candidate for religious leader of the new Turkey". Besides educational institutions, he gives special importance to inter-faith dialogue activities in Turkey and all over the world by stressing the significance of cultural and legal plurality of societies (Unal and Williams, 2000). It is claimed that "Gülen's discourse has had and will have major influences on the future shape of Turkey and the region" (Yilmaz, 2005:394). Probably, the biggest difference between other Islamic movements and the Gülen movement is that his movement is a civil one, rather than a political. As previously mentioned, his main concern could be summarised as ethics and individuals. Considering the institutions and activities of his sympathisers; such as hundreds of schools along with seven universities all over the world, media institutions, inter-faith dialogue centres, college preparation courses; it can be claimed that it is a successful civil initiative. Therefore, this successful movement might be a proper example of how a civil society acquires its autonomy from the state. In other words, the movement plays a crucial role in the empowerment of civil society, which is very important for Turkey's democratization process.

As known, the population of Turkey is overwhelmingly Muslim and the state is strictly secular. From the very beginning of the Turkish republic, the state chose a strict secularism as a lynchpin of its project of modernization. It can be said that it has been successful to some extent. However, the recent emergence of religious businessmen as a phenomenon has been argued by some to be a possible threat for the secular structure, who have dubbed the phenomenon as an attempt by the green or Islamic capital to form an Islamic state, oblivious to the apparent contradiction represented by the combination of capitalist greed and ideological orientation. This contradiction appears to be resolved by an understanding that the Gülen movement uses democracy not out of a normative commitment, but rather instrumentally, as a useful tool for seeking power to establish an Islamic state (Baskan, 2005). Yavuz (2003), away others, considers this sort of readings as superficial. On the contrary, some studies have showed that the religious people in question are well adapted to the rational way of doing business and show strong "Protestant work ethic" values (Arslan, 2001; Ozdemir, 2006).

However, in this paper, we are not interested in the work ethic values of the people in question; whether they are hard workers, or whether they are honest or not. Rather we intend to focus on the dynamics of the emergence of this phenomenon. According to the Weberian reading of society, every social order requires particular type of individuals. In the Turkish context, we propose that Anatolian Islam, in particular the Gülen movement as the typical representative of it, plays a vital role in creating a certain type of individuals. However, the role of this new approach is not only in creating sympathisers of a particular movement, but it also shapes a new interpretation of Islam which is more suitable for worldly activities and, a more rational way of living. In a sense, it might be considered as combining secular and religious values together. For example, educational institutions inspired from Gülen's ideas are not traditional medrese schools; rather they are secular institutions that meet the necessities of the modern world. According to Voll (2003: 243), "it is a new synthesis of elements of the older modern secularism and religion". Therefore, it can be claimed that the new generation religious people grow up within this particular interpretation of the religion. We argue that this new approach, in other words the transition, can also affect the understanding of business and economy. In order to understand the religious businessmen phenomenon in Turkey, we will draw on a particular interpretation of Weber's Protestant work ethic thesis. Then, the phenomenon will be evaluated within that particular interpretation.

Max Weber's Protestant Ethic Thesis

Max Weber's "Protestant work ethic" thesis has been a widely studied subject for many years by considerable amount of researchers from a variety of fields. Naturally, we encounter many different interpretations of Weber's study with different perspectives. Most of the researchers agree about his claim: that ascetic Protestantism played a vital role in the formation of modern, rational capitalism (Weber, 2001). However, this claim might seem vague in itself, and may need to be elucidated by the question how? For this reason, we face many different interpretations explaining how Protestant ethic shaped modern capitalism, and under what circumstances it happened. In this respect, it is extremely important that we use a proper interpretation to explore resembling developments or changes in different cultural settings, such as religious businessmen activities in Turkey.

It is a gripping point that Weber stresses: all of the economically developed countries have already done a series of requisite reformations in relation to the Catholic Church (Weber, 2001). When we examine ascetic Protestantism, we can easily see that ascetic Protestantism shaped a frugal life style, strongly encouraging people towards hard work. Studying Weber on Protestant work ethic (PWE), we encounter two main aspects: one that in psychological, and another that in sociological. In management and psychology literature there are plenty of studies regarding psychological aspect of PWE. This body of literature is mainly about work related values, attitudes, job satisfaction etc. In this respect, the PWE seems to have been converted to personality dimension separated from its socio-political and religious background that Weber proposed (Niles, 1999). In other words, we can assume that the PWE has become secularized, and it can be considered as "work ethic" itself without its religious aspects. Furnham (1990:32) explain this situation as follows: "...so it could be claimed that the PWE is not exclusively Protestant, about only work, nor exclusively concerned with ethics. It may therefore be more accurate to talk about work values and beliefs rather than the PWE itself". Therefore, in a sense, it is understandable that some use such terms as "Muslim Calvinists" or "Islamic puritans" while studying different cultural settings, such as Muslims, in the academic literature. But, of course, it does not suggest any correlation between different religions or social settings. For instance, in an insightful study, Mahmut Arslan (2001) compares work ethic values of Protestant British, Catholic Irish and Muslim Turkish managers in terms of PWE. According to his research, Muslim Turkish managers (specifically selected from the Nur movement[2]), show higher PWE values than their Protestant and Catholic counterparts (Arslan, 2001). The author explains his findings with the minimisation of the Ottoman despotism through democratic reforms and transformation of traditional Sufism into a kind of entrepreneurial ideology (Arslan, 2001:335). In another important study utilising a qualitative and hermeneutic perspective, Ozdemir (2006) focuses on the members of a religious businessmen association, MUSIAD (Association of Independent Businessmen). She interprets this phenomenon as an attempt towards creating an indigenous Muslim ethic compatible with the necessities of the modern world (Ozdemir, 2006).

It is a very common opinion that the Gülen movement is the largest faith-based movement in Turkey, with a strong influence on the mainstream religious way of living. Here, this paper proposes that Gülen's new interpretation of Islam promotes a particular type of individuals; and in so doing, it might assist Turkey's efforts towards economic development. We presume that PWE values such as thriftiness, hardworking, honesty are also important values for secular businessmen in Turkey. Therefore, it is hard to claim that religion, in particular "Islamic work ethic"[3] (if there is such a thing), is the only reason for the emergence of successful religious businessmen. However, doing business in a rational and modern way is a new attitude for religious people in Turkey, and this is what we really need to explain. In this regard, we intend to focus on Hennis's interpretation of Weber on the influence of religion on individuals' way of living in terms of economic activities.

Understanding Weber's Main Concern (Hennis's Interpretation)

As a starting point, we should be able to distinguish between personal change, social change and social development, due to the fact that Weber's study concerns the changes in the social order by individuals' particular way of living. In this respect, personal changes should be considered within the social context. Therefore, we intend to take individuals within the social order, because every social order requires a particular type of individuals (Hennis, 2000). However, there is a nuance between social change and social development. According to Schluchter (1981), social changes occur when a social order is transformed into another, but still manages with the same basic social configuration, such as from patrimonialism to sultanism. On the other hand, social development occurs when the basic configuration changes, for instance transition from tradition to modernity (Schluchter, 1981). Gülen movement should be considered within the concept of "social development", because it seems that the main concern of the movement is not to achieve changes in social order, but in relation to individuals.

When examining PWE, Weber's historical problem should be underlined by distinguishing between Western capitalism and Western rationalism. From the very beginning, Weber takes capitalism in historical perspective. He copes with the origin and organizational structure of

---

2 The Nur (Light) movement is an influential Islamic movement guided by Said Nursi (1878-1960) in Turkey and all over the world, from which the Gülen movement sprang. "It differs from other Islamic movements in terms of understanding of Islam and its strategy of transforming society by raising individual consciousness." (www.religion. info, 2007)

3 According to Yousef (2001:154) "both the Islamic work ethic (IWE) and the Protestant work ethic (PWE) place considerable emphasis on hard work, commitment and dedication to work, work creativity, avoidance of unethical methods of wealth accumulation, cooperation and competitiveness at the work place. However, unlike the PWE, the IWE places more emphasis on intention than on results. For example, Prophet Mohammed stated 'actions are recorded according to intention, and man will be rewarded or punished accordingly'".

legal institutions that shaped the development of a specific form of capitalism, which is the modern production-oriented capitalism (Schluchter, 1981). According to Weber, the main characteristic of the capitalism of the modern business firm is driven from a separation of business and personal assets and on an arrangement of risk and responsibility (Weber, 2001). These peculiarities of modern capitalist firms differ from the traditional medieval trading companies. He notes that only this differentiation between types of assets made possible the organizational separation of household and enterprise (Weber, 2001). On the other hand, according to Weber, rationalism is not limited to the West, like capitalism. He claims that rationalisation has existed in all civilizations in very different forms with very divergent viewpoints. Therefore, Weber takes the Western rationalism in its specific manifestation and seeks to explore its distinctiveness. In this respect he tries to explain the historical origin of the Western rationalism by indicating "who rationalizes which spheres of life in what directions and which historical kinds of social order result there from" (Weber, 2001). In other words, Weber tries to explain the emergence of a new bourgeois class based on the Western rationality by specifically emphasising on individuals and their particular way of living.

Obviously, the Western capitalism and rationalism are key terms. However, we should go further to understand the spirit of modern capitalism, and how it is related to religion in particular the Calvinist puritan sect of Protestantism in 17th century Europe. Probably, the first things we could notice, when we look at the Western capitalism as it historically unfolded are legal and commercial transformations such as new types of organizational structures, the development of double entry bookkeeping or newly emerging mechanical techniques. However, Weber does not accept that capitalism is the only reason for these transformations. He tries to show how the way of life shaped by Calvinist puritans "based on rational, legal acquisition through individual endeavour and self-discipline revolutionized the European economy" (Lewis, forthcoming). According to Giddens (2001:xviii), the "emergence of modern capitalism was an outcome of historically specific conjunction of events". Clearly, we could say that Weber's intention is to explain the historical genesis of "the manner of leading one's life" (Hennis, 2000), rather than develop a causal relationship between religion and modern capitalism. Weber explains his real concern as follows:

> In order that a manner of life so well adapted to the peculiarities of capitalism could be selected at all, i.e. should come to dominate others, it had to originate somewhere, and not in isolated individuals alone, but as a way of life common to whole groups of men. This origin is what really needs explanation (Weber, 2001:20).

Hennis (2000) appears to offer a distinct interpretation of Weber in this regard. According to this reading, every social order requires a certain kind of individuals. Consequently, Hennis claims that Weber's investigation centres around, not a 'spirit' at all, but a 'habitus'. Habitus is a complex concept "referring primarily to the non-discursive aspects of culture that bind individuals to larger groups" (wikipedia.org, 2007), particularly manner of leading one's life (Lebensführung)[4] within the social orders of life, such as family, community and economic activities in life. Weber considered all these as 'sphere' which means a particular aspect of life or activity. Hennis explains the ideas behind this term as follows:

> The 'sphere' which Weber stressed was that of the 'vocation' of acquisitive activity (Erwerbsleben).

---

4   The German term 'Lebensführung', which is critical in Weber's theory of social stratification, inspires various ideas among English speaking sociologists, as Abel and Cockerham (1993) argue. According to the authors, Lebensführung means life conduct or managing one's life; applied to the individual; it refers to the self-direction of one's behaviour, not life style.

> The puritans had brought the great 'internal tensions' between vocation, life and ethics into a 'characteristic equilibrium'; for them there was no 'on the one hand and on the other', 'theory and practice', they rather conducted lives 'totally', harnessed, consciously, 'methodically', at one with their God and themselves – presupposing the corresponding Lebensführung (Hennis, 2000:17).

Similarly, creating an Islamic ethic as a manner of conducting individual's life is the main objective of Gülen and his close circle. According to Özdalga (2003:61) his goal is to promote an ethic that is very close to what Max Weber defined as worldly asceticism, "an activist pietism with a tendency toward the rationalisation of social relationships". It is also possible to see noticeable similarities between the activities of Gülen movement and those of Protestant missionaries. Özdalga (2003:66) summarizes these parallels in the following manner:

> ...belief in the individual study of holy scriptures; the urge to live a life of piety and self-sacrifice; the enthusiasm for knowledge in general and knowledge of the natural sciences in particular; the urge to carry this knowledge to others through various educational projects; an enterprising spirit; the urge to do good deeds (activism); and a strong impulse to break open the borders of one's own national milieu to reach out to other countries and places around the globe.

Weber also states in an earlier debate with Fisher, that his "investigations concern only the analysis of the development of an ethical life-style adequate to emergent modern capitalism" (cited in Hennis, 2000:14). Therefore, it could be concluded that his central interest is the development of modern rational capitalism and how it was most deeply influenced by a particular combination of circumstances (Hennis, 2000). As it is clearly seen, there is no direct link between modern rational capitalism and Protestantism. The primary issue here is how a certain kind of belief system determines the lives of individuals who are born into a particular society. With this point in mind, we can talk about the assistance of Protestant asceticism in building the tremendous cosmos of the modern economic order (Hennis, 2000).

Unlike many others, Hennis (2000) suggests that we must see Weber's starting point first, which is the 'economic ethics of world religions'. In his short life time, Weber tried to look at the world's different religions and their influences on economic activities. He examined, for instance, the religion of China and its effects on economic activities, beside his studies on Protestant ethic in Western Europe. For him, therefore, Protestantism, especially its Calvinist branch, was just a sample of his argument, rather than his central question or focal point. As a common opinion, Weber's fundamental problem was the question of 'what is the meaning of rationality?' However, according to Hennis (2000), it was just an introduction and does not cover everything; and he argues that Weber's thesis has been misunderstood for a long time as a causal hypothesis on the origin of capitalism. To see the process of rationalization as Weber's fundamental theme is certainly not incorrect, he suggests; but, he also adds that it is misleading to read everything in its terms and see it everywhere (Hennis, 2000:7).

Today's prevailing opinion is to focus on the term Weber frequently used: "selective affinity" between 'Protestant ethic' and the 'spirit of capitalism'. Turner (1974) also argues that Weber was not saying that Calvinism created modern capitalism in his study, the Protestant ethic and the spirit of capitalism. By contrast, he claims that one can find many evidences supporting the idea that Calvinism did not create capitalism (Turner, 1974). In this respect, some scholars think that it is also possible to interpret Weber's study in an economically determinist way. Aktay (2004) proposes that it is all about the coexistence of 'Protestant ethic' and 'spirit of capitalism'. This simultaneous meeting of the protestant ethic and the spirit of capitalism together helped for development of modern capitalism. For this reason, Weber might have used the term 'selective affinity' to explain the relationship between Protestant ethic and capitalism. Weber offers a clarification by stating:

> I therefore take no responsibility for the misconceptions upon which in my opinion the foregoing 'criticism' is based. I will, however, try again on occasion of a separate edition of the essays, which for technical publishing reasons cannot be long postponed, to remove each expression which could be misunderstood in terms of derivation (falsely attributed me) of economic forms from religious motives, and to make it if possible even clearer that it is the spirit of a 'methodical' Lebensführung which should be 'derived' from 'asceticism' in its Protestant transformation and which then stands in a cultural-historical relation of 'adequacy-equivalence' which is in my opinion very important. I am grateful to my critic for this stimulus [(PE II, p.31) cited in Hennis (2000)].

In a sense, Weber's study might seem similar to Sombart's important book The Genesis of the Capitalism, which first appeared in 1902[5]. In this study, Sombart explains material developments as the result of an ethos, for instance, the role of Judaism in the development of capitalism (Sombart, 1902-2001). Hennis argues that "if Weber wished to present something new then it could not be in terms of the significance of Protestantism for the rise of capitalism" (Hennis, 2000:14). Considering the fact that, at that time Sombart had already characterised that Protestantism, especially in its Calvinist version had played an important role in the development of capitalism; Weber's problematic must be something quite different (Hennis, 2000). As Weber states, his whole investigation involved, not a 'spirit' at all, but rather a Habitus, in other words, the unfolding of a particular kind of Lebensführung 'within the orders of the world: family, economic life, social community' (Weber, 2001). Therefore, his only concern is the analysis of the development of an ethical life-style adequate to an emergent modern capitalism, according to Hennis (2000). In other words, he is interested in the emergence and development of a Lebensführung (conduct of life) which made modern capitalism achievable, stressing the relationship between a specific type of individual and a specific form of social order (Lewis, forthcoming). Therefore, it can be said that the Calvinist sect was only a sample of Weber's study. In Weber's reading, it provides the moral power and drive of the capitalist entrepreneur, according to Giddens (2001).

In the Turkish context, we can claim, at the most, that the Gülen movement supplies a similar moral energy and drive for Turkish entrepreneurs. The perception of religious people towards worldly, in particular economic, activities seems have been transformed into a more rational and modern way by the new interpretation of Islam in Turkey. Arguably, it can be said that this new approach has similar effects on Anatolian society, as in the effects of Protestant reformation over the Western Europe. It is only because of this theoretical similarity, such terms as "Calvinism" or "Puritanism" are sometimes being used to describe resembling developments in different cultural settings. In a sense, some aspects of the Gülen movement, with their focus on hard work, a disciplined life motivated by traditional and religious values, make comparing it to Protestantism[6]. Therefore, we suggest that in the relevant literature, such concepts as "Muslim Calvinists" or "Islamic puritans" should be read in this perspective. Therefore, interpreting these developments as a Protestantisation of Islam would not correctly be reflecting the transition in question, we propose.

A New Form of Sufism and Economic Activity

Religious sphere, although traditionalist and conservative, has the potential for change and innovation through interaction between its doctrinal dimensions and social reality (Worsley,

---

5   It was before Weber published his study, *the Protestant Ethic and the Spirit of Capitalism.*
6   See Aras, 2000; Ozdalga, 2003; Yavuz, 2003 and ESI's report on www.esiweb.org

1969; Ozdemir, 2006). Protestant reformation is a good example of a religion's transformative potential. As known, Protestant reformation had played an important role in creating a particular way of living in Europe. It was that particular way which had important effect in the emergence of modern rational capitalism.

According to Ozdemir (2006), the growing number of religious businessmen in Turkey is a sign of the rebirth of an indigenous Muslim ethic which was suppressed for a long time after the establishment of the Turkish republic. It can also be described as struggle for creating an internal code of ethics for all aspects of the local life. As in Calvinism, it is not only related to religious individuals, it also affects many different aspects of the public sphere. In this context, the emergence of religious businessmen could be considered as carriers of a new indigenous ethic. Gole (1997) considers these businessmen as a newly emerging secondary elite group. Whether they are named a secondary elites or a new bourgeoisie, we propose that they could play a vital role in Turkey's development process.

In a sense, some studies (Rodinson, 1973; Arslan, 2001; Turkdogan, 2005) seem to prove that Islamic values and capitalism are not incompatible. However, it is a paradoxical situation as well. It does not explain the underdevelopment of Muslim countries, considering the fact that these values have existed for fourteen centuries. Kuran (1997) suggests that the reason for the underdevelopment of Muslim countries should be sought internally rather than externally. By saying internal reasons we understand the different perceptions and interpretations of the religion. For a long time, in Turkey among the other Muslim countries, Western civilisation and rational values were seen as non-compatible for the Muslim societies. Gülen and his close circle "go a step further accepting Western civilisation as a suitable foundation for material life while considering Islamic civilisation suitable for spiritual life" (Aras, 2000:39). For this reason, this paper focuses on a particular interpretation of Islam in Turkey.

Presumably, local and traditional values should shape the understanding of religion. As known, Sufism has had a crucial impact on Turkish understanding of Islam. Spiritual teaching of Sufism can be expressed as: "to help to refine the individual's consciousness so that it may reach the Radiances of Truth, from which one is cut off by ordinary activities of the world" (Shah, 1990:1). The most common motives of Sufism could be summarized by the following terms: "*tevekkul*" (reliance; putting oneself in God's hands), "*dunya*" (worldliness) and "*zikr*" (remembrance of God). However, the perception and the interpretation of these terms have changed over time. Regarding the relations between Sufi ideas and economic activities, Sabri Ulgener is the first scholar, that comes to minds. He is also known as the "Turkish Weber". According to Ulgener (1991) the concepts mentioned had separated from their original meaning as being otherworldliness. In the early years of Turkish republic, many Sufi institutions had been closed by Atatürk on the ground that those institutions (*Tekkes*: Dervish schools) were encouraging laziness, indolence and were open to abuse. At the same period, Turkey chose a strict form of secularism for its development and modernization project. Ulgener finds understandable the reasons for closing *tekkes* down. The misinterpretation of Sufism which defined the late Ottoman tekkes, according to him, was one of the reasons for the economic disintegration of the Ottoman Empire (Ulgener, 1991).

However, Ulgener (2006) also stresses the necessity of investigating the main concern of Sufi ideas. He claims that Sufism is not necessarily against worldly activities. The concept of "*dunya* (worldliness)" is a key notion in Sufi literature. In many Sufi sayings and poems we can see that a negative meaning applied to the concept, in terms of leaving everything in the world. In general meaning, Sufis define the concept of "world" as everything in the world except the love of God. According to Ulgener this is what people misunderstood for long time. He proposes that the meaning of "*dunya*" should be sought within individuals' intention, rather than within the material dimensions of the world (Ulgener, 2006). As Ulgener explains, Sufis consider the "dunya" as nothing else than forgetting of devotion to God. In this respect, Sufis claim that none of the usual suspects such as women, money, or business career, are the "*dunya*". Ulgener makes his argument stronger by citing some sayings of the prophet: "The world is something that keeps you busy from remembrance of God" "Work for this world as if you will never die; and work for the other world as if you will die tomorrow" (2006: 64). Therefore, it can be said that the crucial thing for Sufism is not the worldly activity itself, but the intention of the individual. Engaged in work overall, Ulgener's studies show his optimism regarding a regaining of the power of Sufi ideas in an economic sense.

In this regard, it can be said that Gülen has also been reinterpreting Sufi teachings within the contemporary framework[7]. The ideas of Ulgener, who is an historian of economics, show high compatibility with those of Gülen. When explaining such Sufi terms as isolation (*tecrid*) or asceticism (*zuhd*), Gülen stresses that these terms do not mean that one should leave worldly activities; and he puts great emphasis on rearing Muslim individuals not isolated from the world (Gülen, 2004). Unlike political Islamic movements in Turkey, the priority of the Gülen movement is education towards a reconstruction of the daily lives of people in Turkey (Piricky, 1999). Thus, it can be claimed that his tenets influence many aspects of daily life, including economy and business. In an interview Gülen, gives us some evidence regarding how this new interpretation of Islam contributes to a more rational way of living in terms of economic activities:

> Today, our troubles are ignorance, dissension and poverty. The solution for these problems is organizing rich people and learning how to conduct work. ...Even today, I definitely wish them (Turkish entrepreneurs) who come to see me, to do something (in business sense) here. And, I ask them: Have you done a proper market analysis? Do you know about your competitors? (Akman, 2004:52)

As it is seen, rather than direct relations between religion and economic activities, such as Islamic business principles; his contribution very much values the secular premises of business. In this respect, just as Protestantism in shaping a capitalist entrepreneurial mentality within the Christian world, Gülen is thought to play a comparable role within the modern Turkish society (Piricky, 1999). Therefore, the phenomenon of religious businessmen in Turkey should be explained within the social context which that particular way of living shapes. However, the emergence of religious businessmen in Turkey should not only be applied to the new interpretation of Islam. After 1980s, Turkey's economy politics changed radically and it was shifted from a state-oriented economy to a free-market liberal economy. It can be said that this transformation in economy politics has encouraged private business sector and it has facilitated the emergence of enterprise culture. Historically, the transition both in economics and religion has occurred at the same time period. Aras (2000:40) summarizes it as follows:

> In the 1990s, however, policies oriented towards greater liberalisation and a shift to export-oriented industrialisation have led to the emergence of new, dynamic, export-oriented, small and medium-sized business, many based in traditionally conservative Anatolian cities. This segment of society has been mobilized by Gülen's movement. The newly emerging export-oriented economic class is likely to challenge the existing economic structure and pressure the state bureaucracy to

---

7 For further information about Gülen's reading of Sufi terms, see: Gülen, F. (2004), *Key Concepts in the Practice of Sufism*, The Light Inc: NJ.

end the unequal treatment. It might also be said that the economic activities linked to Gülen's movement as well as the educational activities of Gülen's community have become part of an alternative economy.

In almost every Anatolian city, Gülen's sympathisers have established local businessmen associations. Among these local institutions, they have also established two national businessmen associations: TUSKON (Confederation of Businessmen and Industrialists of Turkey), and ISHAD (Business Life Cooperation Association). These associations work as NGOs (Non-Governmental Organizations) and aim to provide suitable atmosphere for gathering Turkish private business sector together and stress the importance of cooperation and ethics. They arrange business trips all over the world to seek new opportunities for Turkish entrepreneurs. The businessmen of these associations are also financing the educational institutions of Gülen Movement, considering it as a social (or, in a sense a religious) responsibility of their own. In this respect, we can claim that religious businessmen in Turkey have started to work in a more rational way which requires full adaptation to free market and the capitalist system.

Purportedly, we can assume that combining traditional values and modernity might assist Turkey's modernisation project. Talal Asad, in his insightful study entitled Genealogies of Religion, notes that tradition and modernity are not entirely different entities, and he claims that modernity emerges out of tradition (Asad, 1993). In the Turkish context, the Gülen movement seems a new paradigm for acquiring the level of modern developed countries. According to Yilmaz (2005:400) the movement "is generally deemed to be moderate" and it "can be considered 'modern' in the sense that it espouses a worldview centred around the self-reflexive and politically participant individual's ability to realise personal goals while adhering to a collective identity, and seeks to shape local networks and institutions in relation to global discourses of democracy, human rights, and the market economy" Yavuz (1999:195).

Conclusion

It is a common opinion that Muslim world is in transition. As previously mentioned, this paper's focal point is economic aspects of this transition, in the case of religious businessmen in Turkey, and the contribution of the Gülen movement to this transition. While evaluating the emergence of religious businessmen in Turkey we tried to use a Weberian approach by distinguishing the different interpretations of Weber.

In short, this paper proposes two major points. First, we suggest that the phenomenon at issue should be read in the way that, following Hennis, Weber's central concern is all about (which is the conduct/manner of one's life), as opposed to setting up causal relationships between religion and economic activity. We suggest that Gülen's new interpretation of Islam has crucial impacts on mainstream understanding of Islam in Turkish society. In particular, it seems that religious people in Turkey has modified their views towards business activities into a more rational way. Secondly, we suggest that the new interpretation of Islam with its flexible ideas and its high compatibility with the modern world might come handy in Turkey's modernization project that the Turkish state has been trying to achieve from the very beginning through an uncompromising secularism inimical to religious sentiments. Additionally, we propose that this new interpretation of Islam which integrates modernity with tradition might set up an example for the other Muslim countries.

SOCIAL AND SPIRITUAL CAPITAL OF THE GÜLEN MOVEMENT

Talip Kucukcan

Abstract

This paper examines the Gülen movement from the perspective of social and spiritual capital theory. It argues that, in an increasingly globalised world, this movement has been distinguished by its consistent ability to convert its social network and spiritual capital into creative projects that contribute positively to the transformation of Islamic thought and practice in many different settings and socio-political contexts. In the past, traditional spiritual and religious movements remained largely indifferent to the new forms of transformative agency such as civil society organisations, the media, modern educational establishments, corporations and global networking. Social capital theory is derived from the idea that social networks have both importance and power as civil actors in modern democratic societies. The Gülen movement was able to adapt to the modern conditions and successfully turned its spiritual, intellectual and human resources into effective social capital. Three areas of that adaptive success are examined: education (establishment of institutions from primary school to university level, attracting students of diverse backgrounds); the media (a wide range of products in print and audio-visual communication, from a mass circulation daily to TV and radio channels); and civil society organisations (foundations and associations to promote democratic participation and dialogue among various sections of the society). The paper concludes that the Gülen movement has built up a huge social capital and turns it into a number of transformative agents informed by Islamic spirituality.

Introduction

I would like to begin my paper by pointing to the rationale and significance of employing social and spiritual capital theory in the analysis of social and religious movements. I argue that modern social transformations and developments with a significant bearing on current social, cultural and spiritual movements which are inspired by religiously oriented world view requires us to employ social and spiritual capital theory as analytical tools to understand current trends. In the last two decades, sociologists discovered the importance of what is called "the social capital" which broadly refers to values, beliefs, views, ideologies and common concerns shared by a group, nation or a social movement. Social capital generates alliances, unity, solidarity, trust, networks, power and a transformative force which strengthens collective identities, claim makings, resistance to the hegemony of dominant agents. Strong and well organized social capital may play a significant role in various areas of social, cultural, economic and political domains.

The social capital as a theory and a perspective has emerged as one of the salient concepts in social sciences in various forms and contexts in the last twenty years. Today, there is a growing intellectual interest and enterprise in the concept of social capital. (Lin, 1999: 28) Drawing upon the works of theorists of social capital, social scientists who understand the significance of religion in contemporary societies started to work on spiritual capital theory. Here in this paper I will use both of these concepts as the theoretical framework in analyzing the Gülen movement in its diverse forms and contexts. Before moving on to the parameters and foundational elements of social and spiritual capital theory, I would like to argue that these approaches provide an analytical framework to examine institutional innovations and impacts of the Gülen movement. I would like to underline in the beginning my paper that the Gülen Movement differs from many of its counterparts in turning its social network and spiritual capital into creative projects which contribute to the transformation of Islamic thought and practice in an increasingly globalised world. Traditional spiritual and religious movements largely remained indifferent to the new forms of transformative agents such as civil society organizations, the media, modern educational establishments, corporations and global networking in the past. However, the Gülen movement was able to adapt to the modern conditions and successfully turned its spiritual, intellectual and human resources into an effective social capital.

This paper analyses institutional embodiments of the social and spiritual capital of the Gülen Movement in three broad categories: Civil Society Organizations, Education and Media. In the area of education, the Gülen movement succeeded to open educational establishments from primary school to University levels attracting students of diverse backgrounds. In the area of the media, print and communication, a large number of products and institutions emerged including TV and radio channels, newspapers and magazines in Turkish and in other languages. The Gülen Movement has also mobilized its resources to establish civil society organizations such as foundations and associations to promote democratic participation and dialogue among various sections of the society such as Abant Meetings which successfully brought together many intellectuals and activists from different backgrounds both in Turkey and outside to discuss local and global issues.

Theorizing Social Capital

Although the notion of capital can be traced to Karl Marx as expounded in his seminal work Das Kapital, theoretical modifications and refinements were made subsequently. Notions of human capital, cultural capital, social capital and spiritual capital were introduced as variants of classical theory of capital. Here we will focus on social capital first and the spiritual capital second. Debates and clarifications in social sciences concerning the notion of capital suggest that "social capital, as a concept, is rooted in social networks and social relations" and it "can be defined as resources embedded in a social structure which are accessed and/or mobilized in purposive actions". This definition indicates that the notion of social capital contains three elements: resources in a social structure, accessibility to such social resources by individual members and mobilization of such resources for a purpose. (Lin, 1999: 35) Membership in groups and networks facilitates the formation of social capital to achieve goals by individuals. (Sobel, 2002: 139)

Pierre Bourdieu distinguishes between three forms of capital: economic capital, cultural capital and social capital. Bourdieu asserts that social capital can be described as "the aggregate of the actual or potential resources which are linked to possession of a durable network of more or less institutionalized relationships of mutual acquaintance and recognition." (Bourdieu, 1983:249) For Robert Putnam, who is the author of Bowling Alone and the concept's leading advocate, the notion social capital "refers to the collective value of all 'social networks' and the inclinations that arise from these networks to do things for each other". Putnam argues that social capital is a key component to building and maintaining democracy. After Bourdieu and Putnam many other definitions of social capital are made which emphasize different dimensions of the concept. For example, Nahapiet and Ghoshal defines social capital as "the sum of the actual and potential resources embedded within, available through, and derived from the network of relationships possessed by an individual or social unit. Social capital thus comprises both the network and the assets that may be mobilized through that network" (1998: 243).

For Knoke on the other hand, it refers to "the process by which social actors create and mobilize their network connections within and between organizations to gain access to other social actors' resources" (1999: 18). Fukuyama, however, adopts the following definition: "social capital is an instantiated informal norm that promotes co-operation between two or more individuals. The norms that constitute social capital can range from a norm of reciprocity between two friends all the up to complex and elaborately articulated doctrines like Christianity or Confucianism". (2001: 7)

In the theorization of social capital we come across following elements as far as meaning and the core components of this notion: Social energy, social zone, community spirit, individual's networks and institutional affiliations, various kinds of contacts, social obligations, institutionalized relationships, ability to work together, existence of a set of informal values, norms shared among members of a group, resources derived from social structures and a culture of trust. As the conceptualization and definitions indicate social capital theory is derived from the idea that social networks have both importance and power in modern and democratic societies as civil actors. From a sociological perspective, social capital points to the totality of collective values created by the involvement of people who share similar beliefs, spiritual values and moral concerns with a tendency towards doing positive things for one another in their networks. Broadly speaking three forms of social capital are identified: 1) obligations and expectations which depend on the trustworthiness of the social environment, 2) information flow capability of the social structure and 3) norms accompanied by sanctions. (Coleman, 1988: 119)

At this point one might ask the relevance of social capital theory to the Gülen Movement.

I would like to argue that the social capital theory provides a comprehensive framework to analyze the Gülen Movement as far as local, regional and global networks, educational and media establishments are concerned which are inspired by Fethullah Gülen's views and vision drawing upon intellectual and spiritual legacy of Islam and its modern interpretation. Significance of Gülen Movement as a social movement in modern Turkey can be understood better through social capital theory given the status of democracy and civil society, civil-military relations and empowerment of citizens and recent debates on public sphere in the country. Later in the paper, I will demonstrate the relevance of social capital theory to the analysis of the Gülen Movement based on specific cases which show us that the Gülen Movement displays many of the qualities and components as described above.

From Social to Spiritual Capital

As pointed out earlier, there are several variants of the notion of capital in social science research such economic, cultural, human, social and financial capitals. The concept of spiritual capital can also be considered as one of the variants of notion of capital. In social sciences the concept of "religious capital" is also used by some scholars to indicate the symbols, norms, beliefs and obligations inspired by or derived from religion and religious affiliation. To Stark and Finke, for example, religious capital consists of the degree of mastery of and attachment to a particular religious culture" (2000: 120) Finke (2003) argues that emotional attachment and the mastering of a religion become investments that build up over time and constitute religious capital. However in recent years there is a shift towards replacing this with the concept of spiritual capital because of its supposedly limited meaning.

As Peter L. Berger and Robert W. Hefner point out, the role of religion in economic development and in the creation of democracy has been analyzed not only by contemporary sociologists but also by Max Weber, German theorist of modern economy and society who argues that "religion was the pivotal determinant of actors' rationality and behaviour". Berger and Hefner (2003) define spiritual capital as "a sub-species of social capital referring to the power, influence, and dispositions created by participation in a religious tradition". Woodbery (2003) defines spiritual capital "as resources that are created or people access to when people invest in religion as religion" and argues that spiritual capital differs from other forms of capital. He asserts that like those who have social capital, religiously motivated social groups have also "material resources, skills, trusting relationships, and cultural –valued knowledge- that is financial, human, social and cultural capital". Moreover, religious groups have an additional concern which derives from their stress on their relationship with the Supreme Being. As Woodbery concludes, the concept of social capital does not fully encompass religious groups the spiritual capital they generate.

Prophesy of Secularization Thesis and Global Rise of Spiritual Capital

The prophesy of secularization thesis regarding the gradual disappearance of religion from social and political lives seems to have failed because the current revivalism and recent events suggest that religious symbols, language, rhetoric and discourse can play an important role in the reconfiguration of the modern world. Recent social and cultural transformations under the forces of globalization also indicate that the traditional secularization thesis seems to have failed to capture the ongoing influence of religion. Proponents of secularization theory such as Bryan Wilson, Peter Berger, Thomas Luckmann and Karel Dobbledare established an unavoidable and casual connection between the beginning of modernity and the decline of traditional forms of religious life.

Many scholars accepted secularization as uncritical dogma and failed "to recognize multiple roles that religion does play in public life" (Bane, Coffin & Higgins: 2005:6). Generally speaking theorists of secularization process argued that religion would lose its influence on social and political life once the society absorbs the values and institutions of modernization For Wilson (1982:149) for example "secularization relates to the diminution in the social significance of religion". Shiner (1967: 209-216) on the other hand, identifies six types or areas of secularization with several predictions about the future of religions. Before we move onto the analysis of whether these predictions came through or not in the real world, it will be a useful exercise to remember the range of prophecies. Shiner's first type of secularization is the decline of religion, which pointed out that "the previously accepted symbols, doctrines and institutions lose prestige and influence. The culmination of secularization would be religionless society". (p. 209). The second type of secularization "conformity with this world" predicted that "the religious groups or the religiously informed society turns its attention from the supernatural and becomes more and more interested in this world" (p. 211). The third type of secularization "disengagement of society from religion" claimed that "society separates itself from religious understanding which has previously informed it in order to constitute itself an autonomous reality and consequently limits religion to the sphere of private life." (p. 212) The fourth type described as "transposition of religious beliefs and institutions" prophesized that functions of religious knowledge, behaviour and institutions would have a world-based outlook. "Desacralisation of the world" as the fifth type of secularization predicted that the world would gradually be deprived of its sacral character and become an object of rationally explained sphere and rationality would replace supernatural beliefs and mysterious approaches. The sixth type of secularization in the form of "movements from sacred to a secular society" on the other hand refers to a social change, which indicates that the secularization will be completed when the all decisions in society are based on rational and utilitarian considerations rather than religious principles. (p. 216)

Contemporary developments in the globe and recent debates in social sciences indicate that such comprehensive claims and predictions of the secularization theory have only limited validity and success, mostly confined to Western Europe which Davie (1999: 76; 2000:25-26) describes it as en exception rather than the rule where the old thesis seem to hold evidencing that in the last two hundred years secularization has made an immense progress. (Rémond, 1999:187)

Although modern societies have by nature a corrosive effect on traditional forms of religious life and lead to decline in the scope and influence of religious institutions and in the popularity of religious beliefs (Bruce, 1996:26), as Bell (1977: 448) notes existential questions of culture remains inescapable and "some new efforts to regain a sense of the sacred point to the direction in which our culture –or its sentient representatives- will move." After observing the global rise of religion, Peter L. Berger (1999: 2), who was once the proponent of secularization theory, admits "that the assumption that we live in a secularized world is false. The world today, with some exceptions.... is as furiously religious as it ever was, and in some places more so than ever". He argues that the whole body of literature explaining secularization and its repercussions is essentially mistaken. Modernization did not necessarily lead to the decline of religion. Even in highly modernized societies like European countries, religion succeeded to preserve its presence especially in individual consciousness if not institutionally.

Regarding the relation between religion and secularization in Europe, Daniéle Hervieu-Léger makes a strong point in her acclaimed book Religion as a Chain of Memory where she argues that a chain connects an individual believer to a community and the tradition (or the collective memory) constitutes the basis of the existence of this community. Hervieu-Léger (2000: 123) contends that "by placing tradition, that is to say reference to a chain of belief, at the centre of the question of religion, the future of religion is immediately associated with the problem of collective memory." Modern European societies, especially France, she argues have experienced a crisis of collective memory to some degree which led to a break in the chain depriving the memory of religion. She (2000: 141-162) concludes however that the chain that connects memory to religion is being re-invented in modern European societies. Recent developments and contemporary social, cultural and political transformations clearly show that religion is an important force today. There is an increasing tendency towards religion in USA, the Middle East, the East Asia, the South America, the Eastern Europe and numerous other places. This means that spiritual capital embedded in and derived from religion is on the increase on a global scale despite the opposite expectations of rationalist discourse of modernity and secularization theory.

All these developments invite us to look religion and its role modern world more closely. At this point in time the notion of spiritual capital may open new theoretical avenues to understand how religiously inspired resources can be mobilized to improve the human condition. It is argued that religion can at least six interrelated roles or functions in a democracy: fostering expression of beliefs and identity; forming identities shaping organizations; creating and sustaining social bonds; shaping moral discourse; enabling participation and civic engagement; and providing social services. (Bane, Coffin & Higgins: 2005:6). The spiritual capital theory in this context provides very useful perspective to test such claims.

The Turkish Context: State and Religion in Public Domain

Modern Turkey is one of these countries where Islam provides a deeply rooted spiritual capital. Yet, neither Islam nor religiously motivated social and political movements have a monolithic structure in Turkey. Taking the variety of religious expressions in Turkey one can see convergences and divergences among these groups inspired by religious rhetoric and discourse. Turkey provides an excellent context and cases for a comparative study of the varieties of spiritual capital and its influence on democracy, economy, education, media, networking and the politics. Despite all modernizing reforms Islam remained as a strong source of shared identity, morality, co-operation, networking, opposition and expression of solidarity.

Turkey occupies a unique place among the modern nation states. Not only from a geopolitical point of view, but also from cultural and religious points of view, Turkey lies at the crossroads between eastern and western interests. The political and cultural identity of modern Turkey emerged under the influence of domestic and external forces that existed in and around Turkey throughout the centuries. The establishment of a modern Turkey based on Western political models was a watershed in Turkey's history. The early republican elite distanced themselves from the cultural and ideological heritage of the Ottoman Empire and laid the foundational elements of modernization and westernization. The establishment of a modern nation-state in Turkey crystallized the ideology orientation of the republican elite aimed at reshaping the state and its institutions on the basis of a secular model inspired by the West. Political, social, and religious developments in modern Turkey were influenced by the ideals of modernism and secularism. Since its foundation, Turkey's political elites voluntarily attempted the most radical secularization among the Muslim countries. The principle of democracy was secondary to that of state secularism.

Inspired by the principles of modernization, founding political elite in Turkey, introduced sweeping changes in Turkish society. Their main aim in the process of modernization during the early years of the Turkish Republic was to change the basic structure of Turkish society and redefine the political community. The republican tried to remove society from an Islamic framework and introduce society to a sense of belonging to a newly defined "Turkish nation." To achieve this goal, they launched a movement of cultural westernization to provide the Turkish nation with a new worldview that would replace its religious worldview and culture.

The elite treated separation of religion and politics as a prerequisite step to opening the doors to Western values. Therefore, secularism became one of the central tenets of this program to accomplish modernization. As a part of this secularization policy, major campaign was launched against the Islamic institutional and cultural basis of society. This attempt to disestablish Islam as the state religion would prepare the climate for the introduction of secularism in the Turkish Constitution during the single party period of the Republican People's Party (RPP) (Cumhuriyet Halk Partisi).

Secularization reforms, which were undertaken during the first decade of the new republic, founded in 1923, aimed at minimizing the role of religion in every walk of Turkish society. The motive behind the secularization program was to reduce the societal significance of religious values and eventually disestablish cultural and political institutions stamped by Islam. Despite the secularization efforts and the restrictions on religious practices, Islam has remained one of the major identity references in Turkey and it continues to be an effective social reality, shaping the fabric of Turkish society. Spiritual capital remained vibrant in Turkey despite efforts to eliminate it from the public and political spheres. (Kucukcan, 2003).

The Gülen Movement and its Social and Spiritual Capital

A number of religious/social/political movements emerged in modern in the last two decades in Turkey which draws upon a social and spiritual capital that leads to wide range of networking, solidarity and co-operation. For example, one can see rise of organizations to address human rights and democratization in Turkey to represent and defend "Muslim" victims, using the spiritual capital for democratization, empowering civil society and strengthening political liberalization. One of the most striking movements drawing upon and mobilizing the spiritual capital in and beyond Turkey is the Gülen movement which is at the core of this paper.

As pointed by Yilmaz (2005:394) the Gülen Movement can be described as "a faith-inspired collectivity" with numerous followers and sympathizers which constitute one of the largest civil movements drawing on Islamic spirituality and teaching. I argue that the Gülen Movement has a potential of generating significant degree of social and spiritual capital as manifested through its national, regional and global networks, various civil associations, the media outlets, educational institutions which are inspired by the teachings of Fethullah Gülen. Effective resource accumulation and mobilization is one of the key methods and means of the Gülen Movement to spread its message. This is done through and for the service (*hizmet*) to the faith. For the Gülen community there is an urgent need for hizmet and resource mobilization. (Bilici, 2006: 10; Yavuz, 2003: 186) Broadly speaking the Gülen movement emphasizes foremost education and therefore invests in schools, networking and volunteering. The second area of emphasis seems to be on the media ranging from national newspapers to TV and radio stations. The third emphasis seems be to be placed on global networking within and outside the movement through several well established activities.

The Gülen Movement and Democratization

Research on social capital and democracy demonstrates that there is a relationship between social capital and democracy. The vibrant associations help create, consolidate and maintain democracy. Based on testing the impact of social capital on democracy, Paxton (2002:272) argues that social capital promotes democracy, especially connected associations exerts "a strong positive influence on democracy". Fukuyama (2001:7) goes a step further and argues that social capital "is the sine qua non of stable liberal democracy".

As far as religion and democracy are concerned; Fethullah Gülen sees no contradiction between the values of Islam and democratic system. For him Islam and democracy as a political system are compatible. Therefore "Gülen argues that democracy, in spite of its shortcomings, is now the only viable political system, and people should strive to modernize and consolidate democratic institutions in order to build a society where individual rights and freedoms are respected and protected, where equal opportunity for all is more than a dream" (Yilmaz, 2005: 396).

Stevan Voight (2005: 59) draws our attention to a widely circulated claim "that Islam threatens the values and institutions of free societies". In this context he argues that "whether Islamic values are compatible with the institutions of free societies is relevant most importantly for the future of Muslim countries. Yet it is also of immense practical relevance for the West…" In its various institutional forms and intellectual manifestations which form a large social and spiritual capital, one can see that the Gülen Movement demonstrates the compatibility of Islamic values and institutions with the core values and institutions of modern free societies, described as the rule of law, constitutional democracy, civil society, human rights, pluralism and market economy. As far as Turkey is concerned, he stresses that retreat from democracy is impossible for Turkey. (Kuru, 2005: 265)

Civil Society Organizations and the Making of Democratic Culture

In modern times, democratic and free societies have a large room for civil society organizations such as associations, foundations, trade unions and think thanks. These organizations contribute to the consolidation of democracy and improvement of civil liberties and representative political system where transparency, accountability and culture of negotiations are valued and respected. Among the civil organizations contributing to deliberative democratic culture in Turkey, intercultural dialogue within and beyond Turkey through organizing national and international seminars, panels, conferences and workshops, the Journalists and Authors Foundation provides a very good example of how social and spiritual capital of the Gülen Movement are generated and mobilized. The Journalists and Authors Foundation (JWF) was established in 1994 to promote democratic civility in the face of diversity, to facilitate intercultural, intercivilisationnal and interreligious relations, to emphasize cultural richness by challenging and abandoning official and memorized statements that marked previous eras.

In order to achieve its aims and to fulfil its mission JWF has established three main areas of activity. The one which is a well known forum known as the Abant Meetings has been gathering intellectuals, academics, journalists, politicians and representatives of civil society organizations from diverse backgrounds and affiliations to discuss local, regional and international issues of common concern. Since 1988 the Abant Meetings facilitated the discussion of issues such as Islam and Secularism; Religion, State and Society; Democratic Rule of the Law; Pluralism and Social Reconciliation; Globalization; War and Democracy, Islam; Democracy; Secularism, the Turkish experience and Culture; Identity and Religion during Turkey's European Union (EU) Accession Process with the participation of fairly diverse people. In 2007, the Abant Meetings focused on Islam, the West and Modernization which brought Turkish and Egyptian intellectual together; on Turkey-France Conversations held in Paris; and Alevism and its Historic, Folkloric and Contemporary Dimensions in Istanbul. The 13th Abant Meeting which focused on Alevism, is a remarkable one as far as dialogue among various social groups and freedom of religion are concerned in Turkey. This meeting brought together experts, representatives of Alevi organizations and the Directorate of Turkish Religious Affairs around the table which is a rare event in Turkey given the nature of cultural and religious polarization as a result of modernization project in the country. Range of issues discussed and diversity of participants involved in Abant Meetings and the manner in which these meetings were conducted indicate that Abant Meetings become a noticeable practice in the evolving democratic life of Turkey with increasing connections outside such France, Egypt and the US. One can argue that Abant Meetings contribute to the establishment and dissemination of civil and democratic tradition of discussion and negotiation of contentious issues on the one hand and to the participation of various actors in the making of democratic culture by providing a public forum to represent diverse views. JWF published most of the proceedings of Abant Meetings to disseminate views, discussions and conclusions of the forum.

Similar to that of Abant Meetings, The Intercultural Dialogue Platform as an activity of the JWF also aims at contributing to the development of democratic culture by promoting respect, mutual acceptance and establishing a working dialogue with members of other faith communities. Fethullah Gülen believes that "God wanted to teach Muslims, among other things, to be compassionate and merciful in their relations with fellow human beings." (Saritoprak & Griffith, 2005: 333) For Gülen "tolerance of others and genuine interfaith dialogue are not simply a pleasant ideal that will be fulfilled in some future paradise but is something at the core of what it is to be a Muslim in the here and now". (Kurtz, 2005: 375) Gülen's views on interreligious dialogue led him to establish contacts with leaders of minority religious communities in Turkey and to meet the late Pope John Paul II in February 1998.

This Platform clearly reflects the view of Fethullah Gülen about co-existence of different religious communities in the same social order and a dialogue of world religions. The Intercultural Dialogue Platform works towards regional and global peace through raising awareness among followers and believers of different cultures and religions in an age where some political scientists such as Samuel Huntington prophesizes "clash of civilizations". Muslims, Christians and Jews are encouraged to participate in events organized by the Platform to find solutions to various problems on the basis of common moral values of three Abrahamic religions. Given the scope of the issues and problems that are discussed and the variety of people participating from diverse religious traditions in a conflict ridden era, The Intercultural Dialogue Platform should be considered as an important initiative reflecting social and spiritual capital of the Gülen Movement.

The third area where considerable social and spiritual capital is invested in is the Dialogue Eurasia Platform which emerged from the idea that Europe and Asia, even though two different worlds in history, only have socially and politically constructed borders. The Dialogue Eurasia Platform aims to establish a bridge between the culture and people of Europe and

Asia to foster dialogue, better understanding and mutual appreciation of differences. Several International meetings were organized by this platform in order to increase the level of awareness about the common values and legacies on the one hand and the contribution of Europe and Asia to the world civilization on the other hand.

Gülen witnessed the painful consequences of conflicts in Turkey where more than 30 000 people lost their lives and he himself was imprisoned for his views. He saw that such conflicts damage the very social fabric of the society thus dedicated himself to peace and non-violence and advised his followers to avoid involving in conflicts "even he was killed". (Saritoprak, 2005: 422) All these platforms and activities that contribute to the culture of co-existence, mutual respect and understanding, dialogue among cultures, religions and civilizations are inspired by Gülen's philosophy of peace and non-violence.

Education and Democratic Citizenship

The Gülen Movement invests in education more than any other social movement in Turkey informed and inspired by Islamic spirituality. Education is seen as the most influential agent of inculcating a sense of responsible citizenship, cooperation and dialogue among individuals, groups and nations. The Gülen Movement has a diverse interest in educational establishments which range from primary to secondary schools and from high schools to universities both in Turkey and beyond. Moreover, followers of this movement have also considerable steak in preparatory courses for college and university exams as well as in language teaching courses. Instead of engaging in daily politics the followers of Fethullah Gülen "successfully mobilized material and human resources, and built schools and colleges both in Turkey and abroad." (Şimşek, 2004: 122) Especially after 1983, Yavuz (2003: 183) notes, "the privatization of the education system opened it up to competition, and the movement capitalized on the need and desire to establish a better education system". Today, in almost every town and city in Turkey, there are such educational establishments. These schools and courses provide jobs for hundreds of people generating economic income for both the employers and the employees. Educational establishments create a large network of students and teachers all over the world adding substantial human capital to the movement.

The rational behind establishing courses, schools, colleges and universities cannot be reduced to economic interests only. Financial institutors established by the followers of Gülen generate employment and large economic capital. In addition to such powerful financial institutions, investing in education has more than economic motivation. It is reported that by 2003, followers of the movement also known as entrepreneurs have established 149 schools with more than 27 000 students, employing 3209 teachers outside Turkey. (Balci, 2003: 157) In addition to high schools, seven universities were established (Yavuz, 2003: 193), one in Turkey, the rest in Turkic-Muslim republics. The current figure is even higher because more schools were opened in the US, Europe and Africa. As far as schools outside Turkey are concerned, it is claimed that "special importance is given to areas where ethnic and religious conflicts are escalating, such as Albania, Kosovo, Macedonia, the Philippines, Banda Aceh, Northern Iraq". These schools are believed to "have played remarkable roles in decreasing levels of conflict in these areas" (Saritoprak, 2005: 423) These observations demonstrate that social and spiritual capital invested in educational establishments lead to changes in perceptions and attitudes of people involved as envisioned by Fethullah Gülen who advocates peace and non-violence as important elements of democratic political order. As far as history of modernization, nation-state formation, social, economic and political problems that emerged in the formative period of Turkey and continued until today are concerned, the

Gülen Movement provides intermediary networks that contribute to the integration of individual citizens to state which the latter has not been able to do so. (Özdalga, 2005: 433)

The Media and Representation of Diversity

As I have argued before, one of the most important institutions of a sustainable democracy is the existence of free and diverse media which provide a forum for the critical analysis of government policies as well as for the reflection of various voices, including the dissidents' ones, in an open society.

In order to disseminate their message and provide an extensive forum, followers of Fethullah Gülen mobilized their economic and human resources and successfully established nation-wide media institutions. Broadly speaking these media institutions range from magazines (Sızıntı, Aksiyon, Yeni Ümit, Diyalog Avrasya and the Fountain)) to radio stations (Burc FM) to newspapers (Zaman and Today's Zaman) to TV stations (Samanyolu and Mehtap TV). Publication houses such as DA Publications and Ufuk Books and Cihan News Agency should also be added to the range of media outlets of the followers of Fethullah Gülen.

Among these media institutions, Zaman newspaper deserves a special mention which has more than half a million daily circulation in Turkey. The newspapers is also printed and distributed globally including in the US, Europe and Eurasian region. Zaman provides an important forum for the discussions that aims at contributing to democratization of the Turkish political system. Hence, most of its columnists and commentaries seem to support reforms to join the European Union and preparation of a civil constitution, a project of the ruling Justice and Development Party. As a sister institution, Today's Zaman in English started to be published in 2007. Today's Zaman has columnists from various political and ideological backgrounds yet with a seemingly common ground based on defending democracy, human rights, civil society and critically engaging in social and political developments in Turkey and abroad. The columnists include, Turkish authors such as Beril Dedeoglu, Cem Ozdemir, Dogu Ergil, Etyen Mahcupyan, Ihsan Dagi, Ibrahim Kalin, Murat Yulek, Omer Taspinar, Suat Kiniklioglu, and non-Turkish contributors such as Hugh Pope, Nicole Pope, Charlotte McPerson, Amanda Akcakoca and Pat Yale. The newspaper supports a democratic and liberal agenda such as Turkey's accession to the EU, improving human rights record, democratizing the state in Turkey with accountability and transparency and replacing its constitution which is the legacy of the 1980 military coup with that of a civil constitution.

TURKISH MUSLIMS AND ISLAMIC TURKEY: PERSPECTIVES FOR A NEW EUROPEAN ISLAMIC IDENTITY?

Shanthikumar Hettiarachchi

Abstract

The paper discusses the potential of Fethullah Gülen's thinking on the revival of core socio-ethical tenets of Islam to influence an emerging European Islamic identity. The long absence of any substantial Muslim population from the religious landscape of western Europe in the modern period began to end with the post-War immigration of Muslims from South Asia to the UK and other parts of Europe. But Muslims from other parts of the Islamic world have also established communities in Europe with their own, different expressions of Islam. The presence of Muslims represents a religio-cultural counterpoint to the projected 'post-Christian society of Europe', since they are now permanently settled within that society.

The encounter of 'Turkish Islam' (Anatolian & other) and the majority 'South Asian Islam' (with its diverse strands, Barelvi, Deobandi and others) in western Europe hints at the building of a new 'European Islamic' identity. Arguably, this twenty-first century 'European Islam' might be a synthesis of the 'Turkish' and the 'South Asian' expressions of Islam. Any disharmony, on the other hand, might kindle yet another rivalry in the heart of Europe. This paper considers whether Gülen's thought on community education based on the fundamentals of Islam could help build a positive and fresh expression of Islam that may reform the prevailing image of it as a cultural tradition that resorts to violence in order to redress grievances.

Introduction

It is a fact that societies have evolved in human history both in most edifying and shameful ways. There are significant references for the edification when humans first found fire, then the wheel and most recently the chip with which they have revolutionised their thought and behaviour, progress and creativity. However, the shameful historical data bring back the horrors of just the last century from holocaust to the Balkan conflict and the Rwandan genocides to the on going epicentres of conflict in the Middles east, Kashmir, Sri Lanka, Afghanistan and Iraq to name a few. These polarities of creativity and dishonour glued to violence continue to mystify communities, demanding new routes to form society and community practice and to adapt to the rapidly changing world on a daily basis. Gülen's contribution to formation of community and society based on dialogue and tolerance, self sacrifice and altruism, avoidance of political and ideological conflict, taking action on a positive and harmonious way and taking responsibility[1] have had an infectious influence [2] on individuals and groups.

Fethullah Gülen has evoked a thought changing mechanism over the last three decades as a movement[3] both within Turkey and several other parts of the world[4] and has potential to

1 See Understanding of community within the Glen Movement, http//fetaullahGülenconference.org.houston/ prodeedings/mhermansen.pdf, An interview of Enes Ergene by Mercia Hermansen (University of Chicago). Sighted on 18 August 2007.

2 An overview of these activities and influence of Gülenian thought recorded by Hakan Yavuz some years ago is of rare significance to be footnoted here. (I am thankful to Yavuz for this impressive list). He views that Gülen's community is based on a complex web of business networks and controls a large media empire. It owns Sizinti (a scientific monthly), Ekoloji (an environment-related magazine), Yeni Omit (a theological journal), Aksyon (a weekly magazine), Zaman (a daily newspaper), The Fountain (English language religious publication), Samanyolu TV (I made a visit to this creatively established TV station and witnessed for myself the interest based channels consumable both to the local communities and Turkey's large Diaspora in Germany, US, Australia and the rest of Europe), and Burc FM Radio station. In addition to these media outlets, the community controls one of the fastest growing financial institutions, Asya Finans, which is backed by sixteen partners and has over half a billion US dollars in capital. Moreover, a powerful association of businessmen, ISHAD (Hayatı Dayanışma Derneği), which includes over 2000 businessmen and merchants, supports Gülen's educational activities. This infrastructure also includes universities and colleges, high schools, dormitories, summer camps, and over 100 foundations. Day-to-day activities are organized by a hierarchical management based on the tenets of trust, obedience and duty to the community. This structure is composed of businessmen, teachers, journalists, and students". See. Yavuz, M. Hakan, (1999) Towards an Islamic liberalism? The Nurcu movement and Fethullah Gülen, Middle East Journal, 53, 4 Autumn, 584-605.

3 In my reading of Gülenian community movement both in Turkey and in the Diaspora simultaneously has Islamic, nationalist, liberal, and modern characteristics. Its ability to reconcile traditional Islamic values with modern life and science has won a large, receptive audience. The group has even brought together divergent ideas and people, including the poor and the rich, the educated and the illiterate, Turks and Kurds, as well as Muslims and non-Muslims. Gülen's movement could be a model for the future of Islamic political and social activism and has created an archetypal canopy where ideas, thoughts devoid of political ideology, cultural roots, traditions, varying expressions of Islam without historical baggage can seek harmony in a practical way for all who wish to subscribe to a way of life deeply Qur'anic but positively modern.

4 It must be noted that more particularly Central Asia has been a focus in terms of education processes especially since the fall of the Soviet Union. "Statistics show that in January 2001 the movement In Kazakhstan had already 30 high schools and one university, welcoming 5,664 pupils and employing 580 teachers from Turkey. In the same period, 11 high schools and one university were established in Kyrgyzstan, with more than 3,100 pupils and 323 Turkish teachers. In Turkmenistan, the community controls 14 high schools and one university for 3,294 pupils and 353 teachers. Finally, in Uzbekistan (until September 2000, when all were closed because of a diplomatic crisis) 17 high schools and one international school, employing 210 teachers and welcoming 3,334 pupils, had been founded". Balci, B., (2002), Central Asia: Fetuallah Gülen's Missionary Schools, ISIM Newsletter, 9, p.2. see.www. Religiocope.com, sighted on 24 August 2007.

redefine what it rationally means to be Islamic and European at the same time. The current European Islamic voice which seems to be predominantly of South Asian heritage since World War II, requires encountering a different cultural manifestation of Islam in the Turkish heritage if a new phase and shape of Islam were to be evoked within the European Union into which Turkey's entry is a probability. This encounter is fundamental to the life of the 21st century Europe as it expands both as a demographic unit and an economic power even though there are visible and stark cultural, political, ethnic and epistemological differences embedded within.

Europe of Yesterday looking to Future

Today's Europe is associated with a geographical area, stretching from the Atlantic Ocean in the West to the Ural Mountains in the East, to the Black sea, the Hellespont and the Aegean sea in the South east and from the Arctic Ocean in the North to the Mediterranean Sea in the South. Europe's Eastern borders continue to move and for many centuries. River Don remained the border until in the 18 cc. and it was pushed back to Ural Mountains subsequently. However, there is no specific category as to why a certain border may remain as the defining factor for the East-West geopolitical demarcation. Edward Said contentiously reiterates in his Magnum Opus, Orientalism, moves from East-West debate to Orient-Occident essentiality and its operationalism. He observes that "men make their own history, that what they can know is what they have made, and extend it to geography: as both geographical and cultural entities – to say nothing of historical entities – such locales, regions, geographical sectors as 'Orient and Occident are man made. Therefore as much as the West itself, the Orient is an idea that has a history and a tradition of thought, imagery and vocabulary that have given it a reality and presence in and for the West. The two geographical entities thus support and to an extent reflect each other".[5] In fact the Eastern border could have easily being drawn at any point between 'Europe' and 'Asia'. There are no political ethnic or cultural differences to give precise indication of where 'Europe' ends and 'Asia' begins. Russia lies to the East and the West of the Ural range and the debate remains that why Russia does or does not belong to Europe. The borders are so fluid that one could even think that 'Europe' is just a Western appendage of Asia which in geographical terms is only as big as India.

Turkey is yet another classic case as the main part of Turkey lies to the east of the Aegean sea, and so geographically belongs to Asia (in fact it was called Asia minor). Its Western part, across the sea around the city of Istanbul, is considered European, and represents the remnant of the former Ottoman empire, that for several centuries encompassed a large part of South East Europe. Karel Blei says, "that the word Europe and Asia probably derive from Semitic or Phoenician words: Europe from ereb (sunset, evening) Asia from acu (sunrise or morning). Asia and Europe belong together, as morning and evening, as Orient and Occident".[6]

Europe and its Plurality

Europe from its very genesis has been a land mass of highly complex geo-political, religio-cultural, socio-economic and ethno-tribal composite. Tribes and nations that settled in Europe brought with them their own cultures, languages and religions and what is Europe today is a conglomeration and a ever changing patterns and behaviours of people, customs and rituals. It's a nation of nations, culture of cultures but over centuries had developed not so

---

5 Said, E., (reprint, 1995), Oreintalism, (Penguin Books), 4-5.
6 Blei,K., (2002), Freedom of Religion and Belief: Europe's Story, (Assen, Royal Van Gorcum) 4.

much as a geographical entity but a cultural entity characterised by values it has formed itself to uphold. If there is an overarching recognisable element that makes this mosaic tenable over several centuries, then it is arguably described as the Greco-Roman culture as the basic determinants of European civilisation with Christianity being the medium through which this Greco- Roman culture was persevered and sustained. It could be argued that Europe came into being out of Athens, Rome and Jerusalem. Athens presenting art, science and Greek culture and other forms of life, Rome the state, law and justice systems and Jerusalem, the Judeo-Christian religious tenants. Christianity invariably becomes a synergy of a faith of historical Israel and with the spirit of Greece mingled with Roman military endeavours and its zest for expansion. The new Europe will now need to respond to the growing and formidable Islamic presence within Europe side by side with the Judeo-Christian paradigm and its centuries old influence on every aspect of life in Europe from art to politics and economics to social welfare.

Difference and Hybridity

Europe's difference is fundamental to its very being and its capacity for hybridisation of its people, cultures, tribes, languages, customs and rituals and is natural to its identity as a land mass infested with skills and innovative behaviours. It is this unique civilisational reconstruction and that Europe can only be understood and grasped in all its divergent facets. It is sociologically acceptable that difference is a direct result of hybridity which is a natural process of societal growth and expansion. Intermixing is still a taboo in certain societies while unknowingly those very societies have undergone serious processes of hybridisation despite socio-cultural and even political pressures. This process too is natural to Europe as previous socio-political engineering projects seeking to establish purity of ethnicity and nationhood have failed historically. Europe's ethnic, national or tribal claims for sense of chosen-ness or purity may be found in individual nation states or in national debates across the borders, but such claims are automatically made redundant as present priorities have been shifted from political nationalism, nuances of statehood or national pride to a new sense of being European. This sense of direction has been enhanced by the processes of globalisation and the unprecedented migrations patterns[7] that Europe is experiencing since the primary migrations in the aftermath of the World War II.

Turkey and Modernity

My recent visit to Istanbul indicated that it is a growing European city. Secularity is rampant even though there are hundreds of minarets to be sighted from a boat ride in the Bosporus as if to signify the possibility within Islam to open a new critical chapter to modernity and its passion for science and advancement. It seems that difference and hybridity is conspicuous not just in Istanbul, but also in other smaller medium size cities like Konya, Izmir, Kayseri and Efes in Kapadokya which were part of my exposure. Turkey and its 'Muslim population' symbolise an acute evidence of hybridity from Istanbul to Efes with a history of vibrant Christian presence and its folk expression and the Konya-based expression of Islam with the 'veneration' of the tomb of Mavlavi Rumi to the similar manifestation of the through

---

7 There is a clear inter- European re-migrations taking place of those who sought after political asylum and refuge in countries like Norway Sweden, Denmark, Finland and the Netherlands to Great Briton, especially of the Somali heritage. Inner city of Leicester of East Midlands in the UK is a good example of these new settlements. My own neighbour is fluent in Finish and perhaps is her second language.

monumental icon of Rumi in the heart of Izmir. Both Konya and Izmir which are now Muslim places of pilgrimage depict a symbiosis of Islam throbbing to give new expression in a modern secular state, even though there are conspicuous democratic deficits in governance and structures which include the military institutions of the present regime. This internal hybridisation is what 'Turkish Muslims' are expressing, and my reading of Turkey in 2007, is Islamic but in a Turkish idiom. These are clear signs of a people in a hybridised disposition despite what their religious and political norms require them to become. Turkey even though is majority Muslim, yet their behaviour and customs indicate that they are no exception to the changing and challenging forms of life which they either adopt by choice or are made to embrace with or without consent as the defining criteria are beyond their control. Gülen in his extensive writing perhaps does not name it this process as hybridisation, however he passionately identifies hybridity and difference in his own unique way that "it is a condition for the development of nations that the individuals of which they consist should have the same aim. It is not possible for a community, although it shows activity, to develop and make progress while some of its members say 'black' and others say 'white' for the same thing."[8] Future of Europe alongside the South Asian and other Muslims and 'Turkish Muslims'[9] no doubt would create such a symbolic and actual difference as Gülen reiterates would positively contribute to the well being of Islam itself and its theological and fundamental ethico-spiritual openness to science and technology, philosophy and politics, culture and art, family and society.

South Asian Islam in Europe, a 'Home Away From Home'

It sounds really awkward to categorise Islam and its heritage with ethno-nationality or any other contemporary divisions. However, it has also become just impossible to define Islam or its traditional heritage without modern socio-cultural tools and mechanisms to fully understand Islam and its progressive developments. If one component is undermined the other looses its meaning and integrity. Hence, this section purposefully deploys the determined regionalism of Islam even though it would campaign for a theological sense of ummah[10] which some consider is yet to be revived or functions as a mere concept or virtually as non existent.

It is in this sense that South Asian Islam is distinctly significant to Europe more specifically since the World War II.[11] There is a conspicuous absence of Islamic presence and activism in

---

8 Gülen, M.F., (1996), Criteria or the Light of the Way 1, (Truestar London Ltd), 44.

9 Turkish contingency demographically out numbers significantly the entire population of other Muslims who have settled in Europe. This phenomenon is unique to Europe. It is my view that Gülen in fact has prepared an infrastructure for the Muslims to deal intelligently and wisely with modernity and its challenges. Invariably, then it would be possible for the Muslims of new Europe to conspicuously counteract the un-Islamic portrayal of Islam and its misrepresentation through martyrdom-paradise concept by suicide-terror tactics. It is the responsibility of the Muslims have to portray themselves as an engaged faith community and to rectify its present image as painted by the media.

10 It is understood as the universal community, house of Islam or more popularly brotherhood of Islamic roots.

11 The main influx of South Asian Muslims is now considered a post World War II primary migration into Europe, particularly to UK. 1.8 million Muslims in UK which is 2.8% of the total population of UK (*Sources: Total population - Office for National Statistics, 2001 figures; Muslim population - Office for National Statistics, 2001 figures*). The second being the Turks into Germany as Guste Arbiter for the reconstruction of its battered infrastructure. 3 million comprising 3.6% of the total population. (*Sources: total population - Federal Statistical Office, 2004 figures; Muslim population - Federal Ministry of the Interior estimate*). France attracted Muslims from most of her former colonies as if returning to the linguistically familiar terrain, comprising 5-6 millions which is about 8.96% of the total French population *Total population - National Institute for Statistics and Economic Studies, 2004 figures; Muslim population - French government estimate*. These figures indicate nearly a 10 million in just three countries

Europe between the fall of the Ottoman Empire and the influx French speaking North African and the South Asian Muslims[12] in the heart of Europe as if surrendered to the socio-political and religio-cultural voices then spearheading the European priorities in the context of the global changes. What I wish to argue here is the fact that the internal tussle between the lofty concept of ummah integral to the theological axiom of tawhid[13] and risalah[14] and the diversity of regionalism of Islamic ways of life. This regionalism is further manifested within the South Asian Muslim community which is predominantly settled in the United Kingdom.

There are three main regional Muslim groups which can be identified now settled in UK. The first the Pahadi-Urdu speaking Kashmiri-Pakistanis and Punjabi speaking Muslims, secondly the Gujarati-Hindi speaking East African Indians and other Indian Muslims and thirdly the Bangladeshi- Bangla-Syelheti speaking Muslims. These three major categories have in them each of their distinctiveness and multiplicity[15] and these differences emerge and subside in varying degrees both within and in responding to the societal influences and cultural assaults to that distinctiveness which they wish to preserve, perhaps more as a survival strategy than a regrouping mechanism even though it not may look so. These patterns of groups behaviour is unique to many religious and cultural groups and is symbolic of settlement period and adjustment to the alien structures and the unknown socio-cultural patterns yet to be fully grasped.

South Asian Muslims were or are still perhaps at crossroads with a view of carving out a 'home away from home' which I think was a strong psychosocial element at least to the first generation of immigrants becoming nostalgic about the 'home' they left and the struggle they have gone through to carve out 'a home' here in Europe. This sense of in-between-ness perhaps is no longer a pain as the first generation has now seen their offspring and the extended families becoming more active and seemingly coping better than them during their early years of arrival in the country. Second, third and fourth generations have no other 'home' except in Europe, they would visit the ancestral village, meet their cousins, distant relatives, enjoy the tasty summer mangoes, but weeks later would be back in Europe for their work and regular way of life. Islam for these new generations is an enigmatic dimension. They are the offspring of a cultural Islam in which the religious Imam was both revered as the chief instructor and the formator of the life of a Muslim. Whereas, even though there are 'home grown Imams' yet most remain prayer leaders and madrassa[16] teachers except a few who have taken a socio-political role. The latter group even though has adopted some mechanism to communicate Islam in the context of Britain and Europe, yet they face a Herculean task to

---

of Western Europe and the present expanded EU perhaps has at least over 12 million without counting the Turkish Muslims who comprise 68 million which is 99% of its total population (*Sources: Total population - Turkish State Institute of Statistics, 2003 figures; Muslim population - US State Department*).

12 These two Muslim groups that populated Europe in my view are culturally distinct, and different in every way. They brought with them a certain continental specifics in their patterns of reasoning, social behaviour, adaptation, settlement and cohesion. They may be all Muslims but very different Muslims in every definable way. What the North African and other Afro-continental Muslims have brought to France is different to what the South Asian Muslim have brought and contributed to the UK. The primary migrations took place between early 1950s until end of 1970.

13 The singularity and oneness of Reality, Allah.

14 The prophethood and the messengership of the last divine emissary, Muhammad Al-Mustafa (S)

15 Some of the sub categories could be identified as Sunni, Shia and other Islamic schools of thought (Berelvi, Deobandi) and other numerous caste, feudal, tribal and linguistic groups

16 Popularly known as schools of early Quranic learning. Some describe them as supplementary classes. These classes are substantially popular among the Diaspora Muslim communities in Europe, both young male female students attend these schools.

convince their own community the importance of diversifying the global portrayal of Islam and to maintain a critical distance to the cultural, linguistic, caste and tribal corridors which are part of the 'baggage' brought with them.

South Asian manifestation of Islam in Europe is distinct for several reasons. Firstly, its immigrant nature and adaptation and settlement process; secondly, the expressive but at times over assertive regionalism with historical and cultural nuances and thirdly is the practice of Islam and its way of life with South Asian roots in the heart of a world of difference in Europe. Fourthly it is clear that some Muslim communities have migrated from being a majority and now having to live both as an ethnic and a religious minority is a psychological trauma which requires a healing process and an acculturation mechanism. These are not simple challenges for any community to undergo, socially, culturally and religiously. It is in this context that I argue that there is an astute possibility of a critical but enriching mutually beneficial encounter between South Asian idiom of Islam and the Turkish manifestation of Islam as Turkey begins to interact more with Europe, which is a flight from pressed upon and self-imposed isolation from the geopolitical and religio-cultural activities of the world to the West of Istanbul.

South Asian Muslims now have to recognise that nearly 70 million Muslim population had been just concentrated in one single country which will invariably impact upon the more known Islamic way of life in Western Europe since World War II. Islamic Turkey has a new responsibility to encounter this sister Muslim community or communities that have settled to embrace the life of Western Europe now over a half century. There would hardly be any no-go areas for these two culturally different Muslim families. It is my view that the celebrated mystical strand expressed in Sufi tradition within Islam would be one great bridge builder between these two worlds of Islam as both Turks and South Asians have had access to Sufi tradition and their revered spiritual masters across all schools of thought within Islam.

Rediscovering and Redeeming Islam in Europe

Islamic presence in Europe was a constant historical factor since 717CE when the Arab armies under the command of Tariq ibn Ziyad crossed the Mediterranean and invaded Europe. Many fierce battles and conflicts have been a regular feature to assert one's space and political claims. However, its 'golden age' in par with the Spanish Jewry and their intellectual and spiritual growth mark the religious freedom and coexistence within the continent and the mixture of coexistence and rivalry is a hallmark. There is a perceived fear and designated danger bestowed on Islam and Muslims since 9/11 as the enemy of the West. Historical rivalries between and among the Abrahamic traditions and the vilification of both the prophet of Islam and its Bedouin origins have been rejuvenated in political rhetoric and slandering which has supported the gross generalising Huntington thesis of clash of civilisations, igniting bitter memories of past wars and untold sufferings inflicted on one another. Some sections of the European Muslim community are torn apart culturally in a situation of in-between-ness. It's a politico-cultural uncertainty[17] either to be belonged in Europe or to continue to live like an

---

17 It is my view that Both South Asian Muslims and the Turkish Muslims live in this *politico-cultural uncertainty*. South Asian Muslims are perplexed about the complexity of integration processes in the adopted land without compromising their core beliefs and attached values, even though individual Muslims may have embraced certain aspects of European life and even values uncritically. Turkish Muslims are torn between their historical Islam and the new demands of the politically assertive secular state and promotion of its values. These two issues are at the heart of the European Muslim struggle to live and express themselves both as Europeans and Muslims.

alien, an immigrant with a 'myth of return' but without an idea where to return to. It is this context that Islam in Europe requires a rediscovery of its historical credentials as a religious faith glued to a system of law, governance and social care. It is Muslims who need to engage alongside their allies in this soul searching self discovery and Islamic selfhood in Europe.

Gülenian thought is a key to this self-discovery as he does not portray Islam as a political project to be implemented at one's own whim and fancy. For him it depicts a repository of discourses and encounters that are spiritually charged and ethically motivating to build strengthen and fortify a society with justice and compassion. He is genius in 'redeeming' Islam and Muslims from historically inbuilt sense of undue protectionism, as if a burden and a feeling of guilt bestowed on them by their bygone generations.[18]

The future of Europe is a complex reality. Islam and its current manifestations challenge all institutions to seek avenues to understand it as the second most influential faith, alive and active in Europe but in most diverse capacities. There are two positions seemingly functional. Firstly, while Islam is well rooted in an inspirational and a formative way for its adherents from its inception, yet secondly there are some operational waves led by groups of Muslims within contemporary history, seemed to have (mis)used and indulged in un-Islamic ways, bringing destruction, suspicion, political rivalry and shame on itself with terror tactics. This challenge from within Islam must be critically appraised not only just as a sloganised political assault on the West as the sole enemy of Islam but also such acts have evoked a deconstruction of Islam, Islamic theology, practice and invoked interpretation of Islam to suit group agendas. The first position must be rediscovered to portray Islam's way of life as a positive to contributor to the life and progress of Europe which has been covered with misunderstanding and years of intellectual neglect by the Western academia The second wave of Islam must be redeemed as this position is untenable even as a structure to redress grievances with recourse to violence. Europe of tomorrow can no longer be a battle field as it now contained world's most diverse societies with extensive human resourcefulness, competence, heritage and wealth that can be shared with the rest of the world.

Gülen's faith based movement contains vital ethico-social parameters that can set out a new discourse between Islam and modernity. Gülen was also influenced by Said Nursi[19] who was of the opinion that certain dimensions of non believers may be harmful to human progress. However, Gülen goes beyond and offers tolerance positively towards secularists and non-believers in Turkey. This act is not just about promoting multiculturalism but an act of incessant campaign for an inclusive society where baseless religious rivalry leading to conflict and instability which for him is the root cause of institutional decay and failed states of the present day.[20] Gülen revisits the fundamentals of Islam, offers an ethical basis for governance and justice, economics and trade, international relations and political maturity.

These socio-anthropological ingredients are fundamental to an integrated functionality of a society. Is there anything rediscovered in Turkish Muslims or Islamic Turkey with this duality of the secular state with its throbbing religiosity beneath the surface? If Islam is to be

---

18 An interview with Fethullah Gülen, (2005) Translated from original Turkish version by Zeki Saritoprak and Ali Unal, The Muslim World pp. 447-467. See this entire interview for a substantial exposition of Gülen's proposition of the self discoveryof and redeeming Islam and that I suggest in above paragraphs.

19 Born in1878, village of Nurs, Bitlis Province, passed awayin March 1960, Urfa was an Islamic thinker from Turkey of Kurdish origin and the author of the Risale-i Nur Collection, a Qur'anic commentary exceeding five thousand pages. He was also known as Bediüzzaman by his followers, which means "the wonder of the time.

20 Aras B., & Caha O., (2000) Fetuallah Gülen and his Liberal "Turkish Islam" Movement, MERIA, Vol.4 No. 4, p. 4

rediscovered and redeemed in Europe then Turkish model through the thought processes of Gülen and the faith-based movement need to be taken seriously as it offers and outshines as a living precursor to this antinomy.

Self search, a Path to Rediscovery of Identity

Rediscovering the self-identity is the roadmap for a progressive path of understanding the whole in which the self is a unique participant and not necessarily an absolute icon of power, prestige and hegemony. The construction of the other is healthy as long as the other remains a criterion for the self to be reminded that the self has meaning and usefulness with the active existence of the other. The construction of the prominence of the self has been a key to the dominance of the self over the other, creating a 'purity theory', absolutising truth claims, exclusive ethnic roots and determined territoriality.

Europe is no exception to these dynamics even within liberal democratic dispensations. The notion of the self and the other is fundamental to the rediscovery of both the European Islam and Europe itself as a political unit, without which Europe will remain a fortress Europe mindset. Self rediscovery therefore is significant for Islam as a reactivated presence especially within the context of current global events in order to portray itself as a politically and economically productive element. They together can even challenge the trade-politics and economic agendas of the financial institutions and their designs for world development and global governance. Such would be the calibre of cooperation and mutuality that new European communities are able to muster for a Europe with a soul, wiser and generous.

Islam as a faith tradition must also be redeemed from it's self imposed apathetic sense of aloofness which it sometimes portrays without a healthy critique of modernity in this age of globalisation and to shun the disparaging levels of victim syndrome. There are three apparent issues for the European Muslims. Firstly, how best the Muslims themselves disassociate the gross misrepresentation of Islam which is a religion of peace being used to redress grievances and its recourse to violent means to achieve designed objectives? Secondly how best the South Asian, North African and Arab Muslims in Europe are able to relate to their fellow Turkish Muslims, living in a secular state, who have links to Western apparatus of governance and style of living. Thirdly, it is a fact Muslims of South Asian whether migrated from India, Pakistan, Bangladesh, East and North Africa or the Arab world who have now settled in Europe have come from societies either they have been a majority or a minority. Depending on their majority-minority social consciousness of pre migration situation has largely contributed to the adaptation mechanisms of these early immigrants and determined the processes of their behaviour and other cultural patterns distinct to each group.[21]

Ihsan Yilmaz observes that "Turkey is one of the very first Muslim countries that encountered the modern West and attempted to respond to the challenges posed by the Western power and

---

21 An example would the case of Kashmiri- Pakistanis who were the majority whose population is largely concentrated in Northern cities with exception to Luton in Bedfordshire, UK. They hail from the two district of Mirpur and Kotly (Pakistani part of Kashmir, also designated by some as Azad Kashmir (free). They migrated as the dominant group and suddenly found themselves as a minority which required a massive psychosocial adjustment apart from being socially and culturally relocated even though by choice. Whereas, the East African Indians who migrated during and the post Idi Amin regime already lived, adjusted as a minority within their African situation. Their remigration to different parts of Europe, more particularly to UK seem to made their adaptation processes with a less baggage of a majority-minority consciousness.

civilisation".[22] Was or was it not the Republicans that paved the way to understand cultural Muslims of Turkish society? If they did attempt then was Islam undermined or was Islam gained a Turkish flavour? A good example was that Qur'an was translated into vernacular Turkish instead of its use in traditional Arabic version. Was Turkey then an exception? It was obvious that a secularisation process might have been accelerated by the staunch Republicanism for a state to function in their vision for governance distancing both Islam and Sharia.

I found in my sojourns that the 'official Islam in Turkey' cold and numbed to dialogue and encounter the mixture of intense folk religious practices perhaps institutionalised in some cohesive way via Sufi expression from Istanbul to Konya, Efus, Izmir and Kayseri. Would it be the modern Turkish state with its secular project that is capable of changing Islam or is it the collective religiosity of the masses that would be the key to humanising the secular state, naturalising it to hear the different voices of the collective? Aras and Caha jointly in their analysis reiterates that "Gülen's goals are simultaneously to Islamize the Turkish national ideology and to Turkify Islam"[23] which is a creative way of distancing both political nationalism and political Islam and their ideologisation processes which according to him is not true to the spirit of Islam.

Religiosity and Transition

Islam in Europe is the second largest faith tradition, and the proposition to rediscover Islam may sound as if it has lost its identity as a faith in Europe. Currently it appears to be embroiled in a state of flux, transition and definitive change, hence creates an obvious opportunity to seek with wisdom and spiritual maturity. It is in this sense that Islam as a European institution required now to plunge into a fuller engagement in being not so much competitive and reactive, instead to constructively contribute to the expanding socio-political, religio-cultural, economic and business life of Europe. Theological Islam contains sufficient material within not only to comment on these strata of life but also to abundantly and critically dispense its value based principalities not just for Muslims but for the well being of all.

Europe even though claims that its foundations are built on Judeo-Christian patterns of thinking and a framework, but in practice it's by and large currently is a post Christian society. It also struggles to carve out its own European-ness and identity with a rapid expansion of the membership of the European Union with its ever growing radical migratory patterns which the current European governments have mismanaged most times both at policy level and also in practical terms. In this sense its not only the Muslims or other minorities that struggle to locate their identity amidst the majority but also the majority is at crossroads for a self-definition. It is known that a time of transition is a time of threat and fear but also an opportune time for positive change and hope.

European Muslims are almost demanded by history to seize the moment as every nation state, culture, nationality, ethnic group and religious community is at a critical juncture repositioning each within the context of rapidly changing society. Defining a group, identity and perhaps its very survival is now determined by the existence and the productivity of the other. Self can define itself and have meaning in relation to the other. Hence the majority requires

---

22 Yilmaz, I., State, Law, Civil Society and Islam in Contemporary Turkey, The Muslim World, 95,3 July 2005, 385. (I am thankful to Yilmaz for this well research article as it provides a key overview to the post 1923 developments in Turkey).

23 Op.cit. Aras & Omer (2000) p.3

a minority, Muslims in Europe will rediscover their potential in relation to the potentialities that they discover in their fellow European religious and ethnic communities vis-à-vis.

Gülen's Social Formula

Gülenian thought and perspectives on istighrag (immersion) which means "absorption, diving into, becoming deeply involved in, denotes transportation by joy, oblivion of the world, the cleansing of the heart of worldly worries", [24] with which he says that one is filled with wonder, and one travels between love and witnessing truth that finally rest in the divine command. Gülen sums up his view on immersion with hurriaya (freedom) as being freed from selfishness and self-conceit or the evil commanding self which always pursue evils is to 'die before you die'[25] The real falah (enshrining success) of an individual or collective pursuits are imbedded in goodness and virtue. Gülen suggests a new social behaviour which can be found in fundamentals of Islam, not exclusively for Muslims, but for all who pursue honourable social interaction. The South Asian Muslims in a geopolitical sense may feel that they would be dominated by Turkish Muslims which need not be a fear but could well be a counterpart to a revival of a new spirituality of East-West encounter in the West.

Gülen in a radical way attempts to instil into this encounter a character formation through processes of education at all levels of society. It seems to me that he is articulating that it's neither the Ottomans nor the Moguls and their expression of Islam that Europe needs now to resuscitate a social conscience, religious faith, intellectual acumen, economic justice and moral principles and to help evolve a society that can deliver respect, honour and freedom. South Asian Islam has taken its roots now in the European soil and time is right to feel 'at ease and homely' and its encounter with the Turkish form of Islam (Anatolian) would be historical in Europe and fascinating sociologically.

Gülen and Democracy

The historical burdens continue to shadow them in their new found lands in which they have settled and some seem to attempt to rectify the past which is long gone. As I perceive Gülen's proposition of 'democracy education' becomes crucial as he believes that democracy is the only viable system for governance and structural development of a polity. Democracy essentially means the rule of the people, therefore meaningful democracy must be based on "an organisational structure that permits isolated individuals to enter the domain of decision making by pooling their limited resources, educating themselves and others formulating ideas and programmes that they can place   in the political agenda and work to realise it. In the absence of such organisation, political democracy is the domain of elite groups that command resources, based on ultimately on their control of the private economy".[26] However, Gülen view of democracy goes a step further than Chomsky, when he points to the soul of democracy that is " based on righteousness and reality"[27] which I view is a typically Anatolian analysis[28] which actually is the nerve centre of the Gülenian thought. Gülen lucidly but firmly

---

24 See. Gülen, F., http://en.fGülen.com/content view/2097/7/, sighted on 05/08/07

25 See Ibid. http://en.fGülen.com/content/view/1990/7/.

26 Chomsky, N., (1987), On Power and Ideology (The Managua Lectures 1986) South End Press, USA, p.3

27 Gülen M. F., (2001) A Comparative Approach to Islam and Democracy, SAIS Review, XXI, 2 Summer-Fall, p.134.

28 I thought footnoting what I mean here. Anatolain analysis (phraseology is mine) is based on an attitude of tolerance, eliminating harsh restriction and rash judgement. It fosters and injects profuse influence to care for freedom to

illustrates his own argument and provides evidence from within Islam beyond Chomsky's analysis of democracy and hegemony, that "Islam does not propose a certain unchangeable form of government or attempt to shape it. Instead, Islam establishes fundamental principles that orient a government's general character, leaving it to the people to choose the type and form of government according to time and circumstances".[29]

Gülenian Bridge-building Approach to the 'Big & Small' in Europe

There was at least a sense of 'big and small nation states' dynamics both in the post World War II period and during the Cold War era causing a real East-West divide, each having public and clandestine whistle blowers supporting each political camp. Hence, it was rightly called the Cold War, potentially at war but never fought a single, even though the political gurus were cocksure that such was eminent during almost a half century. However, Turkey with its enigmatic geopolitical circumstances has remained at least symbolically transcontinental because of its Ottoman residue, yet developing strong links with the West while fostering relations with the East more specifically with its special affinity to the central Asian people.

Turkey has involved in both creating and sustaining many regional and International organisations[30] since its embrace of republicanism in 1923. These European and international associations, Turkey's internal radicalism, the zest for a post-Ottoman political restructuration and the Istanbul-elitism have all shaped a secular society achievable and workable in Turkey. This brand of Turkish secular agenda has publicly distanced itself from the concept of both theocracy and the symbiotic nature of traditional Islam and governance which in theological sense is fundamental to Islam. Gülen states that "the details (relating to Islamic governance) of such issues have been entrusted to the passing of time. The divine commands and the prophetic suggestions about politics, state and the ruling community have been interpreted in diverse ways, resulting in different manifestations and various forms throughout history. Qur'an has addressed all these groups (from Bedouins to others such as Jews, Christians, and perhaps Zoroastrians too) considering their own understanding, approaches, views, evaluations and even lives".[31]

It is with this crucial entry into a world of debate, controversy, opportunity, and discourse on religion, governance and modernity that Fethullah Gülen innovatively introduces views, ideas and praxis[32]. In my view, Gülen speaks intensely of Islamic praxis fundamentally Qur'anic

---

practice all varied democratic forms of life.

29 Op.cit., Gülen (2001).

30 It is a founding member of the United Nations, the Organization of the Islamic Conference, the Organisation for Economic Co-operation and Development and the Organization for Security and Co-operation in Europe, a member state of the Council of Europe since 1949, and of NATO since 1952. Since 2005, Turkey has been in accession negotiations with the European Union, having been an associate member since 1963. Turkey is also a member of the G20, which brings together the 20 largest economies of the world.

31 Op.cit., p.445. N.B. All in italics is added to further understand the quote.

32 The use of the transliterated Greek word 'praxis' indicates rather a complex set of meanings to understand its roots in modern English parlance. Praxis or practice does not mean simply action or activism in opposition to theory. It brings out what modern scholars call for a dialectics of theory and praxis. Paulo Freire, a Brazilian educationist used this word (praxis) as something that falls conceptually in parlance with a word like pedagogy. Pedagogy and praxis make the core of what they articulate. (The liberation theologians of South America use this word extensively in their literary word and in their education processes of basic human communities which may be defunct now (according to conservative estimates) but in fact are vibrant in their own Latino ways which both Europeans and, perhaps Asians may not fully understand. "Praxis is not blind action, deprived of intention or of finality. It is action

but freshly compatible beyond the medieval definitiveness of interpretation of certain fundamentals of Islam. Gülen unequivocally and devoutly respects and honours the primordial religiosity expressed in the Qur'an and the Allah-experience unique to the prophet of Islam. Gülen's genius is that that he roots his discourse within the historical tradition of Islam but introduces a fresh way to understand Islam and to adopt it to the contemporary issues of political, scientific, cultural and social paradigms which he thinks are part of the praxis of Islam. For him Islam without praxis is empty and it must speak to the modern men and women as relevant as it was during the time of the prophet. It is in this sense that Gülenian thought offers a bridge building approach to the difficult issues that Islam is facing under the current more vociferous manifestations of Islam on the world arena.

The unique character of Gülen's movement lies in its attempt to revitalise traditional values as part of modernizing efforts such as the Turkish state's official modernization program. Thus far, it has had some success as it attempts to harmonize and integrate the historically diverse lands of Turkey with its socio-political affinity with central Asian people and reconcile hundreds of years of tradition with the demands of modernity which is not an easy task. In brief, Gülen seeks to construct a Turkish-style of Islam as much as the Ottomans attempted to Islamicise Turkish nationalism, re-create a legitimate link between the state and religion, while Gülen emphasizes democracy and tolerance, and encourage links with the Turkic republics opening them to modernity and its challenges. Gülen aspires for his nation and people to look towards both the East and the West. East for Islam and its spiritual roots, civilisation, and moral code of conduct while he urges to look geopolitically to the West with Islam's own praxis of inquiry, science and the sense of Qur'anic justice. Gülen's socio-spiritual project is simple, not even as complex as that of Gandhi whose socio-political responsibility was enormous and critical on religio-political lines to find a solution for the political mess that was being created purely on religious lines even though his project was a united India, an abortive dream. There were no victors in the freedom project of India. However, all can be participants of a victory if the European dream can be achieved through wise political decisions and cross fertilisation of ideas and views not for a fortress-Europe but a borderless Europe to cultivate critical inquiry and freedoms for all. It's dream worth dreaming in Gülenian sense.

Gülen's movement seems to have no intention to evolve into a political party or seek political power even though his critics suspected of him such community based agitation within Turkey. The militarist elite continue to be varying of the Gülen movement as the Ankara regime abhors any potential socio-political, religio-cultural threat to its survival. On the contrary, Gülen continues a long standing and profound personal affinity with the Sufi tradition of seeking to address the spiritual needs of people to build work ethics, social and moral behaviour and to educate the masses and in fact has provided some stability to the nation in times of turmoil.

Like many previous Sufi figures including the thirteenth-century unique mystic, Jalal ad-Din ar-Rumi[33] for whom Gülen has admiration and devotion has influence in Turkey and become

---

and reflection. Men and women are human being because they are historically constituted as beings of praxis" See. Freire, P., (1985), The politics of Education, (trans.) Macedo, D., (Garvey Publishers, Massachusetts) 154-155.

33 My visit to Turkey included rejuvenated my early years of admiration for Mavlana Rumi and his genius insight into spirituality, poetry and theatrical mysticism. My special visit to Konay and Izmir (Gülen's own place of teaching career for a long time had been also in Izmir) indicated that Islam (but in Turkish manifestation) is very much the heartbeat of the people even though a stark secularity is being portrayed in the public space of Istanbul. I believe that each Turkish province with its own rural-urban cultural juxtaposition will also portray the heterogeneity of Islam

a considerable spiritual force to distance totalisation of political Islam. Sufi expression of Islam has brought understanding and value to pluralism and diversity as found in the Qur'an to the contemporary society. Gülen brings Muslim Turkey to express its Turkish Islam in an inimitable way so that Turkish Islam can be a catalyst in devising a new understanding of a European Islam beyond the traditional definitions of being Arabic, North African or South Asian. It is right time that these three expressions of Islam understand that there is more about cultural expressions Islam than what has been familiar and known to them.

Gülen's fresh approach opens this intra-Islamo interaction and encounter between different expressions of Islam that have found its roots in Europe. It is appropriate that Turkish Islam with its nation state's approach to the secular paradigm and the popular allegiance to Islam become a learning arena for the multifaceted manifestations of Islam, yet struggling to relate to the secular project of Europe since Enlightenment to the end of Cold War and to the War on Terror campaign. Gülen's Islamodernity discourse and praxis is a challenge both to the traditional understanding of Islam and the blind following of modernity project. He is radically critical of both but wishes that both speak to each other with here and now situations and face up to the reality of the contemporary world.

The challenge to the Gülenian groups will be determined by its ability to evolve and expand its strategic and skilful conduct to improve its relations with the Turkish military leadership and secular elites if it proposes reforms within. If these endeavours are successful, then the movement could have a major impact on both the Turkish State and Turkish society[34] and on the changes that take place in Turkey in the coming decades where Gülen himself could become a more important religious figure even though he may shun that position. Gülenian proposals are palatable within a democratic framework which he himself admits is adjustable, sustainable and could provide people the space to be free and deploy their skills for greater good. These propositions can easily be debated and tested now in the wider European context where Turkish understanding of Islam is able to rectify and provide the enlightened core of Islam to counter the Islamist interpretation to instrumentalise the tradition and to oprationalise it to the very denial of its validity as a religion of peace.

Turkish Islam's (Anatolian expression) perennial links with the Sufi tradition and Gülen's own emphasis on its roots, spirituality and the wisdom guided by a chain of erudite Sufi masters have provided a crucial alternative to the 'official state religion of Islam'.[35] It would

---

within one country. This specific Turkish manifestation of Islam is a unique praxis for both the Western European and the South Asians to understand the complex diversity within Islam. Islam is no exception to a complex process of hybridisation in sociological terms, which in the end will retain the spirit and in fact flush out its own colonialist and feudal characteristic. This in my view is what Gülen campaigns for.

34 It must be noted that state of Turkey and Turkish society could easily be two things as the State has been created around a well crafted elitist framework with a highly motivated plutocracy and its long term alliance with the NATO's second largest military(only to second to the United States)

35 There is a clear distinction between the practice of Islam from the ruling elite to the ordinary masses. A good example would be my encounter with the people whom I met in Konya or Izmir, their Islamic practices were very much related to their folk culture they shared historically with many other worldviews. Whereas my meeting with people in Istanbul who were well connected to the republican ideology and its secular agenda were quite different even though were Muslim but they would distance themselves with the tradition as if any contamination would dilute their connection to the allegiance to the state. The preamble to the Turkey's constitution would elaborate this ideological position well. "The recognition that no protection shall be afforded to thought or opinions contrary to Turkish nationals interest, the principle of the indivisibility of the existence of Turkey with its State and territory, Turkish historical and moral values or the nationalism, principles, reforms and modernism of Ataturk and that, as required by the principle of secularism, there shall be no interference whatsoever of the sacred religious feelings in

be an ideal contact position for many Muslims, especially the South Asian Muslims who too have had exposure to a chain of Sufi masters, more particularly those who hail from the be-relvi school of thought and practice as well as non Muslims who wish to devise a global sense of citizenship in which difference is affirmed and respected where the State is not considered sacrosanct and hence cannot be hegemonic but must held accountable and be at the service of the citizens and their freedoms. It is in this sense that the Gülenian movement is definitively a bridge-builder in the expanding European cluster of nations, cultures and plurality to allow contemporary Muslims of Europe to revisit their fundamentals of Islam and its immense provision for justice, other forms of promoting civic life and governance.

Gülen is emphatic that particularly the divine command and the prophetic suggestion about politics, the state and ruling community have been interpreted in diverse ways throughout history.[36] Hence Gülen himself in an interview reiterates this position as crucially important for his fellow Muslims when he makes reference to some Qur'anic semantics like ule-al-amr (those who rule), itaat (obedience to rulers) shura (consultation), harb (war) and sulh (peace).[37] His thesis on a possible new phase of Islam becomes evident when he appeals to Muslims to be involved in finding solutions to the present and future problems as participants of practice of Islam and its Ijtihad (independent reasoning). His invitation is for those muj-tahids (those who are able to perform independent reasoning)[38] to base themselves on "the values that we call major principles (ummahat) such as faith (iman), submission (Islam), and doing what is beautiful (ihsan) and the acceptance of divine morals by the community are references that form the essence of administrative, economic and political issues".[39] Gülen's rootedness in the heart of Islam and anchoring his own sense of Ijtihad on contemporary Islam and what it's experiencing as a faith tradition remains central to his spiritual expression and the intellectual inquiry.

Some Concluding Strokes

The land mass of Turkey with its historical past of Hittite and Hellenic periods and to the Romans, then Constantinople becoming the centre of power in the Byzantine Empire with the 1054CE schism which later succumbed to the Ottomans who named it as Istanbul, the place of Islam, where the skyline describes itself a city of minarets. With waves of change swept through this nation is yet again at a critical juncture of her history when its entry into the European Union is imminent, 27 countries with 494 million citizens already, adding nearly 70 million of Turkey's population.

If the state of Turkey wishes to join the EU then it is imperative that Turkish flavour Islam[40] plus its diverse affiliations, and the secular pragmatism be added to the European polity

---

State affairs and politics". This paragraph enunciates the finest definition of State religion of Islam according to the State of Turkey which should be followed by its people.

36 Op.cit., An interview with Fethullah Gülen, The Muslim World (2005), p.455.

37 Ibid. p.454

38 Ibid. 454.

39 Ibid. 445.

40 This *Turkish flavour of Islam* is best described by Gülen himself where pluralism and diversity as natural developments in any society. He further says that Turkish Islam composed of the main, unchanging principles of Islam found in the Quran and Sunnah, as well as in the forms that its aspects open to interpretation assumed during Turkish history, together with Sufism… this is why Turkish Islam always has been broader, deeper, more tolerant and inclusive and based on love". See Unal, A., and Williams, A., (2005) *Advocate of Dialogue: Fethullah Gülen* (Fairfax, VA: The Fountain,) 43. See. also footnote 23 to compare with the State flavour of Islam.

which has been dominated by the South Asian and North African Muslim immigrants since post World War II. This encounter between the organically heterogenic nature of Islam would invariably produce new relationships in the new EU both with Muslims and non Muslims which will make over 500 million population with Turkey becoming a member. Composition of this Europe with two major religious traditions side by side cannot simple afford to return to historical rivalries and painful memories of the yester years.

Islam in every way will face the challenges of modernity in all its manifestations in Europe. The fear of the other whether manifested in the attitudes and notions of Islamophobia and Westophobia are both negative but are real social practices apparent and alive within Europe. Giving into these would be to accept the Huntingtonian slogan of clash of civilisation which the Gülen movement wishes to transform into a culture of dialoguing communities. According to him the adherents of a religion like Islam, whose principles are supported by reason and science, should not be doubtful or find difficult in dialoguing with adherents of other religions. For him dialogue is not superfluous, but an imperative. Gülen believes that dialogue is among the duties of Muslims on earth to make our world a more peaceful and safer place.[41]

It is in this context that Fethullah Gülen's three decades of work both inside and outside Turkey will be pertinent to intellectual enlightenment, contemporary spirituality with abiding compassion, striving for peace based on justice, will display an identity not through tribal affinities like ethnicity, culture or perhaps even religion. Instead should evoke a sense of a citizen of Europe, responsible and care for not only one's own, the self but the also the other yet to be known in order to own an honourable shared future. This future then will not be a debate of them & us but finding a sense of direction for whole and all among the former them & us. This new understanding of a European citizenship in no way undermines any single faith, ethnicity, race or culture but could become the defining yardstick in order to enhance not the superiority of self over the other but the validity of each to seek identity in a global sense of a citizen, sharing world's resources and productively contributing to their growth and sustainability.

Encounter of 'Turkish Islam' in the Gülenian sense is able to evoke a transition in understanding the core of religion within the post Christian Europe and would certainly awaken a new form of spiritual growth between Christianity and Islam. Gülen is suggestive of a possible transitional encounter and would be crucial to end the historical rivalries between these two traditions lasted over centuries in order to open a new chapter of renewed relations of good will and cooperation as part of the Abrahamic legacy of faith and practice. Cordial alliances between traditions rather than obsessive allegiances and their essentialisation require as a matter of urgency to evolve a new code of conduct among traditions. Such futuristic dreams are possible as the present circumstances compel the religious bodies to revisit each of their core teachings in order to return to a common ground for a shared future where they wish to wrestle with most critical issues that all communities face today, security for people, equal opportunity and justice for all.

41 See. details of Gülen's opinions in Saritoprak, Z. & Griffith S., Fetaullah Gülen and the 'People of the Book': A Voice from Turkey for Interfaith Dialogue, Op. cit, The Muslim World (2005) p.336 (original in Turkish, Gülen F., (1998) Hosgoru iklmi, eds. Selcuk Camci and Kudret Unal, (Izmir, Merkur Yayinlari) 37

THE EMERGENCE OF A NEO-COMMUNITARIAN MOVEMENT IN THE TURKISH DIASPORA IN EUROPE: THE STRATEGIES OF SETTLEMENT AND COMPETITION OF GÜLEN MOVEMENT IN FRANCE AND GERMANY

Emre Demir

Abstract

This paper examines the organisational and discursive strategies of the Gülen movement in France and Germany and its differentiation in Turkish Islam in Europe, with the primary focus on the movement's educational activities. The paper describes the characteristics of organisational activity among Turkish Muslims in Europe. Then it analyses two mainstream religious-communitarian movements and the contrasting settlement strategies of the "neo-communitarian" Gülen movement.

Despite the large Turkish population in western Europe, the movement has been active there for only about ten years – relatively late compared to other Islamic organisations. Mainly, the associational organisation of Turkish Islam in Europe is based on two axes: the construction/sponsoring of mosques and Qur'anic schools. By contrast, the Gülen movement's members in Europe, insisting on 'the great importance of secular education', do not found or sponsor mosques and Qur'anic schools. Their principal focus is to address the problems of the immigrant youth population in Europe, with reintegration of Turkish students into the educational system of the host societies as a first goal. On the one hand, as a neo-communitarian religious grouping, they strive for a larger share of the 'market' (i.e. more members from among the Turkish diaspora) by offering a fresh religious discourse and new organisational strategies, much as they have done in Turkey. On the other hand, they seek to gain legitimacy in the public sphere in Germany and France by building an educational network in these countries, just as they have done in Central Asia and the Balkans region. Accordingly, a reinvigorated and reorganised community is taking shape in western Europe.

This paper examines the organizational and discursive strategies[1] of the Gülen movement in France and Germany and it is differentiation in Turkish Islam in Europe. We seek to analyse particularly the educational activities of this movement which appeared in the Islamic scene in Diaspora of Europe for the last 10 years. We focus on the case of Gülen movement because it represents a prime example amongst Islamic movements which seek to reconcile-or accommodate- with the secular system in Turkey. In spite of the exclusionary policy of Turkish secular state towards the religious movements, this faith-based social movement achieved to accommodate to the new socio-political conditions of Turkey. Today, for many searchers, Gülen movement brings Islam back to the public sphere by cross-fertilizing Islamic idioms with global discourses on human rights, democracy, and the market economy.[2] Indeed, the activities of Gülen movement in the secular context of France and Germany represent an interesting sociological object. Firstly, we will describe the characteristics of organizational ability of Anatolian Islam in Europe. Then we will analyse the mainstream religious-communitarian movements (The National Perspective movement and Suleymanci community) and the settlement strategies of the "neo-communitarian"[3] Gülen movement in the Turkish Muslim Diaspora. Based on semi-directive interviews with the directors of the learning centres in Germany and France and a 6 month participative observation of Gülen-inspired-activities in Strasbourg; we will try to answer the following questions: How the movement appropriates the "religious" manner and defines it in a secular context regarding to the host/global society? How the message of Gülen is perceived among his followers and how does it have effect on acts of the Turkish Muslim community? How the movement realises the transmission of communitarian and `religious' values and-especially-how they compete with other Islamic associations? In order to answer these questions, we will make an analysis which is based on two axes: Firstly, how the movement position within the Turkish-Islamic associational organisation? Secondly, we will try to describe the contact zones between the followers of Gülen and the global society.

The Social Role of Islam in Europe: A Bridge or a Hindrance?

The studies on the social organization of the Turkish immigration in Europe show that the ethnic-religious identity plays an important role amongst the Turkish Diaspora in Europe. In a recent research on Turkish immigrants in France and Germany, two Turkish scholars noticed this accentuated religious identification.[4] The majority of the immigrants defined themselves as "Turkish-Muslim" (40%). This investigation indicates us that the "Turkish-Muslim" identity constitutes the majority amongst Turks of France and Germany. (61% in Germany, 56% in France)

Thus, the religious practice becomes an important identity-maker in the minority situation.

---

1 The term strategy as we use in this article [inspiring from Pierre Bourdieu's usage] indicates the active responses of social actors' vis-à-vis the structural constraints. If we consider "structure" as the rules of the game, strategy is the manner in which a person/group actually plays the game. So, we do not refer to the common usage of this term which signifies the set of systematical actions to reach a long term goal. For more details, see : Pierre Bourdieu, « *Stratégies de reproduction et les modes de domination* », Actes de la Recherche en Sciences Sociales, Numéro 105, 1994

2 Hakan Yavuz, "The case of Turkey", Daedalus (special issue on secularism & religion), June 2003

3 For a detailed information about this notion, see: Farhad Khosrokhavar, "Islam des Jeunes", Paris,Flammarion, 1997

4 Ayhan Kaya and Ferhat Kentel, "Euro-Turks: A Bridge or a Breach between Turkey and the European Union? A Comparative Study of French-Turks and German-Turks." CEPS EU-Turkey Working Papers No. 14, 1 January 2005

Because of importance of the "Turkish-Muslim" identity, Islamic communities of Turkish origin naturally play an extremely active role amongst the Turkish immigrants. These organisations of Turkish origin shape opinions of the Turkish community and play a significant role in transmission of communitarian values to younger generations.[5] Although these various Islamic associations are often regarded as centres of "Islamic fundamentalism" and also as an obstacle for 'integration', the Turkish immigrants who participate in these communal organisations are not generally motivated by such a commitment. These collective initiatives are not only actuated by a certain determination to preserve the ethnic-religious identity. Their reattachment to ethnic-religious organisations appears as an opportunity to establish solidarity networks. Such networks also occur as defensive structures against the everyday life experiences of the socio-economic life in Europe such as racism, social isolation, insecurity and exclusion.[6] We suggest that the emergence of such institutions at the local and transnational level indicates the motivation for a sub-integration[7] to the host society. These organisations offer a socialization opportunity to young people who do not actually have an easy access to autochthon social structures. Lastly, these associations led by Islamic mobility became active agents of socialization in the sedentarisation process of the Turkish community in Europe along with a conservative role of the Turkish-Islamic identity through the religious and ideological transmission. These associations fulfil multiple functions such as disseminating information, finding jobs, facilitating new friendships and allowing access to diverse social networks in the Turkish community.

By the valorisation of the Islamic communities, the first generation of immigrants who are poor- educated and non-speakers of the host country language (German, French etc.), commonly live in suburbs, sought to rebuild an authority on their family. They consider the Islamic associations as an alternative to "vices of the street" such as prostitution, drug consumption and urban delinquency and so on. Owing to the "legitimacy" of these associations, the young generation could meet out of the family enclosure, without concerning their parents. Moreover, the women branches of these associations promote inter-individual relations between women immigrants which constitute the most excluded group of the immigrant population. The existence of such common platforms of meeting relieves the members from social exclusion, isolation and loneliness.[8] In short, Islam is a tool for an integration which refuses assimilation, a way through which young Muslims strive for a public visibility as both a member of the global society and Muslim. Islam provides this young generation with an opportunity to be the part of the society differently, and to do this, they need to make their difference visible in the public sphere in a positive way.[9]

In spite of this fact, we observe a dilemma between two dimensions in the activity fields of these Islamic organizations: a social dimension which consists in dealing with the daily problems of migrants, and other, political activities which are particularly based on anti-western and communitarian vision. In the discourse of the mainstream Turkish Islamic movements

---

5 Manço, Ural, La question de l'émigration Turque : Une diaspora de cinquante ans en Europe occidentale et dans le reste du monde, in « La Turquie » sous la direction de Semih Vaner, Fayard-Ceri, 2005, Paris pg.567

6 *Altay Manço, Turquie : vers de nouveaux horizons migratoires ?, Paris, Turin, Budapest, L'Harmattan, coll. « Compétences interculturelles », 2004, op. cit. 152*

7 The term "sub-integration" indicates an indirect integration to autochton social structures by participating in communal organisations. The indivudal attempts of diaspora members to publicly affirm an identity give birth to an integration process to the host society. Muslim citizens have dialogue with society through their expressions of identity and difference.

8 *Idem, p. 152-153*

9 Farhad Khosrokhavar, Islam des Jeunes

such as Milli Görüş, Suleymanci community and the fundamentalist movements like Kaplanci community etc., the Western influence are always considered as a threat more than a resource or an enrichment. This "mistrust" also comes from historical competition between two religious universes, Christianity and Islam. The essential differentiation of the Gülen movement from the other Islamic communities occurs in this anti-western attitude.[10]

The social role of the Islamic associations led by various cultural, educational and sportive activities which favours a socialization (following a sub-integration to host society) were always defined as a secondary goal by disciples of these organizations. The ultimate goal was "reislamization of the society" or "reestablishment of the shariah regime in Turkey" etc; however, particularly after the "failure of political Islam"[11] in early 1990s, the big ideological goals are replaced by more pragmatic objects. Furthermore, the Islamic associative institutionalization and bureaucratisation process gave birth to an inner-secularisation amongst the members. Recently, these various socio-religious associations however witness a relative secularisation process as a result of the rejuvenation of their administrative staff. The administrative staff of these associations preoccupies more and more with the everyday life problems of Turkish immigrants who are victims of a social and economic exclusion and who suffer from a constant alienation process. As a result, the social, educational and sportive activities of these associations which were always considered as a "medium" to gain more members have become an ultimate goal. [12] During the 1980s and early 1990s, the communitarian functioning of these associations generated an ideological and psychological closure amongst the younger generations. But today we witness the emergence of a new religious discourse in the Turkish Diaspora in Europe. Associations whether they refer directly to "Islam" or not, engage in a social militancy which concerns the activities such as after-school tutoring and political participation etc. In this paper, we seek to analyze the emergent neo-communitarian Gülen movement in Turkish Diaspora in Europe with a comparative method with the other Anatolian Muslim associations.

The Organization of Turkish Islam in France and Germany

We can summarize various discourses developed by the Turkish immigrants in a retrospective way: The first generation in the 1960s and 1970s developed a discourse revolving around economic issues. The second generation in the 1980s generated an ideological and political discourse attached to the political issues in Turkey. Finally, since the 1990s, the third generation has developed a cultural discourse which stresses citizenship, tolerance and multiculturalism.[13] So, we will describe two important representatives of the second generation Islamic associational organizations (National Outlook and Suleymanci community) and the neo-communitarian Gülen movement in the context of the new generation Islamic associational organizations.[14]

---

10 Nadine A Weibel, Pour une ébauche de l'islamisme Turc en Alsace et en Allemagne, Jund Alain, Dumont Paul, Stéphane de Tapia « Enjeux de l'immigration Turque en Europe » Harmattan, 1995, pg. 267

11   Olivier Roy, "L'echec de l'Islam politique", Paris, Seuil, 1992

12   Ahmet Kuru and Ahmet Yükleyen, "Avrupa'da İslam, Demokrasi ve Laiklik:Fransa, Almanya ve Hollanda örnekleri"(Islam, Democracy, and Secularism in Europe: the cases of France, Germany, and the Netherlands), Istanbul, TESEV Yayınları, 2007, p. 59

13 Ayha Kaya and Ferhat Kentel, "Euro-Turks: A Bridge or a Breach between Turkey and the European Union? A Comparative Study of French-Turks and German-Turks." CEPS EU-Turkey Working Papers No. 14, 1 January 2005 pg.57

14   To see more detailed studies on the emergence of the new islamic organizations in Europe: Cesari, Jocelyne.

National Outlook Movement: Politics as a Religious Vocation

Milli Görüş (National Outlook movement), related to a Turkish Islamist political party is the most influential and established in the Turkish community since its inception in 1976. With 32 regional organisations gathering 2230 representations, 550 places of worship, 55 schools and almost 250,000 members all around Europe, Milli Görüş is the most important representative of the non-official branch of the Turkish Islam. Thanks to a well-established solidarity network in Europe, Milli Görüş has a significant human and material infrastructure. In the lawsuit of Turkish sedentarisation, the MG ensured not only religious but also cultural and social services to the Turkish Diaspora.

In Europe, the activities of the community are coordinated by the Islamic Community of National Outlook (IGMG) which is situated in Köln, Germany. In Germany, the associational network of Milli Görüş was created progressively between 1973 and 1975. After the institutionalization of the community in Germany, the movement started to establish sub-organizations in other European countries. The National Outlook opened its first establishment in the north suburban area of Paris in 1978. The movement reached its top point in 1990s which was parallel to the political rise of Necmettin Erbakan's Welfare Party in Turkey. But after the soft coup d'état in February 1997, by the Turkish military, they started to lose popularity amongst the Turkish Diaspora. Today, IGMG is increasingly less involved in Turkish domestic politics albeit it remains active amongst the Diaspora.[15]

Milli Görüş historically holds an anti-Western and anti-globalist position. In Yörünge (Orbit)[16], Milli Görüş politicised systematically certain issues to create a "war against the West" atmosphere in the form of a "struggle" to eliminate the traces of the Kemalist westernization model in Turkey. Related to this main-strategy, Erbakan's Milli Görüş strongly opposed Turkey's accession to the European Union. The movement in Turkey presents the possibility of accession to EU as a danger of dissolution in the Judeo-Christian Europe.[17] This euro - scepticism of Milli Görüş, which is in fact a by-product of its essentialist anti-western attitude, plays an important role on the Diaspora members of the movement. Milli Görüş in Europe accentuates the protection of the identity through the religious transmission and that creates an identical resistance, which does not support a policy of integration.[18]

Especially before the soft coup d'état in February 28, 1997, the MG community in Europe was in a search of a "roof-organisation" /official representative role which collects the other Turkish Islamic movements in MG structure. They always strive for collaboration with the state (especially in Germany and Netherlands) to have a mediator role between the Turkish Islamic organizations and the state. In fact, we observe a double-discourse of MG regarding to other Turkish Islamic movements. On the one hand, they consider themselves as representative and defender of the various Islamic groups in the political field of the host society. On the other hand, they criticised the Suleymanci community and the Nurcu movements due to their detachment from the political Islamism. Furthermore, they are in a competition with DITIB which is considered today as the official representative of Turkish Muslim community

"*European Muslims and the Secular State*", London,Ashgate Publications, 2005

15 Olivier Roy, "EuroIslam: the jihad within?" The National Interest, 22/3/2003

16 This Turkish journal diffused between 1995-1997 represented the political vision of the Virtue Party

17 Deniz Vardar. Le Parti de la Prospérité : L'image de l'Europe dans son discours politique, in « Turkish Islam and Europe, Europe and Christianity as reflected in Turkish muslim Discourse & Turkish Muslim life in the diaspora » sous la direction de Günter Seufert et Jacques Waardenburg, İstanbul, 1999 p.143

18 Caymaz, Birol. "Les mouvements Islamiques Turcs a Paris", Paris, l'Harmattan, 2002, pg.211

in Europe.

The Suleymanci Community: Professionals of Quran Education

The Suleymanci community is the oldest movement installed in Europe. The movement was founded by Suleyman Hilmi Tunahan. He was a follower of Imam-ı Rabbani and he was the leader of the Naqshibandiyya order which is one of the most influential Sufi orders in Turkey. According to the Strasbourg branch coordinator's statistical information, the followers of Suleyman Hilmi Tunahan founded over 1100 student dormitories in Europe, which are linked to the Germany based federation. The activities of Suleymanci community in Europe are co-ordinated by the Union of the Islamic Culture centres of Europe (Islamiches Kultur Zentrum der Europa), which is situated in Köln. The domination of MG in the Turkish Diaspora was counterbalanced by the Suleymanci community. The community has been present in Germany since 1973 and in France since 1979. The Suleymanci movement attracted essentially the rural originated immigrants in the 1980s.

They establish mosques and student dormitories for Quran education. They present the Quran schools as a challenge against the assimilation risk of the Turkish immigrant youth. They appropriated an exclusivist communitarian and hermetic politico-religious ideology regarding to the host society. Perception of the host society is based on some stereotypical ideas and attitudes which causes a detachment from the society.[19] This "mistrust" against to the host society has an important role on the formation of a collective identity among the members. For the community, individual integration indicates assimilation and loss of the Islamic faith.

The Gülen Movement in Germany and France

The Settlement Process of Gülen Movement in Europe

Despite the large Turkish population in Western Europe, the movement took hold relatively late from other Islamic organizations and they have been present in Europe since almost 10 years. After a research on Fethullah Gülen's old sermon records, we learned that Fethullah Gülen frequently visited some French and German cities at the end of 1980s. But the institutionalization process of the movement started after mid-1990s. Contrary to the other Islamic movements, the Gülen community did not follow the Turkish migratory flow. We can explain this late arrival by two essential reasons:

i.   The appearance of the Gülen movement in Turkey is relatively recent from the other mainstream Islamic movements such Milli Görüş and Suleymanci community. When Suleymanci community and Milli Görüş started to institutionalise their European affiliation in 1970s, Gülen movement was a little religious community in Izmir, a city located in the Aegean coast of Turkey. This religious-conservative community transformed to a transnational educational movement in the early 1990s.

ii.   After the demise of Soviet Union, Fethullah Gülen gave a priority to the Turkish world in Central Asia and other Post-Soviet countries. Thus he allocated a major part of social and economic capital of the community to these regions. Especially, Central Asia, as an unoccupied region by the other Islamic movements, was more attractive than Europe. In early 1990s, the Turkish Diasporic Islam scene was largely dominated by Milli Görüş (National Outlook) movement.

---

19 Caymaz, Birol. İdem. Pg.162 and pg. 186

However, in the last years, the followers of Gülen have disseminate their ideas in the Turkish Diaspora which live in the immigrant-populated cities such as Paris, Lyon, Strasbourg, Frankfurt, Stuttgart, Berlin and Köln. In fact, the movement adapted its educational strategy to the European conditions by creating learning centres. Generally, the Gülen-led associations primarily prefer to establish private schools in Central Asia, Africa and Balkan countries. But, due to the difficult administrative procedure of establishment a private school, Gülen community adapted a different settlement strategy in Europe. The first arriving members found a learning centre, and after the institutionalization period, they took initiatives to found a private school. As a result of our observation, we suggest that the community considers the learning centres as a "preparative period" to reach the main goal, i.e. the private school. For instance, as we learned from the community members, the first learning centre "BIL Learning House" (Das Bildungshaus BIL) in Germany was established at Stuttgart in 1995. After the BIL learning centre gained a considerable popularity amongst Turkish families and developed good relations with the local administration, they transformed the BIL learning centre to a private school in 2003.[20]

Organisational strategies of Gülen Movement in Europe

Discursive and organisational strategies of the Gülen movement differ from the other Turkish Islamic communities. Mainly, the associational organisation of Turkish Islam in Europe base on two axes: the construction and sponsoring of mosques and Quran schools. Contrary to two other settlement strategies of Islamic movements, the Gülen movement members in Europe insist on "the great importance of secular education" and they refuse to build or sponsor mosques. They also do not focus on Quran education for the youth like Suleymanci community. The mosques and Quran schools led by Turkish Islamic movements play an important role in transmission of religious and communitarian values to the new generation. Instead of trying to build mosques or Quran schools, the Gülen movement transposed the Islamic mobilisation in the educational, cultural and entrepreneurial field by forming new voluntary associations.

Gülen movement members in Europe have founded a variety of establishments which operate in the major European cities. Essentially, we observe three main types of establishments: 1) Learning centres which offer particular courses in after-school groups to the students of the primary school by the college and private schools 2) "Intercultural dialogue" associations which organise intercultural events and meetings in order to promote the cultural exchanges between the Turkish population and the native society 3) Entrepreneurial associations which assemble Turkish businessmen who financially support the movement. In this article, we especially focus on the educational activities of the movement.

Learning centres, intercultural centres, entrepreneurial establishments and high schools are typically governed by a registered association. The members of the association, typically Turkish immigrant members of the movement, choose a board of directors, generally consisting of seven members.[21]

These centres typically serve about a hundred students at a variety of levels from grades secondary school to college-preparatory class offering courses such as English, French, German,

---

20 Aydın, Ali İhsan, "Dynamiques religieuses et logiques éducatives: Les Centres d'éducation du mouvement de Fethullah Gülen en France", Unpublished M.Athesis, Institut d'Etudes Politiques de Strasbourg, Strasbourg, 2004, p.68

21 Jill Irvine, "Gülen Movement and Turkish Integration" in RobertHunt and Yuksel Aslandogan, " Muslim Citizens of the Globalized World: Contributions of the Gülen Movement" The Light Publication, 2006. pg.59

math, chemistry, physics and biology. In addition, the learning centres offer language courses for newcomer adults. Furthermore, the learning centres try to encounter the needs of the students primarily of Turkish background. The centres organise seminars for the student parents "to make them conscious about the importance of education". The staff at learning centres is composed by paid French/German teachers and volunteer university students of Turkish descent. Although with some exceptions-such as the Horizon learning centre in Mulhouse, France-, the learning centres don't receive direct financial support from the state and local administrative institutions. In the last years, administrative staff of the movement in Germany established good relations with the local and national political leaders. In France, the relations with the local political authorities are in the minimum level because of the secular context of France and modest visibility of the movement in the public sphere. But we observed that learning centres in Strasbourg and Colmar have close relationship with the deputies of their region and local administrative institutions.

Gülen inspired associations possess more than 100 learning centres in Germany and 16 learning centres in France. More recently, Gülen-led associations in Germany established three private high schools in Stuttgart, Berlin and Dortmund. The private schools offer a full college-preparatory curriculum to the students primarily of Turkish origin. These schools offer the same curriculum as public college preparatory high schools with the difference that they offer Turkish as the third language choice, after German and English. The Gülen movement doesn't have any private school in France. Although the movement members express their eagerness to establish a private school in France, the community hasn't reached a tangible size to realise their purpose. [22]

The Islamic organizations are usually managed by a head organization in Köln, the city which became "the capital of Turkish Diaspora in Europe". Unlike the centralist organization of the other Turkish Islamic communities such as National Outlook Movement and Suleymanci community, inter-institutional relations between Gülen-inspired associations is loose and there is not any head organization or federation in Köln for assembling the Gülen educational associations. As a typical character of the movement, the Gülen community in Europe is highly decentralised. In Germany and France, each city or town is responsible for organising and maintaining its own schools and centres. Strasbourg Le Dialogue Learning Centre director Nihat Sarıer says:

> We have no official relation with the other learning centres in France. Furthermore, we don't have a common strategy. Maybe, we are all inspired by the ideas of Fethullah Gülen but we are not controlled by a top organisation which decides everything. Sometimes I discuss my problems with the directors of other centres in Paris, Metz etc. and we share our experiences. But everybody lives in a different region or country, in different social and political circumstances; so everybody works with his own method.[23]

Despite this decentralized structure of the movement, the movement developed a complicated network on country level, continental level and inter-continental level. Firstly, the European edition of Zaman Daily Newspaper[24] which is located at Offenbach, Germany plays a central

---

22 When we compare the settlement degree of movement in Belgium, Denmark and Netherlands with France, we see a relative success of the movement due to the more liberal immigration policy of these countries. The first school of the movement in Europe was founded in Copenhagen, Denmark (HAY Skolen) in 1993. There are also five private schools in Belgium and two in Netherlands.

23 Interview with Nihat Sarıer, 12.05.2007

24 The principal media organ of the community, Zaman (Time) daily newspaper publishes a special edition for Turkish diaspora in Europe. The European edition of Zaman is published in Offenbach (Close to Frankfurt). The

role on the communication between the community members in different European countries. Every day, the journal publishes articles (particularly in the 17th page) about local activities of the Gülen-led associations, the educational achievement of private schools etc. By this way, a member of the movement in Paris gets informed about the activities in other French cities, or in Germany, Netherlands, and Belgium etc. Secondly, members of the movement constantly organise touristic voyages to the other countries in Europe, and even in Asia of Africa. In these touristic voyages, they also visit the Gülen-led educational establishments. For example, the local representatives of Zaman Daily Newspaper in Metz recently organised a visit to Turkmenistan and Kyrgyzstan for the Turkish origin entrepreneurs who financially support the local establishments of the community. They visited also the Gülen-led schools in these countries. Thirdly, according to information given by Hüseyin Gülerce, a columnist in Zaman and Fethullah Gülen's close friend, every city or town in different European countries sponsors the Gülen inspired educational activities in the African countries.[25] As a result of these strategies, the members feel themselves not only as a participant of a local association in his city but also as a part of the worldwide educational movement.

The Learning Centres: Quest for Normalisation?

Different to the worldwide settlement strategy of the movement, the followers of Gülen in Europe encounter some difficulties with the establishment procedure of private schools. It's not only because of the difficult administrative procedure; but also the prejudices against Muslim immigrants and the rise of Xenophobia- Islamophobia in the old continent. The Gülen movement in Central Asia or in Balkans etc. always searched a direct contact with the host society. Differently to the other regions, the followers of Gülen in Europe meet with a sizeable Turkish population; a population who has became an object of negative characterizations and stigmatizations. Therefore, the Gülen community implements a new immigrant-oriented strategy to gain legitimacy in the host societies. We will borrow Erving Goffman's concept of "stigma" to understand the normalisation strategies of Gülen movement and immigration-originated youth in the host societies. Stigma refers to an individual sign, to social information the individual transmits about himself that disqualifies him and creates an obstacle to being fully accepted by society. A stigma therefore designates an attribute that profoundly discredits the individual.[26] But we must emphasize that the "normal" and "stigmatised" are not persons, but viewpoints. These viewpoints are socially constructed by the mainstream values of the society.[27] According to Goffman, ethnic, racial, religious or national identities are also the particularities which can put a distance with the "normal". Goffman named these types of stigmas as the "tribal stigmas". The young population of the Turkish community who are separated from their peers by the denominations such as "the suburban youth", "immigration-originated youth" etc. are marginalised by the majority of the native society. They suffer from a stigmatization due to the negative image (delinquency, drug, urban violence, religious extremism etc) which sticks to the suburbs/ghettos where they live. The majority of the young generation experiences the school failure in an early age and they are oriented towards non-qualified works. Even when they have reached an adequate school level for a qualified employment, they face with discrimination because of the "tribal

---

newspaper is sold more than 45.000 in 12 European countries. Zaman organized a large campaign called as "Football Unites" during the World Cup 2006 in Germany. The daily newspaper made a call to the Turkish community to support the national team of Germany.

25 Hüseyin Gülerce, "Gönüllüler Hareketi", Zaman, 12.03.2005
26 Goffman, Erving. Stigma: Notes on the Management of Spoiled Identity. New York: Touchstone Books, 1963.
27 Ibid., pg.61

stigmas" which they carry.

According to Goffman, stigmatised persons adopt five principal strategies to correct their stigma:[28]

i.   To try to correct the essence of the stigma or to dissimulate the stigma signs and to deny its influence: search for assimilation

ii.   To show that one's difference from "normal" persons doesn't prevent him/her to be successful in society; try to excel in the society (at school, work etc.) to achieve which is difficult even for the "normal" persons

iii.   To perform the personality who is bound to his social, cultural or ethnic identity, as a reaction to the disreputation of normal ones.

iv.   Cash in on from a person's stigma; seek to instrumentalise his/her stigma;

v.   To redefine your difference as reason of pride and advantage on the "normal ones", (assertion of the negritude: i.e. Black is beautiful etc.)

The first and third strategies go through with a process of "self-devalorisation", while the second, fourth and fifth strategies are experienced by a process of "self-valorisation". All the strategies -except the last one- can be lead to a collective action. Moreover, the first, second and fourth strategies can be perceived as manoeuvres by the "normal" persons. We can observe the practice of all these stigma correction strategies by the Turkish immigrant youth. But in our case, the young students who participate in the educational activities of the Gülen movement adapt the second strategy. They try to excel in the host society via educational success and differentiate from their friends, other stigma carriers.

It's the same case for the Gülen movement. The administrative staff of the Gülen inspired institutions, frequently complain about the host society's perception of the learning centres as an "Islamic association", a "communitarian association", or an "ethnic association" etc. During an interview with a responsible of the movement in France noted:

> We did not come to Europe merely for the Turkish immigrants. We want to serve to the French society. But when we talk about our private school project with the local administrative responsible or politicians, they maintain a sceptical attitude to this idea because of the negative image of the Turkish community in France. They evoke the poor situation of Turkish students at the school. It is really very saddening! So, firstly we will focus on the educational problems of our children. If we achieve to break this negative image, we will have a chance to start a dialogue between equals and we can realise our private school project.[29]

The community members think that they are victims of a "racialisation" as a result of juxtaposition of the Turkish community in France and Turkey-originated movement. In spite of the fact that the Gülen-inspired associations which we observed are largely dominated by Turkish origin volunteers, they complain frequently of their "Turkish association" image. For the director of Paris EtudePlus learning centre director, these associations do not target merely the Turkish population, but the whole Parisians. The faith-based movement try to break this accentuated ethnic-racial image of the movement by organising intercultural activities. But because of the particular problems of the Turkish population, the followers of Gülen privilege the problems of Turkish population in Europe. The reintegration of immigrant students to the educational system of the host societies is defined as a "first" goal.

---

28 We borrow Lorcerie's simplified model of the stigma correction strategy classement. See at: Lorcerie Françoise., « L'Ecole et le défi ethnique : Education et intégration », Paris, ESF &INRP, 2003, op.cit., 34

29 Interview at the coulisses of Etude Plus learning center in Paris, 12.04.2007.

So, we observe a double strategy of normalisation: On the one hand, the immigrant youth appropriates the communitarian values of Gülen community which legitimates the second correction strategy. On the other hand, the administrative staff who is disturbed by "stigmatisation" by host society is in a search of success and excellence in their occupation i.e. the educational activities. The movement also adapts the second correction strategy during the settlement process in Europe.

The Invisible Religion: Towards Secularisation in Public Sphere?

During our observation period at the learning centres in France and in Germany, we did not observe any religious propaganda or a visible proselytism in these establishments. This secular education policy in Europe is a by product of the worldwide strategy of the Gülen movement. According to Bayram Balcı who performed a survey at the Gülen-led schools in Central Asia, the school curricula are prepared in accordance with the instructions of the national education of each country and they are totally secular and scientific. Even the Muslim students, who demand a place to practice their prayers in the school, are not authorized to do it. [30]Elizabeth Özdalga notes that:

> The main objective [of the education provided in these schools] is to give the students a good education, without prompting any specific ideological orientation. One basic idea of Gülen's followers is that ethical values are not transmitted openly through persuasion and lessons but through providing good examples in daily conduct.[31]

The total absence of the religious discourse in these educational establishments constitutes the most interesting and paradoxical point of this movement. By borrowing the concept of Pierre Bourdieu, we suggest that the religious manner constitutes the "doxic" experience of the movement. Doxa is the fundamental and unthought beliefs that inform an agent's actions and thoughts within a particular field.[32] A doxic experience is one in which members of a society share a common perspective that is transmitted by a series of implicit assumptions and values that appear as a matter of fact, us a truth.[33] Through the concept of "Hizmet"[34], Gülen sacralise the secular education. What is essential in this "faith-based social movement" exists implicitly in the body of the community.[35]

Despite the relatively weak religious visibility of Gülen inspired activities, the followers of Gülen in Europe do not encounter a big difficulty to multiply their members due to their conceptualisation of *hizmet* (service). Gülen disseminates knowledge to his community as the most effective way to serve the religious cause ensuring the highest religious re-compen-

---

30 Bayram Balcı, Missionnaires de l'Islam en Asie centrale : Les écoles turques de Fethullah Gülen, Maisonneuve & Larose, 2003

31 Elisabeth Özdalga. "Entrepreneurs with a Mission: Turkish Islamists Building Schools along the Silk Road, " Paper delivered at the Annual Conference of the North American Middle East Studies Association, Washington, D. C., November 19-22, 1999. Published in Turkish: "İslamcılığın Türkiye Seyri", İstanbul, İletişim Yayınları, 2007

32 Pierre Bourdieu. Les Meditations Pascaliennes, Paris, Folio Editions, 2003, pg. 22

33 Pierre Bourdieu and Passeron, Jean Claude, La reproduction: Elements pour une theorie du systeme d'enseignement, Paris, 1970 cited in Nilüfer Göle, "Islamic visibilities and public sphere" in Islam in Public: Turkey, Iran and Europe, Istanbul, 2006, Bilgi University Press

34 Movement members use the term 'hizmet' to refer to all educational, social, civil engagements of the Gülen community. From an essentialist point of view, Hizmet can be described as any volunteer service or work done for the community.

35 Uğur Kömeçoğlu, "A Sociologically Interpretative Approach to the Fethullah Gülen Community Movement" Unpublished thesis, Directed by Nilüfer Göle, Bogazici University, 1997

sation.[36] For instance, we observed that some student parents in Strasbourg influenced by the idea of "hizmet" and believing the secular education in Gülen-led establishments will help their children to be successful not only in life but also in thereafter. Hizmet promotes the appropriation of individual piety and Islamic ethic (*adab*) values in private sphere and a militant participation to the modern secularised world in the public sphere. Apparently, this softened religious image of the Gülen-inspired institutions facilitates the emergence and expansion of the movement in the public sphere. However, as a consequence of these strategies, the movement voluntarily or "involuntarily" revalorises a secularisation process amongst the members. They offer a new communitarian identity to the Turkish community by appropriating the secular codes in public sphere and appropriating the religious codes in the private sphere. Consequently, we suggest that the followers and sympathizers of the movement develop a syncretic attitude towards the modern-secularised world in the public sphere. By adopting an attitude as we call "religio-secular" (an expression of Martin E. Marty), they "blur, mesh, meld, and muddle together elements of the secular and the religious, the worldly and the otherworldly". [37]

But the Gülen movement must not forget that Islam for the European Muslims was largely considered as a "clannish"[38] reinvestment.[39] As a characteristic of the Diasporic Islam, "Religion and ethnicity march hand in hand in Europe because they construct the compensatory refoundation of an "us" lost in the difficulties and reversals of immigration."[40] The associative institutionalisation of Islam in Europe fulfils many complementary functions such as a wish for identity, a community-centred life and fidelity to the ethnic group. Therefore, Islam in Europe is "more culture (than faith) and more tradition than belief."[41] Although there is an accentuation of Turkish identity and patriotism in Gülen movement, Fethullah Gülen's conception of Islam is more close to the Universalist orientation of Islam more than this "culturalised" form of Islam. The movement in France and in Germany, "seeks to find a "middle way" between the cultural devastation implied by assimilation and the "ghettoization" of a minority group living apart from the host society culture"[42] But in this search of a "middle way", the community confronts a risk to lose the "fine balance" between the Diaspora's community-oriented conception of Islam and the movement's more universalist Islam and its integrationist stance. This balance is menaced by 2 main factors:

i.   In spite of its relative success in expansion, Gülen movement's relatively liberal interpretation of Islam causes some criticisms from its members. For instance, Director of Le Dialogue Learning Centre Nihat Sarıer tells that parents of secondary school students severely object to mixed education in the learning centre: "When I talk about the importance and necessity of mixed education at class, the parents says (No, This is a Turkish association. We don't want a mixed education

36   Bekim Agai, "The discursive and organizational strategies of the Gülen movement" Paper submitted in Rice University, USA, 12-13 November 2005

37   Martin E. Marty, "Our religio-secular world", Daedalus(Special issue on secularism and religion), June 2003

38   "Clannish" is the approximate translation for the French adjective "communautariste" which refers to a society whose organization tends to consider the affiliation to a specific community (such as religion, foreign origin etc.) as important as the affiliation to the French nation or the "European citizenship" etc.

39   Jocelyne Cesari, Etre musulman en France aujourd'hui, Hachette, 1997, Paris, pg. 26

40   Albert Bastenier, "L'incidence du facteur religieux dans la conscience ethnique des immigres marocains en Belgique", Social Compass, 45 (2), 1998, pg. 197

41   Abdessamad Dialmy, "Belonging and Institution in Islam", Social Compass, 54 (1),2007, pg. 70-71

42   Jill Irvine, pg. 56

here)" [43]

Another example, the visit of Plateforme de Paris, Gülen inspired intercultural dialogue association in Paris, to a catholic church evoked the critics of some community members. [44] These micro-level tensions within the Gülen community reflect rightly the inner confrontation between the members who interiorised the "culturalised" and "universalist" conception of Islam. During our observation in Strasbourg, we noted that the transposition of community values and "know-how" of the movement realises through the intermediary of Turkey-originated graduate students. These students whom have already an experience in the associations and schools of the movement in Turkey play a vertical role in at the expansion of the movement. We observed –in our particular research area- that these students' looks like more tolerant towards a fully secular mixed education or interfaith dialogue meetings at churches etc. This tolerant/pluralistic attitude causes some tensions between them and the immigrant members. (Especially with the members of elder generation) Turkey originated students try to adopt a socio-cultural representation relating to the logic of the French/German associational structure. The elder members of the movement follow an inward-looking life strategy.

ii.   Although a relative retrogression of the community-oriented Islamic movements such as Suleymanci community or fundamentalist movements like Kaplanci community, a large variety of Sunni Islamic associations constitutes a veritable "religious market" in Turkish Diaspora. These associations which maintained their own clientelist networks criticise integrationist, less community-oriented and liberal discourse of Gülen movement. For instance, The Milli Görüş community harshly criticises the interfaith dialogue activities of the Gülen movement in Europe. While the Alevi community and the nationalist groups such as Ulkucus strictly opposes to the Gülen model of integration.

The Discursive Strategies: Gülen Followers in the Lands "Dar al-Hizmet"

Many scholars specialise in European Islam build their analysis on the traditional Islamic contrast between *dar al-Islam* (House of Islam) and dar al-harb (House of war) which presents somehow the historical antagonism of Islam toward non-Muslims. But the conflict is merely one facet of the complex relationship of Muslims with 'Western' society. Contrary, for a great part of the Muslim population in Europe *dar al-Islam* and *dar al-harb* distinction is not a pertinent method to define relationship to non-Muslim societies. In Germany and France, "many religious Muslims have recently undergone a significant shift toward a more 'integrational' stance".[45] Gülen's frequently used term *dar al-hizmet* (country of service) is a new concept in this regard, which helps to his followers to develop a particular discourse for propagation in the Turkish Diaspora. According to Gülen, "If one's intention is to serve Islam by presenting a good example, then one can stay wherever one desires. Gülen stresses a Muslim who lives in a non Muslim society; he or she has to obey the *lex loci*, to respect others' rights and to be just, and has to disregard discussions of dar al-harb and *dar al-Islam*."[46]

---

43   Interview with Nihat Sarıer, Director of Le Dialogue Learning Center, 12.05.2007

44   Erkan Toguslu, "Le difficile équilibre dedans-dehors : les activités culturelles d'un centre musulman comme stratégie d'intégration dans l'espace public et les critiques au projet au sein de leur communauté » Paper submitted in Colloquy « La Religion de l'Autre » 5-6 February 2007, Paris

45   Heiko Henkel, "Rethinking the dar al-harb: social change and changing perceptions of the West in Turkish Islam." Journal of Ethnic and Migration Studies, 9/2004

46   Ihsan Yılmaz, "İjtihad and Tajdid by Conduct» in "Turkish Islam and the Secular State The Gülen Movement by M Hakan Yavuz and John L Esposito (ed), Syracuse University Press, 2003, New York

The conceptualisation and practical use of the term *dar al-hizmet* looks like a "practical solution" offered by Gülen, more than a new politico-legal contribution to the Islamic law.

A separate note is needed here to summarise Gülen's geo-strategic vision and particularly his pro-western attitude. Gülen has always been a strong supporter of economic and political integration with the EU, while he has a sceptical attitude towards cooperation with Iran and the Arabic world. This pro-European attitude represents a differentiation in the Turkish Islamic scene. The other leading Islamic groups such as Erbakan's National Outlook Movement appropriated an essentialist anti-Europe or anti-western discourse since 1970s.[47] Most of the Turkish Islamic community leaders considered the EU membership as a "danger of assimilation in the Judeo-Christian world". But Gülen affirms that Europe represents no danger to the Turkish-Islamic identity:

> We should be comfortable in our outreach to the world. We will not lose anything from our religion, nationality and culture because of developments like globalisation, customs union or membership in the European Union. We firmly believe that the dynamics that hold our unity are strong. Again, we also firmly believe that the Quran is based on revelation and offers solution[s] to all the problems of humanity. Therefore, if there is anybody who is afraid, they should be those who persistently live away from the invigorating climate of Quran. (2003)[48]

Furthermore, in an interview in 1995, he assigns a particular task to the Turkish Diaspora in Europe:

> Our people who live in Europe must come off from their old situation and become a part of the European society. Their children must be oriented to universities more then artisanal high schools. Also, they must transmit our cultural and religious richness to European society. In the future, they will constitute our lobbies which we highly need today. In the past, only the 2 percent of the Turkish immigrant population was fulfilling their religious requirements. But today, 40 or maybe 60 per cent of the young population regularly prays in the mosques. Obviously, our people didn't undergo to an assimilation process, contrary, they impressed the host societies by their conviction and culture.[49]

The essential idea of the Gülen movement regarding to the Turkish Diaspora is to become a recognized part of the main society without losing one's "Turkish-Islamic" identity. During our research, we observed that the concepts such as "*dar al-hizmet*" and "renewal of intention" (*tashih-i niyet*) are frequently used by the disciples of the Gülen community in Europe. As a matter of fact, The Turkish immigrants mainly immigrated for the economic reasons. Therefore, to gain more money may become raison d'être for a Turkish entrepreneur or an employee, in Europe. By these concepts, sympathizers of Gülen movement try to change the mentality regarding to main society.

A Turkish small entrepreneur Kasım A. (age 46), community member who lives in Frankfurt-Germany says:

---

47   Hasan Kösebalaban, "The Making of Enemy and Friend: Fethullah Gülen's National-Security Identity » in "Turkish Islam and the Secular State The Gülen Movement by M Hakan Yavuz and John L Esposito (ed), Syracuse University Press, 2003, New York

48   Fethullah Gülen, "Hoşgörü ve Medya." Available at: http://www.m-fGülen.org/eser/article.php?id-442. Accessed 18 July 2003. Cited in Hasan Kösebalaban, "The Making of Enemy and Friend: Fethullah Gülen's National-Security Identity » in "Turkish Islam and the Secular State The Gülen Movement by M Hakan Yavuz and John L Esposito (ed), Syracuse University Press, 2003, New York

49   Nuriye Akman, "Hoca'nın hedefi Amerika ve Almanya" (Hodja targets USA and Germany) ,Turkish newspaper Sabah, 28.01.1995, http://tr.fGülen.com/content/view/7853/74/

> We all came here (Germany) with an economic motive, to gain more money and have a more comfortable life. Nobody can deny it. But after 30 years, we became the members of this society. We cannot continue to live in our small communal worlds. Fethullah Gülen advises us to renew our intentions. That means we are not here just for a more comfortable life, but also be a good example for our entourage and work for the good of this country.

Despite the "politically correct" aspect of this declaration, it indicates a discursive change regarding the host society.

The Gülen disciples in Europe advise to followers to renew their intentions (tashih-i niyet). The term "*tashih-i niyet*" is partially inspired by the idea of "*hegira*"[50]. With referring to the compulsive immigration of the prophet Mohammed from Mecca to Medina, the Islamic preachers in 20th century created a universal doctrine of "*hegira*", by urging the Muslims to immigrate to non-Muslim countries in order to make Islamic proselytism in these societies.[51] According to Bassam Tibi, this doctrine largely forms the worldviews of the preachers of Muslim Diaspora in Europe. If we return to our case, the reference to the "*hegira*" doctrine is obvious in conceptualisation of "*tashih-i niyet*". But it does not contain a proselyte or missionary connotation. This concept occurs as a resource of motivation for the community members to present a "good example" in their entourage.

Consequently, the term "*dar al hizmet*", by eliminating the contrast between the dar Al harb and dar Al Islam, allows especially the immigration-originated youth to express their will to be recognized individually and collectively in the host society, not only as a Diasporic -passive subjects, but also as "veritable subjects"[52], "who are searching a constructive role in the host society, as the autonomous authors of their trajectory and as the producers of their own existence." [53]

Conclusion

Consequently, the socio-political problems and economic vulnerability of the Turkish Diaspora in Europe transform the strategies of the Gülen movement. If we consider the schools in Central Asia, in the Balkan countries or in Africa, we can assume that the settlement strategy of the movement is not dependent on the Turkish immigration waves throughout the world. In different regions, the disciples of the movement always seek to contact with the host societies. Differently to evolution of the movement in Central Asia or Balkans etc., the movement does not focus on the host societies in Turk-populated Western European countries. As a result of our qualitative research, we observed that the members of the Gülen community acts in two different trajectories. On the one hand, as a neo-communitarian religious community, they strive to have a larger share -more members- within the religious market of Turkish Diaspora by producing a new religious discourse and new organisational strategies, as they did in Turkey. The followers of Gülen inculcate Islamic values and norms in society through sohbets (religious study circles). So, the clientelist perspective and the search for an ethno-

---

50 "Hegira" is an important notion in the Muslim tradition. The prophet Mohammed ordered his followers to make "hegira" i.e. to immigrate and disperse to the different regions of the world in order to propagate the Muslim faith.

51 Bassam Tibi, "Europeanizing Islam or Islamization of Europe" in Timothy Brynes, Peter Katzenstein, "Religion in Expanding Europe", Cambridge University Press, New York, 2006, op.cit 210

52 For a larger explicaiton of the term "veritable subject" see: Alaine Touraine, "Pourrons-nous vivre ensemble ? Égaux et différents", Fayard Editions, 1997

53 Dounia Bouzar, « L'islam entre mythe et religion : le nouveau discours religieux dans les associa-tions socio-culturelles musulmanes », Les Cahiers de la sécurité intérieure, n°54, 2003,pg. 174, www.islamlaicite.org/ article235.html.

religious reference of the community members are not neglected by the Gülen movement. On the other hand, by interiorising the modern-secular codes and by organising around the non-religious, cultural and non-profit associations , they seek to gain legitimacy in the public space in Germany and France in order to build an educational network in these countries, as they did in Central Asia or in Balkan region. In these two different trajectories, the Turkish population appears both as a backing population and as an obstacle. (See p.18, above) As a result of the synthesis of these trajectories; a reinvented and reorganised community took place in Europe. Therefore, the "fine balance", is procured by a reciprocal compromise between the ethno-religious attachment of the Turkish Diaspora and integrationist stance of the movement. This is why the Gülen community became a neo-communitarian movement in Europe.

The moderate, apolitical and dialogue-oriented Gülen movement undertakes a new task in Europe by readapting a particular settlement strategy oriented to the Turkish Diaspora. The lately arrived Gülen movement assigned "the reintegration of Turkish youth to the educational system of the host societies" as a first goal. The community is searching for a mediator role willing to enforce the Turkish youth to a transition from the Diasporic (stigmatized) condition. They aim to establish a fully secular educational system in Germany and in France which can attract the "Banlieue" or ghetto youth to the schools. In contrast with other Islamic organisations, they could gain the confidence of the host society. It's too early today to speak about a success-or failure- of the movement due to the fact that they haven't reached a tangible size in Europe. Nevertheless, the first reason of a possible failure in the future could be the loss of the "fine balance" between inward-looking life strategy of some of the members and their "innovative" and integrationist discourse.

GÜLEN MOVEMENT AS AN INTEGRATION MECHANISM FOR THE EUROPE'S TURKISH AND MUSLIM COMMUNITY: POTENTIALS AND CONSTRAINTS

M Fatih Tedik

Abstract

This paper discusses the potential of the Gülen movement to serve as a mechanism for, in the medium term, the integration of the Turkish community in Europe and, in the long term, the Muslim community as a whole, taking into consideration the obstacles to this process, given the composition of different communities.

Although many of Gülen's ideas are far from conventional theologically, the real novelty of his work is that it motivates people who are at least sympathetic to his ideas to put them into practice: the ideas do not remain theory and aspiration but become a charter or action-plan implemented by members of the movement. The movement's influence on Muslim community is examined from both a theoretical perspective (i.e. the position of Gülen's ideas within Islamic understanding of dar al-Islam and dar al-harb) and a practical perspective (i.e. the activities of the movement in western Europe that have actual and potential effectiveness in bringing about integration).

In order to assess the movement's capabilities, the current situation of Muslims in Europe and their problems in general and the Turkish experience in particular is presented. The movement's potential for enabling integration is then analysed from four complementary perspectives: (1) does the movement propose an alternative view to stimulate the integration process of the Muslim community; (2) has the movement actually operated as a mechanism for integration in western Europe so that its capability is demonstrable; (3) is the European context suitable for the movement to operate effectively; and (4) what does the Gülen movement offer to European member-states by way of a means to sustain a healthy integration process – Turkish community in the medium-run, and the whole Muslim community in the long-run.

Introduction: From Empire's Children to Imported Employees

As a consequence of the two World Wars and following political events created a brave new world for Muslims in which three great empires of sixteenth century carved up to 44 nation-states. This separation caused one third of Muslim population to live as minorities in non-Muslim countries. The number of minorities noticeably augmented after Muslim population have voluntarily migrated to the Western World as well as Australia and New Zealand for expectation of a new and better life.[1] In the European continent Muslim population became an undeniable conglomeration, and according to the estimates of the National Intelligence Council, with contemporary fertility rates, over the next 15 years, European Muslims will double their population.[2] Although European countries experience social-political problems with their minorities and previous figures intensify their anxiety, they have to continue to the 'minority importation' in order to sustain the continent economic growth. In spite of being unwelcomed by Western society, immigration, therefore, seems to be non-stoppable and ir-reversible aspect for the Continent. So to speak, if an effective method could not be implemented to facilitate the integration process, a serious problem, if not a social crisis, impends within the European society.

This paper endeavours to analyse the potential contributions of the Gülen Movement to the integration process of Turkish community in Europe in the medium-run and the whole Muslim community in the long-run and the feasibility of this process with references to the existing restrictions in the composition of aforementioned communities. However, it is necessary at this stage to highlight why Gülen Movement has been selected although Gülen is not the first or sole pioneer of integration in the Muslim World: that is the existence of a movement as an embodiment of the Gülen's ideas and the capability of this movement to change its surrounding environment. In other words, in the Muslim world there have been certain Islamic scholars prior or contemporary to Gülen who have formulated certain ideas related to interfaith dialogue and/or integration. What makes Gülen significant is the presence of a movement or people that are at least sympathetic to his ideas and put them into operation. The ideas do not remain in the world of ideas but become the charter or action plan that is pursued by the members of the movement. Therefore, while initially the personal, then communal, organisational and finally societal acceptance and realisation of these notions are required for the remaining scholars, Gülen's ideas bypass the almost first three phases, i.e. personal, communal and organisational acceptance and realisation, and function in order to be recognized in societal level.

Never-ending Story: From 'Islam and Europe' to 'Islam in Europe'

Although the beginning dates of immigrations may vary from one country to another, we can say that, it, in today's sense, started after the World War II. For some countries, the im-migration was triggered either by the independence of the of the ex-colonies, e.g. India and Algeria, or treaties for worker importation in order to sustain economic growth after the War, e.g. Federal Republic's First Employment Agreement with Turkey in 1961, or with Tunisia in 1965.[3] In the beginning, the majority of the immigrant workers were young men from rural

---

1 Haddad, Y. (1991) *The Challenge of Muslim Minorityness: The American Experience*, in W.A.R. Shadid and P.S. van Koningsveld, eds., *The Integration of Islam and Hinduism in Western Europe*, Kampen: Kok Pharos Publishing House, p. 134

2 http://www.cia.gov/nic

3 Pauly, Robert J, Jr. (2004) Islam in Europe: Integration or Marginalisation?, Aldershot: Ashgate, p .67

regions who had low level of education and very conservative opinions on religious or on other social concepts. They were not only deficient in the knowledge on Islam but also they were very uncompetitive in social issues such as language or culture of their new society.[4] These were, nonetheless, not a trouble for them because their aim was to return home after saving sufficient money for their living expenses in the homeland. They, thus, were only 'guest' workers without any intention to reside in Europe.[5]

By the 1970s, this sense of temporariness started to fade out with the family reunifications. The arrivals of wives and children altered and broadened the context of workers' relationships with their surrounding society. Now, they had to interact with new institutions in the society which they never get in touch with, such as education and social welfare.[6] They were undergoing the 'transformation from foreign worker to immigrant' and to diminish the shock of the process they began to build a number of institutions to defend their traditions.[7] These institutions, nevertheless, were not established to facilitate their integration process or enhance communication with host nation but to protect their society from outside impacts. In other words, Muslims was pursuing an isolationist and defensive policy. For Joly, this was "not simply the predominance of another religion which caused concern to Muslims; they wanted to safeguard Islam from the growing secularisation" of the surrounding European social order.[8] In my opinion, this was not a genuine consciousness for the preservation of their religion, but a reflex to protect their different aspects of their traditions which make them different even if they do not live it. Because as Dash asserts, the immigrants have been hardly educated people whose "own culture, way of life and religious beliefs were mocked, derided or desecrated".[9]

Today, immigrants are concentrated in the *banlieus* of the big cities in the United Kingdom (London, Manchester etc.), the Netherlands (Amsterdam, Rotterdam etc.), and Germany (Munich, Frankfurt etc).[10] With the illegal immigration in the 1980s and 1990s, the refugees from the revolution in Ira, the Iran-Iraq war, Palestinian conflict and of Kurds from Middle Eastern countries, not only the numbers of immigrants but also national and sectarian variety of the immigration amplified drastically. Religion upholds its position in the social milieu by acting as a protector of the cultural identity – or by being protected in the customs – and providing sense of unity and similarity. This characteristic of religion is vital particularly in Western social context, because for a worker with an Islamic background religion is the only support and "it is the only thing that belongs to him and that he can master".[11] For instance,

4   Sander, A. (1991) The Road from Musalla to Mosque: The Process of Integration and Institutionalisation of Islam in Sweden, in W.A.R. Shadid and P.S. van Koningsveld, eds., The Integration of Islam and Hinduism in Western Europe, Kampen: Kok Pharos Publishing House, p. 82

5   Anwar, M., Blaschke, J., Sander, A. (et. all), (2004) State Policies Towards Muslim Minorities: Sweden, Great Britain and Germany, Berlin: Verlagsabteilung im Europäischen Migrationszentrum (EMZ), p. 19

6   Nielsen, Jørgen S. (1991) Muslim Organisations in Europe: Integration or Isolation?, in W.A.R. Shadid and P.S. van Koningsveld, eds., The Integration of Islam and Hinduism in Western Europe, Kampen: Kok Pharos Publishing House, p. 43

7   Pauly, Robert J, Jr. (2004) Islam in Europe: Integration or Marginalisation?, Aldershot: Ashgate, p. 99

8   Joly, Daniel (1988) Making A Place for Islam in British Society: Muslims in Birmingham, in T. Gerholm and Yngve George Lithman, eds., London and New York: Mansell, p. 32

9   Darsh, S.M. (1980) Islam in Europe, London: Ta-Ha Publishers, p. 51

10   Nielsen, Jørgen S. (1991) Muslim Organisations in Europe: Integration or Isolation?, in W.A.R. Shadid and P.S. van Koningsveld, eds., The Integration of Islam and Hinduism in Western Europe, Kampen: Kok Pharos Publishing House, p. 34

11   Elsas, E. (1991) Turkish Islamic Ideals of Education: Their Possible Function for Islamic Identity and Integration

as Yilmaz examined in the daily practises of Turkish community in Britain, "the traditional homeland Turkish culture, identity and diversity are, to a great extent, reproduced and reconstructed in the British context" which even gives rise to the "emergence of the Anglo-Turkish Muslim law".[12]

Being a Muslim in Europe

Due to the socio-political turmoil that Muslims have experienced in both their native countries and new habitats, their economic, cultural and intellectual backgrounds Muslim community struggle with serious set of overwhelming difficulties which deeply damage the integration process: these are high degree of fragmentation, incompetence, guidance crisis, generation gap, perception of '*minorityness*' and reciprocal perspective of "the other".

The Muslim minority in Western Europe suffers from theological (e.g. Sunni vs. Shiite), cultural, national, linguistic, political heterogeneity and "intra- and inter- community rivalry and split".[13] Those problems could not be resolved due to the absence of good 'socialisation agents who would facilitate the integration process. As Pauly rightly describes, in our day, "there are as many as Islams as there are Muslims".[14] For instance, the mosques and prayer halls are organised as national entities. This is partly because chain migration and village transplantation have caused people with same origin gather same area in the Western Europe, but mostly due to sectarian and ideological differences which grounds contention and resentment among Muslim community.

According to surveys and opinion polls in Western Europe, Muslim migrants represent a cluster which is socio-economically marginalised, geographically dispersed and internally split, and has not constructive asset to share with mainstream European community. Although this result evaluated as a prejudice by Muslim scholars, indeed, first generation, and a considerable proportion of their children in particular, proved mostly incompetent in terms of formal education, vocational skills and language of the host country. Two examples from the Netherlands would suffice to illustrate the point: Firstly, the percentage of people who are officially suspected of a crime is 2.9 among first generation non-Western immigrants and 4.0 among second generation non-Western immigrants, but 1.2 for the total population." What is considered especially disquieting about these figures is that second generation immigrants appear to be doing worse in terms of social participation than their parents. Secondly, school drop-out rates among students with a migrant background are more than two times higher than among non-migrant groups. This ratio is particularly important as an indicator of the expected future socioeconomic position of second and third generation migrants. As Ali states "these observations contradict the long-held claim from immigration advocates that immigration is a solution to economic questions and that, with time, the integration problems would solve themselves."[15] Although this exemplification fits for the majority, evidently, this

in Europe, in W.A.R. Shadid and P.S. van Koningsveld, eds., The Integration of Islam and Hinduism in Western Europe, Kampen: Kok Pharos Publishing House, p. 175

12 Yilmaz, Ihsan (2004) Marriage Solemnization among Turks in Britain: The Emergence of a Hybrid Anglo-Muslim Turkish Law in Journal of Muslim Affairs, Vol. 24, No. 1, April 2004, p. 59

13 Sander, A. (1991) The Road from Musalla to Mosque: The Process of Integration and Institutionalisation of Islam in Sweden, in W.A.R. Shadid and P.S. van Koningsveld, eds., The Integration of Islam and Hinduism in Western Europe, Kampen: Kok Pharos Publishing House, p. 81

14 Pauly, Robert J, Jr. (2004) Islam in Europe: Integration or Marginalisation?, Aldershot: Ashgate, p. 147

15 Ali, A H, Islam and the EU's Identity Deficit, Brown Journal of World Affairs, Summer/ Fall 2005, Volume XII, Issue 1, p.57. For the original set of data, please see Verdacht van Criminalireit, Allochtonen en Autochtonen

is not the case for all immigrants. Especially, when the colonial states receive migration for their ex-colonies, the migrating people are more familiar with the language, institutions and values of the new society. Of the Muslims who have immigrated to the UK, for example, a fair number already spoke English; or had university/ higher education from an educational system that, from colonial times, was influenced by the British educational system. Some had also gone through higher education in the UK. This assumption is also valid for some of the ex-colonial powers.[16]

At the dawn of Islam's emergence in the West, the secular elite had been not only the representative of the migrant Muslim communities, but also the associates of the administration in the struggle to integrate minorities. The same secular elite have evaluated the imam as reactionary people operating for the plans of Islamic country of origins rather than exerting themselves for the minorities to gain more legal rights in their society.[17]

In the non-existence of healthy social infrastructure and environment in which Muslims could live their traditions and express themselves to the mainstream European society, the roles of mosques and imams started to rise steadily. Not only with offering religious services but also with generating network of solidarity which lessen the discomfort of isolation, mosques became the indispensable intermediary institutions for Muslims.[18] And in the absence of traditional social settings such as family, acquaintances and neighbourhood, the functions and significance of imams became unquestionable in the community. Nonetheless, the insufficiency in the capacity and number of imams relative to the number of growing Muslim population necessitated the importation of imams from the country of origins. But newly recruited imams couldn't help minorities because they have not necessary double knowledge – about both Islam and the new society – and language. Therefore, new imams have been more helpless than the people who have been supposed to be guided.[19]

In current situation, Western Countries have large number of younger generation trying to live in their new 'homelands'. Wherever their parents come from, they experience Islam in a very distinct manner. Islam was not taken for granted part of the social order, and neither their environments nor their practices justify/affirm it. This situation leads a generation gap between parents with traditional background who fail to transmit Islamic identity in an acceptable mode and children who interact with society and suffer from the incompatibility of conventional values and Western life. At that juncture, they prefer to implement two strategies: increasing religious consciousness to find 'true Islam' or secularise their social life.

As a recent research reconfirmed, 'British Muslims have sought to adjust to and accommodate existing institutions and practices, experimenting and negotiating between the actual and perceived demands and values of British society, and the needs, beliefs and practices of

Nader Bekeken, cahier 2005-2 by Centraal Bureau voor Statistiek and Wetenschappelijk Onderzoeks en Informatiecentrum

16 W.A. Shadid and P.S. van Koningsveld (1991) Institutionalisation and Integration of Islam in The Netherlands, in W.A.R. Shadid and P.S. van Koningsveld, eds., The Integration of Islam and Hinduism in Western Europe, Kampen: Kok Pharos Publishing House, p. 91

17 Leveau, Rémy (1988) The Islamic Presence in France, in T. Gerholm and Yngve George Lithman, eds., London and New York: Mansell, p. 114

18 Leveau, Rémy (1988) The Islamic Presence in France, in T. Gerholm and Yngve George Lithman, eds., London and New York: Mansell, p. 114

19 Elsas, E. (1991) Turkish Islamic Ideals of Education: Their Possible Function for Islamic Identity and Integration in Europe, in W.A.R. Shadid and P.S. van Koningsveld, eds., The Integration of Islam and Hinduism in Western Europe, Kampen: Kok Pharos Publishing House

Muslims (Ansari 2002: 17). While the widely expected assimilation of English cultural patterns has not occurred and Muslims, and many other minorities, are autonomously evolving their own distinctive lifestyles (Ballard 1982: 190; see in detail 1994; see also Joly 1995: 183).

They have reconstructed 'a home away from home (*desh pardesh*)'. The older generation of Muslims and their British-born offspring are continuing to find substantial inspiration in the resources of their own cultural, religious and linguistic inheritance, which they have actively and creatively reinterpreted in order to rebuild their lives on their own terms (Ballard 1994a: 5). They have become an integral part of the British society. However, 'they have done so on their own terms' (Ballard 1994a: 8). As skilled cultural navigators, Muslims, along with other ethnic minorities, have been meeting the demands of different cultures and laws. Ballard (1994a: 31) explains this phenomenon skilfully:

> (j)ust as individuals can be bilingual, so they can be multicultural, with the competence to behave appropriately in a number of different arenas, and to switch codes as appropriate… they are much better perceived as skilled cultural navigators, with a sophisticated capacity to manoeuvre their way to their own advantage both inside and outside the ethnic colony.

After facing with high tension as a result of living their parent's traditional Islam in a modern secular society, they choose to learn genuine Islam from original sources and construct a hybrid identity as a combination of Islam and Western culture. As Elsas aptly expresses it "the majority of Muslim youths choose a bicultural option with regard to integration: to become full members of the encompassing society without complete identification with its norms and values."[20] In France, for example, despite the assumptions of many French sociologists of religion who once forecast secularisation as the inevitable upshot of individual choice, "a number of young Franco-Muslims are choosing strict religious observance, rather than wholesale abandonment of Muslim attachments, as an expression of personal autonomy".[21] They abandon neither Islam nor their social roles; because, on one hand, Islam represents a protection or a shelter from assimilation in secular and foreign culture, and on the other hand, their social roles are everything they have in their new 'homelands'. Features of this hybrid identity vary according to the state's policies towards Islam and public perception of the religion. In minor cases, the search for a 'true Islam' may later channel them to embrace a radical form of Islam if they are guided to this direction.

In the latter case, by more interaction with their surrounding society, young Muslims are influenced by the secular character of the society. They use some institutions such as sports or youth clubs in order to socialise instead of religion. Nevertheless, it should be noted that, while young Muslims secularise at individual level, they perceive religion as sine qua non of their identity. For instance, although over half of the first generation in France performs their daily prayers regularly and this percentage drops to only three percent in second and third generation; the latter group sees Islam as primary element of their identity and downplay French citizenship.[22]

---

20   Elsas, E. (1991) Turkish Islamic Ideals of Education: Their Possible Function for Islamic Identity and Integration in Europe, in W.A.R. Shadid and P.S. van Koningsveld, eds., The Integration of Islam and Hinduism in Western Europe, Kampen: Kok Pharos Publishing House, p. 183

21   Cesari, Jocelyne (2002) Islam in France: The Shaping of A Religious Minority, in Yvonne Yazbeck Haddad, ed., Muslims in the West: From Sojourners to Citizens, New York: Oxford University Press, p. 42

22   Cesari, Jocelyne (2002) Islam in France: The Shaping of A Religious Minority, in Yvonne Yazbeck Haddad, ed., Muslims in the West: From Sojourners to Citizens, New York: Oxford University Press, p. 43

In February 1997, the Runnymede Commission produced a very controversial consultation paper entitled "Islamophobia: Its Features and Dangers". The report begins by describing the nature of anti-Muslim prejudice and draws a key distinction between closed views of Islam on one hand and open views on the other. *Islamophobia* is equated with closed views. Though according to some scholars, it is an objective report revealing the problems of Islam and proves its incompatibility of with European context, for Muslim scholars in particular, it is nothing but an attempt "to demonise Islam".[23] But whatever it aims, it demonstrates some European's perspective about Islam. Apparently, the closed views are not shared by all Europeans as the features of Islam, but they unarguably reflect some of the Western perception of Islam.

Today, not only a number of Muslims evaluate the West with the experiences of colonial times but some European state and individuals consider Islam according to the parameters remained from the Crusades. And both of the perceptions slow down, at best, and obstruct the process of Muslim integration to the West. For West, Islam and Muslims symbolize a very distinctive "other", a religio-political force that has engaged the West for centuries with a heritage of salient confrontations and clashes. European countries continue to be guided by their bitter past experiences with Islam, such as the colonial period, Ottoman Expansion, and the Crusades.[24] The resultant stereotypes have kept negative images of Islam and Muslims alive. These stereotypes which have led European countries to continue to view Islam as "a threat and a problem" make West feel resentment towards Islam that has survived today.[25] The hostile image of Islam has been bolstered and continues to have an effect on the perception of Muslim immigrants and refugees in Western Europe. Moreover, whereas, most immigrants, are employed in particular jobs that individuals in the majority would never consider occupying, after the rising of unemployment in Europe, immigrants as the cheap labour of 30 years ago began to be identified as the reason of job loss of native people.[26] In other words, although it is not completely accurate, the majority began to assess Muslim minority as a menace to their welfare and everyday lives. From this perspective, we can say that, in some degree, the principal cultural puzzle of the West today is not only how different cultures will be integrated into the secular society, but also how secular society will form a relationship with European Muslims.

Allievi, on the other hand, made a remarkable contribution to the problem of perception of Islam by the Western society and by the Muslims themselves. As he portrayed, the situation in Europe does "resembles much more the Meccan than the Medinese situation. Specifically, the society and the situation in Europe nowadays, from the religious point of view, resemble that of Mecca before the *hijra*"[27]. In the Meccan context Muslims were a minority not a dominant clique, or even an influential one. Quite normally, that is the expected situation when

23   Ramadan, Tariq (1999) Islam and Muslims in Europe: A Silent Revolution Toward Rediscovery, in Yvonne Yazbeck Haddad, ed., Muslims in the West: From Sojourners to Citizens, New York: Oxford University Press, p. 159

24   Köse, Ali (1999) "East Is East, and West Is West": Remarks on Muslim Perspectives on Europe and Christianity, in G. Seufert and J. Waardenburg, eds., Turkish Islam and Europe, Istanbul: Kommission Bei Franz-Steiner-Verlag, p. 183

25   Esposito, John L. (2003) Modernising Islam and Re-Islamisation in Global Perspective, in John L. Esposito and François Burgat, eds., Modernising Islam: Religion in The Public Sphere in the Middle East and Europe, London: Hurst & Company, p. 12

26   Pauly, Robert J, Jr. (2004) Islam in Europe: Integration or Marginalisation?, Aldershot: Ashgate, p. 83

27   Allievi, S., Sociology of a Newcomer: Muslim Migration to Italy - Religious Visibility, Cultural and Political Reactions, Immigrants & Minorities, Vol.22, Issue 2&3, July/November 2003, p. 142

the novelty of Muslim settlement is taken into consideration. What he sees as a contextual dilemma is: although the current situation for Muslims is more Meccan than Medinese, "the common comprehension of Islam by non-Muslims, as well as by Muslims, is often much more Medinese than Meccan. The whole idea of *shari'a* (Islamic law) and *fiqh* (Islamic jurisprudence), as well as the idea of political power influenced by religion, and in many respects the entire Islamic theology … simply presupposes that Islam is a majority in the population as well as a majority in power."[28]

When the migrants' responses to being minority in the Western world and integration to the society as its expected outcome, it can be asserted that the responses may swing in a pendulum from absolute rejection through cautious engagement to enthusiastic support. On the other hand, for most of the Muslim immigrants, the reply should be, at worst, absolute rejection and, at best, cautious engagement. To understand the reason behind this attitude, firstly two Islamic scholars should be evaluated. Firstly, according to Mawdudi, minorities deserve to experience the bitter consequences of belonging to a minority faith and that they must expect to be mistreated and marginalized.[29] From this perspective, Muslims, in order to guarantee their safety and the freedom to practice their faith, are expected to live in areas governed by Islam.[30] Secondly, for Kettani, the reason behind this attitude is the sense of 'minorityness'. 'Minorityness' "implies weakness and powerlessness, a condition that he believes is incompatible with Islam." Islam, he argues, "insists on the health and wellbeing of a community, conditions guaranteed by social and political empowerment." Hence, Muslims must not consent with minority status as a long-term situation in which they accommodate and submit to those in power. Their 'minorityness' is to be understood as a challenge to the community in order to seek methods to correct such a condition and surpass it. To Kettani, if a minority Muslim community faces with repression and cruelty and is not tolerated to observe its faith, then its members have the options of either jihad or emigration.[31] In other words, according to this frame of mind, Muslim should never accept being under the rule of non-Muslims. For a part of Muslims in the Western countries, these assertions constitute the intellectual backbone of their resistance. However, particularly for younger generations, contrary to their predecessors, the implication of these perceptions is not isolation or ostracise themselves from the society but adapting to the environment in which they live. They have even redefined their religious doctrines (probably not only for the sake of religion) and reoriented the way they carry out social and cultural activities.

As a matter of fact, in modern times, one motivation for rethinking on *ijtihad* was the situation of Muslims in non-Muslim territories. The juristic discourse on Muslim minorities with regard to whether or not Muslims may reside in a non-Muslim territory and under what circumstances, the relationships of these Muslims to *dar al-Islam* and the ethical and legal duties that these Muslims owe to the Muslim law and to their host non-Muslim polity have been debated since the eighth century. Indeed, the juristic discourse on the issue has not been dogmatic (see in detail Fadl 1994: 141-187; see also Masud 1989: 118-128). Other than the

---

28 Allievi, S., Sociology of a Newcomer: Muslim Migration to Italy - Religious Visibility, Cultural and Political Reactions, Immigrants & Minorities, Vol.22, Issue 2&3, July/November 2003, p. 142

29 Mawdudi's ideas were grounded in the classical Islamic division of the world into dar al-harb, the domain of war, dar al-Islam, the domain of Islam, and dar al-sulh, the domain of treaty.

30 Haddad, Y. (1991) The Challenge of Muslim Minorityness: The American Experience, in W.A.R. Shadid and P.S. van Koningsveld, eds., The Integration of Islam and Hinduism in Western Europe, Kampen: Kok Pharos Publishing House, p. 135

31 Kettani, MA (1979) The Muslim Minorities, Leicester: The Islamic Foundation

mutually exclusive concepts of *dar al-harb* and *dar al-Islam*, the persistent existence of Muslim minorities voluntarily residing outside *dar al-Islam* challenged this dichotomous view. In that regard, Islamic jurisprudence has developed several mechanisms and concepts that facilitate compromise, such as duress (*ikrah*), necessity (*darura*), and public welfare (*maslaha*). As a result, an understanding of *dar al-ahd* (country of treaty, covenant), *dar al-aman* (country of security), *dar al-sulh* (country of truce), and *dar al-darura* (country of necessity) have come to be recognized as situations and environments in which Muslims may live in non-Muslim territories.

Trying To Live As the Outsider: Evaluation of the Integration Process

Family reunions after the 1970s can be considered as the actual commencement of the institutionalisation of Muslim minorities in Europe. With the arrival of the families, minorities began to interact with wide range of social institutions which force them to fell the necessity the preserve their traditions. In other words, the transition from individual workers to families triggered the establishment of safeguarding institutions for traditional values. This formation of traditional and religious bodies, however, is not independent process; on the contrary, existing European political, economic, social and religious structures have a determinative effect on the profiles, nature and stream of this formation.[32]

Although quite distinct categorisations articulated by different scholars, in my opinion, we can sort people with Islamic origins into five types with regard to religious attitude in the European social context. These are first, those who choose to remain distant to the religion and to the religious establishments, second, those who prefer personal piety and devotion but detached from religious organisations, third, those who join to the moderate/mainstream Islamic organisations seeking improvement in the religious consciousness of their members, fourth, those who adhere organised missionary, and fifth, those who adhere militant affiliations.

Today, the Muslims' organisational activities may be classified into three categories according their origins: first, groups which were composed in the new social framework (i.e. groups formed by the immigrants themselves who were concerned with the conservation (or reconstruction) of essentials of traditional culture and collective continuity and reproduction in the European environment), second, groups arose as the branch or the extensions of the movements or the organisations in the country of origin (i.e. groups formed with the same objective of the previous category but opted to operate under tutelage of powerful organisation originated in the country of origin), and third, groups formed by governments or state-led agencies (i.e. groups or organizations formed in order to control national Muslim minority in Europe and prevent them to connect with informal religious movements considered as rivals).

Whatever the mode of organisations and their strategies are most of them have two common aspects: first, they endeavour to respond the same challenges and offer alternative solutions to those of the West (e.g. such as modernity, social welfare, gender relations, democracy, and human rights), express through an Islamic idiom and legitimise with references to the *Qur'an* and the *Sunnah*. Second, when restructuring the religious community into a secular

---

32 LeVine, Mark (2003) 'Human Nationalisms' Versus 'Inhuman Globalisms': Cultural Economies of Globalisation and The Re-imagining of Muslim Identities in Europe and The Middle East, in S. Allievi and J. Nielsen, eds., Muslim Networks and Transnational Communities in and Across Europe, Leiden and Boston: Brill, p. 101

society they try to find an equilibrium point between total assimilation and total rejection. But, even though for some intellectuals they couldn't find effective resolutions for Muslims in Europe yet, we can say that, they are progressively striving to find ways for integration to the European society.

"Turkum... Dogruyum, Caliskanim?"[33]: Turks in the Diaspora

For Turks, as the first respondents of the Gülen movement, the picture is not so bright, either. As mentioned, after the formal immigration era started the first generation were hardly educated population who had rural background of Eastern and Western Anatolia. When they experienced a shock after coming Western countries, with the instinct of protection they began gathering in the Turkish ghettos. They had no intention to stay permanently, thus, they didn't feel the necessity to integrate into the society. At the beginning, religion had not any role in the Turkish community. Especially before the 1980s, parallel to the Turkish politics, the greater part of Turkish associations could be categorised according to their position on the continuum of the extreme poles of Turkish society. Turkish political competition, both official and underground, became reflected among the Turks in Diaspora. But transition from temporary migration to permanent settlement, family reunification and Turkish political developments increased the significance of religion in the Turkish community.

However, religion of Turkish community is neither strong enough to mobilise people nor monolithic entity. Turkish community divided into many parts due to sectarian and ethnic disparities. In terms of sectarian variations, Turkish population is mostly Sunni with 88% and Alevis with 11%, which have no large exchanges between them. No Alevis live in Sunni-dominated areas and as was shown earlier, the distinctions are repeated in the composition of the unions. The Alevis and the laicists are unlikely candidates for Islamic religious movements. Moreover, in ethno-national sense, the chief split occurs mainly among people with Turkish and Kurdish origins.[34]

Whereas total number of Turks in Diaspora reached nearly 4.5-5 million with unofficial migrants, the majority remained surprisingly uninformed and indifferent about them and their religion. Only in Germany are 2400 mosques associations but their cohorts do not feel Muslim in the religious sense of the definition.[35] They are mostly cultural Muslims who adjust their religious practices towards 'folk Islam', and are little interested in the theological/ideological issues. By and large, – contrary to other Muslims – there is a tendency to join the nearest mosque, no matter which view it represents. Their Islamic way if life is a mixture of "popular religiosity, national customs, Islamic rules of conduct, mysticism, folk knowledge, folklore and magic with Islamic elements".[36] Especially members of the first generation define themselves as Muslims but this is not because of their firm adherence to an Islamic faith but they merge the notion of nationality and the Islam. In other words, they are Muslims because Islam was taken granted with 'Turkishness'.

Today, the Turkish community outside Turkey suffers from very serious deficiencies which

---

33 First three words of a passage which is compulsory to recite for Turkish primary schools before the commencement of lectures. Its means "I am Turkish: honest and hardworking" to stress ethical and practical necessities to be 'a Turk'.

34 Başyurt, Erhan. "Gerçekleşmesi Zor Bir Hayal: Euro–İslam." Aksiyon 09/2004

35 Başyurt, Erhan. "Gerçekleşmesi Zor Bir Hayal: Euro–İslam." Aksiyon 09/2004

36 Thomä-Venske, Hans (1988) The Religious Life of Muslims in Berlin, in T. Gerholm and Yngve George Lithman, eds., London and New York: Mansell, p. 78

not only obstruct a healthy integration but also threaten Turkish community itself. Lack of formal and vocational education, critical deficiencies in communication in native language, social isolation, animosity and anxiety towards the societal environment, and involvement to crime[37] have reached very critical level already. For example, 40% of Turks and 60% of Kurds in Britain have no formal educations[38]; 75% percent of Turks in Germany lives in 'ethnic enclaves' without any interaction with the mainstream society and this problem rises as new generations grows; 81% of the Turkish workforce in 1981 were unskilled and the unemployment rates among Turkish community goes up to three times of the average.[39] Even though, Germany's economic and occupational structures have gone through significant changes, most of the Turks that were originally hired as unskilled or semiskilled labour have remained in unskilled or semiskilled jobs. For some, the worst problem, on the other hand, is that Turkish community does not feel the necessity to integrate to the surrounding society and show no effort to realise this. In fact, the situation is not so desperate since fairly small percentage of the second generation and almost total entity of the third generation of the Turkish community are now struggling to diminish this disadvantaged status. Nowadays, for instance, even it is likely to observe "shining examples" of the Turkish youth in Western context who have achieved academic or professional excellence in nationwide examinations.[40]

Trying to Survive without State's Approval: the Gülen Movement in Brief

The Gülen movement is a fairly controversial formation with its philosophies and institutions run by its sympathisers all over the world. They are severely criticized by two groups, hard-line laicists who mainly constitute the dominant state-elite and a minor radical group of Islamists whose support are mostly external and politically oriented. Whilst the former group suspect of organising to takeover the state when the conditions met, the latter group are not keen on their tolerant approach to the non-Muslims.

Besides, Turkey's Kemalist elite who generally keep high posts in the Turkish state has never accepted Gülen movement as legitimate actor in social field. Not political but particularly bureaucratic figures (e.g. members of the military, high judicial organs etc.) see the movement as the most serious threat for Turkey. If military raises the degree of anti-movement claims, the community's status and position may become unstable, not in public sphere but particularly in political system.

In fact, this is not a surprising reaction by the Kemalist elite as the official Turkish ideology was erected as the "vehemently antireligious tradition of the radical, Jacobin-styled" laicism that emerged in the French Republics.[41] And as the westernization project, Kemalist elite pursued authoritarian, nationalist and "top-down" policies rather than liberal ones.

Kemalism attempted to take Islam apart for two aims; firstly to overcome the religion that used to be institutional basis of Turkish life for more than a millennia; and secondly to subordinate

---

37 Only in German prisons are 25000 Turks and more than this number involved to the street mobs.

38 Bradley, Harriet (2005) İlgisizlik ve Dışlanma, Londra Gazete, February17, 2005

39 Pedersen, Lars (1999) Newer Islamic Movements in Western Europe, Aldershot: Ashgate, p. 155

40 This sort of news have become very common particularly for Europe edition of Turkish newspapers such as Zaman and Hurriyet, or local Turkish newspapers such as London based Haber and Olay newspapers. For examples, please visit www.eurozaman.com/euro, www.habernewspaper.com or www.olaygazete.co.uk.

41 Yavuz, M. Hakan (1999) "Search for A New Social Contract in Turkey: Fethullah Gülen, the Virtue Party, and the Kurds" SAIS Review, Vol. 19, No. 1, p. 117

Islam to the interests of the secular nationalist state. Religion was to be decontaminated from its 'backward' constituent and Turkified. Especially, In the 1920s and 30s, to achieve first objective, the Turkish state prohibited all religious institutions assumed as the backbone of Islam in Turkey.[42] Abolition of the Caliphate, Sultanate, Sufi orders, *madrasahs* (or religious schools) and religious law were few of these institutions. To realise the second aim, all of religious institutions and personalities (mosques, imams etc.), foundations, education and worship were all subsumed under 'the Directorate of Religious Affairs'. All religious codes, alphabet, conducts and ceremonies were also changed with the secular ones.[43]

With some exceptions between 1950 and 1960, the situation was pretty much the same for faith based organisations. In the history of Turkish Republic, however, the most critical change initiated with the coup of 1980. After the revolution, Turkey initiated a scheme to implement liberal economic policies, on the one side, and to apply traditionalist policies in the cultural and social fields, on the other. Military regime and the ensuing governments reintroduced Islam as a part of Turkey's official ideology in order to dismiss Marxist and other violent movements of the 1970s. By the late 1980s that Turkey began to tolerate the existence of non-governmental organizations (NGOs) with different cultural and ideological orientations, and their activities. Now, the censored identities such as Islamic and Kurdish organisations found room to operate. The number of the religious institutions, Muslim foundations and schools were increasing with great pace. With change of some significant concept such as Europe, democracy and liberalisation, Islamic groups began approaching Europe and European values with sympathy and criticizing Kemalist regime because of not reflecting European values in real sense. Although Turkish politics experience critical problems even today, the 1980s marks departure from authoritarian-statist attitudes to liberal ones.

Back to the Movement

One of the striking aspects of the movement is its resources administered by the sympathisers to Gülen's ideas. As educational facilities, they run several hundreds of well-known colleges around the world, universities, university preparation and language courses, student dormitories and summer camps. As a media empire, they own a television obtaining high ratings with some of its programs, a radio channel, a daily newspaper that is the leader in terms of the number of circulation, one weekly and four monthly magazines which are the leaders of their genres, as well. Moreover, "the community controls one of the fastest growing financial institutions, Bank Asya (formerly known as Asya Finans).

As Kömeçoğlu argues, the community is not a response of dissidents Muslims of a 'social breakdown' or group of people with lower class background in order to protest social tension.[44] Contrary, the members of the community are mostly university student and large group of small and big businessmen, professionals from all sectors in the country, especially from academics, media, music and the specialized strata that compose the elite as well as middle layers of the society. Altunoğlu determined seven characteristics of the members of the movement; individually pious, culturally ascetic, politically conservative, idealist in the mission of converting souls, disengaged in active politics, success-oriented 'Otherization'

---

42 Bonner, Arthur (2004), An Islamic Reformation in Turkey in Middle East Policy, Vol. 11, No. 1, p. 84

43 Ahmad, Feroz (1993) The Making of Modern Turkey, London: Routledge

44 Kömeçoğlu, Uğur (1997) A Sociologically Interpretative Approach to the Fethullah Gülen Community Movement, Istanbul, Boğaziçi University, p. 46

and adversary component is weak.[45] Yavuz adds four additional attributes to the followers' profile: they are "more predisposed to tolerance, electoral politics, moderation, and a market economy than are other Islamic groups in Turkey."

Even though the devotees are enthusiastic believers of their faith, they formulise their mission with humanitarian parameters and believe that salvation "is not only to be 'saved from' sinful activities, but also to be engaged actively in the improvement of the world." They think that serving the society in the narrow sense and the humanity in the wide sense is the most crucial activity to gain God's favour and consent. They do not try to challenge the modernity but demonstrate how to be both good Muslims and modern. They are willing to live in a secular democratic atmosphere rather than rejecting it when they are trying to live their faith.

Following this concise information about the characteristics of the movement and its members, I'll endeavour to articulate its current and potential contributions to the integration process with references to the Gülen's ideas, and finally I'll portray major constraints that define the movement's efficacy in the European context.

Theoretical Incentives of the Gülen Movement for Integration

Initially –and perhaps the most importantly– Gülen's redefinition of West, Western civilisation and Western context in religious terms is an attempt to replace the conventional dichotomy of *dar al-Islam* (abode of Islam) and *dar al-harb* (abode of war). He does not only attempts to alter the Muslims' assessment of West as a natural enemy and their land as the natural places of destruction; he also seeks to substitute the classifications, which give temporal reconciliation, with an unconditional idea of concord. For instance, besides the dar al-Islam and dar al-harb dichotomy, Islamic jurisprudence has utilised different concepts –such as *ikrah* (duress), *darura* (necessity), and *maslaha* (public welfare)– and produce some concepts –such as *dar al-ahd* (country of treaty, covenant), *dar al-aman* (country of security), *dar as-sulh* (country of peace), and *dar al-darura* (country of necessity) which denotes that "Muslims can live according to their religion in non-Muslim lands perhaps with difficulty but peacefully."[46] Quite the reverse, Gülen's term of *dar al-hizmet* (abode of service) requires Muslims to *ad infinitum* perform peaceful manners in their societies to demonstrate Islam's *'true façade'*.

The term charges new duty to the believer to portray good example in their everyday lives (*temsil*) without any reservation. It stresses not only necessity but also the obligation of a Muslim to obey legal settings of the new country, not only receiving benefits of the political setting (e.g. pensions, but also perform civic duties (e.g. tax), recognition of other's rights and being fair. Gülen stresses that:

> wherever a Muslim is, even outside a Muslim polity; he or she has to obey the *lex loci*, to respect others' rights and to be just, In Gülen's understanding, *umma* is more of a transnational socio-cultural entity, not a politico-legal one. He hopes that this socio-cultural entity will be instrumental in bringing general universal peace.

Thus, by these words, he nullifies the conventional evaluation of the western context, even those giving a conditional status of peace but which are prone-to-change according to conditions. And quite strikingly, he also changes the magnitude of the aforementioned peaceful manner in terms of Islamic theology. Though in the classical dichotomies, the terms do not

---

45 Altunoğlu, Ebru (1999) Fethullah Gülen's Perception of State and Society, Istanbul: Boğaziçi University, p. 86

46 Yilmaz, I, Ijtihad and Tajdid by Conduct: The Gülen Movement, in M. Hakan Yavuz and John L. Esposito, eds., Turkish Islam and the Secular State: The Gülen Movement, Syracuse: Syracuse University Press, p. 234

belong to the essence of the faith; Gülen repositioned the peaceful method and obedience to the host country to the centre of a Muslim's personal and religious life and requires him/her to re-designate the complete way of life similar to the commands of the religion. Hence, for his integration becomes intrinsic or integral part of the religion.

Secondly, and parallel to the first set of logic, values of Western civilisation such as democracy and modernity, and re-evaluation of the West's development occupy a one of the focal points in his logic. He does not observe the West and its civilisation from 'our eternal enemy' perspective, and thus, denies the rejection of its values just because 'they are Western'. He sees Western dominance as the result of their obedience to the Divine laws valid in the nature by pursuing scientific knowledge and by developing well-structured methodology. Gülen emphasizes his concern for the basic, tenets of Islam, but he also professes the backwardness of today's Islamic interpretation and livelihood vis-à-vis the requirements of the era. To him, that's why West dominates the Muslim World, while latter fails to understand and perform Islam properly, and disregards the scientific investigation as done by the former.[47] He promotes this notion with his understanding of *takwah* which mostly understood as the preservation from sins. He sees *taqwah* as a systematic rapprochement to the creation, fulfillment all the requirements of this world (e.g. from science to economics) which concomitant with having a pious and otherworldly character. It seems that this is not a mere justification of modernity and a pursuit of a 'middle way' between being Muslim and being modern; because he accepts Islam itself as the middle way. In this regard, Gülen is searching for an interpretation of Islam that is compatible with and at the same time critical of modernity and tradition. In other words, it is not an effort for grafting Islam with modernity and obtaining a hybrid identity. "What he does is reveal a dynamic interpretation of Islam that is both compatible with and critical of modernity and Muslim tradition."[48]

Thirdly, with his re-reading of dialogue in which dialogue is the natural result of the practice of Islamic ethics falls apart from most of the Islamic scholars. For him, Islam does not reject interaction with diverse cultures and on condition that it does not challenge with the essence of Islam. For all other conditions, dialogue is not a superfluous endeavour, but an imperative which is inherent to the faith. For him "love, respect, tolerance, forgiveness, mercy, human rights, peace, brotherhood, and freedom are all values exalted by religion... [and are the parts of] the messages brought by Moses, Jesus, and Muhammad, upon them be peace, as well as in the messages of Buddha and even Zarathustra, Lao-Tzu, Confucius, and the Hindu prophets."[49] On the contrary, opposition to the diversity or attempts to take measures against the emergence of diverse ideas are, indeed, against God's creation and historical fact.

Gülen Movement in Practice

In the Western context, it appears that, with the theological incentives, physical and intellectual potential, the Gülen movement has the ability to promote integration process of the Turkish people, in the medium-run, and the majority of the Muslim community, in the long-run even this requires a re-identification phase for the minorities. As the religion is the principal identifier for most Muslims, Gülen's re-aligning of individual's role and the re-positioning of host

---

47 Gülen, MF, Essentials of the Islamic, The Light, New Jersey, 2005, p. 251
48 Kuru, Ahmet T. Fethullah Gülen's Search for a Middle Way Between Modernity and Muslim Tradition, in M. Hakan Yavuz and John L. Esposito, eds., Turkish Islam and the Secular State: The Gülen Movement, Syracuse: Syracuse University Press, 2003, p. 130
49 Ünal, Ali and Alphonse Williams, Fethullah Gülen: Advocate of Dialogue, Fairfax: The Fountain, 2000, p.43

countries in religious context would gradually benefit them to have civic values compatible with the prerequisites of modern states. Since they can diffuse to all levels of everyday life, from schools to magazines, they can influence the population more effectively and efficient. Especially when the movement's success in Turkey, where the operation grounds is so limited due to a fierce rivalry by the Kemalist state elite, is taken into consideration, it can be claimed that the movement is fairly promising in Western context that is characterised by democracy and freedom.

For instance, despite having unpleasant experiences with the Muslim minority presence, Danish society has witnessed a profound change among Turkish population. With the intense exertion of the movement, the politically isolated Turkish minority was convinced participating elections. Now, Turks have an MP in the Danish parliament even though they constitute only 0.7% of the population with scattered residential patterns.[50]

With their moderate message which contains tolerant and friendly messages for the Western world, it can lessen the radical messages of radical ideologies coming from Saudi Arabia and Iran. In the larger context, they can also weaken the impact of Islamism in the Muslim world. This process at one hand, contributes the democratisation of Turkey and Islamic World, respectively via Muslim citizens within European states. And in a possible accession of Turkey to the EU, aforementioned community can significantly facilitate Turkey's adaptation process. The democratisation process of whole Muslim world will undeniably take pretty long time, but even in this situation Turkey can function as a buffer between liberal and democratic Europe and the Middle East. A buffer which absorbs the shock coming from the both sides of the alignment and, hence, would lessen the political and cultural resentment for both sides.

The movement's educational principle that favours the integration into the modern world, can assist the second and third generations of Muslim minorities who undergo severe educational, vocational and language problems. In the Netherlands, for example, one of the countries where the movement well established, are tens of civil society institutions founded by Turks whose cooperation definitely affects the integration process. The positive outcome of the movement's course of action contributes also the Turkish participation to the national politics. In Dutch parliament are five MPs with Turkish origin. Additionally two candidates with Turkish origin succeeded to be elected for the European Parliament. Additionally, with their emphasis of education, it is (hopefully) expected that by 2015, the educational level of Turkish minority will be equalise with the native student's level.[51] Therefore, at one side, with their specialisation in education, they can improve the educational level of Turkish children by paying special care to their specific problems; at the other side since they do not refer any religious and ideological orientation in the education progress, the young generations would not be constrained in terms of interaction to the mainstream society. As Özdalga puts the Gülen movement "may be seen as a training ground, a transition zone in the formation of values and identities suitable for integration".[52]

The Gülen movement proved itself successful while we particularly take its educational and dialogue activities around the world. But it is noteworthy that the rest of the world is not Europe vis-à-vis political, social, financial and cultural characteristics. Until recently, with some exceptions, the countries where the Movement opened educational or social institutions

---

50 http://www.turkembassy.dk/mkt2.htm
51 Başyurt, Erhan. "Gerçekleşmesi Zor Bir Hayal: Euro–İslam." Aksiyon 09/2004
52 "Redeemer or Outsider? The Gülen Community in the Civilizing Process" Muslim World, Vol. 95, No. 3, 2003, p. 436

have been relatively underdeveloped to Turkey. Beginning with the 1990, the members of the movement opened have erected many facilities such as colleges, universities and dormitories from Turkic Republics in the former Soviet Union, African countries, to Indo-China. Opening institutions were financially and politically tough, but to be recognised by the host countries were not so testing especially with their successful educational background in Turkey.

The real challenge was to prove the merit of the movement firstly, in Western Europe with a success in education and with a representation of their commitment to the Western values, and secondly, in Muslim world as Muslims. Because in both regions neither states nor societies are expected to be more reluctant to welcome it. In West, not only they have history between the sides or they experience Islamophobia, but also they would fear due to past experiences with Turkish minority in their borders (as happened in Germany) or they simply would not feel the necessity to accept assistance, if not an outsider. So the movement would not be appealing for them. Additionally, Turkish minority's economic, social and intellectually disadvantaged position would cause unwillingness to assist or participate, or their short-comings (such as incompetence in native language) would prevent them from an efficient participation. At that point, it should be noted that, the history of the movement in Europe and in Muslim World is quite short, but as a beginning, they have a good start in the Netherlands with almost all sorts of institutions and activities, in the United States with a striking rise in the amount of state-financed charter schools and in Kurdish controlled Northern Iraq with seven schools and despite a pretty slippery ground.

MODERN IDEALS AND MUSLIM IDENTITY: HARMONY OR CONTRADICTION? - A TEXT LINGUISTIC ANALYSIS OF THE GÜLEN TEACHING AND MOVEMENT

Gurkan Celik, Kate Kirk, Yusuf Alan

Abstract

At the global level there is an urgent need and increasing attention for a new sense of Muslim identity in harmony with modern realities. Fethullah Gülen, an educationalist, a religious guide and a peace maker, is one of the most persuasive and influential Turkish-Muslim voices in the contemporary world putting strong emphasis on peaceful coexistence and the synthesis of faith and reason in Western democracies through spirituality, religious diversity, dialogue and educational initiatives. This paper primarily examines how and to what extent Gülen's teachings and the world-wide volunteer movement inspired by him are contributing to the dynamic and cheerful coexistence of Muslims and non-Muslims. In order to explore and analyse this coexistence, the seven text linguistic principles (cohesion, coherence, intentionality, acceptability, informativity, situationality and intertextuality) are applied to Gülen's teachings and his movement as an empirical case. Secondarily, these text linguistic standards are modelled to social sciences as a new theoretical and methodological approach for exploring and analysing social movements and phenomena. The originality of this study is specified as the correlations between a movement and a text, and the processes of cognition, production and reproduction of knowledge and its dissemination and transition in the Muslim world, multicultural societies and liberal democracies. This research's practical relevance lies in the fact that it helps understand how the Gülen movement has been formed and accomplished, both nationally and internationally. Metaphorically, in this paper Fethullah Gülen has been considered as the writer; by-him-inspired movement refers to the text; and the readers are the transnational community and the whole humanity.

Introduction

The modern world has been undergoing radical, social, economic, political and intellectual changes over the last several decades. Today there are increasing numbers of Muslims in Western democracies offering a model for society that is pluralist, participatory and wealthy in economic terms. However, the need for peaceful coexistence between Muslims and non-Muslims within and between nations has long been recognized (Carroll, 2007; Shadid & Van Koningsveld; 2002; Hunter, 1998; Esposito, 1999; Huntington, 1993). Consequently, both globally and locally, there is a growing need for a new sense of Muslim identity in harmony with modern ideals such as liberty, democracy, equality, justice, human rights, and freedom of thought and speech (Küçükcan, 2004; Kuru, 2003; Göle, 2000; Gülen, 1998, 2001; Heffner, 1998; Izzetbegovic, 1984; Rahman, 1982; Nasr, 1980). While people struggle to balance different, often opposing identities, there have been notable failures in attempts to make the world more integrated.

M. Fethullah Gülen, an educator, a religious scholar and peace activist, is one of the most influential contemporary Muslim voices encouraging peaceful coexistence and the synthesis of faith and reason in Western societies through democracy, citizenship, spirituality, multiculturalism, religious diversity, educational initiatives and intercultural and interfaith dialogue activities in the context of secular modernity (Celik & Valkenberg, 2007; Hunt & Aslandoğan, 2006; Celik, et al, 2005; Yavuz & Esposito, 2003; Sevindi, 2002). He has had a significant influence on the millions of people, especially the younger people with school-aged children, who became committed to the vision of global peace and progress through education and dialogue (Kurtz, 2001:155-160, 2005:380-381; Ates, Karakas & Ortayli, 2005). Nevertheless, Gülen is important to interfaith dialogue because he provides a source of inspiration for a new and cooperative approach to the Abrahamic religions (Valkenberg, 2006; Capan, 2007) and to a dialogue between civilizations (Carroll, 2007; Ünal & Williams, 2000), which aims to support dialogue, harmony and conciliation between people of different cultural and political backgrounds. Gülen's social movement, which concentrates on education, engages with Western society, and promotes dialogue with the adherents of Christianity, Jews and other faiths.

Aim of the Study

This study[1] primarily examines how and to what extent Gülen's teaching and the worldwide movement inspired by him are contributing to the dynamic and peaceful coexistence of Muslims and non-Muslims. First, in order to explore and analyze this concept of coexistence, seven textual linguistic principles (cohesion, coherence, intentionality, acceptability, informativity, situationality and intertextuality) (Bearugrande & Dressler, 1981; Van Dijk, 1998; Demir, 2004; Tas, 2004; Alan, 2005) are applied to Gülen's teaching and movement. Second, these linguistic standards are modelled on social sciences as a new theoretical and methodological approach for exploring and analyzing social movements and phenomena. The originality of this study is specified as the correlation between a movement and a text, and the processes of cognition, production and reproduction of knowledge and its dissemination and transition in the Muslim world, multicultural societies and liberal democracies. In this current study, Fethullah Gülen is—metaphorically—considered as the 'writer'; his teaching and movement refer to the 'text'; and the 'readers' are the members[2] of the Gülen

---

1 The empirical study on which this study is based was carried out during the spring of 2007.

2 To use the term *member* does not imply in the current study a kind of formal organisation, which does not exist.

movement, the transnational community and the whole of humanity. This research's practical relevance lies in the fact that it helps describe the formation and success of Gülen teaching and movement.

Methodology

In our study, we used case research strategy (Yin 2003; Ragin & Becker, 2002) involving an in-depth examination of a single instance or event: the case of the Gülen movement. It is an empirical inquiry that investigates the Gülen movement as a social phenomenon within its real-life context. Our case study includes qualitative evidence, relies on multiple sources of evidence and benefits from the prior development of theoretical propositions of text linguistic analysis. It is a paradigmatic case which may be defined as an exemplar or prototype (Stake, 1995; Yin, 2002), and shows that the basic mechanisms, actors, motifs or background practices of the Gülen movement are studied in terms of 'exemplars' or 'paradigms'.

In addition to a systematic review of the relevant writings and speeches on and by Fethullah Gülen, a number of qualitative interviews with experts and his sympathisers[3] were used for a theoretical modelling. Further, we conducted internet, ethnographic, and participant observation research. The authors spent a total of 24 hours in community sites, and attended in major cultural and religious events like Ramadan Iftar Diners in the Netherlands and abroad, gatherings, conversation groups, and meetings of members. The ethnographic research approach, broadly defined, is becoming an increasingly popular method for studying though the Internet because of the unique way it provides a flexible set of meanings that allowed for feedback, course corrections and discovery (Walcott, 1999). Baym (2000) used an ethnographic approach, grounded in a set of theories termed the practice approach, to study an online soap opera fan group. We used this approach in order to understand a community by looking at the activities in which the community members engage. This approach also emphasizes language activities as a community-substantiating force. Language practices are "microcosm of the communities in which they are used" (Lave & Wenger, 1991:22).

Furthermore, eleven semi-structured interviews were conducted face-to-face or via electronic mail—in either Turkish or English—lasting an average of one hour each. Qualitative interviewing is an excellent tool for the current study in which rich detail about the perspectives of participants is desired (Rubin & Rubin, 1995). Interviewees were randomly chosen from a group of pre-selected experts and followers who know Gülen's movement and are well acquainted with his ideas and initiatives as well. It is of particular interest to investigate what these respondents think about the Gülen's teaching, how they interpret his discourses and actions, and how Gülen inspires and influences individuals in the movement that is associated with him. Interview questions were both open and close-ended and based on the seven text linguistic principles mentioned above. We prepared an interview protocol, and pre-tested the interview by interviewing a religious studies scholar and a member of the Gülen movement. The interview guide was modified according to the suggestions made by these people.

Data Analysis

Directed data analysis was used to analyze the data collected from the qualitative interviews and participatory observations, while our themes and sub-themes served as an initial framework for content analysis (Miles & Huberman, 1994; Hsieh & Huberman, 2005). Firstly,

---

3 In this study, *sympathisers* refer to people who are inspired by Gülen's teaching.

existing literature was reviewed, and field notes were analysed to get a first (general) impression. Secondly, interview data were tape-recorded and transcribed verbatim. Finally, interview contents were characterised and classified, and then discussed in the light of the observations of the authors. To improve our study's reliability and validity, we incorporated other sources, viewpoints and methods to some of the interviewees, and systematically asked them if we have accurately interpreted and recorded what they meant.

We begin with the exposition of some patterns of the Gülen teaching, and then we examine the main transitions in the movement. Next, we apply the metaphorical linguistic principles to by-him-inspired social movement. Finally, the study closes with conclusions and discussion resting on the evidence.

Fethullah Gülen and Some Characteristics of His Teaching

Fethullah Gülen [1941], as a mark of respect, called 'Hodjaefendi' (esteemed teacher) by his followers and associates, has a considerable impact on the millions of participants in a social phenomenon called the Gülen movement (Yavuz & Esposito, 2003; Yilmaz, 2005). According to the respondents and existing literature, Gülen is an influential Muslim intellectual in the contemporary world who inspired an effective and social movement, including transnational education organizations, business networks like ISHAD and HOGIAF,[4] interfaith dialogue forums,[5] and multicultural encounters, and as a social innovator who develops a new sense of religiosity in touch with modern realities (Hunt & Aslandoğan, 2006; Yavuz & Esposito, 2003). He is also known for his contributions to world peace through his dialogue activities and educational initiatives (Michel, 2003). Gülen is of Turkish origin and can be seen as a product of the Republic of Turkey, having been born in Erzurum, in eastern Turkey, and having been formed by Islamic tradition in such a way that it has been a constant and fixed point of reference for his own personal life, his interpretations of the world, his teaching and actions (Weller, 2006:75-6). According to Gülen's (2004e:199), a believer does not hesitate to communicate with any kind of thought and system; while one foot should remain at the centre the other could be with other 'seventy-two nations', like a compass (Rumi's famous metaphor). He accents that Islam does not reject interaction with diverse cultures and change as long as what is to be appropriated does not contradict with the main pillars of Islam.

Gülen, known by some as 'a modern-day' Rumi[6], is not only an individual but, in his life as well as his teaching, is also the inspirational figure for an emerging volunteer movement that originally took shape in his native country, but is now found throughout many parts of the world (idem; Celik, 2007). Influenced by Sufi traditions[7] of Islam, the Gülen movement's interpretation of the Turkish-Ottoman culture of tolerance have been criticized by both extreme

---

4 ISHAD (Business Life Cooperation Association) as a Non-governmental and Non-profit NGO founded by a group of businessmen in 1993 in Istanbul; HOGIAF (Dutch Federation of Young Entrepreneurs) has been established in the Netherlands.

5 www.interfaithdialog.org ; www.rumiforum.org ; www.dialoguesociety.org ; www.interfaithdialogues.org ; www.indialogue.in ; and www.intercultural.org.au are a few of the main community sites in English.

6 A series conference speeches, entitled 'From Rumi to Fethullah Gülen', held on 23, 24, 25, 26, 27 May 2007 in various cities in the Netherlands, discussed Fethullah Gülen as a representative of the Rumi's thoughts in the contemporary world. Mewlana Jalal ad-Din al-Rumi [1207-1273] is an outstanding poet and spiritual teacher of the thirteenth century (see Celik, 2007; Kandur, et al, 2006; Can, 2005).

7 The Sufi Tradition is one of the main channels of the Islamic heritage of thought and learning. The continual process of spiritual development in Sufism along a path of the innate human poverty, helplessness, and powerlessness before God is undertaken in the knowledge that everything comes from God.

secularists and Islamists. For Gülen (2004a:166), Sufism (tasawwuf)[8] is the spiritual life of Islam. It is a form of self-purification leading to inner dimension of Islamic spirituality, a deeper understanding of the divine acts, and a greater knowledge and love of the Divine. Gülen has been considered as a persuasive Muslim scholar who puts the individual and his or her spiritual, intellectual and personal development at the centre of everything (Celik & Alan, 2007; Akman, 2004; Sevindi, 2002; Ünal & Williams, 2000). Gülen proposes that his followers harmonize intellectuality with modernity, tasawwuf, Sufi-oriented spirituality and caring, humane activism (Michel, 2005). He has geared all his energies towards the regeneration of the Muslim spirit and towards evolving a new breed of idealistic Muslim youth who are modern, spiritual and rational, with a deep sense of belief in and love for humankind. Gülen's greatest intellectual achievement is the inspiration of a youth movement that began in the 1970s and developed into a dense web of transnational networks with millions of followers. The Gülen movement has established hundreds of schools and colleges, organized businessmen and entrepreneurs around a common platform, and set up two of the Turkey's largest daily newspapers (Zaman, Today's Zaman)[9], two TV channels (Samanyolu, Mehtap), a radio station (Burc FM), a leading publishing house (Kaynak A.S.), and a number of periodical magazines and journals, such as Sızıntı (on culture and science), The Fountain (on scientific and spiritual thought), Yağmur (on literature), Ekoloji (on environmental issues), and Yeni Ümit (on religious sciences), Gonca (a children's magazine). Internationally, this movement has extended its reach of educational and media efforts to all parts of the globe (Agai, 2004). Gülen has lived in the United States since 1999 because of the repressive political atmosphere in Turkey, and due to personal health problems.

Gülen (1977; 1990) and his volunteer movement have set out to produce, what he calls, "the golden generation": a generation that can integrate Muslim identity with modern realities. Gülen has developed a model for human life whose social aspects have been brought to the fore. For it is impossible for someone who has not acquired an independent character to make a positive contribution to the social sphere. Gülen argues that the individual and collective happiness lie in disciplining three innate faculties (reason, anger, and lust)[10] to produce a young, "golden generation" that will learn theoretical aspects of "the middle way between modernity and tradition" (Kuru, 2003) and will bring it into practice. This generation is supposed to absorb and represent both modern realities and Muslim morality and identities through its mind, its behaviours and its spirituality. Gülen (2000b:7-8) symbolizes human beings as mirrors for God's names and attributes. Therefore, human beings are distinguished from the rest of creation because they have the honour of being responsible for making the Earth prosperous in God's name. In his teaching, Gülen (2005:5-10, 31-42) lays out a broad vision for a society and world led by individuals of spiritual, moral and intellectual excellence. He calls these people "ideal human" and describes their following eight characters and

---

8 Sufism is the English translation of tasawwuf referring to mysticism in Islam. Thus, non-Muslim mystics should not be called Sufis, and expressions such as Islamic Sufism are problematic since Sufism is Islamic mysticism (Gokcek, 2005:357-364).

9 Zaman is a leading highly-qualified daily newspaper with more then ten world language editions, sometimes in a bilingual format. it is also the first Turkish daily to be published on the Internet. Today's Zaman appears in English and is the largest English newspaper in Turkey.

10 Since the time of Ibn Miskawayh (930-1030) human faculties or innate "drives" have been dealt with in three categories: reason, anger, and lust. He is a Muslim moralist, philosopher and historian. His moral treatise Tahdhib al-Akhlaq, influenced by the Aristotelian concept of the mean, is considered one of the best statements of Islamic philosophy. His universal history Kitab Tajarib al-Umam wa Ta'aqub al-Himam (Eclipse of the 'Abbasid Caliphate), was noted for its use of all available sources and greatly stimulated the development of Islamic historiography.

attributes: faith; love; a balanced view of science with the trio of reasoning, logic and con-sciousness; a re-evaluated view of humans, life, and the universe; free thinking and respect for freedom of thought; a habit to consultative and collective consciousness; mathematical thinking; and appreciate for art. Gülen's (2004a:289-302) entire endeavour is to emphati-cally stress the fact that, by virtue of drawing attention to the relationship between God and humankind, humanity's greatest virtue, ethically speaking, will be to attain the model of universal or ideal human (*al-insaan al-kaamil*). In fact, in his teaching, this is an opening that spells his ideal model for human beings who sacrifice their own life's pleasures–who, in a way, live for others (altruism). He argues that such a human being (e.g. Haci Kemal Erimez)[11] can take as his or her basis only positive action in social arena.

Avoiding partisan politics, the movement developed an enlightenment project to combat social ills through a variety of educational, dialogue and media initiatives (Yilmaz, 2003; Saritoprak, 2005:325). Weller (2006:76) affirms that Gülen's teaching has been particularly aimed at encouraging the younger generations to encompass intellectual engagement with spiritual wisdom and to give expression to this through a commitment to serving the whole of humanity. As a result of this approach, his movement has invested heavily in the develop-ment of cultural centres as well as media outlets and educational institutions in Turkey, in the Central Asian regions after the fall of the Soviet Union, but also in Africa and North- and South America (Agai, 2003; Michel, 2003). Gülen is of the firm opinion that Turkish people have interpreted and applied Islam in a certain way so that it could be called 'Turkish Islam' or 'Anatolian Muslimness'[12] (Ünal & Williams, 2000:54–58). He states that:

Turkish Islam is composed of the main, unchanging principles of Islam found in the Qur'an and Sunnah,[13] as well as in the forms that its aspects open to interpretation assumed dur-ing Turkish history, together with Sufism. [...] This is why Turkish Islam always has been broader, deeper, more tolerant and inclusive, and based on love.[...] The Hanafi understand-ing and Turkish interpretation dominates [sic] more than three-fourths of the Islamic world. This understanding is very dear to me. If you like you can call this Turkish Islam. Just as I see no serious canonical obstacle to this, I don't think it should upset anyone. [...] The Turkish nation interpreted Islam in the areas open to interpretation [...] [I]t attained a very broad spectrum and became the religion of great states. For this reason, I think the Turkish Muslimness is appropriate. Another aspect of this is that in addition to profound devotion to the Qur'an and Sunnah, the Turks always have been open to Sufism, Islam's spiritual aspect. (Ünal and Williams 2000:43,52,56).

He speaks of a "Turkish Muslimness" based on love, tolerance, dialogue, forgiveness, Sufism,

---

11 See for more information on the book by Küçük (2006), entitled *Adanmış Bir Gönül İnsanı Hacı Ata*, focussed on his life and altruism.

12 Gülen was one of the first that used the term "Anatolian Muslimness" or "Turkish Muslimness" which was interpreted as a way of distancing Anatolian people's interpretations and experiences of Islam from those of others, especially the Wahhabi (Saudi) or Shiite radical interpretations.

13 Sunnah refers to the way of the Prophet Muhammad. It is the tradition recording his every act, word, and confir-mation. It is the second source of Islamic legislation (the Qur'an being the first one). The Qur'an and authentic pro-phetic traditions enjoin Muslims to follow the Sunnah. It also defines what is stated in general terms in the Qur'an by referring to particular instances, and it defines the general principles underlying statements in the Qur'an that are in themselves specific and particular. Besides, the Sunnah (like the Quran which it embodies) is also concerned with moral guidance, so the Sunnah provides inspirations and the horizons for moral and spiritual instructions in all spheres of life, as well as providing the inspirations and horizons (limits) within which Islamic legislation may be effected. (see Ünal, 2006:1348).

and excluding harsh restrictions or fanaticism, demonstrating that this Islam is not in contradiction with the modern world. Turkish Islam represents the chain of development of the Central Asia-Seljuk-Ottoman and modern Turkey (Ünal & Williams, 2000:54-58).

Gülen's ethic can be summarized in a few key directives or recommendations, such as predicting and teaching peace, love, forgiveness and tolerance; seeking God's approval; remaining awake to your image of death and to your existential broods; doing good deeds (hizmet); and practicing humility, sacrifice, and self-criticism (Özdalga, 2003). In his teaching, he firmly argues that these are the fundamentals of Islam: whilst other things are accidental (Gülen, 2004e:71; 2004b; 2000a). Respondents accordingly indicated that his teaching aims at promoting these universal values to coexist harmoniously in an increasingly inter-dependent and plural world.

Three Main Transitions in the Gülen Movement

The Gülen-inspired movement has undergone several changes and transitions and can be categorized into three main successive development stages since its inception in the 1960s. The first stage encompasses the period spanning the late 1960s and up to 1980. In these nurturing and planning years, Gülen gave numerous talks, sermons[14] and a series of conference-speeches organized by his followers and sympathizers. This enabled him to reach a more representative cross-section of the population and to attract the attention of the academic community, especially the students. In this period, he also concentrated on inspiring of the foundation of student-dormitories and establishing Işık Evler (Light Houses) in various provinces in Anatolia. The objective behind the Light Houses is to provide students with a home, a network of friends and daily routine making it easier for them to abstain from indulging in religiously immoral acts and maintaining a spiritual lifestyle. The Light Houses are rented to accommodate students and have, on average, between 5-7 inhabitants. The second stage of the movement began in 1981 when Gülen retired as a state preacher. Throughout the 1980s, Gülen and members of the new Anatolian bourgeoisie inspired by his teachings began to invest in advancing educational attainment in Turkey by establishing schools and learning institutions across Anatolia (Hendrick, 2006:23). Since his retirement, Gülen has also concentrated his efforts on building an atmosphere resulting in dialogue and peace among the factions representing different ideologies, faiths and cultures The third phase commenced in the 1990s and extends to the present. In the 1990s, political and economic developments in Turkey, the fall of the Soviet Union, the structural weakening of the Turkish state monopoly over information and capital flows, and global developments in communication and transformation technology all contributed to an emphasis being placed on international educational encounters and dialogue activities among the adherents of different religions, nations and civilizations (Kuru, 2005). To this end, Gülen visited and received leading figures, not only from the Turkish population, but from all over the world. Indeed, the dialogue and mutual understanding initiative is one of the cornerstones of evolution for the Gülen movement (Kurtz, 2005; Yilmaz, 2005; Celik & Valkenberg, 2007).

In short, the widening and deepening of the worldwide movement continues by virtue of his inspirational speeches and writings. His movement has gradually evolved and grown in various areas of Turkish life. Respondents stress that the movement has grown not as a

---

14 Most of Gülen's series sermons, talks, public speeches were recorded and transliterated into text format and with minor review published as books. This form of delivery was unheard of in the Muslim scholarly world where custom had it that matters be studied and presented in a rather loose-haphazard-style with no clear boundary.

political movement but as a social and spiritual one. Many respondent defines the movement as the human- and faith-based movement. New non-for-profit organizations in the domains of education, media, academic studies, business, health and dialogue have been founded. With its theoretical and practical aspects the movement—according to some respondents—offers new solutions for many social and cultural problems and attempts to construct a new Muslim identity in the modern era that meets the challenges of secularism and materialism. The style of the movement is accepted and the activities are supported by different ethnic and social groups in modern democracies.

Applying Seven Text Linguistic Principles To The Gülen Teaching And Movement

By applying seven metaphorical text linguistic principles to the Gülen teaching and movement as an empiric case, we examine—in this section—the main assumption that modern ideals and Muslim identity are harmonizing or contradicting. Text is defined as a communicative occurrence that meets seven standards of textuality (Beaugrande & Dressler, 1981; Van Dijk, 1998). After briefly outlining each standard of textuality, we will apply questions regarding the correlation of these standards to the Gülen teaching and movement:

1. Cohesion

"When a text is analyzed in terms of cohesion, the continuity has an important role at a grammatical level. The continuity can be supported by sub-items which help to form and give meaning to a text" (Demir, 2004).

Cohesion refers to the grammatical unity of a text in which different components exist. Here the importance lays in the surface components, which depend on each other according to grammatical forms and conventions (Tas, 2004). The question we will answer is: What are the elements of social cohesion in the Gülen teaching and movement regarding the surface structure. The surface structure in a text is composed of tangible words, clauses and sentences. These explicit factors are interlinked through references, parallelisms or paraphrases. In the context of a social movement, the tacit factors are members, institutions, publications and activities. These elements in the Gülen movement are connected loosely to each other. There are no organic links among the related institutions. Each institution is independent and can survive even if all the rest become "extinct".

The cohesion within this loose network is realized through reading and watching common media sources (Zaman, Samanyolu TV, Mehtap TV, Sızıntı magazine, the books of Gülen), sharing knowledge (correspondences, seminars, conferences), visiting the successful organizations (national and international), and applying the best practices (such as the Science Fairs of the educational centres in Turkey and Europe). With respect to the movement, the social cohesion is also expressed—according to the respondents—in social networks of people who are inspired by Gülen's vision and make efforts on the territory of education, media and dialogue in which they are supported by business people.

On his website "fGülen.com" Gülen is described as an Islamic scholar dedicated to humanity and peace. He preaches and teaches about the importance of understanding and tolerance. According to the respondents, his message embraces all humanity and is deeply averse to atheism, injustice, anarchy and conflict (Bayramoğlu, 1995). His intercultural and interfaith dialogue call for social cohesion and a respect for education and an end to ignorance and dissention. His call for dialogue is bipartite. First, people should learn about the other's cultural identity, religious beliefs and spiritual values, and second, this knowledge should be used to learn more about their own moral and cultural values. One of the most important points in Gülen's texts and speeches is the toleration of differences in order to live together. The significant factors in his teaching are collective consciousness, shared vision, social responsibility, tolerance, respect, spiritual depth. In Gülen's writings (2004c:21; 1987:96-98), speeches and conversations there is no greater religious concept and action than love: "Love is the most essential element of every being, and it is the most radiant light, and it is the greatest power; able to resist and overcome all else." Everyone should make an effort for the well-being of the society in which people live. In order to promote social cohesion in Gülen's teaching, both education (a means developing forbearance) and dialogue are of eminent importance. Gülen stimulates people of different religious and ethnic groups in any society o have dialogues with each other so that they respect, understand each other, and in doing so ultimately cooperating in favour of the well-being of the society in which they live. The respondents characterise the individuals in the Gülen movement as peaceful within themselves (internal peace) and with their environments (external peace). They have an optimistic view for the future and put emphasis on living peacefully.

Endoen's process of the social division of labour can be considered as the Gülen movement's main tenant. In the movement, different groups deal with different voluntary services that complete the surface structure. Different institutions and their functions complete and help each other like the components of a house: door, windows and roof etc together make a house. The sacrifices made by the pioneers of the movement and their responsibility are very important factors for the continuity of the movement. Having no worldly expectations is an effective virtue for the new followers. The transnational aspect of the Gülen movement is regarded as a healthy interaction and dialogue with all peoples without any discrimination. The members of the community have two main goals: to attain the consent of God and to represent the perfect character of Prophet Muhammad.

An alternative explanation of the Gülen movement's social cohesion from a surface structure perspective would come from human basic needs. 'Light Houses' and youth hostels along with dormitory schools and university preparatory courses provide for the individuals' intellectual, spiritual, physiological, safety and belonging needs. Volunteers from around the globe involved in the Gülen movement provide shelter and guidance, and all of this for the sake of friendship and support for each other—regardless of ethnicity, religion or wealth. Furthermore, the international aspect of the movement furnishes a great deal of vision, self esteem, great achievements and dignity.

2. Coherence

Coherence is the continuity of senses in a text. Cohesion deals with the surface structure whereas coherence deals with the deep structure (experiences or thoughts). In this section, we will give an answer to the following question: What are the elements of social coherence in the Gülen teaching and movement regarding the deep structure?

The deep structure of a text is related to intangible concepts such reputation, trust, and social capital. Culture and tradition are not limited to the tangible. Styles of life, customs, aesthetic sensibilities, and ideas are intangible, invisible aspects of culture and tradition. The continuity of sense is the base of coherence. The Gülen movement has a particular shared vision: to serve humanity for the sake of God. "*Hizmet*" (service) is a key concept which binds members and institutions. Gülen frequently used concept of *dar al-hizmet* (country of service). It means, if one's intention is to serve Islam by presenting a good example, the one can stay wherever one desires (Yilmaz, 2003:234). In the countries where sympathizers reside, they utilize this concept and either establish interfaith organizations, associations, and societies or are in close contact with "People of the Book".[15] Without the concept of *hizmet*, which is utterly represented by the personality of Gülen, the movement may keep its cohesion but probably lose its coherence. Being the servants of One God, and the "*ummah*" (community) of one Prophet, reading one Book (the *Qur'an*) and turning to one "*kiblah*" (prayer direction) are the most significant spiritual ties among the members, and of course the whole Muslim global ummah.

The majority of the respondents indicate that there is no contradiction in Gülen's texts, speeches and actions. There is a social coherence between the local and the global. This means that members of the movement experience no serious problem between the local and the global, and have a holistic perspective. Common values unite people. Thus, common concepts such as compassion, love, tolerance, and dialogue are internalized through conversations and common media, and knowledge sharing. One respondent stated:

"Owning to the principles of diversity, love and dialogue, the movement does not focus on instilling Islamic principles, but instead, opts to teach what Gülen consider the 'universal principles', like compassion, generosity, kindness and humility. Gülen's idea is that you change the world and build peace through education, educating others to consider interfaith and intercultural dialogue, to be modern and change the world through the education within an ethical framework. He proposes an education of the heart and soul as well as of the mind and character, aimed at reviving and invigorating the whole being to achieve competence and provide goods and services useful to humanity."

Dialogue, peace, tolerance, compassion, and forgiveness are the key elements of social cohesion in Gülen's teaching and movement. The respondents stress that Gülen's understanding of tolerance is the acceptance of differences that arise from dialogue in order to further the wider goal of cooperation among all strata of the society. To him, tolerance is based on the idea of charity, or love, and therefore is a duty to God (Agai, 2003:64).

Gülen (1997:60) states that a peaceful social life depends on the balance and dialogue between the two non-hierarchical groups of people in the society: elite (rich) and common (poor) people. He contends that this dialogue and balance, which will manifest itself in peace, is based on care and compassion on the part of the elite or the rich, and respect and obedience on the part of the common people or the poor. The unbalance between these two has destroyed social peace for the last several centuries, especially in Europe's social upheavals, all of which are rooted in the century-old struggle between labour and capital. Gülen's followers and experts pointed out that he developed a modern and innovative education model pertaining to the combination of spirituality with intellect, reason with revelation, and mind with heart, which is applied in Turkey but also in many other countries.[16] According to Gülen,

---

15 The term "People of the Book" or *Ahl al-kitab* is mentioned in the Qur'ān twenty-four times, referring to Christians and Jews in particular. The context of these Qur'ānic references varies. Some of these verses praise the People of the Book for their righteousness and good deeds and faith in the Afterlife (Qur'ān 3.113). Other verses rebuke the People of the Book for not following the way of God (Qur'ān 3.99). A group of these verses invite the People of the Book to a common ground between Muslims and themselves (Qur'ān 3.64). Another group of these verses indicates an intimate relationship between Muslims and Christians (Qur'ān 5.82). The relationship between Muslims and the People of the Book, Jews and Christians, has been a subject of discussion among Muslims throughout the centuries.

16 Given the lack to integration between scientific knowledge and spiritual and ethical values, Gülen and his followers introduced a new style of education reconciling these elements.

education is vital for both societies and individuals (Ünal & Williams, 2000:306), and is the best way to serve humanity and to establish a sincere dialogue with other cultures and religions (Michel, 2005, 2006; Bakar, 2005; Gülen, 1987). Gülen's teachings are seen to be, especially by Turkish Muslims, as a new guideline for practicing Muslim morality in modern societies.

Another significant element of social coherence of the movement is consultation which means reaching consensus among followers and to resolve common issues and possible problems. Gülen (2005:43-58) teaches that mutual consultation is the first condition for the success of a decision made on any issue related to society. Before they put one step they talk about all probable consequences. They call their activities "serving" and they see themselves as servants. Servanthood is a central theme in Gülen's teaching (Gülen, 2007a,b,c). A continuous need for a deep spirituality in the movement is also a remarkable aspect of the social coherence. The members of the movement believe that everything they have is a gift of God. Their activities are just a prayer of thanks for those gifts. They believe that social development is only possible when individuals are developed in heart and mind. Love is stronger than hate. For this goal they spend their time and money even if they are without sufficient means themselves.

The deep structure could also be perceived as the backbone of the Gülen movement, the unique explanation as to the degree of dedication and commitment to the voluntary activities. The very basic questions facing humanity have yet to be answered and neither philosophy nor any other field of hard science has been truly successful in answering fundamental questions such as: Who are we? What is our purpose on this planet? Is there an afterlife where the soul will be rewarded or punished for deeds done on earth? The previous section, focusing on the surface structure of the Gülen movement has only portrayed an earth-bound set of explanations; however, the real engine of activity in Gülen movement comes from the above listed question and attempts to provide the most satisfying answers. These activities gave birth to a new understanding of education where spirituality and positivism were brought together and proved that religion and science are not mutually exclusive but perfectly complementary.

According to several respondents, the notion 'identity' lies in the basis of the social cohesion of the Gülen movement. Gülen preaches that a human being develops his or her own identity by attaching importance to his or her own historical background, and that with regard to the Turkish society or nation, mainly to the religious values (e.g. Sufi Islam, tasawwuf), which were playing a prominent role in their history. This identity—resting on historical and religious values—is in two respects of importance for the social cohesion in the surface structure: (a) People who know their own identity, have a strong basis and therefore it is not threatening for them to have a dialogue with the other. Each one shows respect for each other's cultural and religious identity. As people have the idea that their identity is respected and accepted, they are able to go easier into a dialogue and they are rather willing to work together on common interests and issues in the society. (b) Those who have found their identity in religious values, will discover that their goal lies in the obtaining of the approval of God. This approval can be obtained by "love for the creation for the sake of the Creator". Striving for this approval and the understanding that love for fellow human beings is a condition for the tolerance that necessarily is to go in dialogue with the other(s) in their context. It is also a precondition to deploy self for the welfare of the others and of the society; a goal that will ultimately lead to social cohesion and peaceful coexistence.

3. Intentionality

> The writer of a book produces a text to achieve a specific goal. This may be the expression of one-self, informing others, criticizing, and so forth. Whatever the aim is, the text must be produced in a cohesive and coherent way so that it serves for the text-producer's intention (Tas, idem).

Regarding intentionality we will focus on the following questions: a) What is Gülen's intention? b) What is the ultimate ideal behind Gülen's teaching and movement? and c) How does the movement avoid irrelevant messages and/or actions regarding his intentions and vision?

The respondents stress that Gülen's ultimate intention is to be accepted, loved and honoured by God. He frequently states that there is no attractive goal beyond this one (Gülen, 2007a,b,c). In order to reach this goal he serves humanity, encourages everyone to solve universal problems such as ignorance, poverty and disunity, respects the rights of God, the rights of human beings, the rights of creatures, and the rights of his own soul, promotes what is good, right and beautiful, and discourages what is bad, wrong and awful. According to Gülen, belief necessitates a climate of freedom, peace and stability to flourish and breathe. In justification of this point, Gülen states that the Qur'an, in reference to the Hudaybiyah Pact,[17] considers peace as victory for the believers; a believer must always seek to establish peace and stability. Furthermore, the constructive form of activism required the dismantling of discord, disunity and division. In the respondents' opinion, Gülen is of the firm opinion that the existing social tension and ideological rifts in Turkey and abroad need to be overcome and this can only be achieved through dialogue, tolerance and understanding. Therefore, the initial objective behind worldwide dialogue initiatives was to calm public tension, normalize relations and create a sense of mutual trust and tolerance. In addition to the aforementioned arguments Gülen's experts and followers who we interviewed, pointed out that Gülen's intention and ultimate ideal bears primarily on his faith and concerns basic theological foundations:

"Gülen's ultimate aim is to have the consent of God. His teaching is premised on the belief that there is no aim or reward beyond the approval and love of God. The easiest way to acquire this is obeying the rules explained by the Prophet Muhammad, and imitating the Prophet's way of life. Gülen's purpose is not to be or becoming a leader, he would rather be a slave and servant. He has so many followers even he does not have a desire to lead. He regards his 'reputation' as a credit from God, and uses this to motivate people. One who cannot manage his or her worldly desires cannot rehabilitate someone else. Gülen never 'contaminates' the realities, and does not 'shade' the realities with any personal interest. Therefore the messages reflects what is in his mind and heart and illuminates people. Gülen always interrogates himself and never deceives himself. He practices what he preaches. It is this sincere and honest search for reality that has won him millions of followers all over the world. His followers are disciples of sincerity, honesty and compassion."

An overwhelming majority of the respondents emphasised that Gülen's intention is to produce a humane world and to contribute to world peace. All his movement's activities are done for the sake of such a peaceful world and a harmonious coexistence. This peace and harmony can be realized through the cultivation of eternal happiness based on attaining the consent and love of God. Every activity or message should be considered as God's will. In

---

17 Hudaybiyah Pact (Treaty) was signed between the Muslims and Mekkan Polytheists agreeing to a period of peace. Almost a year after the Battle of Trench in 627 C.E., 5 A.H., the Messenger left for Makkah for a minor pilgrimage with his 1.400 and so Companions. However, the Quraysh did not let them do the pilgrimage. After negotiations, a treaty was signed at al-Hudaybiyah 12 miles away from Makkah (Ünal, 2006:1338).

his teaching, Gülen (2004e:52) frequently emphasizes this ultimate goal of attaining the approval of God. The respondents affirmatively say that as a religious intellectual and peace activist, Gülen has influenced a whole generation of Muslims throughout the world, and inspired them to play an important role in charity and education projects and foundations. His aim has always been to profess Islam's universal message; to serve people regardless of faith, colour, or national origin. In other words, Gülen strives for a peaceful society, in which there is space for dialogue and diversity. He has the conviction that reconciliation between modern society and religious values based on the Turkish-Ottoman model of tolerance and drawn from Sufi-Islam is a condition for this peaceful society. To this end, Gülen proposes that education serves as a tool to be used to establishing a culture of peace, stating: "Education is the most effective and common tongue for relations with others. We are trying our best to do this; we have no other intentions" (Ünal & Williams, 2000:331). Indeed, worldwide peace is indicated as his ultimate purpose, and is a long gain. In this regard, education is utilized as a major medium. To one respondent, the short term gain Gülen has in mind is however the birthing of an example generation, a generation of 'role models' who can exert influence on the society in particular, and the world in general. He promotes a holistic education aiming to educate responsible citizens and empathetic human beings who are open to science and rationality, as well as the religious morality (Aslandoğan & Çetin, 2006:31-54).

Gülen's intentions have always been questioned and thus questions concerning his mindset, and convictions were answered in various ways by the respective people include leading journalists, academics, TV personalities, politicians, and Turkish and foreign state authorities (Ünal & Williams, 2000; Ates, Karakas & Ortayli, 2005). Interestingly, a small group, bred by the power of the positions that they occupy, blinded by their 19th century understanding of the state model, accuse Gülen of attempting to "take over state control and bring 'darkness'". However, Gülen, never made choices for "himself" but lived—and thought how to live—for others. If there is an ultimate goal—one that limits itself to this world—that would be none other than truly understanding religion of Islam in its entirety, which enlightens the contested minds and souls of today's Muslims and engaging with other groups. The movement's intention can also be understood and explained through a functionalist approach. The functionalists (Rosamond, 2000) argue that cooperation and coordination in the sectors rather than politics bring new areas of cooperation dependent upon the success of the previous attempts. (Spill-over effect). The movement considers politics as a secondary importance and focuses on technical issues like economic, cooperation and social interaction. Technical issues can be considered as a general framework. Affirmably, one respondent indicates that Gülen's understanding rests upon a tripod encompassing life's 'economic, cultural, and spiritual aspects. The tripod of economics, education, and religion is the main dynamic of his view's vitality.

According to another interviewee, Gülen claims that the modern world is plagued by the individual's lack of faith, and in particular, the failure to adopt scientific methods while preserving moral values and belief in God. Gülen contends that faith can be scientifically proven, and science benefits from, and indeed requires, a moral foundation from religion (Bakar, 2005). In insisting that science not be separated from religion, Gülen (Kiyimba, et al, 1998:32-60) argues that there is no contradiction between religion and science.

With respect to avoiding irrelevant messages and actions regarding Gülen's intention and vision, the respondents stress that his followers do not deal with politics. Common interests are regarded as more important than the personal ones. Self-criticism and self control make the movement's members proactive. They are not busy with the circle of interest, but are focused on the circle of influence. Moreover, the respondents argue that cooperation and collaboration both in his native country Turkey and abroad bring new opportunities for common projects and dialogue. The activities supporting the national and international interests are accepted by different societies. Once again, the members abstain from politics, and for they want to contribute to the well-being of the society in a concrete and practical way. Over the years the movement, has developed a culture of ignorance towards negative publicity or messages. Instead, Gülen calls for putting the best of hearts into action, streamlines each days activities with the light of faith and continue to serve Islam while continuing to fight prejudice and develops a constructive culture of dialogue. This, however, does not mean that the movement keeps quiet on political issues, on the contrary, the media and education tools are used as a way to get in touch with the rest of the world and provide all there is to know in a constructive and a transparent way.

4. Acceptability

"Readers of a text receive that text for various purposes. Reading a text means expecting something from it. Consequently, for the matching of readers' expectations with what is meant in the text, there must be a coherent and cohesive set of components forming it. In this sense, the type of the text and readers' intention as well as the producer's intention must build a whole body. This is, to some extent, dependent on such factors as text-type, cultural setting and the desirability of goals. For example, if the topic is about sports yet the body of the text focuses on some irrelevant subject matters other than sports, then it cannot be acceptable for a reader who wants to read something about a branch of sport" (Tas, idem).

Using this text linguistic principle, the following questions will be answered: a) Who are the "readers" of Gülen's teaching and movement and what do they expect? b) Do the intentions of Gülen and his community's situation build a whole body? c) Are there any unacceptable messages and/or actions?

The readers are both the insiders, the members of the movement from all segments of the society, and the whole of humanity. More precisely, the readers of Gülen's teaching are students, academics, businessmen, alumni of universities, the whole society, and the secular segment in Turkey, Africa, Asia, Australia, America and Europe. Probably, the insider expect to be inspired and motivated by Gülen's preaching, through his example as a guide for their life and activities. Academics and other highly educated people are able to reproduce an image reflecting the nature and characteristics of Gülen's preaching and his movement. Academics thus have the important role of bringing the ideas and teaching to the readers of the movement.

The distinction between "were" and "are" shall be introduced in defining Gülen's 'readers', his movement's members. During the movement's early years, the readers were a rather overlooked minority that the state considered as "harmless" as long as they were "minority" and lacked any capability of intellectualism that would raise critique and give birth to any sort of progressive activity that would foster "the minority values". As the movement proved its sincere intentions over the decades and the fruits of new approach to education became tangible, the readers of Gülen's movement have expanded greatly. Today they constitute a large array of professionals in almost every field, from the business world to academia, and interestingly followers of other beliefs—even agnostics. The main engine of the movement is faith based on the Gülen's teaching of Islam. The movement is like a firm body that can mobilize and adapt itself into new situations rapidly – despite its ever growing size. Those who are inspired by his texts and speeches regard themselves as pious, however there are also other people supporting educational and dialogue activities. A respondent stresses that the members of the movement expect to see the fruits of their efforts (and they have already been seeing those), and the humanity is waiting for the useful solutions of the movement (and so many have already witnessed those). Another respondent indicated that they do not have a common expectation.

The overwhelming majority of the respondents argue that Gülen's intention and the situation of the movement build a whole body:

> Although Gülen's vision is far beyond those of members, the community represents the teaching and ideals very effectively. Especially, the humbleness, sincerity and altruism of the young teachers and businessmen are a significant dynamic in the movement. The movement grows every day, but those who accept the main Gülen's ideas constitute the character of the movement. Readers of the movement include all parts of the society. They are the different segments of the whole body. They expect to learn how to evaluate the teachings of the Prophet and the Qur'an as well as their responsibilities and potential contributions. Representatives of the movement express their understanding and purpose to everybody with whom they are in touch. Readers want to be participant in the process and they act in accordance with Gülen's views.

One unacceptable action within the movement is lying idle, instead of either seeking spiritual endowment or providing it. Further, the movement may sometimes be associated only with Turkish culture and even missionary endeavour, however, it has a broader and global character, which facilitates the integration and social harmony. Another important point is that each member knows only to what he or she is closely related. Nobody knows and deals with every activity. In addition, in such a fast growing movement, personal interpretations may sometimes be wrong, and these cannot be generalized.

Briefly, Gülen's approach to intercultural and interfaith dialogue and peaceful coexistence has been criticised from two diametrically opposed points of view (Celik & Valkenberg, 2007). On the one hand, those who are opposed to dialogue argue that this will lead to the assimilation of Muslim identity and that Muslim distinctiveness must not be compromised even to the degree of giving precedence to matters and grounds of common concern and belief. Gülen's response to this is: "Islam is clear, cogent and coherent and is in no doubt about its values and therefore does not fear integration" (Yildirim, 1998). Not only radical Islamic groups and nationalistic circles in Turkey opposed Gülen's dialogue with members of other religious, the adherents of the Kemalist state ideology in Turkey also see the Gülen movement as a threat to the secular and laicized nature of the Turkish Republic (Modern Turkey) and its political and societal institutions (Yilmaz, 2005:385-411; Saritoprak & Griffith, 2005:336). On the other end of the spectrum, those in favour of celebrating pluralism and cultural diversity have also criticised Gülen for placing far too much emphasis in meeting on common ground issues. According to interviews with Gülen's followers and experts, this common ground approach is not targeted at those in favour of engagement and dialogue but at those who are not. By emphasising matters of common belief and interest, Gülen is attempting—as a role model— to persuade people that human beings have sufficient commonality to build a peaceful future. On the contrary, some respondents stress that Gülen's efforts and underlying philosophy regarding dialogue and tolerance may be seen as a political strategy to avoid convulsive debate on laicism which where introduced by Atatürk in Turkey to create an secular political culture. However, one of these respondents sees Gülen as an important figure who discusses secularism by bringing constantly the importance of dialogue and tolerance to the fore. To many respondents, suspicions that Gülen would want to take over and to establish an Islamic state are completely unfounded. He maintains the conviction that power lies in the practicing a positive influence on the society, through the combining of integrity, spiritual values, and professionalism in the context of modern life.

5. Informativity

> "Informativity is concerned with how unexpected/expected or known/unknown are the occur-
> rences in the text. This is an unnegegligible standard for an effective text, which can be grouped as:
> First order informativity, second order informativity, third order informativity. The first requires
> ordinary trivial knowledge such as articles, prepositions et cetera. It is not about the content, thus it
> receives little attention; the second, normal standards, is content related; the third, is a much atten-
> tion-demanding occurrence which is caused by discontinuity and discrepancies" (Tas, idem).

The questions are thus: a) What makes the Gülen teaching and movement unique? b) How do they manage the balance known/unknown for their "readers"?

According to some respondents, the uniqueness of the Gülen movement can be seen as two fold. On one hand, it provides a new perception of spirituality and science, on the other hand an unprecedented degree of commitment, loyalty and sincerity with no intentions of seeking worldly flattery. Following the enlightenment, "religion" has been criticized for not provid-ing satisfying answers for the new centuries and dismissing scientific endeavours. Gülen's movement seeks for the "best fit" between modernity and spirituality. Gülen (1997)[18] has openly and constantly stated that a committed Muslim shall not only read the book of Islam, but must also "read" the book of universe—since the universe is also a verse, an art work of the Creator. Only then, the true harmony between universe and religion can emerge. The metaphor used for this is that of a bird needing two wings to fly; hence the universe and spirituality are these two wings. Gülen's teaching is not intended just for some intellectual goals, but for spiritual richness. To respondents, Gülen's compassion, sincerity and altruism are unique. Members practice what they preach. People soar intellectually, socially and spir-itually by the support of the movement. The positive developments manifest very quickly. Further, the discourse of "individual and society", and "local and global" makes the Gülen movement unique.

One respondent makes known that it is their clarity and originality of perception of social, scientific, educational and cultural issues that makes the Gülen movement so unique. The fact that the members combine the 'old' and new is also unique to this movement. Dialogue concerns not only accepting and respecting the other in his or her own position, but also shar-ing one's own cultural and religious values in the context of the other. Sharing implies that people should learn about the other's cultural identity, religious beliefs and spiritual values, of religious understandings and scientific results, of the modern man and religious conviction within an individual.

In his teaching, Gülen also (Çapan, 2005) argues: "There is no such thing as a Muslim ter-rorist; a terrorist cannot be Muslim; a Muslim cannot be a terrorist." He declares that from

---

18 Gülen describes and defines Qur'ān in his book, entitled *Fatiha Üzerine Mülahazalar [Considerations on the Chapter Fatiha]*, as follow: "Qur'ān is an eternal translation of the great book of the universe. Yes, the universe is a book. It is needed for a reader to read this book, which is well-organized with all of its verses and pages. The reader is human and the interpretation of this book is Qur'ān. God has sent Qur'ān as a translation of the universe to the human beings who can not grasp the universe's immense, deep meaning and its huge vision. This meaning that we cannot easily understand by looking at the big pages and phrases of the universe, we can see at a first glance in the Qur'ān, the Miraculous. This is a favour for the human beings. God is the one to make the universe book speak. As the others' thoughts upon the universe would be wrong, it is also the same with humans. The Universe is the universe of Allah, Qur'ān is the speech of Allah and humans are the slaves of God. God is the one to establish the interrelation between these three."

the point of view of Islamic criteria nobody can justify or permit suicide and terrorist attacks. Someone whose knowledge of Islam is limited to the headlines of the daily newspapers is likely to believe that this religion teaches terrorism, suicide attacks, oppression of women, and hatred for those outside its community. Gülen's alliance of civilizations—as apposed to the "clash of civilizations" —offers a perspective from which this sustainable peaceful coexistence can be made possible. Gülen's perspective shows that through cooperativeness and dialogue groups can come to see that they share common virtues and ideas not simply incompatible differences (Carroll, 2007).

The respondents indicate that Gülen gives importance to timing. He does not prioritize the matters that the sympathisers of his movement is not ready for where the global conjuncture is not suitable. Thus, the current unknown matters (probably some new projects concerning art and aesthetics) are delayed within the community, and the known enterprises of education, the media and dialogue are prioritized. Everyone can get something from a text depending of his own position. The openness of the movement and the readiness for change reduce the difference between the known and the unknown. The movement is not closed. It interacts with different societies, and consequently develops new discourses according to changing circumstances. In this regard, the members' attitudes towards modernity and globalization are contingent.

In order to understand the balance between the known and unknown within the Gülen movement, one must seek to understand the "destiny" and the way it is portrayed within Islam. What is unknown for mankind is an "absolute knowledge" for the world beyond, therefore a sincere patience is required. However, once again, this patience is an "active patience" as Gülen describes it. In simple words, the knowledge comes to those who seek it. In his teaching, Gülen takes also known elements (e.g., current problems, scientific results) and couples these at a deeper spiritual and religious content, which perhaps was less known (unknown).

6. Situationality

"A text also must be relevant to a situation of occurrence. This is related to the context and the situation the reader is in. Here we can conclude that different people in different situations can take away different meanings from the same text. But what is important here is that the text must present the knowledge to make sense with a minimum use of words (maximum economy). Otherwise, it may even not be received at all" (Tas, idem).

In this section we will answer the following questions related to situationality. a) What is the context for the Gülen teaching and movement? b) How they decide what to do for a specific situation?

As a leading faith-based movement with a universal educational and interfaith agenda, the Gülen movement aims to promote creative and positive relations between the West and the Muslim world and articulate a constructive position on issues such as democracy, multiculturalism, globalization, and intercultural dialogue in the context of secular modernity (Celik & Valkenberg, 2007; Hunt & Aslandoğan, 2006). The Turkish Muslims in particular, and the global community in general, is the context of the movement. The acclimatization of the teaching to the specific cultural environment in each country is realized through sympathisers living in this country. It is a movement in which social cohesion and commitment, an ethical sense of responsibility, a free and critical mentality and a universal view of aesthetic and culture are prerequisites. In sum, Islam, Prophet Muhammad, the contemporary world, and the history of mankind provide the context for Gülen's teaching. The Gülen's discourse and activities should be regarded in a religious context. What gives a sense to the actions of the followers is "belief". Additionally, the movement produces its own role models (Gülen, 2004d), which help to solve new problems and adapt to new environments, by comparing these models and by remaining loyal to the main discourse. The context of the movement is first and foremost the situation around secularisation and modernisation in the Republic of Turkey. In its context the movement is, in first instance, an alternative form of modernization opposite the modernization in which no space is for religion, as through the Kemalism has been proposed.

The respondents stress that the Gülen movement is not based on a one dimensional process. In the movement there are different groups of people with different backgrounds and aims. Some people focus on the educational aspects, some focus on media and others in different sectors. They are the components of the whole pictures. Although the voluntaries of the movements are in different places and position, they have the same purpose: "Assent to God". Because of "Sahs-i Manevi" (Common Spiritual Identity) members focus on their responsibility and aware of commonality of their purpose.

The sympathisers exchange ideas, benchmark and apply best practices. The decision making processes are democratic. The opinions of senior members are regarded. Those who have expertise, merit and talent direct the activities. Nevertheless, since the events of September 11th, the terrorist bombings in Madrid and London, and the murders of Pim Fortuyn and of Theo van Gogh in the Netherlands the loyalty of Muslim citizens and the compatibility of Islam with liberal democracies have come into question throughout world (Celik & Valkenberg, 2007). These incidents have come to symbolize the supposed threat of aggressive Islam to the peaceful West. Muslims have become a dangerous "other" in many discourses, evoking Islamophobia. As an inspiring and leading figure of the movement Gülen's interpretation and clarification related to such a specific situation are significant guidelines for the members about how to react to this volatile situation in which people of different nations, cultures and civilizations now find themselves.

Finally, the context of Gülen movement does not really show great discrepancies in different parts of the world. This is due to the same sources that the movement refers to and the methods of interpretation that is accepted with unanimity. The beauty in the unanimity of the movement is the result from sincere commitment to the sources of Islam. This is due to Gülen himself minimizes his role within the movement and repeatedly underlining the achievements of the movement and any future successes to come cannot be bounded to the few figures within the movement but to the unanimity, brotherhood and faith. The movement constantly refers to the fact that "there are things to be done" and there are "subcontractors" none of the "subcontracting figure" can claim achievements as his or her own but the success of all.

7. Intertextuality

"During the reading process our stored knowledge, experience, previous readings all affects the present reading perception. That is why the production and the reception of a given text depend on the participants' knowledge of other texts. If a text is produced without making use of any particular knowledge which the reader is supposed to know, it may not be an appropriate text. Especially when it refers to well-known texts or things or people, it is much better" (Tas, idem).

From this perspective we will search for answers to the following questions: a) What are the relations of the Gülen teaching and movement with other communities? b) How they produce knowledge and action regarding the current situation of the "readers"? c) What are their references?

The respondents stress that "positive action" is a foremost and guiding principle of the movement. Members naturally eulogize their movement and formulate a positive attitude in all area, but do not disrespect or disregard others by claiming that the only philanthropic and constructive group is theirs. They should move way from all attitudes and behaviours that might lead the public to fight, conflict, pessimism or tension (Ergene, 2005). In his life, Gülen emphasizes an apolitical, proactive and constructive type of activism. Members are open for cooperation and collaboration. They dislike criticizing and insulting the other groups even if they have different priorities. It is also essential to realize sustainable dialogue and cooperation with people from other different persuasions and philosophies to coexist peacefully. Some of Gülen's public initiatives to establish contacts in the field of interfaith dialogue became issues for public debate in the 1990s. Gülen considers dialogue necessary in order to increase mutual understanding. To this end, he has helped to establish the Journalists and Writers Foundation[19] in 1994, that organizes activities to promote dialogue and tolerance among all strata of the society—activities that have been welcomed by people from almost all walks of life. Other Gülen inspired organizations include the Abant Platform, the Intercultural Dialogue Platform and The Dialogue Eurasia Platform, where Turkish intellectuals meet with political and religious leaders from various backgrounds. Gülen visited and received prominent religious leaders, not only from among the Turkish population, but from all over the world. Pope John Paul II at the Vatican, the late John O'Connor, Archbishop of New York, Leon Levy, former president of The Anti-Defamation League are among many leading representatives of world religions with whom Gülen has met to discuss dialogue and take initiatives in this respect. In Turkey, he had frequent meetings with the Vatican's Ambassador, the Patriarchs of the Orthodox and Armenian communities, the Chief Rabbi of the Jewish community and many other leading figures in Turkey. These meetings exemplify his sincere commitment to dialogue between people of faith. Furthermore, his paper on 'The Necessity of Interfaith Dialogue' is of paramount importance for intercultural and interreligious dialogue, since it has been presented at the Parliament of the World's Religions in Cape Town, South Africa, in 1999.

Some of Gülen's ideas are similar to those of other faith-based communities or movements because Islam is a religion of peace and constitutes their ideational framework and basis of solidarity, yet some of them oppose such issues as interfaith dialogue. The ones who disturb peace and brotherhood shall redefine their understanding of religion and the way that it is reflected on their lives. The ones with contested minds and souls shall only seek the bits and pieces of religion that would "justify" their activities. The ones who seek total understanding and endowment of religion and enrichment of spirituality shall only foster peace, not among themselves but among the humanity. This is the defining principle of Gülen's movement in relation to other communities, be it Muslim or any other faith tradition.

Self and the "other' separation can not be observed in the Gülen movement. Instead of ignoring them, the movement prefers to accept 'others' in their own position and try to find common denominators. Some excerpts from the interviews:

> "The movement during their relations with other communities reflects the need for dialogue and common values that all communities should dedicate themselves to protect. The movement produces its knowledge based on teachings of the Prophet and Qur'an itself. In specific cases, Gülen also refers to the Bible and other religious books as well as historical memories that most of the people aware them. The knowledge and logic of action of the movement are not new in nature but the methodology and the language they use is contemporary. The action plan and knowledge

---

19   See: the website of the Journalists and Writers Foundation: www.gyv.org.tr

is produced from and intertwined web of information networks within the Gülen movement, the "readers" come up with their local agenda and ideas that possibly could be realized within a certain time period. Following this, the ways as to "how to achieve the goals" are sought within the local segment and in close consultation with each others and with other parts of the world where the similar ideas have already been realized. As far the references are concerned, the one and only references are the main sources of Islam and the community life that was pursued during the early days of Islam, the era of peace."

One respondent claims that "Necessity is the mother of invention". Physical, mental, social and spiritual needs of the "readers" are nurtured by the movement. Practical needs urge members to find optimal and innovative solutions. Sharing knowledge and meritocracy are basic principles. Wisdom is also a very important aspect of the activities in the movement. So they attempt to develop modern science and religious knowledge. They try to do this via books, articles, universities, institutions, media etc. The primary references are religious. The secondary ones are related to the local and universal values. In sum, The Qur'an, Prophet Muhammad, the universe, science and their consciences are the main references and sources. They also refer to Gülen's texts, speeches and actions very frequently.[20]

Gülen's movement summons Muslims to be aware that Islam teaches the need for dialogue and peace and that Muslims are called to be agents and witnesses to God's universal mercy. As support for his views, Gülen employs his broad knowledge of the Islamic tradition to bring together the Qur'anic Scripture, the hadith reports from Prophet Muhammad, and the jurisprudences—the insights of Muslim scholars down through the ages. Gülen (2004e:214) writes, "The Qur'an urges peace, order, and accord. It aims at universal peace and order and opposes conflicts and dissensions. It is interesting that the Qur'an calls for actions acceptable to God 'sound actions to bring peace and order'" Gülen calls for humanity to begin with tolerance and dialogue because in such an atmosphere peace follows of its own accord. In fact, Gülen envisions a world order and a new civilization growing towards global tolerance. The ever changing and growing structure within the movement facilitates knowledge production and transfer. New information, which was produced in a critical and clever way, also helps to reproduce information. Change of priorities causes change of activities. A more closed and local movement before the 1990s is now an open and global movement.

Conclusion and Discussion

Based on extended research findings, this study challenges in sociological and methodological sense the linguistic analysis of a social phenomenon by applying seven metaphorical principles of textuality to the Gülen teaching and movement. Provided we refrain from over-generalization, our case study research is not methodologically invalid simply because a selected case cannot be presumed to be representative of entire populations. Concretely, we have learned that this metaphorical approach for exploring and analyzing a movement or an activity provides useful pointers and encourages the form of 'out-of-the-box' thinking. Indeed, the theoretical perspective and methodological approach of this study can be used to examine social movements emerging in other countries. The application of the seven

---

20 Gülen derives much strength from leading religious scholars and Sufi masters of the past in whose footsteps he follows. The example of the personalities of the history of Islam, such as Junayd al-Baghdadi [d.910], Imam al-Ghazali [1058-1111], Ahmad Yasawi [d.1166], Mewlana Jalal ad-Din ar-Rumi [1207-1273], Yunus Emre [1238-1320], Imam Rabbani [1564-1624], Niyazi-I Misri [1618-1694], Shah Waliyyullah Muhaddith of Delhi [1702-1762], Mewlana Khalid al-Baghdadi [d.1827] and Bediüzzaman Said Nursi [1876-1960], has had an inspiring effect on Gülen. It is most likely that apart from referring to Prophet Muhammad and his Companions, Gülen is also referring to such religious figures when he is saying that dialogue is not something that he has invented.

textual linguistic principles (cohesion, coherence, intentionality, acceptability, informativity, situationality and intertextuality) to Gülen's teaching and movement is helpful in exploring and describing the impacts and implementations of his movement in different countries. Our analysis shows that Gülen is revealing a dynamic interpretation of Islam that is both compatible with and critical of modernity and Muslim tradition.

We can arguably say that the Gülen movement's global vision has been shaped along with the lines of Gülen's teaching. His teaching is a doctrine of love, peace, dialogue and tolerance and includes—in first instance—ideological lessons that seek to find and enact solutions for Muslim's social problems grappling with modern world, rather than it only contains theological messages that aim at preserving 'Islamic Faith' in the age of secular heresy. The present article contends that this growing faith-based movement constitutes a changing Diasporic community defying clichés and common stereotypes about Muslims and non-Muslims alike. This article also notes that the Turkish community is part of the emerging 'Islam' in the context of secular modernity and has its own diversity in the expression of Turkish-Muslim identity throughout the world. The movement examined here is a social and dynamic movement that is global, human-oriented, faith-based, non-state, non-profit, non-violent, and voluntary. The Gülen's teaching emphasizes an understanding that is based on science and religion, and has now spread through educational institutions, media outlets and dialogical centres in Europe, America, Australia, Asia and Africa. Although the movement's members live in different countries, societies and nations, they share the same values, principles and have formed similar attitudes. In this study, we underscore Kuru's observation (2005) that the Gülen movement demonstrated the contextual change and diversity in the Muslim world as it relates to modernity, liberalism and democracy. This article concludes that the Gülen's movement represents a new expression of Islam, and instigates the art of living together with differences in modern democracies. Gülen and the members of his movement see modern ideals and Muslim identity as compatible and complementary instead of contradictory. Hence, the movement's existence should be seen as an opportunity to establish a bridge between modern ideals and the Muslim identity. "Anatolian Muslimness"[21] as represented by the Gülen movement can be a source of process of dialogue and mutual understanding between Muslims and the West. For instance, the Turkish Cultural Centre, which is located in New York City, organized "The Annual Ramadan Friendship Dinner" on October 5th of 2006 at the Waldorf Astoria.[22] The dinner was dedicated to mutual understanding, dialogue, and tolerance among peoples of different cultures and faiths. This can be seen as a concrete example of this process occurring. Certainly, an ontological and historical examination of "Anatolian Muslimness" is needed to shed more lights on the origins and dynamics of the Gülen movement.

---

21 Gülen was one of the first that used the term "Anatolian Muslimness" or "Turkish Muslimness" which was interpreted as a way of distancing Anatolian people's interpretations and experiences of Islam from those of others, especially the Wahhabi (Saudi) or Shiite radical interpretations. He writes of a "Turkish Muslimness" based on love, tolerance, dialogue, forgiveness, Sufism and excluding harsh restrictions or fanaticism, demonstrating that this Islam is not in contradiction with the modern world. Turkish Islam represents the chain of development of the Central Asia-Seljuk-Ottoman and modern Turkey (Ünal & Williams, 2000:54-58).

22 The Turkish Cultural Center is an institution committed to community involvement. The organization hopes to be a forum of international cultural exchange while promoting Turkish Cultural Heritage. The theme of the night was "Respect to Sacred Values". The speakers at the night were as follows: Hon. Senator Hillary Rodham Clinton; Hon. Omer Onhon, Consulate General of Turkey; Assistant Director of FBI Mark Mershon; Rabbi Arthur Scheiner; Father Thomas Michel; Dr. Gazi Erdem; Hon. State Senator Liz Krueger; and Hon. State Senator Carl Kruger. More than 800 guests had the joy to observe Ramadan Dinner with the performance of Ercan Dereyayla's Turkish Music Group and Whirling Dervishes (http://turkishculturalcenter.com)

Gülen movement that emerged in late 1960s in Turkey and received recognition from the international community for his bold defence of religious tolerance, compassionate love and mutual understanding from an Islamic perspective and his criticism of both bigotry and zealotry in the form of religious extremism. We can arguably say that dialogical forms of understanding remain the best prospects for understanding the other and creating cohesion and a peaceful atmosphere in the societies. Accordingly, Gülen sees dialogue as an essential element of modern conflict management, and proposes universal and multicultural education as a way to achieve feasible dialogue and peace. In addition, his teaching and movement focus on intercultural dialogue as an instrument for alternative dispute resolution, social mediation and peaceful coexistence within the context of cultural, ethnic and religious divisions, hierarchies, rivalries and conflicts that are grounded in socio-economic and political realities.

In conclusion, the Gülen movement that has spread all over the world, is illustrative of the fact that a majority of the Muslim population in European and other countries do not perceive a contradiction between modern ideals (e.g. democracy, equality, justice, human rights, and freedom of thought and expression) and their attachment to Muslim identity. The sociological result of this dialectic is a European-Islamic synthesis, a new identity uniting a Muslim identity with modernity into one subject position, a merging of Islamic values and Western ideals. The concepts of dialogue, love, forgiveness and tolerance are important universal values in Gülen's teaching and movement and are elementary in nature. Gülen also links dialogue to diversity and exchange to achieve coexistence and ultimately, peace, among the world's people. Thus, the movement associated with him can be characterized as a civic peace movement using educational projects, media initiatives and dialogue activities to promote a lasting peaceful coexistence for the sake of a new, 'golden generation'.

ROBUSTNESS AND CIVILITY: THEMES FROM FETHULLAH GÜLEN AS RESOURCE AND CHALLENGE FOR GOVERNMENT, MUSLIMS AND CIVIL SOCIETY IN THE UNITED KINGDOM

Paul Weller

Abstract

The 7/7 (2005) attack on London Transport by Muslims brought up in the UK shocked the Government, many Muslims, and the wider civil society. Subsequently, the UK's 'multi-culturalist' policy consensus has been subject to intensive questioning. Politicians and some parts of civil society have challenged a perceived 'separatism' among Muslims; emphasised a need for shared values and social cohesion; and advocated the promotion of 'moderate Islam' and 'moderate Muslims'.

This paper argues that, in legitimising simplistic distinctions between 'good' (understood as 'liberal' or 'modernist') and 'bad' or 'suspect' (understood as 'traditionalist', 'radical' or 'fundamentalist') Muslims and forms of Islam, there is a risk of eliding the condemnation of terrorist crimes conducted on religious grounds into the criminalisation, or at least social marginalisation, of religious conservatism and/or radicalism. This approach, it is argued, is more likely to undermine the development of inclusive approaches to the common good and that what is needed instead are authentically Islamic approaches that can offer both a resource and a challenge to Government, Muslims and the wider civil society.

Finally, it is argued that such resource and challenge can be found in themes from Fethullah Gülen's teaching. Gülen, on Islamic grounds, condemns terrorism in the name of religion. Further, being rooted in a confident Ottoman Muslim civilisational heritage and having during the period of the Turkish Republic engaged with both ideological 'secularism' and political 'Islamism', he also offers a critique of the political instrumentalisation of Islam while arguing for an active Muslim engagement with the wider (religious and secular) society based on a distinctive Islamic vision characterised by a robustness and civility that could make a positive contribution in the present UK context.

Introduction

This paper takes as its contextual starting point the situation in the United Kingdom (UK) following the 7/7 (2005) attack on London Transport by those claiming to be Muslims and brought up in the UK. This attack shocked the Government, many Muslims, and the wider civil society. Subsequently, the "multi-culturalist" policy consensus that had shaped UK public policy for several decades has been subject to intensive questioning.

Politicians and some parts of civil society challenged a perceived "separatism" among Muslims, in the light of which they began to emphasise a need for shared values and social cohesion and advocated the promotion of "moderate Islam" and "moderate Muslims". However, this paper argues that legitimising simplistic distinctions between "good" (understood as "liberal" or "modernist") and "bad" or "suspect" (understood as "traditionalist", "radical" or "fundamentalist") Muslims and forms of Islam does not ultimately help in combating terror or building a properly inclusive society.

Instead, this paper suggests that such reactions run the risk of eliding the condemnation of terrorist crimes against humanity conducted on religious grounds into the criminalisation, or at least the social marginalisation, of religious conservatism and/or radicalism. It is also argued that this way of framing the issues is likely to undermine the development of inclusive approaches to the common good. In contrast, it is proposed that what is needed are authentically Islamic approaches that can offer both a resource and a challenge Government, Muslims and the wider civil society.

Finally, it is suggested that such approaches can be found in themes from the Turkish Muslim scholar, Fethullah Gülen who, on Islamic grounds, condemns terrorism in the name of religion. But it is also highlighted that Gülen's contribution is not only one of critique. Rather, being rooted in a confident Ottoman Muslim civilisational heritage, it also offers constructive impulses. Importantly, too, for the current situation in the UK, Gülen's contribution - emerging as it does from the context of the modern history of the Turkish Republic - is one that has developed and matured through engagement with both ideological "secularism" and political "Islamism".

Because of all this, Gülen's teaching offers both a critique of the political instrumentalisation of Islam while at the same time providing a basis for active Muslim engagement with the wider (religious and secular) society in ways that are based on a distinctive Islamic vision that is characterised both by an Islamic robustness and an Islamic civility, a combination of which, it is argued, can make an important and positive contribution to the present UK context.

7/7 and the British Bombers

The 7/7 (2005) attacks on London Transport and which resulted in the deaths of 52 people and the injury of 700 others, followed by the failed attempts of 21/7 shocked the UK Government, many Muslims, and the wider civil society. "Mainland" Britain, and especially London, had previously experienced high levels of violence designed to inculcate terror and to advance a political cause – namely that pursued by the Provisional IRA (Irish Republican Army) in pursuit of British withdrawal from the North of Ireland.

But there was a widespread sense that these most recent atrocities were different in nature. First of all, in contrast with the PIRA bombings experienced by Belfast, London, Birmingham,

Manchester and other cities during the 1970s and 1980s, and also as distinct from the 3/11 (2004) Madrid train bombing, in these more recent attacks, the bombers acted without regard to their own personal safety and security. Indeed, from videos later seen and made by those who took part in the 7/7 bombings, it was evident that the fact that the bombings brought death to their perpetrators was something not to be avoided but rather to be embraced, being understood by them as an act of martyrdom. Indeed, these attacks were the first instance of such "suicide bombings" to occur in Europe. They were later officially claimed by Al-Qaeda.[1]

Second, while bombings of this kind had been carried out in the name of Islam in other parts of the world, another dimension of 7/7 that particularly shocked and concerned many people in the UK was that the bombings were perpetrated not by people coming from outside the country and whose experience might have been directly shaped by the horrors of war and destruction experienced by people living in Chechnya, Bosnia-Herzegovina, Afghanistan, Iraq, Gaza, the West Bank and the Occupied Territories. Rather, they were carried out but by young men brought up in the UK and who were, to all outward appearances, integrated members of British society.[2]

On 1st September 2005, a tape featuring one of the bombers, Mohammad Siddique Khan, was broadcast on the Arab satellite TV station, al-Jazeera. In this tape, he explained that:

> I and thousands like me are forsaking everything for what we believe. Our drive and motivation doesn't come from tangible commodities that this world has to offer. Our religion is Islam, obedience to the one true God and following the footsteps of the final prophet messenger.
>
> Your democratically elected governments continuously perpetuate atrocities against my people all over the world. And your support of them makes you directly responsible, just as I am directly responsible for protecting and avenging my Muslim brothers and sisters.
>
> Until we feel security you will be our targets and until you stop the bombing, gassing, imprisonment and torture of my people we will not stop this fight. We are at war and I am a soldier. Now you too will taste the reality of this situation.[3]

This message, and one from Shehzad Tanweer, later broadcast on the eve of the first anniversary of the bomb attacks, had been edited. In editing they were accompanied by statements from Ayman al-Zawarihi, often described as second in command to Osama bin Laden, and who sought to associate the bombers with al-Qaeda. On the second tape, al-Zawarihi claimed that Khan and Tanweer had attended an al-Qaeda training camp, although this claim has not been independently verified.

"Multi-Culturalism" and Social Policy

The realisation that young Muslims brought up in Britain were seeing the world in this way and drawing consequences from it to inform actions of this kind merged with a questioning

---

1 . In a 1st September 2005 video, broadcast on the Arab television network al-Jazeera.

2 The bombers who died were: (Edware Road Tube) Sidique Khan, aged 30, who lived in Dewsbury, Yorkshire, with his pregnant wife and child; (Aldgate Tube) Shehzad Tanweer, aged 22, who lived with his mother and father and worked in a fish and chip shop; (Russell Square) Germaine Lindsay (19), who lived in Aylsbury, Buckinghamshire, with his pregnant wife; and (Tavistock Square), Hasib Hussain (18), who lived in Leeds with his brother and sister-in-law.

3 Khan spoke in English. The text and video is available from Wikisource at http://en.wikisource.org/wiki/Tape_of_Mohammad_Sidique_Khan.

that had, in any case, already begun in relation to "multi-culturalist" policy consensus that had been the basis for UK public policy on ethnic and religious plurality ever since the Labour Government Home Secretary, Roy Jenkins, had brought in Britain's second, 1968, Race Relations Act.

Ahead of the passage into law of the Race Relations Act, Jenkins (1967: 269) set out what became the classic consensus formulation of: "I do not think that we need in this country a melting-pot, which will turn everybody out in a common mould, as one of a series of someone's misplaced vision of the stereotyped Englishman", clarifying that Government policy was aiming for "integration" (understood in those days as the opposite of 'assimilation'), defined as: "….equal opportunity, coupled with cultural diversity, in an atmosphere of mutual tolerance."

However, in the context of The Satanic Verses controversy, an editorial in the generally liberal UK newspaper, The Independent, under the title 'Limits to mutual tolerance' (18.2.89) noted that,

> Roy Jenkins' philosophy was predicated on the expectation that the minorities would also demonstrate tolerance, and the implicit belief that all manifestations of cultural diversity would be benign. It is becoming disturbingly apparent that this is not the case. The time has therefore come for an examination of how a tolerant, multi-cultural society should handle the intolerant behaviour on the part of a minority.

Indeed, at the height of the controversy around Rushdie's book Lord Jenkins (1989) was himself recorded as saying: "In retrospect we might have been more cautious about allowing the creation in the 1950s of substantial Muslim communities here." Such questioning from one of the architects of the previous policy consensus was a sign of things to come.

In the aftermath of the summer 2001 disturbances in the northern English mill towns involving youth of Muslim background, and even more so following the 9/11 attacks on the World Trade Centre and the Pentagon in the USA, such sentiments became more widespread amid heightened security fears (see Allen and Nielsen, 2002). Such fears became intensified especially following the arrest of Richard Reid, the British so-called "Shoe Bomber", who was arrested on 21st December 2001, for an attempt to destroy an American Airlines Flight from Paris to Miami, though setting off explosives hidden in his shoes. This underlined that UK Muslims might also be being caught up in the emergence of a global struggle, as had also the involvement of suicide bombers of Muslim background from Britain, including one from the author's home city of Derby, in the 30th April attack on a bar in Tel Aviv, Israel.

The change of approach to social policy that accompanied these developments was highlighted in a statement released by the Chair of the former Commission for Racial Equality, Trevor Phillips, on September 22nd 2005. In this, Phillips (2005) argued that: "….the aftermath of 7/7 forces us to assess where we are. And here is where I think we are: we are sleepwalking our way to segregation. We are becoming strangers to each other, and we are leaving communities to be marooned outside the mainstream." At a Government level, an emphasis on "cohesion" was gathering pace (see Kundnani, 2007), in some contrast with a former more positive celebration of "diversity" and in this context, the Government announced the creation of its Commission on Integration and Cohesion.[4]

---

4 . The Commission reported in June 2007, under the title of Our Shared Future.

Head Coverings and 'Separatism'

By 2006, many of these general concerns and policy trends had become symbolically clustered around a series of statements by high-profile Labour politicians criticising some forms of head covering worn by some Muslim women – a mater which, until then (and in contrast with the situation in Germany and, especially, in France) when there had been any issues arising in the UK had been handled by relatively low-key negotiations at local level.

This series of statements – which appear to have all the hallmarks of a co-ordinated use of the media rather than a random collection of unrelated initiatives - were initiated by Rt. Hon. Jack Straw, MP, the former Home Secretary, and Member of Parliament for Blackburn, a constituency with a very high proportion of Muslim residents.

In October 2006 Straw suggested to the local newspaper The Lancashire Evening Telegraph, that women wearing a niqab[5] can inhibit good community relations. He explained that he had asked women visiting his constituency surgeries to consider uncovering their noses and mouths in order, in his opinion, to allow for better communication. He made clear that he did not support a legal ban on the wearing of such coverings, but also stated that he wanted Muslim women to abandon the practice.

It is against this background that politicians and some parts of civil society have increasingly engaged in challenge of a perceived "separatism" on the part of Muslims and have emphasised a need for shared values and social cohesion.

'Moderation', 'Radicalism', 'Extremism' and 'Terrorism'

Others have framed the issues as part of the struggle against terrorism and, like the former Prime Minister, Tony Blair, have echoed President George W. Bush's language of a "war on terror". In his speech to the Los Angeles World Affairs Council, the former British Minister, Tony Blair (2006) argued that, "…we will not win the battle against this global extremism unless we win at the level of values as much as force…."

In this context, Blair referred to "an elemental struggle about the values that will shape our future" and argued that: "It is in part a struggle between what I will call Reactionary Islam and Moderate, Mainstream Islam". Against this background, there has been an attempt on the part of Government and other public bodies to promote a "moderate Islam" and "moderate Muslims" and to marginalise by association with terrorism what can be seen as "radical", "fundamentalist" or "extremist" Islam.

A good example of such an approach – and which this paper would argue tends to confuse rather than to illuminate, by eliding different issues into an overall "terror" model - can be found in the kind of public discourse that followed the most recent, July 2007, attack on Glasgow Airport. That attack came as Gordon Brown took over the office of Prime Minister from Tony Blair. Among Brown's new appointments was Admiral Sir Alan West, appointed as Security Minister.

Admiral West's (2007) interview on ITN (Independent Television News) of 8th July was reported in the on-line media service, BT, Yahoo News, under the headline of "Tackling

---

5 . *Niqab* is the term used for a piece of cloth which covers the face and, sometimes, through a transparent part, the eyes also. While *hijab* – which refers to the covering of the rest of the body except face and hands – is generally seen by Muslim scholars as being obligatory, there are differences of view concerning the *niqab*, with only a minority of scholars seeing this as obligatory.

Terror (my italics for emphasis) will Take 15 Years". Having, in its headline, introduced the theme of "terror", the report then went on to say the following, in which it will be seen that while key words are switched, an assumed continuity of reference is maintained: "Tackling radicalisation could take 15 years, Gordon Brown's new Security Minister has warned". The report then went on to say that: "Admiral Sir Alan West conceded the Government was finding it hard to get its anti-terror message across, but stressed that preventing people from being recruited to extremism (again, my italics for emphasis) was central to beating terrorism."

From the above it will be noted how easily the editorial voice slides easily from "tackling terror" to "radicalisation" to "extremism". While it is certainly the case that, through personal, organisational and ideological means there can be some linkage between these phenomena, in general I would argue that it is very important they should be clearly distinguished. This is because failing to do so will result in additional difficulty in trying to isolate those who are prepared to use indiscriminate and criminal terror in pursuit of their goals from those who may share some aspects of their understanding of the world, but would not resort to criminal violence.

In other words, it is very important to be clear that – even taking such words at their face value in terms of popular and general usage – that "radicalised" Muslims are not necessarily "extremists", and that "extremist" Muslims are not necessarily going to undertake terror actions. "Extremism" is a weasel word that pits an assumed "centre ground" as always being the natural and right one over and against those who are perceived to take a position that is "beyond the pale" of the prevailing consensus.

Thus, depending on one's starting point, the designation of others as "extremists" can simply be a way of marginalizing people from engagement, but without recognising or seeking to understand the content of their views. With regard to "radicalism", it could also be argued from a perspective of religious seriousness that this is an entirely appropriate way of being religious.

Etymologically and also in religious reality, "radicalism" can be understood as something that is concerned with going back to the roots, and which entails a critique of traditionalism for its own sake. Thus the question and issue at stake is not "radicalisation" among Muslims per se, but the forms that such radicalisation takes and also in what it results (see Abbas, ed. 2007). In a world where naked power and military violence seem to be stacked against many predominantly Muslim countries and people, is perhaps not surprising, especially among young Muslims in the UK whose own experience of minority status has been one in which religious discrimination and disadvantage (see Weller, 2004, 2006) will also have played a role in their perceptions of the world, that the prevailing economic, cultural and military powers-that-be will be questioned.

Therefore this paper argues that it is important not to legitimate simplistic distinctions between "good" (understood as "liberal" or "modernist") and "bad" or "suspect" (understood as "traditionalist", "radical" or "fundamentalist") Muslims and forms of Islam. This is because such reactions run the risk of eliding the condemnation of terrorist crimes against humanity conducted on religious grounds into the criminalisation, or at least social marginalisation, of religious conservatism and/or radicalism.

Some 'Tendencies' Among Muslims

By contrast, what is needed is a more sophisticated and grounded understanding of the tendencies present among Muslims and in Islam that goes beyond the ephemera of political rhetoric and media reportage. In this connection, the European Muslim scholar and reformer, Tariq Ramadan, in his book Western Muslims and the Future of Islam, identified what he (2004: 24-30) calls "six major tendencies among those for whom Islam is the reference point for their thinking, their discourse and their engagement" - thus excluding "sociological" or "cultural" Muslims for whom, in their own self-understanding, Islam is not a major point of reference.

The trends that Ramadan identifies include what he calls: "Scholastic Traditionalism"; "Salafi Literalism"; "Salafi Reformism"; "Political Literalist Salafism"; " 'Liberal' or 'Rationalist' Reformism"; and "Sufism". These categorisations can, of course, be questioned. Others categorisations for indicating something of the diversity that can be found in Islam could be put forward (see Andrews, 1994) and especially for the diversities among Muslims of South Asian origins (see Robinson, 1988) who comprise the majority of Muslims in the UK.

Those suggested by Ramadan are included, not because they have to be agreed with, but for the illustrative purpose of underlining that there is diversity as well as unity in Islam and among Muslims, and this is one way of attempting to describe that diversity. But they are also included because Ramadan is a Muslim intellectual who has worked on issues concerning the acculturation of Islam in the European context and whose approach has been referred to in a number of debates in Britain post-7/7.

Ramadan argues that what he calls "Scholastic Traditionalists" have a distinct way of referring to Qur'an and Sunnah by strict and sometimes exclusive reference to one of the classical schools of jurisprudence, relying on scholastic opinions that were codified between 8th and 11th centuries. He (2004: 25) says: "There is no room here for ijtihad or for a rereading, which are taken to be baseless and unacceptable liberties and modernizations" and that "They are concerned mostly with religious practice and in the West do not envisage social, civil or political involvement."

Of "Salafi Literalism", Ramadan (2004: 25) explains that, although those from this tendency are often confused with "Scholastic Traditionalists", in fact they reject the mediation of the texts by the interpretation of traditional schools and scholars: "The Qur'an and the Sunnah are therefore interpreted in an immediate way, without scholarly enclaves." Ramadan points out with regard to this tendency that it "refuses any kind of involvement in a space that is considered non-Islamic."

What Ramadan calls "Salafi Reformists" have significant differences among them.[6] However, says Ramadan (2004: 26), what unites them is "a very dynamic relation to the scriptural sources and a constant desire to use reason in the treatment of the Texts in order to deal with the new challenges of their age and the social, economic, and political evolution of societies." In terms of social engagement, Ramadan (2004: 27) observes that: "The aim is to protect the Muslim identity and religious practice, to recognize the western constitutional structure, to become involved as a citizen at the social level, and to live with true loyalty to the country to which one belongs."

---

6 . Ramadan numbers al-Afghani, al-Nursi, Mawdudi, and Qutb among this tendency, although it should be noted that many with a knowledge of Islam in Turkey would challenge Ramadan's inclusion of al-Nursi in this category.

"Political Literalist Salafists" are "Salafi Literalists" of a kind that Ramadan (2004: 27) says is, "…essentially born of the repression that has ravaged the Muslim world" Their approach is "a complex blend that tends towards radical revolutionary action…the discourse is trenchant, politicised, radical and opposed to any idea of involvement or collaboration with Western societies, which is seen as akin to open treason.

'Liberal or 'Rationalist' Reformism is born from the influence of Western thought in the colonial period which, according to Ramadan (2004: 27), "presenting itself as liberal or rationalist, has supported the application in the Muslim world of the social and political system that resulted from the process of secularisation in Europe." Of this approach in relation to the wider society, Ramadan (2004: 27) says, "In the West, supporters of liberal reformism preach the integration/assimilation of Muslims from whom they expect a complete adaptation to a Western way of life."

In relation to "Sufism", Ramadan (2004: 28) says that: "Sufis are essentially oriented toward the spiritual life and mystical experience" and that: "There is a call to the inner life, away from disturbance and disharmony." However, and importantly, Ramadan notes that "This is not to say that Sufi disciples…have no community or social involvement; the contrary is often the case."

An Islamic Resource for Civility

Against such a varied background, it should be clear that defining the issues in simplistic ways is, in fact, more likely to undermine the development of inclusive approaches to the common good. In particular, it can be counterproductive for the Government overtly to try and define and, even more so, to try to create what it might see as a "good moderate British Islam" over against a "bad radical Islam". This is especially so because of the high levels of distrust which exist among Muslims in the context of British foreign policy, and especially the military actions in Afghanistan and Iraq.

But it is also important to bear in mind the evidence that exists concerning the experience among Muslims in the UK of discrimination and unfair treatment on the basis of religion (see Runnymede Trust, 1997; and Weller, Feldman and Purdam, 2004) that can be expressed in fully developed form and specific form in terms of what come to be known as Islamophobia (see Weller, 2006a), as well as the impact (see Fekete, 2004) that a growing security apparatus 'reach' among Muslims in the UK can have among Muslims' own sense of security as well as on the perceptions of them by others and, in turn, their own perception of these perceptions.

Therefore, even from a pragmatic perspective, the best possibility for combating the attraction of young Muslims to understandings that see the world in highly dichotomised ways, is for authentically Islamic approaches to make a contribution that can offer both a resource for civility and a challenge to Government, Muslims and the wider society alike. One such resource can be found in the teaching of the Turkish Muslim scholar, Fethullah Gülen, and in aspects of the practice of the movement and community that has gathered around his teaching (See Hunt and Aslandoğan, eds., 2006)

It is important to understand that Gülen does not fit any of Ramadan's categorisations of Islamic tendencies. While some have argued that he can be seen within the frame of Sufism, as Saritoprak (2004: 169) has argued, "Strictly speaking, Gülen is not a Sufi" although he has what might be called a "*tasawwuf-style*" of living. At the same time, his teaching and the movement that has developed around it are oriented towards tajdid, or the 'renewal' of Islam. As Gülen (in Ünal and Williams, 2000: 53) himself puts it, "Since Islam is misunderstood, implemented incorrectly, and perceived as a simple religion belonging to the past, today the Islamic world is in a pitiful state" and therefore that:

> As Muslims, we must ask ourselves why? Taking the Qur'an and sunnah as our main sources and respecting the great people of the past, in the consciousness that we are all children of time, we must question the past and present. I am looking for labourers of thought and researchers to establish the necessary balance between the constant and changing aspects of Islam and, considering such juridical rules as abrogation, particularization, generalization, and restriction, who can present Islam to the modern understanding.

Thus while rooted in a confident Ottoman Turkish heritage, he does not take refuge in any invocations of an idealised past as a solution to the weakness of Islam in the present. Rather, he seeks to provide a clear analysis of the kind of global and historical context that has led some Muslims into seeing the world in terms of an epic, militarised global struggle of almost Manichean dualism between *dar-al Islam* and *dar-al harb*. Thus Gülen (2004: 239) has observed that:

> Islamic societies entered the twentieth century as a world of the oppressed, the wronged, and the colonized; the first half of the century was occupied with wars of liberation and independence, wars that carried over from the nineteenth century. In all these wars, Islam assumed the role of an important factor uniting people and spurring them to action. As these wars were waged against what were seen as invaders, Islam, national independence and liberation came to mean the same thing.

In describing this historical development, Gülen recognises the factuality of what has occurred in the interaction between Islam and the broad currents of global politics, economics and military power. But he also identifies the roots of a current concern in which, for many, Islam has become a political ideology bringing with it what, he argues, are damaging consequences for Islam, Muslims and the world.

An Islamic Challenge to Terror

Gülen (in Ünal & Williams, Eds., 2000: 248) does not question the objectivity of the current situation in which Muslims often find themselves on the wrong side of right, but he also argues robustly that:

When those who have adopted Islam as a political ideology, rather than a religion in its true sense and function, review their self-proclaimed Islamic activities and attitudes, especially their political ones, they will discover that the driving force is usually personal or national anger, hostility, and similar motives. If this is the case, we must accept Islam and adopt an Islamic attitude as the fundamental starting point for action, rather than the existing oppressive situation.

Gülen argues that without such a robust self-examination and re-evaluation among Muslims, "The present, distorted image of Islam that has resulted from its misuse, by both Muslims and non-Muslims for their own goals, scares both Muslims and non-Muslims" (in Ünal & Williams, Eds., 2000: 248). Indeed, in the adoption of terrorist activities and justification of them, such an ideologised version of Islam has further both distorted Islam and its image in the wider world. On Islamic grounds Gülen clearly condemns terrorism in the name of religion. Thus he says (in Çapan, 2004: 1),

In Islam, killing a human is an act that is equal in gravity to unbelief. No person can kill a human being. No one can touch an innocent person, even in time of war. No one can give a fatwa (a legal pronouncement in Islam) in this matter. No one can be a suicide bomber. No one can rush into crowds, this is not religiously permissible. Even in the event of war – during which it is difficult to maintain balances – this is not permitted in Islam.

In his "Message Concerning the September 11th Terrorist Attacks" Gülen (in Gülen, 2004: 261-262) went further to state clearly that, "Islam does not approve of terrorism in any form. Terrorism cannot be used to achieve any Islamic goal. No terrorist can be a Muslim, and no real Muslim can be a terrorist", while in his piece entitled "Real Muslims Cannot be Terrorists", Gülen (in Gülen, 2004: 179) he explains this further, in the following way:

The reasons why certain Muslim people or institutions that misunderstand Islam are becoming involved in a terrorist attacks throughout the world should not be sought in Islam, but within the people themselves, in their misinterpretations and in other factors. Just as Islam is not a religion of terrorism, any Muslim who correctly understands Islam cannot be or become a terrorist.

Specifically in relation to the Al-Qaeda network, Gülen is quoted (in Çapan, 2004: 4) as saying about Osama Bin Laden that: "….he has sullied the bright face of Islam. He has created a contaminated image. Even if we were to try to repair the damage that he has done, it would take years to repair" and that "Bin Laden replaced Islamic logic with his own feelings and desires." In relation more generally to those who invoke Islam and yet take the pathway epitomised by Bin Laden, Gülen (in Çapan, 2004: 5) argues for a self-critical approach and for the need to recognise that, "It is our fault…..A real Muslim, one who understands Islam in every aspect, cannot be a terrorist….Religion does not approve of the killing of people in order to attain a goal."

British Muslims Post 7/7

In a question originally posed in the Turkish context, but which is likely to touch a raw nerve of sensitivity among the elders of the Muslim community in the UK, Gülen also asks "What kind of responsibility did we take in their upbringing so that now we should expect them not to engage in terror?"

With relevance to this, in a recent piece in The Guardian (9.7.2007) newspaper, the journalist Madeleine Bunting (2007) wrote of the reaction of Muslim leaders gathered in London immediately following the 7/7 bombings. Of these leaders, Bunting said many "refused to accept that it might have been Muslims", and that because of this: "The discussion had the younger generation of professional British-born Muslims grinding their teeth with frustration at the stubborn naivety of an older generation of leadership. Their elders had completely failed to grasp how the community had been swept up in a global political conflict that was interacting with a local crisis of identity and a generational conflict."

Bunting also pointed, however, that by contrast after the attempted central London and Glasgow airport bombings of July 2007, full page adverts were taken out in national newspapers, and on 7th July imams and activists from across the country gathered to tackle extremism. Thus the Islam is Peace organisation's "Not in Our Name" campaign[7] adverts stated clearly that: "The Muslim communities across Britain are united in condemning the attempted bombings in London and Glasgow"; that "Islam forbids the killing of innocent people" and that: "We reject any heinous attempts to link such abhorrent acts to the teachings of Islam."

---

7 . See http://www.islamispeace.org.uk/p.php?id_art=1

In the light of this, Bunting noted that: "Britain's Muslims have launched their most con-certed attempt yet to win the hearts and minds of the public and distance themselves from the activities of violent extremists who claim to act in the name of their faith". Her conclusion is: "What's remarkable is that these subjects are being aired in public and even discussed with non-Muslims; for years the charge of washing dirty linen in public ensured silence. But Britain is now the arena for one of the most public, impassioned and wide-ranging debates about Islam anywhere in the world."

Islamic Analysis

Post 7/7, Muslims in Britain have a very specific place within "Islamic world in transition" that is the leitmotif of this conference. If Bunting is correct, then the opportunity that at present exists for resources such as those offered by Fethullah Gülen and the Gülen commu-nity to make a positive impact is highlighted. What is particularly important about Gülen's contribution on these matters is that it is based not on mere condemnation of terrorist activity, but also on a realistic understanding of the dynamics of the world, and on a deep understand-ing of Islamic tradition.

Thus, while clearly condemning the 9/11 attacks on the USA, Gülen also warned about the kind of response that the USA might make, and of the likely consequences that could flow from that. Addressing this in words, the force and resonance of which are only underlined by what has occurred since then, Gülen (2004: 262) said,

> Before America's leaders and people respond to this heinous assault out of their justified anger and pain, please let me express that they must understand why such a terrible event occurred and let us look to how similar tragedies can be avoided in the future. They must also be aware of the fact that injuring innocent masses in order to punish a few guilty people is to no one's benefit; rather, such actions will only strengthen the terrorists by feeding any existing resentment and by giving birth to more terrorists and more violence.

Sadly, the prescience of Gülen's warning can be seen all too clearly in the continuing instabil-ity of Afghanistan; the quagmire of death and destruction that Iraq has become; the tangled metal and bloody aftermath of the train bomb in Madrid in March 2004; and the London Transport bombings of July 2005. Thus, as Shehzad Tanweer, one of the 7/7 bombers ex-pressed it:

> For the non-Muslims in Britain, you may wonder what you have done to deserve this. You are those who have voted in your government who in turn have and still continue to this day continue to oppress our mothers and children, brothers and sisters from the east to the west in Palestine, Afghanistan, Iraq and Chechnya. Your government has openly supported the genocide of more than 150,000 innocent Muslims in Fallujah.

> We are 100 per cent committed to the cause of Islam. We love death the way you love life. I tell all you British citizens to stop your support to your lying British government and to the so-called war on terror. And ask yourselves: why would thousands of men be ready to give their lives for the cause of Muslims?

> What you have witnessed now is only the beginning of a series of attacks which will intensify and continue to until you pull all your troops out of Afghanistan and Iraq. Until you stop all financial and military support to the US and Israel and until you release all Muslim prisoners from Belmarsh and your other concentration camps. And know that if you fail to comply with this then know that this war will never stop and that we are willing to give our lives 100 times over for the cause of Islam. You will never experience peace until our children in Palestine, our mothers and sisters in

Kashmir, and our brothers in Afghanistan and Iraq feel peace

> In the face of such deep-seated rage, articulated in a way that clearly undermines the Government's oft-repeated mantra that these actions are nothing to do with foreign policy, what is needed is not only a clear differentiation of Islam from terrorism, but also a form of Islamic teaching and, even more so of an embodied practice. It is the kind of practice exhibited by the movement that has grown up around Gülen's teaching that is needed - a practice in which authentic Islam can itself become a resource for Muslims to engage with the issues and challenges of the modern world among themselves, while also being capable of communicating in a serious way with people of other religious faith, as well as those of secular perspectives.

In other words, in order to contribute to the growth of civility in our multi-ethnic, multi-cultural and multi-religious society, the actions and perspectives of those such as Shehzad Tanweer need robust challenge from Islamic resources that draw upon the deep wells of Qur'an and Sunnah; are informed by the rich history of multi-cultural Islamic civilisation; and yet are also fully engaged with the contemporary global realities of modernity.

Gülen's teaching can offer such resources because, as the editor of Gülen's book, Towards a Global Civilization of Love and Tolerance, (M. Enes Ergene in Gülen, 2004: viii) explains it in his Introduction to that book: "Gülen's model is….the essence of the synthesis created by the coming together of Turkish culture with Islam". It is especially a development of the Sufi tradition and that "re-generates this tolerant interpretation and understanding of Muslim-Turkish Sufism within contemporary circumstances, albeit highlighting a broader, more active, and more socially oriented vision…. Gülen opens up this framework and vision to all societies in the world, transforming and broadening it.

South Asian Muslims and Islam with a Turkish Face

Of course, the potentials for, and constraints upon, the influence of Gülen's teaching in the UK are limited by the fact that the primary face of Islam and of the organised Muslim community groups in the UK is a South Asian, rather than Turkish (or an Arabic) one, albeit that these latter groups are quite numerically significant, especially in London.

The predominant South Asian groupings are shaped by a strong minority consciousness and experience arising from British Imperial India. While this can offer resources for living also as a Muslim minority in the UK, it also brings with it particular weaknesses as compared with the heritage of those Muslims whose background is shaped by more a confident majority history. South Asian Muslim movements with a heritage that developed in the British Indian Empire (Hardy, 1972) have been generally less self-confident in interaction with the wider public life, and more concerned with preserving Islam in a sea of alien cultural influence.

By contrast, Islam in the Turkish context, and as reflected in Gülen's teaching and the practice of the community gathered around this, is rooted in a confident Ottoman Muslim civilisational heritage that has allowed the possibility of developing an approach that is characterised by a greater openness towards people of other ways of believing and living. This relative ease with diversity was a part of the Ottoman heritage. But while there was a tradition of dealing with religious diversity, since the Kemalist revolution in Turkey this tradition has also, of necessity, had to learn to engage both with modernity and secularity, and also with currents that go beyond secularity alone into stances that can be characterised in terms of ideological secularism.

During the period of the Turkish Republic and in very polarised social contexts that have included three coups (1960, 1971 and 1980), periods of community violence and military rule, Gülen and the community that has emerged around his teaching have had to chart a course that both engages with, and differentiates from the twin challenges that arise from ideological "secularism" and "political "Islamism". Forged in this crucible, Gülen's teaching offers a critique of the political instrumentalisation of Islam while arguing for an active Muslim engagement with the wider (religious and secular) society in ways based on a distinctive Islamic vision characterised by robustness and civility which could make a positive contribution in the present UK context

Neither Traditionalism nor Reformism

What Gülen's teaching represents and offers is the possibility of finding an alternative path that is reflected in the title of Ahmet Kuru's (2003: 115-130) essay on "Fethullah Gülen's Search for a Middle Way Between Modernity and Muslim Tradition". Of course, steering a 'middle' or 'third' way is a project that is fraught with difficulty. In politics, 'third ways' have often been viewed with a certain scepticism on the basis that, in the end, they have turned out not to have been 'third ways' after all, but rather variants on one or other dominant ideology.

There remains a possibility that this may become the fate of the movement initiated by Gülen. At this point in time the outcome cannot definitively be known. However, what is significant and potentially creative with regard to Gülen and his teaching is that the 'middle way' that he advocates is not a road of mere 'compromise' but is one that is rooted in a particular understanding and application of traditional Islam and in which Islam is itself identified in terms of a 'middle way'. As Kuru (2003: 130) argues: "Gülen does not try to create an eclectic or hybrid synthesis of modernity and Islam or to accommodate the hegemony of modernity by changing Islamic principles. What he does is reveal a dynamic interpretation of Islam that is both compatible with and critical of modernity and Muslim tradition."

So, for example, in relation to debates around the niqab, in Turkish society where the issue of female head covering in the public sphere is extremely divisive, Gülen has made clear that he regards this as a matter that is not an 'essential' but a 'detail' of Islam, which differs in form in relation to its appropriate implementation according to the cultural context in which it is found. Thus, in Gülen's own words: "If a person takes her headscarf off, she does not become an unbeliever. This subject belongs to furuat [secondary methods of jurisprudence]. That is not like the conditions of amentu [basic principles of belief]. It is not the same as not accepting the basic tenets of Islam." (http://en.fGülen.com/content/view/1731/3/)

This should not be misunderstood or misrepresented as meaning that Gülen views head covering as unimportant. However, it is illustrative of the fact that Gülen employs a hermeneutic which is more in line with the classical traditions of the interpretation of Islam, and quite different from the 'flat' approach of modern Islamists. As Hakan Yavuz (2003: 29) summarises matters more generally: "Gülen's views on the precepts of Islam are pragmatic and contemporary without being liberal".

It is precisely because it is not "liberal" in the populist or modernist sense that Gülen's teaching is capable of resonating with those Muslims of more traditionalist orientation, drawing as it does upon a strong commitment to Islamic sources and Ottoman history. At the same time, its contextual focus contributes to the conditions that facilitate the possibility of dialogue between such traditionalists and those of a more contemporary and secular outlook, as well as with those of other faiths. The particular strength of contribution that Gülen can make in relation to the socially and religiously conservative circles that form the majority of the Muslim organisational scene in the UK is that, at one time, Gülen himself was not a stranger to concerns about the impact on Islam of western influence and a perspective in which the 'secular' is almost automatically equated with the 'immoral'.

Thus, in a 2000 interview with Hakan Yavuz (2003: 45), Gülen acknowledged: "We all change, don't we? ......By visiting the States and many other European countries, I realized the virtues and the role of religion in these societies. Islam flourishes in Europe and America much better than in many Muslim countries. This means freedom and the rule of law are necessary for personal Islam." On the basis of this re-evaluation, rooted in an openness to learning from experience, Gülen critiques the kind of superficial reading of religion in European and Western societies that can be found among many Muslim traditionalists, observing that:

> Some people might be tempted to say that religion has no place in the life of society in developed countries such as America and those of Western Europe. We must immediately point out that such a statement is in no way correct and that these countries have been and are attached to their religions. Just as we have expressed earlier, although religious values may have been weakened over the last two centuries throughout the world, humanity today is again searching for religion, and is once again inclining toward it. Even though the population may be indifferent to religion, to a certain extent in Western Europe, those in the administration seem to be, on the whole, rather religious. Among these, there have always been religious people at the highest levels of administration, and there still are today. Moreover, though secularism is the rule in all these countries, there has never been a mentality dictating that the guidance of religion should be abandoned in social or even in the political life of a country.

In making these observations, Gülen contrasts a civil society understanding of the 'secular' that is concerned with the participation of citizens of all religions and none in the public life of a society with an ideological form of secularism that is concerned to promote positivist philosophical positions and their philosophical consequences.[8] In other words, Gülen is arguing for a society in which support for the robustness of a rich and deep-rooted religious integrity is something that can challenge the kind of dichotomous and Manichean views of the world that lead to the perpetration of indiscriminate terror. It is a perspective that is in principle able, though its robust integrity, to promote the development of an inclusive civility. As summarised by Sahin Alpay (1995), "Hodjaefendi opposes the use of Islam as a political ideology and a party philosophy, as well as polarizing society into believers and non-believers."

In this way, Gülen is able to project an image of Islam that facilitates what can then also be the reality of a contribution to civility and the common good that Islam and Muslims can make in a multi-ethnic, multi-cultural and multi-religious society of the kind that the contemporary UK has become. Such a contribution can also challenge the Government and the wider society to continue to work at negotiating a way forward for British society that continues to draw on the distinctive strengths of its component parts rather than requiring them to lose what makes them who they are as a price for full participation.

---

8 . For an exploration of the various and contested meanings of 'secular' in different social contexts, see P. Weller. (2006b). 'Human rights', 'religion' and the 'secular': variant configurations of religion(s), state(s) and society(ies). Religion and Human Rights: An International Journal. 1, 1, 17-39.

Islam for Civil Society, Religious Freedom and Dialogue

Traditionalist Muslims often highlight a tension, if not an outright incompatibility, between what is identified as *dar al-harb* (referring to territory that lays outside the sway of Islam) and what is called *dar al-Islam* (referring to those lands in which Islam has taken root). Others - of which Ihsan Yilmaz (2002) sees the community associated with Gülen's teaching as an example - are more concerned with what Yilmaz identifies as *dar al-hizmet*. This reflects a movement away from an instrumentalisation of religion in politics to a public life of service based on religious motivations, contributing to civil society as one contribution alongside others.

This contrasts with the approach of those of whom Gülen (2006: 40) says: "There are those who are uncomfortable with other people's freedom of conscience and religion. While saying 'freedom of conscience and religion,' there are people who perceive it as only their own freedom. There are such fanatics and bigots." Thus the deep-seated commitment of Gülen's vision, and of the practice of the community formed around his teaching, to inter-religious dialogue is another important resource that is offered. As Bekim Agai (2003: 65) points out:

> Although many Islamic leaders may talk of tolerance in Islam, it may be problematic to put it into practice. Gülen himself has shown that he has no fears of meeting leaders of other religions, including the Pope and the representative of the Jewish community in Istanbul. He also crossed the borders of Islamic discourse to meet with important people in Turkish society who are atheists. These activities were not easy from a religious perspective because Islamic discourse in Turkey has definite boundaries that do not appreciate close ties to the leaders of other religions and nonreligious persons. Also, his support for the Alevis was not very popular among most Sunni-Islamic groups.

In a compact and accessible way, the main contours of Gülen's thinking on dialogue can be found in his article on "The Necessity of Interfaith Dialogue: A Muslim Perspective" (in Ünal & Williams, Eds., 2000b: 241-256) and in his piece on "At the Threshold of a New Millennium" (in Ünal & Williams, Eds., 2000: 225-232), the texts of both of which, it should be noted, were written before the global religious and political shock of 9/11 and its aftermath, thus underlining that Gülen's advocacy of dialogue is not merely reactive and pragmatic, but is also rooted in his vision of Islam and the contemporary world. Thus Gülen stands against ways of thinking and acting that promote what can all too easily promote the illusion that the uncomfortable plurality of the contemporary world can simply be abolished. Against such illusions Gülen (2004: 249-250) warns that:

> ...different beliefs, races, customs and traditions will continue to cohabit in this village. Each individual is like a unique realm unto themselves; therefore the desire for all humanity to be similar to one another is nothing more than wishing for the impossible. For this reason, the peace of this (global) village lies in respecting all these differences, considering these differences to be part of our nature and in ensuring that people appreciate these differences. Otherwise, it is unavoidable that the world will devour itself in a web of conflicts, disputes, fights, and the bloodiest of wars, thus preparing the way for its own end.

Reflecting on the history of violent conflict in Turkey that preceded the military coups in 1971 and 1980, Gülen (in Çapan, 2004: 7) said: "Everybody was a terrorist. The people on that side were terrorists; the people on this side were terrorists. But, everybody was labelling the same action differently. One person would say, 'I am doing this in the name of Islam'. Another would say 'I am doing it for my land and people'. A third would say, 'I am fighting against capitalism and exploitation'. These were all just words. The Qur'an talks about such 'labels'. They are things of no value. But people just kept on killing. Everyone was killing in the name of an ideal."

Towards the Future: Resource and Challenge

Madeleine Bunting's Guardian article previously referred to was published under the headline, "Hearts and minds of young Muslims will be won or lost in the mosques". Bunting pointed out that: "It is estimated that 90% of Britain's male Muslims attend Friday prayers, making it the best place to connect with the core constituency."

In contrast with what she says has been the "self-defeating" approach of those who argued that "the government should withdraw from any engagement with organisations with historical links to Islamism, the broad 20th century movement of political Islam", she cites the work of the Metropolitan Police Muslim Contact Unit, of whom she says they are "well aware that their best chance of drawing extremists away from violence is through those who know how to argue the case on Islamic grounds and redirect the religious fervour of hot-headed young men."

It is the contention of this paper that it is precisely at this time of transition in the particular corner of the world that Fethullah Gülen's teaching can play such an important role. This is because Gülen is one "who knows how to argue the case on Islamic grounds" and thus to have the possibility to "redirect the religious fervour of hot-headed young men" from violent and near Manichean confrontationalism towards a self-critical renewal. Gülen's teaching is not 'modernist', and so it cannot, with integrity, be denounced as a 'sell-out' to secularism. Nor is it "reformist" in the sense that many mean by this.

Instead, what Gülen's teaching offers is a contribution that is devout, and looks for the renewal of Muslims through deeper engagement with the sources of Islam. At the same time, this Islamic depth calls for deployment of an appropriate ijtihad that is directed towards Islamically faithful engagement with the realities of the current historical and geographical and socio-political contexts. All of this, together, is then directed towards tajdid or "renewal" of Islam and of Muslims that can actively develop and enrich both the 'bonding' and 'bridging' social capital (see Weller, 2005) that religions can offer to the wider civil society.

As Yilmaz (2003: 208-237) puts it in the title of a paper on the movement that has formed around Gülen's teaching, what his Gülen's teaching stimulates is an "*ijtihad* and *tajdid* by conduct". As one whose vision and practice of Islam was honed in the cauldron between 'Islamist' and 'secularist' absolutisms in conflict in modern Turkey, Gülen's Islamic integrity, robustness and civility can contribute towards the laying of more secure foundations for civility among Muslims. At the same time, his contribution can also bring to the wider Christian, secular and religiously plural society the challenge of a rich religious and civilisational heritage that is Islam, in the forms that it took shape in the Ottoman Turkish and Sufi Muslim heritage.

In view of the increasingly important role of Turkey vis-à-vis the European continent and its possible future entry into full membership of the European Union (Bilici, ed., 2006), this heritage in itself is likely to play a more important part in emergent Muslim identities in Europe. And in the setting of the transitional context for Islam and Muslims that is Britain post-7/7, the teaching of Gülen can offer a secure and robust Islamic basis for challenging the equation of Islam and Muslims with terrorism and extremism.

In all these circumstances there is, this essay would argue, a conjuncture of factors in which a resonance for Gülen's teaching can emerge. And on the basis of such an emergent resonance, Gülen's teaching and the that is movement associated with it can positively contribute to the development of a 'style' of Islam in the UK in which Muslims are open to being informed by the strengths of the broader British and European culture and inheritance, while also themselves being confident enough to continue to make a distinctively Islamic contribution that is characterised by both robustness and civility.

THE WORK OF FETHULLAH GÜLEN & THE ROLE OF NON-VIOLENCE IN A TIME OF TERROR

Steve Wright

Abstract

We are living in dangerous times. We can anticipate further polarisation between Islam and the West as the official line becomes more focused on achieving military solutions to what are essentially political and cultural issues.

Fethullah Gülen is unusual in adding a distinctly Islamic voice to the calls for a non-violent approach to conflict resolution. The notion of peace through peace has a rich Western tradition from Tolstoy to Martin Luther King. In the East, all of those active in peace movements today acknowledge a debt to Mahatma Gandhi. These writers continue to influence peace activists such as Gene Sharp, whose work was directly channelled to assist in the recent, relatively peaceful, revolutions in former Soviet states such as the Ukraine.

This paper examines the peace-building work of Gülen within wider concepts of non-violence in order to explore their lessons for modern Islam's transition. It is important for the conference to hear something of past voices and experiences, and the lessons learned from them, which can further inspire those in Islam who wish to move towards future peace using peaceful, non-violent activities.

This goal is particularly pertinent in a time of terror when existing counter-insurgency methods readily provoke a violent response, which justifies more violence and repression.

The paper is illustrated to ensure accessibility of the examples for those less familiar with non-violent action dedicated to achieving social change.

Introduction

We are living in dangerous times. We can anticipate further polarization between Islam and the West as the official line becomes increasingly focused on achieving military solutions to what are essentially political and cultural issues. So why focus on the role of non-violence in presenting this paper to such a timely conference?

Well, a short answer is that Fethullah Gülen is unusual in providing a distinctly Islamic voice to the call for a non-violent approach to conflict resolution. But how well do Gülen's teachings on non-violence lead to peaceful transformation on the ground? Is his a static and passive approach bounded by dogma, or are we witnessing an innovative, active and self aware spirit of transformation which really can lead to a new way of defining Islam in action?

The presentation attempts to explore these questions via a comparison with Western writers such as Johan Galtung and Paul Smoker who have deconstructed positive and negative peace and recognized that structural violence is as important as direct violence, both of which need to be eliminated to establish new cultures of peace. Is the teaching capable of being translated via techniques which can action a non-violent belief in change and social justice, in the way that Gene Sharpe has used Gandhi's teaching to formulate an arsenal of non-violent tactics and strategies to challenge injustice and create peaceful transformation? Are Fethullah Gülen's teaching most appropriate for spiritual salvation in the hereafter or are they sufficiently integrated to be used now in a similar way in which Sharp's work was utilized to create a non-violent peaceful revolutions in Romania and the Ukraine?[1]

For sure, Gülen's approach is to work within an Islamic framework and apply the principles of the Qur'an to create positive change based on mutual respect. How does this differ to more Western approaches that share similar outcomes? It is important for this conference to hear something of past voices that share the vision of peace through peace and their similar experiences in telling truth to power. A key question is the extent to which these different approaches converge or diverge and the extent to which learning can be mutual. This goal is particularly pertinent in a time of terror when extant counter-insurgency models incorporating organized violence against innocents can easily provoke responses used to justify even more violent repression. A crucial issue is whether or not Fethullah Gülen's teachings on non-violence, can inspire a new non- violent praxis towards peaceful social change?

Peace by Peace?

The notion of peace by peace has a rich western tradition from Tolstoy to Martin Luther King. In the East, the non-violent tradition is much more ancient. Emperor Asoka, presiding over India the Third century B.C. slaughtered more than a hundred thousand before experiencing a Buddhist conversion which led him to proselytizing non-violence, from a distinctly spiritual and pragmatic perspective.[2]

Middle Eastern spiritual leaders teaching non-violence have had an enormous significance in the West, but it is a truism that there ahs been much less of a "connect" between spiritual theory and earthly praxis. 2000 years of Christianity has not led to a reduction of violence, far

---

1 For a detailed discussion and resource pack on these strategies, see the writings and presentations contained in the 'Force More Powerful' initiative: http://www.aforcemorepowerful.org/

2 For an extensive elaboration, see Seneviratana, A., (ed.) (1994) King Asoka and Buddhism – Historical and Literary Studies, Buddhist publication Society, Kandy, Sri Lanka http://urbandharma.org/pdf/king_asoka.pdf(checked 29 June 2007)

from it since Christians have slaughtered each other for much of that period and most other races as well. And yet the diversity and complexity of the Christian community, as one of the reviewers perceptively highlighted, can not be so easily dismissed in terms of their differing dimensions of tradition, time and space.

We know that many Christian communities, inspired by their faith have successfully attempted to translate their spiritual ethics and a belief in non-violence into a practical set of transformative actions. For example Pax Christie and the Quakers teach peace through service at community, national and international levels. It is not an exaggeration to say for example in the UK, that nearly all the most significant groupings for social change and peace have benefited from the funding of Quaker groups like the Joseph Rowntree Charitable Trust, without which a tremendous set of changes for the good would simply not have happened. However, at a state level, despite the non-violent message of their founder, the practical messages have been much more mixed

Indeed within living memory we have witnessed military chaplains blessing nuclear missiles and a genocide against Jewish people being rationalized on Christian grounds by an avowedly Christian Hitler.[3] During the last war, the Head of the Catholic Church, Pope Pius XII refused to speak out against the German treatment of Jewish peoples and whilst the Vatican has since apologized for this silence as a permanent stain on its ethics.[4] What is of most significance in these debates is the integrity of spiritual teaching on peace and non-violence and the processes by which such beliefs are made manifest in practice. An absence of integrity in such processes suggests either impotence or hypocrisy. But as one reviewer of this paper highlighted, it could also be read as confusion. Just because the Nazis said they were Christians didn't mean they were and there is much other evidence that Nazism as a movement was strongly anti-Christian. Nevertheless, the reviewer agreed that despite the content of their faith's teaching, the so called "German Christian Movement" tried to enlist them into the service of National Socialist approaches to the Volk etc.

And this is my point: believability is the extent to which teaching and practice are one. This is what is so attractive about the Gülen movement to external observers since even to an outsider the motivation is to unify outward behaviour, with spiritual credo.

Peace is of course central to Islamic teaching, the Qur'an refers to it being one of God's names (59:23). Islamic scholars have cogently argued that the sunnah or Prophet's way, can be understood as a deliberate choosing of the of the path of non-violence – a distinctly Islamic approach to non-violence based on dawah or peaceful struggle for the propagation of Islam.[5]

It is in his sense that Fethullah Gülen's contribution might be best understood through the lens of western practices of non-violent action for social change. This remains a slow process

---

3   For example, Adolf Hitler, (in a speech in Passau, 27 October 1928, Bundesarchiv Berlin-Zehlendorf, cited in Richard Steigmann-Gall's The Holy Reich), is quoted as saying "We are a people of different faiths, but we are one. Which faith conquers the other is not the question; rather, the question is whether Christianity stands or falls.... We tolerate no one in our ranks who attacks the ideas of Christianity... in fact our movement is Christian. We are filled with a desire for Catholics and Protestants to discover one another in the deep distress of our own people"

4   https://www.jewishvirtuallibrary.org/jsource/Holocaust/vatrep.html

5   Points made by Maulana Wahiduddin Khan inan undated paper on "Non-Violence and Islam" presented at the Symposium on Islam and Peace sponsored by Non-Violence International and The Mohammed Said Farsi Chair of Islamic Peace at the American University Washington D.C.) See http://www.alrisala.org/Articles/papers/ nonviolence.html

of recognition since it is only in recent years that the larger peace research networks have begun to recognize and assimilate the thoughts of Islamic scholars on non violence and that this form of non-violence is active and transformative.[6] Of course within Islam, Arab elders have used such principles for centuries to resolve family and community disputes and there is a continuum of practice for scholars willing to research it as such. (Abu-Nimmar M., 2003)

Historically, the East has provided us with some of our most inspirational teachers, translating their spiritual beliefs into a philosophy of both peace cultures and peace through non-violent direct action. All of us active in peace movements today will acknowledge their debt to Mahatma Gandhi. His quest was seen as a process of transformation, of tackling the violent injustices of the largest empire ever assembled. He rejected violence as a tactic because in the long term it was counter productive. "I object to violence because when it appears to do good, the good is only temporary; the evil it does is permanent"[7] For Gandhi, "Victory attained by violence is tantamount to a defeat, for it is momentary"[8].

There are certain similarities between Gandhi's deeply practical spiritual teaching and sayings and those of Fethullah Gülen. For example Gandhi's persistent concern with the world of inner spiritual responsibility, crystallized in his often quoted remark: 'As human beings our greatness lies not so much in being able to remake the world ... as in being able to remake ourselves.[9]' Yet for Western peace activists, the power of Gandhi's contribution is that it incorporates dimensions of technique which can be replicated elsewhere. This is the framework that pioneer peace researcher Theodore Lentz once called a "Science and Technology of Peace"[10].

Both Gandhi and Gülen stress the importance of truthfulness and this is an important test for any movement towards peaceful change, does it work in practice. The quest for "testing truth" occupied not only the earliest philosophers but also the earliest scientists. The English 17th century natural philosopher, Francis Bacon, once said, "Truth is so hard to tell, it sometimes needs fiction to make it plausible". But he went on to conceptualise a founding notion of scientific practice, namely that of falsifiability. "Truth emerges more readily from error than from confusion[11]." In other words, all notions of truth should be open to question and testability.

This was an approach which put Copernicus and Galileo into conflict with the Church of Rome, because their astronomical observations and resultant hypotheses contradicted biblical doctrine. The result was a classic story of paradigm challenge and shift[12]. Bacon himself was aware of the dangers of telling truth to power:" Truth is a good dog; but always beware of barking too close to the heels of an error, lest you get your brains kicked out." And yet Francis Bacon's abiding conclusion was that "Truth is the daughter of time, not of authority." Why is this relevant to any comparative discussion of modern notions of "non-violence"

6 See for example Paige G.D, Satha-Anand, C., & Gilliat, S. (2001)

7 Gandhi, M (1925) YI, 21-5-1925, p. 178

8 Gandhi, M. (1919), 'Satyagraha Leaflet No. 13,May 19

9 Recently quoted for example when Leeds Metropolitan's Great Hall was renamed the Gandhi Hall by the great Indian actor, Amitabh Bachchan, in June 2007.

10 For a discussion of Lentz work on peace technology and peace action, see Eckhardt, W. (1971) Symbiosis between Peace Research and Peace Action , Journal of Peace Research, Vol. 8, No. 1, pp. 67-70 (http://links.jstor.org/sici?sici=0022-3433(1971)8%3A1%3C67%3ASBPRAP%3E2.0.CO%3B2-K)

11 Originally from Francis Bacon's aphorisms in Novum Organum (1620) Quoted in Ed. J. Spedding, R. L, Ellis, & D. D. Heath (1896), The Works of Francis Bacon, (New York, p.210

12 Kuhn T., S. (1962) The Structure of Scientific Revolutions, University of Chicago Press.

especially in regard to Turkey?

Well Gülen's approach to non-violence is totally rooted in Anatolian Islamic belief systems, which to an outsider are based on the timeless wisdom of the Qur'an which is viewed as immutable holy writ. A closer reading however reveals that Gülen seems the inspiration of his faith as a work in progress rather than being 'set in concrete'. He values interfaith dialogue and ongoing cultural exchange as evidenced by his role as honorary chair of the" Journalists and Writers Foundation."

By contrast, alternative approaches to non-violence theory such as Gene Sharp's tactics and theories of civil disobedience[13], or Brian Martin's work on 'backfire techniques' are essentially heuristic. They are about learning by doing, Sharp lists 198 methods of what are essentially techniques used as part of a political rather than a spiritual process of non-violent direct action. These include (i) protest and persuasion; (ii) social, economic and political non-cooperation as well as (iii) non-violent intervention. (See Vol II)

Similarly, Brian Martin's work is a study of the dynamics of state power in facing down resistance and how certain tactic of non-violence can use Gene Sharp's techniques as a form of political jiu-jitsu which has the power to make the weak stronger by making repressive policies of the authorities "backfire"[14]. Does that mean Gülen's work on non-violence is ossified by comparison? No, on the contrary, he is open to the scientific process and sees science and religion as complimentary as long as there is a social responsibility amongst the scientists.[15]

What it does mean is that there may be limits on the extent to which the different processes of non-violence in action can cross fertilize. Is such a conclusion deterministic? Again the answer is no, since at the core of Gülen's teachings, is the importance of education. His perspectives on technological innovation are instructive since Gülen emphasizes the importance of society understanding what else is innovated when new technologies are constructed.[16].

In coming to any conclusions about the relevance of such differing paradigms of non-violence in practice and in faith, it is worth being humble. Most authors in this field have to admit to some level of ignorance of one path, or the other or both. The current author is no exception. I am sure that I have only a crude grasp of the writings of Fethullah Gülen, neither may I do justice to key non-violence theorists such as Gandhi or Sharp.

Nevertheless, I think the exercise of comparison is worthwhile. Western voices have stereotyped Islam to a dangerous extent, as a violent, backward system of beliefs which breed a medieval approach to justice and a terrorist approach to world politics. Gülen is aware of these stereotypes which he has addressed in his typical thoughtful way. In the sense that he offers a powerful approach to spiritual change in Turkey and the wider world which is based on a non-violent understanding of core Islamic values, we should listen. However, there are lessons learned from Western non-violent peace activists and theorists that have verisimilitude and their truth content should be shared.

In that humble spirit, the brief analysis of non-violence and peace cultures which follows is compared with some of the teachings of Fethullah Gülen. My hope is that discussion at

13 Sharp, G. (1973) The Politics of Non-Violent Action, Sargent, Boston, Massachussetts, (Available in 3 paperback Vols only: Power & Struggle, The Methods of Non-Violent Action and the Dynamics of Non-Violent Action).

14 For an online list of Brian Martin's publications giving examples of the backfire process, see his website: http://www.uow.edu.au/arts/sts/bmartin/pubs/backfire.html

15 Gülen, F., (200£) Regretting Science and Technology, Website http://en.fGülen.com/content/view/1283/13/

16 http://en.fGülen.com/content/view/1218/49/

conference will enable us to better understand the similarities, the differences and the limits that all such non-violent approaches face, in making any difference in a time of terror.

Gülen has written widely on the Sufi notion of Safa (purity) and the challenge of ridding human hearts from the things that contaminate it, jealousy, hatred, feelings of vengeance and suspicion.[17] His antidote from the Qur'an is mercy, tolerance and forgiveness.[18] Gülen's philosophy is beginning to be understood by non-Islamic scholars as offering a bridge between worlds. It is an inspirational philosophy whose essence is education in action, teaching love, tolerance and mutual cultural respect.[19]

In many senses the Gülen movement is a practical global networking effort for peace and understanding. And yet paradoxically in Turkey is where its essence has been most widely understood and misunderstood. On the one hand by all accounts the moral teaching in Gülen schools offer an exemplary moral and practical training for young people. And yet there are sectors in the military who distrust any pro-Islamist movement of whatever description because of the threat they perceive to Turkeys avowed secular identity. Fethullah Gülen himself has made it abundantly clear that the movement has no interest in seizing economic, political or cultural power either inside or outside of the country. In an interview with Turkish newspaper Zaman he has reiterated his spiritual credo of serving humankind by self-sacrifice:

> As in the past, I am currently maintaining the same distance to all political parties. Even if power, not only in Turkey, but that of the entire world, were to be presented to me as a gift, I have been long determined to reject it with contempt.[20]

Although we might take this at face value, perceptions are often just or even more important than realities. And this is possibly the missing link between our different cultural perspectives on non-violence. It is not enough to simply withdraw from future political challenges to a spiritual movement toward peace, even though that might be necessary, it is not sufficient.

Gülen's expressed philosophy does not falter when it comes to characterizing the unacceptability of terrorism. For him. terrorism is against the very fabric of Islam. On the basis of his erudite understanding of the Qur'an: No Muslim can be a terrorist, no terrorist a Muslim. Western commentators lack the scholarly authority within Muslim communities that Gülen brings when he concludes that suicide bombing, whatever, wherever, whenever is absolutely forbidden in Islam and for those that commit such crimes, the logical prospect is eternal banishment. It is important that such debates over interpretation are had within the Muslim community and that powerful voices are heard that can with full knowledge declare can make an extremely articulate attack on those who would attempt to use religious justification to commit atrocities. "Islam never approves of any kind of terrorism.[21]"

There is no ambiguity there. And yet there is a need for caution. It is possible that a willingness to clearly define position according to faith whilst absolutely necessary may still be insufficient. Those building new communities in turbulent times also need to better understand the dynamics of non-violent action in order to preserve their integrity, even in the

---

17 http://en.fGülen.com/content/view/1809/33/

18 Ibid.

19 For an insight into how some scholars have responded and been deeply inspired by the to the Gülen community, see Carol, J.

20 Quoted in Dr Serif Ali Tekalan' article "A Movement of Volunteers: http://en.fGülen.com/content/view/2139/31/

21 http://www.cam.net.uk/home/aaa315/peace/islam.htm

face of those who seek to either undermine or destroy it. My hope is that participants at this conference might consider this bridge between different but complementary approaches to no-violent progress, one that is worth crossing.

Cultures of Peace

Under the auspices of the International Peace Research Association (IPRA), considerable analytical work has been done on what constitutes a true culture of peace. It is worth reflecting on these elements before moving to the specific question of comparative approaches to non-violence. One of the foremost minds conceptualizing the nature of cultures of peace is former IPRA Director, Professor Paul Smoker, who with his wife Dr Linda Groff, articulated the necessary steps to creating such cultures.[22]

Smoker and Groff emphasize the micro and macro aspects of creating cultures of peace. They identify a "tire" approach to the peace concept:

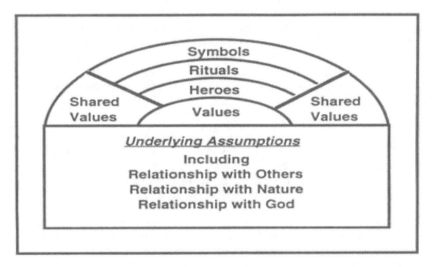

Figure 1: Culture: Visible and Hidden Dimensions

The approach of Smoker and Groff towards cultures of peace is unusual, comprehensive and apt since they are explicitly identifying dimensions that Gülen's identifies as important, namely relationships with others, relationships with nature and relationships with God. Their view is holistic and assumes an inner-outer world relationship towards peace. They explore different levels of the evolution of the peace concept in the west. These can be summarized as follows:

Peace as an Absence of War

Many people and politicians still take this rather primitive view. Nevertheless, an absence of war has to be a precursor for making progress on the other dimensions of non-violent pace building.

---

22 See http://www.gmu.edu/academic/pcs/smoker.htm , for a comprehensive explanation

Peace as Negative Peace (No War) and Positive Peace (No Structural Violence)

The Norwegian Peace Researcher, Professor Johan Galtung articulated the notion of structural violence in his paper of 1969[23]. That is even when there is an absence of overt conflict, the system is still structurally violent if people starve when there is food available, people don't get medical treatment when the society has hospitals to treat them, women and men of equal rank do not enjoy promotion because of gender or ethnic prejudices and so on. Negative Peace is when there is still structural violence: positive peace is the absence of both overt and structural violence. Such notions may have particular bearing within an Islamic context if matters of faith preclude equal opportunities.

Feminist Peace: Macro and Micro Levels of Peace

To quote Smoker and Groff (1994)

> During the 1970s and 80s, a fourth perspective was ushered in by feminist peace researchers, who extended both negative peace and positive peace to include violence and structural violence down to the individual level. The new definition of peace then included not only the abolition of macro level organized violence, such as war, but also doing away with micro level unorganized violence, such as rape in war or in the home. In addition, the concept of structural violence was similarly expanded to include personal, micro and macro-level structures that harm or discriminate against particular individuals or groups. This feminist peace model came to include all types of violence, broadly defined, against people, from the individual to the global level, arguing that this is a necessary condition for a peaceful planet.

Holistic Gaia-Peace: Peace With the Environment

Smoker and gruff compare non-western cultures emphasis on harmony with nature and the western consumer approach that passes certain economic costs on to the environment, endangering the health of future generations and precipitating extinction events for some species. Smoker and Groff conclude:

> It would be a positive development in the environmental area if we could combine the Eastern value of living in harmony with nature with the Western democratic value of taking responsibility for one's own actions based on an internalized value of the need for all of us to be caretakers of planet earth.

Holistic Inner and Outer Peace

Smoker and Groff emphasize the importance of this dimension. They argue that both outer peace making (more emphasized in the West) has to be complemented by holistic inner peace (more practiced in the East).

> Either perspective alone makes it more difficult to achieve the other perspective. For example, if one tries to achieve outer peace in the world only, but does not deal with inner peace, then one's inner conflicts can be projected out onto the world, making it difficult to achieve outer peace--the supposed goal. Likewise, if one tries to achieve inner peace only, but does not pay attention to creating outer peace in the world, then the social injustices and structural violence in the world will make it more difficult for most people experiencing those conditions to be able to find inner peace--the supposed goal. Thus the achievement of either inner or outer peace helps create the conditions necessary for the creation of the other type of peace.

This is a crucial part of Gülen's teaching. Smoker and Groff suggest that multi-cultural visions of peace are required and formally made such an analysis to the UN over a decade

---

23 Galtung, Johan.(1969) "Violence, Peace and Peace Research" in Journal of Peace Research, No. 3.

ago[24]. Conferences such as this can begin to bring these different visions together.

Sharp's Tactics & Politics Of Non-Violence

Vision is one aspect, transformation is another. This author's concern is about how different approaches to Non-Violence can be operationalised at a rate that can make a difference and in a way that is self-reflective, so that new more effective ways of non-violent change can evolve. Gandhi's work on civil disobedience has been a magisterial influence on what has so far emerged in the West and probably the key exponent of tactics of non-violent action is the American Gene Sharp. In his first volume on non violent action he (Sharpe 1973) questions why there is such an inertia amongst populations who put up with cultures of violence and repression when they could enjoy a vastly different system if only they could collectively engage. It is worth quoting some extracts from Volume 1 Sharp's views on why this is the case?

i.   Habit: In my opinion habit is the main reason people do not question the actions their "superiors" expect of them. Habitual obedience is embedded in all cultures. After all, isn't that what culture is—habitual behaviour?

ii.   Fear of sanctions: It is the fear of sanctions, rather than the sanctions themselves, that is most effective in enforcing obedience.

iii.   Moral obligation: This "inner constraining power" is the product of cultural programming and deliberate indoctrination by the state, church and media.

iv.   Self interest: The potential for financial gain and enhanced prestige can entice people to obey.

v.   Psychological identification with the ruler: People may feel an emotional tie with the leader or the system, experiencing its victories and defeats as their own. The most common manifestations of this are patriotism and nationalism.

vi.   Zones of indifference: People often obey commands without consciously questioning their legitimacy.

vii.   Absence of self-confidence: Some people prefer to hand control of their lives over to the ruling class. They may feel inadequate to make their own decisions." (Sharpe 1973)

Some of these lessons are pertinent to the Gülen movement as are the lessons Sharpe elaborated on why a non-violent approach has not been recognized in the mainstream as a legitimate means of struggle for justice and a better world. Sharpe concluded that there is in fact an invisible history and there are a number of reasons why such non-violent philosophies have failed to enter the national psyche:

i.   Rarely have non-violent actionists been romanticized as heroes. Rather, warriors and terrorists and their dramatic acts of heroism are mythologized for future generations.

ii.   Historians have accepted the dominant culture's view that violence is the only legitimate form of combat.

iii.   Historians conspire with the ruling class to keep the people ignorant of their own power.

iv.   Western civilization is "biased toward violence."

---

24   Smoker, Paul, and Groff, Linda (1995). "Spirituality, Religion, and Peace: Exploring the Foundations for Inner-Outer Peace in the 21st Century. "Conference Proceedings, Second UNESCO Conference on "Contributions of Religions to a Culture of Peace," Barcelona, (Conference was Dec. 1994)

v.   It requires a "new way of viewing the world." It is a paradigm whose time has not yet come.

vi.   Non-violence has never been seen as a coherent conceptual system. Consequently, historical examples of non-violent action are viewed as isolated events rather than as different aspects of the same technique of struggle.

vii.   Non-violence is unfairly compared to violence. Non-violence is often used when violence has no chance of success. When non-violence fails, the method is condemned. But when violence fails, strategy or tactics are blamed—not violence as a method. Non-violence successes are written off as flukes. Partial successes are seen as total failures.

Brian Martin & the Dynamics of Backfire

In Volume 3 of Sharp's first book, he examines the dynamics of non-violent action as a means of understanding what works and why. Such analyses are crucial if non-violent processes are to become living heuristic realities rather than dry scholastic or monastic theories. Sharp teaches how the power imbalance between groups can be used to the advantage of the weak by a process of political jiu-jitsu and how these tactics can succeed even in the face of quite brutal repression. This was one of the first efforts to understand how non-violence can disperse power through communities, brining increased self esteem and personal development – a phenomena also being reported in the emergent Gülen communities. Such healing and empowering processes lie in sharp distinction to the use of violence, which creates feelings of callousness and dehumanization which affects victims and victors alike.

The Australian researcher Professor Brian Martin, has taken some of these analyses and techniques further in a theory which he calls backfire.(Martin, 2007) Typically, non-violent activists exposing injustices by the authorities against a weaker group, can precipitate righteous indignation or outrage. Martin examines the dynamics of these processes in order to empower those who would use non-violent action but then face official retribution. He concludes that perpetrators typically use five main methods to inhibit outrage and prevent backfires (Martin, 2007), namely: -

i.   covering up the event;
ii.   devaluing the target;
iii.   reinterpreting what happened;
iv.   using official channels to give the appearance of justice; and
v.   intimidating and bribing the people involved.

He also examines the propaganda and black or grey media operations which typically accompany any official cover up. These have the aim of creating public outrage against the target of the operation, and can be analysed using the same framework. To be effective, a black operation uses deception to foster an interpretation that the victim was actually responsible. The (black) attack is not covered up - it has to be open in order to backfire - but responsibility for it is hidden.

Martin provides invaluable information for countering such attacks, including

i.   expose responsibility for the event;
ii.   validate the target of the operation (the falsely alleged perpetrator);
iii.   interpret the operation as unfair and underhanded;
iv.   avoid or discredit official investigations, at least when they seem likely to dampen

    v.   resist intimidation and bribery.

Such behaviour has spontaneously evolved by many non-violent groups wishing to sustain behaviour consistent with their beliefs. In fact I would argue that the behaviour of Bediüzzaman Said Nursi is a case in point. Nursi used his spiritual insights to follow similar tactics albeit at a substantial personal cost to his health. (Markham and Ozdemir, 2005)

Such response and counter responses can become quite complex. According to Martin and Gray),

> In a conflict between a powerful and a weak side - for example between a group of police and a single suspect, or between a government and a small group of opponents - the powerful side holds many advantages. If the weak side mounts an attack, this can provide the pretext for the powerful group to use its superior resources. The exception is when the powerful side is exposed in a gross abuse, for example when police seriously assault a suspect or troops gun down protesters and this abuse is exposed to a wide audience, leading to a change in public opinion. These are instances of backfire, such as the beating of Rodney King by Los Angeles police and the shooting of peaceful protesters in Dili, East Timor, by Indonesian troops, both in 1991. They are white backfires, because the perpetrators made no attempt to attribute their own actions to their opponents.

> Given this dynamic, it is not surprising that powerful groups sometimes use black operations to give themselves the benefit of public outrage. They want their own actions to be seen as an outrage-generating attack by their opponents, as when police use agents provocateurs to encourage protesters to be violent. These sorts of black operations involve promoting actions that will backfire on their opponents, in what can be called black backfires. (Martin & Gray, 2007)

Despite the fact that Fethullah Gülen has adopted an inspirational spiritual rather than a politically instrumental approach toward implementing non-violent pathways to peace, many of these negative techniques have been used against both him and his followers.[25] So much so that Gülen now lives in exile in the United States. In the sections which follow, the question is put, to what extent do the non-violent philosophies of Gülen match with more Western Implementation and instrumentalist strategies outlined above and can useful bridges be built between these two worlds?

Gülen's Non-Violent Spiritual Paths & Practices

Attempting any reasoned comparison of Gülen's non-violent philosophy with those of more western practitioners is fraught with difficulties, not least because of the way that Gülen's life and work has been moulded by the very specific cultural roots of Anatolian Islam and the specific writings of Said Nursi, though it would be a mistake to think that Gülen's approach is merely a next generation of Nursi's approaches. A more accurate description of the relationship would be that of mentor. And yet there are, some interesting overlaps. Nursi used the tactic of silent withdrawal and non-co-operation in many of his struggles towards resolving conflict without bloodshed. In many ways the maltreatment and imprisonment of Nursi is a classic case of backfire since his repeated representation of the evidence to different tribunals and his unjust punishment actually served as a recruitment engine for his movement and brought about the exact opposite outcome of that desired by the authorities.

---

25   That is not to say that Gülen's followers have not taken an instrumental approach in structuring and expanding the the process of formal teaching. The point here is that the focus of that work has been spiritual rather than political change.

The Gülen movement, from an outsider's perspective, can be considered to have an explicit ambition of eroding structural violence – for example through providing education and shelter to youngsters. But any Western non-violence theorist, taking a purist approach, would find elements within the organization that do not square with classic non-hierarchic theories of peaceful cultures. Such criticisms could be seen as nonsense by the Gülen community. From a Western point of view, the centralization of power via any hierarchy might be seen as evidence of an unequal distribution of power. Then again, most large faith groups operate on some form of hierarchy – the Quakers being some kind of exception but even then there is an elders structure, which is interpreted as simply experienced sets of hands to mentor the process of listening. The buyuk abiler could be considered by some in the Gülen movement to fulfil a similar role. The important strength of the Gülen movement is its transparency – and those who manufacture conspiracy theories around the Gülen movement might be less than forthcoming in being as transparent about there own motives and connections. Many of these confusions will be influenced by cultural differences especially in regard to the traditional role of women in Turkish society and the central and unquestionable bedrock of the Qur'an which cannot be questioned in any way, without attracting counter criticism. Western peace movements adopting non-violent strategies regard them all as a work in progress and not very much is so sacrosanct that it is beyond review.

There are also difficulties in wedding all the prescriptions of the Sharia to a philosophy of complete non-violence. This is a contradiction which is not unique to Islam – Christian and Judaic views on punishment: turn the other cheek versus an eye for an eye, are cases in point. Even the great Emperor Asoka, whose life's work became the promulgation of Buddhist scripture, refused to revoke the death penalty for reason of public order, despite this view being an outright contradiction of the teachings. (Seneviratana, A., 1994).

In many senses, Gülen is following the holistic, spiritual and cultural approaches to peace identified by Smoker and Groff above. It is now a global faith based movement with schools in more than one hundred countries including Kazakhstan, Kenya, Bangladesh, Pakistan, Indonesia, Brazil and Bosnia.

We are informed that today there are more than 300 private high schools and seven universities affiliated with the Gülen community, with over 150 schools in Turkey alone.[26] It is a sign of the health of the Gülen movement that today, that number is undoubtedly far greater.

Why should this matter? Well Gülen's teaching instrumentalises the teaching of the Qur'an towards performing daily acts of service based peaceful social change. Such an approach in a time of terror can make a difference through interfaith dialogue. To my mind, Gülen's Abant platform for dialogue is akin to the Pugwash movement when it first began it's work to prevent nuclear war in the fifties. Pugwash allowed a backchannel for diplomats and scientists to keep talking even during the difficult days of the cold war and led to the processes which not only ended the Vietnam War but the Cold war too. One of the reviewers of this paper said the analogy was pregnant with possibilities.

Such inter-faith dialogue is more important now than ever. The Western stereotypes of Islam need to be constructively challenged by Muslims as well as pundits in the West. Gülen's active compassion for peaceful change based on a precise reading of the Qur'an, can act as a powerful palliative to those who would smear Islam with the label of terrorism. Such work can only be achieved through making a critical mass of thinkers and doers who will engage

---

26   Quoted from Gulay, 2007

in peace in the wider world and that characterises the Fethullah Gülen movement today.

Conclusions

And yet it is wise to be cautious given the turbulent political changes occurring both within Turkey and on its borders with Kurdistan; Iran; Bulgaria; Georgia; Greece; Armenia; Azerbaijan; Iraq and Syria. It could be argued that the Gülen approach to peaceful change from a truly enlightened Islamic perspective, is necessary but not yet truly sufficient. It continues to be a work in progress

The very success of the Gülen movement could be misinterpreted by those with alternative agendas and alliances in the Middle East, during this time of rapid change and potential instability. In some senses this very conference is an act of wisdom by the Gülen community in taking the initiative to broaden the worldwide base of associates who are sympathetic do the credos of the movement and wish its work well. The challenge to us all is to find ways of future collaboration that do not undermine our strengths and differences but complement the project and processes with which we are broadly in tune with.

Just as in previous times, wise authorities made provision for famine and flood when there were no signs that these were inevitable so in this time, it is wise to think through future peaceful responses to challenges which may or may not come. For example, the extent to which the Gülen movement can once again respond to state repression using non-violent means may become the test of the integrity of the movement. Many techniques evolved by non-violent activists elsewhere in the world could then come to be of use and significance to the Gülen movement. This is especially important given the emphasis on self-awareness and wisdom in perusing a pacifist approach without compromising beliefs

The Gülen community is a proselytizing movement in the positive sense in that it is not keeping its beliefs hidden but is actively engaged in widening the base of its activities and is actively engaged in communications with more secular communities of which this conference is just one small but important part.

Inevitably, any new and expanding faith-based movement will draw attention. This is especially so when that movement has the potential to positively influence other Muslims overseas and change the wider perception of what it is to implement the teachings of the Qur'an. In future times such a role may require new notions of non violence and civil disobedience within its heart. So far, the movement has steered an intentional course away from confrontation with the authorities. But this very success may bring about future confrontation as the popularity, educational, business activities and economic independence of the movement grows.

I feel sure that the many teachers, thinkers and proponents encompassed by this movement will already be meditating on how they should behave to ensure future progress towards new cultures of peace on Earth. A central purpose of this conference is dialogue and a useful outcome of our exchanges is to share all the organized knowledge that comes from all our communities to truly bring about peaceful change, despite the current difficulties. We have compatible but different learning resources to share.

COMBATTING TERRORISM IN BRITAIN: GÜLEN'S IDEAS

Asaf Hussain

Abstract

Western policies are focused on fighting terrorist groups rather than terrorist ideology and its roots causes. This paper tries to identify those root causes and the means of eradicating terrorist ideology.

A common misunderstanding is that Islam is prone to violence and extremism, if not itself the cause of terrorism. This misconception is based on ignorance of the many Muslim groups and faith-based movements that work towards peace and better relations in the world because of Islam, not despite it. The Gülen movement is one of the most successful and famous of those faith-based movements. Policy-makers need to become familiar with such movements, their motivations, methods and arguments. The extremist/terrorist ideology must be rebutted; however, of the many interpretations of Islam circulating in the world the most radical ones dominate the media and therefore the attention of younger Muslims. Media and policy-makers have not paid enough attention to the authentic interpretations of Islam embraced by the majority – the interpretations of mainstream Muslim thinkers like Fethullah Gülen. Gülen's teachings and principles and the movement's activities and projects can help inform and shape state policies. This paper explains how the views of thinkers like Gülen can be translated into policy terms to defeat terrorism.

Intoduction

Terrorism has spread like an epidemic disease in the world and is particularly targeting the Western world in which Britain, the USA as well as Europe have suffered terrorist attacks. Obviously, when any country is attacked, it has the right to defend itself. The question is: how should one engage in counter attack? If one begins to think seriously about this then one needs to have additional information about whom one should attack and the nature of the attack? If one were fighting a conventional war on a battlefield, it would be a fight between one army against another. But if terrorist attacks have taken place within the country, it is outside the pail of conventional attack for they are not in a battlefield. One not only has to identify the attackers but to think how did they emerge in the first place and will they emerge in the future or was it a one-off attack? In other words, terrorist attacks in various Western countries have become a very complex subject and often the response may not be effective.

In Britain the terrorist attacks on the underground trains on July 7, 2005 shocked the nation and have raised serious questions. The nation was shocked because the bombers were mainly British born young men of Muslim background. After 9/11 attacks on the USA, the British government was aware that Britain would be targeted. But the assumption was that they would come from abroad and they could then be easily detected and caught. This assumption was proved wrong for they were British born Muslims (BBMs) or raised from early childhood in Britain by their migrant parents.

For the British government, the question was no longer would more attacks follow, given that extremist ideology had appeared to permeate British communities, but when, where and how. The BBMs factor had certainly complicated matters.

Whatever the concern now, the most important task in hand was to devise a workable and useful strategy of engagement and approach. Needless to say, a flawed strategy would only work to the terrorists' advantage, providing them with room and time to continue spreading their ideology.

The contention of this paper is that terrorism has to be combated by Islam as an instrument of counter-terrorism because terrorists are using it for legitimizing their actions. Islamic fundamentalists with their interpretations have equated Islam with terrorism making it a religion which has no moral or ethical codes and allows one to kill innocent people including Muslims (bombing them inside and outside mosques and other places) and non-Muslims (killing them in trains, buses and other places). Since Islam has been reduced to the ideology of terrorism---every Muslim who believes in Islam is or will be perceived as potential terrorists in the future. Islam therefore then has to be re-understood but the question then is, which Islam? This paper attempts to provide an answer to that question. Britain has a large Muslim population and that is the reason that the authorities have to seriously consider this strategy. Radical fundamentalist views circulating in Britain have to be discredited and eradicated. If they are not then the prevention of terrorism will be the only strategy for the British government of terrorism. The answer that will be provided in this paper will be for the eradication of terrorism, it will be an essential supplement and only then will prevention strategies will result in success.

The British government had engaged itself in dealing with Islam by thinking of changing the nature of Islamic Studies in the universities; initiation of a Commission for Integration and Cohesion; or evening supporting some new Muslim organizations like the British Muslim Forum etc. None of these policies have so far succeeded which will be discussed later... It is essential to first survey the preventive strategies.

The Preventive Approach

The Preventive approach is the most spontaneous one by any country in which a terrorist attack has taken place. Britain's preventive approach post-7/7 had many important aspects. First, it had to make all kinds of laws to prevent terrorism. Secondly, it had to increase detection measures. Thirdly, it had to devise measures to contain attacks by terrorists with force. All this operated under the umbrella of Counter-Terrorism strategies. Since 2003, one of the British government's strategy (known as CONTEST) key aims was to "reduce the risk from internationalism terrorism so that people can go about their business freely and with confidence."[1] The counter terrorism strategy had four principle strands which were: Prevent, Pursuit, Protect and Prepare. This was the major strategy of operations to safeguard the lives of the people. Another very important tactic was surveillance for "it was an indispensable way of gathering intelligence against terrorists" (Home Office network) Surveillance tactics therefore meant that legislation was another strategy for preventing terrorism. The "legislative framework" was for "preventing and pursuing terrorist and those who support terrorist organizations."[2]

Furthermore, for preventing terrorism the legislation laws were made under the following acts which were:

i.   The Terrorism Act 2000 (TACT);
ii.   The Anti-Terrorism, Crime and Security Act 2001 (ATCSA);
iii. Prevention of Terrorism Act 2005;
iv.   The Terrorism Act 2006.[3]

Responding to terrorist incidents was done at both national and regional levels. In terrorism decisions the Home Secretary was involved since he was

> responsible for counter terrorism across England, Wales and Scotland". On the regional level, the local authorities and the local governments were involved. The 'Regional Resilience Teams' supported the 'Formation of Regional Resilience Forums which are made up of central government agencies, the armed forces, the emergency services and local authorities and provide a multi-agency strategic direction to civil protection planning at a regional level.[4]

In addition to these processes a number of important bodies were established by the government and its agencies. The Prime Ministers office had its Cabinet Office Contingencies Secretariat (COBRA) which was the emergency coordinating committee comprising the "Ministerial Committees on Defence and Overseas Policy, the Ministerial Committee on Intelligence Services, the Joint Intelligence Committee, MI6, GCHQ, MI5, New Scotland Yard and many other elements". [5]

Gregory and Wilkinson also observed that

> the UK…. had in place an impressive national structure of coordination to deal with terrorism"

---

1 http://security. homeoffice. gov. uk/counterterrorism-strategy/about the strategy
2 http://security. homeoffice. gov. uk/counterterrorism-strategy/about the strategy
3 http://security. homeoffice. gov. uk/counterterrorism-strategy/about the strategy
4 http://security. homeoffice. gov. uk/counterterrorism-strategy/about the strategy
5 Frank Gregory and Paul Wilkinson, Riding Pillion for Tackling Terrorism is a high risk policy. London: Chatham House. ISP/NSC Briefing Paper 05/01. p. 3.

but on the Prevention, Pursuit and Protection and Preparations, they commented that "these broad principles seem eminently sensible but its implementation is problematic in particular areas. A key problem with regard to implementing 'Prevention' and 'Pursuit' is that the UK government has been conducting counter terrorism policy 'shoulder to shoulder' with the US, not in the sense of being an equal decision-maker, but rather as pillion passenger compelled to leave the steering to the ally in the driving seat.... achieving the goals of protection and preparedness in the UK is also not an easy task.[6]

There is no doubt that the counter terrorism strategy was a difficult task and all these preventive measures were necessary. This will not succeed unless Muslims are made the 'pillion passenger' with its first ally (the British Government).

It seemed that most of these counter-terrorism strategies were based on the past experience of the authorities with the IRA which had haunted Britain for many years. But radical Muslim fundamentalism was a very different kind of terrorism for it had religious and not nationalist legitimations. Even the tactic of terrorism used was different from the IRA which had not produced suicide bombers. Recently the agreements between the IRA and the Protestants were made but that was not easy with the Muslim Fundamentalist groups. As Gregory and Wilkinson commented

Al-Qaeda, which is best described as a movement or a network of networks and affiliates with a presence in at least 60 countries, confronts the US and its allies and the whole international system with the most dangerous form of terrorist threat ever posed by non-state actors. Unlike the most traditional terrorists groups formed in the 1970s and 1980s, Al-Qaeda explicitly promotes mass killing, and the 9/11 attacks together with their major assaults in Kenya, Bali, Iraq, Saudi Arabia, Morocco to carrying out deadly and determined attacks wherever and whenever the opportunity arises. The UK is at particular risk because it is the strongest ally of the United States, and has deployed armed forces in the military campaigns to topple the Taliban regime in Afghanistan and in Iraq; and its intelligence services have also been accused of aiding the CIA for using British airports to take its prisoners to Guantanamo Bay. All this negatively reflects the images of Britain.

Moreover, it is well known that radical extremists have been recruited and deployed within the UK's borders and that in an open society such as the UK it is notoriously difficult to prevent it for no-warning comes from suicide attacks, which is the characteristic modus operandi of Al-Qaeda. The attacks on the transport system in London on 7 July 2005 gives an example of the nature of the threat from international terrorism that the UK authorities have been concerned about since 9/11. Furthermore, it is also known that the Al-Qaeda network has been actively seeking the materials and expertise to acquire chemical, biological, radiological and nuclear (CBRN) weaponry, and they may sometimes succeed in acquiring it.[7]

One can see how complex the new kind of terrorism threatening Britain is. Dealing with this new kind of terrorism by force would be ineffective. For example, after 9/11 the US declared its War on Terrorism on Afghanistan. It succeeded in its 'regime change' policy as Mullah Omar was removed. All of them, Mullah Omar, Bin Laden and other terrorists went into hiding. The US collaborated with Pakistan and a number of terrorists were arrested or killed or deported for trials to the USA. This approach of the US War on Terrorism, if evaluated from 9/11 till 2007, has still not demolished the Al-Qaeda and while President Bush and Prime Minister Blair are going out of their offices, Bin Laden, Mullah Omar and Ayman Zawahiri are still in hiding and running the terrorist groups and becoming more dangerous. In fact, the so-called terrorism 'experts' seem to be ignorant of the fact that the more sophisticated the

---

6   Ibid., p. 3.

7   Ibid., p. 2

'preventative' measures become, the more 'sophisticated' terrorists tactics are becoming to cope and bypass these measures .

When the authorities finally became aware of the need to engage with the Muslim community in Britain, Blair raised 12 points to combats radicalism which in the words of Johnston were:

i.   New grounds for deporting undesirables, closing bookshops, negotiating memorandums of understanding with countries to take deportees. ....

ii.   To create offence of condoning or glorifying terrorism here or abroad...

iii.   To refuse asylum automatically to anyone who has participated in terrorism anywhere...

iv.   To consult on powers to strip citizenship and make procedures simpler and more effective...

v.   Maximum time limit o future extradition cases involving terror suspects...

vi.   To examine court procedures to allow pre-trial process; to consider allowing detention to terrorist suspects before charging to be significantly extended...

vii.   To extend the use of control orders for those who are British nationals and cannot be deported...

viii.   To expand court capacity to deal with control orders and other related issues...

ix.   To proscribe Hizb-ut-Tahrir and successor organization al-Muhajiroun and to examine grounds for proscription to widen them...

x.   Set new threshold for citizenship; to establish with the Muslim community a commission on integration...

xi.   New powers to close mosques...

xii.   Securing borders, new visa controls and biometric visas.[8]

An assessment of the 12 point strategy was that "little has come out of it."[9] Blair has also set up a "Muslim task force" and a Labour party peer Lord Ahmed commented that it had achieved "virtually nothing."[10] While all of Blair's policies to combat terrorism have failed the new British government under the Prime Minister Gordon Brown seems to be 'putting more emphasis on winning the battle of ideas while also being tough on security'. A cabinet source explained that

> Gordon Brown believes that this is an ideological war akin to the Cold war. He has directed ministers to come up with ideas by which we can engage minority groups better and make them feel more part of the UK. A senior government source said 'we can't win the battle of hearts and minds from Whitehall: it can be won only in local community but we can provide more support and strategic leadership.[11]

The new government's thinking is correct for its policies can be effective provided the new approach effectively engages in the 'ideological war' which was briefly discussed in the introduction.

The present government of Gordon Brown will be creating a border force, checking all passengers coming into Britain or travelling abroad electronically---but the July 7 bombers were mainly British born from within the country—so will all Muslims be checked daily through

---

8 Philip Johnston, So whatever happened to Blair's anti-terror strategy? The Daily Telegraph. July 3, 2007. p. 6

9 Gadher, D., The Battle for Hearts and Minds, The Sunday Times, July 8, 2007, p. 14

10 Ibid., p. 14.

11 Ibid., p. 14.

electronics in their daily lives? That will not succeed. What will succeed is the 'ideological' and not 'electronic' war and that will be the eradicative strategy of combating terrorism because it has to be a battle for the hearts and minds of Muslims in Britain.

The Eradicative Approach

The eradicative approach has to engage with the Muslim community. The Blair government was also engaged with the Muslim community but its policies failed for it lacked insights into the Muslim community. According to Sayeda Warsi, the Shadow Community minister "the government failed" because "it didn't engage wider and deeper to develop a true understanding of the Muslim community choosing instead to listen to self-appointed leaders" which were considered 'the usual suspects' such as members of the Muslim Council of Britain". [12] Furthermore, according to "Hassan Butt, a former Jihadi, 'most Muslim institutions in Britain just don't want to talk about theology'. They refuse to broach the difficult and often complex truth that Islam can be interpreted as condoning violence against the unbeliever.... scholars must go back to the books and come forward with a refreshed set of rules and revised understanding of the rights and responsibilities of Muslims."[13] These observations are insightful and have to be taken seriously.

The new British government may still find it difficult to understand how to devise the eradicative approach. If they follow the 'usual suspects' mentioned by the Sayeda Warsi, the policies will fail. The reason why Blair's government's communication with the 'usual suspects' failed is that they came under criticism for they belonged to some of the specific Islamic sects. The government has never thought about which sects they are dealing with. Islam like any other religion also has sects and some, not all, people of the sect have become radicalised so one needs to understand the sectarian politics.

Muslims have to be differentiated from each other on the basis of the sects they belong to. Although Islam is a monolithic faith and the Muslims are trying to reconstruct the doctrine of Ummah (Community of Islam) but the existence of sects has divided Muslims into groups such as Sunnis and Shiites as two major sects. Each of the two is divided further into minor sects. To understand Islam then one has classify it into two kinds of divisions emerging from all the sects as Enlightened Islam and Conservative Islam. The foundation of Enlightened Islam was the love of God. Muslims followed the Sunnah (Practice) of the Prophet and tried to cultivate the depth of love for God and His Prophet. The reason why the label of Enlightenment Islam has been used is because one of the most important attributes of God mentioned in the Qur'an was to perceive Him as Light (Nur) and if any Muslims had cultivated depth of love for God in their hearts, the nearer they were to God, the more chance they had of becoming enlightened from God's Nur. This kind of enlightenment expressed itself through their talents and creativity of Muslims which was the instrumental factor for the emergence of the Islamic civilization known as the 'Golden age' of medieval Muslim history.

The inspirational thinking from enlightenment was the gift from God to His believers and the Muslim made original contributions in the field of sciences, philosophy, arts and literature etc. If one reads the Masnawi of Jalaleddin Rumi, one will realises that it was his depth of love of God which inspired the masterpiece. But during the course of history a number of reactionary sects emerged like Wahhabism in the 18th century which damned Enlightened

12 Ibid., p. 14.
13 Ibid., p. 14.

Islam and did not accept any reverence for the Prophet and just gave literal interpretations of Qur'an. A number of other sects which followed the Wahhabism of Saudi Arabian origin were Salafism from Egypt and Deobandism from South Asia etc. What needs to be understood is that all these sects dominate the contemporary Muslim world and are part of radical conservative Islam.

In their locations in various parts of the Muslim world Conservative Islam started its struggle with the contextual factors of politics which it did not accept and developed sub-sectarian versions of Islam which emerged as Islamic fundamentalism. Their struggle was to convert the nation-states into Islamic states and the use of violence became its tactics for eliminating its enemies. One may be confused as to what were the sub-sectarian interpretations of the sects. These sub-sectarian interpretations used Islam to fulfil their ambitions of Fundamentalist leaders and their movements to obtain power. In order to achieve power it engaged in extremist tactics of terror. Three names can be given as examples of those who distorted their sects' through their sub-sectarian interpretations as, Bin-Laden, a Wahhabi who distorted his sect's concepts; Ayman Zawahiri, who did the same from his sect of Salafism and Mullah Omar who also did the same from his sect of Deobandism---all of them creating a base (Al-Qaeda) for declaring war on the West and killing innocent persons including Muslims anywhere in the world through terrorist tactics. All this falls under the category of Fundamentalist Islam which emerged from Conservative Islam. The Muslim community in Britain comprises of people belonging to both Enlightened and Conservative Islam and understanding this sectarian politics is important if the authorities want to combat terrorism in Britain. What needs to be made clear is that combating terrorism is not combating any sect but their sub-sectarian distortions which have produced illusionary and delusionary interpretations to attract recruits for terrorism.

Fundamentalist Islam considers the West as the land of the *kuffar* (infidels) and the whole country to be *dar al harb* (land of war). An important point to be understood here again is that not all the people belonging to the Conservative sects are terrorist but only those who have turned towards Fundamentalist Islam and they could then become potential terrorists and vulnerable to blindly accepting the sub-sectarian persuasions and recruitments from Al-Qaeda or other groups. How does this kind of conversions take place is beyond the purview of this paper but suffice to say that most of the terrorists produced in Britain have all come from Fundamentalist Islam irrespective of whichever sect they belonged. This is where the British government faces the problem of detecting terrorism for it is an internal problem among the Muslim community. The Intelligence agencies cannot be blamed for failure in detecting terrorists for such kind of detection is even difficult for the Muslims from their communities.

The choice which the new British government has is to decide which Muslim group they should work with. If they decide to work with the people from the Enlightened Islam unlike the last government who worked with Muslims from Conservative Islam they would have a better strategy for combating terrorism. There is no doubt that the views of Enlightened Islam would be the best if eradication of terrorism in Britain is the objective through 'ideological war'. But the British government may have reservations in pursuing an ideological war openly for the Wahhabi state of Saudi Arabia will disagree. The last government had to shelve the BAE investigation of bribery on the basis of its being a threat to national security---which meant that it would not please Saudi Arabia. In its war on terrorism it will have to decide how far its battle of ideas will have to go to. This is a problem of the British government and not the Muslim community.

On the other hand, people from radical conservative Islam are not terrorists but when the sub-sectarian versions of their sects from abroad enter into the minds of the BBMs and make them think of taking terrorist actions then they will have to discredit it which is not being done. This process of discreditation has to start to prevent such sub-sectarian ideas preventing the minds of the BBMs and to be effective the whole Muslim community will have to be made aware of how to combat terrorism by discovering its sources from within communities settled in various cities of Britain. This is a battle of ideas and such sub-sectarian groups are circulating in the world and are building their bridges to penetrate British society to fulfil their objective of global terrorism. It is the contention of this paper that Enlightened Islam will help eradicate terrorism through winning the minds and hearts of lay Muslims.

The Islamic Solution

The radical fundamentalists cannot convince the followers of Enlightened Islam that terrorism is the right strategy for it is considered correctly to be outside the pail of Islam itself. So the authorities have to officially think of how to engage with Islam to project its authentic world-view. The world-view of Islam can be best projected through Muslim faith-based leaders, scholars and opinion-makers, such as Fethullah Gülen.

All Muslims may know the name of the radical fundamentalist thinkers—all of whom are either dead of being hunted like Bin Laden and Ayman Zawahiri--- but if they were asked to give the name of one Islamic thinker of Enlightened Islam in the contemporary world, they would struggle. This is the challenge facing the Muslim community, the British government and terrorism experts: how can authentic Islam (Enlightened) overcome inauthentic Islam (Radical Fundamentalism). Inauthentic Islam can never be eradicated unless a new strategy emerges to combat inauthentic interpretations with authentic interpretations and it will have more credibility through the writings of a contemporary Islamic scholar and thinker like Mr. Fethullah Gülen.

Mr. Fethullah Gülen is from Turkey but his nationality does not matter for his world view of Islam is the authentic Islamic interpretation to discredit and combat terrorism. The Fundamentalists have begun to regard Islam only as a political instrument and not spiritual and many studies on Islam label it as 'Political Islam' as if nothing else from the faith emerges. This is a false assumption for as Yilmaz has observed "Islam, for Gülen, is not a political project to be implemented. It is a repository of discourse and practice for the evaluation of a just and ethical society."[14] He reiterates that Islam as a religion should not be reduced to being a political party identity. He is very critical of the 'instrumentalisation' of religion in politics:

> When those who have adopted Islam as a political ideology rather than a religion in its true sense and function, review their activities and attitudes they claim to be based on Islam, especially political ones, will discover that they are usually moved by personal or national anger, hostility, and other similar motives… A Muslim's beginning point must have an Islamic basis. In the present situation, Muslims cannot act out of ideological or political partisanship and then dress this partisanship in Islamic garb, or represent mere desires in the form of ideas. If we can overcome this tendency, Islam's true image will become known.[15]

Gülen's views have little to do with seeking political power or even traditional Islam but

---

14 Yilmaz (2003), p. 225.
15 http://en.fGülen.com/content/view/1336/13/

rather have more in common with Max Weber's ideas about "worldly asceticism." It is based on a paradox because it includes a critical rejection of the world while simultaneously calling for involvement in the world in rationally structured activities. These activities include the building of schools instead of mosques, investing in secular education instead of religious instruction, encouraging economic enterprises and requiring them to invest in education, encouraging educational and economic enterprises to support each other, promoting individual and collective self-criticism, and supporting critically minded planning for future projects.[16]

Islam is a faith which follows the middle path and not extremists paths which the Fundamentalists are following. For Gülen "Islam, being the 'middle way' of absolute balance---balance between materialism and spiritualism, between rationalism and mysticism, between worldliness and excessive asceticism, between the world and the next--- and inclusive ways of all the previous prophets makes a choice according to the situation."[17] The Fundamentalists are either ignorant or deliberately ignore that Islam is a religion of middle way. This is the world-view of Islam which needs to be taught.

The writings of radical fundamentalists are polemical and they do not even know how to engage in discourse or believe in *ijtihad* (independent reasoning) whereas "Gülen's perception of Islam is not based on an abstract model that excludes reinterpretation and thus other interpretations, but it is open to experiences—to the cultural accumulation of this world. Gülen believes that there is a need for ijtihad in our age. He says that he respects the scholars of the past but also believes that ijtihad is a necessity because to freeze ijtihad means to imprison Islam in a given time and space."[18] He puts that:

> Taking the Qur'an and Sunna as our main sources and respecting the great people of the past, in the consciousness that we are all children of time, we must question the past and present. I am looking for labourers of thought and researchers to establish the necessary balance between the constant and changing aspects of Islam and, considering such juridical rules as abrogation, particularization, generalization, and restriction, who can present Islam to the modern understanding.[19]

Muslims have lost their civilization because there is not ijtihad but reliance on taqlid. In modern times, one of the areas that motivates ijtihad is the situation of Muslims in non-Muslim polities. The juristic discourse with regard to such issues as whether Muslims may reside in a non-Muslim polity and under what circumstances, the relationships of these Muslims to Dar al-Islam, and the ethical and legal duties that these Muslims owe both to Muslim law and to their host non-Muslim polity (*dar al-harb*) have been debated since the eighth century.[20] In this regard, Yilmaz explains Gülen's frequently used term *dar al-hizmet* (country of service to humanity) is a new co-existential concept, reflecting his vision:

> If one's intention is to serve Islam by presenting a good example, then one can stay wherever one desires, says Abdullah Aymaz, former editor in chief of the daily Zaman and Gülen's close friend and colleague for more than thirty years. Gülen stresses that wherever a Muslim is, even outside a Muslim polity, he or she has to obey the lex loci, to respect others' rights and to be just, and has to

---

16 Elisabeth Ozdalga, 'Worldly Asceticism in Islamic Casting: Fethullah Gülen's Inspired Piety and Activism,' Critique, 17 (2000): 84–104.

17 Quoted in Ahmet Kuru, Fethullah Gülen's Search for a Middle Way between Modernity and Muslim tradition in M Hakan Yavuz and John Esposito (ed) Turkish Islam and the Secular State: The Gülen Movement. Syracuse: Syracuse University Press. 2003. p. 117.

18 Yilmaz (2003), p. 221.

19 Unal and Williams 2005: 53.

20 Yilmaz 2003: 234-235.

disregard discussions of dar al-harb and dar al-Islam. In Gülen's understanding, Ummah is more of a transnational socio-cultural entity, not a politico-legal one. He hopes that this socio-cultural entity will be instrumental in bringing general universal peace. He formulates a project of cooperation between Islam and the West to reach this desired, almost utopian, universal peace.[21]

Gülen's whole life has been full of teaching, preaching and writing books on Islam in spite of the fact that he comes from a country which follows the path of secularization.

Millions inspired by Gülen put his discourse into practice all over the world. The greatest advantage in the prospect of achieving this is that Gülen has an alim background. It is true that he is an influential leader but he is first of all an expert of Islamic theology (*kalam*), Qur'anic exegesis (*tafsir*), science of *hadith* (*usul-u hadith*) and Islamic jurisprudence (*fiqh*).[22]

Gülen has followed the tasawwuf tradition of Enlightenment Islam and also tried to "address the spiritual needs of the people, to educate the masses and to provide stability in times of turmoil."[23] The Fundamentalists all react to modernity and have produced reactionary thinkers against the West. They fear that Modernity with its westernization and secularization may penetrate the Muslim world. But what they do not think is that it will penetrate their worlds only if they have not alternatives and since they have no solutions from Fundamentalism to fulfil the vacuums, it is not surprising why Western modernization is entering the Muslim world. With all the Fundamentalist show raging in the Muslim world they have not produced an Islamic civilization. According to Piricky,

> Muslim responses to the challenges of our post-modern age are often described in terms of various fundamentalism: The widespread Western view of Islam as a religion conducive to mass anti-Western mobilization is nevertheless one-dimensional, ahistorical and unjust…outside the fundamentalist orientation an Islamic modernism also exists."[24] Islamic modernism has to give the Islamic touch which Gülen has given which makes thinkers like him as being the most important for the Muslim world to develop itself. Thinkers like Gülen "present Islam not as dogmatic religion but as a system which is able to cope with the changes in society and challenges of our new era.[25]

Through his sermons, teachings, books and activities, Gülen has inspired a whole generation in Turkey and abroad. For the peaceful world of the future, Gülen encourages his admirers to establish educational institutions in and outside of Turkey. Gülen's sympathisers are active participants in their society and perform public service by establishing schools and hospitals. Rumi's spirit of love, compassion, tolerance, acceptance of the other, socio-cultural activism and education as the most important method of social innovation to tackle ignorance and improve dialogue lives in the thought of Gülen[26]:

> … if we exclude certain periods and individuals, the Turks' interpretation of what Islam allows to be interpreted is correct and positive. If we can spread globally the Islamic understanding of such heroes of love as Niyazi-i Misri, Yunus Emre, and Rumi, if we can extend their messages of love, dialogue, and tolerance to those thirsty for this message, everyone will run toward the embrace of

---

21 Yilmaz 2003: 234-235.

22 Yilmaz, 2007, Social Innovation.

23 Bulent Aras and Omer Caha, Fethullah Gülen and his Liberal Turkish Islam. MERIA: Middle East Review of International Affairs. Vol. 4. No. 4. 2000. p. 10.

24 Gabriel Piricky, Some observations on New Identities in Modernist interpretations of Islam in Contemporary Turkey: Fethullah Glen Cemaati. Asian and African Studies. Vol. 8. No 1. 1999, p. 83.

25 Piricky, p. 86

26 Yilmaz, 2007, Social Innovation.

love, peace, and tolerance that we represent.[27]Those who perceive religion as being contradictory to science and reason are the afflicted; they are unaware of the spirit of both religion and reason. Moreover, it is absolutely fraudulent to hold religion responsible for clashes between different sections of society. Conflicts between peoples and groups of people arise from ignorance, from ambition for personal advantage and profit, or from the vested interests of particular groups, parties, or classes. Religion neither approves nor condones such qualities and ambitions.[28] In a world becoming more and more globalised, we are trying to get to know those who will be our future neighbours.... One of the most important factors here is to eliminate factors that separate people... such as discrimination based on colour, race, belief, and ethnicity.... Education can uproot these evils. ...We are trying our best to do this.[29]

The community's enthusiasm for establishing secular schools in both the Muslim and non-Muslim world, specifically schools serving people of all faiths and nationalities, is unprecedented among almost all faith-based groups and movements, thus, socially innovative.[30] The movement's schools are non-denominational and follow the national curriculum of the country in which they are based. Many scholars have observed that the Gülen schools endeavour to combine excellence in teaching with the instruction of good morals.[31]

The Gülen movement is presenting a renewed Rumi practice of that emphasise love, mutual respect, understanding, socio-cultural activism, education, social innovation, peaceful coexistence, dialogue and cooperation with all for a cohesive society.[32] With the help of the schools in about 100 countries in North, East, West and South, all over the world, many people, not only Muslims, are getting a good and quality education in a multicultural, multi-faith environment with English primary language of instruction so that in future they will continue to be open to dialogue and they will hopefully attain good socio-economic status within their societies.[33]

Gülen also pioneered in the establishment of the Journalists and Writers Foundation in 1994, the activities of which to promote dialogue and tolerance among all strata of the society receive warm welcome from almost all walks of life. Fethullah Gülen is the Honorary President of the Foundation. The Foundation also works as a think-tank in related issues. The movement tries to bring all scholars and intellectuals regardless of their ethnic, ideological, religious and cultural backgrounds. The Journalists and Writers Foundation also works as a think-tank in related issues. The Abant Platform is a result of the attempt at finding solutions to Turkey's problems by bringing together scholars and intellectuals of all colours. This platform is the first of its kind in near Turkish history where intellectuals could agree to disagree on sensitive issues as laicism, secularism, religion, and reason relations. The Abant Platform is a result of the attempt at finding solutions to Turkey's and world's problems by bringing together scholars and intellectuals of all colours. The Foundation organizes Abant Conventions annually. In

---

27 Gülen, Love and Essence of Human Being, p. 29.

28 http://en.fGülen.com/content/view/1958/12/

29 Ünal and Williams 2000: 329–331.

30 Yilmaz, 2007, Social Innovation.

31 Mandaville states that "in the case of Turkey's Gülen movement... we find elements of Sufi spirituality fused with socio-economic liberalism in a highly successful transnational educational project. Dozens of Gülen-sponsored schools, emphasizing a modernist curriculum against a backdrop of 'non-invasive' Islamic morality, now operate throughout much of the Balkans and Central Asia", Peter Mandaville (2003) "What does progressive Islam look like?". Isim Newsletter. Leiden: ISIM. 33-34. p.34.

32 Yilmaz, 2007, Social Innovation.

33 Yilmaz, 2007, Social Innovation.

2007, the Abant Convention's theme was Alevies in Turkey.[34]

Interfaith dialogue all over the world is on the agenda of the movement. In the countries where they reside utilizing the concept of dar al-hizmet (country of service to humanity), they either establish interfaith organizations, associations and societies or they are in close contact with the men of faith. Thus, for instance, Turkish businessmen in Korea take the Buddhist priests to Turkey to visit historical places where believers of different faiths had lived peacefully. Or, in Thailand, administrators of Fatih College regularly visit Buddhist authorities and priests and report to them the progress of the Thai pupils. In Russia, Romania, Georgia, South Africa, Senegal and so on the theme is the same. They all believe that interfaith and intercultural dialogue is a must to reach a general universal peace (*sulh-u umumi*) and that the first step in establishing it is forgetting the past, ignoring polemical arguments, and giving precedence to common points.[35]

These developments also have led to the establishment of new institutions like the Dialogue Society established in 1998 in London. Through these charities, these volunteers initiate and engage in interfaith and intercultural dialogue with people of different faiths, backgrounds, and cultures. They have been organising events to commemorate Rumi or by hosting whirling dervishes events. Only in the United Kingdom, the Dialogue Society organizes several whirling dervishes programmes each year in perhaps ten different cities of the country, including but not limited to the famous Wembley Arena, Oxford University's Ashmolian Theatre and Hackney Empire.[36]

Gülen strongly emphasizes that acts of violence against innocent civilians including women and children are inhumane. He categorically and without any reservation condemns killing of innocent civilians, elderly, women and children. The following is an excerpt from his condemnation message which was published in Washington Post and New York Times right after the tragedy of 9/11:

> Any terrorist activity, no matter who it is committed by and for whatever purpose, is the greatest blow against peace, democracy and humanity. For this reason, terrorist activities can by no means be approved of. Terror cannot be a means for independence, nor a legitimate route to salvation. The recent terrorist activity, which is by far the most bloody and catastrophic to date, is a sabotage against not only the United States of America but also against world peace and the universal democratic and humanistic values. The perpetrators of this act cannot be but the most brutal of all.

> Terrorism cannot be a means for any Islamic goal, and a terrorist cannot be a Muslim, nor can a true Muslim be a terrorist. Islam orders peace and a true Muslim can only be a symbol of peace and the maintenance of basic human rights. Islam preaches that if there are ten people on board a vessel of whom one is innocent and nine guilty of a criminal act, then the ship may not be sunk in view of punishing the guilty for there is amongst them one innocent. Any right, whatever it's nature, is respected in Islam and it cannot be violated. The right of an individual cannot be violated in the interest of the community. The Qur'an, Islam's sacred Book, declares that one who takes a life unjustly is as if he/she took the lives of all humankind, and that one who saves a life is as if he/she saved the lives of all. In the words of our Prophet, a Muslim is one from who comes no harm, neither from his/her tongue nor hand.

> I strongly condemn the recent terrorist attack on the United States. It is worthy of nothing but condemnation and hatred, and all in the world must condemn it.

---

34 Yilmaz, 2007, Social Innovation.
35 Yilmaz, 2003.
36 www.dialoguesociety.org

I assure the American people that I pray to God Almighty for the victims and share their pain and sorrow from the bottom of my heart. May God give them with patience (Washington Post, September 13, 2001).

Gülen also clearly stated his condemnation of Bin Laden, his accomplices and their actions:

Bin Laden is among the persons in this world that I hate most. Because he has defaced the beautiful face of Islam. He has produced a dirty image. Even if we work on repairing the terrible damage he has caused with all our power, it will take years. We shall speak on every platform everywhere. We shall write books. We shall declare "this is not Islam". Bin Laden replaced Islamic logic with his own desires and wishes and lives as a monster. The men around him are like that as well. If there are people who think like that, they are also locked into monstrosity. We equivocally condemn their perspective.[37]

On this point, Özdalga notes:

Gülen is not suggesting any radically different or heterodox interpretation of Islam, but adopts a solid, conventional Hanafi/Sunni understanding of the religious traditions. So it does not seem to be the content of the religious interpretation as such, but the very existence of a new relatively strong group, filled with religious fervour and claiming a place in the public arena that annoys the establishment in Turkey radical margins who see this as a threat to their ideology. This new element is perceived as being an anomic force, a force that challenges the norms and values, the order of the established hegemonic elite community. Thus, it is not religion per se that is at the root of the conflict. On the contrary, religion has been used as a "false ideology" to displace the real threat. From the Established-Outsider perspective, the key to the problem seems to lie in the threat posed to the existing power balance and established status hierarchy.[38]

The Islamic radical do not study their own civilization history and have focused only on the Caliphate history. They draw the models of their 'Islamic state' from the Caliphate and this is not leading Muslims anywhere for it is based on following the past while the world is changing. According to Gülen "Regardless of changes, advancement in science and technology, and new ways of thinking, the feeling of attachment to a religion always has been the primary factor in forming humanity's scientific and intellectual life, developing human virtues and establishing new civilization with its charm and power, religion is still and will be the most influential element and power in people's lives."[39] As a power in the lives of Muslims Islam created Islamic civilization which emerged to the surface from the 8th till 16th century. It was creative and powerful and it even influenced the West in those times by its knowledge. [40] What is the position of the Muslim world in contemporary times? It is living in a post-Islamic civilization world and the Muslims are lost and confused and for that reason they have been easily persuaded towards fundamentalist thinking assuming that this might regain their lost world.

Gülen's thinking then poses this challenge to the Muslims to develop their selves within their faith and become a powerful innovator of Islamic civilization. It is not surprising then why some Western scholars regard Gülen as "one of the major figures in defining the contemporary global Islamic experience… his work helps to redefine the nature of Islamic discourse in

---

37 Akman, N., Zaman, March 22-April 1, 2004.
38 Ozdalga, Redeemer or Outsider, Muslim World, 2005, pp. 441-442.
39 Voll, pp. 245-246.
40 Eugene Myers, Arabic Thought and the Western world in the Golden Age of Islam. New York: Frederick Ungar Publishing company, 1964.

the contemporary world."[41] Voll observes that

in the clashing vision of globalization Fethullah Gülen is a force in the development of the Islamic discourse of globalised multicultural pluralism. As the impact of the educational activities of those influenced by him attests, his vision bridges modern and postmodern, global and local, and has a significant influence in the contemporary debate that shape the visions of the future of Muslims and non-Muslims alike.[42]

It is this kind of vision from the Islamic world view that has to be internalized by Muslims living in the West. Muslims who hate the Western countries in which they live are vulnerable to Fundamentalist Islam and its sub-sectarian interpretations. It is therefore important to change such Muslims' Fundamentalist world vision to Gülenic world vision of Islam because the "Gülen movement deserves careful study…not just because of the quality of Gülen's ideas but also because it represents one of the few such progressives and inclusive mass-based civil society movement in the world."[43] Gülen believes that Islam is a religion of peace and wherever there were conflicts in countries like Albania, Kosovo, Macedonia, the Philippines, Banda Aceh, Northern Iraq Gülen addressed the problems of ethnic and religious conflicts. His movement opened hundreds of schools for education both in Turkey and abroad for he believed that education for Muslims was necessary for people to have more knowledge. [44]

Gülen also believes strongly in interfaith cooperation and dialogue. He developed relations with Pope John Paul II of the Catholic faith; Patriarch Bartholomew I, the Spiritual leader of Orthodox Christians as well as the Chief Rabbi of Israel "to develop interfaith cooperation on various issues in order to bring peace."[45] Most Muslims from Conservative Islam do not want to have any relations with other faiths. Developing an understanding and respect for other faiths is extremely important when Muslims are living in Britain or other Western countries. Most believers of Conservative Islam do not do this nor want to know about other faiths except their own which is why it is important to make them aware of other faiths from the Islamic point of view. Gülen is very clear about this and states that

Islam recognizes all religions previous to it. It accepts all the prophets and books sent to different epochs of history. Not only does it accept them but also regards belief in them as an essential principle of being Muslim. By doing this it acknowledges the basic unity of all religions.[46]

One of the most important ways of being the ambassador of Islam in the public arena is the development of one's Self of the Muslims with honour and dignity and above all, credibility. This kind of development of their Islamic self identities has to emerge from their spiritually. Gülen's understanding of what kind of Islamic identities Muslims should develop is very important for every Muslim and it means that

True Muslims are people of safety and trust, so much so that other Muslims can turn their backs on

---

41   John Voll, Fethullah Gülen: Transcending Modernity in the New Islamic Discourse in M. Hakan Yavuz and John L. Esposito (Ed) Turkish Islam and Secular state: The Gülen Movement. Syracuse: Syracuse: NJ. University Press. 2003. p238.

42   Voll, p. 247.

43   Paper by Greg Barton, Progressive Islam's thought, Civil Society and the Gülen movement in the national context: Parallels with Indonesia. 8 November 2005, p. 2

44   Zeki Saritoprak, Peace and Non-Violence: A Turkish experience. The Muslim World. Vol. 95. N0. 3, 2005, p. 8.

45   Saritoprak, p. 8.

46   Ihsan Yilmaz, Ijtihad and Tajdid by Conduct: The Gülen Movement in M. Hakan Yavuz and J. L. Esposito. Turkish Islam and the Secular State. Syracuse. Syracuse University Press, 2003. p. 230.

them without doubt or suspicion. They can entrust a family member to such people without fear, for that person will be absolutely safe from the Muslims' hand or tongue. If they attend a gathering together, the person can leave in full confidence that no one will gossip about him or her, and neither will he or she have to listen to gossip about others. Such Muslim are as sensitive to the dignity and honour of other people as they are to their own. They do not eat; they feed others. They do not live; they enable others to live. They will even sacrifice spiritual pleasure for others.[47]

Furthermore, as Saritoprak comments "the victory for Gülen is the spiritual..... He also gives an example from history saying, 'Tariq bin Ziyad the Muslim conqueror of Spain, was victorious not because he defeated the army of the Spaniards, but because of his self-sacrificing when he stood before wealth and said "Be careful Tariq! You were a slave yesterday; today you are a victorious commander; tomorrow you will be under the earth;' In Gülen's teaching, spiritual strength was much more powerful than Tariq's military victory. These are the things that make the theology of non-violence essential in Gülen's understanding. According to Gülen, love is an undefeated weapon, and love for others will bring sacrifice and service to others. Sacrificing oneself for the service of others is an essential part of his teaching. He says that heroes are those who do not live for themselves but live for others. An attribute of peace in Gülen's teaching is compassion and love---not only towards humans, but also towards animals".[48] Muslims have to develop these kinds of identities for radical fundamentalists have demonized Islam with its terrorist actions. Living in Britain with this worldview of Islam, not only the image of Islam will redefine itself in the minds of non-Muslims but Muslims themselves will be considered as assets as 'golden' people who once belonged to the 'Golden age' mentioned earlier. If we can promote the Gülen understanding of what it means to be a Muslim and convert Muslims to authentic Islam, then we will not only save 'Islam' from the clutches of terrorist ideology and rhetoric but also facilitate constructive citizenship among Muslim communities in Britain.

Conclusion

A brief exposition of the authentic Islamic thinking of Fethullah Gülen has been provided in this paper. Clearly his views and school of thought need to be read and made accessible in Britain. Muslims will not react or reject to Gülen's teachings and views since they are not from outside the fold of Islam but from within. The fact that the Gülen movement have not succeeded in spreading their views in the Muslim world to date is because they are not funded by petro-dollar states like Saudi Arabia.

From what has been discussed in this paper some facts which specialists on terrorism or policy makers may not be aware of should be clearly understood. First, preventive measures of terrorism will never be effective when eradicative measures are not given any attention. Eradicative measures reinforce preventive measures and will make it effective to achieve its ends. Secondly, engagement with predictive measures is complex and if corrective approaches are not taken, then it will fail. The sub-sectarian interpretations of Islam are the virus that causes terrorism. They have to be detected and measures have to be taken to eradicate it.

Thirdly, if one embarks on the path to eradicate the virus of terrorism which is emerging from various sects then engagement with Islam becomes necessary. But any engagement with

---

47 Zeki Saritoprak, Peace and Non-Violence: A Turkish experience. The Muslim World. Vol. 95. N0. 3, 2005, pp. 8-9.

48 Zeki Saritoprak, Peace and Non-Violence: A Turkish experience. The Muslim World. Vol. 95. N0. 3, 2005, p. 11.

Islam has to make clear which perspective of Islam one is supporting as the Wahhabi state of Saudi Arabia will be mainly supporting Wahhabi sects; the Shiite state or Iran will be mainly supporting Shiite sects so the engagement discussed above will have to make clear that it is supporting the Sufi sects. Since Fethullah Gülen is the only major thinker of the Sufi tradition in the contemporary Muslim world, then his views must be supported. Some may argue that because he is a Turk why has Turkey not supported him. The answer is that Turkey is a laicist state and does not support any of its great Islamic thinkers like other Muslim countries do. This is the reason why many Muslims from the Sufi tradition may not know about him but about great Sufi thinkers of their past histories. But Fethullah Gülen's interpretation does not contradict any of the past history of the Sufi tradition for it is authentic Islam whose characteristic is not to use Islam for personal motives but for helping humanity.

Lastly, to discover Fethullah Gülen's views is one thing. But to eradicate terrorism it has to be implemented. In order to do this some steps have to be taken which are suggested in the specific recommendations. For translating Gülen's views into action in Britain has to be done in a sophisticated manner.

Recommendations

i. The British government has to come out openly in its support for Islam as one of the great faiths of the world. Misinformation and disinformation has spread, equating Islam with terrorism and this has to be rebutted by all politicians including the Prime Minister and other policy makers. The last Prime minister as well as the American president had made positive statements about Islam but it was done just once or twice. Since the war on terrorism is being fought every day and since it focuses on the Muslim terrorists, it is not surprising that the Global War on Terrorism (GWOT) has been interpreted by terrorist organizations as being war on Islam. Recently, the British government has realized this and advised that the term GWOT should not be used. This is a good step but what is being recommended here is that all governments and authorities involved should make it much more clear that they do not consider Islam to be responsible in any shape or form for the terrorism of some extremist groups. Since GWOT is ongoing should the frequency of this message until common Muslims are convinced that this is not a war against Muslims and that they are as much the victims of this plague as everyone else. It is this kind of projection which is not coming out of the government.

ii. Why the first step is necessary is because the governments cannot combat terrorism with preventive measures unless it joins hand with the Muslim community. The Muslim community will not join hands with the British government if it suspects it of being anti-Islamic. The credibility of the government has been at stake, as stated above for its GWOT has been considered as being a war on Islam. The past history of Britain from the Crusades to Colonialism has not been positive with Islam. Its recent award of knighthood to Salman Rushdie has in fact reinforced the view of its being anti-Islamic. Although the award was given for his contribution to South Asian literature, those who recommended it did not think what its political repercussions will be in the Muslim world. Their ignorance produced consequences that it not only effected the national security of Britain(for threat was made against Britain and the Queen by Al-Qaeda) but Ayatollah Khomeini's fatwa again became activated, monetary awards were raised for beheading Rushdie and some even gave an award of Saif-Allah (Sword of Allah) to Bin Laden!. If such

knighthood was worth being given against the security of the British public—
then such policies have to be rethought for it affects the credibility of the British
government.

iii. Terrorism cannot be combated only in Britain so it has to engage the Muslim
world as well. The British government should know about its low images as well
as that of the USA in the Muslim world. This has to be improved and this can only
be done officially through news policies of Public Diplomacy to raise its image in
the Muslim world for winning the hearts and minds of the Muslims. In order to do
this it has to openly do this as one of the defenders of Islam as a great faith with its
strong support of Sufi traditions. The other sects may oppose it and Britain will be
placed one side of being supporter of the Sufi tradition but would not be accused
of being on anti-Islamic. It will gain support from the Sufi Muslim population and
will develop its own space within the Muslim masses.

iv. There is not doubt that there is a struggle going one between the Muslim world,
between the Fundamentalist and 'Moderate' Muslims. Whatever labels are being
used, the real struggle is between authentic and inauthentic Islam. Authentic Islam
produces enlightened Muslims and because they perceive God as Light (Nur) it
has been labelled as Enlightened Islam against Conservative Islam; in terms of
sects the struggle is between Sufism and Wahhabism and Salafism. The Western
world has to clearly decide whom it supports and it has to support Enlightened
Islam through strong economic and political support both in the Muslim world
and in Britain.

v. Although many more detailed recommendations can be made, for the purposes
of this paper, these four set the general tone and direction the British authorities
need to follow to eradicate extremist elements in society. This will help bring
the Muslim community on board and pave the way towards a collective struggle
against terrorist ideology.

A SUNNI MUSLIM SCHOLAR'S HUMANITARIAN AND RELIGIOUS REJECTION OF VIOLENCE AGAINST CIVILIANS

Y Alp Aslandogan and Bekir Cinar

Abstract

This paper analyses the multi-faceted response of a Sunni-Hanafi scholar, Fethullah Gülen, to the phenomenon of violence against civilians under a religious rhetoric. Gülen's response involves four components: (a) humanitarian, (b) religious, (c) political or realist, and (d) practical/educational. (a) Gülen categorically condemns acts of violence against innocent non-combatants including women and children as inhuman. (b) Gülen sets out the principles of Islamic jurisprudence that invalidate any declaration of war by individuals or groups: hence, such self-declared wars under the banner of Islam cannot be regarded as legitimate. He refutes 'the end justifies the means' argument, calling it a Marxist-Communist rhetoric, with no Islamic justification whatever. (c) While discussing misunderstanding, misrepresentation and abuse of religious texts, Gülen hints at the presence of individuals, interest groups, and other entities that benefit from friction and violent conflict. He suggests that the possibility should be considered that some individuals have been manipulated, perhaps even 'hypnotised' through special drugs, to carry out actions they would otherwise not carry out. (d) Gülen offers practical approaches to rooting out the problem of hate-mongering and violent conflict. The underlying dynamic of this approach is to provide, through education, mutual understanding, respect, opportunity and hope. Only educational institutions that foster interfaith and intercultural dialogue, mutual understanding and respect, and offer hope of upward mobility, can provide lasting solutions. Concepts such as 'love of creation due to the Creator' can be located in every culture and spiritual tradition. Gülen's own emphasis on Islamic spirituality provides an example that is particularly significant for Muslims: his argument against terrorism and for peaceful interfaith relations is based upon the authoritative view of the Sunni tradition, to which 90% of the world's Muslims adhere.

Introduction

This article discusses the unconditional rejection of violence against civilians by an influential Sunni- Muslim scholar, Fethullah Gülen, on humanitarian and religious grounds, as well as the educational response of civil society organizations inspired by his ideas. We first consider forms and contexts of violence. We point out that terrorism that is perpetrated under a religious, ideological or nationalistic rhetoric is part of a larger picture that includes various forms of violence that usually stem from frustration under adverse political conditions and have political goals. We then introduce Gülen as an influential Sunni-Muslim scholar, opinion leader, activist and poet who has consistently voiced his condemnation of terrorism. After reviewing general views of Gülen on violence, we examine Gülen's rejection of violence against civilians that is perpetrated under a religious rhetoric, both on humanitarian as well as religious grounds. We provide both summaries of Gülen's views as well as direct translations of quotations from his works. We briefly touch upon some of Gülen's comments on the political conditions that provide the breeding ground for terrorism. We then highlight educational measures inspired by Gülen's ideas and implemented by civil society initiatives in fragile regions of the world, that inculcate an outlook that embraces and respects diversity. We conclude with a discussion of possible topics for future studies.

Forms and Contexts of Violence

Violence is unwanted physical interference with the bodies of others, such that they experience pain and mental anguish and, in the extreme case, death. In general terms violence is a product of an individual or group who acts unilaterally in order to impose its opinion, where there is no space for negotiation due to power imbalance. Violence can be viewed as the anathema to the spirit and substance of democracy. This follows, almost by definition, because democracy, considered as a set of institutions and as a way of life, is a non-violent means of equally apportioning and publicly monitoring power within and among overlapping communities of people who live according to a wide variety of morals.[1]

Davis comments that 'violence is shown to be negatively related to the availability of alternative means of acquiring political goods and to the availability of alternative economic opportunities.'[2] In other words, one of the aims of the use of political violence[3] is to alter the political and economic status quo, because the latter is seen as maintaining injustice and unfairness. The injustice and unfairness are subjective and not objective. In other words, these are a reflection of the perceptions of people who claim to be suffering from them. They are also relative and not absolute. The 'the deprivation theory of civil violence'[4] suggests

---

1 John Keane, Violence and Democracy, Cambridge University Press: 2004, p.1

2 Gareth G. Davis, 'Repression, Rationality and Relative Deprivation; A theoretical and empirical examination of Cross-National Variations in Political Violence', http://economics.gmu.edu/working/WPE_99/99_04.pdf, accessed on 15 Mar 07

3 Gareth G. Davis, 'Repression, Rationality and Relative Deprivation; A theoretical and empirical examination of Cross-National Variations in Political Violence', http://economics.gmu.edu/working/WPE_99/99_04.pdf, accessed on 15 Mar. 07 and Wilkinson states that 'political violence is either the deliberate infliction or threat of infliction of pysical injury or damage for political ends, or it is violence which occurs unintentionally in the course of sever political conflicts'. In Paul Wilkinson, Terrorism and the Liberal State, Macmillan: London 1977, p.30

4 Paul Wilkinson, Political Terrorism, Macmillan: London, 1974, p. 126. He states that 'there are at least four models of relative deprivation: rising expectations may overtake rising capability; capabilities may remain static while expectation rise; general socio-economic malaise may actually bring about a drop in capabilities while expectations remain constant; and finally there is the classic J-curve phenomenon in which, for a period, capabilities keep pace

that 'political violence results from the social frustration that occurs in the wake of relative deprivation'.[5] Individuals or groups may feel that the deprivation causes the problem, and the use of violence 'becomes more attractive to those that are excluded from the state apparatus– the prize of victory raises with inequality'.[6]

Porta draws a table (Table 2.1) in order to provide some explanations about the origins of violence. These are: the structural conditions, such as 'the level of societal development, the strength of ethnic or class cleavages, the repressiveness of a regime, and cultural traditions'; and what Porta calls the 'conjunctural' explanation, which relates to 'the intermediate stages of economic development, the crises of modernization, period of ineffective state coercion, and rapid cultural changes'.[7]

Whether the structural or the conjunctural explanation has more to say about political violence and terrorism, the essential characteristic of politics itself requires 'conflict between the desires of different individuals,'[8] that helps to find a right balance in the society. This explanation leads us to look at 'socio-economic factors that can potentially contribute to the manifestation of violence, such as social dislocation, urbanisation, modernisation, immigration, unemployment and poverty'.[9]

> When such a dispute involves disagreement about appropriate source of legitimation the conflict may be more than usually intractable, for the standard democratic procedure of majority vote by legitimating 'people' (vox populi, vox Dei) is fatally flawed when the question at issue is who 'the people' are. The more intractable the dispute the more likely, other things being equal, that dissent will take illegal or terroristic forms.[10]

Identifying and analysing forms of violence and responses to forms of violence requires one to focus on the role of representation, sovereignty, and identity in conflict, as well as the role of the state system in reconstructing some of the essential conditions of asymmetric warfare. Without analysing the implications of the conditions and nature of the peace and order, as well as important elements of the violence, one cannot reach a proper result on identifying the violence.

In Table 2.2 forms of violence and responses are shown. There is a very thin line between peace and war. This line consists of political systems and politicians. If the politicians do not react properly in response to political problems, they will make it more difficult to keep

---

with rising expectations and then suddenly drop behind'.

5   Gareth G Davis, 'Repression, Rationality and Relative Deprivation: A theoretical and empirical examination of Cross-National Variations in Political Violence', http://economics.gmu.edu/working/WPE_99/99_04.pdf, and he states that 'Relative Deprivation is said to occur when the outcomes experienced by individuals are inferior to those that: a) they expected to receive or b) felt that they were entitled to receive. It is the inconsistency between outcomes and expectations and/or the prevalence of outcomes that are regarded as unjust that constitutes Relative Deprivation'

6   Carles Boix, 'Political Violence', Paper prepared for the Yale Conference on: Order, Conflict and Violence, April 30th-May 1st, 2004.

7   Donatella Della Porta, Social Movements, Political Violence, and the State, Cambridge University Press: 1995, p.5.

8   Martin Warner and Roger Crisp, 'Introduction', in Martin Warner and Roger Crisp (Ed.), Terrorism, Protest and Power, Edward Elgar: 1990, pp. 1-14.

9   Jason Franks, 'Rethinking the Roots of Terrorism: Orthodox Terrorism Theory and Beyond', http://www.bisa.ac.uk/ 2006/pps/franks.pdf, accessed on 16 March 2007

10   Martin Warner and Roger Crisp, 'Introduction', in Martin Warner and Roger Crisp (Ed.), Terrorism, Protest and Power, Edward Elgar: 1990, pp. 1-14

the peace. This is also the case in the international system, in which states and international politicians become the main actors who represent that thin line. If they have tended to draw on similar simple definitional categories to define and legitimate their responses, they will inflame the political activities of the others, thereby creating more problems. These others may often gain a degree of support and legitimacy when people see their grievances in the media and in public debate.[11]

Frustration, Civil Disobedience and Violence

Civil disobedience is often an effective means of changing laws and protecting liberties. It also embodies an important moral concept that there are times when law and justice do not coincide and that to obey the law at such times can be an abdication of ethical responsibility.[12]

According to the theory of frustration-aggression, 'humans only become violent if they are frustrated in their efforts to attain a particular goal: severe frustration leads to anger and anger to acts of aggressive violence'.[13] This theory 'maintains that aggression is always a consequence of frustration'.[14] Frustration 'results from unfulfilled needs or unresolved problems'.[15] These are 'since ancient times, worsening deprivation, injustice or oppression' which can be seen 'major precondition of political violence'. [16]

Political Violence

Political violence can involve violations of human rights in the society. It occurs whenever the expected net gains from employing it exceed the net gains derived from accepting the status quo among some political actors (such as unions, peasant organizations, a clique of army officers and so on). The status quo is here defined as a situation in which either a section of society holds the (public) monopoly of violence and policymaking uncontested by those that are excluded from the decision-making process or political differences are settled peacefully (through either voting procedures or bargaining) among all parties in contention.[17] In the following table, different levels of political conflict are shown and tried to be distinguished.

In the national scale, political violence becomes unavoidable in an unequal society in which assets are not distributed fairly among people. Then, the potential rebels can apply violence to overturn the existing political and economic system.[18] In the international scale, political violence is perpetrated against real or perceived entities responsible for injustices or suffering. While definitions of terrorism include some common elements such as the use of violence and the aim of inflicting terror on a government or its people, the lack of consensus over the definition "points to its inescapably political nature, perhaps best encapsulated in

---

11 Oliver P. Richmond, 'Realizing Hegemony? Symbolic Terrorism and the Roots of Conflict', Studies in Conflict & Terrorism, Vol. 26 No. 4 (2003): pp. 289–309.

12 Kayla Starr, adapted by Bonnie Blackberry, 'The Role of Civil Disobedience in Democracy' CLMP News Summer '98 Issue at http://www.civilliberties.org/sum98role.html, accessed on 24 May 2007

13 Paul Wilkinson, Terrorism and the Liberal State, Macmillan: London 1977, p.35

14 S O Brien, R Tay and B Watson, 'Situational factors contributing to the expression of aggression on the roads', IATSS Research, 28:1, 2004; http://eprints.qut.edu.au/archive/00002167/01/watson_IATSS.pdf, accessed on 15 Mar 07

15 Random House Webster's Dictionary

16 Paul Wilkinson, Terrorism and the Liberal State, Macmillan: London 1977, p.36

17 Carles Boix, 'Political Violence', Paper prepared for the Yale Conference on: Order, Conflict and Violence, April 30th-May 1st, 2004.

18 Carles Boix, 'Political Violence', Paper prepared for the Yale Conference on: Order, Conflict and Violence, April 30th-May 1st, 2004.

the aphorism (or cliché) that 'one person's terrorist is another person's freedom fighter.'[19] The following table illustrates various forms of political violence perpetrated by individuals, groups or states.

Especially during the last few decades, acts of violence carried out by individuals with Muslim names or groups claiming a Muslim identity have occupied the news numerous times. While each such action or information about their possible perpetrators have made headline news, Muslim reactions to such actions and their tragic consequences were given a disproportionately smaller space by the news media[20]. In the following we will examine the views of an influential Muslim scholar on violence as a case in point. But first a review of indicators of his impact and his significance is in order.

Roots of Terrorism

In the following, we will discuss the political roots of terrorism, and the role ideology or religion might play in the promotion of a terrorist agenda among masses.

Political Roots of Terrorism

Terrorism can be likened to a cancerous cell in an existing political system. If the political system works perfectly, this cancer cell will not be visible within the political system; if the system does not work perfectly, it will be visible and grow and spread into the whole political system.[21] In his parallel views, Wilkinson states that 'revolutionary violence stems directly from conflicts within and between a country's political institutions.

Revolutionary violence is seen as basically the product of conflict about legitimacy, political rights, and access to power. It often results from the refusal or incapacity of a government to meet certain claims made upon it by a powerful group or a coalition of group'. [22]

Roots of conflict and terrorism may feed each other indirectly, and consequently, 'what needs to happen now is a rethinking of terrorism in order to provide alternative approaches that can deal with the root causes.'[23]

No human is born a terrorist and the decision to get involved in terrorism does not happen overnight. Therefore, an important realisation here is that terrorism is a process[24] and 'terrorism is a choice; it is a political strategy selected from among a range of options'.[25] The process of terrorism has an historical background, which involves people who rightly or wrongly perceive that the political system is treating them harshly. This harsh treatment may even stretch back to their ancestors. The action of terrorism is an end product of the process. This process moves through several stages until the overt terrorist action takes place. Only, at the action stage of terrorism does it become noticeable and be named by people. From the initial

19 Ben Golder and George Williams, 'What is Terrorism? Problems of Legal Definition', UNSW Law Journal, 27, 270.

20 As one example of collections of such responses, see the American Academy of Religion's special web site available at http://groups.colgate.edu/aarislam/response.htm.

21 Bekir Cinar, Devlet Guvenligi, Istihbarat ve Terorizm (State Security, Intelligence and Terrorism), Sam Yayinlari: Ankara 1997, p. 247

22 Paul Wilkinson, Political Terrorism, Macmillan: London, 1974, p. 129

23 Jason Franks, Rethinking the Roots of Terrorism: Beyond Orthodox Terrorism Theory - a new research agenda', http://www.st-andrews.ac.uk/intrel/cpcs/papers/Rethinking.pdf, accessed on 12 March 2007

24 Andrew Silke, 'Terrorism', The Psychologist, Vol. 14 No. 11, pp. 580-81.

25 Michael Walzer, 'Five Questions About Terrorism', Dissent, Winter 2002, pp. 5-9.

genesis of terrorism to the action itself, each individual stage requires careful determination and planning. Accordingly, terrorism has many dimensions and each dimension needs to be dealt with carefully in order to understand and prevent it.

Examination of an existing political system and its governance may provide the required information about the root causes of terrorism. Such an investigation, however, should start at least from 40 years before the present day. For example, ethnic terrorism may be a product of a 'nation-state'[26] because nationalism means that the dominant ethnic groups in the country have been prized above others, who have been subordinated in the country's political, economic and social life for a prolonged period. 'Without question, in the most successful revolutionary wars of the last 25 years, the strongest appeal has been to nationalism and patriotism based either on resistance to a conqueror or the gaining of independence from a colonial power'.[27] Today, it is difficult to see any colonial power in any country, but many ethnic groups within the nation-state see the dominant ethnic group or government as a colonial power or occupying power.

In addition to seeing terrorism as the product of the nation-state, one may see it as a product of the political systems of repressive regimes[28], economic systems which are corrupted and produce poverty and no job opportunities, educational systems which are lacking in decent education and training, and the never-ending conflicts within a society.

Another type of political system which is relevant is the international system, in particular the current balance of power. One Middle Eastern academic points out to the imbalance of power in places such as the Middle East, Iraq, Afghanistan, Chechnya and Kashmir as a factor in the escalation of violence.[29]

Ideological Roots

According to Kullberg and Jokinen, 'terrorism is not an ideology as such. It has no united political agenda. In principle, almost any ideology could be claimed by a terrorist'.[30] Terrorism

---

26 'Nation-states exist to deliver political goods-security, education, health services, economic opportunity, environmental surveillance, a legal frame-work of order and a judicial system to administer it, and fundamental infrastructural requirements such as roads and communications facilities-to their citizens'. In Rober I Rotberg, 'The New Nature of Nation-State Failure', The Washington Quarterly, Summer 2002, Vol.25 (3), pp.85-96, and http://www. twq.com/02summer/rotberg.pdf, accessed 15 Mar. 07 and 'A form of state in which those who exercise power claim legitimacy for their rule partly or solely on the grounds that their power is exercised for the promotion of the distinctive interests, values and cultural heritage of a particular nation whose members ideally would constitute all, or most of, its subject population and all of whom would dwell within the borders.' In the online edition of A Glossary of Political Economy Terms by Dr. Paul M. Johnson and http://www.auburn.edu/~johnspm/gloss/nation_state, accessed on 15 Mar. 07

27 Paul Wilkinson, Political Terrorism, Macmillan: London, 1974, p. 74

28 'The region has been dominated by a range of authoritarian political systems, including military regimes, monarchies, theocracies, and one-party states regimes. ... Civil society is weak as a result of the severe legal restrictions and coercive methods that the region's regimes use to stifle political expression. Independent media are largely nonexistent; most newspapers and articles are censored, and those that exist are seen as serving the interests of the regime or particular political parties. In such societies, severe repression drives all politics underground, placing the moderate opposition at a disadvantage and encouraging political extremism'. In Jennifer L. Windsor, Promoting Democratization Can Combat Terrorism', The Washington Quarterly, summer 2003, 26:3, pp. 43–58

29 Ben Mollov, who is lecturer in conflict studies, social studies at Bar-Ilan University in Israel, 'Religion and Religious Extremism', International Summit on Democracy, Terrorism and Security, 8-11 March 2005, Madrid, at http://english.safe-democracy.org/keynotes/religion-and-religious-extremism.html, accessed on 3 March 2007

30 Anssi Kullberg and Christian Jokinen, 'From Terror to Terrorism: the Logic on the Roots of Selective Political

uses ideology as a tool for participating in relations with an audience who believes in that ideology and for influencing the wider public. In other words, 'terrorism needs an all-encompassing philosophy, a religion or secular ideology, to legitimize violence, to win recruits to the cause and to mobilize them for action'.[31] Human beings seek to justify whatever they do. The justification can be done with an ideology or a religion cast into an ideological form[32]. People who belong to different groups in a friction-stricken society feel forced to position themselves in relation to two opposing poles. The opposing concepts of the others have such powerful meanings that they tend to supersede other conflicts and determine how these conflicts are interpreted, mobilised around, and fought over.[33]

The Role of Religion

Popular arguments that overlook the complex historic, political and social factors and link terrorism with religion do not stand scrutiny. But even if religion per se is not a direct cause of terrorism, there is no question that people can find justification for terrorism in religion, just as they do in nationalism, various ideologies and racism. Mark Juergensmeyer says that while religion has been a major factor in recent acts of terrorism, it is seldom the only one[34].

Religiosity itself is not a cause of political radicalism. Appeals to religion are likely to be a way of framing or representing a struggle in terms that a potential constituency will understand rather than the determinants of a strategic choice.

Religious ideologies, goals, and motivations are often interwoven with those that are economic, social, and political. A group's decision to turn to violence is usually situational and is seldom endemic to the religious tradition to which the group is related. Islam does not cause terrorism, nor does any other religion with which terrorist acts have been associated. As John Esposito explained, usually 'political and economic grievances are primary causes or catalysts, and religion becomes a means to legitimate and mobilize'. Ian Reader stated that even in the case of Aum Shinrikyo, the Buddhist movement implicated in the Tokyo nerve gas incident in 1995, the religious factor 'would not have been enough to take the group in the direction that it did'.[35]

Because there are terrorists who claim that they belong to a certain religion, or use religious symbols, they may be easily branded 'religious terrorists' (e.g. 'Islamic terrorists'). But such an attitude overlooks several significant factors that play a role in an individual's getting involved in terrorism, as well as the reactions and condemnations of those who legitimately represent the faith. Terrorism can be the means used in the name of some ideology by terrorist groups, but that ideology is not terrorism.[36] 'Interviews with terrorist often reveal that

---

Violence', *Research Unit for Conflicts and Terrorism*, University of Turku, Finland, The Eurasian Politician, 19th July 2004.

31 Louise Richardson, *What Terrorists Want: Understanding the Terrorists* Threat, John Murray: Great Britain 2006, p.92-93

32 Anthony Shadid, 'Legacy of the Prophet: Despots, Democrats, and the New Politics of Islam', Westview Press, 2002, 228.

33 Tore BJØRGO, Yngve Carlsson, Thomas Haaland, 'Hate Crime or Gang Conflict? Violence between Youth Group in a Norwegian City', at http://www.fpvv.uni-mb.si/conf2004/papers/bjorgo.pdf, accessed on 24 May 2007

34 Mark Juergensmeyer, 'Terror in the Mind of God', University of California Press, 2003.

35 Mark Juergensmeyer, 'Religion', *Addressing the Causes of Terrorism*, The Club de Madrid Series on Democracy and Terrorism, Vol. 1, pp.27-34.

36 Anssi Kullberg and Christian Jokinen, 'From Terror to Terrorism: the Logic on the Roots of Selective Political Violence', *Research Unit for Conflicts and Terrorism*, University of Turku, Finland, The Eurasian Politician, 19th July 2004.

their sense of frustration bred of failure. Religion provides them with a means of dealing with these personal issues in a way that address their particular inadequacies by making them part of a more powerful movement and promising ultimate victory.[37] In short, religion may enable people to deal with their frustrations, but it is not the root cause of those frustrations, or their decision to engage in terrorist action. A striking study supporting this point is the one by Pape[38].

Drawing conclusions from the 23 years of data collected by the Chicago Project on Suicide Terrorism, Prof. Robert Pape of University of Chicago demonstrated that occupation of territories claimed by a group is the best predictor of suicide terrorism, far better than religious orientation. Pape found surprisingly weak correlation between religion and suicide terrorism, even including the case of al-Qaeda related groups. Out of the 315 separate attacks within the 23 years between 1980 to 2003, 301 of them were perpetrated as part of a "large, coherent political or military campaign" against an entity perceived as a "foreign occupier"[39]. Pape lists nine such cases including Lebanon, West Bank and Gaza, Sri Lanka, southeast Turkey, Chechnya, Kashmir, Punjab, Iraq and the Arabian Peninsula that account for 95 percent of the suicide terrorist attacks in the aforementioned period. Pape shows that in the past 20 years groups with an Islamist rhetoric were responsible for less than 35 percent of suicide attacks. The leading perpetrator of suicide attacks, the Tamil Tigers, as well as the Kurdish PKK group are Marxist-Leninist groups that are strictly opposed to religion[40]. Another surprising finding of Pape was that even among the individuals identified with al-Qaeda, religious fundamentalism was a considerably weaker predictor than the presence of foreign troops in the individual's homeland territory. The presence of foreign troops was a ten times stronger predictor of involvement in terrorism than religious orientation[41]. If we consider that "ends justify means" is an essentially Leninist argument[42] and some of the Arab states have been under Soviet influence during the 1950-1980 period, then the impact of Marxist-Leninist ideology can be seen as even greater than these figures suggest.

Gülen: An Influential Sunni-Muslim Scholar

Fethullah Gülen is an authoritative mainstream Turkish Muslim scholar, thinker, author, poet, opinion leader and educational activist, whose ideas carry great significance for Turkish Muslims as well as increasingly Muslims in other countries. A recent study sponsored by the Brookings Institution found Gülen as the top contemporary role model for Turkish youth[43]. Internet opinion polls have consistently confirmed his name recognition and approval as a mainstream scholar by the vast majority of Turkish people[44]. Gülen's readership in Turkey is estimated around several millions. His impact outside Turkey is growing daily as his works are translated into many languages including English, Arabic, Russian, German, Spanish,

37 Louise Richardson, *What Terrorists Want: Understanding the Terrorists* Threat, John Murray: Great Britain 2006, p.91

38 Robert A. Pape, 2005. Dying to Win: The Strategic Logic of Suicide Terrorism, New York: Random House, 23.

39 Pape, Ibid. p. 4.

40 Pape, Ibid. p. 4

41 Pape, Ibid. p.103.

42 Ladis K. D. Kristof, 'Reflections on Angelina Balabanoff's Lenin', Russian Review, 22:4, 1963, 369-376.

43 Akbar Ahmed, 2007, Journey Into Islam, Washington D.C.: Brookings Institution Press, 157.

44 Muhammed Çetin, 2005. Mobilization and Countermobilization: The Gülen movement in Turkey. Proceedings of the Conference on Islam in the contemporary world: Gülen Movement in Thought and Practice, Rice University, Houston, TX.

Urdu, Bosnian, Albanian, Malay and Indonesian. In addition to printed publications, his ideas are accessible to an ever increasing world population through private Radio/TV networks sympathetic to his views.

Gülen has been recognized for his consistent stance against the use of violence with a religious rhetoric. More specifically,

i.   He was the first Muslim scholar who publicly condemned the attacks of 9/11 with an advertisement in the Washington Post.

ii. He helped publish a scholarly book on Islamic perspective on terror and suicide attacks, condemning such acts on humanitarian and religious grounds.

iii. He did not express these views only to western readers but voiced them in mosque sermons among thousands of Muslim audience members. He unequivocally rejects suicide attacks, regardless of location or conditions.

iv. He gave interviews to Turkish, Japanese, Kenyan and American newspapers categorically condemning acts of terror for political, ideological and religious reasons. He appeared on numerous national television shows publicly condemning such acts.

Gülen has been actively promoting interfaith and intercultural dialogue for over a decade, starting long before the tragedy of 9/11. In Turkey, he has been credited for bringing about a positive atmosphere of relationships between the majority Muslim population and the various religious minorities such as Greek Orthodox, Armenian Orthodox, Catholic, and Jewish communities. Outside of Turkey, his ideas on interfaith dialog have inspired many to establish organizations engaging in dialogue with the same objectives of mutual understanding, empathic acceptance, peaceful coexistence, and cooperation. His efforts for dialog and tolerance have been recognized by a personal audience with the late Pope John Paul II, an invitation by the chief Sephardic Rabbi of Israel, as well as meetings with the leaders of various Christian denominations.

Gülen's Opinions on Political Violence

Throughout his career as a preacher and teacher, Gülen has maintained a consistent stance against the use of violence for political means, especially against civilians. In Gülen's view, economic conditions, corruption in the state, or ideological reasons can not justify violence. He is on the record numerous times for encouraging his listeners or readers to respect the rule of law and to find a peaceful solution to any conflict between individuals or between the individual and the state. Besides being illegitimate, Gülen views violence as producing the very opposite of what its perpetrators aim to achieve, especially in the case of inter-group conflicts arising from difference as experienced in Turkey during the 1970s. According to Gülen, 'the problems of difference among people can be solved by means of tolerance. If these differences are respected, there will be a chance of benefiting from everybody's ideas without discriminating against anyone'.[45]

His very fist article on 1 February 1979 in the popular magazine 'Sızıntı[46] states that his

---

45 Filiz Baskan, 'The Fethullah Gülen Community: Contribution or Barrier to the Consolidation of Democracy in Turkey?', Middle Eastern Studies, Vol. 41, No. 6 (November 2005), pp. 849 – 861, In addition to his encouragement on dialogue, he also offer another way too. 'In order to work on various social problems and bring harmony to society, Gülen promoted cooperation with various segments of society, particularly with adherents of religions other than Islam as well as with secularists in Turkey.' In Zeki Saritoprak, 'An Islamic Approach to Peace and Nonviolence: A Turkish Experience', The Muslim World, Vol. 95 (July 2005), pp. 413-427

46 Sızıntı is a monthly magazine on literature, science and story which began its publishing life on 1 February

methods and mission is stopping 'the crying of children by sharing their unhappiness and agony, and helping them to be happy and helping them reach their highest level of human soul'[47]. With this mission, he states one of his principles as 'avoidance of political and ideological conflict.'[48] Institutions which have been established by participants of a civil society movement inspired by his works have made non-violence a key principle in their activities.[49] Altunoğlu states that according to Gülen, whatever is achieved by violent means will inevitably collapse'.[50] Violence cannot be seen as a means of achievement. Moreover, Gülen expresses that 'it is obvious that you could not and cannot achieve anything by violence and bad temper. It is needless to emphasize that when you knock with love, respect and affection, doors to the paths of dialogue are opened and that you can have the opportunity to explain the values that you represent'.[51]

Gülen's Rejection of Violence on Humanistic Grounds

The first component of Gülen's response to violence against civilians is a rejection on humanitarian grounds. As will be illustrated below, Gülen declares acts of violence against innocent civilians including women and children as inhumane. He uses clear statements in categorically condemning killing of innocent civilians, elderly, women and children. The following is an excerpt from his condemnation message which was submitted to Washington Post on September 12th, 2001[52]:

> Any terrorist activity, no matter who it is committed by and for whatever purpose, is the greatest blow against peace, democracy and humanity. For this reason, terrorist activities can by no means be approved of. Terror cannot be a means for independence, nor a legitimate route to salvation. The recent terrorist activity, which is by far the most bloody and catastrophic to date, is a sabotage against not only the United States of America but also against world peace and the universal democratic and humanistic values. The perpetrators of this act cannot be but the most brutal of all.

> I strongly condemn the recent terrorist attack on the United States. It is worthy of nothing but condemnation and hatred, and all in the world must condemn it.

> I assure the American people that I pray to God Almighty for the victims and share their pain and sorrow from the bottom of my heart. May God give them with patience.

During late 1990s Turkey suffered from the terrorist activities of a group who called themselves "the party of God." This group went to such extremes as to torture and kill Muslims who they declared as being hypocrites or conspirers of enemies of faith. The Turkish daily newspaper Zaman, which is known for its sympathetic editorial position toward Gülen used

---

1979.

47 M. F. Gülen, 'Bu Ağlamayı Dindirmek İçin Yavru (For Stopping This Crying of Baby)' Sızıntı, Vol.1 No.1, pp.1-2

48 M. Hermansen, 'Understandings of "Community" within the Gülen Movement', http://fethullahGülenconference.org/ houston/index.php, accessed on 12 August 2007

49 Ebru Altunoğlu, Fethullah Gülen's Perception Of State And Society, Thesis Submitted To The Institute Of Social Sciences In Partial Fulfilment Of The Requirements For The Degree Of Master Of Arts in Political Science and International Relations, Boğaziçi University, 1999, p.60

50 Ebru Altunoğlu, Fethullah Gülen's Perception Of State And Society, Thesis Submitted To The Institute Of Social Sciences In Partial Fulfilment Of The Requirements For The Degree Of Master Of Arts in Political Science and International Relations, Boğaziçi University, 1999, p.94

51 Selçuk Camcı, Dr. Kudret Ünal (ed.). Fethullah Gülen'in Konuşma ve Yazılarında Hoşgörü ve Diyalog İklimi, Merkür Yayıları. İzmir, 1998, p.140

52 http://en.fGülen.com/content/view/968/3/.

a headline that gave a new name to this group: "The party of savagery[53]".

In multiple interviews given to Zaman daily, Milliyet daily, Kenyan and Canadian newspapers, Gülen also clearly stated his condemnation of Bin Laden, his accomplices and their actions[54]:

> Bin Laden is among the persons in this world that I hate most. Because he has defaced the beautiful face of Islam. He has produced a dirty image. Even if we work on repairing the terrible damage he has caused with all our power, it will take years. We shall speak on every platform everywhere. We shall write books. We shall declare "this is not Islam". Bin Laden replaced Islamic logic with his own desires and wishes and lives as a monster. The men around him are like that as well. If there are people who think like that, they are also locked into monstrosity. We equivocally condemn their perspective.

In the above two quotes it is important to note that Gülen both declares perpetrators of terrorist acts as evil as well as questioning their humanity. In other words, in Gülen's views these individuals have lost their inner capacity to function as human beings through their conscious and persistent involvement in acts of terror against humanity. On the one hand, by condemning terrorist acts as cruel as a human and by depicting Bin Laden as a monster, Gülen shows his solidarity with the humanity and his common stance against terror as a fellow human. At the same time he also appeals to the human side of his audience, who are primarily Muslims. But Gülen completes this appeal with a religious component, and for an important reason. After all, the appeal and justifications of the terrorist groups such as Bin Laden's is based on both suffering of individuals and nations, as well as their religious conscience.

Gülen's Rejection of Violence on Religious Grounds

Gülen's opinion towards violence and political violence is based on mainstream traditional interpretations of basic sources of Islam, such as the Qur'an, the prophetic tradition, as well as particular interpretations of certain aspects of those same sources shaped by the Central-Asian and Anatolian experience. His opinion has provided a powerful approach to spiritual change not only in Turkey but also many parts of the world through educational institutions and dialogue activities.

In Gülen's view, any Muslim who correctly understands Islam cannot be or become a terrorist, or a person engaged in terrorist activities can not remain a Muslim.'[55] Misunderstandings and misinterpretations of Islam and Islamic resources need to be corrected. For this reason, Gülen strongly encourages Muslims to engage in education to internalize and convey open and inclusive interpretations of their faith, as demonstrated by the spiritually-oriented Anatolian Muslim experience.[56]

---

53 Zaman daily, 17 January 2001.

54 Akman, N. Zaman daily, March 22-April 1, 2004.

55 M. Fethullah Gülen, 'Real Muslims Cannot Be Terrorists', Turkish Daily News, September 19, 2001

56 Basic Principles of Anatolian Sufism are: We are the avant-garde of love; we don't have time for hostility; Love all the creation because of the Creator; Tongueless to those who curse, handless to those who hit; Self-renewal is the only condition of continues existence; The greatest book to be read is human being; Be an advocate of others, but a judge to yourself; If there is no one left on Earth to build dialogue and love, go to other parts of the universe; Universe is within human, human is within the Universe; Science is the light illuminating roads towards the reality; Our way has been established on science, knowledge and love of human; Do not preach; instead act as a living model; Let us unite together, let us be huge, alive; Do not hurt even if you were offended; Whatever becomes heavy for your own personality, do not make it applied to anybody; Always bear in mind that even your enemy is a human; Everything created by God is placed orderly. In Fahri Karakas, 'Global Peaceful Social Innovation: The Case of

There are three components of Gülen's religious response to violence against civilians. The first is the rejection of self-declared wars. The second is the reiteration of an important principle of Islamic jurisprudence: Individuality of crime and the rejection of harming women, children and otherwise non-combatant civilians under any circumstances. The third is the rejection of "they have no other means" rhetoric and "ends justify means" philosophy. Gülen supports this position by pointing to the Leninist roots of this philosophy and the lack of precedents in the lives of the Prophet of Islam (peace be upon him) and his companions.

Gülen states that 'all kinds of unjust murders are great sins'[57] referring to some of the central concepts justice and peace in the Qur'an, both of which are the current essence of the modern legal system developed to protect life, capital, and reproduction. Other verses Gülen alludes to in this context include 'Deal fairly, and do not let the hatred of others for you make you swerve to wrong and depart from justice. Be just, for that is next to piety, and fear God'[58]; and 'He who kills a soul unless it be (in legal punishment) for murder or for causing disorder and corruption on the earth will be as if he had killed all humankind; and he who saves a life will be as if he had saved the lives of all humankind.'[59] According to Gülen, no political reason could justify killing innocent civilians and causing disorder and corruption on the earth. In contrast, he highlights that 'loving and respecting humanity merely because they are human is an expression of respect for the Almighty Creator. … If we can raise a community upon this perspective, people will eventually recover and they will manage to compensate for whatever they have lost'.[60]

Gülen's first categorical response to violence against civilians is the rejection of self-declared wars. The following quote summarizes this point[61]:

> The rules of Islam are obvious. Individuals cannot declare war. Neither a group nor an organization cannot declare a war. War is declared by the state. You cannot declare a war without a president or an army saying that it is war. Otherwise, it becomes a relative or personal war.

Another quote reiterates this principle and alludes to the rules of conduct during war which we will elaborate below[62]:

> An Islamic authority can do war only within the framework of such definite principles, and only a state, not certain individuals or organizations, can decide a war.

Elsewhere, Gülen states that if a person or group believe that their government does not represent their views, then it is their duty to influence the government or otherwise induce social change through non-violent means[63]. The issue of Iraqi insurgence during the first months of U.S.-led invasion is not addressed in the sources available to the authors of this essay. While

Gülen Network', http://en.fGülen.com/content/view/2242/4/, accessed on 14 August 2007

57 M. Fethullah Gülen (under pen-name Hikmet Isik), 'What does Islam say about killing an innocent person?' The Fountain, October - December 2006, Issue 56, August 2007, available online at http://www.fountainmagazine.com/articles.php?SIN=7808256c10&k=792&840098454&show=part1, accessed on 13

58 The Quran, 5:8,

59 The Quran 5:32

60 M. Fethullah Gülen, 'Respect For Humankind', The Fountain, January – March, 2006 / Issue 53 http://www.fountainmagazine.com/articles.php?SIN=6e31958cbc&k=738&593384988&show=part1, accessed on 13 August 2007

61 Fethullah Gülen. 2004. 'No Islamic World Exists Today.' Interview with N. Akman. Zaman, 22 March.

62 Fethullah Gülen. 2004. Interview with Fethullah Gülen. Daily Nation. 30 July.

63 Fethullah Gülen, 2003, 'Suicide Attacks Can not be Reconciled with the Universal Call of Islam', Zaman daily, 16 November 2003, available online in Turkish at http://tr.fGülen.com/content/view/3885/77/.

some logical inferences can be made based on Gülen's stated views on related topics, we will leave this exercise to another research project.

Gülen also highlights a point of confusion among both Muslims as well as non-Muslims, with respect to those principles that regulate a soldier's conduct during the time of war and encourage active defence toward the protection of five important entities: Life, freedom, family/progeny, property, and sanity/health. Gülen distinguishes between regulation of war and promotion of war[64]:

> Islam has never looked favourably upon war, although it is a reality and one of the most prominent elements in the history of humankind; Islam has bound war first and foremost to the condition of defence, and then, within the framework of the principle "inciting division/rivalry is worse than murder," found in the Qur'an, it has deemed war lawful only to prevent war and disputes which lead to war, to prevent disorder, oppression and subjection. These are the conditions that Islam deems necessary for engaging in war;

Here is the middle part of Gülen's condemnation message after 9/11/01 we omitted above which touches upon the principle of individuality of crime, and the rejection of "ends justify means" approach[65]:

> In relation to Islam's stance regarding terrorism, I can assure that Islam, never approves of any kind of terrorism. Terrorism cannot be a means for any Islamic goal, and a terrorist cannot be a Muslim, nor can a true Muslim be a terrorist. Islam orders peace and a true Muslim can only be a symbol of peace and the maintenance of basic human rights. Islam preaches that if there are ten people on board a vessel of whom one is innocent and nine guilty of a criminal act, then the ship may not be sunk in view of punishing the guilty for there is amongst them one innocent. Any right, whatever it's nature, is respected in Islam and it cannot be violated. The right of an individual cannot be violated in the interest of the community. The Qur'an, Islam's sacred Book, declares that one who takes a life unjustly is as if he/she took the lives of all humankind, and that one who saves a life is as if he/she saved the lives of all. In the words of our Prophet, a Muslim is one from who comes no harm, neither from his/her tongue nor hand.

Earliest recorded stance of Gülen against violence occurred in the midst of ideologically driven armed conflicts in Turkey during the 1970s. Various ideological groups such as communists (Marxist, Leninist, Maoist, as well as sympathizers of Albanian Enver Hodja) and ultra-nationalists used both propaganda as well as violence to pursue their agendas. Clashes among the youth groups claimed the lives of thousands of youth as well as members of security forces, intellectuals, teachers and politicians. Armed groups would demand the students to boycott classes, and the shopkeepers to close down shops to disturb normal life in the country. During this troubled period, Gülen consistently promoted non-violent resistance to the demands of these groups. The Marxist-Leninist-Maoist groups were especially keen on provoking resistance from the faithful and hence drawing them to the armed conflicts. While communist factions marched across the street from the mosque where Gülen was preaching, he is reported to have said the following[66]:

> Those people who chant agitating slogans today may one day come into the mosque and shoot me. If any of you in this audience react violently, let it be known that I do not approve or condone it.

---

64 Nevval Sevindi, "Fethullah Gülen ile New York Sohbetleri" (New York Conversations with Fethullah Gülen and Global Tolerance), Timas Yayinlari, Istanbul, April, 2002.

65 http://en.fGülen.com/content/view/968/3/

66 An account of Gülen's years in Izmir can be found in the biography of his early years, entitled "Kucuk Dunyam" (My Little World), Ufuk Yayinlari, Istanbul, 2006.

If I am assassinated, despite all your angers, I ask you to bury my body and seek for order, peace and love in our society. Regardless to what happens; you should say that 'we, believers should be representatives of love and security[67].

His second noteworthy stance was during the first Gulf war. While Saddam was sending missiles to Israeli cities, Gülen declared publicly in a mosque sermon attended by thousands of Muslims[68]:

Today, I am equally sad for the Israeli children who are under the threat of deadly missiles, as I am sad for the dying Iraqi children. Killing innocent children has no place in our faith.

The Qur'anic references for the principle of individuality of crime are well known and even memorized in its original Arabic by many Muslims[69]:

No bearer of a burden can bear the burden of another [The Qur'an, Chapters An'am, 6:164; Nahl, 16:15; Fatir, 35:18].

The following quote from Gülen combines this principles of the individuality of crime, rejection of suicidal attacks, and harming innocent civilians[70]:

You can not touch innocent civilians even at the time of war. No one can issue a religious verdict condoning such an act either. No one can become a suicide bomber. No one can wrap explosives around his/her body and enter a crowd of innocent civilians. This is religiously unacceptable regardless of the faith of those in the crowd. Such an act can not be condoned even at the time of war.

Islamic rules of conduct during the war tells us not to touch children, those who pray in their places of worship. This is not something that was declared during a certain time period and then forgotten. Instead, this rule has been stated by Prophet Muhammad (peace be upon him) and reiterated by (the first caliph) Abu Bakr, (the second caliph) Omar, and in later times Salahaddeen Ayyoobi, (Seljuk Sultan) Alparslan, Kilicarslan and (Ottoman Sultan) Fatih (Mehmed II).

One example of the prophetic tradition regarding protection of women and children that Gülen alludes to was issued shortly after the conquest of Mecca. Certain polytheist Arab tribes, especially the tribe of Hawazin got worried after the conquest of Mecca and the submission of the tribe of Quraish, the Prophet's tribe. These tribes thought that if they did not strike first, they would be politically isolated among the tribes who accepted Islam or made an alliance with the Muslims. Hence they began assembling a force under the leadership of the Hawazin elite. This culminated in a battle known as the battle of Hunayn. At the end of the battle Prophet Muhammad saw the body of a dead woman among the dead of the pagans. "What is this that I see?" he asked. People around him answered: "This is a woman, killed by the forces of Khaled ibn Walled." The Prophet said to one of them "Run to Khaled! Remind him that the Messenger of God forbids him to kill children, women, and servants." One of

---

67 One of his Sermons, Izmir, 1979, and Sefa KAPLAN, 'Ateist terörist değildir', Hurriyet, 21/04/2004
68 One of the series of sermons entitled "Peygamberimizin Yuce Ahlaki" (The Exemplary Morals and Conduct of Our Prophet) given in 1990, some of which are available online at http://tr.fGülen.com (Multimedia->Vaaz). As an example of criticism Gülen received, see http://f1.parsimony.net/forum789/messages/8354.htm.
69 Ali, A.Y., "The Meaning of the Holy Qur'an," Amana Publications, MD, 2004, Unal, A., "The Qur'an with Annotated Interpretation in Modern English", The Light Inc., NJ 2007.
70 Capan 2004, p.10, Isik Yayinlari, Istanbul, 2004. Translation by the authors. For reference, the Turkish original begins as follows: "... Savaşırken bile suçsuz! insanlara ilişemezsiniz. Hiç kimse bu mevzuda bir fetva da veremez. Kimse intihar komandosu olamaz. Kimse vücuduna bombalar bağlayıp, masum insanların içine giremez. İçine girdiği bu toplum hangi dinden olursa olsun caiz değildir. Savaş halinde bile buna cevaz verilmemiştir."

those present said "Dear Messenger of God! But are they not the children of the pagans?" The Prophet answered: "Were not the best of you, too, once the children of pagans? All children are born with their true nature and are innocent."[71]

The same principle and instruction can be seen consistently reiterated toward the end of Prophet's life. During a time of illness, the news of an imminent attack by an alliance of Northern Arabs and the forces of the Eastern Roman Empire arrived at Medina. The Prophet ordered the preparation of an army under the command of Uthama b. Zayd, and gave the following instructions to Uthama: "Fight in God's way. Do not be cruel to people. Do not go against your covenant. Do not cut down trees bearing fruits. Do not slaughter livestock. Do not kill the pious who are secluded in monasteries, engaged in worship, or children and women...[72]" Another record of Prophet's protest of killing a non-combatant woman can be found in the respected source of prophetic tradition Abu Dawud. The instructions of the Prophet were enshrined in Islamic legal literature, to the effect that the killing of non-combatants such as women, children, the elderly, the disabled is expressly forbidden.[73] Albayrak points out that there is no Islamic text which allows the killing of non-combatant civilians in war, as opposed to a combatant (muharib). Albayrak (Albayrak 2006:137) gives a linguistic analysis of a Qur'anic verse in this context[74]:

> The Qur'an states clearly 'Fight in the cause of God those who fight you (who are liable and able to fight, and who participate actively in the fight) but do not transgress the limits; for God loves not transgressors' (Baqara, 2:190). The Arabic verb yuqâtilûna in the verse is of extreme importance. To explain this in grammatical terms, the mood (reciprocal form) in Arabic denotes 'participation' which, in this sense, means 'those who fall under the status of combatant'. Thus non-combatants are not to be fought against. This must be obeyed rule in war and applies equally stringently when war has not been declared.

Gülen's Historical References

Among Gülen's references in this context are historical incidents that illustrate the consistent interpretation of the same religious sources. The expulsion of Muslims and Jews from Spain by Catholic Christians provides a historic example that shows the continuity of the understanding of the principles of individuality of crime (2006:137).

> It is known that when Muslims in Andalusia (Spain) were expelled from the peninsula, some Muslims asked the Ottoman Sultan Mehmed II to expel his Christian subjects from Istanbul as a retaliation for the Christians' attacks on the Andalusia Muslims. However, the Ottoman Shayk al-Islam Zambilli Jamali Efendi objected, arguing that this practice was against Islamic law concerning the rights of non-Muslim subjects.[75] In brief, Islam forbids reprisal and the frame of every action in war is defined by Islamic law, which nobody may transgress.

The third component of Gülen's religious response to violence is perhaps the most significant. This is the rejection of ends justify means philosophy. In a recorded address after London subway bombings and amidst suicide bombing events in Israel, Gülen criticized an authority

---

71 Abu Dawud, Jihad, 111.

72 Muhammed b. Umar b. Waqid, Kitab al-Maghazi, Oxford 1966, III.117-118; Hamza Aktan, 'Acts of Terror and Suicide Attacks in the Light of the Qur'an and the Sunna', An Islamic Perspective: Terror and Suicide Attacks, New Jersey: Light Pb 2004., 26

73 Tahawi, Sharh al-Maan al-Athar, Beirut: Dar Kutub al-Ilmiyya 1996, III.224; Çapan, Ibid., 83

74 Albayrak, I., "Juxtaposition of Islam with Violence", in Hunt et al., "Muslim Citizens of the Globalized World: Contributions of the Gülen Movement", The Light Inc., NJ 2006.

75 Bekir Karlığa, Kültürlerarası Diyalog Sempozyumu, Erkâm Mat. İst. 1998, 16

who condoned acts of suicide bombings for Palestinians[76]:

> Unfortunately some condone acts of suicide bombing with the rhetoric of "they have no other means". If this (referring to suicide bombings) is the only means Muslims have, let that means be buried deep into ground together with the one who uses it.

Gülen continues that the combination of certain non-religious motives and the lack of a holistic perspective allows people to pick and choose what part of the religious tradition they would use in justifying violent acts[77]:

> The problem today is that Islam is not understood properly, in a holistic manner. Islam has always been respectful of plurality of worldviews and this point needs to be understood well today. Islam is an authentic religion and it should be lived true to its spirit. While striving toward an Islamic life, it is self-contradictory to use illegitimate means. Just as the ends should be righteous, the means should also be righteous. A Muslim can not hope to please God by killing humans. Killing humans can not be a means of pleasing God.

Gülen also offers explanations for misinterpreted verses and prophetic sayings which are abused by those who justify acts of violence. He states that 'the reasons why certain Muslim people or institutions that misunderstand Islam are becoming involved in terrorist attacks throughout the world should be sought not in Islam, but within the people themselves, in their misinterpretations[78] and in other factors.[79]

> The verses in the Qur'an that specify conditions for jihad have been misinterpreted by others and taken as the fundamental aim of Islam. In essence, these people, who have failed to grasp the true spirit of Islam, have been unable to strike a balance between the broad and finer points and this, when coupled with the fact that they have been consumed with hatred, has led them to misinterpret Islam. The heart of a genuine Muslim community is full of love and affection for all of creation.

Albayrak points out Gülen's criticism of context-free reading of the religious sources driven by motives other than religious piety[80]:

> (Gülen) 'argues that some narrow-minded individuals who lack the power of discernment narrow the broad scope of Islam. For this reason Gülen suggests that such people must first change the image of Islam in their mind. Because they have no comprehensive understanding of the sources, they take as reference only some sections of the Islamic sources without exploring the Qur'an and the Prophetic tradition, or the understandings of prominent Muslim scholars. They read these texts literally and mostly out of context without examining what precede or follows them. The results are disastrous: they misinterpret their religion and then put this misunderstood religion into practice; consequently they are misguided and they misguide others'.

Gülen's Opinions on Political Roots of Terrorism

On the political perspective while discussing misunderstandings, misrepresentations and abuses of religious texts, Gülen hints at the presence of individuals, ideology or interest groups, and other entities that benefit from friction and armed conflict. He points out that the possibility of some individuals having been manipulated and deceived or plainly hypnotized,

---

76 "Hosgoru, bombalar ve azinliklar" (Tolerance, bombs and religious minorities), available online in Turkish at http://www.herkul.org.

77 Akman, Ibid.

78 Ismail Albayrak, 'Islam and Terror: From the Perspective of Fethullah Gülen', http://en.fGülen.com/ content/ view/2243/4/, accessed on 14 August 2007

79   M. Fethullah Gülen, 'Real Muslims Cannot Be Terrorists', Turkish Daily News, September 19, 2001

80 Albayrak Ibid.

sometimes through special drugs, to carry out actions they would not carry out otherwise should be given consideration.

Gülen does not deny that political conditions are sources of political violence and terrorism, but he insists that people should not use those conditions in order to justify their unlawful action. He advises that 'Muslims must be legitimate in their intentions when it comes to their goals, thoughts, and actions, for only a straight and allowed way can lead them to their exalted object'.[81] This clearly indicate that Muslim should be legitimate not only their action but also their intentions. Without legitimacy, neither their action nor intention is acceptable even if they gain what they aimed.

We have discussed the secondary role of ideology or religion in communication and recruitment for terrorism. Gülen echoes the findings of researchers who point out diverse conditions that provide a feeding ground for terrorist groups. The recent history of colonialism, tyranny of non-democratic, authoritarian leaders, the presence of various forms of suffering and injustice, and the lack of authoritative scholars provide opportunities for misleading individuals toward violent reactions that serve other interests. He asserts that

> We must realize that no Muslim country, when considered from the viewpoint of administrative, legal, and economic matters, exists. What we mean by that phrase is countries with majority Muslim populations. Many of them have movements for independence and also have to cope with the pressures of artificial and oligarchic governments, poverty, ignorance, lack of accurate religious knowledge, geographical difficulties, and unjust distribution of wealth; continued intervention from outside forces who want to block democracy from taking root; easy imports and the consequent non-improvement in domestic production, export, and economics; and, more than anything else, the role of the media in undermining moral values. All of these problems are confronting the Muslims and make them appear in an unfavourable light. [82]

We have highlighted frustration as a leading cause of terrorism tendencies above. The frustration serves as the turning point toward political violence. According to Gülen, in order to eliminate the tendency toward violence, main focus should be on the individual who lives under those conditions that produce frustration. In some cases, only moral support is enough for many people who are suffering under those conditions. Often, however, a systematic approach centred around education is the only lasting solution. Gülen believes that the humanity is looking forward to the days where individuals endowed with high human values overcome those who favour hostility:

> I have been looking forward to a better world resembling Paradise, where humanity can live in peace and tranquillity. Our world is tired of war and clashes. It direly needs mercy, affection, spiritual well-being, and peace more than air and water. I believe that people in every country are ready for such a world.[83]

The states have been responding to the problem of terrorism through measures such as anti-terrorist legislation, strengthening judicial power, increased state accountability, special

---

81 In M. Fethullah Gülen, 'Respect For Humankind', The Fountain, January – March, 2006 / Issue 53 http://www.fountainmagazine.com/articles.php?SIN=6e31958cbc&k=738&593384988&show=part1, accessed on 13 August 2007

82 M. Fethullah Gülen, 'Respect For Humankind', The Fountain, January – March, 2006 / Issue 53 http://www.fountainmagazine.com/articles.php?SIN=6e31958cbc&k=738&593384988&show=part1, accessed on 13 August 2007.

83 Fethullah Gülen, 'Excerpts from F. Gülen's Answers to Questions on Education and Turkish Educational Activities Abroad', http://en.fGülen.com/content/view/779/2/, accessed on 14 August 2007.

forces, better command and coordination among security forces, direction of media, better intelligence, deterrence, and collaboration among government agencies, as well as reduction of systematic causes. Below, we will examine the civilian response inspired by Gülen's educational philosophy and activism that centres on the individual human.

The Educational Approach to the Problem of Terrorism

Gülen sees the individual human being at the centre of every major problem of humanity as well as its solution. Lasting solutions to social problems such as lack of education, poverty and division can not be achieved without paying enough attention to the individual human. For this reason, the underlying dynamics of Gülen's approach are education, mutual understanding, respect, opportunity and hope. Saritoprak comments that 'for the peaceful world of the future, Gülen encourages his admirers to establish educational institutions in and outside of Turkey. He gives special importance to the areas where ethnic and religious conflicts are escalating, such as Albania, Kosovo, Macedonia, the Philippines, Banda Aceh, Northern Iraq, and South-eastern Turkey'.[84]

Many educational institutions (from nursery to university) have been established in Turkey and some 103 countries of the world by civil society organizations that have been inspired by Gülen. In addition to following the national curricula of their localities, these educational institutions actively foster interfaith and intercultural dialog, mutual understanding and respect, which offer hope of upward mobility, and provide lasting solutions to the problem of violent social conflict.[85] A striking example of generation of hope of upward mobility is the set of educational institutions in south-eastern Turkey. In his soon to be published book, in part presented at this conference, Kalyoncu describes how the people of the region, predominantly Kurdish citizens of Turkey, embrace and support the educational initiatives of organizations inspired by Gülen that give their children an opportunity to become engineers, doctors, lawyers and architects instead of being recruited by terrorist organizations[86]. Other examples of such bridges can be seen in Philippines, where Muslim minority students study with their fellow Christian students in an atmosphere of trust[87]; Bosnia-Herzegovina where children of Bosnian Muslims who have been massacred by Serbians study shoulder-to-shoulder with their children[88], and Macedonia where the fighting Albanian, Macedonia and Serbian factions carry their children to such schools for safety.

Students are not the only beneficiaries of these educational institutions. Increasingly transnational in their outlook, civil society organizations focusing on education 'serve as a bridge between the peoples of the countries where they are and thereby can contribute to the world peace'.[89] In many cases, the educational institutions have started a larger synergy and led to

---

84 Zeki Saritoprak, 'An Islamic Approach to Peace and Nonviolence: A Turkish Experience', The Muslim World, Vol. 95 (July 2005), pp. 413-427

85 Zeki Saritoprak, 'An Islamic Approach to Peace and Nonviolence: A Turkish Experience', The Muslim World, Vol. 95 (July 2005), pp. 413-427

86 Mehmet Kalyoncu, 'The Counter Terrorism Issue In Terms Of Systems Theory; Diyarbakir as a Case Study', presentation at the Second Istanbul Conference on Democracy and Global Security, June 14-16, 2007.

87 Michel, Thomas. 2003. Fethullah Gülen as an Educator. In Turkish Islam and the secular state: The Gülen movement. M. H. Yavuz and J. L. Esposito, eds. Syracuse: Syracuse University Press.

88 Serif Ali Tekalan, 'Monuments of Love and Alturism', in Baris Kopruleri (Bridges of Peace), Istanbul: Ufuk Kitaplari, 2005, 254.

89 Fahri Karakas, 'Global Peaceful Social Innovation: The Case of Gülen Network', http://en.fGülen.com/content/view/2242/4/, accessed on 14 August 2007

the formation of new trade and civic links among communities and nations.

Conclusion

We began by examining origins and root causes of violence, especially political violence. Economic, political, social and cultural factors each play a role in the slipping of individuals into the perilous slope of terrorism. Both governments as well as civic organizations have an obligation in responding to this modern phenomenon which has far reaching consequences for humanity. Recently, religion, and in particular the name of Islam have been juxtaposed with terrorist actions and individuals. Among opinion leaders who respond to terrorism, Gülen is distinguished by three factors. First, Gülen has clearly voiced his unconditional condemnation of acts of violence against civilians and stated that involvement in terrorism can not coincide with commitment to faith. Secondly, Gülen argued both as a human and as a Muslim scholar in systematic and convincing ways to distance his audience from having sympathy with the perpetrators of such actions. Third, lasting solutions to the problem of terrorism in the form of educational institutions inculcating a culture of tolerance and respect, and opportunities for upward mobility have been generated by civil society organizations inspired and encouraged by Gülen. In other words, Gülen's ideas and vision have not remained in audio tapes and books, but instead they have been realized in concrete projects in volatile regions of the world. From the beginning of his career, Gülen has been involved in the establishment of educational institutions and personally tutored some of their first teachers. He has personally experienced whether his proposals to humanity were workable or not. The results have so far been positive and there are tangible indicators of decreased tensions in communities with Gülen-inspired educational institutions in many regions of the world.[90] A review of Gülen's rhetoric and action reveals that he has understood the root causes of violence and political violence (terrorism), paving the way for him to pioneer sustainable ways to combat and prevent them.

We have pointed out to the political and economic roots of terrorism and the role ideology, or religion cast into an ideological form, plays in communicating with the community in order to recruit more support, rather than being itself the root cause of terrorism. Richardson comments that 'broad social, economic and cultural factors may be the underlying causes or rather the risk factors that make a society more or less susceptible to the appeal of terrorist groups'.[91] Economic and other grievances only lead to terrorism if people feel that those grievances are a product of the political system, and they are excluded from that system. Consequently, the response to the complex phenomenon of terrorism involves participation by political institutions, such as governmental agencies, as well as civil society organizations. Gülen's humanitarian, religious as well as educational response to violence against civilians, as implemented by the civil society organizations inspired by his ideas, demonstrates the potential of the civil society organizations in this challenging task.

---

90 Zeki Saritoprak, 'An Islamic Approach to Peace and Nonviolence: A Turkish Experience', The Muslim World, Vol. 95 (July 2005), pp. 413-427

91 Louise Richardson, *What Terrorists Want: Understanding the Terrorists* Threat, John Murray: GB 2006, p. 93

GÜLEN'S CONTRIBUTION TO A MODERATE ISLAM IN SOUTHEAST ASIA

Muhammad Nawab Osman

Abstract

This paper aims to demonstrate the relevance of the Gülen movement as a counter to extremist ideology and an encouragement to inter-religious dialogue in the Southeast Asia region. The movement presents a Middle Way Islam, which can accommodate local cultural differences and make a hospitable space for positive relations between Muslims and non-Muslims.

Following an account of Fethullah Gülen's views on extremism and inter-religious dialogue, the paper turns to case studies of Gülen-inspired organisations in Singapore and Indonesia to show how they have applied his ideas to enable inter-religious dialogue and offer an effective alternative to legalistic teaching of Islam. The case studies allow for comparison of the movement's approach to a Muslim-majority and Muslim-minority context. The paper concludes by charting the trajectory of the movement's role and contribution to the development of a Middle Way Islam in Southeast Asia.

The paper is based on a combination of fieldwork with a qualitative approach and documentary research. The fieldwork comprises data gathered through participatory observation in Singapore and interviews with key members of the two organisations and their local partners. The documentary research comprises data from the movement's publications – books, magazines (Asya Pasifik), newspaper articles, brochures and online materials.

The emergence of Islam as a political force is a recent development in Southeast Asia. Earlier, the impact of the resurgence of Islam had been felt both in the social and cultural realms, through the mushrooming of Muslim organizations attempting to promote a 'purer' form of Islam in the region. In more recent times, however, the expression of religiosity has been brought about by way of participation in political parties and groups. More shockingly, some of these groups, such as the terror network known as Jemaati Islamiyah, have sought to use violence to achieve their aims. This has had severe ramifications for both intra-Muslim relations and Muslim-non-Muslim relations in the region. In this chaotic socio-political climate, a group has emerged in the region advocating peace, tolerance and understanding between people of different races and religions. This group is known as the Gülen movement, or is commonly referred to as the *hizmet*, in Turkey. [1]

This paper will demonstrate how the Gülen movement has addressed the issues facing them and remained relevant by developing a counter-trend through proactive measures to oppose extremist ideology and enhance inter-religious discussion in the Southeast Asian region. Its key thrust is to show that the Gülen movement can reverse the current distorted state of Islam back to its original form. The teachings of Islam which is the teachings of the Middle Way can accommodate the cultural differences in Southeast Asia and enhance inter-religious ties between Muslims and non-Muslims in the region. The paper will first examine Fethullah Gülen's views on extremism and inter-religious dialogue. The paper will then proceed to examine case studies of organizations inspired by Gülen in Singapore and Indonesia and how these organizations utilized his ideas to enhance inter-religious dialogue and provide an alternative to the legalistic discourse on Islam. This section will also attempt to compare and contrast the approach of the organization in a Muslim-majority country (Indonesia) and in a Muslim minority country (Singapore). The paper will conclude by charting a trajectory of the movement's role its potential contributions to the development of moderate Islam in Southeast Asia. It will be argued that these contributions will become an important counter to extremist ideologies and enhance ties amongst Muslims and between members of different faiths in the region.[2]

Fethullah Gülen and His Movement

Fethullah Gülen is an important Turkish scholar, educationalist and popular preacher, influential not only in Turkey but also in other parts of the world. His reach transcends world borders and cultures. He is well respected by many world leaders including those in Southeast Asia. The former President of Indonesia and a prominent Muslim scholar, Abdurrahman Wahid said "it is a must for us to study from Said Nursi and Fethullah Gülen in Turkey who emphasized good moral standard" (PASIAD, 2006, p. 2). His standing as a widely respected religious scholar has inspired many people in Turkey to establish educational institutions. Commonly known as the Gülen movement, the movement is loose in nature. Due to this, it has been difficult for one to assess the real numbers of those involved in the movement. This has led an observer to suggest that, "Gülen has made himself a most likely candidate for

---

1 *Hizmet* literally means service to humanity in Turkish and is often used by followers of Gülen to describe his movement.

2 The research for this paper combines field and documentary research methods with a qualitative approach. The field research component was based on data gathered through participatory observation (in the case of Singapore) and interviews with key figures of the Gülen-inspired organisations as well as local partners of these organizations. The documentary research component of the paper gathers data from the movement's publications, including books, newspaper articles and online materials.

religious leader of the new Turkey"(Bulent, 1998, p. 27). Hakan Yavuz described the Gülen movement as a web of formal and informal relations that constantly activates its members' loyalty. These relations are carried out within a set of networks in which commitment to the goals of the movement are maintained through informal living spaces—the lighthouses, the dormitories, the summer camps—and through regular fund-raising activities (Yavuz, 2003, p. 32). Perhaps, more importantly, these networks are gelled together through a common belief in the ideas of Gülen. In the next section of this paper, a discussion of Gülen's ideas on extremism, tolerance and dialogue will be discussed.

Gülen on Dialogue and Tolerance

Gülen's emphasis on dialogue is on the basis of his belief that Islam is a religion of peace and dialogue. He advocates an Anatolian-Islam that puts an emphasis on tolerance and Turkish modernity emphasizing that this discourse of Islam is not in contradiction with the modern world (Yilmaz, 2005, p. 397) Gülen had written that the Qur'an strongly urges and also calls for tolerance, forgiveness and humility, which he sees as central Islamic ethical values that are also interrelated. For Gülen, those who close the road of tolerance are beasts who have lost their humanity. It is only through forgiveness and tolerance that wounds could be healed (Gülen, 1999, p. 76). Gülen finds the roots of these themes in the teachings of the Prophet Muhammad. He gave the example of the Prophet and Abu Jahl.[3] Once in an assembly where Abu Jahl's son Ikrima was present, the Prophet admonished a companion for insulting Abu Jahl (Ünal & Williams, 2000, p. 196). This is despite the fact that Abu Jahl was strongly opposed to Islam.

For Gülen, dialogue and tolerance must first start amongst Muslims. He exemplified this spirit through his engagements with the Alevi and Kurdish communities in Turkey. Of the Alevies, he noted that the community enriches Turkish culture. He also supported the setting up of Alevi meeting or prayer houses (Ünal & Williams, 2000, p. 70). Gülen's emphasis for dialogue and tolerance is not limited to Muslims but also extends to include non-Muslims. Gülen wrote about this need by citing a story of the great Sufi scholar Mevlana Jalaleddin Rumi and a Christian priest. According to the story, a priest had visited Rumi and wanted to kiss his hands out of respect but Rumi kissed the hands of the priest first. According to Gülen, therefore, dialogue with adherents of other religious traditions is an integral part of an Islamic ethic that has been neglected for a long time (Gülen, 1999, p. 76).

Gülen once again acted upon his own calling by meeting important Christian leaders such as Pope John Paul and the Greek Orthodox Patriarch Bartholomew. The visit was an important step in Muslim/Christian relations. Their efforts bore fruit in the form of an interfaith conference organized by an interfaith dialogue organization, the Foundation of Journalists and Writers in Turkey. This conference, called the Abraham Symposium, was held in southeast Turkey in the city of Urfa, believed to be the birthplace of Prophet Abraham (Saritoprak & Griffith, 2005, p. 336). The meeting with the Greek Patriarch also brought about better relations between Greeks and Turks, two communities long known for their enmity. The spirit that Gülen creates amongst Muslims ensures that the true teachings of Islam, which is moderate and characterized by a path of the Middle Way, are emphasized.

Beyond expressing support for peace, tolerance and inter-faith dialogue, Gülen is also vehemently against violence and extremism. Gülen points to misinterpretation of Islamic

---

3 Abu Jahl or Amr ibn Hishām was one of the chieftains of Makkah during the life of the Prophet. He was known for his cruelty and given the name Abu Jahl or Father of Ignorance for his opposition to the Prophet.

teachings and lack of education as being prime reasons for Muslim extremism and terrorism. He believes that many extremist Muslims read Islamic texts and sources literally and mostly out of context without understanding the Qur'an and the Prophetic traditions or the interpretations of prominent Muslim scholars (Albayrak, 2007, p. 140). For Gülen, in true Islam, terrorism does not exist (Ergün, 2004, p. 1). He stated clearly that in Islam no group or individual could declare war. The prerogative of such an action is that of the state (Ergün, 2004, p. 2). To counter the threat of extremism and terrorism, Gülen has proposed enhancing the reach of education and inter-religious dialogue amongst Muslims. To implement this, Gülen called for the establishment of schools, with a comprehensive educational system, that will produce well educated, cultured people who are cognizant of their religious and civic duties (Ergün, 2004, p. 5). Gülen's vision was achieved when many of his students and supporters started schools all over the world extending from Papua New Guinea in the South Pacific to Tanzania in Africa. The success of these schools in encouraging tolerance and inter-faith dialogue are best encapsulated in the observations made by Thomas Michel, the secretary for Inter-Religious Dialogue of the Society of Jesus in Rome. He remarks that the Philippine-Turkish School of Tolerance in Zamboanga, Philippines offers Muslim and Christian Filipino children a positive way of living and relating to each other (Michel, 2003, p. 71). This is especially important in a country bogged down by more than 300 hundred years of conflict between Christians and Muslims. The school also marks an important step in countering terrorism, as the value system taught in the school prevent students, especially from the Muslim community, from being influenced by Muslim terrorist groups in the region.[4]

Gülen's thinking on the issues of tolerance, dialogue and terrorism have enhanced relations among Muslims as well as between Muslims and non-Muslims in many parts of the world. It has also provided a blueprint for the development of a Middle Way Islam, which is none other than the original and traditional teachings of the Prophet. The case studies of the movement in Southeast Asia will reveal that his ideas are not abstract or theoretical in nature but are in fact practical and easy to implement. The examples of the movement in Singapore and Indonesia will attest to this.

The Gülen Movement in Southeast Asia

One cannot be sure of the exact point in time when the movement began to make a presence in the region. Individuals from Turkey who were influenced by Gülen's idea first arrived in the region in the 1980s. However, it was only in 1993 that the first school was started in the region. Today, the movement has started schools in virtually all the Southeast Asian countries. Interestingly, the movement started a school in Cambodia in the late 1990s, when the country was just recovering from political turmoil following the genocide perpetrated by its dictator, Pol Pot, against the Cambodians. Members of the Gülen movement, through the encouragement of peers, made their way to certain cities after first assessing their needs.

Similar to other parts of the world, the movement in SEA adopts the same method of spearheading and promoting its activities. Businessmen from a particular city in Turkey will concentrate their efforts on a particular Southeast Asian city. For instance, the city of Gaziantep in the South-eastern part of Turkey, partially supports activities of certain cities in SEA, such as Singapore and Manila. Unlike Central Asia, where members of the Gülen community were sent by the movement with the aim of making contact with important companies, bureaucrats

---

4 Conversation with Amina Rasul-Bernardo is the Lead Convenor of the Philippine Council for Islam and Democracy. She is a Senior Research Fellow with the Asian Institute of Management Policy Centre.

and personalities, the followers of Gülen who came to Southeast Asia did so mainly due to self-motivation or due to a sense of duty to serve in places that badly needed assistance.[5] This probably explains why a follower of Gülen from Malaysia subsequently left for Papua New Guinea, a place often linked to cannibalism and a tribal way of life, to set up a school.

An organization that plays an important role in the development of the movement in the region is the Pacific Countries Social and Economic Solidarity Association (PASIAD). PASIAD plays an important linking role. It assists Turkish businessmen and students who are interested to invest or study in a particular Asia-Pacific country by linking them up with the local Gülen movement operating in a particular country. It also plays a 'middle man' role in the disbursement of funds from Turkish businessmen to the respective Gülen movement-school or institution they are supporting.[6] PASIAD does not however oversee or direct activities of the local movements. Its role is merely a supportive one.

The Turkish Cultural Centre in Singapore

Context and Historical Background

Singapore is small country of four million people. Muslims make up about 14% of the population while the remaining populace are Buddhists, Christians, Hindus and Jews. Most Muslims in Singapore are ethnically Malay. Due to historical and political reasons, the Muslim minority in Singapore is often seen to be a 'problematic' community.[7] Their increased adherence to Islam and the emergence of a more puritan version of Islam amongst Singaporean Muslims is often viewed with trepidation by the Singaporean government. Since 1990s, several controversies such as the banning of the headscarf in schools, the government's attempt to reform the madrasas in Singapore, and the arrests of several members of the Jemaati Islamiyah terror network, had created tensions between the Muslim and non-Muslim communities.[8] There was little effort made in formulating any form of inter-religious dialogues among the different religious communities. The ignorance about one another's religion only went on to exacerbate the uneasiness between Muslims and non-Muslims in the country. The emergence of the Gülen movement was timely in easing some of these tensions.

The Gülen movement first found a foothold in Singapore when Mr Sadik Yildiz, a journalist with the Zaman newspaper, first came to the island state in 1997. He was in Singapore as Zaman's representative in Singapore. Similar to other members of the Gülen movement elsewhere in the world, he began to establish relations with members of the Singaporean community. In particular, he made important contacts with members of the ethnic Chinese and Indian communities, who are mostly non- Muslims, as well as with several important politicians including Mr Sidek Saniff, the then Senior Minister of State for Education as well as Mr Harun Ghani, the Senior Parliamentary Secretary for the Ministry of Home Affairs. In addition, he built strong relations with several Singapore based Turkish businessmen including Mr Ismail Cem, owner of a prominent Turkish restaurant (Candemir, 2007). These important links facilitated in the work of the Gülen movement in the country. Yildiz, with

---

5 Refer to Balci, Bayram. (2003), Fethullah Gülen's Missionary Schools in Central Asia and their Role in the Spreading of Turkism and Islam. Religion, State & Society, 31, 2, 151-177 for the Central Asian cases.

6 Conversation with Irfan Tibet, a staff of PASIAD in March 2007 during his visit to Singapore.

7 For more on the problems of Malays in Singapore, see Rahim, Lily Zubaidah. (1998) The Singapore Dilemma: The Political and Educational Marginality of the Malay community, (Kuala Lumpur, Oxford University Press).

8 For more on these issues, see Mohamed Osman, Mohamed Nawab. (2004) Activism of Ulama in Singapore, (Unpublished Academic Thesis, National University of Singapore).

the assistance of the local Turkish community and Singaporeans, formed the Turkey-Central Asia Cultural Centre on the 3rd of April 1999. Later the centre was renamed as the Turkish Cultural Centre (TCC). Since its formation, the TCC has had three directors, Sadik Yildiz (1999), Halit Yuksel (1999-2001) and Necmettin Eskici (2001-present).

Yildiz also encouraged students from the Gülen inspired schools in Turkey to come to Singapore to further their studies. These students began to enrol in several universities in Singapore by 2001 (Eskici, 2007). These students, including Dr Erkan Polatdemir, were to form an important component of the movement in Singapore. The TCC grew in prominence after the 1999 earthquake, when it coordinated the assistance that Singapore gave to Turkey. Subsequently, it also played a more important cultural role, promoting Turkish culture in Singapore. In August 2001, TCC assisted Junction 8, one of the largest shopping malls in Singapore, to promote the movie, 'Accidental Spy', by bringing Turkish folklore dancers to Singapore. TCC also used the promotion period to start booths selling Turkish handicrafts and products, which led to a huge profit for the TCC. In more recent times, TCC has also assisted students from Turkey and Central Asia, most of who were studying in Gülen inspired schools, to acclimatize to Singapore (Polatdemir, 2007). The support for its activities comes mainly through PASIAD, but in recent times TCC has successfully obtained support from local businessmen and partners to support some of its activities.

Encouraging Tolerance and Dialogue

At the initial stage, TCC under the leadership of Yildiz latched on to the Inter-Religious Organization (IRO) to promote inter-religious dialogue in Singapore. However, due to the internal problems of the IRO, TCC started its own initiatives (Polatdemir, 2007). The flagship event that the TCC organizes annually is the iftar dinner, held during the month of Ramadan. The first such dinner was organized in 1999, when about a hundred people, of whom one-third were non- Muslims, attended. A large number of the Muslim attendees were members of the Turkish community in Singapore. The event served as a platform whereby the community could gather and enhance their relations. Some Singaporean Muslims were also invited. These were often family members or friends of Turks staying in Singapore. Among the non-Muslims, the attendees comprised of members of the IRO including its then chairman Venerable Gunaratna, Christian community leaders, Buddhists and Hindus. The Guest of Honour was Mr Sidek Saniff, the then Senior Minister of State for Education. The iftar dinner was a watershed event given the context of the time when it was organized (Eskici, 2007). Firstly, the Muslim community in Singapore was divided along religious and ideological lines. Several issues, such as the ban on the wearing of headscarf and the perceived attempt by the Singaporean government to ban Islamic religious schools, had given rise to differing opinions amongst Muslims. Secondly, these issues had resulted in tensions between Muslims and non-Muslims in Singapore. Both the Singaporean government and the non-Muslim communities perceived the Muslims as being exclusive and failing to integrate with the larger Singaporean society. Most importantly, the iftar was often seen to be an exclusively Muslim event and most Singaporean Muslims were not comfortable with inviting non-Muslims for it. The smooth running of this annual event thus served as an important milestone in bridging the gap between the communities, which otherwise would have widened. Such an initiative is a replica of the larger Abant platform that the Gülen Movement had initiated and utilized in Turkey. The Journalists and Writers Association, an organization inspired by Gülen in 1998, first initiated the Abant platform.[9] It was a platform for the discussing issues considered to be

---

9 For all the declarations for various Abant meeting, see http://www.gyv.org.tr/bp.asp?caid=174

sensitive and divisive in Turkey. Ihsan Yilmaz noted that the Abant Platform has shown the Turkish public that it is possible to bring together intellectuals, academics and civil society leaders from all walks of life, discussing and in most cases agreeing on every single sensitive issue in the country (Yilmaz, *Today's Zaman*, 23 March 2007).

TCC's iftar dinner attendance has since grown larger in number and includes more non-Muslims. When the author attended the iftar dinner in 2005 and 2006, the diverse background of the attendees pleasantly surprised him. The Muslims who attended the dinner were from different ideological types- from the puritan Salafi types to the more Sufi-oriented types.[10] Despite their different religious ideology, they sat at the same table and interacted well. Leaders of all the major Muslim organizations were also invited for this function. More interestingly, members of various religious communities were also present. These included members of the Jewish community and various church communities including representative of the City Harvest Church, a church known for its staunchly conservative and evangelical position. The fact that representatives of the Church even came to the function was a matter of amazement for many of the attendees, and is in fact a big achievement for the TCC.[11] The programs of these iftar also featured non-Muslim speakers, Brother Michael Broughten from the Catholic community and Mr Hsieh Fu Hua from the Methodist community. The success of these iftar was acknowledged even by the Islamic Religious Council of Singapore (MUIS), a government statutory board dealing with affairs of Muslims in Singapore, when they decided to partially sponsor the 2006 iftar dinner (Eskici, 2007).

The next iftar event scheduled to be held on the 25th of Sept 2007 will be another watershed event for TCC. For the first time in its history, the Minister of Muslim Affairs, often seen as the highest office held by a Muslim in the country, Yacoob Ibrahim will be attending the function as the Guest of Honour. The fact that the minister decided to grace the event especially in the month of Ramadan, which is often seen to be one of the busiest months in his schedule is an acknowledgement of the importance of TCC in developing inter-religious dialogue in Singapore. TCC has also invited members of The Rock, an evangelistic Christian movement known for their rejection of inter-religious dialogues for the 2007 iftar.

Perhaps, the most important impact of these iftars is the fact that following the events of Sept 11, other Muslim organizations and several mosques began inviting non-Muslims to their own iftar dinners. This was often seen to be a taboo but learning from the example of the TCC, they began to realize the importance and value of this endeavour. For instance, as a student leader, leading the National University of Singapore Muslim Society, the author himself decided to organize iftar dinners ala TCC and invited non-Muslim students for the function. As such, one could argue that the efforts of the TCC have been significant in creating a new method of inter-religious dialogue. At the same time, many of the attendees, who included prominent religious and community leaders of the Singaporean society, continue to come and even look forward to the iftar. This is a reflection of the importance of the event in enhancing their understanding of the others and of Islam.

Intra and Inter Faith Dialogues

The TCC's inter-faith engagements go beyond these iftar dinners. Imbibing the spirit of Gülen's teachings, they also collaborate with various local partners to organize seminars and

---

10 Personal Observation of Author at the TCC *Iftar* Dinner at Hilton Hotel in Oct 2006.

11 The church has been at odds with the Muslim community and other communities for its aggressive proselytizing techniques. For more on this church, see the website of the City Harvest Church at http://www.chc.org.sg/main_landing.htm

talks aimed at creating a better image of Islam. One such event was a seminar on Islam and Modernity jointly organized with the Ba'alwi Mosque in April 2006. The seminar featured several prominent academics including Prof Ibrahim Abu Rabi from the Hartford Seminary, and Assoc Prof Farid al-Attas from the National University of Singapore .[12] The key message of the speakers was that Islam is a religion of the Middle Way, which was against terrorism and extremism. Prof Farid and Prof Abu-Rabi also spoke about the ideas of Fethullah Gülen in countering extremism. The session, attended by many non-Muslim Singaporeans was significant in trying to create a better image of Islam post Sept 11.

Another approach adopted by the TCC to enhance inter-religious ties was to invite Singaporeans to Turkey for a 'cultural immersion' program. These trips are not only important in so far as they contribute to a deepening understanding of Turkey and its culture but also enhance the participant's knowledge of Islam. In December 2006, the TCC facilitated a trip to Turkey organized by the National University of Singapore's Scholars Program.[13] The students, who were mostly non-Muslims, visited various Islamic historical sites and were hosted by academics from Fatih University in Istanbul. They were also introduced to Turkish Islam and the ideas of Fethullah Gülen. Upon their return to Singapore, a seminar was organized at the Harmony Centre, a centre for inter-faith activities, and they presented their impressions of Turkey. It was obvious that their knowledge of Islam was greatly enhanced and many were clearly moved by their experience. One of the non-Muslim participants mentioned in his presentation that the teachings of Gülen would shape a positive perception of Islam, which will be instrumental in the resurgence of the Muslim World. [14]

TCC also organized another trip to Turkey in June 2007 for Christian community leaders in Singapore. Participants were taken to visit several institutions linked to the Gülen movement. They also met and had dinner with supporters of the Gülen movement. During such events, they developed an understanding of the Middle Way Islam that Gülen is advocating and gained an insight into why many people devoted their time and effort for the movement (Yap, 2007). One of the participants, Reverend Yap Khiam Hoe, former Bishop of the Methodist Church in Singapore and Malaysia said that Gülen is indeed a gifted Muslim renewer who will change the world's impression of Islam through his enlightened ideals (Yap, 2007). After the trip, Reverend Yap has become an even stauncher supporter of TCC. He has promoted the ideas of Gülen to his Muslim friends and has requested the author to address members of the Contemporary Centre for Islamic Studies on Gülen's ideas and on the movement.

The efforts of TCC at enhancing intra and inter-religious dialogue is indeed commendable. Besides being a trend setter in inter-religious dialogue, the TCC was also in the forefront organizing various events to improve the understanding of Islam. Its efforts has led to better relations amongst Muslims and between Muslims and non-Muslims in Singapore. The TCC will soon embark on the next stage of its intra and inter-religious dialogue effort by starting a Turkish school in Singapore. While this seems like an arduous task at this moment due to the Singaporean government educational policies, the positive imprint that TCC has left in the shaping of Singapore's society may lead to the Singaporean government shifting their policy on the Turkish school.

---

12 The author was present at this seminar.

13 Students who are selected for this program are among the best students in Singapore and often occupy important policy making positions upon their graduation.

14 The author himself was also greatly impressed by the Gülen movement. He had visited some of the institutions linked to the movement during his personal trip to Turkey in Dec 2006.

PASIAD Indonesia

Context and History

Indonesia is the world's largest Islamic country, with 190 to 200 million Muslims out of a total population of around 240 million. Historically, Islam in Indonesia is moderate and is known for its pluralistic nature. Yet, since the fall of the former President Suharto in 1998, a more radical form of the religion has emerged. While the vast majority of Indonesian Muslims are moderate, some are now pushing for an Islamic state to be established, violently if necessary. Religious conflict between Muslims and Christians in some parts of Indonesia has led to thousands of lives lost. The proliferation of Islamic groups and political parties in the country also means that Muslims are increasingly divided along the lines of religious ideology.[15] In these difficult times, the Gülen movement in Indonesia remains one of the few moderate Islamic voices advocating for both intra and inter Muslim tolerance and dialogue.

The Gülen movement arrived in Indonesia in 1993 when three students from Turkey came to study in the country.[16] This decision is indeed a strange one given that none of these students could speak Indonesian or even knew anyone in the country. They first approached a contact of an Indonesian friend (who studied in Turkey). This person, Haji Alwi was initially rather surprised to see the Turkish boys, but nevertheless assisted them to obtain places in various universities in Indonesia. Islamoglu secured a place at the University of Indonesia in the Department of Indonesian Literature. In 1994, after about a year of studying in the university, Islamoglu informed Haji Alwi about the Gülen movement and expressed his desire to start a school in Indonesia (Islamoglu, 2007). Haji Alwi introduced him to the Governor of Indonesia state Bank, Burhanuddin Abdullah who assisted Islamoglu in setting up the first school in Indonesia, the Pribadi High School in Depok. Another person who was instrumental in the setting up of the school was Dr Aip Syarifuddin, an Indonesian politician (Islamoglu, 2007). To ensure that the administration of the school was managed professionally, Islamoglu and his friends tied up with several Indonesians, including Dr Syarifuddin and a Mr Firman Kartiman, to start the Yenbu Indonesian Foundation (Islamoglu, 2007). In 1997, another organization, PASIAD Indonesia, was formed to facilitate in the administration of the school.

In 1996, Islamoglu decided to transfer his studies to the Gadjah Muda University in Semarang, a city located in the centre of the island of Java. Islamoglu quickly became close to the Dean of the University, Prof Siti Chamamah Soeratno and invited her to visit the school in Jakarta. Upon seeing the quality of its education, Prof Soeratno was impressed and was inspired to start a similar school in Semarang. This led to the setting up of the Al-Firdaus Semarang Foundation, which then worked closely with PASIAD Indonesia to start the SMP-SMA Semesta Boarding School (PASIAD, 2006, p. 18). In 2002, a school was built in Bandung. Another school was also built following the tsunami of 2005 in Aceh. The most recent school that was built is the Kharisma National School. This school was built with the support of a rich and prominent Indonesian family (Altun, 2007).

Besides educational activities, PASIAD Indonesia also played an important role promoting cultural ties between Turkey and Indonesia. Since 2001, it has published several books with local partners promoting the Turkish language. This includes the publication of a Turkish-Indonesian dictionary in 2006 (PASIAD, 2006, p. 62). They have also played an important

---

15   For a better sense of Indonesian politics and history, see Ricklefs, Merle, (2001), History of Indonesia since 1200c (Hampshire, Palgrave).

16   One of these students is Hakan Islamoğlu who is still in Indonesia till today. Kerim Tursun and Galip Kayar are the two other students.

charity role. Since 1998, PASIAD Indonesia has organized the donation of frozen meat from the Turkish community in Australia to poor Indonesians during the festival of Eid-ul-Adha. During the tsunami crisis that hit the province of Aceh, PASIAD Indonesia coordinated relief work in the region, which included rebuilding schools and houses, assisting in health care and providing food for the victims (PASIAD, 2006, pp. 50-51). In the cultural realm, PASIAD was also involved in organizing a Turkish film festival and being involved in several international cultural festivals (PASIAD, 2006, p. 60-61).

Building Tolerance Through Education

As highlighted earlier, Gülen believed that it is through education that extremism will be curbed and tolerance promoted. It was this philosophy that motivated his followers in Indonesia to build schools in the country. Islamoglu noted that intolerance occurs between the different religious groups in Indonesia due to the lack of education. He cited an incident when he was asked by a Christian priest whether the Islamic criminal laws are applied in Turkey. This is despite the fact that Turkey is one of the most secular Muslim countries in the world (Islamoglu, 2007).

At its initial stage, there were only fifteen students in the school, many of whom being from a rural and poor background. Today, the number of students has increased to about two thousand and many are from a more privileged background.[17] This does not mean that the schools are elitist in any way. The higher fees charge to these more privileged students are partly used to provide scholarships to students from poorer background to study in these schools (PASIAD, 2006, p. 20). The diverse backgrounds of the students allow interaction between students, who often would not meet, due to the segmented nature of different class groups in Indonesia. This allows the richer student to understand better the challenges faced by a fellow student from a less privileged background. At the same time, about 10% of the student population is not Muslim. PASIAD Indonesia also does not discriminate in the allocation of scholarships, and about 20% of the non-Muslim students receive scholarships from PASIAD Indonesia.[18] The presence of non-Muslim students allows for interaction and building of trust and tolerance between Muslims and non-Muslims, in an otherwise stratified society where there is little interaction between the two communities. The universal values taught to the students meant that they tend to look beyond ethnic or religious cleavages in dealing with others. At another level, these schools serve as an excellent cultural bridge between Turkey and Indonesia. The students are exposed to aspects of Turkish culture such as its food and language. Due to this exposure, they have become an important ambassador for Turkey in Indonesia

For many parents, the attraction of these schools lies in their high standard of education, which has produced students who have won international physics and mathematics competitions (Republica, July 2006). More importantly, many parents are aware that the teachers of these schools are good role models for their children and that the schools give the students a good education, without inducing any ideological leanings. Moreover, tolerance and an appreciation for what others do are also values advocated in these schools. In an interview with

---

17 The changing profile of these students are due to high fees that the schools charges. Parents pay an average of about US$100 per month in the school. See Radio Singapore International, Turkish Delight, 3 July 2007. Accessed from www.rsi.org.sg on 4th July 2007.

18 About 13% of Indonesia's population is non-Muslims. Generally, the non-Muslims are stronger economically, which explains the relatively lower number of non-Muslim students receiving scholarships from PASIAD Indonesia.

an alumnus of the school, he echoed Gülen's vision of peace and tolerance when he said that Muslims should cease to have an us against them mindset. There must be a shift in their paradigm to start thinking of everyone as fellow human beings, rather then by their religious affiliations (Riaz, 2007). Mahmud Riaz is an example of the kind of educated, cultured Muslim described by Gülen who will never resort to terrorism or turn to extremism to pursue his aim. The Indonesia government has acknowledged the importance of these schools in countering extremist ideologies. A government leader the author spoke to indicated that the Department of National Education and local governments want more such schools built in Indonesia.[19] This is because they recognize the Islam that Gülen advocates is an important anti-dote to the extremism promoted by radical groups in Indonesia. Interestingly about 70% of the school's alumni, including many non-Muslim students have volunteered to teach in the schools despite their often prestigious educational backgrounds, which could allow them to obtain more lucrative jobs (Altun, 2007). This development would mean that more schools could be built in future as the movement receives more staff support from amongst its alumni.

Intra and Inter Religious Dialogue

Understanding the factional nature of Indonesian Islam and politics, PASIAD Indonesia has sought to maintain good relations with all Muslim groups and political parties in the country. PASIAD Indonesia had paid courtesy visits to the President, Vice-President, various cabinet ministers as well as major Muslim organizations and political parties such as Muhammadiyah, Nahdatul Ulama, The Justice and Prosperous Party (PKS) and Golkar (PASIAD, 2006, pp. 69-82). It is also interesting to note that despite the constant changes in the leadership of Indonesia, PASIAD Indonesia was able to maintain warm ties with all the different leaders of the country. Building intra-Muslim dialogue remains an important focus for PASIAD Indonesia due to the fact that the country is overwhelmingly Muslim.

PASIAD Indonesia does this by initiating various programs such as iftar dinners and Halalbihalal functions. Halalbihalal is a unique Indonesian Muslim cultural practice where Muslims will seek forgiveness from one another for mistakes committed against one another for the year. This often occurs at the end of the fasting month. PASIAD Indonesia adopted this practice and has been organizing Halalbihalal function annually. Staff members of the different PASIAD Indonesia's schools as well as local partners of PASIAD are invited for the function. Interestingly, PASIAD also invites various Islamic community leaders, despite their religious and political ideological differences.

The iftar dinner is another annual event organized by PASIAD Indonesia. Similar to Singapore, iftar functions in Indonesia are overwhelmingly Muslim events. The invited guests include prominent politicians and Muslim community leaders. The event is often graced by the presence of an Indonesian cabinet minister or and was attended by the Vice-President of Indonesia, Yusuf Kalla. Similar to the Halalbihalal function, one could find politicians from secular political parties such Golkar as well as those from more religious parties such as the PKS coming for the iftar. Their religious orientation were also diverse ranging from the more Sufi types to the more puritan types. Non-Muslims were often not invited for these iftar functions. Breaking these norms, PASIAD invites non-Muslim community leaders such as leaders of various churches, Buddhist and Hindu temples to these events so as to bring about inter-religious harmony between the different religious communities (Islamoglu, 2007). For many of these non-Muslim leaders, it is the first time in their lives that they attended such a function and is important in enhancing their understanding of Islam.

---

19 Conversation with a government leader who do not want to be named.

In another effort to increase both intra and inter religious tolerance, PASIAD Indonesia organized overseas trip to Turkey. Once again the leaders of different Muslim organizations are invited to enhance their relations with one another during the trip. Several non-Muslim leaders also accompany the delegation to Turkey (PASIAD, 2006, p. 88-89). In these trips, delegates are taken to various historical sites and are also taken to meet supporters of the Gülen movement to allow them to gain insight into the movement in Turkey. Such trips are important in cementing ties between these community leaders and PASIAD Indonesia.

Perhaps the most important trip organized by PASIAD Indonesia is a trip to Moscow to attend an International Symposium titled "From Terrorism to Global Ethics: Religions and Peace" (PASIAD, 2006, p. 90). The trip saw two Indonesian leaders known for their political differences, Dr Din Syamsudin from Muhammadiyah and Dr Hidayat Nur Wahid from PKS coming together for an inter-religious event.[20] The fact that a leader of an Islamic party, PKS known for its conservative Islamic leanings, such as the imposition of Islamic criminal laws, decided to attend an inter-religious is remarkable. Several leaders of the Hindu, Christian and Confucian communities also attended the event. The participants of the event were exposed to the importance of inter-faith dialogue in a climate where terrorism and extremism could weaken ties between faith communities. (Altun, 2007). The dialogue efforts of PASIAD Indonesia have been crucial in enhancing ties amongst Muslims and between Muslims and non-Muslims. This is especially so at the elite level of the Indonesian society. Such efforts have become essential, especially given the threat of religious strife and extremism that Indonesia faces.

Conclusion

The Muslim World is today in a transition phase. This could be clearly seen from the intolerant and extreme acts of some Muslims. Historically, all major civilizations have undergone this phase where members of these civilizations are insular and weak. Yet, in the midst of these uncertainties, the ideas of Fethullah Gülen emerge to reverse the thinking and attitudes of Muslims. The Gülen movement is a trendsetter movement that has sought to create intra and inter-religious understanding and improve the education standards in the World. As Gülen had highlighted time and again, improving educational standards in the Muslim World is likely to change the mindset and thinking of Muslims leading them to have a more enlightened approach in dealing with their coreligionist and non-Muslims. This development will be especially important where Muslims are in the minority such as in Singapore and Europe. In Europe the misconceptions and prejudices held by Muslims and non-Muslims towards each other are leading to worsening relations. Yet, if Gülen's ideas are imbibed and practiced by the Muslims, such misconception and prejudices will slowly be eradicated.

The case studies of the Gülen movement in Indonesia and Singapore is reflective of how a small group of Gülen followers have successfully impacted the society they are living in. It is also reflective of the important impact Gülen's ideas have had for people around the world. Acting upon his vision of tolerance and dialogue, his followers in both countries began promoting this vision by encouraging dialogues amongst Muslims and between Muslim and non-Muslims. In the case of Singapore, such dialogues were especially encouraged between Muslims and non-Muslims given that Muslims are in a minority in the country. The efforts of the TCC proved significant, as they were able to change the perceptions of Islam and even

---

20 For more on the rivalry between Muhammadiyah and PKS see) Azra, Azyumardi. (1999) Partai Islam Tidak Prospektif, in: Hamid Basyaib & Hamid Abidin (Eds) Mengapa Partai Islam Kalah? (Jakarta, Alvabet).

gained supporters amongst the non-Muslims for their cause. In Indonesia, PASIAD Indonesia focused on the development of relations amongst Muslims due to the overwhelming number of Muslims in the country. In the process they were not only able to lessen tensions among Muslims but also enhanced ties between the Muslims and non-Muslims through the Turkish schools and their inter-religious activities. The schools in Indonesia are likely to chart a new course for Islam in Indonesia, which is moderate and tolerant. The precedence given to universal values in these schools, inherent in all religions, are important in shaping the educated, cultured Muslim who is tolerant and progressive, as Gülen had envisaged. The common values that the Gülen movement emphasizes on are likely to also reverse the shape of Islam in Southeast Asia, which is tolerant and accommodating to other religions. Beyond the Southeast Asian region, the ideas of Gülen on inter-religious dialogue is likely to change the shape of Muslim-non-Muslim relations in places like Europe where misconception and prejudice on both sides have led to conflict between the two groups.

PHNOM PENH'S FETHULLAH GÜLEN SCHOOL AS AN ALTERNATIVE TO PREVALENT FORMS OF EDUCATION FOR CAMBODIA'S MUSLIM MINORITY

Philipp Bruckmayr

Abstract

Following the end of Khmer Rouge rule (1975–79), the Cham Muslim minority of Cambodia began to rebuild community structures and religious infrastructure. It was only after 1993 that they became recipients of international Islamic aid, mostly for the establishment of mosques, schools and orphanages. Now Cambodia boasts several Muslim schools, financed and/or run by Saudi Arabian and Kuwaiti NGOs as well as by private enterprise from the Gulf region, most of which rely on a purely religious curriculum. However, Cambodian Muslim leaders are urging attendance of public Khmer schools and seeking to establish alternatives in the form of Islamic secondary schools with a mixed curriculum, modelled after similar schools in Malaysia. The generally harmonious relations between Chams and Khmers have been affected by the importation of new interpretations of Islam through international Islamic welfare organisations, and the long arm of international terrorism.

The only Cambodian non-religious and non-discriminatory educational facility operated from a Muslim country is Phnom Penh's Zaman International School. It was founded in 1997 and is associated with the Fethullah Gülen movement. Classes are taught in both Khmer and English. Its kindergarten, primary and high schools are attended by Khmers, resident foreigners and a few Chams. For them, apart from the high standard provided by the school, its explicit agenda of instruction on an inter-racial and inter-religious basis, coupled with its prestige as an institution operated from Muslim lands, serves to make the school a valuable alternative to both secular private schools and Islamic schools.

This paper raises and discusses the interesting question of the applicability of Gülen's thought on education and inter-faith relations to the periphery of Southeast Asian Islam.

Introduction

Fethullah Gülen is a former Turkish state imam, who has risen to become Turkey's most famous Islamic intellectual. He is by now widely known as a elaborate supporter of inter-religious dialogue, pluralism, tolerance and democracy[1]. Most important for the present study, the probably most striking aspect of his thought is the conviction, that acquiring and transmitting secular knowledge, as well as supplying people with the means to do so, is in perfect accordance with and in fact demanded by Islamic ideals[2]. Gülen's thought has attracted a considerable following, which has grown into a whole Gülen-inspired movement with an education network as its basis (Yavuz & Esposito 2003; Agai 2004). Starting out by establishing schools and student hostels in Turkey, the movement has since the early 1990s founded Turkish secular schools in many countries in Europe, Asia, America, Africa and Australia[3].

Religiously motivated educational efforts have been and are a outstanding feature of worldwide Islamic resurgence in the past decades. To this one has to add the unprecedented internationalization of these efforts on a global scale in a rapidly globalizing world, first through organizations like the Muslim World League and then through Islamic charities. The case of the Gülen movement is unique as it is an Islamically inspired international actor providing not religious but secular education. What is more, its activities fall into a time of major transitions and upheavals in the Muslim world. A development displaying common patterns like the growth of terrorism in the name of religion and the politicization of Islam from Trinidad to Maluku. Yet, instantly this transitional processes had very different outcomes. Whereas the Taliban regime was just firmly consolidating its rule over most of Afghanistan in 1998, the same year witnessed how Indonesia's long time ruler general Suharto had to give way to a pro-democracy movement largely carried by what was labelled as "civil Islam" (Hefner 2000). For the Chams of Cambodia the time since 1993 was also a major transitional experience, namely from long enduring isolation from the wider Muslim world to an unprecedented sudden onslaught of international Islamic endeavours in the Khmer kingdom.

So-called Gülen schools have been founded in a number of Southeast Asian states, namely in Cambodia, Thailand, Indonesia, Myanmar and in the Philippines[4]. Contrary to the Muslim minorities of the Philippines and Thailand, the Khmer kingdom's Muslim minority is not confined to a specific geographic area. Consisting mostly of Chams interspersed with a much smaller number of Malays, it is dispersed over all 22 Cambodian provinces. Another major point of difference between the Cambodian Chams and other Southeast Asian Muslim minorities is their specific history in relation to the Khmer majority, as there is no long history of inter-religious strife as in southern Thailand, the South Philippines and the Arakan region of Myanmar. It is a major particularity of the Cambodian Chams' case, that they had not been conquered but had instead come to Cambodia as refugees.

While taking into account, that Phnom Penh is not a potential inter-religious powder keg as is Zamboanga on Mindanao, which houses the Gülen network's "Turkish-Philippine School of Tolerance" (Michel 2003, 70), it is important to view the movement's agenda of education and ethics across religious and ethnic boundaries in the contemporary Cambodian context, to assess its possible contribution to both the Khmers' and the Chams' plight in a country which

---

1 On Gülen and important aspects of his thought see Ünal & Williams 2000.

2 On Gülen's education discourse see Agai 2004, 191-260.

3 An incomplete list of schools is to be found in Ibid., 13-15.

4 References to these educational facilities are scattered throughout different sources. See Yılmaz (2003, 236); Agai (2004, 14-15); Michel (2003, 70-71).

still has to recover from the repercussions of Khmer Rouges rule from 1975-1979. This is even more so, if one considers, that a prime field of the movement's activities are countries under former communist rule like the Central Asian republics and Albania (Agai 2004, 272-280; Turam 2003, 184-207, Agai 2003, 66-68). Although, as far as Central Asia is concerned, common Turkic-ness plays a major role in describing the motivations of both Gülen himself and of his movement's activists there (Agai 2004, 224-229; Turam 2003, 188-202), it is nevertheless often stated, that "the moral vacuum left by communism" (Again 2004, 344) is something to be confronted by the movement's efforts in the field of education. Moreover, Gülen's thought on living in non-Muslim lands (Yılmaz 2003, 234-237) should, in the face of worldwide Islamic resurgence, be valuable for all Muslim minorities and immigrant communities around the globe.

In this paper, I am arguing, that the thought of Fethullah Gülen is valuable for the Cambodian Chams in several aspects, including their coexistence with the Buddhist Khmer majority, intra-community harmony, and their quests for both empowerment and identity preservation through education. The latter factor is practically and exemplarily related to the Zaman International School in Phnom Penh.

As a background for the envisaged assessment of Phnom Penh's Gülen School's presumed character as a appropriate alternative to other forms of education for the Cham minority, especially likewise foreign patronized ones, it will be mandatory to present a concise overview of Cham history in Cambodia in relation to the Khmer majority and the field of education. This will be done in the first section of this study. For our purpose it is certainly most important to focus on the period since 1993, when Cambodia emerged from over 20 years of isolation to become a playground for numerous NGOs and private enterprise, often originating from Muslim states and investing into educational programs. Thus, the next section will present an assessment of the different forms of schooling as well as of differing views on education that have emerged among the Chams since then. Getting closer to our main topic, the third section then tries to find convergences between Gülen's thought on the one hand and the efforts and self-images of Cham NGOs in Cambodia on the other. The following two sections deal specifically with the relation of the Zaman International School to the Gülen movement, and secondly, to the Cham community. Finally, the concluding section will, apart from recapitulating prior findings, try to assess the relevance of Gülen's thought for the Cambodian Chams' case in the field of education and beyond.

The Chams in Cambodia and Education in Religious and Secular Spheres

Chams migrated to Cambodia in numerous waves between 1471 and the 1830s, as their homeland, the once powerful Champa, was gradually absorbed by the Vietnamese until its ultimate dissolution in 1832 (Phoeun 1987). Close contact with resident Malays as well as the advance of Islam in Champa in the 16th and 17t century, due to its close attachment to the Muslim dominated maritime trade of the Malay-Indonesian world, led to their Islamisation. In, for the Southeast Asian context, remarkably ethnically homogenous Cambodia, the Chams, with a population of between 400000 and 500000 people, are constituting the only numerically important ethnic and religious minority. The vast majority of Cambodian Chams are adherents of the Shafi'ite school of law, and have underwent a significant Malay cultural influence. Knowledge of the Malay language is wide spread, as most religious literature employed by the Chams is in Malay, and moreover intermarriage and close contacts to resident Malays have been common currency for centuries. However, Cham language is still the native tongue of most Chams, and Khmer is also spoken by most.

A distinct minority within the Cambodian Cham community are the Cham Sot ("the pure Chams"), referred to as Jahed by the majority, which are displaying no traces of Malayisation and are professing a specific form of Cham Islam, characterized by a different conduct with regard to the basic obligations agreed upon by the Islamic mainstream (as to avoid the ten-dentious term "orthodoxy") as well as by an incorporation of traditional pre-Islamic Cham practices (De Feo 2005a; Baccot 1968). Most notably, only this group has preserved tradi-tional Sanskrit-derived Cham script and old manuscripts, whereas the rest has consequently given up Cham script in favour of an adapted version of Malay Jawi script.

For both Khmers and Chams education had for centuries a purely religious character, either provided in the Buddhist monasteries or in Muslim village schools or by itinerant Muslim teachers. However, in both the monasteries and the Muslim village schools, acquiring the ability to read and write was a prerequisite for further religious instruction. Apparently, the majority of Chams eventually came to rely on Malay teaching materials instead of Cham ones. This development was not only triggered by Malay teachers visiting Cambodia, but also by the fact, that the most revered Cham teachers were themselves educated in Malay centres of learning like Kelantan and Patani. That Islamic education was a major ingredient of Cham village life in the middle of the 19th century can be inferred from European travel reports. Thus, the German ethnographer Adolf Bastian, upon visiting Cambodia in 1864, notices that a recently established Cham-Malay village near Battambang, traditionally not a Cham stronghold, already housed a religious school (Bastian 2005, 100). Although educa-tion in spoken Arabic was certainly hardly ever available in such schools, the same author nevertheless remarks, that French soldiers from the Maghreb were able to communicate with certain Chams in the modern-day border region between Cambodia and Vietnam (Bastian 2005, 145).

From the early 20th century were are informed about textbooks used in Cham schools. Then, studies were confined to Qur'anic commentaries (tafsir)[5] and Malay translations of cate-chisms, like those of Abu-l Layth al-Samarqandi (incidentally a Central Asian scholar of the Hanafite school) and Abu Abdullah al-Sanusi (Cabaton 1906, 43-44).

Both cited reports date from French colonial times (beginning in 1863), yet unlike one would suspect, French education initially had virtually no impact on the Chams, and was even in the 1930s still very limited. Generally education in Cambodia has been labelled as "an area of colonial neglect" (Vickery 1999, 19). While traditional pagoda schools declined under French rule, the authorities failed to fill the gap with a modern education system (Kiernan 1999, 6). Although Muslim schools were most probably not subject to such decline, modern education among the Chams was certainly not boosted by the French presence, with full secondary education only available in 1933 (Kiernan 1999, 6) and only 50000-60000 chil-dren enrolled in primary school in 1936 (Vickery 1999, 19). In this respect, the remarks of a French ethnographer are of interest. The author states, that Muslims were hardly frequenting

---

5 Unfortunately there is no mention of the authorships of the commentaries in question. However, by the time of Cabaton's survey, there existed only two Malay commentaries on the entire Qur'an, namely the works by the Acehnese Abd al-Ra'uf al-Singkili (d. ca. 1700) and the Javanese Muhammad Nawawi Banteni (d. 1897) (Feener 1998, 52-55; Riddell 2001, 195-197). Then and now the most widely distributed classical Arabic work of tafsir in Southeast Asia is the concise *Tafsir al-Jalalayn* ("the commentary of the two Jalals") by al-Mahalli (d. 1459) and al-Suyuti (d. 1505).

French schools in the late 1930s (Ner 1941, 188). Instead, he describes a lively religious education system, with informal education and the village schools as basis, and elevated and revered "secondary" schools in Chruy Changvar (Phnom Penh), and most notably Trea in Kampong Cham province[6], as the highest level of education. For further studies the Chams still looked mostly to Kelantan and, by then, even to Mecca (Ner 1941, 189-190). Of major importance for our present discussion is the fact, that Trea in the 1930s already also housed a madrasa providing a mixed curriculum of both religious and secular subjects. Throughout Southeast Asia, the introduction of such balanced curricula was among the major demands of the Islamic modernist movement as well as a symbol of it (Giora 2004, 1-8). However, this innovative institution in Trea was neither destined to last nor to serve as a model for other religious schools in Cambodia at that date.

Naturally, neither the low enrolment of Chams in the French schools nor the failure to establish a network of modern institutions of religious education, as was done by Indonesia's Muhammadiyah modernists in the same period, served to uplift the Chams in protectorate society, where upward mobility through education was even very hard to achieve for Khmers. Whereas Cham enrolment in official schools was even low in the urban milieu (62 students in Phnom Penh and neighbouring Kandal province) in the late 1930s, it was virtually non-existent in the rural Cham strongholds, which is most clearly exemplified by the tiny number of merely four Cham students for the whole of Kampong Cham province[7], which had at least a 33000 strong Cham population by then (Ner 1941, 196). Accordingly, Chams were not to be found in any administrative positions, apart from that of district or village chief in Cham areas.

In independent Cambodia under king Sihanouk the overall educational situation changed dramatically with a rapid increase in availability and attendance up to tertiary level. Unfortunately in the long run, this otherwise laudable and surely well intended development, due to the employed ill-suited curricula and a simple absence of adequate governmental and administrative jobs coupled with a far too slow expansion in the commercial and industrial sectors to absorb the graduates, was to constitute a problem of its own, which contributed to the urban-rural antagonism playing a role in the ascension of the Khmer Rouges to power (Vickery 1999, 19-23). Yet, observers in the early 1960s still lament the Chams' preference for religious schools despite the progress of the public system (Delvert 1961, 23). On the contrary, Chams reminiscing over the Sihanouk era, are criticizing the system's partiality in terms of its availability for minorities and allocation of stipends (Le Front d'Union 1983, 50, 58)[8].

When general Lon Nol deposed Sihanouk in 1970, the country was already a battlefield with both communist insurgency and US bombing in the countryside (Kiernan 1999, 18-19). As the war gradually intensified until the Khmer Rouges victory in 1975, Cambodians were generally occupied with more fundamental issues than educational reform. However,

---

6 On Trea's history as a centre of Muslim learning in Cambodia see Bruckmayr (forthcoming).

7 It has to be kept in mind, that the Chams would have had very little opportunity for official schooling in rural areas like Trea, even if they had wanted to participate. In 1942 Kampong Cham city saw the inauguration of the comparably prestigious Collège Norodom Sihanouk. However students were selected from all over the country, surely to the exclusion of local Chams. Among those first chosen was a farmer's son from Kampong Thom with palace connections named Saloth Sar (Chandler 2000, 17-18). He should gain notoriety three decades later as Pol Pot.

8 Although the source of this information is a publication of the People's Republic of Kampuchea (PRK) government, which was certainly intended to present the conditions of the Chams under previous regimes as unfavourable, it would be misleading to regard the grievances described in the published interviews as mere inventions of the interviewees.

high school and university life continued to function at least in Phnom Penh, where only 24 Cham students were enrolled at the outset of Khmer Rouges rule (Front d'Union 1983, 52). Although the still repeatedly heard view, that education was subject to total destruction in Pol Pot's Democratic Kampuchea, has long been falsified, it is nevertheless firmly established that, due to "romantic peasantism" (Vickery 1999, 185), only the lowest level of primary schooling, providing basic literacy and numeracy, was maintained (Vickery 1999, 183-186). Apart from the general horrible death toll inflicted on the overall Cambodian population under Democratic Kampuchea, its rule proved especially disastrous for traditional religious learning among the Chams. Out of approximately 300 teachers at Muslim schools, only 38 survivors were counted in 1979 (Kiernan 1999, 271; Taouti 1982, 194-195). Even though it is most probable that certain teachers have successfully fled abroad, and might not have returned by then, the general pattern of extermination of generations of Cham teachers is obvious. In 1979 the Chams found themselves with hardly any teachers and almost all their mosques destroyed, not to mention the estimated deaths of 90000 to over 400000 Chams (Kiernan 1988, 30; Osman 2002, 1-3; Bruckmayr 2006, 4-7).

After the Vietnamese invasion, which brought Democratic Kampuchea to a close, the new People's Republic of Kampuchea started to rebuild the country, including its educational system, in the face of a prolonged war against the remnants of the Khmer Rouges and the anti-communist Khmer Serei ("free Khmers"). Its educational efforts are considered as "one of the regime's greatest achievements" (Gottesmann 2002, 74). Moreover participants emphasized its non-discriminatory treatment of the Chams. As far as the Chams are concerned, it has been argued, that they served as a showcase to demonstrate the new regime's tolerance (Hawk et. al. 1995, 11). However, in this respect support was a two-way road, and also important parts of the Chams came out as ostentatious supporters of the new regime, and were suddenly strongly represented in the government and its institutions (Kiernan 1989, 34). Similarly, Cham participation in public schooling was certainly the greatest ever.

These developments were paralleled by Cham efforts to re-establish their religious school system. This was initially only achieved at a minimal scale, due to absence of experienced teachers, and a lack of funds. The regime sought to bring the Chams' plight to international attention, most notably through the efforts of Mat Ly, Cambodia's highest ranking Cham, who just like former party secretary Heng Samrin (1981-1991) and current prime minister Hun Sen had been a second level Khmer Rouges cadre before fleeing to Vietnam, and was now a member of the ruling party's political bureau. Yet, the international rejection of the regime as a puppet of communist Vietnam served to prolong Cham isolation from the Muslim world and its charities in a time, which coincided with US and Saudi-Arab engagement in the anti-communist struggle in Afghanistan.

The first arrival of international Islamic aid used for education, occurred in the early 1980s, when the Islamic Development Bank provided funds for the reconstruction of mosques with annexed class rooms, and school materials including scientific and religious books in Arabic and Malay (Taouti 1982, 200 n.10). After the 1993 elections, which marked a late return to a certain degree of stability not experienced for more than two decades in Cambodia, a great number of Muslim charities started to operate in Cambodia, mainly financing mosques and religious schools, which led to an unprecedented increase of both (Bruckmayr 2006, 10-13; De Feo 2005b, 107-110). Whereas rapid madrasa growth as an indicator of Islamic resurgence was a development starting already in the 1970s in the South Philippines (Milligan 2005, 122), Indonesia and other Southeast Asian states, the Cambodian Chams took no part in this process. However, since 1993 with a variety of Islamic organizations working directly or indirectly in the country, and a renewed attachment to Malaysia, Cambodian Chams quickly caught up with their Southeast Asian peers.

Consequently, the number of Chams having access to religious education has risen dramatically. Yet, a number of Cham leaders are arguing, that more is needed to uplift the still mostly rural, poor and uneducated Chams, whose general situation was apparently little affected by the promising restart of public education in the early 1980s, notwithstanding the obvious success of a number of Cham politicians. Moreover, Islamic resurgence and its side effects have also affected otherwise traditionally harmonious Khmer-Cham relations, and have, in some circles, brought forward the view, that too intimate relations with the Khmers are undesirable.

The Religious, the Secular, the Paralleled and the Combined: Schooling the Chams

Recent research among the Chams has shown, that in the rural villages illiteracy in Khmer, Cambodia's official language, is still a major problem. As the religious school are naturally not concerned with the instruction in Khmer alphabet and language, the over-concern of many Chams and Islamic charities with religious education does nothing to confront this deficiency (So 2005, 5). Moreover, it is obvious, that the public school system has failed even in this basic aspect.

By now, Cambodia boast around 300 Islamic schools. My own fieldwork served to testify to the purely religious curricula relied on in most of these schools. However, independent initiatives are also undertaken to provide useful extra classes to the pupils in several of these schools. Thus, in a school in a Cham village in Siam Reap, which with the ruins of Angkor Wat in its vicinity, is apart from Phnom Penh the tourist centre of Cambodia, English, no doubt of major importance in such an area, is also taught apart from usual classes in Malay[9]. Awareness for the usefulness of English in Cambodia in urban Cham circles, dates back to the UNTAC (United Nations Transitional Authority) era (1992-1993) as is preserved in the report of Strubbe (1993, 15), yet among rural Chams, Malay[10] and even Arabic speakers are still easier to encounter than people fluent in English. Consequently, it is naturally almost impossible to find anybody with sufficient English skills to teach Cham students in the countryside.

Among many Chams former rejection of public schools has given way to an embracement of secular education, however a fear of assimilation to the Khmer majority through education remains. Therefore pupils are often pursuing parallel schooling. Enrolled in both public and religious schools, even children attending primary school are spending a considerable amount of time at school, "in a desperate attempt to ensure a better future [..] while retaining their identity as Muslims", as Milligan has put it, as he observed a similar situation among the Maranao of the southern Philippines (2005, 139-140). Naturally, in rural Cambodia, where children are often needed by the family to participate in fishing, rice farming and the like, this educational double load is often not endurable for long. As the religious village schools are closer to home than the public ones, usually located in Khmer villages, the choice is often made in favour of the former, when the attendance of both proves to be too exhausting or too

9   Interview with the province imam of Siam Reap, Musa Soleh, in Stung Thmey (15-7, 16-7-05).
10   Adding to its importance as language of religious instruction, it has to be noted that, in contrast to Khmer language, Malay, as an Austronesian language and thus related to Cham, is comparably easy to learn for Cham speakers. On Cham language see Thurgood 1999.

time-consuming.

A possible solution to the problems posed by parallel schooling is the establishment of religious schools with a mixed curriculum including core subjects of the public syllabus. Thus, while explicitly Islamic in orientation, its students still have the opportunity to switch to, or to engage in further studies in the public system. Strikingly, whereas rapid madrasa growth in the southern Philippines started two decades before the beginning of a similar process in Cambodia, the introduction of schools with such combined curricula dates to the late 1990s in both countries[11].

A notable advocate of schools with a combined curriculum is the Cambodian Muslim Development Foundation (CMDF), a Cambodian NGO patronized by the grand mufti Kamaruddin Yusof, and headed by the currently most influential Cham in politics, secretary of state (ministry of labour and training) Othman Hassan. Starting in 1999, the CMDF has embarked on building a network of secondary schools for boys and girls, which rely on the same mixed syllabus employed at similar schools in Malaysia (CMDF 2004, 8-11)[12]. Their goal is to provide, otherwise in Cambodia unavailable, standardized Islamic education, without barring its students' way as far as success through secular education is concerned. However, their religious character is emphasized by stressing, that their graduation certificates are accepted by renowned Muslim centres of learning like Cairo's Al-Azhar University and Kelantan's Islamic College. Nevertheless, among the Chams studying at Malaysian universities, many have chosen to study modern sciences rather than in religious fields[13].

Similarly, a number of schools founded and funded by Arab NGOs employ a mixed syllabus. Examples include the school at Choum Chao in Phnom Penh, run by the Kuwaiti Revival of Islamic Heritage Society, which serves for the education of the Chams residing in the annexed largest orphanage for Muslim children in Cambodia (De Feo 2004, 91). Here religious subjects are taught in the morning and secular ones in the afternoon[14]. Generally, such Arab financed schools are credited with providing classical Islamic education as well as general subjects on a high level (De Feo 2004, 92). However, their funding is regarded as controversial as several of the operating NGOs feature on the blacklists of the Bush administration for suspected links to terrorism. Given the intricacies of the situation, a crackdown on and subsequent shutdown of a school of the Saudi Umm al-Qura International Organization in Kendal province caused fierce disputes, as the school was regarded as the only high level institution affordable for Chams in its rural surroundings (Osman 2006). On the other hand it is doubtful whether mixed curriculum schools are having a positive impact on national integration. Thus, it has been argued in the Philippine context, that such schools are implicit symbols of "dissatisfaction, if not outright rejection, [..] of educational alternatives offered [..] by mainstream society" (Milligan 2005, 124).

Notwithstanding the abovementioned efforts to either study at public and religious schools in a parallel mode, and the quest to establish satisfying mixed educational alternatives, there are also currents within the Cham community, which are deliberately rejecting schooling at public schools above the primary level to avoid Khmerization, while strongly opting for purely religious studies. This view is specifically expounded by members of the Cambodian branch

---

11 For the Philippines see Milligan (2005, 107).
12 In 2004 the network had already 14 schools in 8 provinces.
13 Interview with CMDF member and Cambodian Student Association (CAMSA) secretary-general Sos Mousine (14-7-05).
14 Interview with CAMSA vice secretary-general Set Muhammadsis (13-7-05).

of the Tablighi Jamaat[15], an Indian "evangelical" movement and offshoot of the Deobandi school (Metcalf 2002), which lays particular stress on individual conduct with regard to the prophet's example (Masud 2000; Sikand 2002). Arriving in the southern Philippines already in the early 1970s (Milligan 2005, 121), it made its first appearance in the Khmer kingdom only at the end of the 1980s, but has since then become a mass movement, especially among the rural Chams (De Feo 2005b, 110-112; Bruckmayr 2006, 13-14). Schools associated with the movement are particularly concerned with memorization of the Qur'an (De Feo 2005b, 111). The centre of its activities is Trea in Kampong Cham province, which houses a big Tablighi boarding school attached to Cambodia's largest mosque (Bruckmayr forthcoming).

A major problem of exclusively religious studies is, that many religious specialists, which have moreover completed their education in Saudi-Arabia, southern Thailand or Malaysia, now cannot even find a job a teacher as there are hardly any vacant positions in this field anymore, due to the rapid increase in graduates in the last decade. It is most probable, that the considerable number of foreign religious teachers in the country will be reduced in the future, as their presence is a cause for growing uneasiness among the authorities. Yet, it remains questionable, whether future demand will keep up with graduation rates.

Common Agendas of Gülen and Cham NGOs

Greg Barton has recently shed light on the similarities of the Gülen movement in Turkey and the neo-modernist currents in Indonesia as so-called post-Islamist civil society forces outstanding in the Muslim world (Barton 2005, 43). As such they might be rightfully regarded as illustrative, yet rarely recognized examples for the assumption that Islam, civil society and democracy are indeed compatible. Interestingly, although taking Turam's reservations against applying the label "civil society organization" to freely on everything non-governmental and independent (2003, 186-187) into account, I am suggesting, that also Cambodian Muslim NGOs should be regarded as such, as their agendas have many convergences with those of the two aforementioned movements. Organizations like the Cambodian Muslim Development Foundation and the Cambodian Islamic Development Association are indeed supporting democracy, participation and interaction of Chams with the Khmer majority, as well as secular education as a means of community empowerment without necessarily losing one's Islamic identity. More specifically their leaders are mostly politically active[16], which brings them closer to the Indonesian examples of Abdurrahman Wahid and Amien Rais, both formerly leaders of multi-million religious organizations before becoming influential politicians, than to Gülen and Nurcholish Madjid[17], who stayed clear of party politics, while still wielding political influence as the respective states' most prominent religious thinkers and intellectuals.

Although Gülen's ethos of education, with its outstanding element, namely the acquirement of secular knowledge as an Islamic value per se (Agai 2004, 195-196), has so far found no effective counterpart or followers in Cambodia so far, the agenda and activities of a organization like the Cambodian Muslim Student Association (CAMSA) bear many resemblances to Gülen's discourse on education (Michel 2003; Agai 2003). Indeed, according to its own

---

15 Naturally not all of the movement's members are sharing this view.

16 The high ranking members of CMDF are in their majority members of the Cambodian People's Party (CPP), whereas another important NGO, the Cambodian Islamic Development Association, is headed by a parliamentarian of the oppositional Sam Rainsy Party (Bruckmayr 2006, 10-11).

17 On Madjid and his thought see Saleh 2001, 240-292.

presentation[18], CAMSA offers its services to make sure that Cham youths complete their secular education. Moreover, it is providing adult education classes for those, who have been unable to graduate from high school. Another activity is the founding of Muslim hostels to accommodate students from countryside at a low cost or for free, in exchange for community work. Even though such hostels certainly have an exclusive character, it has to be remembered that similar institutions are among the core elements of the Gülen movement in Turkey (Agai 2004, 301-309). Due to the fact, that businessmen sympathetic to its cause are instrumental in funding the Gülen movement's activities, it is also of interest, that CAMSA organizes classes in business administration to foster entrepreneurial activities. Likewise other Cham NGOs openly support secular education. Thus, the Cambodian Islamic Development Association gives financial support to Cham students attending private Norton University in Phnom Penh (De Feo 2005b, 108). Furthermore, its leader Ahmad Yahya had already sent Chams to Turkey, Malaysia and Indonesia to acquire university education in fields like law and economics in the 1990s (Collins 1996, 61).

Another important feature of Gülen's thought, is his call for inter-cultural and inter-religious understanding by emphasizing common values rather than differences (Agai 2004, 256), the basis of which has to be knowledge of the other. In this respect, CAMSA pursues the translation of seminal works on Islam into Khmer and English for distribution to Islamic and public schools to be available to both Muslims and non-Muslims. Inter-religious and inter-cultural understanding is explicitly described as the way to mutual respect and harmonious coexistence. Whereas Gülen is mostly associated with dialogue among Muslims, Jews and Christians (Ünal & Williams 2000, 241-296), members of the Gülen movement are indeed cooperating and interacting freely with Buddhists in Buddhist countries such as Korea or Thailand (Yılmaz 2003, 236) and also in Cambodia. In general, the number of books dealing with Muslim-Buddhist relations from a Muslim perspective, or from a Buddhist perspective for that matter, is certainly very small. However, in CAMSA's library one finds the works of the Trinidadi Maulana Imran Hossein, who addresses this topic in a conciliatory manner. This selection of books seems to suggest, that CAMSA is looking to provide knowledge legitimizing the traditional relation to the Buddhist majority, in times in which it is challenged by certain currents within the Cham community.

The Zaman International School of Phnom Penh and the Gülen Network

The private Zaman International School was founded in 1997 by the Turkish journalist Attila Yusuf Guleker. With over 700 hundred students enrolled, it is educating more boys and girls than similar Phnom Penh private schools like the International School of Phnom Penh or Northbridge International School.

It has already been stressed that, due to the instrumental role played by followers of Fethullah Gülen in the recent spread of Turkish private schools around the globe[19], such institutions are, albeit officially classified merely as "private institutions", automatically associated with the Gülen network by the Turkish state and public, and especially by the network's activists (Agai 2004, 13 n.8). As elsewhere (Agai, 2004, 17), most students of the Zaman school have

---

18 The following information about CAMSA's agenda is derived from an unpublished document of the organization dating to the year 2005, and obtained thanks to Sos Mousine.

19 For Gülen's own reflections about this development and his contribution to it, see Ünal & Williams 2000, 320-322.

certainly never even heard the name of Fethullah Gülen. However, linkages between the Gülen network and the school are easily detected. Founder Yusuf Guleker came to Cambodia as correspondent for the daily Zaman[20], which is closely associated with the Gülen movement at least since 1988 (Agai 2004, 168). Naturally, Guleker is also a member of the Journalists and Writers Foundation (Gazeteciler ve Yazarlar Vakfı), which is, notwithstanding the great number of organizations associated with Gülen, the only organization connected to Gülen on a institutionalized level, as he is acting as its patron (Agai 2004, 172).

Apart from education and media, business and finance networks are considered to be the third important sphere of the Gülen movement's activities as exemplified by the business support agency PASIAD (Society for Social and Economic Solidarity with Pacific Countries), which serves to facilitate trade contacts between Turkish and Asian businessmen. In return, those who profit from its activities are often benefactors of the movement's educational institutions (Barton 2005, 29-30). Similarly, the Kazak-Turk Education Foundation in Kazakhstan serves as central node not only for educational but also for economic endeavours in the area (Turam 2003, 189). In line with this approach, the former director of the Zaman school, Ali Kökten, was involved in PASIAD activities in Cambodia[21]. The same goes for both Kökten and his successor Osman Karaca, in relation to a similar organization named TUSKON[22].

Apart from these typical intra-network relations the connection between the Gülen network and the Zaman school can also be inferred from references to it within the network. Thus, Agai was informed about the existence of a school run by followers of Gülen in Cambodia during his research on the network (Agai 2004, 15). Furthermore, reports about the Zaman school appear in Gülen-related forums and websites[23], and it has also been accorded a standard place in lists of schools of the Gülen movement's world-wide activities in recent scholarly works. However, the school's principal declined discussing idealistic or organizational relations to Gülen[24]. Similarly, Agai reports, that, whereas it was common for teachers and administrators of similar schools in Albania to talk freely about their association with the movement grounded in Gülen's thought, new staff in the following year avoided the issue of Gülen (Agai 2004, 279). Although the efforts of the Gülen movement are widely appreciated (even in the West), negative press and conspiracy theories surrounding Gülen's figure since 1999 (Agai 2004, 162-164) might have contributed their part to the silence about Gülen in communication with outsiders. Moreover, younger members of the educational network might even be unaware, that they are part of a process, which owes so much to the thought of Fethullah Gülen. This especially goes for the great number of non-Muslim native teachers in the schools' staff.

The Zaman School and the Chams

It is obvious, that the Zaman school was not founded with the purpose to provide high level education specifically for the Muslim Chams, but rather for the whole Cambodian public. In line with Gülen's thought, activists in the network emphasize, that good works cannot be limited to Islamic countries (Agai 2004, 335-336) or to Muslims for that matter. Thus,

---

20 For examples of Guleker's work as Phnom Penh correspondent see his contributions in *Zaman* 18-Temmuz-98 and 1-8-98.

21 See www.pasiad.org/haber.php?id=2269

22 See *Zaman International School Newspaper*, IV, no. 46 (5.3.07), p. 1.

23 See for example http::/en.fGülen.com/content/view/2171/20/. The same text also appeared in the E-Gazette *Today's Zaman* (19-1-06).

24 Personal communication with Osman Karaca (13-8-07).

the schools of the network are open to everybody, and although its members often have a specific Islamic agenda motivated by Gülen behind their efforts (Agai 2003), this does not include a distinct agenda towards Muslims in comparison to followers of other religions in multi-religious societies like Kazakhstan, Albania or Cambodia. This equal treatment sets the Gülen network apart from the Islamic charities in Cambodia, which are solely concerned with Muslim affairs. Moreover, Gülen himself stresses the importance of providing adequate education in accordance with local contexts and value systems by saying, that "[A]lthough education is undeniably important for a country's development, the expected results will never be achieved if the young people are not educated according to the country's traditional values", yet with each generation learning from its predecessors' experiences and following its own way (Gülen 2005, 54).

While the schools of the Gülen network are not relying on any confessional instruction, they are instead seeking to transport and expound ethical Islamic values like honesty, hard work, generosity and the like (Michel 2003, 71; Aslandoğan & Çetin 2006, 41) by exemplary conduct. This practice is denoted by Gülen and his followers with the term temsil (propagation of Islamic values by way of individual example) as opposed to common notions of tebliğ[25] (usually meaning propagation of Islam as such, or in the understanding of the Tablighi Jamaat, propagation of proper conduct among Muslims). Interestingly, Gülen uses these two terms interchangeably in his religious works (Agai 2004, 235), which gives tebliğ a considerably broader meaning within the Gülen discourse than in common usage[26]. Obviously the aforementioned values are far from being exclusively Islamic ones, but rather part of a universal ethical system and communicated to people through different cultural and religious traditions, which is also considered by Gülen (Michel 2003, 82).

In fact, currently there are only one or two Chams enrolled at Zaman school according to its principal[27]. Apparently, the staff of the school is not particularly concerned with the Chams. Principal Karaca explains, that he knows only little about them[28], and references to the Chams are neither to be found in Yusuf Guleker's articles in Zaman, nor in the school's newspaper[29]. I am considering the latter instance as a deficiency as the school's newspaper is otherwise presenting a wide range of cultural and historical information on Cambodia, including such about Buddhist and Khmer festivities as well as about those of the Chinese minority.

However, as the school is open to everyone given successful passage of the entrance exams and parents' ability to provide the rather expansive entrance and tuition fees[30], it is not surprising, that a mostly poor minority like the Chams is not well represented in its ranks. To this one has to add the rejection of secular, or at least of purely secular education by parts of the Cham community. Naturally, for the limited number of Chams both desiring private secular education for their children and having the necessary financial means to do so, the Zaman school has to be the prime option, as they will surely find it desirable to have at least some coreligionists charged with the secular education of their children. Furthermore, as Turkish language is also studied at school, it should be remembered that Turkish, like Arabic, Persian, Urdu, Malay and others, is rightfully regarded as an Islamic language.

---

25 Derived from the Arabic verb *ballagha* (to relate, inform).

26 On the usage and relevance of these terms in the Gülen discourse see Agai 2004, 235-243.

27 See n. 21.

28 See n. 21.

29 An article about the ancient kingdoms of Southeast Asia contains two references to Champa, without mentioning its descendents on Cambodian soil. See *Zaman International School Newspaper*, IV, no. 41 (22-11-06), p. 4.

30 Full scholarships are accorded every year to the five most outstanding students.

Whereas the school's presentation is explicitly secular, and also its newspaper is not concerned with Islamic religion at all, contrary to its frequent treatment of Cambodian Buddhism, common religious values are emphasized by the school, as is common currency in the institutions of the Gülen network. The Islamic background of parts of the staff at times reveals itself in the school's English newspaper. Thus, in an article about the relevance of reading for children, a story about Muhammad appears, in which the prophet's name is followed by the common abbreviation of "peace be upon him" (pbuH) without further explanation. For the Khmer reader this practice must be completely unknown, contrary to a Cham reader. Moreover, the judgement attributed to the prophet in this story is presented as having been in the meantime confirmed by modern science[31]. With regard to the Muslim taboo concerning alcohol, it has to be noted, that the dangers of alcohol are discussed at several times[32]. Furthermore, sections about Turkish culture are naturally at times containing information about Islamic culture, such as the history of calligraphy[33].

Moreover, the fact, that the Turkish staff at the school is not displaying a specific interest in the Chams, does not imply, that the latter should not be able to appreciate the advantages of the school with regard to their special situation as a Muslim minority in the country, especially once they have been exposed to Gülen's thought themselves. Thus, in our final section, we will dwell on the presumed relevance Gülen's ideas could have in Cambodia, and their applicability among the Chams.

Gülen's Thought and the Plight of the Chams

For this concluding assessment I intend to focus not only on our main topic education, but also on two more relevant issues in Cham discourse, for which Gülen's approaches seem to be useful. As far as Gülen's thought on secular education is concerned, it is obvious, that the opposition between the secular and the religious is perceived in different terms by Gülen than by those Chams rejecting secular education. Rather than seeing it as a threat to the believer, Gülen regards secular knowledge as prerequisite for better religious understanding and for the ability to falsify those, who claim revelation and reason to be irreconcilable (Agai 2004, 196). That Gülen is not an advocate of purely religious studies at all, is evident in his view, that the closing of Islamic education institutions to positive sciences was a catastrophe for Islamic thought (Ünal and Williams 2000, 324-325). Moreover he stresses, that "avoiding the positive sciences fearing that they will lead to atheism is naivety (sic), and seeing them as contradictory to religion and faith and as vehicles for the rejection of religion is prejudice and ignorance" (Gülen 2005, 49), as the constructed conflict of religion and science is "a bitter struggle that should have never taken place" (quoted in Michel 2003, 75).

Another distinct problem, albeit also belonging to the education debate, is the situation of Cham women, among whom illiteracy and drop-outs after primary schools are even much more virulent than among male Chams (So 2005). At the root of this present problem lies not only the traditional role of women in Cham households, but also the recent spread of the hijab among the Chams. As the headscarf is forbidden in most secondary schools, many Cham females of conservative villages drop out of public schools to continue at purely religious schools (So 2005, 6). Especially in Turkey, but also in many European countries, the Islamic headscarf has proven to be a bone of contention. Gülen's view on the topic is strikingly

---

31 Zaman International School Newspaper, III, no. 31, p. 5.

32 See issues III, no. 27 and IV, no. 43, p. 6-7.

33 See issues III, no. 27. and I, no. 3.

simple and pragmatic. According to him, the Islamic headscarf belongs to the realm of details and not to the essentials of the faith. Therefore treating it as an essential part of Muslim identity would amount to "sacrificing the important for the trivial" (Ünal & Williams 2000, 63). Moreover, the sharp increase in secondary and university education of girls out of religious families in Turkey during the last decade, has also been partly contributed to Gülen's tireless efforts of rallying for equal education for both boys and girls in Turkey among the religiously minded (Yavuz 2003, 30).

It has already been stated above, that Gülen's ideas about Muslims living in non-Muslim lands bear relevance for all Muslim minorities and immigrant communities outside of the Muslim world. Given the Chams history as descendents of refugees, and the long history of peaceful coexistence with their Khmer hosts, the term *dar al-harb* (country of war) seems to be very inappropriate for their place of residence, rather justifying the refined Islamic law term of *dar al-aman* (country of security)[34]. Similarly Gülen stresses, that local laws are to be obeyed by Muslim residents in non-Muslim (as well as in secular) states (Yılmaz 2003, 234). Thus, Muslim minorities like the Chams should rather contribute their part to peace within the country, than jeopardizing it by pressing for a special legal or political status.

The last feature of Gülen's thought to be discussed here in relation to the Chams of Cambodia is of special interest, as it appears to be both rather unique and fitting perfectly into the Cham context. This concerns the relation between the Sunnite Cham majority and the Cham Sot. Albeit generally respected by the other Chams, this minority with its specific traditional practices, at times in outright discord with standard Islamic observance, is not accepted as truly Muslim. Therefore it is excluded from the benefits of international Islamic charities, which are tying aid to proper conduct, and have therefore refused to provide funds to Cham Sot villages (Collins 1996, 50-51; De Feo 2005a, 227). Local NGOs like CAMSA are not closing their doors to them, yet are allegedly also seeking to purify the practices of the so-called Jahed (De Feo 2005a, 235).

The antagonism between the two Cambodian Muslim groups is of course reminiscent of Sunnite-Alevi opposition in Turkey or Sunnite-Bektashi opposition in Albania, Kosovo and Macedonia[35]. The issue of similar Muslim minorities, often regarded as divergent sects, has not been addressed by many Muslim writers so far, especially when compared to treatment of dialogue with other book religions. Given the similarity of the respective cases, what Gülen has to say about Sunnite-Alevi relations appears to be very useful for the Cambodian case. Gülen notes, that the Alevis are in fact enriching Turkish culture, and that the two groups should open up to each other "for the sake of unity and enrichment". Moreover, he argues that "Alevi (sic)[36] prayer houses should be supported" to reflect Islam's inclusiveness (Ünal and Williams 2000, 68-69). With regard to the two specific groups of Chams in Cambodia, Gülen's references to inclusiveness and cultural diversity are particularly important, if one considers, that the Cham Sot are indeed representing traditional Cham culture in Cambodia, and that the eventual consolidation of the two factions as two distinct religious groups is of very recent date, as this process only took place during the 20th century (Bruckmayr 2007, 103-107).

In retrospect it appears that Gülen's thought could provide useful approaches for various current problematic issues among the Cambodian Cham community in this period of transition.

---

34 On this terminology see Yılmaz 2003, 234.
35 On these two groups see Yaman & Erdemir 2006.
36 This spelling invites confounding with the *Alawiyya* of Syria.

Whereas acquaintance with Gülen's ideas is still lacking in Cambodia now, the acknowledgement of the thought of Indonesian Neo-Modernists like Nurcholish Madjid and Abdurrahman Wahid, and its convergences with Gülen's positions might pave the way for the recognition of his efforts as universal and locally applicable instead of being specifically Turkish. As far as the Zaman International School is concerned, it is evident that it remains, at least for the time being, rather a theoretical than an actual option for the education of Cham students. Yet, what is more, certain segments of the Cham community have similar agendas as Gülen and his followers in the field of education, and home grown efforts along similar lines would certainly have a much bigger impact on the community than a single foreign run school.

We have discussed the history of Cham education as well as contemporary positions in the educational debate among the Chams. Evidently, the idea of secular educational endeavours not merely for upward mobility, but also as pursuance of an Islamic ideal, as expounded by Gülen and exemplified by the existence of the Zaman International School, is an entirely new impetus for this debate. Although still widely unknown and of vanishing relevance in Cham discourse in comparison to the agendas of Arab, Malaysian and Tablighi institutions propagating their respective views and ideals, it is indeed important to note, that the Gülen movement has obviously arrived in Cambodia as a completely different type of Islamic internationalism. Its inclusive character is well-suited for the plight of a Muslim minority people with intra-community diversity, and makes it easier to deal with the Cambodian government. On the contrary, the activities of other foreign Islamic groups at times rather serve to provoke intra-community strife between Sunnites and Cham Sot as well as between modern-oriented Muslims and Tablighi Traditionalists, and are moreover in certain instances at odds with governmental demands, when the principled is preferred to the pragmatic[37].

Finally, as an afterthought, I want to put Gülen into a new perspective provided by Milligan's discussion of Islamic identity and education in the Philippines. In an attempt to detect possible solutions to the educational dilemma in the South Philippines, Milligan calls for "prophetic pragmatism"[38]. With the latter he has in mind a creative combination of post colonialism and the pragmatism of a John Dewey (Milligan 2005, 162), yet without eschewing the religious component so decisive in the life and works of social reformers and peace activists like Mahatma Ghandi and Martin Luther King (Milligan 2005, 173-175). Although seemingly unaware of Gülen and the network's schools in the South Philippines, the question has to be raised, whether Gülen could not be rightfully regarded as such a prophetic pragmatist, as both the religious and the pragmatic seem to be the major components in Gülen's thought, and as the reconciliation of progressive energies and religious channels lies at the root of prophetic pragmatism.

---

37 For example, a teacher at RIHS school was reprimanded by his superiors for attending a government AIDS prevention workshop for teachers (personal conversation, Kampong Cham, 1-8-2005).
38 A term coined by the American philosopher Cornel West (1989).

THE CONTRIBUTIONS OF THE SEBAT INTERNATIONAL EDUCATION INSTITUTES TO KYRGYZSTAN

Ibrahim Keles

Abstract

Sebat International Education Institute has been operating for over 15 years in Sebat, Kyrgyzstan, educating and training the Kyrgyz youth. The institution has won a high reputation for quality education through excellent results, demonstrated by its students' high grades in international and domestic scientific competitions. This paper studies the impact of this institution on values among Kyrgyzstan youth, and compares its educational principles, policies and effects with those of other educational institutions in the city and country.

Introduction

Central Asian countries gained their independence in 1991, and a transition period has started not only in political life but in social, cultural and economic lives as well. As a result of this transition, people needed to re-identify their values. Their values were defined under the Soviet System and the result was not so successful. Additionally, there is disunity with Turkic-Islamic values.

Kyrgyz Turkish Schools were opened by Turkish entrepreneurs at that time, and local people met with people who possessed a similar set of values. This closeness resulted in many high schools and universities being established in the region. Sebat International Education Institute (Sebat) is the non-governmental organization founded the Kyrgyz Turkish Schools.

The quality of the education together with positive attitudes of teachers toward the students and parents make these schools very successful. The students learn to speak four languages (English, Russian, Turkish and their local language) as well as computer skills and receive many awards from local and international scientific competitions. These activities improve the quality of their education. In addition, determining the impact of the education given on their social values, democratization and globalization of the Kyrgyz society and country are more difficult to identify.

In this study, the contribution of schools to students' characters with some values such as honesty, tolerance, hard work, responsibility, loyalty, patience, courage, and cooperation between Sebat schools and others is analyzed with the help of a survey instrument that measures values. Also interviews were conducted with students. Data collected from the interviews explores where students see themselves in the global world. Finally, contributions of Sebat to enhance democratization practices of the Kyrgyz society and country will be discussed.

Kyrgyzstan and Turkic World

Kyrgyzstan, formally the Kyrgyz Republic, is located in Central Asia. . Kyrgyzstan is landlocked and very mountainous. It borders China, Kazakhstan, Tajikistan, and Uzbekistan. Its capital is Bishkek.

Kyrgyzstan has a wide mix of ethnic groups and cultures; Kyrgyz being the majority group. In 1999, the population of Kyrgyzstan was estimated at 64.9% ethnic Kyrgyz, 13.8% Uzbek, and 12.5% Russians. The rest of the population is composed of about ninety other nationalities. The population of the Kyrgyz Republic is estimated at 5,284,149 in July 2007 (CIA Fact Book, 2007).

Kyrgyz is the official language, however, Russian is the language of inter-ethnic communication. The total number of people speaking the official language fluently currently comprises 70% of the population of the country (compared with 53% in 1989).

The Turkic world can be geographically described parallel to peoples residing in Northern and Central Eurasia who speak languages belonging to the Turkic family and who, in varying degrees, share certain cultural and historical traits. Turkic languages are considered as a subdivision of the Altaic language group, and are one of the most geographically widespread in the world, being spoken in a vast region ranging from Europe to Siberia. And Kyrgyzstan is nearly at the center of the Turkic world.

Figure 1: Map of Turkic World (Wikimedia, 2007)

The Kyrgyz language is a member of Turkic language family. The Soviet experience of Kyrgyzstan and interaction of Turkish people with Western civilization resulted in some cultural and language differentiation between two Turkic nations. For example, Kyrgyz people use the Cyrillic alphabet whereas the Turks use Latin characters. The logic and grammar of the languages are nearly the same.

Kyrgyz civilization had serious contributions to Turkic-Islamic culture. For example, in 1070, Yusuf Khass Khajib Balasaghuni, the author of the Kutadgu Bilig (Wisdom of Royal Glory), explained the philosophy of life and how to administer a country, and Mahmud Kashgari studied Turkic dialects and wrote the first comprehensive dictionary of Turkic languages, the Dīwān ul-Lughat al-Turk (Collection of Turkic words) in 1072. These two books are two of the oldest examples of Turkic-Islamic literature.

The dominant religion in the country is Sunni Islam (specifically the Hanafi school) - about 70% as of 1994 like most of other Turkic nations.

Sebat International Institute (SEBAT)

Sebat International Education Institute (Sebat), founder of the Kyrgyz Turkish Schools, is a non-governmental organization that established itself in the Kyrgyz Republic in 1991. Since February 1992, Sebat has opened 14 high schools, 4 university dormitories, the International Ataturk Alatoo University, the International Silk Road School, and the Secom Center for language and computer studies. Till today 60 million US$ has been invested in education by Sebat.

Figure 2: Sebat International Education Institutes around Kyrgyzstan

Educational and Administrative Staff Profile1

Nearly all Sebat schools are high schools. In those schools, there are one director and 3 vice-directors. 12 of those directors are Turkish and 4 of them are Kyrgyz. Moreover, there are 27 Turkish vice-directors and 21 Kyrgyz vice-directors. 2 of the Kyrgyz directors and 10 of the Kyrgyz vice-directors were graduated from Sebat schools.

---

1 Sebat keeps staff records depending on their citizenship. Here, citizens of Turkey are named as Turkish and Kyrgyzstan citizens are named as Kyrgyz that comprises Russian, Uzbek, Korean, Ethnic Turkish ethnic groups.

There are 510 teachers working in Sebat schools. 170 of them are Turkish and 340 of them are Kyrgyz (150 of them were graduated from Sebat schools.) In addition, nearly 500 workers are working in these schools and just 10 of them are Turkish.

At International Ataturk Alatoo University there is one Rector and one Vice-Rector (both are Turkish nationals), and one Kyrgyz Vice-Rector as well. All three of the faculty deans are Kyrgyz. There are 3 Kyrgyz and 4 Turkish department heads. 64 of the lecturers are Kyrgyz and 20 of them are Turkish. In the university, there are 46 Kyrgyz and 7 Turkish workers.

Student Selection Process and Student Profile

The significant characteristic of these schools is that they are selecting students through admission tests. There are two-steps in this admission process. In the first step, students take a test to demonstrate their general school knowledge. Approximately 50.000 students enroll annually in this first step. The successful candidates (approximately 10.000) take another test of logic and math's. This is the second step. Students are requested to bring a health report to show that they are physically and mentally healthy to live in a dormitory environment. This system is very objective and there is no corruption.

According to National Statistical Committee (NSC) (1999), the urban/rural population of the country is as 34.8% urban population and 65.2% rural population. The student distribution in Sebat schools is as 51% urban students, and 49% rural students (Ormushev et al. 2007:22). Comparing the education quality of urban/rural areas it is acceptable that rural students do not score as high on admission examinations and also the economic conditions of the rural areas are weaker than the urban areas.

Figure 3: Urban/rural population of Kyrgyzstan, %   **Figure 4:** Urban/rural students of Sebat, %

According to Solberg (2006), these schools are perceived as "elite" schools because they are fee-paying private schools, but they are not elite schools. Their admission exams are opened to all and the fees are affordable for people having average income in the country. Also, the previous statistics about urban/rural population verifies this.

Wage (1 year)	1352,4$
Average High School Fee[1]	600$
Average University Fee	850$

Table 1: Comparative wages of an average employee in Kyrgyzstan and school fees of Sebat in 2007, 1$=37.8KGSom (Source: NSC, NBKR, & Sebat)

Beside this, among 4616 students, 324 students are from crowded families, 34 of them orphans, 204 of them are fatherless, and 47 of them are motherless (Ormushev et al. 2007, p:23).

This system has been providing opportunity to get high quality education for all.

Finally, the national distribution of the students is as follows; 74% Kyrgyz, 13% Russian, 6% Uzbek and 7% others. Comparing the national demographic structure of the country, Kyrgyz student population of Sebat is above the statistical average and Uzbek student population is under the statistical average (NSC, 1999).

Education Style

The main courses are instructed in English. In addition to English; local languages as Kyrgyz and Russian are taught as well as Turkish as a foreign language. By graduation, the majority of students are fluent in all four languages, and are able to use basic computer programs.

Sebat students have also proved their quality education at republic and international and world level olympiads.[2] As a result of success in international area, the education minister of Kyrgyzstan, Ishengul Bolcurova said that "Kyrgyzstan opened to world in education area with Sebat" (Zaman, 06.08.2002).

	Republic				World and International			
	Gold	Silver	Bronze	Total	Gold	Silver	Bronze	Total
2001-02	6	9	8	23	-	2	2	4
2002-03	9	9	6	24	-	-	1	1
2003-04	12	11	18	41	1	4	9	14
2004-05	15	18	10	43	3	2	7	12
2005-06	20	15	10	45	1	2	8	11
2006-07	18	12	10	40	2	6	7	15
Total	80	74	62	216	7	16	34	57

Table 2: Number of Scientific Olympiad Degrees at Republic and World and International Levels Earned by Sebat students, 2001-2007 (Source: Sebat)

Sebat students' success has also been improved by close teacher-parent relationships. At Sebat, teachers interact very closely with parents. Sebat schools usually organize 3 teacher-parent meetings a year[3] and these meetings provide good opportunities to discuss the situation of students in detail and to improve their success at school. In fact, Sebat is encouraging its teachers to perform home-visits as a policy in order to increase quality of education in the schools.

Another thing to see the success of the Sebat Schools is the number of students going abroad for higher studies. In 2006, graduates of Sebat Schools continuing their higher education in 24 different countries. While 1571 graduates (almost 75%) are continuing their university education in Kyrgyzstan, 298 (14%) of them have gone to Turkey for higher studies. Turkey is the top country that has been chosen for higher education because Turkish Government is

2 World scientific Olympiads are those organized regularly by UNESCO. International Olympiads are those, which are organized by a foundation, a country, etc. For example, Mathematics Project Competition organized in Kazakhstan by KATEV and DARIN is this type of Olympiad.

3 These meeting are generally visit-at-home type. Actually, Sebat is encouraging teachers to visit parents at home in order to see home environment.

allocating scholarships. Otherwise this figure might be somewhat smaller. Beside this, 276 graduates of IAAU are working or having graduate education in 16 different countries.

Kyrgyzstan	Turkey	Russia	Kazakhstan	USA	China	Others	Total
1571	298	71	22	21	18	50	2051

Table 3: Allocation of Sebat High School Graduates that is continuing their higher education into Countries, 1996-2006.

Kyrgyzstan	Turkey	Russia	Kazakhstan	Others	Total
212	15	19	8	21	276

Table 4: Allocation of IAAU Graduates into Countries, 2000-2006 (Source: IAAU Career Development Center, 2007)

The reasons for this success can be explained as follows; Firstly, Sebat Schools are selecting good students through admission examinations. Secondly, most of them are staying at dormitories and studying two hours regularly (10 hours in a week) there under the guidance of their tutors. Also, their teachers come to dormitories in the evenings and help students with their homework. Third, according to Sebat, approximately 50% of the students are preparing for olympiads; they are spending more than 10 hours per week. Further, Sebat is organizing *Olympic camps* (extensive preparation for olympiads) at the end of each quarters. At these camps, they are studying for more than 10 hours a day for about 15 days, getting 4 hours of lectures and more than 6 hours of individual study.

This type of hard study and preparation for olympiads naturally result in an impressive success.

One activity to develop one's sociability is participation in clubs. Every school has more than 10 clubs. Some clubs are sports, English, math, chess, internet, drama, etc. According to Sebat, the main purpose of the club activities at Sebat Schools is contributing to the positive development of students' character. Clubs are especially contributing to the increased cooperation, responsibility, respect for one another, rights and determination to succeed.

According to Sebat officials, other factors which contribute to student success include low teacher/pupil ratio and relatively high salaries of teachers at these schools. Presently, there are 510 teachers and 4,616 students at Sebat; the teacher/student ration is approximately 1:9.. Also, Sebat officials claim they are paying higher salaries to both foreign and local teachers than Kyrgyzstan standards, resulting in increased teacher performance and higher per student expenditure. Teachers' education and experience levels are also effective on the student performance. As Sebat acknowledges us that they are organizing countrywide teacher meetings once a year. Further, since each Sebat schools has about 300 students, physical facilities like laboratories, computers, etc. are more readily available for students. Above-mentioned factors are increasing student performance at Sebat.

Social Responsibility

Social responsibility is the obligation to make decisions and take actions that will enhance the welfare and interests of society as well as the organization (Daft, 2000:143). And the discretionary responsibility is the organizational responsibility that is voluntary and guided by the organization's desire to make social contributions not mandated by economics, law, or ethics. It is the highest criterion of social responsibility, because it goes beyond societal expectations to contribute to the community's welfare (Daft, 2000:149). All activities of Sebat can be evaluated in this context. Besides educating students, Sebat is organizing and sponsoring a number of activities such as;

i. Sponsoring ecology olympiads in the country (Baycigitov N., 2007),
ii. Distributing meat at the Feast of the Sacrifice to orphanages, hospitals
iii. Helping victims of disasters like earthquake, torrent, … (Toktorov, M. 12.01. 2007)
iv. Organizing and sponsoring national and international scientific conferences,
v. Publishing course books and dictionaries in Kyrgyz language,
vi. Organizing 'days of Kyrgyz Culture' in European countries in order to introduce Kyrgyzstan and Kyrgyz culture (Sebat web page, 2007),
vii. Organizing annual businessmen tours to Kyrgyzstan named ''Business Dialog" in order to attract investment (Zaman, 24 May 2006).

Opinions about Sebat

At a conference at Georgetown University in 2001, Dr. Thomas Michel, S.J. explained his evaluation related to the IAAU and high schools of Sebat as follows;

i. These schools were one of the most dynamic and worthwhile educational enterprises that he has encountered in the world today.
ii. The students had very good English and seemed equally competent in Russian and Turkish, in addition to their native Kyrgyz language.
iii. Lecturers sought to communicate students with universal values such as honesty, hard work, harmony, and conscientious service.
iv. Demir et al. (2000) in their study of Kyrgyz Turkish Schools in Kyrgyzstan, conducted interviews with parents, students and teachers of the education institutes and they determined the three major characteristics of Kyrgyz Turkish Schools in the region as follows:
v. quality of education which includes positive attitudes of the teachers toward the students and parents
vi. teaching four languages
vii. training well-bred individuals
viii. During the opening ceremony of IAAU Boys Dormitory, President of Kyrgyz Republic, Kurmanbek Bakiyev explained his opinions about the dormitory, IAAU and Sebat are as follows (Zaman, 2006);
ix. I hope that other education institutes in my country will have beautiful and high quality buildings like this.
x. I thank Sebat and sponsors of them because of their assisstance to Kyrgyz Education System.
xi. With 14 country-wide high schools, IAAU and language center, they are educating and training our children.
xii. The generation that you educate is the guarantee of our bright future.

Most of graduates of Sebat and IAAU are working in foreign companies in Kyrgyzstan. Those foreign companies prefer to hire them because they have

i. Foreign and local language skills in a good way.
ii. Computer skills.
iii. Experience with foreign people
iv. Ability to adopt foreign working styles
v. Also in order to determine what makes IAAU different from other higher education institutes in the region, interviews were taken from lecturers. Results of interviews with lecturers are as follows;
vi. A good infrastucture for education.
vii. Harmony between administrative staff and academic staff.
viii. Student oriented education.
ix. Using Western style.
x. Using new technologies, tools and approaches.
xi. Discipline in education
xii. Good education system.

Parallel to these opinions in 2007, Kyrgyz president Kurmanbek Bakiyev has given "High Honor Degree" to the President of Sebat, Orhan Inandi because of the contributions of Sebat to Kyrgyz education system (Zaman, 24.04.2006). Also, in 2004, ex-president Askar Akayev has given "Dank (high honor) Medal' (second most important medal of Kyrgyz State) (Zaman, 08.10.2004).

Democratisation and Globalisation

Democratization

Democracy is more likely to emerge and consolidate in countries with high levels of education (Papaioannou, E.& Gregorios S., 2006:26). Across the world, the correlation between education and democracy is extremely high. Glaeser et al (2007) found that the correlation coefficient between these variables is 74 percent across 91 countries. And also according to Lipsetp (1959:79), education has a positive effect on humans' outlooks, enables them to understand the need for norms of tolerance, restrains them from adhering to extremist and monistic doctrines, and increases their capacity to make rational electoral choices. By this way, education is supporting the establishment of democracy.

Kyrgyzstan has a high level of education. The contribution of Sebat Schools to Kyrgyz education system is not in quantitative form but in qualitative form. The Sebat Schools are adding value to Kyrgyz education system with its quality education and creating a diversification in the system.

Schools prepare people for participation in the economy and polity, giving them the knowledge to make responsible judgments, the motivation to make appropriate contributions to the well being of society, and a consciousness about the consequences of their behavior (Epstein E. H., 2007). Parallel to this opinion, in education system of Kyrgyzstan, there are elected class and school presidents. In actuality, they they are seen as an assistant to the teachers. But in Sebat Schools, the system of class and school presidency seen as a part of education system to teach democracy, to improve responsibility and leadership skills of students, and a communication channel between students, teachers and administration.

In the education system of Sebat Schools, students nearly spend all their time together. They are having lessons in the day and living in the dormitories in the evenings for five years. Also as a result of ethnic structure of Kyrgyzstan, the students have different backgrounds. In this way, during the school years students learn the norms of tolerance.

Globalization

Today, as a result of developments in communication, and transportation we are living in a global village. But in order to maneuver throughout the global network, it is essential that students know how to use the internet efficiency and speak English. The significant differences of the Sebat schools are teaching these tools in a good way. Beside these, students improve their local language skills as Kyrgyz and Russian and learn Turkish.

The students of Sebat schools have lots of Turkish teachers and some from other nations. The diversity of the teachers enhances the students' ability to take their first steps towards a more global environment. Further, they meet with people from other parts of the world who have different histories, habits, languages and behaviors.

Also, students attend different programs in other parts of the world. For example, students attended 'Kyrgyz Culture Days' in European countries several times, and they are attending international Olympiads in different countries.

Beside these contributions to democratization and globalization, Sebat has contributions to establish a well educated staffs for the country. Perhaps this is the most important plus on the state perspective. Before gaining independence, Kyrgyzstan was dependent on skilled workers which were mostly among Russian-speaking minorities, mainly Germans, Russians, and Ukrainians (Mamedov N., 2005:52). In 1980 just 13% of the republic's engineers and technicians were Kyrgyz (Mamedov N., 2005:77). Following independence, huge numbers of Russian speaking minorities began to migrate to Russia. This resulted huge decreases in GDP of the country and created new problems throughout the country as a whole. The country had to educate technical and professional staffs. Some government programmes like Cadry XXI.veka started in order to solve this problem. With the efforts of Sebat, they are hiring qualified administrators and teachers from the country. .

Literature Review

There are certain studies focuses on the Turkish private schools in Central Asia and Kyrgyzstan. For example Demir et al 2000, analyzed the roles of Kyrgyz Turkish Schools in Turkmenistan and Kyrgyzstan; At a conference at Georgetown University in 2001, Dr. Thomas Michel, S.J. explained his evaluation related to the IAAU and high schools of Sebat and then this proceeding was published by Yavuz H.M. & Esposito J.L. 2003. The book named "Advocate of Dialogue: Fethullah Gülen" gives examples of interviews with staff of Turkish Schools in different parts of the world including Kyrgyzstan. Also "Barış Köprüleri/ Dünyaya Açılan Türk Okulları", Ortaylı et al. 2005, contains opinions of Turkish writers on Kyrgyz Turkish Schools.

"Sebat" Bilim Beruu Uyasi written by Ormushev A., Inandi O. & Asan uulu T. (2007) in Kyrgyz, gives a brief history of Kyrgyz Turkish Schools in Kyrgystan. Sagbansua, L.& Keles, I. (2006), "Turkish Higher Education Experience in Central Asia: Managerial and Educational Features of IAAU" illustrates the educational and managerial aspects of the Sebat's university, IAAU.

Methodology

In this study, the importance of values such as honesty, tolerance, hard work, responsibility, loyalty, patience, courage, and cooperation between students of Sebat schools and others is analyzed with the help of a survey instrument. The survey consists of two sections. The first section is mostly based on the survey of World Values Survey. The second section of the survey consists of questions identifying demographic and socio-economic characteristics of the respondents.

The World Values Survey (WVS) is a global network of social scientists who have surveyed the basic values and beliefs of the publics of more than 80 societies, on all six inhabited continents. The WVS is a tool to analyze socio-cultural and political change in a worldwide perspective. It was firstly prepared by the European Values Survey group (EVS) under the leadership of Jan Kerkhofs and Ruud de Moor in 1981. Until today, a total of four waves of the survey have been carried out. The WVS has given rise to more than 400 publications in more than 20 languages (World Values Survey, 2007).

In this study, students of Sebat schools are named as "Sebat". And all other students are named as "others". The data for this study was collected in Bishkek, Kyrgyzstan during the September 2007. Table 13 shows demographic characteristics of the attended students to the survey. Dependent variable of the study is the "students' values" and independent variable of the study is being a graduate student of Sebat schools.

Before starting to survey process, a pre-test of the survey will be done with a small group of students in both groups. By this pre-test process, it is aimed to measure the reliability of the survey and also to check whether the conductors understand the process or not.

In total, there are 8 groups of questions for identifying values and 4 questions for identifying demographic and socio-economic characteristics in the survey.

The survey group consisted of freshmen students at the International Atatürk Alatoo University. %51 of those students are graduted from Sebat schools and %49 of them are graduated from other schools of Kyrgyzstan. At the first day of the school, the survey was done in class environments with the supervisory of lecturers. The surveys distributed to students and approximately in twenty minutes they gave surveys back. 449 surveys were distributed, yet due to incompleteness, only 428 usable questionnaires were obtained.

Results

Culture provides a general set of objectives for members to develop their personal goals and ambitions. Values are these shared concepts of what is considered good, pleasing, and appropriate in culture that indicate what people in a given culture prefer as well as what they find important and morally right. They influence people's behavior and provide as criteria for valuating the others' actions (Schaefer R.T. & Lamm R.P.p:80-81). In this part the survey results will be used to analyze if there is a difference between Sebat students and others on perception of social values.

Firstly, as a result of education, some changes occur on characteristics of the students. It is asked how their schools affect their personal characteristics. A three-point Likert scale was used, "1" being "none" and "3" being "much."

	Sebat	Others
Responsibility	2.77	2.73
Respect	2.83	2.81
Self-Esteem	2.05	2.17
Caring	2.13	1.92
Perseverance	2.22	2.23
Tolerance	2.69	2.57
Honesty	2.83	2.69
Cooperation	2.71	2.60
Courage	2.38	2.24
Loyalty	2.79	2.68

Table 5: How Students Think Their Schools Contribute to Improving Their Characters.

This part of the survey shows the efforts of schools to contribute their students characters. As the nature of education or being a teacher, it is aimed the improve students characteristics. Students of both types of schools said that their schools have contribution to their characteristics. When we compare the results of the survey, the students of Sebat reported higher degree of contribution to their characteristics. The result of this part of the survey means that Sebat schools are spending much more effort to student characteristics improvement comparing to other schools. Beside this, just for the `self-esteem` part of the survey students of Sebat given a lower score that the other students.

Another finding in this part of the survey is, the importance of characteristics for the schools. If students reported higher degree of contribution to their character, it means their school spend more effort and give more importance. The survey resulted that the key characters focused by Sebat are honesty, respect, loyalty, responsibility, cooperation and tolerance. The lowest score was given to 'self-esteem' in Sebat schools. Perhaps, the importance given on 'cooperation' shadows the 'self-esteem'.

	Sebat	Rating	Others	Rating
Honesty	2.83	1	2.69	3
Respect	2.83	2	2.81	1
Loyalty	2.79	3	2.68	4
Responsibility	2.77	4	2.73	2
Cooperation	2.71	5	2.6	5
Tolerance	2.69	6	2.57	6
Courage	2.38	7	2.24	7
Perseverance	2.22	8	2.23	8
Caring	2.13	9	1.92	10
Self-Esteem	2.05	10	2.17	9

Table 6: Rating of Characters by Schools

In the second part of the survey, it was asked to tell the importance of their family, friends, religion, leisure time, and politics. A four-point Likert scale was used, "1" giving "not at all important" and "4" giving "very important."

	Sebat Girls	Other Girls	Sebat Boys	Other Boys
Family	3.99	3.95	3.95	3.9
Friends	3.72	3.5	3.75	3.64
Religion	3.49	3.3	3.5	3.3
Leisure time	3.09	3.08	3.4	3.04
Politics	2.78	2.77	2.67	3

Table 7: Importance of some Indicators in their Daily Life

The sequence of importance of indicators are paralel in each of the groups. The most important indicator is the family, and then friends, religion, leisure time and politics. For the first four indicators both Sebat girls and boys rated more importance than the other school students but for the politics girls rated a similer degree liked the other girls. On the contrary Sebat boys showed a very low degree of importance for the politics. Also, there is a significant difference in giving importance for leisure time among Sebat boys and other boys. Sebat boys are giving too much importance on their leisure time.

In the third part, the participants rated the importance of following sentences on a four-point Likert scale was used, "1" giving "not at all important" and "4" giving "very important."

How important is it to . . .	Sebat Girls	Other Girls	Sebat Boys	Other Boys
Be well off financially?	3.33	3.59	3.5	3.55
To help others in difficulty?	3.8	3.59	3.69	3.58
Develop a meaningful philosophy of life?	3.51	3.34	3.26	3.31
Influence social values?	3.08	3.08	3.05	3.09

Table 8: Importance of some situations

The third part indicates that being well off financially and to help others in difficulty are very important for both groups of students but the Sebat students rated `to help others in difficulty` more important and 'be financially well off' less important than the others.

There are some differences among Sebat students for the ratings of developing a meaningful philosophy of life and influence social values. The Sebat girls rated highest degree of importance in groups and the Sebat boys rated lowest degree of importance. And also it is similar for the `influence social values`.

In the fourth part, it was asked to tell opinions for each of the following actions related to corruption whether it can always be justified, never be justified, or something in between. A three-point Likert scale was used, "1" being "justify" and "3" being "not justify."

	Sebat Girls	Other Girls	Sebat Boys	Other Boys
Avoiding a fare on public transport	2.82	2.7	2.59	2.66
Cheating on taxes if you have a chance	2.85	2.74	2.65	2.65
Someone accepting a bribe in the course of their duties	2.82	2.74	2.63	2.65

Table 9: Sensitivity in corruption

Both student groups are very sensitive in corruption related issues. Perhaps as a result of the coutry agenda, the survey resulted in this way.

In the fifth part, it was asked to tell each of the following actions whether it can always be justified, never be justified, or something in between. A three-point Likert scale was used, "1" being "justify" and "3" being "not justify."

	Sebat Girls	Other Girls	Sebat Boys	Other Boys
Abortion	2.78	2.77	2.73	2.61
Divorce	2.61	2.48	2.55	2.49
Euthanasia	2.82	2.77	2.69	2.72
Suicide	2.93	2.86	2.85	2.88
Polygamy	2.78	2.75	2.68	2.62

Table 10: Justification of some situations

The survey showed that the Sebat students rated more negative opinion on abortion, divorce and polygamy. Also other school students expressed negative opinions about those issues but not as much as Sebat students. For euthanasia and suicide, both boy groups rated less negative opinions but considering all the groups, the Sebat girls rated the highest degree of negative opinion and the Sebat boys rated the lowest degree of negative opinion on those issues.

People have different views about themselves and how they relate to the world. It is asked to tell how strongly they agree or disagree with each of the following statements about them. A four-point Likert scale was used, "1" being "Strongly disagree" and "4" being "strongly agree."

I see myself as a/an....	Sebat Girls	Other Girls	Sebat Boys	Other Boys
...world citizen.	3.33	3.29	3.41	3.16
...part of my local community.	3.35	3.05	3.25	3.06
...part of the Kyrgyz nation.	3.79	3.46	3.67	3.61
...part of the Euroasia.	3.22	2.87	3.31	2.9
...autonomous individual.	3.54	3.45	3.56	3.55

The Sebat/Other girls table show that there are differences in state of belonging to local community, Kyrgyz nation and Eurasia. It can be said that the Sebat girls' degree of state of belonging to world is as much as other girls (the Sebat girls also have a higher degree in world citizen). The Sebat/Other boys table show that there are differences in state of belonging to in all groups.

At the eighth part it is asked how proud they are to be Kyrgyz. A four-point Likert scale was used, "4" being "very proud" and "1" being "not at all proud."

	Sebat Girls	Other Girls	Sebat Boys	Other Boys
Are you proud of being Kyrgyz?	3,90	3,62	3,76	3,66

Table 11: Proud of being Kyrgyz citizen

The results show that both Sebat girls and boys are more proud of being Kyrgyz.

And lastly, what language they normally speak at home was asked.

	Sebat Girls	Other Girls	Sebat Boys	Other Boys
Kyrgyz	65.33	50	57.24	52.87
Russian	17.33	20.18	15.13	20.69
More than one	14.67	25.44	17.76	18.39
Other	2.66	4.38	9.87	8.05

Table 12: Language at home, %

Language at home also approves the previous findings as proud of being Kyrgyz.

Future Research Avenues

The data presented here are static and limited in nature. Here, the perception and opinions of students collected and presented. Therefore, wider researches may be useful for identifying the effects of these schools in daily life. This study shows that Sebat schools are giving more importance on such characters as honesty, respect, loyalty, responsibility, cooperation and tolerance. In order to identify whether they are successful or not some studies must be done. For example a study to identify profile of prisoners in Kyrgyzstan may show this.

Another research area may be the families established by Sebat graduates. This study shows that they are giving more importance on family and have more negative opinions on divorce. A new study to test hypothesis may be done. Also there are some couples as a Sebat graduate and an other school graduate. The effects of Sebat schools on values may be better understand with a research focus on those families.

Conclusions

The Sebat schools have been operating in all regions of Kyrgyzstan for more than 15 years. As a result of their activities, thousands of Kyrgyz students have received a higher quality education. The schools' success in scientific competitions in domestic and international area results a good reputation in the country. Beside this, Sebat schools spend too much effort to develop students' characters.

The education given in those schools support the democratization and globalization of the country. The students meet with democratic practices in their early years and also meet with the global world by having foreign teachers (mainly Turkish), using internet, learning foreign languages and attending scientific olympiads in international area.

Finally, Sebat schools' contributions to students are good education and manner and to Kyrgyzstan are well educated and loyal citizens.

Appendices

Age	Sebat Girls	Other Girls	Sebat Boys	Other Boys	Total
19>	2	7	2	7	18
19	11	11	9	6	37
18	47	63	78	44	232
17	15	29	55	30	129
<17	0	4	8	0	12
Total	75	114	152	87	428
	Sebat Girls	Other Girls	Sebat Boys	Other Boys	Total
Sample Group	78	152	187	111	528
Survey Group	75	114	152	87	428

Table 13: Demographic Characteristics of the Attended Students

Sample Group	265	Confidence Level	99%
Survey Group	227	Confidence Interval	3.25

Table 14: Sample Size Calculations for Sebat Students (CRS, 2007)

Sample Group	263	Confidence Level	99%
Survey Group	201	Confidence Interval	4.43

Table 15: Sample Size Calculations for Other Students (CRS, 2007)

THE GÜLEN MOVEMENT: ITS NATURE AND IDENTITY

Muhammed Çetin

Abstract

The Gülen movement is increasingly visible through the work of a range of institutions across the world. Its visibility has led to the beginning of formal academic inquiry into the nature and identity of the movement and its activities. Such academic study is necessary before one can offer to evaluate the short- and long-term outcomes of the movement and their desirability. While little of an academic nature has been published so far, there have been a number of politicised or journalistic accounts of the movement, characterising it variously as a sect, cult or order. This paper scrutinises a number of those accounts as a way into a more accurate, evidence-based description of the teachings of Fethullah Gülen and of the conduct of the members of the movement inspired by him.

This paper aims to examine the identity and nature of the Gülen Movement. To do this I consider some questions which have been raised about the movement in the academic and political arenas. Specifically, I address whether the movement comprises a sect, cult or religious order by examining the discourse and action of Gülen and the Gülen Movement.

What is a 'Sect' in Islamic Thought?

As a preliminary, it must be highlighted that in the use of this term, 'sect'[1], lies a potential cross-cultural communication problem with significant consequences in the academic and the political world. It is common for academics and journalists commenting on the Muslim world to use such terms with the same import as they have in a European or American context. I shall not compare definitions because for the purposes of this paper how the Western experience is defined is irrelevant. Instead, I will state what comprises a sect within Islamic thinking.

One important science in Islamic is aqida, that is, the statement of belief, or the creed. At its simplest, this is the shahadah, the statement of witness that there is only one God and Muhammad is His Messenger (pbuH). The aqida outlines in more detail the elements of the seen and unseen that Muslims believe in, and is derived from the Qur'an in a quite straightforward manner. A sect arises because the aqida of a group differs from that of the majority, either by addition or subtraction. In the history of Islam, Muslims have generally concurred that there are two sects in Islam, the majority Sunni and the minority Shi'a. It is safe to say that most Muslims feel that this division is regrettable but few would go so far as to say those in the other sect are not Muslims, since Sunni and Shi'a are united by the shahadah and, contrary to current belief in the western media, have lived side by side in peace for centuries. Also, Shi'a Muslims receive permits to visit the holy sites of Islam on the Arabian Peninsula.

Within Sunni Islam, there are then four main madhabs. This word is translated in different ways, sometimes as 'schools of thought', or as 'schools of law'. These are not sects; there is mutual recognition between them. They are traditions which interpret the application of Islamic law to all aspects of life, and while it is necessary to choose one madhab to follow, it is legal and morally acceptable to follow a particular ruling from a different madhab under certain conditions.

The important thing to note is that the division of the Muslim community into sects or sectarian groupings is anathema to canonical Islam. There are warnings against this in the sayings of the Messenger of God (pbuH), and he (pbuH) welcomed differences of opinion in the umma as 'a mercy'. Consequently, Islamic culture is very varied and has made a great contribution to world legal culture (Sykiainen 2007). For these reasons, Muslims avoid breaking off from the main body of Islam into sectarian groupings and are well able to avoid breaking off.

Thus, asking if the Gülen Movement is a sect, means asking if it is enacting a new or deviant form of Islam. If this is not so, it is interesting to ask why the accusation is used, who makes it and what is their purpose.

What is a 'Cult'?

Having looked at the definition of 'sect', it is easy to see that anything which could be termed a 'cult' would immediately and obviously fall outside the boundaries of traditional Islam. So, the word cult is used in the Muslim world in the same way as it is in Western culture for

1 The academic study of religion has tended to move away from the more classical sociological language of 'sect' (in the Weberian sense of intention, which does not necessarily carry negative overtones) to that of 'New Religious Movements' or 'NRMs'. See particularly, Eileen Barker, *New Religious Movements: A Perspective for Understanding Society* (Lampeter: Edwin Mellen Press, 1982); and Eileen Barker, *New Religious Movements: A Practical Introduction* (London: Home Office, 1990).

a religious grouping, usually small, with a number of particular and potentially dangerous characteristics for cult members or for society. To deal with this with respect to the Gülen Movement I will pose a number of relevant questions.

What is an 'Order' in Islamic Thought?

The Gülen Movement has been likened to a Sufi tariqa or order and recently to a Christian lay order. There are a few simple points that can be made about such comparisons. A Sufi order may have some surface similarities with but is quite different from a Christian order.

Tariqas adhere to Islamic teachings so they, for example, demand chastity but not celibacy, unlike most Christian orders, so there is a general expectation in Muslim societies that one will marry. Tariqas are open to men and women equally and though members of tariqas may spend periods of time apart from worldly life, there are no monasteries or convents; members live in society and are expected to make their own living. Since Gülen Movement partici-pants are men and women, live in society, marry, and make their own livings, this leads to the question whether the Gülen Movement is some kind of new tariqa.

The similarities between Christian orders and tariqas lie in some of the processes and hierar-chical structures found within them. So, there may be long novitiates, a high level of commit-ment, and quite a high degree of control over aspects of members' lives.

Why have These Questions been Raised About the Gülen Movement?

These questions were first raised in Turkey and to ascertain the motivations behind them we need to consider the social context of the Gülen Movement.

The Republic of Turkey is a secular state but this term needs some clarification. Çinar (2005: 16) spells out how reality differs from what might be expected:

> The Atatürkist innovation was to bring Islamic authority under the full and absolute control of the secular state. Rather than following the common pattern where all religious affairs are sepa-rated from formal political affairs, the institutionalization of secularism involved bringing all re-ligious activity under the direct control and monopoly of the secular state. In 1924 a Directorate of Religious Affairs was formed to act as the ultimate authority on the knowledge and practice of Islam.

In doing this, the new republic, unintentionally no doubt, created potential for social conflict, as Eickelman (1998: 90) describes:

> The ideals of civil society, democracy, and open debate over basic values-ideals that are explicit in the works of ... Turkey's Fethullah Gülen ... are up against strong vested interests. These ideals threaten the sinecures of many preachers, specialists in religious law, educators, and clerics. Not surprisingly, some efforts at reform have been met with threats of violence.

Lofland (1996: 229) argues that inability or unwillingness of authorities to deal with acute social crisis prepares people to affiliate with Social Movement Organizations. Such organiza-tions would include the educational, cultural and dialogue projects of the Gülen Movement. In a milieu of crisis, religious communities and orders survived and revived though they officially do not exist. Therefore, Alpay (1995) argues that "modern institutionalization and organization in Turkey remain behind, backward, whereas religious brotherhood and solidarity, basic forms of social organization, continue".[2]

Because of this backwardness in institutionalization and organization, politics in Turkey is based on protective relationships[3] in which the very concepts of religion and democracy are misused (Fuller, 2004: 53; Cerrahoğlu, 1995[4]). Yavuz (2000c: 22) argues that "the sharp division between moral community and the political sphere is the source of many problems in Turkey. As the Turkish political domain does not provide an ethical charter, the moral emptiness turned the political domain into a space of dirty tricks, duplicity and the source of corruption".

Consequently, the form of civic, faith-based initiative, or social capital[5] and modernization enacted in the Gülen Movement became a source of worry and a 'matter of state security'[6] for the self-declared statist-elitist-secular bureaucrats, some generals, and state-sponsored businessmen (Yücel, 2002: 23).[7] These people comprise the protectionist vested interest within the establishment. Because religious orders, sects, their leadership, affiliation to and supporting them are outlawed by the Turkish Constitution, many people have been prosecuted for this in Turkey. Just one way for vested interests to countermobilize against what they see as opposition is to refuse to acknowledge the self-identity of any civil society movement, such as the Gülen Movement, and accuse it of being an order or sect. Smith (2001: 3) comments wryly, "Critics further say that Ankara has cultivated a seamless web of internal and external threats – some real some imagined – to keep the enterprise afloat."[8]

Support for statist-elitist-secular criticism of Gülen comes from what might seem a surprising quarter – radical Islamists. Gülen's meeting with John Paul II received wide public support in Turkey, but hard-line secularists and radical Islamists criticized him for it; the former on the grounds that Gülen, by speaking individually to the Pope to promote interfaith dialogue, had revealed his desire for an Islamic state with himself as head; the latter on the grounds that he was degrading Islam by dialogue with a non-Muslim leader (Griffith and Sarıtoprak 2005: 335–6).

---

2 Also Ünal and Williams, 2000: 156–7; Sykiainen, 2006: 116; Yilmaz, 2005: 397.

3 Dorronsoro and Massicard, 2005: 2; Özbudun, 1975: 473–9, 1981: 234, 237–8; Mardin, 1975: 7–32; Kalaycioglu, 1988: 149–79, 1997 at www.biu.ac.il/SOC/besa/meria.html; Çarkoglu, 1998: 544–53; Secor and O'Loughlin, 2004: 11; Ataman, 2002: 122; Aliriza, 2000: 2–5, and 2001: 1–5; Smith, 2001: 17; Babahan, 2006; *Turkish Daily News,* 2000; Hekimoglu 2000; Koru, **2000a;** Pope, 2000; Önis and Turem, 2001: 24–5, 27.

4 Also in Ünal and Williams, 2000: 152.

5 As an example of considering the implications of religion in relation to the notion of "social capital" generated and sustained among civic organizations, see Weller, 2005: 271–89.

6 For the recurrent theme used by the protectionist groups of 'regime under threat' or 'national security syndrome', see Howe, 2000: 39; Ataman, 2002: 122, 150; Hale, 1999; Jung, 1999; Öniş, 2004: 23; Yücel, 2002: 3–4; 2004: 2–6, 23–4; Dumanli, 2006; Alpay, 2007.

7 Also Yavuz, 2003c: 19–23; Yavuz and Esposito, 2003: xxvi.

8 Similar views are expressed in Ülsever, 2001; also Ülsever (2003) argues: "Thus, the so-called 'heritage of the revolutionary leaders of independence', i.e. the ruling military and civilian bureaucracy, have become the keepers of status quo especially after 1980's! ... The claiming heritage [sic] of the once revolutionary elite is now the most reactionary group of the country and they are blocking the way of Turkey before modernity i.e. 'Westernization' in their definition."

Is the Gülen Movement a Sect?

Is there any substantial evidence for this claim? So far, no academic or religious scholar has claimed to find any in Gülen's works. The other place to look is in the practices and beliefs of movement participants. Journalist and author Abdullah Aymaz comments:

> The Gülen Movement has never attempted to form a distinct unit within Islam or Turkey. They are not a distinct unit within the broader Muslim community by virtue of certain refinements or distinctions of belief or practice. Neither is it a small faction or dissenting clique aggregated around a common interest, peculiar beliefs or unattainable dreams or utopia...The Movement has no formal leadership, no sheikhs and no hierarchy. They don't have any procedures, ceremonies or initiation in order to be affiliated or to become a member.

On how participants are regarded by the wider public, Aymaz comments:

> The participants in the Movement, with their words, actions and intentions, have proved themselves not to have any strongly held views or ideology that are regarded as extreme by the majority in Turkey and abroad. They have never been regarded as heretical or as deviant in anyway by the public, in the media or in the courts. They have not been accused of being different from the generally accepted religious tradition, practices or tendencies. All the people in the Movement are highly educated, mostly either graduates or post-graduates, serving voluntarily. These volunteers work by themselves, thousands of miles away from a specific doctrine or a doctrinal leader. So how can anyone call them a sect?[9]

Is the Gülen Movement a Cult?

One of the efforts to delegitimize Gülen, the Movement, and their services is the accusation that they are a sect or cult, backward and thus subversive.

> Though non-political, the movement is controversial in some Turkish quarters. Radical Islamists revile it, saying it is too open to Western ideas and other faiths, and many military officials and secular-oriented intellectuals worry that Gülen and his devotees secretly want to establish an Islamic state in Turkey. (Murphy, 2005)

However, all accusations initiated by protectionist groups or ideologically motivated prosecutors have failed to bring any substantial evidence. After listing almost one hundred lower court hearings and judgments , Webb (2000: 171–8) concludes that " according to the verdicts given, experts appointed by the courts and the courts, the major conclusion is that the allegations and such similar claims" about Gülen "are untrue, baseless and unsubstantiated".

If the Gülen Movement were a cult, most or all of the following questions would elicit a 'yes': Is Gülen a charismatic leader? Has he preached, instructed, led or encouraged anyone into any absurdities, deviations, violence, killings, suicides or abuse of any sort? Are destructive processes ever activated? Does the Movement engender myth, rites, mythical or fantastic enemy, and rebirth? Can the cultural, traditional or spiritual values the Movement is talking about be interpreted as a reactionary call to a kind of regressive utopianism? Does it negate the existence of different levels and different tools of analysis? Does the GM foster among the participants a herd mentality, the character of a flight into militancy, a different theology or drug use and suicide?

Another two questions would require a 'no': Does the Movement value differences in beliefs,

---

9 Excerpt from interview I conducted with journalist and author Abdullah Aymaz in January 2005 as part of my doctoral thesis (unpublished) on the Gülen Movement.

races, customs and traditions for richness and the common good? Is a competitive spirit encouraged?

In expressing their impressions of Gülen, people occasionally use the word 'charismatic', using it not in the Weberian but the popular sense., They mean that "Gülen is so kind, attractive and appealing to all."[10] On this theme, Eileen Barker (2002) talks of:

> the authority that is accorded by the followers being charismatic, in so far as it is not bound by rules or by tradition and the charismatic leader has the right to say what the followers will do in all aspects of their life – whom they will sleep with, whom they will marry, whether they will have children, what sort of work they will do, in what country they will live – perhaps whether they will live – and what toothpaste they will use. It really can cover anything; and it can be changed at a moment's notice.

As this authority is accorded by followers, Barker calls it 'charismatisation'. This makes a leader in the eyes of members, new converts and others interested a very special person, and involves myths about his childhood, holy objects he has used and so on. All stories and things contribute to a picture of this perfect person as out of the ordinary but prepared to come down to the level of ordinary people. Charismatisation makes a leader more unaccountable, unpredictable and power-mad in a number of ways. A leader can change his or her mind at a moment's notice, without referring to or conferring with anyone. (Barker, 2002)

Gülen has been visible in public life since he was sixteen years old as preacher, writer and civil initiator. He has not preached, instructed, led or encouraged anyone into any absurdities, deviations, violence, killings, suicides or abuse of any sort. He has not presented any unaccountability and unpredictability in his thoughts and actions (Woodhall, 2005: 4; Irvine, 2006: 59; Ünal and Williams, 2000: 328; Aslandoğan and Çetin, 2006: 42–4, 51–2). This is one indication that Gülen and the Movement are not like the sects, cults or new religious movements studied by Barker and others.

Is the Gülen Movement a Sufi order?

Hermansen (2005: 9–10) summarizes the arguments against using the tariqa label for the Gülen Movement:

> Bekim Agai concludes that this is a misrepresentation because unlike classical tariqa Sufism, there is no requirement of initiation, no restricted or esoteric religious practices, and no arcane Sufi terminology that marks membership in the Gülen Movement. Enes Ergene also strongly disagrees with the characterization of the Movement as a tariqa in any classical social or organizational sense although he feels that Gülen as an individual thinker could be considered a "contemporary Sufi".

So, what distinguishes the Gülen Movement from Sufi orders, is the fact that no religious processes or hierarchies are found within it. Muslims in the movement respect the opinions of qualified Muslim scholars, but there is no internal religious hierarchy at local levels or transnationally.

What are the characteristics of the Gülen Movement?

It is always difficult to prove a negative, so trying to show what the Gülen Movement is not proves harder than showing what it is. If the Gülen Movement defies characterization as a

---

10 Excerpt from personal correspondence with Dr. Ergun Çapan in 2006 for my doctoral thesis (unpublished) on the Gülen Movement; also see Akman 1995: 16–18.

sect, cult or order, what is special about it? I shall illustrate the more significant and identifiable features of the movement which account for its public visibility and success, while continuing to highlight aspects of its identity which distinguish it from sects, cults and orders.

First of all, the reflexivity of the Gülen Movement is very high. The participants are fully aware of what they are doing and why they are doing it. They have a clear definition of the services, the field of the action, the goals and the instruments used to achieve them.[11] The Gülen Movement also has the necessary accumulated experience and is successful at imparting it to participants and to third parties.[12] The clarity of the general goals, particularity of objectives, the stress on and the observation of legitimacy of means and ends, and the attainability and accountability of the projects they take on demarcate Gülen and the Movement from cults and sects in a clear way (Hermansen, 2005: 4–9, 9–11; Aslandoğan and Çetin, 2006: 43).

In the Movement, direct participation in the services given provides motivation for highly symbolic, cultural, ethical and spiritual values rather than worldly goods or material gains (Hermansen, 2005: 27). Kuru (2003: 123) notes, "Gülen is against the kind of rationalism that focuses on egoistic self interest and pure materialistic cost-benefit analysis." Motivation and incentives are gained through the relational networks and the services given corporately and altruistically. This ties individuals together (Tekalan, 2005: 7–8) and means "living among people by continuously discerning the Divine unity amidst multiplicity" (Gülen, 2004b: 19). Therefore, the Gülen Movement, unlike sects or cults, prefers being with people, rather than avoiding them. Participants do not draw back into themselves, sever relations with the outside, nor renounce all courses of action (Gülen, 2000c: 73).[13]

Quite the contrary, Gülen (2004a: 230) reminds his readers of the current interdependency of communities and that any radical changes in a country will not be determined by that country alone because this is a period of interactive relations, a situation that causes closeness between peoples and nations. Therefore, people should seek ways to get along with each other (Gülen, 2004a: 42). Differences in beliefs, races, customs and traditions are richness, and should be appreciated for the common good through peaceful and respectful relationships (Gülen, 2004a: 249–50).

Gülen (2000d: 73) maintains, "People must learn how to benefit from other people's knowledge and views, for these can be beneficial to their own system, thought, and world. Especially, they should seek always to benefit from the experiences of the experienced." It seems unlikely that individuals in a movement who have been reading and listening to Gülen would be in a sect-like relationship or structure (Kömeçoğlu, 1997: 77–8).

Moreover, the Movement does not designate internal and external scapegoats so as to turn aggressive energies onto itself or any group, so destructive processes are not activated. Far from passivism, though, this encourages a higher motivational level and opens the way for individual and collective responsibility and mobilization. For Gülen (2005: 102), the first and principal way to realize projects is

through the consciousness and the ethic of responsibility. As complete inertia is a death and

---

11 See Irvine, 2006: 59, 66–8; Aslandoğan and Çetin, 2006: 36–7, 40–5; Tekalan, 2005: 6; Ünal and Williams, 2000: 328, 338–47.

12 For further discussions, see Aslandogan and Çetin, 2006: 33; Sykiainen, 2007: 124–6, 128–9. Aslandoğan, 2007: vii; Hendrick, 2007: 12–3, 30-1; Ünal and Williams, 2000: iii; Çetin, 2005: 5.

13 Özdalga, 2005: 434.

disintegration, and irresponsibility in action is disorder and chaos, we are left with no alternative but to discipline our actions with responsibility. Indeed, all our attempts should be measured by responsibility.

This ethic of responsibility nurtures individual upward mobility in the SMOs in the Movement. Tekalan (2005: 8) argues that these "institutions have a corporate identity and their management is in the hands of real people. However, having been appointed as a manager through a social contract, these people are not allowed to utilize the institutions for their own benefits. Those who are now unable to work actively in the movement give over their role to the young people who will carry the torch of the altruistic services of the movement".

Individual upward mobility is always possible for all in the Gülen Movement (Özdalga, 2005: 440) because entry and exit, commitment and withdrawal are always voluntary and always possible.[14] Competitive spirit is encouraged and predominates over primary solidarities (Özdalga, 2005: 435). Individuals are employed at the SMOs for professional qualifications rather than Movement experience (Aslandoğan and Çetin, 2006: 50; Irvine, 2006: 59). These features prevent the rise of dogmatic leaders, ideologues, rites, or exclusivist functions. They also prevent any attempt to construct an ideal self-image with exclusive values and symbolic resources and taking refuge in myth. The Gülen Movement does not create its own sacred texts, or develop rituals and priestly functions. It does not offer rewards unattainable in real life,[15] nor does it seek sacral celebration of the self in an abstract and anachronistic paradigm. In this way, the possibilities for a conflictual mobilization remain very remote (Barton, 2005: 43).

As action is not directed towards a mythical adversary , any shortfall must be socially defined in terms included in the actor's frame of reference. Gülen (2002: 84; 2004a: 199) identifies three major enemies to tackle: ignorance, poverty, and internal schism (social disunity). He (2005: 100) expands on this list:

> Once, our enemies used to be ignorance, illiteracy, poverty, disunity, and bigotry. Now to these have been added cheating, bullying and coercion, extravagance, decadence, obscenity, insensitivity, indifference, and intellectual contamination.

The limits of the reference system do not permit an aggressive and non-institutionalized mobilization, impractical and incompatible demands or expectations, or anything crossing over the Turkish and international threshold that may trigger conflict. (Gülen, 2000: 21)

Another indicator that the Movement is not a cult or sect is that participants perceive their own consistency and continuity[16] and can compare their action in the many different conditions and times since their emergence. As a result, institutions, services given and their success do not belong to anyone alone.

Gülen affirms that "If there is no adaptation to new conditions, the result will be extinction" (Webb, 2000: 86). To Gülen, not only the establishment of justice is hindered by the lack of

---

14 For more on social mobility and professionalism, see Bulaç, 2006: 102; Hendrick, 2006: 25–8; Aslandoğan and Çetin, 2006: 36–37, 40–43, 47;

15 For more on incentives and rewards, see Gülen, 2004a: 200–1; Hermansen, 2005: 4–5; Ünal and Williams, 2000: 276, 326; Turgut 1998; Aslandoğan and Çetin, 2006: 36–7; Stephenson, 2007: 149.

16 The ability to calculate the costs and benefits and make predictions by comparison among successive situations (Melucci, 1999: 293).

well-rounded education, but also the recognition of human rights and attitudes of acceptance and tolerance toward others.[17] If people are properly educated to think for themselves and espouse social justice, human rights and tolerance, they will be agents of change to implement these goals (Michel, 2006: 108–9).

For this to come about, Gülen (2004a: 199; Woodhall and Çetin, 2005: vii) asserts that a new style of education is necessary "that will fuse religious and scientific knowledge together with morality and spirituality, to produce genuinely enlightened people with hearts illumined by religious sciences and spirituality, minds illuminated with positive sciences", who are "cognizant of the socio-economic and political conditions of their time". So, the Movement does not try to limit the curriculum in the educational institutions its participants sponsor. Instead, the institutions follow national and international curricula. Students are encouraged to use external sources of information, such as the internet and universities' information.

Michel (2006: 110) argues that Gülen's use of spirituality includes not only specifically religious teachings, but also ethics, logic, psychological health, and affective openness. He adds that the key terms in Gülen's writings are compassion and tolerance, and such "non-quantifiable" qualities ought to be instilled in students by education in addition to training in the "exact" disciplines. Michel considers that such an education is more related to identity and daily life rather than 'political' and believes that it will yield a new spiritual search and a moral commitment to a better and more human social life. The moral aspects of education are conveyed by example in the teachers' behaviour, rather than proselytizing.

Other terms used frequently by Gülen (1996: 16; 2000b: 35, 44–5) are 'cultural' and 'values': "Little attention and importance is given to the teaching of cultural values, although it is more necessary to education. If one day we are able to ensure that it is given importance, then we shall have reached a major objective." Critics have seen this as a reactionary call to return to pre-Republican Ottoman society, a kind of regressive utopianism, and accused him of being an irticaci, which might be translated as "reactionary" or "fundamentalist" (Michel, 2006: 111). In response, Gülen discusses the term used (Dinç 1998[18]; Webb, 2000: 95):

The word irtica means returning to the past or carrying the past to the present. I'm a person who's taken eternity as a goal, not only tomorrow. I'm thinking about our country's future and trying to do what I can about it. I've never had anything to do with taking my country backwards in any of my writings, spoken words or activities. But no one can label belief in God, worship, moral values and purporting matters unlimited by time as irtica.

Melucci argues that (1999: 104–5) some movements at their inception are characterized by their regressive utopianism. As a group forms, it defines its identity in terms of the past, drawing upon a totalizing myth of rebirth with an almost quasireligious content. Its action involves a utopian appeal with religious connotations. This regressive utopianism reduces reality to the unity of one allembracing principle. It negates the existence of different levels and different tools of analysis, and identifies the whole of society with the sacral solidarity of the group. It translates the reappropriation of identity into the language and symbols of an escapist myth of rebirth. Melucci adds that the predominating religious element in movements makes them susceptible to manipulation by the power structure, to marginalization as sects, and to transformation into a fashion or commodity for sale in the marketplace as a soother of mind. He further argues that contestation in such movements changes into an individual flight, a mythical quest or fanatic fundamentalism.

---

17 Gülen,1999: 4; Ünal and Williams, 2000: 22–3; Woodhall and Çetin, 2005: viii.

18 English version is available at http://en.fGülen.com/content/view/1216/14/ as retrieved on Jan 17, 2007 19:30.

On the other hand, other theorists dub this an overgeneralization. Asef Bayat (2005: 894) draws attention to the reductionism in the understanding of the social theorists on the left, like Alain Touraine and Alberto Melucci, because these consider all religious or revivalist movements, especially Islamist, as regressive utopianism.

With respect to the Gülen Movement, Gülen's historical references show no sign of a cultural politics which attempts to negate any period of history, especially not those moments associated with the origins of modernity (Woodhall and Çetin, 2005: xviii). He has not evoked a past that appears to want to restore a sultanate or monarchy as a paradigm for ideas of unity, order, hierarchy, homeland, religion, and family. Michel (2005: 349) maintains that Gülen does not propose "a nostalgic return to Ottoman patterns". In contradiction to utopian thought, since the origins of the Movement, Gülen has offered models of self-improvement and social transformation (Woodhall and Çetin, 2005: xviii).

Gülen relates to the past to tell us who we were and are. He looks for examples to follow and mistakes to avoid. He looks for ways to progress beyond that which has remained in the past.

> Today, it is obviously impossible to live with out-of-date conceptions which have nothing to do with reality. Continuing the old state being impossible, it means either following the new state or annihilation. We will either reshape our world as required by science, or we shall be thrown into a pit together with the world we live in. (Gülen, 1996: 74. Italics added.)

Gülen instils in younger generations a historical consciousness which enables them to locate themselves in relation to the past and present in a rigorously modern, progressive way. He clarifies the concepts of the present that are mostly shaped by the concepts and events of the past. To him, knowing history is a feeder to an innovative and successful future. Gülen says, "If keeping your eyes closed to the future is blindness, then disinterest in the past is misfortune" (Sevindi, 1997a, 1997b; Ünal and Williams, 2000: 38).

Çinar's (2005: 140). analysis of the state control of 'history' indicates how this more inclusive and continuous view of the people and the nation, that is, how references to 'our long history' and 'the saints of our past', challenge the way in which some militant secularists conceptualize Turkey as a modern state:

> [T]he writing of the official national Turkish history, which was written by a committee convened under the leadership of Atatürk, inscribed the Turkish nation into time, defamed the Ottoman and Islamic past, established Atatürk as the founder of the Republic, and set the founding moment as 29 October 1923.

However, Gülen does not impose on his audience an ideal of citizenship which reflects a certain kind of racial, ethnic, cultural and religious homogeneity based on any past society (Gülen, 1996: 86). He sees such homogeneity as inconsistent with the pluralist character of the historical and contemporary culture of Turkish society. He deems that consoling oneself with re-telling the heroic deeds of others indicates the psychological weakness of those who have failed to discharge their responsibilities to the present society (1996: 52–3). He argues:

> Of course, we should certainly commemorate the saints of our past with deep emotion and celebrate the victories of our heroic ancestors with enthusiasm. ... Each scene from the past is valuable

and sacred only so long as it stimulates and enthuses us, and provides us with knowledge and experience for doing something today. ...Today, our duty is to offer humanity a new message composed of vivid scenes from the past together with understanding of the needs of the present. (Gülen, 1996: 53)

The Gülen Movement endows individuals progressively with a capacity for action. Identity is constructed by each individual in her or his capacity as a social actor. Altruistic services always relate to human sociability and to social relationships.[19] Relationship is formed at the level of the single individual, awakening the enthusiasm and capacity of the individual for action. Through such sociability people rediscover the self and the meaning of life.[20] Herein lies all the distinction of the Gülen Movement. It does not lead to a flight into the myth of identity or an escapist illusion that one is magically freed from the constraints of social action or behaviour. It reaffirms the meaning of social action as the capacity for a consciously produced human existence and relationships.

Gülen (2005: 21) frequently talks about a renaissance, yet never of a magical rebirth. Woodhall and Çetin (2005: xv) argue that this renaissance is an active process, hard work to "prevent illnesses like passion, laziness, seeking fame, selfishness, worldliness, narrow-mindedness, the use of brute force" and replace them instead "with exalted human values like contentedness, courage, modesty, altruism, knowledge and virtue, and the ability to think universally". Acknowledgement of diversity, multiplicity, the necessity of division of labour, and the power relationships within society, subscribe the Gülen Movement to a form of rationality geared to assessment of the relationship between ends and means, and to protecting people from the imbalances and divisions created by the forms of power required to govern complexity.

> Gülen's work is a constant exhortation to greater effort, greater knowledge, greater self-control and restraint. (Woodhall and Çetin, 2005: xiv–xv)

Cults and cult-like sects refuse to accept people as different, diverse and interdependent. They lack a solution for handling difference within complexity. Their totalizing appeal does not take into account that people are simultaneously living in a system interdependently (Melucci, 1999: 189). The Gülen Movement does not deny the interdependence of the social field in its values, worldview or actual organizational frame. It does not have a totalizing ideology that possesses and controls the social field and thus identifies those who do not belong to the group in negative terms. Gülen (1998; 2000: 279) says:

> Islam has banned all ethnic, colour and racial discrimination. We have a long history during which many peoples of different beliefs, races, colours and languages existed together in peace. Without giving priority and prominence to such 'natural' differences and by being awakened to the common factors which they share to live together, we hope different ethnic groups can live together.[21]

The Gülen Movement acknowledges the true social character of such conflicts, and therefore

---

19 For more on collective social altruism and participation, see Nevval Sevindi (1977a), *Yeni Yüzyil*, 'The New York Interview with Fethullah Gülen', July 20–29, 1997a; also at http://en.fGülen.com/content/view/783/13/ and http://www.nevvalsevindi.com/oku.php?id=347; and also Çetin (2006), 'Voluntary Altruistic Action: Its Symbolic Challenge against Sinecures of Vested Interests, presented at "Second Annual Conference on Islam in the Contemporary World: The Fethullah Gülen Movement In Thought and Practice" Norman, Oklahoma, 4–5 November, 2006.

20 Excerpt from interviews I conducted with Ergun Capan, Enes Ergene and Abdullah Aymaz in January 2005.

21 Gülen's Message to the President of the Angels' Movement, 02.26.1998 at http://en.fGülen.com/content/view/970/14/ as retrieved on Jan 20, 2007 11:10; and also in Ünal and Williams, 2000: 279.

does not produce unpredictable forms or expressions of collective action. It responds to the specificity of individual and collective demands, without allowing them to cancel out one another. It does not escape into a reductionism that cancels out the individual for the appropriated identity of the Movement.

The Gülen Movement shares with the rest of society a set of general issues and seeks common grounds and references. Gülen (1998) says:

> We believe that peoples, no matter of what faith, culture, civilization, race, colour and country, have more to compel them to come together than what separates them. If we encourage those elements which oblige them to live together in peace and awaken them to the lethal dangers of warring and conflicts, the world may be better than it is today.[22]

On the other hand, a sect simply breaks any such connection, ideologically and ontologically creating division and rupture that cannot be overcome. Its identity politics and appeal cover up or deny the fundamental dilemma of living a social life in complex systems (Melucci, 1999: 189). As an exclusive organization, a sect demands a long novitiate, rigid discipline, high level of commitment and intrusion on every aspect of its members' lives (Barker, 2002; Della Porta and Diani, 1999: 145). The worldview or collective action of the Gülen Movement is not an isolationist withdrawal into a pure community-based or sect-like structure (Gülen in The Fountain, 1996: 1–3; Kömeçoglu, 1997: 77–8). Gülen says (1996: 86):

> We should know how to be ourselves and then remain ourselves. That does not mean isolation from others. It means preservation of our essential identity among others, following our way among other ways. While self-identity is necessary, we should also find the ways to a universal integration. Isolation from the world will eventually result in annihilation.

If the search for fulfilment within specific closed networks or a society is unable to handle information flow, it withdraws from social life and transforms spiritual needs into intolerant mysticism. Identity claims are pushed too far and evolve a movement into a conflictual sectarian organization with an intolerant ideology. The movement fragments into selfassertive and closed sects.

However, the Gülen Movement with its participation in education, interfaith and intercultural issues, and transnational altruistic projects and institutions, proves itself able to process information and emergent realities. Abdullah Aymaz therefore holds that the Gülen Movement helps to contribute to addressing global concerns.

> The Gülen Movement acknowledges the fact that the common points, grounds, references and problems affecting humanity in general are far more than the differences which separate us. ... People can come together and cooperate around a universally acknowledged set of values. The way to do so is through education, convincing argument, peaceful interaction and negotiation.[23]

Aymaz emphasizes that the Movement does not engage itself with identity politics. It does not seek ethno-religiously, culturally or geographically to be different from other people. Participants abide by Turkish and international regulations and law, share concerns common to people all over the world and work to contribute to their resolution. The intention, worldview and efforts of the Movement are accepted by the overwhelming majority in Turkey and others who know its work outside Turkey.

The Gülen Movement acts as a reconciliating agent between diverse communities around the

---

22 Ibid.
23 Excerpt from interview I conducted with Abdullah Aymaz in January 2005.

world through legal and institutionalized means. The Movement is already defined in terms of its social and multicultural relations. The intention to seek consensus among communities legitimates its transnational projects[24], so it does not deviate into or let others be led into fundamentalism or sectarianism.[25]

Ergene argues that the Gülen Movement does not reduce reality to a small number of truisms. It does not attempt to mask anything from the larger environment. Its openness and transparency make it effective and strengthen faith in it. Turam (2007: 74–75), an independent researcher, contrasts this openness with the behaviour she encountered among the marginal groups opposing the movement:

> STKB's[26] negative attitudes and discouragement of the study of Islam, especially the Gülen movement, stood in sharp contrast to the Gülen movement's openness and encouragement for being a subject of social research. . . I tried numerous times to get in touch with several STKB organizations in order to hear their adherents' views on the issue. Like most of my calls, these efforts to communicate were often left without a response. The adherents were often too busy fighting the movement, which did not leave much time, energy and recognition for "understanding" it.

In contrast to such intellectual rigidity, in the Gülen Movement the spirit of cultural innovation and the spiritual quest in one's own faith, along with other faith community members, dispense security to others. Though everyone who comes into contact with Gülen acknowledges and respects his knowledge, asceticism, piety, expertise and scholarliness on religious, spiritual and intellectual matters, this does not result in any sacral recognition or charisma for Gülen, as discussed earlier. The common description of him as the leader of the Movement, which he has never accepted (Akman, 1995)[27], has not resulted in the emergence of an authoritarian personality or personalities. He is instead very much in favour of collective reasoning, consultation and consensus which cannot foster a herd mentality among Movement participants (Gülen, 2005: 43–8).

Çapan points out that in over forty years there has been no case of crisis, greed, or drug use and suicide within the Movement because people do not feel a situation of frustration, isolation, disappointment and exploitation within the Movement; quite the contrary, they feel and find hope, a true human and humane identity, communication, compassion and peace.[28]

Conclusion

In this paper, I have illustrated the nature and identity of the Gülen Movement and shown how it cannot be matched against recognized definitions of sects, cults or orders. I have illustrated how accusations that it is a sect, cult or order are raised within the Turkish context by particular interest groups, that is, the militant secularist elite or other vested interests in the state apparatus and radical Islamists, groups, all of which appear to be largely opposed to more widespread and equal participation in the public space. In contrast to these two groups the Gülen Movement also has widespread public support both inside and outside Turkey, and thus provides a symbolic challenge to the ideology, authority and control of the groups which

---

24 *Fountain*, 2002: 5; BBC, 2000; Stephenson, 2006: 30–1; Benard, 2003: 38; Aslandoğan and Çetin, 2006: 45–8; Irvine, 2006: 55–74; Hendrick, 2006: 29, Ateş, et al., 2005: 14; Özdalga in Akman 2003; Weller, 2006: 86–8.

25 Excerpt from interview I conducted with Enes Ergene in January 2006.

26 Sivil Toplum Kuruluşları Birliği (United Civil Society Organizations), a secularist umbrella organization.

27 Also at http://en.fGülen.com/content/view/760/13/ as retrieved on Jan 22, 2007 10:11; also in Ünal and Williams, 2000: i, 328;. Irvine, 2006: 66–7; Gülen in Gündem, 2005: 83–4

28 Excerpt from interview I conducted with Ergun Çapan in January 2006.

countermobilize against it.

The Gülen Movement has proved that it acts lawfully within the system in the pursuit of shared objectives. This has had two major outcomes which have sparked opposition from those vested interests in Turkey. The first is that the movement has provided incentives for modernization of the political system, consolidation of civil society and pluralistic democracy, and institutional reform in Turkey. The second is that the movement has shown previous conceptual frameworks to be inadequate and highlighted the shortcomings of categorical and biased approaches to faith-based communities, especially to peaceful, mainstream Muslims, and cultural Islam.

ISLAMIC PROSPECTS FOR INTERRELIGIOUS DIALOGUE: THE CONTRIBUTION OF FETHULLAH GÜLEN

Douglas Pratt

Abstract

Countering extremist ideology may be a problem primarily for the Muslim world, but it has major implications for, and so the interest of, the wider world. Although it might seem that it is the strident militant voices that are gaining ground in the Muslim world, there are also strong voices from within Islam seeking to proclaim the Muslim priority for peaceful and harmonious relations with the wider world, including with religious neighbours. Such a voice is that of Fethullah Gülen.

This paper seeks to understand the prospects and appropriate contexts for dialogue: what enables, and what hinders, good interfaith relations? The paper addresses the issue of Islamic paradigms for inter-religious relations and dialogue, then analyses and critically discusses the views of Fethullah Gülen. The intention is to identify a perspective that will encourage future inter-religious dialogue and enhance the relations of Islam to other faiths, a perspective indicative of transitions within the Muslim world and one that gives cause to be hopeful for the recovery of the true way of peace.

Introduction

It goes without saying that we live at a time where "the importance of dialogue among people of faith for the effective pursuit of peace" is without parallel.[1] The dialogue of civilisations, which is in effect a dialogue of religions, is an imperative which is laid upon us in an unprecedented way. Into this context, as Fr Tom Michel has observed, Fethullah Gülen has emerged as one "of the most persuasive and influential voices in the Muslim community" calling for dialogue as a step toward peace.[2] Indeed, he offers "a way to live out Islamic values amidst the complex demands of modern societies and to engage in ongoing dialogue and cooperation with people of other religions".[3] And the faith-based movement inspired by him promotes "truly spiritual values like forgiveness, inner peace, social harmony, honesty, and trust in God" as the basis for inter-communal peace and interreligious dialogue.[4] At times a controversial figure, Fethullah Gülen has had, and continues to have, a considerable impact upon the thinking and sensibilities of Muslims throughout the Turkish Islamic world and beyond. As Paul Weller has observed, Gülen's teaching "has particularly aimed at encouraging the younger generation to aspire to a combination of intellectual engagement and spiritual wisdom, and to give expression to this combination through concrete commitments in the service of humanity".[5]

Without doubt "one of the major figures in defining the contemporary global Islamic experience", Fethullah Gülen's work "helps to redefine the nature of Islamic discourse in the contemporary world".[6] Poet, philosopher and educator, Gülen has "inspired many people in Turkey to establish educational institutions that combine modern sciences with ethics and spirituality".[7] Indeed, Gülen and the movement that bears his name may be primarily known in some quarters in respect to such educational activities.[8] Yet it is educational priority that has lead into interfaith advocacy. And, as well, "Gülen insists … the basic Islamic sources advise Muslims to engage in dialogue with other faiths".[9] In this paper I seek to address, in a somewhat overview fashion, the matter of Islamic interfaith relations and dialogue – the patterns, drivers, and paradigms that we can discern from history – and then identify and discuss some of the unique perspectives of Fethullah Gülen on interreligious dialogue and relations of Islam to other faiths. In what way does Gülen signal new perspectives and transitions for contemporary Islam in a world of manifest religious plurality? But first, who is Fethullah Gülen and what is his significance to interreligious dialogue?

---

1 See Tom Michel, SJ., 'Two Frontrunners for Peace: John Paul II and Fethullah Gülen' (http://en.fGülen.com/content/view/1944/13/)

2 *Ibid.*

3 *Ibid.*

4 *Ibid.*

5 Paul Weller, 'Fethullah Gülen, Religions, Globalization and Dialogue', in Robert A. Hunt & Yüksel A. Aslandogan, Muslim Citizens of the Globalized World: Contributions of the Gülen Movement, Somerset, NJ: The Light, Inc., & IID Press, 2006, 76.

6 John O. Voll, Fethullah Gülen: 'Transcending Modernity in the New Islamic Discourse', *in* M. Hakan Yavuz and John L. Esposito, eds., *Turkish Islam and the Secular State: The Gülen Movement*, Syracuse, NY: Syracuse University Press, 2003, 238.

7 Ihsan Yilmaz, *Muslim Laws, Politics and Society in Modern Nation States: Dynamic Legal Pluralisms in England, Turkey and Pakistan.* Aldershot: Ashgate, 2005, 175

8 Cf. Thomas Michel, 'Fethullah Gülen as Educator', *in* Yavuz and Esposito, *op. cit.*, 69-84

9 Ismail Albayrak, 'The Juxtaposition of Islam and Violence' in Hunt and Aslandogan, op cit., 127; cf. M. Hakan Yavuz, 'The Gülen Movement: The Turkish Puritans', in Yavuz and Esposito, op. cit., 19-47.

Fethullah Gülen: A Champion of Dialogue

It was Said Nursi who introduced the young Gülen to the idea of dual divine revelation: the Qur'an (or Book of God) and the Universe (or Book of Nature), on the one hand; and also the need to reconcile "the spirituality of the heart (*tasawwuf*) and the intellectual reasoning of the mind" on the other.[10] From the inception of his own teaching and preaching career, Gülen sought to emphasise "the importance of mutual understanding and tolerance" and to stress the need "to harmonise intellectual enlightenment with wise spirituality and a caring humane activism".[11] Gülen is pre-eminently a reconciler: material and spiritual values; positive sciences and religion; the ideologies and philosophies of East and West. The way of civilisation is the way of democratic persuasion, not the imposition of force. Democracy not a perfect system, but it is the only viable political system and process appropriate to the modern age: its aim is to "consolidate democratic institutions in order to build a society where individual rights and freedoms are respected and protected".[12]

Fethullah Gülen is a man of many facets. Over the years he "has become increasingly committed to affirming the possibility of and need for inter-civilizational and interreligious dialogue".[13] Furthermore, his promotion of dialogue "is not merely reactive and pragmatic, but is rooted in his vision of Islam and the contemporary world".[14] He is thus a true champion of interreligious dialogue. For Gülen, "what people have in common … is far greater than what divides and separates them"; thus his approach is holistic: inner harmony and peace of humankind "only occurs when the material and spiritual realms are reconciled".[15] Indeed, it is of the essence of faith to bring things together, to reconcile rather than divide: "Religion reconciles opposites: religion-science, this world-the next world, Nature-Divine Books, material-spiritual, and spirit-body".[16] Furthermore, in the face of rising secularism and widespread unbelief (or loss of the religious sense) Gülen believes that Muslim–Christian dialogue is indispensable.

In the context of human intellectual interaction, the most common form of interchange is that of debate. However, the context and purpose of debate will most likely set the tone and parameters for the interchange. In the political arena, for example, debate is highly adversarial with, very often, a view to belittling one's opponents and in the process asserting the superiority of one's own policies and actions. Public debates on social or religious issues can likewise be intensely polemical, very often generating more heat than light. Yet debating an issue can be an occasion of enlightenment, as when there is the courteous – but no less intentional and focussed – proffering of evidence, probing of perspective, and critical examination of premises and argumentation, all with a view to expanding the horizons of understanding and deepening the wells of knowledge. As Gülen has remarked, "Debate should not be for the sake of ego, but rather to enable the truth to appear".[17] In this context the art of debate merges with the desire of dialogue. For Gülen, dialogue means "the coming together of two or more people to discuss certain issues, and thus the forming of a bond between these people. In that

---

10 Emre Celik, 'Advocate of Dialogue: Fethullah Gülen'. Paper presented to the Annual Conference of the AASR, July 2003.

11 *Ibid.*

12 *Ibid.*

13 Weller, *op. cit.*, 86.

14 *Ibid.*, 87.

15 F. Gülen, 'The Necessity of Interfaith Dialogue', *The Fountain*, July-September, 2000.

16 *Ibid.*

17 F. Gülen, *Dialogue with the People of the Book* (http://en.fGülen.com/content/view/1812/33/)

respect, we can call dialogue an activity that has human beings at its axis".[18] Thus dialogue is no rarefied academic pursuit: it is itself a *praxis*; a methodology; a struggle – even an *ijtihad* – in the pursuit of peace, harmony and justice. Gülen

> ... uses interfaith cooperation and dialogue to prevent future clashes and violence between the adherents of religions... He believes that interfaith cooperation is imperative today... He regards interfaith cooperation as compulsory for Muslims to support peace and harmony.[19]

Islam and Interfaith Relations: Context and Perspective

When it comes to Muslim interfaith relations with Peoples of the Book there is a legacy of shared fundamental convictions, as well as a history of divergence. Distinctions are real, and so too are the prospects for peaceful co-existence. There are, of course, deep issues to be addressed and resolved. One starting place, I suggest, is with the underlying paradigms that each side in any relationship holds with respect to the other. But before attending to the matter of paradigms as such, I want to present an overview of the dynamics of Islamic interfaith activity from an historical perspective.[20] Jean-Marie Gaudeul has offered a useful review of the history of the relationship between Islam and Christianity in which the mutual challenge and response that has engaged the attentions of each may be tracked through broad ages or epochs.[21] These 'epochs', which I denote for heuristic and hermeneutical purposes as *expansion, equilibrium, exhortation, enmity, emancipation* and *exploration*, do not just arbitrarily mark out historical eras. Rather they serve to delineate the ebb and flow of a relationship of encounter, particularly that of intellectual engagement. But as well as indicating the state of play in the relationship between Islam and Christianity at particular times in history, these terms also indicate modes of relationship and interaction *per se*. While each may have dominated a particular historical period, it could be argued that they are always part of the wider picture of interreligious encounter. They certainly persist into the present day so far as the interaction between Islam and Christianity are concerned.

Expansion stands for the expansiveness of self-confidence, embracing self-righteousness on the one hand and magnanimity on the other. Religion in the expansion mode is determined and assertive. This can be seen today in both Islam and Christianity, for instance. But there is also more than a hint of *equilibrium* that shows through in the hesitancy to be overly self-assertive: an inclination to humility that properly counterpoints self-righteousness; a measure of openness that marks a balanced approach to the religious 'other'. Mutual *exhortation*, the proclamation and witness which, in its more extreme forms, seeks to declare an exclusive truth and engages with the 'other' in order to win, is certainly very much evident in some quarters. And, as well, there is evidence aplenty of *enmity*: of dismissive, derogatory and deprecatory prejudice that makes of the religious other an enemy to be fought and vanquished. At the same time, the cultural and socio-political expressions of, and concomitant realities in respect to, the religions of Islam and Christianity, as well as Judaism I would suggest, are ever engaged in the quest for *emancipation*: that seeking for self-determination and finding a rightful place in the affairs of the day, of finding and asserting meaningful identity as

---

18 F. Gülen, The Two Roses of the Emerald Hills: Tolerance and Dialogue (http://en.fGülen.com/content/view/1806/33/)

19 Zeki Saritoprak, 'An Islamic Approach to Peace and Nonviolence: A Turkish Experience', *The Muslim World*, Vol 95, July 2005, 423.

20 Cf. Douglas Pratt, *The Challenge of Islam: Encounters in Interfaith Dialogue*. Aldershot: Ashgate, 2005.

21 Jean-Marie Gaudeul, *Encounters and Clashes: Islam and Christianity in History*. Rome: Pontifico Instituto di Studi Arabi e Islamici, 1990.

communities, and for the individuals who comprise those communities; of seeking socio-economic justice, and of sustaining unique ways of life and cultural expressions.

Interpretive perspectives on the past notwithstanding, perhaps we might say that the under-pinning feature of the early twenty-first century of the Common Era, and that holds all these dynamics together in some sort of creative tension, is the motif of *exploration*. For, despite evidence of resistance and instances of opposition, there seems to be abroad in the world today intimations of a spirit of sincere, tentative, open and honest questing to know the religious other – for Christians, Jews and Muslims to come together in a variety of forums, for instance – and to do so in a climate of mutual recognition of integrity and validity, even as there is recognition of real difference and diversity. But in order for the exploration to proceed, it is necessary to identify not only the patterns of the past, but also the predominant paradigms that influence the present which, if not properly understood and possibly modified, will predetermine the future of interfaith relations.

Islamic Paradigms for Interreligious Relations and Dialogue: An Analytical Review

In seeking to discern Muslim paradigms governing interfaith relations, we need to begin at the beginning, with the life and times of the Prophet Muhammad himself. What may be called 'originating paradigms' emerge out of the life and times of Medina and the revelations given in the Holy Qur'an. What I refer to as 'historico-legal paradigms' emerge around the phenomenon of dhimmitude; the rules and protocols governing the so-called 'Peoples of the Book', the dhimmi communities. Finally, in an attempt to discern dominant contemporary paradigms, the focus is on what may be termed the emergence of an Islamic Exclusivism.

Originating Paradigms: Medina and the Qur'an

Although Muhammad was born in Mecca in the year 570CE, received his calling and be-gan his preaching task there, his founding of the Islamic community proper—the Ummah—occurred after the flight (*al-hijra*) in 622CE from Mecca to the northern city of Yathrib. This city was renamed Medina (in full, Medina-al-Nabi, the 'City of the Prophet') in honour of the presence of Muhammad and the rights granted to him to undertake sweeping social and political reforms. The town's leaders and people desired strong political and religious lead-ership in order that internal dissension and disputes might be resolved. Medina is the place where the structures, policies and ideology of the Islamic theocracy were inaugurated. In the process, two developments occurred that were to determine the essential shape and dynamic of the religion: political consolidation that provided the power base, and religious practices that were to become the 'pillars' of Islam. The mandate for this development was given in a treaty document, the Constitution, or Covenant, of Medina.[22] Significantly, when it was first promulgated it upheld and promoted the peaceful co-existence of Muslims and Jews. Later this attitude of acceptance and incorporation would be extended to Christians. Indeed, as Esposito remarks, "Muhammad discussed and debated with, and granted freedom of re-ligious thought and practice to, the Jews and the Christians, setting a precedent for peaceful and cooperative interreligious relations".[23]

---

22 See Muhammad Husein Haykal, The Life of Muhammad, trans. Ismail Raji al-Faruqi. Kuala Lumpur: Islamic Book Trust, 1993, 180-183.
23 John Esposito, *What Everyone Needs To Know About Islam*. New York: Oxford University Press, 2002, 73.

As the new community developed, alliances with local Jews and neighbouring pagan Arabs for the purposes of defence and security within Medina were secured. The city of the Prophet was by no means made up wholly of Muslim Arabs. Furthermore, the Muslims of Medina were themselves by no means a single homogeneous group. In fact, Medina comprised for the most part Arabs who were either Muslims or non-believers together with three tribes of Jews. Also, Arab Muslims were either immigrants from Mecca (the *Muhajirun*) or those who originated from Medina (called the *Ansar*, or 'helpers'). These had previously converted and so assisted the Meccan Muslims at the time of the *hijra*. Muhammad had initially been asked to arbitrate in a bitter feud between the two main Arab tribes. But soon tensions arose between the original Meccan Muslims and those originally of Yathrib, as well as between some of the Jews and the Muslim newcomers.[24]

The socio-political context in which Islam came to birth was decidedly diverse. But in this context the founding Islamic attitudes toward religious plurality were positive. Significantly, as one Muslim commentator has noted of the situation at Medina, it "was absolutely necessary that the Muslim, the Jew, and the Christian have an equal opportunity in their exercise of religious freedom as well as in their freedom to hold different opinions and to preach their own faiths".[25] However, in the establishment of the new Islamic *Ummah* (community), nothing less than a far-reaching socio-political upheaval was required. This involved, at least on the part of Arab converts, the relinquishing of the ways of old and *becoming* 'muslim', that is, subscribing and submitting to a political and social order which was "carefully established and observed in the here and now as a road to the afterworld".[26] Arabic personal and societal identities were to undergo an immense upheaval. Of course, this was not possible for everyone to undertake, and certainly not for the three Jewish communities initially resident in Medina. By the time of Muhammad there were certainly considerable numbers of Jews in Arabia who were, by and large, well integrated into the life and culture of the peninsula.[27] They "spoke Arabic, were organized into clans and tribes, and had assimilated many of the values of desert society. They formed alliances and participated in intertribal feuds".[28] Yet, even though there was a relatively high degree of assimilation into Arabian society, "Jews were still viewed as a separate group with their own peculiar customs and characteristics".[29] As it happened, when in 624CE Muhammad moved against one of the Jewish tribes, evicting it from Medina after a short siege, the others offered no assistance.[30]

At this stage, the precipitating issues were tribal, not religious or in any sense 'ethnic'. In the following year, when a second Jewish tribe failed to support Muhammad in battle (the fight took place on the Jewish Sabbath and the Muslim forces were at this time defeated), Muhammad moved decisively against them. When Medina was besieged by the Meccans in 627CE, the remaining Jewish tribe in Medina assisted with the erection of defensive fortifications, but then vacillated about active participation in aiding the Muslims against the Meccans. In essence they trusted neither side. This marked the end of the prospect of Jewish

24 Fred M. Donner, 'Muhammad and the Caliphate: Political History of the Islamic Empire up to the Mongol Conquest' in John L. Esposito, ed., The Oxford History of Islam. Oxford: Oxford University Press, 1999, 9.

25 Haykal, op. cit., 175.

26 Abd al-Rahman Azzam, The Eternal Message of Muhammad. Leicester: The Islamic Texts Society, 1993, 22.

27 Cf. Bernard Lewis, The Middle East: 2000 years of History from the Rise of Christianity to the Present Day. London: Weidenfield and Nicolson, 1995, 47.

28 Norman A. Stillman, The Jews of Arab Lands: A History and Source Book. Philadelphia: The Jewish Publication Society of America, 1979, 4.

29 *Ibid.*, 4.

30 See Ibid., 13.

participation, let alone assimilation, within the emerging Islamic Ummah. If there had been an early anticipation that Jews, and then Christians, might simply conjoin with Muslims this expectation had to be re-thought: Jews and Christians would continue as distinct, even in some sense rival, religious communities.

The political problem posed by the relations between Muslim and non-Muslim was already clear in the lifetime of the Prophet, and the principles for its solution are contained in the Qur'an. As chief magistrate and later ruler of the community of Medina, the Prophet had Jewish subjects; as sovereign of the Islamic state he had relations with both Christian and Jewish neighbours in other parts of Arabia.[31]

Thus it was that, at the birth of Islam, in the city of Medina the first intimations of the nascent religious system were positive so far as relations with both Christians and Jews were concerned, but as developments unfolded things tended changed for the worse. As Esposito has remarked,

> ... [the resulting confrontation] became part of the baggage of history and would continue to influence the attitudes of some Muslims in later centuries. Recently, this legacy can be seen in official statements ... (that amount to reiterating) ... an age-old conflict dating back to the Jews' 'rejection and betrayal' of Islam and the Prophet's community at Medina.[32]

If the problem of the relationship between Muslim and a non-Muslim who was yet a theistic believer (as in being a Jew or a Christian, for example) was evident during the lifetime of the Prophet, what are the clues to the Quranic solution? What, indeed, can we say are the paradigms of Islamic attitude toward, and relationship with, non-Muslim People of the Book that have been bequeathed to Islam from out of the Medinan context and the resulting formulation of the Qur'an? A careful reading of the Qur'an, especially in the light of the biography of Muhammad, indicates an early Medinan period in which Judaic and Christian elements and issues loomed large, albeit generally in a favourable light. The emerging Muslim faith seems to have been viewed as relating positively to these forebears. Muslims, Jews and Christians were to be honoured as co-equally 'People of the Book', even though, from an Islamic theological point of view, Jews and Christians may have gone somewhat astray.[33] So, the principal originating paradigm of Muslim interfaith engagement could be said to that of 'contending with ambiguous otherness' denoting a need to relate to faith communities with which there is an awareness of affinity, but also difference and distinction.

As Arabia came under Muslim rule Jews and Christians both paid the *jizyah*, initially a tribute, then later, from 632CE, a poll tax. This taxation was understood to have received divine sanction in 630CE with the revelation of Sura 9:29, which speaks of both the payment and the humility of the one paying. The ambiguity of the other is thus ideologically contained – the ambiguous other is subservient – and the groundwork was laid for a perspective of divine legitimacy for the Muslim superiority over, thence humiliation of, non-Muslim Peoples of the Book as a tool of reinforcing a modality of relating governed by the paradigm of the 'subservient ambiguous other'.

The injunction was clear and unequivocal ... The non-Muslim was to be subjugated. He was made to be a tribute bearer, and he was to be humbled. Just how he was to be humbled was to be more explicitly defined as time went on. But the basis for his position in Muslim Arab

---

31   Bernard Lewis, The Jews of Islam. London: Routledge Kegan Paul, 1984, 11.

32   Esposito, *What Everyone Needs To Know About Islam*, 81.

33   See Michael Lecker, *Muslims, Jews and Pagans: Studies in Early Islamic Medina*. Leiden: E. J. Brill, 1995.

society was permanently established by the eternal word of Allah.[34]

The late Medinan period is noticeable for a hardening of attitude to Judaism and Christianity, and a series of proclamations of the final triumph of a distinct teaching, namely that which Muhammad had been commissioned by God to convey. The late Medinan Quranic suras are also marked by a pronounced legislative tone; they are less combative and often convey a sense of dominating authoritative pronouncement. There is, clearly, a negative portrayal in the later suras which arguably reflect Muhammad's own interaction with Jews and Christians.[35] There was a corollary of political and theological perspective at play, and the juxtaposition of these two dimensions would redound through the ages in terms of other contexts of Muslim interfaith engagement with others.[36]

We need to remember that, from out of the early Quranic material and the Covenant of Medina, there were certainly paradigms of positive predisposition and relationship. Historically, however, it would seem that such originating paradigms were for the most part eclipsed by a relatively negative perspective, namely that of regarding interfaith relations with Peoples of the Book in terms of a requirement to contend with an ambiguous other in the context of a belief in the divinely-ordained socio-political subservience of that other. Arguably, this set the scene for the development of Islamic theological and legal perspectives and paradigms with respect to dealing with the ambiguous other.

Historico-legal paradigms: dhimmi regulations

The Prophet Muhammad arguably came to regard himself as a political and military leader on a divinely sanctioned mission. He thus "became a statesman in order to accomplish his mission as a prophet, not vice versa, and it is clear that the more strictly religious aspect of these relationships was also a prime concern".[37] The primary task, given the context of religious plurality of the day, was to assert the dominance of the one true religion over all others such that "political classification was between those who had been conquered or who had submitted themselves to the power of Islam and those who had not".[38] From out of this context there arose regulations of protection, submission and deference applied to communities of those religions that were also 'of the Book', such as Christianity and Judaism – the so-called *dhimmi* communities.[39] But the Quranic injunction to honour such co-religionists was tempered by the motif of submission. Muslim superiority to both Jews and Christians soon became asserted in overt political terms. During the reign of the Caliph Umar (634–44CE) a treaty between the People of the Book and the Muslim state was enacted. Known as the 'Pact of Umar', it was

> ...a writ of protection (*amaan* or *dhimma*) extended by Allah's community to their protégés (*ahl al-dhimma* or *dhimmis*). In return for the safeguarding of life and property and the right to worship unmolested according to their conscience, the *dhimmis* had to pay the *jizya* (poll-tax) and the *kharaj* (land-tax). They were to conduct themselves with the demeanour and comportment befit-

---

34 Stillman, *op. cit.*, 20.

35 Robert S. Wistrich, *Anti-Semitism: The Longest Hatred*. London: Mandarin, 1992, 199.

36 Cf. Bruce Feiler, *Abraham: A Journey to the Heart of Three Faiths*. New York: William Morrow, 2002.

37 Lewis, *op. cit.*, 12.

38 *Ibid.*, 21.

39 Cf. Bat Ye'or, *The Dhimmi: Jews and Christians under Islam*, Cranbury, NJ: Associated University Press, 1985.

ting a subject population.[40]

Many of the provisions and restrictions of the pact were only elaborated with the passage of time. It is clear that terms imposed upon the conquered peoples varied greatly, and this variation depended upon the conditions surrounding their surrender. So, the principal originating paradigm of the subservient ambiguous other was re-cast as the paradigm of dhimmitude. But it was not the only historical paradigm in respect to Muslim interfaith relations that applied.

Although, together with Christianity, there is a distinctive influence upon Islam that can be traced to Judaism, the historical and prophetic lineage of the religion of the Jews clearly meant Judaism ranked as the primary 'other' over against which Islam, in its formative years, had to distinguish itself. Furthermore, linguistic affinity meant that some Jewish terms and concepts crossed over into the speech of Arabs. Similarly, religious ideas, ethical notions, and the like were disseminated among Arabs who came into close contact with Jews. So, in the very process of determining its own identity and points of reference, Islam found itself drawing upon various types of literature which Muslim scholars attributed primarily to Jewish sources.[41] The Oxford scholar, Ronald Nettler, has concluded that the "presence of the *Isra'iliyyat* within Islam constitutes an important example of traditional Islamic–Jewish cultural interaction and symbiosis which implicitly overrode the built-in monotheistic exclusivism on both sides …"[42] This suggests one very positive paradigm of Muslim interfaith relations, namely that of an enriching cultural interaction. Nevertheless, the predominating paradigm throughout much of Muslim history was that of dhimmitude.

Clearly Islamic authorities were concerned that taxes be paid and that dhimmi subjects acknowledge in a variety of ways, some more and some less humiliating, the superiority and domination of Islam. "As long as the non-Muslims complied, they were accorded a good measure of internal self-rule. However, even in the conduct of their own communal affairs, they were not entirely free of government supervision and, at times, downright interference".[43] At best dhimmi communities would enjoy considerable communal autonomy "precisely because the state did not care what they did so long as they paid their taxes, kept the peace, and remained in their place".[44] Nonetheless, the scene was set for a problematic history of interaction. A lot would depend on local circumstances. Clearly, a paradigmatic line was established: limits to dhimmi autonomy would be determined down the centuries of Islamic rule by Islamic expectations. Non-Muslims would know themselves to be a people submitted to those who themselves live in submission to Allah. If the originating Islamic paradigm of interfaith relations was on the basis of a concept of the "ambiguous other", and the historical paradigm has been largely that of subservient dhimmitude, what appears to be the case at present?

Contemporary Paradigms: Islamic Exclusivism

With the dawn of the modern era, and the early penetration of European influence and colonisation with respect to Islamic lands of the Middle East, there was a weakening of traditional

---

40 Stillman, *op. cit.*, 25.

41 Ronald L. Nettler, 'Early Islam, Modern Islam and Judaism: The Isra'iliyyat in Modern Islamic Thought' *in* Ronald L. Nettler and Suha Taji-Farouki, eds, *Muslim–Jewish Encounters: Intellectual Traditions and Modern Politics*. Amsterdam: Harwood Academic Publishers, 1998.

42 *Ibid.*, 3.

43 Stillman, *op. cit.*, 38.

44 *Ibid.*, 39.

Islamic norms of society and a concomitant improvement in the lot of dhimmi communities. Although reforms were slow, eventually the Ottomans, for example, abolished the *jizya* tax. On the other hand, in Iraq, and particularly Baghdad, throughout much of the nineteenth century relations between Muslims and non-Muslims were most often quite tense. There were, for instance, "numerous anti-Jewish and anti-Christian riots, some limited and some on a large scale" often because "Jews and Christians were especially vulnerable to accusations that they had blasphemed against Muhammad or that they had once converted to Islam and thereafter apostasized. Capital punishment was called for in either case".[45] Furthermore, the late nineteenth century saw the appearance of European-type antisemitic literature within the Arab world, especially within communities under French influence. Stillman remarks that, in general, the inception of antisemitism in the Arab world could be seen

> ...as part of the struggle of one partially emancipated minority – the Christians – to protect itself against the economic competition of another partially emancipated but less assimilated minority – the Jews. The vast majority of Muslim Arabs did not yet perceive the Jews as an economic or political threat. This would come in the twentieth century with the confrontation of opposing Jewish and Arab nationalisms.[46]

While political and ideological elements play a part, the underlying paradigmatic driver is, arguably, theological or religious. For example, from a Muslim perspective "Islam didn't supersede Christianity and Judaism, it preceded them. Islam, in fact, was the faith of Abraham, which his descendants twisted for their own purposes".[47] First and foremost of the descendants doing the twisting is, of course, the Jews; but today, often, Christians may be viewed as not too far behind. Sadly, the twentieth century has also seen a distinct upsurge of anti-Jewish – i.e., antisemitic – literature within the Islamic world, most disturbingly with the coming together "of archetypes fixed in the consciousness of early Islam with the theories of a 'world Jewish conspiracy' adapted from modern European antisemitism".[48]

Arguably there is both a theological and metaphysical dimension to the clash between Islam and the Jews.[49] The Arab–Israeli conflict is not simply territorial and political. It is inherently religious. Palestinian anti-Zionist rhetoric earlier in the twentieth century tended to focus on the desire to protect the Islamic and Arabic character of Palestine and its people from a perceived secular threat.[50] A report of some field research, involving an interview with a local Imam in East Jerusalem, is most telling. Although, of course, hard-line exclusivist perspectives can be found to a degree in all religions, the point is made that, in this context at least, the viewpoint of the Imam does rather represent wider and more generally held popular Muslim perspectives. Jews and Christians are alike dismissed as inferior to Muslims in their devotion and correct worship of God.[51] Of course, in the context of contemporary Israel-Palestine, such profoundly negative views come as no surprise. But that does not lessen the problematic, nor diminish the thesis, of interfaith paradigms I am here exploring.

Contemporary attitudes have contemporary referents; but in this case they also have a

---

45 *Ibid.*, 103.

46 *Ibid.*, 107.

47 Feiler, *Abraham*, 176.

48 Wistrich, *op. cit.*, 222.

49 *Ibid.*, 223.

50 *Ibid.*, 242.

51 These People of the Book are given "opportunity to submit … and follow the rule of God. But you ignore him because you have become strong. … You do the opposite of what God wants. … God gives you many chances, but of course we know you are not going to follow". Feiler, *op. cit.*, 179.

paradigmatic history. And what much contemporary Muslim rhetoric seems to suggest is that a predominant interfaith paradigm is that of Islamic Exclusivism: an exclusive and excluding portrayal of Islam is found in many quarters. But is it the only contemporary paradigm? As I have argued elsewhere,[52] the exclusivist paradigm can itself be construed in three modes – open, closed, and rejectionist – denoting a development that ranges from a clearly held exclusive understanding that nevertheless allows for some measure of relational, if not exactly dialogical, engagement with other faiths; through an exclusivism that prefers to ignore, or at best mutely tolerate, the presence of other faiths; to an extremism that takes active steps to curtail or even eliminate what is perceived to be a dangerously threatening 'other'. All three can be found within Islam today. Patterns and paradigms are instructive. We need to be aware of them and to appreciate them in terms of both their historical significance and their contemporary impact. But we are not bound by them: innovative religious thinkers who appreciate the traditions of the past can offer illuminating insight an interpretation that yields fresh appreciation and even novel application. Thus a new future can be envisioned. Fethullah Gülen, as we have already noted, is just such a thinker. It is to his perspectives on Islam and interfaith dialogue that we now turn to see what contribution can be made that could complement the past and open up the future.

Fethullah Gülen on Interreligious Dialogue and Islamic Interfaith Relations

Fethullah Gülen is absolutely correct in noting that desire for mutual understanding, a dedication to justice, and a priority on mutual respect are requisite are requisite principles for engaging in interreligious dialogue.[53] Gülen is of the view that, in today's world, the task of "representing faith with its true values has gained an even greater importance than before".[54] Indeed, he regards interfaith engagement as a function of the "necessity of increasing the interests we have in common with other people".[55] He and the movement seeking to promote his teachings and views within the Islamic world and beyond are firmly committed to the cause of interreligious engagement and dialogue. In the light of my general analysis of the paradigms and dynamics that have pertained to Muslim interfaith relations, what might be the paradigmatic perspective and prospects that are embedded in the thought of Fethullah Gülen? Lester Kurtz, noting that, for Gülen, "spiritual practice and morality are … more important than ritual and dogmatism" speaks of four pillars of dialogue – love, compassion, tolerance and forgiveness – as descriptive of Gülen's understanding.[56] Indeed, it is this perspective "that opens the way for dialogue with other faith traditions" for Muslims.[57] My own reading of Gülen expands this threefold analysis. I suggest that, from Gülen, we may derive some seven elements for a possible contemporary Islamic paradigm for interreligious relations and dialogue.

---

52 Douglas Pratt, 'Pluralism and Interreligious Engagement: The Contexts of Dialogue', *in* David Thomas with Clare Amos, eds., *A Faithful Presence, essays for Kenneth Cragg,* London: Melisende Press, 2003, 402-418.

53 F. Gülen, *The Two Roses of the Emerald Hills: Tolerance and Dialogue* (*http://en.fGülen.com/content/view/1806/33/*)

54 F. Gülen, *Dialogue in the Muhammadan Spirit and Meaning* (http://en.fGülen.com/content/view/1811/33/)

55 *Ibid.*

56 Lester R. Kurtz, 'Gülen's Paradox: Combining Commitment and Tolerance', *The Muslim World*, Vol 95, July 2005, 377.

57 *Ibid.*, 378.

1. Distinction of Values: Primary and Secondary

Arguably, love is a primary word in Gülen's vocabulary of dialogue.[58] Love, he says, "exists in everyone as a seed. This seed germinates under favorable circumstances and, growing like a tree, blossoms into a flower, and finally ripens, like a fruit, to unite the beginning with the end".[59] Indeed, it is clear that, for Gülen, primary values such as "peace, love, forgiveness, and tolerance are fundamental to Islam" whereas values such as jihad are regarded as a secondary matter.[60] Keeping these categories of primary and secondary value distinguished and in proper perspective is critical for, as Gülen avers, "failure to establish a proper balance between what is primary and what is secondary leads others to conclude that Islam advocates malice and hatred in the soul, whereas true Muslims are full of love and affection for all creation".[61]

2. Intentionality: A Principal Perspective

Intentionality is also an important element of Islamic thought and a key to Gülen's perspective: "In every task undertaken, there should be a certain meaning, sincerity should be sought, and reason and good judgment should be the priority".[62] Gülen remarks that the "Prophet of God said: 'Deeds are judged by intentions', and he emphasized that the intention of the believer is more important than the act itself".[63] Intentionality is applied naturally to the sphere of interfaith engagement. And noting the "Qur'an calls people to accept the former Prophets and their Books", Gülen avers that "having such a condition at the very beginning of the Qur'an seems very important … when it comes to starting a dialogue with the followers of other religions".[64]

3. Tolerance: An Inherent Element

Gülen argues that "Society has to uphold tolerance. If we don't announce jihad for anything else, we should announce it for tolerance".[65] Tolerance, properly understood, is inherent to dialogue for, as well as "being commanded to take tolerance and to use dialogue as his basis while performing his duties", Muhammad was guided toward things in common with the People of the Book (Jews and Christians), as the Holy Qur'an (Al-Imran 3:64) bears witness: "O People of the Book! Come to common terms as between us and you: that we worship none but God; that we speculate no partners with Him; that we take not some from among ourselves for Lords other than God".[66] Tolerance – together with forgiveness – is a virtue enjoined throughout the Qur'an such that, in the contemporary context of today, Gülen is quite clear: Muslims are to "behave with tolerance and forbearance" in the interfaith arena.[67] In his critique of certain Muslim propensities he asserts that "the method of those who act with

---

58 Albayrak, *op. cit.*, 127; cf. F, Gülen, *Toward a Global Civilization of Love and Tolerance*, Somerset, NJ: The Light, Inc., 2004.

59 F, Gülen, *Pearls of Wisdom*, Somerset, NJ: The Light, Inc., 2005, 21.

60 F. Gülen, *Dialogue in the Muhammadan Spirit and Meaning* (http://en.fGülen.com/content/view/1811/33/)

61 F. Gülen, *Islam-A Religion of Tolerance* (http://en.fGülen.com/content/view/1808/33/)

62 F. Gülen, *Sports and the Process of Dialogue* (http://en.fGülen.com/content/view/1813/33/)

63 F. Gülen, *The Two Roses of the Emerald Hills: Tolerance and Dialogue* (*http://en.fGülen.com/content/view/1806/33/*)

64 F. Gülen *in* Ünal & Williams, *op. cit.*, 251

65 F. Gülen, *in* Ünal & Williams, *op. cit.*, 206

66 F. Gülen, *Tolerance and Dialogue in the Qur'an and the Sunna* (http://en.fGülen.com/content/view/1810/33/)

67 Cf. F. Gülen, *Tolerance and Dialogue in the Perspective of the Qur'an and Sunna* (http://en.fGülen.com/content/view/1340/13/)

enmity and hatred, who view everyone else with anger, and who blacken others as infidels is non-Islamic, for Islam is a religion of love and tolerance".[68] Yet Gülen is positive overall: "We are rediscovering tolerance, something that is inherent in the spirit of Islam and something that was explained to us in the Qur'an and by Prophet Muhammad".[69]

Of course, tolerance is not to be equated with attitudes of 'passive putting-up with' that which we would prefer to have nothing to do. This is often the default perspective that we find in our societies – what might be better called 'mere tolerance'. The tolerance to which Gülen alludes, on the other hand, is far more active and intentional, for it has to do with an underlying aim of dialogical engagement: the fostering of that peace and harmony to which the Qur'an refers and for which Islam stands: "peace is better" (Al-Nisa 4:128). Gülen asserts that "Muslims will lose nothing by employing dialogue, love, and tolerance," and that, indeed, there are many verses in the Qur'an that extol these virtues.[70]

4. Dialogue: An Expression of a Divinely-Inspired Love

Fethullah Gülen arguably regards interfaith dialogue as an expression of a divinely-inspired love, for the primary theological verity that binds together all peoples of the Book – Jews, Christians and Muslims especially – is the belief in God as Creator. The act of creation is not that of arbitrary whim but intentional love of the Creator for the creature. As Gülen states, "Love is the reason for existence and its essence, and it is the strongest tie that binds creatures together. Everything in the universe is the handiwork of God".[71] Love issues in practical actions, and at the level of inter-communal and inter-religious relations, love is expressed in terms of dialogical engagement: thus "dialogue is the real remedy for terror, chaos, and intolerance".[72] Gülen is himself succinct and to the point: "those who seek to build the happy world of the future on foundations of spiritual and moral values should arrive first at the altar of belief, then ascend to the pulpit of love, and only then preach their message of belief and love to others".[73]

The complementarity of tolerance and love as being not just human virtues but in reality indicators of primary values which the Creator imbued the creation underscores an essential oneness of human existence that itself suggests dialogue is the right and proper mode of interaction. "Even though we may not have common grounds on some matters", says Gülen, "we all live in this world and we are passengers on the same ship. In this respect, there are many common points that can be discussed and shared with people from every segment of society".[74]

5. Reconciliation: The Essence of Religion

The motif of religion as a force for and of reconciliation is very strong with Fethullah Gülen. Indeed, love, compassion, tolerance, and forgiveness are at the heart of all religions.[75] It is

---

68 F. Gülen, *Islam-A Religion of Tolerance* (http://en.fGülen.com/content/view/1808/33/)

69 F. Gülen, *Making the Atmosphere of Tolerance Permanent* (http://en.fGülen.com/content/view/1801/33/)

70 F. Gülen, *The Two Roses of the Emerald Hills: Tolerance and Dialogue* (http://en.fGülen.com/content/view/1806/33/)

71 F. Gülen, Making the Atmosphere of Tolerance Permanent (http://en.fGülen.com/content/view/1801/33/)

72 Albayrak, *op. cit.*, 129

73 F. Gülen *in* Ali Ünal & Alphonse Williams, eds., *Advocate of Dialogue*, Fairfax, Virginia: The Fountain, 2000, 107

74 F. Gülen, *Tolerance in the Life of the Individual and Society* (http://en.fGülen.com/content/view/1800/33/)

75 F. Gülen, *Love, Compassion, Tolerance, and Forgiving: The Pillars of Dialogue* (http://en.fGülen.com/content/view/1339/13/)

thus of the nature of religion to promote the values and virtues that engender reconciliation. Specifically, for Islam, the Qur'an itself enjoins reconciliation with the wider religious context of the Peoples of the Book, a view that Gülen derives directly from Sura al-Baqara.[76] Allah commands against disputing one with another; instead the reconciling interaction of dialogical debate is encouraged. In particular, Gülen notes that there are "many common points for dialogue among devout Muslims, Christians, and Jews".[77] The imperative to dialogue is therefore strong, and must be conducted in a context of "giving precedence to common points, which far outnumber polemical ones".[78]

6. Hermeneutical Authority for Dialogue

Gülen recognises the need to read the Qur'an carefully and intelligently when it comes, for example, to the issue of specific relations with Jews and Christians. Some expressions in the Qur'an regarding Christianity and Judaism are indeed very sharp and rather negative, even hostile in some cases. At best there seems to be a measure of revelatory paradox. But such paradox may be the effect of taking things out of context, or at least not taking context sufficiently into account. Thus, on the one hand "verses condemning and rebuking the Jews and Christians are either about some Jews and Christians who lived in the time of the Prophet Muhammad or their own Prophets", as opposed to all Jews and Christians at all times; or on the other hand they are about "stubborn unbelievers who lived during the Prophet's lifetime and insisted on unbelief" who happened to be Jews or Christians.[79] Such verses cannot be taken to refer to all Jews and Christians since, for it was never Jewish or Christian belief and believing at such which was being criticised, but the presence of unbelief – Jews and Christians ignoring their own heritage wherein they, together with Muslims, are together believers in the one God. As Gülen himself remarks, it was not Christianity or Judaism that was the subject of condemnation but rather "the Qur'an goes after wrong behaviour, incorrect thought, and resistance to the truth, creation of hostility, and non-commendable characteristics".[80] Rather than counting against dialogue, a careful and correct contextual reading of the Qur'an would seem to be advocated by Gülen. In this way a proper interpretive Muslim authority for dialogue may be discerned.

7. Ijtihad: The Struggle for Dialogue

The final element in a possible Islamic paradigm for interreligious dialogue and relations has to do with the notion of *ijtihad* as meaning a proper intellectual and spiritual struggle. Ihsan Yilmaz argues that

> Gülen believes that there is a need for *ijtihad* in our age. He says that he respects the scholars of the past but also believes that *ijtihad* is a necessity: to freeze *ijtihad* means to freeze Islam and to imprison it in a given time and space. He argues that Islam is a dynamic and universal religion that covers all time and space, and renews itself in real life situations; it changes from one context to another, and *ijtihad* is a major tool in enabling this.[81]

The struggle to live a life of true faith, to follow the way of peaceful submission to God,

---

76 Cf. F. Gülen, *Dialogue with the People of the Book (Jews and Christians)* (http://en.fGülen.com/content/view/1341/13/)

77 *Ibid.*

78 F. Gülen, *Dialogue Is a Must (http://en.fGülen.com/content/view/1336/13/)*

79 F. Gülen, *Jews and Christians in the Qur'an* (http://en.fGülen.com/content/view/1342/13/)

80 *Ibid.*

81 Ihsan Yilmaz, *Muslim Laws, Politics and Society in Modern Nation States: Dynamic Legal Pluralisms in England, Turkey and Pakistan*. Aldershot: Ashgate, 2005, 175.

has led Fethullah Gülen into significant arenas of social and educational action, not the least of which is the promotion of interfaith dialogue and interreligious relations. Such dialogue inheres to the agenda of the Gülen movement because Gülen juxtaposed the struggle to live as a good and true Muslim with the task of engaging with the religious neighbour. This contrasts with forms of ijtihad coming from other quarters in the Islamic world that result in advocating jihad against the religious other. Thus Lester Kurtz can speak of Gülen's "paradoxical fusion ... of intense faith commitment with tolerance", for example, thus resulting "in a paradigm of Islamic dialogue".[82] The essence of Gülen's paradigm is nothing less than the application of ijtihad to the question and challenge of Muslim interfaith relations. Hence, "tolerance of others and genuine interfaith dialogue are not simply a pleasant ideal that will be fulfilled in some future paradise, but ...(are)... at the core of what it is to be Muslim in the here and now".[83] Indeed, Gülen argues that dialogue is demanded by the very nature of religion as such.

Conclusion

Yilmaz notes that "Gülen has found a wide audience for his ideas, which are described as reformative by some scholars", yet the thrust of reformation, interestingly, is that in "exercising *ijtihad* without flagging it as *ijtihad*, Gülen reinterprets Islamic understanding in tune with contemporary times and develops a new Muslim discourse".[84] Today, Fethullah Gülen "continues to practice the theology of dialogue, since he believes that his teachings are well grounded in the principles of Islam".[85] A relatively cursory reading of some representative works of Gülen yield elements for a paradigmatic perspective that is indicative of new possibilities for Muslim interpretation of, and sensibilities toward, interfaith relations and dialogue. Where these values, patterns and perspectives on dialogue are not put into place, the outcome is quite dire. Gülen himself avers that "The present, distorted image of Islam that has resulted from its misuse by both Muslims and non-Muslims for their own goals scares both Muslims and non-Muslims".[86] In reality, at the heart of Islam is the call to dialogue.[87] Peace also lies at this heart; "war and conflict as aberrations to be brought under control" with security and world harmony the underlying divinely desired goal.[88]

It must be remembered that for any faith-based movement there is a dialectical tension in respect to its ongoing relationship to its founder: on the one hand it always stands open to the criticism of not living up as fully as it might to the standards, demands, or expectations of its founder; on the other hand neither must it remain bound by the inevitable limitations that any human founder brings. Rather, the trick is to proceed along the path in the direction pointed to by the founder, cognizant of the values and insights supplied, but capable of applying and developing them as new circumstances and contexts arise. This is the stuff of the inherent and internal dialogical dialectic of all faith-based movements. The Gülen Movement is no

---

82 Lester R. Kurtz, 'Gülen's Paradox: Combining Commitment and Tolerance', *The Muslim World*, Vol 95, July 2005, 373.

83 Kurtz, *Ibid.*, 375

84 Ihsan Yilmaz, 'Inter-Madhhab Surfing, Neo-Ijtihad, and Faith-Based Movement Leaders' *in* Peri Bearman, Rudolph Peters and Frank E. Vogel, eds, *The Islamic School of Law: Evolution, Devolution and Progress*, Cambridge, Mass: Harvard University Press, 2005, 200.

85 Saritoprak, *op. cit.*, 424.

86 F. Gülen, *Jews and Christians in the Qur'an*

87 Cf. F. Gülen, *Islam's Ecumenical Call for Dialogue* (http://en.fGülen.com/content/view/1337/13/)

88 Cf. F. Gülen, *How to Interact with Followers of Other Religions* (http://en.fGülen.com/content/view/1338/13/)

exception. Paul Weller has rightly observed that Fethullah Gülen himself affirms

> ... the existence of a fundamental continuity in the issues faced by human beings in relation to
> their behavior with one another and their place in the universe. At the same time, he recognizes the
> specific nature of the challenges of diversity and plurality – challenges which have previously been
> present in individual historical societies but which, in the 21st century, have been elevated onto a
> global stage. ... Gülen stands against ways of thinking and acting that promote the illusion that the
> uncomfortable plurality of the contemporary world can simply be abolished.[89]

In respect to the issue of relations between Christians and Muslims, or more broadly speaking
between the West and Islam, and prospects for the ongoing dialogue between those two faiths
and their respective cultures, we might agree with Charles Kimball that:

For many people in both communities the basic theological issues constitute the primary
agenda.... Understanding different orientations is an important step, but it does not resolve
the seemingly inherent conflicts. Thoughtful, creative, and persevering efforts are required
in order to bridge some of the real and perceived differences in foundational theological understandings. ... Although we all carry the cumulative baggage provided by our deep-rooted
heritage, developments in the past 150 years have challenged traditional assumptions and
prompted the vexing questions confronting people of faith today.[90]

Religious prejudice, expressed in forms of claims to superiority and exclusivity of one over
another, is an issue that ever needs to be addressed. Parties to any Muslim interfaith dialogue
– be that Jewish, Christian, Muslim or any other "religion of the book" – need to recognise
that, indeed, "each religion is an interpretive venture".[91] The 'book' is ever a text requiring
interpretive understanding and application. Triumphalism must be countered if there is to be
any genuine eirenical advance. As Rabbi David Rosen, a leading Jewish figure in the cause of
interfaith relations, has commented: "We should indeed keep the differences ... and learn to
respect them. Each religion has its *particular* approach to God. But we also have a *universal*
dimension to our traditions that we share, and we must emphasize that as well".[92] By pursuing the challenge of dialogue we seek to comprehend better the respective faiths in which we
live, and move, and have our being.

In dialogue with Fethullah Gülen Muslim and non-Muslim alike are moved "beyond prejudice, suspicion, and half-truths so that they might arrive at an understanding what Islam is
really about" and to see that "tolerance, love, and compassion are genuinely Islamic values
that Muslims have a duty to bring to the modern world".[93] The call of Islam is a call to dialogue. Fethullah Gülen certainly offers "Muslims a way to live out Islamic values amidst the
complex demands of modern societies and to engage in ongoing dialogue and cooperation
with people of other religions".[94] Dialogue with Gülen and the movement that bears his name
is an avenue wherein the non-Muslim can join with Muslims in the greater journey of the
dialogical quest.

---

89   Weller, *op. cit.*, 88.
90   Charles Kimball, *Striving Together: A Way Forward in Christian–Muslim Relations*. Maryknoll, New York:
Orbis Books, 1991, 48.
91   Feiler, *Abraham,* 202.
92   Cited in Feiler, 204.
93   Michel, 'Two Frontrunners' *op. cit.*
94   *Ibid.*

M FETHULLAH GÜLEN'S RESPONSE TO THE "CLASH OF CIVILIZATIONS" THESIS

Richard Penaskovic

Abstract

Part I contains an exposition of Sam Huntington's thesis about the clash of civilisations according to Gülen. Huntington's writings are far from being realistic evaluations regarding the future. Rather, they are more like a self-fulfilling prophecy. Gülen argues that by creating new enemy fronts, Huntington actually sows the seeds for a clash of civilisations on the basis of religious and cultural differences. Part II looks at Gulen's response to Huntington's thesis and has three parts: tolerance, interfaith dialogue, and compassionate love. Tolerance means closing our minds to the faults of others, respecting ideas with which we disagree, and when attacked verbally, responding with mildness or as the Qur'an says, with 'gentle words.' Interfaith dialogue involves stressing the commonalities between the world religions, rather than past polemics and historical differences. In regard to compassionate love Gülen calls the universe a symphony of compassion because without compassion everything is in chaos. Souls filled with love are in Gülen's view, the greatest heroes in the cosmos. The way of love is the way of the prophets. Part III contains my own views on the clash of civilisations. Written in the spirit of Gülen, I argue that in contradistinction to Huntington, the Muslim world is not monolithic, that many of the past wars and clashes were within the same civilisation, and that the real clash is between extremists of all types and moderates within the same culture or civilisation. I also highlight the ecumenical message of Islam, namely, that all religion deserve respect and courtesy, that followers of different religious traditions should compete with one another in piety, and that the rope that links us to God also links us to one another (Qur'an 3:103).

"The differences of opinion among the learned within my community are (a sign of God's) grace." (The Prophet Muhammed)
"The variety of religions belongs to the beauty and richness of the human situation because it is only the entire rainbow that provides a complete picture of the true religious dimension of Man."(Panikkar 1999: 17).

Introduction

Like Caesar's Gaul my essay may be conveniently divided into three distinct parts. Part I presents the thesis of Samuel P. Huntington about the clash of civilizations as found in his 1993 article, "The Clash of Civilizations?" published in the journal, *Foreign Affairs,* and then expanded and qualified in his seminal book, *The Clash Of Civilizations and the Remaking of World Order,* published in 1996. Particular attention will be given to his remarks on the relationship between Islam and the West.

Part II contains M Fethullah's Gülen's response to Huntington's now famous thesis. If Mr. Huntington is a protagonist for Western civilization, then Mr. Gülen is his counterpart, serving as a spokesperson or champion for moderate Islam. The differences between them are like night and day. Mr. Gülen argues that by creating new enemy fronts Huntington actually sows the seeds for a clash of civilizations on the basis of cultural and religious differences. Moreover, in contradistinction to Huntington, Gülen comes out strongly in favor of a rapprochement between Islam and the West based on his understanding of tolerance, interfaith dialogue, and compassionate love.

Part III consists of my own reflections on the controversy, written in the spirit of M. Fethullah Gülen. I argue that Huntington is guilty of semantic ambiguity in his use of the terms "civilization" and "culture." I point out that neither the Western world nor the Muslim world is monolithic, that many past wars and clashes were within the same civilization, and that a dichotomy should not be made between Islam and the West. I also argue that Christianity and Islam have shaped each other, that all religions deserve courtesy and respect, and that the main problem today between Islam and the West has to do more with power rather than with religious issues.

Part I: Huntington's Thesis

Huntington's work on the clash of civilizations presents a paradigm or model for interpreting global politics after the Cold War, meaningful to some academics and useful to some policymakers in the West, particularly in the United States. In spite of the examples that he gives, Huntington's thesis about a clash of civilizations derives from the internal problems of the United States. More specifically, they take their origin from Huntington's critique of multiculturalism during the Clinton administration and the immigration of Mexicans into the United States (Halliday 2005:123). Huntington's thesis goes like this: culture and cultural identities are shaping the patterns of cohesion, disintegration, and conflict in the post-Cold war world. This central thesis finds further elaboration and amplification in five corollaries:

i. For the first time in history global politics is multipolar and multiciviizational. Contacts between civilizations were either nonexistent or intermittent for most of human history. Beginning with the modern era circa 1500, the nation states of the West mainly Europe and the United States constituted a multipolar international system, interacting and fighting wars with each other within Western civilization. During the Cold War global politics became bipolar with the world divided into First World nations such as Europe and the United States, and Second World nations, namely the Communist bloc led by the Soviet Union. However, most of the conflict between these two blocs occurred among Third World nations which were for the most part poor, politically unstable, recently independent, and nonaligned (Huntington 1996: 24).

In the post-Cold War world the most important distinctions among peoples are cultural as people define themselves in terms of religion, language, history, ancestry, customs, values, and institutions. The world's eight major civilizations (Western, Latin American, African, Islamic, Sinic, Hindu, Orthodox, and Japanese), are the most significant groupings of states with nation states remaining the main actors in world affairs. Whereas in the Cold War we had the United States and its allies pitted against the Communist bloc countries, today we have a clash of civilizations. Cultural factors will spark future conflicts with the most dangerous cultural conflicts occurring among the fault lines between civilizations. Local conflicts which have the greatest probability of escalating into broader wars are those between groups and states from different cultures with power shifting from the long predominant West to non-Western civilizations (Huntington 1996: 29).

ii. In regard to the power of the West Huntington juxtaposes two pictures. In the first picture the West has almost total dominance over other civilizations while simultaneously possessing substantial interests in every other civilization. Huntington observes that the West has the ability to affect the economics, politics, and security of every other civilization or region. In the second scenario Huntington sees the balance of power shifting with the West declining in influence and, concomitantly, Asian civilizations (Sinic, Japanese, Buddhist, and Muslim) expanding their political, military, and economic strengths.

Huntington notes that indigenization and the revival of religion are global phenomena and are most evident in the cultural assertiveness and challenges to the West that have come from Asia and from Islam. Whereas Asian assertiveness has its roots in economic growth, Muslim assertiveness arises mostly from population growth and social mobilization. In regard to the former, expansion of the fifteen to twenty-four year old age cohort in the Muslim countries provides recruits for terrorism, migration, fundamentalism, and insurgency. Population growth along with economic stagnation drives Muslim migration to Western and other non-Muslim societies, making immigration an issue in these societies (Huntington 1996: 119). Both Asians and Muslims see their culture as superior to that of the West but, interesting enough, says Huntington, other non-Western civilizations (African, Hindu, Orthodox, and Latin American) while affirming the distinctive character of their cultures, do not proclaim their superiority to Western culture (Huntington 1996: 102). Huntington does not see a bright future arguing that we will see in the beginning of the twenty-first century an ongoing resurgence of non-Western power and culture and the clash of the non-Western civilizations with those of the West (Huntington 1996: 119).

iii. Huntington pictures the emergence of a civilization-based world order with emerging societies sharing cultural affinities cooperating with one another. The effort to shift societies from one civilization to another will not work and countries will group themselves around the core or lead states of their civilization.

Huntington believes that the Muslim world has a very difficult time in terms of unity and cohesion. Islam remains fractured because competing power centers try to capitalize on Muslim identification with the *ummah* or Muslim community in order to further Islamic unity under its leadership. The difficulty comes down to this: a Muslim lead or core state must possess the military power, economic resources, organizational competence, and Islamic commitment to provide religious and political leadership to the *ummah*. Six countries (Indonesia, Egypt, Iran, Pakistan, Saudi Arabia, and Turkey) are often mentioned as candidates for a core state yet presently no one of them has all the requisites to be one (Huntington 1996:177).

iv. Huntington argues that division and intense conflict will occur between the West and the rest, particularly in Muslim and Asian societies. A major factor in this conflict concerns the efforts of the United States to promote a universal Western culture and its declining ability to do so. The United States believes that non-Westerners should commit themselves to such Western values as democracy, human rights, individualism, and the rule of law, free markets, and limited government. Non-Western nations observe a double standard in this regard. Nonproliferation of weapons is preached for Iran and Iraq, but not for Israel. Human rights may be violated in Saudi Arabia but not in China. Democracy is promoted but not if it brings Islamic fundamentalists to power (Huntington 1996:184).

There are three main issues that divide the West and Muslim and Asian societies. First, the efforts of the West to keep its military superiority by means of policies of nonproliferation and conterproliferation in terms of biological, chemical, and nuclear weapons and the means to deliver them; second, the attempt by the West to promote its own political institutions and values by pressuring other societies to respect human rights and adopt the Western view of democracy; and third, the desire of the West to protect its cultural, ethnic, and social integrity by restricting the number of non-Westerners admitted as refugees or immigrants (Huntington 1996: 186).

In the twentieth century a number of factors have escalated the conflict between Islam and the West. Muslim population growth has increased the number of the unemployed and disaffected youth, who migrate to the West or join Islamist causes. The Islamic Resurgence has given Muslims pride in their own identity and culture and values vis-à-vis the West. The Western world's efforts to make universal its institutions and values, to maintain its economic and military superiority, and to intervene in conflicts within the Islamic world, generate intense resentment among Muslims. As long as both Islam and the West refuse to change, the conflict will go on in the future as it has for the past fourteen centuries (Huntington 1996: 212).

v. The final corollary deals with the future of civilizations. Huntington maintains that the central issue for the West is whether it can renew itself or will sustained decay (in the form of moral decline, political disunity, and cultural suicide) accelerate its demise and possible subordination to more dynamic civilizations. Huntington accuses the Clinton administration in the 1990s of rejecting the cultural heritage of the United States by opting for multiculturalism. For Huntington the future of the West depends upon America reaffirming its commitment to Western civilization, rejecting the illusory calls to identify the United States with Asia, and both preserving and renewing the unique qualities of Western civilization (Huntington 1996: 311).

vi. Huntington sets down three requirements for peace in order to avoid major inter-civilizational wars. First, core states must not intervene in conflicts in other civilizations. Second, core states must dialogue and negotiate with each other in order to halt fault line wars between states from other civilizations. Third, the requisites for cultural coexistence demand a stress on the factors various civilizations share. Different civilizations must learn from each other and be willing to live side by side in peaceful exchange. Clashes between civilizations are the greatest threat to world peace. The best preventative of a global war is an international order based on civilizations (Huntington 1996: 321).

Part II: M Fethullah Gülen's Response to Huntington's Thesis

Unlike Huntington Mr. Gülen is not an academic. Rather, he writes as

> a preacher, a journalist, a visionary, and as an activist. His thoughts are simple yet profound, poetic rather than pedestrian. He finds his inspiration in the Qur'an, the *hadith*, the Sufi mystics, particularly Rumi the poet, and in the ideas of Said Nursi. (Valkenberg 2006: 313). Gülen was greatly influenced by Nursi and is accepting of Western modernity, defending such modern ideas as dialogue, democracy, and tolerance. Gülen's ideas on the clash of civilizations are not found in a lengthy treatise but only in a short article of about 1400 words. (Gülen 2004a: 254-257).

What does Gülen say about the clash of civilizations? Gülen does not mince words. He fears that such talk about a clash of civilizations might become a self-fulfilling prophecy. Gülen notes that as a consequence of such a claim readers may form expectations in the very same way they expect an answer to prayer. By arguing that the future will involve a clash of civilizations, Huntington converts such an expectation into a purposeful goal. Gülen fears that with such a goal in mind, various policies and strategies will then be marshaled to reach and attain such a goal.

Gülen also has a different vision of the future than does Mr. Huntington. Where Huntington speaks of conflict between civilizations and variant cultures, Gülen is much more sanguine and upbeat about the future. For example, Gülen speaks to the importance of knowledge and education, which if done properly can avert any clash of civilizations. Mr. Gülen equates knowledge and power. Everything in the future will be in the orbit of knowledge.

In the first phase of his life Gülen, the visionary activist, gathered his students into a quasi-religious community which aimed to form them into a generation of pious and educated Muslims. The atmosphere in these dormitories or lighthouses was greatly influenced by Sufism, although Gülen himself was a not a Sufi, strictly speaking. In these *dershanes* or learning centers of the neo-Nur movement university students prayed, developed a Muslim ethic, and discussed both social issues and the reconciliation between Islam and modern science. Gülen saw these communities as a way of building a new generation of morally superior persons. These lighthouses reminded one of the ideals of the first Muslim *ummah* or community, while they were also pointers to a better Muslim community in the future (Valkenberg 2006: 310).

Gülen believes that Islam has been neglectful of the scientific knowledge obtained during the tenth and eleventh centuries based on the Qur'an. He laments the fact that the *madrasas* or religious schools did not teach Sufism or Islam's spiritual heritage and lost interest in the experimental sciences, thus falling behind the scientific developments in Europe. Gülen feels strongly that Islam must make up for this deficiency today and in the future. He notes that our tomorrows will be constructed on the basis of knowledge since knowledge is power (Gülen 2004a: 255). In this connection Gülen is thinking of knowledge in the sense of *'ilm* or knowledge understood as what God desires from us on earth. Gülen takes this concept from the Qur'an where the word, *'ilm*, is the second most used word in that sacred text. Unfortunately, scholars in some Muslim countries are chased out of their homes, threatened by ignorant Mullahs, or silenced so that they are unable to guide rulers and policymakers. Gülen possibly has in mind the Prophet's *hadith* that says that the death of a scholar is the death of knowledge (Ahmed 2005:109).

Gülen would like Islam to take a new approach to the sciences and develop a new way of thinking. Rather than imitating the ancient, worn-out ways educational institutions must blaze new paths. In this regard Gülen would like to see a new philosophy of life developed. The new generation should be educated at every step of the way from kindergarten to the university level in a creative way. In this connection creativity means the ability to go beyond the confines of convention (Gülen 2004d: 255).

Second, Gülen observes that Huntington's thesis on the clash of civilizations takes conflict as its fundamental presupposition. During the Cold War there was indeed a clash between two opposing power blocks, viz., the NATO countries versus the Warsaw Pact countries. With the breakup of the Soviet Union, however, a clash of civilizations based on religious and cultural differences is being prepared. The creation of these new enemy fronts lays the foundation for the rule of the power blocs in the West. These power centers in the West have put their populations on alert against a conjectured and feared enemy, namely, Islam. In this way the masses are being prepared for war (Gülen 2004d: 256).

In contradistinction to Huntington Mr. Gülen notes that no religion has ever been based on conflict. In the early centuries of Christianity war was condemned and many Christians were pacifists, e.g., Tertullian. From time immemorial Christianity did not lay down any rules regarding war until St. Augustine in the fourth century elaborated the just war theory. The Islamic religion has likewise been based on peace, world harmony, and security. The Arabic term, *jihad*, from the root j-h-d means spiritual warfare or using all one's strength, moving toward an objective with all one's power and resisting every difficulty. The primary meaning of *jihad* is this: keeping one's carnal instincts and drives under control so as to make progress in the interior or spiritual life. Only in its secondary meaning does *jihad* mean war (Juergensmeyer 2000:81). Islam believes in *jihad* as a right to self-defense only in exceptional cases, just as the human body attempts to fight against the germs that have attacked it. (Gülen 2004d: 33).

Gülen notes that Islam has always breathed goodness and peace and has considered war a secondary event. War can only take place in accordance with certain rules and principles, analogous to the criteria for the doctrine of the just war in Christianity. These principles and rules have served the purpose of limiting war, mindful of the words in the Qur'an 5:8. In short, Islam developed a line of defense so that property, life, and freedom of belief can be protected.

Terrorist groups such as Al-Qaeda hijack the Qur'an for their own malevolent purposes and are guilty not of *jihad* or a defensive war (that can only be declared by a legitimate ruler), but of *hirabah* or terrorism (Sullivan 2005: 149). Gülen states that one ought to seek Islam through its own sources and its own true representatives throughout history rather than through the actions of a small minority that distort it (Gülen 2002b:96.)

Gülen's positive response to the clash of civilizations thesis consists of three parts encapsulated in the words, tolerance, interfaith dialogue, and compassionate love. The term, tolerance, appears about sixty times in Gülen's book, *Love & Tolerance*, not to mention the many times it appears in Gülen's *oeuvre* as a whole. Gülen finds the notion of tolerance and forgiveness deeply rooted in the Qur'an and *sunnah* or the customs/traditions of Muhammad (Qur'an 25:63; 25:72; 28:55). The servants of God say nothing unbecoming when they have ugly words thrown in their face. They also know how to ignore ugly or bad behavior. They take the high road bypassing negativity by acing with dignity. Gülen calls such people "heroes of tolerance." Their characteristic marks are tolerance, gentleness, and consideration for others. Gülen point out that when God sent Moses and Aaron, to the Pharaoh who claimed to be a divinity, God ordered them to speak softly and behave tolerantly (Qur'an 20:44). Mohammad, may his name be blessed, was tolerant toward Abu Sufyan, who persecuted the Prophet throughout his lifetime.

The Qur'an in 45:14 orders those whose hearts are filled with love to show tolerance and forgiveness to those who deny belief in the afterlife. Muslims are enjoined to be tolerant and forbearing toward others, expecting nothing in return. Like Yunus, the Turkish poet, true Muslims should not strike back against those who hit them. If attacked, a Muslim has the right to strike back with equal force. However, the Muslim who forgives the attacker has a higher level of faith than the one who exercises the right of self-defense. Muslims should not hold grudges against those who abuse them either (Gülen, 2000a: 258). Tolerance means we can benefit from ideas with which we disagree. Those who disagree with us, have something to give us provided we are truly open to what they say.

Gülen directs attention to the fact that if we do not forgive others, we in return have no right to expect forgiveness. All human beings are part of the same human family in the sense that we are fellow passengers on the ship called planet Earth. Gülen exhorts all of us to pull together to construct a better world built on tolerance. His optimistic and hopeful view of the future leads him to say that the twenty-first century will be called the age of tolerance. And he wants this tolerance to become permanent, that is, to last for all ages. His views about the future stand diametrically opposed to those of Mr. Huntington (Gülen 2004d: 49).

Gülen remains convinced that interfaith dialogue is sorely needed in today's world, one which is torn apart by conflict (Crane 2005:177). Dialogue for him means the coming together of two or more persons to discuss common issues. In the process of dialogue the partners form a close bond (Gülen 2004d: 50). On this score Gülen probably has in mind the Quranic word for dialogue, viz., *jidal* which means to be intimately engaged in a discussion or debate with another person (Ayoub 2007: 201).

Gülen notes that religion acts as a balm reconciling opposites: religion and revelation, this world and the next, the material world and the spiritual one. Optimally, the natural sciences ought to be steps of light leading people to God but instead have become a source of unbelief particularly in Western civilization. Islam, on the other hand, has always emphasized spirituality and spiritual matters. Since Christianity has been the religion most influenced by unbelief, Gülen envisions dialogue between Muslims and Christians as indispensable and exceedingly necessary (Gülen 2000a: 242).

Gülen argues that the very nature of religion demands a dialogue between all the major world religions This dialogue has particular urgency for the three Abrahamic religions, Judaism, Islam, and Christianity. There are as many reasons for Muslims and Jews to engage in interfaith dialogue as there are for Jews and Christians to come closer together. Historically speaking, the Muslim world has a solid record of dealing with the Jewish people. Jews have always been welcomed in times of troubled water, e.g., when the Ottoman Empire embraced Jews after their expulsion from Andalusia. Furthermore, Muslims were not involved in the *Shoah* or Holocaust, and Muslims have neither discriminated against them nor denied them their basic rights (Gülen 2000a: 243).

For historical reasons Muslims are and have been reluctant to enter into dialogue with Christianity. Western powers have killed more Muslims in the last century alone than all the Christians killed by Muslims in the history of the world. Today even liberal and educated Muslims feel that Western policies are designed to weaken Muslim power. Muslims wonder whether the West is continuing its thousand year systematic aggression against Islam with far more sophisticated methods than it has used in the past. No wonder Muslims are cold to the idea of entering into dialogue with Christians (Gülen 2000a: 243).

One of the main points Gülen makes repeatedly about interfaith dialogue is this: for interfaith dialogue to succeed we must forget the past, ignore polemics, and focus on common points (Gülen 2002b: 34). Some of the common points are these: both religions take their lineage from Abraham and the prophets. Both are monotheistic religions, that is, they believe in the oneness (*tawhid)* of God, revere Jesus and Mary, believe strongly in the power of faith, and call upon their followers to lead holy lives by means of prayer, fasting, almsgiving, and, in some Christian denominations, pilgrimage. It would be mutually beneficial if Islam and the West could enter into dialogue with one another (Fitzgerald 2006:141). Whereas the West possesses economic, military, scientific, and technological strength, Islam has a powerful, uncorrupted, and living spiritual tradition rooted in the Qur'an and *sunnah* or way the Prophet lived.

Gülen speaks forcefully about the power of compassionate love. This notion of compassionate love appears in many of Gülen's writings and sermons (Gülen 2002b: 42).Where does he derive this idea? His sources seem to be the Qur'an itself, the *hadith* or stories about what Muhammad did, and in his reading of the Sufi tradition, particularly Mevlana Rumi, the poet and mystic (Gülen 2004b:149). Gülen considers the love of God to be the purest source of compassionate love in the world. On the individual level we may call compassionate love the sultan that reigns on the throne of the human heart. On the social level there exists nothing more real or more lasting than love in any nation or society. Gülen waxes poetically in speaking of love describing it as the most radiant light, the greatest power in the world, and the chain or link that binds one person to another (Gülen 2004a:1). For Gülen it is axiomatic that our love should be as vast as the ocean and we should take every soul to our bosom (Gülen 2004d: 31).

These three entities-- tolerance, interfaith dialogue, and compassionate love-- are Gülen's positive response to Huntington's clash of civilizations thesis. Where Huntington sees conflict, Gülen sees peace. Where Huntington has a decidedly pessimistic view of the relationship between Islam and the West, Gülen speaks of hope and optimism. How do we account for the difference between the two perspectives? My answer would be this. If Huntington views the world as a political scientist, Gülen looks upon the same world through the lens of his Muslim faith (Gülen 2004d: 138).

Gülen's faith may be compared to a glass of water, without color, without odor, without taste, yet when held up to the light of day it is a prism that reflects and captures all the beauty, mystery, and wonder in the universe. Reality does not change. But our view of reality does change depending on the vantage-point from which we approach it. Faith gives us "new eyes." Faith is akin to the plastic lens we put on to see a movie in three dimensions. If we take off this lens during the movie, the screen looks blurred. With them on, reality appears the way it is. Mr. Gülen would remind Mr. Huntington that there are many more things under the heavens than are thought of in his political philosophy.

There are several practical implications to what Gülen proposes. First, one must distinguish between Islam as a religion and global Islamism which is a political ideology dressed in religious imagery and apocalyptical language (Desai, 2007, 96). As a religion Islam stands for tolerance, peace, dialogue, and compassionate love. However, ideologically, global Islamism is decidedly similar to secular ideologies of terror such as Leninism, the Baader-Meinhof Gang, and the Red Brigades, who were prepared to unleash violence against their own people.

Second, Gülen would remind us that if we want to start a revolution, we must begin with ourselves. We must eliminate from our vocabulary such words as "hatred," "enemy", and "revenge." Rather than striking back at others, we must 'retaliate' against others using gentleness and forgiveness as our *modus operandi*. We are called, says Gülen, to reach out in love to others with whom we interact on a daily basis. Thus we will be agents of change within our own circle of friends. In this way we will bridge the gap between Islam and the West in an infinitely small but important way.

Part III: Some Reflections on the Debate

The differences between Huntington and Gülen are stark. Where Huntington thinks in terms of polarities, Islam *or* the West in conflict with one another, Gülen opts for a more holistic view of global politics. Gülen sees Islam and the West working together in a harmonious fashion. In this connection the operative term for Gülen is dialogue. I would also point out that Huntington as a representative of the Western mind-set takes a wholly secular view of global politics. Gülen, on the contrary, takes a transcendent point of view, that is, he looks at global politics through the lens of his Islamic faith.

In this final section I raise the question "where does the truth lie?" Will there be a clash of civilizations as Huntington suggests or should we look forward in the twenty-first century to a "dialogue of civilizations," that is, to a more hopeful view of global politics in accordance with the vision of Gülen? My sympathies are decidedly much more in alignment with those of Gülen for these reasons:

i. In my opinion Huntington thinks too much in terms of dichotomies, for example, Islam vs. the West, and he does not make the necessary distinctions and shades of nuances. Huntington speaks of "Islam" and the "West" as if these are monolithic entities. Are not the terms, Islam, and the West, emaciating abstracts? I would argue that cultures and civilizations are not distinct boxes (Halliday 2005:126). For example, Japanese culture borrows substantive elements from China, India, and lately the United States. Christianity is the largest religion in the West yet where does Christianity take its origin if not from the Middle East? Every civilization, every culture, every religion, every language interacts with other civilizations, cultures, religions, and languages. Religions, for instance, do not exist in hermetically sealed chambers. Tibetan Buddhism had a symbiotic relationship with the Bon culture, so that Buddhism in Tibet differs greatly from Mahayana Buddhism as found in Korea.

Is not Islam today in and of the West, just as the West is in and of Islam? Are there not twenty million Muslim faithful in the West, six million of who live in the United States? There are over 1.6 million Muslims living in the United Kingdom, 38% of whom live in London, which has over 1,070 mosques, Muslim centres, and organizations. And do not many Muslim countries have a large and in some cases an equal number of Christians? Islam is no longer the religion of strangers in the West but the religion of next door neighbors. Muslims share with Christians such things as neighborhoods, schools, athletic facilities, hospitals, and cemeteries (Ayoub 2007:67).

I would note that both China and India maintain that the West is one civilization block derived from three parts, viz., Europe, Byzantium, and the world of Mediterranean Islam (Sullivan 2005:141). Finally, I would observe that the Ottomans were more European than Asian. The sultans very often married European women and the elite government officials in the Ottoman Empire were all converts from Europe. In fact, some nationalist Turks today still blame the Ottomans for suppressing Turks living at the time of their rule.

ii. Were not many past wars intra-civilization or intra-cultural ones? Were not the most violent conflicts of the twentieth century between Christian nations in Europe? The Iran-Iraq war was within the same Islamic civilization. This war lasted from 1980-88 and was very bloody. Two other examples may clarify matters. For years there has been a serious tension in Southeast Asia between China and Japan. However, both countries have deep roots in the Confucian tradition. On the border of Iran we have Armenian Christians in a dispute with Azerbaijani Shiites over the region of Karabakh. Yet Turkey, a Muslim country, supports the Azerbaijani Shiites because Iran, its strategic rival, supports the Armenian Christians. Would anyone want to call this a *sidam al-hadharat* or a clash of civilizations? (Halliday 2005:126).

iii. Mr. Huntington observes that the relationship between Islam and the West has been conflictual for the past fourteen centuries. Hence he argues that this adversarial relationship will continue on into the future. I have a different take on history. I would not deny that Christians and Muslims have been at odds over the centuries, going back at least to the time of the Crusade against Islam in Spain and in West Asia, or the annual Ottoman campaign in Europe (Robinson 2005:86). There have been times, though, when Islam and Christianity have interacted in a mutually beneficial way, yet Mr. Huntington seems to ignore this part of history. There are some Christian monasteries today in Anatolia, in the Tur Abdin region which go back to the year 570. In these monasteries the monks and laity still speak Aramaic, the language of Jesus. These monasteries have survived until now thanks to the often forgotten tolerance of Islam vis-à-vis its Christian subjects (Dalrymple 2005: 94).

When first confronted by the armies of the Prophet Muhammad, the early Byzantines thought that Islam was a variant of Christianity. This is not altogether surprising when both religions have prophets, accept the New Testament as a sacred scripture, speak of Jesus and Mary, place a premium on holiness of life, and stress such spiritual practices as almsgiving, fasting, and daily prayer. For this and other reasons the early Muslims treated Jews and Christians with respect. For example, when the second caliph, Abu Bakr, stood on the borders of Syria he instructed his soldiers that they would find monks in their cells but please do not bother them, because they have secluded themselves for the sake of God (Dalrymple 2005:95).

When the third caliph, Umar ibn al-Khattab visited Syria, he stayed with the bishop of Ayla and made a point of meeting with the Christian holy men in the town. Umar ibn al-Khattab did not pray in a church, fearing that if he did, Muslims would convert the church into a mosque after he left the town. Muslims and Christians prayed side by side for many years in the great churches of the Middle East. At Damascus, for example, Muslims and Christians used the basilica of St. John for worship, though, fifty years later the building became known as the great Umayyad mosque (Dalrymple 2005: 95). I would also note that Muslims, Christians, and Jews living in Spain created a rich cultural synthesis which saw its acme in terms of high quality architecture, art, and literature, which lasted under Muslim rule until 1492 (Ahmed 2005:106). And Arab-Muslim knowledge transmitted through Spain and Italy greatly benefited and enriched medieval Europe. Up until the nineteenth century many Europeans measured themselves against the world of Islam (Robinson 2005:87).

Mr. Gülen has written a very perceptive book on Sufism. Islamic mysticism or Sufism (*tasawwuf*) refers to a lifelong process of spiritual development. I contend that Sufism has been greatly influenced by Christianity. The word, *suf*, means wool, the distinctive clothing material of Eastern Christian monks adopted by Islam's early mystics and holy men. Sufism has always had an affinity with the desert, stressed miracles, visions, and mortification of the flesh all of which show remarkable similarities to the mystical strands of Eastern Christianity. In fact, Mevlana Rumi tried to reconcile both religions. Moreover, the more radical Sufis and Eastern Christian mystics wore heavy chains. By punishing the flesh both groups of ascetics endeavored to induce spiritual ecstasy and visions (Dalrymple 2005:97).

The point I draw from this is that Christian and Muslim worlds have shaped each other. As Francis Robinson has demonstrated, the roots of Islamic civilization are found in the monotheistic and Hellenistic traditions of the Eastern Roman Empire. He argues that Islam's universalism comes from the religious and political universalism of Constantine's Byzantine Empire (Robinson 2005: 87). William Dalrymple has shown that the Muslim prostrations and bowings in the Muslim *salat* or prayer seem to have their roots in the older Syrian Orthodox tradition still practiced in churches without pews in the Levant, particularly in Syria, Lebanon, and Israel (Dalrymple 2005:96).

iv.   Part of the tension between Christianity and Islam at least historically has been the exclusive truth claims both religions have made (Knitter 1995:26). Scholars in religious studies today are beginning to realize that no religion has a total monopoly on the truth and salvation. (Knitter 2002: 216). Rather, each religion has its own tradition and spiritual heritage. Some Muslims now understand that religious diversity is divinely ordained (Qur'an 5:48). Muslims believe that all the biblical prophets and Prophet Muhammad were sent by the very same God. Muslims have an obligation to understand and respect other religious paths in the interests of justice, love, peace, social harmony and in the interest of truth. The Declaration on Non-Christian Religions from the Second Vatican Council (1962-65) gives a theological basis for a fruitful dialogue between Muslims and Catholics (Hinze 2006: 222). Mr. Gülen understands how beneficial such a dialogue can be since Islam and Christianity have between them over two billion followers, more than any other two religions in the world.

v.   Theological and religious reasons may have been a large part of the conflict between Islam and Christianity in the past. Today that is less the case. The problem between Islam and the West has little to do with the Qur'an or the New Testament. Rather, it concerns power, both global and local. I see the so-called clash of civilizations as a conflict with multiple, conventional causes (Pfaff 2006:13). Some observers believe that the central driver in global tensions concerns the conflict between Israel and the Palestinian territories (Bennis 2003: 50). This does not mean that it is the overt cause of all tensions between Western and Muslim societies. However, the Israeli-Palestinian issue has symbolic value, coloring political and cross-cultural relations that transcend its limited geographic scope. It would be beyond the parameters of this paper to fully make this argument. I mention it only to move on.

Gülen is absolutely correct in his assertion that cultures need not clash. They can co-exist. We need to accept, yes even rejoice in diversity instead of rejecting it. God made us in his own image yet we all came out differently. Our challenge is this: we must somehow find God's image in someone whose color is different, who speaks a different language, or worships God differently than we do (Sacks 2005: 134). I am reminded of the words of Imam Abd al-Raouf who said: "We earnestly urge (our friends in the West) to go back to God, to turn their face to Him... What was morally right for Noah, Abraham, Moses, Jesus and Muhammad must be the same for us whether we live in America, Europe, Asia, or Africa. We all should remember that we are brothers, members of the (same) human family. (Therefore) let us live together in peace" (Boase 2005:154).

GIVING PRECEDENCE TO COMMON POINTS: THE LIMITS OF THE OTHERNESS IN FETHULLAH GÜLEN'S DIALOGIC METHODOLOGY FOR INTERFAITH ENCOUNTERS

Irina Vainovski-Mihai

Abstract

This paper examines Fethullah Gülen's teaching on interfaith encounters highlighting his dialogic methodology proposed for a globalised world in which Samuel Huntington's idea of the 'clash of civilisations' (Clash of Civilizations and the Remaking of World Order, 1997) is still prominent. This idea, concludes Gülen, stems from the lack of trust in the religion of the "Other" and, rather often than not, from easily passing over the common points. According to Gülen, dialogue is not a superfluous endeavour, but an imperative ("Dialogue is a must") and it should start by "Giving precedence to common points". Gülen holds that the tendency toward factionalism exists within human nature. A meaningful and nonetheless necessary goal, he says, should be to make this tendency non-threatening and even beneficial. To fully appreciate the significance of Gülen's accomplishments, one must understand the perspective from which he approaches the subject of interfaith dialogue. Based on his thinking as noted above, the purpose of this paper is to set out in some detail the way in which this renowned Islamic thinker limits the "domain" of the Otherness (Homi Bhabha, The Location of Culture, 2004; Nation and Narration, 1990) to make dialogue possible through overcoming both Orientalism (Edward Said, Orientalism, 1978) and Occidentalism (Ian Buruma and Avishai Margalit, Occidentalism: the West in the Eyes of its Enemies, 2004). Challenging the discourse of conflict and focusing on common points may be an important strategy when mutual suspicions are still prevalent and when the field of postcolonial studies stand witness to conflicting processes of refraction (Patricia Crone, Medieval Islamic Political Thought, 2005; Amin Maalouf, Les Croisades vues par les Arabes, 1986).

Those who act according to what they have seen are not as successful as those who act according to what they know. Those who act according to what they know are not as successful as those who act according to their conscience. (Gülen 2005:106)

This article aims to explore Fethullah Gülen's teaching on interfaith encounters highlighting his dialogic methodology proposed to a globalized world in which models and theories of clashes are still prominent. These theories, concludes Gülen, stem from the lack of trust in the religion of the "Other" and, rather often than not, from easily passing over the common points. According to Gülen, dialogue is not a superfluous endeavor, but an imperative ("Dialogue is a must") and it should start by "Giving precedence to common points". Gülen holds that the tendency toward factionalism exists within human nature. A meaningful and nonetheless necessary goal, he says, should be to make this tendency non-threatening and even beneficial. To fully appreciate the significance of Gülen's accomplishments and the challenges he is facing, one must understand the perspective from which he approaches the subject of interfaith dialogue. Based on the above-mentioned landmarks of his viewpoints regarding the representation constructs, the purpose of my paper is to investigate the way in which this renowned Islamic thinker limits the "domain" of the Otherness or dilutes many of the apparently instituted boundaries.

My paper starts from the assumption that recognizing the Other on common grounds is a prerequisite of dialogue. The first section of the essay focuses on conceptual frameworks of defining the "relevant" alterity (Orientalism, Balkanism, Occidentalism) and theories of conflict (models of clashes, competing meta-narratives). The second section looks into identity markers expressed or implied by Sufi thinkers (Al-Ghazali, Rumi, Nursi). The third section discusses Gülen's awareness with the Other and, consequently (as detailed in the fourth section) his identification of common grounds for dialogue.

To achieve the aim of my study, throughout all the four sections, Gülen will be presented in a textual exchange of ideas with other thinkers and authors.

In Search of the Other

The first question regarding the possibility or impossibility to establish a dialogue revolves around the issue of the Otherness and the way in which the representation of the Other is construed. From the mere cognitive category (that generally separates the world into "us" and "them"), to the more intricate pattern of exclusion (in-group, out-group) and to the confrontational mentality (*us*-versus-*them*), the discourse on identities assumes different statuses and has distinctive implications. "… For the nation to exist, it is presupposed that there is some other community, some other nation, from which it needs to distinguish itself." (Triandafyllidou 1998:594) Furthermore, the relevance of the identity is valued in terms of alienation: "(…) la culture des autres est perçue essentiellement comme un écart par rapport à la nôtre, non dans sa propre cohérence." (Todorov 1989: 342).

For Edward Said (in his book first published in 1978 and then reprinted in 1995 under the title *Orientalism: Western Conceptions of the Orient*) "Orientalism" is a discursive system and a cultural creation through which the West imagined the East as its immature Other. Orientalism, he asserts is "a style of thought based upon an ontological and epistemological distinction made between 'the Orient' and 'the Occident'". (Said 1995:8) Said's notion on the modes of making if not an entirely conflictual Other, at least a problematic one, is brought further conceptually and extended geographically by Larry Wolff (*Inventing Eastern Europe: The Map of Civilization on the Mind of the Enlightenment*, 1994) and Maria Todorova (*Imagining the Balkans*, 1997). An attempt of a mirror image came in 2004, with Ian Buruma's and Avishai Margalit's *Occidentalism: The West in the Eyes of its Enemies*. The representations of the West are equally biased and stereotyping, Buruma and Margalit show, and even more, they formulate the conflicting identities already in the title. It is beyond the scope of this paper to evaluate the terms *Occidentalism* and *West* as set forth by the two authors in a rather unsystematic way. Nonetheless, they offer a counter-reflection to the other imagined identities (Orientalism and Balkanism), a partial one in as much as Buruma and Margalit identify the roots of Occidentalism (hostility to the city, repulsion to the material life, adherence to commercial rather then heroic models, etc.) in both the East and Europe.

All the above-mentioned authors achieve, to paraphrase Fethullah Gülen's words, to sum up an entire book and theory in a title. Literally, Gülen says that "sometimes the sun appears in an atom, a flood in a drop, and a book in a sentence" (Gülen 2005:108), after he warns that "every flood comes from tiny drops whose existence and size are neglected. Gradually, it reaches a level that cannot be resisted. A society's body is always open to such types of flood." (Gülen 2005:107)

Religion remains a strong cultural signifier embedded with many layers of meaning and a crucial dimension in the representation of the Other. (Vainovski-Mihai 2000:192) In so far as identity turns out to be meaningful only through the distinction from the alterity, the 'significant others' (Triandafyllidou 1998:595) thus conceived, invented, imagined (to use Said's, Wolff's and Todorova's terms) may shape up the construction of the in-group individuality itself (Appollonia 1996:138) and draw a clear-cut borderline between the in-group of *Us* and the out-group of *Them*. Nowadays religion is no more a mere marker of the otherness in tune with the overtones of travel literature, in which the author's homeland "serves as organizing center for the points of view, the scales of comparison, the approaches and evaluations" (Bakhtin 1990:103) neither is it a label for exoticism. "Exoticism presupposes a deliberate opposition of what is alien to what is one's own, the otherness of what is foreign is emphasized, savored, and elaborately depicted against an implied background of one's own ordinary and familiar world." (Bakhtin 1981:101)

Currently much intellectual effort, in academic circles as well as in the larger political and cultural arena, is devoted to probing many of the world's problems in terms of a clash between secular modernity and religious tradition. At the center of this controversy is a critique of Islam, treated as a more or less coherent culture, civilization, or historical tradition. Typically, Islamic 'fundamentalism' is seen as the prototype of religious extremism. And Islamic 'civilization', according to scholars such as Bernard Lewis and Samuel P. Huntington, has remained 'backward' in comparison with 'the West', because 'something went wrong' earlier in 'Islamic history' (Matin-Asgari 2004:293). In fact, less smoothly than in Matin-Asgari's paraphrase, Huntington claims in all-encompassing terms that "the underlying problem for the West is not Islamic fundamentalism. It is Islam". (Huntington 1996:217) Huntington's article "The Clash of Civilizations?" appeared in the Summer 1993 issue of *Foreign Affairs* and then developed into a book published three years later. His theory of clashes stands on the assumption that people define their identity by what they are not and makes, among others, the dichotomy between Western "*homo economicus*" and Eastern "*homo Islamicus*". (Bilici 2006: 16) He puts forth the same belligerent way of thought with regard to the Western multicultural communities, within which the viable solution for co-existence is not the respect for differences as part of our nature (Gülen 2004:249), but assimilation: "Western Culture is challenged by groups within Western societies. One such challenge comes from immigrants from other civilizations who reject assimilation and continue to adhere to and to propagate the values, customs, and cultures of their home societies." (Huntington 1996:304).

On his turn, Edward W. Said stands far from denying the theory of global cultural conflict, only that he plants it on other ground and labels it as "The Clash of Ignorance". (Said 2001) "In fact, Huntington is an ideologist, someone who wants to make 'civilizations' and 'identities' into what they are not: shut-down, sealed-off entities that have been purged of the myriad currents and countercurrents that animate human history, and that over centuries have made it possible for that history not only to contain wars of religion and imperial conquest but also to be one of exchange, crossfertilization and sharing. This far less visible history is ignored in the rush to highlight the ludicrously compressed and constricted warfare that 'the clash of civilizations' argues is the reality." (Said 2001:12)

Thomas Michel implies, too, that conflicts, tensions, and misunderstandings proceed from ignorance. The visibility of Islam in the last decades is often due to sensational events complemented by a certain disinterest or suspicion towards non-violent forms of Islam and the strives in finding common grounds for dialogue. "Someone whose knowledge of Islam is limited to the headlines of the daily newspapers is likely to believe that the religion teaches terrorism, suicide attacks, oppression of women, and hatred for those outside its community." (Michel 2004:i-ii)

In the same vein, Philip Marfleet argues: "Among the many criticisms of Huntington, one is central: that in order to construct global cultural blocs he has imposed uniformity upon a vast range of people of diverse beliefs and practices. This homogenization of cultures serves to simplify to an extreme degree the complexity of human experience. It denies the fluidity of cultural forms – the complex processes of appropriation and modification of ideas which have taken place for millennia across all manner of borders." (Marfleet 2003:83)

Among the theories of conflicts, a third one is gaining preeminence, with Stanley Hoffmann's "clash of globalizations". (Hoffmann 2002) His model is not grounded on the conflict between separate civilizations, but between different visions of globalization like secularism, fundamentalism or multiculturalism and the sharing of commonly acceptable values. "How can one make the global house more livable? The answer presupposes a political philosophy that would be both just and acceptable even to those whose values have other foundations." (Hoffmann 2002:109)

On account of Hoffmann's model, John O. Voll includes Gülen among the designers of bridges arching over the clashes of globalizations: "In the clashing visions of globalizations, Fethullah Gülen is a force in the development of the Islamic discourse of globalized multicultural pluralism. As the impact of the educational activities of those influenced by him attests, his vision bridges modern and postmodern, global and local, and has a significant influence in the contemporary debates that shape the visions of the future of Muslims and non-Muslims alike." (Voll 2003: 247)

Meanwhile, Michel is regarding Gülen's thinking and deeds as an alternative to the theory of the "clash of civilizations": "The need for dialogue among people of faith has been underscored by the events of the past few years. Interreligious dialogue is seen as an alternative to the much-discussed 'clash of civilizations'. Those who do not subscribe to the theory that a civilizational clash is inevitable are proposing instead a dialogue of civilizations, an exchange of views aimed at mutual enrichment, a sharing of insights that can lead all to a deeper understanding of the nature of God and God's will for humankind on this planet." (Michel 2004:i).

As for Gülen himself, the clash is a matter of deep awareness and accountability both for the Self and the Other: "Humanity is a tree, and nations are its branches. Events that appear as heavy winds hurl them against each other and cause them to clash. Of course, the resulting harm is felt by the tree. This is the meaning of: 'Whatever we do, we do it to ourselves.'" (Gülen 2005:106) On the other hand, confrontation may result from turning a deaf ear to the seemingly contradictory ideas of the Other: "People who do not think like you might be very sincere and beneficial, so do not oppose every idea that seems contradictory and scare them off. Seek ways to benefit from their opinions, and strike up a dialogue with them. Otherwise, those who are kept at a distance and led to dissatisfaction because they don't think like us will form huge masses that confront and smash us. Even if such dissatisfied people have never achieved anything positive, the number of states they have destroyed is beyond counting." (Gülen 2005:89)

Gülen makes here a good point in the appeal to dialogue and in showing the possible conse-quences of the "competing meta-narratives", a phenomenon appreciated by Robert A. Hunt as one of the main problems facing the interfaith dialogue in the contemporary world. "It is the problem of Western civilization claiming to provide the paradigm within which it can understand all other civilizations better than they understand themselves. It is the notion that science can understand religion better than religion understands itself. It is the notion that Christianity understands other religions better than they understand themselves, or that Islam understands Christianity and other religions better than they understand themselves. In the face of such meta-narrative claims, all dialogue essentially ceases because from within a meta-narrative there is no need to listen to the other." (Hunt 2006:6)

Maintaining the dichotomy between Western "*homo economicus*" and Eastern "*homo Islamicus*" reinforces the monistic conception of modernity as a Western product. The sub-stitution of "homo Islamicus" with "Muslim homo economicus", on the other hand, implies a multiplicity of modernities and the existence of commonalities. Emphasis on such com-monalities enables interaction and cooperation rather than competition between these two identities (Cf. Bilici 2006:16). Or, as Gülen puts it into words: "We were in friction with one another. We separated in order to solve the problem, but we didn't attain what we expected to. As a result, we lost our own paradise." (Gülen 2000a:218)

Sufi Perceptions of the Other

"Although a term comes into popular or academic usage at a certain given historical period, this does not mean that the concept itself is new. The idea may have been discussed in previ-ous ages, but other terms were used to describe it. [Terms like] 'tolerance', 'engagement with the other', and 'future of dialogue' are good examples of this." – marks out Michel (2002:5) in his analyzing Said Nursi's views on the engagement with the Other and assumes the task to identify Bediüzzaman's ideas couched in the popularly accepted terminology of the day. Michel points out the nine rules of sincerity spelled out in *Risale-i Nur* as a summing up of Nursi's principles of tolerance towards alterity (defined as a "particular otlook"):

 i. To act positively, that is, out of love for one's own outlook, avoiding enmity for other outlooks, not criticizing them, interfering in their beliefs and sciences, or in any way concerning oneself with them.

ii.   To unite within the fold of Islam, irrespective of particular outlook, remembering those numerous ties of unity that evoke love, brotherhood and concord.

iii.   To adopt the just rule of conduct that the follower of any right outlook has the right to say, "My outlook is true, or the best," but not that "My outlook alone is true," or that "My outlook alone is good," thus implying the falsity or repugnance of all other outlooks.

iv.   To consider that union with the people of truth is a cause of Divine succour and the high dignity of religion.

v.   To realize that the individual resistance of the most powerful person against the attacks through its genius of the mighty collective force of the people of misguidance and falsehood, which arises from their solidarity, will inevitably be defeated, and through the union of the people of truth, to create a joint and collective force also, in order to preserve justice and right in the face of that fearsome collective force of misguidance.

vi.   In order to preserve truth from the assaults of falsehood,

vii.   To abandon the self and its egoism,

viii. And give up the mistaken concept of self-pride,

ix.   And cease from all insignificant feelings aroused by rivalry." (Nursi 2000:203)

Moreover, Nursi ranks the designation of the relevant Other on terms of moral values and ethics when he speaks about "the collective personality of Europe": "It should not be misunderstood; Europe is two. One follows the sciences which serve justice and right and the industries beneficial for the life of society through the inspiration it has received from true Christianity; this first Europe I am not addressing. I am rather addressing the second corrupt Europe which, through the darkness of the philosophy of Naturalism, supposing the evils of civilization to be its virtues, has driven mankind to vice and misguidance. As follows: On my journey of the spirit at that time I said to Europe's collective personality, which apart from beneficial science and the virtues of civilization, holds in its hand meaningless, harmful philosophy and noxious, dissolute civilization." (Nursi 2000:160)

J. B. Schlubach (2005) steps further back along the Sufi tradition in quest of the representation of the Other. Although, when he is evaluating al-Ghazali's and Jalaluddin Rumi's thinking, he is not setting up his textual methodology like Michel, he is ultimately finding the perception of the Other standing implicitly in the discourse of tolerance. He concludes that identity markers are entirely melt away and "tolerance does more than just hinder hostilities. In this sense of tolerance, the boundaries between Other and One become indistinct and lose focus." (Schlubach 2005:6)

Pertaining to the generation following Nursi, Gülen engaged in Nursi's call for dialogue taking up equally an entire rich and generous Sufi heritage. "Gülen must be located and understood squarely within that Sufi tradition indicated by al-Ghazali and Rumi. Both the latter insist on non-belligerence in love and do not prescribe strategies for foreign affairs. Both move toward the ultimate end of dimming distinctions between Self and Other, not of prescriptions for peaceably protecting borders. Both lean away from the possibility of defining each other as "other." Both look on the world of humankind as oriented to eternity, not hegemony. Both define Gülen." (Schlubach 2005:17)

Gülen's Constructs of Otherness

In a broad overview of Gülen's and his movement's national-security identity, Hasan Kösebalaban (Kösebalaban 2003) distinguishes three perceptions of the Other defined by varying degrees of separation: (1) a strong degree of common identification with the Turkic world (a Kantian Other in which the distinction between the Self and Other is weak, where the Self perceives the Other as part of its own group), (2) a lack of common identification with the West but a desire to integrate with Western institutions (an approximate of the Lockean Other, where the Self perceives the Other as a peaceful rival), (3) a strong lack of common identification with Iran (an identity shaped in terms of a Hobbesian culture of anarchy in which not only the distinction between Self and Other is clear, but also the Self perceives the Other as a security threat). (Cf. Kösebalaban 2003:172-173).

Although Kösebalaban applies his research primarily on national-security identity, further on he reformulates Gülen's Lockean Other with a view to religion and leaves aside the expression of antagonism: "For him [Gülen], 'it cannot be imagined that a devout person would be against the West', as the West became supreme following universally applicable rules and principles." (Kösebalaban 2003:177) Thus, we come upon the irenism characteristic to Gülen's facts and words, like the following: "To devotees, the value of their ideals transcends that of the earthly ones to such an extent that it is almost impossible to divert them from what they seek – God's gratuitous consent – and lead them to any other ideal. In fact, stripped entirely of finite and transient things, devotees undergo such a transformation in their hearts to turn to God that they are changed because they recognize no goal other than their ideal. Since they devote themselves completely to making people love God and to being loved by God, dedicating their lives to enlightening others, and, once again, because they have managed to orient their goal in this unified direction, which in a sense contributes to the value of this ideal, they avoid divisive and antagonist thoughts, such as "they" and "we", "others" and "ours". (Gülen 2004:100)

Deliberation as social learning is meant to develop an understanding of various ideational worlds. "Once participants acknowledge that they are interacting with representatives of other traditions, the purpose of deliberation becomes one of appropriation and evaluation of other perspectives by mastering the skills of putting oneself into others' shoes." (Kanra 2005:516) The awareness with the Other, the dialogical approach may transform the experience of the Other into an experience of the Self. "Different positions mean different understandings. Once you accept that, you can benefit from others' thoughts and ideas." (Gülen 2000a:206) The hermeneutic exercise of accepting the difference, as a prerequisite to communication, broadens one's ideational scope, without sweeping away the original perspective. "In the fusion of horizons, nobody is fully detached from his/her subjective views, yet arrives at a new juncture…" (Kanra 2005:517).

In today's global village, differences (beliefs, races, customs, traditions) increase in visibility and interact more and more. The desire of leveling the differences means wishing for the impossible, points out Gülen, because each individual is like a unique realm unto himself/herself, therefore a peaceful coexistence "lies in respecting all these differences, considering these differences to be part of our nature and in ensuring that people appreciate these differences. Otherwise, it is unavoidable that the world will devour itself in a web of conflicts, disputes, fights, and the bloodiest of wars, thus preparing the way for its own end." (Gülen 2004:250) The respect for the Other is equaled by Gülen to the respect for the Self: "When interacting with others, always regard whatever pleases and displeases yourself as the measure. Desire for others what your own ego desires, and do not forget that whatever conduct displeases you will displease others. If you do this, you will be safe not only from misconduct and bad behavior, but also from hurting others." (Gülen 2005:59) Frustrations might be a result of somebody's own (mis)conduct, because "Deserving what we expect is very important." (Gülen 2004:34)

Common Points and Shared Responsibilities

I believe and hope that the world of the new millennium will be a happier, more just, and more compassionate place, contrary to the fears of some people. Islam, Christianity, and Judaism all stem from the same root; all have essentially the same basic beliefs, and are nourished from the same source. Although they have lived as rival religions for centuries, the common points between them and their shared responsibility to build a happy world for all of the creatures of God make interfaith dialogue among them necessary. (Gülen 2004:231)

Gülen rejects conflicting attitudes, prejudice and half-truths and entirely understands the growing interdependencies of today. Establishing and maintaining dialogue should be rooted in giving precedence to the common points and in avoiding the divisive issues. Completely aware that "globalization is rapidly making dialogue between holders of meta-narrative claims a near existential necessity" (Hunt 2006:6), Gülen invites to a emotional coexistence through dialogue across differences and on the basis of joint ethical criteria. A famous verse of the Qur'an calls the People of the Book to a common ground with Muslims:

Say: Oh People of the Book! Come to an agreement between us that we will not worship other than God, and that we shall ascribe no partner unto him, and that none of us shall take others for lords beside God... (Qur'an, 3:64)

All the great universal religions share the same ethical values. "Regardless of how their adherents implement their faith in their daily lives, such generally accepted values as love, respect, tolerance, forgiveness, mercy, human rights, peace, brotherhood, and freedom are all values exalted by religion. Most of these values are accorded the highest precedence in the messages brought by Moses, Jesus, and Muhammad, upon them be peace, as well as in the messages of Buddha and even Zarathustra, Lao-Tzu, Confucius, and the Hindu prophets." (Gülen 2000b:4) Thus, Gülen limits the distance between the Self and the Other and defines dialogue as "an activity that has human beings at its axis" (Gülen 2004:50) forming a bond between people. Meanwhile he rejects confrontational models of dialogue as detrimental. In support of this approach he is quoting Bediüzzaman Said Nursi: "'Those who are happy about their opponent's defeat in debate have no mercy.' He explains the reason for this: 'You gain nothing by defeating someone. If you are defeated and the other person is victorious, then you would have corrected one of your mistakes.'" (Gülen 2004:74).

As Hunt aptly remarks, the Muslim Sufi tradition offers Gülen a generous resource for overcoming the problem of competing meta-narratives and "it allows him, and it can allow those inspired by him, to come to fellow humans not just as bearers of truth, but as seekers of truth." (Hunt 2006:9) Through him, Muslim practice and traditions are preserved and brought into consonance with the timely need for interfaith encounters meant to draw understanding and sharing of interpretations.

Conclusions

This paper showed that the images built on the *Us-Them* disparity tend to create a perceptual gap much larger than the real one, stimulating divergence. Discourses on imagined entities like "Islam", "The Orient", "Europe", "The West" threaten to become a significant obstacle to setting up a dialogic methodology. Our findings in this paper higlight that the drawbacks of such conflicting or competing images and meta-narratives are felt equally by both entities. "Whatever we do, we do it to ourselves." Or, to use the terminology of post-colonial studies, one is both the subject and the object.

This study pinpoints Fethullah Gülen's methodology fundamentals for interfaith encounters, in a hermeneutical approach. Gülen's concrete interaction with the Other deserves a further study on its own.

Finally, I shall use Gülen's own words in which he is condensing his notion of dialog and is setting out its main pillar: "I believe that interfaith dialogue is a must today, and that the first step in establishing it is forgetting the past, ignoring polemical arguments, and giving precedence to common points, which far outnumber polemical ones (Gülen 2000b:6).

TOLERANCE IN THE THEOLOGY AND THOUGHT OF A. J. CONYERS AND FETHULLAH GÜLEN (EXTENDED ABSTRACT)

David B Capes

In his book *The Long Truce* (Spence Publishing, 2001) the late A. J. Conyers argues that tolerance, as practiced in western democracies, is not a public virtue; it is a political strategy employed to establish power and guarantee profits. Tolerance, of course, seemed to be a reasonable response to the religious wars of the sixteenth and seventeenth centuries, but tolerance based upon indifference to all values except political power and materialism relegated ultimate questions of meaning to private life. Conyers offers another model for tolerance based upon values and resources already resident in pre-Reformation Christianity. In this paper, we consider Conyer's case against the modern, secular form of tolerance and its current practice. We examine his attempt to reclaim the practice of Christian tolerance based upon humility, hospitality and the "powerful fact" of the incarnation. Furthermore, we bring the late Conyers into dialog with Fethullah Gülen, a Muslim scholar, prolific writer and the source of inspiration for a transnational civil society movement. We explore how both Conyers and Gülen interpret their scriptures in order to fashion a theology and political ideology conducive to peaceful co-existence. Finally, because Gülen's identity has been formed within the Sufi tradition, we reflect on the spiritual resources within Sufi spirituality that make dialog and toleration key values for him.

Conyers locates various values, practices and convictions in the Christian message that pave the way for authentic toleration. These include humility, trust, reconciliation, the interrelatedness of all things, the paradox of power--that is, that strength is found in weakness and greatness in service—hope, the inherent goodness of creation, and interfaith dialog. Conyers refers to this latter practice as developing "the listening heart" and "the open soul."

In his writings and oral addresses, Gülen prefers the term *hoshgoru* (literally, "good view") to "tolerance." Conceptually, the former term indicates actions of the heart and the mind that include empathy, inquisitiveness, reflection, consideration of the dialog partner's context, and respect for their positions. The term "tolerance" does not capture the notion of *hoshgoru*. Elsewhere, Gülen finds even the concept of *hoshgoru* insufficient, and employs terms with more depth in interfaith relations, such as respect and an appreciation of the positions of your dialog partner.

The resources Gülen references in the context of dialog and empathic acceptance include the Qur'an, the prophetic tradition, especially lives of the companions of the Prophet, the works of great Muslim scholars and Sufi masters, and finally, the history of Islamic civilization. Among his Qur'anic references, Gülen alludes to verses that tell the believers to represent humility, peace and security, trustworthiness, compassion and forgiveness (The Qur'an, 25:63, 25:72, 28:55, 45:14, 17:84), to avoid armed conflicts and prefer peace (4:128), to maintain cordial relationships with the "people of the book," and to avoid argumentation (29:46). But perhaps the most important references of Gülen with respect to interfaith relations are his readings of those verses that allow Muslims to fight others. Gülen positions these verses in historical context to point out one by one that their applicability is conditioned upon active hostility. In other words, in Gülen's view, nowhere in the Qur'an does God allow fighting based on differences of faith.

An important factor for Gülen's embracing views of empathic acceptance and respect is his view of the inherent value of the human. Gülen's message is essentially that every human person exists as a piece of art created by the Compassionate God, reflecting aspects of His compassion. He highlights love as the *raison d'etre* of the universe. "Love is the very reason of existence, and the most important bond among beings," Gülen comments. A failure to approach fellow humans with love, therefore, implies a deficiency in our love of God and of those who are beloved to God. The lack of love for fellow human beings implies a lack of respect for this monumental work of art by God. Ultimately, to remain indifferent to the conditions and suffering of fellow human beings implies indifference to God himself.

While advocating love of human beings as a pillar of human relations, Gülen maintains a balance. He distinguishes between the love of fellow human beings and our attitude toward some of their qualities or actions. Our love for a human being who inflicts suffering upon others does not mean that we remain silent toward his violent actions. On the contrary, our very love for that human being as a human being, as well as our love of those who suffer, necessitate that we participate actively in the elimination of suffering.

In the end we argue that strong resonances are found in the notion of authentic toleration based on humility advocated by Conyers and the notion of *hoshgoru* in the writings of Gülen.

GÜLEN'S RETHINKING OF ISLAMIC PATTERN AND ITS SOCIO-POLITICAL EFFECTS

Fabio Vicini

Abstract

Over recent decades Islamic traditions have emerged in new forms in different parts of the Muslim world, interacting differently with secular and neo-liberal patterns of thought and action. In Turkey Fethullah Gülen's community has been a powerful player in the national debate about the place of Islam in individual and collective life. Through emphasis on the importance of 'secular education' and a commitment to the defence of both democratic principles and international human rights, Gülen has diffused a new and appealing version of how a 'good Muslim' should act in contemporary society. In particular he has defended the role of Islam in the formation of individuals as ethically-responsible moral subjects, a project that overlaps significantly with the 'secular' one of forming responsible citizens. Concomitantly, he has shifted the Sufi emphasis on self-discipline/self-denial towards an active, socially-oriented service of others – a form of religious effort that implies a strongly 'secular' faith in the human ability to make this world better. This paper looks at the lives of some members of the community to show how this pattern of conduct has affected them. They say that teaching and learning 'secular' scientific subjects, combined with total dedication to the project of the movement, constitute, for them, ways to accomplish Islamic deeds and come closer to God. This leads to a consideration of how such a rethinking of Islamic activism has influenced political and sociological transition in Turkey, and a discussion of the potential contribution of the movement towards the development of a more human society in contemporary Europe.

From the 1920s onwards, in the context offered by the decline and collapse of the Ottoman Empire, Islamic thinkers, associations and social movements have proliferated their efforts in order to suggest ways to live a good "Muslim life" under newly emerging conditions. Prior to this period, different generations of Muslim Reformers had already argued the compatibility of Islam with reason and "modernity", claiming for the need to renew Islamic tradition recurring to *ijtihad*[1]. Yet until the end of the XIX century, traditional educational systems, public forms of Islam and models of government had not been dismissed. Only with the dismantlement of the Empire and the constitution of national governments in its different regions, Islamic intellectuals had to face the problem of arranging new patterns of action for Muslim people.

With the establishment of multiple nation-states in the so-called Middle East, Islamic intellectuals had to cope with secular conceptions about the subject and its place and space for action in society. They had to come to terms with the definitive affirmation of secularism and the consequent process of reconfiguration of local sensibilities, forms of social organisation, and modes of action. As a consequence of these processes, Islamic thinkers started to place emphasis over believers' individual choice and responsibility both in maintaining an Islamic conduct daily and in realising the values of Islamic society. While under the Ottoman rule to be part of the Islamic *ummah* was considered an implicit consequence of being a subject of the empire.

Not many scientific works have looked at contemporary forms of Islam from this perspective. Usually Islamic instances are considered the outcome of an enduring and unchanging tradition[2], which try to reproduce itself in opposition to outer-imposed secular practices. Rarely present-day forms of Islamic reasoning and practice have been considered as the result of a process of adjustment to new styles of governance under the modern state. Instead, I argue that new Islamic patterns of action depend on a history of practical and conceptual revision they undertake under different and locally specific versions of secularism[3].

From this perspective I will deal with the specific case of Fethullah Gülen, the head of one of the most famous and influent "renewalist" Islamic movements of contemporary Turkey. From the 1980s this Islamic leader has been able to weave a powerful network of invisible social ties from which he gets both economic and cultural capital. Yet what interests me most in this paper, is that with his open-minded and moderate arguments, Gülen has inspired many people in Turkey to live Islam in a new way. Recurring to *ijtihad* and drawing from secular epistemology specific ideas about moral agency, he has proposed to a wide public a very attractive path for being "good Muslims" in their daily conduct.

After an introductive explanation of the movement's project and of the ideas on which it is based, my aim will be to focus on such a pattern of action. Particular attention will be dedicated to Gülen's conception of a "good Muslim" as a morally-guided agent, because such a

---

1 In Islamic jurisprudence the practice of referring directly to primary fonts of the Law (Qur'an and *Sunnah*) and to make an independent reasoning on them with the aim of interpret these same fonts in order to resolve current practical problems. For an account on *ijtihad* in relation to Fethullah Gülen's thought see Yılmaz 2003.

2 This reading of Islam has informed an entire tradition of works in the anthropology of Islam. For a general assessment see Asad Talal, 1986, *The Idea of an Anthropology of Islam*, Occasional Paper Series, Washington, D.C.: Georgtown Univ. Center for Contemporary Arab Studies. For a recent critic of more subtle contemporary forms of "neo-Orientalism" see Kandiyoti 1997 and Navaro-Yashin 2002.

3 Secularism as a political doctrine is not a monolithic object and has different historical realizations in different countries and periods. Yet, as I am going to show, secular as an ontology and an epistemology implies specific ideas about the subject, reason, human agency and history (see Asad 1993, 2003).

conception reveals underneath secular ideas on both responsibility and moral agency. These considerations will constitute the basis from which we can look at the transformation of Islam – and more generally of "the religion" – in the contemporary world.

Then a part will be dedicated to defining the specificity of Gülen's proposal, which will be compared with that of other Islamic revivalist movements in other contexts. Some common point between them will merge from this comparison. Both indeed use the concept of responsibility in order to push subjects to actively engage in reviving Islam. Yet, on the other hand, I will show how Gülen's followers distinguish themselves by the fact their commitment possesses a socially-oriented and reformist character.

Finally I will consider the proximity of Gülen's conceptualisation of moral agency with that the modern state has organised around the idea of "civic virtues". I argue Gülen's recall for taking responsibility of social moral decline is a way of charging his followers with a similar burden the modern state has charged its citizens. Thus I suggest the Islamic leader's proposal can be seen as the tentative of supporting the modernity project by defining a new and specific space to Islam and religion into it. This proposal opens the possibility of new and interesting forms of interconnection between secular ideas of modernity and the so-called "Islamic" ones. At the same time I think it sheds a new light over contemporary "renewalist" movements, which can be considered a concrete proposal about how to realise, in a different background, modern forms of governance by reconsidering their moral basis.

Gülen's Rethinking of the Islamic Tradition

At the beginning Gülen is an influential interpreter of Sufism and a theorist of the disciplinary path a person should accomplish to reach the virtuous condition of *al-insan al-kamil*[4]. Then from the 1980s onwards he has significantly widened its conceptual views and ideas. Urged by the perception that society is affected by a general moral decline, he has promoted a series of activities directed at reforming individual inner selves. Gülen has directed his followers toward the promotion of such activities, putting less emphasis over the need to respect traditional Islamic practices and refusing political Islam. This attitude involved both recall for renewal (*ijtihad*) and a critic of other approaches to Islamic tradition in Turkey and abroad.

The emphasis Fethullah Gülen places over the need for renewal in Islamic tradition comes from his idea that Islam should be able to offer people the resources they need to overcome the present condition of social dissipation and moral decline. Indeed his basilar assumption is that with the advent of modernity, humanity has turned its attention to technological and scientific progress, taking them as valid teleology for action. In his opinion individuals have put aside the spiritual dimension of human existence to be progressively attracted by consumer society values, research for material satisfaction and individualism. In this sense the general improvement of individual welfare has caused a moral and intellectual decline which could lead modern society to collapse. For this reasons Gülen claims for the need to spread anew moral Islamic values all over society.

But in order to accomplish such a duty Islam has to undertake a radical process of renewal. According to him traditional forms of Islam have not been able to realise this transformation. Therefore he criticises both old Islamic schools (*medrese*) and Sufi brotherhoods (*tarikat*). In

---

4 In Sufism an individual state of spiritual perfection characterised by a total carelessness toward material desire and by a sense of proximity respect to God (Gülen 2004:xx, *Key Concepts in the Practice of Sufism. Emerald Hills of the Hearth* (1st published edition 1998), The Light, Inc. & Işık Yayınlari, New Jersey.)

his opinion the former were too much concerned with legal aspects of Islam, neglecting the spiritual inner dimension of religious experience. Whereas, Sufism has not been able to confront with the challenges technology and scientific thinking have posed to modern society. According to Gülen it has lost the aspect that has permitted it to survive and to stay close to people, that was its dynamism[5]. Instead he wants to cope with modernity and to advertise for a kind of Sufism that does not limit itself to mystic contemplation of God (Gülen 2004).

Even Gülen arrives at criticising the Nur movement. From the 1920s this movement has always been concerned with the safeguard of Islamic practices within the Turkish Republic. The movement's leader Said Nursi thought that the new national state had taken control of the educational system, strictly reducing the opportunities of the population to learn about Islam. Consequently, its followers' efforts were directed at imparting lessons over correct Islamic practices in private houses. Yet they distinguished themselves from other Islamic groups in the country by approving theological, spiritual and scientific knowledge unity (Agai 2003:53). Indeed Gülen has drawn from Nursi's ideas about the relationship between science and religion, and the role of education in shaping society. Even from the 1960s until the end of the 1970s Gülen took part in Nurcu initiatives. However, he soon realised that confining educational ideals to Islamic circles, the Nurcus would not have success in bringing Islam to shape society. In this way they could not challenge the antireligious leftists' hegemony over state education.

Gülen thinks that in order to spread its beneficial effects, the religious message should reach as many members of society as possible. Anyway he rejects any political use of Islam. He argues religion cannot be yielded to party needs because it cannot be reduced to an ideological instrument. In his words politics "darkens religion's spirit, for religion belongs to everyone."[6] This does not mean he is refusing secular forms of governance. In his discourses he upholds democracy, which in his opinion is the most fair form of political organisation known to men. He also defends secularism, at least as a political project that should not reject religion but should grant tolerance toward it. In turn he has always awarded a significant historical role to the state in the preservation and defence of Islam[7]. He simply argues religions should not care about power but about human aspects of life.

From this perspective the fact that Gülen does not consider the veil or the beard as essential elements of Islam, is significant. We know that from the mid-1980s onwards, the public use of such outward signs has became an object of dispute between Islamist movements and both the state and secular public opinion in Turkey. Distinguishing himself from other Islamic thinkers Gülen has affirmed he does not consider those signs as indispensable to the accomplishment of Muslim life[8].

---

5 Even Said Nursi – one of the Islamic thinkers that more influenced Gülen – had criticised *tarikat*'s teaching methods (*sohbet*). He thought they did not leave enough space for individual interpretation because they were based on repetition and memorization of ritualised speech formulas. According to him, *sohbet* mechanically reproduced an a-critical knowledge which was unable to cope with modernity (see Yavuz 1997).

6 Ünal & Williams 2000:168, taken from Riza Zeylut, *Aksam*, April 19th 1997.

7 In particular Gülen thinks at Ottoman period as an example of tolerance and coexistence of different believes under the same state.

8 "I see the robe, turban, beard, and loose trousers as details. Muslims shouldn't be drowning in detail. [...] Choosing not to wear [them] shouldn't be constructed as weakening the Muslim Turkish identity. [...] no one should be categorized as a sinner because of such things." (Ünal & Williams 2000:62-3, taken from *Akman*, "Fethullah Hoca Anlatiyor") Therefore responding to a question about the veil the he says: "This issue is not as important as the essentials of faith and the pillars of Islam. It's a matter of secondary importance in fiqh." (Ünal & Williams 2000:63,

Many secularists in Turkey argue that hidden underneath the moderate character of Gülen's ideas are the leader and his followers' intentions of changing the country into a Iran-like one. On the contrary, I suggest that Gülen's theories depend on a reconfiguration of the space Islam must have in an individual's life and on new ideas about how a "good Muslim" should act in society.

According to Gülen, renewal of Islamic tradition must occur in order to adapt it to the needs of the time. This is why he criticises other approaches to tradition. If they have tried to re-interpret Islam, they have failed in the moment they have not been able to do it accordingly with the requirements of the modern forms of governance and the present condition of moral decline. Instead, Gülen thinks of Islam as the spiritual dimension of life. Consequently, religion has to furnish a guide for individuals independently from socio-political changing conditions.

In his opinion it is no longer important how strictly a person accomplishes traditional Islamic practices or shows signs of Islamic belonging. What matters is that religion helps people to address the problems of contemporary society. This is why in his thinking Islam must push people to actively operate in society in order to overcome the general situation of moral dissipation. When he blames both traditional Islamic education and Sufism for having not been able to reform itself or political Islam for using Islam as an ideological instrument, Gülen is claiming that religion should have an active role in society.

The Educational Project of the Movement

When he criticises traditional forms of Islamic education for not having been able to adapt to modern conditions, Gülen expresses something more than a simple dissatisfaction with old methods of teaching. Instead he blames other Islamic scholars because they had not understood that the decline of Islam was not solely due to its incompatibility with modern forms of governance, but to the hegemony of Western-inspired secularist ideology. Gülen has realised that the battle is a cultural one, and that in order to oppose Kemalist intellectuals' hegemony it is necessary to challenge their monopoly over education. This is why he thinks the solution to society's moral decline could be in the promotion of a particular kind of education that even if teaching secular subjects at the same time could instil in students Islamic ethics and morals.

Gülen's commitment to educational activities started in the 1980s, when he took advantage of changing political conditions to intervene in the public sphere and in particular in the cultural industry[9]. He utilised both his charisma and his religious authority to attract a wide number of people and capital in educational activities. Indeed he used his web of informal ties to get financial resources and to direct them to the opening of a great number of such ethically-oriented schools.

He began to stress in his discourses that schools concentrating on non-religious subjects could serve religious needs and that Turkey needed elite secular schools rather than mosques

---

taken from *Özkök*, "Hoca Efendi Anlatiyor")

9 Gülen's access to public life was favoured by the Özal government overture toward Islamic associations in early 1980s. In that period Islamic associations and sufi brotherhoods could take advantage of a 1983 law which enabled the formation of new foundations (*vakiflar*), provided that they had not political objectives. By the foundations system Islamic groups could organize educational, religious and charitable activities around informal networks (Zubaida 1996). Yet, as aforementioned, Gülen differentiated himself from other Islamic groups by investing foundations' money in the opening of state-like schools, rather than *imam-hatip* ones.

or *imam-hatip* schools. He did not simply argue that religion and science were compatible between themselves, as Nurcu teachings did[10]. In Gülen's educational philosophy science accomplishes a central role not only because of its connection with revelation, but because it is considered a great instrument in the hands of men to make a better world. From this perspective Gülen shares with Western thinkers the connection between science and the idea of progress. That is why he has never rejected either science or progress, but only the assumption of them as a transcendental teleology[11].

But if Gülen considers science a useful instrument in the hands of humanity, at the same time he thinks that it alone cannot constitute a guide for society. In his opinion science is not a positive value in itself. In order to really contribute to the welfare of society it has to be possessed and used by morally-guided individuals. The scope of Gülen's educational project is exactly this: to form individuals with a strong inner Islamic ethics which can guide society toward the correct use of scientific discoveries.

This is the core of the project of the movement. Even if in the schools of the movement teaching is conducted on state-programmed subjects and in environments responding to secular rules of appearance, it is considered a good means to instil people with Islamic ethos. Clearly Gülen has drawn from Nursi ideas about education. Yet differently from Nurcu circles, in Gülen's schools the teaching of Islamic principles and daily practices have completely disappeared. What matters is the transmission of the spiritual dimension of Islam - that is its inner ethics – adding to it the knowledge of "secular" education. This is precisely the scope of what has been called Gülen's "Islamic ethic of education": to give Islamic-inspired education a new meaning and function (Agai 2003:51).

In this perspective education becomes a process that is not limited to the transmission of religious knowledge from one person to another (*temsil*). At the same time it cannot be simply reduced to the transmission of notions from a teacher to his pupil. Instead, it must contribute to shape the student's personality. Indeed according to Gülen the goal of education must be to built student's character (*terbiye*) by enabling him to interiorise qualities of self-discipline, tolerance and sense of mission (Ünal e Williams 2000:312, Michel 2003:78).

The importance Gülen attributes to such a kind of education is intimately connected to the final scope of the movement, that is to reform society. Indeed according to him, education will permit to shape a new generation of people (*the golden generation*) which will be able to use scientific knowledge according to Islamic ethics and to lead society along the right path. Armed with the tools of science and religion, this generation shall be able to solve dilemmas of present and future society. Therefore committing to both education of other people and activism in society, these people will shape other individuals' inner ethics and will definitively transform society into a paradise.

---

10   Effectively Gülen took from Nursi the idea that science is one of the ways that conduct to God, because by showing the complexity of nature it reveals His greatness. For an analysis of the 4 ways to understand the existence of God described in the *Risale-i Nur* (The epistles of Light), the collection of Said Nursi's writings, see Mermer Ali 1997.

11   In Gülen's words the real problem consists in the fact "we have been unable to assign a true direction to science, and thus confused revealed knowledge with scientific theories and sometimes scientific knowledge with philosophy [...]. One result is that the younger generations became alienated from their society. After a while, these inexperienced generations lost their religious and moral values, and the whole nation began to decline in thought, ideals, art, and life [...] and evil aspects of modern civilization were propagated." (Ünal & Williams 2000: 97, taken from *Akman*, "Fethullah Hoca Anlatiyor").

Thus Fethullah Gülen's renewal of Islamic tradition is strictly dependent on his ideas about the role religion should have in the society. Indeed he thinks Islam should constitute a guide for people. But in order to accomplish this duty it has to undermine other dominant ideologies. This implies to change traditional methods of education and to adopt a new educational philosophy which contemplate at the same time both scientific knowledge and Islamic ethics.

Yet it seems to me that here Gülen has done something more than giving Islam a new role in society. By inserting Islam into an educational project he has given it both a new public form and a new aim, and consequently a new life. The emphasis he poses on education as a way of transmitting an Islamic ethos reveals underneath an "essentialised" idea of Islam. As I will discuss further this idea is central in Gülen's conception of the Islamic subject as an ethically-guided agent. Therefore the assimilation of Islam to morals implies a redefinition of those that can be defined Islamic practices. This will be the argument of the next paragraph.

The Sanctification of Daily Life

As it has been observed, contemporary Islamic intellectuals often take certain legal concepts from the Islamic tradition in a selective and arbitrary way (Moosa 1999, Yılmaz 2003). Then they give these concepts new functions and values by inserting them in their personal discursive frameworks. Gülen too has adapted some Islamic traditional concept to activities related to his project. Inserting the life of a vast number of people in Turkey into the educational project of the movement, Gülen has offered them the possibility of embedding their daily work in a transcendental framework.

According to Gülen there are two main ways to take part in the movement's project. People can directly engage in education by becoming teachers in one of the schools connected to the community, or can simply decide to finance the activities of the movement in education and media sectors. The former is the way that certainly indicates a closer engagement to the pattern asserted by Gülen. Indeed teaching is considered by Gülen a holy duty (*kutsi vazife*) that only people with a strong moral can adequately perform (Agai 2003:58). In achieving the aim of building a new society in which individuals will act accordingly with Islamic ethics, teachers have the most important role. In fact they have the duty to instil in students Islamic principles and to shape their character. Overall they have to accomplish this deed following a specific pedagogical pattern.

As I have already said according to Gülen education is not a simple passage of contents from one person to another. Instead, it is a process by which the student incorporates a series of Islamic values by taking an example from his educator. In this perspective the teacher must be a model (*temsil*) for the student. In his daily actions he has to show his pupils how to combine an Islamic moral of action with the study and practice of science. Indeed the role of the teacher consists in assisting his students in acquiring character. In this sense he gives "guidance" (*irşad*). This term usually refers to guide pupils in the learning process of Islamic traditional practices. Yet Gülen has extended its meaning to include teaching in secular schools provided that it is done according to a specific ethics[12]. Consequently being a

---

12 That is why teachers are requested to be of the utmost integrity. In Gülen's words "those who want to reform the world must first reform themselves. In order to bring others to the path of travelling to a better world, they must purify their inner worlds of hatred, rancour, and jealousy, and adorn their outer world with all kinds of virtues" (*The Necessity of Interfaith Dialogue: A Muslim Approach*. Speech given at the Parliament of the World's Religions, Capetown, 1-8 December 1999, quoted in Michel 2003:78). As I have explained elsewhere (*Essere Sufi*

dedicated teacher (in one of the schools linked to the movement) becomes a kind of religious merit (Agai 2003:59).

Instead a person who is not a teacher can take part in the movement's project by working in other activities linked to it, such as journals, foundations, or even school dormitories. Therefore, even people with other occupations can sustain the project by financing its activities. These people participate in the movement only in an indirect way. Yet Gülen inserts their activities in the scope of the movement and make them became "Islamised" as well.

Indeed making use of Islamic concepts Gülen inserts his followers activities - both teaching and working to finance the movement - into a transcendental framework. A central concept Gülen extrapolates from tradition is *hizmet*, which generally refers to religious service. According to his socially-oriented idea of Islam he has extended this concept to every act of serving the benefit of others. Therefore, because the educational project of the movement is finalised at overcoming the present situation of moral decline and transforming this world into a better one, acting in order to support such a project serves the benefit of others. Consequently it becomes a kind of "religious act". At the same time he uses other concepts like those of *himmet* (giving donations and protecting good work) and *ihlas* (seeking God's appreciation for every action) which generally refer to Islamic traditional duties, to define respectively people financing the movement and people acting according to the ethics prescribed by the movement.

Gülen has extended the meaning of different traditional concepts in order that they can include every act that is even indirectly connected with the realisation of the project of the movement. In this way he has given these actions a religious dimension. Therefore, he has strongly widened the number of people who can consider themselves part of the movement. This move can be seen as strategic. Surely it permits the institutions of the movement to obtain money from a large number of wealthy businessmen. At the same time, from Gülen's perspective it can be read as a way of further extending the range of his message and make it accessible to the highest possible number of people. If working can enter into a transcendental framework, many people can start to think of inserting their life in a religious dimension. I suppose this can be considered another manner by which Gülen hopes that Islamic morals can spread all over society.

Aksiyon Insani: The New Islamic Path

After this introductive – but necessary – dissertation about the project of the movement, I will now focus on the topic of my paper. As I have shown, Gülen has been able to offer the chance to insert their daily life into a transcendental framework to a wide number of people. Recurring to traditional concepts he has "made Islamic" the work of different individuals. Yet I think he has done even more: he has given to religious experience a new dimension which is not solely suitable for modern forms of governance, but also overlaps secular conceptions. Indeed the emphasis he poses on education as a way of transmitting an Islamic ethos reveals underneath an "essentialised" idea of Islam, which is in tune with secular ideas about the space religion should occupy in society. Yet moreover, the idea this ethos should push people to act in society reveals underneath a conception of the "Muslim subject" as an ethically-

---

nel movimento neo-Nur di Fethullah Gülen, M.A. Thesis at University of Milano-Bicocca) more devoted members of the movement follow a disciplinary pattern of practices directed to incorporate a series of virtues by which they continuously oversee their moral integrity. Yet here I am interested in the effects of Gülen's message over a larger public.

guided agent which recalls the Western concept of moral agency.

Here my scope is to better define the specificity of Gülen's path of Islamic conduct. I will do this by discerning secular ideas that I think the path reveals. Yet, my aim is not to demonstrate that in reality Gülen is a "secular" thinker instead of a "religious" one, but to describe how Western hegemonic discourses have affected local forms of Islamic action.

Gülen says the ideal person taking part in his project must be *aksiyon insani* (man of action). This person is one who must spend most of his time working in order to turn the world into a paradise. Indeed, according to the religious leader a "good Muslim" should be continuously engaged in accomplishing good deeds. This is why he always appeals to people to hurry up in order to accomplish actions that can contribute to the common good. For example, there are statements where Gülen says that people who perform *hizmet* sleep three hours, reserve one or two hours for other necessities and devote the rest of the time to *hizmet* (Agai 2003:61). Now consider this quotation:

> Man of service must, for the sake of the cause he has given his heart to, be resolved to cross over seas of "pus and blood". [...] He knows himself first of all to be responsible and answerable for work left undone. He has to be considerate and fair-minded to everyone who comes to his aid and support the truth. He is extraordinarily resolved and hopeful even when his institutions have been destroyed, his plans upset and his forces put to rout. He is moderate and tolerant when he has taken wing anew and soared to the summits and so rational and sagacious that he admits in advance that this path is very steep. So zealous, persevering and confident that he can pass through all the pits of hell that he may encounter on his way. So faithful to the cause to which he has devoted his life that, deeply in love with it, he can sacrifice his life and all that he loves for its sake. So sincere and humble that he will never bring to mind all that he has accomplished.[13]

According to these words, only people who have awareness of the problems of society and of how the world is progressing feel the need of being continuously engaged in work. The followers' will to change the present situation must derive from such an awareness. This view is perfectly in tone with Gülen's ideals of education. Only people whose minds have been enlightened by science and whose motivation derives from faith are able to realise what problems afflict society. Only so moulded people are motivated to act in order to resolve such problems.

Surely awareness here recalls for a particular connection between reason and action. Indeed individuals are requested to rationalise their daily life in order to better accomplish the assigned duty. This is why different authors have affirmed that the activities of Gülen's followers resemble the ideal type of Max Weber's "inner-worldly asceticism" (Özdalga 2000, Agai 2003). According to Weber, in this typology of asceticism "the world is presented to the religious virtuoso as the assigned duty. The ascetic's task is to transform the world in accordance with her/his ascetic ideals." Again, "[...] the order of the world in which the ascetic is situated becomes for her/him a 'vocation' which s/he must 'fulfil' rationally" (Weber 1980:329, quoted in Agai 2003:60).

However, I argue Gülen does not simply prescribe or order the accomplishment of specific actions to his followers. That is, the believer's task is not solely to act in order to follow a determined aim. Awareness requires something more than a simple submissiveness. Indeed Gülen asks his followers to undertake the burden of moral responsibility for the problems of contemporary society. To be a "good Muslim" does not consist simply in a rationalistic accomplishment of a prescribed path. According to him, Islamically-oriented work must be

---

13 Gülen Fethullah, *Criteria or the Lights of the Way* - Vol. 1.

a consequence of both rational thinking and an Islamic inner sense of ethics. This is why individuals have to feel responsible for work they have left undone. Indeed to sacrifice most of one's proper time in work and to continuously strive in action respond to a sense of responsibility and culpability for the problems of the world.

I argue it is exactly here that Gülen links his Islamic ethics to secular morals. To explain this point better I will draw your attention to the connection Gülen usually establishes between the sense of responsibility and endless activism. Indeed I think the way Gülen conceives responsibility has a lot in common with secular theories about the subject and its agency.

In Western philosophical tradition a "moral agent" is usually defined as somebody that can be held responsible – and consequently credited or blamed – for his decisions and actions. Central to this definition is the notion of responsibility and in particular responsibility toward an authority. This concept implies not only an idea of a person as "a single subject with a continuous consciousness in a single body"[14] and modern scientific ideas about objective knowledge and causality etc., but – what interests us more – the inner capability of feeling guilty for having disobeyed the Law (Asad 2003). In this theory, morality is considered as the intellectual human ability people must have to realise if their actions agree with a specific set of outer-imposed rules and to feel guilty if they are not.

In a similar way according to Gülen, men of action must be conscious of their duties and have to accomplish them in order not to be blamed, by God in the hereafter and by their conscience immediately. Following secular conceptualisation of morality Gülen argues activism is a direct consequence of an inner sense of responsibility that faithful people must interiorise in order to be "good Muslims". This conceptualisation implies that action derives from a moral choice individuals autonomously make on the basis of the awareness they have obtained through to education.

Thus activism is the outcome of choices of educated people who are conscious of the contemporary world's evil aspects thanks to reasoned and faithful thinking. Having embodied through education such a sense of responsibility, morally-guided people are urged to take charge of the world's moral corruption and act in order to overcome it.

By saying this I am not arguing disciplinary aspects disappear from Gülen's view on Islam. Firstly, because Gülen is a strenuous defender of Islamic pillars and the need to accomplish them. Adherents to the movement – overall people who aim at becoming educators – perform *namaz* five times per day and often even perform the meritorious one during the night[15]. Secondly, because as I am going to show, volunteers of the movement, by endlessly engaging in activism, really follow a very disciplined life.

At the same time I am not arguing Gülen's proposal is essentially "secular". Instead, the path he prescribes maintains its transcendental character at the moment it is connected to human salvation. However the assimilation of Islam to a particular ethos renders Gülen's path something very similar to the philosophical concept of moral agency. This aspect differentiates this path from others in the Muslim World. But before continuing on this issue, I

---

14 T. Asad here refers to Locke's definition of a person as a "forensic term, appropriating actions and their merit, and so belongs only to intelligent agents, capable of law, and happiness, and misery. This personality extends itself beyond present existence to what is past, only by consciousness, whereby it becomes concerned and accountable, owns and imputes to itself past actions, just upon the same ground and for the same reason as it does the present" (An Essay Concerning Human Understanding, Book Two, Essay XXVII, Section 26) in Asad T. 2003:74:n.14.

15 See Fabio Vicini, *Essere Sufi nel movimento neo-Nur di Fethullah Gülen*, M.A. Thesis at University of Milano-Bicocca

will give a brief example of how Gülen's followers subject themselves to the pattern of action he proposes.

An Ethnographic Excerpt

How do Gülen's discourses really affect community members' lives? How do they put into practice their master's prescriptions? My theoretical assumption is that authoritative discourses construct religion in the experiential world of individuals by defining and interpreting correct meanings and excluding some practices in favour of others (see Asad 1993). What I mean is that patterns of religious action are not simply rules faithful people have to follow, but powerful discourses that make them a specific kind of individuals, with specific emotions, desires and sensibilities (see Asad 1993, Mahmood 2001, 2005, Hirschkind 2001). In line with this approach, I argue that by suggesting a specific pattern of action Gülen constructs the religious experience of his followers.

The members of the movement I met and frequented in Istanbul during my brief fieldwork in summer/autumn 2005, are all teachers in a school linked to the movement. There they prepared high school graduates to the entrance exam to Turkish state university. All of them live in a dormitory not very far from the school. They teach physics, chemistry and biology, that are very "secular" subjects, but the way they conduct their daily life makes this compatible with Gülen's requirements.

They spend most of the time between the dormitory and the school. They usually wake up at 6 a.m. in the morning to perform the *namaz*, and until 8 they prepare their lessons or read a book. Then they go to school, where they spend most of the day giving lessons, individual additional teachings, or optional courses. Usually they go back to the dormitory around 7 p.m., change their clothes, go out again to the mosque, pray and have something to eat. Then if they do not have to attend a collective meeting[16] they return to dormitory. Here they read again, receive students for additional explanations or meet informally. Finally they perform the last *namaz* and go to bed.

In their daily schedule, having a rest, relaxing, or satisfying more vital needs such as eating and sleeping, are some of the less contemplated aspects. The discussions I had with my interlocutors reveals they were trying to eat the least possible. Often they told me they had eaten nothing during the day, or they said that they should not have eaten even the little they did. About sleeping, they told me how Gülen in his writings often recommends one to sleep the least possible, because there are many other things to do instead. Therefore, they were trying to sleep very few hours, around 5, per night[17].

For my interlocutors, being a teacher is a real mission to accomplish. They spend all their time performing this task, continuously looking for something more to do. They do everything they can to be busy and they are very active. If they are not teaching, they are very concerned about learning more in order to perfect themselves and to have more knowledge to pass on to their students.

Dedication and self-sacrifice are central aspects of their daily life, and activism is at the same

---

16 These meetings are finalized at organizing teachings and other administrative questions relative to schools and dormitories.

17 Komeçoğlu (1997) says that from interview with persons living in the houses of light came they were trying to sleep less and to reduce meals. They even told him they fast two days per week, as it seems the Prophet did according to one *hadith*.

time both the outcome and the way to embody these values. Indeed according to my observations, by being active the members of the community feel themselves fully dedicated to the project of the movement. It is the way they perceive that they are accomplishing a good deed according to Gülen's ideas. Therefore, it is also the way of embodying important virtues such as humility and self-sacrifice, that are central to the constitution of a morally-responsible Islamic subject.

If their striving in action without a rest is the outcome of an embodied sense of responsibility toward society, at the same time it is also a form of discipline by which adherents construct their religious experience. Indeed the virtues of humility and self-sacrifice are central to community members' life because they continuously remind them of their responsibility. In this sense those virtues are at the basis of their religious experience too.

Being Islamic, Being Citizen

Surely volunteers of the movement are pushed by a strong faith in the accomplishment of their daily tasks. However this does not impede their actions to have a very mundane character. What is singular about Gülen's proposal is that the pattern of action he prescribes is not only based on secular ideas of responsibility and morals. Even the scope of these activities is socially-oriented. That is, they aim at improving the welfare of society in its totality and not, as usual in Islamic tradition, only of the Islamic *ummah*. What I suggest is that Gülen movement has a very worldly preoccupation, which is to turn *this* world into a paradise.

From this point of view the movement seems to pay peculiar attention to "secular matters" – where with secular matters here I intend the preoccupation the state has to grant common welfare to its population. These considerations open the possibility for debate over Gülen movement's potentialities in the development of a more civil society. Yet contributions in this direction are not unique to it. Even in other Middle Eastern countries Islam has became a public arena from which to debate over current issues.

For example, some authors have connected the appearance of new Islamic patterns of action to the definitive affirmation of "public Islam", a concept they use to indicate the fact that traditional forms of "Islamic reasoning" have acquired a public dimension. According to them virtuous Muslim subjectivity is no longer connected to the question of soul salvation. Instead Islam has became the subject of public debates about how to conduct a virtuous life under the umbrella of a modern state and how to contribute to both common good and fair government[18]. New Muslim intellectuals criticise both the reduction of public dimension to an interacting process between single people's interests and the implicit ban of morality from public space. Instead they suggest how to cultivate and maintain Islamic virtues and how to use them in order to promote positive initiatives for society. Therefore, Islamic public sphere has became the place from which to address new and alternative ideas of civil society and of public virtues both built upon religious legitimising principles and practices (Salvatore A. 1998, Hirschkind 2001, Eickelman D. E. & Salvatore A. 2002).

However according to both Salvatore (1998) and Hirschkind (2001), Islamic public sphere in Egypt is a space that is parallel to the secular one. Indeed it has its own rules, modes and

---

18 As Salvatore argues Islamic jurisdiction (*fiqh*) has always been interested in a wide set of social issues and has always aimed at the community's prosperity. However, a general discourse in favour of the "common good" and the collective welfare in relation to modern state's institutions has consolidated only with the collapse of the Ottoman Empire (Salvatore A. 1998).

public. There practices of Islamic reasoning "locates themselves within the temporal frame of Islamic *ummah* and in relation to the succession of events that characterise its mode of historicity". They do not take place within, or serve to uphold, that domain of associational life usually called civil society. In its present form these practices do not play a mediatory role between state and society (Hirschkind 2001:17).

In the Egyptian context Islamic reasoning concerns how to conduct a virtuous Muslim life and how to obtain common good for the Muslim community. Here believers are mostly charged with the duty of overseeing if their own actions and feelings are in line with the requirements of the Islamic authoritative discourses. Even if these discourses become subjects of dispute, the temporal frame and the terms of the discourse remains that of the Islamic *ummah*. Instead for Gülen, religious conduct consists of acting in this world in order to change it. Gülen's pattern of virtuous Muslim life is concerned with how to spend a life in order to improve the welfare of all society both in Turkey and in the world.

Secondly, Gülen's view of the subject understands a radically different conceptualisation of the Islamic duty. Individuals must feel themselves responsible for the problems of the world. They are charged with the burden of the problems of society. According to the ethics they have embodied they feel the necessity to strive in action. Here Islam assumes the form of ethics and fulfils the role of inner moral guidance for individuals over how to construct a fair and just society. Usually Muslim Intellectuals charge the components of the Muslim community with the responsibility to preserve Islamic practices against the process of corruption of society (see Utvik 2003). Yet they do not suggest a general programme of reform for all society. Neither do they push individuals to act according to a pattern of endless activism in order to realise such a project.

It is the mix composed of this "essentialised" idea of Islam and the search for the common good for all society that makes Gülen's proposal very peculiar. Even here I argue that this couple renders this mix similar to the secular concept of "civic virtues". The connection Gülen places between action and transforming this world into paradise indeed have similarities with the duties of citizenship in modern states.

Even if secularism has located human agency in rational mind, it has left some space for morals into so-called "civic virtues". According to historian Gordon S. Wood, in the eighteenth century, republics distinguished themselves from monarchies for the fact that therein the law had to be obeyed for the sake of conscience, rather than for fear of the ruler's wrath. People was persuaded to submit their own interest to the government operating for the collective common good. It was this voluntary submission that constituted the eighteenth century notion of civic virtue.[19] In this perspective citizens of modern states were not only requested to limit their freedom in accordance with the needs of public interest, but even to contribute to the common good by exercising their civil rights. From this point of view voting and discussing political issues was a right that depended on a specific duty of citizenship. Therefore according to classical definition of secular morality, in some cases individuals should renounce their egoistic interests in order to pursue a higher public interest. The modern concept of civil society stands on this basis.

From this perspective it seems to me that Gülen community's project in some points overlaps the secular one directed at shaping good and responsible citizens. The moment that Islam pushes people to act in society in order to create a better future for everyone, Gülen's

---

19 See Wood, Gordon S., 1969, *The Creation of the American Republic, 1776-1787*, University of North Carolina Press.

project of education would seem to be effective in instilling citizens with commitment toward society.

From this point of view I argue that Gülen community is not simply contributing to the construction of an Islamic informed public. Instead, I think its aim is to propose an alternative model to the secular project on how to build a modern, democratic and fair society. Postnational states seem to have lost their force in proposing an adequate and coherent project of civil discipline for their citizens. Gülen has seen the consequences of this weakening in the dominance of materialistic and hedonistic inclinations in modern society. This is why he claims for the need to educate society to Islamic ethical values and secular sciences.

Concluding Remarks

After the failure of explicitly "anti-Western" forms of radical Islamism, such as pan Arabism and Islamic nationalism, only a part of the Muslim world continues to see the necessary condition for the constitution of a more fair and good society in the establishment of an Islamic state. Instead, nowadays most Islamic intellectuals underline the need for a bottom-up kind of society reform. Indeed according to them the decline of Islamic values does not depend on modern forms of governance in themselves, but on the spreading of commodity values, new styles of life, and hedonism that accompany them. The emphasis they place over the need of reforming society starting from the individual, seems to be the result of a kind of anxiety in face of such a situation.

Consequently Muslim intellectuals' first aim has became that of offering patterns of action which permit Muslim people both to revive and maintain Islamic virtues and to be not affected by deviating forces of modernity. Such patterns have the declared common scope of aiming at regenerating traditional Islamic values, but they have different local applications. Indeed how they interact with the dominant secular discourse and have been affected by it, differs from context to context.

As I have shown, Fethullah Gülen has been able to propose a path that does not startle secular sensibilities, at least not immediately and not in its public forms. Adherents are not required to bring any outward sign that marks their Islamic inclination. In places linked to movement's activities – from schools to dormitories, to administrative centres of foundations – no sign of Muslim faith is present. Rather, there we can find – at least in Turkey – Atatürk busts and Turkish flags. From this point of view Gülen has given to Islam a public form that is suitable for secular rules of appearance.

Yet the fact that Gülen's proposal respects the private/public divide is not sufficient. By delinking Islam from the accomplishment of traditional practices and dressing styles, Gülen has transformed it into a kind of moral essence that should push individuals to act in a socially-oriented responsible way. The intrusion of religion into individual choice causes some problems to the secular. Indeed according to classical definition of secularism, religion is seen as inimical to the assignments of modern life. Apart from the forms of its public appearance, it is usually associated with private feelings, emotional and irrational forces. Secularism relegates religion to the private inner self of individuals, that is in the place of morality. However, faith must remain a question of personal belief that must affect neither rational choice nor moral agency. Neither can it address worldly matters, because it would lead to conflict with people with different beliefs. According to this view, in order to be "free" the agents must act only following their reason.

From this perspective Gülen's proposal could be seen by secularists as an unwanted intrusion into the privacy of others, because it allows personal religious beliefs to influence rational choice. The point is that Gülen's call for responsibility and activism subsumes an "essentialised" idea of Islam which overlaps secular notions of moral agency. By assimilating Islam to morals the Islamic leader creates relevant difficulties to the secular project. If as Talal Asad argues "in order to protect politics from perversion by religion, in order to determine its acceptable forms within the Republic, authority must identify religion and police it"[20], secularists in Turkey and abroad shall find it difficult "to police" Gülen's proposal. Due to its proximity with morals Gülen's Islam is not only difficult to locate for secularists, it even attempts to take the place of secular moral agency.

Indeed if at the beginning Gülen's primary scope was that of protecting Muslims in Turkey against the prominence of hedonistic values, then he has elaborated a path which shares many values with "modernity". It seems that proceeding along his own way, Gülen has discovered he has more things in common with universal values elaborated within Western tradition, than with other expressions of Islam. Then, inspired by such arguments, he has re-elaborated his thinking in order to offer an Islam that intends to contribute to the building of a more human society.

From this perspective I suggest Gülen is not simply offering an alternative kind of modernity. Rather he wants to take part in the construction of *this* modernity. And, in line with his anxieties and those in general of the religious world, he intends to contribute to the modern project by re-evaluating its moral basis. By putting emphasis over the moral aspects of religion and recalling to civic principles, he is claiming a specific role in society for Islam. That is, of addressing the progress of human beings without lose of their moral dimension. Thus he cuts a specific space to religion and attributes it a role of guide for society.

Clearly here I am not stating religion should and could aim at this role in the contemporary world. This is a problem that concerns more our personal believes and convictions than scientific analysis. Yet it seems to me, in Western contexts religions are acquiring a medialised form. Even there they are progressively dismissing their practical aspects to become something more close to morality. Indeed eminent figures from the Christian and Orthodox world are making efforts to go beyond the boundaries of their traditions and to agree on some common basilar points. Even Gülen has made significant steps in this direction. I think beyond these changes we can see common anxieties about moral decline in the contemporary world. These anxieties are the common basis on which religions seems to agree on claiming more voice over global moral issues.

I think the secularist discourses should be able to renew themselves in order to face the challenges that renewed religious discourses on modernity pose to it. From this perspective, I argue Gülen's example opens up the possibility for such a rethinking. Indeed it permits of reconsidering the basilar dichotomy on which the secularists have founded their discourse on modernity. Looking at compatibilities between Gülen's project and the modern one should lead us to refuse the aprioristic secularists' exclusion of Islam from the modernist project. I think that if religion continues to be marginalized inside modernity it is not because of an intrinsic incompatibility with it, but because the secularists' have founded their idea of modernity on this opposition.

---

20 Asad Talal, Reflections on Laïcité and the Public Sphere, Keynote address at the "Beirut Conference on Public Spheres", October 22-24, 2004 (Excepts). Source: Social Science Research Council, Items and Issues, Volume 5, Number 3, 2005. (http://www.ssrc.org/publications/items/v5n3/index.html)

GÜLEN'S THEORY OF *ADAB* AND ETHICAL VALUES OF GÜLEN MOVEMENT

Erkan Toguslu

Abstract

This paper seeks to explore and explain the prominent place of '*adab*' (roughly, good manners) in the description and building of Muslim identity and personality, and the implications for Muslim individual and collective behaviour in contemporary societies. In particular, the paper examines the role of ethical values in the formation of character, through Fethullah Gülen's discourses addressed to, and successful in inspiring, Muslim youth: the definition of moral character on the basis of religion provides the movement's members with the ideal and a roadmap to the ideal of the 'perfected human being' (*insan-ı kamil*). Gülen seeks to reshape modernity through the concept of moral character informed and made stable by religious consciousness. As a result, attitudes to the 'other' and the frontiers between 'outward' and 'inward' are reconfigured. The concept of *insan-ı kamil* encourages self-transcendence through service of others (*hizmet*), and the patient, peaceful resolution of tensions between different ideologies such as 'Islamic' and 'secular'. The Gülen movement conceives of and, through the practice of its members, presents the ethical domain as the common ground of shared values.

Derived from the Arabic words of *khuluq* which means to create, to shape and to give form; *Akhlaq*; corresponds to ethic, is a subject of *Ilm al-akhlaq*. *Akhlaq* embraces all of the details of human character and life. It describes not only the religious injunctions containing the beliefs, but also gives a map of social behaviour Muslims adhere to. *Adab*, which the practical dimension of *Ilm al-Akhlaq*, is the base of morality, prescribes a way of living according to the Islamic rules of ethics involving every aspect of daily life. It reflects the good manners, education and self-training that indicates a high valuation of correct order, behaviour and taste. The term is understood by moral formation which is going with *akhlaq* (ethics).[1] *Ilm al-Akhlaq* is a branch of knowledge, which deals with the rules and norms to increase human values and virtues, to avoid misconduct and to do what is correct. There is also the other meaning; that the knowledge which leads to cultivation of intellectual culture, Arabic literature and poetry. In this paper, I examine the discipline, training and self-cultivation through *adab* rules and its relationship with knowledge that makes up "Muslim anthropology of man".

This paper has two central objectives: First, it aims to recover the ethical theory among the Islamic scholar and Gülen's views, to defining *adab* in relating with Islamic morality. We give such views of adap interesting implications for religious morality. Second, it aims to analyze how ethical norms as *adab* rules play a central role in identifying Muslim behaviour and character creating new universal discourse of human ideal. The Islamic manner and body are reshaped by this universal ethical discourse, one claims that the rationalization and secularization affects[2] Thus, Gülen's view of *adab* identifies and formulates some new theoretical and practical options imitate by the Muslim young generation and lead the articulation between secular and religious ethical models. As Yilmaz argues, Gülen's definition of *adab* and ethical body can be explained as a new *tajdid* by conduct.[3] My interest is to understanding the conceptualization of *Adab* and morality in Gülen's followers and sympathizers and different modalities of ethical action which create new modern Islamic subjects, in other terms *Islamic habitus*. My intention is to understand how Gülen reformulates and urges the ethical imperatives which set up behavioural norms connecting ideal Muslim personalities. Arguing Talal Asad, the behavioural set has some relation with moral structures of the self in which emotional, behavioural, repetitive ritual play a crucial role to achieve.[4] He does not represent classical theories and debates among the Muslim thinkers; however he also does not attain to disconnect the "cumulative tradition" of Islamic ethical views.[5] This ethical formulation with drawing up the Islamic conscience is changed and appropriated in different ways and contexts as Hodgson remarks that the Muslim conscience is manifested differently in every case to survive God's commitment by Muslims.[6] In different centuries, Muslim

---

1   B. D. Metcalf, *Moral Conduct and Authority: the place of "adab" in South Asian Islam*, Berkeley, University of California Press, 1984, p. 3, F. Gabrielli, *"Adab"*, in E.I.

2   Elizabeth Özdalga, "Secularizing Trends in Fethullah Gülen's Movement: Impasse or Opportunity for Further Renewal", in *Critique: Critical Middle Eastern Studies*, Spring 2003, v. 12 (1), pp.61-73

3   İhsan Yılmaz, " *Ijtihad* and *Tajdid* by Conduct, The Gülen Movement", in M. Hakan Yavuz and John L. Esposito (eds), *Turkish Islam and Secular State, The Gülen Movement*, New York, Syracuse University Press, pp 208-237

4   Talal Asad, *Genealogies of Religion, Discipline and Reason of Power in Christianity and Islam*, London, John Hopkins University Press, 1993, p. 65

5   The cumulative tradition means "… a change in the way the whole tradition is to be understood". p. 6. I took this term from W. C. Smith, *The Meaning and End of Religion*, New York, MacMilian, 1963 cited by Sheila McDonough, *Muslim Ethics and Modernity, A Comparative Study of the Ethical Thought of Sayyid Ahmad Khan and Mawlana Mawdudi*, Ontario, Wilfrid Laurier University Press, p. 2

6   M. Hodgson, *The Venture of Islam: Conscience and History in a World Civilization*, London, University of Chicago Press, 1974

thinkers emphasizes on requirement of the Muslim conscience with using the Islamic words and concepts. In this modern age, facing modernity, Muslim world research an answer to live how Muslims should coexist with others without laying theirs manners. The need for an ethical character is underlined by Gülen is an embracing response for his symphatisants. Gülen is not only interpreter of Qur'an and an Islamic thinker, he emphasizes to correct individual's ethical life by raising such values as humility, loyalty, altruism, devotion, trust and repentance. This non politic message can easily entice new symphatisants.

I'm interested bodily expressions of ethical conception that Gülen underlines in his speeches. He remarks the importance of representative role (*temsil*) rather than speeches and argumentation (*tebliğ*). This bodily act constitutes the transformation of our perception on Islamic subjects and the meaning of the life. Mahmood argues that gestures and behaviours donate also the meaningful of the world with body shaped some values inherent self.

> ...bodily behavior does not simply stand in a relationship of meaning to self and society, but it also endows the self with certain kinds of capacities that provide the substance from which the world is acted upon.[7]

In this sense, the emotional and bodily performance is proper realization of ethical values that award the substance of world. Some of the values like humility, ascetism, devotion that I follow in this paper provide us to understand how the performatif acts produce and form not only Islamic subjects but give a critical approach in modern society and civilization. Issues raised by Elias, in his book The History of Manners; show us the behavioural and physical changes shifting in a *civilized* direction in the course of Western history. For Elias, these gradually changes resulted the civilizing process marked by new emotional, behavioural feelings. The new conducts are interrelated with the organization of society.[8] Norbert Elias refers to habits and manners to understand how the civilized process developed in modern Europe. He also describes various meanings of civilization, but he brings the habits and the development of good manners to clarify their role in the formation of civilization. However Elias's historical sociology neglects the influence of religious factors in civilized process. My argument is broadly that Gülen's adap theory in which religiously oriented good manners and etiquette come to dominate social interactions is parallel to the civilizing process in which civil norms of self-restraint come to dominate social interaction as Elias describes in the "court society". These two similar civilizing processes have similar functions as a personality that is cultivated through education and discipline. We get the adap as an element of revealing the Muslim manners linking with the civilization. The question of how we can have a well-mannered character depends on the realization of *adap*. Gülen's morality, gives us the ideal of Islamic civilization related to the *adab* rules. He develops the idea of faith oriented from morality to encourage a revival in Islamic activism.

We can interpret the notion of personality guided by *adab* rules and make some comparisons with Foucault's 'technologies of the self'.[9] Foucault takes the ancient Greek ethical conceptions Religion disciplines the person through ascetic practices and creates a perfect human being, in point of Weber; it regulates instinctual life in the interest of social order.[10] Gülen's pedagogical model concerning altruism associated always with devotion, self-criticism is

---

7 Saba Mahmood, *Politics of Piety, The Islamic Revival and the Feminist Subject*, Princeton, Princeton University Press, 2005, p. 27

8 N. Elias, *The Civilizing Process, The History of Manners*, Oxford, Basil Blackwell, 1978

9 M. Foucault, "Technologies of the Self" in *Ethics: Subjectivity and Truth*, London: Allan lane, pp. 225-251

10 B. S. Turner, "The Rationalization of the body: reflections on modernity and disciplines" in S. Whimster and S. Lash (eds), *Max Weber, Rationality and Modernity*, London, Allen&Unwin, pp. 222-241

thought in this paper as technologies of the self in which the objective of taking care body and soul is achieved. Pursuit of this pedagogical model of morality permits Gülen's sympathizers to transform themselves in a state of happiness, purity, wisdom, perfection that shaped ideal human being.

My objectif is to show how, as argued Brown, the Islamic *adab* and morality originated from religious injunctions which lead to the internalization of Islamic rules and norms that give an inner world and spiritual dimension to an ascetic person with outlined religious principles, the human soul which is cultivated by the efforts of one self.[11]

The essential purpose of *adab* is to nurture the human morality. To reach the goal of raising the human character, Muslim's behaviour is determined by the religious recommendation and obligation which gives him a map of cognition. *Adab* is regarded as the practical morality of Islam. Muslims internalize these practices and rituals in order to rear a perfect human being (*insan-ı kamil*). According to a *Hadith*, "the best amongst you are those who have the best manners and characters, the good behaviour are central to the performance of Muslim's personality."

Debates on Ethical Issues

When Islam emerged in the Middle East with the conquests, Islamic literature, the exegetic studies had not been formulated until the 10th century as seen with the separation between the basic sciences of Quran interpretation, *hadith*, theology and *kalam*. As the scholars mention, the elaboration of moral and spiritual literatures dates back to the tenth and the thirteenth centuries.[12] Ten centuries before, we could describe pre-ethical discussions and doctrinal conflicts, consequently determined as some values for Muslim's individual and collective every day life.[13] Later centuries followed the first Islamic expansion, we see the overlapping issues related on human responsibility, free will and divine omnipotence that later raised the ethical debates and ethical theory of Islam as Fakhry wrote "a reasoned account of the nature and grounds of right actions and decisions and the principles underlying".

Islamic thinkers focused on distinguishing the Islamic disciplines as theology, *kalam* and *hadith* literatures, which furnish ethical theories in Islam and every discipline offers Muslims different aspects of ethical fundaments as well as the fiqh recommends the regulation of Muslim daily life according the law, the Sufis develop vital questions that strengthen the inner dimension of Muslims. The major debate in ethics is distinguished between rationalist and scriptural and non rationalist morality theories characterized by different dialectical and methodological ways in which the disputes promote the refurbishment of Islamic ethical rules regarding theological questions about predetermination (*qadar*), obligation (*taklif*), the political duties.[14] The Mu'tazilite school sees the freedom of the will as a fundamental element of Islamic morality. Islamic thinkers and philosophers had been influenced by Greek philosophers whose ethics conceptions had a numerous affects. The contact with Christian theologians and Greek philosophers permit to the Mu'tazilites to apply theirs methods in theirs ethical conceptions. Wasil ibn Ata was the first who started to promote the radical turning of the Mu'tazilite. In this period, al-Kindi refers to Greek philosopher's writings about ethic. He wrote many ethical treatises revealed Socratic understanding. An other Islamic

---

11 Peter Brown, "Late Antiquity and Islam: Parallels and Contrasts", pp. 23-37, in Metcalff, op. cit.

12 Ira M. Lapidus, *A History of Islamic Societies*, Cambridge, Cambridge University Press, 2002, p. 192

13 Majid Fakhry, *Ethical Theories in Islam*, Leiden, E.J. Brill, 1994, p. 3

14 The debates between Ash'arites and Mu'tazilites schools influence the issues of ethical debates.

philosopher is ar-Razi, in his writings we can establish some parallelism on division of parts of the souls, following a hedonistic life with Platonic Socratic themes. The contribution of al-Farabi's on ethical discussion is also profoundly influenced the later Islamic thinkers and scholars. He interpreted the *Nicomachean* Ethics of Aristotle. He followed Aristotle's division on intellectual and practical virtues in other terms moral virtues. In his theory of justice, he claims that the distribution of common good assures the equity among the people. These common goods consists the security, wealth, dignity and other virtues.

Ibn Miskawayh set up the most essential ethical issues dealing with platonic suggestions in his *Tahdhib al-akhlaq* (The Cultivation of Morals).[15] His ethical works explains how acquire the correct way of moral through the harmony of soul, correct manners. Emphasising on human rational that guides humanity to decide and chose between good and bad, led to consider him a humanist. In fact that his use of rationality in his writings, he was criticized by other Islamic thinkers like Al-Ghazali who treatises the worldly and otherworldly happinies. He lays down virtues like wisdom, courage, temperance, justice and divine virtues. He refers Qur'an and Hadith which is a central and basic element in his ethical theory. For Ghazali, human's acts and manners must be governed by divine virtues and the purification of soul. He describes good manners that Muslim imitates in their life.

Nevertheless, the study of Islamic ethics is understood in the Quran which provides Muslims with the way of life which means doing good deeds, acting generously, being charitable, having an altruistic character, restraining from his ardour. We assume that the ethical theories of Islam are the Islamic code of daily conduct which contains also the *adab* having a fundamental role in determining the ethical principles to be divided into three categories: responsibility for God, duties that a Muslim presents to those with whom he lives, and finally the manners to have in daily routines.

The first category is mentioned obviously both in the Qur'an and in the Hadith[16], which includes actions and measures that are the attributes expected from a Muslim to fulfil a responsibility for good behaviour which is good in itself such as sincerity, honesty, altruism, generosity, modesty, tolerance and its opposite is considered grave sins that must be avoided. Secondly, being kind to parents, helping others, showing kindness to all human beings ignoring racial and religious differences. Manners observed in daily life as sleeping, eating, talking, entering into the washing room, posture when sitting, which invoke every aspect of life which Muslims mostly refer to *Hadiths*, are included in the third category of *adab*. All of them codify how Muslims must act by searching for a practical realization of God's commands to attempt an inner self and self-realization as well as the commitment to the revelation and *hadiths*. These practical *adap* principles relate to the Sufis experiences in which a person finds piety and ascetic behaviour.

Gülen's Ethical Views

The discussion among different Islamic ethical theories considered rationalist and anti rationalist does not help us to define Gülen's theory of *adap* and ethic. He underlines the importance of behaviour as play crucial role to identify ethical norms. According to importance the behaviours; "Morals were once thought of as virtues. Today they are regarded as a collection

---

15 See M. Arkoun, Contribution à l'étude de l'humanisme arabe au IV/Xe siècle (Contribution to the Study of Arab Humanism in the 4th-10th Centuries), Paris, Vrin, 1970

16 Hadith literature consecrates some chapters on the ethical comportments.

of rules for social behaviour."[17]

He attempts to define a practical reason, not in Kantian way, and practical knowledge that articulates through body and behaviour. Marcel Mauss describes that body is not only formed, shaped but it is a learning process how act.

Gülen does not mean to refurbish the debates between these two main current discourses on Islamic morality; instead, he gives a practical aspect on morality. He says:

> Morality is the essence of religion and a most fundamental portion of the Divine Message. If being virtuous and having good morals are to be heroic-and they are- the greatest heroes are, first, the Prophets and, after them, those who follow them with sincerity and devotion. A true Muslim is one who practices a truly universal, therefore Muslim, morality.[18]

Lacking a political dimension, his sermons affect the fulfilment of Muslim's morality through the formation of personality. Gülen's movement opposes to violence and does not favour the protest but the aim of movement is to develop the inner life of all Muslim communities. Gülen gives moral advice to the ordinary people. For Gülen, individual self-control and self-renewal are determined through *adab*. The political criticism and responsibility come after the personal responsibility which is the first duty. He emphasizes on Muslim's character how he or she controls, acts:

> ...who sees, thinks, and acts with all the faculties of such a conscience; whose sitting and standing are mercy, whose words and speech are mildness and agreement, and whose manners are politeness and refinement.[19]

In his sermon, the prophetic model to which Gülen attributes a decisive role and a central place is represented as a figure to absolutely imitate. The pious, ascetic and devoted religious practices are expected from the Muslim generation. Stemming ultimately from two central authorities, the Qoran and the life of the Prophet, Gülen underlines the divine aspect of morality. For Gülen, the Prophet is the example of goodness as well as the revelator of high human quality. Following Nursi,[20] the morality is based on *Qoranic* concept and the prophetic manner.

Demonstrating the negative dimension of human character, Gülen identifies the danger of nihilism to man and Muslim consideration that is seen as a fundamental reason of decline of Muslim morality, to grasp the demoralization of human values by materialism and nihilism.[21] This danger of nihilism is at the core of ethical crises in the Muslim world. He criticizes the existentialism of Sartre, the deism of French philosophers, and the atheism injected into the young Muslim generation. Opposing the disjunction between the morality and religious faith, the idea entrusted from the Enlightenment, especially the French thinkers had a more critical and anti-clerical but not anti-religious position that they thought the religion is an obstacle for human emancipation and for developing a moral sense. As for perceiving the religion as the reason of disunity and clashes between people and nations, Gülen finds that those considerations are fraudulent.[22] As to the fact that the misunderstanding and ignorance deriving from different religious faiths, attitudes as a reason of conflicts, however religions recommend the

17 Gülen, Criteria or Lights of the Way, Izmir, 1998, Vol.2, (12th edition), pp. 59-61
18 F. Gülen, Towards the Lost Paradise, London, Truestar, 1993, p. 30
19 F. Gülen, The Statue of Our Souls, Revival in Islamic Thought and Activism, New Jersey, The Light, 2005, p. 91
20 Nursi, *Lemalar, 11. Lema, Sözler Yayınevi*, 1998, p. 49 See Nursi's influence on Gülen Hakan Yavuz
21 F. Gülen, *Işığın Göründüğü Ufuk, Mefkure İnsanı*, Nil Yayınları, 2005, p. 137
22 F. Gülen, *The Statue of Our Souls...*, p. 20

same value, gaping the belief and sincerity, without self-control, Gülen defends that "the virtue with faith cannot approve of nor lead to such calamities. Indeed, the only way to avoid falling into such misfortunes is to integrate the religion with all institutions into our daily life..."[23]   The formation of secular morality which has influenced the Muslim consciousness has turned into crises as a deviation from the Islamic model. Gülen intends to formulate the Muslim consciousness from the Islamic perspective and to examine the events from the Islamic point of view and reasoning without falling down into contradiction with modernity. Gülen has also influenced by occidental intellectuals as Bergson, Kant, Eddington, Pascal. He claims that many Muslim intellectuals "who blindly imitate and import what they see as Western despise" and neglect the spiritual and metaphysical dimension of Western thought.

> it is difficult to accept that Western scientific thought, although primarily materialistic, has always been separate from spirituality and metaphysics. Modern Western civilization is based on the trinity of Greek thought, Roman law, and Christianity. This latter, at least theoretically, contributes a spiritual dimension. The West never completely discarded Platonist thinking, although it failed to reconcile it with positivistic and rationalistic philosophy. It also has not pretended that such thinkers as Pascal and J. Jeans never existed, or excluded Bergson's intuitivism.[24]

There was undoubtedly some tension between reason and faith in current morality debates, but at the same time Gülen contributes to these disputes by invoking the reconciliation of two spheres. In his understanding of Islam, inspired more by Nursi's idea, the reason and the revelation is not in conflict. He refuses the idea that lacking of morality with religious principles permits the humankind to avoid the domination of religion which restrains the liberty of man and he asserts that the human essence, using language of Sufism, combines the soul/body, the mystical dimension/rationalist, the reason/faith refusing the materialistic vision of human substance. Humankind as describing a character owning good manner and ethical codes that built this human substance is the essential purpose of Gülen who doesn't say that the non believers don't have morality, but he argues that the efficiency can be sustained with values as a religious character, because people need a metaphysic thought and transcendental obligation to act or not in daily life. Sufis writings has more influnce on Gülen's view's on ethics and the most persuading and influential teachings about human manner and virtues are described by sufis and they are more acceptable among the Muslims.[25] Gülen states the importance of spirituality on human virtues and manners:

> Morals are a set of noble principles that originate in high spirituality and govern human conduct. For this reason, people who neglect spirituality, and are therefore lacking in spiritual values, cannot sustain conduct in accordance with these principles.[26]

The central argument of Gülen's morality is the necessity of religion in the construction of morality and the utility of practices in daily life for a moral life. In Gülen's writings that we can identify numerous connections of kinship between morality and religion as seen in Durkheim's approach[27], he outlines the role of religious universal ethical principles in

---

23 Gülen, ibid, p. 21

24 Gülen, "The Horizon of Hope: Spiritual or Metaphysical Thought", *http://en.fgülen.com/content/view/805/17/*

25 Anne Marie Schimmel, *The Mystical Dimension of Islam*, Chapel Hill, University of North Carolina Press, 1978 The Sufis lodges offers the cultivation of virtues, the self-control, the treatment of body, manners concerning the devotional exercises.

26 Fethullah Gülen, Criteria or Lights of the Way, Izmir, 1998, Vol.2, pp. 59-61

27 In his major work, *The Elementary of The Religious Life*, Durkheim set out the social origin of religion and he argued that the religion reinforced the morality and social norms. His argument is based on that the religion is provided social control, social cohesion.

reinforcing the morality of society. There is no separation between this world and the hereafter, the body and the soul, the mind and the heart.[28]

Ethical Self and Body

The ethical ideas that Gülen describes for this generation result from an ethical body and soul disciplined with the prevention from some illnesses and by advancing on human values like altruism, virtue, wisdom, love, tolerance, devotion and responsibility. The ethical soul can emerge by returning to revivification of these general assessments idealized by Gülen's followers in schools, media and dialogue activities and in daily life. Gülen summarizes this temptation of cultivation of body and soul in both sides: in the inner structure (hearts and souls) and the outer structure (knowledge). Besides, he supposes that the followers strive to be moral in accordance with universal religious values in their life thereby to promote their inner self, in other terms, realize the progress of human virtues in social relationships.

The gestures, the attitudes which are socially acquired, are formal imitations and indications of a moral significance. They are the parts of the common good of a society and a culture. A reflection on the gestures leads us to deal with the question of modesty and ethics "which seeks to define a gestural standard, say, the good and the bad gesture..."[29] The gesture is exhibited also from inside (soul-spirit) towards outside (physical)[30]. In other words, the expressivity of the gesture creates the function to determine the fundamental element for the construction of the personal and social identity. All the body gestures and behavior are identified by such rules as decency and civility in daily life. The daily prayer, the avoidance of the prohibited food, the manner of clothing and greeting, abstention from the illicit things and respect for one's parents become principles to keep the spirit of *haya*. All of these daily practices produce the technologies of self. The implementation of his daily obligations and religious practices that contain the *adab* rules and ethical codes allows the believer to acquire these ethical manners to train soul and body.

The choice of some food or a drink depends on the moralistic finality. The elimination of excesses is carried out since the sympathizer professes his faith by exteriorizing his religious *adab* rules. The abstinence from the alcoholic drinks, reducing his sleeping, his eating and speaking that are some of the sufistic principles speak less, sleep less, eat less *(killat-i kelam, killat-i menam, killat-i taam)*, having a respectful language without obscene words are required to obtain a holy life, particularly the one which occurs with a virginity. In the lives of the sympathizers, all acts generate a hedonist life. In the spaces like the schools, the houses, dormitories created by the movement, the hearts are emancipated so that no one talks about the hedonism, individualism and the fashionable life. Thus, the prohibition of alcohols and certain food falls under this logic. It is necessary to have a spirit and a holy, pure body away from the desires.

In order not to realize an activity which creates a mental confusion disturbing his spirit and his heart, the behavioural codes, *adab* rules are defined according to Islamic life regulations which evoke also the Islamic subject.[31] This becomes a question of how to accommodate in public sphere with his *adab* rules that contribute them to acquire a good manner and to act

28 Eyüp Can, *Fethullah Gülen ile Ufuk Turu*, Ad Yayıncılık, 1996 and Gülen, *The Statue...*, p. 20

29 Jean-Claude Schmitt, "La morale des gestes", in *Parure, Pudeur, Etiquette*, Revue Communication, Paris, Editions de Seuil, no. 47, p. 31

30 ibid, p. 32

31 Nilufer Göle, « l'émergence du sujet islamique », in Penser le Sujet, Autour d'Alain Touraine, F. Dubet and M. Wieviorka, (dir.), Paris, Fayard, 1995, p. 221

with the pre-disposed comportments. The sympathizer does not seek pleasure and the satisfaction of the mundane needs which contradict with his finality. These types of body and gestural obligations are registered in the formation of the Islamic subject which refers to the characteristics as mentioned above in Gülen's terms. The self-discipline is carried out among the followers in order to mobilize people and the pietism reinforces the ethical soul and body which is accompanied by asceticism and altruism which nourish Sufism.

The question of *haya* [32] (modesty) and esthetics represented by male sympathizers let us grasp the articulated Gülen's formulation on *adab* and morality. One can, as follows, describe the manner of being modest follow-up with the sympathizers: "the envoy of God was more modest than a girl in his cabin. When it saw a hateful thing, for him, we knew it according to his face"[33]

Gülen recommends his followers to be always humble (*tevazu*) with people. In his writings, he refers to his eminent master *Muhammed Lutfi Efendi* "everybody else is good but I am bad; everybody else is wheat, but I am chaff"[34], to be modest and having self-criticism are significant terms in the Gülen's formulation of *adab*.[35] Humility is seen as a portal of good conduct characterized by the Muslim identity.

Prophet says concerning the humility: God has told me that you must be humble, and that no one must boast to another; shall I inform you of one whom Hellfire will not touch? Hellfire will not touch one who is near to God and amiable with people, and mild and easy to get along with; God exalts one who is humble.

Among the followers, to maintain theirs qualities preserve their modesty and keep himself away from any kind of celebrity, they consider the celebrity and ostentation like "the fane as hypocrisy and a venomous honey"[36]. In Gülen's definition modesty is

"seeing oneself as devoid of all virtues essentially originating in oneself, treating others humbly and respectfully, seeing oneself as the worst of humanity (unless being honored by a special Divine treatment), and being alert to any stirring of the ego and immediately suppressing it."[37]

He recommends his followers to escape the attractive power of the ostentation in public which constrains believers to disorient their essential objective.

Modesty is required in different situations as the sympathizer purifies his words from the obscenities, has shame to mention the defects of the others. Ghazali points out that "impoliteness is to release indecent remarks without being concerned too much about their effects and their consequences"[38], while following a *hadith* of the prophet. The sympathizer purifies his language not to utter vain remarks, keeps his sight not to look at the source of carnal pleasure and his hearing not to seek what is hidden. In this case, modesty embraces a whole life. With others, the sympathizer strictly controls his attitude while speaking with measurement and acting with precaution. Sometimes being timid is a good solution for preserving the modesty

---

32 Decency is central in Islam. However the prophet known as: "Each religion has its own morals, and the morals of Islam it is decency" (Malik) and "decency and the Faith go hand in hand. If one is removed, the other is also "(Al-Hakim)

33 Mohammad Al Ghazali, *l'ethique du musulman*, Paris, Al Qalam, Paris, p. 218

34 Gülen, *Key Concepts in the Practice of Sufism*, V. 1, *tawadu,* Fairfax, The Fountain, 1999

35 Gülen, *Prizma, vol.1*, İzmir, Nil, 1996, p. 14

36 Said Nursi, *Mesnevi Nuriye*, Istanbul, Sözler Yayınevi, p. 71 Nursi describes the desire of celebrity and ostentation in contradiction to sincerity.

37 F. Gülen, Key Concepts …, Tawaddu.

38 Ghazali, op.cit., p. 220

and his good manner. He keeps his silence when he seizes that he is caught by the *impudic* situation. The followers' lives are marked by humility which is the strongest communication and expression; prefer tears rather than laughter and keep silent when they hear an obscene and excessive language.

Self-control is applied to oneself even in the details of the life of the follower. Self controlling guides the attitudes of the sympathizers and rules the places and the practices of every sympathizer. The self-control, discipline of the body and managing places include the decency of the sympathizer. He tries to be a modest man by avoiding behavior to excess, because "the *impudic* man is indeed an *impudic* body ... the *impudic* body is *an excess body*, makes projections, going beyond, and excrescence."[39] He keeps measurement according to virtuous principles' which he acquired in spaces like schools, foundations supported by the movement. The sympathizer represents an ascetic body or as does Bourdieu say, "what is learned by the body is not something that one has, as a knowledge that one can hold in front of oneself, but something which one is".[40] Self-control goes with self-criticism (*muhasaba*) through which the sympathizer analyzes and observes his or her deeds, thoughts. He tries to obtain good manner which requires an intellectual effort to acquire moral values to distinguish the borders between good and bad, beneficial and harmful. These moralistic values with self-interrogation help the followers to manage these borders and become a condition. As Gülen indicates that "this condition enables a believer to make amends for past mistakes and be absolved in the sight of God, for it provides a constant realization of the self-renewal in one's inner world".[41]

Secondly, Gülen movement establishes the new possibilities of connection between body and soul through the knowledge with Islamic interpretation in schools founded by the people who spread Gülen's notions. *Adab* is interrelated with knowledge which leads to understanding God's guidance and describes his commands.

Education and *Adab*

Defined as an education movement,[42] since 1980, the movement has entered educational activities by creating schools all over the world with the help of the *adab* rules. In general terms, the ethical codes empower the students to form an ethos of good manner. This primarily results in the creation of a modern self-characterized idealistic human attached to the movement formulation. Although these schools do not give religious courses, the essential orientation is based on the teaching of ethics[43]. Gülen stresses on education inspired an "ethical vision rooted in Islam but not limited in its expression to sympathizers of the *umma* (community)."[44] The Gülen's inspired schools' education style aims to respond the question of how to generate an ethical human with common values. Teaching is considered a holy duty[45] to achieve the finality to demonstrate the right way of ethical dimension of life with

---

39 Jean-Jacques Courtine, Georges Vigarello, "La physionomie de l'homme impudique, Bienséance et "impudeur": les physiognomonies au XVe et XVIIe siècle", in Communications, p. 84

40 Bourdieu, Le Sens Pratique, Paris, Minuit, 1980, p. 123

41 Gülen, Key Concepts..., op. cit, chapter: Muhasaba

42 John L. Esposito, M. Hakan Yavuz, Turkish Islam and The Secular State, The Gülen Movement, New York, Syracuse University Pres, 2003, p, 35 and Bayram Balcı, Missionnaires de l'Islam en Asie Centrale, Les ecoles turques de Fethullah Gülen, Paris, Maisonnneuve Larose, 2003

43 Bekim Agai, « The Gülen Movement's Islamic Ethic of Education », in Esposito and Yavuz, op.cit, p. 49

44 Thomas Michel, "Fethullah Gülen as Educator", in Esposito and Yavuz (edts), p. 82

45 Agai, op. cit, p. 58

daily conduct as many scholars indicate the methods applied in schools.[46]

As arguing Nasr, the role of education is not only to transmit the knowledge, but it attends to achievement of human character.

Islamic education is concerned not only with the instruction and training of the mind and the transmission of knowledge (*ta`lim*) but also with the education of the whole being of men and women (*tarbiyah*). The teacher is therefore not only a *mu`alim*, a 'transmitter of knowledge' but also a *murabbi*, a 'trainer of souls and personalities'. The Islamic educational system never divorced the training of the mind from that of the soul.[47]

The methodology of teachers to transmit the good manners is interesting: "Being a good example through one's deeds"[48] is a method of pedagogy and communication that we can see in Gülen's inspired schools. According to Özdalga and Balcı, a good Muslim representative without constraint and obligation becomes a model and example of teachers amongst pupils (*misal-temsil*). Transforming the students' character needs teachers who represent the qualities they want to inculcate into the students. We intend to develop an ethos of school that "entails the self-sacrifice, abnegation and the personal conviction to transform life"[49] by which the students achieve their inner life that does not exclude the spiritual dimension of every pupil. It is also the character of Gülen's schools that the material and spiritual realms are reconciled for bringing out the ideal human character.[50]

In Gülen's schools, teachers are inspired to give and impart wisdom as well as some qualities such as devotion, simplicity, trust, loyalty, fidelity to his friends, humility, modesty, contentedness, which are the result of the role of exemplarity of teachers. They are interested not only in the opportunity of education that gives a status in life, but also in the aim of these schools forming a modern self-character? when it comes to good manners dealing with civic moral values. Gülen asserts that the students need a solid character focusing primarily on ethics and virtue. Education and knowledge (ilm) are the bases of the action which is *adab*-oriented. Education and learning are not sufficient to provide a moral and truly human if only they carry out the morality through by their high values.

> "Just because you are learned does not mean that you are truly human. Learned people are freed from carrying the burden of superfluous information and attain greatness to the extent that they serve humanity and set a good example for others through their high morals and virtues. Otherwise, they are no more than people who have wasted their lives. Those with high morals and virtues, even if they lack learning and are as dense as iron, sometimes may prove to be useful and valuable, and even as good as gold."[51]

The Major Jihad: Struggle Against Ego (*Nafs*)

Gülen divides Jihad in two: the internal and the external. "The internal one can be described as the effort to attain one's essence; the external one as the process of enabling someone

---

46 Özdalga, Elisabeth, "Worldly ascetism in islamic casting Fethullah Gülen's inspired piety and activisms", in.Critique:Journal for critical studies of the Middle East, n. 17, septembre 2000 and Balcı, op.cit, p. 221

47 Seyyed Hossein Nasr, Ideals and Realities of Islam, New York, ABC International Group, 2001, p. 56

48 Özdalga, "Following in the Footsteps of Fethullah Gülen", in Esposito and Yavuz (edts), p. 86

49 Esposito and Yavuz, op.cit, p. 34

50 Fethullah Gülen, "At the Threshold of a New Millennium", in *Essays, Perspectives, Opinions*, The Fountain, 2002, p. 30

51 Gülen, *Criteria or Lights of the Way*, op. cit., p. 60

else to attain his or her essence. The first is greater jihad; the second is the lesser jihad."[52] Following this definition, the essential enemy is ego's destructive and negative emotions. The first characteristic of a believer's action, for Gülen, has to do with the notion of the greater jihad, the struggle against one's carnal desires and worldliness. Literally, it means doing all one's abilities and skills to materialize an objective and resist all difficulties. Following Gülen's distinction, the sympathizers of movement seek to struggle with their inner world and ego. Every effort and attempt is oriented towards God's contentment destruction of *nafs* with alienation of his or her *nafs*. In followers' discourse, this objective is summarized as action. In Gülen's thought, the jihad contains believers' good manner and such *adab* rules as to act and control their anger, treat their intelligence, dominate their negative emotions, passions and drives which prevent the Muslims from attaining the achievement of ethical and spiritual perfection.[53]

To make the religion part of life, Gülen and his followers insist on acting minutely and show the easy way that does not contain constraint but they prefer to show good examples as doing good deeds to the others. This primarily non violent and voluntary approach is the fundamental method of the Gülen movement's action which is based on the construction of the self.

Ascetic Self and Body: Being with "Other"

Being with the others and uniting one's wishes with the others' desires and capability of integration with the whole existence in the universe is principal action as he states:

> "The real world of the person of action and thought and their real happiness in it are colored with the tones of universality and engraved within the frame of eternity."[54]

Inspired by the Sufistic terminology, the followers elaborate a language to strengthen their good conduct. One is an ascetic body, consciously or unconsciously, that affects one's acts such as eating, drinking, going to bed and getting up, talking and keeping silent, remaining in solitude or with people. Fashioned and displayed, the ascetic *adab* rules govern everyday life of the believers. The pleasure in this world is considered ephemeral and the followers do not pursue the hedonism because they believe that they are sent to this world to enhance his devotion and seek God's contentment. He has the idea that he will not stay for a long time here in this world for the reason that the essential duty is in the terrestrial world, therefore, it is necessary to move away from cheerfulness, joy, and temporary happiness to live the eternal life. The hedonism kills the idealism of the sympathizers. Against the hedonism, the sympathizers follow the value of altruism which Gülen regards as the criteria of life according to the ideal man which requires the effort of follower as developing the detachment from the pleasure and seductive needs, except that the intellectual and aesthetic dimension is allowed and accepted.[55] Gülen's followers do not abstain from the social life, the pleasure and entertainment like going to the cinema or theatre, listening to the music. But as I mentioned above, they like to live meaningfully an aesthetic Muslim life. Paradoxically, these ascetic body and soul which participate actively in daily life are considered better than the ascetic who is absent from worldly life. The sympathizer is in search of *esthétiser* his life according to his religious obligations which make him detach from the voluptuous desires.

According to Özdalga, who describes the community by the term "secular asceticism", the

---

52 Gülen, Essays, op.cit. p. 51-52

53 Gülen, ibid. , p. 53

54 Gülen, The Statue..., op.cit, p. 60

55 Fethullah Gülen, *İkindi Yağmurları*, İstanbul, Gazeteciler ve Yazarlar Vakfı yayınları, 2006, p. 187

Gülen movement rests on the pietism with which the self-control is realized.[56] By the participation in the mundane activities, the sympathizer does not go further with the religion as Weber suggests in Protestant Ethics and the Capitalism of Spirit: "asceticism had become a method of control rational… to withdraw the man from the power of the instincts, to release it from his dependence with regard to the world and… to subject his actions to a permanent control and a conscientious examination of their ethical range".[57] The formulation of "ascetic inner world" offers us to explain how a religious oriented practice is transformed into an ascetic rational good manner as responsibility and self-sacrifice. *Hizmet* for Gülen, implies that a person excessively devotes his life to humanity, is interested in the others needs and prefers their happiness rather than his own needs. He assume that the altruism the essential moral principle that the educators must to have for the humanity.

Conclusion

The self control and self discipline exercised through the individuals' knowledge are inculcated by different methods. The internalization of the norms is laid down by the *adab* and its function is a monitor itself in an effort to conform to these norms. Thus, the believer controls not only his body and soul which are obtained as character and good manner by the ethical formulation, but also a Muslim modern pious self is created. *Adab* rules offer a disciplined body conforming to the religious restrictions and obligations by which we establish an ethical self as Foucault calls this treatment as "aesthetics of the self"[58] which is required for the development of self and subject. As Foucault formulates, *l'esthétique de l'existence* is associated with *éthique*.[59]

We underline a subject tamed that recognizes *adap* rules as an object of morality problematized by some particular ground, divine commands in our example. The Muslim individuals transform themselves into ethical subjects via some sets of techniques as ascetics in sufistic terminologies, meditation and consciousness raising through *adab* manners. Finally, Gülen proposes his followers and believers to pursue an ethos of self control, self discipline, and a lifestyle according the good manners described in *Adab* manuscripts. The aim is to create a practical way of self-making which consists of the purification of body to create a moral self. This ethical subject recognizes the development of new Islamic believers who stress on establishing a form of civilized manners by willing submission to the *adab* rules.

Seeking religious fulfilment has resulted secular behaviour in daily life to manage the relationship with the whole society.[60] In humanistic terms, it is an effort to overcome the divisions and differences among others. This effort requires putting into order the followers' lives, channelling their thoughts and feelings and having a respectful language which is oriented by the leitmotifs as dialogue, tolerance, recognition and pluralism.

The social function of daily conduct and *adab* rules is to preserve morality. Besides, it defines and influences the transmission of ethical values. The trace between good/bad, normal/abnormal is determined by the threshold of *adab* which has the goal to transport the inside towards

56 Elizabeth Özdalga, « Worldly ascetism…, p. 19

57 Max Weber, Ethique Protestante et l'esprit du Capitalisme, Paris, Plon, p. 136

58 M. Foucault, *Histoire de la Sexualité*, 3 volumes, Paris, Gallimard, 1984

59 "Et si je me suis intéressé à l'Antiquité, c'est que, pour toute une série de raisons, l'idée d'une morale comme obéissance à un code de règles est en train, maintenant, de disparaitre, a déjà disparu. Et à cette absence de morale répond, doit répondre une recherche qui est celle d'une esthétique de l'existence." M. Foucault, Dites et Ecrits, Vol. 4, texte n. 357

60 Özdalga, "Secularizing trends…, op. cit.

the outside, on public sphere. The tastes and the gestures produce the control of public space. The appearance of Gülen's followers with their gestures, their ethics also generates the participation of the grammar of this public sphere.

REVIVING THE *SUFFA* TRADITION

Rıfat Atay

Abstract

In Islamic history, one of the most intriguing questions has been the termination of the *Suffa* School immediately following the Prophet's demise. As is well known, the *Suffa* Companions were comprised of mostly single young men who did not have anywhere else to go to. They were provided with shelter and food in the Prophet's Mosque in Medina. Their sole occupation was to spend all their time with the Prophet, learning and studying. They became so well versed in Islam that most of them were sent as teachers and/or governors to new provinces.

The paper claims that today Gülen is seeking to revive the *Suffa* tradition in two ways. First, by resembling the first *Suffa* Companions himself. The four guiding principles traced in the lives of the *Suffa* Companions (single, simple, humble and pious) can be found in the daily life of Gülen. Thus, this paper suggests that Gülen is often mistaken as a Sufi when in fact he can be considered a member of the *Suffa*. Secondly, Gülen has been consistently providing personal tutelage over the last two decades to hundreds of theology graduate students. Students gain admission to Gülen's informal school by passing a rigorous exam in Islamic sciences and Arabic. Thereafter awaits them extensive study and an ascetic lifestyle. Students can remain as long as they wish, some for even as long as ten years. Gülen has been known to have had up to 40 students at times, although given his ill-health this number has dropped to 15 in recent years. In their lifestyle, daily programme and efforts post 'graduation' these students resemble the first *Suffa* Companions.

"Human beings to whichever world they are tuned in are deaf to the other one."[1]

Introduction

Civilization is a continuous process in which institutions do interact with each other. Like other educational initiatives, the Gülen movement probably has its roots at the very beginning of Islamic educational history and the rarely studied first Islamic educational institution, the *Suffa* School. This paper will attempt to show these direct or indirect roots and connections.

It is maintained by Muslims that when societies start deteriorating, especially in moral standards, God sends messengers to them to put them right. The messengers come sometime with a special revelation and mission and sometime with the mission only by following the message revealed to the previous prophet. When the seventh century Arabia was in total decay, the former was the case with them, too. The Prophet Muhammad was sent primarily to them, then to all humanity, with a special revelation and mission to restore the society to the godly rules expected of them. After ten years of struggle and partial success in Mecca, the Muslim community was ordered by Allah to migrate to Medina to start anew and afresh- in fact, this move, technically termed *Hijra*, was later rightly considered to be as a new era in Islamic history and taken to be the beginning of Islamic lunar calendar by the second caliph 'Umar b. al-Khattab. Muslims gradually left in small groups up to the point when only a few remained at Mecca. Then, the Prophet himself was ordered to departure to Medina with his closest companion, friend and an ally of the Muslims, Abu Bakr, the first caliph to succeed Muhammad.

When the Prophet reached at Medina after a long, arduous journey, the first thing he decided to do in the new Muslim settlement was to build a mosque both as a place of worship and a centre for all formal and informal gatherings. The masjid was later to be called the al-Masjid al-Nabawi, the Mosque of the Prophet, the second holiest/sacred place in Islam after the Holy Ka'ba. The Prophet himself not only designed this original mosque but also physically worked in building it alongside his companions. The mosque was divided into three separate parts: **(i)** in the northern direction situated a large section for praying opposite to which was placed **(ii)** the *Suffa* or *Sofa* in the southern direction and **(iii)** at the eastern direction, took place the rooms for the wives of the Prophet.[2]

The Suffa School[3] and *Ahl al-Suffa* (The *Suffa* Companions)

The Arabic word *suffa* literally means *shed, bench* or *banquette*; it was even adapted by some other languages such as Turkish and English as *sofa* or *divan*. In Islamic literature, it came to mean "a long, covered portico or vestibule,"[4] initially, forming part of the newly built mosque at Medina, then in later periods transformed into the antechamber of any mosque in Islamic

---

1 Özel, I, Erbain: Kırk Yılın Şiirleri (Forty: The Poetry of Forty Years), Istanbul, Şule Yay., 2005, 100.

2 Hamidullah, M, İslam Peygamberi (The Prophet of Islam), trans., Tuğ, S, İstanbul, İrfan Yayımcılık, 1990, v. II, 768; Baktir, M, İslam'da İlk Eğitim Müessesesi: Ashab-ı Suffa (The First Educational Establishment in Islam: The Companions of Suffa), İstanbul, Timaş, 1990, 20.

3 Throughout the paper, I shall mostly shorten the phrases as the Suffa for reasons of i) convenience and also ii) prevent confusion that it was like a modern day school of our times.

4 Watt, W M, "Ahl al-Suffa", Encyclopaedia of Islam, New Edition, Leiden, E J Brill, 1960, v. I, 266.

architecture. Although some orientalists assume that both the *Suffa* and *Ahl al-Suffa*[5] were probably ungrounded legends,[6] some Muslim scholars fittingly consider the *Suffa* as the first archetypal Islamic university, even providing an accommodation facility.[7] As will be much clearer in the following pages, it is probably a serious gaffe to suppose such a common, well-known, societal event as legend for it appears not only in historical sources but also in the Qur'anic commentaries (*tafsirs*) and the authentic *hadith* collections.[8] For the time being, it suffices to remark that the *Suffa* was the first Islamic educational institution consisted of a mosque as its classroom, the *Suffa* as dormitory, the *Suffa* Companions as students and above all, the Prophet as the teacher and mentor.

The companions who used to live in the *Suffa* were called *Ahl al-Suffa* or the *Suffa* Companions. Although, in the original plan of the mosque, the *Suffa* section at the mosque was allocated in the southern direction, when the direction of praying (*qibla*) was changed from Jerusalem to Mecca, the mosque had to be rearranged in order to accommodate the new situation. With this new decree, the praying section and the *Suffa* had to be replaced asymmetrically, which meant that the *Ahl al-Suffa* had to be removed to the northern side of the mosque whereas the praying area had gone to the Southern direction towards Mecca.

After their migration, *hijra*, to Medina, the majority of the companions took up either trade or agriculture. Some others, however, made an otherworldly choice by deciding to devote their lives by remaining right next to the feet of the Prophet Muhammad. They were comprised of mostly single young men who did not have anywhere else to go to or relatives and acquaintances to safeguard them.[9] With one exception about 'Abdullah b. Mas'ud who, according to Ibn Sa'd, was given special permission to live in the *Suffa* with his family,[10] whoever has got married left the *Suffa*. Nevertheless, newcomers kept flowing since there are reports putting their numbers as high as 400[11] or even 700 at some points.[12] The *Suffa* Companions took shelter under the *Suffa* where, from time to time, they were also catered for either by the Prophet Muhammad himself or some wealthy companions,[13] such as Sa'd b. Ubade.[14] Often, the Prophet used to take some of the *Suffa* Companions as guests to His rooms and strongly recommended His companions to invite as many of them as possible to their houses at meal-times.[15] Hence, the *Suffa* Companions were nicknamed as the *guests of Muslims*.[16]

One should not get the wrong idea that the *Suffa* Companions were a burden on the Muslim community as far as their day-to-day living is concerned. It has been reported that they themselves had also struggled to earn their living by collecting wood from the jungle and selling it

---

5 The common Turkish expression is Ashab-ı Suffa

6 Watt, "Ahl al-Suffa", 266.

7 Hamidullah, İslam Peygamberi, v. II, 768-769.

8 See e.g.: Baktir, Ashab-ı Suffa, 30-47 (footnotes n.: 41-74).

9 Another exception to the general character of the Suffa Companions was the son of the second caliph Umar, 'Abdullah, better known as Ibn 'Umar, who was so keen on learning the religion and wisdom from the Prophet that he chose to stay at the Suffa rather than the far away family home (Sahih Muslim, "Fadhail al-Sahaba," 140).

10 Yilmaz, H K, "Tassavvufi Açıdan Ashab-ı Suffa" (The Suffa Companions from the Mystical Aspect), Tasavvuf İlmi ve Akademik Araştırma Dergisi, v. 3, n. 7, 15 (Ibn Sa'd, Tabakat, v. III, 152).

11 Hamidullah, İslam Peygamberi, v. II, 769.

12 Yilmaz, "Tasavvufi Açıdan Ashab-ı Suffa", 13.

13 Baktir, Ashab-ı Suffa, 26 (Ibn Sa'd, Tabakat, v. I, 255).

14 Hamidullah, İslam Peygamberi, v. II, 769.

15 Bukhari, "Manakib," 25.

16 Tirmidhi, "Sıfat al-Qiyama," 36.

off or by carrying water for other people.[17] The Prophet was very careful about making sure that the *Suffa* Companions were fed and clothed properly for Allah ordered Him and Muslims in the Qur'an to do so in several verses. Here is one verse in the *Sura al-Baqara*, the second chapter of the Holy Qur'an:

> (Alms are) for the poor who are straitened for the cause of Allah, who cannot travel in the land (for trade). The unthinking man accounteth them wealthy because of their restraint. Thou shalt know them by their mark: They do not beg of men with importunity. And whatsoever good thing ye spend, lo! Allah knoweth it.[18]

In this respect, the general rule followed by the Prophet was that if something was brought to Him, He used to ask whether it was charity or gift. If it was charity, He used to send it directly to the *Suffa* Companions; if it was gift, he used to accept it for Himself but spare a share for the *Suffa* Companions. Like all the previous prophets did, Muhammad, too, always refused charity but accepted gift.[19] Even then, most of the time, the *Suffa* Companions had neither enough food nor proper clothing[20] to the extent that they had to survive without food for two days in succession. As a result, some of them used to fell down in the middle of congregational prayers due to weakness. The Bedouins who witnessed this thought they were mad but they were not mad; they were only hungry.[21] The Prophet, however, had always a great concern for the *Suffa* Companions, sometimes even at the price of refusing his beloved daughter Fatima's wishes. Once she asked a maidservant to be employed at her house by complaining that her hands were bruised because of corn grinding. The Prophet rejected her wish outright with this statement:

> O my daughter. I can give you nothing before I satisfy the needs of the people of the *Suffa*. However, let me teach you something that is better for you than having a servant. When you go to bed, say: 'Glory be to God (*Subhan Allah*), All praise be to God (*Alhamdu li'llah*), God is the Greatest (*Allah Akbar*),' 33 times each.[22] This is better for your next life.[23]

Although the *Suffa* Companions had a difficult life vis-à-vis the material world, their educational and spiritual development was extremely fruitful. Since they neither had a family to feed for nor any other worldly worries to look after, such as camel flocks or beautiful date gardens, their sole business was either to sit next to the knee of the Prophet to gather the treasures he was distributing day by day or keep themselves busy with praying or spiritual cleansing. Certainly, in Islam, learning and teaching are considered both duties and worship. Thus, contrary to the common misperception, the emphasis put on education and learning is far greater than even on *jihad*, the holy struggle. This verse in *Sura al-Tawba* is reported to have been revealed about the *Suffa* Companions:

> And the believers should not all go out to fight. Of every troop of them, a party only should go forth, that they (who are left behind) may gain sound knowledge in religion, and that they may

---

17 Muslim, "'Imara," 147.

18 Qur'an 2/273; for other verses related to the Suffa Companions, see also: 2/267-268, 6/52-54, 9/122 and 18/28.

19 Muslim, "Zakat," 175.

20 Bukhari, "Salat," 58.

21 Tirmidhi, "Zuhd," 39.

22 In Turkish Islamic practice, these three are usually repeated five times a day after each daily prayer regardless of performing either in congregation or alone.

23 Bukhari, "Fada'il al-Sahaba," 9.

warn their folk when they return to them, so that they may beware.[24]

In addition to the Prophet, the *Suffa* had other teachers assigned especially for them by the Prophet Himself. 'Abdullah b. Sai'd b. al-As and Ubade b. Samit were teaching them reading and writing while 'Abdullah b. Mes'ud, Ubay b. Ka'b, Muaz b. Jabal, Salim b. Mua'z and Abu al-Darda were giving Qur'anic studies and religious knowledge. As they grew well informed in Islam, most of them were either assigned for special duties or sent as teachers and/or governors as the new religion reached to the surrounding regions. Bilal al-Habashi and 'Abdullah b. Umm al-Maktum, for instance, were responsible for calling *al-azan*, the prayer time,[25] while Mua'z b. Jabal was sent to Yemen as teacher and governor.[26] Besides other well-known examples, Abu Hurayra can probably be considered the most famous graduate of this school as far as the *hadith* collection is concerned. When some people complained that, as a Yemeni, he was narrating too many *hadiths* some of which might not be sound, he retorted that while they were busy with their businesses or crops, he always remained with the Prophet to memorize the divine wisdom He was delivering.[27]

Besides improving their intellectual capabilities, the *Suffa* students were educated spiritually and morally as well. They passed most of their nights in worship and prayer for their philosophy of life was to eat less and sleep less. Because of their total renouncing attitude towards the world, classical Islamic scholars like al-Ghazali and Ibn Taymiyya established close connections between them and the *Sufis*[28] and sought to originate many of the *Sufi* principles in their lives, such as living in *tekkes* next to the mosques, asceticism, piety and seclusion. Especially Ibn Taymiyya, who severely opposes to most of the *sufi* practices, is highly appreciative of the *Suffa* Companions.[29] Nonetheless, one should not assume that the *Suffa* Companions had an ascetic, secluded life in their own corner, like some of the *Sufis* who are sometime criticised for leading a monastic life totally devoid of social contact. As we have already noted, the *Suffa* Companions were being educated for special missions such as teaching, administrational duties and official representation. Hence, when the circumstances required, they were sent away to accomplish these duties. Probably, this is the reason why the *Suffa* School ceased to exist after the passing away of the Prophet.

As to moral and behavioural education and training, the Prophet, as their prime mentor, used to warn them when they committed a wrong deed and encouraged them when He saw their good behaviours. I shall end this section with a significant anecdote related to teacher training aspect of the *Suffa* School. Ubade b. Samit, as indicated earlier, was a *Qur'an* and writing teacher at the *Suffa*. One of the students gave him an arch as a present but he was unsure about accepting or refusing it. The Messenger of God disapproved of it and warned: "If you would like a ring of fire to be hung on your neck, take it."[30] I consider that this moral code has the utmost importance since, in terms of piety and asceticism; it forms one of the basics of the Gülen educational initiative.

In short, I believe that the *Suffa* Companions had some essential characteristics apparent in their day-to-day lives that can be labelled as the *Suffa* spirit. They are *asceticism, piety,*

---

24 Qur'an 9/122.
25 Muslim, "Sıyam," 38.
26 Abu Dawud, "Aqdhiya," 1.
27 Bukhari, "I'tisam," 22; cf.: Tirmidhi, "Manaqıb," 46.
28 Watt, "Ahl al-Suffa," 266.
29 Yilmaz, "Tasavvufi Açidan Ashab-ı Suffa", 17-27.
30 Abu Dawud, "Buyu'", 36.

humility and *dedication to good deeds* (*al-'amal al-salih*). Particularly the latter, *al-'amal al-salih*, is a general term that covers a wide range of affairs such as *tamsil, tabligh, al-amr bil-ma'ruf wa al-nahy an al-munkar* (commanding good and preventing bad) and serving people in general. What is more, the *Suffa* School created an organisational climate, primarily for the companions staying there and for others in general, that supported to develop and activate these qualities not only in their close environs but also in other places where they went to.

Can Gülen himself and his theology graduate students be related to the members of the *Suffa* School in sharing the *Suffa* spirit in any way? Let us try to discuss this question in the following section.

The Need for Change

With the fall of the so-called "sick man of Europe", the Ottoman State, at the beginning of the 20th century, the last super power came out of the Islamic civilization had also come to an end. This situation presented a grim picture and a possible destiny for Islamic world due to the fact that many people in the Islamic world used to see the Ottomans as their saviour and protector. When this guarantor had ceased to exist, the main picture of the Islamic world looked rather bleak in real disarray and deterioration. Islamic thinkers and scholars were all looking for a way out of this dismal state. In this regard, having studied three different scholars from three different continents, Namik Kemal of Turkey, Muhammad Abduh of Egypt, Sayyid Ahmad Khan of India, Fazlur Rahman drew our attention to the similarity in their conclusions despite the fact that they "hardly met each other." They seem to have agreed on four important pronouncements for the Islamic world in order to stand up on its feet and become a leader in the world stage again:

> **(1)** that the flowering of science and scientific spirit from the ninth to the thirteenth century among Muslims resulted from the fulfilment of the insistent Qur'anic requirement that man study the universe-the handiwork of God, which has been created for his benefit; **(2)** that in the later medieval centuries the spirit of inquiry had severely declined in the Muslim world and hence Muslim society had stagnated and deteriorated; **(3)** that the West had cultivated scientific studies that it had borrowed largely from Muslims and hence had prospered, even colonizing the Muslim countries themselves; and **(4)** that therefore Muslims, in learning science from afresh from the developed West, would be both recovering their past and refulfilling the neglected commandments of the Qur'an.[31]

It is a well-known fact that the Turkish response to the problems of the Islamic world was not limited to Namik Kemal's. The line opened by N Kemal and others was furthered by Said Nursi and other like-minded scholars. Nursi was a scholar and activist strongly suggesting to preserve and revive the religious essentials like faith, fate and the objectives of Allah.[32] It is usually assumed that the Nursi thought fathered several renewalist movements in Turkey and the Gülen Movement is one of them.[33] However, Gülen himself denies the assertion that

---

31 Rahman, F, Islam and Modernity: Transformation of an Intellectual Tradition, Chicago and London, The University of Chicago Press, 1982, 50-51.

32 Michel, T, "Four Frontrunners In Peace: People Who Have Devoted Their Lives To Peace", Academic Resources on the Gülen Movement CD, www.GülenConference.org.uk, 2007, 66 (Michel, T, Bediüzzaman'a Göre Müslümanlık-Hıristiyanlık Münasebetleri (Said Nursi's Views on Muslim-Christian Understanding) trans. Taşkın, C, İstanbul, Etkileşim Yay., 2006, 54).

33 See, Bilici, M, "Context, Identity and Representational Politics of Fethullah Gülen Movement in Turkey," Academic Resources on the Gülen Movement CD, www.GülenConference.org.uk, 2007, 66

"he is a follower of Nursi in any sectarian sense"[34] and would like to put a distance between Nursi and himself, in a way, to establish the movement's own identity. He wholeheartedly acknowledges the spiritual inspiration and indirect contributions of the Nursi intellectual heritage both to himself and the movement but stresses the fact that his primary goal has always been to become a good believer and to live as God commands Muslims to live rather than following this or that scholar.[35] To clarify the identity of the movement more evidently, some of Gülen's articles have been put together as a book under the title *A Movement Originating Its Own Models,* highlighting the article that carries the same name.[36] Despite the boldness of the title, the original article follows a softy softy approach and does not directly deals with the identity problem of the movement. It rather focuses on praising how much of a momentous job the volunteer of the movement are accomplishing both at home and abroad. Certainly, in between the lines, the article also asserts that the movement is unique in many areas and this is one of them and a very important one. Addressing the issue more directly has been left to another author close to the movement, Enes Ergene. Having conducted a thorough study of the movement, Ergene concludes bravely that the movement has produced "all its tradition, visionary, organizational, expansive and missionary objectives, societal and moral values, educational and preparatory institutions on its own. In reaching this level, it was supported by neither political and ideological, nor socio-cultural and Islamic any legacy that existed before itself."[37] Certainly, Ergene is not aiming at cutting bonds with the Islamic heritage. His main intention is to put a barrier between the Gülen Movement and the Nursi Group against the claims of an organic linkage existing between the two. According to Ergene, the movement receives its momentum and success solely from the charismatic personality, scientific and scholarly spirit, strong rhetoric and social activity of Gülen and also from the strong social and spiritual effect of the masses that support his cause. The role of Nursi in the movement is neither is organic and nor direct but remains within the spiritual and psychological sphere by means of the Nursi collection.[38]

The Gülen Movement came to the forefront when it started to gain momentum during the 1980s and became more publicised and got even stronger during the 1990s throughout Turkey. The movement's key philosophy or operating principles can be summed up as "remaining awake to your image of death and to your existential broods; doing good deeds (*hizmet*); and practicing humility, sacrifice, and self-criticism."[39] The traces of the *Suffa* spirit are visible in these principles, such as *humility, asceticism* and *dedication to good deeds (al-'amal al-salih).* In fact, Gülen's worldview is based on a harmonious mixture of activism (establishing charities in many spehres of life and economic enterprises) and pietism.[40] He declares that "our three greatest enemies are ignorance, poverty, and an internal schism." Out of three, the most serious problem is ignorance and the solution lies in education, which has always been "the most important way of serving" one's country in particular and humanity in general. It is also a good way of creating "dialogue with other civilizations," which has become a must

---

34 Michel, T, "Fethullah Gülen as Educator," in Turkish Islam and the Secular State, ed., Yavuz, M H and J L Esposito, Syracuse, NY, Syracuse University Press, 2003, 81.

35 Michel, "Fethullah Gülen as Educator," 81.

36 Gülen, M F, Örnekleri Kendinden Bir Hareket (A Movement Originating Its Own Models), Istanbul, Nil Yay., 2004, 110-115.

37 Ergene, E, Geleneğin Modern Çağa Tanıklığı (Tradition Bears Witness to the Modern Age), Istanbul, Yeni Akademi Yay., 2005, 106-107.

38 Ergene, Geleneğin Modern Çağa Tanıklığı, 107.

39 Özdalga, "Following in the Footsteps of Fethullah Gülen," 85.

40 Özdalga, "Following in the Footsteps of Fethullah Gülen," 85

in the Gülen thought for more than a decade now. Gülen believes that the most crucial thing to remember in education is that it is "a humane service" through which we can learn and be perfected.[41]

Gülen's understanding of education more or less covers the four points Rahman summed up above from the three different Muslim scholars. Gülen presupposes that education rests upon three basic premises. The first one is **(i)** to learn and lead "a commendable way of life" which is a "sublime duty" as "the manifestation of the Divine Name *Rabb* (Educator and Sustainer)." The second and the third rely on this as the results of the first since when one fulfils the first, one is **(ii)** "able to attain the rank of true humanity" and to **(iii)** "become a beneficial element" for one's society,"[42] that is, dedication to good deeds. Hence, according to Gülen, as Michel accurately put it, education should "give a strong scientific grounding, together with character formation in non-material values, which includes cultural, ethical, religious and spiritual training."[43] Gülen, too, is a firm believer in the importance of "the sciences and its centrality to a wholistic educational program which blends faith and science"[44] together. Gülen takes the Qur'anic decree of *contemplating* on "the creation of the heavens and Earth"[45]

> As an invitation to discover the Divine mysteries in the book of the universe and through every new discovery that deepens and unfolds the true believer, to live a life full of spiritual pleasure along a way of light extending from belief to knowledge of God and therefrom to love of God; and then to progress to the Hereafter and God's pleasure and approval – this is the way to become a perfect, universal human being. Studying God's creation is thus a natural consequence of an individual's faith in and love for Him, leading to deeper knowledge of matters of the mind and the spirit and ultimately to 'annihilation in and subsistence with God.'[46]

It is obvious that Gülen concurs with the three scholars in their claim that studying nature is God's commandment and a requirement of faith, though Gülen's reading has a strong flavour of *Sufism*.[47] More significantly, as Yılmaz appropriately observes, another revolutionary transforming contribution of Gülen in the Muslim educational discourse is to take "it from its traditional form as practiced in the *madrasah* and *Qur'an*ic literacy courses to the modern high school and university format."[48] In other words, Gülen has chosen to take up the bold step of carrying out his educational initiative outside of the religious sphere, even if he were to be criticized at times by the pious Muslims for not putting enough effort in creating and preserving the religious educational institutions, such as Imam Hatip High Schools in Turkey. It can be suggested that this Gülenian transformation of education from traditional forms into "the modern high school and university format" can also be a model to other Islamic countries such as Malaysia, Indonesia, Pakistan, etc.

---

41 Gülen, M F, Toward a Global Civilization of Love and Tolerance, New Jersey, The Light Inc., 2004, 198.

42 Gülen, Toward a Global Civilization of Love and Tolerance, 205.

43 Michel, "Four Frontrunners In Peace: People Who Have Devoted Their Lives To Peace" 70 (in Turkish 62).

44 Afsaruddin, A, "The Philosophy of Islamic Education: Classical Views and M. Fethullah Gülen's Perspectives" Academic Resources on the Gülen Movement CD, www.GülenConference.org.uk, 2007, 19.

45 Qur'an 3/190.

46 Afsaruddin, "The Philosophy of Islamic Education", 19.

47 For a detailed analysis of Gülen's educational philosophy, see: Aslandoğan, Y A and M Çetin, "The Educational Philosophy of Gülen in Thought and Practice" in Muslim Citizens of the Globalized World, 31-54, Academic Resources on the Gülen Movement CD, www.GülenConference.org.uk, 2007.

48 Yılmaz, I, "Muslim Laws, Politics and Society in Modern Nation States: Dynamic Legal Pluralisms in England, Turkey and Pakistan" 177 in Academic Resources on the Gülen Movement CD, www.GülenConference.org.uk, 2007.

Gülen's personal life resembles to that of the *Suffa* Companions in many aspects. The four guiding principles traced in the lives of the *Suffa* Companions and put forward previously can also be found in the daily life of Gülen. He leads a single, simple (poverty), humble and pious life dedicated to God in all aspects.[49] Considering the fact that he has not received a formal *Sufi* training, that is, does not belong to a *tarikat*, one can even claim that he might be closer to the line of the *Suffa* Companions than many *Sufis*.[50] In short, he does what he preaches.

The primary concern of the *Suffa* School was to teach religious sciences to young Muslims in order to make them good Muslims for their society. Similary, Gülen also runs an informal school whenever his ill-health permits. For more than the two last decades, Gülen regularly teaches *kalam* (theology), tafsir (Qur'anic exegesis), *usul-u hadith* (science of hadith) and *fiqh* (Islamic jurisprudence) to theology graduate students.

In every 3-4 years, a group of volunteer and eager 15-20 theology faculty graduates from all over Turkey are selected with the help of informal examination by former students of Gülen. It is known that to be selected many theology faculty students start studying extra while they are still at the University level. After selection, these prospective students of Gülen are introduced to him and they start studying under his tutelage.

Every year Gülen teaches different *kalam, tafsir, hadith* and *fiqh* books. The students study next day's lesson wherever they reside either their homes, dormitories or in some cases, as guests where Gülen resides. Needles to say, they all share his ascetic lifestyle as well. Every day, after the morning prayer, they study together with Gülen. They read and discuss a variety of texts from classical to modern. Gülen also interpret these texts in tune with the Zeitgeist while they are studying. In some cases, inspired by these texts he shares his ideas with his students. Students ask him questions regulary too. After studying with Gülen for 3-4 years, these students both emulate their teacher, become truly ascetic similar to him and also become more knowledable having studying many major Islamic sciences texts. It is obvious that Gülen also refreshes his knowledge while teching and also re-reads texts in the light of the current developments, his experiences and so on.

After their informal graduation, these students go on to become academics, writers, journalists, editors, imams and preachers. In almost every sphere of life, they continue teaching and more importantly presenting (*tamsil* instead of *tabligh*)[51] Gülenian undersanting of Islam.

Their teaching climate then encircles in successive waves colleagues, friends, families, cities, countries and civilizations. The important clue here is Gülen's understanding of *servanthood* and *service*. By establishing a link between the two concepts, he encourages his followers

---

49 For more on his life, see: Sarıtoprak, Z, "Fethullah Gülen: A Sufi in His Own Way," in Turkish Islam and the Secular State, 156-169; Ünal, A, Bir Portre Denemesi: M Fethullah Gülen (An Essay in Portrait: M Fethullah Gülen), İstanbul, Nil Yay., 2002; Erdoğan, L, Fethullah Gülen Hocaefendi: "Küçük Dünyam" (Fethullah Gülen Hocaefendi: My Small World), İstanbul, AD Yay., 1995.

50 For Gülen's understanding of Sufism, see: Gülen, Toward a Global Civilization of Love and Tolerance, chap. 4, esp. pp. 164-168; Sarıtoprak, Z, "Fethullah Gülen: A Sufi in His Own Way," in Turkish Islam and the Secular State, 156-169; Michel, T, "Sufism and Modernity in the Thought of Fethullah Gülen," The Muslim World, v. 95, n. 3, July 2005, 341-358 and Gökçek, M, "Fethullah Gülen and Sufism: A Historical Perspective" in Muslim Citizens of the Globalized World, 165-175, Academic Resources on the Gülen Movement CD, www.GülenConference.org. uk, 2007.

51 See for instance: Özdalga, "Following in the Footsteps of Fethullah Gülen," 85-114; Agai, "The Gülen Movement's Islamic Ethic of Education," 48-68; Michel, "Fethullah Gülen as Educator," 69-84; Yilmaz, I, "Ijtihad and Tajdid by Conduct: The Gülen Movement" in Turkish Islam and the Secular State, 208-237.

to serve God by serving, respectively, "families, relatives, and neighbors," and then their "country and nation, with finally humanity and creation being the object" of focus.[52] In other words, they struggle to revive the Suffa spirit.

The *Suffa* Climate

We need to focus on Gülen's students to have a better understanding of their relationship with the *Suffa* Companions vis-à-vis the revival of the *Suffa* spirit. The first thing that should be pointed out in this regard is the perception of work (*hizmet*) as a holy duty,[53] which is similar to what we have noted above as *dedication to good deeds* in the case of the *Suffa* Companions. It should be noted that the Gülenian ethics of vocation consists of total dedication. Agai, by borrowing the Weberian language, terms this state as the "inner-worldly asceticism" and describes the person "who performs *hizmet*" is someone "who sees his or her occupation as given from God."[54] Almost all of Gülen's students are visible in the public sphere –especially the volunteers of the movement see them as beacons- and they are observed as having this sense of duty and set it as the guiding principle of their life. They create a Suffa climate around them.

Gülen utilizes the religious language well in shaping up the hearts and minds of his students, surely not to turn them into religious zealots but into social workers who strive for the betterment of humanity in general. He describes them as *dervishes*,[55] angels, philosophers, ascetics, holy mentors[56] and the altruistic Companions of the Islamic Golden Age (*Asr-ı Saadet*).[57]

Considering the number of the volunteers and the widespread activities of the movement, it can be inferred that Gülen has conveyed his message quite successfully to his sympathisers and followers.

There are numerous accounts exemplifying how the mind setting of the volunteers operates but I will only cite a few instances to illustrate the point. A group of Turkish businessmen were visiting Azerbaijan during the time of which one of them asked casually to a young volunteer when he would be returning to Turkey. The volunteer replied promptly that they did not come to return to the homeland but came to die in that country.[58] It is worth remembering here that Gülen frequently remarks that the number of the Companions who took part in the Prophet's Farewell Pilgrimage (*al-Hajj al-Wada'*) was about a hundred thousand but the books mention only about ten thousand because many of them had migrated to other countries to convey the message where they met their destiny. Such was Abu Ayoub al-Ansari's case, who is believed to have come to Istanbul in an army to conquer it and buried there when he passed away as a result of his wounds. The neighbourhood where his tomb is located was named after him, Eyüp, in Turkish spelling, which is a famous site for visitors.

---

52 Gülen, Toward a Global Civilization of Love and Tolerance, 201.
53 Agai, "The Gülen Movement's Islamic Ethic of Education," 58-61.
54 Agai, "The Gülen Movement's Islamic Ethic of Education," 60-61.
55 Ünal, I, Fethulalh Gülen'le Amerika'da Bir Ay (A Month in America with Fethullah Gülen), Istanbul, Işık Yay., 2001, 14.
56 Tuncer, F, "Gülen'in Eğitim Anlayışı ve Zihni Oluşum Temelleri" (Gülen's Educational Understanding and Bases of His Intellectual Formation) in Barış Köprüleri: Dünyaya Açılan Türk Okulları, 262.
57 Gülen, M F, Örnekleri Kendinden Bir Hareket, 90, 114, 120; see also Özdalga, "Following in the Footsteps of Fethullah Gülen: Three Women Teachers Tell Their Stories," 85-114, which will be dealt with shortly in detail in the following paragraphs.
58 Tekalan, "Sevgi ve Fedakarlık Abideleri: Türk Öğretmenleri", 236-255.

A young female biology teacher, interviewed for a recent research, has solid resolutions about the importance of teaching and of the science in particular and its relation to good deeds. She comments that teaching is "the profession ascribed to the Prophet Muhammad himself; it means learning and conveying knowledge; the knowledge at hand is science oriented and thus has a sacred dimension; and it involves conveying sacred knowledge to others, which means doing good deeds."[59] As regards to science, she believes that "for a Muslim, studying or learning science is equivalent to worship. The same is true of teaching science." [60] She further elaborates what exactly science means by saying that "sciences such as physics, biology, chemistry, and mathematics—that is, the positive sciences. To teach these subjects is equivalent to worship. And that is also the reason we have to teach these courses very carefully: because science is essential."[61] Özdalga, who conducted the research, infers that such an approach to the teaching profession is "based on a combination of intellectual considerations (learning and teaching) and religious considerations (the ethics of giving)," which she takes to mean "the project of becoming an active believer."[62]

The project of becoming an active believer forms one of the founding principles of the Gülen-inspired initiatives in creating learning climates. It has several dimensions, such as pursuing non-formal education, performing *temsil* rather than *tebliğ* and bringing together colleagues, friends, families, businessmen, sponsors and the locals in building up a world of peace, love and tolerance through the individuals who achieved bridging the gap between their hearts and minds.

In order to attain character formation by "cultural, ethical, religious and spiritual training," as Michel rightly observes, the movement engages in "non-formal education through television and radio channels, newspapers and magazines, cultural and professional foundations."[63] Non-formal education, on the one hand, fortifies the Suffa climate while, on the other, eases up the *temsil* (representation) responsibility.

The most important duty of a volunteer –like Gülen's students- in the Gülen movement in society is to become a good example of *temsil* rather than *tebliğ* (proselytism). Gülen compares the two concepts and robustly advises his followers to stick to *temsil* instead of *tebliğ*. He analyses the life of the Prophet and of the Companions and the Apostles in terms of *temsil* and *tebliğ*. He reads the life of the Prophet as comprising of 9 *temsil* out of 10.[64] He comments that the Apostles and the Companions who conveyed religion to foreign countries did not speak the language of those countries but spoke the universal language of *temsil*: demonstrating in person by living what they were preaching.[65] His frequently repeated motto is this: "There can be no room for language, explanation next to showing by living (*hal*)! Once *temsil* speaks, there can be no need for *tebliğ*!"[66] In Gülen's understanding, "*tebliğ* creates a gap between the man who knows and the other who does not know a complex of superiority and inferiority between the preacher and those he is preaching to, and complicates the mission of Muslims."[67] *Temsil*, on the other hand, is "the best way of preaching," and a preacher

59 Özdalga, "Following in the Footsteps of Fethullah Gülen," 102-103.
60 Özdalga, "Following in the Footsteps of Fethullah Gülen," 102.
61 Özdalga, "Following in the Footsteps of Fethullah Gülen," 102.
62 Özdalga, "Following in the Footsteps of Fethullah Gülen," 103.
63 Michel, T, "Four Frontrunners in Peace," 70.
64 Ünal, Fethulalh Gülen'le Amerika'da Bir Ay, 217.
65 Ünal, Fethulalh Gülen'le Amerika'da Bir Ay, 206-207.
66 Ünal, Fethulalh Gülen'le Amerika'da Bir Ay, 113.
67 Balcı, B, "Fethullah Gülen's Missionary Schools in Central Asia and their Role in the Spreading of Turkism and

practicing it will "live an Islamic way of life at all times wherever he is, but will never utter the word 'Islam' or other 'dangerous words'. As "*temsil* missionaries," volunteers ought to "set a good example, embodying their ideals in their way of life rather than preaching about them."[68] In Afsaruddin's words, "exemplary, loving conduct towards others is the best witness one can provide for one's moral integrity and fidelity to God."[69] Therefore, *temsil* is a must for all the volunteers of the Gülen movement.

Nonetheless, working in secular environments does not always permit one to project one's religious affiliations. The Gülenian response to such a problem is to be a faithful Muslim while even imparting secular knowledge[70] because knowledge itself becomes an Islamic value when it is imparted by individuals with Islamic values and who can present an example of employing knowledge in the right and beneficial way.[71] Again, one cannot but stress how huge and important a role the volunteers have in creating the right environment and attitude that support the development of tolerance, love and morality.

As an indicator of the high moral standards I mentioned earlier about the *Suffa* teacher who was advised not to accept a gift from his student, I will refer to another anecdote from the movement. A young entrepreneur, settled in Turkmenistan to support the educational institutions operating there, was returning from a business meeting late at night. When he stopped at the red light, he heard a harsh knocking at his car and opened the window. A lady outside asked him to take her wherever he wanted to. He responded in a rather friendly way that he did not come there to seduce women, which surprised the woman a lot. She asked him who he was. He said he was a Turk who came from Turkey and advised her not to stay there at that time of night. He offered a lift to her house and gave her his card. Later, he introduced her to his wife and they become very close family friends.[72]

Last but not the least, to illustrate the depth and the breadth of the change that the Gülen-inspired initiatives contribute to love, peace and tolerance, I shall finish with an observation by a Turkish columnist writing in a liberal Turkish newspaper, Bugün (Today) Daily. In an article entitled "The Whole World Met in One Scene",[73] Mehmet Harputlu starts by lamenting on the process of Englishizing of the Turkish language. He states that it is very common to hear the Turkish youth using English phrases like "What's up, O.K., Of course, Bye, etc." in their daily conversations. Harputlu observes that the emotional patriotic nationalistic reaction to this inculturation process is to take up the Turkish flag and run to the demonstration arenas. Whereas the Gülenian response, he maintains, is to bring together different youths from 102 countries and organise a multilingual, multicultural event. The author quotes the ex-speaker of the Turkish Great National Assembly, Bülent Arinç, in his saying that "those writing books and preparing scenarios after scenarios on the fight and clash of civilizations must come and see this love." Harputlu adds that despite their differences in religion, language, colour, the young people who hugged each other in one act demonstrated to the whole world what peace and love are all about. He concludes by remarking that what can be more proud than hearing a Vietnamese student saying "Greetings to my second homeland."

Islam", Religion, State & Society, Vol. 31, No. 2, 2003, 162-163.

68 Balcı, B, "Fethullah Gülen's Missionary Schools," 163.

69 Afsaruddin, "The Philosophy of Islamic Education", 20.

70 Afsaruddin, "The Philosophy of Islamic Education", 20.

71 Agai, "The Gülen Movement's Islamic Ethic of Education," 62.

72 Tekalan, "Sevgi ve Fedakarlık Abideleri: Türk Öğretmenleri", 256.

73 Harputlu, M, "Bütün Dünya Tek Bir Sahnede Buluştu" (The Whole World Met in One Scene), Bugün Gazetesi, 6th June 2007, 14.

An outsider, like me, might think that the Gülen Movement is mostly comprised of young, eager, Turkish volunteers with limited capabilities that will probably cool down and eventually die away after the earthly life of Gülen himself. Because of the fact that I am not a trained sociologist to answer properly such a question, I will only repose on it in passing. It is rather difficult to count the movement as an only Turkic-supported activity, since there can be and seem to be several ways of extending it beyond the Turkish frontiers. The first and common one is marriage conducted by volunteers, businessmen and the like in the host countries.[74] The second reason is the support available from the local administration and public in general. The third one is the local graduates themselves who can come back as volunteers either as teachers or governors or businessmen, who can in turn also inspire the public around them. And finally and most significantly, the emphasis put on high moral standards and interfaith and intercultural dialogue by the movement forces it to expand beyond the limits of the Turkish population.[75] These and other possible connections mean that the Movement will most likely keep on broadening its developments both vertically and horizontally by building up institutions that serve to love, tolerance, humanity and friendship.

Conclusion

Many of the thinkers in Islamic world have been and still are of the same opinion that the way-out for the Islamic world from its misery can only be possible through a smooth transition from the Middle-Ages mentality to the modern times we live in. This, however, is an easier to be said than done job. Therefore, I believe that Gülen's successes are very significant at this juncture for he revived the old *Suffa* Tradition and Spirit to provide solutions to the problems of the Muslim world in particular and of humanity in general. By utilising the characteristics of the *Suffa* Companions, he created a movement of volunteers devoting their lives to turn the people around them into respectful good citizens and to transform the society in which they live into a more humane society. Instead of preaching about good and bad (*tebliğ*), these volunteers set good examples (*temsil*) for their fellow travellers, colleagues, friends, companions, families and even acquaintances. Thus, it can be claimed that Gülen's innovative renewal model can be a good example applicable, at least, in the other Muslim countries due to the fact they share the same heritage and the same problems, too.

It can also be inferred that, like the *Suffa* Tradition, the Gülen Movement is also an asceticism-based voluntary organization. The possible effects of both are that they do extend in a wave-like manner and show a snowball type development. In other words, they started out with a small number of men from a certain nationality in a rather small part of the world but gradually multiplied not only quantitatively with the inclusion of other nationalities but also spatially by spreading to other geographical locations. Although the *Suffa* Companions and the volunteers in the Gülen Movement share certain qualities like *humility, asceticism, pietism* and *dedication to good deeds*, they differ slightly in their aims. While the companions were almost purely religious missionaries, the volunteers are rather workers striving for a humanitarian cause that aims to serve for the benefit of humanity in total.

It seems to me that the volunteers who work passionately and tirelessly day and night with a consciousness of worship constitute one of the most, if not the most, important triangle of the successes of the Gülenian initiatives. They may or may not be, but I think many are, aware of their resemblance to the *Suffa* Companions in their *dedication, sacrifice* and *piety* in

---

74 Tekalan, "Sevgi ve Fedakarlık Abideleri: Türk Öğretmenleri", 245, 252.
75 Yilmaz, "Ijtihad and Tajdid by Conduct," 236.

performing their duties. I hope this paper has provided enough evidence of this similarity. In this sense, the volunteers of the Gülen movement are the modern day *Suffa* Companions serving to spread peace, love and toleration in this very divided world. If the accomplishments of the Gülen movement regarding to the transition of the Muslim world are to be continued in the places where they are and/or spread to other unknown neglected parts of the world, one should always bear in mind this model of dedicated volunteers who actively engage in this world without losing their primary target of serving God by serving humanity as a whole. Hence, the better the volunteers are, the closer the Muslim world will be to recover from the current dismal situation and be integrated with the modern world with its positive contributions to the betterment of humanity.

IN DEFENCE OF UNIVERSAL ETHICAL VALUES AND PRINCIPLES

Ali Paya

Abstract

In the past few decades a new approach to ethical principles known as 'particularism' has become fashionable among moral philosophers. According to the particularist the progress in the field of ethics, is from monism (the view that there is only one moral principle), through pluralism (the view that there are many), to particularism (the view that there are none). Jonathan Dancy advocates a radical particularist theory: arguing against a variety of universalist–pluralist doctrines, he maintains that there are no moral principles; and, even if there are, our ethical decisions are highly context-dependent, made case by case, without the support of such principles.

In this paper, drawing on a number of theoretical concepts used in science as well as the philosophy of science, and making use of Fethullah Gülen's insights, I try to develop a moderate universalist–pluralist model in defence of universal ethical values and principles. This model, I argue, is less vulnerable to Dancy's criticisms and better equipped, in comparison to Dancy's own model, to deal with particular moral cases. While particularism in ethics leads to relativism and leaves moral agents with no clear guidelines, the model developed here could serve all moral agents, regardless of credal or cultural association and socio-political outlook, in making sound and commendable moral judgements.

Gülen vs. Dancy on Universal Moral Principles and Values

As moralists, Fethullah Gülen, a Muslim philanthrope, and Jonathan Dancy, a secular philosopher, are poles apart. Gülen believes in universal moral principles and values. He maintains that: 'Morals are a set of noble principles that originate in high spirituality and govern human conduct. ... These principles are worth the sacrifice of many new things, even though people try to present them as outdated.' (Gülen 1998) As a Muslim Sufi, Gülen also subscribes to a plurality of universal (general) moral principles and values. (Gülen 2007) Principles and values which are shared by many people in different cultures albeit under different names and rubrics.

Dancy begs to differ with Gülen on the issue of moral and ethical principles. In a series of publications, which appeared over a period of two decades, Jonathan Dancy has sought to argue against ethical monism and ethical pluralism (both varieties of generalist ethical theory) and to propound a particularist theory. (Dancy, 1980, 1983, 1985, 1993, 1999, 2000, 2001, 2004) The main ingredients of his own particularist model, which has undergone changes over time and has become more nuanced and pointed, can be summarised as follows:

i. There are no general or universal moral principles; and even if there are 'the possibility of moral thought and judgement does not depend on the provision of a suitable supply of such principles'. (2004)
ii. Moral judgements are made on a case-by-case basis.
iii. Ethical particularism is based on 'holism of reasons': what is a reason for moral action in one case may be no reason at all in another, or even an opposite reason in another. (2004)

Against this backdrop, Dancy builds up his case to counter the generalist monist and pluralist theories, though his main target is the latter since he regards the former as more or less a non-starter. In Dancy's view monist moral theories, like Utilitarianism, which uphold just one universal moral principle, are simply false: there is more than one sort of relevant property involved in moral considerations.

As for the generalist-pluralist theories, which subscribe to a number of general or universal moral principles of the sort Gülen advocates, Dancy has raised three inter-related objections, namely:

i. How is it possible for an agent with two ethical principles whose recommendations conflict in a particular case to retain both of them after the struggle?
ii. How do the general moral principles come to be known?
iii. What is the relevance of the ethical decisions made by the virtuous agents in particular situations to the general moral principles? In other words, what sort of relation exists between the particular ethical decisions/duties and general moral principles? Is it, for example, logical, causal, token-type, or counterfactual?

There are some, more or less, standard responses by the generalist-pluralists (G-Ps for short) to these objections, which Dancy discusses and finds wanting. For example, as for the second objection, some G-Ps might claim that general moral principles are self-evident. But Dancy is quick to point out that: 'the longer the list of principles, the less the likelihood that all of them are self-evident.' (1983)

Some other G-Ps might say that they derive moral principles by ordinary induction from a number of particular cases, i.e., by empirical generalisation. Dancy rejects this approach on three grounds:

i. General moral principles if there are any, should both determine what is true in particular cases and explain it. In contrast, empirical generalisations or theories at most explain what is true in such cases.

ii. The particular cases cannot be seen as *tests* for the evaluation of principles. But this is counterintuitive.

iii. Moral principles are able, when defeated in a particular case, to linger or have residual effect, whereas, empirical generalisations, once falsified, do not have residual effects.

Yet other G-Ps may say that they 'see' the principles in particular cases by *intuitive induction*. Dancy holds that this account, like its counterparts, is not working: 'The question is how this is supposed to work. What is that is discernible in one case and tells us that what we have here must repeat in all other cases?' (2001)

Gülen's position on the status of universal moral principles and values, as can be gleaned from his writings, as I shall try to further explicate later in this essay, appears to be a modest one. He does not dwell either on the 'self evidence-ness' of these principles or their derivation by means of ordinary or intuitive induction. Gülen, as a Muslim moralist who is steeped in Sufi teachings, believes in the reality and objectivity of moral principles and values. He maintains that the more the individuals immerse themselves in the 'objective moral universe and the sphere of moral activities' the more adept they become in discerning and discovering objective moral principles. Of course, their grasp of the true meaning of these principles directly corresponds to the extent they have persisted in living a genuine moral life. Those who do not live a moral life, lose their grasp of moral principles. To quote Gülen: 'people who neglect spirituality, and are therefore lacking in spiritual values, cannot sustain conduct in accordance with these principles.' (Gülen 1998) On the other hand, those who do try to live in accordance with moral principles are not all in the same position as far as their understanding of moral principles are concerned: since no individual could claim perfection in epistemological and axiological matters, people's grasp of objective moral principle remain conjectural and subject to (never-ending) further elaboration. In this respect, there is a perfect analogy between individuals' grasping of objective moral principles and scientists understanding of laws and secrets of nature.

The question which can now be asked is: what is the position of a modest G-P theory like the one advocated by Gülen vis-à-vis Dancy's objections? Perhaps we can better answer this question in the context of a real moral case which provides an opportunity to further explain our model and assess its worth in comparison to Dancy's model. The following piece of news from Washington Post could serve this purpose:

Police Torture Threat Sparks Painful Debate in Germany

Peter Finn (Washington Post Foreign Service)

Saturday, March 8, 2003; Page A19

Berlin - In September, 11-year-old Jakob von Metzler, son of a prominent banker, was kidnapped in Frankfurt while on his way home from school. Three days later, police watched a man collect a ransom equivalent to about $1 million that had been placed at an arranged drop-off point. They moved in and arrested him.

But a serious problem developed: The suspect, law student Magnus Gaefgen, 27, wouldn't reveal where the boy was. For hours, he toyed with police, sending them down one false trail after another.

Wolfgang Daschner, deputy police chief in Frankfurt, has recounted that he feared the boy was dying in some makeshift cell known only to the suspect. So Daschner told his officers that they could torture the suspect, and he put that order in writing. They could extract information 'by means of the infliction of pain, under medical supervision and subject to prior warning.'

Daschner's decision last year has only just become public, and it has plunged Germany into a tormented national debate: Is there ever a circumstance under which torture is permissible?

Daschner has said that in this instance, just the mention of torture had the desired affect. 'After Magnus [Gaefgen] was threatened with pain, it only took about 10 minutes for him to tell us where the child was,' he said in an interview with the magazine Der Spiegel. But when police went there they found that the boy was already dead.

Gaefgen has been charged with murder, and Daschner is under investigation for employing the threat of torture, a crime that carries a 10-year sentence in Germany.

How do G-P theories react to this situation? Dancy has distinguished between two forms of G-P moral theories with respect to general moral principles. The first form, which in Dancy's terminology subscribes to an 'absolutist conception' of moral principles, takes these principles to be universal claims which state that all actions of a certain type are overall wrong or right. According to Dancy absolutist G-P moralists are faced with real difficulty when they encounter cases like the above one. Conflicting moral principles would bar such moralists from coming to a clear-cut decision. This is because, Dancy claims, conflicting absolute principles cannot be reconciled and therefore one of them must be abandoned. However, being absolute, they, presumably, cannot be thrown away, hence the impasse. For example, according to Dancy, had Mr Daschner, deputy police chief in Frankfurt, been an absolutist G-P moralist, he would have hopelessly vacillated forever between the two absolute principles of 'helping an individual whose life is in danger' and 'not torturing a suspect'.

The second form of G-P moral theory, according to Dancy, is the one that regards each moral principle as a partial or 'contributory' rather than an absolute reason: it specifies how things are only in a certain respect. Dancy points out that some subscribers to this theory suppose that the principles themselves can be ranked in order of importance. Others suppose that there is no available lexical ordering of such a sort. Dancy believes that these two sub-groups of 'contributory' G-P moralists like their 'absolutist' peer cannot rise to the challenge of real-case moral situations like the above case.

According to Dancy a 'contributory' moralist supposes, qua generalist, that a feature that makes a difference in one case will make the same sort of difference in every case. Dancy calls this aspect of generalist approach 'atomism' in contrast to his own 'holism'. (2004) He also maintains that for a contributory G-P there will be a contributory principle specifying its regular contribution. Dancy also calls this feature, perhaps somewhat misleadingly 'atomism'. He mentions W D Ross as a major proponent of this view and offers three reasons, variants of his three main reasons against G-P theories cited above, to reject it. His first reason involves producing counter examples. He says in his (1983, 539):

> The moral principle 'Do not forget your obligations' is consistent with an action's being the better for its agent having forgotten his obligations. For instance, if I promise to help you move house and fail to turn up, it is better if I have forgotten my obligations than if I have not.'

Dancy's second and third objections flow from the first:

> The second prong of the particularist attack is to ask why we should suppose that a feature that counts in favour in one case must count the same way wherever it appears. ... The third prong of attack on contributory generalism involves asking for an appropriate epistemology. How are we to tell, from what we can discern case by case, that this feature will function in the same way wherever else it appears? (2001)

A Leaf or Two from the Field of Philosophy of Science

What can a modest G-P, like Fethullah Gülen, say in response to Dancy's charges and how can he respond to the moral case introduced above? The modest G-P model that I intend to develop and defend in this essay, while inspired by the Sufi teachings and moral principles to which Gülen subscribes, makes use of some analogies from the fields of science/philosophy of science. In particular, I focus on the views of Ian Hacking and Nancy Cartwright. Incidentally, Dancy himself has alluded to 'interesting similarities' between his own views and those of Cartwright's. In a footnote in his 'The Particularist's Progress' (2000) Dancy observes that, 'My views on the nature of explanation in general bear interesting similarities to those of Nancy Cartwright.' And he goes on to cite Cartwright's *How the Laws of Physics Lie* (1983) as the relevant source in Cartwright's works.

Cartwright is an entity-realist, i.e., one who maintains that many of the theoretical entities posited by more mature sciences actually exist, even though the descriptions provided by these sciences, in the shape of fundamental (as against phenomenological) laws or theories, may not be quite accurate (Cartwright, 1983; Paya, 1995, 2000a).

It is not difficult to see 'interesting similarities' between Cartwright's (1983) views and Dancy's. Both writers are interested in the particular cases/phenomenological laws as against general principles/fundamental laws. Both maintain that each case should be decided on its own, locally, as it were, rather than universally. Cartwright, for example, in her subsequent publications, has made it clear that she subscribes to a doctrine which she dubs, 'metaphysical nomological pluralism' according to which 'nature is governed in different domains by different systems of laws not necessarily related to each other in any systematic or uniform way, by a patchwork of laws.' (1994, pp.288-9)

Dancy, too, in a more or less similar vein, denies G-Ps' claim that similarities between morally relevant aspects of moral situations enable one to apply general moral rules to particular situations. Dancy maintains that since moral properties of each case result from its non-moral properties, each moral situation is unique and governed by different set of moral considerations from other situations/cases. To claim that two situations are similar with regard to their moral properties, we must, according to Dancy, make sure that the two situations are similar in all their other respects. But this is impossible, because only two *identical* situations are similar in all their constitutive aspects. In any other case, one situation may contain further properties which holistically may alter the overall similarity between the two otherwise similar situations. (Dancy, 1981, 1983, 2001)

The similarities between the views of these two writers from the two different fields of philosophy of science and moral philosophy provide an interesting opportunity to make use of a theoretical machinery which has been used in the former to discuss the latter.

Among the useful aspects of this theoretical machinery are notions such as tendency, causal power, propensity, disposition, liabilities and their ilk which play a significant explanatory role in the realm of science and the philosophy of science. However, it must be emphasised that this cluster of notions, which for the sake of brevity I mostly denote by either 'tendency' or 'power' in the rest of this essay, is not the exclusive preserve of science/philosophy of science. In fact, many philosophers of different persuasions (realist, anti-realist, rationalist, empiricist) and in different fields of philosophy have used these notions in their theoretical discussions. (Andrew Wright, 1990)

Tendencies/powers and their related cluster of concepts are applied to all physical entities (including, with some qualifications, to human beings) but not to categories like events. According to the realist philosophers of science, the world is full of powerful entities, or entities with tendencies, which routinely exercise their powers. Interactions between these entities give rise to various phenomena at both the macro and the micro (quantum) levels. (Bhaskar, 1978)

Harré and Madden, among others, have defined the concept of the causal power in the following way: 'X has power to A' means 'X will/can do A, in the appropriate conditions, in virtue of its intrinsic nature.' (1975, p.28) The following is a definition of the same concept in terms of disposition: 'X has the disposition (power to) $A =_{def}$ if X is subject to stimuli or conditions of an appropriate kind, then X will do A, in virtue of its intrinsic nature (which may well be - at the sufficiently basic levels - identical with the disposition'. (Paya, 2002) In the above definitions, the concept 'intrinsic nature' refers to what is known in the philosophy of science as 'conjectural essence'. (Popper, 1974) It should therefore be clear that notions such as tendency/power presuppose the existence of conjectural essence or nature for the entities in question.

Drawing on the analogy with science/philosophy of science, I conjecture that tendencies/powers can be ascribed to moral agents, e.g., the behaviour of the virtuous agents in particular situations can be explained by means of these two notions and their counterparts. For example, one can talk of the tendency of the agents to show mercy towards the needy, to not lose their tempers, to not become blind by greed, to help people in distress, to not be seduced by lust and so forth. More detailed accounts of these tendencies and their effects on man's moral behaviour can be seen in the works of great Sufis and eminent Muslim scholars. Gülen in his own works on Sufism has referred to a host of such moral tendencies. (2007)

Tendencies/powers can also be ascribed to man-made or socially constructed institutions, in view of the fact that such institutions are the product of what Searle (1996) has dubbed 'collective intentionalities'. However, it is important to note that since actions are species of events, tendencies/power cannot be attributed to the acts performed by the moral agents. Any such attribution would be metaphorical or figurative. What is being unfolded in actions/events is the result of interactions between powerful entities/things in particular situations. Nevertheless, in the course of this essay, and as a matter of convenience, I attribute tendency/power to both entities and acts. I talk of 'acts having right (wrong) making tendencies' in lieu of 'agents' tendencies to act in right (wrong) ways'.

It is useful to make a distinction between the two notions of causal power and tendency. A tendency is a power which may be exercised unrealized or without being manifest in any particular outcome. (Bhaskar, 1978). This distinction, as we shall see below, can help to overcome a number of misinterpretations concerning the use of the notion of causal power and tendency. Later on in the essay, I shall make the definition of the notion of tendency more watertight. It is also useful to bear in mind that the notion of causal power does not refer to a tie that binds objects and events together. The exercise of causal power is not a force or power that has some existence of its own but refers to *forceful or powerful objects at work*.

There are not both things and causality in nature, but only causally active things or objects or persons. (Harré & Madden, *op.cit*)

Closely related to the above cluster of notions, there are two other important concepts used by scientists/philosophers of science, namely, open and closed systems. Open systems are various parts of Nature where there are many different causal powers/tendencies at work simultaneously. The sheer number of the powerful entities in the open systems makes it impossible for us to determine particular powers/tendencies of any of the entities involved. This is why scientists, in order to measure the causal powers of various entities or determine their tendencies, resort to closed systems, i.e., the tidier environment of their laboratories, which are under the jurisdiction of *ceteris paribus* clause.

Closed systems, contrary to open systems of Nature, are where our models of reality are being used. These models are inevitably and to varying degrees idealised, approximate, or abstract representations of phenomena, entities, and processes which we encounter in Nature. We use these less than perfect models or representations to measure the causal powers/determine tendencies of various entities. These powers are being measured indirectly and through the effects they make upon certain observable phenomena. The greatest advantage of a closed system over open systems is that within the confine of closed systems, scientists are able to cancel the effects of the unwanted causal powers and isolate the effect due to the one causal power they are interested in. For example, the falling autumn leaves fly in the air under the influence of a number of causal factors or operating mechanisms; gravitational, thermodynamical, fluid mechanical, and perhaps other factors. To measure the effect of each of these conjectured mechanisms, we have to eliminate the effects of other operating factors, and this can only be done by means of well-arranged experiments within the confine of laboratories (closed systems).

Another set of relevant concepts from the field of science/philosophy of science is the contrast between the so-called fundamental laws and phenomenological/technological laws. Fundamental laws of physics which are universally applicable form the bare backbone of the applied and/or phenomenological laws of applied sciences and technology which can only be used in particular contexts. The former laws are paradigm cases of *ceteris paribus* laws. They are our best conjectures concerning some fundamental aspects of the physical world. However, the exact effect of these laws can only be shown in closed systems. The latter laws which are context-sensitive i.e. applicable to the particular messy situations in the real world are obtained from the former by what is technically known as 'approximate derivation'. (Maxwell, 1993) The name is appropriate because although we make lots of simplifying amendments to go from the fundamental laws to phenomenological laws, there is always enough common ground between the simplified (idealized) model (which allows us to apply the phenomenological law(s) to particular case) and the original theory (which furnishes us with the fundamental law (s)) to warrant us to talk about refutation of the original theory should the predications of the modified model fail.

It must be pointed out, as Cartwright has argued in her 1983, that there is a difference between the theoretical and the actual outcome of a real physical system. The theoretical outcome is obtained by means of using appropriate phenomenological laws and applying simplifying assumptions. However, for this very reason, i.e. making use of simplifying assumptions (based on approximation and idealisation) the actual outcome may not exactly match this theoretical result. In such cases, engineers and technologists usually revert to further approximations and local adjustments which are only applicable to the cases at hand and are highly context-dependable.

Nevertheless, even this actual outcome is in the end and in a real sense an 'approximate derivation' of the phenomenological laws which are in turn the results of 'approximate derivations' of the fundamental laws. In other words, the physical quantities calculated by engineers/technologists or scientists in particular contexts, are dependent, on the final analysis, on the fundamental laws of physics. All row data, observations and measurements are theory laden, and all theories, in the final analysis rely on the most fundamental theories. Needless to say, all theories, fundamental and otherwise, are just our fallible conjectures for making sense of some aspects of the reality. (Popper, 1963)

As a real case example for the above discussion consider the calculation of the midband gain of an amplifier which Cartwright has discussed at some length in her 1983. Here electronic engineers use approximate models applying the so-called Kircheoff voltage and current laws to calculate the required quantity. These are well-known phenomenological laws. However, due to the approximations and idealisations used in the construction of these models the theoretical value for the required parameter usually does not match the real value obtained by direct measurement on the actual amplifier. To bring the outcome of the approximate models closer to the actual value, engineers make a number of adjustments/alterations to the approximate model. The important point here is that the final relation/equation for calculating the parameter in question can be 'derived' in an approximate way from the phenomenological laws governing the operation of different parts of the electric circuits. These laws in turn, are based on the basic laws of electromagnetism. (Paya, 2000a)

The last set of notions which needs to be introduced before going back to the realm of ethics is the pair of 'initial conditions' and 'Boundary conditions'. Scientists distinguish the so-called 'initial conditions' and 'boundary conditions'. The instantiation of the initial condition warrants the application of the features (i.e. tendencies or the laws which govern them) whether the system is closed or open. For example, the laws of physics or the universal constants of Nature could have been different had there been a different set of initial conditions at the Big Bang. The boundary conditions, on the other hand, are the conditions for the experimental testing of those features (i.e. tendencies or the laws which govern them) and not their applicability. These are conditions which only apply to the closed systems.

Before going further, let us take stock of our exploration in the field of science/philosophy of science so far. The following table provides a list of key concepts in the field of philosophy of science and their counterparts in ethics. Some of the terms/notions in the table shall be explained in due course.

Ethics	Science/Philosophy of Science
Moral tendencies	Physical tendencies
Moral power	Causal power
Particular situations where only one morally-relevant factor or characteristic is present	Closed systems
Particular situations where many morally-relevant factors or characteristics are present	Open systems
Most basic moral principles (duties)	Fundamental laws of Nature (physics)
Prima facie duties (principles)	Phenomenological/technological laws
Actual duties (principles)	Theoretical outcome of an appropriate model of a subsystem operating in Nature based on the effects of phenomenological laws

Ethics	Science/Philosophy of Science
Final decision/judgement/act in a real situation	Actual outcome of a sub-system operating in Nature
Moral intuition	Scientific intuition

Modest G-P vs. Dancy's Particularism

As indicated in the above table, from my point of view, moral principles can be categorized under three headings: the most basic or fundamental principles, *prima facie* principles, and actual principles. The most general moral principles are like the fundamental laws of physics. Such laws are conjectured to be universally valid. This feature however, does not make them incompatible with each other. For example, Maxwell's laws and Newton's laws, assuming they are valid, are both regarded as universally valid. They are not incompatible though, because each governs a different tendency/power in physical entities. The behaviour of a charged particle in an electric field in the open system is governed, among other things, by both Newton's and Maxwell's laws. Likewise, basic moral principles which are conjectured to be universally valid, as I shall explain, would retain their validity even when they are operating simultaneously in real life cases. For example, two fundamental moral principles like 'thou shall not lie' and 'thou shall not kill' can both be operative in a real-life case without giving rise to an inconsistent situation.

In a way analogous to the fundamental laws of nature which are our best fallible conjectures of the fundamental aspects of the physical universe, the most basic moral principles, are our best fallible conjectures concerning the fundamental aspects of man's moral universe. The exact effect of each of these principles, in a similar fashion to the fundamental laws of nature, can only be shown under the application of *ceteris paribus* clause.

Prima facie duties (principles) are like the phenomenological/technological laws used in applied science and technology. The notion of *prima facie* duty (principle) is due to William David Ross. He writes:

> If, as almost all moralists except Kant are agreed, and as most plain men think, it is sometime right
> to tell a lie or to break a promise, it must be maintained that there is a difference between *prima
> facie* duties and actual or absolute duty. (Ross, 1930, 28)

I would like to define the notion of actual duties (principles) in a way which might be slightly different from Ross' definition. I define an actual duty (principle) as the fallible outcome of the deliberations of the agent, based on his application of appropriate *prima facie* duties (principles) as he understands them, in a real case situation. It must be emphasised that the above does not mean that the conscientious moral agent, as a result of his deliberation, will definitely come to a right moral judgement with regard to his actual duty. In fact, it is conceivable that the agent may make a mistake in deciding about his actual duty in a particular circumstance. It is also possible that, the agent, given his understanding of the *prima facie* principles at a particular time and in a particular context, might fail to come up with a clear cut decision concerning his actual duty in that circumstance.

The agent's decision in a particular situation, however, can be critically assessed by other moral agents. Such processes of assessment as well the processes of moral deliberation (by the moral agents in particular circumstances) can be assisted by what Popper has termed as 'situational logic' (Popper 1957, 1994; Paya 2003a, 2006) or by making use of thought experiments. (Sorensen, 1992; Paya, 2003b) Of the latter of these two analytic tools I shall say some more later on.

Based on the analogy with the cases in science/philosophy of science, I distinguish between the agent's actual or absolute duty (in Ross' sense) and his actual final moral action. The agent's final moral action is based on his final decision/judgement which in turn is a fine tuning of the actual duty he has come to through his deliberations, which take into account the complexity of the situation he finds himself in.

The above distinction can be explicated in terms of the case of the kidnapped boy discussed above. Wolfgang Daschner, deputy police chief, had to weigh two *prima facie* principles of immorality of torturing the suspect and immorality of not taking the proper course of action for saving the life of the kidnapped boy. 'I thought, I can sit with my hands on my lap and wait until Gaefgen maybe, at some point, decides to tell the truth and in the meantime the child is long dead,' Daschner told the *Frankfurter Neue Presse* newspaper. 'Or I do everything I can now to prevent just that.'

After due deliberation, Daschner came to the conclusion that under the particular circumstances he is faced with, he should resort to torture in order to save the life of the boy. This outcome is tantamount to his actual (absolute) duty in Ross' terminology. Note that, the two *prima facie* duties (principles) he weighed against each other in order to reach his decision were based upon his understanding of two basic moral principles, namely, immorality of harming others and the sanctity of human life. The outcome of Dashner's deliberation is an 'approximate derivation' from the *prima facie* duties operative in the case at hand. This can be compared with the analysis of the outcome of a physical system in a particular situation which is based on the consideration of the effects of a number of phenomenological laws operative in that situation.

Particular cases for moral decisions are similar to particular cases in engineering and technology. The moral agent finds himself in a complex situation in which many factors, e.g. other actors, institutions, physical entities, are playing their roles. Given actor's cognitive and physical limitations, he has no choice but to make a simplified model by using the usual processes of idealisation, approximation and abstraction. This means that he has to omit or ignore the effects of many factors which he deems insignificant. Of course, at each stage, the moral agent can make adjustments to his model by adding further factors. Factors which he had deliberately ignored in his earlier deliberation while using his earlier, cruder models. These factors pertain to social actors (including the moral agent himself), institutions and other elements which, in view of the moral agent, play some role in the particular context under consideration. Adding these new factors may result in drawing the attention of the moral agent to some aspects hitherto hidden from his view. This new understanding may, in turn, encourage the moral agent to take into consideration some other moral principles or to re-adjust the weight he had given to the principles he had already considered. However, the match between the two, i.e., the model, with the help of which he is trying to come to a moral decision with regard to a particular context, and the real situation in that context, remains, forever, approximate. After all, a human agent, being human, is not omniscient and has no other choice but to concentrate on a small number of factors he considers to be the most important ones. Whereas an omniscient being who is, by definition, aware of all factors and their significance and bearing on the case under consideration can make a judgement which is objectively the most appropriate one in that particular context. Let's call the judgment passes by such an omniscient being on each moral case 'the ideal moral judgement' for that case. Such an ideal, like the ideal of truth for scientific theories, can serve as a regulative sign-post towards which the non-ideal judgments of the mortal moral agents, who are deliberating on that case, are directed. The ideal judgement for a particular case in a particular context can be regarded as the outcome of proper weighing of the basic moral principles and all the relevant factors involved in that case within the context in question by the omniscient being.

To achieve the goal of approaching the ideal moral judgment in a particular context and therefore to increase the degree of objectivity of the judgment issued in that context, the virtuous agent tries to relate particular moral considerations that he has found relevant to the case at hand to general moral principles he is equipped with. In other words, he tries to show that his judgement is based on (derivable from) most basic moral principles. For example, in the case of the kidnapped boy, two apparently relevant principles were wrongness of harming others and rightness of saving lives. By taking into account the basic moral principles relevant to the case, the moral agent could explore, in an objective way, the relative weight/ power of each of the relevant actions which were open to him in that particular situation. In this way, the chief of the police, in the light of the above two principles and other relevant information about the case, could consider whether he should torture the suspect in order to increase the chance of obtaining vital information about the whereabouts of the victim and therefore increase victim's chances of survival or whether he should refrain from resorting to such a means.

The analogy between the ideal of truth in scientific theories and the ideal moral judgement in moral cases would imply that just as in the case of science where a more competent and better informed scientist can produce a more verisimilar model for understanding some aspects of reality, in the case of moral judgements, the experienced moral judge, in comparison to a moral agent who is not well versed in weighing various factors and does not have extended experience in these matter, is better placed to assess ways in which a feature can contribute to determining how to act in a particular situation. Moreover, these judgements are fallible and in the light of further information (i.e., more realistic models of the situation) may alter. The fact that a virtuous agent who has had a long lived experience of a genuine moral life has a higher chance of approaching ideal moral decisions in various moral situations is an important point, which as Gülen has pointed out, has been emphasised by all great Sufis and true moralists. (2007)

This last point deserves a bit more explication. Gülen, along with many moralists and Sufis, does not insist on exact formulation of moral principles. As a virtue ethicist with the realist outlook of a G-P and a good knowledge of Sufi teachings he knows that to acquire good moral judgement one does not need to bookishly or blindly follow the letter of moral principles. What one needs is to develop his sensitivity, expand his experience, and fine tune his discernment by observing, in a critical manner, the most basic commonsensical moral teachings and understandings which are found in all cultures. Responding to these teachings would gradually enable the individual to better grasp the richer meaning of the moral principles, and use his imagination and judgement in a more competent way to discern in a particular case which features are more relevant and how they interact with each other and what weight should be given to each and how they should be related to relevant moral principles. In other words, mastering moral principles is a matter of combining and harmonising theoretical and practical efforts and this is what that lies at the heart of spiritual teachings of the type Gülen subscribes to. (More on moral laws in section 8.)

Tendencies and Moral Principles

Having explicated the relationship between various types of moral principles, we need to say something about the nature/status of these principles. Philosophers of science spell out the laws of nature in terms of tendency/power of physical entities. Ross has tried to do the same for the moral principles. In an important passage Ross says:

Tendency to be one's duty may be called parti-resultant attribute, i.e., one which belongs to an act in virtue of some one component in its nature. *Being* one's duty is a toti-resultant attribute, one which belongs to an act in virtue of its whole nature and of nothing less than this. … Another instance of the same distinction may be found in the operation of natural laws. *Qua* subject to the force of gravitation towards some other body, each body tends to move in a particular direction with a particular velocity; but its actual movement depends on *all* the forces to which it is subject. It is only by recognizing this distinction that we can preserve the absoluteness of the laws of nature, and only by recognizing a corresponding distinction that we can preserve the absoluteness of the general principles of morality. (Ross, 1930, 28-29)

Dancy is not in favour of notions such as tendency/causal power. In his discussions of the deficiencies of the G-Ps' position, Dancy refers to W.D. Ross' works as a special case of a G-P theory which has anticipated (and tried to respond to) the objections raised by him against generalist theories by appealing to the notion of tendency. Dancy dismisses such an appeal to the notion of tendency/causal power as misguided. (1983, 1993) He writes: 'Ross offers two accounts of a *prima facie* duty. The first is in terms of tendencies; an action is a *prima facie* duty in virtue of being ø iff ø actions tend to be duties proper. It is obvious, I think, that talk about tendencies can only be cashed at the general level. For particular acts do not have tendencies to be duty proper; they either are so or not.' (1983, 539) Again in his (1993) Dancy writes:

> … [T]he official definition of prima facie duty is not the only one to be found in Ross. There is a less formal account in terms of tendencies, which may seem more promising. Ross sometimes speaks of a property which makes an action a prima facie duty as one which *tends* to make any action that has it a duty proper. So here is a different definition of a prima facie duty: an action is a prima facie duty in virtue of having a property F iff actions that have property F tend to be duties proper. One's first thought here is that talk about tendencies can only be cashed at the general level, in a way that would completely distort the role of moral principles as we understand it. (pp.98-9)

It seems Dancy has been led astray in his rejection of Ross' use of the notion of tendency because of a narrow reading of this notion. His conception of this notion is nearer to the statistical definition of tendency which is in turn close to the meaning of the word 'trend'. There is however, another definition of tendency, as we have seen above, in terms of disposition or other related concepts. Almost all the writers who have used tendency or its synonyms in this sense have ascribed them, in the first instance, to individual entities.

From the passages quoted above it is clear that Ross himself has this second meaning of the word 'tendency' in mind. It is also clear that what he terms as parti-resultant attribute is tantamount to the outcome of a particular tendency within the confines of a closed system whereas, what he calls toti-resultant attribute is similar to what happens in the open system.

Dancy's narrow reading of Ross' notion of tendency has apparently led him to a second misinterpretation. As noted above, he maintains that Ross has offered two different definition of his basic notion of '*pima facie* duty'. In his 1983, having discussed Ross' 'first definition' he turns to his 'second account' and says, 'But Ross' second account of *prima facie* duty (perhaps his official one) is better: 'I suggest '*prima facie* duty' or 'conditional duty' as a brief way of referring to the characteristic … which an act has, in virtue of being a certain kind, … of being an act which would be a duty proper if it were not at the same time of another kind which is morally significant (Ross, 1930, p. 19)' & (Dancy, 1983, p.539)'[1]

But Ross, having introduced both notions of 'tendency' and '*prima facie*' goes on to clarify a point which he thinks may cause some confusion. He is worried that his use of the term 'tendency' may imply a sort of causal relation between an act and its moral value. For this reason he suggests to replace the term 'tendency' with the term '*prima facie*': '… if the word 'tendency' is thought to suggest too much a causal relation, it is better to talk of certain types of act as being *prima facie* right or wrong (or of different persons as having different and possibly conflicting claims upon us), than of their tending to be right or wrong.' (Ross, *ibid.* 29)

Perhaps what has made Dancy think that Ross has introduced a second account of '*prima facie* duty' is that Ross has also called this sort of duty as 'conditional duty'. This might imply that what Ross has had in mind was a counterfactual/subjunctive account of these types of duties which, presumably, is different from the account of duties as tendencies. But this does not seem to be the case. Ross' new terminology is not a new account or definition but only an oblique way to refer to the distinction between the closed and open systems. What Ross is trying to make clear, which can be better understood in the light of what has been discussed so far, is that *prima facie* duties qua tendencies are expressed in terms of counterfactual statements which their actual instances can be seen within the confines of the closed systems, where we assume that the act under consideration has only one characteristic, and therefore this very act would determine the duty proper in that (counterfactual) situation. In other words, these are parti-resultant attributes or duties.

Dancy however, thinks that the point made by Ross *qua* a moderate G-P that a feature is relevant iff in any case where it is the only relevant feature or factor, it would decide the issue is both false and incoherent: 'It would be incoherent because the idea that a feature could be present alone, without any other features whatever, is surely nonsense. … Further, there may be some features that can be relevant if some other feature is also relevant. … If this can occur, any 'isolationist test' for reasons must miss some reasons. Finally, trying to isolate the contribution of a feature by asking how things would have been if no other feature had made any contribution is, when one comes to think of it, a rather peculiar enterprise. It is … like trying to determine the contribution made by one football player to his team's success today by asking how things would have been if there had been no other players in the field.' (2001)

Now, it should be clear from our discussion above that Dancy has been misled by an incorrect reading of the notion of tendency/power. The notion of moral relevance needs some careful considerations. In the first place, isolating the effect of one powerful individual within the confines of a closed system and omitting the unwanted effects of the other factors in that situation is something which is going on all the time in science. However, a closed system is not a situation 'without any feature whatever' but a situation in which the so called *ceteris*

---

1 Dancy seems to have changed his mind about the relative effectiveness of what he claims to be Ross' two different definitions. In his (1983) he refers to what he calls Ross's definition in terms of tendency as Ross' first definition. He also calls this Ross' unofficial and the less satisfactory account. In his (2001) however, Dancy refers to this very definition as a more promising one than the other account. But this change of heart does not seem to be of any significance for our present discussion.

paribus clause is operating.

Morally relevant features are dependent on non-moral features. The role of these latter features can be likened to the role of catalysts in chemistry. Without their interference the tendency/power of the entities involved in the reactions cannot be manifested, and yet these catalysts themselves are not part of the relevant features of those reactions. In all such cases the same method of closed system is used to find out about the required tendencies/ powers. I shall further discuss the issue of moral relevance in Section 6 below.

In the case of an 'isolationist test', these non-moral features which act as catalysts are not absent. It is true that for various single outcomes, different catalysts might be needed. In fact, here the two notions of 'initial conditions' and 'boundary conditions' can be used to clarify the above point. To this end, we first need, as indicated earlier, to make our definition of the notion of tendency/power more watertight. We defined power as ' 'X has power to A' means 'X will/can do A, in the appropriate conditions, in virtue of its intrinsic nature.' We can now add that the appropriate conditions mean the satisfaction of the initial conditions and the absence of intervening or countervailing causes. Initial conditions, as we remember from above, are conditions for the applicability of the features in question. To *test* them we also need the boundary conditions. It is with the help of the boundary conditions which we will be able to 'see' X's power. The 'isolationist test' is therefore done under the assumption of the presence of appropriate initial and boundary conditions.

The fact that Dancy, has been misled in his argument against G-P's approach can be best seen from the way he misinterprets the analogy of the football player: contrary to what Dancy has suggested a football coach *can* test, to some extent, the basic abilities/qualities of a football player in an empty field. He can, for example, observe whether the player is good at controlling the ball, precise shooting, fast running, quick manoeuvring, physical endurance, and the like. These are boundary conditions for a professional footballer. In a real football match, i.e. in the open system, these abilities are not lost, though they may pale in comparison with the abilities of much abler players.

To recap, if an act has a right (wrong) making tendency/power, it will always retain this property and it will always exercise its tendency in the same way, should the appropriate conditions become available. Even under those conditions where a prima facie duty is overridden/outweighed, it typically manifest itself in the appropriateness of regret, compunction, or reparation, but always in the continuing presence of a reason to perform the act which the person has decided to be his duty in that particular situation. It is the task of the closed systems to help bring about or realize or make manifest in full such tendencies which are overridden/outweighed. In these systems, there is only one relevant feature or property or tendency in operation, and therefore, it is this very feature or property/tendency which decides the case. In real cases, each action preserves its right (wrong) making tendency. The actual duty of the virtuous agent is the outcome of weighing these various tendencies (*prima facie* duties) against each other. For a moral agent to take a moral decision/act in a moral way, initial conditions for the exercise of his tendencies must have already been satisfied. To *test* or *examine* an existing feature (tendency/law) we resort to isolating cases where boundary conditions and the *ceteris paribus* clause is at work. Such an 'isolationist test' can be done by means of thought experiments or situational logic. Dancy, however, dos not think that thought experiments can be used in ethics. But see section 6 below.

Let us apply the above to instances of moral situation. Take the case of a person who has promised his friend to help him move house. According to a modest G-P forgetting one's promise always count as morally unwelcome and it will always exercise its tendency or realize its power in this (unwelcome) way. In real case situations (open systems) many factors with various tendencies/powers are at work. Here, some tendencies/powers might be far more powerful than others to the extent that they can put those other tendencies in the shade, just as the powerful rays of sun would make the rays of a small torch bulb virtually invisible.

In the case of the man who has forgotten to keep his promise, if it turned out that he had been involved in a severe car accident in which he had had to rush the victims to hospital and this has caused him to forget his promise, then in view of the fact that saving the lives of the victims of a horrible accident is of great importance, the right-making power of this act would overshadow the wrong-making power of forgetting promises and would mitigate the case against the person in question.

It was said that if an act has a right (wrong) making tendency/power, it will always retain this property and will always exercise its tendency in the same way, it should be added that it is quite possible that in a particular situation where the choice is between, for example, two wrong-making tendencies/powers, the one with less degree of wrong-making power would become the preferred moral act. A case in point is breaking a promise. Here, we think better of a person if he breaks his promise because he has forgotten it than he breaks it knowingly.

Likewise, in the case of the kidnapped boy, according to a modest G-P torturing a suspect, or telling lies to him, in order to obtain confession/information is always regarded as morally wrong, whereas rescuing the life of an innocent victim is always a good moral act. However, in a particular situation where both these factors and perhaps many others are at work, each exercises its tendency or moral power and the final outcome is the product of the interaction between these different tendencies. It is here that the relative or apparent power of each tendency in comparison to the other tendencies and in view of the overall situation alters, whereas its power in absolute terms remains unchanged.

To torture a suspect or telling lies to him, for the sake of extracting information from him always counts as morally wrong. However, in a particular circumstance where the overriding moral concern is to rescue an innocent victim, the wrong-making tendency of torturing a suspect, or telling lies to him, though exercised, may be overridden: in view of the moral agent its power may pale in comparison to the power of the act of rescuing the life of the innocent victim. However, in this case, as in all other cases, the moral agent must provide his reason for his decision. These reasons can be objectively and critically assessed by other moral agents in the light of the moral principles and the context in which the agent has found himself.

Moral Deliberations, Thought Experiments and Holism of Reasons

It was mentioned that a moral G-P uses, amongst other things, thought experiments for his moral deliberations. In such deliberations, the moral principles, as we expect, play an important role. Dancy is against the idea that thought experimental cases resemble the actual ones in all morally relevant respects, but are simpler and better manageable. Dancy, of course, is not against the use of *all* types of analogical arguments. He wisely observes that if we were to do this, 'we would leave ourselves rather short of resources (1985, 143)

Dancy has produced four arguments against the use of thought experiments in moral deliberations. These arguments, notwithstanding his claim to the contrary (1985, 148), are not entirely independent of each other. The gist of the four has been captured in the following quotation:

The moral properties of a right action are *parti-resultant*, in Ross' sense. The action has an enormous number of non-moral properties, only some of which are reasons why the action is right. ... One property results from another when the first exists in virtue of the existence of the second. So the relation of resultance, which holds between moral properties and reasons, continues down what I call the resultance tree. ... The question then is this. If we have been told the properties which *de facto* constitute the reasons why the action is right, and nothing much more than these, can we reasonably be expected to form a sound view on the question whether the action is right or wrong? ... It would be misguided to suppose that, if there is a difficulty here, it could be resolved by provision of a bit more 'information' about the imaginary case. The problem will remain; we will still be in the business of determining a matter which is indeterminate.' (1985, 144-5)

Dancy maintains that imaginary cases are ontologically indeterminate but epistemically determinate (since the nature of an imaginary case is exhausted by its description); actual cases are ontologically determinate, but they may well always be epistemically indeterminate to some degree.

In a later publication (1993), Dancy appear to have given some concession to the use of imaginary cases. In his discussion of moral principles as a kind of 'reminders' he says that some properties are more commonly important than others and therefore consideration of imaginary cases can provide inductive support for *some* moral generalizations (especially if people normally or typically are not manipulated or tricked into making promises, etc.). However, his main problem with imaginary cases concerns using them to establish conclusions about the moral behaviour of features in *all* other cases. His holism concerns what may always happen to moral reasons; what actually or typically happens, and what tools are useful for finding that out, is hostage to further facts about the world.

From a modest G-P's point of view of the kind Gülen would subscribe to, Dancy's concern over the use of thought experiments does not seem to be justified. On the one hand, Dancy seems to have committed the so-called fallacy of 'high standards': He is demanding something extraordinary from the conceptual tool of thought experiment. What he expects is something that cannot be fulfilled even by real experiments, i.e., filling the gap between our descriptions and the reality. On the other, there seems to be a conceptual flaw in his model of 'holism'. Let me take these two points in turn.

Suppose in the case of A (the imaginary case) the properties relevant to its F-ness are R^1, ..., R^n. Now, according to Dancy, for an agent to claim that A and B (the actual case) are similar he must first decide whether properties R^1, ..., R^n which are, *ex hypothesi*, shared by A and B, are all the properties that are relevant to the F-ness of A and B. Let us call this, 'static similarity stage 1'. Next, the agent must assume that A's other properties will, in no way, affect the moral relevance of R^1, ..., R^n. This can be called 'static similarity stage 2'. But for Dancy even this is not enough to licence the use of an analogical argument. The moral agent, according to Dancy, needs to show that A and B also enjoy what can be called the 'dynamic similarity', namely the agent should show he knows that A works out in a way which coincides with the detailed truth about B. Otherwise, B may contain further properties which affect the relevance of R^1, ..., R^n and therefore spoil the overall relevance of A to B.

Thought experiments or imaginary cases are our constructs intended mostly to falsify or challenge our conjectures concerning the agent's moral action in a particular situation. Like all our theoretical constructs and conjectures, they are constantly revised in the light of new evidence or information. We conjecture that R^1, ..., R^n are the properties relevant to rightness (wrongness) of an act both in an actual and an imaginary case. However, in light of further deliberation we may decide against our initial conjecture. For example, in the case of the kidnapped boy, suppose that the deputy police chief is using an imaginary case to weigh his various options. He may imagine a case in which a harsh physical punishment would loosen the tongue of the kidnapper and on that basis he may initially decide that such a course of action is right. But then, upon further deliberation, he may come to the conclusion that perhaps the kidnapper may die if physical punishment is administered. Such a possible outcome which is not desirable may force the deputy police chief to reconsider his initial decision concerning the rightness of the imagined course of action.

Dancy maintains that moral properties of an action (or situation) result from some non-moral properties. (1993) One upshot of his holism is that being right (wrong) making is just one species of being morally relevant. As Dancy puts it in his more recent publications (e.g. 2004), whether a feature is right-making depends on the presence of 'enabling conditions' whose instantiation is independent of the instantiation of that feature. Conditions whose presence enable (and absence disable) a feature to be right-making clearly are morally relevant, but they are no part of the right-making feature when present. For example, a right-making feature of an act (say, promise keeping) is a hugely complex feature containing, as a part, any feature that is relevant to the prima facie rightness of the act in question. It is very plausible that issues such as whether the promise was extracted by manipulation, coercion or trickery, whether the promisor was insane, or under the influence of drugs when making the promise, and much else besides, are all relevant to whether having promised generates any prima facie duty at all. The sort of complex feature that is in question will also include negative conditions, and it will be hugely heterogeneous, since the same feature will have to be possessed by any instance of the act in question.

But a G-P has no qualms about the effects of all these factors which are at work in any situation, what he questions is Dancy's dual use of the notion of 'resulting from' in developing his particularist case and defending his conception of holism. On the one hand, Dancy talks about the relation between the moral properties of an action and the reasons why it has them. In this sense action's rightness emerges or results from only a part of its non-moral properties. For example, kindness, generosity, thoughtfulness, unselfishness. On the other, he introduces another type of 'resulting from' which is mostly material evidence for the rightness of an action. For example, assisting charities with large sums of money. While the first type of 'resulting from' is a logical one, the second type is a causal or counterfactual one. This latter type is relevant to moral acts in an extended sense.

Dancy maintains that because of all these other relevant factors (in the extended sense) or the 'enabling conditions', even if the real case does have the narrow relevant moral properties similar to the imaginary case, it cannot be concluded that the two cases are genuinely similar enough to warrant us to apply an analogical argument.

But Dancy's argument, despite its initial plausibility, is not accurate and cannot establish the point he has in mind. It was explained in the previous sections that concepts such as 'closed system,' 'open system,' and 'tendency' are useful tools to make the task of analysis of complex real situations more manageable. In other words in using 'closed systems' we stipulate that out of infinitely many factors which are operating in a real situation, only a handful, which we deem to be important for the case we are interested in, are important, i.e., have bearing on the situation under consideration and its outcome. Thought experiments are, in an exact sense, a class of instances of the application the notion of 'closed system' to real situations. In the case of moral deliberations, we conjecture that $R^1, ..., R^n$ are properties relevant to the rightness of an action in both the imaginary and the real cases. We then use the imaginary case mostly for the purpose of challenging some proposed list of relevant properties by considering a hypothetical case satisfying the list, but lacking the target property.

As explained above, an important tacit assumption of the concept of 'closed system' is that while operating within the confines of a closed system we assume that other factors, unknown to us or as yet not considered by us, do not have appreciable effect on the situation at hand. Of course, we may be wrong about this particular use of the *ceteris paribus* rule and for this reason we are open to revise our model in the light of new evidence or new information. However, it is important to further explore the significance of this tacit assumption and show its relevance to Dancy's two conception of 'resulting from' and his understanding of 'holism of reasons'.

Consider the case of an action being right in virtue of its benevolence. According to Dancy the benevolence of this action must result from something else, for example, active participation of the agent/actor in raising fund for a charity. Now, Dancy maintains that in the imaginary case, we consider the rightness of the action by trying to provide a reason for it, say, its benevolence. However, the real case is much more complex and unexpected surprises may hamper our reason-giving exercise in the thought experiment. For example, it may turn out that the benevolence in question has actually resulted from a purely selfish intention: the actor has had in mind to impress his fiancé and wins her heart or to convince the voters in his constituency that he is the best candidate for the local city council.

However, it seems Dancy's conception of 'holism of reasons' has misled him. According to a G-P within the confines of a closed system, if an action is right, it is right not just in virtue of being R^1, but also because R^1 is 'derivable' from fundamental moral principles and this in turn means that among the more substantial 'reasons' for ascribing rightness to the action in question, 'not being a selfish intention' is also included. According to G-Ps if an act has a right-making power, it would always manifest that power/tendency. In the cases where an act with wrong-making power temporarily and provisionally gains the status of the action of choice for a moral agent in a particular situation, he should be able to provide 'reasons' for such a choice.

However, Dancy may object to this argument by reiterating his disapproval of the use of moral principles in ethical deliberations. It is to this point we should now turn.

Can Particularists Do Away with the General Moral Principles?

As pointed out earlier, Dancy is not fond of general moral principles. He maintains that particularists have no need for such non-existent principles: 'As paricularists, we give no sense to the notion of a property being generally morally relevant, since we cannot relate this satisfactorily to our epistemology; and hence we fail to understand the possibility of moral principles.' (1983, 542)

In his subsequent publications, Dancy has fine-tuned the same theme by distinguishing between the 'more trenchant' and 'more cautious' forms of particularism. The latter, which apparently include Dancy's own version, hold that 'though there may be some moral principles, still the rationality of moral thought and judgement in no way depends on a suitable provision of such things; ... Moral principles are at best crutches that a morally sensitive person would not require, and indeed the use of such crutches might even lead us into moral error.' (2001)

The question which inevitably arises at this juncture is this: how can a moral particularist, if he is not going to make use of general moral principles, decide about particular moral cases. Dancy has a ready answer to this important question: 'I suggest that what the experienced moral judge knows is a range of ways in which a feature can contribute to determining how to act. … in understanding the practical purport of a concept such as cruelty, what one knows is the sort of difference it can make that what one proposes to do would be cruel, in a way that enables one to see new differences made in situations rather different from those one has encountered so far.' (2001) Dancy goes on to liken the particularists knowledge of the practical purport of a concept to the knowledge of a competent language users of semantic purport of a term and the grammatical rules.

Dancy's use of analogy with language is interesting. This is because the phenomenon of language provides a powerful argument in defence of G-P's position. There is a similarity between the basic moral principles and the standards of an advanced language like English. Without these standards making sense of the many different dialects which comprise the large family of English language will be impossible. Different forms of English, e.g., British English, American English, Australian English, Indian English, and the like, are constantly deviating from the standard English, and yet their common aspects make it possible for speakers of these variants of English to be able to understand each other. The English language is larger than its standard version but the standard version, like a backbone keeps its various parts together. Moral principles are similar to the standard English. Moral acts, to be counted as moral, require moral principles, although the set of these acts is larger that the set of the moral principles.

Dancy's position own moral principles however, suffers from a deeper flaw which is not dissimilar to the position of the entity-realists who are claiming that 'experimental work, and not theoretical knowledge, provides the strongest evidence for the reality of a postulated or inferred entity'. This is because, so the argument goes, 'we can measure or otherwise understand its causal power'. Furthermore, as Hacking has pointed out: 'The best evidence, in turn, that we have this kind of understanding is that we can set out, *from scratch*, to build machines that will work fairly reliably, taking advantage of this or that causal nexus. Hence engineering, not theorizing, is the best proof of scientific realism about entities.' (1983, p.170, emphasis added)

Hacking's claim concerning the ability of the engineers 'to set out from scratch' and without the aid of general theories 'build machines that work reliably' bears striking resemblance to Dancy's claim that moral agents are capable to come to moral decisions in particular situations without recourse to moral principles.

However, Hacking's position is, as I have argued elsewhere (2000b), untenable: to build sophisticated machines or instruments in order to invoke the causal powers of the theoretical entities which in turn provide good grounds for the existence of the entities in question, we need to rely on two types of theories. One type puts us in a position to be able to claim that we have '*well understood* the causal powers' of these entities. The other enables us to construct sophisticated machines, purpose built to manipulate these powers. Contrary to what Hacking says, it is impossible to set out *from scratch*, without prior theoretical knowledge, to build machines which work reliably and make use of this or that causal power. To paraphrase Lakatos: technological and practical knowledge without theoretical knowledge are blind (1971, p.91).

To be of any help to scientific realism about electrons, technologists and engineers must first determine whether *their* term 'electron' which they have used to refer to the entity whose causal power they are using has the same referent as the theoretician's term. However, any attempt on the part of entity-realists to show the co-referentiality of the two terms will result in establishing the realist theoreticians' case - that the experimental argument is not an *independent* support for scientific realism. This is because either the entity-realist would succeed in establishing the co-referentiality of the two terms, in which case what they would show is that the theorists have been right in their insistence on the reality of the posited entity, or the entity-realists would fail to establish the co-referentiality of the two terms, in which case, what they would discover is (possibly) a new theoretical entity which requires the help of theorists to produce an acceptable model of its behaviour and properties.

Now, it seems that many of the objections raised against the entity-realists can be re-framed in such a way as to be able to be equally raised against Dancy's particularism. For example, it can be asked that how can an experienced moral judge come to know 'a range of ways in which a feature can contribute to determining how to act' without the benefit of a general knowledge about that very feature and its various ways of contribution to an act. How can the moral judge know whether humiliating a child in situation A, lying to an old mother in situation B, throwing stone at a dog in situation C, generously satisfying the appetite of an unwell friend with not quite healthy dishes in situation D, and … are instances of acting cruelly or benevolently? Without general knowledge we cannot even make analogical inferences from familiar cases to the 'situations rather different from those one has encountered so far.'

Like Hacking, Dancy cannot appeal to 'well-understood properties' or 'setting out from scratch' or 'relying on a modest number of homely truths' for forming moral decisions. To claim that the experienced moral judge would use his 'knowledge' for making such decisions is to beg the question: the agent can only relate his disparate experiences in different situations to each other if he subsumes them under a general principle, since otherwise the experiences will remain unconnected and cannot illuminate his decisions in different situations.

The Status of General Moral Principles

Dancy has challenged the G-Ps on the ontologic and epistemic status of the general moral principles which the G-P theorists maintain to be the main guiding light for our moral decisions/actions. As we have seen above, Dancy rejects the appeal to induction and self-evidence as means of epistemic access to these principles. He also rejects Ross' use of inductive intuition. Above all, he casts doubts on the very existence of such principles (1983). To explain the status of the moral principles, I should, once again, make use of my analogy with the fields of science/philosophy of science and draw upon the insight provided by Gülen's Sufi understanding of moral principles and values.

In my view the basic general moral principles which govern the moral universe of mankind can be likened to the fundamental laws which govern Nature. The notion of moral principles governing our moral universe is not something extraordinary. Laws, rules, and instructions which give rise to structures or shape forms at various levels of inorganic, organic, biological and social reality are widespread. They are emergent properties of complex systems which appear at various stages of development of these systems. Like the fundamental laws of physics which since the Big Bang have allowed non-equilibrium structures to be formed in the universe, the basic moral principles which have emerged since the appearance of the human societies have made moral decision-making possible. Moreover, like the fundamental laws of physics that apply universally and yet can endanger non-universal behaviour if they act within different environments, basic moral principles can give rise to different decisions/judgements/actions in different situations.

What entitles us to talk about general or universal moral principles such as the one formulated by Kant, namely, 'one should regard the other as an end in itself and not means' or the one suggested by Gülen, 'Never deceive anyone, even if they deceive you' is the fact that human beings, despite all their differences due to historical, cultural, and geographical factors, share a common nature, a set of shared innate capacities or dispositions. These shared capacities manifest themselves in various ways: in man's desire for self-preservation, his thirst for acquiring knowledge about his physical and social environment, his fascination with power, his love of freedom and justice, his ability for self-reflection and thinking about thinking, his power to form normative judgments, and so on. All such manifestations can be regarded as the ways we, human beings, as organisms capable of adapting to new environments by invading as well as inventing new environmental niches, use our inherited capacities to face with certain pressures or challenges or problems in our natural and social environments. (Popper, 1994)

In response to these challenges, we, amongst other things, try to capture the universal moral principles which govern our social milieu in the same way we strive to find out about the laws of nature. That is, by means of bold conjectures which are assisted by our intuitions. Moral intuitions just like scientific intuitions, in the sense of non-inferential, un-reflected, untutored and yet fallible beliefs can help us formulating moral principles or criticizing them. (Popper, 1963; Paya, 2003b) Our understanding of moral principles, like our understanding of the laws of nature, is ever-changing and can become richer by the passage of time as human beings collectively acquire more knowledge and accumulate more experience. However, at the same time, just as we can remain ignorant of the laws of nature, sometime to our detriment, we may also not have proper grasp of the moral principles which sustain the fabric of our moral universe, and as a result experience undesirable consequences. In the domain of ethics, as in the domain of science, ignorance is not bliss. Here, too, the achievements of the past generations in terms of better understanding of these principles should be constantly transmitted to the present and particularly the younger generations by means of proper education and training. It is in this context that the significance of teaching general moral principles which go beyond the confines of exclusive forms of life becomes apparent. Here, the value of the views promoted by Institutions such as Gülen Movement can be better appreciated. In the absence of a concerted effort to *teach*, in a rich sense of the word, the general moral principles, the younger generations will be forced to acquire them the hard way with, possibly, huge personal and social costs.

STRIVING IN THE PATH OF GOD: FETHULLAH GÜLEN'S VIEWS ON *JIHAD*

Asma Afsaruddin

Abstract

Jihad ('struggle', 'striving') in the Qur'an and *Sunnah* is a term with multiple inflections. The reiterated Qur'anic phrase *al-jihad fi sabil Allah* ('striving in the path of God') allows for that striving to be accomplished in myriad ways. After surveying a range of exegeses of relevant Qur'anic verses and early hadith works, the paper shows how fully Fethullah Gülen's emphasis on jihad as a means of personal, moral, spiritual and social renewal and transformation is in line with the earliest meanings found in exegetical and hadith works. Such a traditional, historical understanding runs counter to recent, polemical assertions that jihad is a monovalent term requiring unremitting armed combat against non-Muslims. The paper demonstrates that contemporary Muslim thinkers like Gülen, who offer a more expansive and multi-faceted reading of what it means to 'strive in the path of God', are harking back to earlier, and thus more historically authentic, understandings of jihad and its moral purview.

The Arabic term *jihad* has primarily come to mean "armed struggle/combat" and is frequently translated into English as "holy war." And yet a close scrutiny of the occurrence of this term in the Qur'an and early *hadith* literature in particular demonstrates that this exclusive understanding of the term cannot be supported for the formative period of Islam. In the Qur'an the phrase "*fi sabil Allah,*" meaning "in the path of God" or "for the sake of God," is frequently conjoined to *al-jihad*. The full Arabic expression "*al-jihad fi sabil Allah*" means "striving/struggling in the path of God" in the broadest sense. In the supporting *hadith* and exegetical literature, this human struggle for the noblest purpose – that is, to win God's approval– is manifested in multiple ways.

This paper will discuss the multiple meanings of *jihad* as evident in the Qur'an, exegeses, and *hadith* literature, particularly from the early period. After having established the broad range of meanings assigned to *jihad* in these sources, I will then proceed to discuss Fethullah Gülen's understanding of *jihad* and its relevance for contemporary Muslims. It will be argued that his understanding of *jihad* replicates the polyvalence of this term in Qur'an and *hadith* literature and that his emphasis on both its spiritual and physical dimensions is timely and relevant today, especially in the wake of the appropriation of this term as a relentlessly militant activity by contemporary extremist groups.

Jihad in the Qur'an

According to the Qur'an, human beings should be constantly engaged in the basic moral endeavor of enjoining what is right and forbidding what is wrong (Qur'an 3:104, 110, 114; 7:157; 9:71, 112, etc.). The "struggle" implicit in the application of this precept is jihad, properly and plainly speaking, and the endeavor is both individual and collective. The means for carrying out this struggle vary according to circumstances, and the Qur'an frequently refers to those who "strive with their wealth and their selves" (jahadu bi-amwalihim wa-anfusihim; for e.g., Qur'an 8:72) and exhorts believers to continue to struggle in this manner throughout their lives (cf. Qur'an 9:20). This specific Qur'anic locution thus semantically and interpretively allows jihad to be carried out in many ways: through the performance of charity, expenditure of one's wealth for licit purposes, waging a spiritual struggle against the base desires of the carnal self, and verbal and physical, including armed, resistance to social and other forms of injustice.

Actual fighting or armed combat as one aspect of *jihad* is designated by the specific Qur'anic term *qital*. *Qital* is a component of *jihad* in specific situations. *Harb* is the Arabic word for war in general. The Qur'an employs the term *harb* four times: to refer to illegitimate wars fought by those who wish to spread corruption on earth (5:64); to the thick of battle between believers and non-believers (8:57; 47:4); and, in one instance, to the possibility of war waged by God and His prophet against those who would continue to practice usury (2:279).[1] This term is never conjoined to the phrase "in the path of God" and has no bearing on the concept of *jihad*.

The cultivation of patience or patient forbearance, in Arabic termed *sabr*, is also an important aspect of *jihad*, as clearly evident from the Qur'an. During the period known as the Meccan period (that is, between roughly 610-622 of the Common Era), the Muslims were not given permission by the Qur'an to physically retaliate against the pagan Meccans who persecuted them for their faith. Verses revealed in this period counsel the Muslims rather to steadfastly endure the hostility of the Meccans. While recognizing the right to self-defense for those who are wronged, the Qur'an maintains in this early period that to bear patiently the wrong-doing of others and to forgive those who cause them harm is the superior course of action in resisting evil. Three significant verses (42:40-43) reveal this highly significant, non-combative dimension of struggling against wrong-doing (and, therefore, of *jihad*) in this early phase of Muhammad's prophetic career. These verses state:

> The requital of evil is an evil similar to it: hence, whoever pardons and makes peace, his reward
> rests with God –for indeed, He does not love evil-doers.

---

1 These are the only instances when the word harb is employed in the Qur'an, and, therefore, hardly a common Qur'anic usage as Reuven Firestone maintains in his Jihad: The Origin of Holy War in Islam (Oxford, 1999), 140, n. 23.

> Yet surely, as for those who defend themselves after having been wronged– no blame whatever attaches to them: blame attaches but to those who oppress people and behave outrageously on earth, offending against all right; for them is grievous suffering in store!

> But if one is patient in adversity and forgives, this is indeed the best resolution of affairs.

In Qur'anic discourse, patience is thus an important component and a manifestation of the *jihad* of the righteous; quietist and activist resistance to wrong-doing are equally valorized. For example, one Qur'anic verse thus (16:110) states "As for those who after persecution fled their homes and strove actively (*jahadu*) and were patient (*sabaru*) to the last, your Lord will be forgiving and merciful to them on the day when every soul will come pleading for itself. Another (47:31) states, "We shall put you to the test until We know the active strivers (*al-mujahidin*) and the quietly forbearing (*al-sabirin*) among you." Quietist, non-violent struggle is not the same as passivity, however, which when displayed in the face of grave oppression and injustice, is clearly marked as immoral in the Qur'anic view. "Those who are passive" (Ar. *al-Qa'idun* in Arabic) earn divine rebuke in the Qur'an (4:95).

The conscious inculcation of patience and forbearance is an act of great religious merit for the believer. Thus, Qur'an 39:10 states that "those who are patient will be given their reward without measure;" and Qur'an 25:75 states "They will be awarded the high place [in heaven] for what they bore in patience ... abiding there forever." It should be stressed that no other activity or quality is described in the Qur'an as meeting with divine approval to the same extent.

Jihad in the *Hadith* Literature

The variegated meanings of the broad term *jihad* as spiritual, moral, and physical struggle find considerable reflection in *hadith* compilations from the eighth century of the Common Era onwards. It is true that the *hadith* literature contains many prophetic and non-prophetic reports in praise of the combative *jihad*, undertaken with the right intention and for a just cause. The individual who perishes on the battlefield under such conditions is considered to be a martyr and promised generous rewards in the next world for his heroic self-sacrifice. Thus one of the best known reports on the issue of compensation in the hereafter for the military martyr is recorded by Muslim and Ibn Maja (d. 886) in their two authoritative *hadith* collections which states that all the sins of the martyr will be forgiven except for his debt.[2]

Taken in isolation, however, such reports convey the erroneous notion that no other aspect of *jihad* is valorized in the *hadith* literature. This would be patently untrue; a number of reports contained in various *hadith* compilations underscore various dimensions of *jihad* and martyrdom other than the military. Thus a report attributed to the late seventh century scholar al-Hasan al-Basri (d. 728), recorded by 'Abd al-Razzaq (d. 827) in his early *hadith* collection known as *al-Musannaf*, quotes al-Hasan as saying, "There is nothing more arduous or exacting (*ajhad*) for a man than the money which he spends honestly or for a right cause and the prayer that he says deep in the middle of the night."[3] Al-Hasan's use of the Arabic superlative *ajhad* related etymologically to the term *jihad*, stresses the greater moral excellence of basic, non-militant personal acts of piety. Advocacy of the superiority of the spiritual struggle is reflected in another prophetic statement found in the relatively early authoritative *hadith* works of Ahmad ibn Hanbal (d. 855) and al-Tirmidhi (d. 892), which states, "One who

---

2 See A. J. Wensinck, Concordance et indices de la tradition musulmane (Leiden, 1936-69), 2:165.

3 Abd al-Razzaq, al-Musannaf, ed. Habib al-Rahman al-A'zami (Beirut, 1970-72), 11:105.

strives against his own self is a *mujahid*, that is, carries out *jihad*."[4] A report recorded in the famous standard compilation of *hadith* by Muslim b. Hajjaj (d. 875) similarly emphasizes the internal, spiritual aspect of striving for God; it affirms, "Whoever strives (*jahada*) with his heart is a believer."[5] Reports such as these highlight the general signification of *jihad* as striving to better oneself morally and spiritually. Therefore, the emphasis is on spiritual acts of self-purification and on charity and prayer.

In tandem with these multiple inflections of *jihad*, *hadith* collections also record various meanings of the term *shahid*. Thus the early, eighth century *hadith* work titled *al-Muwatta'* of Malik b. Anas (d. 795, the eponymous founder of the Sunni Maliki school of law), records that the Prophet identified seven kinds of martyrs, in addition to those who died from fighting on the battlefield. Thus, "He who dies as a victim of an epidemic is a martyr; he who dies from drowning is a martyr; he who dies from pleurisy is a martyr; he who dies from diarrhoea is a martyr; he who dies by [being burned in] fire is a martyr; he who dies by being struck by a dilapidated wall falling is a martyr; and the woman who dies in childbed is a martyr."[6] This report and the one cited above assigns martyrdom to the believer who suffers a painful death from a variety of debilitating illnesses, from a difficult labor in the case of women, or from falling victim to an unfortunate accident, such as being crushed to death by a falling wall, in addition to falling on the battlefield.

Other reports proclaim that those practicing the virtues of veracity and patience and showing compassion for the disadvantaged are equivalent in moral status to those who undertake the combative *jihad*. Three of the most authoritative Sunni *hadith* compilers —al-Bukhari (d. 870), Muslim (d. 875), and al-Tirmidhi (d. 892)— report that the Prophet declared that "the one who helps widows and the poor are like fighters in the path of God."[7] A report recorded by the pious, ascetic scholar Ibn Abi 'l-Dunya (d. 894) states, "A statement affirming the truth (*al-qawl bi'l-haqq*) and patience in abiding by it is equivalent to the deeds of the martyrs."[8] Such non-combative acts of courage – for example, on speaking the truth even at the cost of imperiling one's life or facing other negative consequences – as well as simple acts of charity are important manifestations of striving in the path of God. All these meanings are consistent with the famous prophetic *hadith* which describes the various means of carrying out *jihad*: by the hand, by the tongue, and by intent (that is, silently with the heart).[9] Another perhaps equally well-known *hadith* quotes the Prophet as remarking on his return from a military campaign, "We have returned from the lesser *jihad* (sc. physical, external struggle) to the greater *jihad* (sc. spiritual, internal struggle)."[10] This later *hadith* underscores the two principal modes of carrying out *jihad* and a hierarchical ordering of their merits, with the internal, spiritual struggle valued more than the external, physical one.

---

4 Wensinck, Concordance, 1:389.

5 Ibid., 5:455.

6 Malik b. Anas, Al-Muwatta', ed. Bashshar 'Awad Ma'ruf and Mahmud Muhammad Khalil (Beirut, 1994), 1:366-67.

7 Wensinck, Concordance, 1:389.

8 Ibid., 116.

9 This is a hadith reported by Muslim and included by al-Nawawi in his Forty Hadith, tr. Ezzeddin Ibrahim and Denys Johnson-Davies (Cambridge, U.K., 1997), 110.

10 This hadith, which appears to have emanated from Sufi circles, is recorded by al-Ghazali, "The book of invocation," Ihya' 'ulum al-din, translated by Kojiro Nakamura as Ghazali on Prayer (Tokyo, 1975), 167. For further attestations of this hadith, see further John Renard, "Al-Jihad al-Akbar: Notes on a Theme in Islamic Spirituality," Muslim World 78 (1988): 225-42.

Striving to acquire knowledge is another highly laudatory aspect of *jihad*. Al-Tirmidhi (d. 892) records the following report in his authoritative collection of *hadith*: "Whoever departs in the pursuit of knowledge is in the path of God (*fi sabil Allah*) until he returns."[11] Accordingly, one who died while engaged in the pursuit and dissemination of knowledge was considered a martyr. Thus a report emanating from the two Companions Abu Hurayra and Abu Dharr quotes the Prophet as saying, "When death overtakes the seeker of knowledge while he is so engaged, then he dies a martyr."[12] The high moral valence assigned to knowledge in the Qur'an, which is the ultimate criterion distinguishing the believer from the unbeliever,[13] is unambiguously signaled in this report. But more importantly, within the competing discourses regarding the purview of *jihad* and martyrdom, it is a valuable proof-text which underscores the self-sacrifice and effort inherent in intellectual and rational pursuits, and thus their religiously meritorious nature.

Later ethical and mystical literature composed by Sufi authors after the fourth/tenth century would further emphasize these spiritual and non-combative aspects of *jihad*, but it is important to recognize that these aspects find considerable emphasis in various sources already from the first three centuries of Islam and do not constitute a later development, as some have polemically asserted in recent times.[14]

Fethullah Gülen's Views on *Jihad*, Peacemaking, and Violence

M. Fethullah Gülen's views on *jihad* and peaceful co-existence of different faith and cultural communities are strongly grounded in Qur'anic and sunnaic perspectives and represent a mimetic continuity with them. As a practitioner of *tasawwuf*, he emphasizes the importance of the greater internal *jihad* without disavowing the necessity of the lesser external *jihad* in specific situations. Thus in his explication of the distinction between these two forms of struggling in the path of God, Gülen says:

> The internal struggle (the greater *jihad*) is the effort to attain one's essence; the external struggle (the lesser *jihad*) is the process of enabling someone else to attain his or her essence. The first is based on overcoming obstacles between oneself and one's essence, and the soul's reaching knowledge, and eventually divine knowledge, divine love, and spiritual bliss. The second is based on removing obstacles between people and faith so that people can choose freely between belief and unbelief.[15]

The effort to attain one's essence, as Gülen puts it, is therefore a perennial one and the greater *jihad* is waged daily by the individual to fight against one's carnal self (*nafs*) which, unchecked, prompts to wrong-doing. The acquisition of knowledge which leads to love for God and one's fellow beings is an important part of this process of self-realization, as Gülen emphasizes.[16] As we recall, the Qur'an and *hadith* stress the pursuit of knowledge as part of the overall human struggle to achieve their full potential on earth.

---

11 Cited by Ibn Qayyim al-Jawziyya, Fadl al-'ilm wa-l-'ulama', ed. Salih Ahmad al-Shami (Beirut, 2001), 99.

12 Ibn 'Abd al-Barr, Jami' bayan al-'ilm wa-fadlihi, ed. 'Abd al-Hamid Muhammad al-Sa'dani (Beirut, 2000), 49; Ibn Qayyim al-Jawziyya, Fadl al-'ilm, 100.

13 Thus the Qur'an (39:9) asks, "Are those who know and those who do not know to be reckoned the same?" The Qur'an further describes knowledge as a great bounty from God bestowed upon His prophets and their followers through time (2:151-52; 4:113; 5:110;12:22; 28:14, etc.).

14 See, for example, David Cook, Understanding Jihad (Berkeley, 2005).

15 M. Fethullah Gülen, Toward a Global Civilization of Love & Tolerance (Somerset, New Jersey, 2004), 171.

16 Ibid.

Gülen's definition of the lesser or external *jihad* as "the process of enabling someone else to attain his or her essence" is rather unique and worthy of note. As he explains further,

> The lesser *jihad* is not restricted to battlefronts, for this would narrow its horizon considerably. In fact, the lesser *jihad* has such a broad meaning and application that sometimes a word or silence, a frown, or a smile, leaving or entering an assembly – in short, everything done for God's sake – and regulating love and anger according to His approval is included. In this way, all efforts made to reform society and people are part of *jihad*, as is every effort made for your family, relatives, neighbors, and region.[17]

The lesser *jihad*, in Gülen's understanding, has important social and, one may add, global dimensions and challenges those who would primarily construe it as a military endeavor in defense of Islam. Every human act undertaken with noble intentions which redounds to the benefit of society and promotes the common good, leading to a genuine transformation of society, is part of the external *jihad*. The external *jihad* must therefore be waged alongside the internal *jihad* to achieve a desired balance, for Gülen says, "If one is missing, the balance is destroyed."[18]

Such a holistic view of what it means to struggle constantly in the path of God is fully consonant with the wide-ranging Qur'anic and sunnaic conceptions of *al-jihad fi sabil Allah*. As we mentioned earlier, the Qur'an's insistence that the individual strive with his or her self and wealth in the way of God allows for this striving to be accomplished in myriad ways. The multiple meanings of the phrase *fi sabil Allah* ("in the way of God") is clear from a noteworthy report recorded in 'Abd al-Razzaq's *Musannaf*, which relates that a number of the Companions were sitting with the Prophet when a man from the tribe of Quraysh, apparently a pagan and of muscular build, came into view. Some of those gathered exclaimed, "How strong this man looks! If only he would expend his strength in the way of God!" The Prophet asked, "Do you think only someone who is killed [sc. in battle] is engaged in the way of God?" He continued, "Whoever goes out in the world seeking licit work to support his family he is on the path of God; whoever goes out in the world seeking licit work to support himself, he is on the path of God. Whoever goes out seeking worldly increase (*al-takathur*) has embarked, however, on the way of the devil" (*fa-huwa fi sabil al-shaytan*).[19] This report contains a clear rebuttal of those who would understand "striving in the way of God" in a limited, military sense. This range of meanings is to be expected since the daily struggle of the individual to live his or her life "in the way of God" infuses even the most humdrum of licit activities with moral and spiritual significance and thus meeting with divine approval.

Gülen's understanding of *jihad* as also including the struggle to ensure the religious freedom of people to believe as they please is particularly noteworthy. Such a view seems less unexpected when compared to the Qur'anic perspective on religious freedom and the freedom of human choice in this critical matter. The facile translation of *jihad* into English as "holy war," as is common in some scholarly and non-scholarly discourses today, has conveyed to many that *jihad* is the instrument for achieving the religious and political hegemony of Muslims over others. Such an understanding constitutes in fact a gross misrepresentation and misunderstanding of the term's Qur'anic usage. The term "holy war" primarily implies a battle waged in the name of God to effect the forcible conversion of non-believers, and often

---

17 Ibid., 172.
18 Ibid.
19 'Abd al-Razzaq, Musannaf, 5:272.

a "total, no-holds barred war" intended to annihilate the enemy,[20] both of which objectives are doctrinally unacceptable in Islam. Qur'an 2:256 states categorically that "There is no compulsion in religion;" while another verse (10:99) asks, "As for you, will you force men to become believers?" With regard to righteous conduct during war (*jus in bello*), the Qur'an prohibits initiation of aggression against the enemy (2:190) and resorting to unjust behavior prompted by anger and desire for revenge (5:8).[21] There is no scriptural warrant, therefore, for waging war (or employing other means) to compel non-Muslims to accept Islam.

Furthermore, an important constellation of verses in the Qur'an indicate that the combative or lesser *jihad* may be undertaken in the defense of all peoples, Muslim and non-Muslim, who face injustice and especially on behalf of those who are persecuted for their religious belief. These verses (Qur'an 22:39-40), which have formed the basis for the formulation of an Islamic ethics on war and peace, state:

> Permission is given to those who fight because they have been oppressed, and God is able to help them. These are they who have been wrongfully expelled from their homes merely for saying 'God is our Lord.' If God had not restrained some people by means of others, monasteries, churches, synagogues, and mosques in which God's name is mentioned frequently would have been destroyed. Indeed God comes to the aid of those who come to His aid; verily He is powerful and mighty.

There is widespread consensus among the exegetes that these were the first verses to be revealed granting Muslims permission to fight in the Medinan period. The specific historical reason given for resorting to physical combat at this specific juncture is the wrongful expulsion of Meccan Muslims from their homes by the pagan Meccans for no other reason than their avowal of belief in one God. Furthermore, the Qur'an asserts, if people were not allowed to defend themselves against aggressive wrong-doers, all houses of worship – it is worthy of note that Islam is not the only religion indicated here – would be destroyed and thus the word of God extinguished. These verses therefore clearly suggest that Muslims may resort to defensive combat even on behalf of non-Muslims who are persecuted for their faith, reminding Muslims that their fellowship extends to righteous people of all faith communities, not just their own.

Early Qur'an exegetes recognized the ecumenical thrust of these verses, although a number of later exegetes from after the ninth century read them in a more particularist way. In his exegesis of Qur'an 22:39-40, the early Umayyad exegete Muqatil b. Sulayman (d. 767) says that permission was given to Muslims to fight in the way of God because the Meccan unbelievers were persecuting them and as a consequence God lifted the prohibition against fighting that had existed for the first thirteen years after the beginning of the Prophet Muhammad's mission. The verse explains the nature of this persecution. It consisted of the Muslims being expelled from their homes, and that a segment of the Muslims were physically tortured and others were verbally abused, so that they eventually had to escape from Mecca to Medina. The pagan Meccans had treated the believers in this way only because of their belief in God and affirmation of His oneness. If God had not constrained the unbelievers in this way

---

20 For various definitions of holy war, see, for example, Ronald Bainton, Christian Attitudes toward War and Peace (Nashville and New York, 1960), 158; the collection of essays in The Holy War, ed. T. P. Murphy (Columbus, Ohio, 1976); and Cross, Crescent, and Sword: the Justification and Limitation of War in Western and Islamic Tradition, ed. James Turner Johnson and John Kelsay (New York, 1990).

21 The later juridical literature developed these Qur'anic notions further and enumerated a list of proscribed actions during combat, including the killing of non-combatants, the chopping down of trees, etc.; see Khalid Abou el Fadl, "The Rules of Killing at War; an Inquiry into Classical Sources," Muslim World 89 (1999): 144-57.

through the agency of the Muslims, Muqatil comments, then they would have prevailed over the believers. Subsequently the monasteries of the monks, the churches of the Christians, the synagogues of the Jews and the mosques of the Muslims would have been destroyed. All these religious groups (al-milal), comments Muqatil, mention the name of God profusely in their places of worship and God defends these places of worship through the Muslims.[22] Similar views are recorded by other exegetes, such as al-Tabari[23] and al-Wahidi.[24]

Given this interpretive trajectory, Gülen's understanding of the external *jihad* to include the struggle to guarantee an individual's freedom to believe as he or she pleases is reflective of the Qur'an's own concern for the protection of this basic human right.[25]

The high valuation in the Qur'an and *hadith* of *sabr* or patient forbearance as an important component of *jihad*, as we stressed earlier, also finds strong reflection in Gülen's writings. Gülen identifies five categories of patience, which are:

> enduring difficulties associated with being a true servant of God or steadfastness in performing regular acts of worship; resisting temptations of the carnal self and Satan to commit sins; enduring heavenly or earthly calamities, which includes resignation to Divine decrees; being steadfast in following the right path and not allowing worldly attractions to cause deviation; and showing no haste in realizing hopes or plans that require a certain length of time to achieve.[25]

According to this comprehensive definition of patience, it is clearly the single most important component of the internal or greater *jihad* whose inculcation transforms ordinary human beings into God's true friends and worshipers. As a Sufi, he invokes the concept of the final station (*maqam*) or point in one's life to which only "those believers who are the most advanced in belief, spirituality, nearness to God, and who guide others to the truth" attain.[26] "Patience," Gülen affirms, "is an essential characteristic" of these believers during their journey towards God.[27]

Through the patient endurance of all the setbacks and misfortunes in one's life, the individual achieves knowledge of his or her true essence, which as we recall, was described by Gülen as the primary purpose of the greater *jihad*. Each individual must be repeatedly "sieved" or "distilled," he says, in order to develop one's fullest human potential.[28] He borrows evocative imagery from the well-known Sufi poet Jalaleddin Rumi (d. 1273) to describe this process of evolution and maturation. In reference to the growth of a grain of wheat from a seed into a loaf of bread which humans may consume for their sustenance, Rumi remarked that "it must be kneaded, baked in an oven, and, finally, chewed by teeth, sent into the stomach, and digested." The process of moral maturity is a long and arduous one and only the patient successfully endure it through the constant waging of the spiritual *jihad* against "one's carnal desires and the impulses of one's temperament."[29]

Finally, Gülen warns against the phenomenon of arbitrary violence and aggression against civilians, that is terrorism, which has no place in Islam and which militates against its very foundational tenets of reverence for human life and for all of God's creation. In an article

---

22 Muqatil, Tafsir, 3:130.
23 Al-Tabari, Tafsir, 9:161-64.
24 Al-Wahidi, Wasit, 3:272-73.
25 M. Fethullah Gülen, Key Concepts in the Practice of Sufism (Fairfax, Virginia, 1999), 100.
26 Ibid., 102.
27 Ibid.
28 Ibid., 103.
29 Ibid., 100.

that he wrote for the *Turkish Daily News* a few days after the horrific events of September 11, 2001 titled "Real Muslims Cannot Be Terrorists," Gülen lamented the deplorable hijacking of Islam by terrorists who claimed to be Muslims and acting out of religious conviction. He counseled that "One should seek Islam through its own sources and in its own representatives throughout history; not through the actions of a tiny minority that misrepresent it."[30]

Gülen is outraged by the current nihilistic disregard of terrorists for the strict rules in classical Islamic jurisprudence which mandate, for example, the formal declaration of a legitimate *jihad* by the state or government and humane conduct during its undertaking. He attributes this alarming state of affairs to a general breakdown in moral, holistic education in Muslim-majority societies today and the rise of a self-serving attitude even among, he says, "ordinary Muslims who live Islam as it suits them." He sorrowfully remarks further that "in the countries [where] Muslims live, some religious leaders and immature Muslims have no other weapon to hand than their fundamentalist interpretation of Islam; they use this to engage people in struggles that serve their own purposes."[31] The violence that such unscrupulous and unselfish behavior may eventually induce may be combated by reforming and strengthening educational systems in the Islamic world so as to emphasize Qur'anic values of compassion and mercy for others.

The antidote to hatemongering and exclusion, Gülen stresses, is the cultivation of the qualities of forgiveness and tolerance enjoined in the Qur'an. He focuses our attention on Qur'an 3:134, which describes righteous people as, "Those who spend benevolently during ease and straitened circumstances, and those who restrain their anger and pardon people; and God loves those who do good to others." Gülen comments that this verse clearly counsels believers to behave with restraint and civility and forgive their adversaries, even in the face of great provocation, and not to resort to hostile behavior.[32] The Prophet Muhammad exemplified such behavior in his daily interactions with people. The external *jihad* that he carried out in his life, Gülen comments, was "an armed struggle ... tied to special conditions," and "was the kind of struggle that is sometimes necessary to carry out in order to protect such values as life, property, religion, children, homeland, and honor."[33] Fighting in the path of God under such highly restricted conditions can never degenerate into the unprincipled and relentlessly hostile acts of terrorism perpetrated by today's extremists.

Conclusion

Even this brief survey cogently demonstrates that Fethullah Gülen's views of *jihad* and its role in our lives is fundamentally shaped by the Qur'anic and sunnaic definitions of this critical term. *Jihad* in the path of God is the perennial human struggle against internal and external enemies in order to be fully human, and as such, defines the very essence of human life and experience. Against the debasement of this concept by militants in the name of Islam, Gülen and many others like him, have steadfastly held to the Qur'anic vision of striving with our selves and our resources, material and spiritual, to constantly better ourselves and the world around us as exemplifying *jihad*. Such views deserve greater amplification and need to be more widely disseminated. I am truly glad to be part of this public forum which is making a valuable contribution to this end.

---

30 Reprinted in Gülen, Toward a Global Civilization, 179-83.

31 From an interview Gülen gave to Nuriye Akman, published in Zaman between March 22-April 1, 2004.

32 .Gülen, Toward a Global Civilization, 182.

33 .Ibid., 178.

TOWARDS AN UNDERSTANDING OF GÜLEN'S METHODOLOGY

Oliver Leaman

Abstract

There is an apparent paradox at the heart of the Gülen approach. On the one hand there is a determination to present a version of Islam that is rational, inclusive, progressive and tolerant. The broad aim is to show Islam to be a universal faith, one that has no difficulties in coexisting with other religions and indeed with those who have no religion at all. On the other hand, Islam is definitely portrayed as the superior form of belief, often because it is seen as incorporating in the best possible ways rational and spiritual virtues present in many other approaches to understanding the nature of the world. Yet how can Islam be represented as one among many and also as the first among many?

This interesting feature of the Gülen methodology is shown to rest on a basic aspect of the *Hanifi/Murji'i* theological approach, which can also be seen as paradoxical. The inability to define precisely the nature of belief and who is a believer suggests an uncertainty about what the Muslim actually believes in. It also implies a difficulty in identifying who is a Muslim and who is not, and that might be regarded as a basic issue in religion.

The lack of definition in the *Hanafiyya* is precisely its strength. This is something taken up well by the Gülen movement. Religious boundaries are often blurred, and believers may wish to hold onto a variety of beliefs not all of which fit neatly into a particular traditional faith. In prioritising Islam the Gülen movement expresses clearly its opinion that within the parameters of Islam is likely to be found the most truth and the best regimen as to how to live. Yet those parameters are not themselves strictly defined and allow for much change and development.

When considering the thought of Gülen it is important to try to classify the sort of approach that he adopts in his writings and speeches. What methodology is he using? This is a question that can be raised about any significant thinker. We need to know how they shape their material, and as we shall see, what sort of audience they design their material for. It is not easy to classify Gülen's thought, in just the same way that his mentor Bediüzzaman Nursi is also difficult to place in a neat category of intellectual life. It is the purpose of this discussion to at least start the process of developing a model of how to understand Gülen, since his work is deceptively simple and direct. It will be shown that despite its attractive and apparently unsophisticated flavour, it embodies a complex hermeneutic, and a very interesting one at that.

Gülen as a Turkish Thinker

One of the observations that people often make about the thought of Gülen is that he is a very Turkish thinker. This is not meant in a narrow sense, but to bring out the fact that he often uses examples from Turkish thought and literature, and of course many of his illustrations come from his experiences as someone religious living in Turkey when the state was constructed in a determinedly secular manner. Another observation follows from this and links him firmly to the *Hanafi/Murji'i madhhab* (legal school). This was the major school of Islamic jurisprudence in the Ottoman period, and as a result has gained considerable traction throughout the Islamic world, and not only in those places that were part of the Ottoman Empire. The status of the Turkish sultan as caliph undoubtedly gave this particular legal approach in Istanbul considerable global force, and this system has continued to be popular as far away from Turkey as Pakistan and beyond.

One of the features of the *Hanafiyya* that immediately strikes a resonance with Gülen is its generally laid back attitude to a whole range of legal issues, and in particular the issue of the nature of *iman* or belief. Some theological and legal schools take a pretty strict line on the nature of belief, and on the status of rulers who have problems with being orthodox, according to those schools. Should or could we be subjects of a ruler who is not a "proper" Muslim, for instance, or would such a ruler debar himself through his beliefs and/or behaviour from political authority? More relevant to us today perhaps is how we should regard other people. Can we know from what they say and/or what they do whether they are really Muslims? The *Hanafi/Maturidi* tradition tends to argue that we cannot really get into deciding such issues, since only God knows how genuine someone's beliefs are, and that knowledge only really comes into play when their lives are finished, since then God can sum up their lives, how they lived and what they thought, and can make an accurate judgement on what their lives amounted to. This is really a position that was acquired through the long-dead theological movement of the *Murji'i*, who based their views as their name suggests on the notion of *irja'*, delay, in judging an individual's religious status.

The Status of Non-Muslims

We find this approach a great deal in Gülen, in the sense that he sees Islam as more of an open than a closed system. Islam encompasses wide varieties of people and beliefs, it is not seen as something narrowly confined to just a few specific forms of belief and action. Non-Muslims, and especially People of the Book such as Jews and Christians, are regarded as believers in something significant, although perhaps not quite as advanced in their religious thinking as might otherwise be accomplished. Alternative views, even views hostile to Islam, are to be tolerated and not persecuted, and their adherents respected, he argues. Violence is anathema to him and any form of terrorism in support of religious aims is ruled out without reservation.

This is not actually the position of the *Hanafiyya*. Certainly they draw the boundaries of belief less sharply than many alternative schools, but once the boundaries are drawn, and they have to be drawn somewhere, they are to be rigorously enforced and patrolled. Gülen's approach is more Ottoman than *Hanafiyya*, in the sense that a large multi-cultural empire such as that of the Ottomans had to make concessions and allowances to differences unless it was going to be at war all the time with its subjects to ensure a high level of religious conformity. But what is the relevance today of the Ottoman empire many decades after its final demise? The caliphate ended over ninety years ago, and the Empire in its material state is no more than a distant memory.

Education and Empire

The relevance of the Ottoman Empire is that it represents a realm of ideas that has replaced the realm of facts on the ground. Empires today exist more in cultural space than as actual colonies with imperial rulers. Different systems of thought try to affect the thinking of parts of the world, and they no longer have to dispatch soldiers or warships to ensure their dominance. More often, and more effectively they send out ideas and through those ideas they seek to ensure the hegemony of their attitude to the world, and also of course their material along with their cultural products. One of the reasons why empires fall is because their military and political strength wavers and declines, and they become overwhelmed by those opposing them. Yet in the empire of ideas what counts is not physical but intellectual strength, the attractiveness of ideas and how far an audience may feel part of a virtual community with common aspirations and experiences.

We can see how Gülen's approach fits into this notion of empire, with his emphasis on the significance of education, communication and ideas. The new Ottoman Empire is one of brains, not brawn, and extends over a far wider area than its predecessor. There is something very apposite about his approach in the modern, or indeed postmodern, world, and that lies in his presentation of Islam as a rather relaxed religion. Gülen selects *hadith* in particular that go along with his approach to Islam, and of course the Qur'anic passages he quotes also stress the Meccan rather than the Medinan revelations, presenting a view of a gentle, kind and non-coercive faith, one that fits in well with modern Western life in the twenty-first century. This might seem as though Gülen does not really consider the whole range of Islamic texts before arriving at his particular interpretation, which in an internal theological debate would be problematic. It is like coming to a conclusion on the basis of only some of the evidence. But what is at issue here is not a debate between knowledgeable Muslims about the appropriate interpretation of Islam. The debate is more schematic and works from the premises that a particular interpretation of Islam is valid, that of Gülen, and we can work from those premises to certain conclusions. His conclusions are inevitably attractive, and link up nicely with each other in presenting a view of the faith that is coherent, moderate and rational. Here we find the ethos of the Ottoman Empire reborn, this time not as an empire in physical territory, but in virtual space.

The Issue of *Iman* (Faith)

It is worth considering an objection to his approach, and we are more concerned here with his methodology than with the actual conclusions that he reaches, or even the premises from which he works. The objection is one very much based on the arguments between the *Hanafiyya* and their opponents a thousand or more years ago which dealt with the implications of the view that one could not tell who an unbeliever really is. Those inimical to the *Hanafiyya* argued that surely there are cases where we can know what someone believes through observing his actions. It is one thing to be tolerant, and quite another to accept any sort of behaviour at all as potentially acceptable, even if it is clearly unacceptable. Could people pray in an inappropriate way and yet argue that what they were doing was acceptable since their motives and intentions were honourable, for example? In some cases the answer is obviously yes, yet if the only thing of significance is the intention of the individual, then we would need no religious rituals or laws. If for example any direction I thought was Mecca was Mecca as far as the ritual of the *qibla* is concerned, then I could be facing in any direction to pray. One direction actually is Mecca, but the others are not, yet it does not matter since I think they are, and want them to be. I have the right intention, but get it wrong. Now, it is one thing to say that God will reward us for trying to get it right, and quite another to say that he will reward us for only trying to get it right. If intention is all that matters then I might read the Qur'an and the *hadith* and *fiqh* and try to get my behaviour right in line with what I take Islam to be, but unless I acknowledge some authorities and rules that help me interpret the texts we end up with an extreme antinomianism. That is, we abandon laws and rituals and just do things that seem right to us. This is the main burden of argument between the *Hanafis* and their theological enemies on the nature of belief. It seemed to the *Hanafis* that to insist on a narrow interpretation of belief was to fail to do justice to the idea that God will decide, eventually, who is a believer and who is not. To their enemies this seemed like the creation of Islam Lite, where anything goes so long as we are trying to get it right.

The Islam Lite Issue

Where is Gülen in this debate? A casual acquaintance with his views suggests that he is in the Islam Lite league. He emphasizes tolerance and love, and stresses the gentler side of religion, indeed all religion, not just Islam. The detractors of Islam see it as a violent and vengeful set of beliefs, and they are wrong, he argues, since it is far from that. But it does not follow from his argument that anything goes. Muslims are called upon to do certain things, and forbidden from doing other things. In his response to 9/11, for example, he does not say that terrorism should not be associated with Islam; he argues rather that terrorists cannot be Muslims, that there is a total incompatibility between violence towards innocent people and Islam. This is not Islam Lite but an account of the religion as a fully-fledged lifestyle with rules and demands.

Yet how can he say that a terrorist cannot be a Muslim? Shouldn't that decision be left to God? Only God can see into the heart of the terrorist, and if the latter's actions are determined by noble motives, we may disparage the actions but nonetheless respect what lay behind them. Not according to Gülen, and here we should distinguish him sharply from the *Hanafi* tradition on these sorts of issues. It is not enough for our motives to be correct, Gülen argues, they must also result in the right sort of actions, and that is a profoundly anti-*Murji'i* idea.

On the other hand, there are places where Gülen seems to interpret Islam so broadly that action becomes unimportant, or even inevitable. For example: "Even a person who refuses to believe in God or who follows another religion has to be a Muslim perforce as far as bodily existence is concerned" (*Toward a Global Civilization* p. 223), based on the idea of human beings submitting (*muslimun*) to natural laws which God has established. So then action becomes insignificant since all action is Muslim, and nothing can rule a person out. Yet when he comes to discussing terrorism he takes an entirely different line "no one - and certainly no Muslim - can approve of any terrorist activity" (*ibid.* p.261). He goes on to say on the same page "No terrorist can be a Muslim". So breathing and walking is no longer enough to define someone as a Muslim. It looks as though there are actions for Gülen which rules someone out as a member of the *ummah*. Yet he also argues that we should not put the emphasis on actions since everyone could be considered a Muslim anyway, so how could anything debar them?

It looks like we are back to Islam Lite here, but this is not the case. All religions have figures who in a short summary of the religion ignore all aspects of the religion except for what they take its essence to be. The famous rabbi Hillel was asked by someone who wanted to be told "while he stood on one leg" (i.e. quickly) what Judaism was all about, and Hillel replied that it was treating someone else as you yourself would be treated, everything else is commentary (Talmud *Shabbat* 31a). People often forget that Hillel then said the enquirer should go next and study the commentary! Judaism Lite looks like it is all about love and community, but in fact Judaism, like all other religions, is far more complicated than that. Exactly the same remarks may be made about Christianity, where people often pick out a few of Jesus' sayings and construct the religion around them, a bit like Gülen's way of using Qur'anic passages, while not taking account of a whole range of sayings from the same text that go in precisely the opposite direction.

Arguing for Islam or for Religion?

What we should notice about Gülen's strategy is that he is not really arguing for Islam against other religions. He is really arguing for religion against secularism. It is here that the Turkish location for his work is so significant, since of course Turkey has in the modern period been an officially secular country battling internally for the minds of its citizens, who are largely religious. In the world as a whole modernity is supposed to lead to the decline of religion as science and technology progress, but as we know this is not what has happened. Yet at a deeper level perhaps it has, and this is where Gülen and a thinker who was very important for him, Said Nursi, are so perceptive. They sense the creeping secularism of the modern world and how it impinges on the religious consciousness even where secularism acts surreptitiously. Do we really, in a scientific age, believe that God brings things about, or do we ascribe what happens to causality and natural law? We may talk about God but really mean science, we may talk about Islam but really mean our social community, and it is the task of Gülen and others to remind people of their origins in a divinely-created reality and their consequent responsibilities. This is not an entirely intellectual enterprise since it is designed to stimulate our emotions and feelings, and so Gülen often uses Sufi vocabulary and talks in terms of love and passion. What he is trying to do is not present a neat theological argument which proves a particular conclusion, but rather help his audience discover or rediscover their spiritual roots in religion. Although to a degree this way back to religion is rational, to a degree it is not and the language he uses calls sometimes for an emotional response by his audience, a response that will help them see the secular world as the limited environment that it is and reconnect them with their spiritual roots in God.

This connection with Sufism is something that Gülen quite rightly sees as a distinctive Turkish or at least Central Asian contribution to the global appeal of Islam. Certainly it was in the Arabian Peninsula that Islam first became established in Medina and Mecca, but it was the Central Asian milieu and the thinkers who lived there such as *Bukhari*, *Tirmidhi* etc. who did so much to shape the original message into a form that enabled it to become ubiquitous. Here he pointed to the *Hanafi* tradition, especially in its *Maturidi* aspect, and in particular to its relative tolerance of existing legal and social frameworks, and the notion of *istihsan* or public welfare as a constraining concept in jurisprudence. Once we have a form of Islam that involves both interior psychological states such as Sufism and exterior general conditions of welfare such as we find in the *Hanafi* School, we have a combination of positive factors that really powers a religion along. According to Gülen, this is one of the explanations for the early and continuing success of Islam.

Identifying the Enemy, Identifying the Audience

Within the modern world Gülen rightly identifies secularism as the major enemy of Islam. Of course, he may well have been thinking of his own local context in a Turkey that in the last century set out determinedly on a secular path, on a route to becoming yet another European country. But over time the power of the secular urban elite in Turkey has been weakened by the influx of more religious people from the countryside, and indeed Europe now looks far more Muslim than it did a hundred years ago, with the large-scale immigration of Muslims and their high birth rate into Europe. The main struggle lies over education, something that was grasped immediately by the secular authorities in Turkey when they wrested education away from religious groups and established a dual system of education, forbidding those attending religious schools to participate in general education. The policies of the present AKP government in Turkey are designed slowly and gradually to reverse this divorce between religion and education, and all ideological groups now appreciate the significance of education and its control in a world where knowledge and how it is viewed and utilized have become major rallying points for competing groups in society.

Before we can assess Gülen's methodology, we have to try to understand his audience. If we think of his audience as theologians then his material is often unsatisfactory, since it skirts a great deal of theological complexity and detail, and appears rather naive in its directness. Theologians require far more of an argument, and a real attempt to show why alternative points of view are invalid. If we think of his audience as committed Muslims who are deeply within a particular Islamic school that rejects his approach, we are also going to be unimpressed by his arguments. To argue with a *Hanbali*, for instance, one needs to compare and contrast their use of *hadith* and what implications may be drawn from those *hadith*. We would need to discuss which notion of *iman* or faith was better, the strict *Hanbali* notion based on action or the looser *Hanafi* notion based on the intentions of the individual. One could see how this argument might go, and of course within the tradition of *fiqh* (jurisprudence) there are many such arguments on both sides. Gülen does not really enter this sort of debate in most of his works.

The audience he sees himself as confronting are those who have an interest in religion and perhaps think they are Muslims but have difficulty in seeing how to make religion part of their daily lives in a world of science and technology. Or they might be people in no religion at all who hear vaguely hostile comments made about Islam and wonder if it is as bad as it is made out to be. Or they are people who regard themselves as interested in spirituality but not in any specific faith, a very common attitude of Europeans today. As the Catholic writer G K Chesterton is said to have remarked, when people lose faith in God they do not then believe in nothing; they believe in anything. Gülen wants to show such an audience that there are good reasons for respecting the contribution that Islam can make to what is sometimes referred to as our modern spiritual crisis, and the way to do this is to concentrate on those aspects of Islam that are in tune with contemporary democratic life. This means stressing the role of tolerance and freedom of thought, the equality of the sexes and love, all ideas that are widely popular and can be shown to have links with aspects of Islam. These ideas are also not those generally associated with Islam in the mind of the public, and Gülen wants to show that there is nothing essentially stern and forbidding about Islam. On the contrary, it is a faith quite capable of reinventing itself and adjusting to modern times and new situations, although this is certainly not how he phrases it.

I think Gülen has another audience in mind, and this is a specifically Turkish audience, but one that has parallels elsewhere. This is an audience that is secular in the sense that it finds no place for God in its heart. This audience is not confined to those without religion, for plenty of nominal believers do not really act as though God were of significance, and their thought processes are not clearly different from those without faith. Like his mentor Bediüzzaman Said Nursi, Gülen is set on creating an *ihya'*, a revival of enthusiasm for religion and Islam in particular, to re-establish religion and God in particular at the centre of our daily life and thought. This is difficult to do since so much in modern life conspires to drive God away from our thinking, and we are often particularly resistant to acknowledging His role in our lives. So in the appropriate Sufi way so popular in Turkish Islam Gülen assembles reminders (*dhikr*) of the role of God designed to return us to an understanding of this very basic notion.

The modern *Ummah* (Community)

In the past the community (*ummah*) of the believers was often a stable and geographically proximate group of individuals. Behaviour was regulated by tradition and parents and grandparents passed on their traditional ways of doing things to their descendants. There were other people around who did not share each other's precise customs, but they often lived in their own communities and did not interact much with those of different beliefs and behaviour. It was not then difficult to continue with the traditional way of doing things, since there were few alternatives and huge social costs in choosing them. But this is not the situation in modern times, and has not been for some time. People move around a lot, the old stable communities have often been uprooted and links with the past severed. The implications of this are everywhere to be seen in Turkey, for example, where many people have moved from the countryside to the city, bringing their traditional beliefs with them, but also raising the possibility that without the support of their rural social environment they will stray from religion. This possibility is only magnified by the phenomenon of migrating away from Turkey entirely, sometimes to a different continent and environment. Within this new situation the individual may feel that new ways of thinking are appropriate, and so abandon what had previously been done in a natural and automatic manner.

Although the Turkish example is important, what is important about it is that it is not limited to Turkey and its citizens. We all live in a context in which we may have left our homeland and travelled far away to set up lives elsewhere. Globalization is a phenomenon which today affects everyone, not just people in one or two countries. So we are all potentially deracinated in the ways that Gülen think of his audience. Once we understand his view of his audience, we can understand how he structures his arguments. He is trying to remind people that wherever they live, they live under the watchful eye of God, that however successful they feel themselves to be, their success is ultimately in the hands of God and not themselves. Gülen wants to remind those who call themselves Muslims of the importance of valuing life and democracy, and of how Islam is a religion based on love and peace. Again, people who live in a new environment may be thrown back on a simplistic approach to Islam which divides up the world into believers and their enemies, and which allows the former to carry out gratuitous acts of violence and terror on the latter. They need to be reminded that this is not in fact what Islam is about, and so we see him highlighting those aspects of Islam which regulate behaviour in socially acceptable ways.

But is not this a poor sort of argument? After all, there are theological views in Islamic culture that go in different directions, and Gülen surely does not refute those views merely by quoting and emphasizing alternative interpretations and Traditions (*ahadith*). This was the approach that we characterized above as that of defending Islam Lite, where we interpret Islam as a rather wishy-washy religion unable to take a strong line on any issue.

Gülen is not guilty of defending such an anodyne version of Islam, though. Here we need to take seriously the recourse to the language of Sufism which is so significant for him. The language of Sufism does not operate by presenting a fully-fledged version of religion. Rather, it brings to our attention important aspects of our lives and our relationship with God, in much the same way that Wittgenstein characterizes philosophy as "assembling reminders for a particular purpose" (*Philosophical Investigations* para.127). These reminders do not in themselves establish a detailed and final view of anything, and certainly not of a religion. What they do is bring out some core facts and experiences which Gülen thinks we are aware of despite the veneer of modernity and secularism that may hide them from us. We may need a nudge in the right direction, and that is the point of his writings. Sometimes the nudge is provided by an argument, or part of an argument, and sometimes by an example, something that grabs our imagination and moves us in a certain direction. Here he confirms to a very traditional pattern of literary work in Islamic thought, yet now transformed and made appropriate for a very different modern audience. For a new sort of world we need a new sort of rhetoric, Gülen suggests, yet the ideas which are presented are not new at all. They are the traditional principles of faith, and although the world and the audience may change, the principles themselves stay the same. Gülen is very effective in reconciling these two ideas that seem to pull in opposite directions, and it is here that his main contribution to the rediscovery of religion in modern times lies.

PREACHERS OF DIALOGUE[1]: INTERNATIONAL RELATIONS AND INTERFAITH THEOLOGY

Turan Kayaoglu

Abstract

While the appeal of 'civilisational dialogue' is on the rise, its sources, functions, and consequences arouse controversy within and between faith communities. Some religious leaders have attempted to clarify the religious foundations for such dialogue. Among them are Jonathan Sacks, the Chief Rabbi of the United Hebrew Congregations of Britain and the Commonwealth, Edward Idris, Cardinal Cassidy of the Catholic Church, and Fethullah Gülen.

The paper compares the approach of these three religious leaders from the Abrahamic tradition as presented in their scholarly works – Sacks' *The Dignity of Difference*, Cardinal Cassidy's *Ecumenism and Interreligious Dialogue*, and Gülen's *Advocate of Dialogue*. The discussion attempts to answer the following questions: Can monotheistic traditions accommodate the dignity of followers of other monotheistic and polytheistic religions as well as non-theistic religions and philosophies? Is a belief in the unity of God compatible with an acceptance of the religious dignity of others? The paper also explores their arguments for why civilisational and interfaith dialogue is necessary, the parameters of such dialogue and its anticipated consequences: how and how far can dialogue bridge the claims of unity of God and diversity of faiths? Islam's emphasis on diversity and the Quran's accommodation of earlier religious traditions put Islam and Fethullah Gülen in the best position to offer a religious justification for valuing and cherishing the dignity of followers of other religions.

---

1   I thank Jessie Dye, Ahmet Kuru, and Kate Marshall for their comments on earlier drafts of this paper.

The plea for a dialogue of civilizations is on the rise among some policymakers and politicians. Many of them believe a dialogue between Islam and the West has become more urgent in the new millennium. For example following the 2005 Cartoon Wars,[2] the United Nations, the Organization of the Islamic Conferences, and the European Union used a joint statement to condemn violent protests and call for respect toward religious traditions. They pled for an exchange of ideas rather than blows:

> We urge everyone to resist provocation, overreaction and violence, and turn to dialogue. Without dialogue, we cannot hope to appeal to reason, to heal resentment, or to overcome mistrust.[3]

Globalization disperses people and ideas throughout the world; it brings families individuals with different beliefs into close contact. Today, more than any period in history, religious diversity characterizes daily life in many communities. Proponents of interfaith dialogue claim that, in an increasingly global world, interfaith dialogue can facilitate mutual understanding, respect for other religions, and, thus, the peaceful coexistence of people of different faiths.[4] One key factor for the success of the interfaith dialogue is religious leaders' ability to provide an inclusive interfaith theology in order to reconcile their commitment to their own faith with the reality of religious diversity in their communities. I argue that prominent leaders of the Abrahamic religions (Judaism, Christianity, and Islam) are already offering separate but overlapping theologies to legitimize interfaith dialogue.

A balanced analysis of multi-faith interactions is overdue in political science. The discipline characterises religious interactions solely from the perspective of schism and exclusion. The literature asserts that interactions among believers of different faiths will breed conflict, including terrorism, civil wars, interstate wars, and global wars.[5] According to this conventional depiction, interfaith cooperation is especially challenging to Judaism, Christianity, and Islam due to their monotheism; each claims it is "the one true path". The so-called "monotheistic exclusion" refers to an all-or-nothing theological view: you are a believer or you are an infidel. Judaism identifies the chosen people, while outsiders are gentiles; Christians believe that no salvation is possible outside of Jesus; Islam seems to call for a perennial *jihad* against non-Muslims. Each faith would claim 'religious other' is a stranger to God. Political "us versus them" thinking evolves from this "believer versus infidel" worldview. This mindset, in turn, initiates the blaming, dehumanizing, and demonization of the believers of other religious traditions. Eventually, it leads to inter-religious violence and conflict.

Disputing this grim characterization of religious interactions, scholars of religion offer a tripartite typology of religious attitude towards the 'religious other.' They are: exclusivism, inclusivism, and pluralism. Exclusivism suggests a binary opposition of religious claims: one is truth, the other is falsehood. In this dichotomy, salvation requires affirmation of truths of one's particular religion. Inclusivism integrates other religious traditions with one's own. In

---

2 Cartoon Wars refer to the controversy and protest following the Danish newspaper Jyllands-Posten's publication of a dozen cartoons of the prophet Muhammad in December 2005.

3 For the text, see http://www.un.org/apps/sg/offthecuff.asp?nid=837

4 One recent interfaith meeting the author attended was Seattle Interfaith Creation Festival aiming to create an interfaith dialogue for environmental protection. At this event Jewish chanting, Christian prayers, and Quran recitation filled the sacred spaces throughout the Capitol Hill neighborhoods of Seattle including First Baptist Church, Temple De Hirsch Sinai, and Saint Mark's Episcopal Cathedral. More information about the Interfaith Creation Festival is available at http://www.interfaithcreationfest.org/. For a comprehensive picture of interfaith projects and groups in the United States, see http://www.pluralism.org/interfaith/. For a recent study on interfaith activities in the United States, see McCarthy (2007).

5 For example, Huntington (1996)

this integration, one's own religion represents the complete and pure, while other religions represent the incomplete, the corrupted, or both. Pluralism accepts that no religious tradition has a privileged access to religious truth, and all religions are potentially equally valid paths.[6]

This paper examines the theology of interfaith dialogue (or interfaith theology) in the Abrahamic religions by means of analyzing the works of three prominent religious leaders, a Rabbi, a Pope, and a Muslim scholar. First, Jonathan Sacks, the Chief Rabbi of the United Hebrew Congregations of Britain and the Commonwealth, offers a framework for the dialogue of civilizations in his book *Dignity of Difference: How to Avoid the Clash of Civilizations*. Rather than mere tolerance and multiculturalism, he advocates what he calls the dignity of difference—an active engagement to value and cherish cultural and religious differences. Second, Pope John Paul II's *Crossing the Threshold of Hope* argues that holiness and truth might exist in other religions because the Holy Spirit works beyond the formal boundaries of Church. Third, the Turkish Islamic scholar Fethullah Gülen's *Advocate of Dialogue* describes a Muslim approach to interfaith dialogue based on the Muslim belief in prophecy and revelation.

I analyze the interfaith theologies of these religious leaders in five sections: First, I explore variations on the definition of 'interfaith dialogue' in their works. Second, I examine the structural and strategic reasons for the emergence and development of the interfaith theologies. Third, I respond to four common doubts about the possibility and utility of interfaith dialogue and theologies. Fourth, I use John Rawls' overlapping consensus approach to develop a framework with which to analyze religious leaders' support for interfaith dialogue. Fifth, I discuss the religious rationales of each religious leader as it relates to interfaith dialogue.

What is Interfaith Dialogue?

The leaders I examine initiate and support interfaith dialogue. More importantly, they articulate religious foundations for interfaith dialogue. While they emphasize the deliberative, formal, and theological nature of interfaith dialogue, distinguishing it from everyday religious encounters and conversations, their notions of dialogue vary. For example, Gülen defines dialogue procedurally and consequentially: dialogue is the "coming together of two or more people to discuss certain issues, and thus the formation of a bond between these people."[7] Gülen's minimalist approach aims to facilitate interfaith dialogue both in order to search for the commonalities between different faiths and to stimulate development of an interfaith framework out of interfaith practices. Privileging the practice (Kantian 'practical reason') over the speculative (Kantian 'pure reason') in religious epistemology is common in Gülen's teaching.[8]

The Catholic Church's notion of dialogue stresses religious 'witnessing.' It is more than a verbal act; it is the co-witnessing each other's faith for mutual growth and enrichment. Witnessing connotes a deeper engagement involving a more spiritual experience than intellectual communication. Furthermore, unlike Judaism and Islam, ecumenical dialogue has become a significant part of the Catholic Church's approach to dialogue in addition to the interfaith. The Second Vatican Council's *Unitatis Redingtegration* (Restoring Christian Unity) attempts to accommodate and integrate non-Catholic Christian Churches into Catholic

---

6 Race (1983), Aslan (1998), Eck (1993).

7 Gülen (2004).

8 Carroll (2007)

theology. *Nostra Aetate* (the Declaration on the Relationship of the Church to Non-Christian Religions) emphasizes shared belief and practices between the Catholic Church and non-Christians.[9]

Last, according to Sacks, interfaith dialogue is not a debate about winning an argument or changing one's own beliefs, but a deliberation for an inclusive identity formation with the 'other'. In this identity formation process, dialogue participants make their "views intelligible to someone who does not share them" and listen to enter "into the inner world of someone whose views are opposed to" their own. The aim of dialogue is not "to change one's beliefs but make space for another deeply held belief".[10] This facilitates respect for differences and makes globalization humane. To this end, Sacks envisions two simultaneous dialogues with complementary functions: an interfaith dialogue and a faith-globalization dialogue.

What explains the growing appeal of interfaith dialogue among some religious leaders? The answer lies with global political developments; the religious leaders in question seek a peaceful coexistence in a global world.

Need for Interfaith Dialogue

Religious leaders and their teachings are not immune to the effects of global development. The theme of globalization, either as cause of increasing inequalities (particularly in Sacks), or as an inevitable process (particularly in Gülen), permeates religious discourse on interfaith dialogue. The Catholic Church's *Nostra Aetate* (literally, 'in our age') starts with a statement that links interfaith dialogue to globalization: "In our age, when the human race is being daily brought closer together and contacts between the various nations are becoming more frequent...."[11]

Globalization prompts these leaders to see the whole world—a common humanity and a shared physical environment—as visible support for the existence of a single creator. However, globalization creates two challenges for faith communities. First, people of different faiths are meeting each other. Continuing religious diversity undermines the naïve religious expectation that if one is exposed to the message of Jesus or Quran, s/he will embrace the truth. Furthermore, the religious diversity may incite a reflexive fear on the part of some religious leaders and followers that if one is exposed to the teachings of other religions, s/he will turn toward that religion. Worse, the global unification of markets and the homogenizing consumer culture has created a backlash among some religious leaders who have embraced exclusivist identity based claims.[12] Dialogue-oriented religious leaders share a view that globalization is an unstoppable process that shrinks the world and makes isolation impossible. This leaves dialogue or conflict as the only two options. Interfaith dialogue is then a peaceful alternative to solve the religious problems of a common humanity made manifest by globalization.

Second, globalization intensifies economic inequalities and environmental degradation. Increasingly, similar problems force faith communities to connect in order to moderate the pervasive influences of globalization. Three religious leaders I examine share a belief abut the importance of interfaith dialogue and its ability to add a moral dimension to globalization.

---

9   Cassidy (2005)
10   Sacks (2002; 83)
11   Flannery (1996; page)
12   Barber (1996), Huntington (1996)

For example, Sacks argues that, although the dialogue of civilizations has always been laudable, new political and economic developments such as economic inequality, environmental destruction and climate change, the spread of information technology, and the increasing power of civil society make this dialogue indispensable for future peace and human welfare.

Facing these huge international challenges, the religious leaders I study seem to believe that economic and political solutions are not enough. These religious leaders are sceptical of such solutions because they feel that economic and political approaches empower the rich and powerful at the expense of the poor and weak, leading to the erosion of human dignity. Among the religious leaders, Rabbi Jonathan Sacks offers the most refined analysis of globalization and its religious implications. According to Rabbi Sacks, lacking a moral dimension, globalization is doomed to remain fragile. Furthermore, the injustices associated with globalization can create anger and resentment among the poor and weak.

However, conflict between the losers and winners in globalization can be avoided. The religious leaders I examine claim that there is a religious authority and responsibility to add a moral dimension to globalization by voicing what Rabbi Sacks describes as "the silent cry of those who today suffer from want, hunger, disease, powerlessness and lack of freedom."[13] For Rabbi Sacks, while interfaith dialogue should focus on finding religious justifications for the dignity of difference, the faith and globalization dialogue should offer ways to enhance the economic justice for a more equitable sharing of world resources. Religious communities' participation is imperative in this process because religious individuals feel a particular moral responsibility to alleviate suffering of the poor and the oppressed.

More than Rabbi Sacks and Pope John Paul II, Gülen underlines the need of an interfaith dialogue to combat the materialism that, Gülen believes, is the root of all evils including wars, conflicts, environmental problems, poverty, and the loss of morality.[14] He claims that the Western-oriented materialist assault on religion damages all religions, particularly Christianity. Under this materialist attack, Christianity can fend off materialism only by allying with Islam.[15] According to Gülen, their similar and powerful teachings can balance a hunger for material gains with service, love, and peace-making. If the two faiths united to advocate for this on the world stage, this cooperation would create a strong foundation for a just and compassionate globalization, rather than one of unequal distribution and unsustainable consumption.

While the structural factors of globalization and materialism contribute to the religious leaders' commitment to interfaith dialogue, urgent political incidents also cause these leaders to call for dialogue. These religious leaders maintain that religion is integral to global politics. According to Rabbi Sacks, belying the Enlightenment predictions that religion would become "mute, marginal, and mild,"[16] resurgence in religiosity is sweeping across the globe. But religious leaders also realize that the in creasing global religiosity does not necessarily contribute to an ever-increasing peace due to the politicized and potentially violent nature of some forms of religious resurgence. To contribute to peace, religions should engage in interfaith dialogue to find ways to "acknowledge the integrity of those who are not of our faith"

---

13 Sacks (2002; 11). Jonathan Sacks expands some of his arguments in Sacks (2005).
14 Gülen (2000; 241)
15 Gülen (2002; 242)
16 Sacks (2002; 11)

and to "hear the voice of God in a language, a sensibility, [and] a culture not our own."[17]

Specific historical events become catalysts of interfaith activities by symbolizing the consequences of a lack of dialogue and the necessity of removing the misconceptions about other religions. For example, the Holocaust and following the Nuremberg trails forced the Catholic Church to take steps to change its anti-Semitic image. Thus, the Holocaust became a catalyst for Jewish-Catholic Church dialogue.[18]

Similarly, post-Cold War developments, concerns about Islam as a new threat,[19] predictions about a clash of civilizations,[20] the terrorist attacks of Al-Qaeda and similar radical groups, and the rise of Islamophobia in Western Europe and the United States increase religious groups' desire to engage in interfaith activities. The subtitle of Rabbi Jonathan Sacks' *The Dignity of Difference: How to Avoid the Clash of Civilizations*' reflects a shared concern among religious leaders. For the proponents of interfaith dialogue, such dialogue can create a unified interfaith stand against the alleged clash of civilizations. Rabbi Sacks stresses that, for a unified stand, religious leaders should cultivate their capability to "see the presence of God in the face of a stranger,"[21] like the Good Samaritan in Christian teaching. Rabbi Sacks warns that if religious leaders fail to accommodate other religions, with the increasing salience of religion in international politics, religions will continue to be a source of discord, not harmony. Rabbi Sacks is firm in his beliefs about integrating faith into the solutions of global problems: "If faith is enlisted in the cause of war, there must be an equal and opposite counter-voice in the name of peace. If religion is not part of a solution, it will certainly be part of the problem."[22] Proponents of interfaith dialogue suggest that their goal is to re-cast religion in the name of peace.

Critique of Interfaith Dialogue and Theologies

Reasons of structural (globalization) and strategic (international politics) factors explain religious leaders' interest in and support for interfaith dialogue. These reasons are external to religion. If external reasons alone explain religious support for interfaith dialogue, a change in these conditions may decrease the support of the religious leaders. In other words, religious leaders' endorsement of interfaith dialogue may reflect individual or group interests consistent with the current political environment rather than a moral commitment to the principle of dialogue.

There are four questions sceptics can raise against the possibility, sustainability, and benefit of interfaith dialogue. First, have these religious leaders the proverbial Atlantis. No. Rabbi Sacks, the late Pope John Paul II, and Gülen have been important Jewish, Catholic, and Muslim leaders. Their commitment to their respective religions and their influence on their co-religionists would prevent them from compromising their religious doctrines. Their explanations rely on religious doctrines and authoritative interpretations of their scriptures. These explanations, rather than significant re-interpretation, identify and magnify what is already in their tradition. Their justifications are anchored in their respective religious traditions and the earlier interpretations of leaders from their religion as opposed to fundamental, marginal,

---

17 Sacks (2002; 83)
18 Barnes (2002)
19 Esposito (1999)
20 Huntington (1996)
21 Sacks (2002; 59)
22 Sacks (2002; 9)

and controversial reinterpretations of their Scriptures.

Second, is the interfaith dialogue just rhetoric to hide the ugly face of religion and religious violence? No. These religious leaders are not developing theology for the sake of subterfuge, but are actively practicing what they preach. Jonathan Sacks, Pope John Paul, and Fethullah Gülen have been initiators and supporters of the interfaith dialogue. No pope before Pope John Paul II ever visited a mosque or synagogue; He visited both. Fethullah Gülen's activities have brought religious leaders, starting in Turkey and now with a global reach and influence, together in countless occasions.

Third, is this a monotheist conspiracy against non-Monotheists? No. While the interfaith theologies of Rabbi Sacks, Pope John Paul II, and Gülen accommodate Abrahamic religions more easily, their interfaith theologies can be generalized to other religions. In Rabbi Sacks' argument, all religions are particular languages God spoke to different communities. The Christian Holy Spirit can work in monotheistic as well as non-monotheistic faiths. In Gülen's case, prophecy and prophets existed in all communities of belief.

Fourth, is interfaith dialogue a faith-based coalition to undermine secularism? Are supporters of interfaith dialogue in search of an interfaith theocracy? No. While concerned about the pervasive influence of politics on religion and vice versa, the religious leaders I examine do not engage with political issues directly. Each is avowedly apolitical. They share an apolitical religious position and express a common concern about the danger of the politicization of religion. Gülen is especially critical of the manipulation of Islam for politics:

> When those who have adopted Islam as a political ideology, rather than a religion in its true sense and function, review their self-proclaimed Islamic activities and attitudes, especially their political ones, they will discover that the driving force is usually personal or national anger, hostility, and similar motives.[23]

A Religious Overlapping Consensus on Interfaith Dialogue

In addition to the problems with each of the sceptics' critique, there is an even further reason to be hopeful for the possibility, sustainability, and benefit of interfaith dialogue: religious leaders are offering overlapping religious rationales accommodating the 'religious other' to substantiate such a dialogue. These internal (religious) rationales are more meaningful than external (globalization and international politics) reasons for religious leaders in their endorsement for interfaith dialogue. These leaders' justifications are tied to their religious doctrines of what mainstream Jews, Christians, and Muslims already believe. If religious leaders offer theologically sound and religious convincing rationales to accommodate the presence of the divine in a religious other, that rationale will connect to the religious creed. Interfaith theologies reflect these religious leaders' commitment to interfaith dialogue as religious value, and not as self- or group interest.

John Rawls' concept of overlapping consensus provides a plausible framework with which to analyze religious leaders' interfaith theologies. An overlapping religious consensus on interfaith dialogue is emerging as Jewish, Christian, and Muslim leaders develop different underlying reasons, consistent with their religious doctrines, to accommodate the religious other and support interfaith dialogue.

Rawls develops the concept of overlapping consensus within political liberalism to explain

---

23   Gülen (2000; 243-244)

how "there can be a stable and just society whose free and equal citizens are deeply divided by conflicting and even incommensurable religious, philosophical, and moral doctrines."[24] An overlapping consensus means that groups with incommensurable comprehensive doctrines can agree to set of principles (in Rawls' case this principle is what he calls 'Justice as Fairness') and can support those principles on moral grounds through their respective comprehensive doctrines. An overlapping consensus materializes when what Rawls considers "stability for the right reasons" emerges to "establish and preserve unity and stability" of a plural society without compromising its plural character.[25] Stability for the right reasons in a society exists when its citizens can agree to some principles of justice out of a moral, not practical or self- or group-centred, reasons.[26] Rawls expects that a reasonable plurality of conflicting and incommensurable doctrines will emerge through practical reason over time under enduring free institutions.

Although John Rawls' develops his overlapping consensus approach for the domestic politics of constitutionally liberal states, his argument has significant implications for religious interactions in domestic as well as international society. For example, scholars of international relations try to explain how justice and stability can be achieved in a plural society with conflicting and incommensurable (religious) doctrines.[27] While Rawls' uses his overlapping consensus concept to explain the possibility of consensus on a political concept (Justice as Fairness), there is no inherent reason to limit its application. Applying the lens of overlapping consensus is particularly useful in explaining religious consensus because it does not impose any value judgment about respective religious truths.

The religious threat to the stability of international society can be removed or mitigated when many of these religious doctrines are consistent with or supportive of the reality of the religious plurality of international society.[28] The existence of strong religious motivations for endorsing interfaith dialogue can contribute toward long-term support for, and thus the stability of, domestic liberal institutions as well as a peaceful coexistence in international society.

In what fallows, I describe how Rabbi Jonathan Sacks, the late Pope John Paul II, and the Muslim scholar Fethullah Gülen develop an overlapping consensus that accommodates 'the religious' other from their own religious doctrines to substantiate their support of interfaith dialogue.

Overlapping Theologies of Interfaith Dialogue

The separate interfaith theologies of Rabbi Sacks, Gülen and the late Pope John Paul II aim to reconcile Jewish, Catholic, Muslim belief in the unity of God with the reality of religious diversity. In his own way, each religious leader leads, inspires, and encourages his co-religionists to join in interfaith dialogue. While these three leaders agree on the importance of this dialogue, they offer different religious justifications for it, reflecting the differences of their religious doctrines.

---

24 Rawls (1996; 133)
25 Rawls (1996; 133-134)
26 Rawls (1996; 142-143)
27 Rawls (1999) develops international implications of his overlapping consensus, but his state-centric approach does not fit for interfaith dialogue because interfaith dialogue is being developed and advocated by religious leaders/ groups outside of public realm.
28 Rawls (1996; 169)

Rabbi Sacks' Theology of Difference

The distinctive aspect of Rabbi Sacks' interfaith theology is his emphasis on the divine nature of religious plurality. He argues that the complexity of nature is the best proof of God's preference for diversity over uniformity, particularity over universality. God sent different Prophets with varying messages to different communities. Despite this diversity of revelations, a core set of tenets revealed in the Noahide Covenant should establish universal standards to prevent moral relativism.

Partially due to their Diaspora and minority experience, Jewish philosophers and scholars have been active in developing an interfaith theology. For example, the most important Medieval Jewish philosopher, Moses Maimonides, offers an inclusivist Jewish theology. In his theology of religions, Islam and Christianity are imperfect but important faiths nonetheless. Maimonides links Christianity to Judaism through the Christian acceptance of the Jewish Scripture as authentic and intact. Maimonides notes that Christians, unlike Muslims, misinterpret monotheism through trinity. He links Judaism and Islam through their rejection of idolatry, but acknowledges that, unlike Christians, Muslims do not accept Jewish Scripture as authentic or intact. Despite these imperfections, Maimonides stresses that Christians and Muslims are important for the fulfilment of the universal reign of the Messiah and the triumph of monotheism.[29]

While drawing on the Jewish tradition to develop his interfaith approach, Rabbi Sacks' interfaith theology differs from Maimonides' as Sacks' argument is not teleological in that it does not envision an end of history with the commencement of Messianic reign. In fact, quite contrary to Maimonides' vision for the convergence of faiths under the Messianic reign, Rabbi Sacks contends that a diversity of faiths is the Divine Will. Rabbi Sacks suggests that monotheism is compatible with the diversity of religions. One God has created natural and religious diversity. In this way, by emphasizing distinctiveness of Judaism—its rejection of religious uniformity—he acknowledges the religious foundation from which other religions can be constructively engaged.

For Rabbi Sacks, the danger lies with universalist ideologies (a notion he traces back to Plato's *Republic*) which can have non-religious as well as religious roots. Rabbi Sacks identifies the Western universalist cultures that propagated the idea of the existence of one universal truth: ancient Greece and Rome, medieval Christianity and Islam, and the Enlightenment. In addition to these five universalizing cultures, the world is going through a sixth—global capitalism. These attempts to unify the world under one truth are not compatible with the Divine Will that has been revealed by the diversity and complexity of the natural and social world. In other words, by creating complexity and plurality in the universe, God is teaching humans a lesson on the dignity of difference.[30]

Despite his criticisms of universalist ideologies and support of particularism, Rabbi Sacks is not a moral relativist. He believes that some universal moral truths exist. One important set of universal truths is the Biblical 'the covenant with Noah.' Like some earlier Jewish scholars, including Maimonides, Rabbi Sacks argues that Noahide Covenant creates a theological space within Judaism to accommodate people of other faiths. The Noahide Covenant includes seven commandments: avoid idolatry, blasphemy, sexual immorality, bloodshed, theft, and

---

29 Novak (1989); Coward (2000)
30 Sacks (2002; 50)

animal cruelty, and obey the rule of law.[31] Going even further, Rabbi Sacks suggests that the Noahide Covenant sanctions the modern understanding of human rights. In this way, Rabbi Sacks is able to establish universality on secular —not religious— grounds. The existence of these secular and moral universal precepts of human rights is compatible with a diversity of faiths. Beyond this moral universal, diversity is the Divine Will, and Rabbi Sacks is firm in his rejection that one God requires "one faith, one truth, one way."

According to Rabbi Sacks, Judaism represents the best example of a monotheistic accommodation of religious pluralism. In contrast to the universalistic monotheisms of Christianity and Islam, Judaism is a particularistic monotheism that "believes in one God, but not in one religion, one culture, [or] one truth." The God of Abraham is the God of all mankind, but the faith of Abraham is not the faith of all mankind. God and religion are uncoupled: "God is universal, [but] religions are particular" translations of God in a "specific language in the form of a specific life, nation, and community of faith."[32] One God shows majesty and mercy though diversity in nature and faiths.

While criticizing Christian and Muslim universalism, Rabbi Sacks' account puts the Abrahamic religions on an equal ground. Stressing that Judaism, Christianity, and Islam are all religions of revelation, Rabbi Sacks argues that

> In the course of history God has spoken to mankind in many languages: through Judaism to Jews, Christianity to Christians, and Islam to Muslims. Only such a God is truly transcendental—greater not only than the natural universe but also than the spiritual universe articulated in any single faith, any specific language of human sensibility.[33]

Rabbi Sacks does not answer how God actually 'spoke different languages to different communities' to sustain his claim of God's hand in religious diversity. Such a theology would require a theology of revelation and prophecy. Rabbi Sacks has an implicit theology of revelation, but he fails to clarify and substantiate it within Judaism. Lacking a clear theology of revelation as a foundational theology for God's speaking to different communities with different religions, Rabbi Sacks' claim for God's complex creativity in nature and religion remains fragile. His pluralist interfaith theology, placing Judaism, Christianity, and Islam on *equal theological* grounds, incited criticisms from other Jewish scholars.

These criticisms led him to rephrase and remove statements of Abrahamic equality. [34] For example, in the subsequent editions of his book, Rabbi Sacks removed this statement included in the first edition: "Judaism, Christianity, and Islam are religions of revelation—faiths in which God speaks and we attempt to listen." He also revised the statement "God has spoken to mankind in many languages: through Judaism to Jews, Christianity to Christians, Islam to Muslims" to read

> "As Jews we believe that God has made a covenant with the singular people, but does not exclude the possibility of other peoples, cultures and faith finding their own relationship with God within the shared frame of the Noahide laws."[35]

These omissions and revisions suggest that Rabbi Sacks' interfaith theology moved from a pluralist (equality of faiths) to an inclusivst (there-is-divine-truth-in-all-religions but mine

---

31 Solomon (2005)
32 Sacks (2002; 55)
33 Sacks (2002; 55)
34 Harries (2004). For a sympathetic review of Sacks (2002), see Dallmayr (2003).
35 Harries (2004)

is superior) theology. From an interfaith perspective, these criticisms and Rabbi Sacks' response indicate interfaith dialogue may require an *intra*-faith dialogue in order to clarify interfaith relevant concepts such as revelation and prophecy.

In conclusion, Rabbi Sacks' interfaith theology goes beyond emphasizing shared beliefs and practices, as it also offers a divine origin for religious differences. Voices for interfaith dialogue from Judaism are particularly important for religious and political reasons. As the representatives of the oldest living monotheistic religion, Jewish scholars' accommodation of other religions may influence the followers of other Abrahamic religions. Politically, it is important because Jewish voices for interfaith dialogue can moderate the ongoing tensions in the Middle East and reduce anti-Semitism and Islamophobia.

The Pope's Hope through the Holy Spirit

Compared to Judaism's traditional quest to develop interfaith theologies, the Catholic Church's attempts are rather recent. The recent attempts are mostly related to Church efforts to respond to charges of anti-Semitism at the Second Vatican Council (1962-1965) following the Holocaust. The political concerns of bishops working in Muslim states prevented a Catholic attempt to prepare a document solely on relationship between the Church and Judaism.[36] The result was *Nostra Aetate*: an authoritative and comprehensive interfaith document. The Catholic Church's formal, hierarchical structure facilitates the preparation of authoritative, binding statements on its members. Lacking a formal hierarchy, Jewish and Muslim leaders attempt to offer authoritative statements based on scholarly and sectarian credentials.

Nostra Aetate shaped the late Pope John Paul II's understanding of the purpose, conduct, and goal of interfaith dialogue. A turning point for the Church's relations with non-Christians,[37] the document stresses shared beliefs and practices with the aim of interfaith dialogue and cooperation, rather than an emphasis on the differences for the condemnation of the other. *Nostra Aetate* consists of five articles. The first article explains the rationale for fostering unity and charity in an increasingly global community by stressing shared principles among religions. The second article refers to Hinduism and Buddhism, and proclaims: "the Catholic Church rejects nothing that is true and holy in these religions." Following this statement, the declaration then encourages the members of the Church that "through dialogue and collaboration with the followers of other religions, carried out with prudence and love and in witness to the Christian faith and life, [the followers will] recognize, preserve and promote the good things, spiritual and moral, as well as socio-cultural values found among men". The third article identifies shared beliefs (monotheism, the virgin birth, and the judgment day) and practices (prayer and fasting) with Muslims without commenting on the authenticity of Quran or prophecy Muhammad. The fourth article extols Judaism as Christianity and Judaism share a common spiritual heritage. It also condemns anti-Semitism. The fifth article makes a general plea for religious tolerance.

Following *Nostra Aetate* (and unlike Rabbi Sacks, but similar to Gülen), the late Pope John Paul II's *Crossing the Threshold of Hope* emphasizes similarities between religious traditions.

---

36 Barnes (2002)

37 Race (1983; 45) suggests: "As official statements by the Roman Catholic Church the documents of Vatican II do not submit a detailed theory of the relation between Christianity and the other faiths. Their role in the catholic theology has been to a signal a change from exclusivism to inclusivism in the approach to other faiths at a fundamental theological level." For the text, see Flannery (1996)

[38] He argues that diversity of religions should not hide the commonalities that unite these religious traditions:[39] "Instead of marvelling at the fact that providence allows such a great variety of religions, we would be amazed at the number of common elements found with in them." The most important common element in these religious traditions is functional: they all try to answer humankind's question about eternity and ultimate destiny.[40] Honouring these various religious attempts, the late Pope cites *Nostra Aetate* which emphasized that the "Catholic Church rejects nothing that it true and holy in these religions."[41] This blanket statement, however, does not offer a theological argument about what and how truth and holiness may be part of non-Christian religions.

Rabbi Sacks implicitly, and Gülen explicitly, link the faith traditions through the notion of revelation—God's speaking to different communities through a variety of prophets. Yet, the Christian notion of Incarnation dominates the concept of revelation. Reducing revelation to God's self-revelation in Jesus (a particular time and space bound self-revelation) limits revelation as a tool to link the religious traditions. [42] One way that John Paul and *Nostra Aetate* circumvent this limitation and link religious traditions is to rely on the notion of Holy Spirit. Revelation in the form of Jesus does not 'travel' across time and space, but the Holy Spirit works "effectively even outside the visible structure of the Church." The Holy Spirit places truth and holiness in other religions, bringing them to Jesus Christ—whether members of this religions are aware or not (anonymous Christians). By linking other religions to Jesus Christ through Holy Spirit, the Catholic Church creates an inclusive interfaith theology. In the late Pope John Paul II's terms,

> The Church is guided by the faith that God the Creator wants to save all humankind in Jesus Christ, the only mediator between God and man, inasmuch as He is the Redeemer of all humankind.[43]

Furthermore,

> Christ came into the word for all these peoples. He redeemed them all and has His own ways of reaching each of them in the present eschatological phase of salvation history. In fact, in those regions, many accept Him and many more have an implicit faith in Him.[44]

More than Judaism and Islam, Christianity puts salvation at the heart of its theology. Thus, for its interfaith theology to succeed, Christianity must have an interfaith theology of salvation. Different religions may include elements that are true and holy, but could the followers of other religions be saved for an eternal life in the (Christian) hereafter? The answer is a qualified yes: other religions can provide help along the way toward eventual salvation, but they are not an independent way of salvation. This view was clarified with other Church proclamations on interfaith dialogue (*Dialogue and Proclamation*):

> Concretely, it will be in the sincere practice of what is Good in their own religions traditions and by following the dictates of their conscience that the members of other religions respond positively to God's invitation and receive salvation in Jesus Christ, even while they do not recognize him as

---

38 John Paul II (1994)

39 John Paul II (1994; 77)

40 John Paul II (1994; 78)

41 John Paul II (1994; 80)

42 John Paul II (1994; 92). Among other factors, the problem of revelation makes it difficult for the Church to accept Muhammad as a prophet and Quran as revelation. Paul II (1994; 94) refers to the fundamentalism and persecution of Christians in Muslim states as an obstacle with dialogue with Muslims.

43 Paul II (1994; 81)

44 Paul II (1994; 83)

their saviour.

An interfaith theology of salvation is the weakest link in the Catholic Church's interfaith theology.

Starting with Vatican II and under the leadership of the late Pope John Paul II, the Catholic Church has been active in seeking common ground with other religions. The Church's formal and authoritative nature facilitates interfaith documents like *Nostra Aetate*. While conceding the possibility that other religions can contain what is true and holy, the Church only narrowly opens the door of heaven to non-Christians.

Gülen's Interfaith Theology through Revelation and Prophecy

Unlike Rabbi Sacks and the late Pope John Paul II, Fethullah Gülen does not have an official status; His authority is based solely on his religious and scholarly credentials. Gülen bases his interfaith approach on Turkish Islamic tradition such as the medieval Sufi poet and theologian Rumi (1207-1273), the Ottoman Empire's religious tolerance (such as the Empire's community self-governance, or Millet, system), and the twentieth century Islamic revivalist Nursi (1878-1960). Growing out from this tradition, Gülen's interfaith approach has three religious bases: a history of revelation and prophecy, the commonalities among faiths, and the Qur'an's explicit sanction of interfaith dialogue.

First, Gülen is unequivocal about his commitment to the interfaith dialogue simply because "the very nature of religion demands this dialogue." According to Gülen, Judaism, Christianity, and Islam, and even Hinduism and other world religions accept the same source for themselves, and including Buddhism, pursue the same goal."[45] This accommodating approach to other faiths is rooted in Gülen's understanding of the spiral history of religion. Embedded in an Islamic understanding of religion and history, this spiral history suggests that God sends prophets and revelations to re-establish the universal principle of the existence of God. The spiral history of religion assumes the "oneness and basic unity of religions." While there may be some variations, the divine revelation establishes an axis for religious unity. In Gülen's words, any religion reflects the universality of religion, which is "a system of belief embracing all races and all beliefs, a road bringing everyone together in brotherhood."[46] Using this singular and inclusive conceptualization of religion, Gülen relates all major religions to each other via the same divine revelation.

Second, the basic unity of religions derives its existence from the chain of prophecy and scripture, and is reflected in the similarity of religious teachings:

> Regardless of how their adherents implement their faith in their daily lives, such generally accepted values as love, respect, tolerance, forgiveness, mercy, human rights, peace, brotherhood, and freedom are exalted by religion. Most of them are accorded the highest precedence in the messages brought by Moses, Jesus, and Muhammad, as well as in the messages of Buddha, and even Zoroaster, Lao-Tzu, Confucius, and the Hindu Scholars.[47]

The fundamental universal values of love, compassion, tolerance, and forgiveness are the basis of all religions.[48] According to Gülen, the similar teachings of these religious leaders, but not necessarily practices of their followers, indicate the presence divine in other religions.

---

45 Gülen (2000; 243)

46 Gülen (2002; 243)

47 Gülen (2000; 242)

48 Gülen (2000; 253)

Gülen, over-emphasize these shared common denominators across religions to establish the foundations of an Islamic interfaith theology and to offer a rationale for interfaith dialogue for common goals of humanity such as peace and justice.

Third, according to Gülen, the Quran is a universal call for dialogue. The call primarily—but not exclusively—targets Abrahamic religions:[49] The dialogue between Judaism, Christianity, and Islam is the first pillar of interfaith dialogue. The Quran provides scriptural support for a Muslim dialogue with the People of the Book (Jews and Christians), saying

> O people of the Book! Come to common terms as between us and you" that we worship non but God; that we associate no partners with Him; that we take not, from among ourselves lords and patrons other than God. "If then they turn back, say you: Bear witness that we are Muslims (surrendered to God's Will).[50]

The Qur'an's twenty four references to Jews and Christians as "People of the Book" sanctions the Islamic accommodation of them.[51]

Fethullah Gülen stresses that Muslims are required to believe "…in what is sent to you and what was sent before you…"[52] From this particular verse, Gülen argues that, in the beginning, the Qur'an calls Muslims to accept "the former Prophets and their Books." By establishing a belief in former prophets and revelations, Islam establishes the foundation of interfaith dialogue. Believing in early prophets is supported by procedural encouragement given to Muslims in the Qur'an: "And discuss you not with the People of the Book, except with means better (than mere disputation)." Gülen suggests that the Quran establishes that dialogue that should concentrate on finding common points rather than refuting others religious beliefs.[53] Gülen's approach does not address to what extent and how to legitimize religious differences.[54]

The unity of the chain of prophecy, revelation, and commonalities of the religious traditions do not necessarily translate into dialogue, particularly between Muslims and Christians. Gülen gives four reasons for Muslim difficulties in this situation: Western assault on Muslims since the crusaders; domestic political repression of Muslims; politicization of Islam; and the misrepresentation of Islam in the West.[55] These mostly political factors are compatible with the general scepticism Gülen has about politics. Politics, with its focus on the allocation of (mostly material) resources, divides people, while religion unites them. These difficulties should not discourage the faithful from participating in dialogue, but, rather, motivate them to advocate for it more strongly.

In conclusion, the Muslim scholar, Fethullah Gülen, develops an interfaith theology using resources within the Islamic tradition. Gülen's interfaith theology establishes a theology of revelation and prophecy as an axis to link faith traditions. The existence of this axis is supported by shared beliefs and practices across faiths. He also relies on the Quran, particularly the Quran's positive references to "Peoples of the Book," to support his inclusive interfaith

---

49 Gülen (2000; 249)

50 Quran (3: 64)

51 Saritoprak and Griffith (2005)

52 Quran (2: 3-4)

53 Gülen (2000; 251)

54 One reason for this may be his emphasis on the practical reason of interfaith dialogue that he expects what is religiously acceptable to Muslims with regard to other religious doctrines to emerge in the practice of interfaith dialogue.

55 Gülen (2002; 243-244)

theology. Gülen emphasizes the shared beliefs and practices among religions to substantiate both of his claims: the divine origins of all major religions and possibility of interfaith cooperation. He is silent about differences among faiths, reducing the religions to a least-common dominator for an interfaith agenda.

Conclusion

There are three caveats about my argument for the growing presence, possibility, and promise of interfaith theologies. Interfaith dialogue presents the glass of religious diversity half-full rather than half-empty. There are preachers of hate as well as preachers of dialogue. This paper explicitly focuses on the latter. My partiality reflects my displeasure with the political science literature that over-emphasizes and over-predicts religious violence and hostility. I have drawn attention to selected religious leaders who preach and support interfaith dialogue. While showing inclusive interpretations of Abrahamic religions, I ignored the exclusivist interpretations of these religious traditions. An intra-religious debate exists within religions between proponents of exclusivist and inclusivist interpretations of religions. Each religious tradition holds the seed of war and the seed of peace. The competition between the preachers of hate and the preachers of dialogue will certainly not end any time soon.

Second, overlapping consensus is not the combination or homogenization of religions. There are multiple roads taken by religious leaders I examine toward an understanding of the value of interfaith dialogue. Given the tendency that religious people reject attempts for the homogenization or unification of religion, taking different routes is natural. Each of these religious leaders takes a separate route, anchoring their rationales within their own faith doctrines. The better justified one's interfaith theology is within its broader religious doctrine, the more it will appeal to the believers, and the greater its chances of success will be.

Third, these religious leaders reject exclusivist (all-or-nothing) interpretations but they do not support pluralist (all-equally-valid) interpretations. While they are not the preachers of exclusion and hate, they are not prophets of cosmopolitan ethics either. They do not support relativism. First, they emphasize the superiority of their traditions. Second, they establish minimum universal standards for what counts as divine truth. What they develop is a theologically acceptable (reasonable) religious pluralism.

These reservations about interfaith dialogue do not invalidate its vitality, possibility, or promise of a global peaceful co-existence. Interfaith activists claim that religion can and does bring people together and fosters shared values rather than creating inevitable division and fear. Works of such prominent Jewish, Christian, and Muslim religious leaders as Rabbi Jonathan Sacks, late Pope John Paul II, and Fethullah Gülen indicate interfaith dialogue is not a spiritual whim but has a rigorous theological framework and value.[56] Their theological leadership thus validates, accommodates, and humanizes the 'other' in order to open up religious space for interfaith activities and to establish religious grounds to complement humanity's quest for peace, tolerance, and care for God's creation.

---

56 Gülen. (2000)

THE PLACE OF THE GÜLEN MOVEMENT IN THE INTELLECTUAL HISTORY OF ISLAM, PARTICULARLY IN RELATION TO ISLAM'S CONFRONTATION WITH POSTMODERNISM[1]

Bruce Eldridge

Abstract

The world is changing at an unprecedented rate. Established religions are struggling to come to terms with societies that are increasingly secular and sceptical about the certainties of the past. They are struggling to come to terms with the new modes and speeds of communication and the moods and ideas that can now be spread so fast. How Islam will eventually respond to the post-modern world is still to be determined. Some want nothing to do with that world, others understand the need to take the opportunities and rise to the challenges. Fethullah Gülen is one of the latter.

This paper places the Gülen movement and Fethullah Gülen himself in particular, within the context of Islam's confrontation with modernity and post-modernity. It demonstrates Gülen's awareness of Islam's intellectual legacy and the extent to which he utilises the methodologies of earlier scholars. Gülen interprets Islam's foundational texts in a way that picks out their relevance to today's world. He is unafraid to engage with other philosophies and faith communities. The schools established by his followers have developed curricula designed to produce the next generation of leaders. Gülen envisions a world where people are deeply grounded in a moral and ethical tradition, where humility and service are highly valued and where reason, science and technology are fully utilised for the benefit of all. This paper shows that when confronted by the uncertainties and relativities of postmodernism, Gülen has located a middle way able to sustain itself in a globalised, postmodern world while remaining true to its Islamic heritage.

---

1 This paper began life as a graduate essay entitled, it seems that Islam has the resources to develop and come to terms with modernity / post-modernity, on its own terms, if only it is allowed to. Discuss. My sincere thanks to Dr. Jennifer Herrick and Suzanne Dooley for encouraging me to develop the essay further.

Introduction

The events of September 11, 2001 changed the world in many ways, but equally, those events confirmed and reinforced many prejudices. They vindicated those commentators, journalists, theologians and politicians who believe there is a fundamental divide between the West and Islam. For those people, the collapse of the New York Twin Towers gave the lie to the postmodern view that all beliefs are equally valid and that there are no objective truths. September 11 took many people in the West back half a century to the ideals of modernity where the West knew that they had the mortgage on objective truth and morality. It can be argued that, the same events had the same effect on many Muslims. The response of the West confirmed all the anti-Western rhetoric of the extreme elements among Muslims. September 11 has changed the landscape and almost inevitably becomes part of the context for any discussion of Islam's relationship with the West since that time. With this in mind this paper will discuss Islam's confrontation with the postmodern world and the place of the Gülen Movement in coming to terms with that world. It will discuss what is meant by the Gülen Movement, Islam, modernity and postmodernity. It will briefly discuss the intellectual history of Islam with emphasis on the role of *ijtihad* (the use of reason in Qur'anic interpretation) in both historical and contemporary Islam and it will situate Fethullah Gülen within that history. It will look at the challenges facing contemporary Muslim intellectuals and argue the Gülen Movement is ideally placed to be part of meeting these challenges.

The Gülen Movement

M Fethullah Gülen was born in Erzurum, Eastern Turkey, in 1941 where he received a classical education. Following exposure to the writings of Said Nursi, Gülen became committed to an educational philosophy which sought to combine theological, spiritual and scientific knowledge. He became concerned that in a strongly secular, state education system, Turkish youth were losing touch with their Islamic heritage. Beginning with holiday camps, Gülen and those who were attracted to his ideas sought ways to provide an Islamic education which would compliment the secular education that the state was providing. The holiday camps led to community houses and dormitories for student teachers of religion and secondary school students. The journal Sızıntı was established to promote the synthesis of scientific knowledge and Islam. As a movement grew up around him, Gülen's educational philosophy moved away from its Nurcu roots. "His main goal [at this time] was to raise a new Turkish elite with an Islamic and modern orientation to lead the country." (Agai, 2002, p33) Following the 1980 coup in Turkey, his followers began to establish elite secular schools, staffed by religiously motivated teachers. Subsequently, schools were established beyond Turkey's borders throughout Central Asia and in the West. Through these schools, Gülen now seeks to build a world wide, 'Golden Generation' characterised by faith, love, idealism and selflessness. (Agai, 2002, p36)

The movement which developed around Gülen and his teachings has grown from its beginnings in the establishment of schools, to include involvement in a wide range of activities. Ihsan Yilmaz (Yilmaz, 2005, p203-4) describes the extent of this movement. Fethullah Gülen's followers, (the Gülen Movement), control a television network, two radio channels, a daily newspaper with a Turkish circulation of 300,000, which is also published in 16 countries and is available on-line, a news agency, a number of specialized periodicals, an Islamic bank and an insurance company. Schools have been established in over 50 countries and there are six universities in Turkey and Central Asia. Gülen's thoughts, sermons, speeches and Qur'anic interpretations are widely disseminated though the media networks established and owned by members of his movement. Gülen has encouraged his followers to become involved in subjects as diverse as "genetic engineering, organ transplantation, music, art, modern theology, Qur'anic exegesis, Muslim-Christian dialogue and secularism." (Yilmaz, 2005, p203-4) Enes Ergene sums up the Gülen Movement thus:

> The Gülen movement is a rare development that brings the social and cultural components of the Islamic tradition face-to-face with modern values and encourages engagement in a positive interaction. It has produced a wide process of dialogue in educational, religious, and social arenas, throughout regions with different cultures and civilizations. ... [Gülen] leaves all ideological concerns aside and proposes a model that is based on man being the basic element of all ideologies. The man or woman in this model is an altruistic person who has been created by God to inherit this world, who can put aside all his personal needs and desires in the name of divine love—love for mankind and all of existence. As a result, this person can be put at the basis of all sorts of interaction, societies and leadership. (Ergene, 2006, p7-8)

The influence of Fethullah Gülen rests on two pillars, the breadth of his thinking and vision, and the size of his constituency (numbered in the millions in over a hundred countries). It is arguable that few if any other moderate, contemporary Muslims have access to as many educational and media opportunities and outlets for the dissemination of their ideas as Fethullah Gülen.

Nature of Islam

Is Islam a religion, a culture or a civilization? Certainly, most non-Muslims, particularly in the West, would regard Islam as a religion. Muslims worship a God, pray and have a book of Holy Scriptures. However, Islam is clearly much more than a religion. In "A Statement by the Islamic Council of Europe, 1976" the authors write, "Islam is not a religion in the Western understanding of the word. It is a faith and a way of life, a religion and a social order, a doctrine and a code of conduct, a set of values and principles and a social movement to realize them in history." (Beckerlegge, 2001, p188) Azyamardi Azra, in discussing the breadth of cultural Islam, identifies "at least eight cultural realms among Muslims". He lists these as, Arab, Persian, Turkic, Sudanic (Black Africa), the Indian Sub-continent, Malay-Indonesian, Sino-Islamic, and the Western hemisphere. (Azra, 2006, p230) Ahmet Karamustafa describes Islam as

> ...a sprawling civilisational edifice under continuous construction and renovation in accordance with multiple blueprints (these are the numerous Islamic cultures at local, regional and national levels encompassing innumerable individual, familial, ethnic, racial and gender identities) all generated from a nucleus of key ideas and practices ultimately linked to the historical legacy of the Prophet Muhammad. It is vital to realize that nothing about this edifice is ever fixed or frozen in either space or time and that the construction itself is in constant flux. (Karamustafa, 2003, p108)

This is a broad, but nevertheless, comprehensive definition.

It is clear that Islam is unable to be placed easily into a neat pigeon-hole for convenient study. Ziauddin Sardar has pointed out that studying the various aspects of Islam in isolation is useful, but restrictive. The various aspects of Islamic life "are [regularly] treated ... as though they had no real bearing on the others." (Sardar, 2003a, p35-47) Yet each aspect of life **does** have a bearing on the others. For example, unlike most Western countries, in Islam there is little or no distinction between culture and law, a law which finds its source in religion. (Hussain, 2004, p28)

Gülen acknowledges this problem in defining Islam:

> On the one hand, religion is an inwardly experienced and felt phenomenon, one that, for the most part, is related to the permanent aspects of life. On the other hand, believers can see their religion as a philosophy, a set of rational principles, or mere mysticism. The difficulty increases in the case of Islam, for some Muslims and policy-makers consider and present it as a purely political, socio-logical, and economic ideology, rather than as a religion. (Gülen, 2004, p 219)

Confining Islam to a convenient definition is therefore a problem. This paper will agree with Karamustafa and accept that Islam consists of a diverse group of people who acknowledge "a nucleus of key ideas and practices ultimately linked to the historical legacy of the Prophet Muhammad."

Modernity

Defining modernity and postmodernity is an exercise described as impossible by a great many writers who then proceed to offer their own idiosyncratic definitions. Clinton Bennett, rather than attempting to define modernity, briefly discusses its history as an intellectual movement from Spinoza in the seventeenth century to today. He describes a number of characteristics which he says are representative of this movement. (Bennet, 2005, p24f)

i.   With the discovery of the laws of physics and the development of the theory of evolution, God was no longer needed as an explanation for the created world.
ii. With the rise of reason, morality could be based on social values rather than on a divine law-maker.
iii. Freed from the legalistic restrictions of God, people could fully utilize their reason and become fully autonomous.
iv. Utilizing science and reason, knowledge could be discovered and continually ex-tended, rather than be confined to the Bible, or in the context of this paper, the Qur'an.
v.   Science and reason were the final arbiters of truth.
vi. Religion was marginalized and tolerated provided it was an activity confined to the privacy of ones own home or church.

This elevation of reason above religion to the point where religion was no longer needed was not a conclusion to which Islamic philosophers were drawn. Leaman argues that rather than finding that rational argument resulted in conclusions contrary to their faith, Islamic philosophers used reason and rational argument to defend their faith and to attack opposing positions. (Leaman, 1999, p14) The rejection of religion in favour of reason and science is a Western response and resulted in an implication among Western rationalists, that other civili-zations were somehow not as intellectually advanced and therefore inferior. This implied superiority of the West became a justification for many of the excesses resulting from European expansion and imperialism.[2] Thus, as Gülen has pointed out "modernity in ideological terms [is] perceived by people coming from different cultures and civilizations as connoting past conflicts and unsettled scores." (Gülen, 2004, pvi)

The separation of religion and science, the reliance on humanity rather than on God, the trust in reason rather than revelation, all of which are characteristic of modernity, have been at-tacked by many non-Western writers. Enes Ergene for example writes,

---

2 The taking of slaves from Africa and genocide in the Americas and Australia are but two examples of such excesses.

> There is no denying that modernity has encouraged man's innate egotism. It has seduced him into a position of such overweening confidence that he can no longer properly appreciate the deep truths of life. (Ergene, 2006 p4)

For Gülen, this separation of science and religion is artificial:

> …there can be no conflict [he writes] among the Qur'an, the Divine Scripture, (coming from God's Attribute of Speech), the universe (coming from His Attributes of Power and Will), and the sciences that examine them. (Gülen 2004, p 196)

Gülen's view coincides with that of the philosopher Oliver Leaman, who argues that the logical conclusion for a theistic religion like Islam, of separating science and religion, is to regard science as equal to, if not higher than religion. In a world brought into existence by God and whose constitution is formed by God, nothing can be completely independent of religion. (Leaman, 1999, p53) Nevertheless, Gülen has suggested that many Muslims have been seduced by the attractions of Western modernity. He believes

> …metaphysical thought and spirituality have been discarded almost entirely by many Muslim intellectuals. In the name of certain notions reduced to such simplistic slogans as *enlightenment, Westernization, civilization, modernity,* and *progress,* metaphysical thought and spiritual life have been denigrated and degraded. Such slogans also have been used to batter traditional Islamic values." (Gülen in Ünal and Williams, 2000, p355)

Such criticism of modernity notwithstanding, the belief in the validity of science over religion allowed Western colonialism and triumphalism to flourish into the latter half of the twentieth century.

Postmodernism[3]

By the mid 1960s, the social analyst Peter Drucker was arguing that at "some unmarked point during the last twenty years we imperceptibly moved out of the Modern Age", and even at that stage, Drucker was beginning to speak of a "postmodern world". (Drucker in Voll, 2003, p239) A sense was developing that this belief in the power of the social narrative that was represented by Science and Reason, had outlived its usefulness. According to the postmodernists, in the late twentieth century and the early twenty-first century there are no longer any great truths. Everything is relative.

Postmodernism a very slippery term and it is much easier to describe than define. Akbar Ahmed describes a number of characteristics of postmodernity. The five characteristics which are most relevant to the present discussion are:

i.   Postmodernity assumes a 'questioning, or a loss of faith in, the project of modernity'. It embraces pluralism, rejects previously accepted orthodoxies, 'a view of the world as a universal totality' and the possibility of 'final solutions and complete answers'. In this view, Islam, like any other ideology, is but one option among many alternatives.

ii.   Ethno-religious revivalism or fundamentalism' feeds on postmodernity… since 'Where nothing is sacred, every belief becomes revisable'.

---

3   It should be noted that though the existence of a phenomenon called 'postmodernism' is recognised by many writers, there is not unanimous agreement as to it what it is, or even whether it exists. Nicholas Fearn for example derides Derrida and his ilk by suggesting that "[p]ostmodernism appeals to thinkers who respect ideas more for their aesthetic qualities than their veracity." (Fearn, 2005, p143)

iii.   An intricate connection between postmodernity and the role of the media as the 'central dynamic' of the present age.

iv.   The postmodern project is driven by those who have access to the media and to means of communication – an educated elite.

v.   Postmodernism celebrates and encourages hybridity, the mixing and mingling of styles and ideas.[4] (Bennet, 2005, p33ff)

Ahmed is equivocal about the postmodern world, for "therein lies the Muslim predicament: that of living by Islam in an age which is increasingly secular, cynical, irreverent, fragmented, materialistic and, therefore, for a Muslim, often hostile." (Forward, 1998, p139) At one level he sees its cynicism as a threat, but he also acknowledges its tolerance of diversity. He retains however, a respectful caution about the West's capacity to put its behaviour where its verbal espousal of tolerance is. Similarly, Ziauddin Sardar, has described the task of remaining true to the values of Islam while confronting the challenges of postmodernity, as a "mega-task", that will "necessarily lead to considerable strife and conflict", but which, he believes, will eventually result in "a saner, safer society." (Sardar (b), 2003, p121-126)

The Christian theologian Kevin Vanhoozer, writing on postmodernism, refers to the "loss of faith in … grand narratives", the denial of universal rationality and reason, and suspicion of claims to the truth. There is, he writes, an "[incredulity] towards narratives that purport to recount universal history" and a rejection of the "notion that the self is an autonomous individual with a rational consciousness". (Vanhoozer, 2003, p12) He continues,

> [p]ostmodern incredulity thus undoes H. Richard Niebuhr's three stranded cord: 'To be a self is to have a God, to have a God is to have a history, that is, events connected in a meaningful pattern; to have one God is to have one history.' In this respect, postmodernists agree with Nietzsche that 'God' – which is to say, the supreme being of classical theism – has become unbelievable, as have the autonomous self and the meaning of history. (Vanhoozer, 2003, p12)

This clearly presents a challenge to any religion or civilization which finds its identity in its history and relationship to God.

For Fethullah Gülen and other Muslims, there **is** a grand narrative that gives meaning to life. Gülen, writing of the Qur'an, describes it as "the strongest and immutable source of religious rules and pillars." (Gülen, 2006) Elsewhere he writes, "Islam, is the religion of the whole universe. That is, the entire universe obeys the laws laid down by God; everything in the universe is 'Muslim' and obeys God by submitting to His laws." (Gülen, 2004, p223) In similar vein, Tariq Ramadan writes of a fundamental body of principles that point humanity towards the divine will:

> This corpus of principles ... is a fundamental given of the Islamic universe of reference, which asserts, in the midst of postmodernism, that all is not relative, that there does indeed exist a universal, for it is a God, an only God, who has revealed timeless principles, which, while not preventing reason from being active and creative, protect it from getting bogged down in the contradictions and incoherencies of the absolute relativity of everything. (Ramadan, 2004, p32)

Gülen and Ramadan are affirming their belief in the unity of their Islamic faith, a faith that is not merely *a* truth, but *the* truth. It would seem on the surface therefore, that there is a fundamental incompatibility between postmodern scepticism and relativity, and Islam. Given the breadth that is Islam, it is not surprising that Muslims are meeting the challenge of

---

4 Ahmed also suggests that another characteristic of postmodernism is that while postmodernity sees itself as 'accessible', its language is often paradoxical and enigmatic, thus compounding the difficulties of definition.

postmodernity in a variety of ways.

Meeting the Challenge of Postmodernity

Islam has a number of resources available in its endeavour to meet this challenge.

i.   There is its history of innovative and radical interpretation of its foundational texts or *ijtihad*. Many contemporary scholars including Gülen are prepared to critically examine the classical commentaries on Islam's foundational texts and are revisiting those texts in the context of contemporary problems.[5]

ii.   There are an increasing number of contemporary Islamic intellectuals who are challenging traditional understandings of Islam.[6] Dialogue with faith groups outside of Islam is increasing. Gülen and others, while remaining true to their own faith, are nevertheless increasingly looking beyond Islamic tradition and are prepared to accept that Islam is not the sole repository of wisdom.

iii.   There is the media, television, and the internet, which provide a capacity to disseminate ideas and promote discussion in a way that has not been seen previously. The internet in particular has given 'ordinary' Muslims, who may not have received theological training, access to scholarly works that enables them to undertake their own *ijtihad*.

Ijtihad

Qur'anic exegesis has a long history. Interpretation of (*ijtihad*), and commentary on (*tafsir*), the Qur'an began during the time of the Prophet Muhammad when he was called upon from time to time to explain the Qur'an. Qur'anic exegesis was subsequently carried on by the Companions. As the early Islamic community grew numerically and spread geographically, there was a continual call for further exegesis, and by the ninth century,[7] distinct schools, legal, theological and religio-political had made their appearance in Islam. By this time it was possible to identify distinctly Sunni, Shi`i or Khariji *tafsir*. Interpretation, despite the range of approaches, tended however to be legalistic and literalistic, as these were considered to be the least error prone methodologies. As the bodies of works grew, *tafsir*, and *ijtihad*, were gradually replaced by *taqlid* (imitation). For most scholars, the gates of *ijtihad* closed during the late ninth century. (Bennet, 2005, p21)

Part of the problem was the status of the Qur'an itself. A major issue in classical Islamic discourse was the status of the Qur'anic text. There was little disagreement as to the divine origin of the text, but was it created at a point in history, or is it eternal, having always existed in the mind of God? If it is eternal, then it cannot be located at any point in history and it therefore cannot have a temporal context. It must stand alone, divine and immutable. Thus argued the *Muhaddithin*, the traditionalists. If on the other hand, the text was created at a point in history then it would be linked to the context of that history. Believers would then be able to use their God-given ability to reason, and to make decisions about how to act in other times and places. (Bennet, 2005 p95) This was the view of the *Mu'tazalites* and their followers. Their use of logical argument (reason), and rationalistic ethics became factors in the development of the methodology of Islamic philosophy. (Esposito, 2003a, p222) In the

---

5 For example, Sayyid Ahmad Khan, Shibli Nu'mani and Muhammad Iqbal from India, and Muhammad Abduh, Rashid Rida and 'Ali 'Abd al-Raziq from Egypt.

6 For example, Rashid Ghannoushi, Anwar Ibrahim, Fathi Osman, and Tariq Ramadan.

7 All dating in this paper uses Common Era (CE) dates.

twelfth century, Al Ghazali, despite his attacks on philosophy, did not hesitate to argue the case for reason in establishing agreed interpretations of a particular text. He believed that scholars should agree on criteria for assessing texts, "for if they do not agree on the scale by which a thing is to be measured, they will not be able to terminate disputes over its weight." (Barlas, 2006, p247) Reason must be the servant, not the master of Qur'anic exegesis.

Just as Medieval scholars argued for the use of reason, so too in modern times, in part as a response to the rise of Western influence and the accompanying decline in Muslim power, "Muslim advocates of renewal, reform, and revival … argued for a return to the right to exercise *ijtihad* to facilitate reinterpretation and to renew the Islamic heritage." (Yilmaz, 2005, p192)

Muslim intellectuals such as Sayyid Ahmad Khan, Shibli Nu'mani and Muhammad Iqbal from India, and Muhammad Abduh, Rashid Rida and 'Ali 'Abd al-Raziq from Egypt who have argued that modern methods of intellectual inquiry are not only compatible with Islam, but that Islam anticipated modernity. Moosa points out that "in their definition, modernity was synonymous with innovation and openness to new knowledge. … Innovative thinking *(ijtihad)* and renewal *(tajdid)*, they argued were emblematic of Muslim discourse." (Moosa, 2003, p117)

In the twenty first century, many contemporary Islamic scholars are calling for a renewed effort to re-examine the Qur'anic texts and review which texts are indeed timeless in their application, which are related to the specific historical context in which they appeared and which are genuinely ambiguous. Abdullah Saeed refers to this group as "progressive ijtihadists". (Saeed, 2006b, p150) Esposito describes "a diverse group of Muslim intellectuals and activists [who] have produced a growing body of literature that re-examines Islamic traditions and addresses issues of pluralism both at the theoretical and practical level." (Esposito, 2003b, p95) For these progressive ijtihadists, continued interpretation and reinterpretation of the foundational texts is not only allowed, but necessary. Postmodernity, with its recognition of the validity of all points of view potentially provides an environment where recontextualization could legitimately take place. Nevertheless, these scholars would not claim the encouragement of postmodern pluralism as their justification for reinterpreting the Qur'an. Their justification lies in the historical precedents of Islamic interpretation. For them, the gate of *ijtihad* did not close.

Fethullah Gülen stands firmly in this intellectual tradition. In many respects a traditionalist, Gülen believes deeply in the relevance of Islam for today. He is not so much concerned to preach to the unconverted, as to provide an example of a moral and spiritual life. It is in the practical effect of his teaching on his followers, that Gülen's employment of *ijtihad* can be best observed. It is a practical *ijtihad* that produces a transformation that takes place within the individuals of the Gülen Movement, then moves beyond the movement to the wider society. (Yilmaz, 2003, p209) Though Gülen often argues for contemporary understandings of the Qur'an, he does not always use traditional discourse in his cause. Yilmaz suggests: "By exercising *ijtihad* without flagging it as *ijtihad*, Gülen reinterprets Islamic understanding in tune with contemporary times." (Yilmaz, 2005, p200) Yilmaz describes Gülen's message as seeking to promote an integration of Islam and science, an acceptance that there is a relationship between reason and revelation and an acceptance of democracy. Stated briefly, Gülen's interpretation of Islam seeks a compromise with the modern living world. In using *ijtihad* to affect this compromise, Gülen claims a precedent for employing *ijtihad* in the secular world from the Seljuqs and Ottomans. Using the results of *ijtihad,* they enacted laws and decrees to respond to the challenges of their times. (Yilmaz, 2005, p201) Just as Muslims through the ages have sought to make Islam relevant to their time, so Fethullah Gülen seeks to make Islam relevant to our time.

Pluralism

Pluralism is fundamental to postmodernism in the sense that postmodernism sees all points of view as valid. If Islam is to come to terms with postmodernism without sacrificing its own integrity, one can argue that it must not only accept the validity of other points of view, it must be prepared to dialogue honestly and respectfully with those points of view.

Islam has a long history of respectful interaction with the world in which it moves. From the time of the *hijra* and the contact with the Jewish communities in Medina, Islam has engaged in dialogue with people and ideas outside its immediate faith boundary. Hazrat 'Ali, the first Shi'a Imam and the first Sunni Caliph, believed that what a person said, was much more important that who said it. (Safi, 2003, p14) In the ninth century, the philosopher Al-Kindi wrote, "We should not be ashamed to acknowledge truth and assimilate it, ... even if it is brought to us by ... foreign peoples." (Safi, 2003, p14)

The problem of innovation, borrowing and continuity in Islamic tradition has divided Muslim intellectuals from the inception of Islam. The question of "the legitimacy of borrowing knowledge and insights from the Greeks, Indians or Persians," occasioned furious debate in the formative years of Islam. (Moosa, 2003, p112) Many scholars, such as al-Farabi, al-Baaqillani, Ibn Sina, al-Juwaynial, al-Ghazali, Ibn Rushd and others believed that knowledge was knowledge, and its provenance did not detract from its legitimacy. They followed the maxim that "foreign knowledge" was the "lost camel of the believer". Wherever knowledge was found, the finder was deserving of it. (Moosa, 2003, p112) Likewise, scientific enquiry was for some time a contentious issue. al-Biruni, Ibn Sina and others were enthusiastically pro-science, while other scholars like al-Shafi'i, Ibn Hanbal, Ibn Salah, argued that any knowledge which had its source outside the teachings of the Qur'an and words of the Prophet, was dangerous and corrupting. (Moosa, 2003, p112) It was a belief in the value of knowledge whatever its source, that allowed for the borrowings from Greek science which drove the explosion of scientific achievement that characterised medieval Islam. (Turner, 1995, p26) Insights from mathematicians in India, and from Jewish and Christian theologians, poets and philosophers in al-Andalusia all contributed to the glories of Medieval Islam.

The late nineteenth and twentieth centuries have produced many significant Islamic voices calling for reform. In addition to their political activities, Muhammad Iqbal argues for a religious pluralism as does Ghannoushi. Likewise, Abd al-Karim Soroush and Hasan Hanafi argue that there is no conflict between science and Islam or between reason and revelation. (Jackson, 2006) Said Nursi "stressed that having contact with the West and Christianity is not harmful to the believer but, on the contrary, may even profit him." (Agai, 2002, p31) Omid Safi suggests that in the twenty-first century, Muslims need to be familiar, not just with the foundational texts of Islam, but with writers both inside and outside Islam, who are not afraid to engage other faiths. Along with many others he suggests, Ibn Sina, Rumi, Chomsky, the Dalai Lama, Malcolm X, and Bob Dylan as being worthy of study. (Safi, 2003, 15)

Among all these names, one must include that of Fethullah Gülen. Gülen is a pluralist. He encourages his followers to become involved in "genetic engineering, organ transplantation, music, art, modern theology, Qur'anic exegesis, Muslim-Christian dialogue and secularism." (Yilmaz, 2005, p203-4) As an intellectual, Gülen is able to draw on a wide range of intellectual traditions. The breadth of his reading is considerable. In the context of stressing the importance of metaphysics for example, he writes, "The whole ancient world was founded and shaped by such sacred texts as the Qur'an, the Bible, the Vedas, and the Upanishads. Denying or forgetting such anti-materialistic Western thinkers, scientists, and philosophers as Kant, Descartes, Pascal, Hegel, and Leibniz means ignoring an essential strand of Western thought." (Gülen, 2004, p140) In the area of religion, he has met with the Pope, and with the Chief Rabbi of Jerusalem, and he continues to advocate dialogue with other faith communities. If pluralism is a characteristic of postmodernity, then Fethullah Gülen, is actively engaging with postmodernity.

Education

Education according to Gülen, is a key tool in the development of society. For Gülen, education is an all-encompassing lifelong process. As an educationalist, Gülen does not confine his understanding of education to one particular facet of life. A proper education includes religion. "If [a thing] is a fundamental principle of religion, then [he believes] it should be taught in education." (Gülen, 2004, p190) But religion on its own is only part of ones education. "We contend", he writes, "that every requirement of life should be met in schools." (Gülen, 2004, p188)

> Making correct decisions is dependent on possessing a sound mind and being capable of sound thought. Science and knowledge illuminate and develop the mind. For this reason, a mind deprived of science and knowledge cannot make the right decisions.(Gülen, 2004, p205)

He argues that we live in a 'global village' and that "education is the best way to serve humanity and to establish a dialogue with other civilizations." (Gülen, 2004) p198)

In developing his educational philosophy, Gülen places heavy emphasis on those passages from the Qur'an and the Hadith that place the pursuit of knowledge as a religious duty, on an equal footing with prayer and charity. (Afsaruddin, 2005) Though a deep believer in the truth of the Qur'an and of its authority as the final arbiter in matters of morality and science, Gülen has been able to accommodate both modernity and post-modernity. While he accepts that extreme modernity and fundamentalist Islam are likely to be incompatible, there is, he believes, a middle way. Just as reason's excess is demagogy and its deficiency is ignorance, its middle way is wisdom. (Kuru, 2003, p118) Gülen has been able to find that illusive middle way between traditional Islam and the modern, globalized scientific world. He believes that for Islam to survive, it needs to live in the Westernised, globalized world as an equal partner and player. Muslims need to be able to rise to leadership positions in industry, in politics and in the bureaucracy, and to this end, he has encouraged the development of schools which emphasise science, language skills and academic excellence. He envisages a 'golden generation', able to lead a personal and community life that will showcase Islam and encourage others to follow. Gülen teaches that:

> Education through learning and a commendable way of life is a sublime duty that manifests the Divine Name *Rabb* (Upbringer and Sustainer). By fulfilling it, we attain the rank of true humanity and become a beneficial element of society. (Ünal and Williams, 2000, p308)

In a very real sense, the Gülen Movement's schools are engaged in building "social capital". (Agai, 2002, p29) In these schools Islam is not always emphasised, though there is an emphasis on the teaching of ethics "which is seen as a unifying factor between different religious, ethnic and political orientations. (Agai, 2002, p27) In many ways, Gülen's educational mission has been likened to that of the nineteenth century Protestant missionaries in Turkey who were often not so much concerned to preach and convert, as to live lives of service and good works, so that they might be a witness and an example to others. Elizabeth Özdalga found a belief among teachers in Gülen Movement schools

> that God's will has to be worked out in silence." (Özdalga, 2003, p67) She quotes one teacher as saying, "I think that religious believers essentially are carriers of universal values. That is also perhaps the reason why parents prefer to send their children to our schools. (Özdalga, 2003, p70)

An example of one of these schools is in Melbourne, Australia. Isik College was established in 1997 by local Turkish migrants. Its website makes no reference to the Gülen Movement, but it describes the school's aims and philosophy in terms that have been taken directly from Gülen's writings. Quoting from their website:

> The name of Isik College derives from the Turkish word meaning 'light' or 'illuminate'. The aim of Isik College is that our graduates will be the representatives of 'The Golden Generation', illuminating the minds and hearts of many. …
>
> Our strength lies in the passion and care we have towards the raising of a new generation – the adults of tomorrow. Our devotion and commitment to this duty is based on the firm belief that our students will be raised as the golden generation – the generation with the nobility of mind and spirit and who have the strength to shape the future.

The use of the expression 'golden generation' is a clear echo of Gülen's vision for the future.

At the academic level, Isik College is clearly succeeding. In 2007, 100% of the 2006 Year 12 girls at Isik College are now studying at university, as are 95% of the boys – the remaining 5% of the boys having been offered places but having deferred. These are outstanding results and were reported to be the best results of any school in the Australian state of Victoria. (*The Age*, 19 June, 2007, 4) The goal of preparing a golden generation of leaders of the future would seem to be being met at least in the academic sense.

Dar al-Cyber Islam[8]

In the thirteenth century, Europeans learned how to make paper from rags. In the fifteenth century, they learned to print using moveable type. These two innovations paved the way for the Protestant Reformation by providing ordinary people (at least those who could read) with their own copies of the Bible as well as commentaries on the sacred text. Ordinary Christians could now read the scriptures and make up their own mind as to what they believed. (MacCulloch, 2003, p71) The advent of the World Wide Web has resulted in an access to knowledge which is no less significant. As more texts are transferred into digital format, more and more people are able to access those texts and form opinions about them. Islamic legal and theological texts are no exception. Ihsan Yilmaz predicted in 2000, that it would not be long before the traditional books of the various legal schools would be available on the internet and on DVDs (Yilmaz 2000, p194). He noted that already, newspapers and journals, radio stations and television channels have their own muftis and question-answer programs. Through these media and through e-mail discussion lists, Muslims can obtain

---

8 The expression Dar al-Cyber Islam is taken from: Kort, A. (2005) Dar al-Cyber Islam: Women, Domestic Violence, and the Islamic Reformation on the World Wide Web, where she uses the expression to refer to the World of Islam as found on the World Wide Web.

answers and *fatwas* for any particular problem. (Yilmaz, 2000, p195) Bernadette Andrea has noted that "since the 1990s, in particular, Gülen's views have been disseminated to Western, and especially English-speaking, audiences via the internet and international publishing ventures." (Andrea, 2006, p148)

Alexis Kort examined the role of the World Wide Web in discussing the question of domestic violence perpetrated on Muslim women. She compares the potential effect of the development of the internet on Islam with the effect of the development of the printing press on sixteenth century Catholicism. The internet she argues, has already opened the gates of *ijtihad* and has brought access to scholarly discourse within reach of anyone with access to the World Wide Web. Her paper concludes:

In my exploration and analysis of websites, I did find evidence that traditional Islamic notions of *ummah, ulama*, and of course *ijtihad* are changing. ... While it is difficult to prove just how far reforming trends in Islam, through the Internet, will succeed in directly changing such tangible things as reactions to and prevention of domestic violence, my research and analysis does indicate that the possibility exists, in Dar al-Cyber Islam. (Kort, 2005, p380)

Gülen is aware of the potential for a postmodern plethora of different views, all claiming legitimacy. He has advocated the formation of *ijtihad* committees. He argues that it is no longer possible for individuals to be able to do justice to the huge amount of learning which would be required to be a *mujtahid*s on all matters. In Gülen's view, scholars from a wide range of disciplines will be able to come together in committees to advise on particular issues. In keeping with his commitment to scientific progress, Gülen believes that they should avail themselves of all the latest technological tools available to them, including computers, the internet, and DVD-ROMs. (Yilmaz, 2000, p202)

Dar al-Cyber Islam is a reality which reflects all the ambiguities of postmodernism. It is a world that Islam at all levels is going to have to come to terms with.

Conclusion

In the twenty-first century, Islam is living in a world that no longer accepts the great truths of the past. Faith communities that rely for their identity on their history and on their relationship to a God who is no longer fashionable, are being challenged to come to terms with this new, globalized, postmodern world. As part of the world wide faith community of Islam, the movement which has developed around Fethullah Gülen and his ideology is making a serious attempt to come to terms with that world.

The Gülen Movement is not new in the sense that its ideology is new. Gülen had grounded his teaching in the precedents of historical Islam. Gülen recognizes that throughout its history, individual Muslims and the movements that have developed around them, have sought to extend the boundaries of Islam's intellectual influence and contemporary relevance. From the *Mu'tazilites* who argued for the introduction of reason into Qur'anic interpretation, to Ibn Rushd who borrowed from Aristotle, to Said Nursi, who believed that contact with Christianity may be profitable, Muslims have been prepared to move outside the square. Mediaeval Islamic mathematicians borrowed from India, and in al-Andalusia, scientists, theologians and philosophers freely exchanged ideas with their Jewish and Christian colleagues.

Fethullah Gülen stands firmly within this tradition. While remaining a theologically conservative Muslim, he believes deeply in the value of reason, science and technology. He has engaged intellectually with Western thinkers and he has personally shared his desire for inter-religious harmony with leaders of other faiths. It is true that these things have been done before. What makes Gülen unusual is the range of activities in which his followers have become involved, the breadth of his vision, and the opportunities he has created to enable his ideology to be disseminated. Gülen envisions a world where people are deeply grounded in a moral and ethical tradition, where humility and service are highly valued and where reason, science and technology are fully utilized for the benefit of all. His use of interpretation to demonstrate the relevance of the Quran in the world today is significant to the attainment of that goal. So too is his readiness to dialogue with non-Muslim philosophies and faiths. The schools established by his followers have developed curricula which will develop adults capable of bringing his vision to fruition. The media outlets owned by his followers allow for the wider dissemination of his ideas.

At present, Gülen's influence is strongest in those Asian countries with cultural ties to Turkey, although this is changing as his movement's schools extend into other parts of Asia and the rest of the world. Gülen is not as well known in the West as he is in Asia, nevertheless, his international profile is increasing. The decision to create the Fethullah Gülen Chair in the Study of Islam and Muslim-Catholic Relations at the Australian Catholic University is not only an indication of his increasing profile, but a recognition of the role Gülen and his movement are playing on the world stage.

The Gülen Movement stands firmly within the intellectual history of Islam. It presents a vision, both for the future of Islam and for the world, a vision that is mindful of the vagaries and relativities of postmodernism while remaining true to its Islamic heritage.

FUNDING GÜLEN-INSPIRED GOOD WORKS: DEMONSTRATING AND GENERATING COMMITMENT TO THE MOVEMENT

Helen Rose Ebaugh & Dogan Koc

Abstract

The projects sponsored by the Gülen-inspired movement are numerous, international and costly in terms of human and financial capital. Critics of the movement often question the financing of these initiatives – with some convinced of collusion with Middle Eastern governments, others (within Turkey) suspicious that Western governments are financially backing the projects. Aware of these criticisms, in a recent comment to a group of visiting followers, Fethullah Gülen indicated greater financial transparency must become a priority for the movement.

This paper addresses the financing of Gülen-inspired projects, based on interviews with business leaders in Turkey, as well as local businessmen throughout Turkey who constitute the financial infrastructure of the movement. In addition, the paper presents data from one local Gülen movement organisation in Houston, Texas, that collects thousands of dollars annually from local members, mostly students on small educational stipends.

The paper is framed sociologically in terms of organisational theories of commitment. Beginning with Kanter (1972;1977) and including subsequent major figures in the organisational field (e.g. Reichers 1985; Meyer and Allen 1991; Hall 2002; Scott 2003), scholars have demonstrated a positive correlation between sacrifices asked of members and degree of commitment to the goals of the organisation. Using this perspective, the paper argues that the financial contributions made by members in the Gülen movement both demonstrate commitment to the ideals espoused by Fethullah Gülen and generate commitment to the movement. The paper presents empirical evidence, based on interviews with financial supporters both in Turkey and the U.S., of how financial resources are generated, the initiatives being supported and the impact of financial giving on the commitment of supporters.

The Gülen movement is a civil society movement that arose in the late 1960s in Turkey, initially composed of a loose network of individuals who were inspired by M. Fethullah Gülen. As a state-approved mosque preacher, Gülen delivered sermons in cities throughout Turkey, beginning with a handful of listeners and gradually drawing tens of thousands of people. His sermons focused not only on religious texts but included a broad array of such topics as religion and science, social justice, human rights, moral values and the importance of education. Gülen repeatedly stressed the importance of educating the youth of society by establishing first-rate schools that expose students to the latest scientific knowledge in an atmosphere of moral values. The projects sponsored by Gülen-inspired followers today number in the thousands, span international borders and are costly in terms of human and financial capital (Woodhall 2005). These initiatives include over 2000 schools and seven universities in more than ninety countries in five continents (Yavuz and Esposito 2003; Baskan 2004; Tekalan 2005), two modern hospitals, the Zaman newspaper (now in both a Turkish and English edition), a television channel (Samanyolu), a radio channel (Burc FM), CHA (a major Turkish news agency), Aksiyon (a leading weekly news magazine), national and international Gülen conferences, Ramadan interfaith dinners, interfaith dialog trips to Turkey from countries around the globe and the many programs sponsored by the Journalists and Writers Foundation. In addition, the Isik insurance company and Bank Asya, an Islamic bank, are affiliated with the Gülen community. In 1993 the community also established the Business Life Cooperation Association (ISHAD) which has 470 members (Baskan 2004).

Questions regarding the financing of these numerous and expensive projects are periodically raised by both critics of the Gülen Movement and newcomers to the movement who are invited to Gülen related events. Because of the large amounts of money involved in these projects, on occasion people have raised the possibility of a collusion between the movement and various governments, especially Saudi Arabia and/or Iran, and including the Turkish government. There has even been suspicion that the American CIA may be a financial partner behind the projects (Kalyoncu, forthcoming). Aware of these criticisms, in a recent comment to a group of visiting followers, Fethullah Gülen indicated that a priority must be proactive financial transparency.

In this paper, we address directly the issue of the financing of Gülen inspired projects based on the little that is available in published sources, including an interview with Gülen himself, and supplementing that information with interviews with business leaders in Turkey who constitute the infrastructure of the movement. In addition, we present data from one local Gülen organization in Houston, Texas, that regularly collects over half a million dollars from local members, mostly students on small educational stipends. Our analysis is framed sociologically in terms of organizational theories of commitment. We argue that the contributions made by rank and file movement members, as well as by wealthier sponsors, both demonstrate commitment to the ideals of the movement and simultaneously generate commitment to the movement.

An analysis of Gülen-inspired financial contributions must include the ideological and religious motivations inherent in the concepts of *hizmet, himmet, sohbet, istisare, and mutevelli.* For an understanding of these concepts, we are most indebted to the superb work of Mehmet Kalyoncu whose study of the Gülen movement in Mardin, a city in southeastern Turkey, was very helpful both in understanding these ideas and in demonstrating their applicability to the financing of local projects in the city.

Theoretical Framework

Commitment to an organization or movement means "the willingness of social actors to give their energy and loyalty to social systems, the attachment of personality systems to social relations which are seen as self-expressive" (Kanter 1968). Simply stated, commitment involves identifying one's personal fate with the success or failure of the collectivity. Commitment is typically examined in terms of the mix of personal and organizational characteristics which increase the willingness to exert high levels of effort, to remain a member in the organization, to accept its major goals and values, and to value the organization as worthwhile (Buchanan 1974). Rosabeth Kanter's research in the late 1960's and early 1970s on commitment within U.S. communes (Kanter 1972) remains a classic statement on organizational mechanisms that generate member commitment. She was interested in how groups maintain cohesion and she focused on the organizational requirements that influence individuals to feel that their own self-interest is indistinguishable from that of the group—their sense of commitment. She argued that a person is committed to a relationship or group to the extent that he/she sees it as expressing or fulfilling some fundamental part of himself and identifies group goals as nourishing one's own sense of self. A committed person is loyal and involved; has a sense of belonging, a feeling that the group is an extension of himself or herself and he is an extension of the group. Through commitment, person and group are inextricably linked.

A major empirical finding of Kanter's study of American utopias, and one that has subsequently influenced the commitment literature, is that for a community to survive, three basic challenges of commitment have to be addressed. First, individuals come to see their own interests as sustained by group participation (Konovsky and Pugh 1994; Rioux and Penner 2001); secondly, individuals feel an affective solidarity with the group (Van Vugt. and De Cremer 1999; Fine 1986; Jacobsen 1988) and thirdly, the individual experiences a moral, transcendent authority in the group (Hales 1993; Cetin 2006). These mechanisms can be summarized as strategies by which the group attempts to reduce the value of other possible commitments and increases the value of commitment to the group, in other words, processes both detaching the person from other options and attaching him to the community. In particular, Kanter's research showed a positive correlation between sacrifice and investment in terms of generating commitment. The more costly the sacrifice, the greater the value placed by the individual on the goals of the group. Data in this paper support Kanter's contention by showing that financial contributions to Gülen-inspired projects not only manifest belief in the goals of the movement but that the giving itself is a commitment mechanism for involvement in the group.

Organizational studies (e.g. Knoke 1981; Joireman, et.al. 2006; Axelrod 1984; Cardona, Lawrence and Bentler 2004; Van Vugt and De Cremer 1999) also show consistently that open avenues of communication in a group and decentralized decision making result in higher levels of member commitment than highly bureaucratized, formal decision making strategies. Members feel a stake in the group to the extent that they participate in setting goals and being part of affecting them. Likewise, establishing personal relationships that are high in trust on the part of group members is also characteristic of effective organizations (Nugent and Abolafia 2006; Cardona, Lawrence and Bentler 2004; Brewer and Kramer 1986). These trusting relationships are demonstrated by a high degree of consideration for one another in the group and generate a sense of shared communal goals. The fact that Gülen-inspired projects are always locally based and embedded in local circles of supporters locates authority and decision making within horizontal relationships rather than a vertical, bureaucratic structure. Being responsible for projects, not only financially but in terms of planning, decision making and accountability, is also a powerful force in involving people in the movement.

Raising Money for Gülen-inspired projects

During his preaching years in mosques throughout Turkey, Gülen stressed education as the center of modernization and social progress. He emphasized continuously that peace, social justice and respect for diverse cultures and religions can be achieved by educated people who are grounded in modern science, strong morality and practical altruism. In his own words, Gülen maintained:

> The main duty and purpose of human life is to seek understanding. The effort of doing so, known as education, is a perfecting process through which we earn, in the spiritual, intellectual, and physical dimensions of our beings, the rank appointed for us as the perfect pattern of creation (Unal and Williams, 2000:34).

While Gülen did not limit education to the formal instruction that schools provide for the youth of society, he advocated the establishment of schools, especially high schools, that would provide the best scientific training along with solid moral values. He realized that the building and maintaining of these schools would require people who believed in the value of education and who could provide financial and human resources. This would require sacrifice and commitment from many different people including dedicated teachers, principals with a strong vision for the schools, politicians and local officials, and local businessmen who were willing to contribute the finances to build and support the schools.

Throughout the 1970s and 1980s in mosques, town squares, public conferences, and any-where people would listen, Gülen advocated first for the establishment of dormitories where students could live and study together under the tutelage of sincere, dedicated teachers. The next step would be sponsoring college-preparatory courses that would enhance students' chances to attend university. Finally, Gülen promoted the establishment of secular, private schools that would offer state of the art education, thus preparing students for the annual university entrance exams (Cetin 2006). His listeners were mostly low-to middle-income businessmen, with a small number of wealthy ones, and university students who would soon be sponsors of and teachers in the Gülen movement's education network (Kalyoncu 2007).

By 1982 the first two goals were realized with dormitories and college preparatory courses being offered in many cities throughout Turkey. In that same year, the first two private secondary high schools opened in Izmir and Istanbul, followed by another in Ankara. These projects were envisioned and financed by circles of local businessmen in each of the cit-ies who set up educational trusts that supported the projects until they were able to raise their own revenues through school fees. Some schools were completely built and funded by businessmen in the local communities who established trusts for this purpose while others were joint ventures between the state and the trusts. In some instances, the state provided the building, electricity and water while the trusts provided the teaching staff and all educa-tional materials and resources (Woodhall 2005). Some of the schools are eventually totally funded by student fees that are deposited into non-profitable trusts and invested back into the school to support teaching materials and new facilities such as labs, gyms and residence halls (Woodhall 2005).

In the late 1980s and throughout the 1990s, Gülen also encouraged the opening of schools in the Central Asian countries that gained independence during the disintegration of the Soviet Union. He convinced his followers to go to these countries to encourage the religious enlightenment of their fellow Turkic speakers who were dominated by atheism for over 70 years of Soviet rule. In Kazakhstan, for example, the Gülen community built one university, 28 secondary schools and one primary school. In Uzbekistan, they established 18 secondary schools (Baskan 2004). Many of the students in these schools, like students in Gülen-inspired schools in Turkey, compete successfully in the International Science Olympics and score very highly in the national university entrance exam. The host countries usually provide the buildings for the schools and modest fees are collected from students. However, Turkish businessmen, many of them with interests in these countries, cover the majority of the costs.

In November, 2004, Gülen was asked by a reporter "where the water for this mill comes from," a Turkish expression meaning what is the source of all the money behind the Gülen inspired projects. Gülen admitted that he has been asked this question many times by Turkish people who assume that there are self interests or hidden plans behind the movement's projects. He says that there are many people who would not give you a cup of tea without guaranteeing that they will get two cups of tea from you in return. However, Gülen contrasts these people with those who are devoted to supporting the good works inspired by his teachings. Of them, he says, "Those are our people who give and give. You could say they are addicted to giving. If you say 'not to give' to them they will be sad and unhappy." He goes on to tell the story of a retired man to whom he spoke before a fundraiser. The man could not give anything because he had very little. When Gülen was leaving the building, the man caught him on the stairs and handed him a set of keys and said, "These are the keys of my house. I don't have anything to give other than that house, please take these keys." Gülen gave back the keys and told him not to worry but to give when he had something to give. Gülen went on to praise the people of Anatolia as miraculous people who support projects that they see as worthwhile and that help to solve the problems of the world and the future of their nation. He commented that the leaders of Turkey have not been able to use this potential in their people.

Gülen himself has never had personal wealth to be able to sponsor projects. Gülen was so poor that for a number of years he lived in a corner of a local mosque with barely enough space to lie down. In addition to never having any personal wealth, he prayed for his relatives to remain poor so as not to raise any suspicions of gaining from his influence (Aslandogan and Cetin 2006). He has appeared at many fund-raising dinners and visited wealthy individuals to try to convince them to support excellent and modern education. Apart from encouraging people to donate money, Gülen has remained distanced from all financial involvements and instead has encouraged those who sponsor projects to oversee the use of their contributions. This stance has built trust and confidence in Gülen's honesty and integrity (Aslandogan and Cetin 2006).

The success of Gülen projects relies on the numerous circles of businessmen in Turkish cities, towns and rural areas. Many of these businessmen are very successful, hence the Gülen movement is known as the richest religious community in Turkey (Baskan 2004). These circles typically consist of businessmen and professionals from the same line of business who meet together once a week to share ideas, discuss the works of Gülen and consider local projects that they might sponsor. As one businessman explained,

> "Being in the same type of business means that we have a strong basis for coming together and understanding one another. We also network and refer customers among us. Then we have a basis for discussing projects that need doing in our community and how we can help with these projects. We also see the results of our efforts which encourage us to be even more generous."

Every school has its own independent accounting system and accountants who manage the budget and financial books. They are all accountable to the local and state authorities, as well as to the trust's sponsors. The local sponsors are knowledgeable about the status of the ongoing projects at any given time, for they are personally responsible for many of them, either as construction contractors, accountants, serving on the board of directors, teachers, principals, etc. It is quite easy, therefore, for them to monitor how the donations are used, thereby achieving transparency in financial issues. Moreover, as one businessman explained, "First of all, I want you to know that people in the Gülen movement have gained the trust of people in every strata of life. People who support the activities of this movement do not worry about whether the support reached its destination, they don't chase it. However, if we want to look at it, all kinds of information is available in every activity, we can be sure by looking at them." Likewise, a local businessmen in Houston who finances Gülen related projects commented, "Even if I don't know the details of their activities, I know these people very well and I trust them. Therefore I make donations knowing they are well used."

In Mardin, for example, a circle of local businessmen met over a three year period (1988-1991) and came to realize that the state was unable to provide the necessary education for students not only in their city but throughout southeastern Turkey to compete on university entrance exams. Most of the businessmen had been attending Gülen's public sermons, in which he emphasized the importance of education and called for the building of modern schools. These businessmen were inspired by the success of the Gülen schools in Izmir, Istanbul and Gaziantep in distinguishing themselves from their counterparts by their research-based education and unprecedented success in international science competitions. During visits to these schools, the men witnessed that the people who donated to the schools included not only businessmen, but also workers, teachers, and civil servants.

Upon their return to Mardin, they reached out to more and more people with whom they shared the educational vision and whose help they solicited in sponsoring the schools. Some pledged money, some promised to seek individuals who would pledge to contribute money, others offered to procure construction materials and equipment as donations from their suppliers, and still others committed an amount of physical work in the construction effort. Currently in the Gülen-movement schools in Mardin, every teacher supports the monthly expenses of at least one secondary or high school student (Kalyoncu, forthcoming).

In a focused interview with a dozen businessmen involved in the small textile industry in Ankara we heard many stories about how the businessmen first became involved with Gülen-inspired projects. For example, in 1985 an imam came to a local mosque and asked the businessmen there for help to open a school for children in the city. After he left, the men gathered together twice every week to discuss the matter. The group made a commitment to assist with the building of the school. Some gave money, others solicited pledges of financial support from other businessmen in the city and others provided goods and services such as concrete, desks, and even volunteer labor. Within a short time, Samanyolu College opened its doors to the first high school class. The group of businessmen continued to meet routinely, to monitor the needs in the school and to initiate additional projects that they supported. For example, in 1991 after the collapse of the Soviet Union, there was a massacre in Azerbaijan. People there needed help. The Gülen community in Ankara responded; 18 businessmen from different parts of Ankara went to Azerbaijan to deliver money and goods that they had gathered from Gülen-inspired people in Ankara. As one of the businessmen said in the interview,

> "That was an important trip for me. I learned a lot from those people in our group. They were very different people, most of them were not educated like me, but they all affected me in their understanding of Gülen's teachings and in their lifestyles. Since that trip I am very involved in the

Gülen movement."

Another businessman in the focus group told a story that typifies the way in which many people get involved in the movement. One day in 1988 he met a law student who was being financed by one of the businessmen that he knew in his living complex. He asked the businessmen to introduce him to some of these underprivileged law students who could not afford law school. Several days later a group of law students showed up at his store. However, they did not ask for money but talked about country and world problems. A few weeks later they invited the man to their house where there were 10 law students gathered from all over Turkey, most of them from poor families. Still there was no talk of money. Some of the students again visited his store and met his son who was having difficulty in school. They offered to tutor the son whose grades improved dramatically with tutoring. There was still no talk of money. The man, after a year of knowing these students personally, initiated scholarships to help them complete law school. He continues since 1988 to provide such scholarships to needy law students.

The above story typifies actions of Gülen himself in the 1970s and 1980s when he lived on or near university campuses throughout Turkey. He served as a teacher for a time and spent many years supervising students in high school and university settings. In Bursa we interviewed a gentleman in his 60s who, along with his brother, shared a house with Gülen while he was attending university in the 1960s. He recalled the many university students who would visit Gülen in his second story apartment for tutoring and encouragement. He commented that, in his opinion, this cadre of university students who gathered around Gülen was the beginnings of the Gülen movement in Turkey.

We asked the group of a dozen businessmen in Ankara whether each of them contributes financially to Gülen-inspired projects and, if so, approximately how much they give each year. Each of the 12 men said that they contribute as they can to the movement projects. Amounts of contributions varied from 10%-70% of their annual income, ranging from $20,000-$300,000 per year. One man, in particular, said he gives 40% of his income every year which is about $100,000; however, he said he would like to give 95% but is not able to do so and still maintain himself and his family. Another man said, "We wish we could be like the companion of the Prophet and give everything we have. But it is not easy." This group of businessmen consisted of older men who have been together as a group for many years and have accomplished numerous Gülen-inspired projects in Ankara as well as in other countries. Currently, each of them has managers in their stores who carry on the daily business affairs. The business owners spend 2-3 hours in their stores every day and then come together almost every day to discuss issues related to the projects they are supporting. The group, therefore, provides a tight community of like-minded individuals working for common causes. Cetin (unpublished dissertation) maintains that

> "the solidarity of the group is inseparable from the personal quest and from the everyday affective and communicative needs of the participants in the network…Yet, it is epiphenomenal, not the ultimate aim or end in itself, by itself, but it accompanies action naturally as a result of the accomplishment of the service projects."

Another very successful businessman in Istanbul whom we interviewed provided insight into the sums of money being contributed by the supporters of the Gülen Movement to local projects. He is 48 years old and is in the textile business. He contributes 20% of his 4-5 million dollar yearly income to movement-related projects. 80% of his good friends are also members of the movement and contribute as they can to projects. He says he has established very sincere and fortunate friendships through participation in activities in the movement. He learned of the movement when a friend in 1986 invited him to a sohbet where people come together and have discussions, both about Gülen's writings and about local projects that need support. Asked what benefits a person gets from supporting Gülen inspired projects, he replied,

> "I do not get any worldly benefit by supporting the Gülen Movement. If I receive anything in the hereafter, we will see that over there. I hope that I will be able to please God through these activities and the time that I spend with these beautiful people. Other than this, neither I nor other volunteers have any other expectations. After giving your heart to these charitable activities, God never leaves you in trouble. We give and he gives more back to us. He multiplies what we have in our hands. I don't think my contributions are big and enough, however, in the sight of God, there is nothing small and valueless if you do that for Him and for humanity."

The 48 year old businessman in Istanbul had this to say,

> "People in the Gülen movement turn their ideas into projects, they tell how they accomplished their success. People trust them, if they ask for a project, they expect it from the Creator, not from creatures, and that's why I believe they reach success. If anybody from the movement comes to my city and asks for help, I try my best to help them and I encourage my friends around me to do the same."

He went on to say that such giving is done in a spirit of serving the Creator by serving his people and that often a result of such giving is that strong ties are developed among the givers. As Cetin (unpublished dissertation) maintains,

> "Participation in services takes relatively permanent forms of networks. Individuals come and go and replace one another but the projects are always there and continue. Individual needs and collective goals are not mutually exclusive; they are one and the same thing. These two and the action of the Gülen Movement coincide and interweave closely with one another in daily life… The participation in services around a specific goal and the tangibility of the products yield and strengthen solidarity."

Aymaz (2006) exemplifies the connections between individual and collective goals in the following way:

> "The multiple, mutable, and overlapping relations of belonging to service projects form the basis, solidarity, cohesion and continuity of the Gülen Movement. In these network relations, belongings, individual needs and collective goals, and individual and collective interests, are constantly negotiated and served. Individuality and collectivity are not mutually exclusive, they are one and the same thing…people commit themselves to service projects both within leisure time and committed time. The continuity between leisure and commitment, by presupposing a close connection between self-fulfillment and participation, expresses and enhances a great deal of feeling and meaning, forms the basis of material and immaterial resources and their utilizability in collective action."

Through the networks of relationships in the Gülen Movement, individuals feel part of a common unity, a social coherence and cohesion.

Financing Projects in the Institute for Interfaith Dialog, Houston, Texas

There are numerous local groups in the United States that consist of individuals who are inspired by the teachings and life of Gülen. These groups are independent organizationally even though members across groups may know another and share ideas and projects in. mally. The Institute of Interfaith Dialog for World Peace, Inc. (IID) was established in Augu 2002 in Austin, Texas. One year later the headquarters moved to Houston. IID organizes activities in more than 16 cities in the southern states, including Texas, Louisiana, Oklahoma, Kansas, Arkansas and Mississippi. The purpose of the nonprofit institute is to promote interfaith dialogue and understanding.

To achieve this purpose, the institute organizes and supports numerous activities in each of the cities in which it has members. These include an annual Ramadan interfaith dinner, a yearly award dinner to honor people in the local communities who make major contributions to interfaith dialog, workshops throughout the year, an annual retreat and numerous interfaith trips to Turkey. These activities are supported financially by contributions on the part of members committed to the institute, most of them Turkish Muslims who are inspired by the teachings of Gülen. Many of them are Turkish students attending universities in the southern United States, even though there are a handful of businessmen and professionals who are also involved.

Based on the Turkish model of local circles that support Gülen-inspired projects, a large percentage of IID's budget is provided by relatively small contributions on the part of over 500 Turkish and Turkish-Americans in the southern states of the U.S. who support projects of IID. About half of these supporters are local students. In terms of financial donations IID collects over half million U.S. dollars every year. Numerous graduate students, many of them on small stipends from Turkey or from their American universities, pledge $2,000-$5,000 every year even though such pledges means great sacrifice on the students' part. It is not unusual for a student on a $1500 per month stipend to give $100-150 per month to IID which amounts to roughly 10% of his/her income. Some of the students also work in second jobs in order to contribute some money to the activities of IID. And many of them look forward to graduating, having good jobs and being able to contribute more of their income at that point. As one student said, "Being a graduate student it is hard to donate big amounts, but hopefully after I graduate, I will be able to make bigger and better donations."

Approximately 50% of IID members are professionals and businessmen in the community, many of whom have completed education in the United States and have opted to work there for the time being. It is the contributions of these individuals which constitute the largest proportion of IID's income. One local businessman, for example, who is an engineer and has some real estate investments, said that he gives $50,000-$70,000 every year to IID which is 40% of his income. He single-handedly finances an Iftar dinner each year. In 2006 he also paid for the tickets for twelve Americans to visit Turkey in an interfaith trip sponsored by IID. He regrets that his busy schedule prohibits him from greater involvement with IID activities; however, he feels he can make an impact in IID projects by providing substantial financial support. In addition, he joins friends every week at sohbet (group meetings) to discuss the ideas of Gülen and how to operationalize them in local projects.

Direct financial contributions do not capture the full picture of donations to Gülen projects. Followers donate time, talents and food to the various activities sponsored by IID. For example, dinner and luncheons are frequently organized by IID. Women in the organization are continuously asked to prepare Turkish food for these gatherings, both small and large, and neither the cost of the food nor the labor involved in preparing it is financially compensated. The design and maintenance of websites, designing fliers and brochures, creating videos related to the activities of IID, organizing events, leading interfaith trips to Turkey, hosting

faith communities into their homes during Ramadan and networking in
ınity are done by volunteers of the movement. It is not unusual for many
d 20-30 hours a week in Gülen movement activities, and many of these
₂ students in local universities. If these activities were outsourced or
₂osts, the donations from IID members would be well over a million
₄ year.

Islamic Concepts Underlying Movement Projects

To fully understand and appreciate the financial structure of the Gülen movement projects, it is imperative to locate contributions within the Islamic concepts of: *hizmet, himmet, sohbet, istisare and mutevelli.* These are the religious, Islamic ideals that provide motivation for member contributions, including not only financial giving but also involvement of time, energies, volunteer work on projects, etc.

Hizmet is an overarching concept that denotes service to one's fellow human beings and is rooted in the Islamic belief that every individual will be held accountable for the way he or she has lived in this world. In Gülen's words:

> Therefore, the worldly life should be used in order to earn the afterlife and to please the One who has bestowed it. The way to do so is to seek to please Allah and, as an inseparable dimension of it, to serve immediate family members, society, country, and all of humanity accordingly. This service is our right, and sharing it with others is our duty (Unal, 267).

Gülen frequently recalls meetings during the time of the Prophet Muhammad who praised his companions for their passion for giving. Gülen reminds his followers of the examples of the first two caliphs, Abu Bakr who donated everything he owned and Omar who donated half of his material goods to support those in need (Kalyoncu, forthcoming). One of the Ankara businessmen commented that

> "commitment and dedication in this movement is very unique, that's why the movement is successful. And also sincerity, people in this movement do not do things for themselves, they do it for others and most importantly to please God. We have a saying in Turkish: 'Service to people is service to God-Halka hizmet, Hakka hizmettir'-that's what this movement is doing."

Sohbet is the medium through which the need for hizmet is shared among individuals. It is a structure where individuals find the opportunity to socialize, chat, and exchange ideas about their projects, either educational or business-related, but devoid of politics and divisive subjects. The sohbet meetings reinforce the Gülen's movement's philosophy and educational vision that permeates the practical projects that are discussed. The Gülen movement seeks to use the sohbet forum to cultivate a sense of community, address common needs and goals and communicate the necessity of hizmet or service for the good of others.

The sohbet is usually organized according to the participants occupation or place of residence; for example, public servants, health care workers, dentists, teachers, businessmen or construction contractors. The purpose of such groupings is to facilitate commonalities among the sohbet meetings' participants so that they can better socialize and network with each other in terms of potential business partners, customers or suppliers. Participants often study passages from Gülen's works and relate them to needs in the community. It is the sohbet meetings that afford the platform to discuss projects and ways to sponsor them.

Gülen emphasized the doing of good deeds through collective action. He encouraged men and women to meet together to build communal ties and to plan and execute good works (Ozdalga 2000). Hizmet, he argued, like all such religious duties conscientiously performed, also has secondary beneficial effects on the individual and the community. This is especially true for education which was always a primary concern and goal for Gülen. As he said in one of his sermons, "Education is vital for both societies and individuals" (Unal and Williams, 2000, p. 306).

Istisare, the collective decision making that occurs within the sohbets in regard to collective projects, results in each person's taking responsibility for making sure that the projects are funded and executed. It is this structure that enables the movement to operate horizontally rather than vertically or bureaucratically. Every institution that is established, whether in Turkey or in the ninety other countries that now have Gülen schools, is a corporate nonprofit entity that is independent of the others and is managed by those people who are supporting the school. The only connection among these institutions is the exchange of ideas that arise from a commitment to the same goals (Tekalan 2005).

In addition to establishing schools, the many other Gülen-inspired projects are organized on the same model of grassroots support from people in the Gülen movement. Typically, before the movement launches its educational and cultural activities in a new country, the people in the movement identify and make contact with local figures through personal visits. These local figures are influential people, such as bureaucrats, civil servants, clerics, intellectuals, and businessmen. The purpose of such visits is to solicit help from people who have an ability to mobilize their society and access resources, both human and financial. Also, these contacts build trust with the local authorities (Kalyoncu forthcoming).

The *mutevelli* is essentially a board of trustees or sponsors who have volunteered to take on more responsibility, whether overseeing more projects or donating more money than others. What is important is that the mutevelli circle is open to anyone who consistently carries out the responsibilities that he or she takes on.

Finally, *himmet* refers to one's personal commitment to carrying out whatever needs to be done to better one's community. In this sense, commitments of money, time or effort identifies one with the movement and the project at hand. Himmet often turns into a passion for giving for those who have willingly taken on the responsibility not only to donate but to procure resources from others. In an interview in Bergama, a wealthy industrialist who is a major sponsor of local Gülen schools commented that people should not be afraid to approach wealthy individuals to support worthwhile projects. Approximately eight years ago, he was approached by members in the Gülen movement, all who were strangers to him, for financial assistance in establishing the first local school. He began attending their meetings, was inspired by the altruism of the group, was convinced of their sincerity regarding education and offered to finance the first school until it could become self sufficient. Today he is helping to fund schools in Afghanistan and Uzbekistan and commented that the more he gives, the better his businesses seem to thrive. He believes that wealthy people want to do their share in helping to create a better world and are looking for projects that they see as being influential in that direction.

We asked a number of businessmen and professionals whether financial contributions to Gülen-inspired projects is part of zakat, one of the five pillars of Islam. We were told that zakat represents the minimum expected of Muslims in order to help their needy neighbor. Those committed to the Gülen movement routinely give many times over the required 2.5% of their yearly earnings. This type of giving is called *sadaqa,* or voluntary charity, and is based on an individual's needs and excess wealth. The above five concepts provide the motivation for going above and beyond this minimum contribution, something that characterizes millions of people in the Gülen movement around the world.

Conclusions

Based on the scant literature that exists on the funding of Gülen-inspired projects and our own interviews conducted with members of the Gülen Movement both in Turkey and in Houston, Texas, it is evident that the money behind the movement is provided by millions of people the world over who are committed to the ideas and ideals promoted by Gülen. The basic money-raising strategy in the movement consists in the establishment of local circles of businessmen, teachers, principals, professionals, and students who meet together regularly to discuss the works of Gülen and consider how his ideals can be applied in their local communities. In the course of initiating and building Gülen-inspired projects, the group evolves into a tightly-knit community where individuals find meaning and support. In Kanter's conceptualization, the goals of the group become fused with one's own sense of purpose and meaning in life. Group goals nourish one's own sense of self and the group becomes an extension of oneself, thus inextricably linking person and group, thus meeting the first of Kanter's basic challenges for group survival and success.

The affective bonds that evolve in the group in the course of working together on meaningful projects fulfills Kanter's second organizational challenge. The fact that many local circles are based on individuals who share occupational or business interests further adds to the solidarity created in the group. The more closely an individual is integrated into a group, the greater will be the degree of his/her participation (Klandermans 2006). Participation is an expression of belonging to a certain social group and receiving individual rewards for being part of the larger collective. Also, the more intense the collective participation in a network of relations, the more rapid and durable will be the mobilization of a movement (Melucci 1999). The Gülen Movement facilitates and thus increases an individual's willingness to get involved in service projects through his/her relationship with other like-minded, similarly intentioned people.

The third challenge, the experience of a moral, transcendent authority in the group is provided by the continuous discussions of Gülen's teachings as well as sharing readings from the Qur'an and the *hadiths* of the Prophet. Thus, the goals and motivations behind the service projects are more than just helping other people. Rather, they are rooted in the notion that they are part of Allah's continuous creation and caring for his people.

Kanter argues that a further mechanism for individual commitment to group life and group goals is that of sacrifice. The giving of one's time and resources to the group not only indicates commitment to the group but also creates that very commitment. As people in the Gülen movement give of their personal resources to group life and group projects, the very act of giving has the consequence of intensifying commitment to the group and its ideals.

The five basic Islamic ideals (i.e. *hizmet, himmet, sohbet, istisare and mutevelli)* that motivate members of the Gülen movement to contribute time, energy and financial contributions to Gülen-inspired projects function, simultaneously, to build strong commitment on the part of individuals to the movement. A major strength of the local circles is the constant discussions of these concepts based on the Qur'an and the works of Gülen. The circles, therefore, provide the spiritual motivation for giving and remain far more than simply money raising venues. Whether consciously or not, the structure that has evolved within the Gülen movement is rooted in sound organizational principles and is reflected in the growth of the movement worldwide.

Yilmaz (2003) foresees an impact of the Gülen Movement not only within Turkish society but also on a global level. As a matter of fact, he states that changes are already happening in Turkish society in regard to certain issues in the direction of what Gülen has been advocating. The Gülen Movement sets an example in the Muslim World not only with its activities but also how it generates financial support for these activities. Usage of the five basic Islamic ideals (i.e. *hizmet, himmet, sohbet, istisare and mutevelli),* and examples from the lives of the companions of the Prophet, strengthens the Gülen Movement's position and impact within the Muslim World. Even though the movement started in Turkey within the Turkish population, in a short time it has grown in other parts of the world within non-Turkish populations, not only with educational projects but also in terms of interfaith dialogue activities.

THE EDUCATIONAL THEORY OF FETHULLAH GÜLEN AND ITS PRACTICE IN SOUTH AFRICA

Yasien Mohamed

Abstract

This paper deals with the educational thought of Fethullah Gülen and its application in a school in South Africa. It will attempt to demonstrate the effectiveness of the school, both academically and in the promotion of universal moral values. The Gülen school provides an alternative both to the Muslim private school and the general private school. Unlike the latter, it gives more attention to moral values, and unlike the former, it is open to all learners irrespective of religious persuasion. It provides a service to society in the transmission of knowledge to humanity, and in cultivating moral values such as responsibility, tolerance, respect, reliability and compassion.

The paper is divided into three parts: First, it introduces the problem of educational dichotomy within the Turkish context since 1924, and how Fethullah Gülen attempted to reconcile science and religion, at least theoretically. Second, it presents the educational philosophy of Fethullah Gülen, especially his moral philosophy as inspired by Miskawayh's (d. 1030) psychology of the soul and his view of the role of the teacher, both in the transmission of knowledge and moral values. Third, it discusses the practice of Gülen's educational philosophy in South Africa, with special reference to Star International School, Cape Town, covering the religious motivations of the teachers, the moral ethos of the school, and educational problems and challenges.

Introduction

This paper will deal with the educational thought of Fethullah Gülen and its practice within the South African context. Gülen's educational philosophy is comprehensive; it is concerned with both the cognitive and moral development of the child. The paper will attempt to illustrate the effectiveness of the school at both these levels.

The Gülen schools have opened in South Africa, and they are bound to flourish in the next five years, due to the excellent academic performance of their learners in recent years. These schools will soon become an alternative to the established private schools and Model C schools in South Africa. Muslim parents are wary of the liberalism and permissiveness of the secular private schools, and some are critical of the elitism of the Islamic private schools. The Gülen schools are secular, but they try to maintain a balance between the needs of the individual and the society. They stress the building of character and cultivating universal moral values, and at the same time, they provide an excellent education in order to prepare learners to become useful citizens of the society. These schools are open to all learners, irrespective of religious persuasion, cultural background or socio-economic status.

This paper is divided into three main parts: First, it introduces the problem of educational dichotomy in Turkey since 1924, and it touches upon how Fethullah Gülen attempted to reconcile science and religion. Second, it deals with the educational theory of Fethullah Gülen, especially his moral education, with focus on the teacher as the transmitter of knowledge and moral values to humanity. Third, it will deal with the practice of Gülen's educational theory, with reference to Star International High School, Cape Town; examining the motivations of the teachers, the moral ethos of the school, and educational problems and prospects.

The first Turkish school, Star International High, was established in Cape Town in 1999. Since then two more were established, one in Durban (Star International) and one in Johannesburg (Horizon International School). These are private secular high schools, they follow the curriculum of the Department of National Education, and they are open to all children, Muslim or non-Muslim. One of the reasons for their great success in Turkey is that the educators have a vision inspired by Fethullah Gülen. This paper will elaborate on this vision and show how it is being implemented in South Africa. The Turkish inspired schools embrace learners from a diverse religious, ethnic, class, and cultural background. The school fosters social virtues such as respect, co-operation and tolerance; preparing learners to integrate into a pluralist, democratic society. For the Muslim minority, the school provides an opportunity for learners to cultivate moral values in a secular environment; assisting in their integration into a society that is a Christian majority. This model could be replicated in other countries where Muslims are a minority. It demonstrates that it is possible to retain one's distinct Islamic identity and at the same time integrate into the broader society.

Moral values are not taught as special subjects such as 'Right living' or 'Guidance'. Relegating morality to a subject taught in a period once a week is already a sign of moral failure. Morality has to shape the vision and ethos of the school, and has to be integrated into classroom lessons; moreover, it has to be lived and practiced by the teachers.

The Educational Dichotomy in Turkey

Since 1924 the Kemalist regime identified the problem of Turkey to lie within religion, which it believes to have been the cause of the neglect of science and the backwardness of Turkey. Consequently, it promoted the pursuit of science, but at the expense of religion and the humanities. The secular state kept religion out of the domain of politics, and public education. Religion had to remain a private affair, and the educational system had to be secular. However, one period a week was left for religious instruction in the school curriculum, in case parents demanded it.

The religionists, on the other hand, had no faith in the new secular system of education, and kept out of it, and continued to promote religious education, but their graduates were marginalized and could not make a significant contribution to civil society. Said Nursi (d. 1960), a Turkish Islamic philosopher, realized the problem of conflict and dichotomy between the secular and religious, and sought to remedy it by harmonizing religion with science. There is no reason why a religious Muslim cannot also have a deep interest in science; after all, Islam encourages study and reflection on nature. Nursi's *risale—nur* (Treatise of Light), devoted to reconciling science with religion, opposed the blind positivistic conception of science, but promoted an indigenous understanding of science for Muslims. He promoted science as a study of the laws of nature, a study of God's art.

Fethullah Gülen, a younger contemporary of Nursi, was inspired by the *Risale-i Nur*, and so also promoted the harmony between science and religion. He sees scientific education and Islamic education as compatible and complementary. Although he was educated in traditional institutions, he has urged his sympathizers to open modern schools rather than traditional madrasas and mosques. For him, as with Nursi, an ideal education combines modern science with Islamic knowledge. Scientific knowledge without religion could lead to atheism, while religious knowledge without science could lead to bigotry and fanaticism. When combined, they urge a student to research further, and deepen both his belief and knowledge (Kuru, 2003:120; Yilmaz, 2005: 203-204).

> He argues that science and technology cannot explain the meaning and the purpose of life, and they may be harmful for humankind if unjust and irresponsible people manipulate them. Science can neither provide true happiness nor replace the role of religion. Moreover, he emphasizes that the development of physics in the twentieth century shook positivist science (Kuru, 2003: 120)

But unlike Nursi, Gülen promoted this harmony through schools all over the world. This did not imply the Islamization of knowledge as we know it today.[1] There was no attempt to infuse Islamic elements into the secular curriculum. All he wanted was for committed Muslim teachers to excel in the sciences. Through education they could "raise a generation both deeply rooted in Islam and able to participate in the modern scientific world. He aspires to create an educated elite within the Islamic *umma* in general and within the Turkish nature in particular" (Agai, 2003: 50). High quality education will prepare religious Muslims for careers previously reserved for the Kemalist regime. This brought Gülen into trouble with the secular state. How could a religious man harmonize science with religion? This was an affront to the secular Turkish state that had tried to undermine the role of religion in public affairs for almost a century.

Modern secular schools, Gülen holds, have been unable to free themselves of the prejudices and conventions of modern ideology, whereas the madrasas have shown little interest or capability to meet the challenges of technology and scientific thought. These madrasas lack the

---

1 Since the 1980's the "Islamization of Knowledge" became popular, first among the Muslims of America, and then the rest of the Muslim world, where Islamic schools and universities mushroomed with the aim of Islamizing knowledge, including science. Gulen, in my view, was not preoccupied with Islamization; his focus was on natural science (not the social sciences), and it was important to pursue science, provided it could be combined with faith and ethics.

flexibility, vision, and ability to break with the past, to enact change, and to offer a relevant education for today. The challenge today is to integrate the strengths of the traditional education with the modern education. The youth must rise above the current education that diverts them from knowledge and reason. Gülen also encouraged greater accessibility and a higher standard of education for women (Michel, 2003: 72; Yilmaz, 2005: 203-204).

With a balanced education learners can become agents of positive change; but if they do not have ideals, and are only taught marketable skills, they will add to the crises of the society. Intellectuals seem to prefer "the spiritually impoverished and technologically obsessed modern culture to a traditional cultural foundation that grew in sophistication and subtlety over the centuries" (Michel, 2003:74). Teacher training is essential; not only in methodology, but also in nurturing the whole person. Teachers should lead by example, otherwise they cannot hope to reform others. Gülen states: "In order to bring others to the path of traveling to a better world, they must purify their inner worlds of hatred, rancor, and jealousy, and adorn their outer world with all kinds of virtues" (Michel, 2003:78). Thus, teachers have to combine the study of science with character development. Success must be measured by scientific progress and moral progress. Material advancement without morality will destroy humanity.

The overall aim of overcoming the dichotomy of education is to create a "golden generation" armed with the tools of science and religion. By combining knowledge and human values, this new generation (*yeni nesil*) will solve the problems of the future (Agai, 2003: 57). Faith teaches what is good and beneficial, and combined with science, can benefit humanity. This idea gained support after 1980, and this integrated approach was (Agai: 2003: 57) considered to be a better alternative to the Kemalist education, which tended to undermine religion and alienate the modernised elite from their traditional roots (Agai, 2003: 58).

Yilmaz refers to the official state version of Islam as 'Lausannian Islam', which means that state and religion are to be kept separate, but the Turkish character of 'Lausannian Islam' is somewhat contradictory in that it attempts to keep religion out of public life by having it under the supervision of the state. Thus, although the constitution allows for religious instruction, it controls its transmission to learners (Yilmaz, 2005:389). Thus, the Kemalist regime does not remove religion entirely from the curriculum, but monitors it to its own advantage. Gülen schools, by contrast, operate independently of the state; indirectly challenging it; showing that progressiveness is not the monopoly of the secularists, and that religious teachers can also be progressive.

Although the educational theory comes from Fethullah Gülen, the curriculum and management of the schools are left to the educators. Turkish merchants also play no role in the management of the school; they leave all educational decisions to the principals and teachers. Funding comes from Turkey, from local Turkish merchants living in South Africa, and from some South African companies (Interview, Kemalettin Ozdemir, and May 2006). For Gülen, education should prepare learners to be useful citizens and good persons. Good schools cultivate virtues in their pupils, and lead them to achieve nobility of mind and spirit. The real teacher is one who sows the pure seed and preserves it. It is his duty to be occupied with what is good and wholesome, and to guide the child accordingly.

Since the Gülen schools have a scientific orientation, they make sure they are equipped with the best laboratories and computer rooms. They want the learners to excel in these areas; enhancing the scientific character of the school. Literature and the humanities, however, have been neglected.[2]

For Gülen, there is no conflict between the Qur'an and the universe; the universe is a mighty Qur'an, reflecting the signs of God's existence. Religion does not oppose or limit science and scientific work; it guides the sciences, determines their goals, and infuses human values in them (Gülen, 2002: 80-81). Thus, the pursuit of science is consistent with the Qur'an, and can enhance faith, provided it is directed by religion. However, religion is superior to science as it prepares one for the eternal world, but science prepares one for this transient world. For science to benefit humanity, it has to be guided by faith. Religious truths are superior because they are absolute; but scientific truths are relative as they are changing all the time. The scientific truths in the Qur'an are not meant to be ends in themselves, but they serve a higher purpose which is to serve religion, a source of spiritual and moral guidance to humanity. If a scientific truth conflicts with a religious truth, and reconciliation has failed, we should favour the religious truth. The absolute truth of religion is the deciding factor in judging the scientific truth (Bakar, 2005: 362-363).

The Educational Philosophy of Fethullah Gülen

Gülen emphasized character building as an integral part of his educational philosophy, and his concept of character is based on a classical humanist conception of the soul.

The Psychology of the Soul

The key to the nurturing of moral character is knowledge of the soul. Gülen adopts the classical Platonic tripartite division of the soul as the foundation for explaining human psychology, and his moral education is based on it. Inspired by Miskawayh (d. 1030), he identifies the three faculties of the soul; the rational, the irascible and the concupiscent, representing reason, anger and lust. When moderated, these virtues give rise to courage, wisdom and temperance respectively. When these three faculties are moderated, the virtue of justice emerges. These four virtues are the core content of the internal morality of the soul. The rational faculty controls the two lower faculties of the soul. If properly nourished, it will moderate (not obliterate) lust and anger, which have a useful purpose.[3] In keeping with this optimistic view

---

2 The school wants its matriculants to study science at a higher level, and will offer scholarships in the hope that the graduate will serve the school for a few years before working in their own professions. Mr Mejit Yaman, for example, graduated from a Gülen school in Turkey; did his degree in science, and taught in a Gülen school in Cape Town. He completed his Masters and Doctoral degrees at the University of Cape Town while teaching at the school. He is now back in Turkey, currently doing his military service. Gülen apparently has a personal bias for the humanities, but for pratical reasons, his schools gave more attention to science. He is now urging educators to also give attention to literature and the social sciences.

3 On Miskawayh's psychology of the soul, and its comparison with al-Raghib al-Isfahani (d. 1060) and Abu Hamid al-Ghazali (d. 1111), see Yasien Mohamed's The Path to Virtue: The Ethical Philosophy of al-Raghib al-Isfahani. Gülen was inspired by these Muslim philosophers, who all adopted the Platonic tripartite division of the soul, and made it the basis for their ethical philosophy. Although Gülen might not identify with modern humanism, he was inspired by classical Greek and Islamic humanism; he had an open mind, and accepted ideas from any source, provided they could be harmonized with the Qur'an.

His attitude to humanism might have changed after he migrated to America. There is perhaps an attempt to reconcile

of human nature, Gülen states:

> We must not seek to annul our drives, but to use our free will to contain and purify them, to channel and direct them toward virtue. For example, we are not expected to eliminate lust, but to satisfy it lawfully through reproduction. Happiness lies in confining our lawful bounds of decency and chastity, not in engaging in debauchery and dissipation. Similarly, jealousy can be channeled into emulation free of rancor, which inspires us to emulate those who excel in goodness and good deeds. Applying the proper discipline to our reason results in the acquisition of knowledge, and ultimately of understanding or wisdom. Purifying and training anger leads to courage and forbearance. Disciplining our passion and desire develops our chastity (Gülen, 2002, 60; Gülen, 2006:203-204).

The teacher educates the whole child, mind and soul. When we rise above our animal self, through reason, we are exalted to the state of humanity. Man stands midway between animal and angel; he is not completely animal because he has reason, nor is he completely angel because he has desire. To be human, he rises above his animal nature, and this leads him to happiness in this world and the next. For this, he needs knowledge, which is an innate desire. Unlike the animal, who learns through instinct, man only matures with knowledge through the passage of time. Gülen states:

> We are born helpless as well as ignorant of the laws of life and must cry out to get help we need. After a year or so, we can stand on our feet and walk a little. When we are about 15 we are expected to have understood the difference between good and evil, the beneficial and the harmful. However, it will take us our whole lives to acquire intellectual and spiritual perfection. Our principle duty in life is to acquire perfection and purity in our thinking, conceptions and belief. By fulfilling our duty of servanthood to the Creator, Nourisher and Protector, and by penetrating the mystery of creation through our potentials and faculties, we seek to attain to the rank of true humanity, and become worthy of a blissful, eternal life in another, exalted world (Gülen, 2002: 58; Gülen, 2006:202).

It may take us 20 years to acquire what a sparrow does in 20 days. The animal is not born to learn, but humans are, and it may take a life-time to "reach clarity of thought, imagination, and belief" (Gülen, 2002, 79; Gülen, 2006: 195). As mentioned, the discipline of our lower faculties is the key to our humanity. This requires the perfection of the soul in order to escape from the "dungeon" of our lower desires. Education, which includes belief and worship, is the key to perfecting the soul.

> We are creatures composed of not only of a, body or mind or feelings or spirit; rather, we are harmonious compositions of all of these elements. Each of us is a body writhing in a net of needs, as well as a mind that has more subtle and vital needs than the body, and is driven by anxieties about the past and future to find answers to such questions as: "What am I? What is this world? What do life and death want from me? Who sent me to this world, and for what purpose? Where am I going,and what is the purpose of life? Who is my guide in this worldly journey?" Moreover, each person is a creature of feelings that cannot be satisfied by the mind, and a creature of spirit, through which we acquire our essential human identity. Each individual is all of these. When a man or a woman, around whom all systems and efforts revolve, is considered and evaluated as a creature

---

tasawwuf (Sufism) with modern science; the former providing the path to moral perfection (seyr ul suluk). Sufi teaching is connected to his educational theory because Sufism gives so much attention to nurturing moral values. Gülen's reference to Miskawayh (who was also influenced by Plato and Aristotle) is a clear indication of his affinity to the classical Islamic humanistic philosophical tradition. See

Afsarudin, 'The Philosophy of Islamic Education: Classical Views and M. Fethullah

Gülen's Perspectives', for more details on Gülen in the context of classical Islamic thought.

with all these aspects, and when all our needs are fulfilled, we will reach true happiness. At this point, true human progress and evolvement in relation to our essential being is only possible with education (Gülen, 2002, 78; Gülen, 2006:194).

Home Education

Education begins at home, and the school is merely an extension of the home. Teachers do not merely provide information, but also nurture the whole personality, both intellectual and emotional aspects. Sound characters produce a sound society, but parents and teachers should set the example. The preparation begins with knowledge.

> A nation's future depends on its youth. Any people who want to secure their future should apply as much energy to raising their children as they devote to other issues. ...The reasons for the vices observed in today's generation, as well as the incompetence of some administrators and other nation-wide troubles, lie in the prevailing conditions and ruling elite of 25 years ago. Likewise, those who are charged with educating today's young people will be responsible for the vices and that will appear in another 25 years. Those who wish to predict a nation's virtues future can do so correctly by taking a full account of the education and upbringing given to its young people. "Real" life is possible only through knowledge. Thus, those who neglect learning and teaching should be counted as "dead" even though they are living, for we were created to learn and communicate to others what we have learned. Right decisions depend on having a sound mind and being capable of sound thought. Science and knowledge illuminate and develop the mind. For this reason, a mind deprived of science and knowledge cannot reach right decisions, is always exposed to deception, and is subject to being misled (Gülen, 2002, 62; Gülen, 2006:205).

Parents have the responsibility of nurturing the minds of their children. It is therefore important to consider choosing the proper partner for marriage. Moral character should be considered above that of wealth and physical charm.

> Children can receive a good education at home only if there is a healthy family life. Thus marriage should be undertaken to form a healthy family life and so contribute to the permanence of one's nation in particular, and of the human population in general. Peace, happiness, and security at home are the mutual accord between the spouses in thought, morals, and belief. Couples who decide to marry should know each other very well and consider purity of feelings, chastity, morality, and virtue rather than wealth and physical charm. Children's mischief and impudence reflect the atmosphere in which they are being raised. A dysfunctional family life increasingly reflects upon the child's spirit, and therefore upon society. Parents must feed their children's minds with knowledge and science before their minds become engaged in useless things, for souls without truth and knowledge are fields in which evil thoughts are cultivated and grown. (Gülen, 2002, 72; Gülen, 2006:207).

The Teacher: his Morality and Industry

Teachers should have an integrated perspective so that they are able to nurture the heart and mind of learners in a balanced way. The idea is not to make a radical break with the traditional past, for this will lead to modernity without morality. It is not enough to have material success for the global market, but also non-material values such as clarity of thought and moral character. The school should not produce people who are greedy, but people who are generous. There is nothing wrong with a salary, but the main motive should service to humanity.

In Western countries such as the USA, the focus of the curriculum has been to prepare students for a career that will make them money, but not to prepare them to be religious or moral. Wealth accumulation for its own sake is wrong. Knowledge should not be guided by utilitarian aims, but should nurture character. School should not be a place where moral values are taught in a certain period in the week; but they should be part of the school ethos, and teachers should transfuse them to their students.

Gülen asserts throughout his writings that knowledge should be combined with love. Knowledge is the province of the sciences and provides students with the intellectual abilities to benefit others; but it will only benefit humanity if it is combined with love, which is a "person's most essential element" (Gulen, 2002: 41). By love, he means self-sacrificing love that initiates action by absolute obedience to God, and out of concern for others, rather than for utilitarian gain. This love entails abnegation and the conviction to transform life on earth (Yavuz, 2003: p. 34). Such a love is the foundation of pedagogy. Consequently, not all teachers are educators. Gülen (2004) asserts, "Education is different from teaching. Most people can teach, but only a very few can educate" (p. 208). Teaching merely conveys information, but educating includes giving knowledge and moral guidance. True teachers are preoccupied with what is good and wholesome (Gülen, 2004: 208). Teaching is a "sacred" activity that brings about positive change. Teachers transmit knowledge with wisdom, and moral guidance with personal example. The goal is to produce a "Golden Generation" that integrates spirituality and knowledge, heart and mind (Gülen, 1998; Gülen, 1996)

The teachers are carefully selected. Those who had a Gülen schooling are preferred as they are more likely to sacrifice their time and talent. Certain countries attract teachers from certain parts of Turkey. The Turkmenistan school, for example, attracts teachers from the prestigious Turgut Özal High School in Turkey.

Focus should be on *temsil* (example), not *tebligh* (preaching). Preaching alienates, not attracts people (Balci, 2003: 10-16). Representation, not presentation, attracts people. Teachers should embody universal values, know their learners well, and appeal to their heads and their hearts (Aslandoğan and Çetin: 2006: 37).

A Kyrgyz student said that he prefers the school as it develops his morality and a positive attitude to religion. Turkish teachers want to serve Turkmenistan/Kyrgyzstan; they identify with, and adapt easily to the common language and culture of the learners. Parents support the school because of the high academic standard, and dedication of the teachers who share a common culture with them (Balci, 2003:10).

Teachers should refine their own minds and hearts so that they can help students acquire a penetrating vision into the reality of things. Knowledge should lead the learner to an appreciation of the creation, and through this, an appreciation of God.

These schools have been established on the model of Anadolu high schools, with superior technical equipment and laboratories. Lessons are given within the curriculum prepared by the Ministry of National Education. Religious subjects are not even taught. Activities take place within the framework of each country's current laws and educational philosophy. For example, in Uzbekistan, after students learn Turkish and English in the preparatory class, they study science in English from Turkish teachers and social subjects in Uzbek from Uzbek teachers. Giving religious knowledge or religious education is not the goal (Gülen, 2002: 87).

For Gülen, a teacher's work is holy; he is blessed, albeit that he is teaching secular subjects. The world is sacred; even a school where so-called secular subjects are taught (Gülen 1998b, 17). The teacher performs one of the highest duties in Islam, *hizmet*, which implies both religious and national service (Agai, 2003: 59). This service for others is also beneficial for life after death. However, the religious motivation behind this service must be projected with discretion. The projection of moral values should not be confused with the projection of religion. Teachers should apply discretion and prudence in their teaching (*tedbir*). [4] Prudence is not only applied to the teaching of a subject, but also to promoting moral values. Without it, people will get the wrong impression, and think that the teacher is preaching Islam.

In Johannesburg, the pupils are mainly Christian Africans; in Durban they are mainly Hindu Indians, and in Cape Town, half the learners are coloured Christians and about half are Muslims. As a secular school, with pupils from a diverse religious background, it would not be prudent to promote Islam overtly. This would alienate non-Muslim learners and parents, and the school would lose its non-Muslim support. Moral values are shared by all religions, and so their promotion would not alienate the non-Muslim learners. The moral ethos of the school is then a distinctive feature of the school.

Teachers are inspired by Gülen's educational theory, but there is no organic link with him as the schools are managed autonomously. Naturally, there is a degree of consultation with Turkish educators at the national level, but this is intended to help improve administrative efficiency and academic excellence.

A moral concept that is applied to teachers is that of *hijrah* (migration). A true believer is always ready for migration. After several years of service, a teacher may be asked to move to a school in another province or country. The reason for this could be academic or moral. A physics teacher may be asked to move to a school where he is more needed, or because of his complacency and boredom, he is placed in a school that is more challenging and reinvigorating. The moral reason fits in with the concept of migration. If a teacher stays in a school for as long as a decade, he is more likely to develop material attachments to his school, house, and friendships. If he is required to move to another school he will be most reluctant. But if his stay is for only five years, he will be able to make the *hijrah*.

Work is a religious duty (*hizmet*) as one is providing for one's family and giving charity to the community. It is called *hizmet*, holy duty; for God is the one who grants the craft one is suited to. Money from one's work should not be wasted on luxury and amusement.

The school benefits from this work-ethic in two ways. The merchants help the school from outside, and the teachers from the inside. The dedicated teachers perceive their profession as a duty to God (Agai, 2003: 59-61).

Teachers who transmit knowledge, even to non-Muslims, are serving Islam as they benefit humanity. Pupils can learn from Turkish teachers how to employ knowledge in a correct and beneficial way. Parents trust the teachers as pious Muslims who teach their children knowledge in a manner that is not perceived as contrary to Islam. Parents are happy with the school because they have a good reputation regarding both their technical skills and their moral qualities. The parents appreciate teachers who neither smoke nor drink, and are willing to make sacrifices for the sake of others.

---

4 When teaching evolution, for example, the teacher should give all views, the creationist, the evolutionist, and the scientific critique of evolution.

The Gülen Schools in South Africa

The Gülen schools have become the elite high schools in Turkey, the former Soviet republics, and in Africa. These are secular private schools inspected by state authorities and sponsored by parents and entrepreneurs. They follow secular, scientific, state-prescribed curricula and internationally recognized programs. For want of a better word, we use the term "Gülen schools". This could be misleading as there is no organic link between Gülen and the schools, only a spiritual connection. The educators are inspired by Gülen's educational theory, which has world-wide popularity. Parents are particularly impressed, by their achievement in the sciences and their stress on the exemplary moral character of teachers (Aslandoğan and Çetin: 2006:32-33).

While the South African educational system during Apartheid used to rest on a rather Christian monolithic world-view; there were private schools that took on an explicitly secular, Islamic or Jewish character, These schools generally conformed to a national curriculum, even if it meant that they introduced Arabic, Hebrew or German, subjects which were part of the national curriculum, but was offered either as part of the school's requirement, or by parents demand. However, with the Post-Apartheid South Africa, the Christian character of the national curriculum was obliterated by the new democratic constitution, and schools now follow a secular curriculum that does not favour a particular religion. The new democracy allows for religious private schools, but they are required to follow the national curriculum. Obviously, they are free to add subjects to the approved curriculum; if it is an Islamic school, Arabic might be offered as an optional or compulsory subject, and if it is a Jewish school, Hebrew might be made compulsory.

Over the last fifteen years there has been a mushrooming of Islamic private schools in the country. During Apartheid, many public schools became unstable due to school boycotts and political unrest. This caused parents to send their children to secular and Christian private schools. With the establishment of the Islamic private school a new alternative was created.

Since 1999, the first Turkish private High school was introduced in Cape Town, The Star International High School, to provide a secular education based on the national curriculum, but with emphasis on moral values. This became an alternative school for Muslims, Christians, Africans and Hindus. For Muslims the Turkish school became an alternative to the Islamic schools because of its stress on moral values and its affinity to religion. It offers Muslim learners an opportunity to pursue a modern education with a moral orientation.

In the Gülen School, the Muslim child maintains an Islamic identity in a secular environment. This is not possible in the liberal state school, where religion or moral values are not respected and encouraged; nor is it possible in the Islamic private schools, where a Muslim laager mentality is nurtured, making it difficult for them to adapt to a secular culture and pluralistic context. It is this balance between preserving moral values of an Islamic identity, (but which are also shared by pupils of other religions), and adapting to a secular school context, that attracted many parents to send their children to these schools.

For many South African Muslims, the Islamic private schools were too elitist. They might have Islamic subjects such as Arabic and Islamic studies, but they have cultivated an attitude of materialism, not one based on morality and spirituality.[5] Gülen schools have also been ac-

---

5 My cousin's daughters are at an Islamic private school in Durban. They used travel to school with the BMW, but when he bought a new Toyota Corolla, they did not want to drive in it. It struck him that they are imbibing material values at an Islamic school! He took them out, and put them in a normal public school. My cousin has no problem

cused of elitism, but we shall return to this question later below.

There are three Star International High Schools managed by Horizon Educational Trust (HET); one in Cape Town, one in Durban and one in Johannesburg. They follow the state curriculum, but include Turkish as a language up till grade 11. The Fountain Education Trust (FET), also inspired by Gülen, also follow the state curriculum (Interview, K. Ozdemir, 31 May 2006), but they are in charge of the Islamic schools called the "Sama" schools. This paper will confine itself only to the schools managed by Horizon Educational Trust.

The Star Schools are distinguished by their emphasis on science, physics, biology and technology. The Trust ensures that they have the best science laboratory and computer rooms. Turkish teachers teach scientific subjects, and South African teachers teach English, Afrikaans, Geography and History.

The school is open to learners of various religious persuasions, and it is different from the Turkish state schools. In the Turkish state schools, religious instruction is offered, but not respected; but in the Gülen schools religious instruction is not offered, but respected.

In the Star International High, Cape Town, there is an equal number of Muslim and Christian learners, and so it is not possible for the school to promote a particular religion. However, there is no problem with teaching moral values, which are shared by other religions. Teachers would teach the moral values of peace and reconciliation, and would sometimes mention the examples of Nelson Mandela and Mahatma Ghandi. The school promotes sound Muslim-Christian relations, [6] and prepares learners to become citizens of a pluralist society. The school promotes faith, but it is tempered with respect and tolerance for other religions.

The school also has a Turkish character: the Turkish national anthem is sung, the Turkish flag is in some classrooms, and the Turkish language is taught. But this is not the purpose of the school; South African learners should be proud of their own national identity. Gülen's vision is that Turkish teachers should serve humanity, not only Turks. Thus, the learner's identity is also shaped by a humanitarian vision.

Do South African pupils feel alienated by the Turkish character of the school? This is not likely. About the Turkish anthem one pupil said: "No, I do not feel uncomfortable about it. It is like learning a Turkish poem or song, and adds to the special flavour of the school. We also sing the South African anthem; so there is no bias towards one national identity."

The Educational Background of the Teachers

The Turkish teachers are practicing Muslims, and share in the educational philosophy of their teacher, Fethullah Gülen. However, they do not impose Islamic values and practices on the learners. They believe that moral example, not moral preaching, influences the learners. As mentioned, they do not teach religion, but moral values are imbibed in the school. One moral value is identified as a theme for each month.[7]

---

taking them to school in the Toyota Corolla.

6   The Fountain Educational Trust has a Dialogue Centre next to the Claremont Main Road Mosque, Claremont. The Trust arranges Iftar functions and group tours to Turkey. In the tour this year they visited Konya, Istanbul, Izmir and Cappadocia. Cappadocia is an ancient district in East –Central Anatolia. Professor Stanley Ridge, a Christian academic and vice-Rector of the University of the Western Cape, was part of the group. Mr Khalil, head of the Dialogue Centre, said: "The purpose of the tour is to build bridges among people of different religious persuasions". I selected the academics from the University of Cape Town, University of Stellenbosch and the University of the Western Cape.

7   I visited the school in Sybrand Park. It is located in a middle-class area, centrally connected to the N2 that takes

The Turkish teachers are science graduates and have attended a school in their country. New teachers adapt easily to the school as they share in the vision and mission of their leader, Fethullah Gülen. Academically, they know they must dedicate themselves to service of the school, and socially they mix easily with fellow Turks who share the same religious and moral values. They know that their service at the school takes on a form of sacrifice: the sacrifice to leave one's country, to give of one's time, to share one's talent, and teach for an average wage.

Teachers sacrifice their time weekends by giving extra tuition to the learners, especially the matriculants. They participate in national workshops twice a year, and contribute to it by sharing their teaching experiences with a view to improving on their methods (Interview, K. Ozdemir, 31 May 2006).

Teachers are expected to be frugal; they are not permitted, or encouraged, to live in expensive apartments, drive expensive cars, and wear expensive clothes. It is believed that such extravagances could blemish the image of the school and damage the trust of the funders. However, teachers do not live in poverty; they earn a decent salary, receive hospital care and obtain a pension upon retirement. In Cape Town most Turkish teachers live in a middle-class area called Pinelands. In Durban they live in an upper-class area called Westville. This does not mean that they live in luxury homes; nor does it mean the school building in the area is elegant. In fact, the school is made of prefabricated structures, and it is not as attractive as the Cape Town one. Thus, the teacher's place of residence is determined by the proximity to the school, and not determined by class or social status. The health and pension benefits apply only to Turkish teachers. A frugal life-style is expected of the Turkish teachers only.

Religious instruction is not taught, but religious values are discernable in the teacher's example. However, moral values are taught, but not in a moralizing, preachy tone. More attention is given to the practice of moral values.[8] The teacher does not project his Islamic identity in the classroom; neither does he conceal his identity outside the classroom. For example, when it is time for prayer, he prays. The teacher, instead, will direct his attention to moral values inside and outside the classroom. Values such as responsibility, accountability, self-control and forgiveness are emphasized. Each month has a different moral theme. The moral virtue for the month is pasted on the walls of the classroom and school, and the principal will remind parents about the moral virtue for the month or the term. The teacher's duty is to emulate the Prophet's mission captured in the Prophetic Tradition (*hadith*): "Verily I have been sent to perfect character."

---

one straight into the city. The area is green, with trees on both sides of the spacious roads. The school is clean, and well-maintained. In the Grade 8B classroom, I saw a South African flag and a Turkish flag on the wall. I read the following values on the classroom wall:

March: Respect: Yourself, Family, community, country

May: good hope, perseverance, compassion, love

July: thankfulness, gratitude, appreciation

August: unity, loyalty, solidarity, peace, friendship

These words are also on the wall of the school. I saw the principal one Saturday put them up himself.

8   Learners will probably notice the teachers praying, and if they should ask a teacher about it, he should not hesitate to say: "We are Muslims and this is our prayer time". But this comes only in response to a question. Focus should be on example (tamsil), not preaching (tebligh).

Turkish university graduates, who obtained a scholarship from the Trust, may feel morally obliged, but not legally compelled, to teach in a Gülen School before working in their own area of specialization (Interview, Ilhami Demirtaþ, May 2006). Turkish teachers are qualified academically for the subject that they teach; some have MA or MSc degrees. Not many, however, have a teacher's diploma or a Degree in Education. This can be a drawback in the system as the teachers may not be able to cope with the less intelligent child. Nevertheless, the school is not aimed at the struggling child, but a child with average or above average intelligence. In this sense the school may be regarded as elitist, but it is only academically elitist; for the norm is to be selective with admission on academic grounds.

Star International High, Cape Town, arranged and hosted the Star Maths Competition for several years, and has attracted learners from different schools to participate. This aught to have been good exposure for the school, but it has not helped in increasing the school enrolment. So far, the matriculation results were not good, and since the inception of the school, only two matriculants obtained distinctions.

Transformation took place in 2005 when the school moved to a new building in Sybrand Park. It used to be a Jewish school, but it is now rented out to the Turks. The new school building is larger, greener and safer. It is now attracting a better class of learners at the Grade 8 level, which is the first year of high school. This year it had a big enrolment, and two Grade 8 classes had to be formed. One class is composed of brighter learners, and five years later, they will be the cream of the crop to obtain excellent results. Currently, there are only three matriculants, but they are excellent learners, and the school is expecting them to obtain distinctions and merit passes. This could be a turning point in the positive publicity of the school.

The Support of the Turkish Merchants

For Gülen, the whole world is sacred; so merchants should donate, not only to a mosque, but also to schools. They will be blessed in this world and the next world. The merchants know the power of knowledge, especially science and technology, but they also know that it should be linked to religion. The focus on science led to the neglect of the humanities; hence, Gülen has recently announced that attention should also be given to the social sciences, including history, human geography and literature.[9]

The total number of Turkish schools world-wide exceeds 500, and most of them are self-financing. New schools require financial backing, usually from Turkish voluntary organizations made up of Turkish merchants (Baydar, 2007:2).The merchants of a particular region in Turkey take responsibility for funding the school in Cape Town. Student fees also provide income, but no profit can be made as the school is not well-established. Local Turkish merchants and South African commercial companies also support the school, especially for the school functions and the Olympiad competitions.

Inasmuch as Turkish teachers share their Turkish culture with the pupils, they also learn

---

9 I attended a conference last year in Johannesburg on Islamic Civilization in Africa, and Dr Khalid Iren of ISRICA announced that scholarships are available for those who want to study the social studies in Istanbul. This coincided with my paper, which was on the neglect of the humanities in the Gülen schools.

Mr. Ilhami said: "Gülen's personal bias is for literature and the humanities, but his focus on science was in response to the challenges in Turkey. Today, science subjects are important to fill the need for careers in these fields. In South Africa, it is imperative to offer science subjects; otherwise parents will not support the school. Equal attention can be given to social studies, but not at the expense of the natural sciences".

from the positive elements of South African culture, and return to their country enriched as educators (Baydar, 2007:2). Tahsin Tumer, the head of the Gülen schools in South Africa, said: "We educate a total of 1, 400 learners now. Fifty one of our teachers are from Turkey, 71 are from South Africa. [We have good relations] with the local authorities are very good" (Baydar, 2007:2). Turkish teachers live in rented flats; earn a salary (with benefits) of 1, 300 dollars a month. One third is married to Turks (Baydar, 2007:2).

Turkish teachers are dedicated. They earn a small, but decent salary, and are not focused on the material goods of this world, but the spiritual goods of the next world (Gülen, 2002: 86). They earn less than local teachers, but if married, they earn more than teachers who are bachelors. Principals earn a bit more, but have more responsibilities. Local teachers are paid on time, but Turkish teachers sometimes wait for their salaries placidly. They know that their purpose is not material gain, but to provide a service. They do not have the mind-set of the local teachers who are in the routine of working only from 8am to 3pm. Turkish teachers have a work-ethic that transcends working hours, and consider themselves on duty for 24 hours a day. With an average of 6 000 Rands a month, they can live decently, but not extravagantly. Even if they can manage to be extravagant, perhaps on account of parental support, they feel morally constrained to remain within the limits of moderation and frugality. Immoderation in the acquisition of material goods is frowned upon by the organization.[10]

The Turkish merchants opened up the Gülen schools in Africa either for humanitarian reasons or for trade (Interview, K. Ozdemir, 31 May 2006). Nowadays, Gülen is urging them to become as rich as they can. If they are wealthy, they will not only be able to give more in the form of *zakah* and *sadaqah*, but will also be in a position to allocate ten percent of their turnover to the organization. Some merchants give half their profits to the schools! Merchants are now working harder than before, not only to provide for their families, but also for the Trust. One merchant is donating virtually all his money for a major school project in Johannesburg.[11]

The organization ensures that teachers maintain a decent standard of living. To allay any anxiety about future material insecurity, provision is made for medical care and a pension when they retire. If a teacher needs to be hospitalized, or should have an operation, the organization is there to take care of all the expenses. They are not subject to a medical aid, and the anxieties associated with it; especially when there is a strict limit to the use of medicines, and when they have to pay out of their pockets for medical service that charge more than the medical aid rates.

It is important that funders maintain the trust in the Turkish educators, and be assured that all monies will be used for what it was intended; be it the payment of rent, salaries or computer facilities. A decent, but frugal, life-style among teachers is important to sustain this trust and

---

10 Most Turkish teachers live in Pinelands, a middle-class, predominantly English area. They stay in two-bedroom spacious apartments. They adapt to each other very well even though they never met before in Turkey. They share a common vision, and so get along with each other, including their wives who belong to the same organization.

11 Mr Ali, a seventy- one year old wealthy Turkish merchant, visited Cape Town in the first week of August 2007, and met the Premier Ebrahim Rasool. His wish is to build a school (with a mosque attached) in Johannesburg before he dies. He says: " I am like a fruit on a tree that will fall any time, so I should not be a wasted fruit, and therefore I want to see the school come up as soon as possible". Mr Ali is donating 15 million dollars for the project in the Midrand. The mosque should have a Sinan architectural style. The project should be built on a ground of 130 000 square metres. It will have shopping malls that will bring in rental income to maintain the complex (Interview with Ilhami, 9th August 2007). A similar project might be built in Cape Town if land is made available.

to allay any possible suspicion.[12]

The Academic Standard and the Admission Policy

The Gülen schools pride themselves in maintaining a high academic standard, having highly qualified educators, providing individual attention, and keeping close communication with parents.[13] The mission statement of the Cape Town school reads as follows:

> We accept it as our mission to offer high quality education with appropriate facilities, equipment and infra-structure to enhance the learning experience of our students. In order to implement this we constantly strive to improve and achieve more in all aspects. This is being conducted even faster in our new location [in Sybrand Park]. The school also practices the latest available teaching methods as well as a set of universal values that will build the character of the learners. Through imparting these values we aim to help them to become respectable and distinguished members of the society.[14]

Star International Cape Town is a private school, but cannot compete with the historically well-established private schools such as Bishops.[15] The educators are aware of this, and so their ambitions are tempered with realism, and they are setting their target on competing with the Model C schools such as Westerford High.[16]

The Model C schools are the historically white public schools that have had better facilities during the Apartheid era, but are now open to all races. The school fees are much higher than the public schools, but they are on par with the cheaper private schools such as Star International High and Islamia College. The matriculants of the Model C schools obtain better results than those coming from the public schools. Star

International aims at academic excellence, so they do not aspire to compete with the public schools, but will rather make the Model C its yardstick for comparison. So far, it is not yet at the academic level of the Model C school, but it has the potential to equal it, or surpass it. Already, the Durban Star learners obtained better Matriculation results than many Model C learners.

---

12 The first group of Turkish teachers came to Cape Town, and shared a house in Claremont (two persons per room). The school started in Retreat. When it moved to Athlone, the teachers came to live in Pinelands, the first English garden town. From here it is easy to commute to school, it is against the traffic, and quick into Klipfontein Road. The teachers live in two bed-room spacious apartments with an average rent of R 3 500 per month. It is decent and affordable. The sub-economic standard of the school in Athlone attracted learners from Manenburg, Athlone and Mitchells-Plane. In 2005 the school moved to Sybrand Park, a middle-class area. The school spent R 200 000 to improve the gardens and build computer rooms and a science laboratory. The change was significant. Middle-class families supported the school, and in 2007, there was a large enrolment, and two classes of Grade 8 pupils were opened (Interview, Ilhami, 9th August, 2007).

13 See Star International Primary-High School (est. 1999) brochure: Other special features mentioned in the school brochure (printed 2007) are: recreational opportunities, fully equipped science lab, computer room with internet, special camps, trips and excursions, annual student shows, extra-mural and club activities, disciplined and caring environment, secure and safe atmosphere, latest educational policies and practices.

14 See Star International Brochure, Cape Town, 2007.

15 Bishops is an independent boys' school situated in Rondebosch in Cape Town, which provides instruction from Grade 0 to Grade 12 (ages 6 – 18), with a post-matric unit as well. The school was founded by Robert Gray, Bishop of Cape Town, in 1849. The school's formal name is the Diocesan College, but it is widely known as 'Bishops'. The school's character arises from its Christian foundation, its history, its position in southern Africa and the values which it strives to embody and to impart to its pupils.

16 Westerford is a co-educational High school located close to the Newlands Rugby Ground and Table-Mountain, and was established on 21st January 1953.

The Gülen schools have a reputation for good results, but this is not the only reason why parents send their children to these schools. They are also impressed by its moral ethos. The Cape Town school has not done as well academically as the Durban school. The matriculants of the latter school obtained 100% distinctions. The reasons for this are as follows: Firstly, Mr. Yasar[17], the principal, established the school in Westville, an upper-class area in Durban. The location itself attracted the middle-class families to enroll their children. With the increasing demand, the school could afford to be stricter in their admission of learners. Secondly, the senior learners stay in the school dormitory under the supervision of a tutor and some teachers, who ensure that they do their schoolwork from sunset till midnight. Thirdly, they have a team of dedicated teachers who have a passion for the subject they teach, and who can teach it with clarity and effectiveness. Teachers will also sacrifice their time at the week-long study camps[18] and weekend-tuition.

By contrast, Star International High, Cape Town, did not perform as well as Durban. The first Gulen school was established in Cape Town, and so this was a first experience for the Turkish teachers. They soon came to realize that the learners have a different cultural background to the learners in Turkey and Russia where they have been very successful. The pupils are not as docile as they expected, and much more was required to maintain the discipline of the learners. So far, the school only obtained two distinctions in the matriculation level. Let us review the main reasons for their poor academic performance. Firstly, the school was in Athlone, a sub-economic area.[19] The school was rundown and had a shabby appearance, and so attracted mainly working class and lower-middle class families. A school should not be judged purely on the grounds of its physical appearance, but a school which is unknown to the public is bound to be judged simply on that basis. The principal said: "The parents were not so co-operative; they hardly attended the meetings and school functions. A reason for this could be the inadequate public transport and lack of safety at night (Interview, Ilhami, August, 2007). Secondly, there is the problem of the English communicative ability of the Turkish teachers. Generally, teachers who are science graduates have a reading ability in English, but mainly for scientific subjects. When they come to Cape Town they become fluent in English, and this is only after five or seven years, depending also on how much they mix and practice with non-Turkish friends.

While they are still improving their English, they are not effective communicators, and this is what undermines the efficacy of their teaching. Hence, the learning and discipline of pupils are affected.[20] Thirdly, the rotation of teachers proved to be more disadvantageous than advantageous. The disadvantage is that just when the teacher has acquired English fluency, perhaps after five years, he is then posted to another school. The new teacher has to now also

---

17　Former principal of Star International, Cape Town; later moved to Durban to start the school there. He learnt from the failure of the Cape Town experiment, and adopted a strict admission policy in Durban.

18　At these week-long camps pupils revise Science and Mathematics under the guidance of teachers. Nabil Mohamed went to Durban this year twice to participate in the Week-study camp. Board and lodging are provided at the school dormitory. He said: 'I benefitted greatly from Mr Binder, the mathematics and physics tutor; he has years of experience and an excellent method of teaching. I was also inspired by the Durban learners who have high aspirations; some are aiming for seven A's".

19　The school was first located in Retreat, which is on the outskirts of the city, and therefore quite far to travel. It moved its premises to Athlone, which is much more central, with easy access into town.

20　English fluency is imperative, even for the teaching of science subjects. For Gülen, the educator is concerned with the whole child, not only the subject being taught. A Turkish teacher said: "I teach mathematics, I do not need to be fluent in English". I disagreed, and said: "In what language do you discipline the child?" He replied: "In English". Discipline suffers when there is a failure to communicate.

adapt to the new environment, not only in building up his English skills, but also in adapting to the culture and background of the learners. The pupils in turn also have to adapt to the new teacher. This rotation undermines the stability and regularity of the school, and so, the school is not able to develop its unchanging character and image. The teachers make up the backbone of the school; they determine the character and ethos of the school; parents come to associate the school with its teachers and not with the physical building or location of the school.

It is inevitable that a new school will have its initial problems, but we have to judge it ultimately for its final outcomes. Thus, we turn to its achievements and future prospects. The school made major progress since it moved to Sybrand Park in 2005. The new location and more attractive physical structure of the school made an instant difference to the enrolment of learners from middle-class families. In 2007, on account of the large enrolment of grade 8s, the school was compelled to form two separate classes. This reflects the increasing support and demand for the school.

The matriculants of 2007 are expected to do exceptionally well. Judging from the June reports, half the class is expected to obtain distinctions. In future, the school can be choosy as to the quality of learners it wants to admit. Admission will be based on academic standards, not class or creed. Strict admission is not the policy of the school, but Mr Ilhami, the principal, indicated that is important in the South African context. He said: "Although not ethical, we have to adopt a strict admissions policy, otherwise we cannot ensure merit and distinction passes. Olympiad competitions and medals have worked elsewhere, but not in South Africa, where the school is judged purely on the basis of matriculation results (Ilhami: Interview, August, 2006).[21]

This new realization led Mr Ilhami to adopt a stricter admission policy, which excluded more of the working class families, not because of the class they belong to, but because they happen to be less anxious to see their children aspire towards excellence. Thus, it is not elitism on the basis of class that determines the admission criteria, but pure academic performance. The school wants to ensure that there is a reasonable through-put, and that even if they subsidize the child's education, they must know that there is a greater chance of academic accomplishment and completion by the end of Grade 12. The school cannot admit learners purely on the basis of compassionate grounds, but only on academic merit.

The stricter admission policy will eventually do more for the publicity of the school than any Olympiad competition or gold medal awards. The fruit of it will be seen five years later when those learners are in Grade 12 and their names appear in the newspapers showing that they have obtained distinction and merit passes.

It is usual for Gülen schools to obtain gold and silver awards in Mathematics, Science, Computers and English in the Olympiad competitions held in various countries. This has created a sense of achievement and prestige, [22] but not in South Africa. Since the inception of the

---

21 At a conference in September, 2006, Johannesburg, I presented a paper on Turkish education in South Africa, and one person asked a question: " How is it that the Turks are Muslims but they do not offer Islamic subjects such as tawhid, hadith, Qur'an reciting etc." I said that this was a secular school, but they were still sceptical, until I said: "The Star International in Durban obtained 100% distinctions in grade 12." I suddenly received a positive response, and some parents wanted to enroll their children at the Durban school.

22 To maintain high standards, weekend and holiday skills training for staff are provided. The school seeks to cultivate a competitive spirit, which is evident by sending children to the academic "Olympic" contests for high-school students all around the world. The pupils have returned with Gold and Silver medals.

Cape Town school, it has attained 23 gold medals; but they have no real meaning as parents' decisions are based mainly on academic results at the matriculation level. The proximity to the school, numbers in the class, and the moral ethos of the school, also play a role in the decision to enrol the child.

There were years when the Star matriculants performed worse than the matriculants of the better public schools. This should not happen. Star International must perform better than the public school; otherwise there is no substantial reason for parents to enroll their children at Star.[23] Presumably, Muslim parents support the school because it is managed by a Muslim trust, and because it discourages social vices such as dating and drinking parties. But this is not a main reason for their support. Like the non-Muslim parents, they support the school mainly for the better education it can provide for their children (Interview, Ilhami, and 8th August, 2006). The notion of a better education became more alive in the consciousness of the parents when the school moved to Sybrand Park. Since the change to a new location, more middle-class parents supported the school. Thus, since last year, better quality learners have enrolled at the school.

The Gülen school has a bias for the science subjects, including mathematics, physics and technology. It tries its best to acquire the latest technology, depending on the funds available (Interview, K. Ozdemir, and 31 May 2006). Turkish educators teach the sciences and South Africans teach the social subjects and languages. Obviously, a Turk teaches Turkish as a language, and South Africans teach English, Afrikaans, Xhosa and Zulu. The Johannesburg school has mainly African learners (Africans make up the majority in the country) and the Durban school is composed of Indian learners (Indians are a minority in the country).[24] The Cape Town school has an even mixture of coloured Christians and "coloured" Muslims.

Ilhami Demirtas, a biology teacher, who graduated from Middle East Technical University from Ankara, and principal of the Star International Primary and High School, Cape Town, said there are 200 pupils; half girls, attending the co-educational primary school. The High School is for boys only. One South African said: "These schools are a model for other Islamic private schools. Here is great respect for science and an eagerness to share universal values" (Baydar, 2007:2).

This year, the High school has fitted the latest equipment for the science and computer labo-ratories. The principal indicated that applications having been streaming in since last year, and now they can afford to be more selective with enrolment. The idea is to create a positive image for the school in an average middle class area. At a later stage, they could open up schools in up-market areas such as Rondebosch and Newlands. Once these schools become profitable, they will be in a position to subsidize Gülen schools in the poorer areas. Thus, the

---

23 The school does not intend to compete with public schools such as Livingstone High School and Belgravia High, but with private schools and model C schools. Nor does the school want to compete with the top private schools in the country; they are established for many years and too expensive. The school will rather compete with Model C schools such as Westerford High and Rondebosch Boys (historically White public schools), which have facilities on par with Star International and their fees are affordable to the average middle-class child (Interview, Ilhami, 7 August, 2007).

24 Durban is a humid and hot coastal city. The school is composed of pre-fabricated structures, which used to be a Christian missionary school before 1999. It has a big field and basket-ball court. There are two hundred students here, and they pay 2 000 dollars per year. They can get a scholarship of 200 dollars to supplement their fees. The school is modest compared to the one in Cape Town, but the learners are from affluent homes, and have high aspira-tions for their future careers.

idea to open up a school in an affluent area has nothing to do with elitism[25]. The idea is to build self-sustaining schools that are profitable, and which can then be of assistance to the school that requires more financial support.

Generally, children from affluent homes have higher aspirations and learning ability than children from poor families. This is because they have had more opportunities and not because of any innate superiority. If children from affluent homes are attracted to a good school, it does not make the school elitist in terms of social class. The school will provide a bursary for a talented boy from a poor home, and not discriminate against him on the grounds of his lower socio-economic class.

As mentioned, elitism is a relative concept; a Gulen school in a poor area will be regarded as elitist, but not in an affluent area. Elitism is also relative to the cost of schooling; the less affordable the school the more elitist it is. The Gülen schools are affordable to the middle-class family, but not the working class. However, bright learners from the working class are also given the opportunity of a better education as their schooling is usually subsidized.

For middle-class standards the Gülen school is not elitist; but for working class standards it is elitist. The Gülen school in Durban is located in an area that is affluent, but the school building is rather modest. The learners are mainly from the middle-class; but as pointed out above, this does not mean that it is a socially elite school, but only academically elite.

Conclusion

Gülen promoted moral values in a secular school environment, which would work within the state's framework of unified education. Parents send their children to the Gülen schools because their graduates have been accepted in reputable colleges and universities, and their learners are less susceptible to the negative influences of drug and alcohol abuse.

For Muslims, a key question that arose is: "Why should I send my child to a secular school instead of an Islamic school"? The standard answer is that the school's teachers embody universal values such as truthfulness, trust, respect for parents, respect for the elderly, respect for one's heritage, and love for human beings. Muslim parents identify with these values and want this to be imbibed in their children (Ünal and Williams 2000:348).

We have discussed the educational philosophy of Fethullah Gülen, and showed how both the academic and moral aspects of his thought have been applied in the South African context, with special reference to Star International High, Cape Town. We have described the schools' achievements, shortcomings, and future prospects.

The school provides an alternative to the private and model C schools. Although secular, it promotes moral values and respects the religious diversity of South African society. For Muslim learners, it is an alternative to the Islamic private schools. The Turkish teachers are morally upright and religious-minded, and this inspires them. At the same time, the Muslim child learns to interact with his Christian class-mates and teachers, and he comes to know that there is a universal set of moral values that they all share. This prepares him to integrate into the pluralist South African society.

---

25 Elitism is a relative concept; a school that is regarded as elitist in one area may not be elitist in another. A Gülen school in a poor area like Manenburg will be regarded as elitist, but not if it is located in affluent Rondebosch. The school is not elitist in terms of social class, but only in accord with academic worth. Thus, funding and subsidization of learners will be in accordance to their learning ability and not social class.

The Gülen schools have a Turkish character: it is inspired by the educational philosophy of a Turkish religious thinker, Fethullah Gülen; the principal is a Turk, the science teachers are Turks, the foreign language taught is Turkish, the Turkish national anthem and Turkish songs are promoted at school functions.

Since the school moved to Sybrand Park, it has gained more support from middle-class families, and this is evident in the large intake of learners this year. Five years from now, the cream of the crop of the current Grade 8 classes will be matriculating, and we predict that most of them will obtain distinction and merit passes.

TURKMENISTAN'S NEW CHALLENGES: CAN STABILITY CO-EXIST WITH REFORM? A STUDY OF GULEN SCHOOLS IN CENTRAL ASIA, 1997-2007

Victoria Clement

Abstract

In the 1990s, Turkmenistan's government dismantled Soviet educational provision, replacing it with lower quality schooling. The Başkent Foundation schools represent the concerted efforts of teachers and sponsors to offer socially conscious education grounded in science and math with an international focus.

This case study of the Başkent Foundation schools in Turkmenistan establishes the vitality of Gülen schools outside of the Turkish Republic and their key role in offering Central Asian families an important choice in secular, general education. The paper discusses the appeal of the schools' curriculum to parents and students, and records a decade-long success both in educating students and in laying the foundations of civil society: in Turkmenistan the Gülen movement offers the only general education outside of state provision and control. This is particularly significant as most scholars deny that there is any semblance of civil society in Turkmenistan.

Notes: The author has been conducting interviews and recording the influence of Başkent schools in Turkmenistan since working as Instructor at the International Turkmen-Turk University in 1997. In May 2007 she visited the schools in the capital Ashgabat, and the northern province of Daşoguz, to explore further the contribution Gülen schools are making. The recent death of Turkmenistan's president will most likely result in major reforms in education. Documentation of how a shift at the centre of state power affects provincial Gülen schools will enrich this conference's broader discussion of the movement's social impact.

The history of Gülen-inspired schools in Central Asia reveals as much about the Gülen movement as it does about transition in the Muslim world. While acknowledging that transition in the 21st century includes new political and global considerations, it must be viewed in a historical context that illustrates how change, renewal and questioning are longstanding inherent to Islamic tradition.

In the former Soviet Union, the Gülen movement contributed to the Muslim people's transition out of the communist experience. Since USSR fell in 1991, participants in Fethullah Gülen's spiritual movement have contributed to its mission by successfully building schools, offering English language courses for adults, and consciously supporting nascent civil society throughout Eurasia. Not only in Turkic speaking regions, but also as far as Mongolia and Southeast Asia, the so-called "Turkish schools" have succeeded in creating sustainable systems of private schools that offer quality education to ethnically and religiously diverse populations. The model is applicable on the whole; Gülen's movement has played a vital role in offering Eurasia's youth an alternative to state-sponsored schooling.[1]

Recognition of the broad accomplishments of Gülen schools in Eurasia raises questions about how these schools function on a daily basis and how they have remained successful. What kind of world are they preparing students for? How do the schools differ from traditional Muslim schools (*maktabs or madrasas*)? Do they offer an alternative to Arab methods of learning?

Success in Turkmenistan is especially notable due to the dramatic politicization of education under nationalistic socio-cultural programmes in that Central Asian country. Since the establishment of the first boarding school, named after Turkish Prime Minister Turgut Ozal, in 1991 the Gülen schools have prospered despite Turkmenistan's extreme political conditions and severely weakened social systems. How did this network of foreign schools, connected to a faith-based movement, manage to flourish under Turkmenistan's capricious dictatorship? In essence, Gülen-inspired schools have been consistently successful in Turkmenistan because a secular curriculum partnered with a strong moral framework appeals to parents and students without threatening the state.[2]

This hypothesis encourages further consideration of the *cemaat*'s ethos and Gülen's philosophies such as the imperative of activism (*aksiyon*), the compatibility of Islam and modernity, and the high value Islamic traditions assign to education.[3] Focusing on this particular set of "Turkish schools" in Turkmenistan provides details and data from which we can consider broader complexities of the movement as a whole. In particular, the study illustrates that current transitions in the Muslim world have long, complex histories that extend beyond today's immediate questions about Islam, modernity, or extremism.[4]

---

1 One scholar calls the schools in Kyrgyzstan "to be among the most dynamic and worthwhile educational enterprises I have encountered in the world." See Thomas Michel, "Fethullah Gülen as Educator," in Turkish Islam and the Secular State: The Gülen Movement, M. Hakan Yavuz and John L. Esposito eds. (Syracuse: Syracuse University Press, 2003), p. 70.

2 I have been conducting interviews and recording influences of Başkent schools in Turkmenistan since I was an Instructor at the International Turkmen-Turk University in 1997. My most recent visit was in May 2007 and included one school in Dashoguz.

3 The importance of activism is underscored by the movement's Turkish magazine of that name Aksiyon (Action). Ahmet T. Kuru, "Search for a Middle Way," Yavuz and Esposito, 2003, p. 126; Bayram Balçı, "Central Asia: Fethullah Gülen's Missionary Schools," ISIM Newsletter, September 2002.

4 Ihsan Yılmaz, "Ijtihad and Tajdid by Conduct," in Yavuz and Esposito, 2003, pp. 208-237; John Voll, "Renewal and Reformation in the Mid-Twentieth Century: Bediüzzaman Said Nursi and Religion in the 1950s," The Muslim

Post-Soviet Turkmenistan

When Turkmenistan gained independence in 1991, adult literacy was near 99%. However, the educational system, left over from the Soviet-era, was utterly inadequate. School textbooks still featured the Bolshevik leader Lenin and university level institutes continued to rely on Russian vocabulary for technical, scientific, and medical studies. Curriculum content was neither current to the post-Soviet order nor free from Moscow's influence. Nevertheless, the institutions were in place and they functioned. Moreover, teachers and administrators were eager to continue their work. Despite all this, the new government's policies ruined the educational system as part of an anti-Soviet backlash that left stark voids in social and cultural spheres. Gülen schools played a major role in filling the instructional and institutional vacuums President Niyazow's programmes created.

From October 1991, when Turkmenistan gained independence and came under sole rule of Saparmurat Niyazow, until 11 February 2007, when Gurbanguly Berdymukhammedow assumed the presidency, Niyazow's personal whims governed the educational system.[5] Instead of linking Turkmenistan to the larger world by building upon systems and personnel in place, President Niyazow reduced the educational system to a shell of what it had been during Soviet times. As part of his *Milli Galkynyş Hereketi* the state cultivated policies to support the "Turkmenification" of social spheres that had been Russified during the Soviet era.[6] The government dismantled Soviet education systems, replacing them with lower quality schools and curricula. Learning became tightly linked to nation building and Niyazow's ideology became codified with the introduction of his *Ruhnama* into the schools in 2002.[7] Rather than move away from political ideology, which had saturated education during the Soviet Union, classroom content further weakened under the weight of Niyazow's cult of personality and state-controlled anti-Russian cultural programs. Moreover, classrooms became sites for ethnic discrimination. Turkmen displaced Russian as a language of instruction in schools; ethnic divisions permeated school lessons as state-employees who did not speak Turkmen—including teachers—were fired; and applications to institutes for higher education required students to identify their ancestry in a veiled attempt to keep non-Turkmen out of universities. Under Niyazow's leadership, the state-sponsored education system suffered from such acute deterioration that it threatened a generation of human capital in that country.[8]

Turkmenistan's citizens felt as if they were moving backward and feared their children might become a "lost generation" rather than the "golden generation" or *Altin Nesil* as Niyazow

---

World, Vol. 89, No. 3-4, 1999, pp. 245-59; Filiz Başkan, "The Fethullah Gülen Community: Contribution or Barrier to the Consolidation of Democracy in Turkey," Middle Eastern Studies, Vol. 41, No. 6, November 2005, pp. 849-861.

5 Saparmurat Niyazow was appointed head of the Turkmen Communist Party in 1985, elected president in 1990, and named "President for life" in 1999. Although he employed the title "president" and the state had the trappings of a parliamentary system it was no secret that all power emanated from Niyazow. His self-chosen title "Türkmenbaşy" meant "leader of the Turkmen."

6 Adrienne Edgar, Tribal Nation: the Making of Soviet Turkmenistan (Princeton: Princeton University Press, 2004); Victoria Clement, "Türkmenistanyň Milli Galkynyş Hereketi [Turkmenistan's National Revival Movement]," Central Asia: Perspectives from the Field, Central Asia Research Network (CARN) SOAS, University of London, November 7-8, 2003.

7 Ruhnama or "Book of the Soul" was a pseudo-philosophical-historical text that came to dominate public discourse throughout 21st century Turkmenistan and supported Niyazow's cult of personality.

8 Victoria Clement, "Bilimli Nesil—the Learned Generation in Niyazov's Turkmenistan, 1999-2005" Paper delivered at Advancement for the Association of Slavic Studies, Boston, December 4-7, 2004.

labeled the post-Soviet youth.[9] In interviews I conducted with parents between 2001-4, one of the most frequent unsolicited comments was that families wished to see Turkmenistan's educational system restored to Soviet levels—at a minimum.[10] In later interviews, in 2006 and 2007, families continued to express this dissatisfaction despite the risk of speaking critically about the state with a foreigner.

It is both because of the extreme local conditions and the continuous success of the Turkish schools that Turkmenistan provides an edifying case study of the Gülen movement's contributions to Central Asian societies. The odds were against success, yet during the past decade, members of the Gülen community have offered Turkmenistan's youth the only means of attaining a quality education within that country. The details of the day-to-day administration and the consistently cooperative approach to dealing with the local government (typical of Gülen-schools everywhere) illustrate aspects of this school system that work well and make the system applicable outside of the Turkic speaking world.

Gülen Schools in Turkmenistan

In 1990 *perestroika* made it possible for Turkmenistan's Ministry of Education to begin formal discussions with Turkey's Başkent Educational Firm over the possibilities of cooperation in the educational sphere. This dialogue led to agreement to develop a network of Turkmen-Turkish schools in Turkmenistan.[11] At the beginning of the 1991/92 academic year the Turkmen-Turkish Boarding School named after Turgut Özal opened in Aşgabat. Two years later, in 1993/94 the network of joint Turkmen-Turkish boarding schools opened institutions in seven cities: Mary, Baýramali, Çarjew, Daşoguz, Nebitdag, Türkmenbaşy and Könyaürgenç. Later that same year the network expanded to include an economic-technical school (*lise*) in Ashgabat, boarding schools in Tejen, Büzmeýn, and Kerki, and the International Turkmen-Turkish University in Aşgabat. In the 1997/98 school-year in Aşgabat a new Turkish Center began offering courses in languages and computers, while a school for girls opened.[12] The schools experienced near continuous expansion and unwavering political support from the Turkmen leadership, even after the death of the Turkish president Turgut Ozal who had played such an imperative role in bringing Turkish culture to post-Soviet central Asia.[13]

The schools' curricula emphasized the natural sciences and mathematics. Languages played a major role in instruction as well as communication within the schools. Study of English, Turkish, Turkmen, and Russian languages was obligatory. Special attention was given to English for which preparatory classes were organized. Designed to reach talented and gifted

---

9 The origin of this moniker is unknown. Niyazow may have borrowed it from Fethullah Gülen, who also speaks of the "golden generation". Beýik Saparmyrat Türkmenbaşynyň Altyn Bilim Syýasaty [Saparmyrat Turkmenbashy the Great's Golden Education Policy] (Aşgabat: Turkmenistan's Ministry of Education, 2003). Victoria Clement, "Education in post-Niyazov Turkmenistan," paper delivered at School of Oriental and African Studies, University of London, January 25, 2007.

10 Victoria Clement, "Rewriting the Turkmen 'Nation': Literacy, Education, and Power in Central Asia, 1904-2004" Ph. D. dissertation, The Ohio State University, Columbus, 2005, chapter 5.

11 Zeki Pektaş, Sovmestnye turkmeno-turetskie shkoly-internaty v Turkmenistane: etapy stanovleniia i razvitiia (Aşgabat: Ylym, 1999), p. 10.

12 Türkmen-Türk Mekdeplerinde Buýsançly 10 Ýyl (Aşgabat, n.d.)

13 Türk Cumhuriyet Bakanlıklığı ve Turkmenistan arasında Eğitim İş Protokolı,1992; "Birleşik Devletlet Topluluğu'nda Türkçe," TÖMER Dil Dergisi, sayı 4, Ocak 1992. See also TIKA (Turkish International Cooperation Agency) journal in general.

children, the Gülen schools offered an education fairly typical to the locality, but with standards higher than in most public schools.[14] The pedagogy is based on the program for private schools in Turkey in correspondence with the requirements of schools in Turkmenistan.[15] In the earliest years, most teachers and staff traveled from Turkey out of their personal interest in the Gülen movement and a sense of *dawah* or mission.[16] Some Turkish citizens worked in Central Asia because schools there afforded religious freedom they could not access in Turkey, such as wearing headscarves. Still others found good jobs with salaries that allowed for a comfortable life, especially considering the low-cost of living in the former Soviet Union in the 1990s. Local teachers, conducting courses in such subjects as Turkmen language, Russian language, and the history of Turkmenistan, sought out work in the Turkish schools for the high-level of pay as well as for better working conditions. These instructors received salaries at least three times that of teachers in Turkmenistan's public education system and many have maintained their positions over the past decade.[17]

Finances

The schools cover expenses with monies received from Turkey, primarily Ankara, or from Turkish businesses in Turkmenistan.[18] The school administration had initially intended to take care of costs down to the clothing of the students; each pupil receives a uniform, shoes, and sports clothes.[19] In fact, some students receive full scholarships, some pay nominal fees, and others pay tuition in the range of $1000 per year.[20] According to Lester Kurtz,

> The movement has mobilized and involved prominent intellectuals and even set up a non-interest bearing bank—with $125 million capital—Asya Finans, to promote economic development in the Turkish-speaking Central Asian republics of the former Soviet Union.[21]

The Bashkent Educational Firm (*Başkent Eğitim Şirket*) is the Gülen community's financial and administrative umbrella organization in Turkmenistan. The *Baskent Bilim Merkezi* (*Başkent Educational Center*) is the Gülen community's administrative and pedagogical center. The Center also houses space for youth interaction that is typically filled with young people spending free time with friends, playing table tennis, or using computers—an important offering in the days before the internet cafes of 2007. Locals refer to the Center as "Başkent" or the "Turkish Center" by association with language and identity of the teachers. Nevertheless, Başkent operates as an independent administrative and legal entity certified in Turkmenistan by that state.

Funded and staffed by members of the *cemaat*, Başkent opened a university in 1993/4 and began to build primary and secondary schools around the country.[22] Başkent has maintained

---

14 Pektas, p. 11.

15 Pektas, p. 12.

16 Interviews with teachers 1997-2007.

17 On human resources at Gülen schools see Thomas Michel, "Fethullah Gülen as Educator," Yavuz and Esposito, 2003, p. 70.

18 "Fethullah Gülen's Missionaries, " Turkish Daily News, September 14, 2001. Monies to schools in Kazakhstan tend to come from Turks in Izmir.

19 Pektas, p. 13. See also

20 Silova, forthcoming, p. 6.

21 Lester B. Kurtz, "Gülen's Paradox: Combining Commitment and Tolerance," The Muslim World, Special Issue: Islam in Contemporary Turkey: the Contributions of Fethullah Gülen, Zeki Sarıtoprak, ed., vol. 95, No. 3, July 2005, p. 381.

22 Clement, 2005, pp. 142-162.

the schools, 11 departments within 3 colleges (*fakultet*) at the university, and the Center itself, which offers 5 courses in foreign languages and computers. Since the earliest days of Turkmenistan's independence, the Center has offered English language classes for a nominal fee. At that time, the office and classroom occupied a small rented space, which though located near the center of the city, was hidden behind the old Soviet Circus. It was a challenge to find. Today, Baskent offices occupy a large building to house all of the classes, administrative offices, and social spaces. Located on a main street in Turkmenistan's capital city Aşgabat, its accessibility and its good reputation doubtlessly encourage the young people who drop in and the adults attending night courses in English.

Başkent's schools and students in have grown in number consistently. In 1997/98 there were 13 schools in Turkmenistan with 3,294 students. In 2006/07 those numbers had grown respectively to 16 schools and 5,250 students.[23] Moreover, the local population recognizes these schools as the best alternative form of education in Turkmenistan. Every year 9-10,000 students compete for 750 places. At the university 4,000 applications were submitted for 200 places. In the first ten years the elementary schools graduated 2,803 pupils, the language and computer program awarded 10,710 certificates, and more than 500 students have graduated from the International Turkmen-Turkish University.[24] This consistent growth is due both to the administration of the institutions, as well as to Turkmenistan's citizens' ever-increasing interest in enrolling their children in superior schools.

Publicity and Growth

How was the *cemaat* able to advertise their new schools in a country without a free press? They began by sending representatives to visit schools to announce the entrance exams. Soon word of mouth among families was enough to build the reputation of the schools among the populace.[25] A few years later, the newspaper *Zaman* began publishing a Turkish-Turkmen language version in Aşgabat. Today it has that country's highest subscription rate for a periodical.[26] *Zaman* originated in Istanbul and is today printed separately in a handful of countries with a *cemaat* presence. For those who cannot obtain print copies, an electronic version of the Istanbul issue is accessible via the Internet. It announces local and international news, local school events and happenings within the Turkish school system, such as the scheduling of university entrance exams. A method for combining news and promoting the schools is to publish articles about such prestigious student events as a competition of language sponsored by Başkent and the Turkish and Afghanistan embassies' cultural attaches.[27]

The reputation of the Turkish schools is their most powerful form of advertisement and recruitment. In conversations with graduates of the Turkmen-Turkish University I asked how Turkmen people generally perceive a graduate of a Turkish school. They explained that they encounter some envy because they have had opportunities that are available to only a handful of the young population. Knowledge of English and Turkish, as well as Russian

---

23 Iveta Silova, "Reclaiming the empire in post-Soviet Asia: Turkish education initiatives towards Central Asia and Azerbaijan," in L. Chisolm & G. Steiner-Khamsi (eds.), South-south transfer: Cooperation and unequal development in education (forthcoming), p. 5.

24 Türkmen-Türk Mekdeplerinde Buýsançly 10 ýyl, 2005, p. 12.

25 Interview with Ahmet Çopursan June 7, 2007 in London, England.

26 This fact is a cause for concern within Turkmenistan's Democratic Party. Interview with member of Democratic Party, May 30, 2007.

27 Ibrahim Asalıoğlu, "ÖSS'deki sayısal sorular bu sene daha kolay olacak," ZAMAN, 14 Haziran 2007, p. 1; "Aşgabat dil sergisi," ZAMAN International Newspaper, May 8, 2004, pp. 1-2.

and Turkmen, make them competitive on the job market. Graduates from state schools may have studied one or two of these languages, or may know a smattering of each, but that cannot compare with the level of acquisition the Turkish schools' programs provide. Moreover, graduates reported that they are viewed as trustworthy and dependable because of the strict discipline of the Gülen schools. Any parent should be instilling a sense of *terbiýä* (upbringing) in their children, but it is never guaranteed that they do. A degree from a Turkish school certifies that the individual has been introduced to the traditional concepts of *adab* (enlightenment, culture, etiquette) and *terbiýä*, in addition to having received an internationally recognized education.[28]

If there is one aspect of the Başkent schools that is foreign to Turkmen students it is the gender separation in middle schools and the university. While Turkmen do practice separation of the sexes during religious events and some family gatherings, it is not typical of their modern educational spaces. Despite this, no one named it as a reason to avoid Başkent schools.[29]

There are families that will not send their children to the Turkish schools, or have even removed them from the schools, due to a perceived influence of Islam on the students. Some parents have complained that their children suddenly developed an interest in visiting the mosque or "developed a more religious attitude."[30] Even though there are no explicit lessons about Islam, "implicit cues about their Islamic orientation" can be detected in the behavior of teachers and in cultural programs on campuses.[31] This handful of dissatisfied families saw in the model living of teachers or in *terbiye* degree of spirituality that they could not reconcile with their expectations of secular education. Despite this minority attitude, a far greater number of families wish to enroll their children in the Turkish schools, even families who are not Muslim.[32]

Measuring Spiritual Influence

The Gülen schools have been successful in terms of education, but the extent of their spiritual influence is difficult to measure. Parents respect the Turkish schools for providing a broad curriculum with high standards, and they appreciate the technical advantages of these well-funded institutions and the level of discipline extolled by committed teachers. However, Turkmen families choose to send students to these schools not in search of Islamic enlightenment but as a means of gaining qualifications for employment.[33]

While independence in 1991 allowed for a surge in religious practice, Turkmenistan did not re-establish an Islamic-based system of public education like that which existed prior to their

---

28 Interview with ethnic Turkmen, male graduates of International Turkmen-Turk University, May 30, 2007. The fact that the Turkish schools meet international standards is most significant in Turkmenistan where the state had reduced the number of years of education available so that high-school graduates could not meet the requirements for international universities.

29 Victoria Clement, "Secular and Religious Trends in Turkmen Education," unpublished study for Eurasia Policy Studies Program, National Bureau of Asian Research, August 2004.

30 Interviews with Turkish graduates of ITTU, in Istanbul, Turkey, June 2007.

31 Engin Demir, Ayşe Balcı, and Fusun Akkok, "The Role of Turkish Schools in the Educational System and Social Transformation of Central Asian Countries: The case of Turkmenistan and Kyrgyzstan," Papers from the Central Asia Regional Literacy Forum, accessed at http://www.literacyonline.org/products/ili/webdocs/carlf_dem.html on 5/15/ 2007.

32 Ethnic Russian families report that they would rather have their children influenced by Turkish schools that teach international languages and business than Turkmenistan's schools which focus on the Ruhnama.

33 Private discussions with parents from varied economic backgrounds between 1997-2004. Clement, 2004.

incorporation into the Russian empire.[34] Rather, the government took steps to ensure that an official Islam, one overseen and limited by the state, was the public Islam. Firstly, academics and government officials replaced the Cyrillic script with a Latin-based alphabet rather than an Arabic-based writing system, thus separating them symbolically as modern or westward looking. Secondly, around the country citizens raised their own funds to build mosques in cities and villages, but prayer remained primarily a private pursuit in the home. Thirdly, a few *madrasas* (Islamic colleges) reopened in the earliest years of independence, but secular schooling remained the primary source for general education. Lastly, Islamic rituals were revived or practiced once again in public, but at no point did anyone suggest the state adopt more Islamic approaches. The thirst for spiritual growth and general education did not overlap explicitly.[35] Appreciative of secular, Soviet education, both citizens and the state eagerly maintained the separation between public education and Islam. Thus, in Turkmenistan, lessons with religious content are found only in a limited number of places such as the Ylahyýet fakultet at Magtumguly State University or in private classes that meet in mosques or the homes of Islamic scholars (*mollas, ahuns*). With an obvious interest in maintaining a separation between secular education and religion, how do Turkmen reconcile that view with the fact that the *cemaat*'s mission is rooted in Islam?

Turkmen parents view general education not as a means for spiritual development, but as path to getting a job. They expect schools to impart knowledge that will allow citizens to function in globalized or international society. Any contradiction between this conceptualization of education and the Gülen movement's faith-based goals is superseded by the fact that the Turkish educational institutions provide the best educational opportunity in Turkmenistan. Ultimately, Turkmen families do make allowances for an overlap between secular enlightenment and Gülen's faith-based initiative in acknowledging that education guided by a moral framework (*terbiýä*) would provide their children with better material opportunities. In that respect their expectations fit well with Gülen's belief that a good Muslim is one who is committed to the world. He clarifies this intersection of education and material advancement in today's world.

> I encouraged people to serve the country in particular, and humanity in general, through education.
> I called them to help the state educate and raise people by opening schools. Ignorance is defeated
> through education; poverty through work and the possession of capital; and internal schism and
> separatism through unity, dialogue, and tolerance.[36]

One of the Turkmen assistant principals asserted the practical aspect of the schools' curricula saying,

We need 'know how' for the development of our country. Those schools provide hope for us in achieving our purposes, because they train qualified people who are familiar with universal standards."[37]

---

34 See Adeeb Khalid, Islam after Communism: Religion and Politics in Central Asia (Berkeley: University of California Press, 2007). Non-Muslim groups also struggled with questions about social development and new expressions of local epistemology in the post-Soviet era. Alexia Bloch, Red Ties and Residential Schools: Indigenous Siberians in a Post-Soviet State (Philadelphia: University of Pennsylvania Press, 2004).

35 Olivier Roy, Globalized Islam: The search for a New Ummah (NY: Columbia, 2004), pp. 80, 190, 227-228.

36 M. Fethullah Gülen, 2005, p. 85.

37 Demir, Balcı and Akkok, Literacy Online, p. 6 of 10.

Making the Global Local: Gülen School's Adaptability to Local Contexts

In each country, the *cemaat* creates a "network" of schools.[38] This term does not imply that a singular overarching association or administration governs the members and schools around the world. Gülen inspires his followers. He is the teacher (*Hocaefendi*) and the author of influential writings, but there is no single formal entity to which the schools are responsible. Each school must consider local political and social conditions when creating a curriculum, admitting students, even in choosing the languages of instruction. For example, in Turkmenistan the Russian language was a part of all Gülen schools' curriculum until 2003, when Turkmenistan's president decreed that Russian should no longer be a language of instruction in schools. According to a former teacher, President Niyazow made an official announcement and the schools complied.[39] While the Turkish schools pride themselves on teaching foreign languages—indeed it is a fundamental aspect of Gülen's philosophy—they adhered to the policy immediately. Yet in Kazakhstan, where the tone is far less nationalistic, Russian remains in the Turkish schools. While a driving principle of the schools and related media is to encourage the spread of English (the international language of technology) and Turkish (language of the founder and most adherents) local languages demonstrate the movement's "state-oriented" inclination to work within systems.[40] The adaptability the Gülen system allows it to flourish beyond the Turkic language world. Moreover, the schools can be, and are, located in countries without a Muslim majority. There are as yet no schools in Arab speaking countries, but the flexible nature of the model makes it at least theoretically possible to use the Gülen educational system in any country.

Hakan Yavuz describes the "movement" as a "loose network system" consisting primarily of shared values as well as methods of teaching and organizing schools, for example, drawing teachers and administrators from within the core community, relying on similar texts and curricula, and the concept of a teacher living as a model. Each set of schools is organized separately within a particular country, in cooperation with that country's government, and is funded through a locally established company or foundation. The sources of funding are critical clues to demonstrating the independence of each school system. Businessmen living in Kazakhstan provide financial support to the *Kazakh-Türk Eğitim Vakfı* which then oversees the institutions in that country. Monies from schools in the Balkans are not shared with those in Kyrgyzstan. In Turkmenistan it is the *Başkent Bilim Şirketi* (Bashkent Educational Firm) that organizes funding, while successful businessmen (*işadamı* and *esnaf*) fund the movement and its schools.[41] Donations to such foundations allow the middle class to contribute to the shaping of society, fulfill an act of piety (*zakat*), and aid in building an active community. Turks living abroad, in Central Asia for example, also assist in the creation of schools at which their children can receive a quality education.

The firms or foundations represent the concerted efforts of teachers and sponsors to offer

---

38   Jean-François Mayer, "Gülen Movement: Modern Expression of Turkish Islam. Interview with Hakan Yavuz," Religioscope, 21 July 2004. http://religion.info/english/interviews/article_74.html.

39   Interview with Ahmet Çopursan June 7, 2007 in London, England. Ahmet Bey was a teacher and head of the Department of History at the boy's koleg in Konya Urgenç—2 years, Abadan (former Buzmeýin)-2 years, Ata Murat (formerly Kerki)—2 years, as well as the Başkent Education Center in Aşgabat—3 years. He lived with his wife and children, one of whom was born in Ashgabat (at the Turkish hospital).

40   Bayram Balci uses the term "state oriented" to describe the cemaat's tendency to cooperate with local governments.

41   M. Hakan Yavuz, Islamic Political Identity in Turkey (Oxford: Oxford University Press, 2003), p. 189.

socially conscious education grounded in teaching modern sciences (*talim*) with an international focus. Yet course offerings do not include religious instruction. "Gülen's group differentiates itself from other Islamic movements by stressing the importance of ethics in education and the business world."[42]

> These schools don't give religious education or encompass educational activities with a religious environment...Activities take place within the framework of each country's current laws and educational philosophy. For example, in Uzbekistan, after students learn Turkish and English in the preparatory class, they study science in English from Turkish teachers and social subjects in Uzbek from Uzbek teachers. Giving religious knowledge or religious education is not the goal.[43]

The aim of the schools is not to teach religion per se, but to stress such values as community service (*hizmet*) and ethics (*ahlak*), which are seen as "unifying factors between different religious, ethnic, and political orientations."[44] *Terbiyä* (character building) is critical to raising good Muslims and is the principal concept by which the schools are organized. Using the phrase "bilim we terbiyä" no less than eight times in a single presentation, Seyit Embel, the Chair of the Başkent Educational Center in Aşgabat wrote that "enlightenment and character building are the main aims" of the combined Turkmen and Turkish efforts.[45]

The underlying methodology of conveying *terbiyä* has been for the teachers to embody spiritual ideals and impart them through model living (*temsil*).[46] Gülen has addressed this methodology writing,

Those who lead the way must set a good example for their followers. Just as they are imitated in their virtues and good morals, so do their bad and improper actions and attitudes leave indelible marks upon those who follow them.[47]

Teachers, administrators and sponsors follow Fethullah Gülen's example of teaching students how to live a life deeply rooted both in Islam and in the modern scientific world via education.[48] Model living covers a range of moral behavior such as restraint from smoking, drinking, or gambling.[49] Teachers make themselves available to students outside of school.[50] After school activities (sports, movies, lectures) and informal relations with staff are designed to encourage character building. Women's reading circles meet in the homes of families to allow for congregation and study. These typically involve the mothers and older women in the Turkish community, but students and local mothers are welcome.

Throughout Central Asia the Gülen schools play an important role in fledgling civil societies in that they operate outside of the state. They offer opportunities for social interaction and experimentation such as student newspapers, women's reading circles, film festivals (in

---

42 Yavuz, 2003, p. 186.

43 Ali Bayramoglu's observations cited in M. Fethullah Gülen, Essays, Perspectives, Opinions (Rutherford: NJ, The Light Inc, 2002), p. 87.

44 Bekim Agai, "The Gülen Movement's Islamic Ethic of Education," in Yavuz and Esposito, 2003, p. 49.

45 "Bilim we terbiyäniň asyl maksady..." in Seýit Embel, "Ata Watanda buýsançly on ýyl," Türkmen-Türk Mekdeplerinde Buýsançly 10 ýyl (Aşgabat: Türkmen-Türk mektepleriniň baş müdirlgi, 2005), p. 11.

46 Elisabeth Özdalga, "Following in the Footsteps of Fethullah Gülen: Three Women tell their Stories," in Yavuz and Esposito, 2003, p. 85. While an Instructor at ITTU, I lived in the on-campus dormitory with the female students.

47 M. Fethullah Gülen, Essays, Perspectives, Opinions (Rutherford, NJ: The Fountain, 2002), p. 72.

48 M. Hakan Yavuz, "Turkish Identity Politics and Central Asia," in Sagdeev and Eisenhower, Islam in Central Asia: An Enduring Legacy or An Evolving Threat? (Washington, D.C.: CPSS, 2000), pp. 193-211.

49 Interview with Ahmet Çopursan June 7, 2007 in London, England.

50 Interview with teachers and students, 2004.

Turkmenistan all cinemas were shut down in 2002), study abroad programs and use of the internet. Most importantly, these private schools offer families a choice in education. One difference between the schools in Central Asia and some other regions—South Asia for example—is that former Soviet regions had high literacy rates but little opportunity for civil society building.[51] In Turkmenistan, a country with arguably the most seriously deficient education policy in the region and one of the worst records on allowances for civil society, the contributions of the Gülen movement are especially impressive. Moreover, because of deficiencies within Turkmenistan's educational system, the graduates of the Turkish schools in Turkmenistan are the only youth in a generation to receive a high-school education that meets international standards.[52]

Another aspect of the Gülen schools in Turkmenistan that sheds light on the movement more broadly is the community's interaction with that country's government. Until recently, it was understood that Turkish businessmen often contributed to the financing of these schools in Turkmenistan as a necessary step in the bidding process for contracts with that Niyazow's government. "It was understood during the trip that Turkmen officials stipulate that businessmen first make a financial contribution to the Turkish high schools in order to be able to win contracts from the Turkmenistan government."[53] This comments perhaps more on Niyazow's methods of governing than it does on the Gülen schools more generally. It does illustrate the "state-oriented" nature of the movement. The privileged place of Turkish businessmen in Turkmenistan has continued under the new presidency of Gurbanguly Berdymukhmedow

In Turkmenistan engaging that state has meant actually placing Turkish members of the *cemaat* in high-level government positions. Muammer Turkyılmaz, Turkmenistan's Deputy Education Minister (*Turkmenistan Bilim Ministerligiň Orunbasar*) and Seyit Embel, Head of the Bashkent Educational Center (*Başkent Bilim Merkeziniň Baş Ugrukdyryjysy*), have been critical to Başkent's success and demonstrate the movement's adaptability. In the initial years Turks held most administrative posts. As part of Turkmenistan's *Milli Galkynyş Hereketi* (National Revival Movement) President Niyazow mandated in 2004 that only ethnic Turkmen could be heads of schools. Today the Rector of the International Turkmen-Turkish University is an ethnic Turkmen as are the principals of the schools. Turks occupy only assistant principal or secondary administrative positions. However, Embel and Türkyılmaz remain in their positions demonstrating that there is flexibility in the relationship with the state. In fact, in March 2007 the new president of Turkmenistan, Berdymuhammedow, confirmed the state's appreciation of Türkyılmaz's work in Turkmenistan by reappointing him as Deputy Minister of Education.[54] Overall, the *cemaat's* success owes much to a long-term view of its goals and its avoidance of postures that could be interpreted by local authorities as antagonistic. As Hakan Yavuz and other scholars have indicated, this *modus vivendi* is seen not only in Turkmenistan, but also in the movement's approach globally.[55]

51 Mohamed Nawab Mohd Osman, "Turkey's Gülen movement and global Islamic activism," Rajaratnam School of International Studies reprinted http:www.isn.ethz.ch/news/sw/details.cfm?id=17551.

52 Clement, 2005.

53 "Fethullah Gülen's Missionaries, Turkish Daily News, September 14, 2001.

54 "Türkmen Milli Eğitimi, Türk Okullarının Kurucusuna Emanet," Haberler, March 2007, p. 1.

55 M. Hakan Yavuz and John Esposito, Turkish Islam and the Secular State: The Gülen Movement (Syracuse: Syracuse University Press, 2003).

Conclusion

Professor John Esposito writes that today's *ummah* is engaged in a process of "Islamisation or re-Islamisation." That is, they seek ways to apply "Islamic principles and values to personal and public life."[56] While the Muslim community may today be experiencing a transition, it is not the *ummah*'s first encounter with change. Introspection, debate, reform (*ijtihad*), and renewal (*tajdid*) are natural and historically significant aspects of Islam. Since its inception the Muslim community has debated such questions as how the community would be shaped, whether it was acceptable to borrow aspects of other cultures, or how they could live as Muslims in the material, modernizing world. Scholars view the Gülen movement as part of this tradition, calling it "*neo-ijtihad*" or "search for a middle way."[57]

The Gülen movement strives to demonstrate the compatibility of Islam and modernity through intellectual and spiritual pursuits. Calls for "A*ksiyon*" and morality based living have encouraged followers who are motivated to actively pursue charitable roles in building successful Muslim societies. The Gülen schools are a manifestation of that motivation.[58] The Gülen school system has been successful in so many different countries because of its flexibility and adaptability to local conditions.

Any contributions of the Gülen movement must be measured not only according to the standards of the movement, but also to the relative conditions of each specific locality in which members expand the *cemaat*, as well as within a historical context. Overall, the Gülen schools in Central Asia are comparable to Gülen schools around the world.[59] With the exception of occasional foreigners teaching languages or locals teaching social subjects, teachers are hired from within the predominantly Turkish *cemaat* or from among the schools own graduates. The privately-funded schools remain independent of any state but do adhere to legal and educational requirements of the host countries; curricula are based on integrating quality education, emphasizing science and languages, with *terbiyä* (upbringing within a moral framework); and religion is never part of curricula. Graduates play a great role in staffing the schools and Turkish businessmen make up the majority of donors.

This case study of the schools in Turkmenistan illustrates how Gülen's philosophy plays out *in situ*. While a vital part of a faith-based movement, it is critical to acknowledge that Gülen-inspired schools offer families a choice in secular education thereby making contributions to civil society building as well as education. Turkmenistan's parents feel that their children receive better education, through high quality teaching, including use of Turkish, English, and Russian, in addition to the local language.[60] They also note that the Turkish schools are better equipped than state schools and have more advanced facilities (comfortable dormitories, good cafeterias, access to technology).[61]

---

56 John Esposito and Francis Burgat, eds. Modernizing Islam: Religion in the Public Sphere in Europe and the Middle East (New Brunswick: Rutgers University Press, 2003), p. 2.

57 John Voll, "Transcending Modernity," Ihsan Yılmaz, "Ijtihad and Tajdid by Conduct," and Ahmet T. Kuru "Fethullah Gülen's Search for a Middle Way between Modernity and Muslim Tradition," in Yavuz and Esposito, 2003, p. 246, 208-237, and 115-130.

58 John Voll, "Renewal and Reformation in the Mid-Twentieth Century: Bediüzzaman Said Nursi and Religion in the 1950s," The Muslim World, Vol. 89, No. 3-4, 1999, pp. 245-59.

59 Bayram Balci, "Fethullah Gülen's Missionary Schools in Central Asia and their Role in Spreading of Turkism and Islam," Religion, State & Society, Vol. 31, No. 2, 2003, pp. 151-177.

60 For comparable views see Yasar Sari, "Turkish Schools and Universities in Kyrgyzstan," The Times of Central Asia, June 8, 2006, p. 22.

61 A. Apay's analysis of parents' opinions of Turkish schools in Uzbekistan and Kyrgyzstan concur with my

Muslim and non-Muslim families want high quality education that is not politicized and remains secular. States want institutions to respect their authority. The government in Uzbekistan closed the 18 Gülen schools there as well as the Turkish state schools. The atmosphere in Kyrgyzstan is simply more tolerant and allows for diversity in education. The Kyrgyz-Turkish schools sponsored by the *Sebat* Company have grown from 12 to 15 from 1997-2007.[62] In Kazakhstan the schools have played a role in the population's hunger to revive a Turco-Islamic heritage that was weakened by its Soviet experience. The Foundation for Kazak-Turkish Education (*Kazak-Turk Egitim Vakfı*) acts as both a cultural center and an organization of civil society.[63] Turkmenistan's government has kept the schools on a short leash but it nevertheless allows them to operate as long as they pay homage to the state. This works because Turkish administrators attend Turkmen state functions and a small percentage of the curriculum gives the obligatory nod to state demands, such as including Niyazow's writings in coursework.

Başkent schools continue to function in Turkmenistan because the *cemaat* preserves a modern, secular curriculum content, takes an unobtrusive approach to imparting *terbiyä*, and does not threaten the state, but rather engages it. In offering a quality education based in foreign languages (English, Turkish, Russian, and local) and natural sciences, the Gülen Movement provides Turkmenistan's youth an opportunity to prepare themselves as citizens of the new (post-Soviet) world order.[64] The success of these private, foreign schools, founded on Islamic values (*terbiye, ahlak, adab*) in a country where state-controlled, political idolatry had supplanted pedagogy, is perhaps the Gülen movement's greatest accomplishment in Eurasia.

---

own conclusion about Turkmenistan. See his "Turkish Higher Education Initiatives toward Central Asia," in The Challenge of Education in Central Asia, Stephen P. Heyneman and Alan J. DeYoung eds, (Greenwich, CT: InfoAgePub Inc, 2004), p. 82. See also Engin Demir, Ayşe Balcı, and Fusun Akkok, "The Role of Turkish Schools in the Educational System and Social Transformation of Central Asian Countries: The case of Turkmenistan and Kyrgyzstan," Central Asian Survey, 19, no. 1, 2000, pp. 141-55.

62 Demir, Balcı and Akkok, 2000, p. 149; Silova, forthcoming, p. 5.

63 Berna Turam, "National Loyalties and International Undertakings," Georgetown University, April 26-27, 2001. While the number of schools in Kazakhstan went down from 29-23 from 1997-2006, they still remain active and important. In 2006/07 5,613 Kazakh students graduated from schools run by the Turkish company Feza et Şelale. See Silova, forthcoming, p. 5.

64 M. Aydin "Turkey and Central Asia: Challenges of Change" Central Asian Survey, Vol. 15, No. 2, pp. 157-177.

"A STATION ABOVE THAT OF ANGELS": THE VISION OF ISLAMIC EDUCATION WITHIN PLURALISTIC SOCIETIES IN THE THOUGHT OF FETHULLAH GÜLEN - A STUDY OF CONTRASTS BETWEEN TURKEY AND THE UK

Ian Williams

Abstract

Gülen cites 'Ali ibn Abi Talib as saying, '... if a person's intellect dominates his or her desire and ferocity, he or she rises to a station above that of angels ...'.

Both historically as well as in modern contexts Muslim education is not characterised by uniformity but rather by a plurality of actors, institutions, ideas and political milieus. The two central questions are: What is required to live as a Muslim in the present world? Who is qualified to teach in this time? The debate over the nature and purpose of Islamic education is no recent phenomenon. It has been conducted for the past two centuries throughout the Islamic world: the transmission of both spiritual and empirical knowledge has always been dependent upon the support of religious, social and political authorities.

Based on fieldwork in Turkey and the UK amongst schools associated with the Gülen movement, examination of national government policies and on readings of contemporary Muslim educationalists, this paper seeks to examine the ideals of Fethullah Gülen on contemporary Islamic and religious education. It reports critically on the contribution of these schools to social cohesion, inter-religious dialogue and common ambitions for every child and student.

We should accept the fact that there is a specific way of being Muslim, which reflects the Turkish understanding and practices in those regions [which] stretch from Central Asia to the Balkans. [Ocak 1996 79]

Islam, a rich and strong tradition in many diverse societies is both a living faith and in every generation has been the means of enabling Muslims to address social developments, justice, and both corporate and individual questions of identity and ethics. Drawing on the Qur'an, *Hadith*, *Sunnah* and *fiqh* new Islamic social movements have constantly formed fresh public spaces in which new identities and lifestyles could emerge. Some of the finest expressions of Islam have occurred in the most pluralist religio-social circumstances when intellectual discourse, educational achievements and social harmony have flourished. Amongst contemporary Islamic thinkers who are professedly concerned to interpret the sources and their practice in an "Islamically correct" manner is Fethullah Gülen [b. 1938], the spiritual father of what is probably the most active Turkish-Islamic movement of the late 20th and early 21st centuries. In considering this movement however, one soon realizes that Fethullah Gülen is neither an innovator with a new and unique theology nor a revolutionary. His understanding of Islam is oriented within the conservative mainstream and his arguments are rooted in the traditional sources of Islam. They stand in a lineage represented as I shall argue through al-Ghazali, Mevlana Jalal ud-Din Rumi, Bediuzzaman Said Nursi, and in company with Muhammad Asad and Muhammad Naquib Syed Al-Attas, and Seyyed Hossein Nasr. Nonetheless, in less than thirty years his followers as Islamic activists have made significant contributions to inter-communal and national peace, inter-religious dialogue, economic development, and most certainly in the field of education out of all proportion to their numbers. Moreover, this is a de-centralised polymorphic social movement.

A Classical and a Contemporary Model of Education

In the classical period of Islam's expansion in the 10th and 11th centuries ce one of that era's significant scholars and educators and indeed regarded as such throughout the history of Islam was Imam Abu Hamid Muhammad al-Ghazali [1058 - 1111]. According to Al-Ghazali,

> …knowledge exists potentially in the human soul like the seed in the soil; by learning the potential becomes actual…. [Al-Ghazali, 1995 167]

The child, Al-Ghazali wrote,

> …is a trust (placed by God) in the hands of his parents, and his innocent heart is a precious element capable of taking impressions. [Al-Ghazali, 1998. 145]

The way the child relates to the world at large occupies a large concern in Al-Ghazali's mind. In concert with Ibn Al-Hajj [1258 – 1336], he stresses the moral and spiritual development of a child. So, alongside and in harmony with his or her development intellectually and in expertise there is the nurturing and flourishing of *tarbiyya* i.e. the development of correct manners, etiquette, attitudes towards parents, elders and teachers and spiritual observances. Thus as a child grows he or she understands that to love money is fruitless; he or she learns to respect rules of cleanliness; to begin fasting in Ramadan; and to avoid ostentatious clothes and jewellery. *Tarbiyyah* involves speaking with courtesy; and living towards God as he has revealed the ways for faithful people to act; and consequently to regard every human as he or she would like to be treated.

The perspective of Al-Ghazali centres upon personal effort in the search for truth; and this presupposes, he insists, a received education and the direction of a master. Education (*tarbiyyah*), Al-Ghazali states in *Ayyuha l-walad* is like "the labour of the farmer, who uproots the weeds, trims wheat so as it grows better and gives a better harvest." [1995: 267]. Every pupil needs a teacher to guide him or her in the right direction. To try to do so without leads to the worst illusions. In *Ayyuha l-walad* the pupil's outward respect for his or her teacher is evidence of esteem for such a person in their heart.

Even more on this matter, in *Ihya Ulum al-Din*, the teacher, Al-Ghazali holds, carries eight duties. Primarily he or she is a parent for a pupil. Teaching is for the sake of God. Prudence should be the mark of counsel for a student. Any reprimand must be moderate and in private rather than in public. In addition, one other duty of the teacher is to make sure that what he or she teaches is pursued in his or her own life and that their actions do not contradict their words.

In a similar fashion Fethullah Gülen as a modern Muslim thinker has reflected upon the ideals of an Islamic education, the character of the teacher and the demeanour of the pupil and student. In his writings, he seeks conciliation between the empirical sciences, which are concerned with the material world, and *tarbiyyah, which* is the focus of the spiritual realms. According to Gülen this reunion occurs with the presence of knowledge and love. Knowledge is the province of the sciences and provides students with the intellectual abilities to benefit others. Alone, however, the sciences are insufficient in leading people to benefit others. Love is essential.

For Gülen [2002. 41], "Love is a person's most essential element" By love, Gülen means self-sacrificing love that initiates action by absolute obedience to God and out of concern for others rather than individual reward or utilitarian calculations for one's happiness. This love entails self-sacrifice, self-denial, and a personal conviction to transform life on earth [Yavuz, 2003, 34]. Such a love is the basis of true pedagogy.

Consequently, not all teachers are educators in Fethullah Gülen's perspective as he asserts "Education is different from teaching. Most people can teach, but only a very few can educate" [2004, 208]. Teaching, in other words, is merely the conveying of knowledge; whilst education involves giving knowledge but also imparting self-sacrificing love and moral guidance:

> True teachers sow the pure seed and preserve it. They occupy themselves with what is good and wholesome, and lead and guide the children through life and whatever events they may encounter. [Gülen, 2004, 208b.]

Thus, teaching is a spiritual activity and to enable students to embrace change and to be transformed is a teacher's "foremost duty" [Gülen, 1998 & 2004]. Teachers are responsible for providing knowledge with the wisdom to use it and for providing moral guidance by embodying spirituality and love.

The objective of Gülen's educational vision is to raise a "Golden Generation," a generation of ideal universal individuals, individuals who love truth, who integrate spirituality and knowledge, who work to benefit society [Gülen, 1998]. Such a person is *zul-cenaheyn* "one who possesses two wings," exhibiting a "marriage of mind and heart" [Gülen, 1996b] with a merging of spiritual and ethical values with contemporary science and understanding [Gülen,

2004] This will create a "genuinely enlightened people" [Gülen, 1996a] who will altruistically be servants to others. [Gülen, 2000].

> If we really wish our children to have faith, all our attitudes and sensitivities in certain subjects, the way we go to bed and get up, the way we exert ourselves in prayer, the way we spread our affectionate wings over our children, must all reflect our faith in Allah and their hearts must be filled with such faith. We should always try to be the ideal for them, to avoid any kind of behaviour, which might make them feel contempt for us.
>
> We should always try to maintain dignity and to remain elevated in their view, so that what we tell them will influence their hearts and they will not rebel against our wishes. In this respect, it can be said that a father who lacks seriousness can probably be the friend of his children; but he can never be their teacher, and he will fail to bring them up the way he wants. [Gülen, Bringing up a Child with Multiple Abilities, http://en.fgülen.com. 11.26.2004a]

This vision has led Gülen and his followers from the 1980's have to initiate an educational project of building institutions in different parts of the world. In Turkey, the Caucuses, Africa, Russia, and the Philippines amongst several socio-geographical contexts hundreds of schools with seven universities have been founded serving diverse religious communities and those of no faith affiliation [Agai 2007. 159].

These institutions resemble other schools in terms of curriculum and resources, IT and laboratory facilities, language teaching and expertise are of a high standard, which result in creditable achievements by students. This is acknowledged by a range of observers and certainly in my fieldwork examination of such schools in Turkey, the USA and Africa. [Agai, 2003; 48-68; Balci, 2003; 151-176; Özdalga, 2000; Yavuz, 2003]. Michel [2003. 70] comments that the student in these schools and higher education institutions have outstanding performance in academic competitions in the natural sciences, information sciences, and languages, and he considers them "to be among the most dynamic and worthwhile educational enterprises ... in the world"

Two Contemporary Contexts in Contrast

The two foci of this paper viz the UK and Turkey have and are both witnessing and forging changes within their respective educational systems to meet the demands of modern economies, globalization, and the creation of socially cohesive if pluralist societies

In the UK we have as the means of education for children and young people from the age of four to eighteen years a "dual system". In essence, a hybrid model of both state, independent, and faith sector provision. A further refinement of this system however, is that whilst we may refer to the "UK" as a single entity state it is also with devolved government to Scotland [1998], Wales [1998], and Ulster [2007] a "four nations state". Powers are devolved in education and other areas to the respective national assemblies in Edinburgh, Cardiff, and Belfast. Consequently, whilst my research focuses upon the English and Welsh contexts of educational provision it is still applicable to the wider "UK" with its common structure of state, independent, and faith schools. Arguably, in the UK we face continuing debate and government initiatives to create a holistic model of education i.e. a broad and balanced curriculum and ethos based on an understanding of the full potential of the human being and a system of pedagogy designed to awaken and develop that potential.

However, a process has also faced us since 1988 with bureaucracy, league tables, school inspection regimens, target setting and quantification. In essence, these are managerially controlled objectives with a narrow prescriptive content. Behind these policies is an agenda of education that until recently has been aligned to a utilitarian concept of schooling with a reduction of truly holistic education to a narrow band of skills for the workplace. The goals have been centered upon economic performance, competition, and efficiency above all else.

The then DfES [Department for Education and Skills] proposed in a White Paper, *Schools: Achieving Success* [DfES, 2001] such a policy and openly stated it in the document's introduction.

> The success of our children at school is crucial to the economic health and social cohesion of the country, as well as to their own life chances and personal fulfillment. [DfES. 2001. 8]

We need to note the priorities which are placed first in the sentence.. The response from the Church of England's Board of Education was salutary.

> The Church of England's Board of Education has welcomed the Government White Paper, Schools achieving success, published today, but warned against any erosion of the place of religious education and spiritual development in the curriculum.

> On plans to develop 'Education with Character', Canon Hall welcomed the idea but warned, "We shall be particularly interested in the introduction of flexibility into the 14 to 19 curriculum, to ensure that the place of religious education and spiritual development is not eroded. [http://www. cofe.anglican.org/news, 05/09/2001]

Certainly, the 1988 Education Reform Act introduced by the then Conservative Government of Mrs. Margaret Thatcher had stated that the newly instituted National Curriculum would

> ...promote the spiritual, moral, cultural, mental and physical development of pupils at the school and of society... [and that]... the curriculum for every maintained school shall comprise a basic curriculum which includes - (a) provision for religious education for all registered pupils at the school. [http://www.opsi.gov.uk/acts/acts1988].

During the period of Conservative Governments from 1979 – 1997 faith based schools were perceived as integral to the "dual system" partnership of education especially as they seemed to respond to parental i.e. client demand for such a model of education in a free market economy [Parker-Jenkins, Hartas & Irving 2005]. Significant debate continued through this time however, on the definition of "spiritual" and "spirituality" as aspects of the curriculum. Did they suffuse the programmes of study in the empirical sciences, aesthetic and creative arts, and the humanities, or were they the preserve of Religious Education?

In Religious Education for example, there may be a moment when "learning about religion" in beliefs, rituals or places of pilgrimage is transformed into "learning from religion" with silence, music, art, personal affirmations of faith, or accounts of visits to significant places. This is the transition from the objective teaching and study of religion to an inward experience, addressing existential questions of ultimate concern, and encounter with mystery. Tillich notes "...such an experience presupposes that the spiritual life is taken seriously, that is as a matter of ultimate concern." [Tillich 1962. 54]. Education in this perception becomes spiritual whenever a lesson that is being delivered irrespective of the subject moves beyond the mundane into the supramundane and faces issues of the fundamental meaning and purpose of life. Fethullah Gülen writes in a similar vein,

> Those believing souls who are capable of considering the location and the position of the world with its place and importance before God can acquire oceans as wide as the universe from this droplet; possess the stars and the sun through this miniature universe; transform the limited time

spent on it into an eternal life time. All of these are possible, if all the abilities entrusted to or hidden in the essence of the human being are used rightly without being squandered.

> In reality, for those who can see with the light of faith, all these beauties folded into one another are only clear signs of His Divine Being, and the human being is an interpreter who can read and understand those signs. The matter shows the path to the secrets beyond the seen to those believers who can filter events through intellect, consciousness, and feelings within a balance. Through time divine secrets diffuse into their souls, and their hearts become observatories of the Divine Attributes. In this way, the torments originating from not knowing the Creator are torn away and they disappear; light covers all. [Gülen 2004c]

Gülen is arguing for a distinction between "ordinary" and "extraordinary" knowledge that is implicit in the ideals of UK education but explicit in the Turkish foundation schools sponsored by his communities. Thus, "everyday education" is transformed into "unexpectedly spiritual" education when learning ceases to glide over the surface facts of a subject and commences to come to grips with issues of ultimate significance and truth that frame the very marrow of our humanity and eternal destiny. Without such ultimate concerns Gülen argues that our lives lack passion, focus, seriousness, selfless service and creativity; with such passion however a new generation,

> ... will pour out to the needy hearts the purest inspirations of their hearts, which are nourished in the higher realms and they will bring forth the newest formations in all sections of society. The inauspiciousness and waste, the insanity, obsessions, and delirium of successive generations in our near past occurred, to a great extent, because they had not met such a generation of hope. [The Generations of Hope – I   http://en.fgülen.com 2005]

This is evident in the "Turkish" schools that I have visited in the USA, Turkey, and the Transcaucasian states where a generation of gifted Turkish graduates are teaching a curriculum in a spiritual way without overt reference to religious propositions and explicit religious education.

Prior to the 1997 UK General Election the then leader of the [new] Labour Party Mr. Tony Blair who was to become Prime Minister had promised that "Education, Education, Education" would be the "number one" priority for a new government under his leadership. In 2002, five years later after another successful election victory that year Mr. Blair as Prime Minister reiterated his commitment to education. Nevertheless, it might be asked what kind of education? In an interview reported in the *Times Educational Supplement* of July 5, 2002, Blair stated that

> Education is and remains the absolute number one priority for the country because without a quality education system and an educated workforce, we cannot succeed economically.

> He defended the "ladder" of schools outlined by Ms Morris with strugglers at the bottom of five categories and beacon and specialist schools at the top. "It is not a hierarchy. It is an escalator. It is not a case of penalising schools that are not specialising. We are increasing funding for all. [TES, 05 / 07 / 2002.]

The real priority was clear and identified with the previous year's White Paper viz. that economic power governed educational policy.

In John Taylor Gatto's work *Dumbing Us Down: The Hidden Curriculum of Compulsory Schooling*, David H. Albert refers to the words of the social philosopher Hannah Arendt that "The aim of totalitarian education has never been to instill convictions but to destroy the capacity to form any." [Gatto 2000. 46]

Gatto questions both the suppositions and configurations which underlie modern state education in his case within the USA but which are also present in UK government educational policy. It is a process, which stresses economic goals and moulding children who are dependent, conforming, materialistic, and lacking in curiosity, imagination, self-knowledge, and powers of reflection.

Supporting the utilitarian agenda in the United Kingdom, and also fuelled by pressure to do well in league tables of performance, is a vigorous testing regime of schools and curriculum delivery. A research project however, initiated by the National Union of Teachers and the University of Warwick's Institute of Education in 2003 revealed,

> Respondents felt most strongly that testing narrowed the curriculum, and distorted the educational experience of children. They felt that excessive time, workload, and stress for children were not justified by the accuracy of the test results on individuals. [Neill 2003. 3]

Almost half the weekly timetable in schools in England and Wales can now taken up by numeracy and literacy teaching with children as young as seven are being tested every week on their reading. The disproportionate emphasis on the teaching and perpetual testing of a narrow band of literacy and numeracy skills, which are deemed essential for economic survival, removes the heart and soul out of education. Neill concluded that teaching each day did not allow for a broad and balanced curriculum, and that creative subjects such as art, drama, and music were being increasingly eroded out of the classroom [Neill 2003. 9]. Subsequent government policy statements have reiterated these practices and broadened the purview of education to embrace additional dimensions of children's well-being [DfES 2003a and 2003b].

The development of education in modern Turkey since 1922 may be cryptically summarized in words of Hannah Arendt,

> The quest for meaning, which relentlessly dissolves and examines anew all accepted doctrines and rules, can at any moment turn against itself, produce a reversal of the old values, and declare these contraries to be new values. [Arendt, 1978. 176]

Following the demise of the Ottoman Empire one of the first legislative proposals of the new republic was the "Law of Unification of Instruction". The pluralism of the empire it was thought had prevented the Turkish people from realizing their nationhood; thus by placing all educational institutions but the military academies under the Ministry of Education a single national identity would be attained.

Drawing upon theories of corporate solidarism and collective consciousness the sociologist Ziya Gokalp [1876 - 1924] propounded ideas that remain influential in Turkish pedagogy. Essentially, he argued that the decline of the Ottoman sphere was a result of unequal and incompatible systems of knowledge. Civilisations and cultures could be placed in an evolutionary typology with Western / European modernity as the zenith.

> In this country there are three layers of people differing from each other in civilization and education: the common people, the men educated in medreses, the men educated in modern [secular] schools.............That means that one portion of our nation is living in an ancient, another in a medieval, and a third in a modern age. How can the life of the nation be normal with such a threefold life? How can we be a real nation without unifying this threefold education? [Gokalp 1959. 278.]

For Gokalp this unification of education in order to coalesce the new nation's citizens involved combining the best aspects of each civilisational stream and rejecting their respective weaknesses. These would embrace the Turkish national myth and a rational Islam together with Western empirical science and technology. Moreover, Gokalp reinterpreted two established concepts of knowledge viz, *terbiye* and *talim* respectiely until that time representing moral behaviour as understood by al-Ghazali and Qur'anic focused knowledge. For Gokalp they would now mean national culture within which Islam would reside as an aspect and empirical knowledge. This pedagogical understanding suffused subsequent state educational policy under Mustapha Kemal Ataturk [1881 – 1938] the republic's first President except that religion was no longer seen as an instrument of creating a Turkish national identity.

In contrast to developments in the UK, in this period the early Turkish republican implementation of educational policies undertook a descralisation process. This course of action reached its peak between 1933 – 1935 when the Hagia Sofia in Istanbul was converted symbolically into a museum, religious titles were abolished, wearing of distinctive religious dress outside places of worship was prohibited, Sunday became the satte day of rest, and texts connected with religion were proscribed from libraries. It would only be during the 1939 – 1945 global conflict when Turkey adopted a neutral stance until early 1945 that religion and Islam in particular re-entered the public domain [Kaplan 2006. 86].

With the reintroduction of multi-party politics from 1950 advocates and opponents of either the teaching of Islam or the involvement of observant Muslims in Turkish education would become a considerable area of debate. The history of the Turkish Republic however, is a series of defining moments and dates, which was exemplified on 18th September 1990 with the publication of a report on the state of Turkish education [Baloglu, 1990]. Sponsored by the prominent Turkish Industrialists' and Businessmen's Association [*Turk Sanayici velis Adamlari Deregi*: TUSIAD] it drew attention to the shortcomings of the curriculum and the brevity of compulsory education. Equally, however, the report questioned how the reappearance of the Imam Hatip middle and high religious schools could enhance national unity and educational achievement.

Paradoxically, even the secular ideology of education in Turkey uses discourse that reflects Qur'anic and historic Muslim ideals. A school is a second home, fellow pupils and students are akin to brothers and sisters, and teachers are compared to parents in their status [Gil'adi 1992. 83]. Opponents and sceptics of religious schools have emphasised the importance of Turkey entering the Western / European area of liberal capitalism and scientific-technological advance; whilst promoters of religious schooling have stressed the values of Islam as keys to national renewal and stability. The Turkish national elections of 2007 embraced such a debate in the area of education amongst others as signifiers of national unity and character in a diverse society.

Such a debate as I will now consider also continues about UK education and its strategic place in framing a national identity of citizenship. In this context as in Turkey the place of religion and the participation of faith traditions in education and their framing of social capital is both contested and promoted. In both situations, the Gülen sponsored model of schools and higher education offers a pedagogic praxis and a dialogic instrument of an alternative middle way.

"Faith Schools" or Schools With "Faith"?

The existence of "Faith Sector" schools in the UK dates back to the introduction of state education in 1870, when state-funded schools supplemented, and state funding assisted, the existing provision of schools by churches and other groups. This 'dual system' has continued until today, with several categories of state funded faith schools: 'voluntary controlled', where the local education authority provides all of the funding in return for control notably over the governing body; and 'voluntary aided', where the voluntary organisation provides 10% of the budget in return for having more control over religious education and governing body. Christian [Church of England and Roman Catholic] and Jewish Faith traditions adopted this cooperative existence. A complex history therefore, lies behind the current situation. Not all Christian traditions however, accepted this pattern; members of the Free Churches in the late 19th c preferred to face legal penalties rather than support Anglican or even Roman Catholic schools by local taxation [Chadwick 2001. 475-487].

An additional complexity was introduced in 1998 when schools with a religious foundation other than Christianity and Judaism could enter this system and in particular Muslim schools. A survey of articles and letters to the educational and general press during 2001–2002, given the significant events that occurred during that period, revealed an element of racism and Islamophobia in the objections to state-funded faith schools (Cush, 2003. 10-15).

For example, a MORI poll conducted for the *Times Educational Supplement* in November 2001 revealed that only 27% opposed the increase in Church schools, whereas the figure rose to 43% when Muslim and Sikh schools were added to the question [Jackson 2001.2-6 & 2003. 86–152] Although it might seem to be an issue of marginal importance compared with other debates about education today, the 'faith schools' discussion provides a case study that soon leads into fundamental questions about the aims and purpose of education, views on human nature, ultimate reality, truth and the meaning of life, and the education policies of a government.

This same MORI poll also reported that the main reasons given for parents supporting faith schools in the UK are a desire for their children to be educated in the same values and beliefs as their family [35%]; good discipline [28%]; and religious ethos [27%]. Only 10% cited good exam results. It is also vital to note the reasons given by parents for sending their children to faith schools, which concern family values and beliefs and religious ethos and identity. The best Islamic education will ensure this breadth of education is added to their ethical and spiritual appeal.

An Islamic education encompasses the two traditional categories of knowledge, and the hierarchical relationship between them: revealed knowledge, attained through the religious sciences; and acquired knowledge, attained through the rational, intellectual, and philosophical sciences. In the worldview of *tawheed* [divine unity], knowledge is holistic and there is no compartmentalisation of knowledge into religious and secular spheres. Both types of knowledge contribute to the strengthening of faith, the former through a careful study of the revealed word of God and the latter through a meticulous, systematic study of the world of humanity and nature. Bediuzzaman Said Nursi's [1878 – 1960] writings such as the *Risale i-Nur* and the Nurcu movement he stirred were formative in Gülen's own spiritual and intellectual development. Nursi wrote,

> We Muslims, who are students of the Qur'an, follow proof. We approach the truths of belief through reason, thought, and our hearts. We do not abandon proof for blind imitation of the clergy like some followers of other religions. Thus, in the future when reason, science, and technology prevail, the Qur'an will surely then rule, which relies on reasoned proofs and makes the reason confirm its pronouncements. [Nursi 1960. 77]

In similar terms Seyyed Hossein Nasr explains

Islamic education is concerned not only with the instruction and training of the mind and the transmission of knowledge (ta`lim) but also with the education of the whole being of men and women (tarbiyah). The teacher is therefore not only a mu`alim, a 'transmitter of knowledge' but also a murabbi, a 'trainer of souls and personalities'. The Islamic educational system never divorced the training of the mind from that of the soul. [Nasr, 2001. 56]

Gülen endorses this perspective,

Preferring the sacred cause over all worldly and animal desires; being steadfast in truth, once it has been discovered, to the degree that you sacrifice all mundane attachments for its sake; enduring all hardships so that future generations will be happy; seeking happiness, not in material or even spiritual pleasures, but in the happiness and well-being of others; never seeking to obtain any posts or positions; and preferring oneself to others in taking on work but preferring others to oneself in receiving wages—these are the essentials of this sacred way of serving the truth. [Gülen 2000. 84]

Syed Muhammad Naguib Al-Attas [b.1931][1997. 98] prefers to regard Islamic education as *ta'dib*, a word related to *adab*. He defines this term in its true sense (before its restriction and debasement of meaning to "a context revolving around cultural refinement and social etiquette") as "discipline of body, mind and soul" which enables man to recognize and acknowledge "his proper place in the human order" in relation to his self, his family, and his community. This order is "arranged hierarchically in degrees (*darajat*) of excellence based on Qur'anic criteria of intelligence, knowledge, and virtue (*ihsan*)." In this sense, *adab* is "the reflection of wisdom (*hikmah*)" and "the spectacle (*mashhad*) of justice (`adl*)."

In a recent paper on the application of religious models to educational administration, Aref Atari [2000. 29–56] has shown how the implementation of both the Christian model of "Service-Stewardship" and the Islamic "Khalifah" model "entails a radical transformation in management, thought and practice" away from a hierarchically organized bureaucratic Western model. The goal he describes as a "caring and sharing spirit." In this climate, trust, love, sympathy, mercy, cooperation, tolerance, and altruism are at least as important as efficiency, effectiveness, competition, professional ambition, and achievement. The outcome is an organisation, which is both "virtue-based and excellence-oriented." *Shurah*-based management, empowering and working with others, replaces a top-down approach, which manipulates, controls, and works through others.

From such a brief excursus it is evident that Gülen in his own field is offering an Islamic representation of Islam faithful to the origins and applicable to modern conditions.

Teachers should know how to find a way to the student's heart and be able to leave indelible imprints upon his or her mind. They should test the information to be passed on to students by refining their own minds and the prisms of their hearts. A good lesson is one that does more than provide pupils with useful information or skills; it should elevate them into the presence of the unknown. This enables the students to acquire a penetrating vision into the reality of things, and to see each event as a sign of the unseen world. [Gülen 1982. 39]

Cross-Cultural and Inter-Faith Education

Following the 11th September 2001, and the 7th June 2005 Europe and the West with all the hazards that accompany a polarisation of an "Us and the Other" *weltanschauung* should never forget one of the founding principles of its civilisation. The affirmation by Plato that philosophical dialectic, the testing process of critical enquiry through discussion and dialogue, is utterly distinct from and immeasurably superior to rhetoric. This inheritance has ensured that in the contemporary usage of modern European languages, the word "rhetorical" almost invariably has negative connotations, implying the abuse of language for self-serving ends.

At the same time, Muslims need to recall that one of the founding principles of Islamic civilisation was a dynamic spirit of open-minded enquiry, which Muslim scholars communicated to the Christian, Greek, and Jewish communities in their midst. Muhammad Asad [1900 – 1992] comments,

> [The Qur'an], through its insistence on consciousness and knowledge ... engendered among its followers a spirit of intellectual curiosity and independent inquiry, ultimately resulting in that splendid era of learning and scientific research which distinguished the world of Islam at the height of its vigour; and the culture thus fostered by the Qur'an penetrated in countless ways and by-ways into the mind of medieval Europe and gave rise to that revival of Western culture which we call the Renaissance, and thus became in the course of time largely responsible for the birth of what is described as the 'age of science': the age in which we are now living. [Asad 1980. 23]

Similarly, for Gülen the Qur'an is the source, which provides the qiblah or orienting point of reference around which all modes of knowledge and all diverse traditions revolve and cohere. With an allusion to Mevlana Jalal ud-Din Rumi he affirms,

The Qur'an is the Divine Word or Speech sent down to humanity, the best pattern of creation that is uniquely qualified to receive it. Despite the Qur'an's weight and gravity, most people cannot feel and appreciate its significance, for they have closed their senses and faculties to it. Those who alienate themselves and their inner life from the Qur'an receive nothing from it.

> For one who is a good "diver"
>
> The Qur'an is an ocean replete with jewels;
>
> While one indifferent to it
>
> Has nothing to receive from it. [Gülen, The Holy Qur'an, http://en.fgülen.com, 14 / 09 / 2001]

Cross-cultural and inter-faith dimensions of education and the inter-cultural and inter-faith sensitivity they promote are of the greatest importance at this time. Despite all the talk about globalisation, there is evidence of entrenched parochialism, increasing xenophobia and Islamophobia, racial and cultural prejudice and injustice isolationism, cross-cultural communication breakdown, profound misconstructions of other cultures.

A curriculum which acknowledges whether implicitly or explicitly the contribution of Islam to the development of Western civilisation, not in the sense of dwelling nostalgically on "past glories," but in the deeper sense of finding common ground between Islam and the West is truly,

> .....a community of the middle way..... [Surah 2. 143]

The *ummatan wasatan* represents a connecting relationship and a centre of significance in the midst of a world polarised between competing power blocs. Islamic education will renew that essentially Islamic capacity to integrate and accommodate diverse traditions in a spirit of pluralism, as embodied in the historical legacy of Al-Biruni, Ibn Al-Haytham, Al-Ghazali, Ibn Rushd, Razi, and Suhrawardi.

Conclusion: Synthesis not Syncretism

Pluralism is an environment in which to advance core Islamic values, including the genuinely Islamic concept of human dignity. These values are the same universal values that promote unity in the "secularist" world such as seeking knowledge, equality, freedom, human rights, justice, and selflessness. The principles of a just world order are embedded in the pluralistic vision of Islam and were embodied however imperfectly in the prototypical Islamic societies from Madinah to Andalusia, from periods in Mughal India to the Ottoman fusion, a vision capable of reconciling the demands of multiplicity and concord in a humane framework. This is the vision, which raises humankind to the "station above that of angels".

However, it must be stressed that such a vision encompasses not only the openness that characterises living traditions, but also a strong commitment to a particular expression of tradition and community. A view of pluralism, which entails commitment as well as openness and respect for diversity, seeks synthesis in relation to a stable, integral core of knowledge, but this is not the same as a syncretic view. This would attempt to blend and mingle different traditions of incompatible principles or beliefs into a new system.

> As every human, unlike animals, represents the whole of humanity, individual rights cannot be sacrificed for society, and social rights should depend on individual rights. This is why the basic human rights and freedoms found in the revealed religions were taken on board by a war-weary West. These rights are given priority in all relations. The primary right is the right to life, which is granted by and can only be taken by God. To accentuate the importance of this right in Islam, a basic Qur'anic principle is that:

> If one person kills another unjustly, it is the same as if he has killed all of humanity; if one saves another, it is the same as if he has saved all of humanity. [Surah 5:32] [Gülen, At the Threshold of a New Millennium, http://en.fgülen.com.11.04.2004]

From the writings and example of Fethullah Gülen the social and educational movement which has thus evolved in association with his name offers a paradoxically non-religious but yet profoundly Islamically motivated movement with the transformation of human society as its objective. These schools and universities emerge from a specific expression of Islam, which is at once conservative, Sufi inspired and innovative in *ijtihad* and *tajdid* religious reasoning and religious reform respectively. Evidence from respondents in dissimilar circumstances attest to a flexible renewalist movement, rational in its expressions of historic Islam yet untrammeled by rigid patterns, a community of the "middle way" uninhibited by political constrictions, and one marked by the spirit of servanthood to humanity.

BUILDING CIVIL SOCIETY IN ETHNO-RELIGIOUSLY FRACTURED COMMUNITIES: "THE CASE OF THE GÜLEN MOVEMENT IN TURKEY AND ABROAD"

Mehmet Kalyoncu

Abstract

Civil society is generally associated with the presence of voluntary, non-governmental civic and social organisations, which are run by informed citizens and assume responsibility for monitoring state bodies and operations and mobilising available resources to maintain order and efficiency in the functioning of both state and society. Early civil society theorists argued the relevance of such voluntary associations to achieving a stable and functioning democracy. But what if the local conditions prevent the formation of such associations – if the social landscape is characterised by communal conflicts stemming from deeply entrenched ethno-religious differences? The reality of such conditions makes it imperative that strategies are re-formulated in ethno-religiously fractured societies, where what divides different segments of the population is more than what unites them.

This paper argues that it is possible to develop such strategies. The argument is based on field research in Mardin on the activities of the faith-based Gülen movement. This group has succeeded in forging policies and programmes that bring different ethno-religious communities together as a necessary first step towards civil society: common problems facing the different ethno-religious communities are identified, then solid services to address those problems are provided, requiring collaborative effort by the different ethno-religious communities. In this way the social potential of those communities is mobilised and channelled to achieve shared goals which enrich the society as a whole.

Introduction

Civil society is generally associated with the presence of voluntary civic and social organizations that function as the basis of a given community. Run by the informed citizens or the groups, these non-governmental organizations assume responsibility of monitoring governmental organizations and mobilize the available resources to maintain order and efficiency in functioning of not only the governmental organizations but also of the society in general. According to Alexis Tocqueville, the civic organization, or the ability of the citizens to organize through associations for common purpose, constitutes the basis of civil society. Critique of the American individualism, Tocqueville suggested that coming around common causes would create a civic consciousness for American nationhood which is far more important than fulfilling selfish individual desires.[1] Moreover, Gabriel Almond and Sidney Verba found a direct correlation between civil society and democracy arguing that political civil society organizations increase civic awareness which respectively generate informed voting choices, participation in politics and holding the government more accountable.[2] Along the similar lines with Almond and Verba, Robert Putnam argues that not only political but also non-political civil society organizations are crucial to democracy because they build social capital, trust and shared values, which are transferred into political sphere and help to hold society together, facilitating an understanding of the interconnectedness of society and interests within it.[3] What is common of all four students of civil society is their conviction that the coming together of citizens within either political or non-political organizations for a common purpose is crucial to achieve a full functioning civil society and as such a healthy democracy. They all compare the merits of civic organization over its absence in terms of achieving a stable and functioning democracy.

What if the community does not have ability to organize at the first place? What if there are ongoing intra-communal conflicts stemming from deeply entrenched ethno-religious differences? How is it possible to convince the different ethno-religious groups within a community to come together around a common cause as Tocqueville suggests, which would eventually generate a common identity and as Almond, Verba and Putnam suggests, a functioning democracy? The very reality that the contemporary societies still suffer from ethno-religious conflicts makes it imperative for the students of civil society to reformulate their strategies to attain civil society in ethno-religiously fractured communities where what divides different segments of the community is mote than what united them.

I argue that it is possible to develop common practical methods to foster civil society and democracy in communities that are traditionally divided along the ethno-religious fault lines and have been experiencing conflict over those ethno-religious differences. My earlier field research in the city of Mardin, which is located on the Syrian border of Turkey and populated by ethnic Turks, Arabs, Kurds and well as Assyrian Christians, about the Gülen movement, a faith-based civil society movement, suggests that it is likely to develop common strategies to bring together different ethno-religious groups within a community to organize toward achieving civil society. Addressing the common problems facing the different ethno-religious communities within a given society, providing solid services to eradicate those problems, and seeking collaboration of those ethno-religious communities along the way constitute the

---

1 For a brief discussion of civil society and democracy relationship, see http://en.wikipedia.org/wiki / Civil_society#_note-8
2 See Almond, G.; Verba, S; The Civic Culture: Political Attitudes and Democracy in Five Nations; 1989; Sage
3 See Putnam, R.; Making Democracy Work: Civic Traditions in Modern Italy; 1993; Princeton

crux of mobilizing social potential which is possible to channel to adopting a civil society's values and practices.

A Glance at the Gülen Movement in Southeast Turkey

The Gülen movement has been able to mobilize Turks, Kurds, Arabs, and Assyrian Christians in Mardin to cooperate on tackling their common problems. The city has been heavily affected by the ensuing insecurity, infrastructural and economic deprivations due to the conflicts between the Turkish security forces and the terrorist organizations such as the Marxist PKK and the Islamist fundamentalist Hezbollah respectively since early 1980s and 1990s. The ongoing conflicts and insecurity have not only deprived the city of basic infrastructures, investments and educational facilities, but also deepened the ethnic fault-lines, less so the religious ones.

Against this background, the affiliates of the Gülen movement first established personal contacts with the local people from different ethnic groups in the late 1980s. Their conversations focused on such common problems facing all groups regardless of their ethno-religious allegiance as the lack of education of the youth, increasing unemployment, the consequential falling prey of the youth to either PKK or Hezbollah, and ensuing problem of terrorism and economic deprivations. The movement has not only preached about these issues but also mobilized the local people to tackle these problems together. The local people's cooperation seems to have yielded tangible outcomes which has changed the earlier attitudes and practices of the ethno-religious groups in Mardin, thereby preparing the ground for fostering participative civil society. These tangible outcomes include educational and cultural institutions which continue to build the human capital for a stable and democratic Mardin.

Gülen Movement Institutions in Mardin

Sur Dersanesi: University Preparatory Courses

Sur Dersanesi is a pioneer in Mardin in preparing the local youth for the national university entrance exam. Before Sur Dersanesi, a few organizations had attempted to run university preparatory courses in Mardin. However, they had ceased their operations either because of financial hardship or the security problems caused by the PKK and Hezbollah in the 1980s. In other words, they fled Mardin without fulfilling their promises to the local people to prepare their children for the national university entrance test.[4] This unfortunate precedent made it difficult for the movement's local representatives to obtain the necessary official endorsement from the local government. The Gülen movement opened its first university preparatory course, which was also its first local institution, in Mardin in 1992. Ever since then, the movement's expansion in Mardin has been focused on opening university preparatory courses. Currently, the movement runs four university preparatory courses in the surrounding counties of Kızıltepe, Derik, Nusaybin, and Midyat. These courses serve the students not only in their own counties but also in nearby counties. For instance, since there is no university preparatory course in Dargeçit yet, the students commute to the closest county (Midyat) to attend the course. Opening another branch of Sur Dersanesi is always one of the top items on the movement's agenda in Mardin. In that regard, Mardin's *mütevelli* (board of trustees composed of local Mardinian businessmen) is currently negotiating with the local

---

4 I obtained this information through my interviews with the local people who helped the movement open its first university preparatory course in Mardin in 1992.

authorities of Savur, another county in Mardin, to obtain a license and rent a building to open a university preparatory course there.

The growth of Sur Dersanesi in Nusaybin is similar to that of its branches in the other counties. According to Murat Salim, a local store owner and resident of Nusaybin, the city has been heavily influenced by both the PKK and Hezbollah: "Between 1989 and 1993, the region was under the complete control of the PKK. For instance, if there was an incident that required a judicial process, the parties had to first see the regional administrator of the PKK. If they went directly to the official court, then the PKK punished them for that wrongdoing."[5] He suggests that Hezbollah, the counter-guerilla movement, took over control of Nusaybin from the PKK after 1993. About this time, the Gülen movement opened its first university preparatory course in Nusaybin. Murat Salim notes: "Sur Dersanesi in Nusaybin had about ten to fifteen students in 1996, but the number of the students has grown every year. The number was 280 in 2004, 480 in 2005, and 900 in 2006."[6] This growth has mirrored the growth in the other counties, such as Kızıltepe and Derik, which are under heavy PKK influence. Today, even though Kızıltepe is still a PKK stronghold, the local people send their children to Sur Dersanesi to prepare for national college entrance test.

ATAK Koleji - Private School (Elementary-Secondary-High School)

Atak Koleji is the first and only private school in Mardin. Its construction, which is still ongoing, started in 1996. In the meantime, however, the school has registered students and provided an education. The school's construction has been funded solely by a wealthy Mardinian family (the Ataks) that has been residing in Istanbul since 1974. The family decided to build the school upon the encouragement of a group of Mardin's local businessmen and a teacher who share Gülen's educational vision and believe that increased educational facilities are the only remedy for Mardin's underdevelopment and the way to solve southeastern Turkey's terrorism problem. When the Atak family visited Mardin and saw that non-Mardinian teachers, despite all the deprivations they suffered there, were dedicating themselves to educating Mardin's children and youth at the university preparatory courses, the family was stimulated to contribute to the Gülen movement's educational projects in Mardin. They are still contributing.[7]

Just as it is the first institution being funded solely by a civic initiative, Atak Koleji is a pioneer in terms of other characteristics. It has become a meeting place for the area's different ethno-religious groups, most notably Kurds and Arabs. The school is located halfway between Kızıltepe (Mardin's largest county) and the city center of Mardin, both of which are, respectively, strongholds of ethnic Kurdish and ethnic Arab populations. According to reports made by Atak Koleji teachers, even if the Kurds and Arabs have not engaged in an active conflict, they have not quite intermingled either.[8] In addition to Kurdish and Arab students, the school also has Assyrian Christian students and follows a secular curriculum approved (and periodically inspected) by the Turkish Ministry of Education. Atak Koleji is a co-ed school and has about three hundred and fifty students taught by thirty teachers, fourteen of whom are women.[9]

---

5 Excerpt from the author's interview with Murat Salim on February 9, 2006, in Nusaybin, Mardin.

6 Excerpt from the author's interview with Murat Salim on February 9, 2006 in Nusaybin, Mardin.

7 See chapter 3, "Genesis and Development in Mardin."

8 This information is based on my interview with the Atak Koleji teachers on February 3, 2006, in Mardin. Several other respondents of both Kurdish and Arab origin confirmed this information at different times and places.

9 This information is based on my notes from my trip to Atak Koleji on February 3, 2006.

The school is unique in Mardin for its education system and the opportunities it provides to its students. Beside teaching natural sciences and math, English as a second language, computer science as well as arts and humanities, the school prioritizes the students' development in terms of not only academic skills, but also of social and physical skills. Throughout the year, the students organize science fairs, exhibitions, theater plays, music performances, chess tournaments, and such sporting events as soccer and basketball tournaments. The teachers encourage each student club to organize own event and participate in those of the other clubs. The school principal Oğuz Ozan explains: "At the end of every school year, a fair is held among the student clubs; these clubs present the activities and accomplishments they have achieved in that year. The local people are invited to the fair and are asked to vote for the best clubs. The students are free to invite as many people as possible, including those with no affiliation to the school, in order to increase the number of votes for their club. Last year, the students brought about five thousand people from the city to visit the fair, and sought to increase the number of their votes."[10] Ozan believes that this voting application helps familiarize students with democratic election practices.

Moreover, the school organizes public seminars and social gatherings with the local people. Through these public seminars, the school shares its future projects with the local people, and seeks their involvement in carrying out these projects. The schools engagement with the local people has not only changed some rooted traditions such as not sending girls to school, but also attitudes toward them. A mother from Surgucu village laments, "I was not allowed to go even to elementary school and was married at a very early age. She continues, "I did not have much say in my immediate family, let alone the extended one, but I am quite happy for Hatice [her daughter] because she is going to high school now in Balikesir [a western city]. Even now, her father consults her for her ideas on issues. She has the opportunity to influence her father's decisions. She will be a strong woman and a good mother."[11]

MOSDER (Mardin Reading Halls Association)

MOSDER has several branches in Mardin, one of which is in the highly impoverished and isolated Dargeçit province. Dargeçit does not even have a bank despite its more than seven thousand inhabitants, and has one entrance, which also serves as an exit and a military checkpoint. The main reason for such deprivation and heavy military control seems to be a combination of the local people's implicit support for the PKK terrorist organization, frequent clashes between the PKK and the Turkish security forces in the vicinity of Dargeçit, and the resulting absence of investment. MOSDER's reading hall opened in February 2005 and serves about one hundred and fifty students. The students are encouraged to spend as much time as possible there reading or studying for the national college entrance test. The students stress that the reading hall has helped them organize their preparation for the university admissions test by providing them with a study place and test books, and that without these they would not be able to prepare very well in their impoverished houses. While the ultimate goal of the reading halls is to help local students get educated and go to college, the most immediate function is to keep them off the street where they easily fall prey to either PKK or Hezbollah recruitment.

MARKOYDER (Mardin Village Development Association)

Compared to MOSDER, MARKOYDER has a more comprehensive scope for its activities, from providing educational facilities to distributing food and clothing to poor villagers. The

---

10 Excerpt from the author's interview with Oguz Ozan at Atak Koleji on February 3, 2006.

11 Excerpt from the author's interview with a groups of women from Surgucu village on February 2, 2006.

operational relation between the two organizations is such that MOSDER goes into a village if MARKOYDER identifies a need for a reading hall in that village, and they cooperate in opening the reading hall. In addition, MARKOYDER, in partnership with the teachers from Atak Koleji, visits families in the villages and tries to convince parents to send their children to school, especially their daughters, since the indigenous conservative culture impedes girls from going to school. MARKOYDER has reportedly been in contact with hundred and fifty villages so far.

What the Movement's Institutions Mean to the Local People

According to my interviewees' responses, Atak Koleji seems to be matchless in Mardin in terms of the education it provides the students. Similarly, Sur Dersanesi, the university preparatory courses, and the reading halls seem to provide the locals with opportunities that the state cannot offer and that perhaps only a small percentage of Mardinians could afford on their own. The material value of these services is clear. However, the local people also seem to attribute a special meaning to these institutions, for they view them as being more than just schools. There are contextual reasons for this special meaning: the local realities of severe unemployment, terror, a conservative culture, and a chronic shortage of schools and teachers. These correspond almost perfectly with what Atak Koleji and the university preparatory courses are committed to eradicating. Therefore, the fact that each of these contextual reasons is important to the parents, although to varying degrees, makes Atak Koleji, as well as other movement-associated educational institutions, something more than what such institutions, by common definition, are.

The local people who have placed their children in these institutions comment that they see the Gülen movement institutions as a way to keep their children immune to the influence of both the PKK and Hezbollah. Although they do not reflect the entire Mardin community, those parents who send their children to the university preparatory course view it as a way to rescue their children from the recruitment pool of both the PKK and Hezbollah. Based on this proposition, one cannot argue that the movement's activities have decreased local support for the PKK and Hezbollah, but we can conclude, based on the parents' statements, that their main motivation is not necessarily to help their children go to university but to keep them away from the streets, which constitutes the main recruitment pool for both the PKK and Hezbollah.

Is the Gülen Education Model Applicable to the International Arena?

So, the question is whether the sociological approach introduced and practiced by the Gülen movement in Mardin, which focuses on communal perfection through individual perfection, and mobilizes different segments of the society to tackle their common problems putting aside their differences, is applicable to alleviating ethno-religious conflicts in diverse communities around globe, and to fostering civil society within these communities?

The field research about the impact of the movement's services in Mardin which is not only ethno-religiously divided but also suffers from terrorism and economic deprivations, suggests that the movement is able to prepare the preliminary conditions for a civil society to flourish from that community. First, the educational facilities established and run by Turks, Arabs, and Kurds together have minimized, if not eradicate, the perception of Turk-Kurd enmity through which PKK has garnered popular support. Second, these institutions, be they college prep courses or reading halls, took the unemployed youth off the streets, who constituted otherwise the main recruitment resource for both PKK and Hezbollah. Third, Gülen's ideas about Islam conveyed through both human interactions and media have convinced the public that radicalism conflicts with the very essentials of Islam. Fourth, Gülen movement's solid education services help rationality override nationalist and ethno-religious sentiments, and create a public opinion against violent means of conduct such as terrorism.

i.   I argue that with its proven capabilities in Mardin, whose ethno-religious diversity and socio-economic problems are representative of the global map where similar problems are experienced, the Gülen movement can contribute to eradicating ethno-religiously driven conflicts and to fostering civil society by mobilizing the indigenous different ethno-religious groups to tackle their common problems. That is, the reconciliatory approach of the Gülen movement can help to greatly appease, if not totally eradicate, social conflicts continuously experienced in various parts of the world provided that the following hypotheses are true for any given community.

ii.   The parties of a given ethno-religious conflict are rational actors. As such, they recognize their interests in peace and stability, and in obtaining tangible results toward bettering their socio-economic situation.

iii.   The Gülen movement's philosophy is that the absence of education, dialogue and tolerance is the source of all likely conflicts.

iv.   It envisions societies that consist of idealistic and patriotic individuals who share common values with their counterparts with different ethno-religious backgrounds. These values are mainly dialogue, tolerance, individual perfection through education, and altruism.

v.   The movement's vision of dialogue, tolerance, and search for common grounds between different cultures is what enables the movement to communicate to a wide range of different communities.

vi.   The movement's strict avoidance from politics and from being politicized makes it able to communicate communities that are radically distant from each other on the political spectrum.

vii.   The movement's activities within any community start with personal contacts with the individuals in that community. That is, the affiliates of the movement share the vision of the movement with individual(s) in the given community.

viii.   Once inter-personal relations are established between the affiliates of the Gülen movement and the local figures, and the necessity of dialogue and education is agreed upon in a particular community; the schools and related educational institutions become media where a vision of dialogue and tolerance are realized through raising individuals who believe in the importance of intercultural dialogue and tolerance.

ix.   The quality education provided by the schools and the joint-cultural activities held in cooperation with the local people become non-relational channel for communicating the vision of the Gülen movement, and they help the movement take further root in a given society.

Based on my previous field research about the impact of the Gülen movement, a faith-based civic movement, on an ethno-religiously highly fractured and socio-economically deprived community of Mardin, I contend that examining the Gülen movement's educational activities in the global conflict zones would enable us to develop strategies that may be helpful in minimizing ethno-religious conflict and fostering civil society in these very zones. These cases studies, which include the movement's impact on the conflicted communities of Bosnia, Northern Iraq, Afghanistan and Philippines, and will be further discussed in the following section, constitute more or less the global map of ethno-religious conflict in general. The case studies, each of them unique in the sense of their socio-political context and their underlying cause of conflict, present a representative sample of the population of ethno-religious conflicts around the globe.

The Gülen movement has been actively operating in all these four places for more than a decade, and has been successful to mobilize the indigenous ethno-religiously distinct communities to put aside their differences and cooperate together to tackle their common problems. Identifying the norms and practices that enable the movement to accomplish such an endeavor may help us identify common and effective strategies to minimize, if not eradicate, ethno-religious conflicts in general.

The Gülen Movement in the Global Conflict Zones

In order to fully assess the ability of the Gülen movement to appease social conflicts and contribute to building civil society in ethno-religiously fractured communities, it is imperative to select a sample or a set of samples, which reflects the notion of ethno-religious fracture with all aspects. That is, the sample examined should be representative of communities that divided along the lines of ethnic differences, religious differences, and ethnic and religious difference. Similarly, the set of samples should also take into account the political framework of the ethno-religiously fractured community under scrutiny. Since it is the concept of civil society and a social movement's ability to contribute to building civil society in a given community, the indigenous political culture of the local people should be taken into account as an indicator of availability of pre-conditions for civil society to develop. In this regard, Bosnia, Northern Iraq, Afghanistan and Philippines provide a unique combination of various sorts of ethno-religiously fractured communities.

First, Bosnia presents a case of community which is composed of Muslim Bosnians, Christian Serbs and again Christian Croats. Despite their common ethnic identity, and more or less, similar political cultures due to their common Yugoslavian background, these three different communities had as recently as a decade ago engaged in the bloodiest conflict due to nationalistic aspirations. Their religious differences had exacerbated, if not caused, their nationalism-driven conflict.

Second, Northern Iraq presents a unique case with highly fractured community along the ethno-religious differences, whose political culture rests in secular authoritarianism of the Baathist ideology. As it goes through a political formation lately, the community composed of Kurds, Sunni Arabs, Turcoman, Shiites, and Assyrian Christians experiences conflicts along the line of these ethno-religious differences. That neither of these ethno-religious groups inherently possesses democratic political culture further minimizes the prospect of easy development of civil society in Northern Iraq.

Third, Afghanistan presents an example of community which is highly diversified with various ethnic groups sharing the same religious background. The ethnic groups include respectively Pashtun, Tajik, Hazara, Uzbek, Aimak, Baluchi, Kyrgyz, Turkmen, Nuristani and Pamiri among other small ethnic groups. After a decade-long war caused by the Soviet invasion, these ethnic groups whose political organization is based on tribalism continued their infighting thereby diminishing the prospects of developing civil society in Afghanistan. In the meantime, emergence of the radical Islamist groups such as Taliban further blockaded any possible progress toward a civil society.

Finally, Philippines provides a unique example of community which is stigmatized with an enduring Muslim-Christian fighting. Like the Christians of Northern Iraq, Muslims, in other words Moro Muslims, constitute the minority in Philippines and are populated in the autonomous region of Mindanao in Southern Philippines. The Moro Muslims have politically organized themselves along the Muslim nationalist movement, which they describe as both Islamic and anti-colonial. As such, the main mobilizing force for the Moro Muslims has been their historical resistance against the Spanish colonialism, and that resistance currently continues as their struggle against the Christian Manila's attempts to assimilate the Muslim Philippines. In a way, after the end of the colonialism threat, the conflict in Philippines has transformed into an enduring one between the Muslim minority and the Christian majority. Yet, despite the earlier attempts to form a unified nationalist Muslim identity (Bansgsamoro), the Philippine's Muslims have been organized along three distinct political groups, which are respectively the Moro Liberation Front (MNLF), the Moro Islamic Liberation Front (MILF), and Abu Sayyaf. Despite their different political orientations, what brings these distinct groups together is their common uprising against their common "other"; the Christian majority.

What is interesting about the Philippines, where Muslim-Christian conflict is still vivid, and the contribution of the Gülen Movement in Philippines is articulated by Thomas Mitchell, the former representative of Vatican on interfaith dialogue for Northern Africa and the Middle East. Mitchell describes the Gülen schools running in Philippines as "peace islands in the sea of conflict" pointing to the fact that the schools bring together both Christian and Muslims students together in a peaceful atmosphere, whose fathers have been fighting each other outside the school campus for more than half a decade because of their religious differences.[12] It is certainly interesting to see a platform in Philippines where Christians and Muslims peacefully join together. What is more interesting though is to see that it is a platform brought about by Muslims affiliated with a faith-based civil society movement while the local Muslims are partially the cause of the conflict. The situation is pretty much the same in Bosnia, Northern Iraq and Afghanistan. In spite of sharing the common ethnic and/or religious background with the parties of the ongoing conflict in either of these places, those inspired and/or affiliated by the Gülen movement tend not to take part in, or not to continue if have taken previously, the conflict. Instead, they prefer to identify common grounds where they get together and cooperate to tackle their common problems.

Conclusion: Gülen Schools as a Means to Social Development and Civil Society

Finally, given the specific example of what the Gülen movement has achieved in the ethnoreligiously diverse Mardin to maintain social consensus among different communities who had previously engaged in a conflict in one way or another and mobilize them to counter their common challenges, what are the prospects for the movement and its schools to do the same in other ethno-religiously conflicted communities? I have argued that the analysis of the Gülen movement's activities in such unique global cases as Bosnia, Northern Iraq, Afghanistan and Philippines would demonstrate that the movement is able to bring together the indigenous ethno-religiously different communities in these respective countries by addressing their

---

12 See Thomas Michel, "Fethullah Gülen as Educator", in M. Hakan Yavuz and John L. Esposito, eds., Turkish Islam and the Secular State: The Gülen Movement

common problems, providing a solid vision and services to address those problems and mobilizing the local people to cooperate in solving those problems. It is certainly imperative to
conduct a field research in all these countries to verify whether the Gülen movement is able to
attain what it did in Mardin. Nevertheless, the accounts of those who have visited the schools
in these countries like that of Thomas Mitchel, who visited the Gülen schools in Philippines,
suggest that the movement is able to bring together the ethno-religiously different communities together in a peaceful environment.

This observation entails a broader question about the Gülen movement's ability to contribute
to developing human capital, the fundamental pre-condition of civil society formation, in
the socially deprived and ethno-religiously conflicted countries such as those in Africa. The
continent provides numerous examples of countries which have plunged into ethno-religious
conflict and chronic political turmoil due to the lack of human capital which will enable civil
society, political stability and economic prosperity.

The Republic of Nigeria, with its diverse ethno-religious popular structure, vast natural resources (particularly oil) and recent step into democratic political system, is representative of
majority countries in the continental Africa. The country's religious distribution consists of
50 percent Muslims, 40 percent Christians, and 10 percent traditional beliefs. Even more diverse ethnic map of the country consists of 29 percent Hausa and Fulani, 21 percent Yoruba,
and 18 percent Ibo with other various ethnicities making up the rest of the population.[13]
Since its independence from the United Kingdom in 1960, ethnic struggles have dominated
Nigeria's politics. Religious differences, inequalities in oil resources among regions, and
pervasive corruption and poverty have only intensified the conflict.[14] The contemporary challenges that Nigeria faces include reconciling antagonistic Muslim Hausa/Fulani in the north
(the majority), Christian Yoruba in the south, and Christian Ibo in the east; evenly distributing
the oil revenues among all the states and local governments; and halting pervasive corruption
in both public and private sector.

Despite the efforts of both the Nigerian governments to maintain a smooth transition from
dependency to independency and from authoritarian to democratic rule, Nigeria has suffered
and is likely to continue to suffer ethno-religious and regional conflicts. Religious differences among the ethnic groups, uneven distribution of oil revenues among the ethno-religious
groups and of the natural resources among the regions, are likely to exacerbate the ethno-
religious and regional conflicts in years to come.

Nigeria's contemporary socio-economic and ethno-religious structure provides a fertile
ground for such parties as international arms dealers who would be interested in supplying
arms to the parties of a possible ethno-religious conflict, and the entities who might be interested in an invasion on the ground of preventing a possible ethno-religious conflict from turning into genocide. As such, Nigeria remains vulnerable to both internal and external impacts
thereby diminishing the prospect for developing a civil society and achieving both economic
and political stability.

An immediate and sustainable solution to such possible threats is to attain human and social development which will consequently enable the Nigerians regardless of their ethno-
religious identity to compete for available political and economic opportunity spaces in their

13 See CIA World Factbook – Nigeria, available at https://www.cia.gov/library/publications/the-world-factbook/
geos/ni.html#People
14 See "Nigeria" in How Governments Work: The inside guide to the politics of the world, London, New York,
Melbourne, Munich and Delhi: Dorling Kindersley Limited 2006, p.162

potentially rich country. Developing an able human capital will also entail a thriving civil society since the educated population will participate in the country's political process, and monitor and hold the government responsible for its policies.

The improvement and reform of the education system with a great emphasis on secondary and post-secondary education is crucial to civil society building in any given country according to the World Bank civil society development program. Unlike the early civil society theoreticians who associate the possibility of civil society formation with the will of the people, the World Bank civil society program recognizes the reality that the will itself would not suffice to form a civil society if the human capital to do so is not present. With its proven experience and capability in Mardin and other conflict zones to help the ethno-religiously diverse local population develop human capital, the Gülen movement and its schools can contribute to developing the human capital not only in Nigeria but also in other African countries which possess similar demographic and socio-economic structure.

The case of Mardin has demonstrated that the Gülen movement has been able to mobilize the individuals of Turkish, Kurdish, Arab and Assyrian origins, who were previously fractured and isolated from one another, to tackle their very own common problems with their own resources. Based on this example, one can deduct that the Gülen movement emphasizes the role of human agency and the autonomy of society and individuals from the state. That is, the individuals organize together and mobilize their resource to meet their common needs. Consequently, the necessity of law and order to sustain what has been achieved as a result of the collective action cultivates both individual and communal quest and respect for the rule of law, which constitutes the backbone of a sustainable civil society.

REFLECTING ON THE GÜLEN MOVEMENT'S INTERFAITH DIALOGUE WORK THROUGH THE ACTIVITIES OF NITECA, A GÜLEN-INSPIRED SOCIETY BASED IN NORTHERN IRELAND

Jonathan Lacey

Abstract

Until the peace agreement of 1998 the Catholics and Protestants of Northern Ireland were pedantically focused on what separates these two identities. Following the end of the decades-long 'civil war', reconciliation has led to increased migration to the region, which now hosts more than 20,000 people from ethnic minority backgrounds. This means that there are now more than just two identity communities in Northern Ireland.

This paper focuses on an unlikely actor in this peace-building endeavour, a Turkic religio-cultural organisation, the Northern Ireland–Tolerance, Educational and Cultural Association (NI-TECA), inspired by the Turkish Islamic scholar Fethullah Gülen. The paper relies on ethnographic work and qualitative interviews conducted with members of NI–TECA, and draws on the writings of Fethullah Gülen and others to explain the organisation's principles and policies as implemented by NI–TECA. The paper also reflects on the global influence of Fethullah Gülen's ideas, of which the existence and work of NI–TECA is an illustration.

Introduction

> Did you hear the one about a Muslim man who entered Northern Ireland?
>
> The policeman stopped him and asked: "Are you a Catholic or Protestant?"
>
> To which the man replied, "I am a Muslim".
>
> The policeman then asked, "Are you a 'Catholic Muslim' or a 'Protestant Muslim'?".

The above 'joke' serves to illustrate the traditional division in Northern Ireland between Catholics and Protestants. The society has been so pedantically focused on the two separate primordial articulations of identity, that it was difficult, until recent years, to think outside of this dual paradigm. For so long the two communities lived separately and antagonistically. Thousands have been killed in a 'civil' war that has spanned decades.

A peace agreement was signed in 1998, which has led to relative peace in the region. This more benign environment is pregnant with potential for lasting peace. The reconciliation has also led to increased migration to the region, which now hosts more than 20,000 people from minority ethnic backgrounds, including roughly 300 Turkish people. This means that there are now more than just two identity communities in Northern Ireland. This paper focuses on an unlikely actor in this peace-building endeavour, a Turkic religio-cultural society, namely the Northern Ireland-Tolerance, Educational and Cultural Association (NI-TECA). This society was inspired by the Turkish Islamic scholar Fethullah Gülen.

I am interested in exploring the Gülen Movement through the endeavours of this association, as well as drawing on the written word of Fethullah Gülen and an array of different authors. I also use their presence in Northern Ireland as an example of the global scope of this Movement. This article draws on ethnographic work and qualitative interviews I conducted with members of NITECA.

I begin by describing the current situation in Northern Ireland. I argue that the form of democracy practiced in this region, namely consociational democracy, is a flawed system and has served to entrench ethnic divisions further in Northern Ireland. Along with an increase in racist incidents, this is the situation in which NITECA is attempting to bring its style of dialogical practice. This section is followed by a brief description of the work and ideas of Fethullah Gülen. I then introduce the core principles of NITECA before describing some of their activities. This latter section will predominantly be drawn from interview excerpts with members of NITECA. This is followed by an analytical section that links the local endeavours of NITECA with the global endeavours of the wider Gülen Movement.

Describing the Current Situation in Northern Ireland

I find it necessary at this early juncture to describe the current situation in Northern Ireland in order to situate NITECA in the appropriate context. In 1998, after three decades of violence in Northern Ireland, the Good Friday Agreement (GFA) was signed by the elites of the two major opposing parties in an attempt to bring stable governance to the region. Consociational Democracy was adopted as the model for governance. At the heart of this system is the 'grand coalition'. This entails a number of various antagonistic segments (potentially hostile) sharing power in a grand coalition and attempting to cooperate and run the government together. One of the architects of consociational theory, Arend Lijphart maintains that because the stakes are so high in a plural society (i.e. winner takes all) 'a grand coalition is therefore more appropriate than the government-versus-opposition pattern' (i.e. British model) (1977: 27). Presently Sinn Fein and the Democratic Unionist Party (DUP) represent each community in the grand coalition in Northern Ireland.

There are disputes by academics and politicians as to whether this form of government is a step forward or a missed opportunity. It is my contention that it was a missed opportunity as it institutionalises the notion of primordial identities which necessarily perpetuates the conflict (albeit in a largely non-violent form). Literary theorist Declan Kiberd praised the GFA, claiming that '…it offers a version of multiple identities…open rather than fixed, as a process rather than a conclusion?' (cited in Finlay, 2004: 4). In this sense Kiberd is claiming that there is recognition in the GFA that identities are constructed and open to change. However, Andrew Finlay (2004) rightly points out that Kiberd's reading of the GFA is selective. Read as a whole, the document promotes 'parity of esteem' for two communities only, namely 'British or Irish, unionist or nationalist' (Finlay, 2004: 5). Furthermore, Finlay insists that "parity of esteem' [necessarily] depend[s] on an implicit essentialism' (2004: 23). This echoes the logic of consociational theory which fixes, reifies and objectifies identities that in reality are much more fluid and changing.

There is evidence to suggest that since the signing of the GFA in 1998, there has been an augmenting abyss developing between communities in Northern Ireland. By 2004, there were 37 'peace walls' dividing potentially antagonistic 'communities'. In 1994, the year of the Irish Republican Army (IRA) cease-fire, there were only 15 such 'peace walls'[1] (Wilford and Wilson, 2004: 8). There is no suggestion here that consociational democracy (epitomised by power-sharing by two conflicting 'segments' in society) has created this abyss between the two 'communities'. Of course, these problems were already in existence. However, it is my contention that this form of democracy has led to its exacerbation and consolidation. The people of Ireland, particularly Northern Ireland, were exhausted with the violence and havoc of the previous 30 years. They were ready for radical transition in 1998 when the GFA was signed. However, the adoption of consociational democracy represents a missed opportunity and in my view was myopic. The physical barriers of the 'peace walls' are mirrored by a growing pessimism towards the possibility of concordance amongst the different 'communities'. This has been documented by the Northern Ireland Life and Times Survey of Public Attitudes which discovered that the people of Northern Ireland are very cynical about the future of peace (cited in Wilford and Wilson, 2004: 8).

So, Finlay is correct to suggest that the GFA (guided by the tenets of consociational theory) 'remains resolutely bicultural in the way that it privileges the rights of two indigenous communities, each of which is presumed to have its own cultural identity, conceived in essentialist terms' (2004: 24). In this context one must ask what is the affect on other ethnic groups in Northern Ireland that do not fall into the bicultural model of the GFA. Lentin and McVeigh (2006) note that regardless of Northern Ireland's slack economy, it is attracting a sizeable number of migrants. Whilst the GFA caters and promotes the two 'segments' in society, it ignores other minority ethnic groups. McGarry and O'Leary (2004) dispute this claim, insisting that provisions are made for individual human rights complaints through the European Convention of Human Rights in Northern Ireland Law and the Northern Ireland Act (1998). In theory, of course, they are right. However, it is my contention that due to the state sanctioned divisions and institutionalising of mistrust between the two major 'segments' in Northern Irish society, mistrust of all ethnic groups has penetrated throughout the region.

---

1 'Peace Walls' are a euphemistic name for walls of up to and over 1 kilometre in length and up to 20 feet high in Northern Ireland built specifically to keep apart "warring factions" (www.geographyinaction.co.uk)

Deepa Mann-Kler (2002) is an Indian woman living in Belfast and a community activist in Northern Ireland. She maintains that 'One of the many legacies of the Troubles has been the denial of the existence of racism in Northern Ireland' (2002: 63). She notes that there are over 20,000 people of minority ethnic background living in Northern Ireland and they are largely 'non-recognised' (Taylor, 1994) by the state and consequentially inequality towards these groups is endemic. More recently, Gabriele Marranci (2005), Ronit Lentin and Robbie McVeigh (2006) and Robbie McVeigh and Bill Rolston (2007) have pointed out the rise in racism in Northern Ireland. In 2005 the prominent German magazine Der Spiegel claimed that Belfast was 'the most racist City in the world' (cited in Lentin and McVeigh, 2006: 145). Lentin and McVeigh (2006) make the point that this claim is both complex and disputed. Nevertheless, the aforementioned commentators provide evidence for growing intolerance in Northern Ireland.

Bottom-up Approach

Though I have outlined several criticisms regarding the model of democracy practiced in Northern Ireland, ruefully I am unable to offer a solution. I do, however join Cochrane and Dunn (2002: 4), who insist that there is a dire need for an empirical focus on the bottom-up approach of actors involved in peace-building. They recognise that the overwhelming majority of research focuses on the top-down approach of the elite representatives rather than those working on the ground.

Cochrane and Dunn provide some interesting research vis-à-vis grassroots organisations in Northern Ireland. Their focus is on indigenous groups such as the 'Families Against Intimidation and Terror' (FAIT) and 'Quaker House' (QH). My focus is somewhat different, focusing on a non-indigenous group, namely NITECA, who amongst other things offer an island of dialogue amongst a tense post GFA ethnic climate. Before focusing on the principles and activities of this group, I give some brief biographical details about the man who inspired this association, namely Fethullah Gülen.

Fethullah Gülen

The Gülen-inspired publishing company, Fountain, describes Gülen as follows: 'An intellectual with a distinctive spiritual charisma, a prolific writer and poet, M. Fethullah Gülen has been an extremely effective and popular scholar of Islam for the last three decades' (Fountain, 2002: i). This type of description is echoed by other scholars, including the political scientist, M. Hakan Yavuz (2003) and the Islamic theologian, Zeki Saritoprak (2005). Gülen was born in Turkey, where he eventually became a licensed Imam and subsequently an esteemed writer and orator. As well as being educated in Islamic theology, he is also well versed in the natural and social sciences and has reportedly 'tried to synthesize positive science with religion, reconcile their apparent differences, and bring the ideologies and philosophies of East and West closer together' (Fountain, 2002: 4). Though he has largely been influenced by the Sufi tradition, and indeed wrote a best-selling book (Gülen, 2004a) on its major principles, he never established anything like a Sufi order (Gokcek, 2005).

Gülen's emphasis on tolerance in Islam and adherence to the secular state gained him favour with several important Turkish politicians and his charisma, heart-felt speeches, ascetic lifestyle and his prolific writings gained him millions of followers amongst the Turkish public. Gülen offers his supporters a worldview that is grounded in Islam and more specifically in the Sufi tradition. Fethullah Gülen is an advocate of interfaith dialogue between different

Muslim groups and different religions. In his pursuit of this goal, he has met with several world religious leaders, including the former Roman Catholic Pope, John Paul II, the leader of the Orthodox Church, Patriarch Barthalemeos; Turkey's Chief Rabbi, David Aseo; Israel's Sephardic Head Rabbi, Eliyahu Bakshi Doron. He has also met with and influenced Turkish presidents and academics. These endeavours have arguably made Gülen an important religious figure both in Turkey and around the world.

With a belief in the necessity of Dialogue between different cultures and religions he helped establish the Journalists and Writers Foundation in 1994. He is the honorary president of this organisation. This Foundation consistently organises conferences and meetings to promote dialogue and tolerance between different sections of Turkish society. In early 1995, they initiated a Ramadan Dinner (Iftar) which included representatives from many different strata of Turkish society. Yilmaz tells us that 'In terms of diversity of the participants, it was the first of its kind' (2003: 230). Early in 2000, they also held an interfaith conference that focused on the celebration of Abraham, as the common figure amongst Jews, Christians and Muslims (Yilmaz, 2003). In 2004, on the 10th Anniversary of the Journalists and Writers Foundation, they held a conference in Istanbul, named 'The Common Moral Values in the Three Monotheistic Religions and Terror', where members from different faiths congregated to discuss the relationship between religion and terrorism. These are just some of the many conferences organised by this Gülen-inspired foundation.

The Journalists and Writers Foundation represents the largely structured part of the Gülen movement. Most of the movement is however much more fragmented and grassroots, which is perhaps the reason for its success. Organisations have been set up all around the world, inspired by Fethullah Gülen, though he appears to have little knowledge and control over them. Ihsan Yilmaz (2003: 235) notes that Gülen encourages his followers to migrate in order to become ambassadors for the Turkish state around the world. This idea is encapsulated in the concept of *dar al-hizmet* (country of service), which Gülen interprets as meaning that Muslims are not obliged to live in Muslim countries but wherever they go they must respect the law of the land they are in and serve their faith by respecting those in their host country (Yilmaz, 2003: 234). Gülen further motivates his followers to mobilise by insisting that the mere aversion of transgressions is not sufficient to being a 'good Muslim'. One must also become socially active in order to improve the conditions in the world. Islam, according to Gülen's articulation, is action-oriented. He argues that to become an integral Muslim one must live to serve the benefit of others in order to be satiated in the next world (see Agai, 2002: 38; Komecoglu, 1997: 52). This principle has inspired the establishment of a multitude of organisations around the world devoted to interfaith dialogue, peaceful co-existence and conflict resolution. One such organisation is based in Northern Ireland and goes by the name of NITECA. I intend to use this group as an example of the real and practical contribution of Fethullah Gülen.

Introducing NITECA

NITECA was initiated in 2004 by a number of Turkish residents living in Northern Ireland. Amongst its principal goals are to help integrate Turkish people living in Northern Ireland into the host society. This does not mean assimilating but promoting their own culture whilst learning from their host country's culture. They promote a wide range of activities aimed at promoting tolerance and respect for different communities, as well as demonstrating aspects of their own culture. Their pursuits include a strong focus on interfaith and intercultural dialogue. More will be said about this in the next section. At this stage it is enough to note that these include, conferences celebrating the commonality amongst the Abrahamic Religions, subsidised trips to Turkey and a range of other events promoting Turkish culture.

NITECA was established by a few Turkish academics and business-people living and working in Northern Ireland, several of whom had experience of working in Gülen-inspired associations in different countries. As the group grew, however, they recruited several university graduate students from Turkey and other Central Asian[2] nations, who were committed to their ideals, in order to consolidate their association in Northern Ireland.

I asked one member of NITECA how he felt about coming to Northern Ireland. He admitted that he had heard that it was a troubled place. Some of his friends exclaimed "oh it's not a good place in Northern Ireland. It's not safe". Despite this warning he made the trip to Belfast and has now been working voluntarily with NITECA for three years. The important point is that he believed Belfast to be an unsafe place to live and he still showed the courage to go there to work voluntarily. He now feels that these warnings were naïve and feels very safe living in Belfast.

Another member from Turkey speaks humbly about his experiences working in troubled spots around the world such as Albania and Kosovo, where he was director of a Gülen-inspired school. He claims that these Balkan countries share hundreds of years of history with Turkey from the Ottoman era and he therefore felt at ease in these regions despite the conflictual situations surrounding him. He also noted that there were still many Turkish-speakers there. Many other members of the Gülen Movement have entered into war-thorn regions, especially in Central Asia and the Balkans over the years in order to promote their ideals. Given the experiences of these volunteers they were largely unflustered by the violent history of Northern Ireland and the thought of entering into an apprehensive post GFA atmosphere.

The work undertaken by members of NITECA is voluntary. I asked members of the association what motivated them to give up their time to engage in these social endeavours. One member said:

> I think it is a responsibility. It is not a hobby... If I don't do it I will be irresponsible according to my religion. It is one of the major requirements of my religion... You can't sit down in your house all the time. If Islam is good you have to live it... You must be proactive, especially in this part of the world... [where] dialogue is needed.

This opinion is widespread in NITECA. Members believe it is their responsibility as "good Muslims" to carry out good works. They insist that though prayer, pilgrimage and asceticism are core components of Islam, so is engaging in social endeavours to make the world a more peaceful place. They do this through the promotion of dialogical activities. This echoes Gülen's action-oriented Islam which is grounded in social engagement with other faith and cultural groups. It further illustrates the impact of his conceptualisation of dar al-hizmet previously referred to. Gülen (2005) describes organisations like NITECA that promote interfaith dialogue, as 'Peace Islands'. These 'Peace Islands' he argues promote "understanding" and "tolerance" and must be designed to encourage 'universal human virtues' and draw together those of different beliefs and orientations in a mutually respected milieu. I now illustrate the manifestation of these principles by describing some of the projects NITECA has initiated.

---

2 See Turam, B. (2003) for a discussion on Gülen's emphasis on the ancient ethnic affinity between Turkey and the Turkic countries of Central Asia

NITECA's Activities

Interfaith dialogue is a must today, and the first step in establishing it is forgetting the past, ignoring polemical arguments, and giving precedence to common points, which far outnumber polemical ones (Gülen, cited in Unal and Williams, 2000: 244/5)

In an era when Huntington's (2002) mediatised thesis arguing for the inevitable clash of civilisations is gaining strength, Gülen insists that dialogue should replace the potential clash. This can only be accomplished, he argues, by side-stepping the most antagonistic and apparently irreconcilable differences and instead focusing on the similarities amongst different groups, which he insists far outweigh the differences.

This attitude threads all the activities of NITECA. One member explains their dialogical practice. He insists that dialogue must begin at the most basic level and proceeds to give an example:

> ...in the Kurban festival, we sacrifice the sheep and then we have meat, fresh cooked meat and we shared [it] with all the neighbours in [the area we live in Belfast]... And at first they were surprised... For 20 minutes we explained [to a local man] and he was very suspicious and then at the end he said "Is it possible to get one more plate?". And these are the reasons – to know each other...but also we celebrate Christmas and then they celebrate our festivals. It is very good samples for dialogue.

This anecdote is illustrative of the humble and small-scale attempts by NITECA to begin dialogue in Northern Ireland. They begin by sharing what they know and then attempt to learn from their ethnically and religiously different neighbours. From basic acts like these, NITECA has built up many relationships with different faith groups, including, Jewish, Catholics, Protestants and Bahai'is. Following the lead of Fethullah Gülen and the Writers and Journalists Foundation, they have organised Ramadan dinners (Iftar), whereby they invite different faith groups to share a meal together, hosted by NITECA. A NITECA member notes that though it is common for Muslims to share food with others during the month of Ramadan;

> ...inviting different faith groups to the dinner is a new idea and it started in Turkey in the 1990's again by Fethullah Gülen.

This dinner has taken place for the last two consecutive years and the members claim it was a great starting point to get to know different groups in the area. They acknowledge that some Muslims believe that Ramadan is only about sharing with other Muslims but insist that those people misinterpret the spirit of the festival. They further maintain that the Koran specifically calls "people of the book" (i.e Jews, Christians and Muslims) to come together. Inspired by this principle, these dinners play host to Catholics, Protestants, Jewish, and different Muslim groups, all seated around the same table.

One senior member of NITECA pays tribute to the work of Gülen and his close associates for their extraordinary work. However, he recognises that NITECA cannot accomplish such massive feats as meeting the Pope and Head Rabbis. He does, however, point out the importance of the dialogue, not only between the faith leaders, but also between the 'participants of different faiths' (which he means non-clerics – lay-people). Without this commitment to the ordinary man and woman, he argues, dialogue between the faith leaders will come to nothing. This is very much a bottom-up approach which engages at the community level. He mentions that he has organised a table-tennis competition between different faith groups and insists that this is a form of dialogue that is every bit as important as any conference.

Celebration of the Commonalities in the Abrahamic Religions

The insistence on the ubiquity of commonalities between the Abrahamic religions is one of the keys to Fethullah Gülen's thought. He claims:

> As a Muslim, I accept all Prophets and Books sent to different peoples throughout history, and regard belief in them as an essential principle of being Muslim. A Muslim is a true follower of Abraham, Moses, David, Jesus, and all other Prophets. Not believing in one Prophet or Book means that one is not a Muslim. Thus we acknowledge the oneness and basic unity of religion, which is a symphony of God's blessings and mercy, and the universality of belief in religion.
> (Gülen, cited in Unal and Williams, 2000: 242)

One must believe in all the prophets of the Abrahamic religions in order to be "true Muslim", he argues. Though there are clearly differences between the beliefs in the different personalities of the Prophets, Gülen encourages Muslims to embrace all religions but pays most attention to the Abrahamic ones as they have most obvious things in common. In an effort to bring peace he encourages his followers to embrace the similarities and ignore the differences between the different faith groups.

The most explicit promotion of interfaith dialogue by NITECA comes in the form of the interfaith symposiums they organise. In 2006 they held a conference focusing on the 'Mercy in the Abrahamic Religions', inviting speakers from the Jewish and Christian community in Northern Ireland. In 2007 they organised a symposium, namely 'Fundamentals of Peace', where there were speakers from the three faiths again, who talked about the universal principles of 'truthfulness and trustworthiness'. There was also a professional storyteller from the Baha'i community. These conferences attracted up to 100 attendees from a variety of religious backgrounds, including Jewish, Catholic, Protestant and Sunni and Shi'a Muslims. One member of NITECA explained the reasoning behind these conferences:

> ...it is important to share and discuss the common values... We believe in the Abrahamic religions. At the basic principles all the religions are the same. As a Christian you cannot tell me that being a thief is good behaviour, no you cannot say this...the Muslim people believe that all of these Abrahamic religions... are from the same light... The origin is the same. We invited a professional story teller. She was of the Baha'I community... She read from stories of the Bible and the Koran... each religion was represented... at the conference... When we are organising this [conference], the aim is not to compare the religions and it is not to talk about the differences. I think if we come together and talk about the differences we will not solve our problems. You are a Christian. If you are a good Christian you are happy and I am happy. You should be a good Christian and I should be a good Muslim. But while I am being a good Muslim, I should be aware of you and learn about you and your traditions... the aim is not to convert or to make them Muslim or Christian...

Again this echoes Fethullah Gülen's work with an insistence on the certain compatibility of the different Abrahamic religions. This volunteer argues that focusing on the differences will lead to more conflict. One must, he argues, learn and appreciate each other's culture and traditions in order to live in harmony. Members of NITECA acknowledge that they did not 'invent' these themes but they just replicate the annual conferences going on in Turkey. Indeed the same conferences with the same theme are replicated in many different countries around the world, inspired by organisations belonging to the Gülen Movement.

The dialogical approach of this Gülen-inspired association sounds quite simplistic especially in the context of Northern Ireland with its violent past. Indeed it is a straightforward approach and in the current climate whereby the guns have largely stopped firing in Northern

Ireland, this simple approach appears to be having some impact, although modest. The sight of Catholics, Protestants, Jews and Muslims, sitting around the same table in a peaceful milieu bodes well for the future.

Another example of NITECA's ideas on dialogue can be explained by a recent visit they had from an academic who was interested in understanding their perspectives on education. She asked one of the leading members if he thought that Islam should be incorporated into the curriculum. He replied, to her surprise, in the negative and insisted that Islam should not be taught in schools but should be left to the parents direction. This principle is consistent with the ethos of the Gülen-inspired schools around the world. Islam is not taught or privileged in these schools (Turam, 2003). This came as a surprise to the Jesuit academic Thomas Michel who visited several of these schools and studied Gülen's education vision. He noted the ethnic and religious diversity of these schools and insisted that proselytising was never a factor as students from different faiths and ethnic backgrounds studied harmoniously (Michel, 2003). Journalist Nicole Pope (1998) found similar results in the Gülen-inspired schools in Turkmenistan. In another of these Gülen-inspired schools in Kazakhstan, Turam was taken aback at finding Turkish Jews opening high schools in the name of Gülen. Furthermore she discovered through interviewing students and students' parents that they were unaware of any Islamic association with these schools or aware of Fethullah Gülen.

Returning to the NITECA respondent mentioned above, instead of teaching Islam in schools, he proposed that there ought to be 'dialogue classes' incorporated into the curriculum which would 'teach people to live together'. This would serve all the people of Northern Ireland. He suggests piloting it in a few schools to begin with to see if it works. This indeed is an interesting proposal in an attempt to deschool society of prejudices. NITECA made similar recommendations at another conference organised with the Police Service of Northern Ireland (PSNI).

PSNI Conference

Muslims should say, "In true Islam, terror does not exist." In Islam, killing a human is an act that is equal in gravity to unbelief. No person can kill a human being. No one can touch an innocent person, even in time of war. No one can give a fatwa (legal pronouncement in Islam) in this matter. No one can be a suicide bomber. No one can rush into crowds with bombs tied to his or her body. Regardless of the religion of these crowds, this is not religiously permissible (Gülen, 2004b: 1).

The above is an unambiguous condemnation of terrorism by Fethullah Gülen. One cannot be a Muslim and a terrorist, he insists. Shortly after the 9/11 attacks in New York, Gülen wrote an article in *The New York Times*, expressing a similar sentiment. This attitude inspired NITECA to organise a conference, named 'The Necessity of Dialogue to Prevent another 7/7' with the Police Service of Northern Ireland's (PSNI) Community Safety Branch. It was a closed conference whose attendees were solely from the PSNI, including, the Chief Constable of Northern Ireland and a number of police officers working in the field of community relations. The main speaker was Ozcan Keles of the London Centre for Social Studies. He reportedly spoke about the key factors that caused the attacks in London on the 7th of July 2005 which resulted from 'prejudice, preconception, misunderstanding, fear, suspicion and animosity' (www.NITECA.org.uk). He subsequently went on to argue that the interfaith dialogical approach promoted by Fethullah Gülen serves as a possible way to prevent another such terrorist attack. One member of NITECA noted that though this was a small conference, it was effective.

Given that the PSNI has always had major difficulties dealing with the largest minority group in Northern Ireland, namely Catholics, for reasons too complex to discuss here, it is a progressive move to see that they are embracing other minority groups in this increasingly diverse region. It appears to be a sincere attempt to help understand the situation of Muslims living in Northern Ireland. From the decades of troubles in the region perhaps the legally armed forces of this disputed territory have finally realised that dialogue is the answer to peaceful coexistence. The conference also served to raise the profile of NITECA amongst state officials and other minority ethnic groups in Northern Ireland.

Cultural Events Organised by NITECA

Much of the discussion above has focused on conferences organised by NITECA, which are typically aimed at elites in society; those who can make changes at an official level. However, NITECA is also engaged in a variety of cultural pursuits which are aimed at the general public. Each year they distribute a dessert known as 'Noah's Pudding'. In collaboration with Catholic and Protestant churches, they dispense the puddings to those leaving church on Sunday mornings. They also include a leaflet describing the reason for distributing this pudding and also detailing the ingredients. The leaflet narrates that when the Prophet Noah survived the flood, his family gathered all the remaining food on the ship and made a pudding. NITECA members replicate this symbolic gesture in order to remember the Prophet Noah. This endeavour is also an act of dialogue. They claim that:

> Sharing food offers a way to re-affirm unity and the essential relationship of humans to one another, regardless of faith background and belief (www.niteca.org.uk)

Other cultural events organised by NITECA include a trip to Turkey, subsidised by business associates of the Gülen Movement in Turkey. This trip is articulated as an intercultural event. They also organised the Whirling Dervishes to come to Belfast. This group has its roots in the work of the famous sufi poet, Mevlana Jalal al-Din Rumi, whose work has been very influential on Fethullah Gülen. Rumi is renowned for his emphasis on tolerance and dialogue.

Analysis

The examples of NITECA'S activities discussed in the previous section illustrate its declared commitment to tolerance and dialogue. They are different to the traditional organisations working for dialogue and peace in Northern Ireland in many ways. They are obviously non-indigenous, whilst the vast majority of groups engaged in dialogical practice in Northern Ireland are natives to Ireland. The most important difference, however, is the difference in outlook. Indigenous groups in Northern Ireland act locally and think locally. They work at a grass-roots level to try and bring peace to the region. Their thoughts are on peace in their local area and region and they are unlikely to envision their modest work as having a global impact.

NITECA on the other hand engages in an explicit form of what sociologists refer to as glocalization. This concept has its origins in marketing culture whereby global corporations adapt their products and managerial practices to local conditions and tastes (Robertson, 1997). Roland Robertson (1997) generalises this concept to refer to the interpenetration of the global and local in any given context. In a very practical way members of NITECA act locally and think globally, always positioned delicately and concurrently in the two contexts without incongruence. By thinking globally (in their capacity as NITECA volunteers) they always pay heed to the messages and principles of Fethullah Gülen and are loosely connected to other Gülen-inspired groups around the world in a global circuit. They largely work in unison with the same aims and objectives but adapt their dialogical methods to local situations. As shown in the previous section NITECA are keen to work with anybody who is willing to engage with them. This has included, faith members of all the Abrahamic religions, including Catholics and Protestants. They have also adopted a conscious strategy of inviting local academics and clerics to speak at their conferences, whilst at times electing to draw from their international reservoir of 'sister organisations' to bring in spokesmen to represent the Muslim opinion on a variety of issues.

Their emphasis on localism largely extends to funding also. NITECA members insist that they get most of their funding from local Turkish business-people and other funding from the City Council, though they also have collection boxes in local shops to help with their fundraising. They maintain that finances are regularly tight but they do not let these obstacles deter them. They do however sometimes 'go global' in an attempt to gain funding for some activities. Members acknowledged that they get some financial assistance from business-people in Turkey to help subsidise a yearly trip they organise to Turkey for indigenous people of Ireland. This trip, as mentioned above, is a continuation of their promotion of intercultural dialogue. It also serves to promote Turkish culture in Northern Ireland.

Having spoken in-depth to several members of NITECA, as well as attending conferences and a trip to Turkey, I am of the opinion NITECA's main aim is to promote a positive version of Islam and Turkey. However, as previously mentioned, guided by their faith in Islam, they also feel an obligation to serve humanity in order to be rewarded in the hereafter. Following the lead of Fethullah Gülen, they attempt to endorse a tolerant version of Islam that is grounded in the Sufi principles of love and tolerance. They claim that fundamentalist Muslims have, to an extent, 'hijacked' Islam. They further maintain that the image of Muslims and Islam as violent is reinforced by a disproportional and sensationalist focus by the media on this minority of Islamic fundamentalists. This view is supported by the author of the ground breaking book, *Orientalism* (1979), Edward Said. He has taken up this theme in his book, *Covering Islam: How the media and the Experts Determine How We See the Rest of the World* (1997). This volume attempts to illustrate how the majority of opinion-makers in Europe and America, both journalists and academics, have predominantly portrayed Islam as a monolithic group determined to challenge the West through terrorist activities. Said claims that:

> Malicious generalizations about Islam have become the last acceptable form of denigration of foreign culture in the West; what is said about the Muslim mind, or character, or religion, or culture as a whole cannot now be said in mainstream discussion about Africans, Jews, other Orientals, or Asians. (1997: xi/xii)

In any other context, such denigration would be rightly regarded as racism. However in the context of Islam, such vilification appears acceptable as it has become part of the 'common sense thinking' of many people in the Western world, particularly since the September 2001 attacks on New York and Washington. In the absence of a collective effort to portray positive representations of Muslims by western opinion-makers, it is only the negative depictions that filter down to the general media consumer. Said (1997) notes that for every book written fairly on the subject of Islam, there are numerous written with an unbalanced orientation towards depicting Muslims as terrorists. The corollary of this, according to Said, is that 'the average reader comes to see Islam and fundamentalism as essentially the same thing' (Said, 1997: xvi). For the average person, Islam becomes synonymous with terrorism, violence and atavism. Muslims in the West have thus been racialised in this derogatory manner. Said's position was articulated before the terrorist attacks in New York (2001). A variety of authors have since shown that the denigration of Islam by Western opinion-makers has intensified since the attacks in New York (Modood, 2005; Anwar, 2005; Parekh, 2006; Ishay, 2004; Wu, 2004).

Members of NITECA feel a duty to help remedy this situation through the various conferences and cultural projects they organise which emphasise dialogue as the key to peaceful coexistence. However, though I maintain that a key element of NITECA's activities include the promotion of a positive image of Islam and Turkey, it is important to note that their events help bring different faith groups together and their presence is conducive to the project of lasting peace in Northern Ireland. Furthermore their activities may contribute to the formation of an antidote to the growing racialisation of migrants and ethnic minorities in post GFA Northern.

Given the difficult history of ethnic and religious intolerance in Northern Ireland and the current nervous post-GFA environment, one may question whether another ethnic and faith group in Northern Ireland could exacerbate tensions rather than acting as a potential antidote. In response, it is clear that we now live in a globalised world and one corollary of this is an increase in migration and furthermore an unprecedented mixture of cultures and religions. As aforementioned there has been a dramatic increase in migration to Northern Ireland in recent years. The Turkish community are amongst these migrants. They do not claim to represent all Muslims in the region but do espouse views of tolerance and through Gülen's conceptualisation of *dar al-hizmet*, they obey the laws of the land and offer a contribution to the society based on their system of beliefs which avowedly has service to humanity at its core. By hosting various functions and inviting different ethnic and faith groups, including Catholics and Protestants, NITECA has acted as a conduit by setting up a platform which may be interpreted with suspicion if it was initiated by either of the aforementioned Christian groups. In this sense the neutrality of Islam vis-à-vis the different Christian groups may serve as their strongest asset in promoting their dialogue platforms. Furthermore it has been well documented that some migrants isolate themselves in their host country. This is often exacerbated by restrictive and assimilationist tendencies of the host government. NITECA have shown that they are willing and indeed actively engaged in integrating into the mainstream in Northern Ireland, combating potential problems of isolation and discordance.

Cochrane and Dunn (2002: 178) note that it is difficult to assess the quantitative influence of small bottom-up organisations working for peace in Northern Ireland. They claim that it is only when you see the cumulative affect of all of these organisations that you realise the importance of each small group. NITECA is amongst these associations whose contribution is humble, though noteworthy. In the same light NITECA is but a small organisation inspired by Gülen. Their input to the Movement is certainly humble though added to the hundreds of other Gülen-inspired associations around the world, the cumulative affect is considerable and has helped turn a social movement peculiar to Turkey into a global social movement with peace and tolerance as their avowed core principles.

Conclusion

This article attempted to evaluate the contribution of Fethullah Gülen by focusing on an organisation inspired by his teachings. I believe my methodological approach helps the reader to understand the very practical and grounded contribution of Fethullah Gülen to interfaith and intercultural dialogue. Using the backdrop of Northern Ireland, I illustrated the commit-ment of the Gülen Movement members by entering into an uncertain post-conflict territory that was named in 2005 by Der Spiegel magazine as 'the most racist City in the world' (cited in Lentin and McVeigh, 2006: 145). A focus on Northern Ireland also demonstrates the global reach of Fethullah Gülen's ideas. I found it necessary near the beginning of this article to discuss the current situation in Northern Ireland. Some people may be under the illusion that since the GFA was signed in 1998, ethnic tension has ceased. I argued that instead of ending, it may have exacerbated and indeed created a milieu whereby there is a widespread distrust of all ethnic groups. With growing migration to the region, the potential for ethnic tension is ominous. I argued that the dialogical activities of the Gülen-inspired NITECA may contribute to the antidote to this ethic tension and their presence is conducive to peace-building in the region.

Largely using the words of NITECA members I displayed several of their activities and clearly showed the influence of Fethullah Gülen's thought on all of their projects. These endeavours include conferences focusing on the celebration of the Abrahamic religions, Iftar dinners for different faith groups and a seminar with the PSNI in order to discuss ways to pre-vent terrorist attacks. These activities are oriented towards the elites in society, in an attempt to influence academics and important state institutions. Other endeavours target the general public. These include more basic and simple elements such as playing games and picnicking with other faith groups, as well as the distribution of Noah's pudding and organising subsi-dised trips to Turkey. NITECA members insist these are good ways to begin dialogue.

Analysing their activities I argued that NITECA embrace the process of glocalization. They act local but think global. I explained that NITECA adapt the philosophy of Fethullah Gülen to local conditions but concurrently think of the global impact of their work and are al-ways connected to the global circuit of the globalised Gülen Movement. I further argued that amongst NITECA's aims are to promote a positive image of Islam and Turkey, whilst also offering a service to humanity. I thus concluded that their presence in Northern Ireland is conducive to a peaceful milieu in the region. Though their contribution is modest, they are challenging the racialisation of minority ethnic groups in Northern Ireland by engaging in constructive dialogue. NITECA can be understood as a 'Peace Island' that may indeed replace the so-called 'peace walls' in Northern Ireland.

Professor of Philosophy, Bhikhu Parekh (2006) argues that there are many powerful groups in Europe that insist that the values and practice of the 15 million Muslims residing there are incompatible with European values. However he importantly notes that there is little evidence to corroborate this proposition. By focusing on the Gülen-inspired NITECA, this article has shown how a group of Muslims have adapted to one of the most difficult situations in Europe (i.e. post GFA Northern Ireland) and have indeed found their niche in this region on the edge of Europe.

In conclusion as the title of this conference indicates, the Muslim world is in transition. It now has to deal with extremists within the *Ummah* as well as with the portrayal of Islam as inherently radical and its members as an undifferentiated group, by the majority of opinion makers in the West. With the hyperbolic claims of the inevitability of the 'clash of civiliza-tions' permeating the general consciousness, there is a need for a counter-discourse from both Muslims and non-Muslims alike. John Esposito notes that

> While a minority of extremists focus on revolution in their own countries and abroad, others
> concentrate on more peaceful political and social "revolutions" and reforms dedicated to the

incorporation and expression of Islamic values in both the public and private spheres. (2003: 1)

Fethullah Gülen and the Movement that has surrounded him have discursively and practically contributed to peaceful participation in civil society. I hope that this paper has illustrated this point. There is need for a more balanced investigation of the variety of expressions of Islam and a need for academics to focus more on the peaceful movements and movements promoting moderation. I hope I have contributed to this endeavour by focusing on the dialogical relations practiced by the Gülen Movement at a very micro level.

A BRIDGE TO INTER-RELIGIOUS COOPERATION: THE GÜLEN-JESUIT EDUCATIONAL NEXUS

Michael David Graskemper

Abstract

The Gülen movement's educational mission is, at its core and in its praxis, remarkably similar to the centuries-old Jesuit educational tradition. It can be argued that both educational movements are united in a *shared* mission today –a deep concern for the spiritual freedom of the individual and a commitment to the betterment of the world.

Both movements seek to instil values such as honesty, dedication, compassion and tolerance. To achieve this goal, students are offered a narrative of the past as a foundation on which to build an understanding of the modern world. Furthermore, they are educated holistically – in ethics and social justice as well as the sciences – what Gülen calls a 'marriage of mind and heart'.

This paper focuses on four shared values of education: commitment, responsibility, virtue and service. Within this framework, themes found in the Gülen educational movement, such as the Golden Generation and the concept of *hizmet*, are compared to similar Jesuit notions such as A.M.D.G., *cura personalis*, and 'Men and Women for Others'. Differences and nuances are also addressed in the paper. The discussion aims to highlight the importance of values-oriented education in the modern world. The Gülen–Jesuit educational nexus is one positive bridge to inter-religious understanding and, importantly, collaborative action.

The educational endeavors associated with the Turkish-Muslim Gülen movement have popularized, possibly more than any other facet of the group, Fethullah Gülen's mission to promulgate and cultivate an individually transformative Islam in the modern world. As the teachers and business partners of the Gülen movement continue to work to form conscientious, open-minded and just students in different cultures across the world, they will continue to be challenged and influenced by a myriad of different perspectives, religions, and socio-political groups; and, in turn, they will succeed in positively influencing those same cultures, as they have in many cases already. Of the many groups with which the Gülen movement has interacted in its ever-expanding intercultural milieu, this paper will focus on one: the educational charge of a Roman Catholic religious order called the Society of Jesus, a group more commonly known as the Jesuits.

This paper shows that the educational mission of the Gülen movement is, at its core, remarkably similar to the mission of the centuries-old Jesuit Catholic educational tradition. In fact, it can be argued that the Gülen and Jesuit educational missions are, in theory and in praxis, united in a *shared* mission today; one that is rooted in a deep concern for the spiritual freedom of the individual and dedicated to the betterment of the world. In analyzing this shared mission, this paper aims to discuss the importance of values-oriented education; particularly by addressing how the Gülen-Jesuit educational nexus can act as one positive bridge to interreligious understanding and, importantly, cooperation and action in our transitioning world.

In order to achieve this end, this paper begins with a short analysis of each movement's background with regard to education. Afterwards, the each movement's notion of religious education is discussed. Finally, the focus turns to the mission themes the educational movements have in common. While there is a plethora of shared mission traits from which one could choose, for practical purposes this paper uses as its foundation for comparison four themes distilled by William J. Byron, S.J., from a mission statement from Georgetown University, the Jesuit university in Washington, D.C., which reads:

> Georgetown seeks to be a place where understanding is joined to commitment; where the search
> for truth is informed by a sense of responsibility for the life of society; where academic excellence
> in teaching…is joined with the cultivation of virtue; and where a community is formed which
> sustains men and women in their education and their conviction that life is only lived well when it
> is lived generously in the service of others (Byron 1997, 653).

The first of these themes is a *commitment* to the understanding that God works in the world through people. The second is a *responsibility* to raise individual students to act justly in and for the world. The third is *virtue*, with the understanding that the way to achieve the mission of these schools is through educating students to be morally upright. Finally, the fourth theme is the need to be actively engaged in *service* to make the world a more peaceful, tolerant and just place to live. Commitment, responsibility, virtue, and service are, significantly, foundational for not only Jesuit schools, but Gülen schools as well.

Mission & Background

Both the Gülen and Jesuit educational movements seek to instill in students values such as honesty, dedication, conscientiousness, compassion and tolerance. To achieve this goal, students are offered a narrative of the past as a foundation on which to build an understanding of the modern world and their individual roles in making it more peaceful and just. Furthermore, students in Gülen and Jesuit schools are educated holistically in the sciences as well as ethics and social justice; a "marriage of mind and heart," as Gülen says (Michel 2003, 84). Each movement strives to create people of genuine freedom and authenticity who can be active and sincere voices of dialogue and action in an increasingly-divided world.

However, while the Gülen and Jesuit missions are strikingly similar, it ought not to be assumed that these movements are the *same*. After all, Gülen education, like Jesuit education, is far from monolithically expressed: both traditions are vast, have many layers, and are often as diverse as the cultures in which they thrive. Furthermore, each movement is involved in communities in ways that are broader than just their educational initiatives. For instance, while it can be said that the Jesuit circles have some political clout in many countries[1] and, in times past, held major political sway, the Jesuits today do not have the same cultural base and political aspirations as the Gülen movement in Turkey does. But, nuances aside, the educational movements are separated by two prominent, albeit basic, differences worth mentioning: the fundamental scriptural inspirations for each, and the teaching—or not—of courses in religious education. The paper will now look at the first of these differences.

The Gülen movement is comprised of Muslims, mainly, who look to the life and teachings of the Prophet Muhammad for practical inspiration; whereas Jesuits, as Roman Catholic Christians, primarily, look to the life and teachings of Jesus. While Jesus is without a doubt greatly revered in the Islamic tradition, Jesus' role in the Christian tradition is fundamentally different than the Jesus of the Qur'an. This is based on a significantly different theology that is beyond the scope of this paper. However, Muhammad and Jesus are not the only two inspirations upon which these movements were founded. The Jesuit educational movement finds its spiritual heritage in the life and writings of Ignatius of Loyola (1491-1556), while the Gülen movement owes much of its heritage to the life and thought of Bediüzzaman Said Nursi (1878-1960).

Ignatius of Loyola did not originally envision himself as the leader of a religious order whose major ministry was education. When the Society of Jesus was founded in 1540, the Protestant Reformation was sweeping Europe. In that milieu Ignatius believed that his order would be a missionary movement the aim of which would be to recall people to the Catholic faith. In some ways this vision was fulfilled, in no small part, by the spread of Jesuit schools around the world. In the end, "education was a ministry to which Ignatius, intent on saving souls and defending the Catholic church, was drawn not because he planned it but because so many of his contemporaries, seeing his success in training his own men, wanted it for themselves and their sons" (Troy 1991, 606-7).

Quite similarly Fethullah Gülen did not envision himself as the "leader" of an educational movement when he was a student. Even now, Fethullah Gülen finds this title somewhat imprecise, saying, "I am tired of saying that I do not have any schools" (Aslandoğan and Çetin 2005, 32; from Webb 2000:106). Yet, much like Ignatius was drawn into the realm of education by the spirit of the times and his skill as an educator, Gülen too has found that his schools are perhaps the greatest success of his movement. Furthermore, as Ignatius' original movement grew in Counter Reformation Europe, the Gülen movement has grown in response to the modernization and secularization of Turkey and acts, in many ways, as a moderate yet dedicated challenge to the more radical Islamist movements arising in many parts of the world (Yavuz 2003a, 4).

The Jesuit movement spread because at its core "lies a determination to make education not just a next-step commodity for the privileged, but a powerful tool for transforming society

---

1 "While the twenty-eight [American Jesuit universities] are independent, they work together through the Association of Jesuit Colleges and Associations, an effective Washington lobby" (Troy 1991, 607).

as well" (von Arx 2005, 317). This is based on the Jesuit understanding of "recognizing the God-given dignity of each person; acknowledging that each had God-given gifts and talents that could bless our world; and deciding to assume moral agency in helping those gifts to bear fruit, through education" (von Arx 2005, 318). Likewise, Gülen's concept of education is rooted in the deeply rich Islamic traditions of Rumi and Nursi, who also understood the inherent dignity of each individual, being inspired by the Qur'an. Gülen himself ascribes to the "Sufi model of self-cultivation," which "teaches followers to internalize values of tolerance, patience, dignity, self-esteem, and self-sacrifice for the sake of the community," and which recognizes the gifts of every person (Yavuz 2003b, 34).

Although Fethullah Gülen never personally met Nursi, his understanding of education was greatly influenced by his teachings, among others (Michel 2003, 81). Of those teachings that influenced Gülen were Nursi's three goals for his community of followers:

> (1) To raise Muslims' religious consciousness (self-transformation very important); (2) to refute the dominant intellectual discourses of materialism and positivism; and (3) to recover collective memory by revising the shared grammar of society, Islam. This faith community empowers communal life by stressing the power of knowledge, freedom, and initiative to build stable Muslims selves and communities (Yavuz 2003a, 5).

Gülen, however, departed from Nursi in several important ways. M. Hakan Yavuz writes that, "Gülen leads a different form of movement [than Nursi], one that is more praxis oriented and seeks to transform society and institutions by expanding its circles of sympathizers" (Yavuz 2003a, 3). This focus on praxis, especially through educational initiatives, is very different from Nursi's original faith movement:

> Although Nursi was focused on personal transformation, Gülen has focused on personal and social transformation by utilizing new liberal economic and political conditions. As a combined ulema-intellectual persona, Gülen not only preaches inner mobilization of new social and cultural actors, but also introduces a new liberative map of action. His goals are to sharpen Muslim self-consciousness, to deepen the meaning of the shared idioms and practices of society, to empower excluded social groups through education and networks, and to bring just and peaceful solutions to the social and psychological problems of society (Yavuz 2003b, 19).

Bekim Agai argues that the main reason for this departure from Nursi's faith movement is "Gülen's perception of education and of the effects resulting from engagement in the educational sector" (Agai 2003, 54). Due to the spread and popularity of Gülen schools, the movement has become more than just a faith-based movement battling localized issues. It has instead become a world-wide educational movement that seeks to build a more peaceful world through dialogue and cooperation.

Religious Education

Before this paper turns to the four common mission themes of Gülen and Jesuit schools, it should be noted that Gülen schools, while certainly faith-based initiatives, often do not teach religion as an academic subject. In Turkey, for instance, Gülen schools teach only one hour of religion per week, and even that is a constitutional prescription. In other countries religion is often not taught at all (Agai 2003, 51). In fact, Gülen schools make the choice not to teach religion to avoid proselytizing. This has been a major reason for the movement's success, especially in areas and cultures where communities are religiously diverse, such as Germany or the Philippines, or antagonistic towards religion, such as some formerly Communist Central Asian countries. Gülen has made it a point to clearly state that Gülen schools are not *madrassas*, but it should be remembered that they are not secular schools in the traditional sense of the concept either. Rather, Gülen schools seek to lead students to live ethically by the example of their teachers, not by teaching doctrinal Islam. For example, Thomas Michel, S.J., noticed that because Gülen schools in places like the Philippines and Kyrgyzstan were religiously diverse, the values teachers "sought to communicate were universal Islamic values such as honesty, hard work, harmony, and conscientious service rather than any confessional instruction" (Michel 2003, 70).

On the other hand, Jesuit schools do teach religion and Catholic doctrine in the classroom and this is often a major reason why many people send their children there. However, just as a large part of religious education in Jesuit schools takes place outside of the classroom--i.e., through service opportunities, faith sharing groups, and other religious community activities--so too do Gülen schools find ways to bring religion to their students. Bayram Balci acknowledges that education extends beyond the classroom saying that the methods of the Gülen schools are similar "th[ose] of the Jesuits in that the pupils are permanently being educated regardless of whether they are in the classroom or the dormitory" (Balici 2003, 160). This does not diminish the fact that Gülen schools find their greatest strength in leading others to faith by the example of their teachers. In fact,

> ... even without teaching Islam explicitly, their schools serve Islam because they deliver knowledge. From Gülen's perspective, knowledge itself becomes an Islamic value when it is imparted by teachers with Islamic values and who can show students how to employ knowledge in the right and beneficial Islamic way (Agai 2003, 62).

Commitment

This paper now turns its attention to the four common mission themes Gülen and Jesuit schools share in common. The first marker of Gülen and Jesuit educational philosophy that this paper addresses is the virtue of *commitment*. In the Jesuit context, William J. Byron, S.J., describes commitment in the following way:

> Jesuit education focuses on the care of the person and the cultivation of one's personal human potential. Jesuit alumni are persons who are taking a voyage of self discovery. They have a place to stand. They have a sense of place in the human community and the world of ideas. They hold common ground from which they can exercise 'their conviction that life is only lived well when it is lived generously in the service of others' (Byron 1997, 654).

Embodied in this concept of commitment are two Jesuit ideals that are also held by the Gülen movement, albeit named differently. The first of these is the motto of the Society of Jesus, *Ad Meiorem Dei Gloriam* (or, as it is abbreviated, A.M.D.G.). Literally, this translates from the Latin as "For the Greater Glory of God." The second concept within commitment is that of *cura personalis*, which translates to "care for the person."

The first of these concepts, A.M.D.G., can be understood to mean that one ought to glorify God's greatness in everything one does in life. In this understanding of God and the world, everything in all of creation is filled with the Spirit of God, and one's actions should reflect this truth. God should be remembered constantly and acknowledged with every choice one makes in life.

Fethullah Gülen's writings on education indicate that this theme of commitment is a vital part of his movement's mission as well. Gülen's understanding of morality approaches this ideal of A.M.D.G.: "to learn to live in the presence of God" (Yavuz 2003b, 25). In fact, Gülen's usage of a quote from the Turkish poet and mystic Yunus Emre also comes fairly close to the ideal of A.M.D.G.: "We love the created for the sake of the Creator" (Agai 2003, 64-5). Furthermore, and maybe most importantly, Gülen firmly believes that "dialogue rests on the premise that all kinds of humans share values because they have the same Creator; dialogue is able to show these shared values" (Agai 2003, 65). Both the Gülen and Jesuit communities understand that this common creator to Whom people call out is the One that binds people together and strengthens them in their commitment for justice.

The understanding that God permeates all of creation is embodied in the notion of *cura personalis* as well. Kevin O'Brien, S.J., says that,

> God labors in and through us. If God works with each of us so tenderly, patiently and lovingly, then teachers must aspire to emulate these same qualities in their relationship with students. This is what Jesuit educators mean by cura personalis: caring for each student in mind, body and spirit (O'Brien 2003, 9).

This is exhibited most strongly in Gülen's writings about the relationship between teacher and student. Gülen says that, "A young person is a sapling of power, strength, and intelligence. If trained and educated properly, he or she can become a 'hero' overcoming obstacles and acquire a mind that promises enlightenment to hearts and order to the world" (Gülen 1996d, 51). Michel expands upon this, saying:

> Teachers in Gülen schools must be committed to cultivating virtue in their students because, Gülen warns, 'when [people] are left with no ideals or aims, they become reduced to the condition of animated corpses, showing no signs of distinctly human life....Just as an inactive organ becomes atrophied, and a tool which is not in use becomes rusty, so aimless generations will eventually waste away because they lack ideals and aims' (Gülen, 1996d, 51; Michel, 174-75).

The knowledge that all actions ought to be made for the Greater Glory of God must be nurtured by caring and religiously grounded teachers. This ensures, in Gülen schools and Jesuit schools alike, that students will be committed to making choices out of freedom to act with justice and love in the world. As O'Brien says, teachers encounter the same grace they give when their "students stretch their minds to realize their God-given potential, wonder about new ideas, marvel at the intricate beauty of the world, strive for a more just and gentle world, and grow in love for themselves and others. This is what makes desks like altars, and all of us like sacraments pointing to the divine" (O'Brien 2003, 12).

This commitment is not easy, however, and Ignatius memorialized this struggle in a prayer of his, the *Memorare,* part of which reads that a person should serve God and in doing so, "To give and not to count the cost, to fight and not to head the wounds." Gülen reiterates this sentiment in his own words, saying, "People of service must resolve, for the sake of the cause to which they have given their heart, to cross over seas of 'pus and blood'" (Gülen 2000, 83; Nelson). Similarly, he says that one must remain committed to:

> Preferring the sacred cause over all worldly and animal desires; being steadfast in truth, once it has been discovered, to the degree that you sacrifice all mundane attachments for its sake; enduring all hardships so that future generations will be happy; seeking happiness, not in material or even spiritual pleasures, but in the happiness and well-being of others; never seeking to obtain any posts or positions; and preferring oneself to others in taking on work but preferring others to oneself in receiving wages—these are the essentials of this sacred way of serving the truth (Gülen 2000, 84; Nelson).

Responsibility

The second shared trait of Jesuit and Gülen education is *responsibility*. With regard to this value, Byron describes the spirituality of Jesuit schools as,

> a spirituality of choice. The Jesuit heritage offers centuries of evidence of informed action follow-
> ing upon deliberate choice. And all action, in the Jesuit tradition, is for the greater glory of God.
> God, in the Jesuit view, is to be found and served in the work of building not the Tower of Babel,
> but a New Jerusalem, a better society. And this construction project is undertaken by exercising
> responsibility for the life of society (Byron 1997, 654-5).

Those involved in Jesuit and Gülen education undertake the responsibility of building a better world, one student at a time. The way the Jesuit mission fosters this is by creating what Pedro Arrupe (1907-1991), a Father General of the Society of Jesus, called, "Men for Others," or in modern parlance, "Men and Women for Others." At a meeting of Jesuit Alumni in Europe in 1973, Arrupe stated that, "men who cannot even conceive of love of God which does not include love for the least of their neighbors; men completely convinced that love of God which does not issue injustice for men is a farce"[2] (Byron 1997, 653). Pedro Arrupe's ideal of 'education for others' was a "compromise between education and Christian activism," and a vision of responsibility (Troy 1991, 607).

Fethullah Gülen's concept of the "Golden Generation" (*yeni nesil, altin nesil*), a generation "armed with the tools of science and religion," is strikingly similar to the Jesuit concept of "Men and Women for Others" (Agai 2003, 57). The Golden Generation is Gülen's,

> description of a future generation that is educated in all respects and that forms the basis for the
> perfect future, the 'Golden Age.' This generation will be educated 'representatives of the under-
> standing of science, faith, morality, and art who are the master builders of those coming after us'
> (Gülen 1998k, 128)—that is, the movement's teachers. Combining knowledge and human values,
> this new generation will solve the problems of the future (Agai 2003, 57).

This Golden Generation is achieved through responsibly educating youth in acquiring the "freedom to realize the power of God, and through this realization…in turn be freed from man-made oppression and persecution" (Yavuz 2003a, 6).

The Golden Generation is characterized by faith, love, idealism, selflessness and action (Agai 2003, 57). Faith is vital in the raising of this generation because it is only through remem-brance and knowledge of God that one comes to understand what is beneficial for humanity. From faith comes love, idealism and selflessness, virtues that are made true only through ac-tion (Agai 2002, 37). This action is a responsibility of the Golden Generation and, in fact all of humanity. In this action is the need to,

> to rekindle the altruistic desire to let others live in the hearts of our fellow citizens…In such an
> activism, there is a need to identify a set of shared values that will form the trajectory of such a
> broad social action which will include all segments of the society, the villager and the city dweller,
> the intellectual as well as the merchant, the student as well as the teacher, the lay person as well as
> the preacher (Gülen in Ergene 2006:330; Aslandoğan and Çetin, 35).

The Golden Generation is comprised of "ideal universal individuals, individuals who love truth, who integrate spirituality and knowledge, [and] who work to benefit society" (Gülen, 1998; Nelson). Gülen describes such a person as "*zul-cenaheyn,*" that is, "one who possesses two wings," and that demonstrates a "marriage of mind and heart" (Gülen, 1996b; Nelson),

---

2 Tenth International Congress of Jesuit Alumni of Europe, Valencia, Spain, July 31, 1973.

between faith and scientific knowledge (Gülen, 2004). The Golden Generation is comprised of "genuinely enlightened people" (Gülen, 1996a; Michel 2003) who serve humanity (Gülen, 2000; Yildirim & Kirmizialtin, 2004) (Nelson).

However, Gülen says that,

> Until we help them through education, the young will be captives of their environment. They wander aimlessly, intensely moved by their passions, but far from knowledge and reason. They can become truly valiant young representatives of national thought and feeling, provided their education integrates them with their past, and prepares them intelligently for the future (Gülen; Michel 2003, 72-3).

Educators in the Gülen and Jesuit educational movements have the responsibility to help students "fuse religious and scientific knowledge together with morality and spirituality," in order "to produce genuinely enlightened people with hearts illumined by religious sciences and spirituality, minds illuminated with positive sciences...[who are] cognizant of the socio-economic and political conditions of their time' and willing and prepared to work for positive change in the world" (Gülen, 1996a, 39; Michel 2003, 76).

Virtue

The third of the educational virtues that the Gülen and Jesuit movements have in common is "virtue" itself. In the context of values-education, this somewhat nebulous word means moral cultivation and strength. Although Byron is speaking of Jesuit education here, his words certainly encapsulate the mission of the Gülen educational movement as well: "Jesuit education is education of the heart, cultivation of the will, development of the mind; it is a celebration of the person—body and soul, mind and heart—striving for excellence" (Byron 1997, 655).

This "striving for excellence" is integral to Gülen's understanding of virtue because he argues that "Islam is not about 'being' but rather 'becoming' a moral person by internalizing the Muslim model of...a perfect human being'" (Yavuz 2003b, 26). For Gülen, "the main duty and purpose of human life is to seek understanding," and one does this through perfecting one's morals and growing in knowledge through education (Ünal and Williams 2000:305; Aslandoğan and Çetin 2005, 35). True "Islam" is the embodiment of virtue for which Gülen education strives; and morality is a major component of his vision of Islam (Michel 2003, 82). With regard to morality, Gülen states that it,

> is the essence of religion and a most fundamental portion of the Divine Message. If being virtuous and having good morals is to be heroic—and it is—the greatest heroes are, first, the Prophets and, after them, those who follow them in sincerity and devotion. A true Muslim is one who practices a truly universal, therefore Muslim, morality (Gülen 1996d, 30; Michel 2003, 82).

However, one must be diligent about being virtuous. Gülen continues, saying that,

> Those who want to reform the world must first reform themselves. In order to bring others to the path of traveling to a better world, they must purify their inner worlds of hatred, rancor, and jealousy, and adorn their outer world with all kinds of virtues. Those who are far removed from self-control and self-discipline, who have failed to refine their feelings, may seem attractive and insightful at first. However, they will not be able to inspire others in any permanent way, and the sentiments they arouse will soon disappear (Gülen, 1999a, 30; Michel 2003, 78).

The essence of virtue, for Gülen, is the transformation of the self through the cultivation of virtue and living a moral life. To achieve this knowledge of how to live morally, education in ethics and the practice of discipline are necessary (Yavuz 2003b, 26). Education leads one to make right decisions and,

> Right decisions depend on having a sound mind and being capable of sound thought. Science and knowledge illuminate and develop the mind. For this reason, a mind deprived of science and knowledge cannot reach right decisions, is always exposed to deception, and is subject to being misled (Gülen 1998a).

Education can effectively help to foster virtue in the individual because teachers in Gülen and Jesuit schools work with individual students on a person by person basis. Yavuz says that, "Gülen's immediate concern is not to achieve changes on the macrolevel; rather, he focuses on the spiritual and intellectual consciousness of the individual" (Yavuz 2003b, 29). By cultivating virtue at the level of the individual the Gülen and Jesuit educational movements work to build a virtuous generation outfitted with firm moral foundations onto which they can build a better society.

Service

According to Gülen, action "should be the most indispensable element or feature of our lives" (Gülen, 1996b, 85; Nelson), for he believes that "moral consciousness toward other cultures can be raised only through participating in action" (Yavuz 2003b, 27). This final and immensely vital component of both Gülen and Jesuit education is found in the virtue of service which is at the core of "the Jesuit conception of education as pursuit of knowledge in service of the world" (Byron 1997, 655). It is only after knowledge of God and one's own self is obtained that one is free to "searc[h] out and mee[t] human need" (Byron 1997, 655).

To highlight this point, Gülen argues that,

> if you wish to keep masses under control, simply starve them in the area of knowledge. They can escape such tyranny only through education. The road to social justice is paved with adequate, universal education, for only this will give people sufficient understanding and tolerance to respect the rights of others (Gülen, 1996a, 4; Michel 2003, 74).

The teacher who frees his or her pupil from the oppression of ignorance performs a great service, *hizmet*, to all of humanity. For Gülen, *hizmet* is devotion to Islam through serving others (Agai 2003, 59). A major aspect of *hizmet* for Gülen is this service in honor of God through teaching (Afsaruddin 2005, 18). Through teaching, the teacher has the ability to serve humanity by influencing the hearts and souls of their students. The service of education is "a cure for resolving identity conflicts…a bridge between the people inside and outside Turkey, and…the basis for an interreligious dialogue" (Gulen 1997d, 214; Agai 2003, 55).

Quite possibly, the greatest service the Gülen movement is giving to the world now is opening the doors to true and authentic dialogue between Islam and other faiths.

On account of his schools, as Gülen says, "we have more to give humanity than we have to take" (Ünal and Williams 2000, 318). Gülen calls those in his movement to "Be so tolerant that your bosom becomes wide like the ocean. Become inspired with faith and love of human beings. Let there be no troubled souls to whom you do not offer a hand and about whom you remain unconcerned" (Gülen 1996, 87). This is a call that those in Jesuit education strive to hear and answer as well.

Conclusion

In many ways, the Gülen movement's pairing of Islam with universal education has challenged the contention of pundits and bloggers that Islam and modernity are incompatible with one another (Yavuz 2003b, 2). In fact, the Gülen movement has become for many in the West sound evidence that Islam and modernity are not divergent philosophies; rather, the Gülen movement can be "the way in which they can interact with and transform each other" (Yavuz 2003b, 2). As the Gülen movement's schools spread, they will continue to interact with non-Muslim groups such as Jesuit institutions—and this is already starting to occur. In the end, the dialogue between like-minded—and in the case of the Gülen-Jesuit nexus—like-spirited groups, is vital in order for there to be a just and equitable transition from the concept of a "Muslim world," i.e., in opposition to a "non-Muslim world," to a new world in which those in faith-based communities work together with a shared mission toward common goals.

This paper has shown that in theory, as well as in praxis, the Gülen and Jesuit educational missions have similar hopes and desires for the individual and the world. Furthermore, and perhaps most importantly, these two movements share a common understanding of how God works in the world—through individuals being committed to cultivating virtues such as responsibility, love, tolerance, and service to humanity in themselves and in their students. It is this confluence, above all the others, that gives the greatest hope for cooperation and collaboration between these two educational movements. And collaboration, in the end, is the hope for the Gülen-Jesuit educational nexus; that students of the Golden Generation and Men and Women for Others will be able to help make the world a more peaceful and just home through shared dialogue, prayer, and service to humanity. A bridge to inter-religious understanding, cooperation and action already exists between these two educational movements; one merely needs to find a way to cross it.

GÜLEN AND HIS GLOBAL CONTRIBUTION TO PEACE-BUILDING

Zeki Saritoprak

Abstract

Fethullah Gülen is one of the most influential scholars and thinkers in the contemporary Islamic world, particularly in Turkey. Although recent studies have put forward Gülen's ideas on various topics, Gülen's approach to peace building is one of the less studied. Given the contemporary reality of wars and ethnic/religious strife, this is a neglect that needs to be corrected. Fethullah Gülen stands up for peace and for the prevention of any clash of civilisations, not only through his speeches and writing, but through his actions as well. This paper examines the concept of peace building through Gülen's writings and activities with reference to the main sources of Islam and Gülen's commentary on them. In focusing on Gülen's activities, the paper emphasises certain American institutions, notably the Washington D.C. based Rumi Forum for Interfaith Dialogue (of which Gülen is the honorary president), and its contribution to peace-building through interfaith activities.

> *"O Lord, you are peace and peace comes from you. Give us, our Lord, a life full of peace." (Prophet Muhammad (pbuH))*

Our world has become a global village, where people are more interconnected than ever. Technological progress continues in an amazing speed. The emergence of human beings' awareness of their place in the universe increases human sharing in one another's happiness and sorrow; this consciousness is unique to our time and carries risks as well as benefits. No nation or ethnicity in the world can claim complete isolation, even the most primitive of societies. As a result of increased interaction and access to faster channels of communication, human beings have greater need than ever for the maturity of mind and spirit to coexist peacefully. In contrast to the high speed of technological development, the building of human relationships appears to be slower than ever. Where greater communication should foster real relationship between members of the human family; today's world instead faces conditions in which two-thirds of the world's population suffers from interpersonal violence and war.

In this paper, I will examine a sampling of Fethullah Gülen's views on peace and peace building, and the roots of these views in the Qur'an. This does not claim to be an exhaustive study of Gülen's writings on peace.

Building peace among human beings is the most important task, though one of the most difficult of all tasks required of the human family. Peace is one of the names of God (al-Salam). Many Muslims carry the name Abd al-Salam (the Servant of Peace). Humans must live peacefully in order to reflect the divine name, Peace.

The Qur'an makes hundreds of references to peace. The root word for peace is s-l-m, which carries connotations of both "peace" and "submission." The words "Islam," "Muslim," "Muslimun" (plural), and "Salam" all come from this same root. The word "Salam" is mentioned many times in the Qur'an, for example, when describing the quality of the servants of God, who are defined by their peaceful response: "The servants of God are those who walk on the earth modestly, and when certain foolish people address them, their answer is "salam" (25:63). Another Qur'anic verse says, "When the servants of God pass near negative behavior, they pass by with dignity and kindness" (25:72).

Considering the violence in today's world, and the proliferation of weapons capable of rendering the human species extinct several times over, it is urgent that both Muslims and non-Muslims must follow the instructions of the Qur'an for human relationship: "Peace is better" (4:128). Even in the midst of war, on the battlefield, if there is an opportunity for peace, the Qur'anic injunction is "if the enemy inclines towards peace, you should incline toward it too" (8:61).

The very beginnings of Islam were marked by successful peaceful resolutions to ongoing conflicts. The Prophet was known for his peaceful response to violence and persecution in Mecca. His peace building skills were so well known that he and his followers were invited by the leaders of Medina to build peace among rival tribes that had been fighting for centuries. Under his leadership, a peaceful society was successfully established in Medina, and later, even Mecca.

Islamic civilization is based on two essential principles: mutual cooperation, and the loving interrelatedness of creation. In the first principle, the planet depends upon all creatures helping one another: rain helps grass to grow; grass helps animals to grow; and animals help human beings to grow. In the second principle, all members of creation are considered brothers and sisters. This principle requires all human beings to reject anything that does damage to this essential relationship; in Islam all forms of chauvinism (including racism and nationalism) are unacceptable.

The Islamic view of human society is based on the principles of harmony and peace: wars and violent actions, while part of the history of every major world religion, have no place in the essence of Islam. The ideal society described in the Qur'an is Paradise, *Dar al-Salam* (the Abode of Peace). It is required of believers that they make this world as similar as possible to this ideal society.

The Qur'an acknowledges the reality of human nature and the possible conflicts that may arise between peoples. However, it constantly encourages believers to incline towards peace in any situation of dispute. First of all, all human beings should assume the responsibility of making peace, in accordance with the divine principles: "be fearful of God and make peace among yourselves" (8:1). A similar Qur'anic verse speaks of the responsibility of political authorities to make peace and stop violence if it occurs: when fighting occurs between two rival groups, it is incumbent upon the Islamic authority to make peace between the two.

> If two groups of believers fight against each other, make peace between them. If one party does wrong to the other, you fight that which does wrong until it return to the ordinance of God. If it returns, make peace between them justly, and act equitably; God loves the just. (49:9)

Since God has put no limitations on the devastating capacity for human anger, building peace is one of the most difficult tasks for human beings. It requires steadfastness, resolve and patience. It is a long process, and may take generations in order to build a worldwide peace. The Qur'an encourages peace-builders in this struggle by reminding them of the eternal rewards they will receive. Even if they are not fully successful, still they will be rewarded for their works, and therefore they should not be lose hope in the work of peace: even the angels in paradise will greet such peacemakers with joy. "Peace be with you," they will say, "because of your patience in the life of the world" (13:24).

Peace is such a central notion to Islam that the very greeting among the people of paradise is "Peace," or *Salam* (10:10). The righteous will be told, "enter paradise peacefully and safely forever" (15:46). Muslims in their daily greetings use the same language: *as-Salamu Alaikum*, "peace be with you."

Some scholars suggest that the five pillars of Islam have a direct relationship with the work of peace building and non-violent action. Obeying God and the Prophet (and disobeying others if needed); discipline through daily prayer; social solidarity thorough compulsory charity (*zakat*); self-sacrifice, suffering, and patience through fasting; and finally unity and friendship through pilgrimage are all elements through which one is prepared to make peace and to accept peace.[1]

The Prophet himself dealt with building peace between tribes as well as individuals. One example of the Prophet's peace-building is the famous story of the black stone, in which he solved a dispute among several Arab tribal leaders in such a way that all were able to equitably share in the honor of placing the sacred stone. On another occasion, the reconciliation of

---

1 See Abu-Nimer, Non-violence and Peace Building in Islam: Theory and practice, p. 45. Also see Chaiwat Satha-Anand, "Core Values for Peacemaking in Islam: the Prophet's practice as paradigm" in Building Peace in the Middle East, ed. Elise Boulden, (Boulder: Lynnne Rinner, 1993).

two individuals took precedence over even the Prophet's prescribed daily prayer; this occasion is recorded in certain Islamic references which indicate that Abu Bakr led the prayer in the Prophet's absence. *Sahih al-Bukhari*, the most authentic collection of the sayings of the Prophet, contains an entire book on the Prophet's sayings about peace-building, or reconciliation (*sulh*).

Nowadays, the majority of the world's population is suffering the effects of global conflicts and wars. The victims are mainly the vulnerable: children, women and the elderly. The world experienced one of its most devastating wars just decades ago, and there is fear that history may repeat itself. The very building in which this conference is being held was, only 60 years ago, in the midst of intense bombing. According to one account, as many as 35 million people were killed during World War II, which can be considered a collective suicide of Europe. Enlightenment and civilization did not help prevent the civilized world from engaging in such destruction.

When describing the effects of the two World Wars, the world agrees, "never again." However, the current trend of our world is unfortunately not peace-oriented; every indication is that we are headed for much more horrible destruction. Therefore, Muslims, Christians, Jews, Hindus, Buddhists, and adherents of all other religions should make all efforts for the dominion of peace.

In the Islamic world one can see some important efforts in this direction. The focus of this paper will be on the efforts of Fethullah Gülen (b. 1941-), as one of the most influential personalities of our time. As elaborating on Gülen's biography is beyond the scope of this paper, suffice it to say that Gülen's passionate pursuit of peace began at a young age, in a time when anarchy and chaos were dominating Turkish society. In the 1970s, college students, teachers, and even some professors were highly influenced by Marxism. Marxist and nationalist groups were in armed conflict with one another. More than 10,000 people in Turkey were killed in two decades in these clashes. Even families were not immune to this violence and tragedy; members of the same family could be found fighting on opposite sides. Gülen made all efforts to extinguish the fire of conflict amidst this chaos, and made great impact in building peace. Gülen in one of his statements narrates the following:

> My admirers know that when anarchy was everywhere in our country, I called for calmness and controlling of anger. I had received death threats, yet, I called upon my admirers to continue working for peace, 'If I am assassinated, despite all your anger, I ask you to bury my body and seek order, peace and love in our society.' Regardless of what happens, we believers should be representatives of love and security. I continue saying the same today.[2]

Gülen's efforts were mainly educational. It can be argued that he did not directly stop the armed conflict, but his efforts equipped young people with values that prevented them from engaging in such conflicts. Gülen believes that the new generation should be equipped with qualities such as wisdom, compassion, and knowledge. As an inspired Muslim scholar, he has spiritually influenced thousands of people through his educational efforts as well as his public speeches. He continues to influence millions in Turkey and around the world.

It is a tradition among Turkish intellectuals to work for the creation of an "ideal generation." For example, Mehmet Akif, the writer of the Turkish National Anthem, spoke of a generation that he named the "Generation of Asim" (*Asim'in Nesli*). Bediüzzaman Said Nursi spoke of the "New Generation" (*Nasl-i Jadeed*, in Turkish: *Nesl-i Cedid*). Necip Fazil,

---

2 Hurriyet daily, 4.21.2004 (an interview given to Safa Kaplan).

another prominent Turkish poet and author, idealized his generation as the "Faithful-Youth Generation" (*Imanli Genclik*). Gülen, having read the work of his predecessors, looked for his own generation and found the lack of proper education to be the essence of the problems they faced. Through his writings and educational institutions, he has attempted to create such a generation, which he has coined the "The Golden Generation" (*Altin Nesil*). The aim of the Golden Generation is to provide a perfect education for a perfect generation in order to obtain a perfect society. The Golden Generation also requires the young people of the community to show a great respect for religious and national values.[3] Gülen hopes that a lasting peace can be achieved through the work of a generation which is peaceful, made up of individuals who are living examples of peace, who will build bridges of dialogue and mutual understanding to make peace among people. To Gülen, the Golden Generation has certain specific qualities: knowledge, faith, love, idealism, altruism, and action.[4] In the last decade, when some political scientists spoke of a "clash of civilizations," Gülen ardently urged the building of "wave-breakers" in order to prevent such a clash.

It is not an exaggeration to assert that the endeavors of Gülen have, and will continue to have, a global impact on building peace. Gülen's philosophy of peace and his efforts are not considered isolated instances in Islam; in fact, as briefly mentioned above, the entire heritage of Islam is considered to be the foundation of Gülen's understanding of peace. He counts among his role models, certainly, mystics such as Hasan al-Basri, and Abu-Talib al-Makki; scholars and mystics such as Abu Hamid al-Ghazzali, Jalal al-Din Rumi, Ahmet Sarhandi, and Bediüzzaman Said Nursi; and most importantly, the companions of the Prophet. One can argue that if any of these Muslim personalities had lived in our time, they would be involved in the same work as Gülen.

Contemporary scholars of peace-building have elaborated on certain elements that are essential for making peace in any part of the world. Two of these elements are education and knowledge. There is no doubt that Gülen's greatest efforts and contributions are related to these two fields. Bediüzzaman Said Nursi, in the beginning of the twentieth century, stated that "there are three major enemies of Muslims: ignorance, poverty, and internal division."[5] If we take a closer look at our modern world, we can easily understand the importance of education, particularly for Muslims, who constitute 22% of the world's population. Population growth is faster among Muslims than any other population, while literacy rates remain significantly low.[6] Gülen considers lack of education to be a disease requiring a cure; he wants to cure the diseases that were diagnosed by Nursi. Education, according to Gülen, will result in peace.

Today in Turkey, Central Asia and many other parts of the world, the educational institutions that were established by admirers of Gülen have continued to contribute greatly to the education of people of different religions and ethnicities. In fact, his Golden Generation has already contributed, through educational endeavors, to the building of peace in many areas of conflict, including the Balkans, northern Iraq, Northern Ireland, and the Philippines.

Thomas Michel, in his article on Gülen, speaks of a school established by the admirers of Gülen on the Philippine island of Mindanao, which he visited in 1995. Michel visited an area

---

3   Bayram Balci "Fethullah Gülen's Missionary Schools in Central Asia and their Role in the Spreading of Turkism and Islam." Religion, State & Society. 31:2, 2003. pp 151-169.

4   Begim Agai, The Muslim World, 2003, Vol. 57

5   Nursi, Hutbe-i Samiye, in Risalei Nur, II, p. 1976.

6   Akbar Ahmed, Islam Under Siege: From Clash to Dialogue of Civilisations, p5.

of the island where kidnapping, guerrilla warfare, and armed conflict was constant between Moro separatists and the state. Michel states, "The school [which is named the Philippine-Turkish School of Tolerance] offers Muslim and Christian Filipino children an excellent education and a more positive way of living and relating to each other."[7] Michel found, in this school, students from all backgrounds, and described it as a "heaven of peace" in this area of conflict.[8]

Another example comes from my own experience, when I visited Skopje, Macedonia in the summer of 2004. I had a chance to visit a school established by some Turkish businessmen who were supporters of the Gülen movement. I was told that when civil war was going on in the region, members of different ethnicities were sending their children to this school. Their parents were fighting, but the children were living peacefully under the roof of the same school.

In order to contextualize Gülen's peace building philosophy, I would like to draw upon the famous Muslim sociologist Ibn Khaldun's understanding of building peace. In Ibn Khaldun's philosophy, individual efforts and sacrifices remain essential. He says, "peace in society is possible through willingness of an individual to subordinate [the individual self] to the group. Without this, peace and social development are not possible."[9]

Ibn Khaldun addresses the development of urban society in the term *Asabiyya,* or "group solidarity," in a way which he empties of its original connotations of racism and nationalism, both of which are prohibited in Islam. I would like to borrow this term from Ibn Khaldun to indicate solidarity around a value or an idea that is shared by members of society. Gülen's "Golden Generation" exemplifies Ibn Khaldun's idea of the establishment of peace in society.

Gülen believes in the integrity of the individual; his approach to social restoration and peace building, therefore, is one of "bottom-up" social change. It should be noted that Ibn Khaldun's concept of *Asabiyya* carries its own risks of an excessive group loyalty, which can be dangerous for a harmonious society. Ahmad Akbar points to such a danger. Gülen solves this problem by emphasizing the quality of individuals, since his ideal Golden Generation is based, not on ethnicity, but on moral and ethical dimensions. Gülen describes his Golden Generation as "selfless people, sincerely thinking of others rather than themselves." He says:

> Who knows? Maybe in the near future some selfless people, who sacrifice themselves to make others live, will unite hearts and minds through their efforts. The conscience and logic will become two different, deeply rooted dimensions of their lives that will complete each other. Physics and metaphysics will abandon the fight between themselves: in order to give the opportunity for the beauty of everything to express itself in its own language, each will return to its own field. These selfless people will discover the interconnectedness of the divine command and the laws of nature. People will repent for their previous meaningless fights with one another. An atmosphere of serenity will be built and be felt in homes and in schools. No dignity will be stepped on. The hearts will be full of respect to the extent that no one will trespass on the properties or the dignities of others. The powerful will act justly so that the weak and the poor will have a chance to live humanely. No one will be arrested just because of an assumption. No one's house or business will be attacked. No innocent's blood will be shed. No oppressed person will cry out. Everyone will love human beings as a duty towards God. It is exactly this time when the world, which is a corridor to Paradise, will

---

7   Thomas Michel. "Fethullah Gülen as Educator." Turkish Islam and the Secular State: The Gülen Movement. Ed. M Hakan Yavuz and John L. Esposito. Syra Cruz, Syra Cruz University Press, 2003. pp 69-84.

8   Ibid.

9   Ibn Khaldun, The Muqqadimah

become a paradise-like place that will always be enjoyed.[10]

He strongly advocates selflessness and living for others as the most essential qualities of the builders of peace. He calls them "sacrificed souls" (*adanmış ruhlar*). By living for others, he says, an individual should always prefer the advantages of others over his/her own. This is in fact a description of the believers in early Islam, namely the companions of the Prophet as the Qur'an speaks of them. The verse says: "They prefer others over themselves even if they are in need." Without a generation with such qualities, Gülen, like Ibn Khaldun, argues that peace would not be possible. This is why he constantly asserts the need for faithful and selfless individuals to dedicate themselves to the establishment of peace. Educational institutions should serve to bring up such individuals from the realm of imagination to the realm of realization. All of Gülen's educational efforts work towards this realization.

Despite the overwhelmingly negative and violent state of the world, Gülen remains hopeful about the future of humanity. He believes that the efforts of building peace in the world and attempting to create a harmonious society will bear fruit. This great hope is exemplified in the following statement:

Once upon a time, despite intercontinental obstacles, through the teaching of the Qur'an, a permanent love, respect, and dialogue was achieved. These days, I have full faith that through the efforts of these *holy people* a new atmosphere, new understandings and dialogue will be achieved. Even now, through the *immigrants* who carry this idea around the world, the rivers of love have started to flow. Now they are heard in every corner of the planet. The breezes of tranquility and happiness have started to be felt. And in every corner of the world, they are creating *islands of peace* for stability and harmony.[11]

According to Gülen, his ideal Golden Generation will always think of positive steps to build peace. His Golden Generation will not be distracted by historical mistakes. He would say, despite some negative historical experiences like the Crusades and colonization,

> We are resolved not to remember those events and not to give an opportunity for the rebirth of animosity. We strongly encourage the constraint of historical mistakes within the limits of the history books so as not to resurrect the feelings of animosity among people.[12]

Describing his ideal generation further, Gülen says:

> there is no bullying, no greed, no quarrelling, no distrust, no lies, no oppression, and no deception. On the contrary, there is chivalry, tenderness, the efforts of revival, the love for life, kindness and dialogue, respect for truth, trust, acknowledgement of kindness and generosity, the spirit of righteousness, justice, and the following of the straight path.[13]

To Gülen, the Golden Generation can be an important instrument for establishing such a world of peace where "people love love and hate hatred." Gülen compares hatred to a destructive flood which destroys trust among segments of society. This hatred brings baseless accusations against the people who strive for peace. Through hatred, words can be taken out of their context and even the most innocent statement can be used against an individual.[14]

---

10 M. Fethullah Gülen, Örnekleri Kendinden Bir Hareket (A movement whose samples are from within itself) (Cag ve Nesil Serisi, N.8), (Izmir: Nil Yayinlari, 2006), p110

11 Ibid., p111

12 Fethullah Gülen, Isigin Gorundugu Ufuk (Cag Ve Nesil Serisi-7) (Izmir: Nil Yayinlari, 2006), pp158.

13 Fethullah Gülen, Yeseren Dusunceler (Cag ve Nesil 6) (Izmir: Nil Yayinlari, 2006), p88-92.

14 Fethullah Gülen, Ornekleri Kendinden bir Hareket, p. 75.

One has to acknowledge that building a global peace is not an easy task. Gülen suggests that the individuals who dedicate themselves to working for humanity and building peace have to be patient and uninfluenced by the trend of quick and sloganeering politics.

Gülen insists that people should light candles in their communities in order to enlighten society: it is the duty of the ideal generation to enlighten people rather than sulk in darkness. Gülen is aware of the fact that it is difficult to do this without the power of the media. For this reason, during the 1980s, his movement worked towards the establishment of a newspaper, and later, the establishment of a television channel. Both projects became highly successful both within and outside of Turkey. Through these, as well as through monthly and weekly journals, the Gülen movement successfully established a powerful media presence, which directly and indirectly contributes to the building of peace. *Zaman* ("Time"), which started in 1986, is regarded as one of the best newspapers in Turkey, with a circulation of more than 600,000 copies per day. With its many correspondents around the world, it is now published in many different languages and countries, including Australia, Azerbaijan, Bulgaria, Germany, Romania, Kazakhstan, Kyrgyzstan, Macedonia, Turkmenistan, and the United States of America.[15]

Gülen suggests that his admirers should invest first in human beings. Any investment in human beings takes years, so people must be patient in their expectation of results. His own experience indicates some of the difficulties that peace builders face: in the 1990s, when Gülen promoted dialogue between different ethnicities and adherents of different religious traditions, both some extreme secularists and some extreme Muslims opposed him. Eventually, he left Turkey, ostensibly for medical reasons, but also to avoid this conflict.

Gülen was confident about his approach and its compatibility with the core teachings of Islam. He compared his opponents in Turkey to the Kharijites of early Islam, saying:

> similar to the logic of Kharijites, this destructive group destroys everything positive; like an anarchist under the control of hatred and revulsion, they attack everything. They run from one wildness to another, destroying the bridges of understanding and making the roads of dialogue impassable, causing despair in the loving spirits and injecting violence and hatred into hearts that beat with love.[16]

These thoughts express his deep concern and fear for the future of peace in his country. Despite this, he has never lost hope and has always believed that the efforts for building peace will eventually bear fruit. When all doors were closed against him, the media and the secular elite pronounced him *persona non grata* to the extent that his life was under threat.[17] Despite the hardships that Gülen faced during the process of accusations, spiritual persecution and exile, he never sought revenge. "We are going to be respectful for our character," he says.

> "We will not harm those who persecuted us. We will not seek an eye for an eye. We will never curse them. We will not break hearts and, in the manner of Yunus [the famous 14th century Turkish poet], we will invite everyone to love. . . . As a believer, I promise that I will never shun any person

15   Greg Barton, "Turkey's Gülen Hizmet and Indonesia's neo-Modernist NGOs: Remarkable Examples of Progressive Islamic Thought and Civil Society Activism in the Muslim World," in Political Islam and Human Security, eds. Fetih Mansouri and Shahram Akbarzadeh (Cambridge: Cambridge Scholars Press, 2006), pp140-160.
16   Fethullah Gülen, Ornekleri Kendinden bir Hareket, pp75-82.
17   For the details of Gülen's feelings, see ibid pp75-82.

and I will not prosecute those who transgressed against me."[18]

For Gülen, forgiveness is an essential element to building peace. When a woman accused of committing adultery was brought to Jesus, he said, "Let the person who is without sin, cast the first stone." Gülen says of this, "Those who understand the deep sense in this statement cannot throw stones at others while they deserve to be stoned themselves." Self-criticism, for Gülen, is an important step towards forgiveness. "In fact, we will never be able to make a right decision, neither on behalf of ourselves nor on behalf of others, until we break, with courage such as Abraham's, the idols within us."

There is no doubt that forgiveness is one of the most important elements for building peace. Therefore, according to Gülen, the most important gift for the coming generation is to teach them how to forgive. Gülen states, "today's generation's greatest gift for their children and for their grandchildren is to teach them how to forgive even the most offensive behaviors and nauseating actions."[19] He calls forgiveness a heavenly medicine that can cure the many wounds of society.

For Gülen, another effective element to build peace is love. He considers love to be an effective weapon; he embraces this weapon of love against all violent actions:

> In a time when people are defeated by their sense of revenge and animosity, when masses are driven into struggles and wars, when truth is silenced before force, when those who wield power behave against their dissidents as tyrants, when dictators and oppressors are applauded and promoted, while the oppressed are treated badly, we once again say: love. I believe that love has the capacity to change the rhythm of our life.[20]

According to Gülen, once one is equipped with love and compassion, there will be no difference between "you," "we" and "others." Gülen believes that for building peace, love is essential. Furthermore, today "we need love and compassion more than water and air."[21] Gülen describes those who love others and live for others as heroes. He says, "happy are those who make love their guide in their journey. How unfortunate are those who do not perceive the love that is grounded in their spirit and who spend an entire life blind and deaf."[22]

In recent years, Gülen's admirers have started building bridges between adherents of different religious traditions. In the United States where I live, I know of dozens of institutions that promote inter-faith dialogue. In major cities of the United States such as Los Angeles, New York, Chicago, and Washington D.C, one can find many such institutions. For example, I lived for five years in the Washington D.C. area, where I participated in the establishment of the 'Rumi Forum for Interfaith Dialogue.' In 1999, two years before 9/11, a group of Turkish-American Muslims who admire Gülen's idea of dialogue approached me and asked me to help establish a forum for interfaith dialogue. I witnessed the foundation of this institution and the dedication of the members of the Turkish-American community in the greater D.C. area, when they voluntarily came and painted the doors and walls, cleaned the floors, and did whatever was necessary to make the center function. I asked myself, what was the motivation

---

18 Fethullah Gülen, Isigin Gorundugu Ufuk (Cag ve Nesil Serisi-7) (Izmir: Nil Yayinlari, 2006), p217.

19 Fethullah Gülen, Sag ve Nesil (Cag ve Nesil Serisi-1) (Istanbul: Nil Yayinlari, 2006), p77.

20 Fethullah Gülen, Yeseren Dusunceler (Cag ve Nesil 6) (Izmir: Nil Yayinlari, 2006), p. 113. For further reading on Gülen's understanding of love for human beings, see Isigin Gorundugu Ufuk (Cag Ve Nesil Serisi-7) (Izmir: Nil Yayinlari, 2006), pp. 34-38.

21 Fethullah Gülen, Ornekleri Kendinden bir Hareket, p. 184.

22 Fethullah Gülen, Yitirilmis Cennete Dogru (Cag ve Nesil Serisi-3) (Izmir: Nil Yayinlari, 1997), p. 98.

behind this? These people would not receive any material benefits from such an institution; on the contrary, they gave of their own funds to support it.

Having witnessed this communal solidarity, I was reminded of Ibn Khaldun's concept of 'solidarity of group,' which emerged in a remarkable way in this local community. The motive for a computer engineer, who volunteered as a painter at the center, was evident in his statement: "solidarity with other people to build peace." In fact, their efforts became so fruitful that within a year, the institution became one of the most well-known organizations of inter-faith dialogue in the area.

Dr. Ali Yurtsever, the current president of the Rumi Forum, responding to my request for information regarding their recent endeavors, states that in recent years, the institution has reached thousands of people, including Muslims, Christians, Jews, Hindus and Buddhists, as well as adherents of other faiths. As for the institution's goal, he reminded me of the Qur'anic verse: "human beings are created to know each other" (49:13). When asked how these events would contribute to the building of peace, he said: "knowing each other is the first step to eradicate hatred."

What attracted me most to the people of the forum was their great sense of devotion to their work. Dr. Yurtsever categorizes such activities into six groups: establishing relationships with churches, planning trips to Turkey, organizing conferences and seminars, presenting cultural activities, organizing *iftar* programs for Ramadan, and participating in peace building work with community leaders.

Yurtsever states that the Forum members have communicated and become familiar with approximately 150 leaders in a variety of Christian churches. By organizing common events and building relationships, they have overcome prejudices and hatred on both sides. At many of their gatherings, he says there are over 50 differing ethnicities and nationalities present.

The Forum organizes trips to Turkey to build friendships between the members of the Turkish and American communities. They have already invited over 150 community leaders to Turkey to develop such friendships. Yurtsever says, "We have successfully managed to establish beautiful relationships between Turkish and American people during these trips."

The Rumi Forum plans conferences, seminars, and other academic events, through which they inform and educate the public and students about various cultures and religious traditions. They also publish booklets and leaflets in order to establish bridges between peoples.

The Forum's cultural activities are designed to develop friendships and peace among people through music. These include cultural and religious events such as performances of the Whirling Dervishes and picnics through which they introduce the cultural diversity of their society.

The Forum also organizes *iftar* programs in the month of Ramadan, in order to recognize those who contribute to the establishment of dialogue and peace in their community, wider society, and world. The purpose of these programs is to inform Washington, D.C.'s elites, such as congressmen, senators, and think-tank scholars, about what is going on in the realm of building peace, and to recognize the efforts of those who work hard towards this goal.

Finally, the Forum meets regularly with political leaders to inform them of developments in the work of peace around the world, and to prevent misunderstandings regarding the religion of Islam. By this, the Forum makes a connection between members of Muslim society and the leaders of the local community, including law enforcement agents.

Alongside these six categories, the Rumi Forum website indicates further activities. Such activities include monthly gatherings with Georgetown University scholars to discuss certain themes of Islam and Christianity. I personally heard very positive remarks from many attendees of such inter-faith activities, who benefited from them immensely. None of these activities are financed by any government; rather, they are developed and run by the efforts of individuals.

Fethullah Gülen has no worldly possessions and he is celibate. One cannot imagine that Gülen receives any material benefits from any activities inspired by his teaching. The benefit here, rather than material, is a spiritual one, which encompasses all.

The concept of compassion in the teachings of Gülen is one of the most important principles in Gülen's understanding of peace. His own compassion can be seen in his physically drained reaction to the plight of innocent human victims of chemical weapons in northern Iraq, to a deep respect for the life of such an insignificant creature, like an insect.

In the tradition in which Gülen was brought up, his understanding is that no matter how small, every creature praises God in its own tongue, and therefore deserves its proper respect and compassion. As Yunus Emre, the famous Turkish poet, said, "we love creatures for the sake of the Creator." Therefore, compassion can be read frequently in the writings of Gülen:

> Compassion is the beginning of being; without it everything is chaos. Everything has come into existence through compassion and by compassion it continues to exist in harmony. . . . Everything speaks of compassion and promises compassion. Because of this, the universe can be considered a symphony of compassion. All kinds of voices proclaim compassion so that it is impossible not to be aware of it, and impossible not to feel the wide mercy encircling everything. How unfortunate are the souls who don't perceive this. . . human beings have a responsibility to show compassion to all living beings, as a requirement of being human. The more one displays compassion, the more exalted one becomes, while the more one resorts to wrongdoing, oppression and cruelty, the more one is disgraced and humiliated, becoming a shame to humanity.[23]

Gülen reflects the Qur'anic teaching of compassion in this statement, which is confirmed by Akbar Ahmed as an important component of peace building:

> Search for global solutions to common global problems confronting human society, and the quest for a just, compassionate, and peaceful order, will be the challenge human civilization faces in the twenty-first century. To meet the challenge is to fulfill God's vision to embrace all humanity. Doing so is to know God's compassion.[24]

---

23 M. Fethullah Gülen, Towards the Lost Paradise, (London: Truestar, 1996), 40-2; see also M. Fethullah Gülen, Fatiha Uzerine Mulahazalar (Considerations on the Chapter Fatiha), (Izmir: Nil Yayinlari, 1997), 90-95.
24 Ahmed, ibid, p8.

TURKISH IN THE LANGUAGE OF THE QUR'AN: *HIRA'*

Paul L. Heck

Abstract

When it comes to the Gülen movement, scholarly attention is often given to its attitudes towards non-Muslims, its willingness to operate within secular environments, and its rapprochement with the material achievements of the West, as well as its own network of educational institutions. As a result, less attention is given to its interest in connecting with the larger Muslim community beyond its own internal associations. The Gülen movement is, however, aware of the need to situate itself and publish its ideas within the wider *ummah*.

Hira magazine, a relatively new venture of the Gülen movement (first issue Dec. 2005), is chiefly intra-Muslim in its aims and aspirations. The magazine is published in Arabic and features articles written by both Turkish and Arabic writers; a lead article by Fethullah Gülen opens and sets the tone of each issue. The magazine acts to bring the intellectual outlook of the Gülen movement to the Arab world, serving as a cultural bridge between Turks and Arabs, as a forum in which pressing issues in contemporary Islam can be aired and treated by leading Muslim thinkers, and as a tool for the global Muslim community to consolidate a renewed vision of its relation to the intellectual and socio-political realities of the modern world.

This paper recounts the establishment and development of *Hira* magazine, focusing on the calibre of its themes and contributors, and also its reception in the Arab world as evidenced in local Arab media as well as by the comments of those in charge of the magazine. Finally, a critical assessment is offered of the overall vision of the magazine, its presentation style, material content, and religious perspective, as well as its potential to speak effectively to the global *ummah* as a leading voice for the future of Islam.

In late 2005 the Gülen movement launched a new religious initiative, a magazine by the name of *Hira'*. A quarterly magazine of which seven issues have appeared to date, *Hira'* treats a range of topics: education, science, religion, art and culture, philosophy, civilization, history, poetry, and above all the psychological and spiritual formation of the human soul—all through the lens of Islam. The emphasis on the interior life make sense of the magazine's name, *Hira'*, which refers to the cave near Mecca on Jabal al-Nur—"Mount of Light"—where the Prophet Muhammad would go for meditation and contemplation and revelations from God through the mediation of the Angel Gabriel. The magazine, with offices in both Istanbul and Cairo, is published in Arabic and features art and poetry as well as articles by various Arab and Turkish intellectuals, scholars, and littérateurs. A lead article by Fethullah Gülen opens and sets the tone of each issue. It is worth noting that the Arab figures assembled by the magazine represents some of the most highly respected Muslim voices in the Arab world today.

Here, then, is a Gülen initiative that is intra-Muslim and directed at the global *umma* beyond the movement's own institutions and organizations. It seeks to engage Arab society, Muslim Arabs first and foremost. When it comes to the Gülen movement, scholarly attention often focuses on its willingness and desire to engage non-Muslims and western intellectual and cultural life and, also, its ability to coexist with secularism. This magazine suggests that the movement is also interested in creating a bridge between the Turkish and Arab spheres of the *umma* and that it is aware of the need to bring its outlook to the wider concerns and discussions of the global Muslim community today. Certainly, attempts have been made in the past to build bridges between Turks and Arabs. Muhammad Rashid Rida (d. 1935), for example, proposed a political bridge, i.e. a post-Ottoman caliphate that would embrace Turks and Arabs in a single political framework. It was not feasible, even if a noble idea. In contrast, the bridge that the Gülen movement seeks to build is decidedly spiritual—and, in that sense, more likely to succeed.

The magazine's message, emphasizing the formation of the soul and addressed to Muslims primarily, is at the same time oriented to the world in its global aspects. It is therefore appropriate to locate the magazine, which largely mirrors the thinking of the Gülen movement, alongside three other prominent forms of globalizing religiosity in contemporary Islam.

The first is Wahhabism, which seeks to purify Islam of all human elements and innovations and so guard against the possibility of Islam falling into error and infidelity itself. Modernity is here shunned as a positive source of human achievement.

The second is Tablighism (Tablighi Jama'at), which is related to Deobandism, the madrasa-network in South Asia that seeks to preserve Muslim identity through exact study of hadith, i.e. the reports of the Prophet's sayings, deeds, and decisions as normative model of Muslim life. Tablighism, which is quite active in the Arab context, such as Morocco, is a global revivalist movement that seeks to strengthen Muslim commitment to the ritual practices of the faith, not only prescribed daily prayers but also collective reading and identification with the lifestyle of the first Muslims. Although dissimilar to Wahhabism in many respects, Tablighism also has a negative view of human history, its realities and its imperfections, leading to disconnect between Islam's religious experience and the challenges of the current human condition.

The third is Jihadism, a religiosity of conflict. Fighting infidel enemies of God, identified with today's global powers, is the highest religious virtue, and Muslims who do not fight the enemies of God—or ally themselves with them—are reclassified as enemies of God themselves.

This brief summary of globalized Islam is not to overlook 1) the many other Muslim movements that operate largely within a national or regional context or 2) the bulk of Muslims who do not align themselves with any movement at all but simply do their best to follow the teachings of Islam as passed down by their predecessors in the faith. The point is transition in the Muslim world on a global scale. The Gülen movement can be generally classified as a fourth form of globalizing Muslim religiosity, which I call reformed Sufism.

Sufism has many sides to it and has undergone development over the centuries. Historically, as a social institution in Muslim society, it has focused on a saintly character whose function was not only to instruct his disciples in the ways of noble character (*makarim al-akhlaq*) and to model them himself but also to mediate heavenly mysteries to them and even intercede for them before the throne of God. Networks of this kind of Sufism still exist and even flourish regionally and trans-regionally. The Barelwi movement is one example, with origins in the shrine culture of South Asia and a significant presence in the UK. Sheikh Nazim is another example, with followers in both the Middle East and Europe. This kind of Sufism, however, has faced a degree of criticism from contemporary Muslims who look askance at its hierarchical concept of religious authority. This is not to say that Sufism in its traditional form is anti-modern in outlook but that its structure, a hierarchy of intercessory saints, has been challenged in this democratic age.

The Gülen movement—and other examples of reformed Sufism—have for the most part abandoned this hierarchical structure while retaining the spiritual knowledge (*'ilm laduni*) of Sufism along with the doctrine (*'aqida*) and law (*shari'a*) of Islam. The concept of human guidance (*irshad*) is not rejected but rather the idea of human intercession (*shafa'a*), obviating the need for a saintly hierarchy in a formalized sense. Also, reformed Sufism has responded to modernist and fundamentalist charges against Sufism—of being antiquated and anti-modern in its otherworldly preoccupations—by refashioning itself as rational and activist but still spiritual. In other words, the essential religiosity of Sufism that operates both within and beyond the visible boundaries of Islam is still intact. The world beyond the pale of Islam may be problematic but it is not condemnable per se. Islam in its particular beliefs and practices is still the central departure point and central reference point, but it is not the only one or perhaps even the final one. The religious goal here is not at all the discarding of the very particular ritual and moral duties prescribed by divine law, *shari'a*, but rather the attainment of insight into divine reality, *haqiqa*, which is unbounded and informs all existence. Thus, in contrast to Wahhabism, Tablighism, and Jihadism, Sufism as advanced by the Gülen movement has a positive view of the world entire. The internal workings of the universe—science, history, politics, art and culture, philosophy—are not something Muslims should fear or stuff into an Islamized box but rather engage positively in view of the spiritual insight of Islam.

In line with the reformed Sufism of the Gülen movement, *Hira'* aims not to discuss the latest developments in the various branches of learning, knowledge, and science directly. Rather, it seeks to inform the Muslim mind with a spiritually enriched perspective of the world, which, in turn, can be brought to bear on the various branches of learning, knowledge, and science. The Moroccan scholar Farid al-Ansari sums this up (no. 1): "How much we need a rereading of Islam today… a reading that brings the Muslim to God before a reading that leads him to criticizes himself, social injustice, and political tyranny and that makes him in his religiosity an enemy of religion whether he realizes it or not." Here, I believe, al-Ansari is referring to the other forms of globalized religiosity noted above. They all have a religiosity that demands perfection of the world as the standard by which religion is validated. As a result, they invariably end with a negative view of a world that stubbornly refuses to conform perfectly to the ideals of religion.

The prophetic cave of Hira' —and the magazine too (!)— shows that something more is needed for religion to realize its purpose: spiritual insight that rejects the notion that material reality is final measure of the worth of religion. This is not to say that religion is to have no impact on worldly life. The spiritual insight that a religious formation of the soul affords believers is to be brought to bear on *all aspects of existence*, so as to inform them with an otherworldly perspective that does not violate their autonomy but rather enhances understanding of their purpose. Islam is to touch all things human and worldly but is not reducible to them, in line with the qur'anic teaching that God's signs (*ayat*) are to be discerned in human souls (*anfus*) and worldly horizons (*afaq*) and not only in scriptural verses. It is about a dynamic engagement of the heavenly with the earthly realm and not the collapse of the two into a single entity.

Again, the central goal of *Hira'* is to move Muslims beyond defensiveness by teaching a religiosity that can confidently interact with modernity. This is what Gülen means by *rabbaniyya* (no. 7), the engineering of the soul for the sake of its harmonious integration with others and society as a whole, effecting its salvation *within* the sometimes troubling specificities of modernity and endowing it with a prophetic heart that puts concern for others before self. The failure of this mission, *rabbaniyya*, would be a betrayal of the *umma*, and the furthering of its spiritual activism will permit the *umma* to rediscover itself, restore its global relevancy, and make Muslims worthy to be God's caliphs, i.e. His delegates on earth (Gülen, no. 4).

Such a mission, however, is not meta-religious but arises within the boundaries of Islam. The particulars of Islam—Ramadan, Hajj, etc.—are not mere ceremony and ritual but occasions filled with divinely inspired sounds and images meant to awaken the spiritual consciousness of Muslims (Gülen, no. 1 and no. 2). Key to Muslim life is the ability not simply to undertake religious duties but to experience the foretaste (*dhawq*) of the hereafter that they anticipate, ensuring existential satisfaction as opposed to dissatisfaction even amidst the realities and imperfections of this world. The point is that religion is not just about divine command but also symbolic meaning, such that the duties of religion become indispensable vehicles for the spiritual transformation of the soul and the dispersal of its egoistic tendencies.

Islam here is not just about *shari'a* as standard of Muslim actions but also *haqiqa* as standard of Muslim souls. Indeed, realization of *haqiqa* is a necessary preliminary to correct performance of *shari'a*, lest one's religiosity be driven by materiality instead of spirituality. It is for this purpose that Gülen dwells on the necessarily pre-existential nature of the Prophet Muhammad as revealer of *haqiqa* and not only conveyor of *shari'a* (no. 5). The fact that here the Prophet is mediator and intercessor of divinely imbued existence gives all Muslims a sense of responsibility before divine truth but also raises questions that it would seem Gülen has only begun to explore about the inherently hierarchical nature of religion. It is not only the case that divine truth must be prophetically revealed. It must also be manifestly preserved by those worthy of inheriting the heavenly mystery (*warathat al-sirr*) and of assuming authority (*walaya*) over its correct expression in this world.

The production of this heavenly-earthly dynamic is possible only with the formation of the soul. *Hira'* does not therefore focus on theological disputes, which never end decisively. There are articles, e.g. by the Egyptian Zaghlul al-Najjar, proposing that the latest findings of science confirm the revelations of Islam, such as the statistical improbability of the world, in all its minutely complex detail, coming into existence on its own (no. 7; see also his article in no. 6, which comes close to collapsing religion and science into a single framework with the claim that modern science is proof of the Qur'an's divine origin). Also, given the common allegation that Sufism did not form part of the religious heritage of the first generations of Muslims (*al-salaf al-salih*), it is important—for *Hira'* to communicate its message credibly across the *umma*—to demonstrate the place of Sufism in early Islam. *Hira'* accomplishes this task convincingly with the pen of a scholar of impeccable shari'a credentials, the Syrian Muhammad Sa'id Ramadan al-Buti (no. 5), who links his argument for Sufism's place in early Islam to the example of Badi' l-Zaman Sa'id Nursi, a figure whose commitment to the cause of Islam is indisputable.

Still, the approach of *Hira'* is not so much to convince the mind with theological argumentation as to evoke a heavenly horizon in the human psyche (*wijdan*), addressing readers at the visceral more so than the rational level. As suggested by Farid al-Ansari in an article on the doctrine of Islam (no. 5), there is inherent deficiency in a religiosity limited to scholastic disputation and theological definition. The tendency among Muslims today, he claims, is to engage in doctrinal debate about the implications of monotheism without actually entering into a dynamic engagement with it in their hearts. Allah—monotheism—is not simply object of rational speculation, which invariably falls short in its attempt to capture the ineffable character of divinity in human words, but more fundamentally object of passions and emotions. It is not enough to know monotheism but rather to identify with it psychically in what al-Ansari calls a covenant of love between God and His servants. This, he says, is the secret of the hadith that states that those whose confession of monotheism is backed by a *desire* for the face of Allah are assured of entering paradise.

The presentation of the magazine and not only the content of its articles seeks to appeal to the Muslim psyche and remind it of the heavenly desire within that can only be fulfilled in a realm beyond the material one. The visual image is a highly effective means of mediating spirituality in a way words are not, even for the highly educated and not only for the illiterate. *Hira'* devotes important space for pictures that bespeak heavenly aspirations, stirring not simply intellectual rumination but psychic identification, awakening the soul to its desire for spiritual reality as reflected in the visual imagery and assisting it in the process of finding contentment and satisfaction not in material reality per se but rather in a spiritually transfigured view of it. Indeed, as Farid al-Ansari demonstrates in an article on aesthetics in Islam (no. 1), this is the goal of religious art in contrast to the elitist and self-referential tendencies of modern art: to induce through calligraphic, geometric, vegetal and other forms of mosque design a sense of being in the heavenly court. As he argues elsewhere (no.2), the beauty of the world and the beauty of humanity have a place within the spectrum of religion and cannot therefore be set in opposition to it—and that on the basis of evidence from the Book of God and Sunna of the Prophet. In this sense, things worldly and human—art and architecture, emotions, intellect, psyche—can act as sites for the manifestation of divine beauty (*jamal*). It is, of course, highly significant that al-Ansari and other contributors to *Hira'* show the revealed basis for the place of worldly and humanly beauty in the divine economy, since it is exactly this that the other forms of globalized religiosity noted above reject—the idea that existence has a positive place in Islam. Again, this is reformed Sufism, advancing not by hierarchical fiat but *'ilm*-based argument, i.e. demonstration rooted in Qur'an and Sunna.

There are other compelling ways that *Hira'* presents its unique religiosity by appealing to the psyche and not only the intellect. For example, much use is made of poetry and poetic imagery.

Scattered across the pages of *Hira'*, for example, are several poems of the Moroccan Hasan al-Amrani that speak of prophecy and love in a single breath. In a very interesting article, the Turkish Isma'il Lutfi Joqan analyzes the different ways in which the Prophet Muhammad experienced sorrow (*huzn*), offering believers a model by which to link human feeling to religious experience, binding the psyche more closely to God (no. 5). The Moroccan Ahmad 'Ibadi goes so far as to suggest a science of identification (*'ilm al-ta'assi*) with the Prophet, complete with rules and conditions (no. 7)—something with significance at a moment when many a Muslim seek to identify with the Prophet in a very literal sense, resulting in disconnect with modern realities.

Two critical observations: Several articles exhibit a bit of the obsessive antagonism towards the West that can be found in some Muslim circles. The West as a whole is characterized as a black hole of materialistic impulses with no appreciation for spirituality or religiosity of any kind. This anti-westernism might be a strategy for *Hira'* to appeal to the strongly anti-American sentiment in the Arab world, but it risks undermining the universal religiosity that the magazine claims for Islam. Why not speak simply of materialism without attributing it to the West as source, since, after all, it is no longer possible, if it ever was, to identify it exclusively with the West? There is currently a great need to get beyond reducing others to categories. Materiality is not exclusive to the West no less or more than spirituality is exclusive to the East, and one can find various forms of corruption in eastern societies no less than in western ones. There are materialistic and spiritualistic impulses in both East and West. It is more truthful to abandon tendencies to divide East and West into antagonistic categories.

It is certainly permissible—even vital—to criticize the moral shortcomings of government policies, whether governments in the West or governments in the East. In this globalized age, however, western civilization can be tagged as spiritually and ethically bankrupt no less or more than eastern civilization. Muslim attempts to locate the tyranny of the West—real or perceived—in its cultural and spiritual heritage are no less hypocritical or unfounded than non-Muslim attempts to link democratic shortcomings and terrorist activities—real or perceived—in the East in its cultural and spiritual heritage.

Second, *Hira'* is silent on politics. Why? Its religiosity is well-grounded in the heritage of Islam and could offer a welcome contribution on Muslim understanding of the nature and purpose of politics by recovering the great insights of Islam's tradition of political thought. By avoiding politics, *Hira'* risks irrelevancy for an Arab audience that desperately seeks a way for Islam to guide it beyond authoritarian rule, sectarian conflict, and Jihadist activity. One important element in Islam's tradition of political thought is mercy (*rahma*) as a public interest (*maslaha*) and not only a spiritual virtue. Forgiveness, as the moral fruit of mercy, has vital import for the public welfare of Arab society today. The aim of *Hira'* of speaking Turkish in Arabic, i.e. the language of the Qur'an, is highly relevant in this sense. Arab society still has a strong feeling of injustices committed by Ottoman rule. This is not at all to connect these injustices to the religious outlook of *Hira'* but rather to suggest that backing this outlook by *aksyon* would connect the magazine and its purpose more dynamically to the concerns of Arab society. Fethullah Gülen could effectively do this, devoting an issue of *Hira'* to this theme, including a statement of apology and hope for forgiveness for the excesses of Ottoman rule. Or, alternatively, the magazine could devote some of its articles on history to a careful treatment of some of the problematic sides of Muslim history and the place of Ottoman rule in it. (Two articles on Ottoman history seem to be defensive of Ottoman rule). Seeking forgiveness by exploring history is a strategy that has been used by other religious leaders, including popes, and can be an effective way to mediate a profound religiosity of the type represented by *Hira'*. The evidence suggests that the ideas of Nursi have been favorably received in Arab society, from Morocco to Syria. It may be useful to think of a way to consolidate these ideas with *aksyon* as heralded by the appearance of *Hira'*.

This has been a general overview of a new Gülen initiative. The magazine has caught the attention of the Arab press and Arab intellectual circles to a degree, but it is still too early to assess its impact on Arab society as a whole. Is it having effect? It has to—for the sake of the Muslim world it addresses but also for the entire world. It represents the type of religiosity that must succeed for the sake of global solidarity. And to judge from the history of the Gülen movement, it will.

PREACHING BY EXAMPLE AND LEARNING FOR LIFE: UNDERSTANDING THE GÜLEN *HIZMET* IN THE GLOBAL CONTEXT OF RELIGIOUS PHILANTHROPY AND CIVIL RELIGION

Greg Barton

Abstract

The Gülen movement, or *hizmet*, is often misunderstood, and this is in large measure because it is unlike anything else in the Muslim world, though the Muhammadiyah and Nahdlatul Ulama mass-based organisations of Indonesia do bear some resemblance.

However, there is no good reason to limit comparisons to the Muslim world. As a social movement motivated by religious values and the ideals of selfless service, engaged in philanthropic endeavour and active in the civil sphere, the Gülen *hizmet* deserves comparison with other such movements around the globe.

This paper looks outside the geographic and cultural context of the Muslim world to demonstrate that the Gülen *hizmet* shares much in common with many Western, Christian, philanthropic initiatives in education and public discourse of the past three centuries, particularly in North America. The utility of this comparison is that it helps us to understand better aspects of the Gülen *hizmet* that cannot be easily understood in the limited context of the Muslim world. It also helps break down some of the 'us and them' barriers that divide Christians and Muslims, and east and west, by allowing us to recognise common concerns, values and shared experiences.

The paper also explores the concept of civil religion in the twenty-first century, examines ways in which religious philanthropic activity can contribute to the development of non-exclusivist civil religion and apply these insights to the Gülen *hizmet* to argue that the *hizmet* models an interesting modern Islamic alternative to Islamism.

A New and Different Kind of Islamic Movement

The Gülen movement, or *hizmet* (the word literally means 'service' but is also used by some to describe the Gülen movement and will be used interchangeably with the 'Gülen movement' in this paper) a vast loosely connected network of autonomous schools, universities, NGOs and media and publishing enterprises, is often misunderstood.[1] This is in large measure because it is unlike anything else in the Muslim world. It looks, superficially, somewhat like a Muslim Brotherhood social movement but closer examination of its core doctrine and values soon reveals that it is in no respects an Islamist movement. Whereas Islamist movements like the Brotherhood are convinced that the application of *shari'ah* through radical (that is to say, from the roots up) political and legislative transformation of the state represents a panacea to the ills of modern secular society the Gülen *hizmet* has no desire for a religious state. Speaking of Islamism Gülen counters:

> This vision of Islam as a totalising ideology is totally against the spirit of Islam, which promotes the rule of law and openly rejects oppression against any segment of society.[2]

Rejecting the coercive application of *shari'ah* the Gülen *hizmet* believes instead that the best way to achieve a better society is by the personal development of individuals through education and by the setting of a positive example (*temsil*).[3] Like the Muslim Brotherhood, Fethullah Gülen and the movement around is openly committed to *tadjid*, or renewal, and *ijtihad*, or the continuing interpretation of the Qur'an and Sunnah. Speaking of his own position Gülen observed that:

> The community members are required to obey the laws that one can identify as "higher principles" as well as laws made by humans. Islam has no objection to undertaking *ijtihad* (independent reasoning), *istinbat* (deductive reasoning), and *istikhraj* (derivation) in the interpretation of *Shari'ah* principles.[4]

Unlike most associated with the Brotherhood, however, Gülen and his followers are deeply committed to tolerance, the embracing of pluralism and the pursuit of dialogue, and as a result is much more progressive in outlook and much more productive in *ijtihad*.[5] Indeed, as Ihsan Yilmaz has so evocatively put it, the Gülen movement achieves *ijtihad* and *tadjid* by conduct.[6]

---

1 Bekim Agai (2003) 'The Gülen Movement's Islamic Ethic of Education in M. Hakan Yavuz and John Esposito (eds.) Turkish Islam and the Secular State: The Gülen Movement, Syracuse, New York: Syracuse University Press, p.53-4, 60-1, 67.

2 M. Fethullah Gülen (2005) 'An Interview with Fethullah Gülen (translated by Zeki Saritoprak and Ali Unal)', The Muslim World Vol. 95 no. 3 July 2005, pp.452.

3 On temsil refer to Yavuz, M. Hakan (2003) 'The Gülen Movement: The Turkish Puritans, in M. Hakan Yavuz and John Esposito (eds.) Turkish Islam and the Secular State: The Gülen Movement, Syracuse, New York: Syracuse University Press, p.41; and to Elisbeth Ozdalga (2003) 'Following in the Footsteps of Fethullah Gülen' in M. Hakan Yavuz and John Esposito (eds.) Turkish Islam and the Secular State: The Gülen Movement, Syracuse, New York: Syracuse University Press, p.86.

4 M. Fethullah Gülen (2005) 'An Interview with Fethullah Gülen (translated by Zeki Saritoprak and Ali Unal)', The Muslim World Vol. 95 no. 3 July 2005, p.450.

5 John O. Voll (2003) 'Fethullah Gülen: Transcending Modernity in the New Islamic Discourse', in M. Hakan Yavuz and John Esposito (eds.) Turkish Islam and the Secular State: The Gülen Movement, Syracuse, New York: Syracuse University Press, p.245-7.

6 Ihsan Yilmaz (2003) 'Ijtihad and Tadjid by Conduct: The Gülen Movement', Gülen' in M. Hakan Yavuz and John Esposito (eds.) Turkish Islam and the Secular State: The Gülen Movement, Syracuse, New York: Syracuse University Press, p.208-37.

Although there really is nothing quite like the Gülen *hizmet* in the Arab 'heartland' of the Muslim world the giant mass-based Islamic organizations of Indonesia - Muhammadiyah and Nahdlatul Ulama - do bear some resemblance. Like Nahdlatul Ulama the Gülen *hizmet* is a modern articulation of rural, Sufistic, traditional Islam. It is more like the urban Islamic modernist Muhammadiyah, however, in its approach to professional philanthropic endeavour, including modern non-religious education.[7] Similar movements, though not so extensive, can be found elsewhere on what some might call the periphery, and others the leading edge, of Muslim world. There is no good reason, however, to limit comparisons only to the Muslim world. As a social movement motivated by religious values and the ideals of service and selflessness, engaged in philanthropic endeavour and active in the civil sphere the Gülen *hizmet* deserves comparison with other such movements around the globe, both in the present and over the past several centuries.

This paper examines the thinking of Fetullah Gülen as demonstrated in the social movement that he has inspired. In particular it examines the approach of Gülen and the *hizmet* to learning and to modernity. It concludes by arguing that to fully understand the movement we need to look outside the geographic and cultural context of the Muslim world. It seeks to demonstrate that the Gülen hizmet shares much in common with many of the western, Christian, philanthropic initiatives in education and public discourse of the past three centuries, particularly those found in North America. Hakan Yavuz has described the members of the Gülen *hizmet* as being Turkish Puritans.[8] It is easy to dismiss such phrases as being throw-away lines, especially when they are used by the media without any great insight into who the 18th century New England Puritans were. In fact there are a number of strong parallels between the Puritans in general and the *hizmet* leaders and between Gülen and Puritan thinkers such as Jonathan Edwards, Quaker thinkers such as John Woolman and, to some extent, Anglican thinkers such as John Wesley and Samuel Johnson. There is an even stronger correlation with subsequent movements in Christian education, both Protestant and Catholic, through to the present time. The utility of this comparison is that it both helps us to better understand many aspects of the Gülen hizmet that cannot otherwise be easily understood in the limited context of the Muslim world. It also helps break down some of the 'us and them' barriers of otherness that divide Christians and Muslims, and east and west, by allowing us to recognize common concerns and values and shared experiences. The paper will also briefly explore the concept of civil religion in the Twenty-first Century, examine ways in which religious philanthropic activity can contribute to the development of non-exclusivist civil religion and apply these insights to the Gülen hizmet to argue that the hizmet models an interesting modern Islamic alternative to Islamism.

Islam and the Modern Turkish State

State Islam in Turkey, the official sanctioned expression of religion that Ihsan Yilmaz has dubbed Lausanian Islam, is a direct product of the philosophy behind Turkey's revolution.[9]

---

7 For more on this see Greg Barton (2006) "Turkey's Gülen hizmet and Indonesia's neo-modernist NGOs; remarkable examples of progressive Islamic thought and civil society activism in the Muslim world", in Fethi Mansouri and Shahram Akbarzadeh (eds), Political Islam and Human Security, Newcastle: Cambridge Scholars Press, p.140-160.

8 Yavuz, M. Hakan (2003) 'The Gülen Movement: The Turkish Puritans, in M. Hakan Yavuz and John Esposito (eds.) Turkish Islam and the Secular State: The Gülen Movement, Syracuse, New York: Syracuse University Press, p.19-47.

9 Ihsan Yilmaz, (2005) 'State, Law, Civil Society and Islam in Contemporary Turkey', The Muslim World Vol. 95 no. 3 July 2005, pp.386-90

The modern Turkish state's approach to religion is based on the conviction of the Kemalist establishment, the inheritors of the legacy of Atatürk, that the state is able to shape and direct religious practice and belief through the comprehensive application of law and intervention of state institutions.[10] This means that the state feels that it needs to maintain control over religious expression in the public sphere. As the military remains a very powerful institution of state power in Turkey, and has intervened directly via coups (in 1960 and 1971) and less directly via 'soft coups' (the political upheavals in 1980 and 28 February 1997 are widely understood to be 'soft coups') the democratically elected government represents but one of several elements of the Turkish state.[11] This dynamic is sometimes alluded to by referring to a 'deep state' shadowing and intimidating the elected executive and legislature. The military claims an important role for itself as protector of Turkish secularism and the legacy of Mustafa Kemal Attaturk. The secularism of modern Turkey is directly modelled on French laicism and as such is profoundly different from the secularism of the English-speaking world.[12]

Turkish laicism did not simply call for a separation of 'church' and state but aspired to reserve for the state the right to direct all aspects of religious expression outside of the individual and the family home.[13] On the one hand, certain kinds of religious organizations and social movements in the civil sphere are expressly proscribed, most notably the centuries-old Sufi *tarekat*, or Sufi orders. On the other hand Islamic belief practise is actively encouraged and supported through state agencies. Religious education, through the Imam Hatip is directly controlled by the state through the Department of Religious Affairs. This department oversees the training of state imam and issues and official Friday sermon which is to be read in every mosque across Turkey. It also directs an extensive program of providing *fatwa*, or authoritative religious rulings, on all manner of issues relating to Islam and modern life.[14]

Modern Turkish secularism has proven broadly popular. The overwhelming majority of modern Turks, including the majority of practicing, socially conservative, Muslims, have no desire for Turkey to become an Islamic state. Nevertheless, there are, broadly speaking, two communities that have expressed a degree of concern with, or opposition to, the state's control of religious life.

The first, and largest is the broad community of traditional sufistic Anatolian Muslims from the thousands of villages, towns and small cities across the interior of rural Turkey. Socially conservative, deeply religious and constituting a large portion of all Turkish citizens these 'Anatolian Muslims' had little reason to concern themselves with disputing Turkish laicism when they were living in small rural communities. In recent decades, however, tens of millions of these people have moved to Istanbul, Turkey's mega-city, to Ankara, Turkey's capital,

---

10 Ihsan Yilmaz (2005) 'State, Law, Civil Society and Islam in Contemporary Turkey', The Muslim World Vol. 95 no. 3 July 2005, pp.392-3.

11 Yavuz, M. Hakan and Esposito, John (2003) 'Introduction: Islam in Turkey: Retreat from the Secular Path?' in M. Hakan Yavuz and John Esposito (eds.) Turkish Islam and the Secular State: The Gülen Movement, Syracuse, New York: Syracuse University Press, p. xxiv-xxv.

12 Yavuz, M. Hakan and Esposito, John (2003) 'Introduction: Islam in Turkey: Retreat from the Secular Path?' in M. Hakan Yavuz and John Esposito (eds.) Turkish Islam and the Secular State: The Gülen Movement, Syracuse, New York: Syracuse University Press, p. xx-xxiii.

13 It of course never fully achieved the degree of control that it aspired to. Nevertheless, its claim on the state's right to direct public life gave it a powerful weapon for the repression of social movements that it felt threatened by and gave to the military a useful pretext for intervening in political affairs in the name of upholding Turkish lacism.

14 Ihsan Yilmaz (2005) 'State, Law, Civil Society and Islam in Contemporary Turkey', The Muslim World Vol. 95 no. 3 July 2005, pp.390-2.

and to Turkey's large coastal cities like Izmir. Bringing with them their traditional styles of dress and ways of living to the burgeoning, semi-planned seas of high density suburbs ringing the old cities. Inevitably, there is a degree of friction between the two cultures: the culture of cosmopolitan urbanites and the culture of the recently arrived from the Anatolian interior. The former are accustomed to religion being a largely private affair, the latter experience it as the glue that holds communities together. Many of these new settlers were drawn to the earlier Islamist parties, such as the Welfare Party of former prime minister Erbakan. In recent years, and in much greater numbers, they have been attacked to the post-Islamist phenomenon of Prime Minister Erdogan's Virtue Party (AKP). No doubt part of the appeal of these parties is their advocacy of a more flexible approach to secularism combined with their empathy for Anatolian Islam. A large part of their appeal, however, likely lies in the perception that they are advocates for the interests of the working and lower-middle classes.

The second community uncomfortable with Turkish laicism is comprised of the very much smaller number of people who are drawn explicitly to the ideology of Islamism. Ironically, the Islamists share with the hardline Kemalists the conviction that the state is able to shape and direct religious practice and belief through the application of law and the control of key institutions. And like the Kemalists they not only believe that this is possible they also believe that it is desirable (naturally, however, they have very different views of what role religion should play in public life). This means that the Islamists have focused their long-term efforts on achieving political power in order to be able to use the state mechanisms of law and institutions to create a more Islamic nation and society.

Fethullah Gülen (b. 1941), and those who lead the *hizmet* that puts his ideas into practice, is openly and consistently critical of Islamism. Gülen's criticism of Islamism is deeply rooted in a progressive understanding of Islam that emphasizes rationality and open-minded enquiry marked by tolerance of difference and pluralism and a deep love for humanity.[15]

Given his deeply religious, socially conservative rural background, and the fact that he continues to faithfully hold to an conventional *Hanafi/Sunni* orthodox position in matters of theology, it is remarkable just how broadly ecumenical Fethullah Gülen has become.[16] Inspired by Said Nursi Gülen has long been optimistic about the potential for Muslims to work together with the People of the Book – as Jews and Christians are traditionally recognised to be. Writing recently Gülen implies a respectful appraisal of earlier prophetic books and their adherents well beyond the understanding of conservative Islamic scholars when he remarked:

> Regardless of how their adherents implement their faith in their daily lives, such as generally accepted values as love, respect, tolerance, forgiveness, mercy, human rights, peace, brotherhood, and freedom are all values exalted by religion. Most of these values are accorded the highest precedence in the messages brought by Moses, Jesus, and Muhammad, upon them be peace, as well as in the messages of Budda and even Zarathustra, Lao-Tzu, Confucius, and the Hindu prophets.[17]

As a progressive thinker Gülen believes that the future can be better than the past and that rather than wistfully looking back to a forever lost 'golden age' Muslims, together with other

---

15 The emphasis on tolerance and the practise of dialogue evolved to assume central importance in the thinking of Fethullah Gülen and the work of the movement from the mid-1990s onwards, refer to: Bekim Agai (2003) 'The Gülen Movement's Islamic Ethic of Education in M. Hakan Yavuz and John Esposito (eds.) Turkish Islam and the Secular State: The Gülen Movement, Syracuse, New York: Syracuse University Press, p.64-5,

16 Elisabeth, Ozdalga (2005) 'Redeemer or Outsider? The Gülen Community in the Civilizing Process), The Muslim World Vol. 95 no. 3 July 2005, pp.441.

17 Fethullah Gülen (2004) Toward a Global Civization of Love and Tolerance, New Jersey: Light, pp.75-6.

people of good will, should work to achieve societies that are progressively more just, compassionate and decent. This progressive outlook lies at the heart of the hizmet's focus on education and the development of individual potential through learning and discipline. For Gülen secular democracy represents the best and only appropriate approach to governance in the modern state. He argues that whilst the Qur'an and the Sunnah speak clearly of religious values that should be reflected and upheld in the state they do not contain a blueprint for politics.

> Islam does not propose a certain unchangeable form of government or attempt to shape it. Instead, Islam establishes fundamental principles that orient a governments general character, leaving it to the people to choose the type and form of government according to time and circumstances.[18]

Gülen frequently endorses democracy specifically, arguing that it is the most appropriate form of government for the modern period and one that is entirely compatible with Islam:

> Democracy and Islam are compatible. Ninety-five percent of Islamic rules deal with private life and the family. Only 5 percent deals with matters of the state, and this could be arranged only within the context of democracy. If some people are thinking of something else, such as an Islamic state, this country's history and social conditions do not allow it … Democratization is an irreversible process in Turkey.[19]

Gülen is generally seen to draw directly on the intellectual heritage of the influential and greatly loved Sufi scholar and writer Bediuzzaman Said Nursi.[20] And indeed, an examination of Gülen's writing reveals it to be substantially built upon the foundation laid by Nursi, who in turn drew upon the great Anatolian Sufi Mevlana Jalal ad-Din Rumi (d. 1276) and the Indian writers Ahmad Faruqi Sirhindi (1564-1624) and Shah Wali Allah al-Dihlawi (1703-1762) amongst others.[21] Members of the Gülen hizmet, like hundreds of thousands of other admirers of Nursi meet regularly to read and discuss his multi-volume thematic commentary on the Qur'an, the Risale-i Nur, or Treatise of Light. For this reason the Gülen *hizmet* is seen to represent a significant component of the broader so-called Nurcu movement. Gülen is, however, not simply a follower of Nursi. Rather he is a significant thinker, writer and leader in his own right. Much of Gülen's work essentially takes the form of a synthesis, rearticulation, or fresh application of the earlier work of Nursi and others. And like Nursi and many other Islamic scholars Gülen frequently returns in his writing to the lived example the Prophet Muhammad

---

18 Gülen, M. Fethullah (2001), 'A Comparative Approach to Islam and Democracy', SAIS Review 21, no. 2. p. 134

19 Gülen interviewed in Sabah, 27 January 1995 and quoted in Yavuz, M. Hakan (2003) 'The Gülen Movement: The Turkish Puritans, in M. Hakan Yavuz and John Esposito (eds.) Turkish Islam and the Secular State: The Gülen Movement, Syracuse, New York: Syracuse University Press, p.28.

20 On links with Nursi, refer to: M. Hakan Yavuz, and John Esposito (2003) 'Introduction: Islam in Turkey: Retreat from the Secular Path?' in M. Hakan Yavuz and John Esposito (eds.) Turkish Islam and the Secular State: The Gülen Movement, Syracuse, New York: Syracuse University Press, p. xxvii-xxviii. Yavuz, M. Hakan (2003) 'Islam in the Public Sphere: The Case of the Nur Movement', in M. Hakan Yavuz and John Esposito (eds.) Turkish Islam and the Secular State: The Gülen Movement, Syracuse, New York: Syracuse University Press, p.1-18. Yavuz, M. Hakan (2003) 'The Gülen Movement: The Turkish Puritans, in M. Hakan Yavuz and John Esposito (eds.) Turkish Islam and the Secular State: The Gülen Movement, Syracuse, New York: Syracuse University Press, p.19-47. See also: Ahmet T. Kuru (2003) Fethullah Gülen's Search for a Middle Way Between Modernity and Muslim Tradition', in M. Hakan Yavuz and John Esposito (eds.) Turkish Islam and the Secular State: The Gülen Movement, Syracuse, New York: Syracuse University Press, p.118-9.

21 Zeki Sariotoprak and Sidney Griffith (2005) 'Fetullah Gülen and the 'People of the Book': A Voice from Turkey for Interfaith Dialogue', The Muslim World Vol. 95 no. 3 July 2005, pp.331-2

for inspiration and direction. Nevertheless there are several significant areas where Gülen is a thinker and leader of striking originality and innovation. In general terms Gülen, like Nursi before him, can be described as a Sufi and his thinking is richly infused with Sufi imagery, values and ideas, including most notably focus on the heart, the inward being, the seat of both wisdom and spirituality. Growing up in the small village of Korucuk Gülen, however, is not a traditional Sufi and does not align with any particular Sufi order, or *tarekat*, rather he is, in the evocative formulation of Zeki Saritoprak, 'a sufi in his own way'.[22]

A disciplined child growing up in a pious household Gülen came to religious life at an early age. He recalls that he "began praying when I was four years old and never missed a prayer since."[23] As was the case with many village boys Gülen was first taught to recite the Qur'an by his mother, Rafi'a and his father, Ramiz Efendi, who taught him Persian as well as Arabic, and was only later, at the age of ten, set under the tutelage of his first formal teacher, Muhammad Lufti Efendi (d.1954) who soon succeeded in helping him commit the entire Qur'an to memory.[24] Significantly, Lufti Efendi, a well regarded Sufi poet and teacher was a member of the Qadiri order whilst Ramiz Efendi was a member of the Naqshbandi order. These orthodox Shari'ah-oriented Sufi orders were popular in rural Turkey at the time.

One of the areas where Gülen has made his greatest contribution to Islamic thought is in his exploration of learning. Gülen is a passionate advocate of learning in the broadest sense in every field of enquiry and dialogue. This is reflected both in the *hizmet's* direct engagement with educational initiatives and with a wide range of media and publishing initiatives designed to inform and engage.

Not surprisingly, given that it is a deeply religious movement, the *hizmet* does undertake a significant amount of activity relating directly to religious teaching and encouragement. Indeed the movement's origins are rooted in the regular reading group meetings focusing on Said Nursi's Risale-i Nur referred to above. In most Nurcu communities these reading groups are known as *dershane* but in the Gülen *hizmet* community they are referred to as *isik evler*, or lighthouses. Fethullah Gülen trained as an official state *imam* in an Imam Hatip, an Islamic college run by the Department of Religious Affairs for the training of *imam*. His first appointment as an imam began in 1966 in the large, cosmopolitan, city of Izmir on Turkey's Mediterranean coast.[25] Gülen formally retired from the Department of Religious Affairs in 1981. In the late 1960s Gülen established several *isik evler* in Izmir. These grew steadily in number through the 1970s in Izmir and Istanbul and became the nucleolus for the *hizmet*.[26]

---

22 For an extensive discussion of this refer to: Zeki Saritoprak (2003) 'Fethullah Gülen: A Sufi in His Own Way', in M. Hakan Yavuz and John Esposito (eds.) Turkish Islam and the Secular State: The Gülen Movement, Syracuse, New York: Syracuse University Press, p.156-69. See also Thomas Michel (2005) 'Sufism and Modernity in the Thought of Fethullah Gülen', The Muslim World Vol. 95 no. 3 July 2005, pp.341-58.

23 Quoted in Lester R. Kurtz (2005) 'Gülen's Paradox: Combining Commitment and Tolerance', The Muslim World Vol. 95 no. 3 July 2005, p.375.

24 Zeki Saritoprak and Sidney Griffith (2005) 'Fetullah Gülen and the 'People of the Book': A Voice from Turkey for Interfaith Dialogue', The Muslim World Vol. 95 no. 3 July 2005, pp.330-1. See also Osman Bakar (2005) 'Gülen on Religion and Science: A Theological Perspective', The Muslim World Vol. 95 no. 3 July 2005, pp.360.

25 In Izmir Gülen was attached to the Kestanepazari Qur'anic School. From this base he was able to build a circuit of regular talks in coffeehouses, community centres, private homes and mosques in an around Izmir. Refer to: Yavuz, M. Hakan (2003) 'The Gülen Movement: The Turkish Puritans, in M. Hakan Yavuz and John Esposito (eds.) Turkish Islam and the Secular State: The Gülen Movement, Syracuse, New York: Syracuse University Press, p.20

26 Yavuz, M. Hakan (2003) 'The Gülen Movement: The Turkish Puritans, in M. Hakan Yavuz and John Esposito (eds.) Turkish Islam and the Secular State: The Gülen Movement, Syracuse, New York: Syracuse University Press, p.30-5.

From its earliest days the *hizmet* has been involved with writing and publishing. The movement's first magazine, *Siziniti*, launched in the early 1980s, is a popular publication directed towards a lay audience and intended to promote discussion and learning about science. It aims to foster interest in science and to demonstrate that rational scientific enquiry and religious faith are not incompatible. *Siziniti*, a Turkish magazine, was joined several years later by the English language publication, *Fountain*, edited in Istanbul and printed in New Jersey and aimed at fostering a general interest in religion and spirituality. The Articles in *Fountain* deal mostly, but not exclusively with Islam and generally reflect a tolerant, Sufistic orientation and a modern articulation of tradionalist Islam. A sister publication of Fountain, *Dialogue* (joined in Australia, in 2004, by *Dialogue Australia Asia*) was established specifically to encourage inter-religious dialogue.

In the field of learning the Gülen hizmet is best known for its loosely connected network of more than 500 modern secular private schools and six universities that sprung up across Turkey and throughout Central Asia and some 50, or so, nations around the world, beginning in 1983 with one school in Izmir and another in Istanbul.[27] In addition to these schools there also a handful of well regarded secular colleges and half a dozen universities such as Fatih University in Istanbul and Ankara. These schools, many of which have been deliberately established in some of the poorest and most needy parts of the word, are generally very well regarded and achieve a high standard of scholastic achievement in neighbourhoods, districts and nations not normally accustomed to excellence in education. What makes them so remarkable in the context of the Muslim world is their commitment to secular modern learning open to students of all backgrounds. The schools, regardless of the nation in which they operate and the legislation that pertains to religious instruction in schools, adhere consistently to a secular curriculum. Where the state mandates an hour per week of religious instruction, as is the case in Turkey, the *hizmet* schools, of course, comply, but otherwise the schools are as at least as secular in their teaching program and formal orientation as contemporary mainstream denomination Christian schools. In this respect they are very much like modern Anglican, Presbyterian, Methodist or Catholic schools and as such don't have the overtly religious character of many independent Christian or Jewish schools.

There is no shortage of Islamic leaders calling for the construction of a new mosque in their neighbourhood. There are precious few such leaders, however, who urge their supporters to build schools rather than mosques and then not necessarily in their own neighbourhood but in foreign societies, to the benefit of both non-Muslim and Muslim students.

Although Gülen *hizmet* is becoming increasingly well-known outside Turkey for its schools and passion for education these schools are only one part of the *hizmet's* activism. Magazines *Sizinti, Fountain and Dialogue.* These publications represent modern religious magazines in the style of many contemporary Christian publications, such as *The Catholic World Report,*

---

27 Ahmet T. Kuru (2003) Fethullah Gülen's Search for a Middle Way Between Modernity and Muslim Tradition', in M. Hakan Yavuz and John Esposito (eds.) Turkish Islam and the Secular State: The Gülen Movement, Syracuse, New York: Syracuse University Press, p.116. For a general overview of the schools network and related issues refer to Bekim Agai (2003) 'The Gülen Movement's Islamic Ethic of Education in M. Hakan Yavuz and John Esposito (eds.) Turkish Islam and the Secular State: The Gülen Movement, Syracuse, New York: Syracuse University Press, p.48-68; to Thomas Michel (2003) 'Fethullah Gülen as Educator' in M. Hakan Yavuz and John Esposito (eds.) Turkish Islam and the Secular State: The Gülen Movement, Syracuse, New York: Syracuse University Press, p.69-84; and to Elisabeth Ozdalga (2003) 'Following in the Footsteps of Fethullah Gülen' in M. Hakan Yavuz and John Esposito (eds.) Turkish Islam and the Secular State: The Gülen Movement, Syracuse, New York: Syracuse University Press, p.85-114.

Christianity, The Christian Century, Christianity Today, Guideposts, and *World.* If they represented the movement's primary ventures in journalism and media this aspect of *hizmet's* activities would still warrant serious study but as we will see below there is much more to the movement's publishing activities than just 'religious publishing'. The moderate and generally inclusive approach to discussion of spirituality and modern life of these religious magazines would suggest that the religious character of the movement is comparable to that of the mainstream Christian denominations in the west. These publications portray a religious movement that is socially and doctrinally conservative yet clearly not fundamentalist in the manner of America's Christian right or its Islamist analogues in the Muslim world. The writings dealing with patterns of religious devotion and practise reveal a traditionalist orientation that shares common characteristics, in terms of reverence for places, peoples and events, with traditional Catholicism, Anglicanism/Episcopalianism and Lutherism. At the same time the movement's character is clearly forward-looking: optimistic about the future and the opportunities presented by modernity, and keen to adapt and contribute. There is, in general, in these publications a sense of the sort of values and principles associated with American civil religion and the humanitarianism and common decency of America's mid-west and the world of Norman Rockwell that is also manifested in secular magazines such as *Reader's Digest,* America's best-selling consumer magazine.

Alongside of these religious magazines the movement has published hundreds of books with explicitly religious themes. Isik Publishing, the Istanbul-based publishing house behind *Fountain* magazine is responsible for most of the Gülen movement's religious book publishing. The heart of its catalogue consists of works by Said Nursi, most notably the Risale-i Nur, and Fethullah Gülen. Alongside these are studies of Gülen's thought and devotional works dealing with the life of the Prophet Muhammad and with Ottoman religious life. In certain respects Isik Publishing is comparable to American Christian publishing houses such as Eerdmans, Intervarsity Press, Loyola Press Thomas Nelson and Zondervan.

Although these religious publications, both magazines and books, represent a vitally important aspect of the hizmet's, in terms of broad circulation and, arguably, of influence, the *hizmet's* wide-ranging initiatives in secular media are even more important. And it is these publications which represent some of the most remarkable aspects of the *hizmet's* activism. Here it becomes much more difficult to make comparisons can with western Christian movements. Contemporary Christian media in the English-speaking world, with a few notable exceptions, such as the Christian Science Monitor and some recent developments in radio and new media, tends to be inward looking and primarily concerned with explicitly religious issues.

The Gülen hizmet really began to 'go public' following the 1980 coup and the rise of the moderate, centrist, government of Turgut Ozal in 1982. Remarkably, beginning in the early 1980's, this civil sphere activism was manifested as much, or more, in secular initiatives as it was in conventional religious initiatives such as those in religious publishing noted above. Apart from the schools themselves, these secular activities were, and are, mostly defined by initiatives in intellectual inquiry and dialogue, taking the form of newspapers, current affairs magazines, television and radio stations and dialogue-orientated NGOs. Alongside of these secular initiatives are another kind of activism involving the development of loose networks of businessmen and associated institutions in finance and banking including the business network Is Hayati Dayanisma Dernegi (ISHAD) and the bank Bank Asya.[28] The latter are

---

28 Yavuz, M. Hakan (2003) 'The Gülen Movement: The Turkish Puritans, in M. Hakan Yavuz and John Esposito (eds.) Turkish Islam and the Secular State: The Gülen Movement, Syracuse, New York: Syracuse University Press,

vital in producing support for the school network but the media ventures themselves are self-financing businesses in themselves.

One of the first initiatives on this front was the launching of the daily national newspaper *Zaman* in Istanbul.[29] *Zaman* was founded in 1986 and quickly established a reputation for comprehensive, objective reporting directed by an editorial position that was perceived to be neutral and, unlike virtually every other major newspaper at the time, not aligned to any particular political camp or ideological position. In a market marked by overtly partisan periodicals *Zaman* was welcomed by readers seeking reliable reporting of current affairs and professional journalistic standards. With current circulation exceeding 700,000 copies per day it would appear that many of these readers have no connection with the Gülen movement and do not have a particular interest in its religious outlook. Some of *Zaman's* writers take an overtly socially conservative on the issues that they write about but others are regarded as being relatively liberal and progressive in their stance. From its inception *Zaman* was intended to be a 'newspaper of record' along the lines of London's *The Times*, and *The Guardian, The New York Times, The Washington Post, The Times of India, Karachi's Dawn*, and Indonesia's *Kompas*.

Apart from striving for objective and professional journalism *Zaman* is remarkable for its cutting-edge approach to developing the business of newspaper publishing. *Zaman* launched its online edition in 1996 placing it in an elite group of newspapers worldwide to make the move to cyberspace when usage of the internet was only just beginning.[30] Within several years of its establishment in Istanbul *Zaman* opened operations in four other Turkish cities and began producing regional editions outside Turkey. Today regional editions are printed and distributed in Australia, Azerbaijan, Bulgaria, Germany, Romania, Kazakhstan, Kyrghizistan, Macedonia, Turkmenistan, and the US. *Zaman* also produces special international editions in local languages in Eastern Europe and Central Asia. *Zaman* also employs a remarkably complete array of foreign correspondents and stringers across the world, as reflected in its extensive reporting on world affairs. Zaman is assisted in maintaining this bread of coverage though its association with its sister company CHA, one of Turkey's largest news agencies. Both *Zaman* and CHA are under the control of Feza Publications Incorporated which also has in it's the well-regarded weekly news magazine *Aksiyon* along with *Sizinti* and the theological journal *Yeni Umit*.

The CHA stable of print publications are undisputedly part of the Gülen movement but are remarkable not just for their professionalism but also for their non-sectarian outlook. In this respect they have few parallels in the world of Christian media. In some respects *Zaman* could be compared, for example, with the *Church of England Newspaper* but unlike *Zaman* the venerable *Newspaper*, which has been published since 1828, is largely concerned with matters relating to its particular religious community. So too, to a greater or lesser extent, is the case with the other Christian newspapers and magazines mentioned above. The closest parallel to *Zaman* is probably *The Christian Science Monitor*.

---

p.36-7.

29 Yavuz, M. Hakan (2003) 'The Gülen Movement: The Turkish Puritans, in M. Hakan Yavuz and John Esposito (eds.) Turkish Islam and the Secular State: The Gülen Movement, Syracuse, New York: Syracuse University Press, p.36.

30 The 'internet' only began to be widely known by that name in 1996. Version 1.0 of Mosaic, the world's first widely-used web browser was released in 1993 and by the end of the following year, 1994, public interest in the internet could be said to have begun to spread beyond the technical and academic communities.

Founded in 1879, in Boston Massachusetts, by Mary Eddy Baker, The Church of Christ, Scientist, is a relatively small Christian denomination (its membership is thought to number no more than several hundred thousand strong) that sits uneasily on the outside of main-stream Protestantism. With its unusual emphasis on spiritual healing through prayer and the ultimate 'unreality' of sin, disease and death the church has been viewed with suspicion by many mainstream Christians since its earliest days. It was partly because of this and related general disillusionment with mainstream media that in 1908 Baker launched the *Christian Science Monitor* as a daily newspaper (published Monday through Friday) intended "to in-jure no man, but to bless all mankind". From these unlikely beginnings and despite its name the *Monitor* has become a highly regarded reporter of American and international affairs, winning many plaudits, including seven Pulitzer prizes. The only indications of its religious connections are a single daily religious feature page ('The Home Forum') and a general avoidance of issues relating to medicine and disease.

Zaman and its sister CHA publications compare very favourably with *The Christian Science Monitor* in every respect, and arguably exceed it in several important respects, such as the breadth of outlook displayed by its editorial staff. Like the *Monitor*, *Zaman* was quick to take advantage of the internet, launching its first online presence in 1995, one year before the *Monitor*. Unlike the *Monitor*, however, *Zaman* and its CHA stable mates have met with con-sistently strong commercial success. Whereas the *Monitor* has struggled for years to expand circulation and turn a profit *Zaman* has gone from strength to strength. It is likely that one reason for the greater success of *Zaman* compared with the *Monitor* is that whereas the later was merely adding one more quality newspaper to a market already well-served with such publications *Zaman* was filling a hitherto unmet demand for objective, professional, non-par-tisan reporting and analysis. It is likely that this also is the reason that the Gülen movement has succeeded, where the Monitor has tried and failed, in expanding into electronic media.

Samanyolu Television was launched in January 1993. The initiative represented a finan-cial gamble at a time when private television programming was dominated by tabloid re-porting and entertainment with poor production values and sensationalist content. Like the CHA print publications Samanyolu set out to provide non-sectarian, largely secular content of a high standard. The product soon found a market and the rather undercapitalised ven-ture steadily consolidated its market position and commercial viability. Samanyolu came to achieve the sort of quality in programming for which the BBC (the British Broadcasting Commission) in Britain, PBS (the Public Broadcasting Service) in America and the ABC (the Australian Broadcasting Commission) are well regarded. Unlike the BBC, PBS and the ABC, however, Samanyolu remains an entirely commercial venture, albeit one driven by a similar philosophy of striving for quality and thoughtful programming in both current affairs and in popular entertainment, including drama production and general interest documentary and lifestyle programs.

A separate, but related aspect of the hizmet's activities is found in the Journalists and Writers and Foundation (Gazeteciler ve Yazarlar Vakfi – JWF) established in 1994.[31] This very in-fluential NGO goes beyond straightforward journalistic reporting and analysis to support strategic public intellectual initiatives in the promotion of dialogue. One of the Foundation's most important activities is the hosting of a high level annual summer dialogue forum known as the Abant Platform (named after the lakeside location of its annual meetings) designed

31 Yavuz, M. Hakan (2003) 'The Gülen Movement: The Turkish Puritans, in M. Hakan Yavuz and John Esposito (eds.) Turkish Islam and the Secular State: The Gülen Movement, Syracuse, New York: Syracuse University Press, p.42.

to bring together disparate elements of the political and cultural elite to talk face to face about issues of pressing national importance.[32] Each Abant Platform produces and Abant Declaration summing up the issues discussed. The first Abant Platform was held in July 1998 on the theme of 'Islam and Secularism'. The 1998 Abant Declaration, Ihsan Yilmaz observed:

> attempts to redefine the meaning of laicism in accordance with the way it is practiced in Anglo-Saxon cultures. Moreover the Declaration reinterprets Islamic theology to respond to modern challenges. It was underscored in the declaration that revelation and reason do not conflict; individuals should use their reason to organize their social lives; the state should be neutral on beliefs and faiths prevalent in society; governance of the state cannot be based on the dominance of one religious tradition; secularism should expand individua freedoms and rights and should not exclude any person form the public sphere.[33]

Subsequent Abant Platforms dealt with the related themes of 'Religion and State Relations' (July 1999), 'Islam and Democracy' (July 2000), and 'Pluralism' (July 2001). In April 2004 the Journalists and Writers Foundation to the Abant Platform offshore to America and held a successful forum meeting at Johns Hopkins University in Washington D.C. around the them of Islam and Democracy.[34] Subsequently the Abant Platform has also met in Europe and has planning for an ongoing series of international meetings.

When compared with Islamic movements across the Muslim world the Gülen movement, or *hizmet*, is without equal with the possible exception of Indonesian organizations such as Muhammadiyah and Nahdlatul Ulama, but on certain fronts, media in particular, even these much larger institutions are not a match for the Gülen *hizmet*.

Leaving aside the Gülen movement's unmatched endeavours in the realm of modern media, in many respects the closest parallels to the *hizmet* are found not in the civil sphere of the Muslim world but rather in the western hemisphere in contemporary and early modern Christian civil society movements and organizations. The reasons for this appear to be bound up with the existence of certain social needs in modern Turkish society and the opportunities to meet them that have arisen over the past three decades. Just as importantly, however, is the fact that Fethullah Gülen and his movement share a similar philosophical approach to science and learning. The following statements from Gülen could just as easily have come from John Wesley or Jonathon Edwards or any number of Jesuit brothers:

> Neglect of the intellect ... would result in a community of poor, docile mystics. Negligence of the heart or spirit, on the other hand, would result in crude rationalism devoid of any spiritual dimension ... It is only when the intellect, spirit and body are harmonized, and man is motivated towards activity in the illuminated way of the Divine message, that he can become a complete being and attain true humanity.[35]

A person is truly human who learns and teaches and inspires others. It is difficult to regard as

---

32 Yavuz, M. Hakan (2003) 'The Gülen Movement: The Turkish Puritans, in M. Hakan Yavuz and John Esposito (eds.) Turkish Islam and the Secular State: The Gülen Movement, Syracuse, New York: Syracuse University Press, p.45.

33 Ihsan Yilmaz (2005) 'State, Law, Civil Society and Islam in Contemporary Turkey', The Muslim World Vol. 95 no. 3 July 2005, pp.400.

34 Zeki Saritoprak (2005) 'An Islamic Approach to Peace and Nonviolence: A Turkish Experience', The Muslim World Vol. 95 no. 3 July 2005, pp.423.

35 Gülen, Fethullah (2001) Prophet Muhammad: Aspects of His Life, trans. Ali Unal, Fairfax, Va.: The Fountain, pp. 105-6.

fully human someone who is ignorant and has no desire to learn. It is also questionable whether a learned person who does not renew and reform oneself so as to set and example to others is fully human.[36]

Scientific knowledge without religion usually causes atheism or agnosticism, while religious knowledge without intellectual enlightenment gives rise to bigotry. When combined, they urge a student to research, further and further research, deepening in both belief and knowledge.[37]

As Hakan Yavuz has so acutely observed:

Gülen's conception of identity and morality are interconnected but do not form a self-contained or closed system. Morality translates into identity through conduct and collective action, so acting and engaging in the public and private spheres are part of building the moral self. In short, morality and identity must be put into practice and reinterpreted on the basis of new challenges. "Islam by conduct (hizmet and himmet) and "Islam by product (eser) are the two key concepts of the Gülen movement.

Because Islam, for Gülen, is the constitution of morality and identity, he stresses the role of education for the cultivation of the self. His education project is based on three principles: cultivation of ethics, teaching of science and self-discipline. In his faith-inspired education project, morality and discipline consist of sacrifice, responsibility to others, handwork and idealism. In fact this religiously motivated global education movement is a way of bringing God back to one's life through the ethic of self-sacrifice and hardwork. Muslims constantly are reminded that avoiding sin is not enough; rather, engaging to a create a more human world is require. Salvation means not only to be "saved from" sinful activities but also to be engaged actively engaged in the improvement of the world."[38]

Fethullah Gülen can be truly said to be 'preaching by example' and, on the front of social activism and the greater good through learning and the pursuit of knowledge, his example is one that speaks loudly not just to the Muslim world but also to the west.

---

36 M. Fethullah Gülen (1999) 'The Necessity of Interfaith Dialogue: A Muslim Approach', Speech given at the Parliament of the World's Religion, Capetown, 1-8 December 1999; quoted in Thomas Michel (2003) 'Fethullah Gülen as Educator' in M. Hakan Yavuz and John Esposito (eds.) Turkish Islam and the Secular State: The Gülen Movement, Syracuse, New York: Syracuse University Press, p.79.

37 M. Fethullah Gülen (1997) Understanding and Belief: The Essentials of the Islamic Faith, Izmir: Kaynak, p.302.

38 Yavuz, M. Hakan (2003) 'The Gülen Movement: The Turkish Puritans, in M. Hakan Yavuz and John Esposito (eds.) Turkish Islam and the Secular State: The Gülen Movement, Syracuse, New York: Syracuse University Press, p.26.

PRESENT AND POTENTIAL IMPACT OF THE SPIRITUAL TRADITION OF ISLAM ON CONTEMPORARY MUSLIMS: FROM GHAZALI TO GÜLEN

Y. Alp Aslandogan

Abstract

Western analysts of trends in the contemporary Islamic world often overestimate the impact of contemporary Sufi orders and/or underestimate the impact of the spiritual tradition of Islam. Among the elements of the spiritual tradition conducive to religious pluralism is the 'mirror' concept: every human is seen as a mirror of God in three aspects: reflecting the attributes and names of God as His work of art, reflection through dependence on God, and reflection through actions God commands or commends. Since only the last aspect is voluntary, every human, regardless of creed, is a mirror of God in at least the first two aspects. This is a potent argument for peaceful coexistence in religious diversity. The perspective of the spiritual tradition is emphatically inclusive and compassionate and naturally lends itself to non-violence, going beyond mere tolerance to hospitality and friendship. There are important impediments that prevent this perspective from having a greater impact: (1) the literalist opposition to flexible interpretation of concepts from the Qur'an and the Prophetic tradition, and the wide definition of innovation or heresy ('*bid`a*'); (2) deviations of some Sufi orders and subsequent criticisms by orthodox Muslims; and (3) the impact of the politicisation of religion by some groups and political moves by certain Sufi orders.

This paper argues that the only approach that has a chance of influencing the majority of contemporary Muslims in positive ways without being open to criticism is the 'balanced' spiritual tradition, after the style of the Companions, sometimes called tasawwuf, which strives to harmonise the outer dimensions of Islamic law and worship with the inner dimension of spiritual disciplines firmly rooted in the Qur'an and Prophetic tradition. This paper will present an analysis of this 'balanced' spiritual tradition in Islam, from Ghazali, through Rumi, to Gülen.

The emergence of M. J. Rumi as the best selling love poet in the U.S., thanks in part to the compilations of C. Barks[1], has drawn attention to the spiritual tradition of Islam. El-Zein[2] talks about commercialization of Rumi's works and "how his work is taken nowadays out of the Muslim Sufi tradition into an elusive spiritual movement" which the author calls the "New Sufism". The interest in Sufism was renewed after the tragedy of 9/11 as both Muslims and non-Muslims sought to highlight the inclusive, peace and love-focused essence of this faith[3].

Sufism is sometimes called the esoteric dimension of Islam, as opposed to the exoteric dimension of Islamic law[4]. It does not take long for any researcher of the Sufi tradition to recognize how overloaded the term *Sufism* has become, in part due to its long and complex history and its geographical dispersion. Like an umbrella term over a giant field, it covers various traditions, sub-traditions and branches thereof, that share many essential concepts and differ significantly in others. In recognition of this fact, the late Anne-Marie Schimmel, the noted scholar of Rumi, avoids a definitive description in her celebrated treatise of Sufism, but relates the varying views of the discipline by renowned masters[5]. The core concept of the tradition, *ihsan*, that is living in the constant consciousness of God's presence is described in a famous and authentic prophetic tradition where a stranger[6] appearing as a traveler sits down close to the Prophet and asks him three questions:

> [The stranger] said: "Tell me about *iman* (Faith)."

> [The Prophet] said: "It is that you affirm God, His angels, His books, His messengers, and the Last Day...."

> [The stranger] said: "Muhammad, tell me about *Islam* (Submission to God)."

> The Messenger of God, may God bless him and grant him peace, said: "Islam is that you bear witness, testifying that there is no object of worship aside from God, and that Muhammad is the Messenger of God; and you establish the ritual prayer; and you give the alms-tax; and you fast in the month of Ramadan; and you perform the pilgrimage to the House if you are able to find a way to do so."

> Finally, he said: "Tell me about ihsan (Virtue)[7]."

> [The Prophet] said: It is ... that you worship God as though you see Him, for though you do not see Him, truly He sees You[8].

Georgetown scholar of Islamic studies S. Hossein Nasr sees the strive to live the concept of

1 Barks, C. 1995. *The Essential Rumi*, San Francisco: Harper.

2 El-Zein, A., 2000, Spiritual Consumption in the United States: the Rumi phenomenon, *Islam and Christian-Muslim Relations*, 11:1, 1 March 2000 , pp. 71-85.

3 Baran, Z. (ed). 2004. Understanding Sufism and its Potential Role in US Policy, *Nixon Center Conference Report*, Washington, D.C., March 2004.

4 Nasr, S. H. 2002. *The Heart of Islam*, New York: HarperCollins.

5 Schimmel, A. M. 1975. *Mystical Dimensions of Islam*, U. of North Carolina Press, Chapel Hill, pp:3-22.

6 In the continuation of the tradition we learn that this was ArcAngel Gabriel who appeared in the form of a man to facilitate a learning experience for the companions.

7 Please note that the English word virtue is only an indicator of one of the meanings embedded in this loaded concept.

8 This famous prophetic tradition is related in multiple trusted books of Hadith, namely, Muslim, Iman, 1; Nesai, Iman, 6; Ebu Davud, Sunnet, 17; Tirmizi, Iman, 4. For a digital collection of important books of Islamic prophetic tradition, see *Hadith Encyclopedia*, Harf Information Technology, Cairo, 1996.

Ihsan in one's life as a practical definition of Sufism:

> As for ihsan, it is obvious that not everyone can worship God as if they saw Him. This is the station of the saintly, and ihsan, which means both "virtue" and "beauty", is associated with the spiritual path that leads to sanctity, and is considered practically a definition of Sufism[9].

Elsewhere, he elaborates on the concept:

> The goal of the inward life in Islam is to reach the Divine as both the Transcendent and the Imminent. It is to gain a vision of God as the Reality beyond all determination and at the same time of the world as "plunged in God". It is to see God everywhere[10].

In a brief description of Sufism opening their collection of verses from renown Sufi masters, Fadiman and Frager point to the same concept:

> Sufis are Muslim mystics who can trace their beginnings to the prophet Muhammad. Most Muslims would like to see and be with God after death, but the Sufis are impatient. They want to be with God now. Hence the Sufi path is the discipline and practice towards experiencing God in this very life[11].

Consequently, a Sufi can be seen as a person 'who is completely absorbed in Divine Beloved and does not think of anything but Him.'[12]

Western analysts of the trends in the contemporary Islamic world often exhibit one of two fallacies: Overestimating the impact of contemporary Sufism or underestimating the impact of the deep current of the spiritual tradition of Islam. Hassan, writing for Al-Ahram weekly of Egypt, comments on the diverse paths of developments various Sufi traditions went through in countries or regions such as Egypt, Turkey, Algeria and the Indian Sub-continent:

> American conceptions deal with Sufism either as a movement that forms a single and positive model to be spread, or as a unique, internal state that highly values conviction and human freedom and raises tolerance as a value in dealing with others. Yet Sufism no longer remains as it began, that being a state of asceticism and individual worship. It has developed into massive institutions that cross all continents, some of which strive to play roles in development, politics and society, and others that lose themselves in folklore and celebrations[13].

Turkish, Indian, North African, Syrian, Indonesia-Malaysian and Persian Sufi traditions run deep and wide among contemporary Muslim populations[14]. Akbar Ahmed's recent anthropological excursion into eight predominantly Muslim countries, namely India, Indonesia, Jordan, Malaysia, Pakistan, Qatar, Syria and Turkey, highlight the spiritual tradition as the source of one of the three models of Muslim response to modernity and globalization[15]. After a detailed discussion of both historical and current developments involving Sufi orders, Martha B. Olcott of Carnegie Endowment for International Peace concludes that "Sufism has

---

9 Nasr, S. H. 2002. *The Heart of Islam*, New York: HarperCollins, p.62.

10 Nasr, S. H. 1977. Interior Life in Islam, 3:2

11 Fadiman, J. and Frager, R. (editors) 1997. *Essential Sufism*. New York: Harper-Collins.

12 Schimmel, ibid. 16.

13 Hassan, A. A. 2007. "America's Favoured Islam", Al-Ahram weekly, published in Cairo, Egypt, available online at http://weekly.ahram.org.eg/2007/852/op1.htm.

14 Chittick, W.C. 2000. *Sufism, A Short Introduction*. Oxford: Oneworld Publications.

15 Ahmed, Akbar. 2007. *Journey into Islam: The Crisis of Globalization*, Washington, D.C.: Brookings Institution Press.

a strong potential" in all countries of Central Asia[16].

The influence of the spiritual tradition can be categorized into three: The first is the direct influence in the immediate fellowship of a Sufi order. A Sufi Order (or tariqah) is a fraternity of individuals who follow a particular school of Sufism under the guidance of a *sheikh* (spiritual master). A Sufi order can be seen as an institutionalized version of the individually oriented practices of the early Muslim ascetics. The orders are typically named in reference to their founders, such as the *Naqshbandi* order after Bahaudeen Naqshband or *Chisthi* order after Moinuddin Chisthi. The Sufi orders typically link their sheikh, through a lineage of various Sheikhs, to Ali, the cousin and son-in-law of Muhammad and thus to Muhammad himself, upon whom be peace and blessings. One exception to this is the Naqshbandi order, which traces the chain of their spiritual masters to Abu Bakr, the first Caliph after Muhammad. Every student or seeker, named *mureed* (seeker), *faqeer* (poor), or *dervish*, is assigned a personal daily recitation (awrad), authorized by his guide. The spiritual practice and development of the seekers are supervised[17] by the guide. In most cases the sheikh nominates his *khalīfah* or successor during his lifetime, who might be his son, a relative, or just a qualified member of the order.

The second impact of the spiritual tradition is an indirect, wider influence in the larger community of Muslims through lectures, "sohbets"[18] or companionship circles, and other types of oral tradition. Finally, the third type of influence in the contemporary world on Muslims as well as non-Muslims is through printed literature and other media. Among these three types of influences, the third type, influence through printed literature and media, has been gaining importance in contrast to the decline in direct Sufi order membership in many countries in the past two decades.

Armstrong comments that, Al-Ghazali's masterpiece, Ihya al-Ulum al-Din, 'which provides Muslims with a daily spiritual and practical regimen', is the most quoted Muslim text after the Qur'an the Prophetic tradition (*ahadith*)[19]. Al-Ghazali wrote this book primarily to point out that a more fulfilling experience of faith is only possible through a worship life that leads a believer to deeper spiritual experiences. Ghazali is credited for this presentation of a formal description of Sufism in his works and his successful integration of Sufism with the Islamic Law.

Commenting on the cross-cutting influence of the spiritual tradition over Muslim life, Nasr comments[20]:

> The practitioners of Sufism on all its different levels constitute and important group in Islamic society, even if not sociologically distinct as a class, and they have exercised great influence over the ages on fields as far as apart as the inner life and public ethics, psychology and art, metaphysics and the guilds, poetry and politics.

The Influence of Rumi's works on the cultural lives of Turkish, Persian, Central Asian Muslims as well as Muslims living in the west can hardly be overstated. Lewis comments on

---

16 Olcott, Martha Brill. 2007. Sufism in Central Asia: A Force for Moderation or a Cause of Politicization? *Carnegie PAPERS, Middle East Series, Russian and Eurasian Program*, Number 84, May 2007.

17 Schimmel, ibid, 237.

18 Sohbet, is a spiritual conversation between a guide and student(s) which relies on ancient oral storytelling traditions and practices.

19 Karen Armstrong, 2000, Islam: A short History, New York: Modern Library, 88.

20 Nasr, ibid. 177.

the inclusive and embracive spirit of the Rumi works[21]:

> Any objective western reader who takes the time to compare the Divine Comedia with the Masnavi, which is about twice as long as the former, will have to acknowledge that Rumi, who wrote a half century before Dante, reflects a much more ecumenical spirit and a far broader and deeper religious semsibility.

Works of Rumi are published by Turkish Departments of Culture and Education, the whirling dervishes ceremonies held every year around December 17th, his passing away day, are sponsored by the Konya city government as well as the Turkish national government. According to Lewis, 'in the nearby Islamic Republic of Iran, Rumi has reached new heights of popularity among the modern heirs of his language and culture.'[22]

The First Seekers on the Path of Spiritual Ascension

The first centers of Sufi development in the 8th and 9th centuries (first and second centuries of Islamic calendar) were the cities of Basra, Kufa and Baghdad in Iraq, Central Asia, in particular the city of Balkh in the Khorasan region, the birth place of Rumi, and Egypt. Prophet Muhammad, upon whom be peace and blessings, is regarded as the first spiritual master who passed his esoteric teachings orally to his successors, starting especially with Ali[23], his cousin and son in law. Various Sufi orders trace the lineage of their Sufi masters to Ali and then Prophet Muhammad through an unbroken chain of transmission of special authority.

Sufism developed historically first as a concern over the preservation of the spiritual dimension of Islam, in parallel to the development of other Islamic sciences such as *Hadith* (prophetic tradition) and *Tafseer* (Qur'anic interpretation). During the early years of Islam, only a minority of religious commandments were written down. Practice and the oral tradition allowed Muslims to memorize religious principles concerning belief, worship life and social relationships. These principles, being vital issues in a Muslim's personal and social life, were prioritized by scholars and later systematically collected in authentic books.

The praise-worthy efforts of these scholars facilitated the establishment of authentic resources for many Islamic sciences early on in the development of the Islamic civilization. Amidst these developments, some spiritually-oriented Muslims were concerned about the preservation of the spiritual tradition of their faith in a similar manner[24]:

> While some scholars were engaged in these "outer" activities, Sufi masters were mostly concentrating on the Muhammadan Truth's pure spiritual dimension. They sought to reveal the essence of humanity's being, the real nature of existence, and the inner dynamics of humanity and the cosmos by calling attention to the reality of that which lies beneath and beyond their outer dimension. Adding to Qur'anic commentaries, narrations of Traditionists, and deductions of legal scholars, Sufi masters developed their ways through asceticism, spirituality, and self-purification in short, their practice and experience of religion.
>
> Thus the Islamic spiritual life based on asceticism, regular worship, abstention from all major and minor sins, sincerity and purity of intention, love and yearning, and the individual's admission of his or her essential impotence and destitution became the subject matter of Sufism, a new science possessing its own method, principles, rules, and terms.

---

21 Franklin Lewis, 2000, Rumi: Past and Present, East and West, Oxford: Oneworld, 3.
22 Lewis, ibid.
23 May God be pleased with him, a phrase of respect reserved for the companions of the Prophet.
24 Gülen, M. F. 2004. *Key concepts in the practice of Sufism*, New Jersey: The Light Inc., xviii.

This first century of Islam was also a century of material riches and worldly engagement. Especially during the Umayyad dynasty (661-749) the wealth and luxurious habits of the ruling class were criticized and contrasted with simple lifestyle of the early companions of the Prophet as well as the Prophet himself[25]. The first stage of the development is called the *zuhd* (asceticism) period. The first Sufis were considered ascetics[26] who reflected and meditated on the concepts of death, resurrection, the Day of Judgment and giving the account of one's life to God. Their lives were characterized by the principle of "Little food, little talk, and little sleep," following a prophetic saying in which Prophet Muhammad (peace be upon him) identified obesity, oversleeping and lack of deep faith as his greatest concerns over his community.

Early Sufis such as Hasan Al-Basri (d. 728), Ibrahim b. Adham (d.777), Shaqiq of Balkh (d. 810), Al-Muhasibi (d. 837), Dhun-noon of Egypt (d. 859), Abu Yazid al-Bistami (d. 874) and Junaid of Baghdad (d. 910) are considered examples of the balanced spiritual tradition in which the seeker observes the religious law while pursuing the spiritual path. Mortification of the flesh, denial of carnal-self, willful poverty, abstinence, fasting, sessions of silent or loud remembrance, long nights of prayer, and Qur'anic recitations in early morning were commonly seen as the elements of the path of drawing near to God. The refinement and promotion of the notion of divine love in the Sufi tradition is attributed to a woman from Basrah in Iraq, Rabi'a al-Adawiya (d.801). Rabia yearned to love God only for God Himself, and not for any other concern such as hope of a reward (paradise) nor out of fear of judgement (hell). She also proclaimed that God's love preceded a believer's love of God.

The first tension of the spiritual tradition with the law-focused tradition is seen in the example of Hallaj Mansoor (d. 922) who exclaimed "I am the Truth" and was executed in Baghdad for blasphemy. He is also considered the father of the Wahdat-ul Wojood (Unity of Existence) movement within the Sufi tradition championed later by Ibn Al-Arabi. Later, the theme of divine love was brought to focus especially by a woman Sufi, Rabia Adawiyya, and found a rich expression in Sufi poetry, those of M. J. Rumi's being the most popular representatives.

Later, Sufism also assumed a reactionary role against the rigid interpretations of the orthodox religious scholars and legalists. To the spiritually oriented Muslims, theirs was an unjustified focus on one of the dimensions of the religion, the outer dimension, at the expense of the inner. Sometimes these dimensions are listed as three:

> Religion consists of a dimension which is outward and another which, upon the basis of this outwardness, leads to the inward. These dimensions of the Islamic revelation are called the Shariah (the Sacred Law), the Tariqah (the Path) and the Haqiqah (the Truth), or from another point of view they correspond to Islam, Iman, and Ihsan, or "surrender", "faith" and "virtue"[27].

> To the first Sufis, outward observance of the Islamic laws regarding worship and social life were

---

25   Michael Sells, 1996, Early Islamic Mysticism, New Jersey: Paulist Press, 20.

26   The issue of engagement with the world while pursuing the spiritual ascension ultimately led to different Sufi paths which favor one over the other. An example of an order that prefers seclusion is Khalwatiyya, while the more popular Naqshbandi order emphasizes engagement with the world. It is also argued that both paths have their proper audiences. An interesting anecdote on the reaction of Aisha, (may God be pleased with her), the second wife of Prophet Muhammad, to the early ascetics is as follows: Upon seeing a few men who were walking feebly and talking with a low voice, Aisha asked who they were. She was told that they were Zuhhad (ascetics). She is reported to exclaim, "By God, Umar (the second Claiph) was the real ascetic! When he walked he went somewhere, when he spoke he was heard and when he hit it hurt."

27   Nasr, S. H. 1966. *Ideals and Realities of Islam*, London.

not sufficient to lift a believer to the stage of *ihsan*[28]

Therefore it could be said that there has always been a need to maintain a balance between the outer and inner dimensions of the religion. Figures such as Hasan Al-Basri, and later Al-Ghazali were authorities successful at managing this tension and maintaining a balance appreciated by both the mainstream Muslims as well as the more spiritually focused. The following excerpt from an anonymous poem translated by Godlas illustrates some of the key concepts of the spiritual path as well as the effort by the seekers of spiritual ascension to demonstrate the complimentary role of their endeavor with respect to religious law:

> What is Tasawwuf? Good character and awareness of God.
>
> That's all Tasawwuf is. And nothing more.
>
> What is Tasawwuf? Love and affection.
>
> It is the cure for hatred and vengeance. And nothing more.
>
> What is Tasawwuf? The heart attaining tranquility–
>
> which is the root of religion. And nothing more.
>
> What is Tasawwuf? Concentrating your mind,
>
> which is the religion of Ahmad[29] (pbuh). And nothing more.
>
> What is Tasawwuf? Contemplation that travels to the Divine throne.
>
> It is a far-seeing gaze. And nothing more.
>
> Tasawwuf is keeping one's distance from imagination and supposition.
>
> Tasawwuf is found in certainty. And nothing more.
>
> Surrendering one's soul to the care of the inviolability of religion;
>
> this is Tasawwuf. And nothing more[30].

The main argument of this paper is that the only approach that has a chance of influencing the majority of contemporary Muslims in the aforementioned positive ways without being subject to criticisms is the approach of "balanced" spiritual tradition, which is the early, "companion-style" or "first generation" spiritual tradition. Based on a balance of the outer dimension of Islamic law and worship life and the inner dimension of spiritual disciplines, and firmly rooted in the Qur'an and Prophetic tradition, this approach nevertheless shares many concepts and principles with the more sophisticated Sufi tradition. Exemplified by historic figures such as Al-Ghazali, and contemporary figures such as Gülen, the balanced spiritual tradition holds the highest potential for the education of Muslim youth with an inclusive and tolerant worldview.

---

28 Sometimes also transliterated as *al-ikhsan*.

29 Another name of Prophet Muhammad, upon whom be peace and blessings of God.

30 Godlas, A. 2000. What is Tasawwuf (Sufism)? Translation from Persian by the author.

Inclusive Concepts of the Muslim Spiritual Tradition

In this section we examine three inclusive and egalitarian concepts in the spiritual tradition of Islam which lend themselves well to the increasingly diverse world. These are the mirror concept, non-violence and service discipline.

The Mirror Concept

The spiritual tradition of Islam embodies many concepts that are conducive to religious plurality. The heart of the tradition are the concepts of *hubb*[31], love of the Divine and the concept of *ihsan*, or the state of constant awareness of God's presence[32]. One way of achieving this state is to discipline the body (actions) and the heart (thoughts, feelings) toward a state of spiritual purification[33].

> Tasawwuf [Sufism] is the path of gaining freedom from the vices and weaknesses particular to human nature and acquiring angelic qualities and conduct pleasing to God, and living in accordance with the requirements of knowledge and love of God and in the spiritual delight that comes thereby[34].

The second, somewhat complementary way is to develop the capacity to see signs of God in everything. To a refined and spiritually awakened Muslim, therefore, everything becomes a mirror of God and everything reminds him or her of God. At a higher level, these signs become more than simple reminders as the traveler of the path of spiritual purification ceases to forget God at any moment. The signs then become displays of God's majesty, beauty, grace and other divine attributes at increasingly sophisticated ways. As the highest of the creations of God, humans are the walking displays of God's various attributes. In the words of Gülen, the author of one of the leading contemporary references on Sufi concepts[35], the human resembles a droplet that is small in size yet capable of reflecting the Sun with all its attributes:

> Humans, the greatest mirror of the names, attributes, and deeds of God, are a shining mirror, a marvelous fruit of life, a source for the whole universe, a sea that appears to be a tiny drop, a sun formed as a humble seed, a great melody in spite of their insignificant physical positions, and the source for existence all contained within a small body. Humans carry a holy secret that makes them equal to the entire universe with all their wealth of character; a wealth that can be developed to excellence[36].

Every human is seen as a mirror of God in three aspects: In the first aspect, a human is seen as a masterpiece of art of the Master Artist, the Creator and Fashioner of everything. The face of the human is a display of beauty, order, function, compassion and wisdom. The eye or the brain of a human are equally impressive works of wonder. In every detail of a human's creation, a spiritually oriented Muslim sees opportunities for reflection.

The second way a human becomes a mirror of God is through their reliance on God. When a person becomes hungry and is fed, he/she becomes a mirror of God as the sustainer. When

---

31 In Arabic or *ashk* in Persian.

32 Gülen, M. F. 2004. *Key concepts in the practice of Sufism*, New Jersey: The Light Inc.

33 Murata, S. and Chittick, W. C. 1994. The Vision of Islam. Minnesota: Paragon House.

34 Gülen, M. Fethullah. 2005. The Statue of Our Souls: Revival in Islamic Thought and Activism. New Jersey: The Light Inc., p. 5.

35 Gülen, M. F. 2004. *Key concepts in the practice of Sufism*, New Jersey: The Light Inc.

36 Gülen, M. Fethullah. 2005. The Statue of Our Souls: Revival in Islamic Thought and Activism. New Jersey: The Light Inc., p. 112.

a person becomes ill and is then healed, she becomes a mirror of God as the Healer. When a person seeks knowledge and is bestowed with knowledge, he becomes a mirror of God the Knower of All, the Owner of Infinite Knowledge.

The third way of mirrorship is through actions. For instance, God is compassionate toward His creation. A compassionate person, therefore becomes a mirror of God the Compassionate. God helps all his creation regardless of their belief in, or rejection of God. God's sustenance is indiscriminative. When a person helps every human in need, she becomes a mirror of God the Helper. God forgives the sins of humans who sincerely repent and turn toward Him. When a person forgives the mistakes and mistreatments of others, he becomes the mirror of God the Merciful. A target state in the spiritual tradition is to become a person such that when people see him or her they remember God. They can not help but say that "there must be a Compassionate God that such a person walks this earth."

It is noteworthy that only the third of these three ways of mirrorship is voluntary while the first two are involuntary. Therefore, every human, regardless of their creed is a mirror of God in those two aspects. This is a powerful paradigm and influence for peaceful coexistence in religious diversity. The words of the famous Anatolian Sufi poet Yunus Emre, who is also a source of inspiration for Gülen, resonates in the Turkish population even after eight centuries:

> We love the creation due to the Creator[37].

In another poem he points out the inherent inconsistency of those who claim to worship God but disregard the dignity of the most precious of God's creation, the human:

> If you have broken a heart, then what you are doing is not prayer.

Non-violence

The second influence of the spiritual tradition is the inclusive, emphatic and compassionate perspective that naturally lends itself to non-violence, going beyond tolerance to hospitality and friendship. A quote from Gülen illustrates the non-violence stance of a contemporary scholar who also represents the balanced spiritual tradition of Islam. The context of the quote was the era of ideologically driven armed conflicts in Turkey during the 1970s. Clashes among the youth groups claimed the lives of thousands of youth as well as members of security forces, intellectuals, teachers and politicians. Armed groups would attack each other, demand the students to boycott classes, and the shopkeepers to close down shops to disturb normal life in the country.

> My audience know that when anarchy was everywhere in our country, I have called for calmness and controlling of anger. I had received death threats, yet I requested from my audience to continue working for peace, 'If I am assassinated, despite all your angers, I ask you to bury my body and seek for order, peace and love in our society. Regardless to what happens; we believers should be representatives of love and peace.[38]

Representing love and peace in times of adversity and violent conflict requires a level of *pious transcendence*, which could also be seen as holistic understanding of religious law. A

---

37 Emre, Y., K. Helminski, R. Algan, E. Helminski (trans). 1999. *The Drop That Became the Sea: Lyric Poems of Yunus Emre*. Shambhala Publications.

38 Saritoprak, Z. 2005. An Islamic Approach to Peace and Nonviolence. *The Muslim World*, 95, no.3 (2005): 423.

prophetic tradition illustrates this concept:

> A Muslim man was wounded in a battle. The next morning he needed to have a bath. The people around him were confused. Would they wash the whole body or leave the wound aside? Washing of the whole body being a requirement of ritual, they did so and the man died. Upon hearing the incident the Prophet declared "You killed the man. Could you not just wash the rest of his body and only slightly touch the wounded area?"

This pious transcendence enables a Muslim to choose and apply the appropriate religious law and organize their priorities more in conjunction with the spirit of Islamic faith, especially at times of hardship.

Service Principle

Another principle of the spiritual tradition that is conducive to religious plurality and world peace is the *service* discipline. This can be summarized in the doctrine

> Serving people is serving God.

Connected with the principles of humility, and chivalry, this principle encourages Sufis to serve public, regardless of their creed, in various ways, and especially in ways that are unexpected of one's social rank. Harvesting crops, cleaning toilets or helping handicapped persons with grocery shopping are some examples. Gülen comments on the concept of futuwwa, a composite of such virtues as generosity, munificence, modesty, chastity, trustworthiness, loyalty, mercifulness, knowledge, humility, and piety[39].

> Some have summed up futuwwa in the four virtues mentioned by Haydar Karrar Ali, the fourth Caliph and cousin of the Prophet, upon whom be peace and blessings. They are: forgiving when one is able to punish, preserving mildness and acting mildly and gently when one is angry, wishing one's enemies well and doing good to them, and being considerate of others' well-being and happiness first, even when one is needy.

In Gülen's philosophy this principle is put into the service of education with a new name: "The principle of devotion[40]."

Obstacles to Greater Impact of the Spiritual Tradition

While the inclusive and empathic influences of Sufism are desirable and conducive to interreligious harmony, there are important impediments that prevent the spiritual tradition from having a greater impact. The first of these is the literalist opposition to more flexible interpretations of concepts from the Qur'an and the Prophetic tradition and the strict definition of the notion of invention in religion, or "Bid'a". The second consist of deviations of some Sufi orders and subsequent criticisms by orthodox Muslims. The third consist of political obstacles, namely, impact of politicization of Islam by some groups, politicization of certain Sufi groups and the charge of passivism directed against certain other Sufi orders.

Deviations of certain Sufi orders from the prophetic tradition include Saint and tomb worship, exaggerated veneration of spiritual masters (sheikh or pir), called *pirism* by Muhammad

---

39 Gülen, ibid. 81-82.
40 Çetin, Muhammed. 2005. Mobilization and Countermobilization: The Gülen Movement in Turkey. Proceedings from Islam in the Contemporary world: The Fethullah Gülen Movement in Thought and Practice, Rice University, Houston, TX.

Iqbal[41], statements that are considered *shirk* or associating partners with God, and negligence on obligatory prayers.

Especially important in this context is the notion of *bid'a,* or invention (innovation) in religion. Various forms of *dhikr,* or remembrance of God, such as repeating certain names of God in fixed numbers by controlling breathing etc., are considered by some as innovations.

Politicization of Islam during the late twentieth century has brought upon major influences on Sufism: On the one hand, the political Islamist groups have accused the Sufi orders as being complacent or passive. On the other hand certain governments, suspicious of any organization besides formal-government controlled ones, have suppressed Sufi orders made them illegal. Finally, some other governments have sought to orient Sufi orders as an ally political opposition.

> From the eighteenth century onward, Sufi-led protest movements were often found in societies that were confronted with the encroachment of Western ideas or colonialism. Thus, rulers were either frightened by the political specter posed by Sufis or were eager to make common cause with them, depending on the circumstance. Alliances between Sufis and their rulers (both secular and religious) have also been of varying success, at least from the point of view of the governing class[42].

In the perspectives of many prominent figures of Sufism, such as Al-Ghazali, Imam-I Rabbani Ahmed Sirhindi, a spiritually oriented Muslim can not be called a Sufi, unless he or she first observes the basics of Islamic creed and worship life. According to these authoritative figures, the claims of certain groups and sects that assume the name of a Sufi order should not be accepted at the face value. The Sufi path cannot be condemned because of the errors associated with the behaviors of such groups. In short, one should not throw the baby with the bath water.

Gülen's Criticisms of Contemporary Institutionalized Sufism

While underlining the potential for spiritual development in the Sufi tradition, Gülen voices his own criticism of the deterioration among followers of the discipline, especially around the collapse of the Ottoman Empire. In 1925 Sufi orders were banned in Turkey. Referring to the deterioration of the Sufi centers prior to this era, Gülen commented that by then, the Sufi centers "have closed themselves already." Gülen also alludes to the disengagement of the Sufi centers from the education and development of individuals and busying themselves in insignificant metaphysical discussions:

> At a time when modern schools concentrated on ideological dogmas, institutions of religious education (*madrasas*) broke with life, institutions of spiritual training (*takyas*) were immersed in sheer metaphysics, and the army restricted itself to sheer force, this coordination [of knowledge] was essentially not possible[43].

The third observation of Gülen concerning the Sufi institutions around the country was their failure to adapt themselves to the needs of the society and meet the challenges of the scientific/rational revolutions. Instead of revitalizing themselves, these organizations turned to "console themselves with virtues and wonders of the saints who had lived in previous centuries.[44]"

---

41 Schimmel, ibid., 22.

42 Olcott, ibid.

43 Gülen, F. 1996. Towards the Lost Paradise. London: Truestar. P.11 cited in Michel ibid.

44 Gülen, F. 1996. Towards the Lost Paradise. London: Truestar. P.11 cited in Michel ibid.

It is worth noting that Gülen's criticisms of Sufi orders and centers are historical and institutional in nature and do not pertain to Sufism as a discipline[45]. Each of the three deficiencies Gülen notes, "closing themselves before being closed", "disengagement from educational needs of the society and engagement in useless metaphysical speculation," and "failure to cope with the changing times" are matters of social decay and are not inherent deficiencies in the spiritual tradition.

Just as the beliefs and practices criticized as deviant have formed in an environment of a clash between the legalistic tradition, which represents the outer dimension, and the spiritual or inner dimension, the recovery of the spiritual tradition lies in the reunion of the inner and outer dimensions. In this paper, we call this union the 'balanced spiritual tradition'. In the next section we will discuss its main tenets.

From Hasan Al-Basri to Al-Ghazali to Gülen: The Balanced Spiritual Tradition

A hallmark of the balanced spiritual tradition represented by figures such as Hasan Al-Basri, Al-Ghazali, and Gülen is the balancing of the inner and outer dimensions of faith, that is the Islamic law concerning worship and community life and the principles and practices of the spiritual path. In the eyes of these scholar/masters, faith is incomplete before a person realizes a deeper experience of the faith above and beyond simple following of the rules.

> Sufism leads the way to *shawq*, delight, so that the practice of religious commitment is not some onerous and unpleasant burden that a person is forced to carry, but can rather be conducive to a joyful, loving acceptance of life[46].

Representatives of the balanced spiritual tradition, such as Al-Ghazali and Gülen view Sufism as the inner dimension of the religious law, and consider it jugular that the two dimensions are never separated. Observance of the rules that pertain to externals without attention to their interior transformative power results in dry ritualism[47]. Trying to follow the spiritual path without regard to the religious law is often likened to "trying to build a house on a foundation of sand[48]". A prophetic tradition hints at this perspective:

> There are those who pray for hours during night and all they gain is sleeplessness and tiredness.
> There are those who fast and all they gain are hunger and thirst.

The people described by this prophetic tradition are following the exterior rules perfectly. Yet, their effort is not benefiting them, hence they must be missing something. That something, according to the balanced spiritual tradition, is the observance of the inner dimension.

On the opposite pole, focusing exclusively on the interior dimension and rejecting (or taking lightly) the prescribed ritual prayers and rules of conduct opens the door to relativism and transgression. Only a balance of the exterior law and the inner discipline enables the seeker to proceed in the path of spiritual ascension to the stage of *ihsan*. Consequently, the traveler

---

45   Kuru, A. T. 2003. Fethullah Gülen's Search for a Middle Way Between Modernity and Muslim Tradition. In Turkish Islam and the secular state: The Gülen movement. M. H. Yavuz and J. L. Esposito, eds. Syracuse: Syracuse University Press.

46   Michel, S.J., T. 2005. Sufism and modernity in the thought of Fethullah Gülen. *The Muslim World*, 95(3), 341-349.

47   Michel ibid.

48   Frager. R. Sufism and the Islamic Tradition. Personality and Personal Growth. Longman. p.563.

on the balanced spiritual path never separates the outer observance of the religious law from its inner dimension, and observes both.

Perhaps the most famous representative of the balanced spiritual tradition of Islam is Al-Ghazali. His book entitled "The Revival of Religious Sciences" is considered as a monumental work which "aligned Sufi experiences with Islamic beliefs and practices[49]". He is well read around the world in Muslim communities despite their differences in many aspects.

> The writings of Abu Hamid Muhammad Ibn Muhammad, known as al-Ghazali (A.D. 1058-1111), are among the most widely read Sufi teachings. Because of his influence, many Islamic theologians finally accepted Sufism within formal Islam. Called the Proof of Islam and the Restorer of Islam, he is one of the dominant figures in Islamic theology. His work altered the public view of Sufism from that if suspect, even heretical teaching, to a valued and essential part of Islam.[50]

Al-Ghazali regards the inner dimension as bringing life to religious sciences, while the religious law keeps the believer rooted in the mainstream Islamic tradition[51]. Speaking on the importance of experiential learning in the Sufi discipline, Al-Ghazali comments:

> I acquired a thorough knowledge of their[52] research, and I learned all that was possible to learn their methods by study and oral teaching. It became clear to me ... that Sufism consists in experience rather than in definitions and that what I was lacking belonged to this domain, not of instruction, but of ... initiation[53].

A trend among some of the representatives of the balanced spiritual tradition is the lack of a membership in a Sufi order and guidance by a personal Sufi master. At various times in his life, Gülen clearly stated that the movement inspired by his ideas is not a Sufi brotherhood and he himself can not be regarded as a Sufi master[54].

> The religious orders are institutions that appeared in the name of representing Sufism six centuries after our Prophet, upon whom be peace. They have their own rules and structures. Just as I never joined a Sufi order, I have never had any relationship with one[55].

Combining this statement with the fact that Gülen wrote one of the most authoritative contemporary works on Sufism led some authors to conclude that Gülen belongs to a category of spiritually oriented Muslim scholars who continue the tradition of the first generation Sufism[56]. This observation naturally leads to the question: What elements of the spiritual tradition of Islam are present in the balanced path represented by figures such as Ghazali and Gülen, and whether these elements are subject to the same criticisms leveled at the Sufi brotherhoods.

---

49 Frager, R. ibid. p.559.

50 Frager ibid.

51 Michel ibid.

52 Referring to the teachings of Sufi masters.

53 Frager, ibid. p.560.

54 Saritoprak, Zeki (2005a) 'Introduction', The Muslim World, Special Issue, Islam in Contemporary Turkey: The Contribution of Fethullah Gülen, Volume 95, No.3, July 2005, pp. 325-7 - (2005b) 'An Islamic Approach to Peace and Nonviolence: A Turkish Experience', The Muslim World, Special Issue, Islam in Contemporary Turkey: The Contribution of Fethullah Gülen, Volume 95, No.3, July 2005, pp. 413-27. - (2003).

55 Saritoprak, Z. 2003. Fethullah Gülen: A Sufi in His Own Way. In Yavuz, Hakan and Esposito, John (eds) (2003) Turkish Islam and the Secular State: The Gülen Movement, Syracuse: Syracuse University Press, pp. 156-169.

56 Gokcek, M. 2006. Gülen and Sufism: A Historical Perspective. In Robert Hunt et al. (eds), *Muslim Citizens of the Globalized World: Contributions of the Gülen Movement*. New Jersey: The Light Inc.

How Balanced Spiritual Tradition Avoids Criticisms of Sufism

The first criticism of the Sufi tradition is the exaggerated veneration of spiritual masters, the preferring of sainthood to prophethood ("messengership") and Sufi masters to Prophets and their companions. In various sermons and written works, Gülen clearly underlines the superiority of the Messengers. In particular, he uses a quote by Hasan Al-Basri (d. 110/728), a member of the first generation of Muslims after the generation of Prophet's companions, known as the *tabeen*. This generation is revered and respected due to their having the opportunity to observe and learn from the companions of the Prophet. Al-Basri holds a special place among the tabeen. Al-Basri is credited with the refinement of the concepts of *'irfan*, (personal and accurate knowledge of the divine, gnosis) and *kalam*, (Islamic theology). Born in 642 A.D. (22nd year of the Islamic calendar), Al-Basri spent most of is life in the first century of Islamic civilization. Al-Basri is also a perfect representative of the balanced spiritual tradition, being counted in the Sufi lineages (silsile) as the last element of the chain before Ali, as well as being respected as an orthodox Sunni scholar. His compiled book called *Ri'ayah li huquq Allah* (Observance of the Duties to Allah), a copy of which is reported to exist at Oxford, is regarded by some as the first book on Sufism. Mutahhari relates the following quote from Nicholson on Al-Basri's significance, which also summarizes important stages of the Sufi tradition:

> The first Muslim to give an experimental analysis of the inner life was Harith al-Muhasibi of Basrah ... 'The Path' (tariqah), as described by later writers, consists of acquired virtues (maqamat) and mystical states (ahwal). The first stage is repentance or conversion; then comes a series of others, e.g. renunciation, poverty, patience, trust in God, each being a preparation for the next[57].

> Secondly, the 'urafa' themselves trace their orders back to al- Hasan al-Basri; and from him to 'Ali (A), such as the chain of the sheikhs of Abu Sa'id ibn Abi al-Khayr. Similarly, Ibn al-Nadim, in his famous al-Fihrist, traces the chain of Abu Muhammad Ja'far al-Khuldi back to al-Hasan Al-Basri, stating that al-Hasan al-basri had met seventy of the Companions who had fought at Badr.

> Thirdly, some of the stories related of al-Hasan al-Basri give the impression that he was in fact part of a group that in later times became known as Sufis[58].

Al-Basri compares the later generations of Muslims, including Sufi masters, to the companions as follows:

> The greatest of the later generations of Muslims can not be a piece of dust under the feet of the horse of a companion of the prophet Muhammad (peace be upon him).

On the question of *bid'a*, (innovation in religion) scholars of Islam fall into two camps. The majority, including Gülen, consider new concepts and practices as acceptable as long as they are based on principles outlined in the authentic prophetic traditions and they are not confused with the more authentic prophetic traditions. The other camp, represented by strict literalists argue that any innovation in religion is bad, regardless of its nature.

Michel points out to this phenomena that originate with the numerically small but politically influential circles inspired by the criticism of the famed scholar Ibn Taymiyya, who is seen as the originator of the literalist movement:

---

57 Nicholson, R.A. 1931. *Mysticism in The Legacy of Islam,* London: ed. by Sir Thomas Arnold and Alfred Guillaume pp. 211-212.
58 Mutahhari, M. *An Introduction to the Islamic Sciences*, transl. By Ali Quli Qarai, *Al-Tawhid*, vol II No. 2.

(The Wahhabi perspective) view Sufism as responsible for turning the Islamic *ummah* away from its God-given task of building a society in accord with the ideals of the Qur'an and Sunnah; they accuse the Sufis of encouraging unwarranted and unorthodox innovations and of promulgating a passive, pietistic religiosity[59].

The balanced tradition regards Sufism as one facet of the life of the sincere Muslim who seeks to witness and live fully the essence of the message contained in the Qur'an and the prophetic tradition[60]. However, the balanced tradition does not consider every concept or practice that historically has come out in the name of Sufism as a positive value, practices approaching Saint worship being primary examples.

For the representatives of the balanced spiritual tradition such as Gülen, Sufism and religious law are two aspects of the same truth and two complimentary dimensions. Human spiritual perfection is not possible with negligence in either dimension. The preference of an individual of elaboration in one dimension over the other should be attributed to either lack of knowledge or "it should be viewed as the result of a natural human tendency, which is that everyone gives priority to the way more compatible with his temperament and for which he has aptitude" (Michel 2003).

The tension between the two dimensions is in part due to the extremists such as those who claimed that following the exoteric regulations of the religious law were unnecessary for the seekers of the esoteric path, and those who declared even moderately liberal interpretations of Qur'anic verses or prophetic traditions as outside of the faith.

Another point of criticism, identified by Nursi[61], is confusing inspiration with revelation. This criticism is leveled against the Sufi figures in history who claimed to have received personal inspiration which might apparently contradict the revelation as recorded in the Qur'an and authentic prophetic tradition. In this context the response of the balanced tradition is that the communication of God as the Lord of the Universe with His last messenger Muhammad through the Qur'an is the highest form of communication and is thus superior to all other forms of communication, including inspiration of the Sufi saints.

The Question of the Spiritual Guide

The concept of a Sufi master occupies an important place in the later Sufi literature. The vast majority of the later Sufis discouraged the potential seekers from pursuing the spiritual path without a personal guide. The early Sufis such as Hasan Al-Basri, Rabia, Junayd, Muhasibi, Bishr, Ghazzali, Feriduddin Attar, and even Rumi did not belong to a *tariqah* or Sufi order. While they could each be regarded as a master on their own, a seeker without a personal guide would be seen as problematic from the perspective of institutionalized Sufism. Although we can see the same emphasis on the role of spiritual guide by important figures of the balanced spiritual tradition, another trend is the guidance of the virtual personality of a text:

A minority view has always held that the spiritual guide need not be a living person. Kharaqani, for example, was initiated into the Sufi path by the spirit of Abu Yazid al-Bistami, while 'Attar was inspired by the spirit of al-Hallaj. Other Sufis claimed to have as their guide Khidr, the mysterious companion of Moses mentioned in *Surat al-Kahf* of the Qur'an. Gülen's position is that he is

---

59 Michel,ibid.

60 Michel, ibid.

61 Nursi, S. 1997. 29th Letter. 9th Section, Nine Allusions About the Ways of Sainthood and Sufism, *The Letters*. Istanbul: Kaynak A.S.

guided in his spiritual development by the Qur'an and the Sunnah. In Gülen's view, the Qur'an is not only the best guide, but is the source and font of all Sufi thought and practice. Rooted in the Qur'an and Sunnah, and supplemented by the views and experiences of later Sufis down through the centuries who applied the Qur'anic teachings through their own personal efforts (*ijtihad*), Sufism must be considered not an "alternative" path followed by some Muslims in contradistinction or in contradiction to the Islamic law but rather, one of the basic sciences of Islam.

The Potential Impact of the Balanced Spiritual Tradition

Now we would like to give some indicators that point out that spiritual tradition that is free of deviations identified above has a great potential to influence the Muslim world. The famous Sunni scholar Dr. Yusuf Al-Qaradawi, chair of European Council for Fatwa and Research, whose religious opinion commands great respect among the politically oriented Muslims especially in the Middle East has the following to say about the balanced spiritual tradition:

> By and large, we should try to take from Sufi ideas what corresponds to the teachings of Islam, such as the idea that calls to noble values of mutual love, as well as the idea that teaches one how to get rid of psychological ailments and to attain spiritual grace.

> In fact, there are some examples of good Sufis, with some minor exceptions, from whom one can understand better this form of worship. Imam al-Ghazali is one of such moderate Sufi figure whose ideas go in line with the teachings of Islam[62].

Another example of praise for the balanced spirituality comes from the strong critic of deviant Sufi orders Ibn Taymiyya about Bayazid Bistami, one of the early Sufis famous for his championing of the concept of *fana*, or the annihilation of the carnal self in awe and constant presence of God.

> There are two categories of fana': one is for the perfect Prophets and saints, and one is for seekers from among the saints and pious people (saliheen). Bayazid al-Bistami is from the first category of those who experience fana', which means the complete renunciation of anything other than God. He accepts none except God. He worships none except Him, and he asks from none except Him." He continues, quoting Bayazid saying, "I want not to want except what He wants[63]."

In another place, Ibn-Taymiyya refers to Abd-al Qadir Gilani, the author of Futuh-ul Ghayb (The Conquest of the Unseen) and spiritual founding father of the Qadiri Sufi order, as "our teacher".

> The upright among the followers of the Path - like the majority of the early sheikhs (shuyukh al-salaf) such as Fudayl ibn `Iyad, Ibrahim ibn Adham, Ma`ruf al-Karkhi, al-Sari al-Saqai, al-Junayd ibn Muhammad and others of the early teachers, as well as Sheikh Abd al-Qadir [Gilani], Sheikh Hammad, Sheikh Abul Bayan and others of the later masters - do not permit the followers of the Path to depart from the divinely legislated command and prohibition, even were that person to have flown in the air or walked on water[64].

Haddad comments that other works of Ibn Taymiyya are full of praise for what we call in this paper as the balanced spiritual tradition. He gives the example from Ibn Taymiyya's

---

62 Al-Qaradawi, Y. 2004. Islam's Stance on Sufism, SALAM Magazine, March-April, available online at http://www.famsy.com/salam/Sufism0404.htm

63 Ibn Taymiyya, *Majmoo` fatawi Sheikh al-Islam Ibn Taymiyya*. (The Collection of Opinions of Master Scholar of Islam Ibn Taymiyya), Riyadh. p. 516. Cited in Fouad Haddad, *Ibn Taymiyya on Futooh Al-Ghayb and Sufism*, 1996. Availabile online at http://www.abc.se/~m9783/n/itaysf_e.html.

64 Ibn Taymiyya, ibid.

book entitled "*al-ihtijaaj bi al-qadar*" (Cairo: *al-matba'a al-salafiyya*, 1394/1974 p. 38) as a praise for the Sufi emphasis on love of God and their "voluntarist rather than intellectual approach" to attainment of spiritual improvement:

> As for the Sufis, they affirm the love (of Allah), and this is more evident among them than all other issues. The basis of their Way (tariqa) is simply will and love. The affirmation of the love of Allah is well-known in the speech of their early and recent masters, just as it is affirmed in the Book and the Sunna and in the agreement of the salaf.

Hamza Yusuf, one of the rising leaders of the Muslim youth in North America and increasingly around the world, and the author/translator of the book entitled "Purification of the Heart[65]," commented about the spiritual tradition with these words:

> In fact what Islam is trying to do and what most of the other spiritual religions and in fact from the Muslim perspective all of them have failed to do is to join these two elements in a harmonious and balanced way and this is why in the tradition of Islam Sufism has always been part of the traditional Islamic curriculum in every single Muslim university. I know of no period in the Islamic tradition in which Sufism was not taught in the universities and not seen as an important and fundamental aspect of the tradition of Islam[66].

These two examples illustrate the potential of the balanced spiritual tradition to avoid the criticisms of the strictest of the scholars opposing the deviations of certain Sufi organizations.

According to Ruthven, the intellectual leaders of modern Muslim India as well as Pakistan, such as Sayyid Ahmed Khan, Muhammad Iqbal and Abu'l Ala al-Maududi are indebted to Shaikh Ahmed Sirhindi, also known as Imam Rabbani, a Naqshbandi Sufi reformer who sought to revive the more pure versions of the spiritual tradition of Islam free of Hindu influences[67].

According to P. J. Stewart, the author of Unfolding Islam, 'the future of Islam must lie in a renovated mystical orientation where debt of religious feeling can be yoked to metaphorical understandings of the Qur'an and the Prophetic traditions.[68]' According to Travers[69], 'there are signs that this is already happening' such as the increasing popularity of Sufism in Central Asia, at the expense of political Islamism, and in the West 'despite the media-grabbing clamour' of the actions of politically oriented groups. The late Anne-Marie Schimmel comments about the renewed interest in the teachings of Naqshbandi tradition in Uzbekistan:

> Studies, especially in the Naqshbandi Tariqa have proliferated during the last few years. It is interesting that last year in Bukhara that we have a conference at the mazar of Khaja Naqshband in which German and Uzbek scholars participated and scholars from other Central Asian countries. It was highly interesting to see that here the Uzbek interest in teaching the Naqshbandiyya became very visible because they claimed, and I think they were right, that the old adage 'the hand at work, the heart close to the Divine Beloved' is a very practical way of approaching modern science. It gives you the possibility of constantly thinking of God, remembering God, as it is also taught in the Quran and yet do your daily work successfully. The interest in the Naqshbandiyya has grown

---

65 Yusuf, Hamza (trans.), 2004. Purification of the Heart: Signs, Symptoms and Cures of the Spiritual Diseases of the Heart. Translation and commentary of Imam al-Mawlud's Matharat al-Qulub, Chicago: Starlatch.

66 Yusuf, Hamza. 1997. Tasawwuf/Sufism in Islam, lecture at Stanford University, available online at http://sunnah.org/events/hamza/hamza.htm.

67 Malise Ruthven, 1984, Islam in the World, London: Granta Publications, 2006.

68 In Ruthven, ibid, 429.

69 Writing the afterword for Ruthven, ibid, 429.

considerably[70].

Travers argues that the Muslim Diaspora in the West, increasingly well educated in atmosphere of free association, freedom of expression and religious freedom, is a candidate to promote the spiritual tradition. Another advantage of this Diaspora is its experience in asserting itself 'culturally through the media and politically through the democratic system.' Beyond calls for social justice, the Islamic message of 'man's special responsibility as guardian of this planet' is likely to be relevant and significant for the protection of environment in the centuries to come.

> It is a message which calls on men and women to show gratitude for the world's bounty, to use it wisely and distribute it equitably. It is a message phrased in the language and imagery of a pastoral people who understood that survival depended upon submission to the natural laws governing their environment, and upon rules of hospitality demanding an even sharing of limited resources. In a world increasingly driven by the gap between rich and poor nations, and growing danger of environmental catastrophe, this message has an urgent relevance. It is one we ignore at our peril.

Commenting on his impressions of the hajj pilgrimage he undertook in 2004, Fuad Nahdi, the editor-in-chief of Q News, a prominent British Muslim magazine especially among young Muslims, notes that the atmosphere of the hajj that year was more spiritual than in previous years. Nahdi states[71]:

> Everywhere I find well-produced leaflets focusing on the spiritual aspects of the Hajj. The literature is more inclusive and more tolerant than one used to expect. In the past, this kind of spirituality would have been banned or cursed from the pulpits.

Geaves comments that reading between the lines of Nahdi's words, one can see the influence of more literalist and less tolerant forms of interpretation, as opposed to the more liberal approach of the spiritual tradition, in decline in the Muslim world.

We have alluded above to the increasing popularity of the works of Al-Ghazali and Rumi among Muslim populations of Turkey, Iran, Central Asia and the West. The influence of these towering figures, however, may remain dormant until invoked by contemporary authorities and opinion leaders such as Gülen. In his centerfold pieces for the top selling popular youth magazine of Turkey[72], Gülen discussed key concepts of the spiritual tradition of Islam with references to the works of Al-Ghazali, and Rumi, as well as the other significant figures of the spiritual tradition, in addition to his references from the Qur'an and the Prophetic tradition. Gülen's impact is not limited to his sermons and written works. He is credited with starting a civil society movement focused on education and 'characterized by conscientious effort and tolerance for others.' One example of Gülen's countless comments on the reconciliatory and embracive attitude derived from the spiritual tradition is cited by Horkuc[73]:

> It should be such a broad tolerance, that we can close our eyes to others' faults, show respect for different ideas, and forgive everything that is forgivable. In fact, even when our inalienable rights are violated, we should respect human values and try to establish justice. Even before the coarsest thoughts and crudest ideas, with the caution of a Prophet and without boiling over we should

---

70 Schimmel, Anne-Marie, Sufism and its Influence on Europe, lecture at Stanford University, May 4, 1997, available online at http://www.naqshbandi.org/events/sufitalk/sufismeu.htm.
71 Ron Geaves, 2005, Aspects of Islam, Washington D.C.: Georgetown University Press, 139.
72 The popular scientific and spiritual magazine SIZINTI is estimated to have a readership of over 700,000.
73 Hasan Horkuc, 2002, New Muslim Discourses on Pluralism in the Postmodern Age, American Journal of Islamic Social Sciences, Spring 2002, 19 (2), footnote 62, cited in Michel, ibid.

respond with a mildness that the Qur'an presents as "gentle words."

Hundreds of educational institutions from kindergarten to college level have been established in Turkey and some 103 countries of the world by organizations within the aforementioned civil society movement inspired by Gülen. One characteristic of these institutions is that in addition to their excellence in physical and social sciences, math and language, they foster a culture of interfaith and intercultural respect and harmony.[74] Building bridges of peace among conflict-stricken groups, these institutions serve as trust-havens in fragile regions of the world. Examples of such as bridges can be seen in Philippines, where Muslim minority students study with their fellow Christian students in an atmosphere of trust[75]; Bosnia-Herzegovina where children of Bosnian Muslims who have been massacred by Serbians study shoulder-to-shoulder with their children[76], Southeast Turkey where the Kurdish students get an opportunity to become doctors, scientists, lawyers and artists instead of being recruited by terrorist organizations[77], and Macedonia where the fighting Albanian, Macedonia and Serbian factions carry their children to such schools for safety. In the example of Gülen, and the civil society movement initiated by his ideas, the latent potential of the spiritual tradition of Islam can be observed vividly.

Conclusion

Sufism offers many significant concepts and practices that are indispensable in an age of globalization and religious plurality, such as the *mirror* concept and the universal human dignity, divine love emerging as a love of fellow humans, non-violence, and the service mentality.

The "mirror" concept views every human as a mirror of God in three aspects: Reflecting attributes and names of God as His work of art, reflection through reliance, and reflection through actions. Only the third of these ways is voluntary while the first two are involuntary. Therefore, every human, regardless of their creed is seen as a mirror of God in these two aspects. Consequently, every human is to be loved and admired for those aspects. This is a powerful paradigm and influence for peaceful coexistence in religious diversity in the post-modern world.

Various expressions of the spiritual tradition throughout history of Islam have centered around the concept of love. Since the beginning, divine love and its reflection in the form of love of fellow humans have been characteristic of spiritually oriented Muslims. While carrying the potential of pacifism with it, this concept has traditionally been put into practice in the form of non-violence or at least non aggression. Often, the seekers went beyond tolerance to hospitality and companionship.

Western analysts of the trends in the contemporary Islamic world often exhibit one of two fallacies: Overestimating the impact of contemporary Sufi orders or underestimating the impact of the deep current of the spiritual tradition of Islam. Turkish, Indian, North African, Syrian, Indonesia-Malaysian and Persian Sufi traditions run deep and wide among contemporary

---

74   Zeki Saritoprak, 'An Islamic Approach to Peace and Nonviolence: A Turkish Experience', The Muslim World, Vol. 95 (July 2005), pp. 413-427

75   Michel, Thomas. 2003. Fethullah Gülen as an Educator. In Turkish Islam and the secular state: The Gülen movement. M. H. Yavuz and J. L. Esposito, eds. Syracuse: Syracuse University Press.

76   Serif Ali Tekalan, 'Monuments of Love and Alturism', in Baris Kopruleri (Bridges of Peace), Istanbul: Ufuk Kitaplari, 2005, 254.

77   Mehmet Kalyoncu, 'The Counter Terrorism Issue In Terms Of Systems Theory; Diyarbakir as a Case Study', presentation at the Second Istanbul Conference on Democracy and Global Security, June 14-16, 2007.

Muslim populations. The influence of the spiritual tradition can be categorized into three: Direct influence in the immediate fellowship of a Sufi order, indirect, wider influence in the larger community of Muslims through lectures, "sohbets" or other types of oral tradition, and finally, influence in the contemporary world on Muslims as well as non-Muslims through printed literature and other media. We gave indicators of how especially this third type of influence is attracting larger audiences, especially among younger generations of Muslims.

Despite the presence of the aforementioned positive notions, the impact of Sufism on larger Muslim populations has been limited by three factors: The first is the literalist opposition to more flexible interpretations of concepts from the Qur'an and the Prophetic tradition and the strict definition of the notion of invention in religion, or "*Bid'a*." The second is the deviations of some Sufi orders and subsequent criticisms by orthodox Muslims. The third impediment consists of the political obstacles, namely, impact of politicization of religion by some groups and political moves by certain Sufi orders.

While sharing the aforementioned inclusive and synergistic concepts with the more sophisticated, institutionalized Sufi tradition, the 'balanced' spiritual tradition avoids these criticisms by holding the prophetic tradition higher over any other practice even if based on the framework of the former. This approach, represented by towering historical figures such as Hasan Al-Basri and Al-Ghazali as well as contemporary figures such as Gülen, "emphasizes the central role of the Qur'an and Sunna, it has a tolerant and non-rigid style, and it emphasizes religious activism[78]." By the same token, the balanced spiritual tradition steers clear of negligence in obligatory forms of worship, practices resembling *shirk*, or associating partners with God, such as Saint worship.

We gave examples of fierce critics of the Sufi orders of their time, such as Ibn Taymiyya, as well as contemporary influential Muslim figures, who nevertheless applaud the balanced practice of the early masters of the spiritual tradition. The criticism of passivity is answered by historians of Islam who point out to numerous examples of Sufi orders participating in defensive struggles.

While immediate membership in a Sufi order has declined considerably around the world, the impact of spiritual masters have continued to influence and shape the minds and hearts of Muslim populations. Name recognition and reverence for spiritual personalities as well as affinity for their teachings are clearly observable in many Muslim communities from Turkey to Egypt to India to Indonesia. According to Ahmed, the spiritual tradition is the source and defining tone of one of the three major responses to modernity and globalization that can be observed in the Muslim communities around the world. The works of Al-Ghazali and Rumi remain most read and quoted Muslim literature after the Qur'an and Prophetic tradition.

Analysts point out to the increase in the popularity of the spiritual tradition of Islam at the expense of political Islamism which is declining after decades of semi-successes and profound failures. The failures of the politicized Islam in the past century and the recent tragedies of terror and the subsequent association of Islam with unjustified violence have prepared the Muslim mind for a worldview that could shape a harmonious Muslim response to globalization. The balanced spiritual tradition of Islam holds the greatest potential to be that worldview and help the world steer toward peaceful and harmonious coexistence with religious plurality.

---

78 Gokcek, ibid.

PROMOTING HUMAN RIGHTS VALUES IN THE MUSLIM WORLD: THE CASE OF THE GÜLEN MOVEMENT

Ozcan Keles

Abstract

The premise of this paper is that human rights values are a persistent theme of Fethullah Gülen's thought and *tajdid* and expressed by the Gülen movement through example. That *tajdid* is collectively constructed and communicated by allowing for adaptation and indigenisation in flexible response to different socio-cultural contexts. What is more, Gülen's views on democracy, pluralism, human rights and freedom of belief directly promote human rights values and norms. The paper argues that the Muslim world is very important to Gülen's overall aspiration for an inclusive civilisation and thus the movement is now active in most parts of that world. In time, as in Turkey, Gülen's ideas will enable and empower the periphery in Muslim societies to influence the centre ground and open the way for wider enjoyment of freedom and human rights.

The paper is in three sections. The first looks at the underlying dynamics of Gülen's influence and the nature of his *tajdid*, to assess whether his influence is transferable elsewhere. The second appraises the content of Gülen's *tajdid* arguing that human rights values are an inherent theme of his discourse on Islam. Here, the paper analyses Gülen's views on Anatolian Muslimness, democracy and politics, human rights and freedom of belief, illustrating Gülen's incremental *ijtihad* on temporal punishment for apostasy in Islamic law. The third part traces the movement's activities in the Muslim world, arguing that the movement has now entered a phase of adolescence, and asks whether Gulen's *tajdid* and discourse, through the practice of the movement, can indeed promote human rights values in this world.

Introduction

The premise of this paper is that human rights values are a persistent theme of Fethullah Gülen's thought and *tajdid* and expressed by the Gülen movement through example. That *tajdid* is collectively constructed and communicated by allowing for adaptation and indigenisation in flexible response to different socio-cultural contexts. What is more, Gülen's views on democracy, pluralism, human rights and freedom of belief directly promote human rights values and norms. The paper argues that the Muslim world is very important to Gülen's overall aspiration for an inclusive civilisation and thus the movement is now active in most parts of that world. In time, as in Turkey, Gülen's ideas will enable and empower the periphery in Muslim societies to influence the centre ground and open the way for wider enjoyment of freedom and human rights.

I must stress at the beginning that although there is a growing body of literature and research surrounding Gülen and the movement, there is extremely little, if any, so far concerning his influence in the Muslim world. This is largely due to the fact that the movement has been less visible or active in the Muslim world than elsewhere. More empirical research is required in this field. The challenge this presents therefore is to first contextualise Gülen in the Muslim world, before moving on to look at what influence, if any, he has in promoting human right Svalues in this region.

Thus, the paper is in three sections. The first looks at the underlying dynamics of Gülen's influence and the nature of his *tajdid*. The purpose behind this is simple; in order to predict whether Gülen has any meaningful scope of influence in the Muslim world it is imperative to first understand what makes Gülen influential in the first place, how influential he is in Turkey and whether that influence is transferable elsewhere. The second appraises the content of Gülen's *tajdid* arguing that human rights values are an inherent theme of his discourse on Islam. Here, the paper analyses Gülen's views on Anatolian Muslimness, democracy and politics, human rights and freedom of belief, illustrating Gülen's incremental *ijtihad* on temporal punishment for apostasy in Islamic law. The third part traces the movement's activities in the Muslim world, arguing that the movement has now entered a phase of adolescence, and asks whether Gülen's *tajdid* and discourse, through the practice of the movement, can indeed promote human rights values in this world.

In assessing Gülen's potential influence in the Muslim world, I will refer to Serif Mardin's Centre/Periphery model. I suggest that the current power struggle in Turkey, as manifested by the tip of the iceberg political battle recently unfolding between the newly emerging, previously rural, democratic yet conservative public as represented by the ruling Justice and Development (AK) Party and the militant-secular status quo margins as represented by the Republican People's Party (CHP), is in fact a struggle between the periphery and centre, respectively.

In this paper, I argue that just as Gülen's discourse and the Gülen movement were instrumental in empowering the periphery in Turkey[1], their presence will have a similar effect in the Muslim world.

Finally, any theological discussion in this paper is tangential to the main premise and argument. What is significant for the purposes of this paper is that Gülen is perceived and considered to be working within the traditional framework of Islamic jurisprudence and theology not that he actually is. The argument that he is, helps explain the perception and influence he

---

1 Ozdalga 2005: 441

enjoys in Turkey and increasingly abroad. Whether that is actually the case, is the subject of another study.

Gülen's Influence and *Tajdid*

Gülen is many things at once and it is this combination of characteristics, abilities and quali-fications, some of which have hitherto seemed mutually exclusive, that marks him out from the rest and has provided him with a transformative edge. Gülen is an Islamic scholar, peace activist, intellectual, civil-faith-based movement leader, social reformist, mentor, poet and writer. He has motivated and inspired a whole generation in Turkey and abroad numbering millions (not used lightly) into a multi-ethnic (and even multi-religious) movement, which he calls a 'Community of Volunteers'.

While there is a lot interesting about the Gülen persona and psyche, for the purposes of this paper, I will look at the dynamics that enables him to enjoy an immense influence in Turkey.

The Gülen Trio-Formula: Devout-Intellectual-Alim

I suggest that it is the combination of three particular characteristics that have enabled Gülen to become immensely popular and influential in Turkey, namely being a Sufi-orientated spir-itually-devout Muslim, an intellectual in contemporary reading and thought and an acclaimed Islamic scholar or *alim*.

Ali Bulac, a well-known independent Muslim scholar and columnist, was the first to empha-sise Gülen's intellectual-*alim* credentials and its importance, stating that Gülen is the most recent reviver of the *Ulema* tradition. *Alim* (singular for *Ulema*) is an Arabic title provided only to the most knowledgeable Islamic scholars who have an impeccable command of the traditional Islamic sources, sciences and methodologies. However, Bulac argues that being merely an *alim* renders one insufficient, a mere conveyor. To be effective and relevant one has to be a *janahayn* (the dual wing), in other words an intellectual versed in western sciences and thought as well.

Concerning Gülen, in this respect, Bulac states:

> Of the very few contenders, Gülen is perhaps the foremost representative of *janahayn*. His outlook has several key features: a profound understanding of Islamic sciences; a deep knowledge of bi-ography (*ilm al-rijal*) in Hadith narration; and a thorough understanding of Islamic methodology (*usul*)… His book, Key Concepts in the Practice of Sufism… is an extremely important work in terms of thought and Sufi tradition. Gülen's most important characteristic is that he analyzes contemporary issues and brings forth solutions using the traditional methodology of Islamic juris-prudence and Hadith.[2]

Gülen's appreciation of Western philosophies, history, literature and science is evident from the references he draws from these disciplines and interpretations he makes of contempo-rary issues. In an interview with Eyup Can, Gülen lists Kant, Descartes, Sir James Jean, Shakespeare, Victor Hugo, Tolstoy, Dostoyevsky and Puskin as some Western intellectu-als whose works he has read[3]. We know from his memoirs that he studied Kant, Rousseau, Voltaire, Emile, Schiller and the works of such existentialist philosophers such as Camus,

---

2   Bulac 2006: 101
3   Can 1996: Ref

Sartre and Marcuse during his military service in 1961[4].

In his 14 cassette sermon series delivered in 1978 over several months to a mosque-congregation regarding the existence of God (*Tawheed*), Gülen speaks in some detail about the 2nd law of thermo-dynamics, the big bang, astrophysics, astronomy, probability, atomic physics and biology in substantiating his arguments. Many other sermon-series, structured and methodological in themselves, include this variety of discipline and content. There are legendary stories told among Gülen's followers of how unaccustomed listeners used to sleeping during sermons, or left-wing intellectuals nudgingly persuaded to attend, wake up bemused and disoriented during the sermon to Gülen speaking about protons, electrons and neutrons.

It is Gülen's ability to draw his references from both Islamic and Western philosophies and interpret one within the other that marks him out as a *janahayn*. This dual-wing, allows him to achieve two-things, one draw sympathy and a gathering from those who draw their references from positive sciences and sympathise with the Western Enlightenment thought and two, demonstrate to the "Western-liberal" and "conservative-religious" that there is no inherent contradiction between Islam, science and the necessities of modern age.

However, this duo characteristic is insufficient to explain Gülen's influence. There is another wing missing in Bulac's description and that is Gülen's Sufi orientated spiritual devotion and fervour often manifested through intense emotion and dedication and poetic prose in his speech.

Gülen is perceived by the public as a deeply religious individual who has remained celibate from devotion to God and cause and leads a deeply ascetic lifestyle, sleeping and eating very little and spending most of his time, especially now, in solitary worship and study with his personal students. His unusual religious fervour and zeal is clearly evident in his excitement when delivering sermons in which he often ends up crying, in return causing the congregation to follow suit. Among the wider Turkish public, Gülen is known as the "crying *Hodja*".

Referring to Gülen's religious upbringing, Lester Kurtz notes:

> [Gülen] memorized the Qur'an at a young age and testifies that he "began praying when I was 4 years old, and has never missed a prayer since." He dedicated himself early on to a simple lifestyle devoted to prayer, meditation, religious writing and teaching. Eschewing family life, he chose an ascetic's path, devoting his life to prayer and religious pursuits and owning virtually no possessions.[5]

Or at least that is how Gülen is perceived and perception is extremely important. In fact, without this reputation, Gülen's intellectual-*alim* credentials would win him little influence. Simply put, the common Muslim has become weary of so-called Islamic scholars in recent years, especially those who have an appreciation of Western sciences. Trust is only inspired if scholarly credentials are supplemented with devotion and practice and even then the question of orientation remains, i.e. Sufi, *Salafi*, *Shiite* or secular.

Thus, an accurate understanding of who Gülen is is more important than what he says. The influential Rand think-tank in the United States for example, wrongly identifies Gülen as a "modernist" and states that although modernists are the most suited allies of the West in terms of their discourse and beliefs, they lack the authenticity of the traditionalists and the

---

4 Erdogan 1997: Ref
5 Kurtz, 2005 p375

service-outlets through which to influence the public[6]. The overall observation concerning modernists are correct, categorising Gülen as one is not. The consequence of this is misjudging Gülen's influence. Had Gülen been a modernist as such, he would never have enjoyed the kind of influence he does in Turkey, let alone have any meaningful chance of doing so in the Muslim world. Hence the significance of getting this right.

The question of course is whether Gülen will be able to transfer his influence to the wider Muslim world. The Muslim world is a vast geography made up of over 50 different countries. A crude reply, leaving aside a detailed study of each countries idiosyncratic nature and its relevance vis-à-vis the Gülen movement, is 'yes', since the underlying cultural dynamics and characteristics are similar. If anything, religion is as important in most of the Muslim world as it is in Turkey. Gülen's devotion to faith and cause and fifty year proven track record will exchange as good currency in this part of the world. However, the main determining factor of Gülen's influence in the Muslim world will be the presence and effectives of the Gülen movement in this region.

The Gülen Movement and Tajdid (Renewal of Religion)

Gülen's spiritually-devout, intellectual-*alim* credentials comprises the first field of influence he enjoys among the Turkish Muslims. These characteristics have helped him form a second field of influence, the Gülen movement. Where Gülen's personal reputation fails to reach, this wider movement goes. So one can imagine two concentric circles one within the other. Gülen influences the movement, the movement influences wider society. Since Gülen not only combines but preaches the unification of spiritual devotion with scientific appreciation and religious knowledge, his followers also manifest this trio-quality. An active volunteer of the movement will be a practising Muslim or believer of some tradition, of moral character who seeks to abstain from worldly indulgences, usually at least of graduate level degree, well read in Islamic theology and fairly informed of other religions, thereby becoming a *miniature-Gülen*.[7] Thus, the effective formula of influence replicated throughout the movement to varying degrees.

This characteristic empowers the Gülen-follower with self-confidence and is highly effective in influencing those who find themselves on one or the other side of the religious-secular spectrum.

So although Gülen is influential on an individual basis for the reasons given above, it is the faith based movement he now inspires which allows him to put his views into practice, and which marks him out as a candidate who can effectuate real change at the ground level. Without a mass following and wide influence among the grass roots of society, Gülen would have remained a scholar of great depth but no means of implementation. An elitist, an academic, a thinker who is waiting for the right masses to develop to be heard. With Gülen, the masses are ready, waiting for him to speak.

It is for this reason that Yilmaz argues that Gülen is engaged in *"tajdid* by conduct"[8]. *Tajdid* means to renew, revive and restore religion. It is an authentic Islamic mechanism prophesised by the Prophet himself.[9]

---

6   Benard 2003: 38-40
7   Active volunteers should not be confused with supporters and donors, who make up the backbone of the movement.
8   Yilmaz, 2003
9   Hadith (Ref)

Tajid can only be undertaken by a *mujaddid*. A *mujaddid* in his effort to renew (*tajdid*) religion will use a tool called *ijtihad* (reasoning) and in doing so also become a *mujtahid*. *Ijtihad* is a re-reading and re-evaluation of religious text and sources to deduce and derive a re-understanding of its teachings for contemporary times while keeping within its overall framework and spirit. It too is an authentic mechanism and in accordance with Islamic orthodoxy. *Ijtihad* has its limits, rules and conditions and should not be confused with reform which has neither. All *mujaddids* are also *mujtahids* but not all *mujtahids* are *mujaddids*.

In relation to *ijtihad*, I coin Gülen's efforts in this vein as incremental (*tadriji*)[10] *ijtihad*, since (i) he develops and communicates his *ijtihad* incrementally over many years and different mediums, respectively, and (ii) he does not claim that he is engaged in *ijtihad* at all, thus further delaying the recognition that he is in fact engaged in *ijtihad*. The relevance for this paper is that Gülen is currently engaged in this incremental *ijtihad* regarding the death penalty for apostasy in Islamic law as explored below.

In relation to Gülen's *tajdid*, Yilmaz states that:

> Gülen has reinterpreted Islamic understanding in tune with contemporary times and has developed and put into practice a new Muslim discourse... on religion, pluralism, jurisprudence, secularism, democracy, politics and international relations.[11]

Yilmaz argues that Gülen is undertaking this *tajdid* through conduct, because his ideas are put into immediate effect through the movement and affects the surrounding wider society in *la longe durée*.[12]

I suggest that Gülen's *tajdid* is collectively constructed by the movement's conduct and Gülen's views. If Gülen's *tajdid* is based on conduct, then the movement plays a significant role in the construction of that *tajdid*. What is more, Gülen encourages the contribution of the active player here, namely the movement. Thus, Gülen is aware that his general views and teachings will be locally received, interpreted and adapted in the process of application.

I suggest that the movement's contribution to Gülen's *tajdid* is in the form of (i) its interpretation of Gülen's views on receipt, (ii) its reformulation of those views to meet local realities such as funding and capability on application, (iii) its adaptation of those general views to meet local culture and customs (indigenisation) (iv) new realities formed by local conduct and activities of the movement pose new questions and challenges which Gülen responds to, and (v) the movement innovates new forms of conduct itself which are put to Gülen, to which he replies and the above process renews itself. Thus, there is continuous and interactive dialogue between the movement and Gülen, the net outcome of which is a collective *tajdid*. Some may claim that the same process of interpretation and adaptation is present in other (or all) forms of *tajdid* as well. While that may be true to some degree, since the movement is active in over a hundred countries, the spectrum across which Gülen's views are received, adapted and localised is ever more great. What is more, the fact that the movement's volunteers are well educated, well read and very mobile means they are more critical, analytic and innovative in their dialogue with Gülen. Also, Gülen promotes collectivism within the movement through his emphasis on joint decision making and consultation (*sura*). As such, every

---

10 In Islamic terminology, incrementalism usually refers to the revelation of the Qur'an over 23 years by the instigation of certain events (*sebebul nuzul*). The prohibition of alcohol in the Qur'an in four steps is usually given as an example of incrementalism in Islam.

11 Yilmaz 2003: 209

12 Yilmaz 2003: 220

venture and project of the movement has its own committee responsible for making its own decisions. Locally and collectively made decisions explain the movement's success in vastly different socio-cultural and economic markets across the world.

Thus, Gülen acts more like a chairperson in the construction of this *tajdid*. He sets the guidelines, objectives and principles. But then how those principles and objectives are put into action depend more on the movement than Gülen. Simply put the movement's dialogue efforts tell us much more about Gülen's *tajdid* on Islam and society than any of his essays or interviews on the topic.

The clarification of how Gülen's *tajdid* is constructed and communicated is important since it demonstrates that this *tajdid* is indigenised by the local people influenced by it. This does not mean Gülen's original thought is watered down; clearly it is not. But Gülen's global discourse and teachings are localised to best serve local conditions. The difference of the movement's educational projects in Turkmenistan with, let's say, the United State or Germany helps illustrate this point.

The significance of this regarding the Muslim world (and elsewhere for that matter) is that Gülen's views and discourse demonstrates that it is adaptable, flexible, durable and practical. These are essential qualities if Gülen's ideas and *tajdid* are to influence the Muslim world. Otherwise, without provision for indigenisation, the strong Arab culture would easily reject and react to this new discourse. This is something that will be explored further below.

Gülen Movement's Influence in Turkey

The Gülen movement is "one of the most influential revivalist movements in modern Turkey."[13] On Gülen's influence over his own the movement, Yavuz notes

> A decade ago, this religious community was not even willing to allow their daughters to go to secondary or high schools. They preferred to send female students to the Qur'anic courses or strictly female Imam Hatip schools. For years, Gülen publicly and privately encouraged the community to educate all their children regardless of gender. Today, there are many all-female schools and many of their graduates go onto universities.[14]

Bacik states that the relationship between the Muslim self and Islamic groups has undergone significant change due to, *inter alia*, the Muslim self's understanding of some important concepts such as Europe and democracy and that members of the Islamic community are coming from better educated backgrounds[15]. I argue, that Gülen's contribution to this change is significant as stated by Kosebabalan

> Gülen's pro-Western attitude has played a key role in the domestication and softening of other Islamic groups' anti-Europe and anti-U.S. positions. Although many Islamists eventually came closer to embracing this idea, a majority of them initially criticized Gülen for his pro-Europe views. He was one of the first Islamic leaders to embrace the idea of EU membership and at a time when Islamists in general regarded it as a threat to Turkish security and Islamic culture.[16]

On Gülen and the movement's influence in Turkey, Kosebabalan notes

> Fethullah Gülen and the movement he established and leads comprise two of he most important actors in Turkish social and political life. His ideas, despite a number of complications and

---

13 Ozgalga 2005: 430
14 Yavuz 1999: 125
15 Bacik 2003: 31
16 Kosebabalan 2003: 176

contradictions in them, directly influence Turkish foreign policy and certainly would bring some vivacity to that policy if put to practical application.[17]

Kosebabalan notes how some credit Gülen's intellectual contributions that led to the EU-OIC summit in Istanbul in 2002[18]. Supporting Kosebabalan, Yavuz states that 'Gülen is the engine behind the construction of a "new" Islam in Turkey'.[19]

On Gülen's influence of thought, Yilmaz states

> Preliminary observations indicate that Gülen not only is renewing Muslim discourses and practices, but also transforming the public sphere, without claiming or boasting that he is doing so. In this regard, the movement is evolving into a school of thought based on Gülen's discourse and with the potential to influence the whole Muslim world. This transformation process is definitely a tajdid in the Turkish public sphere.[20]

On Gülen's transformative discourse and evolving a new school of thought, Yavuz states

> In the clashing visions of globalizations, Fethullah Gülen is a force in the development of the Islamic discourse of globalized multicultural pluralism. As the impact of the educational activities of those influenced by him attests, his vision bridges modern and postmodern, global and local, and has a significant influence in the contemporary debates that shape the visions of the future of Muslims and non-Muslims alike.[21]

We have already studied the dynamics of this influence, whether it be the Gülen persona or the movement. Through this influence, Gülen has helped strengthen the periphery in Turkey. The Gülen movement's education, media and business initiatives have empowered and enabled the working-class silent-majority in Turkey who where hitherto unable to contest for the centre ground.

What is more, through this new school of thought, Gülen has helped remove the theological and cultural dogmas, which until recently, prevented the periphery from positively engaging in society and therefore from moving into the centre ground currently occupied by the militant secular margins.

The AK Party phenomena, which has its roots in the pro-Islamic National Outlook movement, owes its evolutionary success in becoming a modern, inclusive and democratic Party, largely to Gülen's transformative discourse. In 1994, when Recep Tayip Erdogan was characterising democracy as a means to an end, Gülen stood up at the Journalists and Writers Foundation and said 'there is no return from democracy; it's not perfect, but is the best system we currently have'. Again, in the polarised Turkey of the 1990's Gülen was the first to speak of dialogue, tolerance, acceptance of each other and peaceful coexistence. It was the Gülen movement's conferences, interfaith fast-breaking dinners, peace awards and so forth that brought together people of opposing ends of the political spectrum. Many expressed pleasant-surprise, even shock, at how they could share the table with once considered archenemies. However, at the time, many criticised Gülen on this, including some members of the current AK Party government and the Religious Affairs Directorate. It is interesting to note that the Religious Affairs Directorate now hosts several interfaith dialogue events itself and

---

17 Kosebabalan 2003: 170
18 Kosebabalan 2003: 181
19 Yavuz 1999: 121
20 Yilmaz 2003: 237
21 Voll 2003: 247

that the current government has adopted Gülen's approach of reconciliation.[22]

Gülen helped ease the ideological rift in Turkey and the resultant community tension. When the Alevis where offended by the Sunnis he made a televised announcement as a Sunni imam, saying, 'if loving reverend Ali makes one an Alevi, then I am an Alevi for I love him dearly'. Regarding communists he is known to have said, 'they love this country as much as you do. You cannot question their patriotism.' Even on secularism, Gülen's announcements that he looks favourably on a Anglo-Saxon-style open secularism (against a French-style militant laicism) has helped ease tensions on this fault line as well.

The Abant meetings which brought together academics, writers, journalists and politicians (including leading members of the current government) to discuss deeply dividing political issues in Turkey and arrive at a consensus reflected in the Abant declarations are efforts in this vein.[23]

Gülen's views on democracy, secularism, pluralism, human rights and modernity have helped empower Muslims in Turkey, who until recently fought to withstand the lure of these values despite their better judgment out of fear that giving in would run contrary to their faith. Muslims in Turkey were now able to socially, politically and more importantly, sincerely and constructively, participate in Turkey's public life and contemporary debates. The fact that the AK Party government has done more during its first term than any other in the past 40 years to achieve Turkey's accession to the EU, is proof of this point.

Gülen's *Tajdid* and Human Rights by Default

Before contextualising Gülen in the Muslim world, I will contextualise human right values in Gülen's discourse. My premise is that Gülen's discourse and the movement's activities are (i) human based and therefore contain an ever present underlying streak of humanistic values, and (ii) help eradicate the cultural and religious-couched objections towards human rights values. This means that, given its normal course, human rights values will spread through and with the movement's influence as a matter of default. I will look at Gülen's discourse on Anatolian Muslimness, politics, human rights and freedom of belief since they best illustrate the above-mentioned two points.

Anatolian Muslimness

Anatolian Muslimness is Gülen's understanding and practice of Islam. It is the underlying bedrock of Gülen's thought and discourse. All of Gülen's views and outlook are essentially based on this. Thus, where this primary understanding and practice of Islam is spread, Gülen's secondary views on democracy, human rights and pluralism will eventually follow.

---

22 Yilmaz 2005: 399-405

23 In 1998 the Abant platform discussed the relationship between Islam and secularism, in 1999 democracy and human rights, in 2000 pluralism and reconciliation.

The 1998 Abant Declaration states that 'revelation and reason do not conflict; democracy and secularism does not conflict with Islam; the state should remain neutral towards every kind of ideology, belief and philosophical view; the state should ensure basic human rights and freedom of belief, conscience and religion and should not seek to exclude nor deprive any person of the right to public participation'. (Ref)

The 2001 Abant Declaration reads: 'Civil and political freedoms, headed by the freedoms of belief, thought and expression, education, and organization, are the prerequisites of pluralism' (Journalists and Writers Foundation 2001: 316).

For Gülen, Islam is by its very nature moderate and therefore the recently popular phrase "moderate Islam" is incorrect as it implies that Islam can be anything but moderate. Gülen believes that moderation is such a central characteristic of Islam that any understanding of it that is not, is not Islam. He states that those who harbour an extremist practice and understanding do so either deliberately, ignorantly or because they have an incomplete grasp of Islam and have taken matters completely out of context.

Gülen states that the manifestation and emphasis of uniform Islamic teachings and tenets of religion can vary according to region and culture. This provides Islam with a degree of flexibility and allows for various "Islamic flavours" to develop which differ with each other in terms of nuances, emphases and aesthetics but remain the same on creed and teachings.

Accordingly, Gülen argues that the Anatolian Muslimness practiced in Turkey is different than the Arab or Iranian Muslimness. Anatolian Muslimness is "broader, deeper, more tolerant and inclusive, and based on love"[24].

Gülen states that he sees no canonical objection to acceding to the fact that different socio-historic conditions produce different emphases of Islam. In fact, Gülen goes a step further and believes in promoting this understanding to the wider world

> Within this framework, if we exclude certain periods and individuals, the Turks' interpretation of what Islam allows to be interpreted is correct and positive. If we can spread globally the Islamic understanding of such heroes of love as Niyazi-i Misri, Yunus Emre, and Rumi, if we can extend their messages of love, dialogue, and tolerance to those thirsty for this message, everyone will run toward the embrace of love, peace, and tolerance that we represent.[25]

Thus, in saying that the Turks have a "broader and deeper" understanding of Islam, given that they have had the opportunity and experiences to interpret and explore Islam in areas that other Muslims have not, he is in fact suggesting that this understanding is more suited for contemporary times.

Turkish Islam or Anatolian Muslimness existed long before Gülen made these coins so widespread. However, it was Gülen's interviews, talks and books that helped communicate this concept to the wider public for the first time. By analysing the underlying dynamics of Anatolian Muslimness he helped define the concept more thoroughly. In doing so, Gülen has legitimised the concept of Anatolian Muslimness and its recognition in the minds of Turkish Muslims. Before, most felt that admitting this would amount to schism in Islam. There are still some Turkish Islamic groups that criticise Gülen for making this idea so widespread. Convincing people to the contrary has helped define, protect and now spread this concept to wider the Muslim world.

What is being spread is not a new religion, but a practice imbued with certain values. Therefore, it is about fine-tuning the more conformist, rigid and didactic Muslimness to a more open, Sufi-orientated and loving practice.

> Others saw in Gülen's discourse a strong neo-Ottomanist taste. But a closer look into the work of Gülen will show that Gülen is using Turkish and Ottoman experience of Islam so as to extract Islam from a pure Arabic religion. The Turkish experience is more of an activist Islam and is coloured with devotion to Islam and yet tolerance to others.

Candar and Fuller state that Gülen can play a strong role "of positively representing Turkey in

---

24 Turgut 1997: 53
25 Camaci & Unal 1999: 196

the Muslim world, and demonstrating the moderate character of Turkish Islam and Islamism that denies neither democracy or good ties with the West". They also add that "Turkish Islamists can assist in moderating other Islamist movements in the region [Muslim world] and in supporting reconciliation through its own successful mode."[26]

Gülen's dialogue theology should also be read as part of his Anatolian Muslimness discourse. Gülen has been bringing out the theological, philosophical and historical teachings, arguments and stories, respectively, surrounding dialogue in Islam to the attention of contemporary Muslims. In developing this theology he refers to the Qur'an and *hadith* and re-tells stories from the Prophet, Ottomans and Sufi masters like Rumi to make his point. This theology informs the movement's dialogue initiatives and sends out a very strong message that Islam necessitates dialogue and constructive citizenship. I argue that this is transforming Muslim understanding of Islam in general and attitude toward society in particular, in accordance with Anatolian Muslimness.

It is clear therefore, that Gülen is promoting Anatolian-Muslimness among Muslims. His primary vehicle in doing so is his dialogue-theology and the movement's dialogue activities. Anatolian Muslimness and Gülen's dialogue theology includes human rights values and culture. Gülen's views on human rights itself is based on his fundamental understanding of Islam as discussed further below.

Islamic State, Political Islam, Democracy and Secularism

In terms of politics, Gülen advises his movement to remain non partisan and apolitical. Unlike other Islamic groups, Gülen argues that there is no such as thing as a puritan Islamic State, and that therefore there can be no ultimate goal to work for its fulfilment. Instead, Gülen argues that states and governments should follow certain fundamental principles as espoused by Islam

> Islam does not propose a certain unchangeable form of government or attempt to shape it. Instead, Islam establishes fundamental principles that orient a government's general character, leaving it to the people to chose the type and form of government according to time and circumstance.[27]

These fundamental principles and values include justice, human rights, freedom of religion and belief, freedom of thought and expression, rule of law, meritocracy in public appointment, public order, balanced approach, consultation and elections[28]. Note carefully how Gülen includes human rights, freedom of belief and elections as Islamic principles that must be upheld by governments and states. In that sense, any form of governance that upholds these principles is in fact "Islamic" even if it is not called so. The logical extension of this point is that Britain is more Islamic than Saudi Arabia or Iran because it is more loyal to the principles noted above.[29] Thus, Gülen is overtly promoting support for human rights values and democracy and undermining any support, albeit miniscule in Turkey, for a theocratic state[30].

---

26 Candar & Fuller 2001: Ref

27 Gülen 2001: 134

28 Gülen 2006: 88-92

29 I don't think that it's any easier to live Islam in another country than it is in Turkey. Supposedly there are Islamic regimes in Iran and Saudi Arabia, but they are state-determined and limited to sectarian approval. (Turgut 1997: 151)

30 "[T]he Qur'an declares that the rule does not belong to holy and infallible spiritual leaders, as in theocracies, nor to any religious institutions under their supervision, nor to any other religious institution organized in any other way. Islam... does not allow any privilege based on family, class, race, color, wealth, or power" (An Interview with

Gülen is also against political Islam or Islamism which seeks to use religion for political means, regardless of whether it seeks to found an Islamic state or not.

In that sense, Gülen is against bringing religion into politics. That does not mean that politics should completely ignore religion or its citizens' religious needs, but that one should not be used for the sake of the other. In some ways therefore, Gülen can be considered to argue for a secular approach in politics.

> If reconciliation is being sought between Islam and secularism, then according to some views of Islam, in fact according to some Qur'anic verses like Your religion for you, mine for me, there's no big problem. If secularism is understood as not basing the state on religion, not interfering in religion or in the believers' religious life, and acting in an unbiased way, there's no problem at all. I don't think secularism is in danger now or that it will be in the future.[31]

On democracy, Gülen states that "democracy and Islam are compatible. Ninety-five per cent of Islamic rules deal with private life and family. Only 5 per cent deals with matters of the state, and this could be arranged only within the context of democracy."[32] Gülen argues that democratization is irreversible, that while not perfect, it is the best model so far, which must be further perfected, providing it with a metaphysical dimension which considers its subjects metaphysical need as well. What exactly Gülen means by this is unclear and is one of Gülen's ideas incubating for now.

On minorities and international law, Gülen states that "[M]ember of minority communities should be allowed to live according to their beliefs. If these sorts of legislation are made within the norms of international law and international agreements, Islam will have no objection to any of these".[33] Thus, Gülen has not only contributed to the internalisation of democratic and human rights values by Turkish Muslims but he is also promoting respect for international law and therefore codification of human rights values.

On democracy in the Muslim world, Gülen states that "despotic rulers in the Islamic world, who see democracy as a threat to their despotism, presents another obstacle for democracy in Muslim nations"[34] He adds that,

> Those who follow a more moderate pattern also believe that it would be much better to introduce Islam as a complement to democracy instead of presenting it as an ideology. Such an introduction of Islam may play an important role in the Muslim world…[35]

Thus, Gülen is aware that democracy can only be introduced in the Muslim world through Islam. This is something that will be explored further below.

Human Rights Values

Gülen looks at human rights from three perspectives: (i) the inherent value of freedom vis-à-vis freedom of choice and willpower, (ii) the contingent value of freedom vis-à-vis personal and social development and (iii) metaphysical human rights (kul hakki in Turkish).

Gülen views man as the centre of the universe. For him, man is the purpose of creation. Following the Islamic tasawwuf (roughly translated as the meaning and spirit of Islam)

Fethullah Gülen 2005: 450)

31 Ref: p185
32 Ref: p28
33 An Interview with Fethullah Gülen 2005: 451
34 An Interview with Fethullah Gülen 2005: 453
35 An Interview with Fethullah Gülen 2005: 452

concept of 'all beauty and fairness require to see and be seen', Gülen states that God is All-Beautiful and All-Fair and that He wanted to see His beauty and wanted His beauty to be seen. It is for this reason that God created humans. Humans have intellectual, emotional and bodily faculties to observe, enquire, understand, admire, praise and love God. Thus, humans were created as intelligent and conscious beings that can travel from the created to the Creator, marvel at the beauty and majesty of God's art and arrive at some estimation and understanding of His attributes, names and qualities. Like Nursi, Gülen argues that all creation manifests God's infinite names and attributes and that humans are "intelligent mirrors" who can turn and look at what creation is manifesting and appreciate their Creator.

However, there is an important 'magical switch' in humans which turns all of this on[36] and differentiates it from angels, who also marvel, worship and love God, and that is the element of choice. This "choice" is what makes humans human. The fact that a person chooses to recognise and worship God changes everything. Gülen explains that with this choice, humans can surpass angels in piety or fall lower than demons in barbarity. God wants humans to "choose" Him. Thus, choice was bestowed on humans as a gift and, simultaneously, test from God.

Once the matter is approached from this perspective, preserving the freedom of choice bestowed upon humans by God becomes an intrinsic, inherent and inalienable right of ones very humanness.

> Being free and enjoying freedom are a significant depth of human willpower and a mysterious door through which man may set forth into the secrets of the self. One unable to set forth into that depth and unable to pass through that door can hardly be called human.[37]

Summarily put, the universe was created for humans; a human is defined by its ability to choose. Choice is protected by freedom. Freedoms therefore allow humans to fulfil their purpose of creation. Hence, for Gülen, human rights which protect freedom of choice have an inherent value and must be promoted at all cost to preserve the balance of creation and purpose of existence.

While this is not a new outlook, and many Islamic scholars share this view, the fact that Gülen is willing to make the logical connection between this religious definition of "choice" and faith-neutral doctrine of "human right norms and practices" is quite significant.

> By visiting the State and many other European countries, I realized the virtues and the role of religion in these societies. Islam flourished in Europe and America much better than in many Muslim countries. This means freedom and the rule of law are necessary for personal Islam.[38]

Gülen's second consideration of freedom is as a contingent value in relation to personal and social development[39]. Gülen states that a human must strive to become an *insan-i kamil* that is perfect person. This perfection is one of belief, thought and practice. However, it does not solely relate to "religious matters" in the conventional sense but includes perfection and piety (*taqwa*) in "worldly" matters as well.[40]

---

36 Gülen 2005: 15

37 Ref

38 Ref

39 Carroll 2007: 28-9

40 Gülen states that God sets the laws of religion and the laws of nature and causality. Thus, a believer must follow both. Failing to follow the laws of nature and causality means failing to obey God's laws in achieving a desired result. Hence, Gülen re-defines *taqwah* (piety) as including, living in accordance with God's *sunnatullah* (God's

Freedom, in this context, therefore is a prerequisite to allow for personal and social perfection and development. Without freedom, the room and dynamic force for perfection and development is non existent. The most pertinent form of freedom in this respect, is freedom of thought and expression:

> True freedom is the freedom of the human mind from all shackles that hinder it from making material and spiritual progress, as long as we do not fall into indifference and heedlessness.[41]

Gülen considers free-thinking as a significant personal attribute of the "inheritors of the earth" or Golden Generation as he refers to elsewhere. These are the new generation of Muslims who have a balanced disposition, appreciation and awareness of this world and the next; who combine reason with revelation; who have love towards humankind and burn with the sensation of altruistic cause and action. For Gülen, this generation will contribute towards stability and eventual peace between not only people and nations but also between faith and science, matter and metaphysics.

> [W]e have to be more free-thinking and free-willed. We need those vast hearts who can embrace impartial free-thinking, who are open to knowledge, sciences and scientific research, and who can perceive the accord between the Qur'an and Sunnatullah (God's pattern of creation) in the vast spectrum from the universe to life.

Free-thinking and freedom of thought is therefore an imperative climatic condition for personal development. Without this freedom, development will stagnate on all fronts. Although Gülen is against the categorisation of "this world" and "afterlife", since he sees the two as inextricably linked, it is clear that according to him, without this freedom, development regresses both in the worldly and in the spiritual and religious sense.

For Gülen, to achieve social development, you must begin from the individual. A group of individuals who have attained a certain awareness and concern for others can then come together to engage in further altruistic works. This way, a virtuous cycle that feeds itself will be born and help strengthen civil society and social infrastructure. Thus, for Gülen, freedom of thought has a direct link with developing society as a whole through developing the individual.

That is what Gülen is trying to achieve through education:

> if you wish to keep masses under control, simply starve them in the area of knowledge. They can escape such tyranny only through education. The road to social justice is paved with adequate, universal education, for only this will give people sufficient understanding and tolerance to respect the right of others.[42]

In this respect, the hundreds of Gülen-schools that provide a broad and balanced curriculum and instil values of tolerance and respect for differences are significant in putting Gülen's views into practice on free-thinking to the wider public. The very notion that education is worthy in itself, regardless of its topic, whether mathematics, geometry or English, is a huge step forward in removing the cultural shackles on freedom of thought in cultural Muslim thinking which in the past only valued Qur'anic or religious teaching.

Secondly, education empowers people to think, reason, listen, research, extrapolate, relate,

---

pattern of creation, laws of nature). As such, Gülen states that the West is more Muslim than Muslims since they have achieved superiority by following God's laws of causality while the religious-Muslims have not.

41 Gülen 2006: 65

42 Ref

argue and learn which is immensely important in enabling individuals to become independent "free-thinkers".

Once the mindset of constantly challenging the modes and mediums of the present is fully internalised, then perhaps the movement will have achieved what Gülen refers to as freeing oneself from the shackles of thought:

> [A]s we draw toward renewal, it is imperative that we should review the historical dynamics of the last thousand years and question the changes and transformations of the last one hundred and fifty years of our past. It is imperative because judgments and decisions are nowadays made according to certain unquestioned taboos.[43]

Finally, metaphysical human rights. For Gülen, human rights include not only the enforceable rights included in law, but also those rights that we hold regardless of enforceability in this world. In that sense, a right is a right and is no less "real" simply because it cannot be enforced. For Gülen, there is no categorical distinction between the right not to be tortured with the right not to be backbitten (*giybah*). From a religious point of view, all transgressed rights will be accounted for on the day of judgement. This is quite significant in Islam, since Muslims are taught that God does not permit Himself to forgive the transgression of another, unless the transgressed forgives first. Thus, Gülen lists *su-i zan* (negative thought about another), *giybah,* slander[44] tax evasion and, even, non payment of utility bills[45], the charge of which will be picked up by others, as transgressions of human rights. For Gülen, they are all one and the same, basic human rights.

Hence, Gülen extends the scope and depth of human rights to include the unenforceable as well. In doing so, however, he also extends the scope of the unenforceable to include tax evasion and illegal use of electricity and water.

Incremental (Tadriji) Ijtihad in the Making: Apostasy in Islam

Freedom of belief has been a tricky topic for the Muslim world. A quick survey of the debates surrounding this freedom during the drafting of art 18 of the Universal Declaration of Human Rights or International Covenant for Civil and Political Rights will prove this point. The exact difficulty relates to the concept inherent in this freedom, namely the right to change religion. The question for Muslim countries has been whether Islamic law allows for Muslims to convert out of Islam. The conventional answer is that it does not and that one who does (*murted*) is punishable by death in Islamic law.

Regarding freedom of belief, Gülen is unequivocal. He clearly states in a number of articles that faith is a matter of choice and conscience and that no one can be coerced into believing or worshipping.[46] In one article[47] on the topic (a transcript of Gülen's response dating back to the late 1970's), Gülen passingly refers to the issue of temporal punishment for apostasy. Whilst he reiterates the conventional position as his own, he treats the matter as political rebellion towards the state and equates it with high treason. This latter comment marks the

---

43 Gülen 2005: 39

44 Gülen 1995: 277

45 Gülen 1995: 280

46 "If individuals cannot live by the principles of their religion freely because of certain obstacles put before them, this means that they have been denied the freedom of belief and conscience." (An Interview with Fethullah Gülen 2005: 448)

47 "Dinde Zorlama Yoktur" Ayetini Izah Eder misiniz? (http://www.asringetirdigitereddutler.com/ index.php/ content/view/470/12/)

beginning of an incremental *ijtihad* on the topic which will eventually manifest itself as part of an evolving *tajdid* on dialogue, pluralism and human rights in Islam.

I claim that Gülen is engaged in incremental *ijtihad*, since (i) he develops and communicates his *ijtihad* incrementally over many years and different mediums, respectively, and (ii) he does not claim that he is engaged in *ijtihad* at all, thus further delaying the recognition that he *is*. [48] His evolving position on the death penalty for an apostate is an example of this incremental *ijtihad*.

Since the aforementioned article, Gülen has not expounded on his position that apostasy is a political act of high treason. Instead, it has been picked up by Dr Ahmet Kurucan, a personal student of Gülen for many years and columnist of the Zaman Daily Newspaper on *fiqh* (Islamic jurisprudence) related issues. Given his expertise, columns and affinity with Gülen, Dr Kurucan is known as the movement's teacher on Islamic jurisprudence.

In 2006, I attended a Conference in Germany in which Dr Kurucan gave a talk on apostasy and punishment. He explained that the death penalty for apostasy was an *ijtihad* itself, not a definitive commandment of Islam, and that therefore it could be superseded by another *ijtihad* today. He argued that the time in which premodern jurists arrived at their decision, communities were deeply divided over Islam and Muslims were under political and physical siege from a number of fronts. Thus, you were either a Muslim defending Islam or a non-Muslim attacking it. For these jurists, apostasy at the time meant rebelling against the State and joining forces against the Muslims. There are a number of incidents at the time when apostates subsequently took arms against Muslims. According to Dr Kurucan therefore, apostasy was treated as high treason by the premodern jurists and their *ijtihad* of execution is in relation to this, not to the mere renouncing of faith.

This is an important observation backed by other scholars today as well:

> Many of the scholars and jurists define apostasy in terms of rebellion against the State, where a Muslim-subject of the Islamic State after denouncing Islam joins with those who take arms against the Islamic State and thus commits a political offence against the State.[49]

Dr Kurucan's PhD thesis (2006), entitled *Freedom of Thought in Islam,* substantiates this argument further. In summary, it argues that the Qur'an makes no reference to temporal punishment for apostasy, that to the contrary it states that *there is no compulsion in religion*[50]; that there are a number of recorded incidents in the Prophet's lifetime when an apostate went without punishment whatsoever; that much of the justification for this *ijtihad* is based on incidents that occurred during the reign of Abu Bakr when whole communities uprose against the central government and that therefore these were political acts of rebellion against the State; that the Hanafi school of thought states that a woman apostate is not punishable by death since she cannot take arms against Muslims, which, coupled with the fact that Islam treats man and women equally in reward and punishment, helps prove the overall point that in the premodern jurists' mind, apostasy was equated with high treason and political rebellion. Dr Kurucan argues that since apostasy can no longer be charged with such meaning today (as imminent physical attack by the apostate) and that times have changed, then this *ijtihad* can be superseded by another.

---

48 See Gülen 1995: 218 for a short discussion about the need to consider the socio-cultural conditions, perceptions and customs of the time.

49 Baderin 2003: 124

50 Qur'an: 2:256

Whether or not one agrees with Dr Kurucan's reasoning is irrelevant for the purposes of this paper, since we are not engaged in a theological study. The point is that Gülen and the movement are using Islamic tools of reinterpretation and renewal to reunderstand Islamic history and teachings. In doing so, they are referring to traditional texts and methodologies and forming a new discourse and school of thought.

Given the importance of the topic and its potential for controversy, it is unthinkable that Dr Kurucan would take such a stance without Gülen's prior approval. Thus, the various incremental stages of this *ijtihad* include Gülen's article dating back to the late 1970's, the overall dialogue works that became a priority for Gülen in the mid 1990's, the various meetings with minority religious leaders in Turkey in same period, the repeated emphasis on freedom of belief and human rights in the Abant meetings in the 2000's and Dr Kurucan's academic work in 2006. All of these comprise a further reason and justification in themselves towards a new position on the issue of change of religion in Islam.

Therefore, what we have here is an incremental development and communication of a hitherto minor opinion through new arguments to change the conventional thinking and attitude towards freedom of belief in general, apostasy in particular in traditional Islamic law. I expect that Gülen will publicly endorse this position in the near future, completing the incremental process of this *ijtihad's* formation. This will then comprise a significant piece of the Gülen *tajdid* on dialogue, pluralism and human rights. [51]

It is true that Gülen does not criticise the punishment for apostasy in the article referred to above or since. However, it should be noted that this was back in the 1970's, that in the same article Gülen hinted at the line of thought that would be later developed by Dr Kurucan and that since then an incremental change of position has taken place in conduct and word. What is more, this is perhaps one of the most sensitive topics in Islamic law and given that Gülen is lambasted by some religious fanatical groups that he is trying to water down religious sensitivity in order to Christianise the Turks and ultra laicist militant margins that he is trying to establish an Islamic State in Turkey and Islamisize the whole world, one can appreciate why Gülen would take a cautious note on this issue.

A number of jurists and scholars have also held that apostasy is not a punishable offence. However, the difference in Gülen's case is that he has the influence to change the thought of a critical mass to make a real difference. In doing so, Gülen and the movement are challenging a religiously-couched cultural reaction to the 'right to change religion' in the Muslim world. Religion is a matter of conscience and many Muslims believe that it is there duty to oppose the freedom to convert out of Islam, because of Islam. It is this which Gülen is incrementally challenging.

This does not mean that opposition to change of religion will immediately crumble, especially in the political circles. For them, controlling the right to change religion is a means to controlling opposition and religious authority. After all, it is they who decide what amounts to apostasy. However, the likes of Gülen's efforts will undermine the religious, cultural and public support for such a stance and in time will influence the thinking of the masses on freedom of belief in the wider Muslim world.

---

51 Other Gülen incremental *ijtihad's* incubating for the time being include "metaphysical democracy" and Islamic art in the modern age.

Gülen's Influence in the Muslim World

What we have examined above are some of Gülen's transformative views on frontline contemporary debates in the Muslim world. The point is to now assess whether Gülen can influence the Muslim world along the lines of the discourse espoused above.

Gülen on the Muslim world

Gülen's goal of universal peace allows us to judge the importance he ascribes to the Muslim, and for that matter, non-Muslim world. In his short English biography, often used as an introduction to most of his translated books, it states:

> Gülen envisions a twenty-first century in which we shall witness the birth of a spiritual dynamic that will revitalize long-dormant moral values; an age of tolerance, understanding, and international cooperation that will ultimately lead, through intercultural dialogue and sharing of values, to a single, *inclusive civilization* (emphasis added).[52]

In one of his early writings, Gülen states that this inclusive civilisation will emerge from the cooperation of the East and West and the respective values and strengths each represent:

> Communities based on the cooperation of science and morality always have established true civilizations. For this reason, Western civilization remains paralyzed because it is based mainly on science, and Eastern (Asian) civilizations are not "true" because, in their present conditions, they have no scientific background. The civilization of the future will have to be established upon a combination of Western science and eastern faith and morality.[53]

In another of his writings, Gülen explains further what those values and strengths are;

> The West cannot wipe out Islam or its territory, and Muslim armies can no longer march on the West. Moreover, as this world is becoming even more global, both sides feel the need for a give-and-take relationship. The West has scientific, technological, economic, and military supremacy. However, Islam possesses more important and vital factors: Islam, as represented by the Holy Book and the Sunna of the Prophet, has retained the freshness of its beliefs, spiritual essence, good works, and morality as it has unfolded over the last fourteen centuries. In addition, it has the potential to blow spirit and life into Muslims who have been numbed for centuries, as well as into many other peoples drowned in the swamp of materialism.[54]

Thus, for Gülen, universal peace and the will of God can only be achieved in an inclusive civilisation that merges the values and strengths of the East and West.

That is how we should read Gülen's request of his students to replace a map on his wall that solely shows the Muslim world, with one that shows the entire world. That is also consonant with the movement's efforts that span four continents and more than one hundred countries.

Therefore, Gülen's primary objective is religion-neutral and includes all people. To achieve this however, the Muslim world must be willing to contribute. To do so, Gülen argues that they must reform and revive themselves.[55] As to the nature of that revival, Gülen explains elsewhere

> With all sincerity, we support a renaissance that would consist of the rediscovery of lost human

---

52 Woodhall & Cetin 2005: viii
53 Gülen 2006: 56
54 Ünal and Williams 2000: 247
55 The Islamic world continues to squirm in the vicious grasp if error...[W]e must work within the Islamic world... which will lead to a comprehensive renewal... The Islamic community needs to be revived... (Gülen 2003: 3)

values and the rapprochement of humanity with universal human morals. Again, we support a renaissance that allows the questioning of dictatorship and the end of dictators, and working towards
a democratic society. A renaissance that fosters great achievement in the fine arts and promotes
a careful reading of the book of the universe, which has been lost for a long time, is greatly ap-
plauded. We support a renaissance that promotes a longing for research, a passion for knowledge,
and the articulation of religion in accordance with the understanding of our century in a new style
and new manner. (Emphasis added)[56]

From another perspective, it is clear from these essays that for Gülen, Turkey is socio-cultur-
ally, historically, geographically and geopolitically very important. Indeed, if we are to judge
Gülen's priority by the scale of the movement's investment, then again -no doubt- Turkey
tops the list. Unlike Hakan Yavuz, who seeks to explain Gülen's emphasis on Turkey, as
nationalistic tendencies originating from his *dadas* spirit or frontier experience[57], I believe
that this is due to Gülen's estimation of Turkey's past and future potential to lead the Muslim
world towards an inclusive civilisation. Turkey is critically important to Gülen, because the
future of Islam, the Muslim world and universal peace are so inextricably linked in Gülen's
mind.

In his essay 'The World We Long For', Gülen speaks of '*our nation may shortly realize a
second or third renaissance*' and his prayer to God to '[s]*ow our people to the ways to revival
in the Muhammadi line*'[58]. In this essay, Gülen is alluding to the leadership role of the Turks
in reviving the Muslim world

> After long ages of crises and depressions, despite all odd, this nation is still capable of such regen-
> eration; it still has the potential to realize a new resurrection... Moreover, it has the advantage of
> the subconscious acceptance by peoples which shared history, a leadership which may possibly be
> of use again in the future.[59]

Thus, Turkey's significance in Gülen's estimation is due to the role it is yet to play in this
Muslim world.

Another clue on the topic is Gülen's ongoing intellectual project since 1991; a compilation
of essays running into four volumes, entitled *Key Concepts of Sufism*. Here Gülen looks at
key terminology and values in the practice of Sufism by locating these concepts within the
Qur'an, the *sunnah* and the lifetime of the Prophet. Gülen oscillates between concepts such
as *ashq, jazba, tevazu, tevekul, vasil, halvet, kurb-buud*, and the Qur'an, Hadith and practice
of great Sufi masters. Thus, in these essays, Gülen is legitimising Sufi practice, thought and
perception. He is meticulously threading a theological and philosophical link between Sufism
and the sharia. In doing so, Gülen is strengthening one of the fundamental dynamics and underlying bedrock of Anatolian Muslimness, namely Sufi appreciation and perception.

These essays were clearly intended for Muslims. Its purpose is to spiritually reform. To do so,
it defines and contextualises Sufi concepts in Islamic sources. Turkish Muslims do not need
to be convinced of the legitimacy of Sufism in Islam. They accept this outright. I therefore
argue that the primary audience of these works are not Turks but the wider Muslim world
which, according to Gülen, desperately needs the Sufi touch. For Gülen, Sufism (or *tassawuf*
to use a better word), is the spirit of Islam and a practice void of this is didactic, rigid and
conformist.

---

56 An Interview with Fethullah Gülen 2005: 458
57 Yavuz 2003: 22
58 Gülen 2005: 28
59 Gülen 2005: 25

Thus, Gülen's intellectual project spanning sixteen-years is, in part, geared towards the Muslim world.

Why then is the movement so much more active in the West than it is in Muslim countries? The answer is practicality. The Gülen movement moved very quickly into Central Asia because it could, and because Gülen wanted to pre-empt Saudi and Iranian influence in the region. As for Europe, there was already an existing Turkish Diaspora there and the movement quickly flourished as a result of this existing base. What is more, for Gülen, Turkey is the most important Muslim country in the Muslim world, with its history, Anatolian Muslimness and ability to bridge the East and West and therefore the movement has always been at the heart of the Muslim world from the very beginning. Pakistan, India, Indonesia, Malaysia, Egypt are some of the other Muslim countries where the movement is also now active.

The main reason why the movement has not, until recently, been active in Saudi and Iran is to do with these countries refusals. Saudi and Iran consider Turkey and Turkish-Islam as a threat to their Wahhabi and Shiite practices, respectively. It is widely known that both countries spend millions of dollars each year to convert Muslims to their Islamic outlooks through Islamic cultural centres, mosques, bookshops, student sponsorships etc.

However, none of this should be taken to mean that Gülen is not concerned with the Muslim world. My contention is that Gülen is seeking to mobilise and influence the Muslim and Arab world through the example and credibility the movement gains in the West. Gülen needs this credibility, since he is seeking to enter a resilient and, at times, hostile market

> Q: What do you say about the attitude: "Forget about Europe, and become the leader of the Muslim world in the East. You're not European anyhow."
>
> A: We have one side in common with Europe and one side in common with the Muslim world. *Our integration with Europe will necessarily bring the other.* (Emphasis added)[60]

The well-known Professor Akbar states in the Forward of *A Dialogue of Civilisations,* "[t]he size and effectiveness of the Gülen movement has grown exponentially over the past thirty years" and adds:

> While conducting a research project for the Brookings Institution entitled "Islam in the Age of Globalization" during the spring of 2006, I travelled to nine Muslim countries, and my research team and I were shown just how influential Fethullah Gülen has become. In an attempt to understand the "mind" of Muslims throughout the Muslim world, we prepared a questionnaire that asked direct personal questions to each participant. The questions posed attempted to gauge reactions towards the West and globalization. We found that many people are following those who seek to put barriers around Islam, and to exclude everything else, especially Western influence. This idea is rapidly gaining popularity across the Muslim world. In Turkey, however, we saw that the most popular contemporary role model was Fethullah Gülen, indicating to us the importance of his intellectual movement and also its potential as a countervailing force to ideas of exclusion that are gaining more traction within the Muslim world.[61]

It is this potential influence of Gülen in the Muslim world that we now turn to appraise.

Gülen's influence in Muslim world

As noted at the very beginning, human rights values are an intrinsic value in the Gülen discourse. For Gülen, human rights are an inalienable part of one's humanness. Gülen's ideas

---

60 Sevindi 1997: 189
61 Akbar 2007: Foreword

surrounding tolerance, acceptance of one another, pluralism, democracy and the West are all connected with human rights and human freedoms. Gülen's Anatolian Muslimness, in particular, is a conveyor of Sufi perception which is favourable to human rights discourse.

Thus, Gülen's influence in the Muslim world on human rights will not be as distinct as some would have thought at the beginning of this paper. Rather, it will part and parcel of the Gülen-package. In fact, as seen above, Gülen will not claim to be changing or influencing anything. That is why he has a greater chance of success. Instead, the movement will concentrate on schools, dialogue efforts, media and intellectual gatherings. In time, the Gülen *tajdid*, ethos and principles will permeate the Muslim world through the example of the movement.

This is in fact what is needed. The problem in the Muslim/Arab world is intricate, complex and deep rooted and no progress can be made on any front unless the solution is encapsulating, incremental and localised or locally driven. The problems that surround the practice of human rights in the Muslim world are vast and complex and cannot be tackled on its own. A wider approach that deals with the underlying cultural, economic, social and political dimensions of the problem is needed. An approach that is not reactive to the problems of the Muslim world, but is positive and proactive.

That is why the Gülen solution is significant. It seeks to empower and enable the common person through education and dialogue which challenges cultural perceptions and overcomes dogmas. It seeks to mobilise the individual and society towards achieving to become *insan-i kamil* which can only progress in a free, fair and just society. Since Gülen's goals and teachings are justified in traditional Islamic sources, they have no problem of legitimacy or authenticity. Just as Gülen's and the movement's efforts have helped strengthen the periphery in Turkey, my contention is that this will be replicated in the wider Muslim world. The pace of this influence naturally depends on the movement's presence in this region.

Since 2005, the Gülen movement have begun a new initiative in the form of an Arabic magazine, called *Hira*.[62] The magazine is published quarterly and includes topics such as religion, theology, culture, education, science and poetry and an editorial article by Gülen for each issue. The magazine is based in Istanbul and Cairo and draws writers from both Turkey and the Arab world. Contributors from the Arab world include very well known and respected writers and scholars. This is a new development; the only Gülen initiative that is exclusively dedicated to engage the Arab world. Clearly this is a medium through which Gülen is seeking to introduce the underlying dynamics of Anatolian Muslimness to the Arab world. The overall ethos of the magazine, reflect the Gülen emphasis and thinking of religion and society. Although the magazine does not engage in politics, its discussion of faith, religion and society will eventually help communicate Gülen's views on these issues. The challenge for the magazine is to catch and maintain the interest of the Arab youth. It is too early to assess whether it is achieving this.

The 12th Abant meeting, entitled 'Islam, the West and modernization', was held in Cairo over two days in February 2007.[63] Intellectuals, scholars and journalists from both countries took part in this two day-long platform. This was the first time the Gülen movement organised a significant conference in an Arab country. The event was co-organised by the prestigious Al Ashram centre for Political and Strategic Studies think tank which publishes a daily newspaper with a circulation of one million. The meeting in Cairo was entitled *Turkey-Egypt Talk I*, signalling that its mark the beginning of a series of events to be organised by the

---

62 http://www.herkul.org/yazarlar/index.php?view=article&article_id=2727.

63 http://www.gyv.org.tr/bpi.asp?caid=336&cid=874

Abant platform. The underlying objective of this meeting was to look at modernisation in the Muslim world; how to overcome common problems among Muslim societies; universal values such as human rights, democracy and rule of law and spreading these notions in the Muslim world through Muslim interpretation. The second of these meetings will be held in February 2008 in Istanbul and it is expected that leading universities from Egypt such as Al-Ezher and Seem University will take part.

Clearly it is very significant that this meeting was held in Cairo and can be taken as a further indication that Gülen is starting to slowly engage the Arab world. The fact that both *Hira* and this Abant meeting was based in Egypt is no coincidence. It is well known that both countries have good relations and share a long history together. Unlike, Saudi Arabia and Iran, Gülen speaks favourably about Egypt. Perhaps Egypt will serve as Gülen's springboard to the rest of the Arab world. If *Hira* and Abant are anything to go by, this certainly seems likely.

Given that the Gülen schools are not centrally coordinated, there is no verifiable data as to the exact number of schools in any given region. Recent estimates suggest six hundred schools in over a hundred countries[64]. The website for the 5th Turkish Language Olympics organised in Istanbul by the movement states that 550 contestants took part in the event in Istanbul from 100 different countries[65]. It is well known that all of these contestants were service-recipients of the Gülen movement in some capacity, often as a pupil in one of Gülen's schools. This confirms previous estimates regarding the number and span of Gülen schools.

The list of contestants from Muslim countries include: Afghanistan, Azerbaijan, Bangladesh, Bosnia-Herzegovina, Algeria, Chad, Indonesia, Ethiopia, Morocco, Philippines, Ghana, India, Iraq, Iran, Kazakhstan, Kyrgyzstan, Kosovo, Maldives, Malaysia, Mali, Egypt, Mongolia, Mozambique, Nigeria, Pakistan, Senegal, Syria, Tajikistan, Tunisia, Turkmenistan, Uganda, Jordan and Yemen. Of the 57 member states of the Organisation of the Islamic Conference, which includes all but a very few countries of Muslim population, the Gülen movement is active in approximately 42 of these. What is more, we know that some of these countries have more than just one school, for example there are seven each in Pakistan[66] and Yemen[67], six in Afghanistan[68], and three in Northern Iraq. Some of these we know about from the Internet[69] others from word of mouth. So at the very least, the Gülen movement is active in over forty Muslim countries; the more credible likelihood is that this activity involves at least one school if not more.

Clearly therefore, there is a Gülen presence in the Muslim world. What is lacking is the Middle East. Attentive readers will have noticed 'Iran' in the above-list of countries. During discussions with volunteers of the movement who have worked in the region, I was told that there are student-dormitories in Iran and in every major city of Saudi Arabia. Apparently, one purpose of these dormitories and hostels are to serve pilgrims. This is very signifi-cant. Conventional research and thinking on the movement has always maintained that the

---

64 Ref

65 http://www.turkceolimpiyatlari.org/

66 http://www.pakturk.org/

67 http://www.tissenior.com/

68 Abdullah Gülen (the then Foreign Secretary), attended the opening ceremony of the Afghan Turkish Girls school with a 1500 student capacity, in Kabul in February 2007. It was later reported that Mr Gul informed Margaret Becket (the then Foreign Secretary of Britain) of these schools and that she encouraged him to make these efforts known to the European leaders: http://www.zaman.com.tr/webapp-tr/haber.do?haberno=522069

69 There are a few websites that list some links to Gülen schools, such as http://www.turkokullari.net/index.php?option=com_weblinks&catid=14&Itemid=22

movement is non-existent in Iran and Saudi. My research suggests otherwise. Whether the movement will set up schools in Iran[70] and Saudi is another question, but they are certainly active there.

What is important to note at this juncture is the pace at which these schools and the span of the movement is growing. If we are to go by the Turkish Language Olympics, the number of countries taking part is growing at a phenomenal speed. In 2006, the number of countries that took part was 87, in 2007 this number reached to 100. Clearly, this is not a definitive estimation of growth, since a Gülen school may have chosen to only take part in 2007 despite being around in 2006. While this is quite possible in theory, it is unlikely in practice, given the importance Gülen places on these Olympics. In this respect, it would not be far off to suggest that the countries and schools that take part in these Olympics reflects the approximate size and scope of the Gülen movement in general and schools in particular.

Another indication of the Gülen movement's pace of growth, for example, is in the media industry. In 2006 there was two international TV stations, Samanyolu and Mehtap. In 2007, three more TV stations came on air: Samanyolu Haber, a 24 hour news channel; *Ebru*, an all-English TV channel based and broadcast from the U.S and finally *Yumurcak*, a children's TV channel. In 2007, Zaman, the movement's Turkish newspaper, became the highest circulating daily at an average of 650,000 copies. In 2006, the movement launched its first English daily newspaper, Today's Zaman which is already the highest selling English newspaper in Turkey.[71]

Gülen's books translated into Arabic include, the *Infinite Light*, a topic based commentary on Prophet Muhammad's life (pbuh); *Key Concepts in the Practice of Sufism*; *The Statue of our Souls – Revival in Islamic thought and action* and *'İrşad Ekseni'*.[72] Gülen's official website is accessible in twenty languages including Arabic, Persian and Urdu.

New Phase: Adolescence and the Muslim World

The founding of an international relief and development charity in 2004, called *"Kimse Yok mu?"* (Is There No One?), which seeks to alleviate suffering and poverty in the world, signals a new phase for the movement, a coming of adolescence. The ambit of this charity is not just the Muslim world but poverty in the South and suffering all over. The charity website explains the various national and international relief programmes and projects carried out by the charity. The charity first undertook national relief programmes and *ad hoc* relief efforts to alleviate poverty and help natural disaster victims (Agri 2004, Bingol 2005, Eastern Turkey 2007). From 2005 onwards, the charity began relief programmes abroad. In January 2005, the charity appealed for donations for the victims of the South Pacific earthquake. With funds collected, the charity provided water sanitation machinery, clothes, food and medical help and support to victims of the Ace province in Indonesia. In 2006[73] and 2007[74] the charity pro-

---

70 I was told that when the movement proposed opening a school in Iran, the Iranian authorities replied "give us the funds and we will open it for you".

71 http://www.Todays Zaman.com

72 Not translated into English

73 Following the 2006 eartquake in Asia, the charity built three tent-villages in Pakistan which accommodated approximately 5000 victims. The charity provided these villages with food and support for six months. The charity also presented the Pakistan authorities with a four million dollar cheque as relief aid to the victims of this earthquake. The charity also built ten pre-fabricated schools, each with a capacity for 350 students, and provided school material and equipment.

74 In 2007, the charity began a campaign entitled 'Hand in hand with the Palestinian and Lebanon People'. This

vided aid and support to Pakistan and Lebonan. The local Gülen institutes helped coordinate the aid and support in these countries.

The efforts of this charity vis-à-vis the Muslim world is important for two reasons: (i) the credibility it will provide the movement in the Muslim world, and (ii) the wider implications of the movement entering a phase of development. The charities efforts to date prove that the Muslim world is important to Gülen and the movement, and is an excellent way to win the "hearts and minds" of the Muslim people in the region. What is more, this is also an excellent means of raising the profile and visibility of the local Gülen movement in the region and use of their local experience and knowledge. Through such relief work, the Gülen movement is gaining the awareness, sympathy and support of the Muslims in the wider Muslim world, enhancing its prospects of success in this region.

The second point is that this relief charity demarcates very clearly a new phase in the development of the Gülen movement.

Crudely put for the purposes of this paper, until recently, the main focus of the movement has always been to build its own capability, credibility and capacity. In that sense, all works and projects were geared around winning over volunteers and support. These works in themselves were always charitable but one unchanging dimension was the contingent gain for the movement. One example is that all donations received would only go to a public cause organised directly by the movement itself. In this sense, the movement was still in its early developmental stage.

What this relief charity does, is clearly mark out what was slowly emerging anyway; that the movement has now entered a stage of adolescence where it undertakes more complex and burdensome projects which do not necessarily benefit the movement itself. The fact that the relief charity collects money from businessman in Turkey, often the same people who fund Gülen projects, and then donates that money to earthquake victims in Pakistan, despite the movement needing that money elsewhere, is a sign that the movement has now entered a new phase where it considers itself capable of making such a donation. Put differently, the Gülen movement's charitable works have moved to a whole new altruistic level defined by "need of society" as opposed to "gain for the movement."

In the past the movement was criticised for remaining indifferent to wider public issues like poverty and human right violations. It appears that Gülen and the movement were not so indifferent to these issues after all, but building the mechanisms through which a meaningful attempt of contribution towards a solution could be made.

I argue that this will mean a more active Gülen in the Muslim world and South. The movement will not only spread as it first did in Turkey, but do so with more authority and greater speed. The relief charity is a clear indication that the movement considers itself to be of sufficient maturity to attempt bigger and more complex issues and that it has turned its energies towards the Muslim world.

In summary therefore, the Gülen movement is clearly present in most parts of the Muslim world. The movement is obviously strongest in Turkey and the Turkic states. However, the movement has clearly moved well beyond this and is now active in approximately 42 Muslim countries. The movement is not so active in the Middle East for reasons more to do with these countries than to do with Gülen. Gülen and the movement have demonstrated that they are

---

involved sending food to Palestine (13 lorries) and Lebanon (14 lorries). The list of other international support programmes undertaken by the charity continues.

now turning their resources to the Muslim world. The *Hira* magazine, conference in Cairo and expanding schools in the Muslim world demonstrates this and proves that this is not just a Turkish movement.

Gülen's view concerning the Muslim world in general and the Middle East in particular has been that much of the non-Arab Muslim world still approaches Turkey with affinity and as their natural leader given the Ottoman past. This "subconscious affinity and acceptance" is significant for Gülen as shown by his repeated repetition of this. I contend that Gülen is now seeking to cash that subconscious credit in the Muslim world. Given that the problems in the Muslim world are complex, deep rooted and intricate and that there is –to some extent- an Arab and Iranian resistance to Turkey, the Turkish-model and the Gülen movement, Gülen has sought to build leadership in the Turkic world and credibility in the West before attempting to permeate the Middle East. That attempt is well underway and I predict a growing number of schools, periodicals, newspapers and eventually TV channel in the Middle East in the next 10 years. Through *Today's Zaman* discussions are already underway with Arab counterparts.

Conclusion

This paper argues that Gülen's infuence is transferable to the wider Muslim world, given its underlying dynamics and nature. The scope and depth of this influence depends on the presence and activity of the movement in this region. All research indicates that the movement is now investing greater energy in the Muslim world, whether through *Hira*, book publications or a growing number of schools.

The movement introduces Gülen's philosophy, views and *tajdid* to the Muslim world through its example. Gülen's *tajdid* proves itself to be adaptable, flexible, durable and practical. Most importantly, it is collectively constructed, based on action and conduct and spread among the grass roots of society. In this way, it lends itself to localisation and indigenisation providing it with a greater chance of success in the Muslim world. An ever-present underlying streak in Gülen's *tajdid* and discourse are human rights values. This is significant since it means Gülen's views, of themselves, promote human rights values by default. Gülen's views are spread through the example of the movement. This is best illustrated in the movement's dialogue activities among Muslims. These activities usher in Gülen's dialogue theology and Anatolian Muslimness. Anatolian Muslimness is Gülen's perception of Islam, which gives prominence to Sufi perception, love, tolerance, forgiveness and peace. Gülen would say that this is Islam in itself. I suggest that Gülen is promoting Anatolian Muslimness among Muslims to fine-tune the rigid, conformist and literal Muslimness in practice in some parts of the Muslim world today. This is significant for the development of human rights values in the Muslim world.

What is more, Gülen promotes human rights directly by internalising democracy, human rights, freedom of belief, pluralism and Anglo-Saxon-style secularism. It is well known among human right lawyers and academics that democracy and pluralism are considered the prerequisites for the enjoyment of human rights. Where there is antagonism towards either, there can never be the enjoyment of the former. Furthermore, by de-politising Islam and replacing the theological support for an Islamic state or theocratic governance with respect for rule of law, elections and other fundamental principles as noted above, Gülen is directly promoting human rights through Islam, or because of Islam. His incremental *ijtihad* –ongoing– on change of religion in Islam is significant in this respect.

The net effect of Gülen's efforts has been to contribute to a new type of Muslim in Turkey, who while a strong believer supports democracy, pluralism and human rights because of his faith not despite it. This has helped strengthen the silent and significant periphery in Turkey, who are now constructively participating in Turkey's public life and contesting for centre ground.

By tracing the movement's presence and growth in the Muslim world, this paper suggests that a similar effect will take place in this world as well. The movement's relief charity proves that the Muslim world is important to Gülen and that the movement has now entered a new phase of adolescence where it is undertaking wider social and more complex issues. One of these, I suggest, is enabling the civil society of the Muslim world. The growing activity and schools in this region bolsters this point further. This runs contrary to conventional thinking on the movement to date, which suggests that the Muslim world is not significant to Gülen. I argue that the Muslim world has always been central to Gülen's vision of an inclusive civilisation but practicality as opposed to philosophy prevented greater prominence to this region. What is more, the strong and resilient Arab culture against a Turkish model could only be countered through significant credibility. I argue that the movement now possesses that credibility through it works and activities in the rest of the world and is now seeking to make use of it in the Muslim world. Based on the movement's project so far and a long history of good relations, it is very likely that Egypt will serve as the springboard to the movement's wider activity in the Middle East.

The fact that Turkey's profile has been on a steady rise in the Muslim world in recent years will only add pace to the movement's efforts here. In time, and as in Turkey, that will lead to a change of culture, perception and mood on points pertinent to human rights enjoyment and contribute to a wider debate in the Muslim world on developing an internally meaningful and effective and externally coherent and consistent set of human right norms and laws.

BIBLIOGRAPHY

Abbas, Tahir (ed) (2005) Muslim Britain: Communities under Pressure (London, Zed Books)

Abbas, Tahir (ed) (2007) Islamic Political Radicalism: A European Perspective (Edinburgh, Edinburgh University Press)

Abd al-Razzaq (1970-72) al-Musannaf, ed Habib al-Rahman al-A'zami (Beirut, 1970-72) 11:105.

Abel, T. & William C. (1993) Lifestyle or Lebensfuhrung? Critical Remarks on the Mistranslation of Werber's "Class, Status, Party", The Sociological Quarterly, 34, 3, 551-556

Abu Dawud. Sunen.

Abu Zayd, Nasr (2006) Reformation of Islamic Thought: A Critical Historical Analysis, Amsterdam, Amsterdam University Press.

Abu-Nimer Mohammed (2003) Non-Violence and Peace Building in Islam: Theory and Practice, University Press of Florida.

Abu-Rabi, Ibrahim (ed) (2003) Islam at the Crossroads. On the Life and Thought of Bediuzzaman Said Nursi. Albany, NY: State University of New York Press.

Ackerly, Brooke (1997) What's in a Design? The Effects of NGO Programme Delivery Choices on Women's Empowerment in Bangladesh, in: Anne Marie Goetz (Ed) Getting Institutions Right for Women in Development (London: Zed Books)

Afsaruddin, Asma (2005) "The Philosophy of Islamic Education: Classical Views and M. Fethullah Gulen's Perspectives", Conference Paper: Islam in the contemporary World: The Fethullah Gulen Movement in Thought and Practice, November 2005, Rice University, Houston. pp. 1-26.

Agai, Bekim (2002) "Fethullah Gulen and his Movement's Islamic Ethic of Education". Critique: Critical Middle Eastern Studies, 11(1) 27-47.

Agai, Bekim (2003a) "The Gulen movement's Islamic ethic of education", in: H. Yavuz & J. Esposito (eds) Turkish Islam and the Secular State: The Gulen Movement (Syracuse, New York, Syracuse University Press) 48-68.

Agai, Bekim (2003b) The education-network of Fethullah Gulen: the flexible implementation of modern Islamic thought. A comparison of three countries. Ruhr-Universität Bochum.

Agai, Bekim (2004) Zwischen Netzwerk und Diskurs. Das Bildungsnetzwerk um Fethullah Gulen" (geb. 1938): Die Flexible Umsetzung Modernen Islamischen Gedankenguts (Hamburg, EB-Verlag)

Agai, Bekim (2005) Discursive and Organizational Strategies of the Gulen Movement, Islam in Contemporary World: The Fethullah Gulen Movement, article présenté dans le Rice University,

Nov 12-13.

Agai, Bekim (2007) "Islam and Education in Secular Turkey: State Policies and the emergence of the Fethullah Gulen Group" in Robert W. Hefner & Muhammad Qasim Zaman [eds] Schooling Islam. The Culture and Politics of Modern Muslim Education. Princeton, Princeton University Press, 2007.

Ahmed, Akbar S. (2005) "Islam and the West: Clash or Dialogue of Civilizations?" in: R. Boase (Ed) Islam and Global Dialogue: Religious Pluralism and the Pursuit of Peace (Hants, England, Ashgate) 119-129.

Ahmed, Akbar S. (2007) Journey into Islam: The Crisis of Globalization, Washington, D.C.: Brookings Institution Press.

AK Parti (2002) Parti Programı. N.p.: AK Parti.

AK Parti (N.D) Siyasal Kimlik. N.p.: AK Parti.

Akdoğan, Yalçın (2003) Muhafazakar Demokrasi. Ankara: AK Parti.

Akman, N. (1995) "I feel extremely uncomfortable. I don't have such a principle". Sabah, January 23–30.

Akman, N. (1995) "Interview". Nokta, February 5–11, 16–18.

Akman, N. (2003) "Gulen Suggests Non-violent Options to Young Activists". An Interview with Elisabeth Özdalga. Zaman, June 10. Available from: <www.zaman.com/default.php?kn=2656>

Akman, N. (2004) Gurbette Fethullah Gulen, Zaman Kitap: Istanbul.

Aktan, Hamza (2004) 'Acts of Terror and Suicide Attacks in the Light of the Qur'an and the Sunna', An Islamic Perspective: Terror and Suicide Attacks, New Jersey: Light Pb, 26

Aktay, M. Hakan (2003) "Islam in the Public Square: The Case of the Nur Movement," in Turkish Islam and the Secular State (ed by M. Hakan Yavuz, John L. Esposito) Syracuse University Press, 2003, p. 11

Aktay, Yasin (1997) Body, Text, Identity: The Islamist Discourse of Authenticity in Modern Turkey, PhD Thesis, 1997, The Graduate School Of Social Sciences of the Middle East Technical University, Ankara

Aktay, Yasin (1999) Turk Dininin Sosyolojik Imkani – Islam Protestanligi ve Alevilik, Iletisim Yayinlari: Istanbul

Aktay, Yasin (2003) "Diaspora and Stability: Constitutive Elements in a Body of Knowledge," in Turkish Islam and the Secular State: The Gulen Movement (Syracuse, NY: Syracuse University Press) edited by M. Hakan Yavuz and John L. Esposito, pp. 131-54.

Akyol, Taha (1999) Osmanlı'da ve İran'da Mezhep ve Devlet Istanbul: Milliyet Yayınları, 1999.

Alam, F. (2006) Blame it on the Burka. Catalyst: Debating Race, Identity, Culture and Citizenship, 20.11.2006 electronically published at: http://www.catalystmagazine.org/Default.aspx.LocID-0hgnew0n2.RefLocID-0hg01b00100k.Lang-EN.htm.

Alan, Yusuf (2005) Lisan ve Insan [Language and Human], Istanbul: Kaynak.

Albayrak, Ismail (2007a) 'Islam and Terror: From the Perspective of Fethullah Gulen', http://en.fgulen.com/content/view/2243/4/, accessed on 14 August 2007

Albayrak, Ismail (2007b) "The Juxtaposition of Islam and Violence", in: Robert A. Hunt & Yüksel A. Aslandoğan (Eds) Muslim Citizens of the Globalized World: Contributions of the Gulen Movement (Houston, The Light) pp. 133-145.

Ali, A H (2005) "Islam and the EU's Identity Deficit", Brown Journal of World Affairs, Summer/ Fall

2005, Volume XII, Issue 1, p.57.

Ali, A.Y. (2007) "The Meaning of the Holy Qur'an," Amana Publications, MD, 2004, Unal, A., The Qur'an with Annotated Interpretation in Modern English, The Light Inc., NJ 2007.

Aliriza, B. (2000) "Turkey's Winter of Discontent", CSIS Report, December 5. Washington, DC, CSIS–Center for Strategic and International Studies, 1–5.

Aliriza, B. (2001) Turkey's Crisis: Corruption at the Core. CSIS Report, March 5. Washington, DC, CSIS–Center for Strategic and International Studies, 1–5.

Allen, C. and Nielsen, J. (2002) Summary Report on Islamophobia in the EU after 11 September 2001 (Vienna, European Monitoring Centre on Racism and Xenophobia)

Allievi, S. (2003) "Sociology of a Newcomer: Muslim Migration to Italy - Religious Visibility, Cultural and Political Reactions", Immigrants & Minorities, Vol.22, Issue 2&3, July/November 2003, p. 142

Almond, G.; Verba, S (1989) The Civic Culture: Political Attitudes and Democracy in Five Nations, Sage.

Alpay, Şahin (1995a) Religion and Politics. Milliyet, February 18.

Alpay, Sahin (1995b) Respect for Hodjaefendi. Milliyet, 29th July.

Alpay, Şahin (2007) Secularism without Democracy is an Illusion. Today's Zaman, April 30. Available from: <www.todayszaman.com/tz-web/yazarDetay.do?haberno=109792>

Altunoğlu, Ebru (1999) Fethullah Gulen's Perception of State and Society, thesis submitted to the Institute of Social Sciences in partial fulfilment of the requirements for the degree of Master of Arts in Political Science and International Relations, Boğaziçi University, p.60

Andrea, Bernadette (2006) Women and Their Rights: Fethullah Gulen's Gloss on Lady Montagu's "Embassy" to the Ottoman Empire, in Robert A. Hunt, R. A. and Yüksel A. Aslandoğan, Y. A. (2006) Muslim Citizens of the Globalized World: Contributions of the Gulen Movement (Somerset N. J., The Light Inc.)

Andrew Silke (2001) 'Terrorism: an Action Plan', The Psychologist, Vol. 14 No. 11, pp. 580-81.

Andrews, A. (1994) The Concept of Sect and Denomination in Islam, Religion Today 9, 2, 6-10.

Anoushiravan Ehteshami (2004) "Islam, Muslim Polities and Democracy," Democratization, Volume 11 No 4, August, p. 93.

Antoun, Richard T. (2000) Civil Society, Tribal Process, and Change in Jordan: An Anthropological View. International Journal of Middle East Studies, vol. 32, no. 4 (November)

Anwar, M. (2005) 'Muslims in Britain: Issues, Policy and Practice' in T. Abbas (ed) Muslim Britain: Communities under Pressure (London: Zed Books)

Anwar, M., Blaschke, J., Sander, A. (et al) (2004) State Policies towards Muslim Minorities: Sweden, Great Britain and Germany, Berlin: Verlagsabteilung im Europäischen Migrationszentrum (EMZ)

Apay, A. (2003) "Turkish Higher Education Initiatives toward Central Asia," in In Stephen P. Heyneman and Alan J. De Young (eds) The Challenges of Education in Central Asia. Charlotte, NC: information Age Publishing.

Appollonia, A. Ch. d' (1996) Les morales de l'autre: les identités nationales, in: B. Badie (Ed) L'Autre: études réunies par Alfred Grosser (Paris, Presses de Sciences Politiques) 137-150.

Aral, Berdal (2001) "Dispensing with Tradition?: The Özal Decade, 1983-1993," Middle Eastern Studies, Vol. 37, No 1 (January 2001) pp. 72-88.

Aras, Bulen (1998) Turkish Islam's Moderate Face, Middle East Quarterly, 5(3)

Aras, Bulent and Omer Caha (2000) "Fethullah Gulen and his liberal 'Turkish Islam' movement". Middle East Review of International Affairs Journal online 4(4) 30-42. www.meria.idc.ac.il/journal/2000/issue4/jv4n4a4

Arendt, Hannah (1978) The Life of the Mind, vol 1, London, Secker & Warburg.

Aristotle (1984) Politics and the Constitution of Athens (Cambridge, UK: Cambridge University Press)

Arkoun M. (1970) Contribution à l'étude de l'humanisme arabe au IV/Xe siècle (Contribution to the Study of Arab Humanism in the 4th-10th Centuries) Paris, Vrin, 1970

Arkoun, M. (2006) Within the Limits of Western Historical Boundaries, in Said, A.A., Abu-Nimer, M and Sharify-Funk, M. (eds) Contemporary Islam: Dynamic, not Static (Abingdon, Routledge)

Armstrong, Karen (2000) Islam: A short History, New York: Modern Library, 88.

Arslan, M. (2001) The Work Ethic Values of Protestant British, Catholic Irish and

Asad, Muhammad (1980) Message of the Quran, New York, New Era Pubns 1980 ed

Asad, Talal (1993) Genealogies of Religion-Disciplines and reasons of power in Christianity and Islam, The Johns Hopkins University Press: London.

Asad, Talal (2003) Formations of the Secular. Christianity, Islam, Modernity, Stanford University Press, Stanford, California.

Aslan, Adnan (1998) Religious Pluralism in Christian and Islamic Philosophy, Surrey: Curzon Press.

Aslandoğan, Y. A. & Çetin, Muhammed (2006) "The Educational Philosophy of Gulen in Thought and Practice", in Robert A. Hunt & Yüksel A. Aslandoğan (Eds) Muslim Citizens of the Globalized World: Contributions of the Gulen Movement (New Jersey, The Light) 31-54.

Aslandoğan, Y. A. (2007) Preface. In: Hunt, R. A. & Aslandoğan, Y. A., vii-ix.

Ataman, M. (2002) "Leadership Change: Özal Leadership and Restructuring in Turkish Foreign Policy". Alternatives: Turkish Journal of International Relations, 1(1) 120–153. Available from: <www.alternativesjournal.net/volume1/number1/ataman.pdf> [February 10, 2006, 14:18]

Atari, A.T.M (2000) "Christian "service-servant" and Islamic "Khilafah": Emerging models in educational administration." The American journal of Islamic Social Sciences, 17(2) 2000.

Atasoy, Yildiz (2005) Turkey, Islamists and Democracy . London: I. B. Taurus.

Ates, T., E. Karakas & I. Ortayli (2005) (eds) Baris Kopruleri: Dunyaya Acilan Turk Okullari – I [Peace Bridges. To the World Opening Turkish Schools – I]. Istanbul: Ufuk Books, Da Publishing.

Attas, Muhammad Naquib Syed Al- (1997) The Concept of Education in Islam, Kuala Lumpur, Library of Islam.

Axelrod, R. (1984) The Evolution of Cooperation. New York: Basic Books.

Aydın, Ali İhsan (2004) Dynamiques religieuses et logiques éducatives : Les Centres d'éducation du mouvement de Fethullah Gulen en France, Unpublished thesis, Institut d'Etudes Politiques de Strasbourg, Strasbourg,

Aydin, M. (1996) "Turkey and Central Asia: Challenges of Change" Central Asian Survey, Vol. 15, No. 2,

Ayoub, M. (2007) A Muslim View of Christianity: Essays on Dialogue/Edited by I.A.Omar (Maryknoll, NY, Orbis Books)

Azra, A. (2006) "Pluralism, Coexistence and Religious Harmony in Southeast Asia", in Abdul Aziz Said, Mohammed Abu-Nimer, and Meena Sharify-Funk (eds) Contemporary Islam: Dynamic, not Static (Abingdon, Routledge) 227-241.

Azyumardi, Azra (1999) "Partai Islam Tidak Prospektif", in: Hamid Basyaib & Hamid Abidin (Eds) Mengapa Partai Islam Kalah? (Jakarta, Alvabet) 307-310.

Azzam, Abd al-Rahman (1993) The Eternal Message of Muhammad. Leicester: The Islamic Texts Society.

Babahan, E. (2006) Andiç Günü. Sabah, 10 May 2006.

Baccot, Juliette (1968) On G'nur et Cay à O Russey: syncrétisme réligieux dans un village cham du Cambodge (Paris, Faculté des Lettres et Sciences Humaines)

Bainton, Ronald (1960) Christian Attitudes toward War and Peace (Nashville and New York, 1960) 158;

Bakar, Osman (2005) "Gulen on Religion and Science: A Theological Perspective". The Muslim World 95:359-72.

Bakhtin, M. M. (1990) The Dialogic Imagination (Austin, University of Texas)

Baktir, M (1990) İslam'da İlk Eğitim Müessesesi: Ashab-ı Suffa (The First Educational Establishment in Islam: The Companions of Suffa) İstanbul, Timaş, 1990.

Bal, Idris (2000) Turkey's Relations with the West and the Turkic Republics: the Rise and Fall of the 'Turkish Model (Aldershot: Ashgate)

Balcı, Bayram (2003) "Fethullah Gulen's Missionary Schools in Central Asia and their Role in the Spreading of Turkism and Islam", Religion, State & Society, Vol. 31, No. 2, 2003 in Academic Resources on the Gulen Movement CD, www.GulenConference.org.uk, 2007.

Balcı, Bayram (2003) Missionnaires de l'Islam en Asie centrale: Les écoles turques de Fethullah Gulen, Maisonneuve & Larose,

Baloglu, Zekai (1990) Turkiye'de egitim sorunlar ver degisime yapisal uyum onileri, Istanbul, TUSIAD.

Bane, J. B, Coffin, B. & Higgins, R. (2005) Introduction. In: Bane, J. B, Coffin, B. & Higgins, R (Eds) Taking Religion Seriously. Cambridge: Harvard University Press.2-17.

Baran, Z. (ed) (2004) Understanding Sufism and its Potential Role in US Policy, Nixon Center Conference Report, Washington, D.C.

Barber Benjamin (1996) Jihad vs. McWorld, New York: Ballantine Books.

Barker, E. (1982) New Religious Movements: A Perspective for Understanding Society. Lampeter: Edwin Mellen Press.

Barker, E. (1990) New Religious Movements: A Practical Introduction, London: Home Office.

Barker, E. (2002) Introducing New Religious Movements, Fathom Knowledge Network. Available from: www.fathom.com/feature/121938 [May 1, 2006, 11.11]

Barks, C. (1995) The Essential Rumi, San Francisco: Harper.

Barlas, A. (2006) "Reviving Islamic Universalism: East/s, West/s, and Coexistance", in Said, A.A., Abu-Nimer, M and Sharify-Funk, M. (eds) Contemporary Islam: Dynamic, not Static (Abingdon, Routledge)

Barnes Michael S. J. (2002) Theology and the Dialogue of Religions, Cambridge: Cambridge University Press.

Barton, Greg (2005) "Progressive Islamic Thought, Civil Society and the Gulen movement" in the National Context: Parallels with Indonesia (Paper presented at the Conference on Islam in the Contemporary World: The Fethullah Gulen movement in thought and practice, Rice University Houston)

Barton, Greg (2006) "Turkey's Gulen hizmet and Indonesia's neo-modernist NGOs; remarkable examples of progressive Islamic thought and civil society activism in the Muslim world", in Fethi Mansouri and Shahram Akbarzadeh (eds) Political Islam and Human Security, Newcastle: Cambridge Scholars Press, p.140-160.

Baskan, Filiz (2004) "The Political Economy of Islamic Finance in Turkey: The Role of Fethullah Gulen and Asya Finans" in The Politics of Islamic Finances. Edited by Clement M. Henry and Rodney Wilson. Edinburg University Press.

Baskan, Filiz (2005) 'The Fethullah Gulen Community: Contribution or Barrier to the Consolidation of Democracy in Turkey?' Middle Eastern Studies, Vol. 41, No. 6 (November 2005) pp. 849 – 861.

Bastenier, Albert (1998) L'incidence du facteur religieux dans la conscience ethnique des immigres marocains en Belgique", Social Compass, 45 (2) ,

Bastian, Adolf (2005) A Journey in Cambodia and Cochin-China (1864) (Bangkok, White Lotus Press)

Başyurt, Erhan (2004) "Gerçekleşmesi Zor Bir Hayal: Euro–İslam." Aksiyon 09/2004

Bayat, A. (2005) Islamism and Social Movement Theory. Third World Quarterly, 26(6) 891–908.

Baycigitov, N. (2007) Taza Tabiat – Den Sooluk Kepili, Kirgiz Tuusu, Bishkek, Kyrgyzstan

Baydar, Y. (2007) "In the Heart of Africa, a meeting of Minds", Today's Zaman, 2.

Baym, N. K. (2000) Tune in, log on: Soaps, fandom, and online community. Thousand Oaks: CA: Sage.

Bayramoğlu, A. (1995) Yeni Yuzyil. 26 August, Turkey.

BBC (2000) Army Chief Demands Islamist Purge. August 31.

Beaugrande, R. de & W. Dressler (1981) Introduction to Text linguistics, London: Longman.

Beckerlegge, G. (ed) (2001) World Religions Reader 2nd ed (London and NY, Routledge)

Beckford, James (2000) "Religious Movements and Globalization," In Global Social Movements, edited by Robin Cohen and Shirin M. Rai (New Brunswick, NJ: Athlone Press, 2000)

Bell, D. (1977) "The Return of the Sacred? The argument on the future of religion", British Journal of Sociology, Vol. 28, No. 4. 419-449.

Benard, C. (2003) Civil Democratic Islam, Partners, Resources, and Strategies. VA: RAND Corporation, pp.88. Available from: <www.rand.org/publications/MR/MR1716/MR1716.pdf> [October 4, 2005, 11:50]

Bennett, C. (2005) Muslims and Modernity: An Introduction to the Issues and the Debates, (London, Continuum)

Bennis, P. (2003) Before & After. U.S. Foreign Policy and the September 11th Crisis (NY, Olive Branch Press)

Berberoglu, E. (2000) Hurriyet (Turkish daily) 10 August 2000.

Berger, P. L & Hefner, W. R. (2003) Spiritual Capital in Comparative Perspective, Unpublished paper. available at http://www.metanexus.net/spiritual%5Fcapital/pdf/Berger.pdf

Berger, P. L. (1999) The Desecularization of the World: A Global Overview. in: Peter L. Berger (ed) The Desecularization of the World, Resurgent Religion in World Politics. Washington: Ethics and Public Policy Center.1-18.

Berlin, Isaiah (1958) Two Concepts of Liberty (Oxford, Oxford University Press,) John Gray, "The Case for Decency (2006) The New York Review of Books , July 13, LIII, No. 12, 20-22.

Bernstein, Mary (1997) "Celebration and Suppression: The Strategic Uses of Identity by the Lesbian and Gay Movement." American Journal of Sociology 103: 531-65.

Bhaskar, R. (1978) A Realist Theory of Science (London, Harvester Press)

Bienséance et "impudeur": les physiognomonies au XVe et XVIIe siècle".

Bilici, Abdülhamit (ed) (2006) Neden Türkiye? Why Turkey? Istanbul: Zaman.

Bilici, Mucahit (2006) "The Fethullah Gulen Movement and Its Politics of Representation in Turkey". The Muslim World, 96, 1-20.

Bilici, Mücahit (2000) "İslam'ın Bronzlaşan Yüzü: Caprice Hotel Örnek Olayı [Tanning Face of Islam: The Case of the Caprice Hotel," In İslam'ın Yeni Kamusal Yüzleri [New Public Faces of Islam], edited by Nilüfer Göle (İstanbul: Metis,)

Bilir, Ünal (2004) "'Turkey-Islam': Recipe for Success or Hindrance to the Integration of the Turkish Diaspora Community in Germany" Journal of Muslim Minority Affairs (24, #2, Oct.): 259-283.

BJØRGO, Tore, Yngve Carlsson, Thomas Haaland (2007) 'Hate Crime or Gang Conflict? Violence between Youth Group in a Norwegian City', at http://www.fpvv.uni-mb.si/conf2004/papers/bjorgo.pdf, accessed on 24 May 2007

Blair, Tony (2007) Speech to the Los Angeles World Affairs Council. 1.8.2006. http://www.number-10.gov.uk/output/Page9948.asp

Boase, R. (2005) Ecumenical Islam: A Muslim Response to Religious Pluralism, in: R. Boase (Ed) Islam and Global Dialogue: Religious Pluralism and the Pursuit of Peace (Hants, England, Ashgate) 247-265.

Boix, Carles (2004) 'Political Violence', Paper prepared for the Yale Conference on: Order, Conflict and Violence, April 30th-May 1st, 2004.

Bonner, Arthur (2004) An Islamic Reformation in Turkey in Middle East Policy, Vol. 11, No. 1, p. 84

Bourdieu, Pierre (1980) Le Sens Pratique, Paris, Minuit.

Bourdieu, Pierre (1983) "Ökonomisches Kapital, kulturelles Kapital, soziales Kapital". In: Reinhard Kreckel (ed) Soziale Ungleichheiten (Soziale Welt, Sonderheft 2) (Goettingen: Otto Schartz & Co.) 183-98.

Bourdieu, Pierre (2003) Les Méditations Pascaliennes, Paris, Folio Editions, 2003

Bouzar, Dounia (2003) « L'islam entre mythe et religion : le nouveau discours religieux dans les associations socio-culturelles musulmanes », Les Cahiers de la sécurité intérieure, n°54, 2003

Bozarslan, Hamit (2004) "Islam, laïcité et la question d'autorité dans l'Empire ottoman et en Turquie kémaliste." Archives des sciences sociales des religions (125): 99-113.

Bradley, Harriet (2005) "İlgisizlik ve Dışlanma", Londra Gazete, February17, 2005

Brewer, M.B. and R.M. Kramer (1986) "Choice Behavior in Social Dilemmas: Effects of Social Identity, Group Size, and Decision Framing." Journal of Personality and Social Psychology, Vol. 50, pp. 543-549.

Brien, S. O, R. Tay and B. Watson (2004) "Situational factors contributing to the expression of aggression on the roads", IATSS Research, 28 (1) 101-107.

Browers, Michaelle and Charles Kurzman (eds) (2004) An Islamic Reformation? (Oxford: Lexington Books, 2004)

Brown, Peter (1984) "Late Antiquity and Islam: Parallels and Contrasts", in Barbara Metcalf (ed) Moral Conduct. Berkeley: University of California Press.

Bruce, S. (1996) Religion in the Modern World from Cathedrals to Cults. Oxford: Oxford University Press

Bruckmayr, Philipp (2006) "The Cham Muslims of Cambodia: From Forgotten Minority to Focal Point of Islamic Internationalism", American Journal of Islamic Social Sciences, XXIII, 3, 1-23.

Bruckmayr, Philipp (2007) The Islamization of Champa (Wien, Universität Wien)

Bruckmayr, Philipp (forthcoming) "Cambodia's Phum Trea as mirror image of religious change". ISIM Review.

Buchanan, Bruce (1974) "Building Organizational Commitment: The Socialization of Managers in Work Organizations." Administrative Science Quarterly, Vol. 19, pp. 533-546.

Buğra, Ayşe (1999) Islam in Economic Organizations (Istanbul, TESEV)

Bulaç, A. (2007) "The Most Recent Reviver in the 'Ulama Tradition: The Intellectual 'Alim, Fethullah Gulen". In: Hunt, R. A. & Aslandoğan, Y. A. (2007) 101-20.

Bulaç, Ali (2000a) "Tarikat ve Cemaat", Zaman, 22.07

Bulaç, Ali (2000b) "Modern cemaatler"

Bulaç, Ali (2000c) "Cemaatin modern karakteri"

Bulaç, Ali (2000d) "Cemaat ve cemiyet"

Bulaç, Ali (2005) "Küresel Bir Açılım Olarak Türk Okulları [Turkish Schools as a Global Opening]," In Barış Köprüleri: Dünyaya Açılan Türk Okulları, [Bridges of Peace: Turkish Schools Opening to the World], edited by Toktamış Ateş, Eser Karakaş and İlber Ortaylı (İstanbul: Ufuk Kitap) pp. 181-98..

Bulac, Ali (2007) "Postmodern Coup," Today's Zaman, March 2.

Buzan, Barry, Ole Waever and Jaap de Wilde (1998) Security: A New Framework for

Byron, William J. (1997) "Living Generously in the Service of Others: Commitment, Responsibility, Virtue and Service". Vital Speeches of the Day, 63:31, 652-55.

Cabaton, Antoine (1906) "Notes sur l'Islam dans l'Indochine française". Revue du Monde Musulman, 1, 27-47.

Caha, Omer (2003) "Turkish Election of November 2002 and the Rise of 'Moderate' Political Islam." Alternatives: Turkish Journal of International Relations. 2: 95-116.

Cakir, Rusen (1997) Devlet Babanin Nurcu Oglu: Kirkinci Hoca, Arti Haber (Dec. 20.1997: 19)

Çakır, Ruşen, and İrfan Bozan (2005) Sivil, Şeffaf ve Demokratik Bir Diyanet İşleri Başkanlığı Mümkün mü? Istanbul: TESEV.

Cambodian Muslim Development Foundation (eds) (2004) CMDF serves the Muslim's community (Phnom Penh, CMDF)

Camcı, Selçuk and Dr. Kudret Ünal (ed) (1998) Fethullah Gulen'in Konuşma ve Yazılarında Hoşgörü ve Diyalog İklimi, Merkür Yayıları. İzmir, 1998, p.140

Can, E. (1997) Fethullah Gulen Hocaefendi ile Ufuk Turu [The Tour d'Horizon with Fethullah Gulen's Hocaefendi]. Istanbul: AD Publishing. (pp.33-34)

Can, S. (2005) Fundamentals of Rumi's Thought. A Mevlevi Sufi Perspective. NJ: The Light, Inc.

Canatan, Kadir (1997) Din ve Laiklik. Istanbul: İnsan Yayınları.

Cantori, Louis J. (2002) "The Dual Arab State and Islamic Radicalism", August 29,2002.

Cantori, Louis J. (2007) "Islamic Republicanism, Hamas and the Emergence of the Palestinian State", American Political Science Association, Chicago, August 29, 2007.

Çapan, E. (2005) (ed) Terror and Suicide Attacks. An Islamic Perspective. NJ: The Light, Inc.

Capan, E. (2007) (ed) Interfaith Dialogue in Islam. Legal and Historical Foundations. NJ: The Light,

Inc.

Cardona, P., B.S. Lawrence and P.M. Bentler (2004) "The Influence of Social and Work Exchange Relationships on Organizational Citizenship Behavior." Group and Organization Management, 29, pp. 219-247.

Çarkoglu, A. (1988) The Turkish Party System in Transition: Party Performance and Agenda Change. Political Studies, 46, 544–53.

Carol, Jill (2007) A Dialogue of Civilisation: Gulens Humanistic Ideals and Humanistic Discourse, The Light Inc.

Carothers, Thomas (1999) Civil Society: Think Again. Foreign Policy, no. 117.

Carr, P. (2000) The Age of Enterprise: The Emergence and Evolution of Entrepreneurial Management, Blackhall Publishing: Dublin, Ireland.

Carroll, Jill. (2007) A Dialogue of Civilizations: Gulen's Islamic Ideals and Humanistic Discourse. New Jersey: Light.

Cartwright, N. (1983/4) How the Laws of Physics Lie (Oxford, Clarendon Press)

Cartwright, N. (1994) "Fundamentalism vs. the Patchwork of Laws". Proceeding of the Aristotelian Society, Vol. XCIV, 279-292.

Casanova, Josâe (1994) Public Religions in the Modern World. Chicago: University of Chicago Press, 1994.

Casanova, Josâe (2001) "Civil Society and Religion: Retrospective Reflections on Catholicism and Prospective Reflections on Islam," p. 1074.

Cassidy, Edward and Idris Cardinal (2005) Ecumenism and Interreligious Dialogue. New York: Paulist Press.

Cavdar, Gamze (2006) "Islamist New Thinking in Turkey: A Model for Political Learning?" Political Science Quarterly. 121: 477-97.

Caymaz, Birol (2002) Les mouvements Islamiques Turcs à Paris, Paris, l'Harmattan.

Celik, Emre (2003) "Advocate of Dialogue: Fethullah Gulen". Paper presented to the Annual Conference of the AASR, July 2003.

Celik, G. & P. Valkenberg (2007) Gulen's approach to dialogue and peace. Its theoretical background and some practical perspectives. International Journal of Diversity in organisations, communities and nations. Volume 7.

Celik, G. & Y. Alan (2007) "Fethullah Gulen as a Servant Leader", International Journal of Servant-Leadership, Volume 3 (1) Spokane, WA: Gonzaga University.

Celik, G. (2007) Van Mevlana naar Fethullah Gulen: Voorlopers van Innerlijke Vrede [From Mevlana to Fethullah Gulen: Frontrunners of in inner peace]. Zaman Nederland, Rotterdam: TMG, 3(20):10-11.

Celik, G., et al. (2005) (eds) Voorlopers in de Vrede [Forerunners for peace]. Damon: Budel,

Cerrahoglu, N. (1995) Differences Should Not Lead to Separation. Interview with Prof. Dr. Ali Yasar Saribay. Milliyet, August 10.

Cesari, Jocelyne (1997) Etre musulman en France aujourd'hui, Paris, Hachette.

Cesari, Jocelyne (2002) "Islam in France: The Shaping of a Religious Minority", in Yvonne Yazbeck Haddad, ed, Muslims in the West: From Sojourners to Citizens, New York: Oxford University Press, p. 42

Cetin, Muhammed (2005) "Mobilization and Countermobilization: The Gulen Movement in Turkey.

Proceedings from Islam in the Contemporary World: The Fethullah Gulen Movement in Thought and Practice. Rice University, Houston, Texas.

Cetin, Muhammed (2006) "Voluntary Altruistic Action: Its Symbolic Challenge Against Sinecures of Vested Interests." Proceeding from Islam in the Contemporary World: The Fethullah Gulen Movement in Thought and Practice. Rice University, Houston, Texas.

Chadwick, Owen (2001) "The Anglican Perspective on Church Schools" in Oxford Review of Education, vol 27, no 4.

Chandler, David P. (2000) Brother Number One: A Political Biography of Pol Pot (Chiang Mai, Silkworm Books)

Chittick, William C. (1982) "The five divine presences: from al-Qunawi to al-Qaysari", Muslim World (72, 2): 107-128.

Chittick, William C. (2000) Sufism, A Short Introduction. Oxford: Oneworld Publications.

Chodkiewicz, Michel (1993) Seal of the Saints: Prophethood and Sainthood in the doctrine of Ibn `Arab'i Cambridge: Islamic Texts Society.

Chomsky, Noam (1987) On Power ad Ideology (The Managua Lectures 1986) South End Press, USA.

CIA Fact Book (2007) https://www.cia.gov/library/publications/the-world-factbook/print/kg.html

Cicero (1980) The Republic and The Laws, Translated from the Latin by Niall Rudd (Oxford, Oxford University Press)

Cinar, A. (2005) Modernity, Islam and Secularism in Turkey: Bodies, Places, and Time. Public Worlds, vol. 14. Minneapolis, London, University of Minnesota Press.

Cinar, Bekir (1997) Devlet Guvenligi, Istihbarat ve Terorizm (State Security, Intelligence and Terrorism) Sam Yayinlari: Ankara.

Cizre, Umit and Menderes Cinar (2003) "Turkey 2002: Kemalism, Islamism, and Politics in the Light of the February 28 Process." The South Atlantic Quarterly 102: 309-32.

Clark, Janine A. (1994) "Islamic Social-Welfare Organizations and the Legitimacy of the State in Egypt: Democratization or Islamization From Below?" unpublished PhD dissertation, University of Toronto, Canada.

Clement, Victoria (2004) "Rewriting the Turkmen 'Nation': Literacy, Education, and Power in Central Asia. PhD thesis.

Cochrane, F. and Dunn, S. (2002) People Power?: The Role of the Voluntary and Community Sector in the Northern Ireland Conflict. (Cork: Cork University Press)

Cohen, Jean L. (1985) "Strategy and Identity: New Theoretical Paradigms and Contemporary Social Movements." Social Research 52: 663-716.

Coleman, J. S. (1988) "Social Capital in the Creation of Human Capital", The American Journal of Sociology, Volume 94, Supplement. 95-120.

Collins, William (1996) The Chams of Cambodia (Phnom Penh, Center for Advanced Studies) Communication, Paris, Editions de Seuil, no. 47.

Cook, David (2005) Understanding Jihad (Berkeley, 2005).

Courtine, Jean - Jacques and Georges Vigarello (1999) "La physionomie de l homme impudique. Bienséances et impudeur : les physiognomonies au XVIe et au XVIIe siècle". In: Communications, vol. 46, Paris.

Crane, R.D. (2005) "From Clashing Civilizations to a Common Vision", in: R. Boase (Ed) Islam and Global Dialogue: Religious Pluralism and the Pursuit of Peace (Hants, England, Ashgate) 159-

177.

Creaser, James (1990) Liberal Democracy and Political Science (Baltimore, MD: Johns Hopkins University Press, 1990)

Creative Research Systems (2007) http://www.surveysystem.com/sscalc.htm

Cush, Denise D. (2003) 'Should the state fund 'schools with a religious character?' Resource, 25(2).

Daft R.C. (2000) Management, 5e, The Dreyden Press, Harcourt Brace College Publishers (USA)

Dağı, İhsan (1998) Kimlik, Söylem ve Siyaset: Doğu-Batı Ayrımında Refah Partisi Geleneği. Ankara: İmge Kitabevi.

Dağı, İhsan (2001) "Human Rights, Democratization, and the European Community in Turkish Politics: The Özal Years, 1983-1987," Middle Eastern Studies, Vol. 37, No 1 (2001)

Dağı, İhsan (2004) Rethinking Human Rights, Democracy and the West: Post-Islamist Intellectuals in Turkey?," Critique: Critical Middle Eastern Studies, Vol. 13, No 2 (2004)

Dağı, İhsan (2005) "Transformation of Islamic Political Identity in Turkey: Rethinking the West and Westernization," Turkish Studies, Vol. 6, No 1 (2005)

Dahl, Robert (1971) Polyarchy: Participation and Opposition (New Haven: Yale University Press)

Dallmayr Fred (2002) Dialogue Among Civilizations: Some Exemplary Voices, New York. Palgrave Macmillan.

Dallmayr Fred (2003) The Dignity of Difference: A Salute to Jonathan Sacks, Kroc Institute Occasional Paper # 24: OP:1

Dalrymple, W. (2005) "Of Saints and Sufis in the Near East: Past and Present", in: R. Boase (Ed) Islam and Global Dialogue: Religious Pluralism and the Pursuit of Peace (Hants, England, Ashgate) 91-101.

Dancy, J. (1981) "On Moral Properties". Mind, 90, 367-385.

Dancy, J. (1983) "Ethical Particularism and Morally Relevant Properties", Mind, 92, 530-547.

Dancy, J. (1985) "The Role of Imaginary Cases in Ethics". Pacific Philosophical Quarterly, 66,141-153.

Dancy, J. (1993) Moral Reasons (Oxford, Blackwell)

Dancy, J. (1999) "Defending Particularism", Metaphilosophy. 30, 25-32.

Dancy, J. (2000) "The Particularists Progress", in B. Hooker & M. O. Little (eds) Moral Particularism (Oxford, Oxford University Press) 130-156.

Dancy, J. (2001) "Moral Particularism", in Edward N. Zalta (ed) Stanford Encyclopedia of Philosophy, http://plato.stanford.edu/.

Dancy, J. (2004) Ethics Without Principles (Oxford, Clarendon Press)

Darsh, S. M. (1980) Islam in Europe, London: Ta-Ha Publishers, p. 51.

Davie, G. (1999) Europe: The Exception That Proves the Rule?. in: Peter L. Berger (ed) The Desecularization of the World, Resurgent Religion in World Politics, Washington: Ethics and Public Policy Center. 65-83.

Davie, G. (2000) Religion in Modern Europe: A Memory Mutates, Oxford: Oxford University Press

Davis, Gareth G. (1999) 'Repression, Rationality and Relative Deprivation; A theoretical and empirical examination of Cross-National Variations in Political Violence', http://economics.gmu.edu/working/WPE_99/99_04.pdf, accessed on 15 Mar. 07

Davison, Roderic H. (1954) "Turkish Attitudes Concerning Christian-Muslim Equality in the Nineteenth

Century", American Historical Review, Vol. 59, No. 4 (Jul., 1954) pp. 844-864

De Féo, Agnès (2004) Les Chams, l'islam et la revendication identitaire (Paris, Mémoire de DEA: EPHE IVe section)

De Féo, Agnès (2005a) "Les Chams sot, dissidence de l'islam cambodgien". Les Cahiers de l'Orient, 58, 115-124.

De Féo, Agnès (2005b) "Le royaume bouddhique face au renouveau islamique". Les Cahiers de l'Orient, 58, 99-114.

Della Porta, D. & Diani, M. (1999) Social Movements: An introduction. Oxford, Blackwell.

Delvert, Jean (1960) Le Paysan Cambodgien (Paris, Mouton)

Demir, C. E.; Balci, A.; Akkok, F. (2000) The role of Kyrgyz Turkish Schools in the educational system and social transformation of Central Asian countries: the case of Turkmenistan and Kyrgyzstan, Central Asian Survey, 19(1) 141-155.

Demir, H. (2004) "Hills Like White Elephants: Analysis according to Seven Standards of Text Linguistics" http://www.ingilish.com/hd7.htm

Demiralp, Seda and Eisenstadt, Todd A. (2006) Prisoner Erdagan's Dilemma and the Origins of Moderate Islam in Turkey (unpublished paper for the Center for Democracy and Election Management, available at http://au-dubai.org/ia/cdem/pdfs/case_study_2.pdf)

Denny Frederick M. (1977) "The Umma" Numen 24: 26-59.

Denny Frederick M. (1985) "Ethics in the Qur'an: Community and World View" in Ethics in Islam (ed) Richard G Hovannisian Pp. 103-121. Malibu: Undena.

Deringil, Selim (2000) "There Is No Compulsion in Religion": On Conversion and Apostasy in the Late Ottoman Empire: 1839–1861," Comparative Studies in Society and History 42: 547-575, Cambridge University Press.

Desai, M. (2007) Rethinking Islamism: The Ideology of The New Terror. London & N.Y., I.B. Tauris)

DfES (2001) Schools: Achieving Success White Paper, London, HMSO / DfES 2001.

DfES (2003a) Excellence and Enjoyment: A strategy for primary schools, London, HMSO / DfES 2003a.

DfES (2003b) Every Child Matters, London, HMSO / DfES 2003b.

Dialmy, Abdessamad (2007) "Belonging and Institution in Islam", Social Compass, 54 (1)

Dinç, A. (1998) Fethullah Gulen: Cevap veriyorum (trans. Claims and Answers in Aksiyon No. 183 (June 6) Available from: <http://en.fgulen.com/a.page/press/interview/a1216p5.html>

Doney, P.M., Cannon, J.P. and M.R. Mullen. (1998) "Understanding the Influence of National Culture on the Development of Trust." Academy of Management Review, 23, pp. 601-620.

Donner, Fred M. (1999) 'Muhammad and the Caliphate: Political History of the Islamic Empire up to the Mongol Conquest' in Esposito, ed, The Oxford History of Islam. OUP.

Dorronsoro, G. & Massicard, E. (2005) "Being a Member of Parliament in contemporary Turkey". European Journal of Turkish Studies, Thematic Issue No. 3, p.30.

Dumanli, E. (2006) "The Only Power that can Spoil the Insidious Plan in the Southeast". Zaman, March 31. Available from: http://zaman.com/?bl=columnistsandalt=andhn=31500

Duyvendak, Jan Willem and Marco G. Giugni. (1995) "Social Movement Types and Policy Domains." Pp. 82-110 in New Social Movements in Western Europe: A Comparative Analysis, Hanspeter Kriesi, Ruud Koopmans, Jan Willem Duyvendak, and Marco G. Giugni, eds, Minneapolis: University of Minnesota Press.

Ebu Davud.

Ecevit, Bülent (2005) "Türk Okullarının Türk Dili ve Türkiye'ye Katkısı [The Contributions of Turkish Schools to Turkey and Turkish Language]," In Barış Köprüleri: Dünyaya Açılan Türk Okulları, [Bridges of Peace: Turkish Schools Opening to the World], edited by Toktamış Ateş, Eser Karakaş and İlber Ortaylı (İstanbul: Ufuk Kitap, 2005) p. 25.

Eck Diana (1993) Encountering Gold: A Spiritual Journey from Bozeman to Banaras. Boston: Beacon Press.

Edgar, Adrienne (2005) Tribal Nation: The Making of Soviet Türkmenistan (Princeton: Princeton University

Eickelman Dale F. & Salvatore Armando (2002) The Public Sphere and Muslim identities, European Journal of Sociology 43, no. 1, 2002, 92-115.

Eickelman, Dale F. (1998) 'Inside the Islamic Reformation, Wilson Quarterly, Winter 1998, Vol. 22 Issue 1, p.80-90.

Eickelman, Dale F. (1999) "The Coming Transformation of the Muslim World", Middle East Review of International Affairs Vol. 3, No. 3 (September 1999) 78-81.

Elias, Norbert (1978) The History of Manners, Oxford, Blackwell.

Elsas, E. (1991) "Turkish Islamic Ideals of Education: Their Possible Function for Islamic Identity and Integration in Europe", in W.A.R. Shadid and P.S. van Koningsveld, eds, The Integration of Islam and Hinduism in Western Europe, Kampen: Kok Pharos Publishing House, p. 175

El-Zein, A. (2000) "Spiritual Consumption in the United States: the Rumi phenomenon", Islam and Christian-Muslim Relations, 11:1, 1 March 2000 , pp. 71-85.

Emre, Yunus (1999) The Drop That Became the Sea: Lyric Poems of Yunus Emre. K. Helminski, R. Algan, E. Helminski (trans). Shambhala Publications.

Epstein E. H.(1997) Globalization of Education - Globalization Theory, The Role of Education, http://education.stateuniversity.com/pages/2010/Globalization-Education.html

Erdoğan, L. (1995) Fethullah Gulen Hocaefendi: "Küçük Dünyam" (Fethullah Gulen Hocaefendi: "My Small World") İstanbul, AD Yayinlari.

Erdoğan, Mustafa (1999) "Religious Freedom in the Turkish Constitution." The Muslim World 89 377-388.

Erdoğan, Recep Tayyip (2004) "Keynote Speech." In International Symposium on Conservatism and Democracy. N.p.: AK Parti.

Ergene, E. (2005) Geleneğin Modern Çağa Tanıklığı (Tradition Bears Witness to the Modern Age) Istanbul, Yeni Akademi Yay.,.

Ergene, E. (2006) M. Fethullah Gulen and His Movement: A Common-Sense Approach to Religion and Modernity, (Accessed from F. Gulen.com 24.8.07)

Esposito, John L. (ed) (1999) The Oxford History of Islam. Oxford: Oxford University Press,.

Esposito, John L. (1999) "Clash of civilizations'? Contemporary images of Islam in the West". In: Muñoz, G.M. (ed) (1999): Islam, modernism and the West. Cultural and political relations at the end of the millennium. NJ: I.B. Tauris Publishers (pp.94-108)

Esposito, John L. (1999) The Islamic Threat: Myth or Reality? Oxford: Oxford University Press (Third Edition)

Esposito, John L. (2002) What Everyone Needs to Know About Islam. New York: Oxford University Press, 2002.

Esposito, John L. (2003a) The Oxford Dictionary of Islam (Oxford, Oxford University Press)

Esposito, John L. (2003b) Islam and Civil Society, in Esposito, J. L. and Burgat, F. (eds) Modernizing Islam: Religion in the Public Sphere in Europe and the Middle East. (London, Hurst and Company)

Esposito, John L. (2003c) 'Introduction: Modernizing Islam and Re-Islamization in Global Perspective' in J.L. Esposito and François Burgat (eds) Modernizing Islam: Religion in the Public Sphere in Europe and the Middle East (London: Hurst and Company)

Esposito, John L. and Hakan Yavuz (eds) (2003) Turkish Islam and the Secular State: The Gulen Movement, New York, Syracuse University Press.

Esposito, John L. and James P. Piscatori (1991) "Democratization and Islam," Middle East Journal, Volume 45 No 3 (Summer 1991) p. 436.

Esposito, John L. and John O. Voll (1996) Islam and Democracy (Oxford: Oxford University Press)

Europe Stability Initiative (2005) Islamic Calvinists: Change and Conservatism in Central Anatolia (Berlin/ Istanbul, www.esiweb.org)

Eyerman, Ron (2002) "Music in Movement: Cultural Politics and Old and New Social Movements." Qualitative Sociology 25: 443-58.

Eyerman, Ron (2006) "Performing Opposition or, How Social Movements Move." pp. 193-217 in Social Performance: Symbolic Action, Cultural Pragmatics, and Ritual, Jeffrey C. Alexander, Bernhard Giesen, and Jason L. Mast, eds, Cambridge: Cambridge University Press.

Eyerman, Ron and Andrew Jamison (1991) Social Movements: A Cognitive Approach. Penn: The Pennsylvania State University Press.

Fadiman, J. and Frager, R. (eds) (1997) Essential Sufism. New York: Harper-Collins.

Fadl, Khaled Abou El (1999) "The Rules of Killing at War; an Inquiry into Classical Sources," Muslim World 89 (1999): 144-57.

Fadl, Khaled Abou El (2004) Islam and the Challenge of Democracy (Princeton: Princeton University Press) See also Khaled Abou El Fadl, "Islam and the Challenge of Democratic Commitment," Fordham International Law Journal, Volume 27 No 4 (2003-2004) pp. 4-71.

Fakhry, Majid (1994) Ethical Theories in Islam, Leiden, E.J. Brill

Fearn, N. (2005) Philosophy – The Latest Answers to the Oldest Questions (London, Atlantic Books)

Feener, R. Michael (1998) "Notes towards the history of Qur'anic exegesis in Southeast Asia". Studia Islamika, V, 3, 47-76.

Feiler, Bruce (2002) Abraham: A Journey to the Heart of Three Faiths. New York: William Morrow, 2002.

Fekete, L. (2004) Anti-Muslim racism and the European security state. Race and Class, 46, 1, 3-29.

Feroz, Ahmad (1993) The Making of Modern Turkey, London: Routledge.

Fine, G.A. (1986) "Friendship in the Workplace." In V.J. Derlega B.A. Winstead (eds) Friendship and Social Interaction. New York: Springer-Verlag. Pp. 185-206.

Finke, R. (2003) Spiritual Capital: Definitions, Applications, and New Frontiers. Unpublished paper. available at http://www.metanexus.net/spiritual%5Fcapital/pdf/finke.pdf

Finlay, A. (2004) 'Introduction' in A. Finlay (ed) Nationalism and Multiculturalism: Irish identity, Citizenship and the Peace Process (London: Transaction Publishers)

Firestone, Reuven (1999) Jihad: The Origin of Holy War in Islam. Oxford.

Fitzgerald, M.L. & Borelli, J. (2006) Interfaith Dialogue: A Catholic View.

Flannery Austin O.P. (ed) (1996) Vatican Council II: Constitutions, Decrees, Declarations. Northport, NY: Costello Publishing

Forward, M. (1998) Faith in the Future? Islam and Postmodernity, in Ursula King (ed) Faith and Praxis in a Postmodern Age (London, Cassell)

Foucault, M. (1984) Histoire de la Sexualité, 3 volumes, Paris, Gallimard

Foucault, M. (1988) "Technologies of the Self" in Ethics: Subjectivity and Truth, London: Allan

Fountain (2002) 'Foreword' in M. Fethullah Gulen: Essays, Perspectives, Opinions (Rutherford: The Light)

Frager. R. (1997) Sufism and the Islamic Tradition. Personality and Personal Growth. Longman.

Franks, Jason (2006) 'Rethinking the Roots of Terrorism: Orthodox Terrorism Theory and Beyond', http://www.bisa.ac.uk/2006/pps/franks.pdf, accessed on 16 March 2007

Fukuyama, F. (2001) Social Capital, civil society and development. The Third World Quarterly. 22 (1) 7-20.

Fuller, G. E. (2004) Turkey's Strategic Model: Myths and Realities. The Washington Quarterly, 27(3) 51–64.

Furnham, A. (1990) The Protestant Work Ethic: The Psychology of Work-Related Beliefs and Behaviours, Routledge: London.

Gabrielli, F. "Adab", in E.I.

Gadher, D. (2007) The Battle for Hearts and Minds, The Sunday Times, July 8, 2007, p. 14

Galtung, Johan (1969) "Violence, Peace and Peace Research" in Journal of Peace Research, No. 3.

Gamson, William A. (1992) Talking Politics. Boston: Cambridge University Press.

Gardet, Louis (1991) "Djamâ'at" in Encyclopedia of Islam II, 411-3 Leiden: E.J. Brill.

Gatto, John Taylor (2005) Dumbing Us Down: The Hidden Curriculum of Compulsory Schooling.

Gaudeul, Jean-Marie (1990) Encounters and Clashes: Islam and Christianity in History. Rome: Pontifico Instituto di Studi Arabi e Islamici,.

Gay, Peter Ed Deism (1968) An Anthology (New York. NYC: Van Nostrand)

Gazeteciler ve Yazarlar Vakfı (1998) İslam ve Laiklik. Istanbul: Gazeteciler ve Yazarlar Vakfı.

Gazeteciler ve Yazarlar Vakfı (1999) Din, Devlet, Toplum. Istanbul: Gazeteciler ve Yazarlar Vakfı.

Gazeteciler ve Yazarlar Vakfı (2000) Abant Platformu: Din, Devlet ve Toplum (Gazeteciler ve Yazarlar Vakfi Yayinlari)

Gazeteciler ve Yazarlar Vakfı (2000) Demokratik Hukuk Devleti. Istanbul: Gazeteciler ve Yazarlar Vakfı.

Gazeteciler ve Yazarlar Vakfı (2001) Çoğulculuk ve Toplumsal Uzlaşma. Istanbul: Gazeteciler ve Yazarlar Vakfı.

Geaves, Ron (2005) Aspects of Islam, Washington D.C.: Georgetown University Press, 139.

Ghannouchi, Rached (1999) Muqarabat fi al-`ilmaniyya w'al-mujtam' al-madani [Papers on Secularism and Civil Society] (London: Maghreb Center for Research and Translation)

Ghazali, Abu Hamid Muhammad ibn Muhammad al- (1975) "The book of invocation," Ihya' 'ulum al-din, translated by Kojiro Nakamura as Ghazali on Prayer (Tokyo, 1975) 167.

Ghazali, Abu Hamid Muhammad ibn Muhammad al- (1995) T.J. Winter [Trans] On Disciplining the Soul and Breaking the Two Desires: The Revival of the Religious Sciences (Ihya Ulum Al-Din)

Cambridge, Islamic Texts Society.

Ghazali, Abu Hamid Muhammad ibn Muhammad al- (1998) T.J. Winter [Ed] T. Mayer [Translator] Letter to a Disciple: Ayyuha'l-Walad. Cambridge, Islamic Texts Society,.

Ghazali, Mohammad (1983) l'ethique du musulman, Paris: Al Qalam.

Giddens, A. (2001) Introduction in The Protestant Ethic and the Spirit of Capitalism, Routledge: London.

Gil'adi, Avner (1992) Children if Islam: Concepts of Childhood in Medieval Muslim Society, New York, St Martin's Press.

Giora, Eliraz (2004) Islam in Indonesia: Modernism, Radicalism, and the Middle East Dimension (Brighton, Sussex Academic Press)

Glaeser E. L., Ponzetto G.& Shleifer A. (2007) Why does Democracy need Education? Harvard University and NBER, http://www.people.fas.harvard.edu/~ponzetto/GPS.pdf

Goddard, Hugh (2002) "Islam and Democracy," The Political Quarterly, Volume 73 No 3 (2002) p. 6.

Godlas, A. (2000) What is Tasawwuf (Sufism)? Translation from Persian by the author.

Goffman (Erving) (1963) Stigma: Notes on the Management of Spoiled Identity, New York, Touchstone Books.

Gokalp, Ziya (1959) Turkish Nationalism and Western Civilisation, London, Allen & Unwin.

Gokcek, M. (2005) "Gulen and Sufism". Conference Proceedings, Islam in the contemporary world: The Fethullah Gulen Movement in Thought and Practice. Rice University Houston, Texas. pp.357-364.

Gokcek, M. (2006) Gulen and Sufism: A Historical Perspective. In Robert Hunt et al. (eds) Muslim Citizens of the Globalized World: Contributions of the Gulen Movemen,. New Jersey: The Light Inc.

Golder, Ben and George Williams (2004) 'What is Terrorism? Problems of Legal Definition', UNSW Law Journal, 27:2, 270.

Göle, Nilüfer (1994) "Towards an Autonomization of Politics and Civil Society in Turkey", in: Metin Heper (Ed) Politics in the Third Turkish Republic (Boulder: Westview Press)

Göle, Nilüfer (1995) "l'émergence du sujet islamique", in Penser le Sujet, Autour d'Alain

Gole, Nilüfer (1997) Secularism and Islamism in Turkey: The Making of Elites and Counter-Elites, Middle East Journal, 51(1)

Göle, Nilüfer (2000) Snapshots of Islamic Modernities. Daedalus 129 (1): 91-117.

Göle, Nilüfer and Ammann Ludwig (2006) Islam in Public: Turkey, Iran and Europe, Istanbul, , Bilgi University Press.

Goodwin, Jeff and James M. Jasper (1999) "Caught in a winding, snarling wine: the structural bias of political process theory." Sociological Forum 14: 27-54.

Gottesman, Evan (2002) Cambodia after the Khmer Rouge: Inside the Politics of Nation Building (New Haven, Yale University Press)

Gregory, Frank and Paul Wilkinson (2005) Riding Pillion for Tackling Terrorism is a high risk policy. London: Chatham House. ISP/NSC Briefing Paper 05/01.

Gruen, George E. (1999) "Defining Limits on Religious Expression in Public Institutions: The Turkish Crisis over Headscarves," The Jerusalem Letter, Jerusalem Center for Public Affairs, CIAO, Columbia International Affairs Online, at <http://www.ciaonet.org/pbei2/jcpa/grg01.html>, accessed May 2 2007.

Guazzone, Laura (1995) Islamism and Islamists in the Contemporary Arab World, in: Laura Guazzone (Ed) The Islamist Dilemma: The Political Role of Islamist Movements in the Contemporary Arab World (Reading: Ithaca Press)

Gulalp, Haldun (2001) Globalization and Political Islam: the Social Bases of Turkey's Welfare Party. International Journal of Eastern Studies, 33. 433-448.

Gulay, E.N. (2007) The Gulen Phenomenon: A Neo Sufi Challenge to Turkey's rival Elite?, Critique: Critical Middle Eastern Studies, Vol 16, No.1, 37-61, Spring 2007.

Gulen, M. Fethullah (1977) Altin Nesil [The Golden Generation]. Conference CD's. Istanbul: Nil.

Gulen, M. Fethullah (1978) 'Bu Ağlamayı Dindirmek İçin Yavru (For Stopping This Crying of Baby)' Sızıntı, Vol.1 No.1, pp.1-2.

Gulen, M. Fethullah (1982) Education from Cradle to Grave, Sızıntı, March 1981–June 1982, Issue No: 26-41.

Gulen, M. Fethullah (1985) "Mukaddes Göç [Sacred Emigration]," Sızıntı, Volume 7 No. 81 (October 1985)

Gulen, M. Fethullah (1990) Cağ ve Nesil [This Era and the Young Generation]. Izmir: T.O.V.

Gulen, M. Fethullah (1992) Truth through Colours Izmir, Nil.

Gulen, M. Fethullah (1993) Towards the Lost Paradise, London, Truestar

Gulen, M. Fethullah (1995) Fasildan Fasila (From Time to Time) 1 & 2 Izmir, Nil.

Gulen, M. Fethullah (1996a) Criteria or the Lights of the Way. Vol. 1. London: Truestar.

Gulen, M. Fethullah (1996b) Inancin Golgesinde. Vols. 1-2. Izmir: Nil.

Gulen, M. Fethullah (1996c) Prizma, vol.1, İzmir, Nil.

Gulen, M. Fethullah (1996d) Towards the Lost Paradise. London, UK, Truestar.

Gulen, M. Fethullah (1997a) Fatiha Uzerine Mulahazalar (Considerations on the Chapter Fatiha) (Izmir: Nil Yayinlari) 90-95.

Gulen, M. Fethullah (1997b) Prizma 2 (Prism 2) Izmir: Nil. "Dünden Bugüne Işık Evler" (Light Houses from Yesterday to Today) http://tr.fGulen.com/a.page/eserleri/prizma/perspektif/a696.html

Gulen, M. Fethullah (1997c) Understanding and Belief: The Essentials of the Islamic Faith, Izmir: Kaynak.

Gulen, M. Fethullah (1997d) Yitirilmis Cennete Dogru (Cag ve Nesil Serisi-3) (Izmir: Nil Yayinlari) p. 98.

Gulen, M. Fethullah (1998a) "Claims and Answers" Aksiyon, 06.06.1998, Claim #19.

Gulen, M. Fethullah (1998b) Criteria or Lights of the Way, Vol. 2, 12th Ed, Izmir: Nil, 59-61.

Gulen, M. Fethullah (1998c) Irsad Ekseni. İzmir: Nil.

Gulen, M. Fethullah (1998d) Message to the President of the Angels' Movement. Available from: <http://en.fgulen.com/a.page/press/messages/a970p2.html>

Gulen, M. Fethullah (1998e) Questions This Modern Age Puts to Islam. Izmir: Kaynak.

Gulen, M. Fethullah (1998f) Ruhumuzun Heykelini Dikerken (Izmir, Nil Publications)

Gulen, M. Fethullah (1999a) 'The Necessity of Interfaith Dialogue: A Muslim Approach', Speech given at the Parliament of the World's Religion, Capetown, 1-8 December 1999.

Gulen, M. Fethullah (1999b) Key Concepts in the Practice of Sufism (Fairfax, The Fountain)

Gulen, M. Fethullah (2000a) 'The Necessity of Interfaith Dialogue', The Fountain, Vol 3/31, July-September 2000, 4-9.

Gulen, M. Fethullah (2000b) "At the Threshold of a New Millennium. The Fountain 3(29) (January-March):7-8.

Gulen, M. Fethullah (2000c) "Buhran Ufku ve Beklentilerimiz [The Scope of Crisis and Our Expectations]," Işığın Göründüğü Ufuk [The Horizon that Light Appears] (İzmir: Nil, 2000)

Gulen, M. Fethullah (2000d) "Forgiveness", The Fountain 3 (April-June):4-5.

Gulen, M. Fethullah (2000e) Advocate of Dialogue. Compiled by Ali Unal and Alphonse Williams. Fairfax, VA. The Fountain Press.

Gulen, M. Fethullah (2000f) Criteria or Lights of the Way. London, UK, Truestar.

Gulen, M. Fethullah (2000g) Pearls of wisdom. Fairfax, VA: The Fountain.

Gulen, M. Fethullah (2000h) Status of our Souls: Revival in Islamic Thought & Activism New Jersey: Light

Gulen, M. Fethullah (2000i) The Necessity of Interfaith Dialogue: A Muslim Perspective, The Fountain, 3, 4-9.

Gulen, M. Fethullah (2000j) Essays, Perspectives, Opinions. Rutherford, NJ, The Light Inc.

Gulen, M. Fethullah (2001a) 'A Comparative Approach to Islam and Democracy', SAIS Review 21, no. 2. p. 133-8.

Gulen, M. Fethullah (2001b) 'Message on the latest Terrorist Attacks', New York Times, 12 September 2001.

Gulen, M. Fethullah (2001c) 'Real Muslims Cannot Be Terrorists', Turkish Daily News, September 19, 2001

Gulen, M. Fethullah (2001d) Prophet Muhammad: Aspects of His Life, trans. Ali Unal, Fairfax, Va.: The Fountain.

Gulen, M. Fethullah (2002a) "M. Fethullah Gulen and Education" in Essays, Perspectives and Opinions: M. Fethullah Gulen, 58-88, (Rutherford, Fountain)

Gulen, M. Fethullah (2002b) Essays, perspectives, opinions. Rutherford, NJ: The Light.

Gulen, M. Fethullah (2003a) 'Suicide Attacks Can not be Reconciled with the Universal Call of Islam', Zaman daily, 16 November 2003, available online in Turkish at http://tr.fgulen.com/content/view/3885/77/.

Gulen, M. Fethullah (2003b) "Altın Nesil" (Golden Generation) Conference 2 CDs. (1977) Istanbul: Nil Productions, 2003.

Gulen, M. Fethullah (2003c) Işığın Görüngüğü Ufuk (The Horizon of Light) (Çag ve Nesil-7) Istanbul: Nil..

Gulen, M. Fethullah (2003d) KırıkTesti (Broken Jug) Istanbul: Zaman Kitap.

Gulen, M. Fethullah (2004a) "'In True Islam, Terror Does Not Exist'" in E. Çapan (ed) Terror and Suicide Attacks: An Islamic Perspective (New Jersey: The Light)

Gulen, M. Fethullah (2004b) 'No Islamic World Exists Today.' Interview with N. Akman. Zaman, 22 March.

Gulen, M. Fethullah (2004c) Bringing up a Child with Multiple Abilities. http://en.fgulen.com. 11.26.

Gulen, M. Fethullah (2004d) Günler Baharı Soluklarken (Cağ ve Nesil 5) Izmir: Nil.

Gulen, M. Fethullah (2004e) Interview with Fethullah Gulen, Daily Nation. 30 July.

Gulen, M. Fethullah (2004f) Key Concepts in the Practices of Sufism. Emerald Hills of the Heart. Vol.1-2. NJ: The Light, Inc.

Gulen, M. Fethullah (2004g) Love and The Essence of Being Human. Istanbul: Da Publication.

Gulen, M. Fethullah (2004h) Ornekleri Kendinden Bir Hareket [A Movement Originating Its Own Models]. Istanbul: Nil.

Gulen, M. Fethullah (2004i) The Necessity of Interfaith Dialogue: A Muslim Perspective. NJ: The Light, Inc.

Gulen, M. Fethullah (2004j) The World and its Contents from the Perspective of a Believer in The Fountain October – December 2004, Issue 48.

Gulen, M. Fethullah (2004k) Toward a Global Civization of Love and Tolerance, New Jersey: Light.

Gulen, M. Fethullah (2005a) 'An Interview with Fethullah Gulen (translated by Zeki Saritoprak and Ali Unal)', The Muslim World Vol. 95 no. 3 July 2005, pp.447-67.

Gulen, M. Fethullah (2005b) 'Fethullah Gulen's Message to the Conference Entitled "Islam in the Contemporary World: The Fethullah Gulen Movement in Thought and Practice"' (www.fgulen. org)

Gulen, M. Fethullah (2005c) "Bu hareket devlete alternatif mi? [Is this movement an alternative to the state?]," Herkül, 14 November 2005, available at: http://www.herkul.org/kiriktesti/index. php?article_id=2418 Last accessed on September 22, 2007.

Gulen, M. Fethullah (2005d) "Himmet: Teveccüh, İnfak ve Gayret [Assiduity: Favour, Charity, and Perseverance]," Herkül, 12 December 2005, available at: http://www.herkul.org/kiriktesti/index. php?article_id=2720. Last accessed on September 22, 2007.

Gulen, M. Fethullah (2005e) Işığın Göründüğü Ufuk, Mefkure İnsanı, Nil Yayınları

Gulen, M. Fethullah (2005f) Pearls of Wisdom (New Jersey, The Light)

Gulen, M. Fethullah (2005g) The Essentials of the Islamic Faith, Somerset, NJ: The Light, Inc.

Gulen, M. Fethullah (2005h) The Generations of Hope – I http://en.fgulen.com..

Gulen, M. Fethullah (2005i) The Messenger of God – Muhammad, Somerset, NJ: The Light, Inc.

Gulen, M. Fethullah (2005j) The Statue of Our Souls. Revival in Islamic Thoughts and Activism. NJ: The Light, Inc.

Gulen, M. Fethullah (2006a) "Diyalog Etrafında Sorulan Sorulara Verdiği Cevaplar." In Diyaloğun Dini ve Tarihi Temelleri, edited by Ergün Çapan. İzmir: Işık Yayınları.

Gulen, M. Fethullah (2006b) 'Respect For Humankind', The Fountain, January – March, 2006 / Issue 53

Gulen, M. Fethullah (2006c) "Demokrasi Yokuşu [Acclivity of Democracy]," Herkül, 2 January 2006 (Online portal to which Fethullah Gulen's speeches are posted) available at: http://www.herkul.org/ kiriktesti/index.php?article_id=2846 Last accessed on September 22, 2007.

Gulen, M. Fethullah (2006d) "Fedakarlıkta Mantığın Ölçüsü [The Limits of Rationality in Altrusim]," Zaman, 10 February 2006.

Gulen, M. Fethullah (2006e) "On the Holy Qur'an and Its Interpretation". The Fountain, Issue 55. (Accessed from http://www.fountainmagazine.com 24 August, 2007)

Gulen, M. Fethullah (2006f) A Comparative Approach to Islam and Democracy, in The Light (compiled) Essays, Perspectives, Opinions: M. Fethullah Gulen (New Jersey, The Light) 13-20

Gulen, M. Fethullah (2006g) Cag ve Nesil (Cag ve Nesil Serisi-1) (Istanbul: Nil Yayinlari)

Gulen, M. Fethullah (2006h) İkindi Yağmurları, İstanbul, Gazeteciler ve Yazarlar Vakfı yayınları,

Gulen, M. Fethullah (2006i) Isigin Gorundugu Ufuk (Cag Ve Nesil Serisi-7) (Izmir: Nil Yayinlari)

Gulen, M. Fethullah (2006j) Kucuk Dunyam (My Little World) Ufuk Yayinlari, Istanbul, 2006.

Gulen, M. Fethullah (2006k) Toward a Global Civilization of Love and Tolerance. Somerset, NJ: The Light,

Gulen, M. Fethullah (2006l) Yeseren Dusunceler (Cag ve Nesil 6) (Izmir: Nil Yayinlari)

Gulen, M. Fethullah (2007m) 'Excerpts from F. Gulen's Answers to Questions on Education and Turkish Educational Activities Abroad', http://en.fgulen.com/content/view/779/2/, accessed on 14 August 2007.

Gulen, M. Fethullah (2007n) Civilization and the Confusion of Conceptions, http://en.fgulen.com/

Gulen, M. Fethullah (2007o) Islam – A Religion of Tolerance, http://en.fgulen.com/

Gulen, M. Fethullah (2007p) Kirik Testi 1-5 [Broken Pitcher]. Istanbul: Journalists and Writers Foundation.

Gulen, M. Fethullah (2007r) Lesser and Greater Jihad, http://en.fgulen.com/

Gulen, M. Fethullah (2007s) Prizma 1-5 [Prism]. Istanbul: Nil.

Gulen, M. Fethullah (2007t) Respect for Humankind, http://en.fgulen.com/

Gulen, M. Fethullah (2007u) The Necessity of Interfaith Dialogue, http://en.fgulen.com/

Gulen, M. Fethullah (2007v) Three Groups Opposing Dialogue – Kharajites, Karmatis, and Anarchists, http://en.fgulen.com/

Gulen, M. Fethullah (under pen-name Hikmet Isik) 'What does Islam say about killing an innocent person?' The Fountain, October - December 2006, Issue 56, August 2007

Gulen, M. Fethullah, and Akman, Nuriye (2005) "In True Islam, Terror does not exist", in Çapan, Ergün An Islamic Perspective. Terror and Suicide Attacks (New Jersey, The Light) 1-8

Gümüşhanevi, Ahmed Ziyauddin (2005) Qulub al-Daria Istanbul: Işık Yayınları.

Gündem, M. (2005) 11 Days with Fethullah Gulen: An analysis of a movement with question-and-answers. 5th ed Istanbul, Alfa. Available in English from: <http://en.fgulen.com/a.page/press/interview/interview.with.mehmet.gundem.of.milliyet.daily/c277.html>

Habermas, Jürgen (1989) "The Public Sphere." In Jürgen Habermas on Society and Politics: A Reader, edited by Steven Seidman. Boston: Beacon Press.

Habermas, Jürgen (1999) The Structural Transformation of the Public Sphere: An Inquiry into a Category of Bourgeois Society. tr. by Thomas Berger. Cambridge: MIT Press.

Hacking, I. (1983) Representing and Intervening (Cambridge, Cambridge University Press)

Haddad, Y. (1991) The Challenge of Muslim Minorityness: The American Experience, in W.A.R. Shadid and P.S. van Koningsveld, eds, The Integration of Islam and Hinduism in Western Europe, Kampen: Kok Pharos Publishing House, p. 134

Hadith Encyclopedia (1996) Harf Information Technology, Cairo..

Haenni, Patrick (2005) L'islam de marché (Paris, Le Seuil/ La république des idées)

Hale, William (1994) Turkish Politics and the Military. London: Routledge.

Hale, William (1999) Turkey's Domestic Political Landscape: A Glance at the Past and the Future. The International Spectator, XXXIV(1) 27–46. Available from: <www.ciaonet.org/olj/iai/iai_99haw01.html> [August 17, 2005, 09:34]

Hales, C. (1993) "Power, Authority and Influence." In A. Harris, N. Bennett and M. Preedy (Eds) Organizational Effectiveness and Improvement in Education. Buckingham, Philadelphia: Open University Press.

Halliday, F. (2005) The 'Clash of Civilizations'?: Sense and Nonsense, in: R. Boase (Ed) Islam and Global Dialogue: Religious Pluralism and the Pursuit of Peace (Hants, England, Ashgate) 119-

137.

Hamidullah, M (1990) İslam Peygamberi (The Prophet of Islam) trans., Tuğ, S, İstanbul, İrfan Yayımcılık, v. I-II.

Handbook of International Ataturk Alatoo University (April 2006)

Handbook of Sebat International Education Institutes (May 2006)

Hanioğlu, Şükrü (2001) Preparation for a Revolution: The Young Turks, 1902-1908, Oxford University Press, p. 305

Hanioglu, Sukru (2007) "Derin Devlet Osmanli Mirasi Mi?," Zaman, February 15, 2007.

Hardy, P. (1972) The Muslims of British India (Cambridge, Cambridge University Press)

Harputlu, M (2007) "Bütün Dünya Tek Bir Sahnede Buluştu" (The Whole World Met in One Scene) Bugün Gazetesi, 6th June 2007.

Harries Richard (2004) Jonathan Sacks's The Dignity of Difference: How to Avoid the Clash of Civilizations. Scottish Journal of Theology. (57)1: 109-115.

Hassan, A. A. (2007) "America's Favoured Islam", Al-Ahram weekly, published in Cairo, Egypt, available online at http://weekly.ahram.org.eg/2007/852/op1.htm.

Hawk, David et al. (1995) Minorities in Cambodia (London, Minority Rights Group)

Haykal, Muhammad Husein The Life of Muhammad, Kuala Lumpur: Islamic Book Trust, 1993.

Heffner, R.W. (1998) Multiple Mondernities: Christianity, Islam and Hinduism in a Globalizing Age. Annual Review of Anthropology 27:83-104.

Hefner, Robert W. (2000) Civil Islam: Muslims and Democratization in Indonesia (Princeton, Princeton University Press)

Hegel, Georg Wilhelm Friedrich (1956) The Philosophy of History . Translator . S. Sibree (New York: Dover)

Hekimoglu, I. (2000) Journalist Çandar: "The media aristocracy resists change". Turkish Daily News, November 11.

Hendrick, J.D. (2006) "The Regulated Potential of Kinetic Islam", in: Hunt, R.A. & Y. A. Aslandoğan (eds) Muslim Citizens of the Globalized World. Contributions of the Gulen Movement. Somerset, NJ: The Light, Inc & IID Press: Somerset, NJ (pp.11-29)

Henkel, Heiko (2004) "Rethinking the dar al-harb: social change and changing perceptions of the West in Turkish Islam." Journal of Ethnic and Migration Studies, 9/2004

Hennis, W. (2000) Max Weber's Central Question, Threshold Press: Newbury, Berks.

Hermansen Marcia (1996) The Conclusive Argument from God: Shah Wali Allah of Delhi's Hujjat Allah al-Baligha Leiden: Brill.

Hermansen Marcia (2005) 'Understandings of "Community" within the Gulen Movement', http://fethullahgulenconference.org/houston/index.php, accessed on 12 August 2007

Hervieu-Léger, D. (2000) Religion as a Chain of Memory. Oxford: Polity Press

Hinze, B. (2006) Practices of Dialogue in the Roman Catholic Church. Aims and Obstacles, Lessons and Laments (NY, Continuum)

Hirschkind Charles (2001) Civic Virtue and Religious reason: an Islamic counterpublic, Cultural Antropology, 16(1): 3-34.

Hoffmann, S. (2002) Clash of Globalizations. Foreign Affairs, 81, 104-109.

Horkuc, Hasan (2002) New Muslim Discourses on Pluralism in the Postmodern Age, American Journal of Islamic Social Sciences, Spring 2002, 19 (2)

Hourani, Albert (1983) Arabic Thought in the Liberal Age, 1798-1939, Cambridge University Press.

Howe, M. (2000) Turkey Today: A Nation Divided Over Islam's Revival. Boulder, Colorado, Westview Press.

Howe, Marvine (2000) Turkey Today: A Nation Divided over Islam's Revival (Boulder, Colorado, Westview Press)

Hsieh H.F. & Shannon, S.E. (2005) "Three approaches to qualitative content analysis". Qual Health Res 2005, 15 (9):1277-1288.

Hunt, R. and Y. Aslandoğan (eds) (2006) Muslim Citizens of the Globalized World: Contributions of the Gülen Movement (Somerset, NJ, The Light Inc and IID Press)

Hunter, S.H. (1998) The Future of Islam and The West. Clash of civilization or peaceful coexistence? London: Praeger.

Huntington, S.P. (1993) "The clash of civilizations?" Foreign Affaires, 72 (3):22-49.

Huntington, Samuel (1984) "Will More Countries Become Democratic," Political Science Quarterly, Volume 99 No 2 (1984) pp. 193-218;

Hussain, J. (2004) Islam Its Law and Society (Sydney, The Federation Press)

Ibn 'Abd al-Barr (2000) Jami' bayan al-'ilm wa-fadlihi, ed 'Abd al-Hamid Muhammad al-Sa'dani (Beirut, 2000) 49;

Ibn Khaldun, The Muqqadimah.

Jawziyya, Ibn Qayyim al- (2001) Fadl al-'ilm wa-l-'ulama', ed Salih Ahmad al-Shami (Beirut) 99.

Ibn Taymiyya, Majmoo' fatawi Sheikh al-Islam Ibn Taymiyya. (The Collection of Opinions of Master Scholar of Islam Ibn Taymiyya) Riyadh. p. 516. Cited in Fouad Haddad, Ibn Taymiyya on Futooh Al-Ghayb and Sufism, 1996. Availabile online at http://www.abc.se/~m9783/n/itaysf_e.html.

Independent (1989) Limits to mutual tolerance. 18.2.89.

Institute for War and Peace Reporting (2005) 'Clampdown on Islamic teaching in Turkmenistan', Reporting Central Asia no.401, 4 August 2005, Institute for War and Peace Reporting, London.

Irvine, Jill (2006) "The Gulen Movement and Turkish Integration in Germany" in Hunt and Aslandogan (eds) (2006) 55-74.

Ishay, M.R. (2004) The History of Human Rights: From Ancient Times to the Globalization Era

Izetbegovic, A. A. (1984) Islam Between East and West. Indianapolis, IN: American Trust Publications.

Jackson, R. (2006) Fifty Key Figures in Islam (Abingdon, Oxon, Routledge)

Jackson, Robert (2001) Faith based schools and religious education within the state system in England and Wales, editorial, British Journal of Religious Education, 24(1)

Jackson, Robert (ed) (2003) The faith based schools debate, British Journal of Religious Education, 25(2) 86–152.

Jacobsen, C. (1988) "Expecting Consideration: Further Insights." Israeli Social Science Research. Vol 6, pp. 83-86.

Jasper, James M. (1997) The Art of Moral Protest. Chicago: The University of Chicago Press.

Jenkins, Gareth (2004) "Non-Muslim Minorities in Turkey: Progress and Challenges on the Road to EU Accession." Turkish Policy Quarterly 3 (1): 53-61.

Jenkins, J. Craig. (1983) "Resource Mobilization Theory and the Study of Social Movements." Annual

Review of Sociology 9: 527-53.

Jenkins, R. (1967) Essays and Speeches (London, Collins) 267.

Jenkins, R. (1989) On race relations and the Rushdie affair. The Independent Magazine.18.3.89.

Jillani, Tassaduq Hussain (2006) "Democracy and Islam: An Odyssey in Braving the Twenty-First Century," BYU Law Review (2006).

John Paul II (1994) Crossing the Threshold of Hope. London: Jonathan Cape.

Johnston, Philip (2007) So, Whatever Happened To Blair's Anti-Terror Strategy? The Daily Telegraph, July 3, 2007, p. 6.

Joireman, Jeff (2006) Denise Daniels, Dishan Kamdar and Blythe Duell, "Good Citizens to the End? It Depends: Empathy and Concern with Future Consequences Moderate the Impact of a Short-Term Time Horizen on Organizational Citizenship Behaviors." Journal of Applied Psychology, Vol 91, pp. 1307-1320.

Joly, Daniele (1988) "Making A Place for Islam in British Society: Muslims in Birmingham", in T. Gerholm and Yngve George Lithman, eds, London and New York: Mansell, p. 32

Juergensmeyer, Mark (2003) Terror in the Mind of God, University of California Press, 2003.

Juergensmeyer, Mark (2004) 'Religion', Addressing the Causes of Terrorism, The Club de Madrid Series on Democracy and Terrorism, Vol. 1, pp.27-34.

Jund (Alain) (1995) Dumont (Paul) and De Tapia (Stéphane) Enjeux de l'immigration Turque en Europe Paris, Harmattan

Jung, D. (1999) Turkey at the Crossroads, March 1999, Copenhagen Peace Research Institute. Available from: <www.ciaonet.org/wps/jud01/> [September 9, 2005, 18:16:44]

Kalaycioglu, E. (1988) "Elite Political Culture and Regime Stability: the Case of Turkey". Journal of Economics and Administrative Sciences, Bogaziçi University, 2, 149–79.

Kalaycioglu, E. (1997) "The Logic of Contemporary Turkish Politics". Meria Journal, 1(3) Available from: <http://meria.idc.ac.il/journal/1997/issue3/jv1n3a6.html>

Kalyoncu, Mehmet (2007) 'The Counter Terrorism Issue In Terms Of Systems Theory; Diyarbakir as a Case Study', presentation at the Second Istanbul Conference on Democracy and Global Security, June 14-16, 2007.

Kalyoncu, Mehmet (Forthcoming) A Civilian Response to Ethno-Religious Conflict: The Gulen Movement in Southeastern Turkey. New Jersey: The Light.

Kanat, Kilic Bugra (2003) Review of 'Turkish Islam and the Secular State: The Gulen Movement', by M. Hakan Yavuz and John Esposito (eds) 2003, Journal of Muslim Minority Affairs, Vol. 25, No. 2, August 2005, 287-290.

Kandil, Amani (1999) "Women and Civil Society", in: Civil Society at the Millennium (Civicus, Connecticut: Kumarian Press)

Kandiyoti Deniz (1997) "Gendering the Modern. On Missing Dimensions in the Study of Turkish Modernity", in Bozdoğan and Kasaba (edited by) Rethinking Modernity and National Identity in Turkey, University of Washington Press, 113-132.

Kandur, J.L., F. Citlak, H. Bingül & K.St, Onge (eds) (2006) Rumi: His Sufi Path of Love. NJ: The Light Inc.

Kanra, B. (2005) "Democracy, Islam and Dialogue: The Case of Turkey". Government and Opposition, 40, 515-539.

Kanter, Rosabeth M. (1968) "Commitment and Social Organization: A Study of Commitment

Mechanisms in Utopian Communities." American Sociological Review, Vol 33, pp. 499-517.

Kanter, Rosabeth M.(1972) Commitment and Community: Communes and Utopias in Sociological Perspectives. Cambridge, Massachusetts: Harvard University Press.

Kaplan, Sam (2006) The Pedagogical State, Education and the Politics of National Culture in Post-1980 Turkey, Stanford, Stanford University Press.

Kara, İsmail. (2003) "Türkiye'de Laiklik Uygulamaları Açısından Diyanet İşleri Başkanlığı." In Devlet ve Din İlişkileri-Farklı Modeller, Konseptler ve Tecrübeler. Ankara: Konrad Adenauer Vakfı.

Karakas, Fahri (2005) 'Global Peaceful Social Innovation: The Case of Gulen Network', http://en.fgulen.com/content/view/2242/4/, accessed on 14 August 2007

Karamustafa, A. (2003) Islam: A Civilizational Project in Progress, in: Safi, O. (ed) Progressive Muslims: On Justice, Gender and Pluralism (Oxford, Oneworld)

Karlığa, Bekir (1998) Kültürlerarası Diyalog Sempozyumu, Erkâm Mat. İst., 16

Karpat, Kemal (2001) The Politicization of Islam: Reconstructing Identity, State, Faith, and Community in the Late Ottoman State, Oxford University Press.

Kassam, T. R. (2003) On Being a Scholar of Islam: Risks and Responsibilities, in: O. Safi (ed) Progressive Muslims: On Justice. Gender and Pluralism. (Oxford, Oneworld)

Katzenstein, Mary F. (1998) Faithful and Fearless: Moving Feminist Protest inside the Church and Military. Princeton, NJ: Princeton University Press.

Kaya, Ayhan and Ferhat Kentel (2005) Euro-Turks: A Bridge or a Breach between Turkey and the European Union?A Comparative Study of French-Turks and German-Turks, CEPS EU-Turkey Working Papers No. 14, 1 January 2005.

Kazancigil, A., & Özbudun, E. eds (1981) Atatürk: Founder of a Modern State. London, Hurst.

Keane, John (2004) Violence and Democracy, Cambridge University Press:, p.1.

Keat, R. (1991) Introduction-Starship Britain or universal enterprise, in Enterprise Culture (Ed Russell Keat & Nicholas Abercrombie) Routledge: London.

Kedourie, Elie (1992) Democracy and Arab Political Culture (Washington, DC: Washington Institute for Near East Policy, 1992)

Kettani, M A (1979) The Muslim Minorities, Leicester: The Islamic Foundation.

Keyder, Çağlar (2004) "The Turkish Bell Jar." New Left Review (28): 65-84.

Khosrokhavar, Farhad (1997) Islam des Jeunes, Paris, Flammarion.

Kiernan, Ben (1988) "Orphans of Genocide: The Cham Muslims of Kampuchea under Pol Pot". Bulletin of Concerned Asian Scholars, XX, 4, 1-33.

Kiernan, Ben (1989) "Kampuchean Muslims: An Uncertain Future". Journal of Muslim Minority Affairs, X, 1, 28-39.

Kiernan, Ben (1999) The Pol Pot Regime: Race, Power, and Genocide in Cambodia under the Khmer Rouge, 1975-79 (Chiang Mai, Silkworm Books)

Kılınç, Ramazan (2005) "Transformative Role of Liberalism in Turkey after 1990s: The Case of Turkish Islamic Groups," Paper Presented at the 7th Annual Kokkalis Program Graduate Student Workshop, Harvard University, Cambridge, MA, 3-4 February 2005.

Kimball, Charles (1991) Striving Together: A Way Forward in Christian–Muslim Relations. Maryknoll, New York: Orbis Books.

Kitschelt, Herbert (1986) "Political Opportunity Structures and Political Protest: Anti-Nuclear Movements in Four Democracies," British Journal of Political Science, Vol. 16 (1986) pp. 57-85.

Kiyimba, A. et al (1998) Knowledge and responsibility: Islamic Perspectives on Science. Izmir: Kaynak.

Klandermans, Bert (1992) "The Social Construction of Protest and Multiorganizational Fields," In Frontiers in Social Movement Theory, edited by Aldon Morris and Carol McClurg Mueller (New Haven and London: Yale University Press)

Knitter, P. F. (1995) One Earth, Many Religions: Multifaith Dialogue & Global Responsibility (Maryknoll NY, Orbis Books)

Knitter, P. F. (2002) Introducing Theologies of Religion (Maryknoll NY, Orbis Books)

Knoke, D. (1999) Organizational networks and corporate social capital in: S. M. Gabbay (Ed) Corporate Social Capital and Liability (Boston: Kluwer) 17 – 42

Knoke, David (1981) "Commitment and Detachment in Voluntary Associations." American Sociological Review, Vol 46, pp. 141-158.

Kömeçoğlu, Uğur (1997) A Sociologically Interpretative Approach to the Fethullah Gulen Community Movement, Istanbul, Boğaziçi University, p. 46

Komecoglu, Ugur (2000) "Kutsal ile Kamusal: F. Gulen Cemaat Hareketi", İslamın Yeni Kamusal Yüzleri, ed Nilufer Göle. İstanbul: Metis Yayınları, pp. 148-94;

Konovsky, M.A. and S.D. Pugh (1994) "Citizenship Behavior and Social Exchange." Academy of Management Journal, Vol 37, pp. 656-669.

Kort, A. (2005) Dar al-Cyber Islam: Women, Domestic Violence, and the Islamic Reformation on the World Wide Web. Journal of Muslim Minority Affairs, 25(3) 363-383

Koru, F. (2000) A Simple Question. Yeni Safak, November 13.

Köse, Ali (1999) "East Is East, and West Is West": Remarks on Muslim Perspectives on Europe and Christianity, in G. Seufert and J. Waardenburg, eds, Turkish Islam and Europe, Istanbul: Kommission Bei Franz-Steiner-Verlag, p. 183

Kösebalaban, H. (2003) "The Making of Enemy and Friend Fethullah Gulen's National-Security Identity", in: H. Yavuz & J. L. Esposito (Eds) Turkish Islam and the Secular State (New York, Syracuse University Press) 170-183.

Kösebalaban, Hasan (2005) "The Impact of Globalization on Islamic Political Identity." World Affairs 168 (1): 27-37.

Kristof, Ladis K. D. (1963) 'Reflections on Angelina Balabanoff's Lenin', Russian Review, 22:4, 1963, 369-376.

Kücük, M. (2006) Adanmış Bir Gönül İnsanı Hacı Ata. Istanbul: Kaynak.

Küçükcan, T. (2004) "The making of Turkish-Muslim Diaspora in Britain: religious collective identity in a multicultural public sphere", Journal of Muslim Minority Affairs, 24(2): 243-258

Kullberg, Anssi and Christian Jokinen (2004) From Terror to Terrorism: the Logic on the Roots of Selective Political Violence, Research Unit for Conflicts and Terrorism, University of Turku, Finland, The Eurasian Politician, 19th July 2004.

Kundnani, A. (2007) "Integrationism: The Politics of anti-Muslim Racism". Race and Class. 48 (4) 26-44.

Kuran, T. (1997) "Islam and Underdevelopment: An Old Puzzle Revisited", Journal of Institutional and Theoretical Economics, 153, 41-71.

Kurtz, L. R. (2005) "Gulen's Paradox: Combining Commitment and Tolerance". The Muslim World. Volume 95 (July) 373-384.

Kurtz, L.R. (2001) "Local Gods and Universal Faiths", 155-160, in: Bradshaw, Y.W., J.F. Healey, & R. Smith (ed) Sociology for a New Century. Boston: Pine Forge Press.

Kuru, Ahmet (2003) Fethullah Gulen's Search for a Middle Way Between Modernity and Muslim Tradition in: Yavuz, A.H. and Esposito, J.L. (eds) (2003) Turkish Islam and the Secular State – The Gulen Movement. (Syracuse, Syracuse University Press)

Kuru, Ahmet (2005) Globalization and Diversification of Islamic Movements: Three Turkish Cases. Political Science Quarterly. 120 (2) 253-274.

Kuru, Ahmet (2006) "Reinterpretation of Secularism in Turkey: The Case of the Justice and Development Party." In The Emergence of a New Turkey: Islam, Democracy, and the AK Parti, edited by M. Hakan Yavuz. Salt Lake City: University of Utah Press.

Kuru, Ahmet (2006) Dynamics of Secularism: State Policies towards Religion in the United States, France and Turkey, unpublished Ph.D. Thesis, University of Washington, Seattle.

Kuru, Ahmet (2008) "Passive and Assertive Secularism: Historical Conditions, Ideological Struggles, and State Policies towards Religion." World Politics (forthcoming)

Kuru, Ahmet and Ahmet Yükleyen (2007) " Avrupa'da İslam, Demokrasi ve Laiklik:Fransa, Almanya ve Hollanda örnekleri"(Islam, Democracy, and Secularism in Europe: France, Germany, and the Netherlands) Istanbul, TESEV Yayınları.

Kurzman, Charles (1998) Liberal Islam: A Source Book (New York: Oxford University Press, 1998);

Lakatos, I. (1971) History of Science and its Rational Reconstructions, in R. Buck and R. Cohen (eds) Boston Studies in the Philosophy of Science, 8, 1970.

lane, pp. 225-251

Lapidus, Ira M (2002) A History of Islamic Societies, Cambridge, Cambridge University Press

Lave, J. & E. Wenger (1991) Situated learning: Legitimate peripheral participation. NY: Cambridge University Press.

Le Front d'Union pour l'Edification et la Défense de la Patrie Kampuchéenne (Eds) (1983) La communaute islamique au Kampuchea (Phnom Penh)

Leaman, O. (1999) A Brief Introduction to Islamic Philosophy. (Cambridge, Polity Press)

Leaman, Oliver (1999) "Nursi's place in the Ihya' tradition" Muslim World, 314-24

Leaman, Oliver (2005) "Is globalization a threat to Islam? Said Nursi's response," Globalization, ethics and Islam, ed I. Markham & I. Ozdemir, Aldershot: Ashgate, 121-26.

Leaman, Oliver (2005) "Tradition and Transformation: Why religion will flourish in the global network', Ethics, Values and Society: Social Transformation, G. Irfan (ed) Karachi: Oxford University Press, xii-xx

Lecker, Michael (1995) Muslims, Jews and Pagans: Studies in Early Islamic Medina. Leiden: E. J. Brill.

Lentin, R. and McVeigh, R. (2006) After Optimism? Ireland, Racism and Globalisation (Dublin: Metro Eireann Publications)

Lerner, Daniel (1958) The Passing of Traditional Society (Glenco, IL: Free Press)

Leveau, Rémy (1988) The Islamic Presence in France, in T. Gerholm and Yngve George Lithman, eds, London and New York: Mansell, p. 114

LeVine, Mark (2003) 'Human Nationalisms' Versus 'Inhuman Globalisms': Cultural Economies of Globalisation and The Re-imagining of Muslim Identities in Europe and The Middle East, in S. Allievi and J. Nielsen, eds, Muslim Networks and Transnational Communities in and Across

Europe, Leiden and Boston: Brill, p. 101.

Lewis, Bernard (1984) The Jews of Islam. London: Routledge Kegan Paul, 1984.

Lewis, Bernard (1995) The Middle East: 2000 years of History from the Rise of Christianity to the Present Day. London: Weidenfield and Nicolson.

Lewis, Bernard (2003) The Crisis of Islam: Holy War and Unholy Terror (New York: Modern Library)

Lewis, Bernard (2003) What Went Wrong?: The Clash between Islam and Modernity in the Middle East (New York: Prennial)

Lewis, Franklin (2000) Rumi: Past and Present, East and West, Oxford: Oneworld, 3.

Lewis, P. (forthcoming) The Protestant Ethic, in International Encyclopaedia of Organization Studies, Stewart Clegg and James Bailey (editors)

Lijphart, A. (1977) Democracy in Plural Societies (London: Yale University Press)

Lilla, Mark (2002) "The New Age of Tyranny', The New York Review of Books , October 24, 2002, XLLI, Number 16, 28-9 .

Lilla, Mark (ed) (2001) The Legacy of Isaiah Berlin (New York City: New York Review)

Lin, N. (1999) Building a network theory of social capital. Connections. 22 (1) 28-51.

Lipset, Seymour Martin (1959) "Some Social Requisites of Democracy: Economic Development and Political Legitimacy," American Political Science Review, 53, 69-105.

Lofland, J. (1996) Social Movement Organizations: Guide to research on Insurgent realities. New York, Aldine De Gruyter.

Lorcerie (Françoise) (2003) L'Ecole et le défi ethnique : Education et intégration , Paris, ESF &INRP.

M. Featherstone, S. Lash and R. Robertson (eds) (1995) Global Modernities. (London: Sage Publications)

MacCulloch, D. (2003) Reformation: Europe's House Divided, 1490-1700. (London, Penguin)

Mahmood Saba (2001) Rehearsed spontaneity and the conventionality of ritual: disciplines of ṣalāt, American Ethnologist 28 (4):827-853.

Mahmood, Saba (2005) Politics of Piety, The Islamic Revival and the Feminist Subject, Princeton, Princeton University Press

Malik b. Anas (1994) Al-Muwatta', ed Bashshar 'Awad Ma'ruf and Mahmud Muhammad Khalil (Beirut) 1:366-67.

Mamedov N. (2005) Ethnocultural Practices in Post-Soviet Kyrgyzstan and Turkmenistan: A Comparative Perspective, Central European University Nationalism Studies Program, Budapest, Hungary

Manço, Altay (2004) Turquie : vers de nouveaux horizons migratoires ?", Paris, Turin, Budapest, L'Harmattan, coll. « Compétences interculturelles ».

Manço, Ural (1999) Discours et Identité Naksibendi Contemporains: de la mystique à la statistique, in: Groc, Gérard (Ed) Formes nouvelles de l'Islam en Turquie (Paris, Les Annales de l'autre Islam) 183-194.

Mandaville, Peter (2001) Transnational Muslim Politics: Reimagining the Umma (London: Routledge)

Mandaville, Peter (2003) "What does progressive Islam look like?" Isim Newsletter. Leiden: ISIM. 33-34.

Mandaville, Peter (2005) "Sufis and Salafis: The Political Discourse of Transnational Islam" In Robert W. Hefner (ed) Remaking Muslim Politics: Pluralism, Contestation, Democratization (Princeton:

Princeton University Press)

Mann-Kler, Deepa (2002) 'Identity and racism in Northern Ireland' in R. Lentin and R. McVeigh (eds) Racism and Anti-Racism in Ireland (Belfast: Beyond the Pale)

Mardin, Serif (1973) "Center Periphery Relations: A Key to Turkish Politics." Daedalus, 102.

Mardin, Serif (2006) "Turkish Islamic Exceptionalism Yesterday and Today: Continuity, Rupture and Reconstruction in Operational Codes." In Carkoglu, Ali and Barry Rubin (eds) Religion and Politics in Turkey. London and New York: Routledge, pp. 3-25.

Marfleet, Ph. (2003) The 'Clash' Thesis: War and Ethnic Boundaries in Europe, Arabic Studies Quarterly, 25, 71-88.

Markham, I and I. Ozdemir (2005) Globalization, Ethics & Islam – the Case of Bediuzzaman Said Nursi, Ashgate, Aldershot, UK.

Marranci, G. (2005) 'Pakistani's in Northern Ireland in the Aftermath of September 11'.

Martin, B. (2007) Justice Ignited: The Dynamics of Backfire (Lanham, MD: Rowman & Littlefield.

Martin, B. And Gray, T. (2007) "Backfires: white, black and grey", Journal of Information Warfare, Vol.7,Issue 1, pp.7-16

Marty, Martin E. (2003) "Our religio-secular world", Daedalus(Special issue on secularism and religion) June 2003

Masud, Khalid Muhammad (ed) (2000) Travellers in Faith: Studies on the Tablighi Jama'at as Transnational Islamic Movement for Faith Renewal (Leiden, Brill)

Matin-Asgari, A. (2004) Islamic Studies and the Spirit of Max Weber: A Critique of Cultural Essentialism. Critique: Critical Middle Eastern Studies, 13, 293-312.

Maxwell, N. (1993) Induction and Scientific Realism, Einstein vs. van Fraassen, British Journal for the Philosophy of Science, 44, 61-101.

McAdam, Doug (2001) Sidney Tarrow, and Charles Tilly, Dynamics of Contention (New York: Cambridge University Press)

McAdam, Doug, John D. McCarthy and Mayer N. Zald (eds) (1996) Comparative Perspectives on Social Movements: Political Opportunities, Mobilizing Structures, and Cultural Framings. Cambridge: Cambridge University Press.

McCarthy Kate (2007) Interfaith Encounters in America, New Jersey: Rutgers University Press.

McCarthy, John D. and Mayer N. Zald (1973) The Trend of Social Movements in America: Professionalization and Resource Mobilization. Morristown, NJ: General Learning Press.

McCarthy, John D. and Mayer N. Zald (1977) "Resource Mobilization and Social Movements: A Partial Theory," American Journal of Sociology, Vol.82 (1977) pp. 1212-41.

McClay, Wilfred M. (2002) "Two Concepts of Secularism." In Religion Returns to the Public Square: Faith and Policy in America, edited by Hugh Heclo and Wilfred M. McClay. Baltimore: Johns Hopkins University Press.

McDonough, Sheila (1985) Muslim Ethics and Modernity, A Comparative Study of the Ethical Thought of Sayyid Ahmad Khan and Mawlana Mawdudi, Ontario, Wilfrid Laurier University Press

McGarry, J. and O'Leary, B. (2004) The Northern Ireland Conflict: Consociational Engagements

McVeigh, R. and Rolston, B. (2007) 'From Good Friday to Good Relations: sectarianism and racism.

Melucci, Alberto (1989) Nomads of the Present. London: Hutchinson Radius.

Melucci, Alberto (1999) Challenging Codes: Collective action in the information age. Cambridge, Cambridge University Press. (Reprinted 1999; First edition 1996.)

Mermer Ali (1997) The ways to knowledge of God in the Risale-I-Nur, 3th International Symposium on Bediuzzaman Said Nursi, edited by Nesil Foundation.

Metcalf, B. D (1984) Moral Conduct and Authority: the place of "adab" in South Asian

Metcalf, Barbara D. (2002) Islamic Revival in British India: Deoband, 1860-1900 (New Delhi, Oxford University Press)

Michel Thomas (2001) Fethullah Gulen as Educator, conference on "Islamic Modernities: Fethullah Gulen and Contemporary Islam", Georgetown University, http://en.fgulen.com/a.page/press/review/a1222.html

Michel, T (2005) "Turkish Islam in Dialogue with Modern Society: The Neo-Sufi Spirituality of the Gulen Movement". Concilium 5:71-80.

Michel, Thomas (2001) Fethullah Gulen and the Gulen Schools. Islamic Modernism: Fethullah Gulen and Contemporary Islam. Georgetown University (26-27 April)

Michel, Thomas (2002) "Gulen as Educator and Religious Teacher" in M. Fethullah Gulen and Education" in Essays, Perspectives and Opinions: M. Fethullah Gulen, . 58-88 (Rutherford, Fountain)

Michel, Thomas (2004) Foreword, in: F. Gulen, Toward a Global Civilization of Love and Tolerance (New Jersey, The Light) i-iii.

Michel, Thomas (2005) "Een analyse over de vrede", Celik, G., P. Cobben, J. van Dijk, P. Valkenberg (eds) Voorlopers in de Vrede [Forerunners for peace]. Budel: Damon (pp.31-44)

Michel, Thomas (2005) "Sufism and Modernity in the Thought of Fethullah Gulen," The Muslim World, v. 95, n. 3, July 2005.

Michel, Thomas (2005) Said Nursi's Views On Muslim-Christian Understanding (Istanbul, Soz Yayinlari)

Michel, Thomas (2005) Two Frontrunners for Peace: John Paul II and Fethullah Gulen. Presented at the Frontrunners of Peace symposia organized by the Cosmicus Foundation, Holland, at universities in Tilburg, Erasmus, and Amsterdam, March 16–18, 2005. Available from: <http://en.fgulen.com/content/view/1944/13/>

Michel, Thomas (2007) "Four Frontrunners In Peace: People Who Have Devoted Their Lives To Peace" in Academic Resources on the Gulen Movement CD, www.GulenConference.org.uk, 2007.

Miles M.B. & Huberman A.M. (1994) Qualitative data analysis: an expanded sourcebook. Thousands Oaks, CA: Sage.

Miller Jr., Kevin (2003) Islam in Kazakhstan and Kyrgyzstan: the Nurcu movement. The Eurasian World www.amerasianworld.com/islam_in_kazakhstan, accessed 19 March 2007.

Milligan, Jeffrey Ayala (2005) Islamic Identity, Postcoloniality, and Educational Policy. Schooling and Ethno-Religious Conflict in the Southern-Philippines (New York, Palgrave MacMillan)

Modood, T. (2005) 'Foreword' in T. Abbas (ed) Muslim Britain: Communities under Pressure (London: Zed Books)

Mohamed Osman, Mohamed Nawab (2004) Activism of Ulama in Singapore (Unpublished Academic Thesis, National University of Singapore)

Mohamed, Y. (2006) The Path to Virtue: The Ethical Philosophy of al-Raghib al-Isfahani: An Annotated translation, with critical Introduction, of Kitab al-Dhari'ah ila Makarim al-Shari'ah.(Kuala Lumpur, ISTAC)

Moldogaziev, Temirlan (2003) World Values Survey of Kyrgyz Republic.

Moosa, E. (2003) The Debts and Burdens of Critical Islam, in: O. Safi (ed) Progressive Muslims: On

Justice. Gender and Pluralism. (Oxford, Oneworld)

Mousalli, Ahmad S. (2001) The Islamic Quest for Democracy, Pluralism, and Human Rights (Tampa: University Press of Florida, 2001)

Mucahit Bilici (2001) "Context, Identity and Representational Politics of the Fethullah Gulen Movement in Turkey," paper delivered at the seminar "Islamic Modernities: Fethullah Gulen and Contemporary Islam," Georgetown University, 26-27 April 2001, unpublished article

Muhammed b. Umar b. Waqid (1966) Kitab al-Maghazi, Oxford 1966, III.117-118;

Muqatil, Tafsir, 3:130.

Murata, S. and Chittick, W. C. (1994) The Vision of Islam. Minnesota: Paragon House.

Murphy, C. (2005) A Modern, Mystic Ramadan. Washington Post, October 4, 2005, B01. Available from: <www.washingtonpost.com/wp-dyn/content/article/2005/10/03/AR2005100301661.html>

Murphy, T. P. (1976) (Columbus, Ohio)

Muslim, Sahih-i Muslim.

Mutahhari, M. (2002) An Introduction to the Islamic Sciences, transl. By Ali Quli Qarai, Al-Tawhid, vol II No. 2.

Myers, Eugene (1964) Arabic Thought and the Western world in the Golden Age of Islam. New York: Frederick Ungar Publishing company.

Nahapiet, J. & Ghoshal, S. (1998) Social capital, intellectual capital, and the organizational advantage. Academy of Management Review. 23: 242.

Narli, Nilufer (1999) The rise of the Islamist movement in Turkey. Middle East Review of International Affairs online 3(3) 38-48. www.meria.idc.ac.il/journal/1999/issue3/jvol3no3in

Nasr, S. H. (1966) Ideals and Realities of Islam, London.

Nasr, S. H. (1977) Interior Life in Islam, 3:2

Nasr, S. H. (1980) Reflections on Islam and Modern Life. Al-Serat 6, 1.

Nasr, S. H. (2002) The Heart of Islam, New York: HarperCollins.

Nasr, Seyyed Hossein (2001) Ideals and Realities of Islam, New York, ABC International Group 2001.

Nasr, Vali (2005) "The Rise of Muslim Democracy," Journal of Democracy, Volume 16 No 2 (April pp. 13-27.

National Bank of the Kyrgyz Republic (NBKR) (2007) http://www.nbkr.kg/web/in-terfeis.buil-der_frame?language=ENG

National Statistical Committee Kyrgyz Republic (2007) http://www.stat.kg/Eng/Ho-me/HLatest.html

National Statistical Committee Kyrgyz Republic (2007) Results of the First National Population Census of the Kyrgyz Republic of 1999 (Bishkek, Kyrgyzstan) http://www.stat.kg/Eng/Home/census.pdf, 14.03.2007

Navaro, Yashin Yael (2002) Faces of the State. Secular and Public Life in Turkey, Princeton University Press.

Nawawi (1997) Forty Hadith, tr. Ezzeddin Ibrahim and Denys Johnson-Davies (Cambridge, p. 110.

Neill, S. R.St. J (2003) National Curriculum Tests, London / Warwick, NUT / University of Warwick Leadership, Policy and Development Unit.

Nelson, Charles (2005) Fethullah Gulen: A Vision of Transcendent Education. Unpublished,

Ner, Marcel (1941) "Les musulmans de l'Indochine Française". Bulletin de l'Ecole Française d'Extrême-Orient, 41, 151-200.

Nesai, Sunan.

Nettler, Ronald L. and Suha Taji-Farouki (eds) (1998) Muslim–Jewish Encounters: Intellectual Traditions and Modern Politics. Amsterdam: Harwood Academic Publishers.

Neuhaus, Richard John (1984) The Naked Public Square: Religion and Democracy in America, William B. Eerdmans Publishing, pp. 80-84

Nicholson, R.A. (1931) Mysticism in The Legacy of Islam, London: ed by Sir Thomas Arnold and Alfred Guillaume pp. 211-212.

Nielsen, Jørgen S. (1991) Muslim Organisations in Europe: Integration or Isolation?, in W.A.R. Shadid and P.S. van Koningsveld, eds, The Integration of Islam and Hinduism in Western Europe, Kampen: Kok Pharos Publishing House, p. 43

Niles, F. S. (1999) Toward a Cross-Cultural Understanding of Work-Related Beliefs, Human Relations, 52, 7, pp.855-867.

Nisbet, Robert (1986) Conservatism (Minneapolis, MI :University of Minneapolis Press)

Nissim, Rejwan (2000) The Many Faces of Islam: Perspectives on a Resurgent Civilization. Gainesville: University Press of Florida.

Niýazow, Saparmurat (2001) Ruhnama, Aşgabat.

Norton, Richard (1995) Introduction, in: Augustus Richard Norton (Ed) Civil Society in the Middle East, Vol. 1 (Leiden: E. J. Brill)

Novak David (1989) Jewish-Christian Dialogue: A Jewish Justification. Oxford: Oxford University Press.

Nugent, Paul D. and Mitchel Y. Abolafia. (2006) "The Creation of Trust Through Interaction and Exchange: The Role of Consideration in Organizations." Group and Organizational Management, Vol. 31, No. 6, pp. 628-650.

Nursi, Said (1960) Said Tarihçe-i Hayati, Sinan Matbaasi, Istanbul.

Nursi, Said (1976) Hutbe-i Samiye, in Risalei Nur, II, p. 1976.

Nursi, Said (1996) "Kastomonu Lahikasi Mektub #121" in Risale-i Nur Kulliyati Istanbul: Nesil Yayinlari, 1569-1677.

Nursi, Said (1997) Letters (transl. Shukran Vahide) Istanbul: Sozler.

Nursi, Said (1998) Rays (transl. Shukran Vahide) Istanbul: Sozler.

Nursi, Said (2000) Flashes (transl. Shukran Vahide) Istanbul: Sozler.

Nursi, Said (2002) The Words (transl. Shukran Vahide) Istanbul: Sozler.

Nursi, Said (2003) Risale-i Nur 1.0 (CD) Turkish/English/Arabic Istanbul: Nesil Yayinlari

Nursi, Said (2005) The Words. The Reconstruction of Islamic Belief and Thought. NJ: The Light, Inc.

O'Brien, Kevin (2003) Jesuit Education and the Example of St. Ignatius: The Classroom as Holy Ground. America, 188:18, 8-12.

Ocak, Ahmet Y. (1996) Turk Sufilig^ine Bakıs,lar (Approaches to Turkish Sufi Orders) Istanbul: Iletisim.

Öğün, Süleyman Seyfi (1995) Modernleşme, Milliyetçilik ve Türkiye. Istanbul: Baglam.

Öğün, Süleyman Seyfi (2005) "Türk Okullarına Dair Gözlem ve Tespitler [Some Observations and Points on Turkish Schools]," In Barış Köprüleri: Dünyaya Açılan Türk Okulları, [Bridges of Peace: Turkish Schools Opening to the World], edited by Toktamış Ateş, Eser Karakaş and İlber Ortaylı

(İstanbul: Ufuk Kitaplari) pp. 99-104.

Öktem, Emre (2004) "Türkiye'deki Gayri Müslim Cemaatlerin Durumu." In Türkiye ve Avrupa'da Din, Devlet ve Toplum: Dinlerarası Barışçı Bir Ortak Yaşam İçin Olanaklar ve Engeller. Ankara: Konrad Adenauer Vakfı.

Olcott, Martha Brill (2007) Sufism in Central Asia: A Force for Moderation or a Cause of Politicization? Carnegie PAPERS, Middle East Series, Russian and Eurasian Program, Number 84, May 2007.

Önis, Z. & Turem, U. (2001) Entrepreneurs, Democracy and Citizenship in Turkey. RSCAS Working Papers, European University Institute, EUI RSC 2001/48, pp.39. Available from: <http://hdl.handle.net/1814/1757>

Onis, Ziya (1997) "The Political Economy of Islamic Resurgence in Turkey: The Rise of the Welfare Party in Perspective." Third World Quarterly 18: 743-66.

Öniş, Ziya (2004) "Turgut Özal and His Economic Legacy: Turkish Neo-Liberalism in Critical Perspective," Middle Eastern Studies, Volume 40 Number 4 (July 2004) pp. 113-34.

Öniş, Ziya (2004) Turkish Modernization and Challenges for the New Europe. Presented at the workshop Beyond the Clash of Civilizations, Trent University, Ontario, Canada, and at a seminar organized by the Department of Near Eastern Studies, Princeton University, USA (September 2004)

Öniş, Ziya (2006) The Political Economy of Turkey's Justice and Development Party, in: Yavuz, Hakan (ed) The Emergence of a New Turkey: Islam, Democracy and the AK Party (Salt Lake City, University of Utah Press) 207-234.

Opportunity for Further Renewal", in Critique: Critical Middle Eastern Studies, v. 12 (1)

Ormushev A., Inandi O. & Asan uulu T. (2007) "Sebat" Bilim Beruu Uyasi, Bishkek

Osman, Mohamed Nawab Mohd (2002) "Turkey's Gulen movement and global Islamic activism," Rajaratnam.

Osman, Ysa (2002) Oukoubah: Justice for the Cham Muslims under the Democratic Kampuchea Regime (Phnom Penh, Documentation Center of Cambodia)

Osman, Ysa (2006) War against Terrorism: Response from a Cambodian Muslim (Paper presented at the Conference on War against Terrorism: People's Response, Malaysia)

Özbudun, E. & Tachau, F. (1975) Social Change and Electoral Behavior in Turkey: Toward a 'Critical Realignment'? International Journal of Middle East Studies 6, 473–9.

Özbudun, E. (1981) The Turkish Party System: Institutionalization, Polarization and Fragmentation. Middle Eastern Studies 17, 228–40.

Özbudun, Ergun and Serap Yazıcı (2004) Democratizing Reforms in Turkey (İstanbul: TESEV Publications)

Özdalga Elisabeth (2000) Worldly Asceticism in Islamic Casting: Fethullah Gulen's Inspired Piety and Activism, Critique 17 (fall):83-104.

Özdalga, E (2003) "Following in the Footsteps of Fethullah Gulen," in Turkish Islam and the Secular State, ed, Yavuz, M H and J L Esposito, Syracuse, NY, Syracuse University Press.

Ozdalga, E. (2003) Secularizing Trends in Fethullah Gulen's Movement: Impasse or Opportunity for Further Renewal?, Critique: Critical Middle Eastern Studies, 12 (1) pp.61-73.

Özdalga, E. (2003) Three women teachers tell their stories. In M. Hakan Yavuz and John L. Esposito (Eds) Turkish Islam and the secular state: The Gulen movement (pp. 85-114) Syracuse, New York: Syracuse University Press.

Özdalga, E. (2005) Redeemer or Outsider? The Gulen Community in the Civilizing Process. The Muslim World. Volume 95 (July)429-446.

Ozdalga, E. 2000. "Worldly Asceticism in Islamic Casting: Fethullah Gulen's Inspired Piety and Activism." Critique: Critical Middle Eastern Studies, Vol 17 (Fall 2000)

Ozdalga, Elizabeth (2007) İslamcılığın Türkiye Seyri, İstanbul, İletişim Yayınları.

Ozdalga, Elizabeth (July 2006) The Hidden Arab: a critical reading of the notion of 'Turkish Islam'. Middle Eastern Studies, 42(4) 551-570.

Ozdemir, S. (2006) MUSIAD: Anadolu Sermayesinin Donusumu ve Turk Modernlesmesinin Derinlesmesi (Musiad: The Transformation of Anatolian Capital and the Deepening of Turkish Modernity) Vadi: Ankara.

Özel, I (2005) Erbain: Kırk Yılın Şiirleri (Forty: The Poetry of Forty Years) Istanbul, Şule Yay., 2005

Paige G.D, Satha-Anand, C., & Gilliat, S. (2001) Islam and Non-Violence, Centre For Global Non-Violence

Panikkar, R. (1999) The Intra-Religious Dialogue (Maryknoll NY, Orbis Books)

Papaioannou, Elias and Gregorios Siourounis (2006) "Economic and Social Factors Driving the Third Wave of Democratization", London Business School.

Pape, Robert A. (2005) Dying to Win: The Strategic Logic of Suicide Terrorism, New York: Random House, 23.

Parekh, B. (2006) 'Europe, liberalism and the 'Muslim question' in T. Modood, A. Triandafyllidou and R. Zapata-Barrero (eds) Multiculturalism, Muslims and Citizenship: A European Approach. (New York: Routledge)

Parker-Jenkins, Marie, Dimitra Hartas & Barrie Irving (2005) In Good Faith. Schools, Religion and Public Funding, Aldershot, Ashgate.

PASIAD Indonesia. (2006) Mengenal Lebih Dekat PASIAD Indonesia (Jakarta, PASIAD)

Pauly, Robert J, Jr. (2004) Islam in Europe: Integration or Marginalisation?, Aldershot: Ashgate, p. 99

Paxton, P. (2002) Social Capital and Democracy: An Interdependent Relationship. American Sociological Review, 67 (2) 254-277.

Paya, A. (1995) Philosophers Against Truth: The Cases of Harré and Laudan The International Studies in Philosophy of Science, 9 255-284.

Paya, A. (2000a) Professor Cartwright and the Fundamental Laws of Nature, The Journal of the Faculty of Letters and Humanities, University of Tehran, 40, 33-55.

Paya, A. (2000b) An Instrumentalistic Defence of Scientific Realism, Falsafeh (Philosophy, Journal of the Department of Philosophy, University of Tehran) 1, 113- 138.

Paya, A. (2000c) Reciprocal Knowledge, Philosophy of Heart, and the Need to Understand the Other, Can Situational Logic and Dialogue Help? in U. Eco & A. Le Pichon (eds) Les Assises de la Connaissance Réciproque, Tomnouctou- Paris – Bruxelles, 94-112.

Paya, A. (2002)) 'Dialogue' in a 'Real World': Quixotic pursuit or sine qua non? International Journal of Applied Philosophy, 16, 201- 222.

Paya, A. (2003a) "Clarifying Situational Logic" (Part I) Nameh-e Ulum-e Ejtemaee (Social Sciences Letters) 21, 271-301.

Paya, A. (2003b) The Role of Thought Experiments in Scientific and Philosophical Investigations in Analytic Philosophy, Problems and Prospects, 473-498.

Paya, A. (2006) "Clarifying Situational Logic" (Part II) Nameh-e Ulum-e Ejtemaee (Social Sciences Letters) 27, 1-25.

Paya, A.(2003) Analytic Philosophy: Problems and Prospects (Tehran, Tarh-e Nou)

Pedersen, Lars (1999) Newer Islamic Movements in Western Europe, Aldershot: Ashgate, p. 155

Pektaş, Zeki Sovmestnye (N.D.) Turkmeno-turetskie shkoly-internaty v Turkmenistane: etapy stanovleniia.

Pettit, Philip (1997) Republicanism: A Theory of Freedom and Government(New York , NY: Oxford University Press)

Peuch, Jean-Christophe (2004) Turkey: Fethullahci schools – a greenhouse for Central Asian elites? www.rferl.org/featuresarticleprint/2004/06/413c394a-c79a-438 accessed 19 March 2007.

Peuch, Jean-Christophe (2004) Turkey: Group seeks to create a new generation of Muslim believers', www.referl.org/featuresarticleprint/2004/06/a6393817-e7d9-4c, accessed 19 March 2007.

Pfaff, W. (2006) Clash of Cultures. Commonweal 133, 13-17.

Phillips, T. (2005) After 7/7: Sleepwalking to Segregation. Commission for Racial Equality. 22.9.2005. http://www.cre.gov.uk/Default.aspx.LocID-0hgnew07r.RefLocID-0hg00900c001001.Lang-EN. htm.

Phoeun, Mak (1988) "La communauté cam au Cambodge du XV au XIX siècle", in Actes du Séminaire sur le Campa organisé à l'Université de Copenhague, le 23 mai 1987 (Paris, Centre d'histoire et civilisations de la péninsule indochinoise) 83-93.

Pipes, Daniel (1983) In the Path of God: Islam and Political Power (New York: Basic Books.

Pipes, In the Path of God: Islam and Political Power, pp. 48-69, 144-47.

Piricky, G. (1999) some Observations on New Departures in Modernist Interpretations of Islam in Contemporary Turkey: Fethullah Gulen Cemaati, Asian and African Studies, 8 (1) pp.83-90.

Polletta, Francesca (1994) "Strategy and Identity in 1960s Black Protest." Research in Social Movements, Conflicts and Change, 17: 85-114.

Polletta, Francesca (1997) "Culture and Its Discontents: Recent Theorizing on the Cultural Dimensions of Protest." Sociological Inquiry 67: 431-50.

Polletta, Francesca (1998a) "'It Was Like a Fever…' Narrative and Identity in Social Protest." Social Problems 45: 137-59.

Polletta, Francesca (1999a) "'Free Spaces' in Collective Action." Theory and Society 28: 1-38.

Polletta, Francesca (1999b) "Snarls, Quacks, and Quarrels: Culture and Structure in Political Process Theory." Sociological Forum 14: 63-70.

Polletta, Francesca (2006) It Was Like a Fever: Storytelling in Protest and Politics. Chicago and London: University of Chicago Press.

Polletta, Francesca.and James M. Jasper (2001) "Collective Identity and Social Movements." Annual Review of Sociology 27: 283-305.

Pope, N. (1998) 'An Ottoman Empire of the Mind' in Fethullah Gulen. http://fethullahgulen.org/a.page/ press/columns/1998/a1205.html. Accessed on July 25, 2006.

Pope, N. (2000) Opposition Deputy Sues Retired General. Turkey Update, November 14. Available from: <www.turkeyupdate.com/andic.htm> [January 21, 2005, 23.55]

Popper, Karl (1945) Open Society and Its Enemies (London, Routledge & Kegan Paul)

Popper, Karl (1957) The Poverty of Historicism (London, Routledge & Kegan Paul)

Popper, Karl (1963) Conjectures and Refutations (London, Routledge & Kegan Paul)

Popper, Karl (1972) Objective Knowledge (Oxford, Oxford University Press)

Popper, Karl (1994) The Myth of the Framework (London, Routledge)

Porta, Donatella Della Social Movements, Political Violence, and the State, Cambridge University Press: 1995, p.5.

Posusney, Marsha Pripstein and Michele Penner Angrist, Eds (2005) Authoritarianism in the Middle East: Regimes and Resistance (Boulder, CO: Lynne Reiner)

Pratt, Douglas (2003) 'Pluralism and Interreligious Engagement: The Contexts of Dialogue', in David Thomas with Clare Amos, eds, A Faithful Presence, essays for Kenneth Cragg, 402-418.

Pratt, Douglas (2005) The Challenge of Islam: Encounters in Interfaith Dialogue. Aldershot: Ashgate.

Przeworski A. Alvarez, M., Cheibub J.A. Limongi F. (2000) Democracy and Development: Political Institutions and Material Well-being in the World, 1950-1990. Cambridge: Cambridge University Press.

Putnam, R (1993) Making Democacy Work: Civic Traditions in Modern Italy; Princeton

Putnam, R. D. (2000) Bowling Alone: The Collapse and Revival of American Community (New York: Simon & Schuster)

Putnam, Robert D. (1995) "Bowling Alone: America's Declining Social Capital", Journal of Democracy (6.1) pp. 65-78.

Putnam, Robert D., Robert Leonardi, and Raffaella Nanetti. (1993) Making Democracy Work: Civic Traditions in Modern Italy. Princeton, N.J.: Princeton University Press.

Qardawi, Y. al- (2004) Islam's Stance on Sufism, SALAM Magazine, March-April, available online at http://www.famsy.com/salam/Sufism0404.htm

Quine, W.V. (1953) From a Logical Point of View (Cambridge, Massachusetts, Harvard University Press)

Race, Alan (1983) Christians and Religious Pluralism: Patterns in the Christian Theology of Religions. London: SCM Press.

Radio Singapore International, Turkish Delight, 3 July 2007. Accessed from www.rsi.org.sg on 4th July 2007.

Ragin, C.C. & H. S. Becker (1992) (eds) What is a Case? Exploring the Foundations of Social Inquiry. Cambridge: Cambridge University Press.

Rahim, Lily Zubaidah (1998) The Singapore Dilemma: The Political and Educational Marginality of the Malay community (Kuala Lumpur, Oxford University Press)

Rahman, F. (1982) Islam and Modernity: The Transformation of an Intellectual Tradition. Chicago: The University of Chicago Press.

Ramadan, Tariq (1999) Islam and Muslims in Europe: A Silent Revolution Toward Rediscovery, in Yvonne Yazbeck Haddad, ed, Muslims in the West: From Sojourners to Citizens, New York: Oxford University Press, p. 159

Ramadan, Tariq (2004) Western Muslims and the Future of Islam (Oxford, Oxford University Press)

Rawls, John (1996) Political Liberalism. New York: Columbia University Press.

Rawls, John (1999) The Law of Peoples. Cambridge, MA: Harvard University Press.

Rémond, R. (1999) Religion and Society in Modern Europe. Oxford: Blackwell Publishers.

Renard, John (1988) "Al-Jihad al-Akbar: Notes on a Theme in Islamic Spirituality," Muslim World 78 (1988): 225-42.

Richardson, Louise (2006) What Terrorists Want: Understanding the Terrorists Threat, John Murray: Great Britain.

Richmond, Oliver P. (2003) 'Realizing Hegemony? Symbolic Terrorism and the Roots of Conflict',

Studies in Conflict & Terrorism, Vol. 26 No. 4, pp. 289–309.

Ricklefs, Merle (2001) History of Indonesia since 1200c (Hampshire, Palgrave)

Riddell, Peter (2001) Islam and the Malay-Indonesian World: Transmission and Responses (Honolulu, University of Hawai'i Press)

Rioux, S.M. and L.A. Penner (2001) "The Causes of Organizational Citizenship Behavior: A Motivational Analysis." Journal of Applied Psychology, Vol 86, pp. 1306-1314.

Robert J, Pauly, Jr. (2004) Islam in Europe: Integration or Marginalisation?, Aldershot: Ashgate, p. 147

Roberts, R. H. (1992) Religion and the "Enterprise Culture": The British Experience in the Thatcher Era (1979-1990) Social Compass, 39 (1) pp. 15-33.

Robertson, R. (1997) 'Glocalization: Time-Space and Homogeneity-Heterogeneity' in

Robinson, F. (1988) Varieties of South Asian Islam (Coventry, Centre for Research in Ethnic Relations, University of Wariwck)

Robinson, F. (2005) Islam and the West: Clash of Civilizations? in: R. Boase (Ed)

Rodinson, M. (1973) Islam and Capitalism, Pantheon Books: New York.

Rosamond, B. (2000) Theories of European Integration, Palgrave Macmillan; NY: St. Martin's Press, Basingstoke.

Ross, W. D. (1930) The Right and the Good (Oxford, Clarendon Press)

Rotberg, Rober I (2002) 'The New Nature of Nation-State Failure', The Washington Quarterly, Summer 2002, Vol.25 (3) pp.85-96, and http://www.twq.com/02summer/rotberg.pdf, accessed 15 Mar. 07

Roy, Olivier (2003) "EuroIslam: the jihad within?" The National Interest, 22/3/2003

Roy, Olivier (2004) Globalized Islam: The search for a New Ummah (NY: Columbia)

Rubin, H.J. & L.S. Rubin (1995) Qualitative interviewing, the art of hearing data. Thousands Oaks, CA: Sage.

Rucht, Dieter (1988) "Themes, Logics, and Arenas of Social Movements: A Structural Approach," pp. 305-28 in From Structure to Action: Social Movement Participation across Cultures, International Social Movement Research, vol.1, edited by Bert Klandermans, Hanspeter Kriesi, and Sidney Tarrow. Greenwich, Conn.: JAI Press.

Rudolph, Susanne Hoeber (2005) "Religious Transnationalism" in Religion in Global Civil Society, ed by Mark Juergensmeyer. Oxford: Oxford University Press, pp. 189-200.

Rule, James B. (2004) "McTheory." Sociological Forum 19: 151-62.

Runnymede Trust (1997) The Islamophobia: A Challenge for Us All (London, Runnymede Trust)

Rushdie, S. (1998) The Satanic Verses (London, Viking Penguin)

Rustow, Dankwart (1970) "Transitions to Democracy: Towards a Dynamic Model"Comparative Politics 2(3) April 1970, 337-363.

Ruthven, Malise (2006) Islam in the World, London: Granta Publications, 2006.

Sachedina, Abdulaziz (2006) The Role of Islam in the Public Square: Guidance or Governance (Amsterdam, Amsterdam University Press, 2006)

Sachedina, Abdulaziz (2008) The Islamic Roots of Democratic Pluralism (Oxford: Oxford University Press)

Sacks, Jonathan (2005) The Dignity of Difference: Avoiding the Clash of Civilizations, in: R. Boase (Ed) Islam And Global Dialogue: Religious Pluralism and the Pursuit of Peace (Hants, England,

Ashgate)

Sacks, Jonathan (2005) To Heal A Fractured Word: The Ethics of Responsibility. New York: Schocken.

Saeed, A. (2006a) Interpreting the Qur'ān: Towards a Contemporary Approach. (Abingdon, Routledge)

Saeed, A. (2006b) Islamic Thought: An Introduction. (Abingdon, Routledge)

Safi, O. (2003) Introduction: The times they are a-changin' – A Muslim Quest for Justice, Gender Equality and Pluralism in: Safi, O. (ed) (2003) Progressive Muslims: On Justice, Gender and Pluralism (Oxford, Oneworld)

Sagbansua, L.& Keles, I. (2006) "Turkish Higher Education Experience in Central Asia: Managerial and Educational Features of IAAU", International Conference on Higher Education Management: International Trends & Local Sustainability, 12 May 2006, Westminster International University in Tashkent, Uzbekistan

Said, E. W. (1995) Orientalism. Western Conceptions of the Orient (London, Penguin Books)

Said, E. W. (1997) Covering Islam: How the media and the Experts Determine How We See the

Said, E. W. (2001) "The Clash of Ignorance". The Nation, October 22, 11-12.

Saleh, Fauzan (2001) Modern Trends in Islamic Theological Discourse in 20th Century Indonesia: A Critical Survey (Leiden, Brill)

Salvatore A. (1998) Staging Virtue. The Disembodiment of Self-Correctness and the Making of Islam as Public Norm, in Islam-Motor or Challenge of Modernity, vol. 1. Yearbook of the Sociology of Islam. Georg Stauth, ed Pp. 87-120. Hamburg: Transaction Books.

Sander, A. (1991) "The Road from Musalla to Mosque: The Process of Integration and Institutionalisation of Islam in Sweden", in W.A.R. Shadid and P.S. van Koningsveld (eds) The Integration of Islam and Hinduism in Western Europe, Kampen: Kok Pharos Publishing House.

Sardar, Z. (2003a) Reconstructing Muslim Civilization, in: S. Inayatullah, and G. Boxwell, (eds) Islam, Postmodernism and Other Futures: A Ziauddin Sardar Reader (London, Pluto Press)

Sardar, Z. (2003b) "When the pendulum comes to rest," in S. Inayatullah, and G. Boxwell, (eds) Islam, Postmodernism and Other Futures: A Ziauddin Sardar Reader (London, Pluto Press) 121-126.

Saritoprak, Zeki (2002) "The Mahdi Tradition in Islam: A Social-Cognitive Approach" in Islamic Studies XLI (# 4): 651-674.

Saritoprak, Zeki (2003) "Fethullah Gulen: A Sufi in His Own Way". In Yavuz, Hakan and Esposito, John (eds) (2003) Turkish Islam and the Secular State: The Gulen Movement, Syracuse: Syracuse University Press, pp. 156-169.

Saritoprak, Zeki (2005) 'Introduction' in The Muslim World, Vol. 95 (2) pp.325-327.

Saritoprak, Zeki (2005) "An Islamic Approach to Peace and Nonviolence: A Turkish Experience". The Muslim World. Volume 95 (July) 413-427.

Saritoprak, Zeki (2005) "Islam in Contemporary Turkey: the Contributions of Fethullah Gulen". Special Issue. The Muslim World 95(3):325-327.

Saritoprak, Zeki (2005) "Peace and Non-Violence: A Turkish experience". The Muslim World. Vol. 95. N0. 3, 2005, p. 8.

Saritoprak, Zeki and Ali Ünal (tr.) (2005) "An Interview with Fethullah Gulen". The Muslim World, 95, 3

Saritoprak, Zeki and Griffith, Sidney (2005) 'Fetullah Gulen and the 'People of the Book': A Voice from Turkey for Interfaith Dialogue', The Muslim World Vol. 95 no. 3 July 2005, pp.329-340.

Satha-Anand, Chaiwat (1993) "Core Values for Peacemaking in Islam: the Prophet's practice as paradigm" in Building Peace in the Middle East, ed Elise Boulden (Boulder: Lynnne Rinner, 1993.

Saufert, Günter and Jacques Waardenburg (ed) (1999) "Turkish Islam and Europe, Europe and Christianity as reflected in Turkish Muslim Discourse & Turkish Muslim life in the Diaspora" Stutgart.

Schaefer R.T. & Lamm R.P. (2000) Sociology, International Edition, McGraw-Hill

Schimmel, Annemarie (1975) Mystical Dimensions of Islam, Durham: University of North Carolina Press.

Schimmel, Anne-Marie (1997) Sufism and its Influence on Europe, lecture at Stanford University, May 4, available online at http://www.naqshbandi.org/events/sufitalk/sufismeu.htm.

Schlubach, J. B. (2005)" Tolerance Is Love: Gulen, Ghazali, and Rūmī", in: Islam in the Contemporary World: The Fethullah Gulen Movement in Thought and Practice (Huston, Rice University, Houston) 1-18

Schluchter, W. (1981) The Rise of Western Rationalism: Weber's Developmental History, University of California Press: London.

Schmid, Alex (1988) Political Terrorism. Amsterdam, North-Holland Publication, pp. 58-59.

Schmitt, Jean-Claude (1987) "La morale des gestes", in Parure, Pudeur, Etiquette, Revue School of International Studies, reprinted http:www.isn.ethz.ch/news/sw/details.cfm?id=17551.

Schwedler, Jillian (1995) "Introduction", in: Jillian Schwedler (ed) Toward Civil Society in the Middle East? A Primer (Boulder CO: Lynne Rienner)

Secor, A. J. & O'Loughlin, J. (2004) "Social and Political Trust in Istanbul and Moscow: A Comparative Analysis of Individual and Neighbourhood Effects".

Selçuk, Sami (1999) "Laiklik ve Demokrasi." Türkiye Günlüğü (56): 45-49.

Seligman, Adam B. (1992) The Idea of Civil Society (New York: The Free Press)

Sells, Michael (1996) Early Islamic Mysticism, New Jersey: Paulist Press, 20.

Seneviratana, A. (ed) (1994) King Asoka and Buddhism – Historical and Literary Studies, Buddhist Publication Society, Kandy, Sri Lanka.

Sevindi, N. (1997a) "Twenty-first Century Utopia and the Dervish tradition". (From the series, 'The New York Interview with Fethullah Gulen', July 20–29) Yeni Yüzyil. English translation available from: <http://en.fgulen.com/a.page/life/commentaries/a783.html>

Sevindi, N. (1997b) Fethullah Gulen'le New York Sohbeti (trans. The New York Interview with Fethullah Gulen) Istanbul, Sabah Kitaplari.

Sevindi, N. (2002) Fethullah Gulen ile Global Hosgörü ve New York Sohbeti. [Global Tolerance and New York Interview with Fethullah Gulen]. Istanbul: Timas.

Shadid, Anthony (2002) 'Legacy of the Prophet: Despots, Democrats, and the New Politics of Islam', Westview Press, p. 228.

Shadid, W. & P.S. van Koningsveld (2002) (eds) Religious Freedom and the Neutrality of the State: The Position of Islam in the European Union. Leuven, Peeters.

Shadid, W.A. and P.S. van Koningsveld (1991) "Institutionalisation and Integration of Islam in The Netherlands", in W.A.R. Shadid and P.S. van Koningsveld (eds) The Integration of Islam and Hinduism in Western Europe, Kampen: Kok Pharos Publishing House.

Shah, I. (1990) Sufi Thought and Action, The Octagon Press: London.

Sharp, G. (1973) The Politics of Non-Violent Action, Sargent, Boston, Massachussetts (Available in 3 paperback Vols only: Vol.1 Power & Struggle, Vol 2 The Methods of Non-Violent Action and Vol. 3 The Dynamics of Non-Violent Action)

Sharp, G. (2005) Waging Non-Violent Struggle:20th Century Practice and 21st Century Potential, Extending Horizons Books, Boston, USA.

Shils, Edward (1992) "The Virtue of Civil Society". Government and Opposition., vol. 26, no. 1 (winter)

Shiner, L. (1967) The Concept of Secularization in Empirical Research, Journal for the Scientific Study of Religion, Vol. 6: No. 2, 13-22.

Shively, Kim (2005) "Religious bodies and the secular state: the Merve Kavakci affair." Journal of Middle East Women's Studies, 3: 20-45.

Sikand, Yoginder (2002) The Origins and Development of the Tablighi Jama'at (1920-2000): A Cross-country Comparative Study (Hydarabad, Orient Longman)

Silova, Iveta, Johnson, Mark S. and Heyneman, Stephen P. (2007) Education and the crisis of social cohesion in Azerbaijan and Central Asia. Comparative Education Review, 51(2) published in printed form May 2007, electronically published 14 February 2007, accessed 19 March 2007.

Simon, Rachel (2003) "Review of 'Turkish Islam and the Secular State: The Gulen Movement" by M. Hakan Yavuz and John Esposito (eds) 2003, Digest of Middle East Studies, Fall 2004, 89-90.

Şimşek, S. (2004) "New Social Movements in Turkey since 1980". Turkish Studies. 5 (2): 111-139.

Singerman Diane (1995) Avenues of Participation: Family, Politics, and Networks in Urban Quarters of Cairo (Princeton: Princeton University Press)

Skinner, Quentin (1998) Liberty Before Liberalism. Cambridge, UK: Cambridge University Press, 1998);

Smidt, Corwin E. (2003) Religion as Social Capital: Producing the Common Good. Waco, TX: Baylor University Press.

Smith, D. E. (1999) "India as a Secular State." In Secularism and its Critics, edited by Rajeev Bhargava. Delhi: Oxford University Press.

Smith, T. W. (2001) "Constructing a Human Rights Regime in Turkey: Dilemmas of Civic Nationalism and Civil society". Presented at the American Political Science association annual conference in San Francisco, August 29–September 2, 2001. Panel 42–1–New Political science/Human Rights, Civil society, and Democratic Justice, pp.24.

Smoker, P. and Groff, L. (1995) Creating Global-Local Cultures of Peace, http://www.gmu.edu/academic/pcs/smoker.htm

So, Farina (2005) "The Study of the Qur-an vs. Modern Education for Islamic Women in Cambodia" (Paper presented at the Short Course on Islam, Gender, and Reproductive Rights, Sunan Kalijaga University Yogyakarta)

Sobel, J. (2002) "Can we trust social capital?", Journal of Economic Literature, Vol. XL, March. 139-154

Solberg A. (2005) "The Gulen schools: A perfect compromise or compromising perfectly?" 2nd Kotor Network Conference, http://www.kotor-network.info/activities/kotor2005.htm

Solomon Norman (2005) "Towards a Jewish Theology of Trilateral Dialogue" in Islam and Global Dialogue: Religious Pluralism and the Pursuit of Peace, ed by Roger Boase. Burlington, VA: Ashgate.

Sorensen, R. (1992) Thought Experiments (Oxford, Oxford University Press)

Stake, R.E. (1992) The Art of Case Study Research. Thousand Oaks, CA: Sage.

Stark, R. & Finke, R. (2000) Acts of Faith: Explaining the Human Side of Religion. Berkeley, CA: University of California Press.

Starr, Kayla (2007) adapted by Bonnie Blackberry, 'The Role of Civil Disobedience in Democracy' CLMP News Summer '98 Issue at http://www.civilliberties.org/sum98role.html, accessed on 24 May 2007

Stauth, Georg Ed (1998) Islam-Motor Or Challenge Of Modernity ? (Hamburg, Germany: Lit Verlag)

Stephenson, A. J. (2007) Leaving Footprints in Houston: Answers to Questions on Women and the Gulen Movement. In: Hunt, A. R. & Aslandogan, Y. A. eds (2007) 145-60.

Stillman, Norman A. (1979) The Jews of Arab Lands: A History and Source Book. Philadelphia: The Jewish Publication Society of America.

Strubbe, Bill (1993) "The People Persist". Aramco World, XLIV, 2, 10-15.

Sullivan, A.T. (2005) Conservative Ecumenism: Politically Incorrect Meditations on Islam and the West in: R. Boase (Ed) Islam and Global Dialogue: Religious Pluralism and the Pursuit of Peace (Hants, England, Ashgate)

Swatos, William H., and James K. Wellman (1999) The Power of Religious Publics: Staking Claims in American Society, Religion in the Age of Transformation. Westport, Conn.: Praeger.

Sykiainen, L. (2007) Democracy and the Dialogue between Western and Islamic Legal Cultures: The Gulen Case. In: Hunt, A. R. & Aslandogan, Y. A. eds (2007) 121–32.

Syracuse University Press, pp. 85-114

Tabari, Tafsir.

Tahawi (1996) Sharh al-Maan al-Athar, Beirut: Dar Kutub al-Ilmiyya 1996, III.224.

Taouti, Seddik (1986) "The Forgotten Muslims of Kampuchea and Viet Nam", in Ahmad Ibrahim et. al. (Eds) Readings on Islam in Southeast Asia (Singapore, Institute of Southeast Asian Studies) 193-200.

Tas, N. (2004) "Analysis of a Text from a Newspaper", http://www.ingilish.com/ned3.htm

Taylor, Charles (1999) "Modes of Secularism." In Secularism and Its Critics, edited by Rajeev Bhargava. Delhi: Oxford University Press.

Taylor, Charles (2004) Modern Social Imaginaries. Durham: Duke University Press.

Taylor, Verta and Nella Van Dyke (2004) "'Get up, Stand up': Tactical Repertoires of Social Movements." Pp. 262-93. in David A. Snow, Sarah A. Soule and Hanspeter Kriesi, eds, The Blackwell Companion to Social Movements, Malden, MA: Blackwell.

Tekalan, Ş A (2005) "Sevgi ve Fedakarlık Abideleri: Türk Öğretmenleri" (The Monuments of Love and Devotion: The Turkish Teachers) in Barış Köprüleri: Dünyaya Açılan Türk Okulları (Bridges of Peace: Turkic Schools Opening Up to the World) eds, Ateş, T and et.al., Istanbul, Ufuk Kitapları.

Tekalan, Serif Ali. (2005) "A Movement of Volunteers." Proceedings from Islam in the Contemporary World: The Fethullan Gulen Movement in Thought and Practice. Rice University, Houston, Texas

Thomas, David with Clare Amos (eds) (2003) A Faithful Presence, essays for Kenneth Cragg, London: Melisende Press.

Thomä-Venske, Hans (1988) The Religious Life of Muslims in Berlin, in T. Gerholm and Yngve George Lithman, eds, London and New York: Mansell, p. 78

Thurgood, Graham (1999) From Ancient Cham to Modern Dialects. Two thousand years of language contact and change (Honolulu, University of Hawai'i Press)

Tibi Bassam (1998) Aufbruch am Bosporus. Die Turkei zwischen Europa and Islamismus Munchen: Diana.

Tibi, Bassam (1998) The Challenge of Fundamentalism: Political Islam and the New World Disorder (Berkeley, CA: California University Press, 1998);

Tibi, Bassam (2006) "Europeanizing Islam or Islamization of Europe" in Timothy Brynes, Peter Katzenstein, "Religion in Expanding Europe", Cambridge University Press, New York.

Tillich, Paul (1963) The Courage to Be, London, Collins 1962.

Times Educational Supplement (2001) Voters oppose expansion of faith schools: MORI Poll, Biddy Passmore and Nic Barnard, London 30/11/2001.

Times Educational Supplement (2002) Judith Judd, Blair says schools come first.   London, 05/07/2002.

Tirmizi. Sunan.

Tocqueville, Alexis (2000) Democracy in America, 2 Vols.Translated by Harvey C. Mansfield and Delba Winthrop (Chicago, Il.: University of Chicago Press)

Todorov, Tz. (1989) Nous et les autres. La réflexion française sur la diversité humaine (Paris, Editions du Seuil)

Toguslu, Erkan (2007)"Le difficile équilibre dedans-dehors : les activités culturelles d'un centre musul-man comme stratégie d'intégration dans l'espace public et les critiques au projet au sein de leur communauté » Paper submitted in Colloquy « La Religion de l'Autre » 5-6 February 2007, Paris

Toktorov, M. (2007) Capa Nekkenderge Cardam, Kut Bilim Bishkek, Kyrgyzstan

Touraine, Alain (1981) The Voice and the Eye: An Analysis of Social Movements. Cambridge: Cambridge University Press.

Touraine, Alaine (1997) Pourrons-nous vivre ensemble ? Égaux et différents", Fayard Editions.

Triandafyllidou, A. (1998) National Identity and the 'Other'. Ethnic and Racial Studies, 21, 593-612.

Troy, Thomas F. (1991) Jesuit Colleges Without Jesuits? Ignatian Identity at Risk. Commonweal, October 1991, 605-08.

Tuğal, C. (2007) NATO's Islamists: hegemony and Americanization in Turkey. New Left Review. 44, 5-34.

Tuncer, F, (2005) "Gulen'in Eğitim Anlayışı ve Zihni Oluşum Temelleri" (Gulen's Educational Understanding and Bases of His Intellectual Formation) in Barış Köprüleri: Dünyaya Açılan Türk Okulları.

Turam, Berna (2001) "National Loyalties and International Undertakings. Islamic Modernism: Fethullah Gulen and Contemporary Islam". Georgetown University (26-27 April)

Turam, Berna (2004) "A bargain between the secular state and Turkish Islam: politics of ethnicity in Central Asia", Nations and Nationalism, 10(3) 353-374.

Turam, Berna (2004) "The Politics of Engagement between Islam and the Secular State: The Ambivalences of 'Civil Society'," The British Journal of Sociology, Volume 55 Issue 2 (2004) pp. 259-281.

Turam, Berna (2007) Between Islam and the Sate: The Politics of Engagement. Stanford, California, Stanford University Press.

Turgut, H. (1997) "Nurculuk". Sabah, January 23-31.

Turgut, Hulusi (1998) "Fethullah Gulen ve Okullar [Fethullah Gulen and Schools]," Yeni Yüzyıl, 22

January 1998.

Turkdogan, O. (2005) Islami Degerler Sistemi ve Max Weber, IQ Yayincilik: Istanbul.

Turkish Daily News (2000) Public Drive Against Corruption. National News. November 14.

Turner, B. S. (1987) "The Rationalization of the body: reflections on modernity and disciplines" in S. Whimster and S. Lash (eds) Max Weber, Rationality and Modernity, London, Allen&Unwin.

Turner, B. S. (1974) Weber and Islam: A Critical Study, Routledge & Kegan Paul Ltd: London

Turner, H. R (1995) Science in Medieval Islam (Austin, University of Texas Press)

Ugur, Etga (2004) "Intellectual Roots of Turkish Islam and Approaches to the Turkish Model," Journal of Muslim Minority Affairs, vol. 24, no. 2, pp. 327-345.

Uğur, Etga (2004) "Political Culture, Civil Society, and Public Religion: Musings on the Gulen Movement" Paper Presented In Second Middle East and Central Asia Politics, Economy, and Society Conference (MECA) University of Utah (September 2004)

Uğur, Etga (2006) "Civic Islam in the Public Sphere: The Gulen Movement, Civil Society, and Social Capital in Turkey," Paper Presented In Second International Conference on Islam, University of Wisconsin-Madison (March 2006)

Ulgener, F. S. (1991) Iktisadi Cozulmenin Ahlak ve Zihniyet Dunyasi, Der Yayinlari: Istanbul

Ulgener, F. S. (2006) Zihniyet ve Din – Islam, Tasavvuf ve Cozulme Devri Iktisat Ahlaki, Der Yayinlari: Istanbul

Ülsever, C. (2001) "Will Turkey demolish her fundamental taboo? The role of the army". Turkish Daily News, August 14.

Ülsever, C. (2003) Status-quo blocking Turkish modernism. Turkish Daily News, February 4. Available from: <www.turkishdailynews.com/old_editions/02_04_03/ulsever.htm> [November 5, 2004, 20:19]

Ulusoy, Ali (1999) "Fransız ve Türk Laikliğinin Larşılaştırılması " Liberal Düşünce (14): 96-101.

Ünal, Ali (2002) Bir Portre Denemesi: M Fethullah Gulen (An Essay in Portrait: M Fethullah Gulen) İstanbul, Nil Yayinlari.

Ünal, Ali (2006) The Qur'ān. With annotated interpretation in modern English. NJ: The Light, Inc.

Utvik Bjorn Olav (2003) The Modernizing Force of Islamism, in Esposito J. L. and Burgat François editors, Modernizing Islam. Religion in the Public Sphere in Europe and the Middle East, Rutgers University Press, New Brunswick, New Jersey.

Vainovski-Mihai, I. (2000) "A Food of Their Kind". The Gastronomic Image of the Eastern Other in a Time of a Tensioned Self-Identification. Annals of the Sergiu Al-George Institute for Oriental Studies, IX-X, 191-200.

Valkenberg, Pim (2006) Sharing Lights On The Way To God: Muslim-Christian Dialogue and Theology in the Context of Abrahamic Partnership (Amsterdam, NY, Rodopi)

Van Dijk, T.A. (1998) Ideology. A multidisciplinary study., London: Sage..

Van Vugt, M. and D. De Cremer (1999) "Leadership in Social Dilemmas: The Effects of Group Identification on Collective Actions to Provide Public Goods." Journal of Personality and Social Psychology, Vol 67, pp. 126-141.

Vaner, Semih (ed) (2005) La Turquie, Paris, Fayard-Ceri.

Vanhoozer, K. J. (2003) "Theology and the Condition of Postmodernity", in: Vanhoozer, K. J. (ed) The Cambridge Companion to Postmodern Theology. (Cambridge, Cambridge University Press)

Vertovec, Steven (2003) "Diaspora transnationalism and Islam: sites of change and modes of research",

Allievi, Stefano and Nielson, Jorgen (eds) Muslim networks and transnational communities in and across Europe (Leiden and Boston: Brill) 312-326.

Vickery, Michael (1999) Cambodia 1975-1982 (Chiang Mai, Silkworm Books)

Victoria, Clement (N.D.) "Secular and Religious Trends in Turkmen Education," Unpublished study for Eurasia.

Viroli, Maurizio (2002) Republicanism. Translated from the Italian by Antony Shugar (New York , New York : Hill and Wang)

Voigt, S. (2005) "Islam and the Institutions of Free Society". The Independent Review, 10 (1) 59-82.

Voll, John O. (1999) "Renewal and Reformation in the Mid-Twentieth Century: Bediuzzaman Said Nursi".

Voll, John O. (2003) "Transcending Modernity in the New Islamic Discourse", in Turkish Islam and the Secular State: The Gulen Movement (Eds M. H. Yavuz & J. L. Esposito) Syracuse: New York.

Von Arx, Jeffrey P. (2005) "Diversity and the Jesuit Education: A Call to Action". Vital Speeches of the Day, 71:10, 317-20.

Wahidi, Wasit.

Walcott, H. F. (1999) Ethnography: A way of seeing. Walnut Creek, CA: AltraMira Press.

Walzer, Michael (2002) 'Five Questions About Terrorism', Dissent, Winter 2002, pp. 5-9.

Warner, Martin and Roger Crisp (1990) 'Introduction', in Martin Warner and Roger Crisp (ed) Terrorism, Protest and Power, Edward Elgar,, pp. 1-14

Watt, W M, (1960) "Ahl al-Suffa" Encyclopaedia of Islam, New Edition, Leiden, E J Brill.

Webb, L. E. (2000) Fethullah Gulen: Is There More to Him Than Meets the Eye? Izmir, Mercury.

Weber, M. (1930-2001) The Protestant Ethic and the Spirit of Capitalism (Translated by T. Parsons) Routledge: London

Weber, Max (2004) Ethique Protestante et l'esprit du Capitalisme, Paris, Plon

Weller, Paul (2005) "Religions and social capital: theses on religion(s) state(s) and society(ies): with particular reference to the United Kingdom and the European Union". Journal of International Migration and Integration. 6, 2, 271-289.

Weller, Paul (2006a) "Addressing religious discrimination and Islamophobia: Muslims and liberal democracies. The case of the United Kingdom", in: The Journal of Islamic Studies. Advanced published, doi: 10.1093/jis/et1001, and 17, 3, 295-325.

Weller, Paul (2006b) "'Human rights', 'religion' and the 'secular': variant configurations of religion(s) state(s) and society(ies)" Religion and Human Rights: An International Journal. 1, 1, 17-39.

Weller, Paul (2006c) "Fethullah Gulen, Religions, Globalizations and Dialogue", in: Hunt, R.A. & Y. A. Aslandoğan (eds) Muslim Citizens of the Globalized World. Contributions of the Gulen Movement. Somerset, NJ; The Light, Inc & IID Press (pp.75-88)

Weller, Paul, A. Feldman and K. Purdam (2004) "Muslims and Religious Discrimination in England and Wales", in: J. Malik (ed) Muslim Minority Societies in Europe: From the Margin to the Centre (Münster, LIT Verlag) 115-144.

Wensinck, A. J. (1936-69) Concordance et indices de la tradition musulmane (Leiden, 1936-69) 2:165.

West II, W. Jefferson (2006) "Religion as dissident politics? Geopolitical discussions within the recent publications of Fethullah Gulen". Geopolitics, 11(2) 280-299.

West, Cornel (1989) The American Evasion of Philosophy: A Genealogy of Pragmatism (Madison,

University of Wisconsin Press)

White, Jenny B. (2001) Islamist Mobilization in Turkey: A Study in Vernacular Politics (Seattle, University of Washington Press)

White, Jenny B. (2005) "The End of Islamism? Turkey's Muslimhood Model", Modern Muslim Politics, Robert Hefner, ed, Princeton University Press

Wilford, R. and Wilson, R. (2003) "Northern Ireland: A Route to Stability", Democratic Dialogue. (http://www.devolution.ac.uk/Wilson_&Wilford_Paper)

Wilkinson, Paul (1974) Political Terrorism, London: Macmillan.

Wilson, B. (1982) Religion in Sociological Perspective. Oxford: Oxford University Press

Windsor, Jennifer L. (2003) "Promoting Democratization Can Combat Terrorism", The Washington Quarterly, Summer 2003, 26:3, pp. 43–58

Wistrich, Robert S. (1992) Anti-Semitism: The Longest Hatred London: Mandarin.

Wittgenstein, Ludwig (1958) Philosophical Investigations, trans. E. Anscombe. Oxford: Blackwell.

Woodbery, R. D. (2003) Researching Spiritual Capital: Promises and Pitfalls, Unpublished paper available at http://www.metanexus.net/spiritual%5Fcapital/pdf/woodberry.pdf

Woodhall, Ruth & Çetin, M. (2005) "Preface". In: Gulen, M. F. (2005) The Statue of Our Souls: Revival in Islamic Thought and Activism. Somerset, New Jersey, The Light Inc, xiii–xviii.

Woodhall, Ruth (2005) "Organizing the Organization, Educating the Educators: An Examination of Fethullan Gulen's Teaching and the Membership of the Movement." Proceedings from Islam in the Contemporary World: The Fethullah Gulen Movement in Thought and Practice. Rice University, Houston, Texas.

Worsley, P. (1969) Religion as a Category. Sociology of Religion, ed By R. Rabortson, Penguin: London

Wright, A. (1990) "Dispositions, Anti-Realism and Empiricism", Proceedings of the Aristotelian Society, XCI, 39-60.

WRR, Netherlands Scientific Council for Government Policy (2004) The European Union, Turkey and Islam. Amsterdam: Amsterdam University Press.

Wu, F.H. (2004) 'Profiling in the Wake of September 11: The Precedent of the Japanese American Internment' in M.K.B. Darmer et al (eds) Civil Liberties vs. National Security In A Post-9/11 World (New York: Prometheus Books)

Yaman, Ali & Erdemir, Aykan (2006) Alevism-Bektashism: A Brief Introduction (London, England Alevi Cultural Centre and Cem Evi)

Yavuz, Hakan (1997) "Political Islam and the Welfare (Refah) Party in Turkey." Comparative Politics 30 (1): 63-82.

Yavuz, Hakan (1999a) "Search for a New Contract: Fethullah Gulen, Virtue Party, and the Kurds." SAIS Review, 19: 1.

Yavuz, Hakan (1999b) "The Assassination of Collective Memory: The Case of Turkey", The Muslim World, 89(3-4) 193-207

Yavuz, Hakan (1999c) "Towards an Islamic liberalism? The Nurcu movement and Fethullah Gulen" Middle East Journal (53, # 4 Autumn): 584-605.

Yavuz, Hakan (2000a) "Being Modern in the Nurcu Way", ISIM Newsletter, 6.

Yavuz, Hakan (2000b) "Cleansing Islam from the Public Sphere." Journal of International Affairs, 54: 1.

Yavuz, Hakan (2000c) "Turkish Identity Politics and Central Asia" in Roald Sagdeev and Susan Eisenhower, eds, Islam and Central Asia (Washington: Center for Political and Strategic Studies, 2000) 193-211.

Yavuz, Hakan (2003a) "Islam in the Public Sphere: The Case of the Nur Movement", in M. Hakan Yavuz and John Esposito (eds) Turkish Islam and the Secular State: The Gulen Movement, Syracuse, New York: Syracuse University Press, p.1-18.

Yavuz, Hakan (2003b) "The case of Turkey", Daedalus (special issue on secularism & religion) June 2003

Yavuz, Hakan (2003c) "The Gulen Movement: The Turkish Puritans", in M. Hakan Yavuz & John L. Esposito (Eds) Turkish Islam and the Secular State: The Gulen Movement (Syracuse, University Press) 19-47.

Yavuz, Hakan (2003d) Islamic Political Identity in Turkey. Oxford: Oxford University Press.

Yavuz, Hakan (2004a) "Is there a Turkish Islam? The emergence of convergence and consensus". Journal of Muslim Minority Affairs, 24(2) 213-232.

Yavuz, Hakan (2004b) Religioscope, 21 July 2004. http://religion.info/english/interviews/article_74.html.

Yavuz, Hakan and John L. Esposito (2003) "Introduction: Islam in Turkey: Retreat from the Secular Path?" in Hakan Yavuz and John L. Esposito (eds) Turkish Islam and the Secular State: The Gulen Movement, Syracuse, New York: Syracuse University Press, pp. xiii-xxxiii.

Yavuz, Hakan and John L. Esposito (eds) (2003) Turkish Islam and the Secular State, Syracuse, NY, Syracuse University Press.

Ye'or, Bat (1985) The Dhimmi: Jews and Christians under Islam, Cranbury, NJ: Associated University Press.

Ye'or, Bat (2002) Islam and Dhimmitude: Where Civilizations Collide (Trans. By Miriam Kochan and David Littman) Cranbury, NJ: Associated University Presses. 2002

Yıldırım, Ergün (1995) Türkiye'nin Modernleşmesi ve Islam. Istanbul: İnsan Yayınları, 1995.

Yildirim, S. (1998) "Fethullah Gulen's Meeting with the Pope". Zaman, Istanbul.

Yılmaz, H. K. (N.D.) "Tassavvufi Açıdan Ashab-ı Suffa" (The Suffa Companions from the Mystical Aspect) Tasavvuf İlmi ve Akademik Araştırma Dergisi, v. 3, n. 7

Yilmaz, Ihsan (2000a) "Muslim legal pluralism in asr al-darura: Surfing on the inter-madhhab-net." Prsented at the III International conference on Islamic Legal Studies, Madhhab, Harvard University Law School (4-7 May).

Yilmaz, Ihsan (2000b) "Changing Turkish-Muslim Discourses on Modernity, West and Dialogue". Paper presented at the Congress of the International Association of Middle East Studies, Berlin (October 5-7).

Yilmaz, Ihsan (2001) "Renewing the religious thought and practice while transforming society: Fethullah Gulen and Tajdid". Presented at the Islamic Modernities Conference: Fethullah Gulen, the Man and His Movement, Center for Muslim-Christian Understanding, Georgetown University, Washington DC, (26-27 April).

Yilmaz, Ihsan (2002) "Dynamic Legal Pluralism in England: The Challenge of Postmodern Muslim Legality to Legal Modernity". In: Journal of Ethnic and Migration Studies. Spring 2002. Vol. 28 No. 2.

Yilmaz, Ihsan (2003) "Ijtihad and Tajdid by Conduct: the Gulen Movement", in: H.Yavuz & J. Esposito (Eds) Turkish Islam and the Secular State (New York, Syracuse University Press) 208-237.

Yilmaz, Ihsan (2004) "Marriage Solemnization among Turks in Britain: The Emergence of a Hybrid Anglo-Muslim Turkish Law" in Journal of Muslim Affairs, Vol. 24, No. 1, April 2004.

Yilmaz, Ihsan (2005a) "Inter-Madhhab Surfing, Neo-Ijtihad, and Faith-Based Movement Leaders" in The Islamic School of Law, Evolution, Devolution and Progress (edited by Peri Bearman, R. Peters, F.E. Vogel) (Cambridge, MA: Harvard University Press). 191-206.

Yilmaz, Ihsan (2005b) "State, Law, Civil Society and Islam in Contemporary Society", The Muslim World, 385-412.

Yilmaz, Ihsan (2005c) Muslim Laws, Politics and Society in Modern Nation States: Dynamic Legal Pluralisms in England, Turkey and Pakistan. Aldershot: Ashgate.

Yilmaz, Ihsan (2006) "Panacea to Neo-Assassin Terror: Nursi's Discourse & Praxis". Presented at the Islam in Contemporary Turkey: Perspectives of Bediuzzaman Said Nursi Conference. John Carroll University, Cleveland, Ohio, USA (November 5 – 6).

Yilmaz, Ihsan (2007a) "Abant Platform, Alevis and Diaspora", Today's Zaman,.23 March 2007.

Yilmaz, Ihsan (2007b) "Rumi's Renewed Social Innovation And Pluralist Activism Today", Paper presented at the International Mawlana Jalaluddin-i Rumi Conference, Tajikistan Academy of Sciences, Dushanbe, Tajikistan. 5-7 September 2007.

Yin, K.R. (2002) Case Study Research. Design and Methods. Third Edition. Applied social research method series. Volume 5. CA: Sage.

Yousef, D.A. (2001) "Islamic Work Ethic: A moderator between organizational commitment and job satisfaction in a cross-cultural context", Personnel Review, 30(2) 152-169.

Yucel, G. (2002) "New Dilemmas of Turkish National Security Politics: Old and New Security Concerns and National Development in the Post-1980 Era". Paper for presentation at the Fourth Kokkalis Graduate Student Workshop at JFK School of Government, Harvard University, Cambridge, Massachusetts, February 8–9, pp.24.

Yusuf, Hamza (1997) Tasawwuf/Sufism in Islam, lecture at Stanford University, available online at http://sunnah.org/events/hamza/hamza.htm.

Yusuf, Hamza (trans.) (2004) Purification of the Heart: Signs, Symptoms and Cures of the Spiritual Diseases of the Heart. Translation and commentary of Imam al-Mawlud's Matharat al-Qulub, Chicago: Starlatch.

Zayd, Nasr Abu (2005) Reformation of Islamic Thought: A Critical Historical Analysis, Amsterdam: Amsterdam University Press.

Zubaida Sami (1996) "Turkish Islam and National Identity", Middle East Report, No. 199, pp. 10-15.